CALIFORNIA

INTEGRATED MATH 1

Edward B. Burger
Juli K. Dixon
Timothy D. Kanold
Matthew R. Larson
Steven J. Leinwand
Martha E. Sandoval-Martinez

Printed in the U.S.A.

ISBN 978-0-544-21670-9

2 3 4 5 6 7 8 9 10 0877 22 21 20 19 18 17 16 15 14 13

4500452985 A B C D E F G

Authors

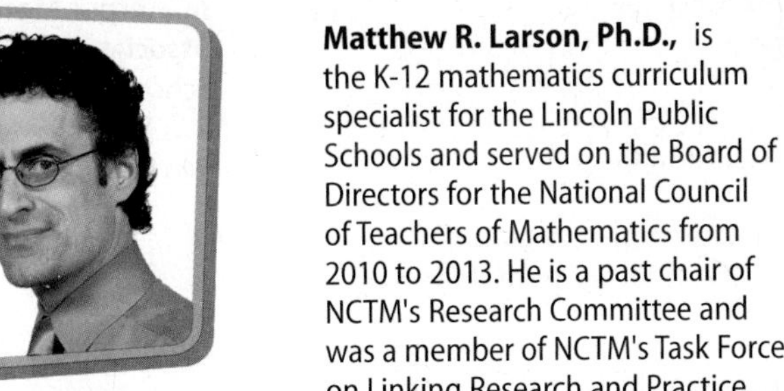

Edward B. Burger, Ph.D., is the President of Southwestern University, a former Francis Christopher Oakley Third Century Professor of Mathematics at Williams College, and a former vice provost at Baylor University. He has authored or coauthored more than sixty-five articles, books, and video series; delivered over five hundred addresses and workshops throughout the world; and made more than fifty radio and television appearances. He is a Fellow of the American Mathematical Society as well as having earned many national honors, including the Robert Foster Cherry Award for Great Teaching in 2010. In 2012, Microsoft Education named him a "Global Hero in Education."

Matthew R. Larson, Ph.D., is the K-12 mathematics curriculum specialist for the Lincoln Public Schools and served on the Board of Directors for the National Council of Teachers of Mathematics from 2010 to 2013. He is a past chair of NCTM's Research Committee and was a member of NCTM's Task Force on Linking Research and Practice. He is the author of several books on implementing the Common Core Standards for Mathematics. He has taught mathematics at the secondary and college levels and held an appointment as an honorary visiting associate professor at Teachers College, Columbia University.

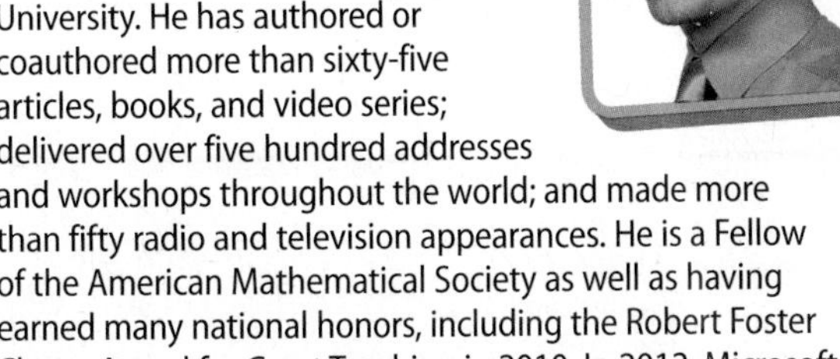

Juli K. Dixon, Ph.D., is a Professor of Mathematics Education at the University of Central Florida. She has taught mathematics in urban schools at the elementary, middle, secondary, and post-secondary levels. She is an active researcher and speaker with numerous publications and conference presentations. Key areas of focus are deepening teachers' content knowledge and communicating and justifying mathematical ideas. She is a past chair of the NCTM Student Explorations in Mathematics Editorial Panel and member of the Board of Directors for the Association of Mathematics Teacher Educators.

Steven J. Leinwand is a Principal Research Analyst at the American Institutes for Research (AIR) in Washington, D.C., and has over 30 years in leadership positions in mathematics education. He is past president of the National Council of Supervisors of Mathematics and served on the NCTM Board of Directors. He is the author of numerous articles, books, and textbooks and has made countless presentations with topics including student achievement, reasoning, effective assessment, and successful implementation of standards.

Timothy D. Kanold, Ph.D., is an award-winning international educator, author, and consultant. He is a former superintendent and director of mathematics and science at Adlai E. Stevenson High School District 125 in Lincolnshire, Illinois. He is a past president of the National Council of Supervisors of Mathematics (NCSM) and the Council for the Presidential Awardees of Mathematics (CPAM). He has served on several writing and leadership commissions for NCTM during the past decade. He presents motivational professional development seminars with a focus on developing professional learning communities (PLC's) to improve the teaching, assessing, and learning of students. He has recently authored nationally recognized articles, books, and textbooks for mathematics education and school leadership, including *What Every Principal Needs to Know about the Teaching and Learning of Mathematics*.

Martha E. Sandoval-Martinez is a mathematics instructor at El Camino College in Torrance, California. She was previously a Math Specialist at the University of California at Davis and former instructor at Santa Ana College, Marymount College, and California State University, Long Beach. In her current and former positions, she has worked extensively to improve fundamental pre-algebra and algebra skills in students who have historically struggled with mathematics.

California Consulting Reviewers

Elizabeth Jiménez, CEO
GEMAS Consulting
Pomona, CA

Erin Bostick Mason, MA.Ed.
Adjunct Faculty
Dept. of Language, Literature and Culture
College of Education, California State University
San Bernardino, CA

Jill Kerper Mora, Ed.D.
Associate Professor Emerita
School of Teacher Education
San Diego State University
San Diego, CA

California Advisory Board

Ashley A. Downing
Eagle Peak Middle School
Ukiah Unified School District
Redwood Valley, CA

Robert Kaplinsky
Teacher Specialist, Mathematics
Downey Unified School District
Downey, CA

Peggy M. Mendez
Charles Wagner Elementary School
Placentia, CA

Melissa Samson
Kraemer Middle School
Placentia, CA

Lori With
BMS Math Teacher
Benicia Middle School
Benicia, CA

UNIT 1 Numbers and Expressions

MODULE 1 Relationships Between Quantities

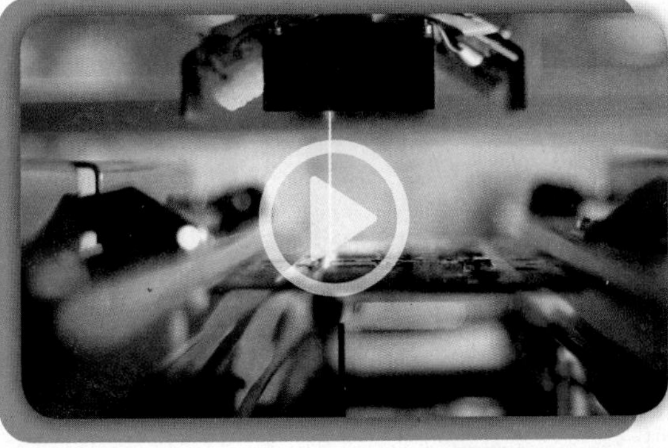

MODULE 2 Expressions

Unit 2 Equations and Functions

MODULE 3 Equations and Inequalities in One Variable

MODULE 4 Equations in Two Variables and Functions

MODULE 5 Absolute Value

CA CC

Linear Relationships

Linear Functions

MODULE 7 Building Linear Functions

CA CC

MODULE 8 Modeling with Linear Functions

CA CC

MODULE 9

Systems of Equations and Inequalities

UNIT 3B Exponential Relationships

MODULE 10 Exponen[...]unctions and Equations

MODULE 11 Modeling with Exp[...] Functions

UNIT 4 CALIFORNIA

Statistics an[d] Data

MODULE 12 Descriptive Statistics

MODULE 13 …a Displays

Transformations, Congruence, and Constructions

MODULE 14 Geometric Terms and Transformations

MODULE 15 Transformations and Congruence

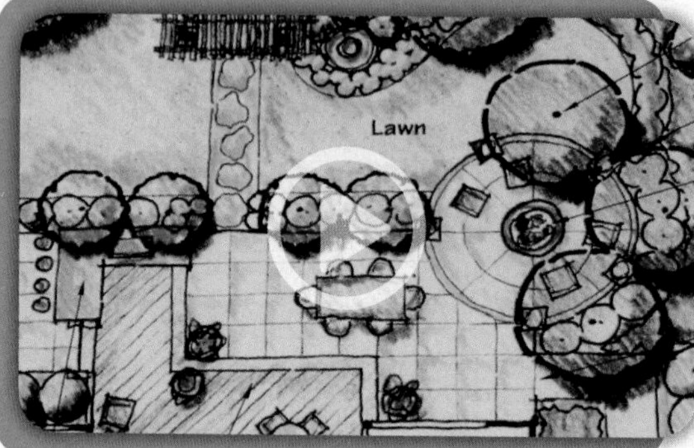

CA CC

MODULE 16 Geometric Constructions

CA CC

Coordinate Geometry

MODULE 17 Coordinate Proofs and Applications

CA CC

California Common Core Standards for Mathematics I

Correlations for *HMH California Integrated Math 1*

NUMBER AND QUANTITY

Standard	Descriptor	Citations
QUANTITIES		**N-Q**
Reason quantitatively and use units to solve problems.		
N-Q.1	Use units as a way to understand problems and to guide the solution of multi-step problems; choose and interpret units consistently in formulas; choose and interpret the scale and the origin in graphs and data displays.	15–22, 29–34, 43–50, 187–192
N-Q.2	Define appropriate quantities for the purpose of descriptive modeling.	43–50, 65–72, 249–256
N-Q.3	Choose a level of accuracy appropriate to limitations on measurement when reporting quantities.	7–14, 17–22

ALGEBRA

Standard	Descriptor	Citations
SEEING STRUCTURE IN EXPRESSIONS		**A-SSE**
Interpret the structure of expressions.		
A-SSE.1	Interpret expressions that represent a quantity in terms of its context. **a.** Interpret parts of an expression, such as terms, factors, and coefficients. **b.** Interpret complicated expressions by viewing one or more of their parts as a single entity.	29–34, 35–42, 43–50
CREATING EQUATIONS		**A-CED**
Create equations that describe numbers or relationships.		
A-CED.1	Create equations and inequalities in one variable including ones with absolute value and use them to solve problems.	65–72, 73–82, 131–138, 361–368
A-CED.2	Create equations in two or more variables to represent relationships between quantities; graph equations on coordinate axes with labels and scales.	179–186, 201–206, 219–226, 331–338, 361–368, 375–380
A-CED.3	Represent constraints by equations or inequalities, and by systems of equations and/or inequalities, and interpret solutions as viable or nonviable options in a modeling context.	65–72, 73–82, 271–278, 279–286, 287–296, 301–304, 305–312
A-CED.4	Rearrange formulas to highlight a quantity of interest, using the same reasoning as in solving equations.	83–88

Standard	Descriptor	Citations
REASONING WITH EQUATIONS AND INEQUALITIES		**A-REI**
Understand solving equations as a process of reasoning and explain the reasoning.		
A-REI.1	Explain each step in solving a simple equation as following from the equality of numbers asserted at the previous step, starting from the assumption that the original equation has a solution. Construct a viable argument to justify a solution method.	**65–72, 73–82, 83–88**
Solve equations and inequalities in one variable.		
A-REI.3	Solve linear equations and inequalities in one variable, including equations with coefficients represented by letters.	**65–72, 73–82, 83–88**
A-REI.3.1	Solve one-variable equations and inequalities involving absolute value, graphing the solutions and interpreting them in context.	**131–138, 139–140, 144–145, 148**
Solve systems of equations.		
A-REI.5	Prove that, given a system of two equations in two variables, replacing one equation by the sum of that equation and a multiple of the other produces a system with the same solutions.	**297–304**
A-REI.6	Solve systems of linear equations exactly and approximately (e.g., with graphs), focusing on pairs of linear equations in two variables.	**271–278, 279–286, 287–296, 297–304**
Represent and solve equations and inequalities graphically.		
A-REI.10	Understand that the graph of an equation in two variables is the set of all its solutions plotted in the coordinate plane, often forming a curve (which could be a line).	**95–100, 101–108**
A-REI.11	Explain why the *x*-coordinates of the points where the graphs of the equations $y = f(x)$ and $y = g(x)$ intersect are the solutions of the equation $f(x) = g(x)$; find the solutions approximately, e.g., using technology to graph the functions, make tables of values, or find successive approximations. Include cases where $f(x)$ and/or $g(x)$ are linear, polynomial, rational, absolute value, exponential, and logarithmic functions.	**101–108, 123–130, 131–138, 139–140, 145, 361–368**
A-REI.12	Graph the solutions to a linear inequality in two variables as a halfplane (excluding the boundary in the case of a strict inequality), and graph the solution set to a system of linear inequalities in two variables as the intersection of the corresponding half-planes.	**227–234, 305–312**

FUNCTIONS

Standard	Descriptor	Citations
INTERPRETING FUNCTIONS		**F-IF**
Understand the concept of a function and use function notation.		
F-IF.1	Understand that a function from one set (called the domain) to another set (called the range) assigns to each element of the domain exactly one element of the range. If *f* is a function and *x* is an element of its domain, then $f(x)$ denotes the output of *f* corresponding to the input *x*. The graph of *f* is the graph of the equation $y = f(x)$.	101–108, 187–192
F-IF.2	Use function notation, evaluate functions for inputs in their domains, and interpret statements that use function notation in terms of a context.	101–108, 187–192
F-IF.3	Recognize that sequences are functions, sometimes defined recursively, whose domain is a subset of the integers.	109–116, 213–218, 347–354
Interpret functions that arise in applications in terms of the context.		
F-IF.4	For a function that models a relationship between two quantities, interpret key features of graphs and tables in terms of the quantities, and sketch graphs showing key features given a verbal description of the relationship.	123–130, 163–170, 171–178, 179–186, 193–200, 339–346
F-IF.5	Relate the domain of a function to its graph and, where applicable, to the quantitative relationship it describes.	101–108, 155–162, 187–192, 331–338, 339–346
F-IF.6	Calculate and interpret the average rate of change of a function (presented symbolically or as a table) over a specified interval. Estimate the rate of change from a graph.	171–178, 179–186, 201–206
Analyze functions using different representations.		
F-IF.7	Graph functions expressed symbolically and show key features of the graph, by hand in simple cases and using technology for more complicated cases. **a.** Graph linear and quadratic functions and show intercepts, maxima, and minima. **e.** Graph exponential and logarithmic functions, showing intercepts and end behavior, and trigonometric functions, showing period, midline, and amplitude.	123–130, 155–162, 163–170, 171–178, 179–186, 331–338, 339–346
F-IF.9	Compare properties of two functions each represented in a different way (algebraically, graphically, numerically in tables, or by verbal descriptions).	187–192

Standard	Descriptor	Citations
BUILDING FUNCTIONS		**F-BF**
Build a function that models a relationship between two quantities.		
F-BF.1	Write a function that describes a relationship between two quantities. **a.** Determine an explicit expression, a recursive process, or steps for calculation from a context. **b.** Combine standard function types using arithmetic operations.	109–116, 201–206, 213–218, 219–226, 347–354, 361–368
F-BF.2	Write arithmetic and geometric sequences both recursively and with an explicit formula, use them to model situations, and translate between the two forms.	116, 213–218, 235–236, 317, 347–354
Build new functions from existing functions.		
F-BF.3	Identify the effect on the graph of replacing $f(x)$ by $f(x) + k$, $k\,f(x)$, $f(kx)$, and $f(x + k)$ for specific values of k (both positive and negative); find the value of k given the graphs. Experiment with cases and illustrate an explanation of the effects on the graph using technology.	123–130, 193–200, 355–360
LINEAR, QUADRATIC, AND EXPONENTIAL MODELS		**F-LE**
Construct and compare linear, quadratic, and exponential models and solve problems.		
F-LE.1	Distinguish between situations that can be modeled with linear functions and with exponential functions. **a.** Prove that linear functions grow by equal differences over equal intervals, and that exponential functions grow by equal factors over equal intervals. **b.** Recognize situations in which one quantity changes at a constant rate per unit interval relative to another. **c.** Recognize situations in which a quantity grows or decays by a constant percent rate per unit interval relative to another.	171–178, 179–186, 213–218, 339–346, 347–354, 381–388
F-LE.2	Construct linear and exponential functions, including arithmetic and geometric sequences, given a graph, a description of a relationship, or two input-output pairs (include reading these from a table).	201–206, 213–218, 219–226, 331–338, 339–346, 347–354, 361–368
F-LE.3	Observe using graphs and tables that a quantity increasing exponentially eventually exceeds a quantity increasing linearly, quadratically, or (more generally) as a polynomial function.	381–388
Interpret expressions for functions in terms of the situation they model.		
F-LE.5	Interpret the parameters in a linear or exponential function in terms of a context.	187–192, 193–200, 219–226, 249–256, 339–346, 375–380

GEOMETRY

Standard	Descriptor	Citations
CONGRUENCE		**G-CO**
Experiment with transformations in the plane.		
G-CO.1	Know precise definitions of angle, circle, perpendicular line, parallel line, and line segment, based on the undefined notions of point, line, distance along a line, and distance around a circular arc.	471–478
G-CO.2	Represent transformations in the plane using, e.g., transparencies and geometry software; describe transformations as functions that take points in the plane as inputs and give other points as outputs. Compare transformations that preserve distance and angle to those that do not (e.g., translation versus horizontal stretch).	479–486, 487–494, 495–502, 503–510, 511–518
G-CO.3	Given a rectangle, parallelogram, trapezoid, or regular polygon, describe the rotations and reflections that carry it onto itself.	495–502, 503–510
G-CO.4	Develop definitions of rotations, reflections, and translations in terms of angles, circles, perpendicular lines, parallel lines, and line segments.	487–494, 495–502, 503–510, 511–518
G-CO.5	Given a geometric figure and a rotation, reflection, or translation, draw the transformed figure using, e.g., graph paper, tracing paper, or geometry software. Specify a sequence of transformations that will carry a given figure onto another.	479–486, 487–494, 495–502, 503–510, 511–518, 525–532, 573–582
Understand congruence in terms of rigid motions.		
G-CO.6	Use geometric descriptions of rigid motions to transform figures and to predict the effect of a given rigid motion on a given figure; given two figures, use the definition of congruence in terms of rigid motions to decide if they are congruent.	511–518, 525–532
G-CO.7	Use the definition of congruence in terms of rigid motions to show that two triangles are congruent if and only if corresponding pairs of sides and corresponding pairs of angles are congruent.	533–540
G-CO.8	Explain how the criteria for triangle congruence (ASA, SAS, and SSS) follow from the definition of congruence in terms of rigid motions.	541–546, 547–552, 553–558
Make geometric constructions.		
G-CO.12	Make formal geometric constructions with a variety of tools and methods (compass and straightedge, string, reflective devices, paper folding, dynamic geometric software, etc.).	471–478, 554–555, 565–572, 573–582, 583–590
G-CO.13	Construct an equilateral triangle, a square, and a regular hexagon inscribed in a circle.	583–590

Standard	Descriptor	Citations
EXPRESSING GEOMETRIC PROPERTIES WITH EQUATIONS		**G-GPE**
Use coordinates to prove simple geometric theorems algebraically.		
G-GPE.4	Use coordinates to prove simple geometric theorems algebraically.	607–614, 615–622, 623–630, 631–638
G-GPE.5	Prove the slope criteria for parallel and perpendicular lines and use them to solve geometric problems (e.g., find the equation of a line parallel or perpendicular to a given line that passes through a given point).	607–614, 615–622
G-GPE.7	Use coordinates to compute perimeters of polygons and areas of triangles and rectangles, e.g., using the distance formula.	623–630, 631–638

STATISTICS AND PROBABILITY

Standard	Descriptor	Citations
INTERPRETING CATEGORICAL AND QUANTITATIVE DATA		**S-ID**
Summarize, represent, and interpret data on a single count or measurement variable.		
S-ID.1	Represent data with plots on the real number line (dot plots, histograms, and box plots).	433–440, 441–448, 449–454
S-ID.2	Use statistics appropriate to the shape of the data distribution to compare center (median, mean) and spread (interquartile range, standard deviation) of two or more different data sets.	425–432, 433–440, 449–454
S-ID.3	Interpret differences in shape, center, and spread in the context of the data sets, accounting for possible effects of extreme data points (outliers).	433–440
Summarize, represent, and interpret data on two categorical and quantitative variables.		
S-ID.5	Summarize categorical data for two categories in two-way frequency tables. Interpret relative frequencies in the context of the data (including joint, marginal, and conditional relative frequencies). Recognize possible associations and trends in the data.	405–410, 411–418
S-ID.6	Represent data on two quantitative variables on a scatter plot, and describe how the variables are related. **a.** Fit a function to the data; use functions fitted to data to solve problems in the context of the data. **b.** Informally assess the fit of a function by plotting and analyzing residuals. **c.** Fit a linear function for a scatter plot that suggests a linear association.	241–248, 249–256, 257–264, 375–380, 385

Standard	Descriptor	Citations
Interpret linear models.		
S-ID.7	Interpret the slope (rate of change) and the intercept (constant term) of a linear model in the context of the data.	**249–256, 257–264**
S-ID.8	Compute (using technology) and interpret the correlation coefficient of a linear fit.	**241–248, 257–264**
S-ID.9	Distinguish between correlation and causation.	**241–248**

MATHEMATICAL PRACTICES

Standard	Descriptor	Citations
MP MATHEMATICAL PRACTICES STANDARDS		
MP.1	**Make sense of problems and persevere in solving them.** Mathematically proficient students start by explaining to themselves the meaning of a problem and looking for entry points to its solution. They analyze givens, constraints, relationships, and goals. They make conjectures about the form and meaning of the solution and plan a solution pathway rather than simply jumping into a solution attempt. They consider analogous problems, and try special cases and simpler forms of the original problem in order to gain insight into its solution. They monitor and evaluate their progress and change course if necessary. Older students might, depending on the context of the problem, transform algebraic expressions or change the viewing window on their graphing calculator to get the information they need. Mathematically proficient students can explain correspondences between equations, verbal descriptions, tables, and graphs or draw diagrams of important features and relationships, graph data, and search for regularity or trends. Younger students might rely on using concrete objects or pictures to help conceptualize and solve a problem. Mathematically proficient students check their answers to problems using a different method, and they continually ask themselves, "Does this make sense?" They can understand the approaches of others to solving complex problems and identify correspondences between different approaches.	***This standard is integrated throughout the book. See, for example:*** **88, 170, 185, 225–226, 233, 388, 425–429**
MP.2	**Reason abstractly and quantitatively.** Mathematically proficient students make sense of quantities and their relationships in problem situations. They bring two complementary abilities to bear on problems involving quantitative relationships: the ability to *decontextualize*—to abstract a given situation and represent it symbolically and manipulate the representing symbols as if they have a life of their own, without necessarily attending to their referents—and the ability to *contextualize*, to pause as needed during the manipulation process in order to probe into the referents for the symbols involved. Quantitative reasoning entails habits of creating a coherent representation of the problem at hand; considering the units involved; attending to the meaning of quantities, not just how to compute them; and knowing and flexibly using different properties of operations and objects.	***This standard is integrated throughout the book. See, for example:*** **162, 186, 226, 256, 286, 554–555, 558**

Standard	Descriptor	Citations
MP.3	**Construct viable arguments and critique the reasoning of others.** Mathematically proficient students understand and use stated assumptions, definitions, and previously established results in constructing arguments. They make conjectures and build a logical progression of statements to explore the truth of their conjectures. They are able to analyze situations by breaking them into cases, and can recognize and use counterexamples. They justify their conclusions, communicate them to others, and respond to the arguments of others. They reason inductively about data, making plausible arguments that take into account the context from which the data arose. Mathematically proficient students are also able to compare the effectiveness of two plausible arguments, distinguish correct logic or reasoning from that which is flawed, and—if there is a flaw in an argument—explain what it is. Elementary students can construct arguments using concrete referents such as objects, drawings, diagrams, and actions. Such arguments can make sense and be correct, even though they are not generalized or made formal until later grades. Later, students learn to determine domains to which an argument applies. Students at all grades can listen or read the arguments of others, decide whether they make sense, and ask useful questions to clarify or improve the arguments. **Students build proofs by induction and proofs by contradiction. CA 3.1**	***This standard is integrated throughout the book. See, for example:*** **206, 234, 367, 528, 531–532, 547, 552, 584, 589**
MP.4	**Model with mathematics.** Mathematically proficient students can apply the mathematics they know to solve problems arising in everyday life, society, and the workplace. In early grades, this might be as simple as writing an addition equation to describe a situation. In middle grades, a student might apply proportional reasoning to plan a school event or analyze a problem in the community. By high school, a student might use geometry to solve a design problem or use a function to describe how one quantity of interest depends on another. Mathematically proficient students who can apply what they know are comfortable making assumptions and approximations to simplify a complicated situation, realizing that these may need revision later. They are able to identify important quantities in a practical situation and map their relationships using such tools as diagrams, two-way tables, graphs, flowcharts and formulas. They can analyze those relationships mathematically to draw conclusions. They routinely interpret their mathematical results in the context of the situation and reflect on whether the results make sense, possibly improving the model if it has not served its purpose.	***This standard is integrated throughout the book. See, for example:*** **84, 87–88, 107, 199, 278, 285**
MP.5	**Use appropriate tools strategically.** Mathematically proficient students consider the available tools when solving a mathematical problem. These tools might include pencil and paper, concrete models, a ruler, a protractor, a calculator, a spreadsheet, a computer algebra system, a statistical package, or dynamic geometry software. Proficient students are sufficiently familiar with tools appropriate for their grade or course to make sound decisions about when each of these tools might be helpful, recognizing both the insight to be gained and their limitations. For example, mathematically proficient high school students analyze graphs of functions and solutions generated using a graphing calculator. They detect possible errors by strategically using estimation and other mathematical knowledge. When making mathematical models, they know that technology can enable them to visualize the results of varying assumptions, explore consequences, and compare predictions with data. Mathematically proficient students at various grade levels are able to identify relevant external mathematical resources, such as digital content located on a website, and use them to pose or solve problems. They are able to use technological tools to explore and deepen their understanding of concepts.	***This standard is integrated throughout the book. See, for example:*** **15, 66–68, 163–167, 178, 193–197, 263, 440, 447, 479, 485, 487, 511, 565**

Standard	Descriptor	Citations
MP.6	**Attend to precision.** Mathematically proficient students try to communicate precisely to others. They try to use clear definitions in discussion with others and in their own reasoning. They state the meaning of the symbols they choose, including using the equal sign consistently and appropriately. They are careful about specifying units of measure, and labeling axes to clarify the correspondence with quantities in a problem. They calculate accurately and efficiently, express numerical answers with a degree of precision appropriate for the problem context. In the elementary grades, students give carefully formulated explanations to each other. By the time they reach high school they have learned to examine claims and make explicit use of definitions.	***This standard is integrated throughout the book. See, for example:*** **7–10, 14, 16, 22, 256, 277, 473–474, 476–477, 607, 614**
MP.7	**Look for and make use of structure.** Mathematically proficient students look closely to discern a pattern or structure. Young students, for example, might notice that three and seven more is the same amount as seven and three more, or they may sort a collection of shapes according to how many sides the shapes have. Later, students will see 7×8 equals the well-remembered $7 \times 5 + 7 \times 3$, in preparation for learning about the distributive property. In the expression $x^2 + 9x + 14$, older students can see the 14 as 2×7 and the 9 as $2 + 7$. They recognize the significance of an existing line in a geometric figure and can use the strategy of drawing an auxiliary line for solving problems. They also can step back for an overview and shift perspective. They can see complicated things, such as some algebraic expressions, as single objects or as being composed of several objects. For example, they can see $5 - 3(x - y)^2$ as 5 minus a positive number times a square and use that to realize that its value cannot be more than 5 for any real numbers x and y.	***This standard is integrated throughout the book. See, for example:*** **30, 170, 218, 248, 355, 360, 497, 540, 545–546, 622, 623, 630**
MP.8	**Look for and express regularity in repeated reasoning.** Mathematically proficient students notice if calculations are repeated, and look both for general methods and for shortcuts. Upper elementary students might notice when dividing 25 by 11 that they are repeating the same calculations over and over again, and conclude they have a repeating decimal. By paying attention to the calculation of slope as they repeatedly check whether points are on the line through $(1, 2)$ with slope 3, middle school students might abstract the equation $(y - 2)/(x - 1) = 3$. Noticing the regularity in the way terms cancel when expanding $(x - 1)(x + 1)$, $(x - 1)(x^2 + x + 1)$, and $(x - 1)(x^3 + x^2 + x + 1)$ might lead them to the general formula for the sum of a geometric series. As they work to solve a problem, mathematically proficient students maintain oversight of the process, while attending to the details. They continually evaluate the reasonableness of their intermediate results.	***This standard is integrated throughout the book. See, for example:*** **36–38, 40, 114, 178, 338, 353–354, 387**

Succeeding with HMH California Integrated Math 1

Actively participate in your learning with your write-in Student Edition. Explore concepts, take notes, answer questions, and complete your homework right in your textbook!

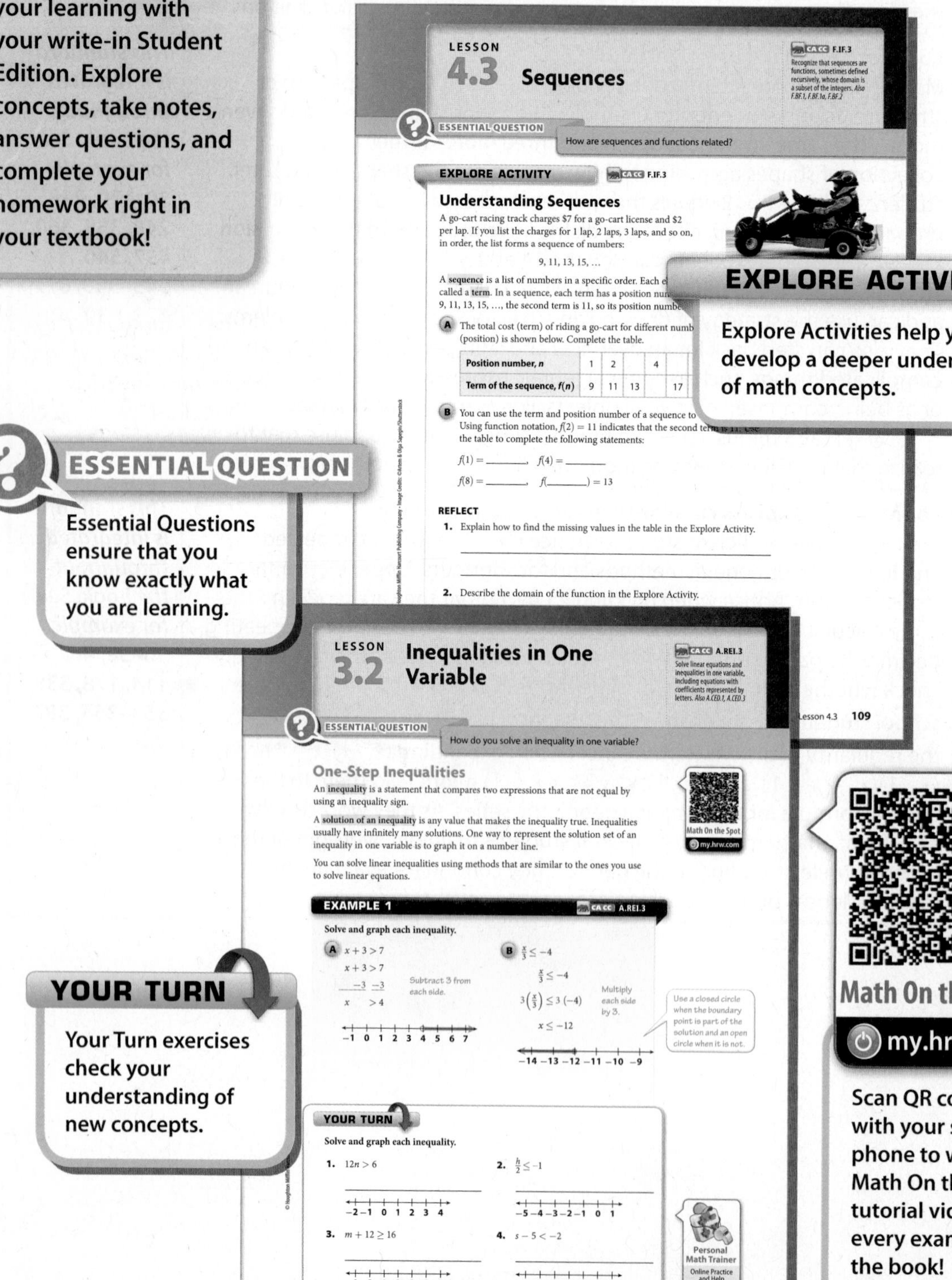

EXPLORE ACTIVITY Real World

Explore Activities help you develop a deeper understanding of math concepts.

ESSENTIAL QUESTION

Essential Questions ensure that you know exactly what you are learning.

YOUR TURN

Your Turn exercises check your understanding of new concepts.

Math On the Spot

my.hrw.com

Scan QR codes with your smart phone to watch Math On the Spot tutorial videos for every example in the book!

Unit Project CA CC F.LE.2, F.BF.1a, F.LE.5

Bank On It

An investor has $5000 to invest for 10 years in one of the banks listed below. Each bank offers an interest rate that is compounded annually.

Bank	Principal	Years	Balance
Super Save	$1000	6	$1173.34
Star Financial	$2500	3	$2684.35
	$4000	5	$4525.63

MATH IN CAREERS ACTIVITY

Statistician When researching data concerning caribou populations in the Arctic, Lee uncovered some archives of old caribou populations, shown in the first two columns of the table. Use a graphing calculator to find an exponential function that models the data. Complete the table and use the data to make an inference about the accuracy of the model.

396 Unit 3B

Unit Project

Apply new skills and concepts to solve real-world problems in Unit Projects and Math in Careers activities.

Reading **Start-Up**

Visualize Vocabulary

Use the review words to complete the case diagram. Write an example for each oval.

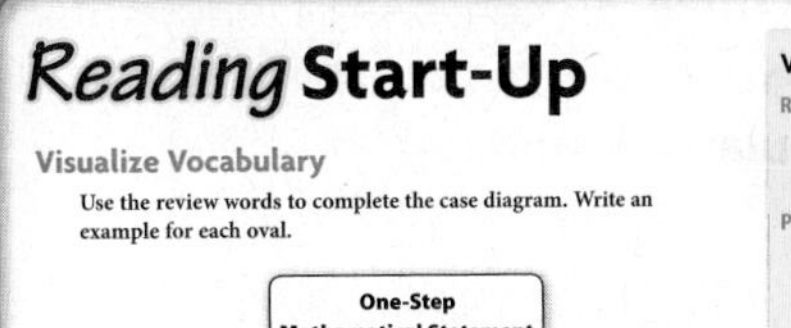

One-Step Mathematical Statement

Vocabulary

Review Words

one-step equation

one-step inequality

Preview Words

equivalent equations

formula

identity

literal equation

solution of an equation

Understand Vocabulary

To become familiar with some of the vocabulary ... the following. You may refer to the module, the g...

1. One definition of identity is "exact sameness." An e... expressions. If an equation is an *identity*, what do you think is true about the expressions?

2. The word *literal* means "of letters." How might a literal equation be different from an equation like $3 + 5 = 8$?

Active Reading

... Before beginning the module, create a ... help you organize what you learn about ...ties. Organize the characteristics of the ... for easy comparison.

Module 3 63

Reading Start-Up

Get vocabulary, language, and note-taking support throughout the book.

UNIT 3A MIXED REVIEW

Assessment Readiness

Personal Math Trainer — my.hrw.com Online Practice and Help

1. Consider each linear function. Does the function have a greater y-intercept than the linear function represented in the table?

x	$f(x)$
2	10
4	18
6	26
8	34

Select Yes or No.

A. $g(x) = 2x + 3$ ○ Yes ○ No

B. $g(x) = 1 + 5x$ ○ Yes ○ No

C. $g(x) = -4(x - 1)$ ○ Yes ○ No

2. The table shows how the price of apples at a store has changed over the past 6 months.

Month, x	Price per pound ($), y
1	1.69
2	1.79
3	1.50
4	1.38
5	1.3[illegible]
6	1.3[illegible]

Choose True or False for each statement.

A. A scatter plot of the data shows a negative correlation. ○ True ○ False

B. The correlation coefficient for the data is closer to 1 than to 0. ○ True ○ False

C. The y-intercept of the best line of fit is greater than 1.50. ○ True ○ False

3. Adult tickets to a play cost $20.50, and student tickets cost $16.00. Ms. Powers can spend no more than $120.00 on tickets. If she buys 3 student tickets, how many adult tickets is she able to buy? Use a linear inequality in two variables to explain your reasoning.

4. A hobby pack of baseball cards contains 9 cards, and a jumbo pack contains 35 cards. Ethan bought 7 packs for a total of 141 cards. Write and solve a syst... of equations to find the number of each type of pack that he bought. State a... justify your solution method.

Performance Tasks

★5. A store rents backpacks and sleeping bags. Backpack rental costs $0.88 per day, plus an initial fee of $24.84. Sleeping bag rental costs are shown in the table. Write the function $f(x)$ to represent the cost of renting both a backpack and a sleeping bag for x days. Explain how you determined your answer.

Sleeping Bag Rental	
Time (days)	Cost ($)
3	18.28
6	20.65
9	23.02

★★6. The table shows data for 6 gas-engine cars.

a. Make a scatter plot of the data in the table.

b. Write an equation of a line of fit for the data.

c. Tell what the slope of the line of fit represents.

d. Predict the mileage for a car that weighs 3000 lb. Justify your reasoning.

3295	27

★★★7. Rita and Chris are making patterns out of tiles. The first 4 figures in each of their patterns is shown. Continuing these patterns, is there a figure for which the number of tiles in Rita's figure will be the same as the number of tiles in Chris's figure? If so, what is the figure number, and how many tiles will be in each figure? Explain.

Rita's Pattern

Chris's Pattern

Assessment Readiness

Prepare for new high-stakes tests with SBAC-aligned practice items and Performance Tasks.

Enhance Your Learning!

...t Edition provides additional ...media resources to enhance your learning. You can write in answers, take notes, watch videos, explore concepts with virtual manipulatives, and get homework help!

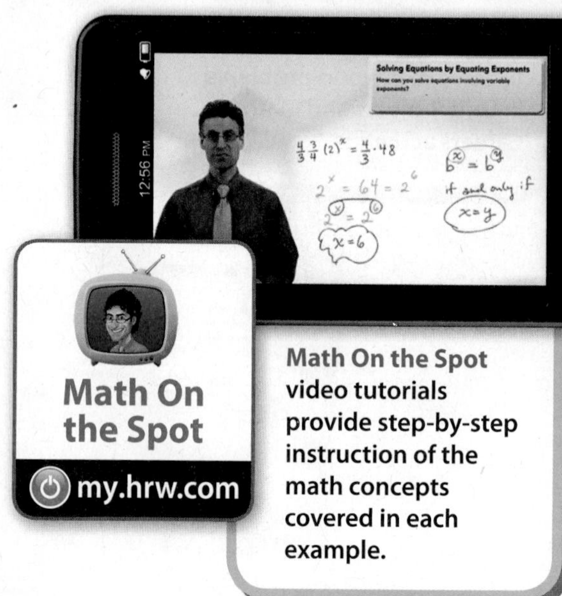

Math On the Spot video tutorials provide step-by-step instruction of the math concepts covered in each example.

Real-World Videos show you how specific math topics can be used in all kinds of situations.

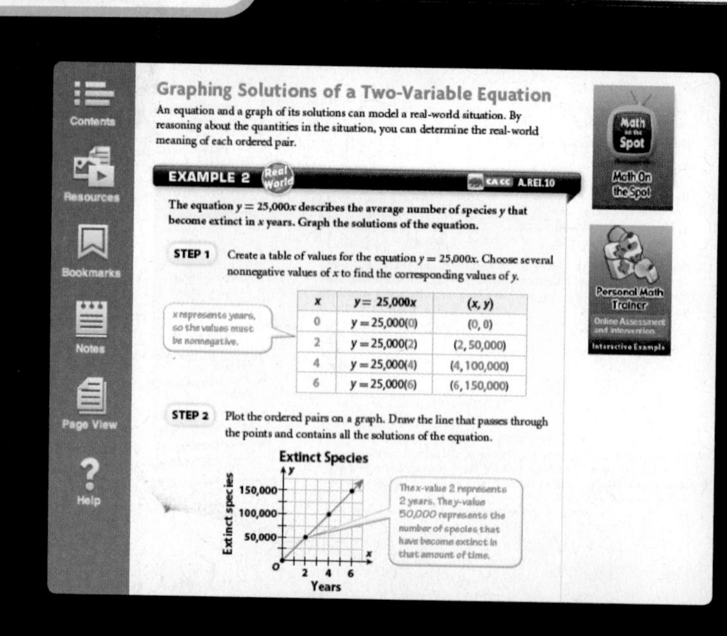

Contents
Resources
Bookmarks
Notes
Page View
Help
Graphing Solutions of a Two-Variable Equation
An equation and a graph of its solutions can model a real-world situation. By reasoning about the quantities in the situation, you can determine the real-world meaning of each ordered pair.
EXAMPLE 2
A.REI.10
The equation y = 25,000x describes the average number of species y that become extinct in x years. Graph the solutions of the equation.
STEP 1
Create a table of values for the equation y = 25,000x. Choose several nonnegative values of x to find the corresponding values of y.
STEP 2
Plot the ordered pairs on a graph. Draw the line that passes through the points and contains all the solutions of the equation.
Extinct Species
Years
Extinct species
Math On the Spot
Personal Math Trainer

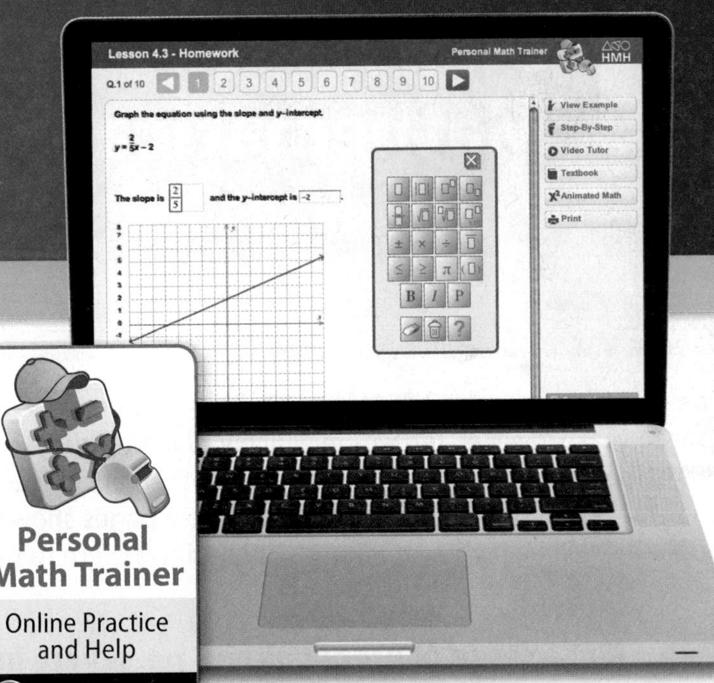

Personal Math Trainer lets you practice, take quizzes and tests, and get homework help with instant feedback!

Personal Math Trainer provides a variety of learning aids, including videos, guided examples, and step-by-step solutions, that develop and improve your understanding of math concepts.

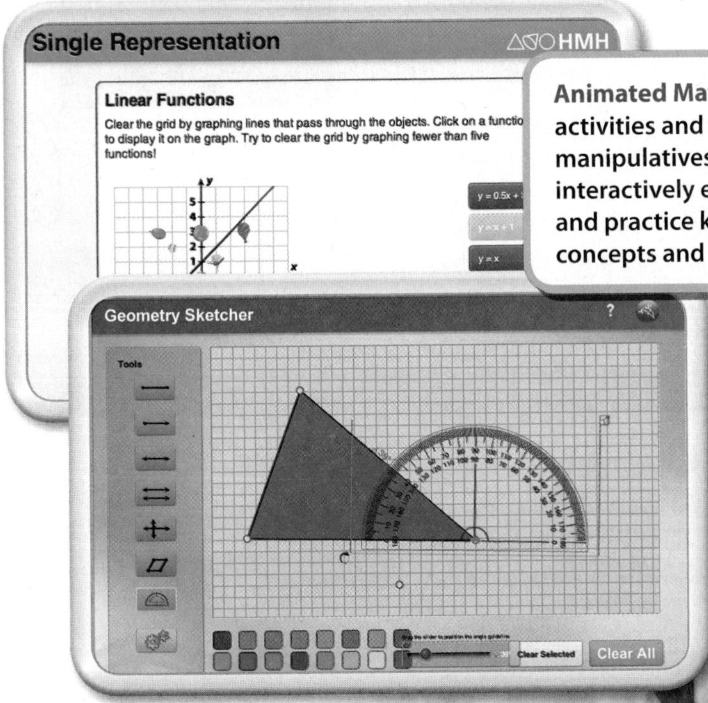

Personal Math Trainer

Online Practice and Help

my.hrw.com

Single Representation

Linear Functions

Clear the grid by graphing lines that pass through the objects. Click on a function to display it on the graph. Try to clear the grid by graphing fewer than five functions!

Geometry Sketcher

Animated Math activities and virtual manipulatives let you interactively explore and practice key math concepts and skills.

Animated Math

my.hrw.com

Standards for Mathematical Practice

The topics described in the Standards for Mathematical Content will vary from year to year. However, the *way* in which you learn, study, and think about mathematics will not. The Standards for Mathematical Practice describe skills that you will use in all of your math courses. These pages show some features of your book that will help you gain these skills and use them to master this year's topics.

MP.1 Make sense of problems and persevere in solving them.

Mathematically proficient students start by explaining to themselves the meaning of a problem… They analyze givens, constraints, relationships, and goals. They make conjectures about the form… of the solution and plan a solution pathway…

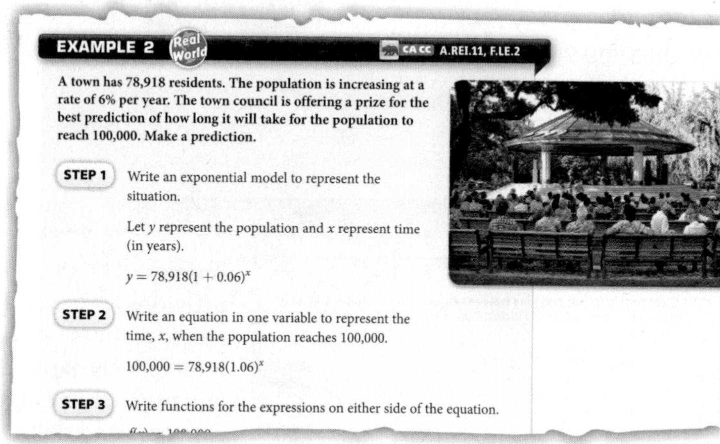

EXAMPLE 2 Real World CA CC A.REI.11, F.LE.2

A town has 78,918 residents. The population is increasing at a rate of 6% per year. The town council is offering a prize for the best prediction of how long it will take for the population to reach 100,000. Make a prediction.

STEP 1 Write an exponential model to represent the situation.

Let y represent the population and x represent time (in years).

$y = 78{,}918(1 + 0.06)^x$

STEP 2 Write an equation in one variable to represent the time, x, when the population reaches 100,000.

$100{,}000 = 78{,}918(1.06)^x$

STEP 3 Write functions for the expressions on either side of the equation.

Problem-solving examples and exercises lead students through problem-solving steps.

MP.2 Reason abstractly and quantitatively.

Mathematically proficient students… bring two complementary abilities to bear on problems…: the ability to decontextualize—to abstract a given situation and represent it symbolically… and the ability to contextualize, to pause… in order to probe into the referents for the symbols involved.

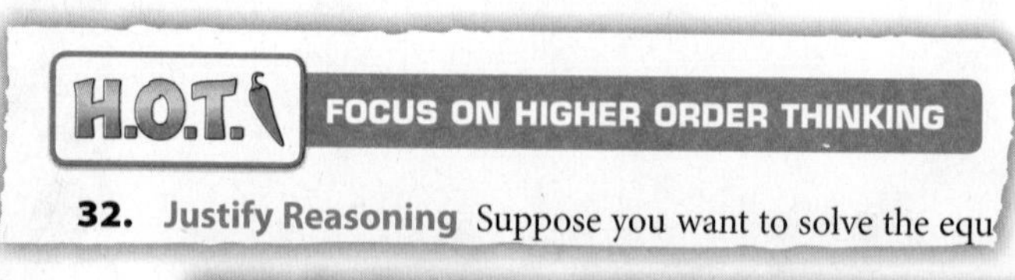

H.O.T. FOCUS ON HIGHER ORDER THINKING

32. Justify Reasoning Suppose you want to solve the equ

Unit Project CA CC F.BF.1a

Focus on Higher Order Thinking exercises in every lesson and a **Project** in every unit require you to use logical reasoning, represent situations symbolically, use mathematical models to solve problems, and state your answers in terms of a problem's context.

MP.3 Construct viable arguments and critique the reasoning of others.

Mathematically proficient students… justify their conclusions, [and]… distinguish correct… reasoning from that which is flawed.

REFLECT

5. **Make a Conjecture** Does multiplying both sides of an inequality by a negative number result in an equivalent inequality? Explain.

Essential Question Check-in and **Reflect** in every lesson ask you to evaluate statements, explain relationships, apply mathematical principles, make conjectures, construct arguments, and justify your reasoning.

MP.4 Model with mathematics.

Mathematically proficient students can apply… mathematics… to… problems… in everyday life, society, and the workplace.

EXAMPLE 2 Real World

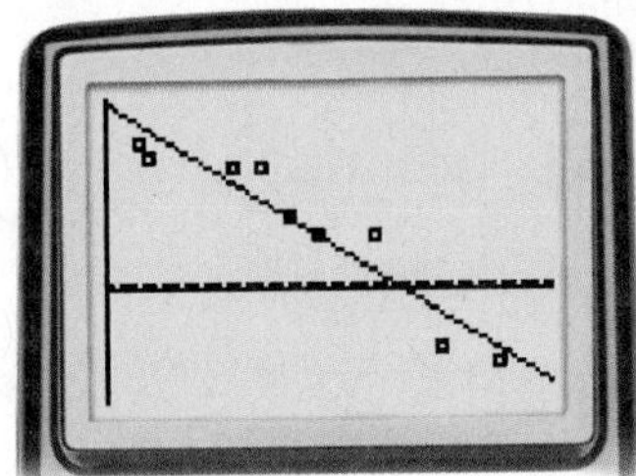

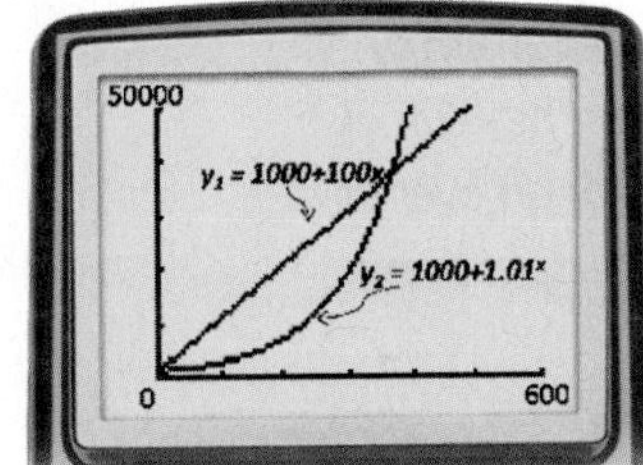

Real-world examples and **mathematical modeling** apply mathematics to other disciplines and real-world contexts such as science and business.

MP.5 Use appropriate tools strategically.

Mathematically proficient students consider the available tools when solving a… problem… [and] are… able to use technological tools to explore and deepen their understanding…

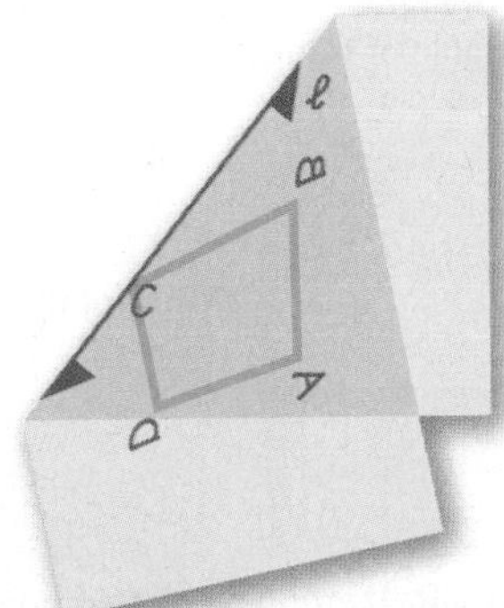

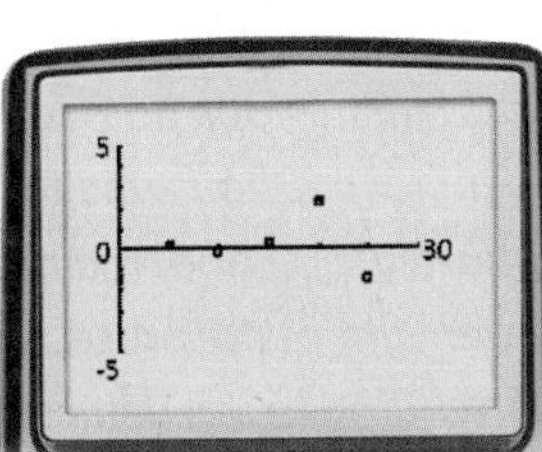

Exploration Activities in lessons use concrete and technological tools, such as manipulatives or graphing calculators, to explore mathematical concepts.

MP.6 Attend to precision.

Mathematically proficient students… communicate precisely… with others and in their own reasoning… [They] give carefully formulated explanations…

REFLECT

1. **Communicate Mathematical Ideas** Which parameter, *a* or *b*, rep the initial value of *y*? Explain how you know

Key Vocabulary

slope *(pendiente)*
The slope of a line is the ratio of rise to run for any two points on the line.

Precision refers not only to the correctness of calculations but also to the proper use of mathematical language and symbols. **Communicate Mathematical Ideas** exercises and **Key Vocabulary** highlighted for each module and unit help you learn and use the language of math to communicate mathematics precisely.

MP.7 Look for and make use of structure.

Mathematically proficient students… look closely to discern a pattern or structure… They can also step back for an overview and shift perspectives.

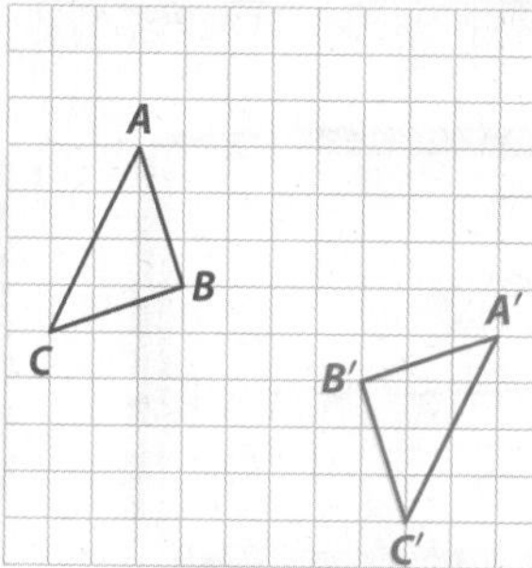

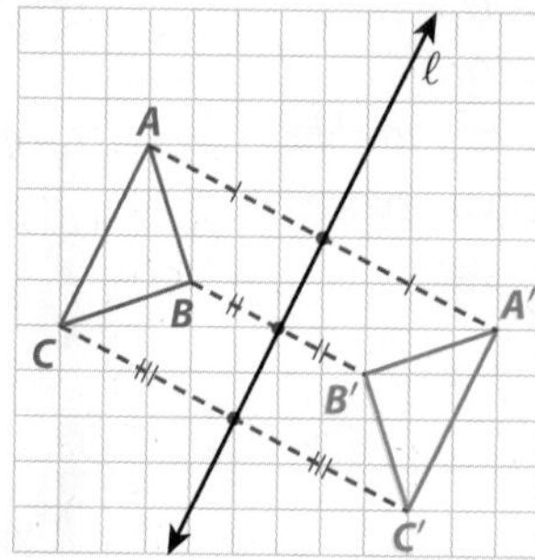

Throughout the lessons, you will observe regularity in mathematical structures in order to make generalizations and make connections between related problems. For example, you can use the structure of a coordinate grid to help locate a line of reflection.

MP.8 Look for and express regularity in repeated reasoning.

Mathematically proficient students… look both for general methods and for shortcuts… [and] maintain oversight of the process, while attending to the details.

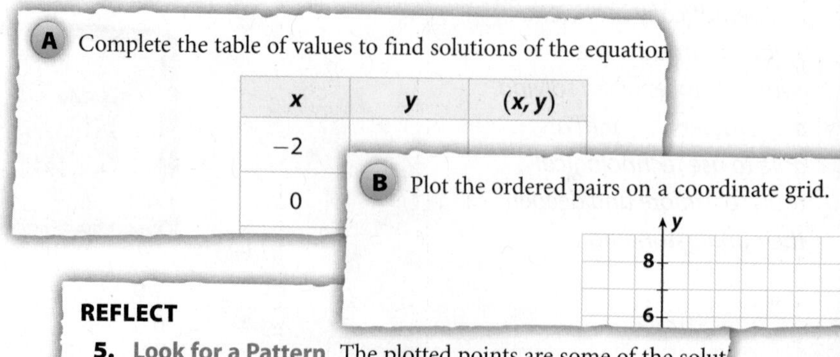

A Complete the table of values to find solutions of the equation

x	y	(x, y)
−2		
0		

B Plot the ordered pairs on a coordinate grid.

REFLECT

5. **Look for a Pattern** The plotted points are some of the solut equation. What appears to be true about them?

Examples in your book group similar types of problems together to allow you to look for patterns and make generalizations.

REVIEW OF GRADE 8 PART 1

Review Test

1. Evaluate $(3^{-4})^6$.

____

2. Simplify $-8\sqrt{-15 + 31}$.

____

3. A passenger plane travels at about 7.62×10^2 feet per second. The plane takes 1.23×10^4 seconds to reach its destination. About how far must the plane travel to reach its destination? Write your answer in scientific notation.

____

4. What linear function describes the relationship shown in the table?

x	$f(x)$
−5	25
−3	13
2	−17
3	−23

____

5. A remote-control airplane descends at a rate of 3 feet per second. After 6 seconds the plane is 89 feet above the ground. Which equation models this situation, and what is the height of the plane after 12 seconds?

____

____

6. Which of the following is a congruence transformation? Select Yes or No.

A. a dilation with scale factor 1

◯ Yes ◯ No

B. a reflection across the y-axis

◯ Yes ◯ No

C. a translation 5 units down

◯ Yes ◯ No

D. a dilation with scale factor 2

◯ Yes ◯ No

7. In the gift shop of the History of Flight museum, Elisa bought a kit to make a model of a jet airplane. The actual plane is 20 feet long with a wingspan of 16 feet. The finished model will be 15 inches long. What will be the wingspan of the model?

____

8. What is the value of n?

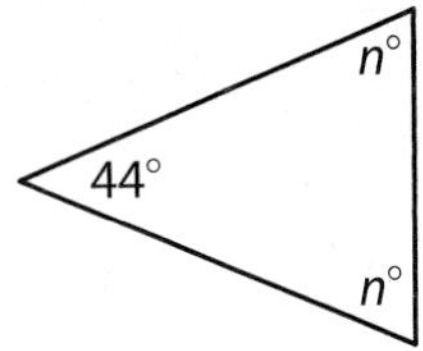

____

9. Melanie is making a piece of jewelry that is in the shape of a right triangle. The two shorter sides of the piece of jewelry are 12 mm and 9 mm. Find the perimeter of the piece of jewelry.

____

10. What is the distance, to the nearest tenth, from $S(4, -1)$ to $W(-2, 3)$?

____

11. Estimate $\sqrt{285}$ to the nearest hundredth.

____

12. Harry and Selma start driving from the same location. Harry drives 42 miles north while Selma drives 144 miles east. How far apart are Harry and Selma when they stop?

____

13. In Hannah's science report, she says that the average distance between the Sun and Earth is about 9.3×10^7 miles. Show how to write this number in standard notation.

____

14. A summer theater pass costs \$24.75. Every time the pass is used, \$2.75 is deducted from the balance. Write an equation to represent this situation.

____

15. Describe a possible situation that could be modeled by the graph.

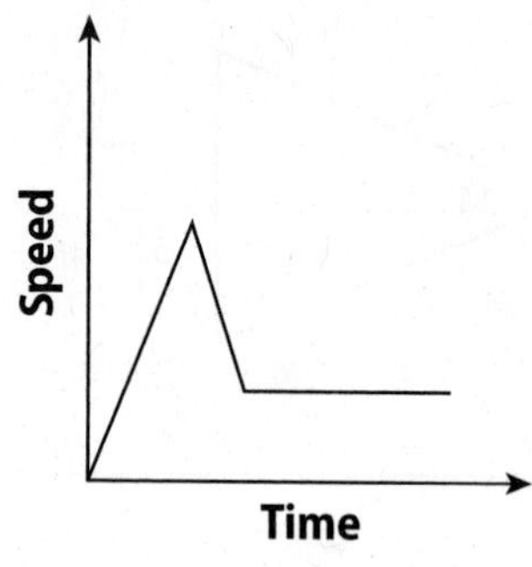

____

____

____

____

____

16. Dilate the figure by a scale factor of 1.5 with the origin as the center of dilation. Graph the new figure below with the original figure.

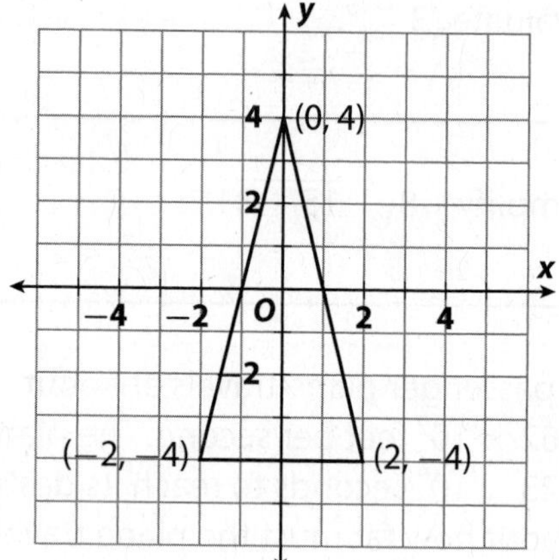

Performance Task

17. Does the following graph display a function? Explain.

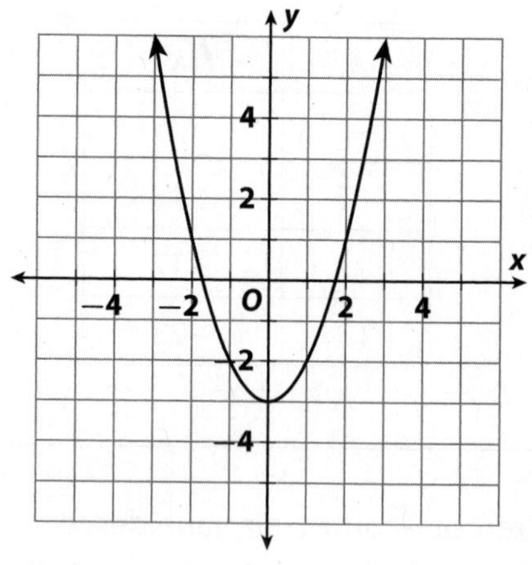

____

____

____

____

____

REVIEW OF GRADE 8 PART 2

Review Test

1. Write the equation, in slope-intercept form, of the line shown in the graph.

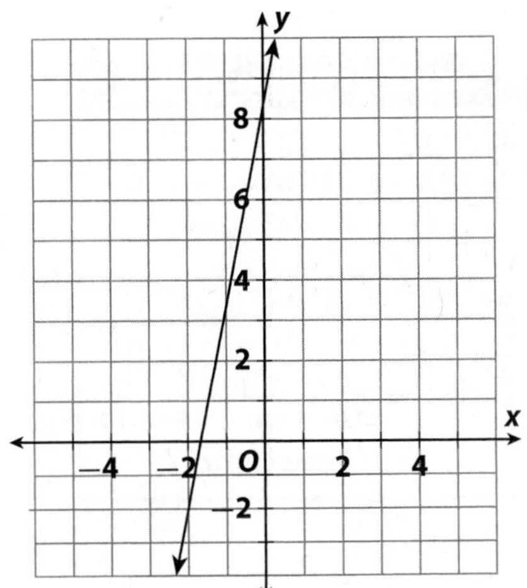

2. What is the solution of $-4c + 10 + 8c = 86$?

3. How many solutions does the equation $c + 2 = c - 2$ have?

4. What is the solution of the system of equations?

$$\begin{cases} y = 3x + 1 \\ y = 5x - 3 \end{cases}$$

5. A bicyclist heads east at 18 km/h. After she has traveled 19.2 kilometers, another cyclist sets out from the same starting point in the same direction going 30 km/h. How long will it take the second cyclist to catch up to the first cyclist?

6. Which of these functions is a linear function? Select Yes or No.

A. $f(x) = 3 - \frac{x}{3}$
◯ Yes ◯ No

B. $f(x) = 3^x + 4$
◯ Yes ◯ No

C. $f(x) = 3^3 - 3x$
◯ Yes ◯ No

D. $f(x) = 3(4 - x) + 3$
◯ Yes ◯ No

7. Which function has the greatest rate of change? Explain.

- $y = 11x - 8$
- A fitness club charges a $200 membership fee plus monthly fees of $25.
- $y = -8x$
- $\{(-1, -2), (1, 2), (3, 6), (5, 10), (7, 14)\}$

8. You buy hats for $12 and sell them for $8 each. Describe the graph of the profits. Is it a line or a curve? Does it go up or down?

9. An artist is creating a large conical sculpture for a park. The cone has a height of 19 feet and a diameter of 28 feet. What is the volume of the sculpture to the nearest hundredth?

10. A cylindrical barrel has a radius of 4.2 meters and a height of 3 meters. Tripling which dimension(s) will triple the volume of the barrel? Select Yes or No.

A. height

○ Yes ○ No

B. radius

○ Yes ○ No

C. diameter

○ Yes ○ No

11. What linear equation best models the data in the scatter plot? Write your answer in $y = mx + b$ form, and round m and b to the nearest integer.

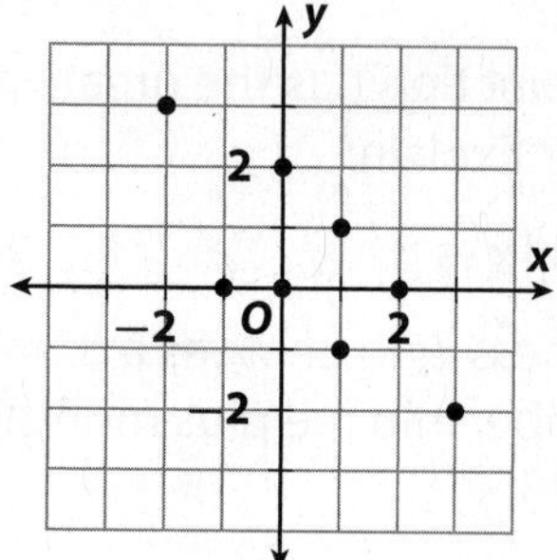

____

12. Write a function that converts x days to y hours.

____

13. Solve $h - 8 = 3h + 3$.

____

14. Solve the system using any method.

$$\begin{cases} 2x - 5y = -22 \\ x + 3y = 11 \end{cases}$$

____

15. Rewrite the equation $2y + 3x = 4$ in slope-intercept form. Then find the slope and y-intercept.

____

16. Find the slope of the line that passes through the points $(-3, 6)$ and $(4, 2)$.

____

17. Describe the correlation in the scatter plot and explain what it means in the given situation.

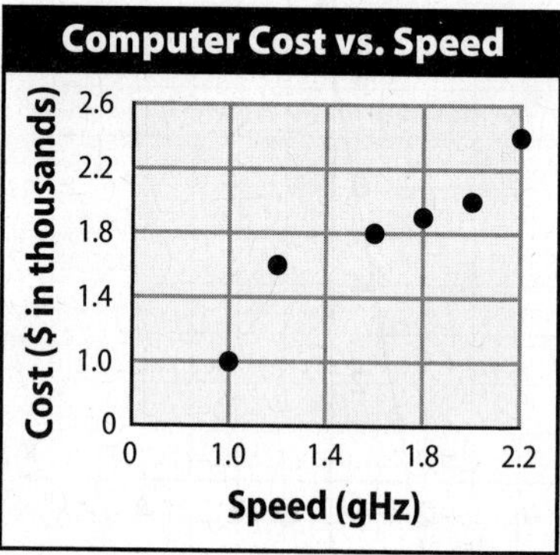

____

____

Performance Task

18. Use the graph to identify the slope and y-intercept. Then explain what each means in the context of the problem.

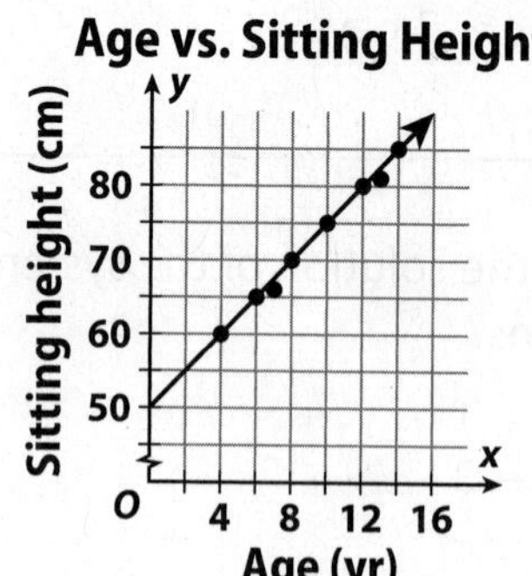

____

____

____

____

MATHEMATICS I PART 1

Benchmark Test

1. A movie theater charges $8.50 for a ticket. To help the local animal shelter, the theater agrees to reduce the price of each ticket by $0.50 for every can of pet food a customer donates. Write an equation that gives the ticket cost y for a customer who contributes x cans.

____

____

2. The population of a Midwestern suburb is growing exponentially. The chart shows its population for four consecutive years. Write a rule that gives the population P_n after n years. Use $n = 1$ to represent Year 1.

Year	Year 1	Year 2	Year 3	Year 4
Population	6500	7800	9360	11,232

____

____

3. Ticket sales for the first 5 nights of a new play form the sequence 400, 399, 396, 387, 360, ... If this pattern continues, what rule gives the number of tickets sold on the nth night?

____

____

4. Write each system of linear inequalities that is graphed.

A.

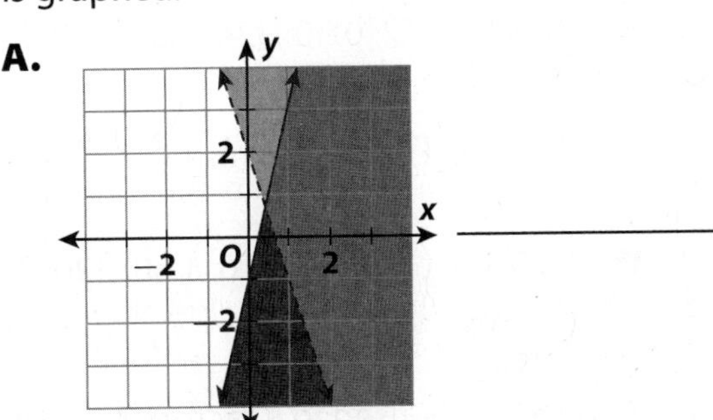

____

B.

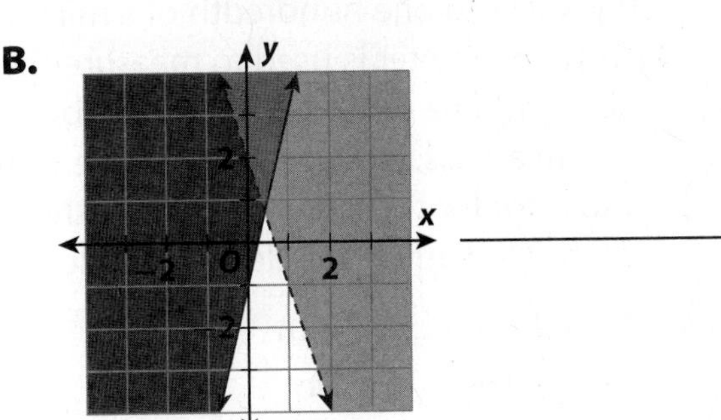

____

C.

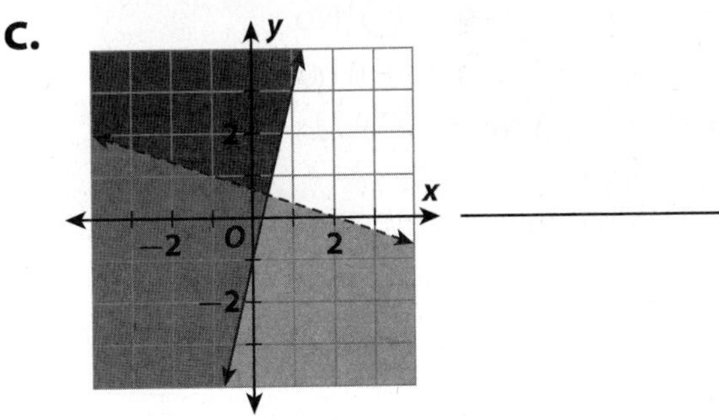

____

D.

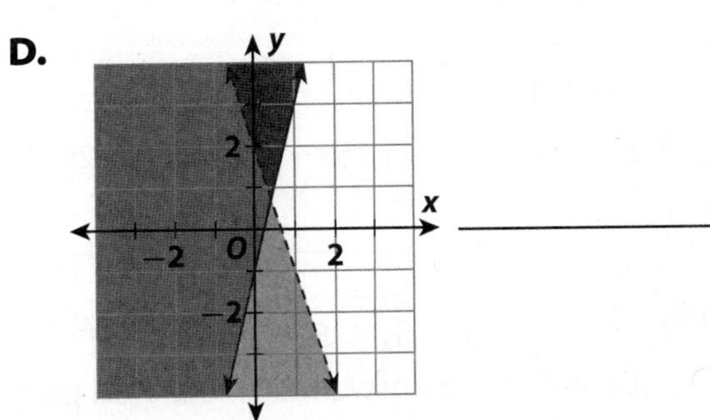

____

5. Do the points represent a price that increases at a constant rate per ounce for ordered pairs in the form (ounces, price)? Select Yes or No.

A. (8, 0.50), (12, 1.00), (24, 1.50), (32, 2.00)
○ Yes ○ No

B. (8, 0.60), (12, 0.90), (24, 1.80), (32, 2.40)
○ Yes ○ No

C. (8, 0.80), (12, 1.20), (16, 1.60), (20, 2.00)
○ Yes ○ No

D. (8, 0.40), (12, 0.80), (16, 1.60), (20, 3.20)
○ Yes ○ No

6. A micrometer used in a factory measures thickness to one hundredth of a millimeter. This micrometer is used to measure the diameter of a ball bearing that is about 1.7 cm across. What is a reasonable value and error for the measurement of the bearing's diameter? Select Yes or No.

A. 2.25 cm $\pm$ 0.05 cm
○ Yes ○ No

B. 1.715 cm $\pm$ 0.005 cm
○ Yes ○ No

C. 1.6713 cm $\pm$ 0.0005 cm
○ Yes ○ No

7. How many terms are in the algebraic expression $2x - 9xy + 17y$?

____

8. Solve $y = \frac{5}{8}b + 10$ for b.

____

9. Solve $-0.25 + 1.75x < -1.75 + 2.25x$.

____

10. Solve $\begin{cases} -7x + 5y = -5 \\ -9x + 5y = 5 \end{cases}$ by elimination.

Express your answer as an ordered pair.

____

11. Write an exponential function to model a population of 390 animals that decreases at an annual rate of 11%. Then estimate the value of the function after 5 years (to the nearest whole number).

____

Performance Task

12. Kristi rides her bike to school and has an odometer that measures the distance traveled so far. She subtracts this distance from the distance to the school and records the distance that remains. What are the intercepts of the function represented by the table? What do the intercepts represent?

Time traveled (min)	Distance remaining (ft)
0	5000
2	3750
4	2500
6	1250
8	0

____

____

____

____

____

____

____

____

MATHEMATICS I PART 2

Benchmark Test

1. Aaron won \$500 in an essay contest. He invests the money in an interest-earning account. The table shows how much money he has in the account. Find an appropriate model for the amount that Aaron will have in the account after t years. Then, use the model to predict approximately when Aaron will have \$1000 in the account.

Aaron's Account	
Year	**Value**
1	\$520.00
2	\$540.80
3	\$562.43
4	\$584.93
5	\$608.33

2. How could you translate the graph of $y = -x^2$ to produce the graph of $y = -x^2 - 4$?

3. Draw the image of $\triangle ABC$ after a reflection across line ℓ followed by a 180° rotation around point P.

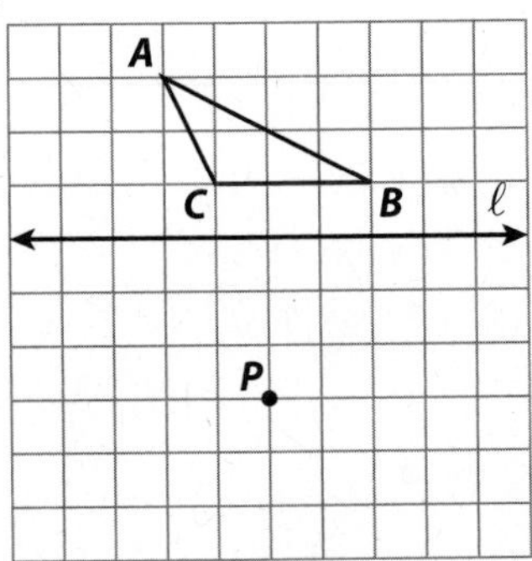

4. Explain whether $p + 4r^2$ will be positive or negative if p is positive. Is this always true?

5. Look for a pattern in the data set. Which kind of model better describes the data, exponential or linear?

Population Growth of Bacteria	
Time (hours)	**Number of bacteria**
0	2000
1	5000
2	12,500
3	31,250
4	78,125

6. A computer animation artist wants to rotate a design in the shape of a regular pentagon less than 360° so that it maps onto itself. What is the least rotation the artist can use? Explain.

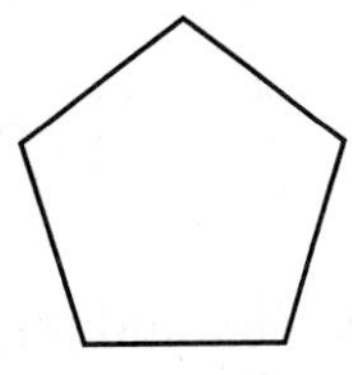

7. The data set shown by the box-and-whisker plot includes a single outlier and no duplicate data values.

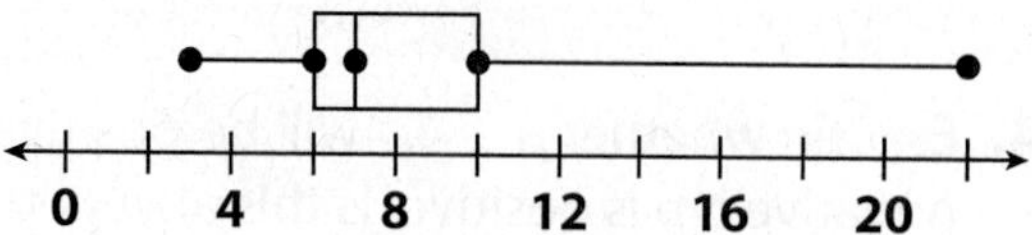

The outlier is removed. Select True or False for each statement.

A. The interquartile range increases.
○ True ○ False

B. The interquartile range decreases.
○ True ○ False

C. The range increases.
○ True ○ False

D. The range decreases.
○ True ○ False

8. What is the coefficient of x in the expression $(5a)x - 17x^2 + 14a$?

____

9. Consider the following box plots.

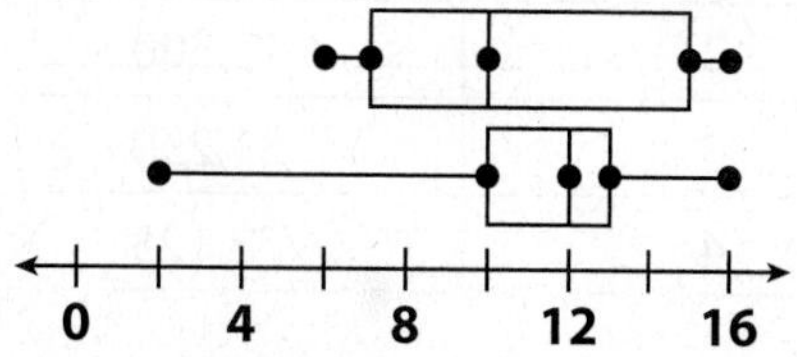

Which data set has the greater median? Which has the greater interquartile range?

____

10. Find the perimeter and area of $\triangle JKL$ with vertices $J(-10, 2)$, $K(-2, -8)$, and $L(3, -4)$.

____

Performance Task

11. The PGA tour is for male professional golfers; the LPGA tour is for female professional golfers. The top-rated golfer on each tour has a rank of 1. As a golfer's rating decreases, his or her rank increases, so that a golfer with a rank of 50 has a much lower rating than a golfer with a rank of 1. Earnings for the 50 top-rated golfers on each tour in 2010 are modeled by the functions in the table and the graph. Compare earnings as a function of rank for the PGA and the LPGA.

PGA Earnings, 2010

Rank	Millions of $
1	4.95
10	3.53
20	2.87
30	2.41
40	1.88
50	1.61

____

Numbers and Expressions

MODULE 1

Relationships Between Quantities

CA CC N.Q.1, N.Q.3

MODULE 2

Expressions

CA CC N.Q.1, N.Q.2, A.SSE.1, A.SSE.1a, A.SSE.1b

MATH IN CAREERS

Cave Geologist A cave geologist uses math from algebra and geometry up through higher-level math to study caves, find resources in them, or organize their excavation. He or she uses math for statistical analysis of the data he or she gathers.

If you're interested in a career in cave geology, you should study these mathematical subjects:

- Algebra
- Geometry
- Statistics
- Calculus

Research other careers that require the use of geometry and statistics.

ACTIVITY At the end of the unit, check out how **cave geologists** use math.

Unit Project Preview

Prices at the Pump

The Unit Project at the end of this unit will ask you to calculate and compare costs of gas at a gas station. You will collect data from a gasoline purchase. To successfully complete the Unit Project you'll need to master these skills:

- Understand precision and rounding.
- Understand and use real numbers.
- Write and evaluate expressions.

1. If the price showing on the pump is \$3.799, what is the price per gallon to the nearest cent?

____

2. If you bought 14.580 gallons, describe how the cost \$55.39 was calculated.

____

____

____

____

Tracking Your Learning Progression

This unit addresses important California Common Core Standards in the Critical Areas of writing and interpreting expressions and using units of measurement correctly when reporting results and performing calculations.

Domain A.SSE Seeing Structure in Expressions

Cluster Interpret the structure of expressions.

The unit also supports additional standards.

Domain N.Q Quantities

Cluster Reason quantitatively and use units to solve problems.

Relationships Between Quantities

MODULE 1

CALIFORNIA COMMON CORE

LESSON 1.1
Precision and Significant Digits

N.Q.3

LESSON 1.2
Dimensional Analysis

CA CC N.Q.1, N.Q.3

ESSENTIAL QUESTION

How do you calculate when the numbers are measurements?

Real-World Video

my.hrw.com

In order to function properly and safely, electronics must be manufactured to a high degree of accuracy. Material tolerances and component alignment must be precisely matched in order to not interfere with each other.

GO DIGITAL
my.hrw.com

my.hrw.com

Go digital with your write-in student edition, accessible on any device.

Math On the Spot

Scan with your smart phone to jump directly to the online edition, video tutor, and more.

Animated Math

Interactively explore key concepts to see how math works.

Personal Math Trainer

Get immediate feedback and help as you work through practice sets.

Are YOU Ready?

Complete these exercises to review skills you will need for this module.

Personal Math Trainer
my.hrw.com
Online Practice and Help

Rounding and Estimation

EXAMPLE Round 25.35 to the nearest whole number.

25.35 *Locate the digit to the right of the whole number.*

25 *Because it is not 5 or greater, do not round up the whole number.*

Round to the place value in parentheses.

1. 3.24 (tenths) ________ **2.** 0.51 (ones) ________ **3.** 35.8 (tens) ________

Compare and Order Real Numbers

EXAMPLE Compare 2.11 to 2.02.

2.11 *Align the numbers at the decimal point.*

2.02 *Compare each place value from left to right.*

2.11 > 2.02 *Because 1 > 0*

Compare. Write <, >, or =.

4. 3.01 ◯ 4 **5.** 80.2 ◯ 8.03 **6.** 9.001 ◯ 9.010

7. 1.11 ◯ 1.01 **8.** 3.2 ◯ 3.2 **9.** 0.154 ◯ 0.145

Measure with Customary and Metric Units

EXAMPLE Measure the line segment in inches and in centimeters.

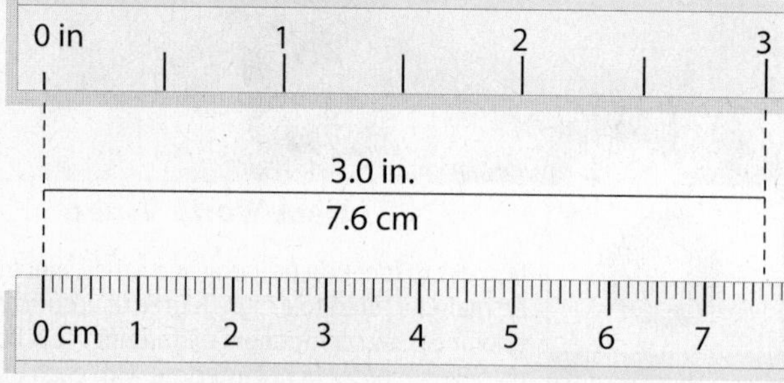

Measure from end to end, starting at 0.

Remember that metric rulers are divided into tens, but customary rulers are not.

Measure each item to the unit in parentheses.

10. the length of your foot (inches) ________________

11. the width of your index finger (millimeters) ________________

12. the height of your desk chair (feet) ________________

Reading Start-Up

Visualize Vocabulary

Use the review words to complete the bubble map. You may put more than one word in each bubble.

Systems of Measurement

- values are related by a base-ten system
- values are related by varying amounts

Vocabulary

Review Words

- customary system of measurement *(sistema usual de medidas)*
- decimal system *(sistema decimal)*
- metric system of measurement *(sistema métrico de medidas)*

Preview Words

- conversion factor
- dimensional analysis
- precision
- significant digits

Understand Vocabulary

Complete the sentences using the preview words. You may refer to the module, the glossary, or a dictionary.

1. The level of detail of a measurement, determined by the unit of measure, is ___________________.
2. ___________________ are the digits used to express the precision of a measurement.
3. ___________________ is a method of determining the proper units in an algebraic solution.
4. The ratio of two equal quantities in different units is a ___________________.

Active Reading

Layered Book Before beginning the module, create a Layered Book for taking notes as you read a chapter. Use two flaps for each lesson from this module. As you study each lesson, write important ideas such as vocabulary, properties, and formulas under the appropriate flap.

GETTING READY FOR

Relationships Between Quantities

Understanding the standards and the vocabulary terms in the standards will help you know exactly what you are expected to learn in this module.

 **CA CC N.Q.3**

Choose a level of accuracy appropriate to limitations on measurement when reporting quantities.

What It Means to You

You will learn to use precision and significant digits when calculating with measurements.

EXAMPLE N.Q.3

Which is the more precise measurement: 5.7 m or 568 cm?
Which measurement uses more significant digits: 5.7 m or 568 cm?

	Precision	Significant Digits
5.7 m	5.7 m = 570 cm is measured to nearest *ten* centimeters.	5.7 has 2 significant digits.
568 cm	568 cm is measured to the nearest centimeter.	568 has 3 significant digits.

568 cm is more precise because it is measured to a smaller unit.
568 cm has more significant digits.

CA CC N.Q.1

Use units as a way to understand problems and to guide the solution of multi-step problems; choose and interpret units consistently in formulas; choose and interpret the scale and the origin in graphs and data displays.

Key Vocabulary

unit analysis/ dimensional analysis *(análisis dimensional)* A practice of converting measurements and checking among computed measurements.

Visit **my.hrw.com** to see all **CA Common Core Standards** explained.

my.hrw.com

What It Means to You

You will learn to convert between measurements that can be used in calculations.

EXAMPLE N.Q.1

Li's car gets 40 miles per gallon of gas. At this rate, she can go 420 miles on a full tank. She has driven 245 miles on the current tank. How many gallons of gas are left in the tank?

STEP 1 Find the number of miles remaining.

$$420 \text{ mi} - 245 \text{ mi} = 175 \text{ mi}$$

STEP 2 Find the number of gallons.

$$x = 175 \text{ mi} \cdot \frac{\text{gal}}{40 \text{ mi}} = \frac{175 \cancel{\text{mi}}}{40 \cancel{\text{mi}}} \text{ gal} = 4.375 \text{ gal}$$

According to these measurements there are 4.375 gallons left in the tank.

LESSON 1.1

Precision and Significant Digits

CA CC N.Q.3

Choose a level of accuracy appropriate to limitations on measurement when reporting quantities.

ESSENTIAL QUESTION

How do you use significant digits when reporting the results of calculations involving measurements?

Precision

Precision is the level of detail of a measurement. More precise measurements are obtained by using instruments marked in smaller units. For example, a ruler marked in millimeters allows for more precise measurements than a ruler that is marked only in centimeters.

A measurement of 25 inches is more precise than a measurement of 2 feet because an inch is a smaller unit than a foot. Similarly, 9.2 kilograms is more precise than 9 kilograms because a tenth of a kilogram is a smaller unit than a kilogram.

EXAMPLE 1

CA CC N.Q.3

Choose the more precise measurement in each pair.

 5.7 m; 568 cm

5.7 m — *Nearest tenth of a meter*

568 cm — *Nearest centimeter*

A centimeter is a smaller unit than a tenth of a meter, so 568 centimeters is the more precise measurement.

 31 oz; 31.32 oz

31 oz — *Nearest ounce*

31.32 oz — *Nearest hundredth of an ounce*

A hundredth of an ounce is smaller than an ounce, so 31.32 ounces is the more precise measurement.

REFLECT

1. **What if?** Suppose that Example 1A asked you to choose the most precise measurement from among 5.7 m, 5.683 m, and 568 cm. Now what would the answer be? Why?

____

____

____

____

YOUR TURN

Choose the more precise measurement in each pair.

2. 2 lb; 31 oz ______ **3.** 4 in.; 0 ft ______

4. 6.77 m; 676.5 cm ______ **5.** 1 mi.; 5,280 ft ______

EXPLORE ACTIVITY

Exploring Effects of Precision on Calculations

My Notes

A Measure the width of a book cover to the nearest centimeter.

Width of book cover: ______ cm

Measure the length of the book cover to the nearest tenth of a centimeter.

Length of book cover: ______ cm

B A measurement given to the nearest whole or fraction of a unit can actually range from 0.5 unit below the reported value up to, but not including, 0.5 unit above it. So, a length reported as 3 cm could actually be as low as 2.5 cm or as high as nearly 3.5 cm, as shown in the diagram. Similarly, a length reported as 3.5 cm could actually be as low as 3.45 cm or as high as nearly 3.55 cm. Find a range of values for the actual length and width of the book cover.

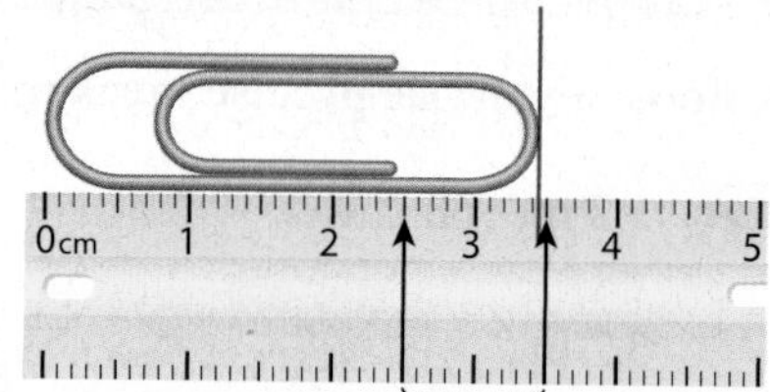

When measuring to the nearest centimeter, lengths in this range are rounded to 3 cm.

Minimum width = ______ Maximum width < ______

Minimum length = ______ Maximum length < ______

C Calculate the minimum and maximum possible areas of the book cover. Round your answers to the nearest square centimeter.

Minimum area = minimum width × minimum length

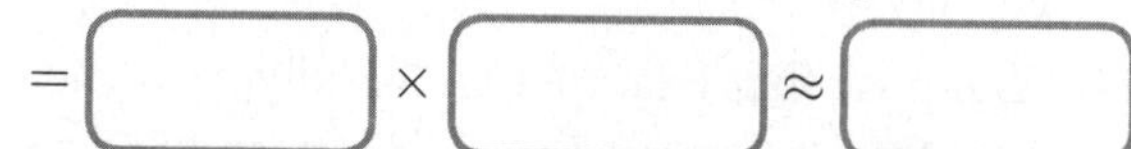

Maximum area < maximum width × maximum length

REFLECT

6. Give a range of possible values for a reported width of 21.0 cm.

______

Significant Digits

In the preceding Explore Activity, there was a wide range of possible values for the area of the book cover. This raises the question of how a calculated measurement, like an area, should be reported. Keeping track of **significant digits** is one way to resolve this dilemma. Significant digits are the digits in a measurement that carry meaning about the precision of the measurement.

Math On the Spot

my.hrw.com

Identifying Significant Digits

Rule	Examples
All nonzero digits are significant.	37.85 has 4 significant digits. 622 has 3 significant digits.
Zeros between two other significant digits are significant.	806 has 3 significant digits. 0.9007 has 4 significant digits.
Zeros at the end of a number to the right of a decimal point are significant.	1.4000 has 5 significant digits. 0.270 has 3 significant digits.
Zeros to the left of the first nonzero digit in a decimal are *not* significant.	0.0070 has 2 significant digits. 0.01048 has 4 significant digits.
Zeros at the end of a number without a decimal point are assumed to be *not* significant.	404,500 has 4 significant digits. 12,000,000 has 2 significant digits.

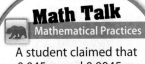

A student claimed that 0.045 m and 0.0045 m have the same number of significant digits. Do you agree or disagree? Why?

EXAMPLE 2

CA CC N.Q.3

Determine the number of significant digits in the measurement 840.090 m.

STEP 1 Find all nonzero digits. These are significant digits.

840.090 *8, 4, and 9 are nonzero digits.*

STEP 2 Find zeros after the last nonzero digit and to the right of the decimal point. These are significant digits.

840.090 *The zero after the 9 in the hundredths place is significant.*

STEP 3 Find zeros between the significant digits found in the previous steps. These are significant digits.

840.090 *There are 2 zeros between the significant digits 4 and 9.*

STEP 4 Count all the significant digits you have found.

840.090 *All the digits in this number are significant.*

So, 840.090 m has 6 significant digits.

YOUR TURN

Determine the number of significant digits in each measurement.

7. 36,000 ft ________ **8.** 0.01 kg ________ **9.** 15.0 L ________

Operations with Significant Digits

When you perform calculations with measurements of differing precision, the number of significant digits in the solution may differ from the number of significant digits in the original measurements. Use the rules in this table to determine how many significant digits to include in the result of a calculation.

Rules for Significant Digits in Calculations

Operation	Rule
Addition or Subtraction	The sum or difference must be rounded to the same place value as the last significant digit of the least precise measurement.
Multiplication or Division	The product or quotient must have no more significant digits than the least precise measurement.

EXAMPLE 3  

A rectangular garden plot measures 16 feet by 23.6 feet.

A Find the perimeter of the garden using the correct number of significant digits.

Perimeter = sum of side lengths
= 16 ft + 16 ft + 23.6 ft + 23.6 ft
= 79.2 ft

The least precise measurement is 16 ft. Its last significant digit is in the ones place. So round the sum to the ones place: 79 ft.

The perimeter is 79 feet.

B Find the area of the garden using the correct number of significant digits.

Area = width · length
= 16 ft · 23.6 ft
= 377.6 ft^2

The least precise measurement, 16 ft, has 2 significant digits, so round to a number containing 2 significant digits: 380 ft^2.

The area is 380 ft^2.

REFLECT

10. **Justify Reasoning** Why must the area have no more than 2 significant digits?

____

____

____

____

11. **Critical Thinking** Can the perimeter of a rectangular garden have more significant digits than the measures of its length or width have? Explain.

____

____

____

YOUR TURN

12. Find the perimeter and area of a sandbox that has a width of 4.5 ft and a length of 3.45 ft. Write your answers using the correct number of significant digits. _______________

13. In chemistry class, Julio measured the mass and volume of an unknown substance in order to calculate its density. It had a mass of 23.92 g and a volume of 2.1 mL. Find the density of the substance in g/mL, using the correct number of significant digits. _______________

Personal Math Trainer

Online Practice and Help

my.hrw.com

Guided Practice

Choose the more precise measurement in each pair. Then state the minimum and maximum possible values for the more precise measurement. (Example 1 and Explore Activity)

1. 18 cm; 177 mm

____

____

2. 3 yd; 10 ft

____

____

3. 71 cm; 0.7 m

____

____

4. 1.5 ft; 19 in.

____

____

Determine the number of significant digits in each measurement. (Example 2)

5. 12,080 ft ____________ **6.** 0.8 mL ____________ **7.** 1.0065 km ____________

A rectangular window has a length of 81.4 cm and a width of 38 cm. Use the correct number of significant digits to write each indicated measure. (Example 3)

8. Find the perimeter.

81.4 cm + 81.4 cm + 38 cm + 38 cm

The unrounded perimeter is ________ cm.

The least precise measurement is ________ cm.

Its last significant digit is in the ________ place.

Perimeter rounded to the ____________ place:

____________________ cm

9. Find the area.

81.4 cm × 38 cm

The unrounded area is ____________ cm^2.

The least precise measurement is ________ cm.

It has ____________ significant digits.

Area rounded to ____________ significant digits: ____________________ cm^2

10. A model car rolls down a 125.3 centimeter ramp, and continues to roll along the floor for 4.71 meters before it comes to a stop. The car's entire trip takes 2.4 seconds. Find the average speed of the car. Use the correct number of significant digits. (Example 3)

Do not round your results before you are finished with the calculation.

STEP 1 Total distance = ☐ cm + ☐ m

= ☐ m + ☐ m = ☐ m

STEP 2 Speed = $\frac{\text{total distance}}{\text{time}}$ = $\frac{\square \text{ m}}{\square \text{ s}}$ = ☐ ... m/s

The measurement with the fewest significant digits is ____________ s,

with ____________ significant digits. So rounding the speed to ____________

significant digits is ____________ m/s.

The car's average speed is ____________.

ESSENTIAL QUESTION CHECK-IN

11. How are significant digits related to calculations using measurements?

____

____

____

Name ______________________ Class ______________________ Date ______________________

1.1 Independent Practice

CA CC N.Q.3

Write each measurement with the indicated number of significant digits.

12. 454.12 kg; 3 significant digits ______

13. 8.45 lb; 2 significant digits ______

14. 9.1 in.; 1 significant digit ______

Order each list of units from most precise to least precise.

15. centimeter, millimeter, decameter, meter, kilometer

______

16. feet, inches, miles, yards

______

17. pints, quarts, cups, gallons

______

18. **Analyze Relationships** How is the precision used in measuring the length and width of a rectangle related to the precision of the resulting area measurement?

______

Express each calculator result using the rules for significant digits.

19.

______

20.

______

21.

______

22.

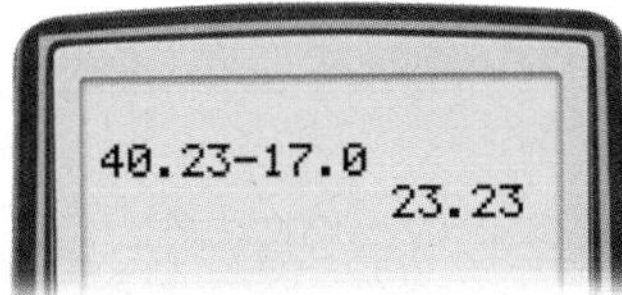

______

23. Write this sum to the correct number of significant digits:
34.01 m + 1940 m + 4.6 m ≈

______

24. Measure the length and width of the pictured book to the nearest tenth of a centimeter. Then use the correct number of significant digits to write the perimeter and area of the book.

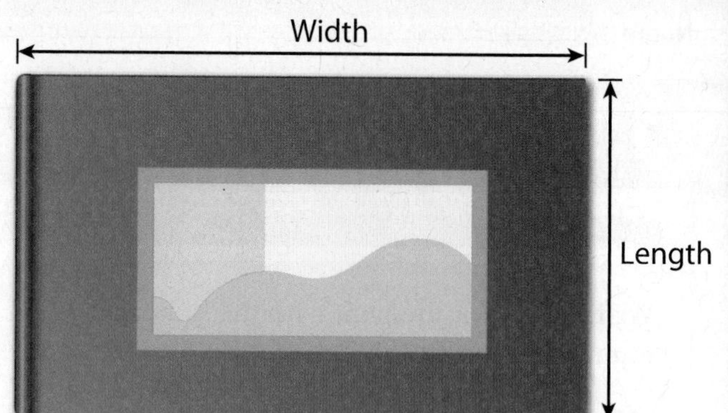

FOCUS ON HIGHER ORDER THINKING

Work Area

25. Justify Reasoning Yoshi is painting a large wall in the park. He is told that the dimensions of the wall are 4 m by 20 m. Yoshi has a can of paint that will cover an area of 81 m^2. Should he buy more paint? Explain?

26. Make a Conjecture If two measurements have the same number of decimal places and the same number of significant digits, is it ever possible for the result of an operation performed using these measurements to have a different number of decimal places or significant digits than the original measurements? Explain.

27. Explain the Error A student found that the side lengths of a square rug were 1.30 m. The student was asked to report the area using the correct number of significant digits. He wrote the area as 1.7 m^2. Explain the student's error.

28. Communicate Mathematical Ideas Consider the calculation 4.3 m $\div$ 16 s = 0.26875 m/s. Why is it important to use significant digits to round the answer?

LESSON
1.2 Dimensional Analysis

CA CC N.Q.1

Use units as a way to understand problems and to guide the solution of multi-step problems; choose and interpret units consistently in formulas; choose and interpret the scale and the origin in graphs and data displays. *Also N.Q.3*

ESSENTIAL QUESTION

How can you use dimensional analysis to convert measurements?

EXPLORE ACTIVITY  

Exploring Measurement Conversions

In the United States, the customary measurement system is used for everyday tasks such as finding the volume of a bottle or the length of a room. However, scientists throughout the world use the metric system of measurement. To convert between these two systems, you need to use equivalent measures such as those shown in the table.

Metric and Customary Measurements

Measurement Type	Metric unit	Customary equivalent
Length	1 meter	3.28 ft
	1 centimeter	0.39 in.
Area	1 square meter	10.76 ft^2
Volume	1 liter	0.26 gal
Mass/Weight	1 kilogram	2.2 lb

Use the equivalent measures given in the table to find the capacity of an 8-liter gas tank in gallons.

8 liters

1 L

1 gallon

A From the table: 1 liter (L) = ______ gallons (gal)

B From the diagram, about how many liters are in 1 gallon? ____________________

C Will the number of gallons in an 8-liter gas tank be greater or less than 8?

Explain. ____________________

____

____

D To convert 8 liters to gallons, do you need to multiply or divide by the conversion factor? ____________________

8 L = ______ gal

REFLECT

1. Analyze Relationships How would you convert from 8 gallons to liters?

____

Converting Measurements

Dimensional analysis is a way of using units to help solve problems involving measurements. You can use dimensional analysis to convert units by setting up ratios of two equivalent measurements, such as $\frac{12 \text{ in.}}{1 \text{ ft}}$. These ratios are called **conversion factors.**

EXAMPLE 1  

CA CC N.Q.1

The body of a large adult male contains about 12 pints of blood. Use dimensional analysis to convert this quantity to liters. There are about 2.1 pints in a liter.

Identify the given unit and the unit you need to find. Use that information to set up your conversion factor. The given unit should be in the denominator of the conversion factor, so that it will cancel out when multiplied by the given measurement.

$$x \text{ liters} \approx 12 \text{ pt} \cdot \boxed{\text{conversion factor}}$$

$$\approx \frac{12 \cancel{\text{pt}}}{1} \cdot \frac{1 \text{ liter}}{2.1 \cancel{\text{pt}}}$$

The pints in the denominator cancel with pints in the numerator.

$$\approx \frac{12 \text{ liters}}{2.1}$$

$$\approx 5.7 \text{ liters}$$

The body of a large adult male contains approximately 5.7 liters of blood.

REFLECT

2. Explain the Error Elena wanted to convert 30 inches to centimeters. She multiplied 30 in. by $\frac{1 \text{ in}}{2.5 \text{ cm}}$ and got an answer of 12. What was her error?

____

____

____

____

____

____

YOUR TURN

Use dimensional analysis to convert each measurement.

3. 3 feet ≈ ________ meters

4. 4 inches ≈ ________ yards

5. 12 kg ≈ ________ lb

6. 4 inches ≈ ________ centimeters

Converting Rates

Sometimes you will need to convert not just one measurement, but a ratio of measurements.

When working with a rate such as 50 miles per hour, you might need to know the rate in different units, such as meters per second. This requires two conversion factors: one to convert miles into meters, and one to convert hours into seconds.

EXAMPLE 2 

A cyclist travels 105 kilometers in 4.2 hours. Use dimensional analysis to convert the cyclist's speed to miles per minute. Write your answer with the correct number of significant digits. Use 1 mi = 1.61 km.

STEP 1 Identify the rate given and the rate you need to find. Use that information to set up your conversion factors.

$$x\,\frac{\text{miles}}{\text{minute}} \approx \frac{105\text{ km}}{4.2\text{ hr}} \cdot \boxed{\text{conversion factor}} \cdot \boxed{\text{conversion factor}}$$

$$\approx \frac{105\,\cancel{\text{km}}}{4.2\,\cancel{\text{hr}}} \cdot \frac{1\text{ mi}}{1.61\,\cancel{\text{km}}} \cdot \frac{1\,\cancel{\text{hr}}}{60\text{ min}}$$

Set up conversion factors so that both km and hr units cancel.

$$\approx \frac{105\text{ mi}}{4.2 \cdot 1.61 \cdot 60\text{ min}}$$

$$\approx 0.2588\text{ mi/min}$$

STEP 2 Determine the number of significant digits in each value: the distance, the time, and both conversion factors:

- 105 km has 3 significant figures.
- 4.2 hours has 2 significant figures.
- 1 mi/1.61 km has 3 significant figures.
- 1 hr/60 min is an exact conversion factor. Significant figures do not apply here, or to any conversion within a measurement system.

The value with the fewest significant digits is the time, 4.2 hr, with 2 significant digits. So the result should be rounded to 2 significant digits.

The cyclist travels approximately 0.26 miles per minute.

My Notes

REFLECT

7. **Communicate Mathematical Ideas** Tell which of the following conversion factors are exact, and which are approximate: 1000 grams per kilogram, 0.26 gallon per liter, 12 inches per foot. Explain.

____

____

____

____

YOUR TURN

Use dimensional analysis to make each conversion.

8. A box of books has a mass of 4.10 kilograms for every meter of its height. Convert this ratio into pounds per foot.

____

9. A go-kart travels 21 miles per hour. Convert this speed into feet per minute.

____

10. A tortoise walks 52.0 feet per hour. Convert this speed into inches per minute.

____

11. A pitcher throws a baseball 90.0 miles per hour. Convert this speed into feet per second.

____

Converting Areas

Dimensional analysis can also be used for converting areas. When converting areas, the conversion factor must be squared because area is expressed in square units.

EXAMPLE 3

CA CC N.Q.1, N.Q.3

The area of a practice field is 45,100 ft². How large is the field in square meters? Write your answer with the correct number of significant digits. Use 1 m ≈ 3.28 ft.

45,100 ft²

Identify the given unit and the unit you need to find. Use that information to set up your conversion factor.

Math Talk
Mathematical Practices
When would you multiply by the cube of a conversion factor?

$x \text{ m}^2 = 45{,}100 \text{ ft}^2 \cdot$ **conversion factor**

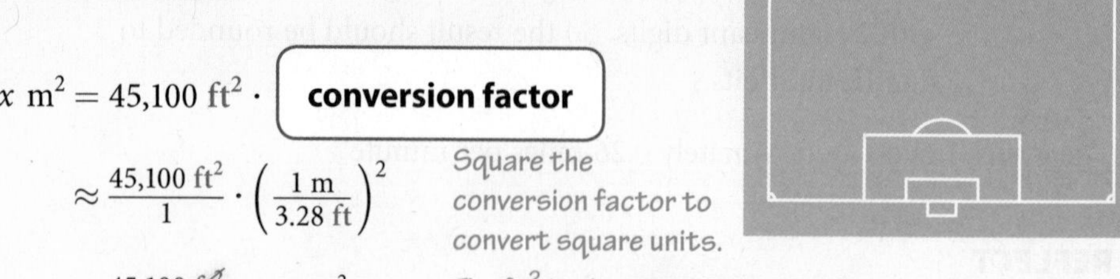

$\approx \frac{45{,}100 \text{ ft}^2}{1} \cdot \left(\frac{1 \text{ m}}{3.28 \text{ ft}}\right)^2$ Square the conversion factor to convert square units.

$\approx \frac{45{,}100 \text{ ft}^2}{1} \cdot \frac{1 \text{ m}^2}{10.7584 \text{ ft}^2}$ The ft² in the numerator cancel the ft² in the denominator.

$\approx \frac{45{,}100 \text{ m}^2}{10.7584}$

$\approx 4192.073 \text{ m}^2$

Because the given measure and the conversion factor both have 3 significant digits, the product should also be rounded to 3 significant digits. The area of the practice field is 4190 square meters.

YOUR TURN

Use dimensional analysis to make each conversion. Use the equivalent measures indicated.

12. The surface area of a swimming pool is 373 square feet. What is its surface area in square meters? (1 m = 3.28 ft) ________

13. A birthday card has an area of 29.1 square inches. What is its area in square centimeters? (1 in. = 2.54 cm) ________

14. A patio has an area of 9 square yards. What is its area in square inches? (1 yd = 36 in.) ________

Guided Practice

Use the diagrams to determine whether you need to multiply or divide by the indicated value to convert each measurement. (Explore Activity)

1. To convert 5 meters to feet, you need to ________ 5 meters by 3.28 feet per meter.

5 meters ≈ ________ feet

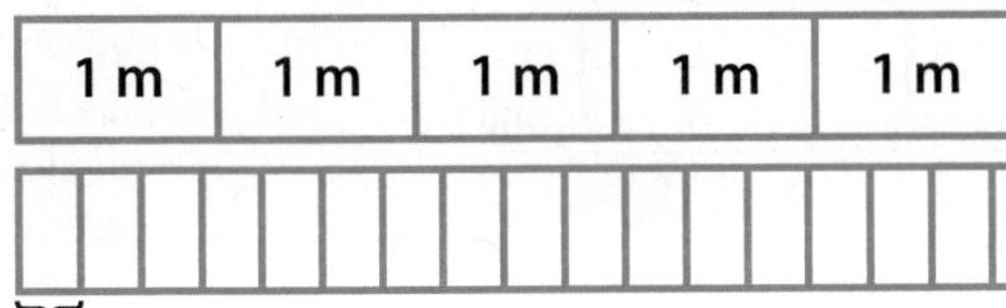

2. To convert 11 liters to gallons, you need to ________ 11 liters by 3.8 liters per gallon.

11 liters ≈ ________ gallons

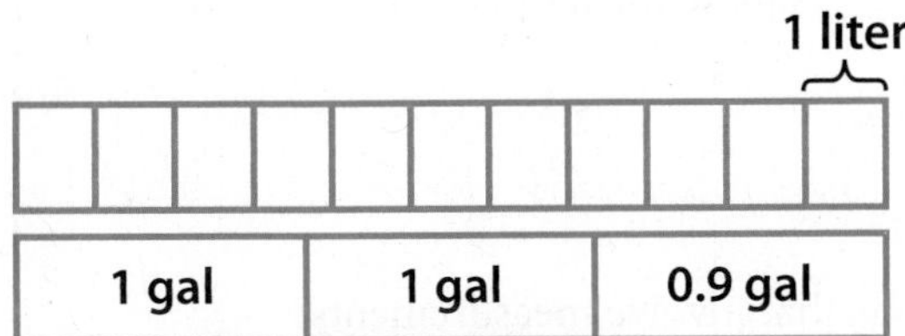

Set up the conversion factor needed for each conversion. Use the table of equivalent measures in the Explore Activity. (Example 1)

3. meters into feet ________

4. gallons into liters ________

5. pounds into kilograms ________

6. A dripping faucet is wasting 0.5 mL of water every second. How many liters of water does it waste per week? Write your answer with the correct number of significant digits. (Example 2)

STEP 1 Identify equivalent measures. 1 L = ____________ mL

1 wk = ____________ days 1 day = ____________ hr

1 hr = ____________ min 1 min = ____________ s

STEP 2 Set up conversion factors, cancel units, and calculate.

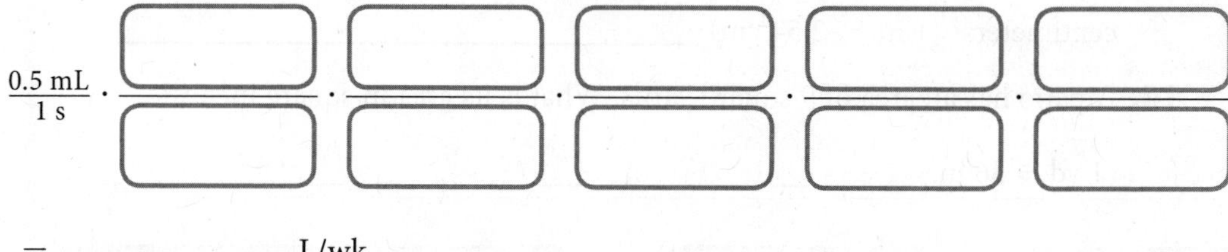

= ____________ L/wk

The answer should have ____________ significant digit(s),

so the final answer is ____________ L/wk

7. If an area can be washed at a rate of 3100 cm^2/minute, how many square inches can be washed per hour? Write your answer with the correct number of significant digits. (Examples 2 and 3)

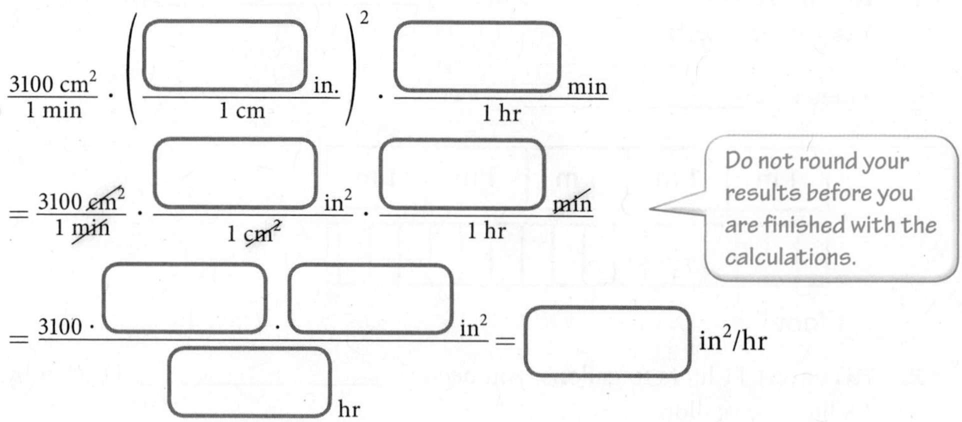

Do not round your results before you are finished with the calculations.

Because the given measure and conversion factor both have ________

significant digits, the equivalent rate is ________ square inches per hour.

ESSENTIAL QUESTION CHECK-IN

8. How is dimensional analysis useful in calculations that involve measurements?

____

____

____

Name ________________ Class ________________ Date ________________

1.2 Independent Practice

CA CC N.Q.1, N.Q.3

For Exercises 9–14, choose the conversion factor you need to multiply by to carry out each conversion.

A. $\frac{3.28 \text{ ft}}{1 \text{ m}}$ **B.** $\frac{0.39 \text{ in.}}{1 \text{ cm}}$ **C.** $\frac{2.2 \text{ lb}}{1 \text{ kg}}$

D. $\frac{1 \text{ cm}}{0.39 \text{ in.}}$ **E.** $\frac{1 \text{ kg}}{2.2 \text{ lb}}$ **F.** $\frac{1 \text{ m}}{3.28 \text{ ft}}$

9. feet to meters ________________

10. meters to feet ________________

11. inches to centimeters ________________

12. centimeters to inches ________________

13. kg to pounds ________________

14. pounds to kg ________________

Use dimensional analysis to make each conversion. Write your answer with the correct number of significant digits. Use the equivalent measures indicated.

15. A bedroom is 5.2 meters wide. Find its width in feet. (1 m $\approx$ 3.28 ft)

____

16. A bag of rice weighs 3.18 pounds. Find its mass in kilograms. (1 kg $\approx$ 2.2 lb)

____

17. A giraffe can run about 14 meters per second. Find its speed in miles per hour. (1 mi = 5280 ft; 1 m $\approx$ 3.28 ft)

____

18. The cover of a photo album has an area of 97.5 square inches. Find its area in square centimeters. (1 cm $\approx$ 0.39 in.)

____

19. A carpet costs $15 per square foot. (When calculating the price, any fraction of a square foot is counted as a whole square foot.) If the area you want to carpet is 19.7 square meters, how much will it cost to buy the carpet? (1 m $\approx$ 3.28 ft)

____

20. Measure the length and width of the outer rectangle to the nearest tenth of a centimeter. Using the correct number of significant digits, write the perimeter in inches and the area in square inches.

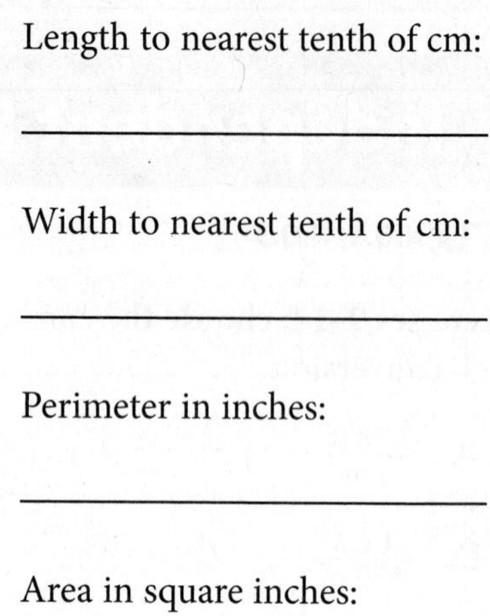

Length to nearest tenth of cm:

____

Width to nearest tenth of cm:

____

Perimeter in inches:

____

Area in square inches:

____

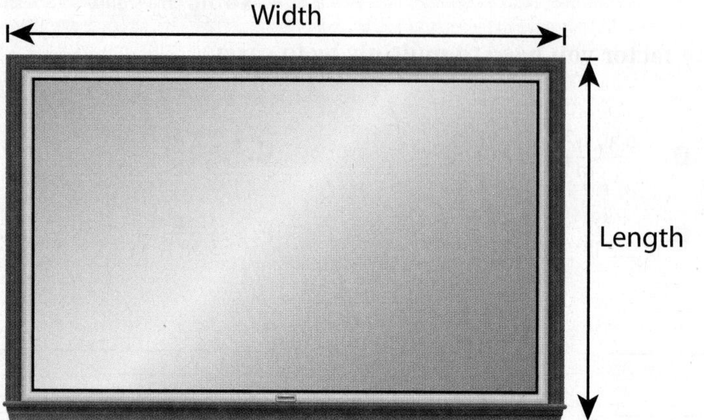

H.O.T. FOCUS ON HIGHER ORDER THINKING

Work Area

21. Represent Real-World Problems Write a real-world scenario in which 12 fluid ounces would need to be converted into liters. Make the conversion, and write the converted measure with the correct number of significant digits. Use 1 fl oz = 0.0296 L.

____

____

____

____

22. Analyze Relationships When a measurement in inches is converted to centimeters, will the number of centimeters be greater than or less than the number of inches? Explain.

____

____

23. Explain the Error A student measured the area of a bulletin board as 2.1 m^2. To find its area in square feet, he multiplied 2.1 by 3.28, getting an answer of about 6.9 ft^2. Explain the student's error. What is the correct area in square feet?

____

____

____

____

Ready to Go On?

Personal Math Trainer

Online Practice and Help

1.1 Precision and Significant Digits

Write each measurement with the indicated number of significant digits.

1. 982.1 m^2 (3) ________________

2. 1.5244 kg (2) ________________

Give the result of each operation with the correct number of significant digits.

3. 170.1 lb + 3.44 lb ________________

4. 1.1 cm × 4.28 cm ________________

5. A circle has a radius of 3.07 inches. Using the correct number of significant digits, find the circumference and area of the circle.

____

1.2 Dimensional Analysis

6. Use dimensional analysis to convert 8 milliliters to fluid ounces.

Use 1 mL ≈ 0.034 fl oz. ________________

Use the table of equivalent measures to answer each question.

Measurement type	Metric unit	Customary equivalent
Length	1 m	1.09 yards
Volume	1 L	2.11 pints
Mass/Weight	1 kg	2.20 lb

7. A designer found the area of a wall to be 3.0 square yards. What is the area of the wall in square meters? ________________

8. Will a stand that can hold up to 40 pounds support a 21-kilogram television? Explain.

____

9. Scientist A dissolved 1.0 kilogram of salt in 3.0 liters of water. Scientist B dissolved 2.0 pounds of salt in 7.0 pints of water. Which scientist made a more concentrated salt solution? Explain.

____

____

ESSENTIAL QUESTION

10. How are significant digits used in calculations with measurements?

____

____

____

MODULE 1
MIXED REVIEW

Assessment Readiness

1. Is each volume greater than 2.5 liters? Use 1 liter $\approx$ 0.26 gallon.

Select Yes or No for expressions A–C.

A. 0.5 gallon ○ Yes ○ No
B. 3 quarts ○ Yes ○ No
C. 5.5 pints ○ Yes ○ No

2. Choose True or False to tell if each measure has exactly four significant digits.

A. 0.0025 millimeter ○ True ○ False
B. 15.04 seconds ○ True ○ False
C. 0.01225 gram ○ True ○ False

3. A silo is composed of a cylinder topped by a half-sphere. The height of the cylinder is 6.2 meters and the radius of both the cylinder and the half-sphere is 1.6 meters. Use 3.14 for π. Find the volumes of the half-sphere, the cylinder, and the entire silo to the nearest tenth. Explain how you found the volume of the silo.

4. A rectangular rug has a length of 231 centimeters and a width of 166 centimeters. What is the area of the rug in square meters? Explain how you determined the correct number of significant digits for your answer.

5. Christina swims 2400 feet in 16 minutes. Gloria swims 12 meters in 15 seconds. Whose average speed is faster? Explain. Use 1 meter $\approx$ 3.28 feet.

Expressions

MODULE 2

CALIFORNIA COMMON CORE

LESSON 2.1
Evaluating Expressions
CA CC A.SSE.1, A.SSE.1a, A.SSE.1b, N.Q.1

LESSON 2.2
Simplifying Expressions
CA CC A.SSE.1, A.SSE.1a

LESSON 2.3
Writing Expressions
CA CC N.Q.1, N.Q.2, A.SSE.1, A.SSE.1a, A.SSE.1b

ESSENTIAL QUESTION

How can you use algebraic expressions to solve problems?

Real-World Video

In a grocery store receipt, some items are taxed and some items are not taxed. You can write an expression that shows a simplified method for calculating the total grocery bill.

my.hrw.com

GO DIGITAL
my.hrw.com

my.hrw.com

Go digital with your write-in student edition, accessible on any device.

Math On the Spot

Scan with your smart phone to jump directly to the online edition, video tutor, and more.

Animated Math

Interactively explore key concepts to see how math works.

Personal Math Trainer

Get immediate feedback and help as you work through practice sets.

Are YOU Ready?

Complete these exercises to review skills you will need for this module.

Personal Math Trainer

Online Practice and Help

Order of Operations

EXAMPLE Simplify $6 + 2(5 - 8)^2 + 7$

$6 + 2(5 - 8)^2 + 7 = 6 + 2(-3)^2 + 7$ Parentheses

$= 6 + 2(9) + 7$ Powers

$= 6 + 18 + 7$ Multiplication and division

$= 31$ Addition and subtraction

Simplify each expression.

1. $7^2 + 3(8) \div 3$ ______

2. $(4 - 9)(13 - 16) + 5$ ______

3. $11^2 - 4(2^3 - 8) + 5$ ______

4. $(5 + 3)^2 \div 16 + 2$ ______

5. $6 + (-9 - 12 + 7)5$ ______

6. $(6 + 2)(28 - 3^3)^5$ ______

Combine Like Terms

EXAMPLE $x - 1 - 2x + 9$

$x - 2x - 1 + 9$ Reorder terms with same variable factors.

$(1 - 2)x + (-1 + 9)$ Add or subtract the coefficients of the like terms.

$-1x + 8$, or $-x + 8$

Simplify each expression.

7. $9y - 2x - 4y + 11x - 3x$ ______

8. $-2x^2 - 12x + 5 - x + 8x^2 - 1$ ______

9. $4a^2 - 9b^2 + a^2 - 1 + 2b^2 + 5$ ______

10. $\frac{1}{2}m^2 - 9n^2 - m^2 - 12 + n$ ______

Connect Words and Algebra

EXAMPLE 12 decreased by a number

$12 \quad - \quad x$

Represent the unknown number with a variable.

Decreased by means subtraction.

Write an algebraic expression for each word phrase.

11. the quantity 9 more than a number ______

12. the difference between 3 times a number and 21 ______

13. the product of 4 and the sum of 7 and a number ______

Reading Start-Up

Vocabulary

Review Words

- Associative Property *(Propiedad asociativa)*
- Commutative Property *(Propiedad conmutativa)*
- constant *(constante)*
- Distributive Property *(Propiedad distributiva)*
- variable *(variable)*

Preview Words

- algebraic expression
- coefficient
- equivalent expressions
- expression
- like terms
- numerical expressions
- order of operations
- simplify
- term

Visualize Vocabulary

Use the review words to complete the diagram. Write an example for each oval.

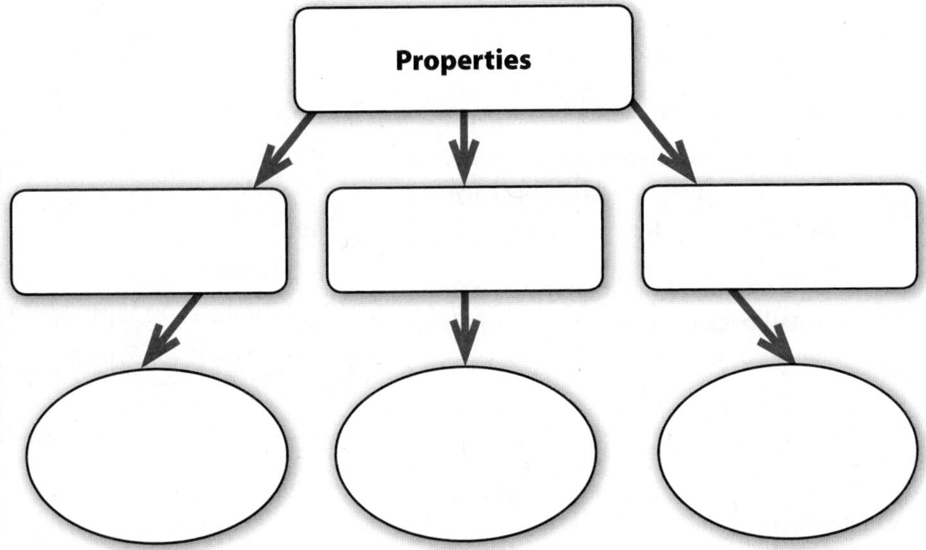

Understand Vocabulary

To become familiar with some of the vocabulary terms in the module, consider the following. You may refer to the module, the glossary, or a dictionary.

1. The word *express* is used when you want to demonstrate that an idea is solid and real. What do you think an **algebraic expression** might be?

____

____

____

____

Active Reading

Trifold Before beginning the module, create a Trifold Note to help you organize what you learn. Write vocabulary terms with definitions on the left and right folds and take notes in the center fold.

GETTING READY FOR

Expressions

Understanding the standards and the vocabulary terms in the standards will help you know exactly what you are expected to learn in this module.

CA CC A.SSE.1

Interpret expressions that represent a quantity in terms of its context.

Key Vocabulary

expression *(expresión)*
A mathematical statement written in terms of numbers, variables, and operations.

What It Means to You

You can translate a real-world situation in words into an expression that represents specific quantities.

EXAMPLE A.SSE.1

Fleetwood Delivery charges \$6.50 per pound to deliver a small package plus a \$12 pick-up fee.

The charge in dollars for delivering a small package weighing p pounds is

Rates:

Under 10 pounds:	\$6.50 per pound
10-30 pounds:	\$4.50 per pound
Over 30 pounds:	\$6.50 per pound
Pick-up fee:	\$12

$$6.5p + 12$$

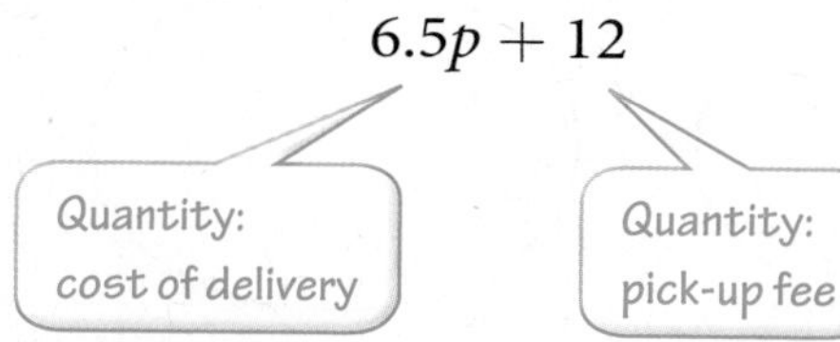

CA CC N.Q.1

Use units as a way to understand problems and to guide the solution of multi-step problems; choose and interpret units consistently in formulas; choose and interpret the scale and the origin in graphs and data displays

Key Vocabulary

unit *(unidad)*
a quantity used as a standard relative to which other quantities of the same type are measured, such as a pound or a centimeter

What It Means to You

Units can help you confirm that you are on the right track when solving a problem. If your units work out right, your answer is probably right.

EXAMPLE N.Q.1

Rina wants to express the time for her 195-second video in minutes rather than seconds. Should she multiply by 60 or divide? Using units guides her to the correct answer.

$$195 \text{ seconds} \cdot \frac{1 \text{ minute}}{60 \text{ seconds}} = 3.25 \text{ minutes}$$

Visit **my.hrw.com** to see all **CA Common Core Standards** explained.

my.hrw.com

LESSON
2.1 Evaluating Expressions

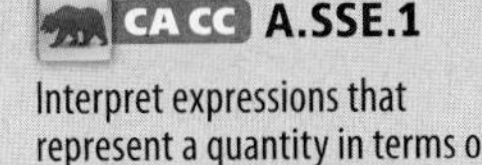

Interpret expressions that represent a quantity in terms of its context. *Also N.Q.1, A.SSE.1a, A.SSE.1b*

ESSENTIAL QUESTION

How do you evaluate and interpret algebraic expressions?

EXPLORE ACTIVITY CA CC A.SSE.1a

Interpreting Expressions

An **expression** is a mathematical phrase that contains operations, numbers, and/or variables. A **numerical expression** contains only numbers and operations, while an **algebraic expression** contains at least one variable.

A An algebraic expression can have both variables and numbers. In the expressions $5b$, $-7k$, and $2q$, the blue numbers are called **coefficients**. Write a definition of *coefficient* in your own words.

____

____

B The expression $8a + 5$ has two terms. The expression $4 - 5x + t$ has three terms, but to identify the terms, you must rewrite it as the sum $4 + (-5x) + t$. Write a definition of *term* in your own words.

____

____

C Compare your definitions in **A** and **B** to those of other students, and discuss any differences between them. If necessary, make changes to your definitions.

____

REFLECT

1. Identify the terms and coefficients in the expression $4p + 5 - 3g$.

____

2. **Communicate Mathematical Ideas** Explain and illustrate the difference between a term and a coefficient.

____

____

____

3. What is the coefficient of n in the expression $n - 9$? Explain your reasoning.

____

Evaluating Algebraic Expressions

To evaluate an algebraic expression, substitute the value(s) of the variable(s) into the expression and simplify using the order of operations.

Recall that **order of operations** is a rule for simplifying an expression.

Order of Operations	
Parentheses (simplify inside parentheses)	$7 - 5(9 - 6) + 4^2 = 7 - 5 \cdot 3 + 4^2$
Exponents (simplify powers)	$= 7 - 5 \cdot 3 + 16$
Multiplication and Division (left to right)	$= 7 - 15 + 16$
Addition and Subtraction (left to right)	$= 8$

EXAMPLE 1

CA CC A.SSE.1b

Evaluate the algebraic expression $n(5n - 13)^3$ for $n = 3$.

$n(5n - 13)^3 = 3(5 \cdot 3 - 13)^3$	Substitute 3 for *n*.
$= 3(15 - 13)^3$	Multiply within parentheses.
$= 3(2)^3$	Subtract within parentheses.
$= 3(8)$	Simplify exponents.
$= 24$	Multiply.

REFLECT

4. **Justify Reasoning** Compare multiplying 5 by 3 within parentheses to multiplying 3 by 8 in the last step. Explain why some multiplication is done first and some multiplication is done later.

___

___

___

___

YOUR TURN

Evaluate each expression for $x = 4$ and $y = 7$.

5. $7x + 3y - 12$ ______

6. $2x(3y - 4x)^2$ ______

Evaluating Real-World Expressions

When evaluating expressions that represent real-world situations, pay attention to units of measurement.

EXAMPLE 2 Real World  CA CC A.SSE.1, N.Q.1

Sheila is riding in a multi-day bike trip. Each day she rides a different distance in a different period of time. On the first day Sheila rides 100 miles.

A On the first part of the first day of the trip, Sheila rode for 6 hours and covered 75 miles. Find the average speed for the first part of the trip. Use the relationship $d = rt$, or distance = rate · time.

Rate is the same as speed.

$r = \frac{d}{t}$ Solve $d = rt$ for r.

$= \frac{75 \text{ miles}}{6 \text{ hours}}$ Substitute 75 miles for d and 6 hours for t.

$= 12.5$ miles per hour

B On the second day of the trip, Sheila rode at the same average speed as the first part of the first day. Her total distance over the two days can be represented by $100 + 12.5t$ where t is the number of hours Sheila rode on the second day. Sheila rode 7 hours on the second day. Find the total distance Sheila rode in two days.

Total distance = Day 1 distance + Day 2 distance
= 100 miles + $12.5t$

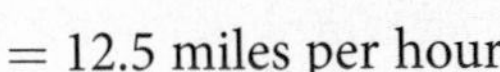

STEP 1 Find the distance for Day 2.

$d = 12.5t$

$= 12.5 \frac{\text{miles}}{\cancel{\text{hour}}} \cdot 7 \cancel{\text{hours}}$ Substitute 7 for t.

$= 87.5$ miles

STEP 2 Find the total distance.

Total distance = 100 mi + Day 2 distance

= 100 miles + 87.5 miles

= 187.5 miles

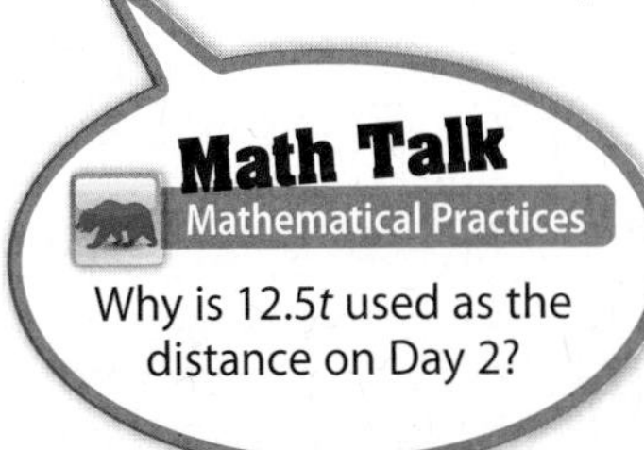

Math Talk
Mathematical Practices
Why is 12.5t used as the distance on Day 2?

YOUR TURN

7. For the second part of the first day of the trip, Sheila rode for an additional 1.5 hours. Find the average speed for the second part of the first day of the trip. Use the relationship $d = rt$, or distance = rate · time.

____

Guided Practice

Identify the terms and coefficients of each expression. (Explore Activity)

1. $7 + 8p - 2r^3$

terms: ______________________

coefficients: ______________________

2. $g^2 - 14h + 10$

terms: ______________________

coefficients: ______________________

3. Evaluate $(4x + y)^2 - 3z$ for $x = 2$, $y = -1$, and $z = 5$. (Example 1)

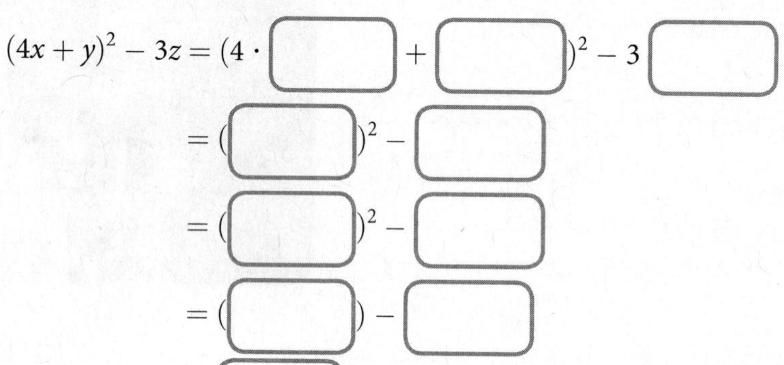

$(4x + y)^2 - 3z = (4 \cdot \square + \square)^2 - 3\square$ Substitute values for variables.

$= (\square)^2 - \square$ Simplify within parentheses.

$= (\square)^2 - \square$ Subtract within parentheses.

$= (\square) - \square$ Simplify powers.

$= \square$ Subtract.

4. As a lifeguard, Sara earns a base pay of $60 per day. If her day involves swim instruction, Sara also earns an additional $9t$ dollars, where t represents the number of hours she gives instruction and $9 is her hourly pay rate. The total amount that Sara earns in a day can be expressed as $60 + 9t$. (Example 2)

a. What does $9t$ represent in this context?

____

b. What are the terms and the coefficients in the expression $60 + 9t$?

Terms: ______________ Coefficients: ______________

c. Rewrite the expression for 5 hours of swim instruction.

____

d. How much will Sara earn in all? ______________________

ESSENTIAL QUESTION CHECK-IN

5. How do you evaluate and interpret algebraic expressions?

____

____

____

Name ______________________ Class ______________ Date ______________

2.1 Independent Practice

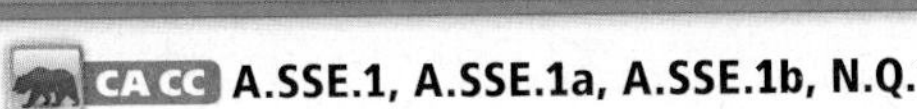

Evaluate each expression for $a = 2$, $b = 3$, and $c = -2$.

6. $7a - 5b + 4$ ______ **7.** $b^2(c + 4)$ ______ **8.** $8 - 2b$ ______

9. $a^2 + 2b^2 - c^2$ ______ **10.** $(a - c)(c + 5)$ ______ **11.** $12 - 2(a - b)^2$ ______

12. $a + (b - c)^2$ ______ **13.** $(a + b) - ab$ ______ **14.** $5a^2 + bc^2$ ______

15. For each of the indicated values given for x and y, determine which expression has a greater value: $(x + y)^2$ or $(x - y)^2$.

a. $x = 5, y = -3$

____

____

b. $x = -5, y = -3$

____

____

16. Analyze Relationships Jared sells square frames of various sizes made of wood. To find the area of a frame, Jared uses the formula $A = s^2 - (s - 2w)^2$, where s is the length of a side of the frame and w is the width of the frame.

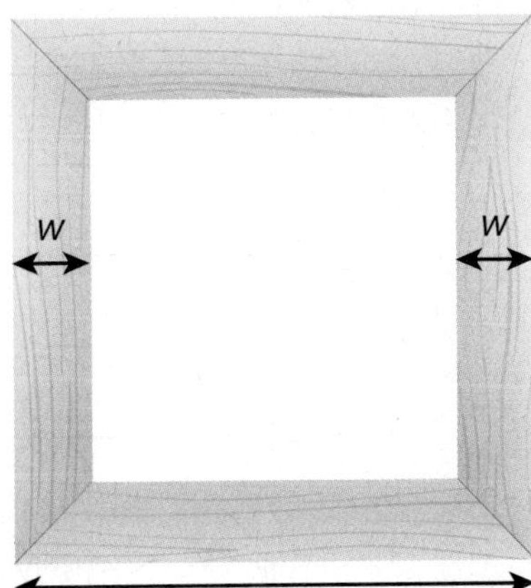

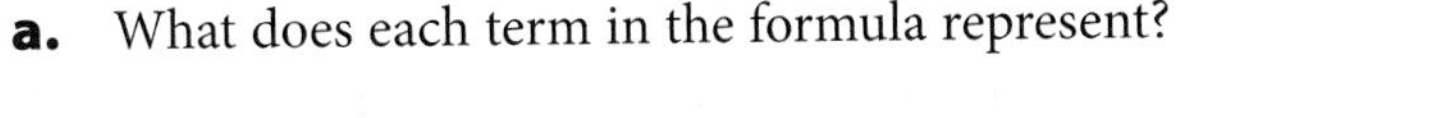

a. What does each term in the formula represent?

____

____

____

____

____

b. Find the area of a frame that measures 20 inches on each side and has a width of 3 inches. ______________________

c. Jared charges 18 cents per square inch for his frames. How much will he charge for a frame that measures 16 inches on each side and has a width of 2 inches?

____

17. At a rate of 25 miles per hour, it takes Henry 15 minutes to drive from the library to his house. Show how to find the distance that Henry traveled. Include units in your calculation.

____

____

H.O.T. FOCUS ON HIGHER ORDER THINKING

Work Area

18. Explain the Error Joan works on commission for a furniture store. She gets a base pay of $80 a day plus 5 percent of the value of any merchandise she sells that exceeds a total of $400. Joan wrote the expression $400 + 0.05(t - 80)$, where t represents her sales total in dollars, to compute the total amount of money that she will make. For sales of $475 Joan calculated that she will make $419.75. Explain Joan's error.

____

____

____

19. Justify Reasoning Nita finds that the expression $(a + 1)^2$ is sometimes, but not always, greater in value than $(a + 1)^3$ when she evaluates both expressions for the same value of a. How do you explain this finding?

____

____

____

____

____

____

____

20. Analyze Relationships Find the values of x and y that make the expression $5 + 4x(x - y) - x$ equal to zero. Explain how you got your answer.

____

____

____

____

____

____

LESSON

2.2 Simplifying Expressions

CA CC A.SSE.1a

Interpret parts of an expression, such as terms, factors, and coefficients. *Also A.SSE.1*

ESSENTIAL QUESTION

How do you simplify algebraic expressions?

EXPLORE ACTIVITY CA CC A.SSE.1a

Expressions

Equivalent expressions are algebraic expressions that simplify to the same value for any value(s) substituted for the variables that they contain. For example, the expressions $2x + y$ and $y + 2x$ are equivalent for any values of x and y.

Determine which of the following expressions appear to be equivalent expressions.

$3(n - 4)$	$3(n - 2)$	$3n + 4$
$3n - 12$	$3n - 6$	$4 + 3n$

A Substitute 5 for n in each expression, and evaluate.

$3(n - 4)$ $= 3(\square - 4)$ $= \square$	$3(n - 2)$ $= 3(\square - 2)$ $= \square$	$3n + 4$ $= 3 \cdot \square + 4$ $= \square$
$3n - 12$ $= 3 \cdot \square - 12$ $= \square$	$3n - 6$ $= 3 \cdot \square - 6$ $= \square$	$4 + 3n$ $= 4 + 3 \cdot \square$ $= \square$

B Which expressions appear to be equivalent?

____

____

____

____

EXPLORE ACTIVITY *(cont'd)*

REFLECT

1. **Communicating Mathematical Ideas** Which of the pairs of expressions in the Explore Activity can be shown to be equivalent using the commutative property? Explain.

____

____

____

2. **Communicating Mathematical Ideas** Which property could you use to show that the expressions $3(n - 4)$ and $3n - 12$ in the Explore Activity are equivalent? Explain.

____

____

____

Combining Like Terms

Like terms are terms with the same variables raised to the same power. If there is no variable associated with a number, then it is called a *constant*. Constants are also like terms. Look at the chart below for examples of like terms and unlike terms.

Like terms	Unlike terms
$2x, 3x, x$	x, y, z
$1, 5, 100, 7$	$1x, 5, 100y$
$3y, 19y, y$	$7a, 5b, 7$
$5n^2, n^2, 12n^2$	$5n^2, n, 12n^3$

EXAMPLE 1 CA CC A.SSE.1a

Combine like terms in each expression.

A $3x + 2x = x(3 + 2)$ Distributive Property

$= x(5)$

$= 5x$ Commutative Property

B $7x - 4x = x(7 - 4)$ Distributive Property

$= x(3)$

$= 3x$ Commutative Property

C $4x - x + 2x = x(4 - 1 + 2)$ Distributive Property

$= x(5)$

$= 5x$ Commutative Property

REFLECT

3. **Communicating Mathematical Ideas** Examine A, B, and C in Example 1. Describe how you combine like terms.

____

____

YOUR TURN

Combine like terms in each expression.

4. $7x + 3x$ ______

5. $17y + 8y$ ______

6. $13r - r$ ______

7. $9z - 8z + 2z$ ______

Simplifying Algebraic Expressions

To **simplify** an algebraic expression you can use the properties of real numbers to combine like terms and eliminate grouping symbols.

EXAMPLE 2 CA CC A.SSE.1a

Simplify each expression.

A $3a + 5b^2 + 2a + 4b^2$.

$3a + 5b^2 + 2a + 4b^2$ — Identify like terms.

$= 3a + 2a + 5b^2 + 4b^2$ — Commutative Property of Addition

$= 5a + 9b^2$ — Combine like terms.

B $4x - (3x + 1) - 2$

$= 4x - 3x - 1 - 2$ — Distributive Property

$= x - 3$ — Combine like terms.

Math Talk
Mathematical Practices

Are $2a$ and a^2 like terms? Explain.

YOUR TURN

Simplify each expression.

8. $7x + 18y^2 - 9y^2 - 5x$

______

9. $6n^3 + 3n^2 - 4n^3$

______

10. $4y^4 - (3y^2 + 3y^4) + y^2$

______

11. $-m^3 - (2n^2 - m^3) + 6n^2$

______

Simplifying Real-World Expressions

You can use algebraic expressions to represent real-world situations.

EXAMPLE 3 

CA CC A.SSE.1, A.SSE.1a

Write and simplify an expression to answer each question.

A Carlos is buying supplies for school. He buys p packages of paper at \$3.50 per package and p packages of pens at \$2.50 per package. What is the cost for paper and pens?

$3.5p + 2.5p$ — Cost of p packages of paper plus cost of p packages of pens.

$= 6p$ — Combine like terms.

B Carlos buys 2 fewer packages of pencils than packages of paper. Pencils cost \$1.50 per package. What is the cost for pencils?

$1.50(p - 2)$ — Cost of pencils.

$= 1.50p - 3$ — Use the Distributive Property.

C What is the total cost for paper, pens, and pencils as described in Parts A and B?

$6p + 1.50p - 3$ — Cost of all items.

$= 7.50p - 3$ — Combine like terms.

My Notes

REFLECT

12. The coefficients from the original expression $3.5p + 2.5p$ in part A represent what unit?

13. What does each term in the expression $3.5p + 2.5p$ represent?

14. Show two ways of finding the total cost of 7 packages of paper and 7 packages of pens.

YOUR TURN

Write and simplify an expression to answer each question.

15. Carly buys t play tickets at \$14.50 per ticket and t choir concert tickets at \$5.50 per ticket. What is the cost for play tickets and choir concert tickets?

____

16. Use your expression from Exercise 15 to find the total cost of 8 play tickets and 8 choir concert tickets.

____

17. Carly buys 3 more band concert tickets than choir concert tickets. Band concert tickets cost \$3.50 per ticket. What is the cost for the choir concert and band concert tickets?

____

Guided Practice

1. Which expressions are equivalent for all values of k? (Explore Activity)

$3(k - 3)$	$9k - 9$	$3k + 3$
$3 + 3k$	$9(k - 1)$	$3k - 9$

____

____

____

Combine like terms. (Example 1)

2. $8x - x =$ ________________

3. $6b + (2b + 4c) =$ ________________

4. $-5r - 3r =$ ________________

5. $2g + 8g - 3g =$ ________________

6. $11x + 4x =$ ________________

7. $6z - 2z =$ ________________

8. $5m - 3n + 2m - m$ ________________

9. $4x + 3y - x$ ________________

10. $-2z^2 + 4z + 2z^2$ ________________

11. $6r^3 + 2r^3 - r^2$ ________________

12. $6 - 3h^2 + 6h^2 + 2$ ________________

13. $4a + 2b^2 + b^2 - a$ ________________

Simplify. (Example 2)

14. $4(m - 7) + 15$

$= \_\_\_\_\_\_\_\_ + 15$

$= \_\_\_\_\_\_\_\_$

15. $10g - 2(4h) + 7g$

$= 10g + \_\_\_\_\_\_\_\_$

$= \_\_\_\_\_\_\_\_$

16. $4(m - 2) + 3m$

$= \_\_\_\_\_\_\_\_ + 3m$

$= \_\_\_\_\_\_\_\_$

17. $4x + 3(5x) + 4y - x$

$= 4x \_\_\_\_\_\_\_\_ 4y - x$

$= \_\_\_\_\_\_\_\_$

18. $12 - 3(4 - t) + 4t$

$= 12 \_\_\_\_\_\_\_\_ + 4t$

$= \_\_\_\_\_\_\_\_$

19. $3g + 3(2 - g) + 4(g + 1)$

$= 3g \_\_\_\_\_\_\_\_$

$= \_\_\_\_\_\_\_\_$

20. In basketball, Carmela's team scored seven 1-point free throws and four times as many 2-point baskets as 3-point baskets. The expression that represents the total number of points that the team scored is $3b + 7 + 2(4b)$ where b stands for the number of 3-point baskets that the team scored. Simplify the expression. (Example 3)

$3b + 7 + 2(4b)$

$= 3b + \square + \square$ Commutative Property of Addition.

$= 3b + \square + 7$ Simplify.

$= \square$ Combine like terms.

21. A rectangle has a width w and a length that is two more than its width. What is the perimeter of the rectangle? Write and simplify an expression. (Example 3)

____

ESSENTIAL QUESTION CHECK-IN

22. How do you simplify algebraic expressions?

____

____

____

____

Name ____________________ Class ____________ Date ____________

2.2 Independent Practice

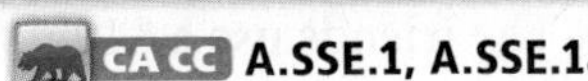
A.SSE.1, A.SSE.1a

Identify each property being illustrated.

23. $6(5x + 2) = 30x + 12$

____

24. $a(9 - 7) = (9 - 7)a$

____

25. $9 + (3b + 8) = (3b + 8) + 9$

____

26. $k + 5k + 8 = (1 + 5)k + 8$

____

Simplify each expression.

27. $a - 4 + 7a + 11$ ____________

28. $11k - (k + 3) + 2$ ____________

29. $6(n - 8) - 4n$ ____________

30. $-2(2x - 5) + 5x + 6$ ____________

31. $8b + 3(2b + c) - 3$ ____________

32. $x - 5(y + 2) + (3y - x)$ ____________

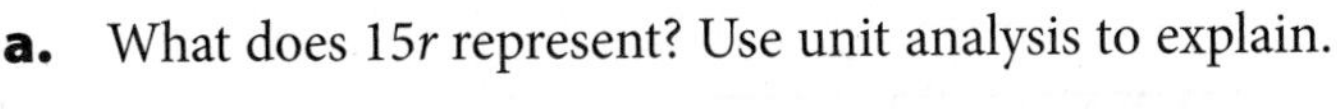

33. **Draw Conclusions** Marina burns calories at a rate of 15 calories per minute when running and 6 calories per minute when walking. Suppose she exercises for 60 minutes by running for r minutes and walking for the remaining time. The expression $15r + 6(60 - r)$ represents the calories burned during the 60-minute session.

a. What does $15r$ represent? Use unit analysis to explain.

____

____

b. What does $60 - r$ represent? What are the units associated with $6(60 - r)$?

____

____

c. Simplify $15r + 6(60 - r)$. What are the units associated with the entire expression?

____

d. Evaluate $15r + 6(60 - r)$ for $r = 20, 30,$ and 40. What conclusion can you draw?

____

____

____

Simplify each expression and identify the units.

34. You purchase n cartons of tennis balls at \$25 per carton from an online retailer that charges 8% tax and \$17 in shipping costs. The expression $25n + 0.08(25n) + 17$ can be used to represent the total cost.

____

35. Six friends all order the same lunch at a restaurant. Each lunch costs c dollars plus 5% tax and 20% tip. The friends use a \$10 gift certificate. The total cost of the lunch is $6c + (0.05 + 0.20)(6c) - 10$.

____

36. **Explain the Error** A student says that the perimeter of a rectangle with side lengths $(2x - 1)$ inches and $3x$ inches can be written as $(5x - 1)$ inches, because $(2x - 1) + 3x = 5x - 1$. Explain why this statement is incorrect.

____

____

H.O.T. FOCUS ON HIGHER ORDER THINKING

Work Area

37. **Represent Real-World Problems** Miguel is baking raisin bread for the bake sale using a recipe that requires flour, raisins, and butter in a ratio of 5 to 2 to 1 by volume in cups. Suppose Miguel uses c cups of butter. His mother tells him to use one cup less of raisins than the recipe requires. Then the expression $5c + (2c - 1) + c$ represents the total number of cups of ingredients that Miguel uses. How many cups of butter would he use to have a total of 27 cups of ingredients? Explain how you got your answer.

____

____

____

____

38. **Analyze Relationships** The gas tank of Michelle's car holds g gallons, and the car does 30 miles per gallon. With 3 gallons of gas left in the tank, Michelle added a bottle of MilePlus, an additive that boosts mileage by 10 percent. Overall, the number of miles she drove on the tank is given by the expression $30(g - 3) + [(30 + 0.1(30)]3$. How many extra miles did Michelle drive as a result of adding MilePlus? Explain.

____

____

____

39. **Explain the Error** A rectangle with sides of length $n + 2$ and n is compared to a square with sides of length $n + 1$. Steve says that the two shapes are equal in area. Explain Steve's mistake.

____

LESSON
2.3 Writing Expressions

CA CC N.Q.2

Define appropriate quantities for the purpose of descriptive modeling. *Also N.Q.1, A.SSE.1, A.SSE.1a, A.SSE.1b*

ESSENTIAL QUESTION

How do you write algebraic expressions to model quantities?

EXPLORE ACTIVITY 1

CA CC A.SSE.1b

Writing Algebraic Expressions

Expressions can be written with constants and variables, or they may be described in words. When given an expression in words, it is important to be able to translate the words into algebraic terms.

There are several key words that indicate that a particular operation is being used.

Key Words for Operations

Addition	Subtraction	Multiplication	Division
• added to • plus • sum • more than	• subtracted from • minus • difference • less than • take away • taken from	• times • multiplied by • product of • groups of	• divided by • divided into • quotient of • ratio of

How can you write the verbal phrase "the quotient of 5 and the quantity 3 more than a number *n*" as an algebraic expression?

A Which words in the expression identify an operation done to two quantities?

____

____

B Complete the expression for the quotient by filling in an operation symbol.

Quantity 1 ◯ Quantity 2

C What key words does Quantity 2 have that identify an operation? Write Quantity 2 as an algebraic expression with an operation.

____

D Write values for Quantity 1 and Quantity 2 in the boxes. Place parentheses around Quantity 2. Fill in an operation sign.

☐ ◯ ☐

EXPLORE ACTIVITY 1 *(cont'd)*

REFLECT

1. **Communicating Mathematics** Why did Quantity 2 require parentheses? Explain.

____

____

____

2. **Justify Reasoning** Use a value for n to explain why the expressions $5 \div (n + 3)$ and $5 \div n + 3$ are not the same.

____

____

____

____

3. **What If?** Suppose the quantities in the verbal phrase in the Explore Activity were reversed. Write an algebraic expression to represent this situation.

____

Modeling with Algebraic Expressions

You can create a verbal model to help translate a verbal expression into an algebraic expression.

EXAMPLE 1

CA CC N.Q.2

Write an algebraic expression to model the following phrase: "the price of lunch plus a 15% tip for the lunch."

STEP 1 Use the verbal phrase to write a verbal model.

Price of lunch	+	15% of price of lunch
Quantity	**Operation**	**Quantity**

STEP 2 Use a variable such as p for the price of lunch.

p	+	$0.15p$

The algebraic expression is $p + 0.15p$.

REFLECT

4. **Communicating Mathematics** What does the expression represent? Include the units in your answer.

______

______

______

5. Use a property to write an expression that is equivalent to the expression you wrote in Example 1. Identify the property and simplify the expression, if possible.

______

______

6. **Justify Reasoning** What could the expression $\frac{p + 0.15p}{2}$ represent? Explain.

______

______

______

______

7. **What If?** Suppose the tip was increased to 20% and then the price p of lunch is divided among 5 friends. What expression could represent this situation?

______

My Notes

YOUR TURN

Write an algebraic expression to model each phrase.

8. "The base price of a car plus 7.5% tax" represents the total cost of the car.

Simplify your expression. ______

9. "The base salary of \$500 per week plus a commission of 10.5% of sales" represents the total salary for the week. ______

10. "The original cost c less a discount of 20%" represents the sale price of the sweater. Simplify your expression. ______

11. "The wholesale price p plus a markup of 33% + \$50" represents the final price of the necklace. Simplify your expression. ______

Using Unit Analysis to Guide Modeling

You can create a model to help translate a verbal expression into an algebraic expression.

EXPLORE ACTIVITY 2

Last month, Lizzie volunteered 20 hours at her town library. In the weeks to come, she plans to volunteer 5 hours per week at the library. Write an algebraic expression to represent the total number of hours she will have volunteered *w* weeks from now.

A Use unit analysis to write a model.

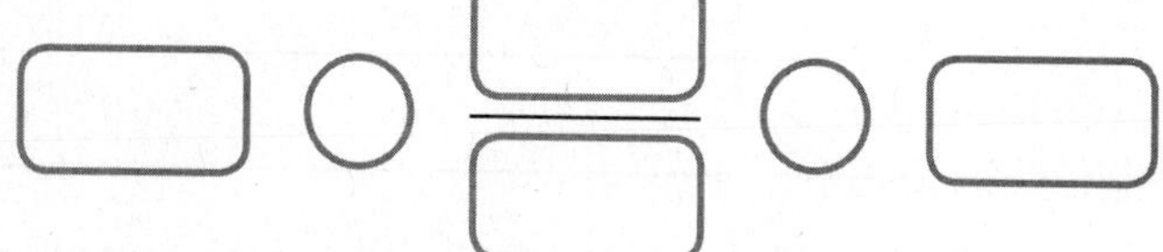

B Express the unit model as a verbal model.

____

____

Math Talk
Mathematical Practices
How would your expression change if Lizzie decided to volunteer 7 hours a week rather than 5?

C Write an algebraic model for the total number of hours volunteered after *w* weeks have passed.

____

D The expression ____________ represents the total number of ____________ Lizzie will volunteer after *w* weeks have passed.

REFLECT

12. Explain why you chose the units you chose in Step A above.

____

____

____

____

13. How many hours will Lizzie have volunteered by the end of 10 weeks? Explain how you solved this problem.

____

____

____

____

Solve each problem.

14. Lizzie plans to volunteer 3 hours a week at an animal shelter in addition to her library work. Rewrite the expression from the example to reflect this.

____

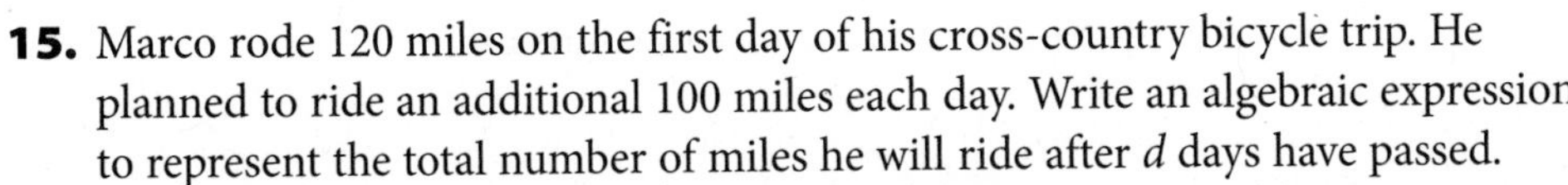

15. Marco rode 120 miles on the first day of his cross-country bicycle trip. He planned to ride an additional 100 miles each day. Write an algebraic expression to represent the total number of miles he will ride after d days have passed.

____

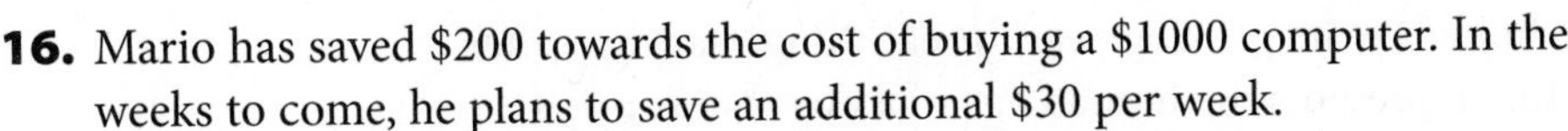

16. Mario has saved \$200 towards the cost of buying a \$1000 computer. In the weeks to come, he plans to save an additional \$30 per week.

a. Write an algebraic expression to represent the total amount he still needs to save after w weeks have passed.

____

b. How much more does he need to save after 8 weeks?

____

17. Irene has 50,000 airline miles in her account. She is planning to redeem the miles on a trip that costs 100,000 miles. In the months to come, she expects to accumulate an additional 2000 miles per month in her account.

a. Write an algebraic expression to represent the total number of miles she still needs to accumulate after m months.

____

b. How long will it take her to reach her goal of 100,000 miles?

____

Guided Practice

Write and simplify an algebraic expression to represent each situation.

1. Alex purchased a phone card for \$30. He has used t minutes of access time at 10 cents per minute. To write an algebraic expression to represent how many dollars Alex has left on his card, fill in the boxes. (Explore Activity 1)

30  

Write your expression. ______________________________

2. It costs $20 per hour to play pool and $3 for a cue stick rental. Write a verbal model and an algebraic expression to represent the cost for n hours of playing pool and identify the units for the expression. (Example 1)

____

____

3. Karla purchased a gym membership for $175. For each hour she uses the gym, she is charged another $5 per hour. Write an algebraic expression to represent the total cost for h hours of gym usage, and identify the units for the expression. (Example 1)

____

4. To convert dog years to human years, count 21 human years for the first two dog years and then 4 human years per dog year for each dog year thereafter. Write an expression that represents the human age of a dog that is y dog years old, where y is greater than 2. (Explore Activity 2)

____

5. Kelsey has saved $35 towards the cost of a $390 video game system. In the weeks to come, she plans to save an additional $10 per week. (Explore Activity 2)

a. Use unit analysis to represent the amount she has saved after w weeks and identify the units for the expression.

____

b. Write an algebraic expression for the amount Kelsey has saved after w weeks.

____

c. Write an algebraic expression to represent the total amount she still needs to save after w weeks have passed.

____

ESSENTIAL QUESTION CHECK-IN

6. How do you write algebraic expressions to model quantities?

____

____

____

____

____

Name ______________________ Class ______________ Date ______________

2.3 Independent Practice

CA CC A.SSE.1, A.SSE.1a, A.SSE.1b, N.Q.1, N.Q.2

7. Two more than 4 times the sum of yesterday's high temperature in degrees Fahrenheit and 7 is equal to the current temperature in degrees Fahrenheit.

a. Write an expression for the current temperature using t as yesterday's high temperature in your expression.

____

b. Simplify the expression.

____

c. If yesterday's high temperature was 3 °F, what is the current temperature?

____

8. Jared earns 0.25 paid vacation day for every week that he works. He also gets 10 paid company holidays per year.

a. Use unit analysis to represent the amount of paid time off Jared gets in a year after working for w weeks, and identify the units for the expression.

____

b. Write an algebraic expression to represent the amount of paid time off Jared gets in a year after working for w weeks, and identify the units for the expression.

____

c. Identify the units of each term in the expression, the variable, and its coefficient.

____

____

9. Tracie buys tickets to a concert for herself and two friends. There is an 8% tax on the cost of the tickets and an additional $10 booking fee for a single order of any size.

a. Write an algebraic expression to represent the cost per person. Simplify the expression, if possible.

____

____

b. Define what the variable represents and identify the units for the expression.

____

____

____

____

10. George claims that he is 3 years less than 3 times as old as his niece Pam will be one year from now. Let p = Pam's age now. Write an expression to represent George's claim. Then simplify the expression. If George is 42 years old now, how old will Pam be next year?

____

____

____

____

FOCUS ON HIGHER ORDER THINKING

Work Area

11. Critical Thinking Physicists measure velocity (speed) in units of distance per unit time. Acceleration is measured as the *change* in velocity per unit time, or velocity divided by time. Suppose you have measured velocity in meters per second. What units would acceleration have, using seconds as your time units? Explain how you got your answer.

12. Make a Prediction Hannah invests money in a fund that promises to provide 10 percent interest each year. Write an expression to show how much money Hannah has in the fund after 1 year, with p representing the principal amount she invests. Simplify the expression. Suppose Hannah invests \$1000 in the fund and leaves it there for 3 years. How much money will she then have? Explain.

13. Justify Reasoning A right triangle has sides of length n, $n + 1$, and $n + 2$. Monica uses the basic formula, area $= \frac{1}{2}$ base · height, to compute the area of the triangle and comes up with an area of $\frac{n^2 + 3n + 2}{2}$. Sunil uses the same formula and comes up with an area of $\frac{n^2 + n}{2}$. Which area is correct? Explain.

14. Represent Real-World Problems Suppose a sports event paid \$1,000,000 for an insurance policy if the event was cancelled due to bad weather. The policy stated that for each inch of snow above the average snowfall of 39 inches, the policy would pay \$75,000, up to a maximum of \$1,500,000. Write an algebraic expression in terms of s, the number of inches of snowfall, that represents how much the policy pays. Estimate how many inches of snow would have to fall before the event receives a payout equal to the cost of the policy. How many inches of snow would have to fall before the policy reaches the maximum payout?

Ready to Go On?

Personal Math Trainer

Online Practice and Help

my.hrw.com

2.1 Evaluating Expressions

Evaluate each expression for $r = 5$, $s = -3$, and $t = 7$.

1. $7 - 3s - 3t$

2. $9r - 5s + 4$

3. $8 + s^2(t + 4 - 3r)$

4. $(r - t)(2t + 5)$

5. $r^3 - 10s^2 + t^2$

6. $23 + 2(r + s)^3$

7. $3(r + s)^4 - rs^2$

8. $12r + (s - t)^2$

9. $5r^3 + st^2$

2.2 Simplifying Expressions

Simplify each expression.

10. $5(n - 8) - 4n$

11. $3b + 2(7b + c) - 3$

12. $-4(3x - 5) + 9x + 4$

13. $7(m - n) - 4(-4m)$

14. $x + 6(y + 3) - (3y - x)$

15. $d - e(3d + 8)$

2.3 Writing Expressions

Write an expression. Simplify if possible.

16. Cruz has d \$10-bills and 3 fewer \$20-bills than he has \$10-bills. Write an algebraic expression to represent how much money Cruz has in dollars. Simplify the expression, if possible.

ESSENTIAL QUESTION

17. How can you use algebraic expressions to solve problems?

MODULE 2
MIXED REVIEW

Assessment Readiness

1. Consider each expression. Is the expression equivalent to $2x + 4(x - 3)$?

Select Yes or No for expressions A–C.

A. $4(x - 3) + 2x$ ○ Yes ○ No
B. $(2x + 4x) - 3$ ○ Yes ○ No
C. $6x - 12$ ○ Yes ○ No

2. The expression $-16t^2 + 60t$ gives the height in feet of a football t seconds after it is kicked.

Choose True or False for each statement.

A. After 0.5 second, the ball is 22 feet high. ○ True ○ False
B. After 1 second, the ball is 44 feet high. ○ True ○ False
C. After 1.5 seconds, the ball is 54 feet high. ○ True ○ False

3. Science fiction novels at a bookstore are on sale for 15% off. Write an expression for the sale price of a science fiction novel with a regular price of r dollars, and explain what each part of the expression represents. Then simplify the expression.

4. The formula for the surface area of a sphere is $S = 4\pi r^2$, where r is the radius of the sphere. The formula for the volume of the sphere is $V = \frac{4}{3}\pi r^3$. If the surface area of a sphere is 36π square inches, what is its volume? Explain your reasoning.

UNIT 1

Study Guide Review

MODULE 1 Relationships between Quantities

Key Vocabulary
precision *(precisión)*
significant digits *(dígitos significativos)*
dimensional analysis *(análisis dimensional)*
conversion factors *(factor de conversión)*

ESSENTIAL QUESTION

How do you calculate when the numbers are measurements?

EXAMPLE 1

A cyclist travels 100 kilometers in 4 hours. Use dimensional analysis to convert the cyclist's speed to miles per minute.

Use the conversion factor $\frac{1 \text{ mile}}{1.61 \text{ km}}$ to convert kilometers to miles, and use $\frac{1 \text{ hour}}{60 \text{ min}}$ to convert hours to minutes.

$$\frac{100 \text{ km}}{4 \text{ h}} \cdot \frac{1 \text{ mi}}{1.61 \text{ km}} \cdot \frac{1 \text{ h}}{60 \text{ min}} \approx 0.2588 \frac{\text{miles}}{\text{minute}}$$

EXAMPLE 2

Sharon is building a wooden crate in the shape of a rectangular prism with dimensions 12 meters by 10.2 meters by 15.5 meters. Find the volume of the crate. Write your answer using the correct number of significant digits.

$$\begin{aligned} A &= l \times w \times h \\ &= 12 \times 10.2 \times 15.5 \\ &= 1897.2 \end{aligned}$$

The least precise measurement is 12 meters, which has 2 significant digits. Round the volume to a number that has 2 significant digits: 1900 m^3.

EXERCISES

1. Shaniqua's bedroom is 12.6 feet long and 8 feet wide. What are the perimeter and area of the room? Give your answers using the correct number of significant digits. (Lesson 1.1)

____

2. Rachel's biscuits require 0.75 cup of milk for 1 batch. Use dimensional analysis to convert this amount into liters. Use the conversion factors $\frac{1 \text{ cup}}{0.5 \text{ pint}}$ to convert cups to pints, $\frac{1 \text{ pint}}{0.5 \text{ quart}}$ to convert pints to quarts, and $\frac{1 \text{ quart}}{0.94 \text{ liter}}$ to convert quarts to liters. Use the correct number of significant digits to give your answer. (Lessons 1.1, 1.2)

____

MODULE 2

Expressions

ESSENTIAL QUESTION

How can you use algebraic expressions to solve problems?

Key Vocabulary

expression *(expresión)*
numerical expression *(expresión numérica)*
algebraic expression *(expresión algebraica)*
coefficients *(coeficiente)*
order of operations *(orden des las operaciones)*
equivalent expressions *(expresión equivalentes)*
like terms *(términos semejantes)*
simplify *(simplificar)*

EXAMPLE 1

Evaluate the algebraic expression $n(5n - 13)^3$ for $n = 3$.

$$n(5n - 13)^3 = [3] \cdot (5 \cdot [3] - 13)^3$$
$$= [3] \cdot (15 - 13)^3$$
$$= [3] \cdot (2)^3$$
$$= [3] \cdot 8$$
$$= 24$$

EXAMPLE 2

Simplify $3a + 5b^2 + 2a + 4b^2$.

$3a + 5b^2 + 2a + 4b^2$

$= 3a + 2a + 5b^2 + 4b^2$ Commutative Property of Addition

$= a(3 + 2) + b^2(5 + 4)$ Distributive Property

$= a(5) + b^2(9)$ Combine like terms

$= 5a + 9b^2$ Commutative Property of Multiplication

EXAMPLE 3

"The price for a dozen eggs plus 8% tax, divided by 12" represents the cost of one egg. Write and simplify an algebraic expression to model the phrase.

Use the verbal model to identify each quantity and the operations.

(Price of a Dozen Eggs	+	8% of Price of a Dozen Eggs)	÷	12 Eggs per Dozen
Quantity	Operation	Quantity	Operation	Quantity

Let d represent the price of a dozen eggs.

(d	+	$0.08d$)	÷	12 Eggs per Dozen

$$= \frac{(d + 0.08d)}{12}$$

$$= \frac{1.08d}{12}$$

EXERCISES

Evaluate each expression for $x = 2$ and $y = 4$. (Lesson 2.1)

3. $\frac{2x^2 + 3x}{y}$

4. $(xy)^2 - x + y$

Evaluate each expression for $a = -3$ and $b = 5$. (Lesson 2.1)

5. $a^3 + 2a - 3b$

6. $(b - a)^2 + ab$

7. $(4a + 2b)^3 + (ab)^2$

8. $(3b^2 - 2a^3) - (6b + 5a)$

Simplify. (Lesson 2.2)

9. $2(x + y - 3) - x$

10. $2 + (6 - x) + 2x$

11. $15g - 3(5h) + 5g$

12. $6(m - 3) + 17$

13. $5x + 3y^2 - 7y^2 - 8x$

14. $5(m^3 + 2n^2) - 8(n^2 - m^3)$

Write an algebraic expression for each situation, and then solve the expression for the given values. (Lessons 2.1 and 2.3)

15. Samuel earns \$10 per hour plus \$1 per T-shirt he sells. Find his earnings when he works 8 hours and sells 20 T-shirts.

16. Claire and Li are evenly sharing the cost of 7 yards of red fabric and 3 yards of blue fabric. Find the amount each pays when red fabric is \$6.50 per yard and blue fabric is \$8.00 per yard

17. Jason is buying 2 hats and 3 scarves for each of his 4 children. Find the amount Jason spends when hats cost \$8.50 and scarves cost \$5.50.

Unit Project

CA CC N.Q.1, N.Q.3, A.SSE.1

Prices at the Pump

Gas stations display prices per gallon to the nearest tenth of a cent. For example, in the price \$3.249 or $\$3.24\frac{9}{10}$, the digit 9 represents \$0.009, or $\frac{9}{10}$ of 1¢.

For this project, collect data from a purchase of gasoline at a gas station. Include the price per gallon, the number of gallons purchased, and the total cost for the gas. Then create a presentation that includes the following:

- The data you collected
- An explanation of how the total cost of the gas was calculated
- An expression relating the price per gallon, p; the number of gallons purchased, n; and the total cost, c

Compare your results in small groups. Write an expression that gives the amount of money that you can save by buying g gallons of gas at the lowest price found among those in the group.

Use the space below to write down any questions you have or important information from your teacher.

MATH IN CAREERS ACTIVITY

Cave Geologist Maria is studying stalactite formation in caves. A stalactite forms when water carrying minerals drips from the ceiling of a cave. Over long periods of time, the water deposits minerals, especially calcium carbonate. The minerals build up to form an icicle-shaped stalactite. Maria finds one stalactite that is 1.2 meters long. Based on data she has collected, she estimates that the stalactite is getting longer at an average rate of 0.13 millimeters per year. Write two expressions, one for the length of the stalactite in millimeters after x years, and one for the length of the stalactite in meters after x years. Then predict the length (in millimeters and meters) of the stalactite after 500 years. Give the lengths to the correct number of significant digits.

UNIT 1
MIXED REVIEW

Assessment Readiness

1. Consider each expression. If $x = -2$, is the value of the expression a positive number?

Select Yes or No.

A. $-2(x - 2)^2$ ○ Yes ○ No
B. $-3x(5 - 4x)$ ○ Yes ○ No
C. $x^3 + 6x$ ○ Yes ○ No

2. A bedroom is shaped like a rectangular prism. The floor has a length of 4.57 meters and a width of 4.04 meters. The height of the room is 2.3 meters.

Choose True or False for each statement.

A. The perimeter of the floor with the correct number of significant digits is 17.22 meters. ○ True ○ False
B. The area of the floor with the correct number of significant digits is 18.46 square meters. ○ True ○ False
C. The volume of the room with the correct number of significant digits is 42 cubic meters. ○ True ○ False

3. A faucet is leaking at a rate of 4.2 milliliters per minute. How many gallons of water does the faucet leak per day? Use $1 \text{ L} \approx 0.26$ gal. Explain how you solved this problem.

4. The delivered power P, in watts, of an electric circuit with voltage V, in volts, and resistance R, in ohms, is given by $P = \frac{V^2}{R}$. Jean set up an electric circuit with a delivered power of 25 watts. If the resistance is 9 ohms, what is the voltage? Explain your reasoning.

Performance Tasks

★**5.** A spice store charges $2.75 for 25 grams of paprika. It also charges 5% of the purchase price for shipping any order.

a. Write and simplify an expression to determine the cost of buying and shipping x ounces of paprika. Use 1 ounce $\approx$ 28 grams.

b. Can a customer buy 2.5 ounces of paprika and have it shipped for less than $8.00? Explain.

★★**6.** A city park planner is deciding between two proposals for a new rectangular playground. One proposal is for a playground with an area of 1930 square feet.

a. The second proposal is for a playground that is 11.5 meters long and 19.5 meters wide. What is the area of this playground? Use 1 m $\approx$ 3.28 ft. Use the correct number of significant digits.

b. The playground will be covered with rubber mulch. Let c represent the cost in dollars to cover 1 square foot with rubber mulch. Write and simplify an algebraic expression for the amount the city will save on mulch by using the first proposal over the second.

c. Rubber mulch costs between $11 and $17 per square foot. Will the city save at least $3000 by using the first proposal? Explain.

★★★**7.** The Cote family car gets between 25 and 29 miles per gallon of gasoline. The fuel tank holds 17 gallons of gasoline, and the Cotes refill the tank whenever it is $\frac{1}{4}$ full. The cost of gasoline will be between $3.47 and $3.69 per gallon.

a. Write expressions to estimate the amount they will pay for gasoline and the number of times they will need to stop for gas for a trip of m miles. Justify the choice of numbers you use in your expressions.

b. Denver is 1004 miles from Chicago. For a round trip from Denver to Chicago, how much should they budget for gas? How many times can they expect to stop for gas on the trip? Explain your reasoning.

Equations and Functions

MODULE 3

Equations and Inequalities in One Variable

CA CC N.Q.2, A.CED.1, A.CED.3, A.CED.4, A.REI.1, A.REI.3

MODULE 4

Equations in Two Variables and Functions

CA CC A.REI.10, A.REI.11, F.IF.1, F.IF.2, F.IF.3, F.IF.5, F.BF.1, F.BF.1a, F.BF.2

MODULE 5

Absolute Value

CA CC A.CED.1, A.REI.3.1, F.IF.4, F.IF.7, F.BF.3

MATH IN CAREERS

Astronomer An astronomer uses equations and functions to calculate models of star and planet movements and to calculate the speed of heavenly bodies. Using a telescope and a computer, an astronomer creates equations to accurately measure things light-years away.

If you're interested in astronomy, you should study mathematical subjects such as:

- Algebra
- Geometry
- Trigonometry
- Calculus

ACTIVITY At the end of the unit, check out how **astronomers** use math.

Unit Project Preview

Round Trip

The Unit Project at the end of this unit involves sketching a map to represent a bicycle trip. You will write and solve an equation to obtain the information necessary to create the map. To successfully complete the Unit Project you'll need to master these skills:

- Define quantities to model a real-world situation.
- Write an equation to represent the situation.
- Solve a one-variable equation.

1. a. If you bicycle 18 miles per hour, how can you find the distance you will travel in 25 minutes?

____

____

b. How far do you go in 25 minutes?

____

2. Write another problem using the rate of 18 miles per hour. Then write an equation to solve the problem.

____

____

Tracking Your Learning Progression

This unit addresses important California Common Core Standards in the Critical Areas of writing and solving equations in one and two variables and working with functions.

Domain A.CED Creating Equations

Cluster Create equations that describe numbers or relationships.

The unit also supports additional standards.

Domain F.IF Interpreting Functions

Cluster Understand the concept of a function and use function notation.

Equations and Inequalities in One Variable

MODULE 3

ESSENTIAL QUESTION

How can you solve an equation or inequality in one variable?

CALIFORNIA COMMON CORE

LESSON 3.1

Equations in One Variable

CA CC A.REI.1, A.REI.3, N.Q.2, A.CED.1, A.CED.3

LESSON 3.2

Inequalities in One Variable

CA CC A.REI.3, A.CED.1, A.CED.3

LESSON 3.3

Solving for a Variable

CA CC A.CED.4, A.REI.3

Real-World Video

my.hrw.com

In some sports, such as boxing and wrestling, the athletes and their competitions are categorized by weight. The weight divisions are defined by specific upper and lower weight limits, which can be efficiently described using inequalities.

GO DIGITAL

my.hrw.com

my.hrw.com

Go digital with your write-in student edition, accessible on any device.

Math On the Spot

Scan with your smart phone to jump directly to the online edition, video tutor, and more.

Animated Math

Interactively explore key concepts to see how math works.

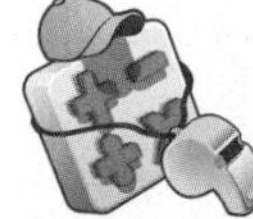

Personal Math Trainer

Get immediate feedback and help as you work through practice sets.

Are YOU Ready?

Complete these exercises to review skills you will need for this module.

Order of Operations

EXAMPLE Simplify: $17 + 3(7 - 5) + 3^2$

$= 17 + 3(2) + 3^2$ Parentheses
$= 17 + 3(2) + 9$ Exponents
$= 17 + 6 + 9$ Multiplication and division
$= 32$ Addition and subtraction

Simplify.

1. $15 - 3^2 + 2(7 \cdot 3)$ ________

2. $5^2 + 4^2 + 3(2 - 10)$ ________

3. $(10^2 - 9^2) + 5 \cdot 7 + 3$ ________

4. $10 \div 5\,(2 \cdot 4) - 5^2$ ________

5. $17 - 5 \cdot 2 \div 5 - 1^2$ ________

6. $18 \div 3 \div 3 \cdot 5^2$ ________

One-Step Equations

EXAMPLE Solve:

$y - 5.5 = 11$
$y = 11 + 5.5$ Isolate the variable by adding 5.5 to both sides of the equation.
$y = 16.5$

Solve each equation.

7. $5x = 100$ ________

8. $-25 = x + 100$ ________

9. $\frac{z}{3} = 17$ ________

One-Step Inequalities

EXAMPLE Solve:

$x + 5 < 14$
$x < 14 - 5$ Isolate the variable by subtracting 5 from both sides of the equation.
$x < 9$

Solve each inequality.

10. $x - 22 < 17$ ________

11. $f - 110 \geq 25$ ________

12. $\frac{z}{12} < -11$ ________

Reading Start-Up

Visualize Vocabulary

Use the review words to complete the case diagram. Write an example for each oval.

One-Step Mathematical Statement

Vocabulary

Review Words

- one-step equation
- one-step inequality

Preview Words

- equivalent equations
- formula
- identity
- literal equation
- solution of an equation
- solution of inequality

Understand Vocabulary

To become familiar with some of the vocabulary terms in the module, consider the following. You may refer to the module, the glossary, or a dictionary.

1. One definition of identity is "exact sameness." An equation consists of two expressions. If an equation is an *identity*, what do you think is true about the expressions?

____

2. The word *literal* means "of letters." How might a literal equation be different from an equation like $3 + 5 = 8$?

____

Active Reading

Two-Panel Flip Chart Before beginning the module, create a Two-Panel Flip Chart to help you organize what you learn about equations and inequalities. Organize the characteristics of the two topics side by side for easy comparison.

GETTING READY FOR

Equations and Inequalities in One Variable

Understanding the standards and the vocabulary terms in the standards will help you know exactly what you are expected to learn in this module.

CA CC A.CED.1

Create equations and inequalities in one variable including ones with absolute value and use them to solve problems.

Key Vocabulary

equation *(ecuación)*
A mathematical statement that two expressions are equivalent.

variable *(variable)*
a symbol used to represent a quantity that can change

What It Means For You

You can write an equation to represent a real-world problem and then use algebra to solve the equation and find the answer.

EXAMPLE A.CED.1

Michael is saving money to buy a trumpet. The trumpet costs \$670. He has \$350 saved, and each week he adds \$20 to his savings. How long will it take him to save enough money to buy the trumpet?

$$\text{cost of trumpet} = \text{current savings} + \text{additional savings}$$
$$670 = 350 + 20w$$
$$320 = 20w$$
$$16 = w$$

It will take Michael 16 weeks to save enough money.

CA CC A.REI.3

Solve linear equations and inequalities in one variable, including equations with coefficients represented by letters.

Key Vocabulary

inequality *(desiguladad)*
A mathematical sentence that shows the relationship between quantities that are not equivalent.

solution of an inequality in one variable *(solucion de una desiguladad en una variable)*
A value or values for the variable that make the inequality true.

What It Means for You

You can apply some equation solving techniques to solve inequalities.

EXAMPLE A.REI.3

Sally has at most \$100 to spend at a fair. She spends \$20 on admission and \$25 on food. If ride tickets cost \$5 each, how many can she buy?

Let x be the number of ride tickets.

$$100 \geq 5x + (20 + 25)$$
$$100 \geq 5x + 45$$
$$55 \geq 5x$$
$$11 \geq x$$

Sally can buy at most 11 ride tickets.

Visit **my.hrw.com** to see all **CA Common Core Standards** explained.

my.hrw.com

LESSON
3.1 Equations in One Variable

CA CC A.REI.1, A.REI.3

For the full text of these standards, see the table beginning on page CA2. *Also N.Q.2, A.CED.1, A.CED.3*

ESSENTIAL QUESTION

How do you solve an equation in one variable?

Solving Two-Step and Multi-Step Equations

Recall that an equation shows that two quantities are equal. Often an equation contains a variable. A solution of an equation is a value for the variable that makes the equation true.

$x + 2 = 5 \leftarrow$ equation

$x = 3 \leftarrow$ solution because $3 + 2 = 5$ ✓

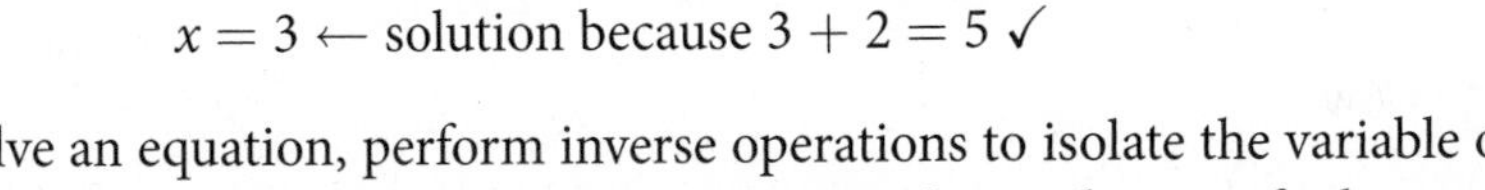

To solve an equation, perform inverse operations to isolate the variable on one side of the equation. The properties of equality can be used to justify the steps taken in solving an equation.

Properties of Equality

Property	Algebra	Numerical example
Addition Property of Equality	If $a = b$, then $a + c = b + c$	$12 = 7 + 5$, so $12 + 3 = 7 + 5 + 3$
Subtraction Property of Equality	If $a = b$, then $a - c = b - c$	$12 = 7 + 5$, so $12 - 3 = 7 + 5 - 3$
Multiplication Property of Equality	If $a = b$, then $ac = bc$	$12 = 7 + 5$, so $12 \cdot 3 = (7 + 5) \cdot 3$
Division Property of Equality	If $a = b$ and $c \neq 0$, then $\frac{a}{c} = \frac{b}{c}$	$12 = 7 + 5$, so $\frac{12}{3} = \frac{7+5}{3}$

You can use the properties of equality to solve two-step and multi-step equations.

EXAMPLE 1 CA CC A.REI.1, A.REI.3

Solve each equation.

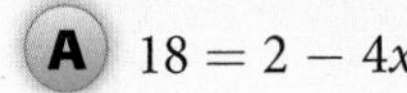

A $18 = 2 - 4x$

$$\begin{aligned} 18 &= 2 - 4x \\ -2 & \quad -2 \end{aligned}$$ Subtraction Property of Equality

$$16 = -4x$$

$$\frac{16}{-4} = \frac{-4x}{-4}$$ Division Property of Equality

$$-4 = x$$

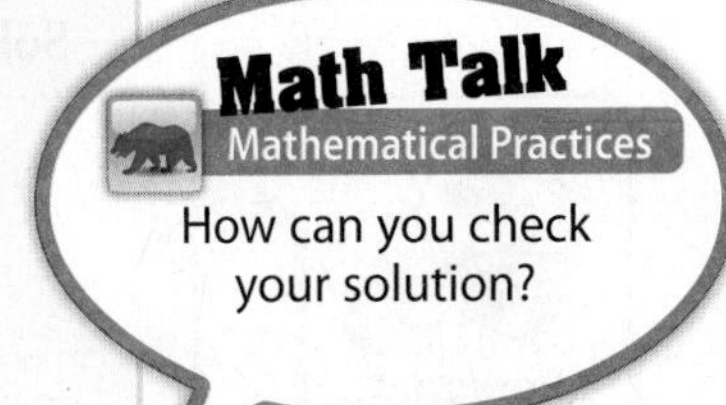

Math Talk
Mathematical Practices
How can you check your solution?

B $\frac{1}{2}z - 12 = 36$

$$\frac{1}{2}z - 12 = 36$$
$$\underline{+12 \quad +12}$$ Addition Property of Equality
$$\frac{1}{2}z = 48$$
$$2 \cdot \frac{1}{2}z = 2 \cdot 48$$ Multiplication Property of Equality
$$z = 96$$

C $\frac{3}{4} = 6w + 1$

$$\frac{3}{4} = 6w + 1$$
$$\underline{-1 = \quad -1}$$ Subtraction Property of Equality
$$-\frac{1}{4} = 6w$$
$$-\frac{1}{4}\left(\frac{1}{6}\right) = 6w\left(\frac{1}{6}\right)$$ Multiplication Property of Equality
$$-\frac{1}{24} = w$$

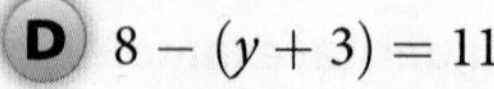

D $8 - (y + 3) = 11$

$$8 - (y + 3) = 11$$
$$8 - y - 3 = 11$$ Distribute the negative sign.
$$5 - y = 11$$ Combine like terms.
$$5 - y = 11$$
$$\underline{-5 \quad -5}$$ Subtraction Property of Equality
$$-y = 6$$
$$\frac{-y}{-1} = \frac{6}{-1}$$ Division Property of Equality
$$y = -6$$

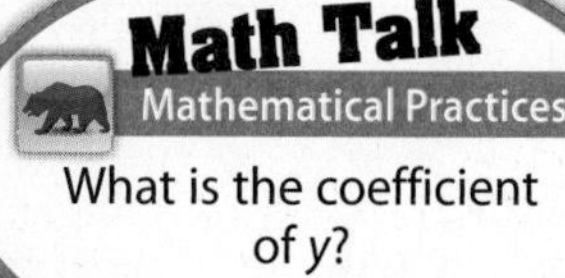

What is the coefficient of *y*?

YOUR TURN

Solve each equation.

1. $6k - 9 = -15$ ______

2. $17 = -5m + 32$ ______

3. $23 = 16 - (2z - 4)$ ______

4. $8 = \frac{1}{2}(-m - 1)$ ______

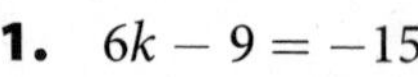

Solving Equations with Variables on Both Sides

In some equations, the variable appears on both sides. You can use the properties of equality to collect the variable terms so that they are all on one side of the equation.

EXAMPLE 2  CA CC A.REI.1, A.REI.3

My Notes

Solve each equation.

A $8n - 7 = 2n + 5$

$$\begin{aligned} 8n - 7 &= 2n + 5 \\ -2n \quad & \quad -2n \\ 6n - 7 &= 5 \\ +7 \quad & \quad +7 \\ 6n &= 12 \\ \frac{6n}{6} &= \frac{12}{6} \\ n &= 2 \end{aligned}$$

Subtraction Property of Equality

Addition Property of Equality

Division Property of Equality

Check: $8n - 7 = 2n + 5$ — Substitute 2 for n in the original equation.

$$\begin{aligned} 8(2) - 7 &= 2(2) + 5 \\ 16 - 7 &= 4 + 5 \\ 9 &= 9 \checkmark \end{aligned}$$

B $-4(3x - 1) = 10 - 4x$

$$\begin{aligned} -4(3x - 1) &= 10 - 4x \\ -12x + 4 &= 10 - 4x \\ +12x \quad & \quad +12x \\ 4 &= 10 + 8x \\ -10 \quad & \quad -10 \\ -6 &= 8x \\ \frac{-6}{8} &= \frac{8x}{8} \\ -\frac{3}{4} &= x \end{aligned}$$

Distributive Property

Addition Property of Equality

Subtraction Property of Equality

Division Property of Equality

Simplify.

Equations are often easier to solve when the variable has a positive coefficient. Keep this in mind when deciding on which side to "collect" variable terms.

YOUR TURN

Solve each equation.

5. $13b = b + 27$ ________

6. $6n + 21 = -3 - 2n$ ________

7. $2p - 9 = 3(2p - 5)$ ________

8. $t - 3 + 4t = 3(3t - 9)$ ________

Infinitely Many Solutions or No Solutions

An **identity** is an equation that is always true, no matter what value is substituted for the variable. The solutions of an equation that is an identity are all real numbers. Some equations are always false. Such equations have no solutions.

EXAMPLE 3 CA CC A.REI.1, A.REI.3

Solve each equation.

A $4d - 5(d - 1) = 3 - d + 2$

$4d - 5(d - 1) = 3 - d + 2$

$4d - 5d + 5 = 3 - d + 2$ Distributive Property

$-d + 5 = 5 - d$ Combine like terms

$\underline{+d} \quad \underline{+d}$ Addition Property of Equality

$5 = 5$ ✓ True statement

The equation $4d - 5(d - 1) = 3 - d + 2$ is an identity. All values of d will make the equation true. All real numbers are solutions.

B $3q + 6 - 5q = 8 - 2q + 1$

$3q + 6 - 5q = 8 - 2q + 1$

$-2q + 6 = 9 - 2q$ Combine like terms.

$\underline{+2q} \quad \underline{+2q}$ Addition Property of Equality

$6 = 9$ ✗ False statement

The solution set contains no elements. This is called the empty set. The empty set can be written as ϕ or $\{\}$.

The equation $3q + 6 - 5q = 8 - 2q + 1$ is always false. There is no value of q that will make the equation true. There are no solutions.

YOUR TURN

Solve each equation.

9. $3h + 6(h - 1) = 9h - 6$ ________

10. $4n - 3 - 5n = 6 - n + 4$ ________

Writing and Solving Real-World Equations

You can write and solve an equation to model a real-world situation. Check that the solution to the equation makes sense in the context of the situation.

EXAMPLE 4

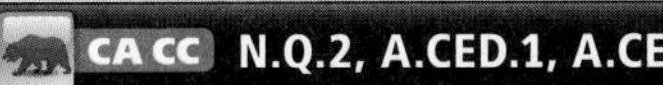

Leon paid \$26.50 for a shirt with a sales tax of 6% included, but he doesn't remember the price without tax. What was the price of the shirt?

Write a verbal model for the situation.

price of shirt + (6% of price of shirt) = total paid

Choose a variable for the unknown quantity. Include units. Write an equation to model the situation.

Let p represent the price of the shirt in dollars.

$p + 0.06p = 26.50$

STEP 3 Solve the equation.

$p + 0.06p = 26.50$

$1.06p = 26.50$ *Combine like terms.*

$\frac{1.06p}{1.06} = \frac{26.50}{1.06}$ *Division Property of Equality*

$p = 25$

So the price of the shirt was \$25.

STEP 4 Check that the answer makes sense in the context of the problem.

6% of \$25 is \$1.50, so the sales tax on the shirt is \$1.50.

\$25.00 + \$1.50 = \$26.50

So the answer does make sense.

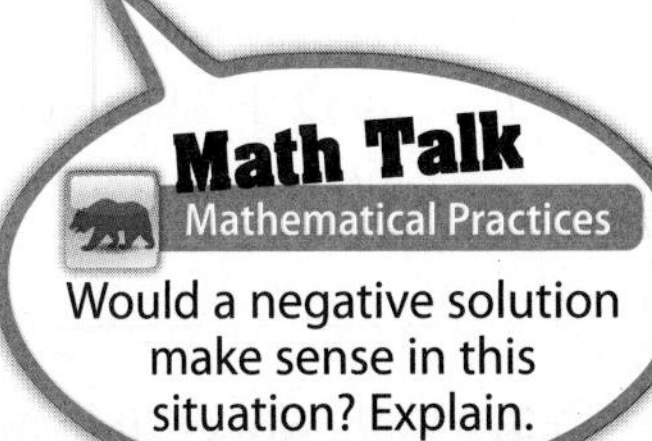

Math Talk
Mathematical Practices
Would a negative solution make sense in this situation? Explain.

YOUR TURN

11. Maria bought a blouse on sale for 20% off the regular price. The sale price was \$28.76. What was the regular price? Write an equation to model the situation. Solve the equation.

____

Guided Practice

Identify the steps you would take to solve each equation. Then solve. (Example 1)

1. $18x + 17 = -19$

2. $7y + 6 + 4y - 13 = 26$

Solve each equation. (Examples 1 and 2)

3. $13 = 4x - 9$

4. $55 - 6(3b - 1) = -11$

5. $2.5k + 5 - 1.5k = 14$

6. $12n + 9 = 6 - 3n$

7. $6z = 4\left(\frac{1}{2}z - 8\right)$

8. $2r - 6 + 5r = 3 - r + 7$

Solve each equation. Determine whether the equation has infinitely many solutions or no solution. Explain. (Example 3)

9. $7t - 13 - 2t = 9 + 5t$

10. $4(2x - 3) = x - 12 + 7x$

11. $6 - 2r + 1 = 3r - 5(r - 2)$

Write an equation to model each problem. Solve the equation. (Example 4)

12. At 12 noon in Anchorage, Alaska, Janice noticed that the temperature outside was 12 °F. The temperature dropped at a steady rate of 2 °F per hour. At what time was the temperature −4 °F?

13. Zelly works 20 hours a week at a food market for $7.50 an hour. She takes home $6.75 an hour after deductions. What is her rate for deductions?

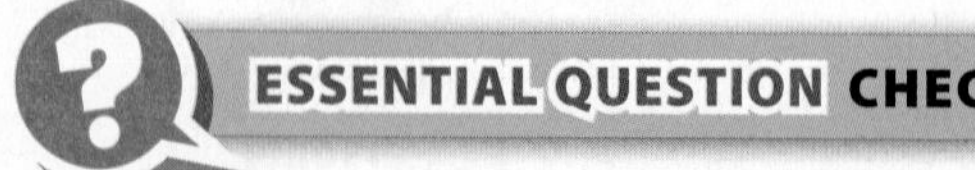

14. How do you use the properties of equality to solve an equation in one variable?

Name ______________________ Class ______________ Date ______________

3.1 Independent Practice

CA CC A.REI.3

Solve each equation.

15. $6y - (2y - 5) = 29$

16. $5x - 9 = 7x + 6 - 2x$

17. $8(3m + 5) = 2m - 4$

18. $15q - 3(4q - 6) = 3q + 9 - 9q$

19. $6z + 10 = 4z + 19$

20. $8b + 12 - b = 8 + 7b + 4$

21. $5a - (8 - a) = 4a - 10$

22. $7n - 2 = 6n - 2n$

23. $8d - \frac{1}{3}(6 - 9d) = 42$

Write and solve an equation to solve each problem.

24. Mari and Jen each work 20 hours a week at different jobs. Mari earns twice as much as Jen. Together they earn $480. How much does each girl earn in a week?

25. David's bowling score is 5 less than 3 times Aaron's score. The sum of their scores is 215. Find the score of each student.

26. **Multi-Step** One month, Jon worked 3 hours less than Chaya, and Angelica worked 4 hours more than Chaya. Together they worked 196 hours. Find the number of hours each person worked.

27. The teacher separated her class of twenty-eight students into two groups. One group has 4 more than twice as many students as the other group. How many students are in each group?

28. An equilateral triangle and a square have the same perimeter. Each side of the square measures 6 cm. What is the length of each side of the triangle?

29. Gaetano spent $37.80, including tax, on a pair of jeans. How much did the jeans cost if there was an 8% sales tax?

30. The temperature at 4 a.m. was $-13\,°$F. The temperature was rising at a steady rate of $5\,°$F an hour. At what time will the temperature be $12\,°$F ?

31. Brian is fencing a rectangular area in the backyard for his dog. He has 25 ft of fence. He does not need fencing on the side that runs along the garage. This side is 9 ft long. What are the dimensions of the kennel?

FOCUS ON HIGHER ORDER THINKING

Work Area

32. Justify Reasoning Suppose you want to solve the equation $2a + b = 2a$, where a and b are nonzero real numbers. Describe the solution to this equation. Justify your description.

33. Persevere in Problem Solving A rectangular garden is fenced on all sides with 160 feet of fencing. The garden is 6 feet longer than it is wide. What is the area of the garden?

a. What information do you need to find the area? How can you find the information?

b. Describe how to find the area of the garden. Include the steps you used.

LESSON 3.2

Inequalities in One Variable

CA CC A.REI.3 Solve linear equations and inequalities in one variable, including equations with coefficients represented by letters. *Also A.CED.1, A.CED.3*

ESSENTIAL QUESTION

How do you solve an inequality in one variable?

One-Step Inequalities

An **inequality** is a statement that compares two expressions that are not equal by using an inequality sign.

A **solution of an inequality** is any value that makes the inequality true. Inequalities usually have infinitely many solutions. One way to represent the solution set of an inequality in one variable is to graph it on a number line.

You can solve linear inequalities using methods that are similar to the ones you use to solve linear equations.

EXAMPLE 1

CA CC A.REI.3

Solve and graph each inequality.

A $x + 3 > 7$

$$x + 3 > 7$$
$$\underline{-3 \quad -3}$$
$$x \quad > 4$$

Subtract 3 from each side.

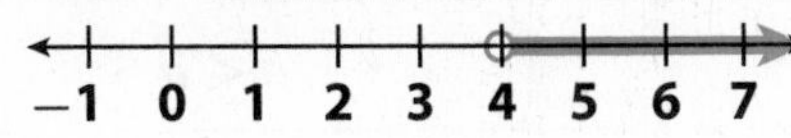

B $\frac{x}{3} \leq -4$

$$\frac{x}{3} \leq -4$$
$$3\left(\frac{x}{3}\right) \leq 3\,(-4)$$
$$x \leq -12$$

Multiply each side by 3.

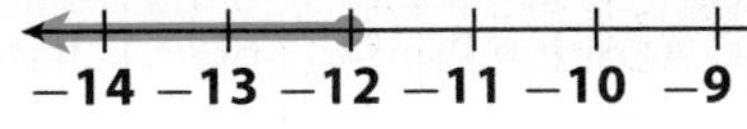

Use a closed circle when the boundary point is part of the solution and an open circle when it is not.

YOUR TURN

Solve and graph each inequality.

1. $12n > 6$

____

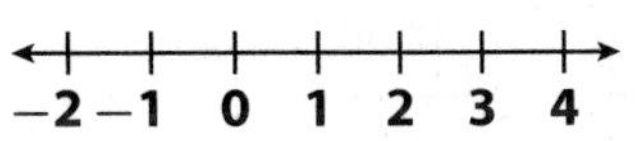

2. $\frac{h}{2} \leq -1$

____

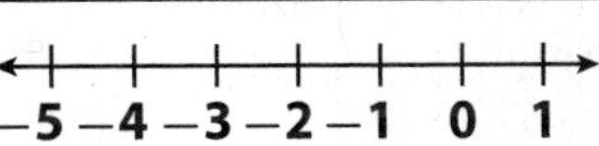

3. $m + 12 \geq 16$

____

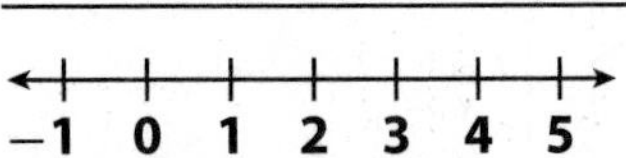

4. $s - 5 < -2$

____

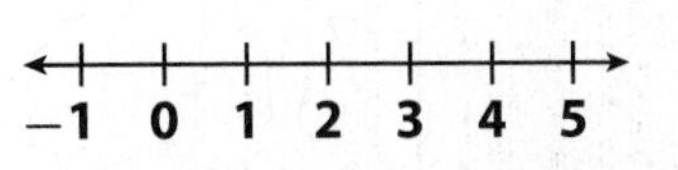

EXPLORE ACTIVITY

A.REI.3

Multiplying and Dividing by a Negative Number

What happens when you multiply each side of an inequality by the same number?

A Multiply both sides of $2 > -1$ by 2. Does it result in a true inequality?

Explain. ______________________________

B Multiply both sides of $2 > -1$ by -2. Does it result in a true inequality?

Explain. ______________________________

C Multiply both sides of $2 > -1$ by -2 AND reverse the inequality symbol from $>$ to $<$. Does it result in a true inequality? Explain.

____

REFLECT

5. **Make a Conjecture** Does multiplying both sides of an inequality by a negative number result in an equivalent inequality? Explain.

____

Solving Multi-Step Inequalities

You can use the Properties of Inequality to help you solve inequalities.

Properties of Inequality

Property	$a > b$	$a < b$
Addition Property of Inequality	If $a > b$, then $a + c > b + c$	If $a < b$, then $a + c < b + c$
Subtraction Property of Inequality	If $a > b$, then $a - c > b - c$	If $a < b$, then $a - c > b - c$
Multiplication Property of Inequality	If $a > b$ and $c > 0$, then $ac > bc$	If $a < b$ and $c > 0$, then $ac < bc$
	If $a > b$ and $c < 0$, then $ac < bc$	If $a < b$ and $c < 0$, then $ac > bc$
Division Property of Inequality	If $a > b$ and $c > 0$, then $\frac{a}{c} > \frac{b}{c}$	If $a < b$ and $c > 0$, then $\frac{a}{c} < \frac{b}{c}$
	If $a > b$ and $c < 0$, then $\frac{a}{c} < \frac{b}{c}$	If $a < b$ and $c < 0$, then $\frac{a}{c} > \frac{b}{c}$

EXAMPLE 2

CA CC A.REI.3

Solve and graph each inequality.

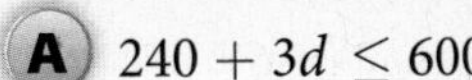

A $240 + 3d \le 600$

$$\begin{aligned} 240 + 3d &\le 600 \\ -240 \quad & \quad -240 \\ 3d &\le 360 \end{aligned}$$

Subtraction Property of Inequality

$$\frac{3d}{3} \le \frac{360}{3}$$

Division Property of Inequality

$$d \le 120$$

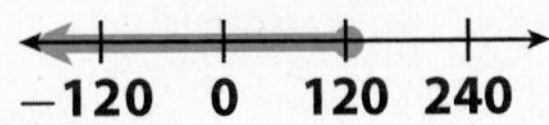

B $12 - 5k > 72$

$$\begin{aligned} 12 - 5k &> 72 \\ -12 \quad & \quad -12 \\ -5k &> 60 \end{aligned}$$

Subtraction Property of Inequality

$$\frac{-5k}{-5} < \frac{60}{-5}$$

Division Property of Inequality
Reverse the inequality symbol.

$$k < -12$$

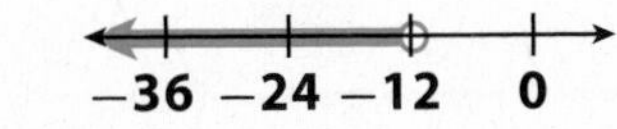

C $6^2 - 1 < -7(y - 3)$

$$6^2 - 1 < -7(y - 3)$$

$$35 < -7y + 21$$

Simplify.

$$\begin{aligned} -21 \quad & \quad -21 \\ 14 &< -7y \end{aligned}$$

Subtraction Property of Inequality

$$\frac{14}{-7} > \frac{-7y}{-7}$$

Division Property of Inequality
Reverse the inequality symbol.

$$-2 > y \text{ or } y < -2$$

When you read an inequality containing a variable, begin with the variable. $-2 > y$ is read, "y is less than -2." You can write $y < -2$.

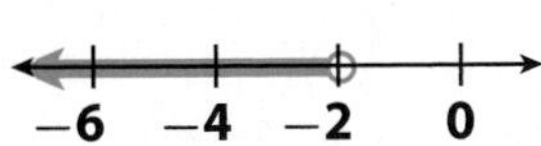

My Notes

D $-\frac{2}{3}x > -\frac{1}{2}$

$$-\frac{2}{3}x > -\frac{1}{2}$$

$$\left(-\frac{3}{2}\right)-\frac{2}{3}x < \left(-\frac{3}{2}\right)-\frac{1}{2}$$ Multiplication Property of Inequality. Reverse the inequality symbol.

$$x < \frac{3}{4}$$

0 1

YOUR TURN

Solve and graph each inequality.

6. $-7t \geq 4.9$

______

−2 −1 0 1

7. $-\frac{5}{6}y < -\frac{3}{4}$

______

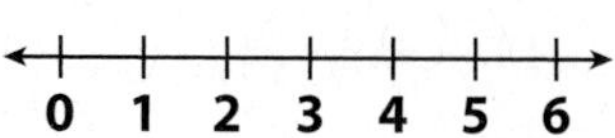

8. $-3(x - 4) < 18$

______

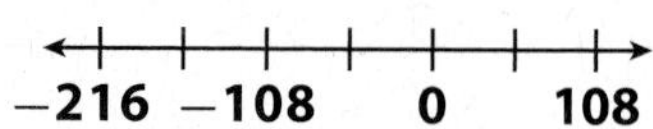

9. $5y + 2(3 - 4y) < 330$

______

Solving Inequalities with Variables on Both Sides

Solving inequalities with variables on both sides is similar to solving equations with variables on both sides. Use inverse operations and the properties of inequality to "collect" the variable terms on one side.

EXAMPLE 3 CA CC A.REI.3

Solve and graph each inequality.

A $17 - 5m \leq 8m - 9$

$$17 - 5m \leq 8m - 9$$

$$\underline{+5m \quad +5m}$$ Addition Property of Inequality

$$17 \leq 13m - 9$$

$$\underline{+9 \qquad +9}$$ Addition Property of Inequality

$$26 \leq 13m$$

$$\frac{26}{13} \leq \frac{13m}{13}$$ Division Property of Inequality

$$2 \leq m \text{ or } m \geq 2$$

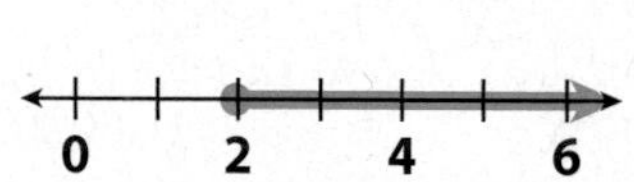

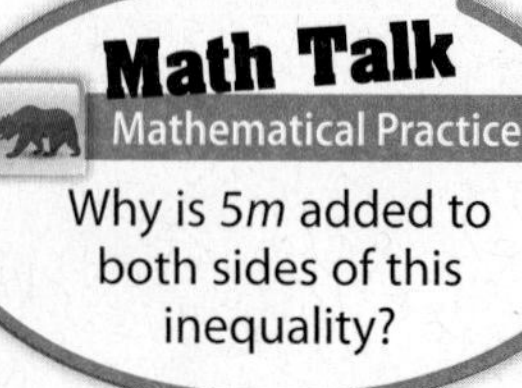

Math Talk
Mathematical Practices
Why is 5m added to both sides of this inequality?

B $24 - 6y - 5y \le -9$

$$24 - 6y - 5y \le -9$$

$$24 - 11y \le -9$$ Combine the like terms

$$\underline{-24} \qquad \underline{-24}$$ Subtraction Property of Inequality

$$-11y \le -33$$

$$\frac{-11y}{-11} \ge \frac{-33}{-11}$$ Division Property of Inequality
Reverse the inequality symbol.

$$y \ge 3$$

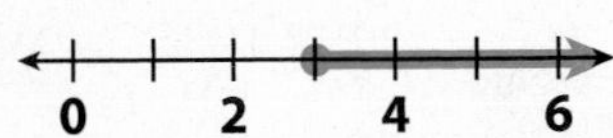

C $6(z - 5) > -5(7 - 2z)$

$$6(z - 5) > -5(7 - 2z)$$

$$6z - 30 > -35 + 10z$$ Distributive Property

$$\underline{-6z} \qquad \underline{-6z}$$ Subtraction Property

$$-30 > -35 + 4z$$

$$\underline{+35} \qquad \underline{+35}$$ Addition Property of Inequality

$$5 > 4z$$

$$\frac{5}{4} > \frac{4z}{4}$$ Division Property of Inequality

$$1.25 > z \text{ or } z < 1.25$$

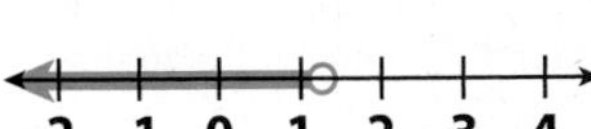

My Notes

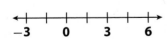

YOUR TURN

Solve and graph each inequality.

10. $10 - k > 5 + \frac{2k}{3}$ ________________

−3 0 3 6

11. $\frac{3}{5}(a + 3) \ge 0.4(2 + a)$ ________________

−6 −4 −2 0

All Real Numbers as Solutions or No Solutions

Some inequalities are always true and some inequalities are always false, no matter what value is substituted for the variable.

My Notes

EXAMPLE 4

CA CC A.REI.3

Solve and graph each inequality.

 $2x - 7 + x < 3x + 10$

$2x - 7 + x < 3x + 10$

$3x - 7 < 3x + 10$ Combine the like terms.

$\underline{-3x} \quad \underline{-3x}$ Subtraction Property of Inequality

$-7 < 10$ ✓ True statement

The inequality $2x - 7 + x < 3x + 10$ is a true statement. Any real number substituted for x will make the inequality true. All real numbers are solutions. The graph represents the set of all real numbers.

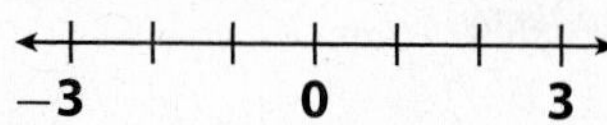

 $5(x + 4) \geq 8x + 25 - 3x$

$5(x + 4) \geq 8x + 25 - 3x$

$5x + 20 \geq 5x + 25$ Combine the like terms.

$\underline{-5x} \quad \underline{-5x}$ Subtraction Property of Inequality

$20 \geq 25$ ✗ False statement

The inequality $5(x + 4) \geq 8x + 25 - 3x$ is always false. There is no value of x that will make the inequality true. There are no solutions. The graph represents the empty set.

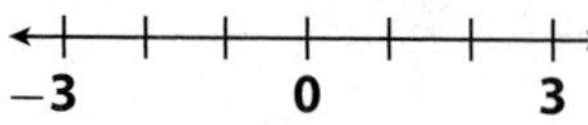

YOUR TURN

Solve and graph each inequality.

12. $3d + 6 < 5d - 2(d + 3)$

____

−3 0 3

13. $18p - 15 + 6p \geq -10 + 24p - 5$

____

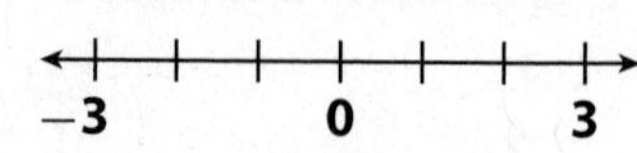

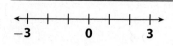

Writing and Solving Real-World Inequalities

You can use inequalities to solve some real-world problems. Phrases such as "no more than" and "at least" imply that there is more than one solution to the problem.

Math On the Spot
my.hrw.com

Kristin wants to spend no more than \$50 for a birthday dinner at a restaurant, including a 15% tip. What is the most that the meal can cost before tip?

STEP 1 Write a verbal model for the situation.

cost before tip $+$15% of cost before tip $\leq$ \$50

STEP 2 Choose a variable for the unknown quantity. Include units. Write an inequality to model the situation.

Let x represent the cost of the dinner before the tip in dollars.

$x + 0.15x \leq 50$

STEP 3 Solve and graph the inequality.

$$x + 0.15x \leq 50$$

$$1.15x \leq 50$$

$$\frac{1.15x}{1.15} \leq \frac{50}{1.15}$$

$$x \leq 43.478260\ldots$$

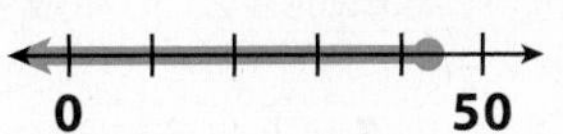

Find the answer to the nearest cent and interpret the result.

The most that the meal can cost before the tip is \$43.47. You also know that the cost of the meal must be more than \$0.

If you round to the nearest hundredth, the value will be more than the maximum cost that you calculated.

REFLECT

14. Why are there no negative numbers in the solution set?

____

____

YOUR TURN

15. Ammon and Nakia volunteer at an animal shelter. Nakia worked 3 more hours than Ammon. They each worked a whole number of hours. Together they worked more than 27 hours. What is the least number of hours each worked?

____

Guided Practice

Complete the steps to solve and graph each inequality (Examples 1 and 2)

1. $4 \leq -9y + y$

$4 \leq$ ☐

$\frac{4}{☐} \geq \frac{-8y}{☐}$

☐ $\geq y$

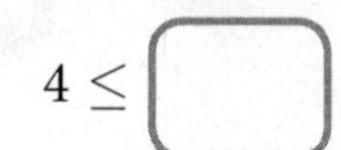

2. $7 - 4x < -1$

7 ☐ < -1 ☐

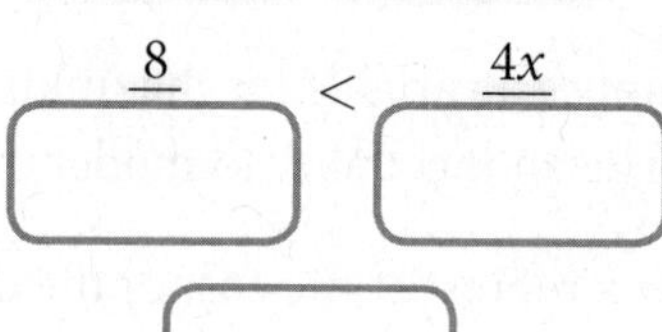

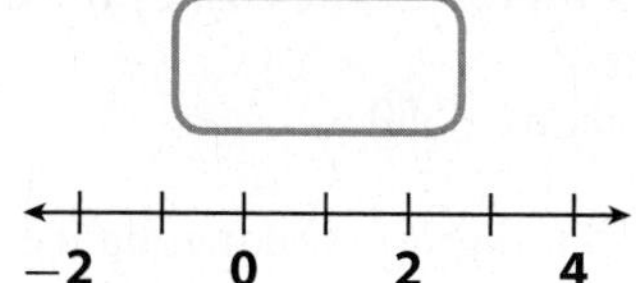

Solve and graph each inequality. (Examples 2, 3, and 4)

3. $3 - 9d < 30$

−3 0 3

4. $k + 3 - 2k > 50$

−51 −49 −47

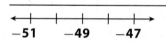

5. $4m \leq 6m - 4$

−2 0 2 4

6. $\frac{1}{5}(30 + a) < 5$

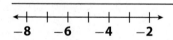

−8 −6 −4 −2

7. $3(x - 4) > 5(x + 2) - 2x$

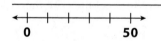

0 50

8. $9y + 4 \geq -2(1 - 3y)$

−4 −2 0 2

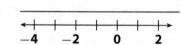

Solve each problem. (Example 5)

9. Mari has a part time job. She earns \$7 an hour. She makes at most \$143.50 a week. What is the greatest number of hours that she works? ________

10. Alexis received an 85, 89, and 92 on three tests. How many points does she need to score on her next test in order to have an average of at least 90? ________

ESSENTIAL QUESTION CHECK-IN

11. How do you solve an inequality in one variable?

Name ____________________ Class ____________________ Date ____________________

3.2 Independent Practice

CA CC A.REI.3

Solve and graph each inequality.

12. $-20x \geq -400$ ____________________

−30 −10 10 30

13. $0 < -10k + 5k$ ____________________

−4 −2 0 2

14. $6 - 5d > 21$ ____________________

−6 −4 −2 0

15. $3(10 + 2m) \leq 96$ ____________________

6 8 10 12

16. $5a - 6 \geq 3a$ ____________________

0 2 4 6

17. $5q \geq 8q - \frac{3}{2}$ ____________________

−4 −2 0 2

18. $2b - 15 > 5b$ ____________________

−8 −6 −4 −2

19. $7 - 6x < 2x + 89$ ____________________

−12 −10 −8 −6

For Exercises 20–22, determine whether each inequality is sometimes, always, or never true.

20. $w + 6 \leq w - 6$ ____________________

21. $12s \geq 10s$ ____________________

22. $3k - 4 < 2k + 1$ ____________________

23. After selling a dozen copies of the daily newspaper, a newsstand had fewer than 75 copies left. How many copies did the newsstand have at the beginning of the day?

____

24. Ken wants to rent a car for a week and to pay no more than $130. How far can he drive if the car rental costs $94 a week plus $0.40 a mile?

____

25. Lana's car averages 25 miles per gallon. What is the greatest number of gallons of gasoline that she will need if she travels no more than 450 miles?

____

26. The length of a rectangle is 4 cm longer than the width, and the perimeter is at least 48 cm. What are the smallest possible dimensions of the rectangle?

____

27. David charges $15 plus $5.50 per hour to mow lawns. Ari charges $12 plus $6.25 per hour to mow lawns. In what situations is Ari's charge greater than or equal to David's charge?

____

____

28. Critique Reasoning David said he charges less than Ari if the job takes 4 hours. Do you agree with David's statement? Explain.

FOCUS ON HIGHER ORDER THINKING

Work Area

29. Draw Conclusions Find a value of b such that the number line shows all the solutions of $bx + 4 \leq -12$. Explain.

−12 −10 −8 −6

30. Explain the Error Is the stepped-out solution correct? Explain.

$17 - 5y < 8y - 9$

$-13y < -26$

$y < 2$

31. Communicate Mathematical Ideas Give an example of an inequality that could be solved by using the Multiplication Property of Inequality where both sides of an inequality are multiplied by a negative number. Show the steps of the solution.

32. Justify Reasoning Given the inequality $3(x - 4) > bx$, for what value of b are there no solutions? Use properties of inequality to justify your solution.

LESSON 3.3

Solving for a Variable

A.CED.4 Rearrange formulas to highlight a quantity of interest, using the same reasoning as in solving equations. *Also A.REI.3*

ESSENTIAL QUESTION

How do you solve formulas and literal equations for a variable?

Solving a Formula for a Variable

A **formula** is an equation that describes a relationship among quantities. You can "rearrange" a formula using inverse operations and properties of equality to isolate any variable in that formula. This is called solving for a variable. The result of solving a formula for a variable is not a number but a variable expression.

EXAMPLE 1

CA CC A.CED.4

Solve the formula for the indicated variable.

A The formula $V = lwh$ is used to find the volume of a rectangular prism with length l, width w, and height h. Solve the formula for h.

$$V = lwh$$

$$\frac{V}{lw} = \frac{lwh}{lw} \quad \text{Division Property of Equality}$$

$$\frac{V}{lw} = h$$

B The formula $E = \frac{1}{2}kx^2$ is used to find the potential energy E of a spring with spring constant k that has been stretched by length x. Solve the formula for k.

$$E = \frac{1}{2}kx^2$$

$$(2)(E) = (2)(\tfrac{1}{2}kx^2) \quad \text{Multiplication Property of Equality}$$

$$2E = kx^2$$

$$\frac{2E}{x^2} = \frac{kx^2}{x^2} \quad \text{Division Property of Equality}$$

$$\frac{2E}{x^2} = k$$

YOUR TURN

Solve each formula for the indicated variable.

1. The formula for the perimeter P of a triangle with sides of length a, b, and c is $P = a + b + c$. Solve the formula for b. ______

2. The formula for the volume of a cylinder of radius r and height h is $V = \pi r^2 h$. Solve the formula for h. ______

Modeling with Formulas

Sometimes you are given a formula solved for one variable, but the formula would be more convenient to use if it were solved for one of the other variables. You can solve for a variable in a formula so that it is more convenient for you to use.

EXAMPLE 2 

CA CC A.CED.4

My Notes

A flower garden is made up of a square and an isosceles triangle with dimensions as shown. Use the formula for perimeter to write a formula for the side length of the square in terms of the perimeter.

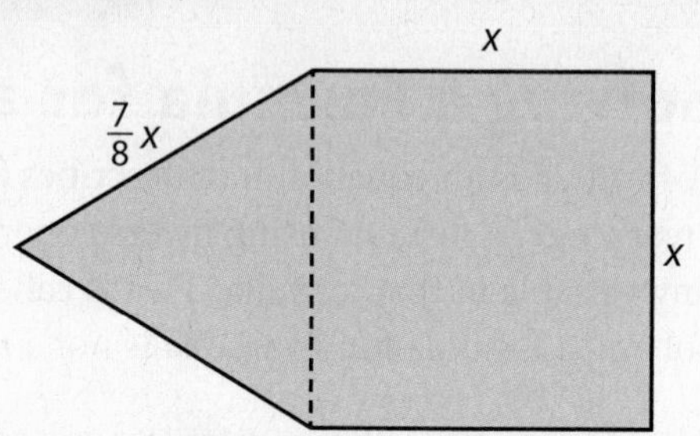

STEP 1 Write and simplify a formula for the perimeter of the garden.

$$P = x + x + x + \tfrac{7}{8}x + \tfrac{7}{8}x$$

$$P = 3x + \tfrac{14}{8}x \qquad \text{Combine like terms.}$$

$$P = 4\tfrac{3}{4}x \qquad \text{Combine like terms.}$$

STEP 2 Solve the formula for x.

$$P = 4\tfrac{3}{4}x$$

$$P = \tfrac{19}{4}x$$

$$\left(\tfrac{4}{19}\right)P = \left(\tfrac{4}{19}\right)\tfrac{19}{4}x \qquad \text{Multiplication Property of Equality}$$

$$\tfrac{4}{19}P = x$$

So the formula for the length of a side of the square is $x = \frac{4}{19}P$.

REFLECT

3. **Communicate Mathematical Ideas** How could you use the formula you derived to find the side lengths of the garden with perimeter 133 feet?

____

____

YOUR TURN

Solve each formula for the indicated variable.

4. Formula for density, $D = \frac{m}{V}$, for V

____

5. Formula for the lateral surface area of a cylinder, $S = 2\pi rh$, for r

____

Solving a Literal Equation for a Variable

A **literal equation** is an equation with two or more variables. A formula is a type of literal equation. To solve a literal equation for a variable, use inverse operations and properties of equality.

EXAMPLE 3

CA CC A.REI.3

Solve each literal equation for the indicated variable.

A $a(x + b) = c$, where $a \neq 0$, for x

$\frac{a(x+b)}{a} = \frac{c}{a}$ Division Property of Equality

$x + b = \frac{c}{a}$ Simplify.

$x + b - b = \frac{c}{a} - b$ Subtraction Property of Equality

$x = \frac{c}{a} - b$ Simplify.

Math Talk
Mathematical Practices
Why are both sides of the equation divided by a?

B $A = \frac{1}{2}h(b_1 + b_2)$, where $h \neq 0$, for b_1

$A = \frac{1}{2}h(b_1 + b_2)$

$2A = h(b_1 + b_2)$ Multiplication Property of Equality

$\frac{2A}{h} = \frac{h(b_1 + b_2)}{h}$ Division Property of Equality

$\frac{2A}{h} = b_1 + b_2$ Simplify.

$\frac{2A}{h} - b_2 = b_1 + b_2 - b_2$ Subtraction Property of Equality

$\frac{2A}{h} - b_2 = b_1$ Simplify.

$b_1 = \frac{2A}{h} - b_2$

REFLECT

6. **Justify Reasoning** Another way to solve $a(x + b) = c$ is to start by using the Distributive Property. Show and justify the solution steps using this method. ______________________________

____

____

YOUR TURN

Solve each literal equation for the indicated variable.

7. $2(k + m) = 5$, for m ______________

8. $ax - b = c$, for x ______________

9. $2x + 10 = 5y - 4$, for y

10. $s = 3(w - s)$, for s

______________ ______________

Guided Practice

Solve the formula for the indicated variable. (Example 1)

1. Formula for distance traveled, $d = rt$, for t

______

2. Formula for the flow of current in an electrical circuit, $V = IH$, for I

______

3. Formula for the surface area of a cylinder, $SA = 2\pi r^2 + 2\pi rh$, for h

______

4. Formula for the area of a trapezoid, $A = \frac{1}{2}(a + b)h$, for h

______

5. Formula for the average of 3 numbers, $A = \frac{a + b + c}{3}$, for c

______

6. Formula for Celsius temperature, $C = \frac{5}{9}(F - 32)$, for F

______

7. The formula $T = p + sp$ can be used to calculate the total cost of an item with price p and sales tax rate s, expressed as a decimal. Describe a situation in which you would want to solve the formula for s. Then solve the formula for s. (Example 2)

______

______

Solve each equation for the indicated variable. (Example 3)

8. $bx = c$, for x

______

9. $kn + mp = q$, for p

______

10. $a = b + rb$, for r

______

11. $A = P + Prt$, for t

______

12. $\frac{y - b}{m} = x$, for y

______

13. $\frac{m}{n} = \frac{p}{q}$, for p

______

ESSENTIAL QUESTION CHECK-IN

14. How do you solve formulas and literal equations for a variable?

______

______

______

______

______

Name ____________________ Class ____________ Date ____________

3.3 Independent Practice

A.CED.4

Solve the formula for the indicated variable.

15. Formula for the volume of a cylinder, $V = \pi r^2 h$, for h

____

16. Formula for the area of a polygon, $A = \frac{1}{2}aP$, for a

____

17. Formula for the sum of the measures of the interior angles of a polygon, $S = 180(n - 2)$, for n

____

18. The Pythagorean theorem, $a^2 + b^2 = c^2$, for c

____

19. Formula for the volume of a square pyramid, $V = \frac{1}{3}\ell wh$, for w

____

20. Formula for surface area of a cone, $S = \pi r^2 + \pi r\ell$, for ℓ

____

21. Formula for Fahrenheit temperature, $F = 32 + \frac{9}{5}C$, for C

____

22. Formula for the volume of a sphere, $V = \frac{4}{3}\pi r^3$, for r

____

Solve each equation for the indicated variable.

23. $km = \frac{m}{2} + p$, for m ______________

24. $\frac{2}{3}c = d$, for c ______________

25. $rs - t = us + v$, for s ______________

26. $\frac{2}{5}(z + 1) = y$, for z ______________

27. $g\left(h + \frac{2}{3}\right) = 1$, for h ______________

28. $a(n - 3) + 8 = bn$, for n ______________

29. Ken purchased a plot of land shaped like the figure shown. How can he find the length of the side labeled x if he knows the area A of this lot?

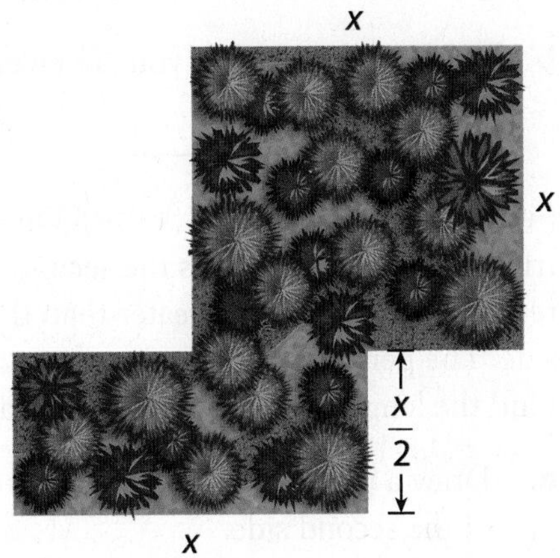

____

____

____

30. An electrician sent Bonnie an invoice in the amount of a dollars for the six hours of work done on Saturday. The electrician charges a weekend fee f in addition to an hourly rate r. Write a formula Bonnie can use to find r, the rate the electrician charges per hour, in terms of a and f. If the invoice amount is \$450 and the weekend fee is \$75, what is the hourly rate?

____

____

31. The formula for the surface area of a cylinder is $S = 2\pi r^2 + 2\pi rh$. The surface area of a cylinder is 112π square inches and the radius is 4 inches. What is the height of the cone?

____

H.O.T. FOCUS ON HIGHER ORDER THINKING

Work Area

32. Marion's dinner at a restaurant came to \$32.40. This included an 8% tax. Marion wants to leave a 15% tip on the cost of the dinner alone. How much should she leave as a tip?

____

33. Multi-Step A rectangle has a perimeter of 48 cm and a width of 6 cm. Use the formula $P = 2l + 2w$ to find the length.

a. Write the formula in terms of l. ______________________________

b. Substitute the values you are given into the rearranged formula. What is the length? ______________________________

34. Persevere in Problem Solving One side of a triangle is twice as long as the second side. The remaining side is 4 cm greater than the second side. The perimeter of the triangle is 24 cm. Find the length of each side of the triangle.

a. Draw a picture. Label each side in terms of the second side.

b. Write a formula for the perimeter of the triangle in terms of the second side. ______________________________

c. Use the formula to find the length of each side of the triangle.

____

35. Communicate Mathematical Ideas Liam receives a basic salary of \$600 a week plus 7% of his sales as a commission.

a. Write a formula for the amount Liam can expect to earn each week.

____

b. Last week Liam earned \$740. How much were his sales last week?

____

36. Make a Conjecture Write a formula for the area of a square in terms of the perimeter.

____

Ready to Go On?

Personal Math Trainer

Online Practice and Help

3.1 Equations in One Variable

Solve the following equations for x.

1. $3x - 2 = 8 - 2x$

2. $7 - 8x = 1 - 5x$

3. $15 + \frac{(5 - x)}{x} = 30$

3.2 Inequalities in One Variable

Solve and graph each inequality.

4. $7x - 20 \leq 3x$

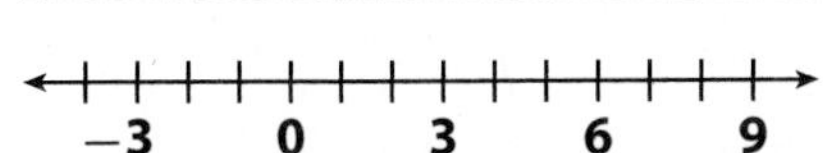

5. $2x + 20 \geq 14$

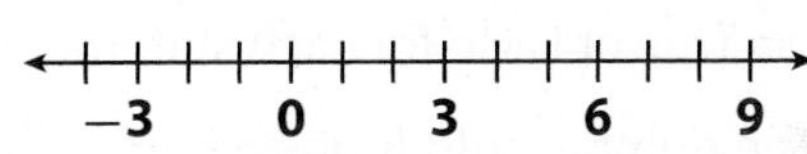

6. $x - 10 \geq 2(x - 4)$

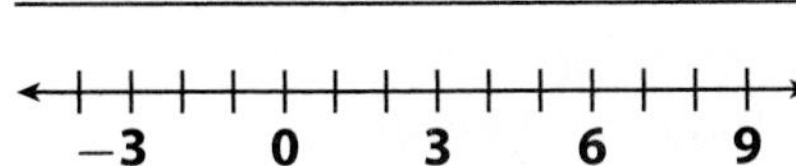

7. $3x - (x + 2) > x - 14$

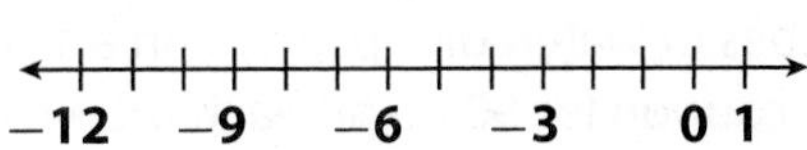

3.3 Solving for a Variable

Solve the formula for the indicated variable.

8. The volume of a cone $V = \frac{1}{3}\pi r^2 h$, for h

9. Surface area of cylinder $S = 2\pi r^2 + 2\pi rh$, for h

10. Damien has enough red paint to cover an area, of 36 square meters. The surface area of the playground tunnel he must paint has a radius, r, of 3 meters. The formula for surface area is $S = 2\pi rl$ where l is the length.

Solve the formula for l and find the length of the tunnel Damien can paint.

ESSENTIAL QUESTION

11. How can you solve an equation or inequality in one variable?

MODULE 3
MIXED REVIEW

Assessment Readiness

1. Consider each inequality. Is the inequality equivalent to $5(x - 4) \geq -3x + 4$? Select Yes or No for expressions A–C.

A. $5x - 20 \geq -3x + 4$ ◯ Yes ◯ No
B. $8x - 20 \leq 4$ ◯ Yes ◯ No
C. $x \geq 3$ ◯ Yes ◯ No

2. The formula $g = sn - (b - e)$ gives a store's monthly gross profit g for selling coffee mugs. In this formula, s is the selling price of the mugs, n is the number sold, b is the value of the inventory of mugs at the beginning of the month, and e is the value of the inventory at the end of the month.

Choose True or False for each statement.

A. The number sold is given by $n = \frac{g + b - e}{s}$. ◯ True ◯ False
B. The beginning value is given by $b = sn + e - g$. ◯ True ◯ False
C. The ending value is given by $e = sn - g - b$. ◯ True ◯ False

3. All tubes of watercolor paint at an art supply store have the same price. An artist has a coupon for \$0.50 off each tube of paint she buys. She buys 6 tubes of paint and pays a total of \$84.30 after the coupon is applied. Write and solve an equation to find r, the regular price of each tube of paint. Explain each step of your solution.

4. Climbing at an indoor rock-climbing gym costs \$8 per hour. Lizbeth has a \$30 gift card to spend at the gym. Write an algebraic expression for the dollar amount Lizbeth will have left on the card after she spends h hours climbing. Can Lizbeth climb for 4.5 hours using only her card? Explain how you know.

Equations in Two Variables and Functions

MODULE 4

ESSENTIAL QUESTION

What is a function and how can a function be represented?

CALIFORNIA COMMON CORE

LESSON 4.1
Equations in Two Variables

CA CC A.REI.10

LESSON 4.2
Representing Functions
CA CC F.IF.1, A.REI.10, A.REI.11, F.IF.2, F.IF.5

LESSON 4.3
Sequences
CA CC F.IF.3, F.BF.1, F.BF.1a, F.BF.2

my.hrw.com

Real-World Video

A function can be thought of as an industrial machine: only accepting of certain predefined inputs, performing a series of operations on what it's been fed, and delivering an output dependent on the initial input.

GO DIGITAL
my.hrw.com

my.hrw.com

Go digital with your write-in student edition, accessible on any device.

Math On the Spot

Scan with your smart phone to jump directly to the online edition, video tutor, and more.

Animated Math

Interactively explore key concepts to see how math works.

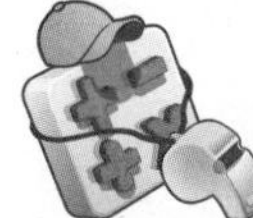

Personal Math Trainer

Get immediate feedback and help as you work through practice sets.

Are YOU Ready?

Complete these exercises to review skills you will need for this module.

Ordered Pairs

EXAMPLE (–3, 1)
Start at (0, 0).
Move 3 units to the left. The *x*-coordinate is –3.
Move 1 unit up. The *y*-coordinate is 1.

Graph each point on the coordinate plane.

1. (–2, 4)

2. (0, –5)

3. (1, –3)

4. (4, 2)

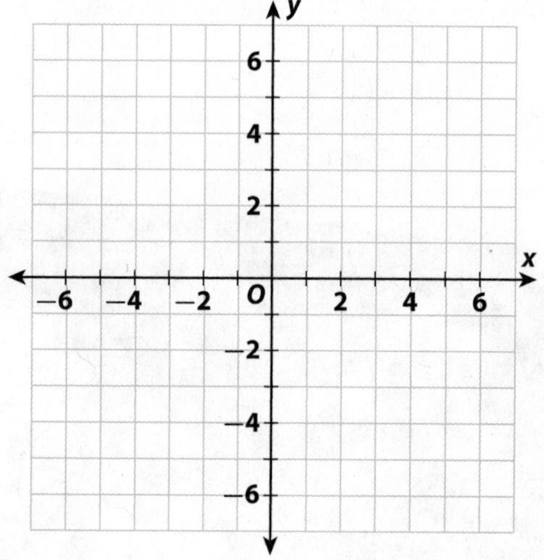

Evaluate Expressions

EXAMPLE Evaluate $4x$ for $x = 3$

$4x = 4(3)$ Substitute 3 for x.

$= 12$ Simplify.

Evaluate each expression for $x = -2, -1, 0, 1,$ and 2.

5. $-2x - 1$ ________

6. $x - 1$ ________

7. $x^2 - 1$ ________

8. $3(x + 2)$ ________

9. $15 - 5x$ ________

10. $2x^2 - 5x + 2$ ________

11. $\frac{1}{2}x + \frac{3}{2}$ ________

12. $0.05x - 0.1$ ________

13. $(x + 1)^3 - x$ ________

Reading Start-Up

Visualize Vocabulary

Complete the graphic using each review word.

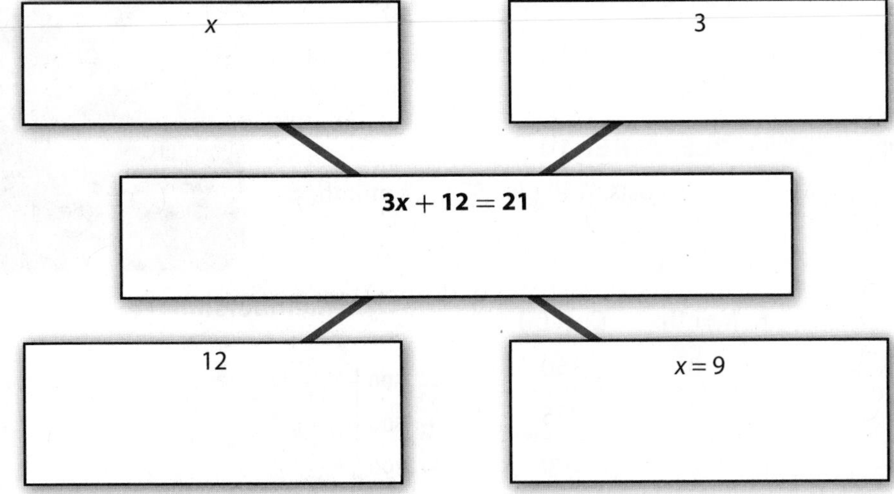

Vocabulary

Review Words

- coefficient *(coeficiente)*
- constant *(constante)*
- equation in one variable *(ecuación en una variable)*
- solution of an equation in one variable *(solución de una ecuación en una variable)*
- variable *(variable)*

Preview Words

- equation in two variables
- solution of an equation in two variables
- function
- domain
- range
- function notation
- sequence
- term
- explicit rule
- recursive rule

Understand Vocabulary

To become familiar with some of the vocabulary in the module, answer each question. You may refer to the module or the glossary.

1. You've learned what a solution of an equation in one variable is. What do you think the **solution of an equation in two variables** is?

____

____

2. Have you heard the term **sequence** before? What do you think it may mean mathematically?

____

____

Active Reading

Key-Term Fold Before beginning the module, create a Key-Term Fold Note to help you organize what you learn. Write a vocabulary term on each tab of the key-term fold. Under each tab, write the definition of the term and an example of the term.

GETTING READY FOR

Equations in Two Variables and Functions

Understanding the standards and the vocabulary terms in the standards will help you know exactly what you are expected to learn in this module.

 CA CC **A.REI.10**

Understand that the graph of an equation in two variables is the set of all its solutions plotted in the coordinate plane, often forming a curve (which could be a line).

Key Vocabulary

solution of an equation in two variables *(solución de una ecuación en dos variables)*
An ordered pair of values for the variables making the equation true.

What It Means to You

You can represent mathematical relationships with words, equations, tables, and graphs.

EXAMPLE A.REI.10

Membership costs \$150 plus \$75 per month.

$$y = 75x + 150$$

Months	Cost (\$)
0	150
1	225
2	300
3	375
4	450

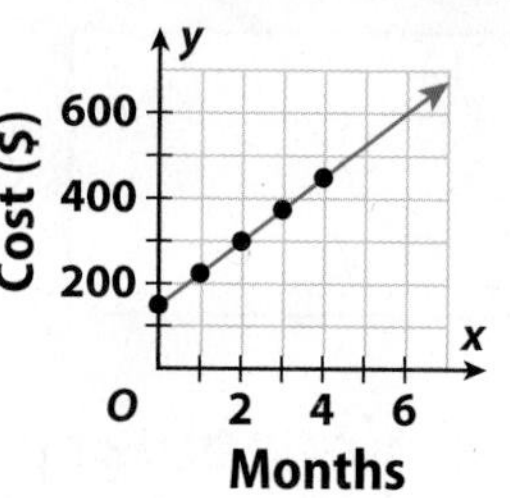

CA CC **F.IF.1**

Understand that a function from one set (called the domain) to another set (called the range) assigns to each element of the domain exactly one element of the range. If *f* is a function and *x* is an element of its domain, then $f(x)$ denotes the output of *f* corresponding to the input *x*. The graph of *f* is the graph of the equation $y = f(x)$.

Key Vocabulary

domain *(dominio)*
The set of all possible input values of a function.

range *(recorrido o rango)*
The set of all possible output values of a function.

What It Means to You

A function model guarantees that for any input value, you will get a unique output value.

EXAMPLE F.IF.1

Categorize each of the following as a function or not a function.

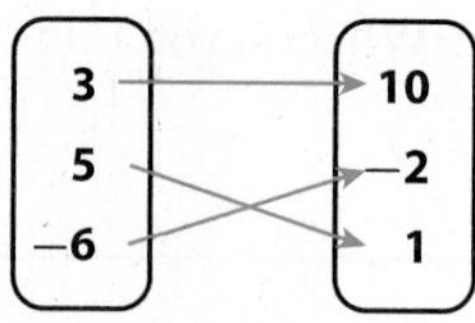

A function: each input number in the left box is matched with exactly one output number in the right box.

$\{(0, 3), (2, -1), (0, 0)\}$

Not a function: the input 0 is matched to two outputs (3 and 0).

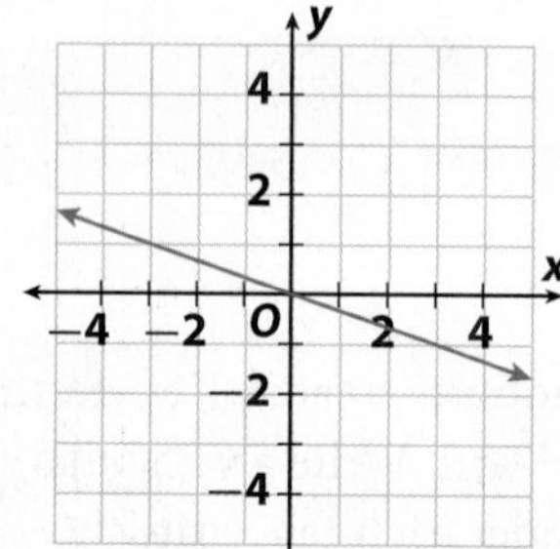

A function: each input (x-value) is matched with exactly one output (y-value).

Visit **my.hrw.com** to see all **CA Common Core Standards** explained.

my.hrw.com

LESSON 4.1

Equations in Two Variables

CA CC A.REI.10

Understand that the graph of an equation in two variables is the set of all its solutions plotted in the coordinate plane, often forming a curve (which could be a line).

ESSENTIAL QUESTION

What is the relationship between the solutions of an equation in two variables and its graph?

Solutions of Equations in Two Variables

Equations in one variable usually have one solution. **Equations in two variables** usually have infinitely many solutions.

A **solution of an equation in two variables** x and y is any ordered pair (x, y) that makes the equation true. To determine whether an ordered pair (x, y) is a solution of an equation, substitute the values of x and y into the equation.

Math On the Spot

EXAMPLE 1

CA CC A.REI.10

Tell whether each ordered pair is a solution of the given equation.

A $3x + 5y = 15;\ (8, 1)$

$3(8) + 5(1) \stackrel{?}{=} 15$ Substitute.

$24 + 5 \stackrel{?}{=} 15$ Simplify.

$29 \neq 15$

$(8, 1)$ is NOT a solution of $3x + 5y = 15$.

B $3x + 5y = 15;\ (0, 3)$

$3(0) + 5(3) \stackrel{?}{=} 15$ Substitute.

$0 + 15 \stackrel{?}{=} 15$ Simplify.

$15 = 15$

$(0, 3)$ is a solution of $3x + 5y = 15$.

C $x^2 - y = 23;\ (-5, 2)$

$(-5)^2 - 2 \stackrel{?}{=} 23$ Substitute.

$25 - 2 \stackrel{?}{=} 23$ Simplify.

$23 = 23$

Remember that squaring a negative number results in a positive number: $(-5)^2$ means $(-5)(-5)$, which is positive 25.

$(-5, 2)$ is a solution of $x^2 - y = 23$.

D $x^2 - y = 23;\ (5, 2)$

$(5)^2 - 2 \stackrel{?}{=} 23$ Substitute.

$25 - 2 \stackrel{?}{=} 23$ Simplify.

$23 = 23$

$(5, 2)$ is a solution of $x^2 - y = 23$.

Math Talk
Mathematical Practices

What do you know about the point (0, 3) and its relationship to the graph of $3x + 5y = 15$?

My Notes

YOUR TURN

Tell whether each ordered pair is a solution of the given equation.

1. $x - 2y = 3$; $(5, 2)$ ______

2. $x - 2y = 3$; $(9, 3)$ ______

3. $2(x + 1)^2 + 3y = 15$; $(0, 5)$ ______

4. $2(x + 1)^2 + 3y = 15$; $(1, -1)$ ______

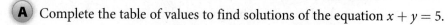

EXPLORE ACTIVITY

CA CC A.REI.10

Exploring the Graph of an Equation

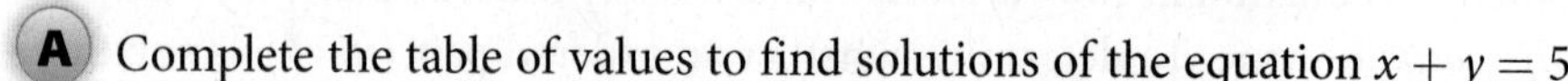
A Complete the table of values to find solutions of the equation $x + y = 5$.

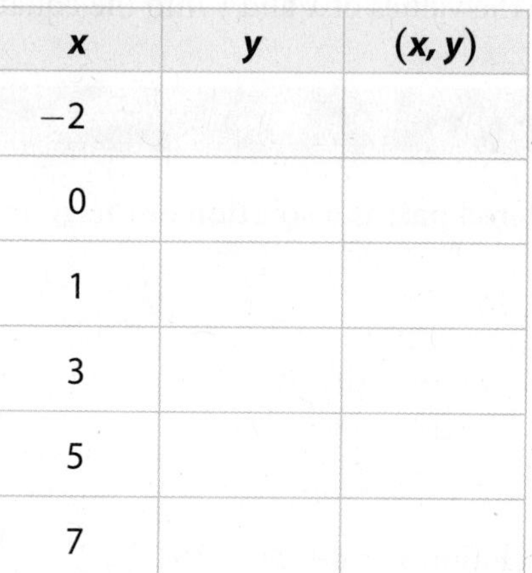

x	y	(x, y)
−2		
0		
1		
3		
5		
7		

B Plot the ordered pairs on a coordinate grid.

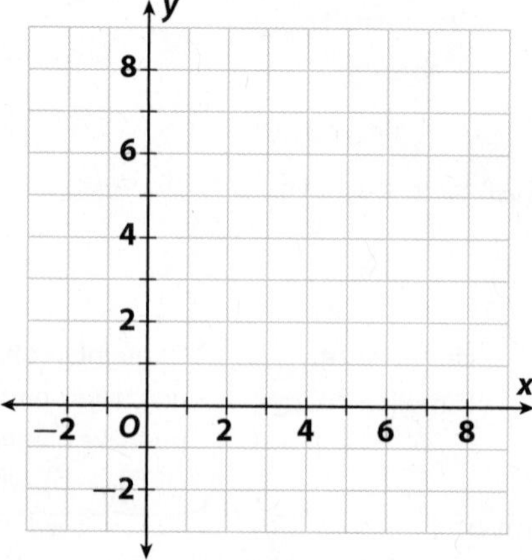

REFLECT

5. **Look for a Pattern** The plotted points are some of the solutions of the equation. What appears to be true about them?

____

____

Graphing Solutions of a Two-Variable Equation

An equation and a graph of its solutions can model a real-world situation. By reasoning about the quantities in the situation, you can determine the real-world meaning of each ordered pair.

The equation $y = 25{,}000x$ describes the average number of species y that become extinct in x years. Graph the solutions of the equation.

STEP 1 Create a table of values for the equation $y = 25{,}000x$. Choose several nonnegative values of x to find the corresponding values of y.

x represents years, so the values must be nonnegative.

x	$y = 25{,}000x$	(x, y)
0	$y = 25{,}000(0)$	(0, 0)
2	$y = 25{,}000(2)$	(2, 50,000)
4	$y = 25{,}000(4)$	(4, 100,000)
6	$y = 25{,}000(6)$	(6, 150,000)

STEP 2 Plot the ordered pairs on a graph. Draw the line that passes through the points and contains all the solutions of the equation.

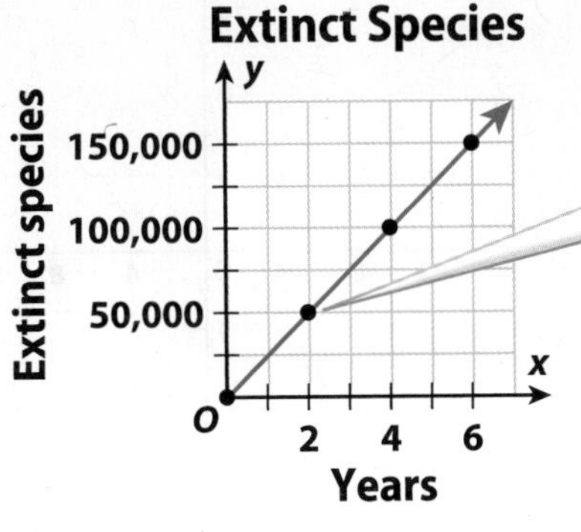

The x-value 2 represents 2 years. The y-value 50,000 represents the number of species that have become extinct in that amount of time.

YOUR TURN

6. Mark wants to have a laser tag party. The cost of the party, y, can be modeled by the equation $y = 20x + 15$, where x is the number of guests. Complete the table and graph the equation.

x	$y = 20x + 15$	(x, y)
3	$y = 20(3) + 15$	(3, 75)
5	$y = 20(\quad) + 15$	( )
7	$y =$	( )
8	$y =$	( )

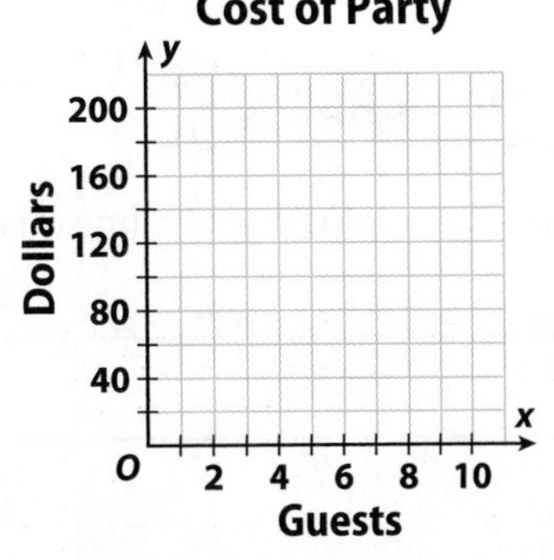

Guided Practice

Tell whether each ordered pair is a solution of $6x - 3y = 24$. (Example 1)

1. (5, 1)

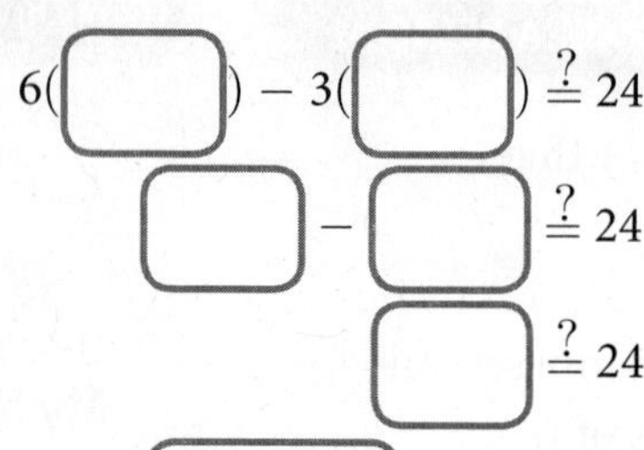

(5, 1) **is / is not** a solution.

2. (0, −8)

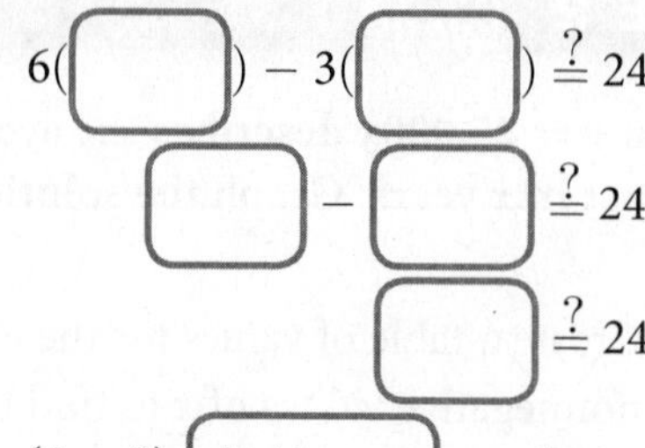

(0, −8) **is / is not** a solution.

Tell whether the ordered pair is a solution of the equation. (Example 1)

3. $2x + y^2 = 10$; (3, 2)

____

4. $\frac{1}{2}x - 4y = 4$; $(10, \frac{1}{2})$

____

5. $x^2 + y^2 = 2$; (0, 1)

____

6. Complete the table of values and graph the ordered pairs to find solutions of the equation $4x - 6 = y$. (Explore Activity and Example 2)

x	$4x - 6 = y$	(x, y)
	4( ) − 6 = y	
	4( ) − 6 = y	
	4( ) − 6 = y	
	4( ) − 6 = y	
	4( ) − 6 = y	

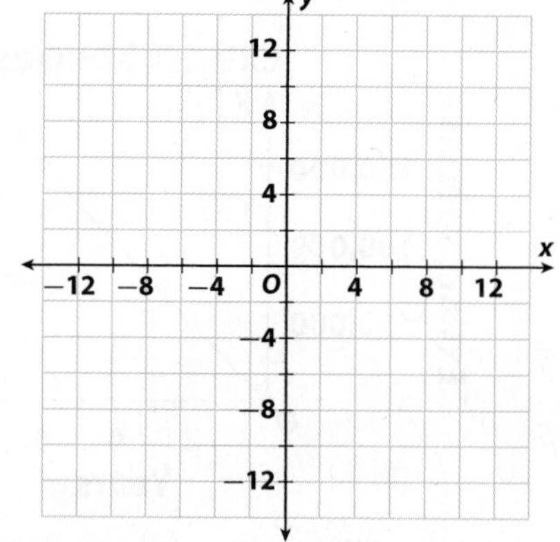

7. Kelly is saving money to buy a concert ticket. Her savings y for x days can be represented by the equation $y = x + 10$. Graph the solutions of the equation. (Example 2)

ESSENTIAL QUESTION CHECK-IN

8. How does a graph show solutions of a linear equation?

____

____

Name ________________ Class ________________ Date ________________

4.1 Independent Practice

A.REI.10

Tell whether each ordered pair is a solution of the equation. Justify your answers.

9. $-5x + 2y = 4$; $(4, 8)$

____

____

10. $2x - 7y = 1$; $(11, 3)$

____

____

11. $\frac{1}{3}x - 2y = 7$; $(9, -2)$

____

____

12. a. Complete the table for the equation $-2x + y = 3$. Then draw the graph.

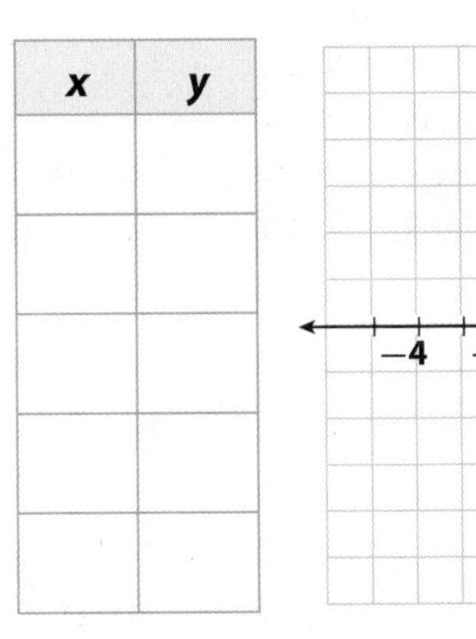

x	y

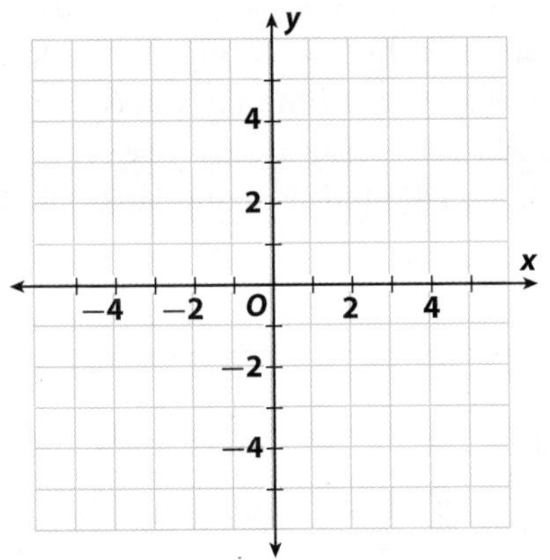

b. Using the graph, locate another solution of the equation. Explain how you can check to see if you are correct.

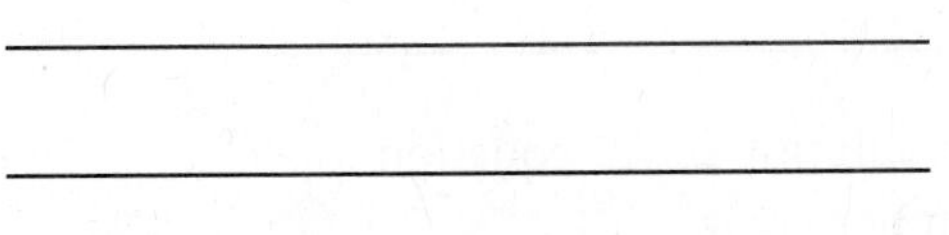

____

____

____

13. Multiple Representations Trish can run the 200-meter dash in 25 seconds. The equation $8x + y = 200$ gives the distance y that Trish has left to run x seconds after the start of the race. The graph of this relationship is shown.

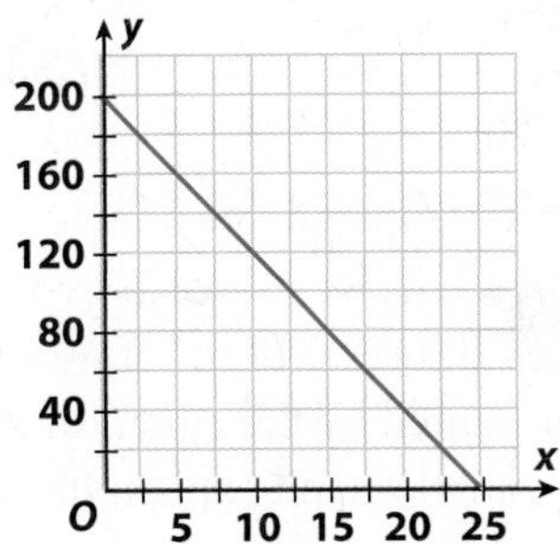

a. Identify three points on the graph and write their coordinates below.

____

____

b. Choose one of the ordered pairs and explain what the values mean.

____

____

____

c. Select one ordered pair. Show that the ordered pair is a solution of $8x + y = 200$.

____

____

d. Select a point not on the line. Show that the ordered pair represented by this point is not a solution of the equation $8x + y = 200$.

____

____

14. Alex is making a rectangular wall hanging from fabric scraps. He has 36 inches of trim to go around the outside border, and he wants to use all of the trim. Let x represent the width of the wall hanging and let y represent the length. The solutions of the equation $2x + 2y = 36$ give the possible dimensions of Alex's wall hanging. Complete the table and graph the solutions.

x	y	(x, y)
2		
4		
6		
8		
10		

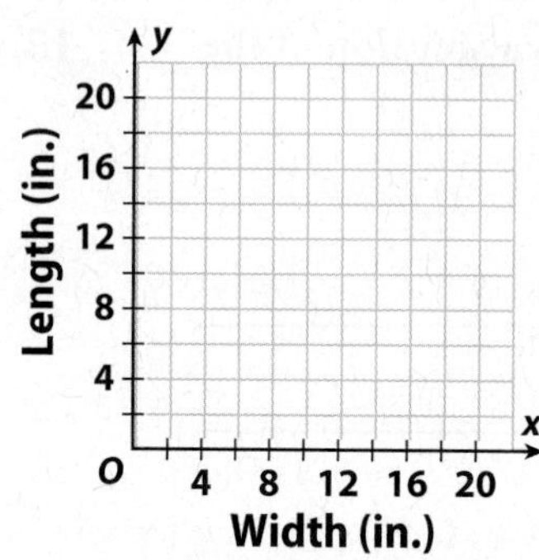

15. Represent Real-World Problems A family swimming pool holds 60 m^3 of water. It loses 0.18 m^3 of water to evaporation each day. This situation can be represented by the equation $y + 0.18x = 60$. Find an ordered pair solution of the equation and explain its real-world meaning.

____

____

FOCUS ON HIGHER ORDER THINKING

Work Area

16. Justify Reasoning Jackie wants to earn $250 this summer by babysitting and dog walking. She earns $20 each time she babysits and $15 each time she walks dogs. This situation can be represented by the equation $20x + 15y = 250$. Use the equation to determine whether or not Jackie will earn $250 if she babysits 8 times and walks dogs 6 times. Justify your answer.

____

____

17. Critique Reasoning Max is asked to find 15 solutions of a linear equation. How could Max use a graph to help him find these solutions?

____

____

____

18. Explain the Error Chanasia thinks that (3, 2) is a solution of the equation $5y + 10x = 35$ because $5(3) + 10(2) = 35$. Explain her error.

____

____

LESSON

4.2 Representing Functions

CA CC F.IF.1, F.IF.2, F.IF.5

For the full text of these standards, see the table beginning on page CA2. *Also A.REI.10, A.REI.11*

ESSENTIAL QUESTION

How do you represent functions?

Understanding Functions

A **function** is a set of ordered pairs in which each value in the *domain* is paired with exactly one value in the *range*. The x-values are the **domain** of the function and the y-values are the **range** of the function. Functions can be expressed as tables, ordered pairs, graphs, equations, and mapping diagrams.

EXAMPLE 1

CA CC F.IF.1, F.IF.2, F.IF.5

A fund-raising program awards \$30 for first place, \$20 for second place, \$10 for third place, and \$5 for fourth place. This function can be written as ordered pairs: {(1, 30), (2, 20), (3, 10), (4, 5)}. Express this function as a table, a graph, and a mapping diagram.

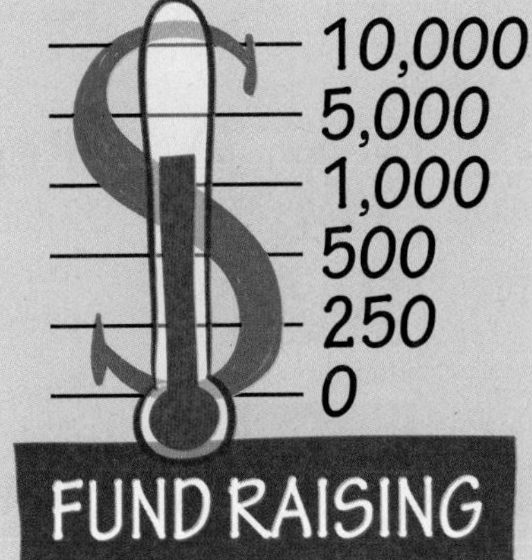

Table

Ranking	Prize in dollars
1	30
2	20
3	10
4	5

Write each x-value under "Ranking" and the corresponding y-value next to it, under "Prize, in Dollars".

Graph

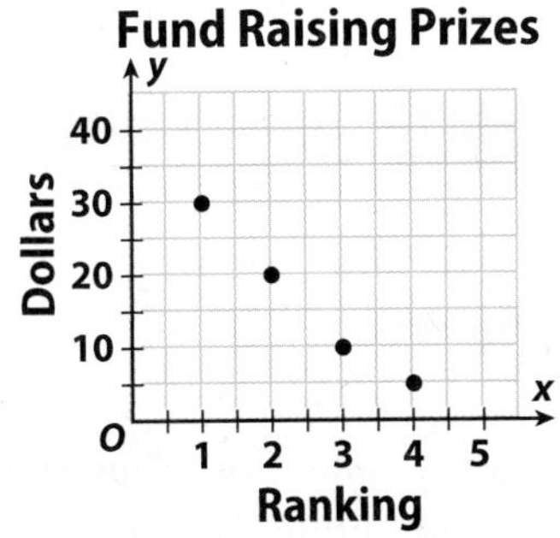

Fund Raising Prizes

(Graph: x-axis Ranking 1–5, y-axis Dollars 10–40; points (1, 30), (2, 20), (3, 10), (4, 5))

Plot each ordered pair represented in the table on the graph.

Mapping diagram

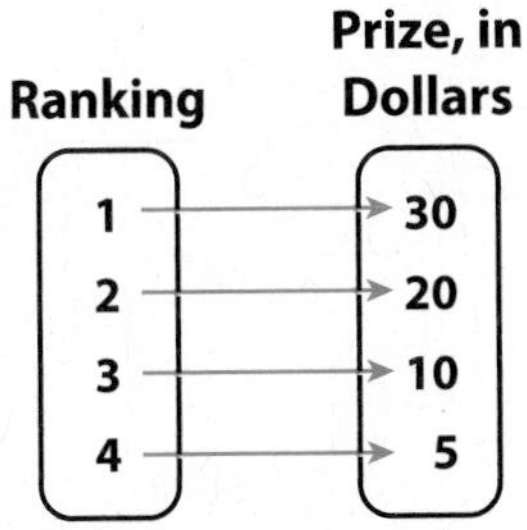

Ranking	Prize, in Dollars
1 →	30
2 →	20
3 →	10
4 →	5

Write each x-value in the region labeled "Ranking" and every y-value in the region labeled "Prize, in Dollars". Use arrows to connect each x-value to the corresponding y-value.

REFLECT

1. The domain of the function in Example 1 is {1, 2, 3, 4}. What is the range?

____

YOUR TURN

2. Suppose each prize for the fundraiser was doubled. Complete the table, graph, and mapping diagram to show the new prize system.

Ranking	Prize, in Dollars
	60
	40
3	
4	

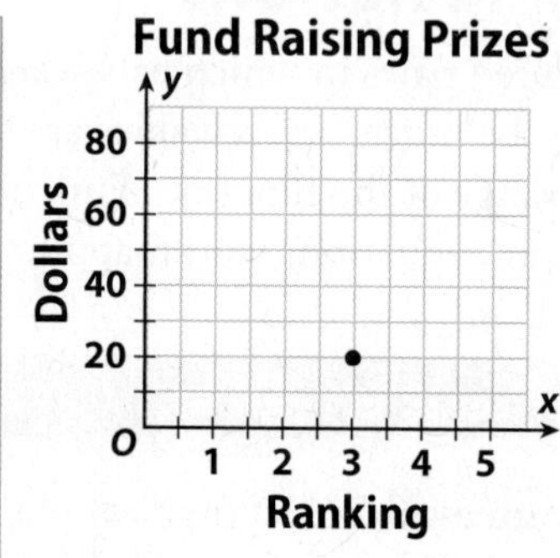

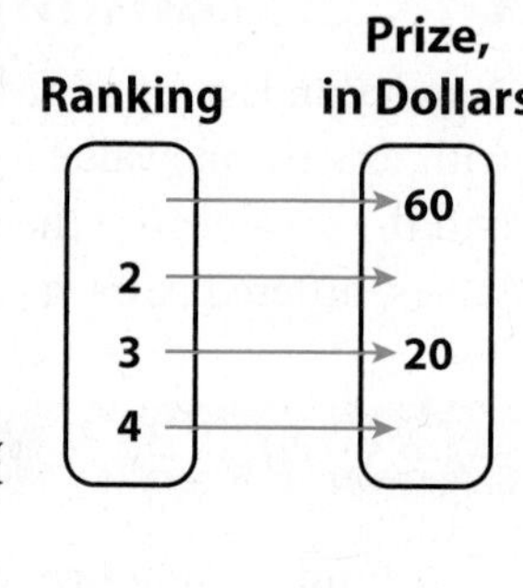

Representing Functions with Equations

Another way to represent a function is with an equation in two variables, like $y = 2x + 8$. The x-value is the input for the function, and after performing one or more operations to the x-value, the output is the y-value.

Since not every equation in two variables is a function, we use function notation to describe functions. To write an equation in two variables using function notation, replace y with $f(x)$, which is read "f of x". In function notation, the equation $y = 2x + 8$ is written as $f(x) = 2x + 8$.

EXAMPLE 2   CA CC A.REI.10

The number of dollars Julio earns for working x hours can be represented by the function $f(x) = 9x$. Graph this function.

STEP 1 Make a table of values. Choose values for x, and substitute them into the function to find the corresponding y-values.

x	$f(x) = 9x$	(x, y)
0	$f(0) = 9(0)$ $= 0$	(0, 0)
1	$f(1) = 9(1)$ $= 9$	(1, 9)
2	$f(2) = 9(2)$ $= 18$	(2, 18)
3	$f(3) = 9(3)$ $= 27$	(3, 27)

Remember that $y = f(x)$.

STEP 2 Graph the function by plotting the ordered pairs. Draw a line through the points to represent all the x-values you could have chosen and their corresponding y-values.

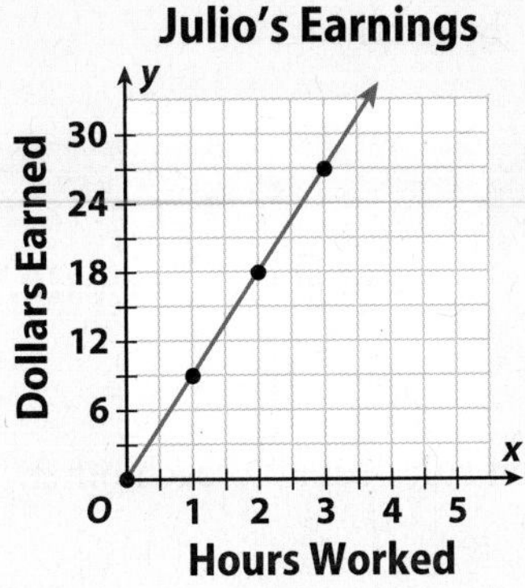

My Notes

REFLECT

3. **Explain the Error** Julio looks at the graph in Example 2 and concludes that the domain for the function is {0, 1, 2, 3}. Explain his error.

____

____

____

YOUR TURN

4. The cost for x gallons of heating oil can be represented by the function $f(x) = 4x + 6$. Graph this function.

x	$f(x) = 4x + 6$	(x, y)
0	$f(0) =$	
2	$f(2) =$	
3	$f(3) =$	
5	$f(5) =$	

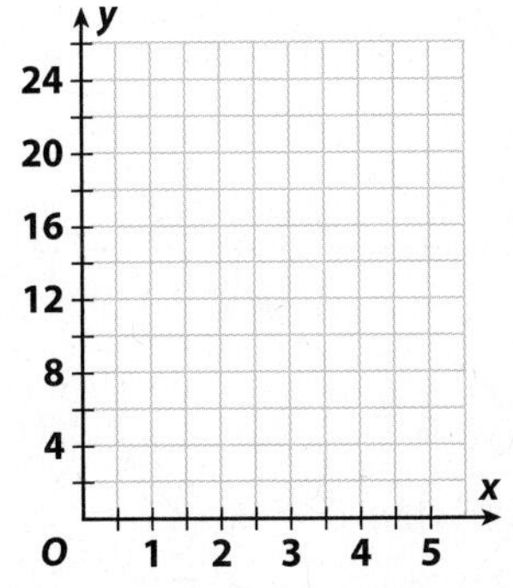

Equality of Functions

When dealing with two different functions, you can use letters other than f to name the function, like the two functions $f(x) = 3x + 2$ and $g(x) = -x + 10$. The function $g(x)$ is read "g of x". You can find values that satisfy both functions by using properties of equality or by graphing.

EXAMPLE 3

Given the functions $f(x) = 3x + 2$ and $g(x) = -x + 10$, find the value of x for which $f(x) = g(x)$.

Method 1 Set the function rules equal to each other. Then solve the equation.

Solving this equation will give you the value of x when the y-values are equal to each other.

$$\begin{array}{rcl} 3x + 2 &=& -x + 10 \\ +x & & +x \\ \hline 4x + 2 &=& 10 \end{array}$$

Add x to both sides.

$$\begin{array}{rcl} 4x + 2 &=& 10 \\ -2 & & -2 \\ \hline 4x &=& 8 \end{array}$$

Subtract 2 from both sides.

$$4x = 8$$

$$\frac{4x}{4} = \frac{8}{4}$$

Divide both sides by 4.

$$x = 2$$

So $f(x) = g(x)$ when $x = 2$.

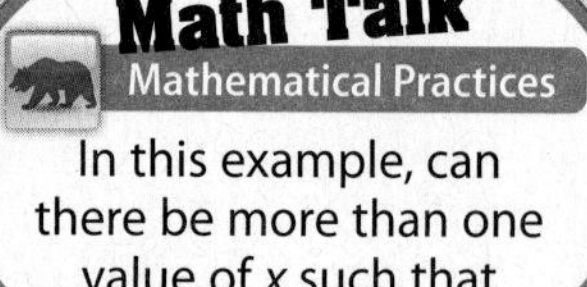

In this example, can there be more than one value of x such that $f(x) = g(x)$?

Method 2 Create tables to find a set of ordered pairs for each function. Then compare the ordered pairs to determine the value of x where the two functions have the same value.

x	$f(x) = 3x + 2$	(x, y)
0	$f(0) = 2$	(0, 2)
1	$f(1) = 5$	(1, 5)
2	$f(2) = 8$	(2, 8)
3	$f(3) = 11$	(3, 11)

If the solution of the equation is not an integer, it may not be in your table. In that case, you can use the tables to find an approximate answer.

x	$g(x) = -x + 10$	(x, y)
0	$g(0) = 10$	(0, 10)
1	$g(1) = 9$	(1, 9)
2	$g(2) = 8$	(2, 8)
3	$g(3) = 7$	(3, 7)

$f(x)$ and $g(x)$ have the same value when $x = 2$.

Method 3 Generate ordered pairs for each function. Then use the ordered pairs to graph the functions and identify where the lines intersect. You can use the ordered pairs from the tables in Method 2.

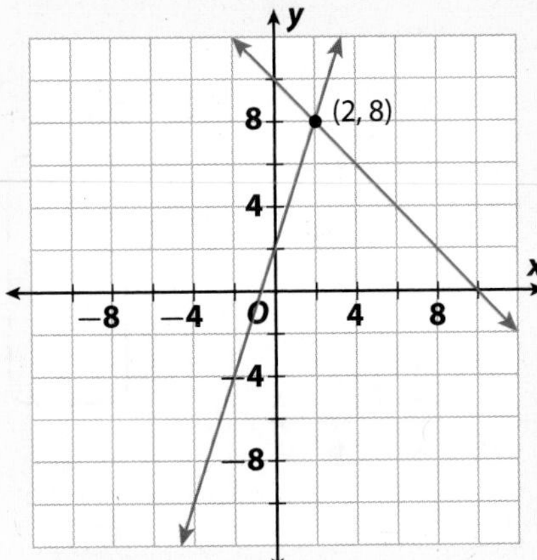

$f(x) = 3x + 2$

$g(x) = -x + 10$

You can check your answer by substituting 2 for x in both function rules. If $f(x)$ and $g(x)$ are equal, the answer is correct.

The x-coordinate at the point of intersection is 2, so $f(x) = g(x)$ when $x = 2$.

REFLECT

5. In Example 3, $f(x) = g(x)$ when $x = 2$. Describe two ways to find the y-coordinate when $f(x) = g(x)$.

____

____

____

6. **Analyze Relationships** What does the y-coordinate of the point of intersection represent?

____

____

7. **What If?** Given two functions m and n, is it possible for there to be no value of x that makes $m(x) = n(x)$? Can all real numbers make $m(x) = n(x)$? Explain.

____

____

____

My Notes

YOUR TURN

8. Given the functions $f(x) = 4x - 2$ and $g(x) = 2x + 4$, find the value of x for which $f(x) = g(x)$. ______________

Personal Math Trainer

Online Practice and Help

my.hrw.com

Guided Practice

Express the function $\{(0, -1), (1, 1), (3, 5)\}$ as a table, a graph, and a mapping diagram. (Example 1)

1.

Domain	Range

2.

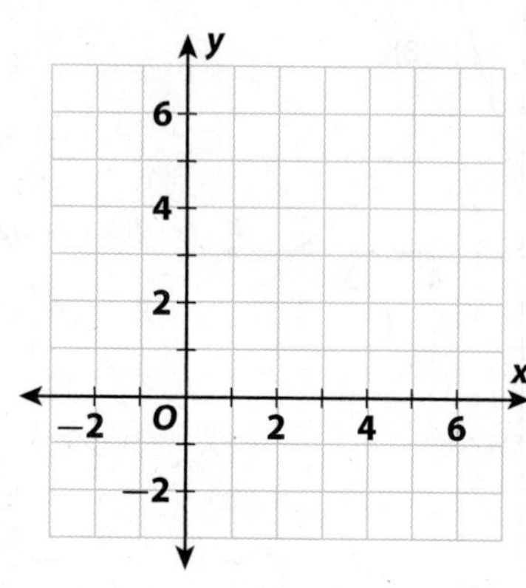

3.

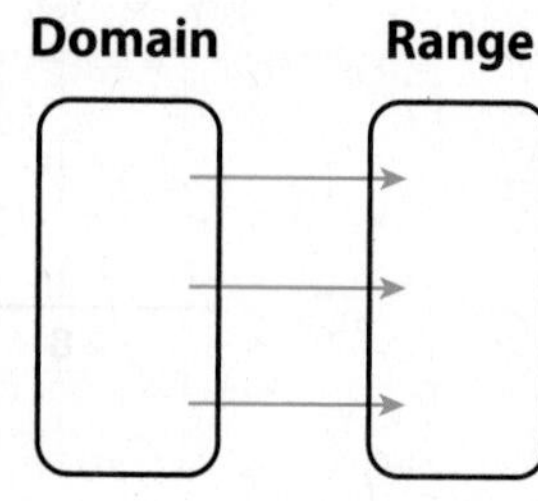

4. Complete the table for the function $f(x) = 2x - 4$. Then draw the graph. (Example 2)

x	$f(x) = 2x - 4$	(x, y)
−2	$f(-2) = 2(-2) - 4 =$	$(-2, -8)$
0	$f(0) = 2(\quad) - 4 =$	$(0, \quad)$
2	$f(2) = 2(\quad) - 4 =$	$(\quad, \quad)$
4	$f(4) = 2(\quad) - 4 =$	$(\quad, \quad)$

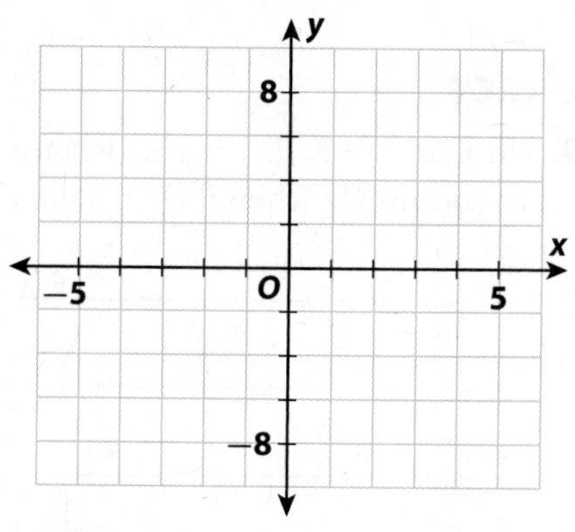

Given the functions $f(x) = -2x + 4$ and $g(x) = 2x - 8$, find the value of x for which $f(x) = g(x)$. (Example 3)

5. Set the function rules equal to each other.

Step 1:

$-2x + 4 = 2x - 8$

$+2x \quad \square$

$4 = 4x - 8$

Step 2:

$4 = 4x - 8$

$+8 = \quad + 8$

$12 = \square$

Step 3:

$\frac{12}{\square} = \frac{4x}{\square}$

$\square = x$

The x-coordinate at the point of intersection is ______.

So $f(x) = g(x)$ when $x =$ ______.

6. Graph the functions.

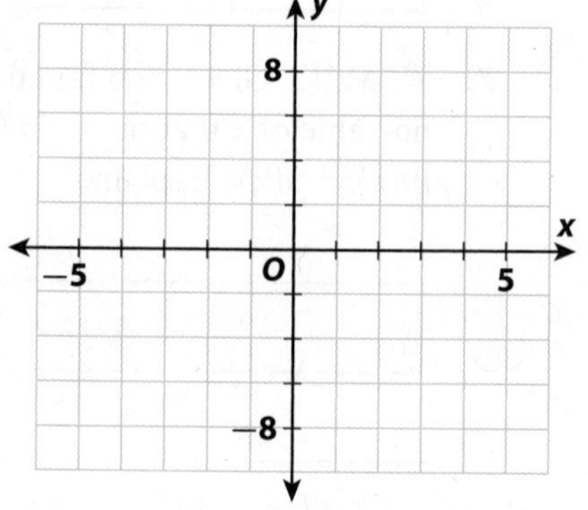

ESSENTIAL QUESTION CHECK-IN

7. How do you represent functions? ____

____

Name ____________ Class ____________ Date ____________

4.2 Independent Practice

 CA CC F.IF.1, F.IF.2, F.IF.5, A.REI.10, A.REI.11

For 8–10, tell whether each pairing of numbers describes a function. If so, identify the domain and the range. If not, explain why.

8. Each whole number from 0 to 9 is paired with its opposite.

____

____

____

9. (36, 6), (49, 7), (64, 8), (36, −6), (49, −7), (64, −8) ____________

____

10. Each even number from 2 to 10 is paired with half the number.

____

____

11. **Multiple Representations** Neal has a $5 gift card for music downloads. Each song costs $1 to download. The amount of money left on the card, in dollars, can be represented by the function $f(x) = 5 - x$, where x is the number of downloaded songs.

a. Use the function to complete the table.

x	0					5
$f(x)$						

b. Graph the function.

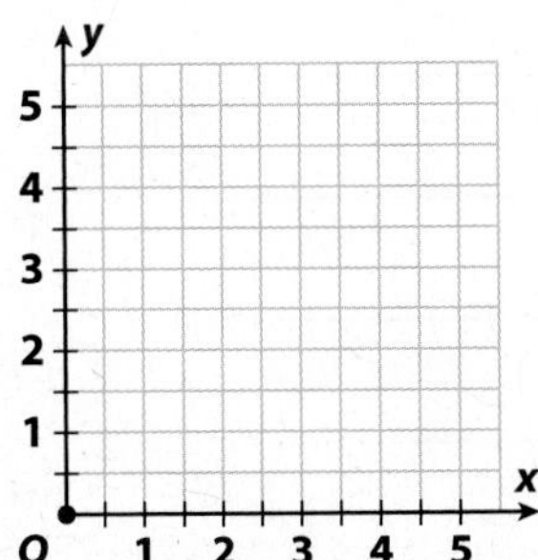

c. Identify the domain and range of the function.

____

____

d. **Explain the Error** Neal decided to connect the points on his graph. Explain Neal's error.

____

____

____

____

____

12. Sam is trying to lose weight, and George is trying to gain weight. Sam's weight in pounds can be represented by the function $f(x) = 240 - 2x$, where x is the number of weeks since Sam started losing weight. George's weight in pounds can be represented by the function $g(x) = 180 + 4x$, where x is the number of weeks since George starting gaining weight.

a. What is the x-value when $f(x) = g(x)$?

____

b. When $f(x) = g(x)$, what does the x-value represent?

____

____

____

c. When Sam and George weigh the same, what will their weight be?

____

13. Represent Real-World Problems Jasmine has \$15 dollars and saves \$2.50 every month. Radha has \$0 and saves \$3.50 every month. Jasmine's savings after x months can be represented by the function $f(x) = 2.5x + 15$. Radha's savings after x months can be represented by the function $g(x) = 3.5x$.

a. After how many months will they both have the same amount in savings? Find the values of x for which $f(x) = g(x)$.

____

b. Explain how to check your work.

____

c. Explain what the graph of the two functions would look like.

____

____

H.O.T. FOCUS ON HIGHER ORDER THINKING

Work Area

14. Critical Thinking Can a linear function be continuous but *not* have a domain and range of all real numbers? Justify your answer.

____

____

15. Justify Reasoning Fred's weekly earnings for mowing lawns can be represented by the function $f(x) = 45x - 40$, and George's weekly earnings for delivering papers can be represented by the function $g(x) = 85x - 110$. Fred says that after 3 weeks they will have earned the same amount. Determine whether Fred is correct. Explain.

____

____

____

____

16. Communicate Mathematical Ideas The whole numbers from 10 to 12 are paired with their factors. Explain why this pairing of numbers does *not* describe a function.

____

____

____

____

LESSON

4.3 Sequences

CA CC **F.IF.3**

Recognize that sequences are functions, sometimes defined recursively, whose domain is a subset of the integers. *Also F.BF.1, F.BF.1a, F.BF.2*

ESSENTIAL QUESTION

How are sequences and functions related?

EXPLORE ACTIVITY 

Understanding Sequences

A go-cart racing track charges \$7 for a go-cart license and \$2 per lap. If you list the charges for 1 lap, 2 laps, 3 laps, and so on, in order, the list forms a sequence of numbers:

9, 11, 13, 15, ...

A **sequence** is a list of numbers in a specific order. Each element in a sequence is called a **term**. In a sequence, each term has a position number. In the sequence 9, 11, 13, 15, ..., the second term is 11, so its position number is 2.

A The total cost (term) of riding a go-cart for different numbers of laps (position) is shown below. Complete the table.

Position number, *n*	1	2		4		6		8	Domain
Term of the sequence, *f*(*n*)	9	11	13		17				Range

B You can use the term and position number of a sequence to write a function. Using function notation, $f(2) = 11$ indicates that the second term is 11. Use the table to complete the following statements:

$f(1) =$ ________, $f(4) =$ ________

$f(8) =$ ________, $f($________$) = 13$

REFLECT

1. Explain how to find the missing values in the table in the Explore Activity.

____

____

2. Describe the domain of the function in the Explore Activity.

____

3. The go-cart racing track records the number of gallons of gas they have at the beginning of each day. The numbers form the following sequence: 25, 21, 17... Predict the next term in the sequence. Justify your answer.

____

Math On the Spot
 my.hrw.com

Using an Explicit Rule to Generate a Sequence

An **explicit rule** for a sequence defines the nth term as a function of n. Explicit rules can be used to find any specific term in a sequence without finding any of the previous terms.

My Notes

EXAMPLE 1

CA CC F.IF.3

A **Find the first four terms of the sequence defined by the explicit rule $f(n) = n^2 + 1$. Assume that the domain of the function is the set of whole numbers greater than 0.**

Make a table and substitute values for n.

n	$f(n) = n^2 + 1$	$f(n)$
1	$f(1) = (1)^2 + 1 = 1 + 1 = 2$	2
2	$f(2) = (2)^2 + 1 = 4 + 1 = 5$	5
3	$f(3) = (3)^2 + 1 = 9 + 1 = 10$	10
4	$f(4) = (4)^2 + 1 = 16 + 1 = 17$	17

The first four terms are 2, 5, 10, 17.

B **Find the 20th term of the sequence defined by the explicit rule $f(n) = n^2 + 1$. Assume that the domain of the function is the set of whole numbers greater than 0.**

$$f(20) = (20)^2 + 1 \quad \text{Substitute 20 for } n.$$
$$= 400 + 1$$
$$= 401$$

The 20th term in the sequence is 401.

REFLECT

4. Explain how to find the 6th term of the sequence defined by the explicit rule $f(n) = 3n - 2$. Assume that the domain of the function is the set of whole numbers greater than 0.

5. The number 121 is a term of the sequence defined by the explicit rule $f(n) = 3n - 2$. Assume that the domain of the function is the set of whole numbers greater than 0. Which term in the sequence is 121? Justify your answer.

YOUR TURN

6. Write the first 4 terms of the sequence defined by the explicit rule $f(n) = 3n + 1$. Assume that the domain of the function is the set of whole numbers greater than 0.

n	$f(n) = 3n + 1$	$f(n)$
1	$f(1) = 3(1) + 1$	
2		
3		
4		

The first four terms of the sequence are ____________________

7. What is the 15th term of the sequence defined by the explicit rule $f(n) = n^2 + n$? Assume that the domain of the function is the set of whole numbers greater than 0. ____________________

8. What is the 8th term of the sequence defined by the explicit rule $f(n) = 2n^2 + 6$? Assume that the domain of the function is the set of whole numbers greater than 0. ____________________

Using a Recursive Rule to Generate a Sequence

A **recursive rule** for a sequence defines the nth term by relating it to one or more previous terms. Unlike an explicit rule, a recursive rule cannot be used to find a specific term directly. To find a specific term's value, you need to know the value of one or more of the previous terms. The following is an example of a recursive rule:

$f(1) = 4$

$f(n) = f(n - 1) + 10$ for each whole number n greater than 1.

This rule means that after the first term of the sequence, every term $f(n)$ is the sum of the previous term $f(n - 1)$ and 10. The function table below shows the first 4 terms of the sequence.

n		$f(n)$
1	1st term	4
2	1st term + 10	$4 + 10 = 14$
3	2nd term + 10	$14 + 10 = 24$
4	3rd term + 10	$24 + 10 = 34$

EXAMPLE 2

CA CC F.IF.3

Write the first 4 terms of the sequence defined by the recursive rule below.

$f(1) = 3$

$f(n) = f(n - 1) + 2$ for each whole number n greater than 1.

My Notes

STEP 1 Identify the domain of the function and the first term of the sequence. Describe the recursive rule.

The domain of the function is the set of whole numbers greater than 0.

The first term of the sequence is 3, and the recursive rule is adding 2 to each term to find the next term.

STEP 2 Create a table to find the first 4 terms in the sequence. Use 2, 3, and 4 as values for n.

n	$f(n) = f(n - 1) + 2$	$f(n)$
1	1st term	3
2	$f(2) = f(2 - 1) + 2$ $= f(1) + 2$ $= 3 + 2$	5
3	$f(3) = f(3 - 1) + 2$ $= f(2) + 2$ $= 5 + 2$	7
4	$f(4) = f(4 - 1) + 2$ $= f(3) + 2$ $= 7 + 2$	9

The first four terms of the sequence are 3, 5, 7, 9.

Math Talk
Mathematical Practices

Describe how to find the 12th term of the sequence.

REFLECT

9. Suppose you want to find the 50th term of a sequence. Would you rather use a recursive rule or an explicit rule? Explain your reasoning.

Personal Math Trainer

Online Practice and Help

my.hrw.com

YOUR TURN

10. Write the first 8 terms of the sequence with $f(1) = 37$ and $f(n) = f(n - 1) - 3$ for each whole number greater than 1.

Guided Practice

Use the table to complete the statements. (Explore Activity)

1. $f(4) =$ ________

2. $f(7) =$ ________

n	1	2	3	4	...	7
$f(n)$	5	8	11	?	...	?

Write the first four terms of each sequence. Assume that the domain of the function is the set of whole numbers greater than 0. (Example 1)

3. $f(n) = (n - 1)^2$

n	$f(n) = (n-1)^2$	$f(n)$
1	$(1-1)^2$	0
2	$(2-1)^2$	
3	$(\quad -1)^2$	
4	$(\quad -1)^2$	

4. $f(n) = 2n - 2$

n	$f(n) = 2n - 2$	$f(n)$
1	$2(\quad) - 2$	
2		
3		
4		

5. $f(n) = \frac{1}{2}n + 3$

n	$f(n)$
1	
2	
3	
4	

Use the explicit rule to find the 25th term of each sequence. Assume that the domain of each function is the set of whole numbers greater than 0. (Example 1)

6. $f(n) = \frac{1}{2}n + 3$

$f(25) = \frac{1}{2}\square + 3 = \square$

7. $f(n) = \frac{n-3}{11}$

$f(25) = \frac{\square - 3}{11} = \square$

8. Complete the table to find the first 4 terms of the sequence with $f(1) = 2$ and $f(n) = f(n - 1) + 6$ for each whole number greater than 1. (Example 2)

The first 4 terms of the sequence are

____

n	$f(n) = f(n-1)_6$	$f(n)$
1	1st term	2
2	$f(2-1) + 6 = f(1) + 6$ $+ 6 =$	
3		
4		

ESSENTIAL QUESTION CHECK-IN

9. Why is a sequence a function?

____

____

____

Name________________________ Class________________ Date________________

4.3 Independent Practice

F.IF.3

For 10–19, assume that the domain of each function is the set of whole numbers greater than 0. Write the first four terms of each sequence.

10. $f(n) = \sqrt{n} - 1$

____

11. $f(n) = 2n(n + 1)$

____

12. $f(1) = 16$ and $f(n) = \frac{1}{2} \cdot f(n - 1)$ for each whole number greater than 1

____

13. $f(1) = 1$ and $f(n) = 2 \cdot f(n - 1) + 1$ for each whole number greater than 1

____

14. $f(n) = 1.5n + 6$

____

15. $f(1) = 6.2$ and $f(n) = 20 - 2 \cdot f(n - 1)$ for each whole number greater than 1

____

Write the 12th term of each sequence.

16. $f(n) = \frac{5}{n}$

____

17. $f(1) = 181$ and $f(n) = f(n - 1) - 17$ for each whole number greater than 1

____

18. $f(1) = 3.5$ and $f(n) = f(n - 1) + 1.5$ for each whole number greater than 1

____

19. $f(1) = 1$ and $f(n) = 2 \cdot f(n - 1)$ for each whole number greater than 1

____

20. Represent Real-World Problems A movie rental club charges \$4.95 for membership and \$18.95 for each month of subscription.

a. Complete the table to represent the fees paid over the first three months.

n	$f(n) = 18.95n + 4.95$

b. What would $f(0) = 4.95$ represent?

____

c. What would the cost be for a year's membership? ________________

d. If the first month were free, what would be the total cost of a yearly membership?

____

e. Determine an explicit rule for the total fees paid to the movie rental club if the first month were free.

____

21. Jessica had \$150 in her savings account on the first Sunday of November. Beginning that week, she saved \$35 each week.

a. Write a recursive rule that describes how much money Jessika had in her savings account at the end of n weeks.

____

____

b. How much money will Jessika have in her savings account at the end of 6 weeks? ________________

22. Copper Creek Pizza is having a special. If you order a large pizza for the regular price of \$17, you can order any number of additional large pizzas for \$8.50 each.

a. Complete the table to show the cost of ordering up to 4 large pizzas.

Number of Large Pizzas	1	2	3	4
Total Cost				

b. Write an explicit and a recursive rule for the cost of placing an order for n large pizzas. ______________________

____

c. What is the cost of placing an order for 20 large pizzas? ______________

d. Five people each make an order for 3 large pizzas. How much money would they have saved if they placed one order for 15 pizzas? Explain.

____

____

23. The 5th term in a sequence is 25, and each term is 3 less than the previous term. Write an explicit rule and a recursive rule to describe the sequence.

____

____

24. An amusement park charges \$12 for one round of mini-golf and a reduced fee for each additional round played. Tom paid \$47 for 6 rounds of mini-golf.

a. What is the price per round for additional rounds of mini-golf?

____

b. Write an explicit and a recursive rule for the cost of playing n rounds of mini-golf. ______________________

____

c. What is the cost of playing 9 rounds of mini-golf? ______________

25. **Represent Real-World Problems** Carrie borrowed money interest-free to pay for a car repair. She is repaying the loan in equal monthly payments. The table shows the loan balance at the end of each month, after she makes the payment.

Monthly payment number	n	1	2	3	4
Loan balance (\$)	$f(n)$	840	720	600	480

a. After 6 months, how much will Carrie have left to repay? ______________

b. How many months will it take Carrie to pay off the loan? ______________

26. Kendall is stacking boxes that are 7.5 inches tall.

a. Explain how to find the height (in inches) of the stack of boxes after Kendall adds the nth box.

______

b. A sequence is defined by the rule $f(n)$ = the height (in inches) of n boxes.

What is the fourth term of the sequence? ______

H.O.T. FOCUS ON HIGHER ORDER THINKING

Work Area

27. The explicit rule for a sequence is $f(n) = 1.25(n - 1) + 6.25$. Determine the recursive rule for the same sequence.

______

28. The recursive rule for a sequence is $f(1) = 8\frac{1}{2}$, $f(n) = f(n - 1) - \frac{1}{2}$. Determine the explicit rule for the same sequence.

______

29. **Analyze Relationships** Determine an explicit rule and a recursive rule to describe the following sequence.

2, 4, 6, 8, ...

______

______

______

30. **Explain the Error** Shane is trying to find the 5th term of a sequence where $f(1) = 4$ and $f(n) = 2 \cdot f(n - 1) + 1$ for each whole number greater than 1. He reasons that he can find the 5th term by calculating $(4 \times 2 \times 2 \times 2 \times 2) + 1$. Explain Shane's error.

______

______

______

______

______

31. Write a recursive rule for a sequence where every term is the same.

______

______

______

Ready to Go On?

4.1 Equations in Two Variables

Complete the table of values to find solutions of the equation $-x + y = 5$. Then graph the ordered pairs.

1.

x	y
−2	
−1	
0	
1	
2	

2.

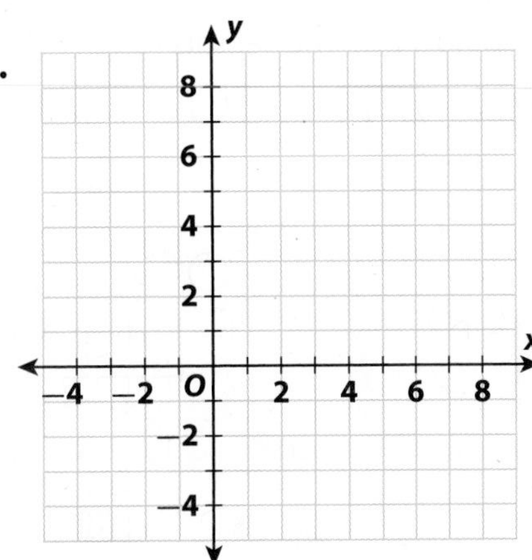

4.2 Representing Functions

3. Marco owed his father \$150 and began paying him back \$20 at the end of each week, beginning November 1. Joni owed her father \$130 and began paying him back \$15 at the end of each week, beginning on the same day. What Marco owed his father in dollars at the end of n weeks can be represented by $f(n) = 150 - 20n$. What Joni owed her father in dollars at the end of n weeks can be represented by $g(n) = 130 - 15n$.

Find the value of n for which $f(n) = g(n)$. What does that value mean in this situation?

____

____

4.3 Sequences

4. Write the first 4 terms of the sequence defined by the rule $f(n) = 2n^2 + 1$. Use the domain in the table.

n	1	2	3	4
$f(n)$				

ESSENTIAL QUESTION

5. What is a function and how can it be represented?

____

____

____

MODULE 4
MIXED REVIEW

Assessment Readiness

1. Consider the function $f(x) = -3x + 1$ for the domain {0, 1, 2}.
Which representation(s) below also model this function? Select all that apply.

○

x	0	1	2
$f(x)$	1	−4	−7

○ 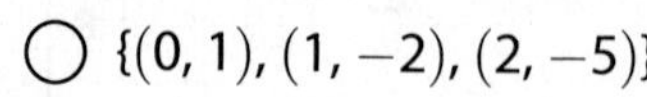
{(0, 1), (1, −2), (2, −5)}

○ 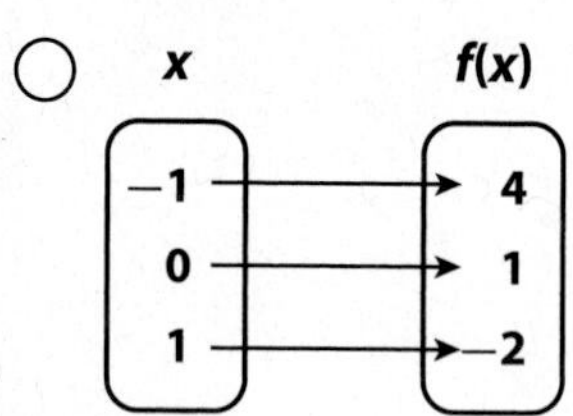

○ 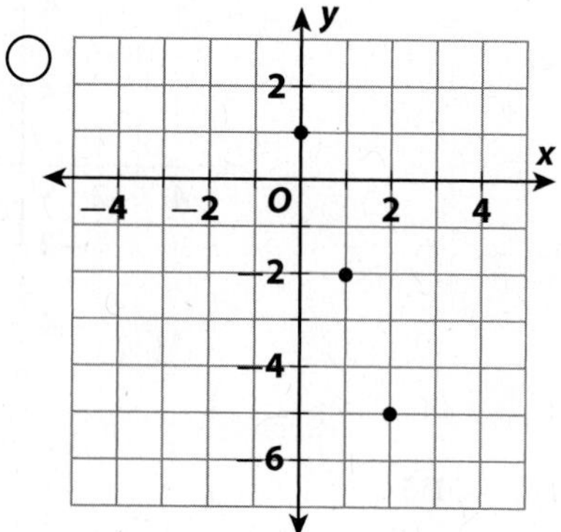

2. A grocery clerk is making a display of oranges. The numbers of oranges in the layers of the display form a sequence, with the top layer counting as layer 1. The explicit rule $f(n) = (n + 1)^2$ describes this sequence, where n is a whole number greater than 0. Will 50 oranges be enough to complete the top 4 layers of the display? Explain your reasoning.

3. Jonathon's suitcase can weigh no more than 50 pounds or he will have to pay an extra fee at the airport. His suitcase already weighs $44\frac{1}{2}$ pounds. Each pair of his jeans weighs about $\frac{7}{8}$ pound. How many more pairs of jeans can Jonathon pack without having to pay an extra fee? Explain your reasoning by writing and solving an inequality.

Absolute Value

MODULE 5

CALIFORNIA COMMON CORE

LESSON 5.1

Absolute Value Functions

F.IF.7, F.IF.4, F.BF.3

LESSON 5.2

Solving Absolute Value Equations and Inequalities

CA CC A.REI.3.1, A.CED.1

ESSENTIAL QUESTION

How do you represent absolute value functions and solve absolute value equations and inequalities?

my.hrw.com

Real-World Video

Gold jewelry is sold with a rating for purity. For instance, 18-karat gold is 75% pure by weight. The purity level has to meet tolerances that can be expressed using absolute value inequalities.

GO DIGITAL

my.hrw.com

my.hrw.com

Go digital with your write-in student edition, accessible on any device.

Math On the Spot

Scan with your smart phone to jump directly to the online edition, video tutor, and more.

Animated Math

Interactively explore key concepts to see how math works.

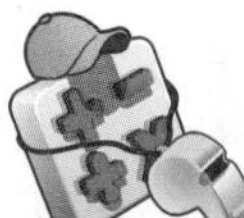

Personal Math Trainer

Get immediate feedback and help as you work through practice sets.

Are YOU Ready?

Complete these exercises to review skills you will need for this module.

Graph Linear Functions

EXAMPLE Graph the function $y = -3x + 5$.

1. Substitute $x = 1$ into the equation.
   $y = -3(x) + 5$
   $y = -3(1) + 5$
   $y = -3 + 5$
   $y = 2$, so the point $(1, 2)$ is on the graph.
2. Repeat step 1 to find other points on the graph. Fill in the table shown.

x	1	0	−1	2
y	2	5	8	−1

3. Graph the points on the scale.
4. Draw a line through the dots.

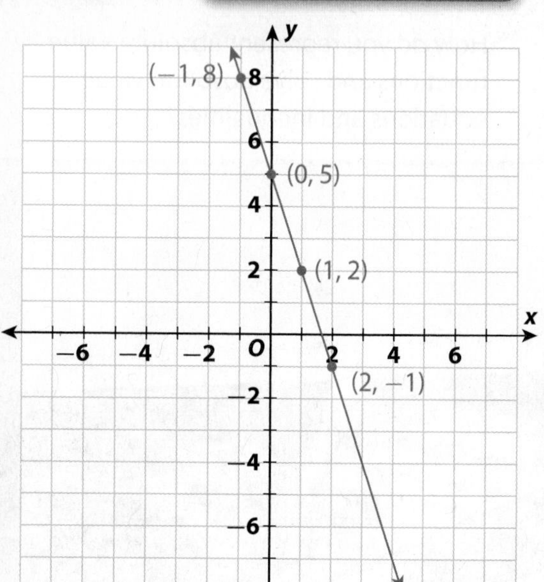

Graph the following functions on the grid shown.

1. $y = 2x + 1$

x	−1	0	1	2
y			3	

2. $y = -4x + 2$

x	−1	0	1	2
y				

3. $y = -2$

x	− 1	0	1	2
y				

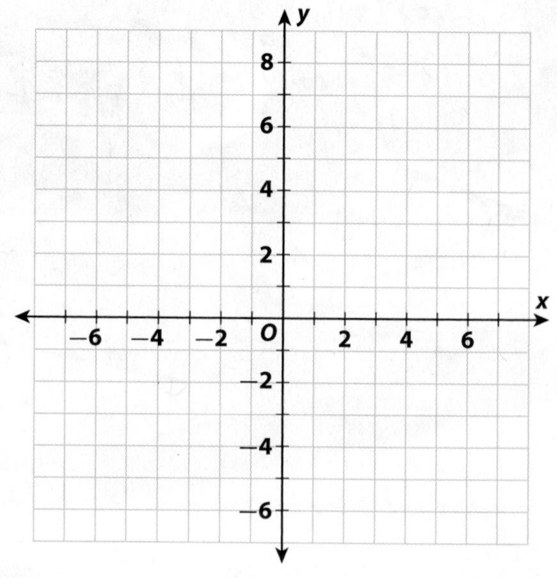

Reading Start-Up

Visualize Vocabulary

Use the Review Words to complete the Pyramid Chart. Write one word in each box.

A ______________ is a relation in which every input is paired with exactly one output.

The ______________ is all of the possible input values of a relation or function.

The ______________ is all of the possible output values of a relation or function.

Vocabulary

Review Words

- absolute value *(valor absoluto)*
- ✔ domain *(dominio)*
- ✔ function *(función)*
- integer *(entero)*
- ✔ range *(rango)*

Preview Words

- absolute value function
- vertex

Understand Vocabulary

To become familiar with some of the vocabulary terms in the module, consider the following. You may refer to the module, the glossary, or a dictionary.

1. The word *absolute* refers to an item that is not reduced or diminished in any way. How do you think this definition relates to an **absolute value function**?

____

2. The vertex of a triangle is the point where two sides meet. What do you think the **vertex** of an absolute value function represents?

____

Active Reading

Three-Panel Flip Chart Before beginning the module, create a three-panel flip chart to help you organize what you learn. Label each flap with one of the lesson titles from this module. As you study each lesson, write important information like vocabulary and examples under the appropriate flap.

GETTING READY FOR

Absolute Value

Understanding the standards and the vocabulary terms in the standards will help you know exactly what you are expected to learn in this module.

F.IF.7

Graph functions expressed symbolically and show key features of the graph, by hand in simple cases and using technology for more complicated cases.

Key Vocabulary

absolute value function

(función de valor absoluto)

A function whose rule contains absolute value expressions.

What It Means to You

You can see what an absolute value function looks like.

EXAMPLE F.IF.7

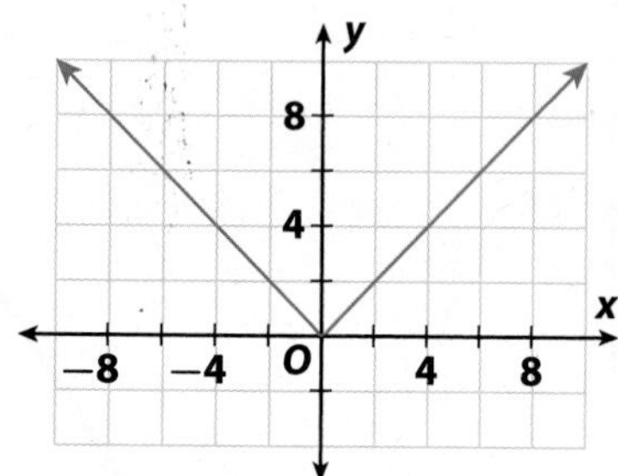

A car is braking at a uniform speed as it nears a stop sign. For this particular car, this reduction in speed can be represented by the equation $y = -x$ for $x \leq 0$. After coming to a stop at the stop sign, the car accelerates at a constant speed. For this particular car, this acceleration in speed can be represented by $y = x$ for $x \geq 0$. Graph both of these functions on the same coordinate grid. Describe the shape of the combined graph.

The graph is V-shaped and opens upward, and the two sides of the V have a common point at the origin.

CA CC **A.REI.3.1**

Solve one-variable equations and inequalities involving absolute value, graphing the solutions and interpreting them in context.

What It Means to You

Before they are used in a game, basketballs must be inflated to a pressure of 8 pounds per square inch (psi) with an error of no more than 0.5 pound per square inch. What are the minimum and maximum acceptable pressures for a basketball?

EXAMPLE A.REI.3.1

The maximum value of the error must equal the absolute value of the expression $x - 8$, or $0.5 = |x - 8|$, where x is the pressure of the basketball in pounds per square inch.

Solve the equation $0.5 = |x - 8|$.

$$0.5 = |x - 8|$$
$$0.5 = x - 8 \text{ or } -0.5 = x - 8$$
$$8.5 = x \text{ or } 7.5 = x$$

The maximum pressure is 8.5 psi and the minimum pressure is 7.5 psi.

Visit **my.hrw.com** to see all **CA Common Core Standards** explained.

my.hrw.com

LESSON 5.1

Absolute Value Functions

CA CC F.IF.7

Graph functions expressed symbolically and show key features of the graph, by hand in simple cases and using technology for more complicated cases. *Also F.IF.4, F.BF.3*

ESSENTIAL QUESTION

What are the characteristics of an absolute value function?

EXPLORE ACTIVITY

F.IF.7

Evaluating and Graphing Absolute Value Functions

An *absolute value function* has different rules for different parts of its domain. Let's explore the properties of the absolute value function, $f(x) = |x|$.

A When $x \geq 0$: $|x| = x$ *Example:* $|3| =$ ________

When $x < 0$: $|x| =$ ____________ *Example:* $|-3| = -(-3) =$ ________

Thus, the **absolute value function** can be defined as $f(x) = |x| = \begin{cases} -x \text{ if } x < 0 \\ x \text{ if } x \geq 0 \end{cases}$.

B Complete the tables.

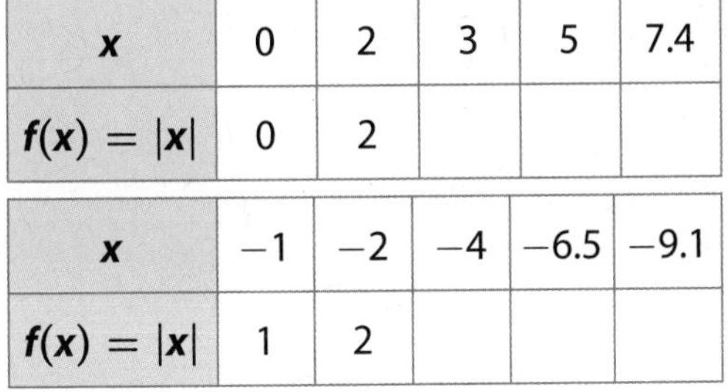

x	0	2	3	5	7.4
f(x) = |x|	0	2			

x	−1	−2	−4	−6.5	−9.1
f(x) = |x|	1	2			

C Graph the absolute value function, $f(x) = |x|$.

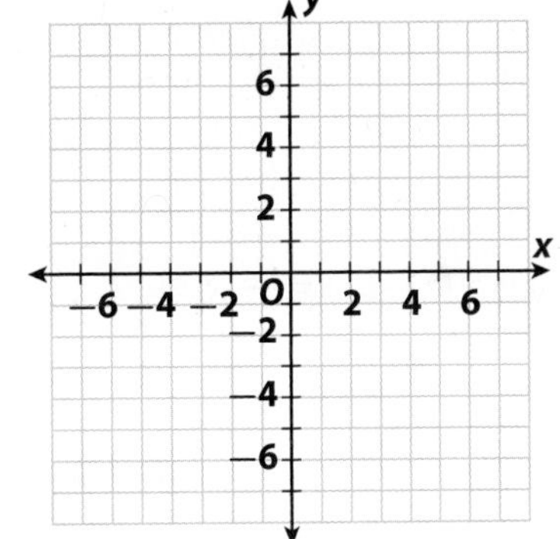

The graphs of other absolute value functions are transformations of the graph you drew in part C. Because of this, the function $f(x) = |x|$ is called the parent absolute value function.

Math Talk
Mathematical Practices

How do you think the "parent function" for absolute value got its name? Discuss.

REFLECT

1. What is the domain and range of the function $f(x) = |x|$? Explain.

____

____

____

2. **Look for a Pattern** With respect to shape and symmetry, what kind of pattern does the graph of $f(x) = |x|$ display?

____

Characteristics of Absolute Value Functions

The graphs of absolute value functions have some features in common.

- The graphs are composed of two rays that meet at a common point, called the **vertex**. The vertex for both of the graphs in Example 1 is (0, 2).
- The graphs are V-shaped and symmetrical across a vertical line passing through the vertex.

EXAMPLE 1

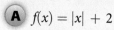

CA CC F.IF.7

Graph each function.

A $f(x) = |x| + 2$

STEP 1 Make a table.

x	0	1	−1	2	−2	5	−5
$f(x) = \|x\| + 2$	2	3	3	4	4	7	7

STEP 2 Graph the points.

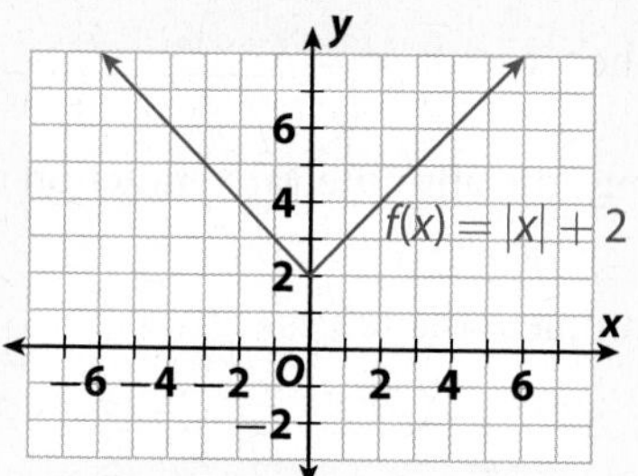

B $f(x) = -|x| + 2$

STEP 1 Make a table.

x	0	1	−1	2	−2	6	−6
$f(x) = -\|x\| + 2$	2	1	1	0	0	−4	−4

STEP 2 Graph the points.

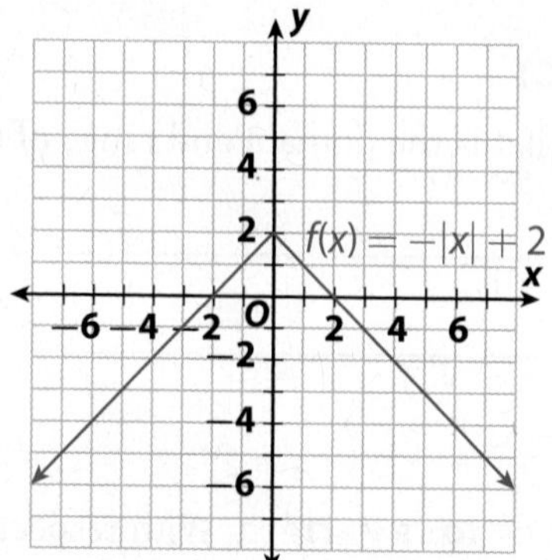

My Notes

REFLECT

3. **Analyze Relationships** How are the graphs in part A and part B related?

YOUR TURN

4. Graph $f(x) = -|x| + 1$.

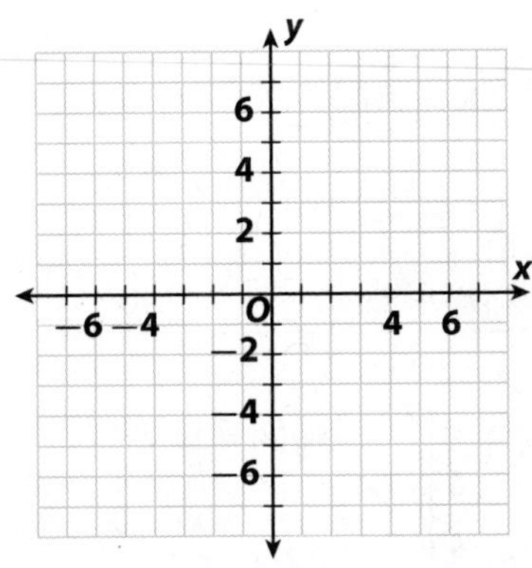

Transformations of Absolute Value Functions

Graphing multiple absolute value functions can help you see how they are related to the parent function $f(x) = |x|$.

EXAMPLE 2  CA CC F.BF.3

Graph each set of functions on the same coordinate plane. Find the vertex, domain, and range of each function.

A $g(x) = |x| + 5$, $h(x) = |x| - 4$, $k(x) = |x| + 1$.

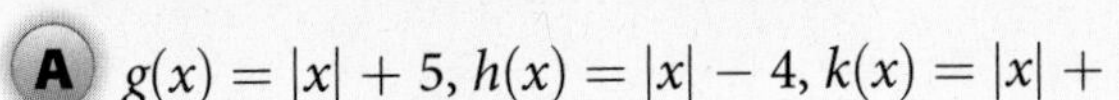

x	0	1	−1	2	−2	7	−7
$g(x) = \|x\| + 5$	5	6	6	7	7	12	12

x	0	1	−1	3	−3	5	−6
$h(x) = \|x\| - 4$	−4	−3	−3	−1	−1	1	2

x	0	1	−1	2	−2	5	−5
$k(x) = \|x\| + 1$	1	2	2	3	3	6	6

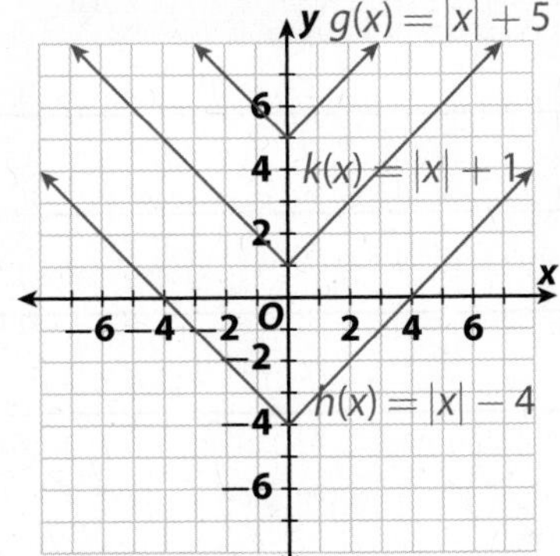

$g(x)$ vertex: (0, 5)
domain: all real numbers
range: $y \geq 5$

$h(x)$ vertex: (0, −4)
domain: all real numbers
range: $y \geq -4$

$k(x)$ vertex: (0, 1)
domain: all real numbers
range: $y \geq 1$

Each graph is a vertical translation of the parent function.

B $g(x) = |x + 4|$, $h(x) = |x - 4|$, $k(x) = |x - 1|$.

x	0	1	−1	2	−2	7	−7
$g(x) = \|x + 4\|$	4	5	3	6	2	11	3

x	0	1	−1	3	−3	5	−5
$h(x) = \|x - 4\|$	4	3	5	1	7	1	9

x	0	1	−1	2	−2	5	−5
$k(x) = \|x - 1\|$	1	0	2	1	3	4	6

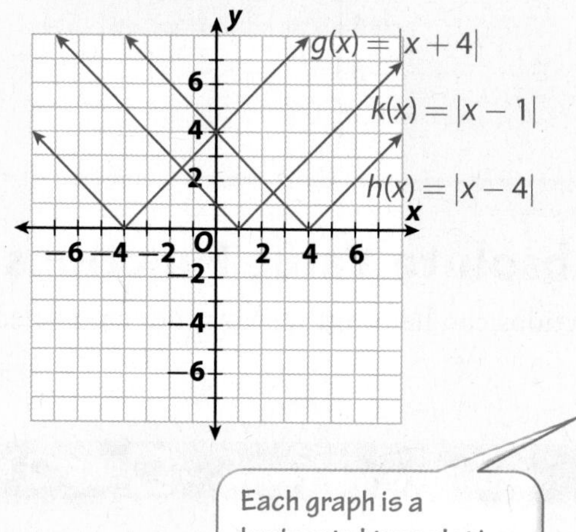

$g(x)$ vertex: $(-4, 0)$
domain: all real numbers
range: nonnegative real numbers

$h(x)$ vertex: $(4, 0)$
domain: all real numbers
range: nonnegative real numbers

$k(x)$ vertex: $(1, 0)$
domain: all real numbers
range: nonnegative real numbers

Each graph is a horizontal translation of the parent function.

My Notes

REFLECT

5. How does adding a value (k) to the parent function affect the graph?

6. How does subtracting a value (h) from x in the parent function affect the graph?

7. **Make a Conjecture** Complete the following statements.

For $f(x) = |x| + k$, the vertex is (0, ☐).

For $f(x) = |x - h|$, the vertex is (☐, 0).

8. Graph $f(x) = |x| + 3$, $g(x) = |x| - 3$, and $h(x) = |x| - 5$ on the same coordinate plane. Give the domain and range of each function.

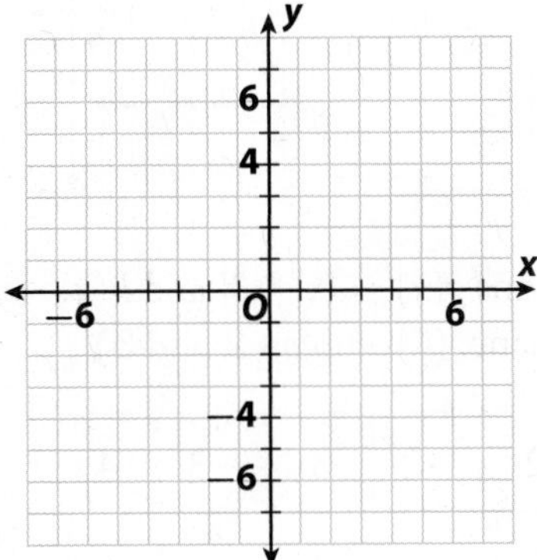

____

____

____

9. Graph $f(x) = |x + 1|$, $g(x) = |x - 5|$, and $h(x) = |x + 5|$ on the same coordinate plane. Give the domain and range of each function.

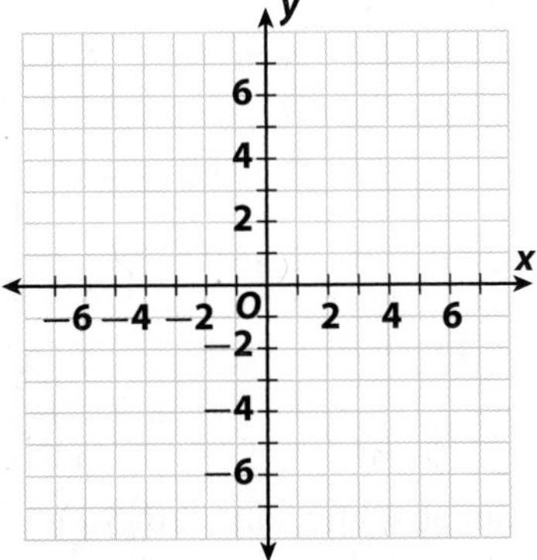

____

____

____

____

Guided Practice

For 1–2, use the same coordinate plane.

1. Complete the table of values for the function $f(x) = |x| + 2$. Graph the function on the coordinate plane. (Example 1)

x	0	1	−1	2	−2
$f(x) = \|x\| + 2$	2		3		

x	3	−3	5	−5	−7
$f(x) = \|x\| + 2$					9

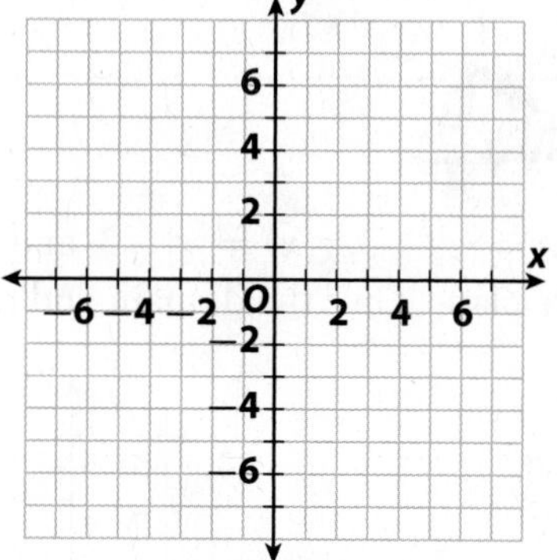

2. Complete the table of values for the functions $g(x) = |x - 3|$ and $h(x) = -|x| + 1$. Graph both functions on the coordinate plane. (Examples 2 and 3)

x	0	1	−1	2	−2	3	−3	4	−4	6
$g(x) = \|x - 3\|$	3									

x	0	1	−1	2	−2	3	−3	5	−5	6
$h(x) = -\|x\| + 1$	1									

3. Find the vertex, domain, and range for the function $f(x) = |x| + 2$ from Exercise 1. (Examples 2 and 3)

vertex: ______________________

domain: ______________________

range: ______________________

4. Find the vertex, domain, and range for the function $g(x) = |x - 3|$ from Exercise 2. (Examples 2 and 3)

vertex: ______________________

domain: ______________________

range: ______________________

ESSENTIAL QUESTION CHECK-IN

5. What are the characteristics of the graph of an absolute value function?

____

____

____

____

Name ________________ Class ________________ Date ________________

5.1 Independent Practice

CA CC F.IF.4, F.IF.7, F.BF.3

Graph each function. Identify the vertex, domain, and range.

6. $f(x) = |x| - 3$

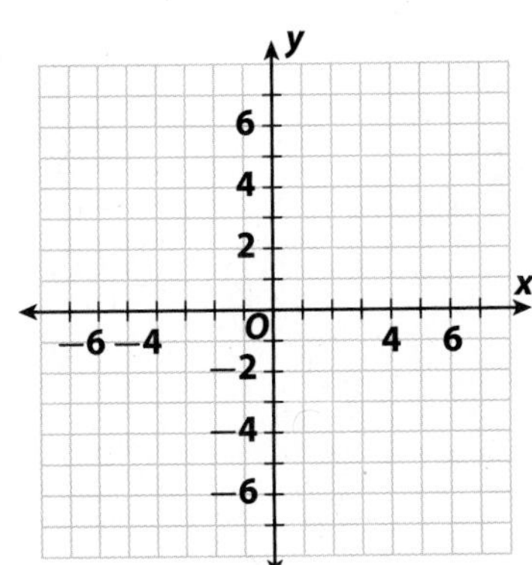

vertex: ________________

domain: ________________

range: ________________

____

7. $g(x) = |x + 3|$

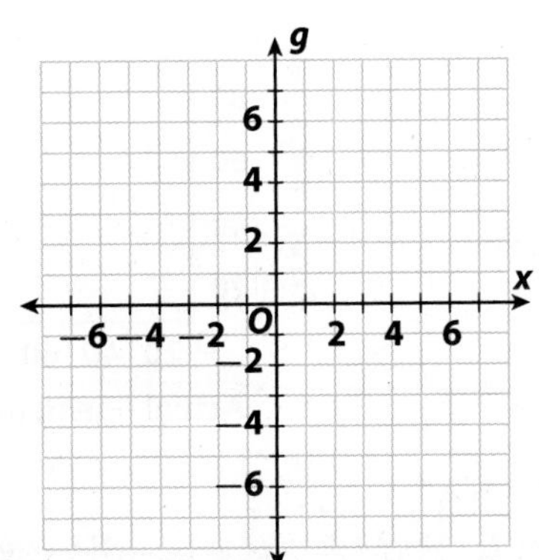

vertex: ________________

domain: ________________

range: ________________

____

8. **Represent Real-World Problems** Montague National Bank is running a promotion in which customers get points for any transaction that can be redeemed for prizes. Each transaction is awarded points equal to double the absolute value of its dollar value plus 100 bonus points.

a. Write an absolute value function where $p(d)$ represents the number of points that are awarded when a transaction of d dollars is made.

____

b. Complete the table of values for $p(d)$.

d	+50	−50	+70	−70	6	−6
$p(d)$						

c. Graph $p(d)$.

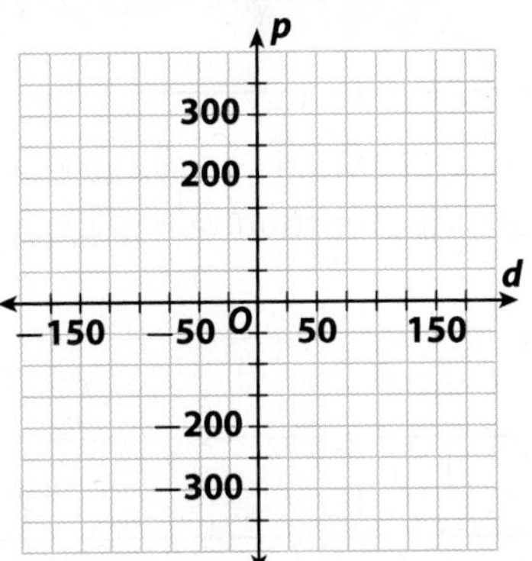

9. The speedometer on a car shows that the car is going 60 miles per hour. The function $e(x)$ defined by $e(x) = |x - 60|$ represents the error in the speed that the speedometer shows, where x is the actual speed of the car in miles per hour. For example, if your actual speed is 70 miles per hour, the error in the speedometer display is $e(70) = |70 - 60| = |10| = 10$ miles per hour. Graph the function.

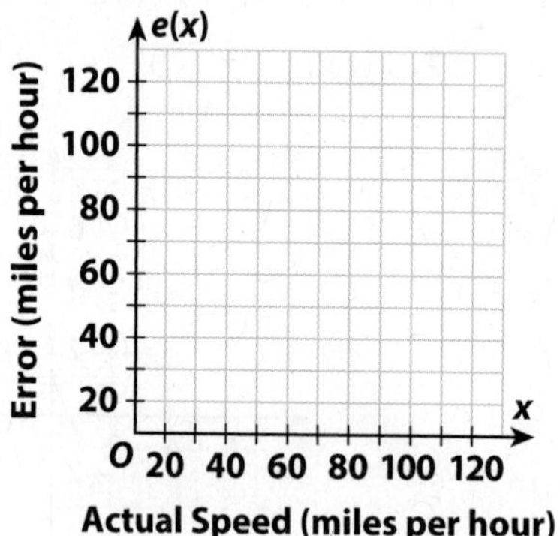

FOCUS ON HIGHER ORDER THINKING

Work Area

10. Explain the Error Terry is checking Randi's work. His comments are in red.

Name: Randi Manietti

#7 $f(x) = |x| - 5$

$f(3) = -2$

Incorrect! Absolute value functions have no negative values.

Which student is correct? Explain.

____

____

____

____

11. Critical Thinking Give an example of an absolute value function that has only negative function values. Explain why all function values are negative.

____

____

____

____

LESSON 5.2

Solving Absolute Value Equations and Inequalities

CA CC A.REI.3.1

Solve one-variable equations and inequalities involving absolute value, graphing the solutions and interpreting them in context. *Also A.CED.1*

ESSENTIAL QUESTION

How do you solve equations and inequalities that involve absolutevalue expressions?

EXPLORE ACTIVITY CA CC A.REI.3.1

Solving Absolute Value Equations Graphically

The graphs of three absolute value functions are shown.

Graph A is $f(x) = |x|$.

Graph B is $h(x) = |x - 2|$.

Graph C is $j(x) = |x + 3|$.

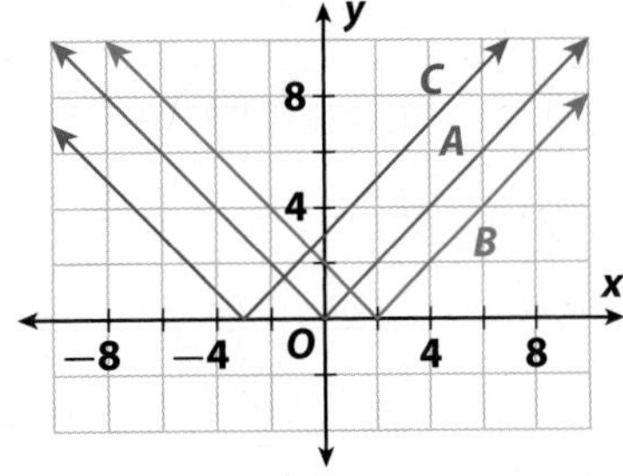

A On the same coordinate grid, graph the function $g(x) = 5$. What type of function is this? Describe its graph.

____

B At how many points does the graph of $g(x)$ intersect each graph?

Graph A: ______ points of intersection

Graph B: ______ points of intersection

Graph C: ______ points of intersection

C Use the graph to find the x-coordinate of each point of intersection of the graphs of $h(x)$ and $g(x)$. Show that each x-coordinate satisfies the equation $|x - 2| = 5$, which is obtained by setting $h(x)$ equal to $g(x)$.

____

D Use the graph to find the x-coordinate of each point of intersection of the graphs of $j(x)$ and $g(x)$. Show that each x-coordinate satisfies the equation $|x + 3| = 5$, which is obtained by setting $j(x)$ equal to $g(x)$.

____

REFLECT

1. Describe how you could solve an equation like $|x + 4| = 9$ graphically.

____

____

____

EXPLORE ACTIVITY *(cont'd)*

2. How many points of intersection exist for the graphs of $m(x) = |x| + 3$ and $n(x) = 3$? How many solutions does the equation $|x| + 3 = 3$ have? Explain.

3. How many points of intersection exist for the graphs of $p(x) = |x| + 10$ and $q(x) = 2$? How many solutions does the equation $|x| + 10 = 2$ have? Explain.

Solving Absolute Value Equations

To solve absolute value equations, perform inverse operations to isolate the absolute value expression. Then you must consider two cases.

Solving an Absolute Value Equation

1. Use inverse operations to isolate the absolute value expression.
2. Rewrite the resulting equation as two cases that do not involve absolute values.
3. Solve the equation in each of the two cases.

EXAMPLE 1 CA CC A.REI.3.1

Solve each equation.

A $|x| = 4$

$|x| = 4$ Think: What numbers are 4 units from 0?

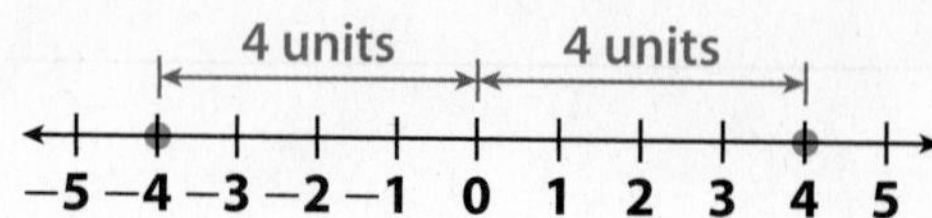

Case 1	**Case 2**
$x = -4$	$x = 4$

Rewrite the equation as two cases.

The solutions are −4 and 4.

B $4|x+2| = 24$

$$\frac{4|x+2|}{4} = \frac{24}{4}$$ Divide both sides by 4.

$$|x+2| = 6$$ Think: What numbers are 6 units from 0?

Case 1	Case 2
$x + 2 = -6$	$x + 2 = 6$
$\underline{-2 \quad -2}$	$\underline{-2 \quad -2}$
$x = -8$	$x = 4$

Rewrite the equation as two cases. Subtract 2 from both sides.

The solutions are −8 and 4.

YOUR TURN

Solve each equation. Check your answer.

4. $|x| - 3 = 4$ ________________

5. $8 = |x - 2.5|$ ________________

Special Cases of Absolute Value Equations

Not all absolute value equations have two solutions. If the absolute value expression equals 0, there is one solution. If an equation states that an absolute value is negative, there are no solutions.

EXAMPLE 2

CA CC A.REI.3.1

Solve each equation.

A $|x+3| + 4 = 4$

$$|x+3| + 4 = 4$$
$$\underline{\quad -4 \quad -4}$$ Subtract 4 from both sides.
$$|x+3| = 0$$

$$x + 3 = 0$$
$$\underline{-3 \quad -3}$$ There is only one case. Subtract 3 from both sides.
$$x = -3$$

B $5 = |x+2| + 8$

$$5 = |x+2| + 8$$
$$\underline{-8} \qquad \underline{\quad -8}$$ Subtract 8 from both sides.
$$-3 = |x+2| \; ✗$$ Absolute value cannot be negative.

This equation has no solution.

YOUR TURN

Solve each equation.

6. $2 - |2x - 5| = 7$ ________

7. $-6 + |x - 4| = -6$ ________

Solving Absolute Value Inequalities

Absolute value inequalities are solved using the same steps as for solving absolute value equations. However, if you divide by a negative number, you must reverse the inequality symbol.

EXAMPLE 3

CA CC A.REI.3.1

Solve each inequality. Graph the solution.

A $|x| + 3 < 12$

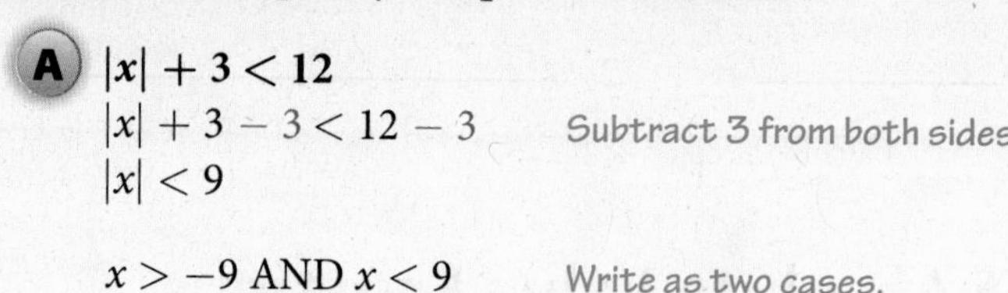

$|x| + 3 - 3 < 12 - 3$ Subtract 3 from both sides.

$|x| < 9$

$x > -9$ AND $x < 9$ Write as two cases.

$-9 < x < 9$

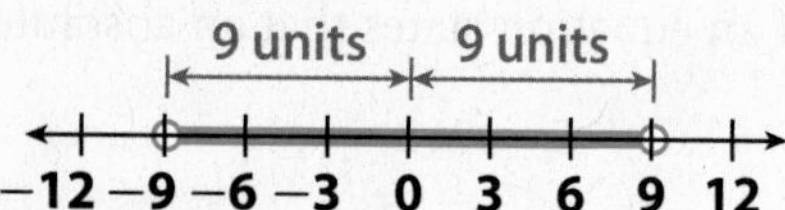

B $|x - 8| + 5 \geq 11$

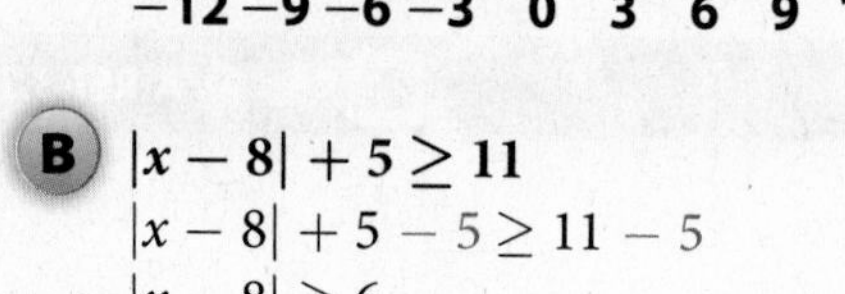

$|x - 8| + 5 - 5 \geq 11 - 5$ Subtract 5 from both sides.

$|x - 8| \geq 6$

$x - 8 \leq -6$ OR $x - 8 \geq 6$ Write as two cases.

$x - 8 + 8 \leq -6 + 8$ OR $x - 8 + 8 \geq 6 + 8$ Add 8 to both sides.

$x \leq 2$ OR $x \geq 14$

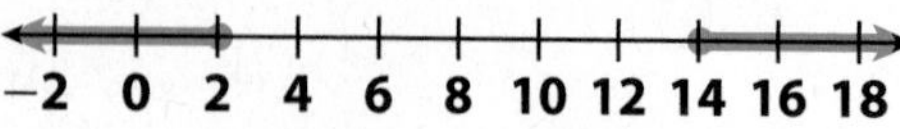

YOUR TURN

Solve each inequality.

8. $2|x| \leq 6$ ________

9. $|x| + 10 > 12$ ________

Solving Real-World Problems

Absolute value equations can be used to model and solve real-world problems.

Math On the Spot
my.hrw.com

EXAMPLE 4 CA CC A.REI.3.1, A.CED.1

Sydney Harbour Bridge in Australia is 1149 meters long. Because of changes in temperature, the bridge can expand or contract by as much as 420 millimeters. Write and solve an absolute value equation to find the minimum and maximum lengths of the bridge.

First convert millimeters to meters: 420 mm = 0.42 m.

The length of the bridge can vary by 0.42 m, so find two numbers that are 0.42 units away from 1149 on a number line.

You can find these numbers by using the absolute value equation $|x - 1149| = 0.42$. Solve the equation by rewriting it as two cases.

Case 1	Case 2
$x - 1149 = -0.42$	$x - 1149 = 0.42$
$+1149 \quad +1149$	$+1149 \quad +1149$
$x = 1148.58$	$x = 1149.42$

Add 1149 to both sides of each equation.

The minimum length of the bridge is 1148.58 m, and the maximum length is 1149.42 m.

YOUR TURN

10. Sydney Harbour Bridge is 134 meters tall. The height of the bridge can rise or fall by 180 millimeters because of changes in temperature. Write and solve an absolute value equation to find the minimum and maximum heights of the bridge.

____

____

11. The diameter of a valve for the space shuttle must be within 0.001 mm of 5 mm. Write and solve an absolute value equation to find the minimum and maximum acceptable diameters of the valve.

____

____

Personal Math Trainer
Online Practice and Help
my.hrw.com

Guided Practice

Solve each equation by graphing. (Explore Activity)

1. $|x + 1| = 3$

Graph the functions $f(x) = |x + 1|$ and $g(x) =$ ________.

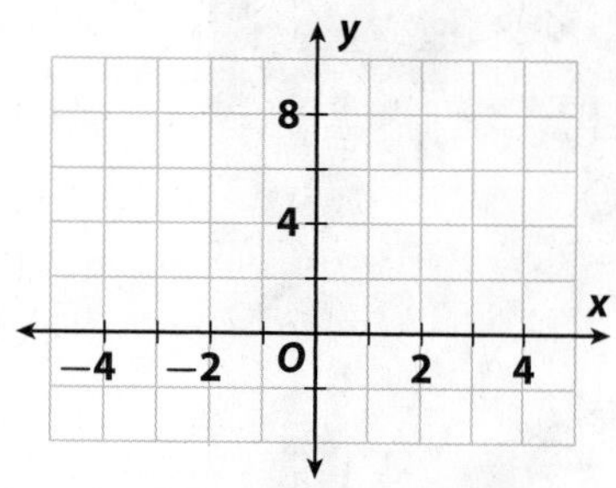

The solutions are $x =$ ________.

2. $2|x| = 4$

Graph the functions $f(x) =$ ________ and $g(x) =$ ________.

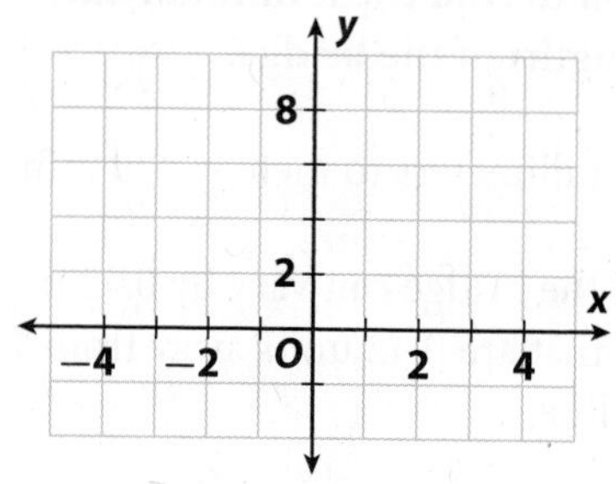

The solutions are $x =$ ________.

Solve each equation. (Examples 1 and 2)

3. $9 = |x + 5|$

____

4. $|3x| + 2 = 8$

____

5. $|x - 3| - 6 = 2$

____

6. $|x + 4| = -7$

____

7. $7 = |3x + 9| + 7$

____

8. $5|x + 7| + 14 = 8$

____

Solve each inequality. (Example 3)

9. $|3x| + 2 \leq 8$

____

10. $|x + 2| > 7$

____

11. $|x - 3| + 2 \geq 4$

____

12. Communication Barry's walkie-talkie has a range of 2 mi. Barry is traveling on a straight highway and is at mile marker 207. Write and solve an absolute value equation to find the minimum and maximum mile marker from 207 that Barry's walkie-talkie will reach. (Example 4)

____

ESSENTIAL QUESTION CHECK-IN

13. How do you solve absolute value equations and inequalities?

____

____

____

Name ______________________ Class ______________________ Date ______________

5.2 Independent Practice

Personal Math Trainer
my.hrw.com
Online Practice and Help

CA CC A.REI.3.1, A.CED.1

Solve each equation or inequality.

14. $|2x - 4| = 22$

____

15. $18 = 3|x - 1|$

____

16. $3|x| - 12 = 18$

____

17. $|x| + 6 = 12 - 6$

____

18. $|x - 3| + 14 = 5$

____

19. $3 + |x - 1| = 3$

____

20. $|x| - 6 > 16$

____

21. $|x + 1| - 7.8 \leq 6.2$

____

22. $|x - 5| + 1 \leq 2$

____

23. The two numbers that are 5 units from 3 on the number line are represented by the equation $|n - 3| = 5$. What are these two numbers? ______________

24. Write and solve an absolute value equation that represents two numbers x that are 2 units from 7 on a number line.

____

25. A brick company guarantees to fill a contractor's order to within 5% accuracy. A contractor orders 1500 bricks. Write and solve an absolute value equation to find the maximum and minimum number of bricks guaranteed.

____

26. Fill in the missing reasons to justify each step in solving the equation $3|2x + 1| = 21$.

Statements	Reasons
1. $3|2x + 1| = 21$	**1.** Given
2. $|2x + 1| = 7$	**2.**
3. $2x + 1 = -7$ or $2x + 1 = 7$	**3.** Definition of absolute value
4. $2x = -8$ or $2x = 6$	**4.**
5. $x = -4$ or $x = 3$	**5.**

27. A machine prints posters and then trims them to the correct size. The equation $|l - 65.1| = 0.2$ gives the maximum and minimum acceptable lengths for the posters in inches. Does a poster with a length of 64.8 inches fall within the acceptable range? Why or why not?

____

____

28. A nutritionist recommends that an adult male consume 55 grams of fat per day. It is acceptable for the fat intake to differ from this amount by at most 25 grams. Write and solve an absolute value inequality to find the range of fat intake that is acceptable.

29. The thermostat for a sauna is set to 175 °F, but the actual temperature of the sauna may vary by as much as 12 °F. Write and solve an absolute value inequality to find the range of possible temperatures.

30. The minimum and maximum sound levels at a rock concert are 90 decibels and 95 decibels. Write an absolute value equation to model the situation.

H.O.T. FOCUS ON HIGHER ORDER THINKING

Work Area

31. Analyze Relationships Tell whether each statement is sometimes, always, or never true. Justify your answer.

a. The value of $|x + 4|$ is equal to the value of $|x| + 4$.

b. The absolute value of a number is nonnegative.

32. Critique Reasoning Do you agree with the following statement: "To solve an absolute value equation, you need to solve two equations." Why or why not?

33. Critical Thinking Is there a value of a for which the equation $|x - a| = 1$ has exactly one solution? Explain.

Ready to Go On?

Personal Math Trainer

Online Practice and Help

5.1 Absolute Value Functions

1. Graph $f(x) = |x - 3|$.

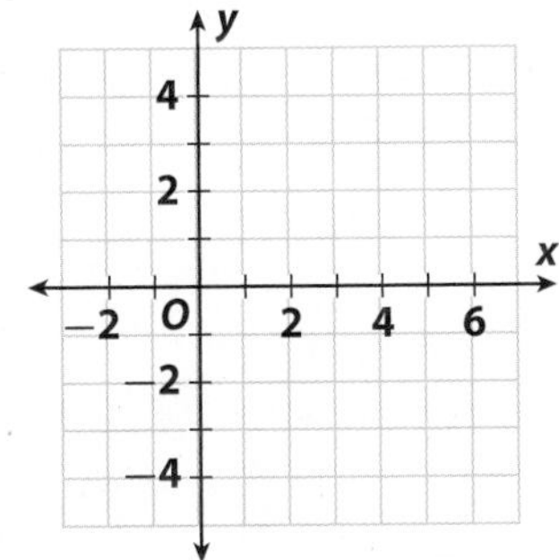

2. Graph $f(x) = |x + 3|$.

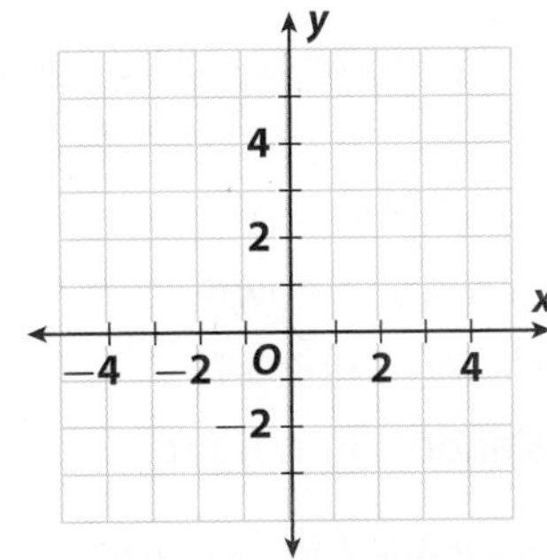

3. Graph $f(x) = |x| + 5$.

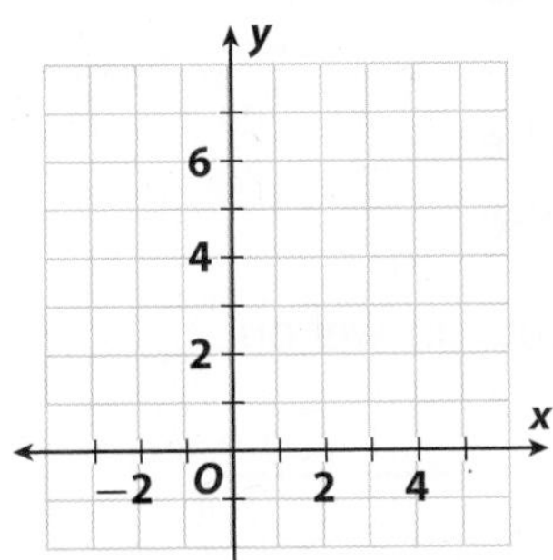

4. Graph $f(x) = -|x| + 2$.

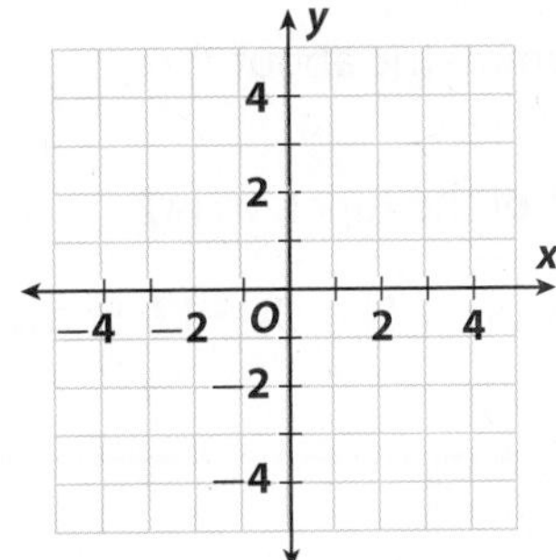

5.2 Solving Absolute Value Equations and Inequalities

Solve each equation or inequality.

5. $|2x - 1| = 11$

____

6. $3|x + 5| < 24$

____

ESSENTIAL QUESTION

7. How does solving absolute value equations and inequalities differ from solving other equations and inequalities?

____

____

____

MODULE 5
MIXED REVIEW

Assessment Readiness

1. Consider the functions $f(x) = |x|$ and $g(x) = |x - 1|$.
   Which transformation(s) below could be applied to the graph of $f(x) = |x|$ to produce the graph of $g(x) = |x - 1|$? Select all that apply.
   - ◯ vertical translation 1 unit up
   - ◯ vertical translation 1 unit down
   - ◯ horizontal translation 1 unit left
   - ◯ horizontal translation 1 unit right

2. Consider the absolute value function $f(x) = |x + 2|$.
   Choose True or False for each statement.
   A. The minimum value of the function is 2. ◯ True ◯ False
   B. The graph is symmetric about the line $x = 2$. ◯ True ◯ False
   C. The y-intercept of the function is 2. ◯ True ◯ False

3. Solve the inequality $2|x - 5| + 3 \geq 17$. Show all your steps. Graph your answer on a number line.

4. A sequence is given by the explicit rule $f(n) = 5n + 15$. Complete the table to give the first ten terms. Then write a recursive rule for the sequence.

n	1	2	3	4	5	6	7	8	9	10
***f*(*n*)**										

Study Guide Review

MODULE 3 Equations and Inequalities in One Variable

Key Vocabulary
equation *(ecuación)*
identity *(identidad)*
inequality *(desigualdad)*
solution of an inequality *(solución de una desigualdad)*
formula *(fórmula)*
literal equation *(ecuación literal)*

ESSENTIAL QUESTION

How can you solve an equation or inequality in one variable?

EXAMPLE 1

Francine opens a savings account with $150. At the end of every week, she adds $35 to her account. After how many weeks will Francine have $360 in her saving account?

Let w represent the number of weeks Francine has been saving.

$$\begin{aligned} 150 + 35w &= 360 \\ -150 \quad\quad &\quad -150 \\ 35w &= 210 \\ \frac{35w}{35} &= \frac{210}{35} \\ w &= 6 \end{aligned}$$

EXAMPLE 2

A test car has a velocity of 280 miles per hour minus five times the gear setting. The track has a speed limit of 150 miles per hour. What are the gear settings that can be used for the car in this trial?

Let x equal the gear setting.

$$\begin{aligned} 280 - 5x &\le 150 \\ -280 \quad\quad &\quad -280 \\ -5x &\le -130 \\ \frac{-5x}{-5} &\ge \frac{-130}{-5} \\ x &\ge 26 \end{aligned}$$

EXERCISES

1. Megan has $25 to buy groceries. She has $15 worth of groceries in her cart, and would like to buy some melons that cost $1.25 each. Write an equation that describes the situation, and determine how many melons Megan can afford. (Lesson 4.1)

____

2. Is 20 a solution for $2x - 5 > 30$? Explain your answer. (Lesson 4.2)

____

MODULE 4 Equations in Two Variables and Functions

Key Vocabulary
equation in two variables *(ecuación en dos variables)*
solution of an equation in two variables *(solución de una ecuación en dos variables)*
function *(función)*
domain *(dominio)*
range *(rango)*
function notation *(notación de función)*
sequence *(sucesión)*
term *(término)*

? ESSENTIAL QUESTION

What is a function and how can a function be represented?

EXAMPLE 1

Graph the solutions of the equation $y = 2x + 4$.

Make a table.

x	y
−4	−4
−3	−2
−2	0
−1	2
0	4
1	6

Graph the ordered pairs.

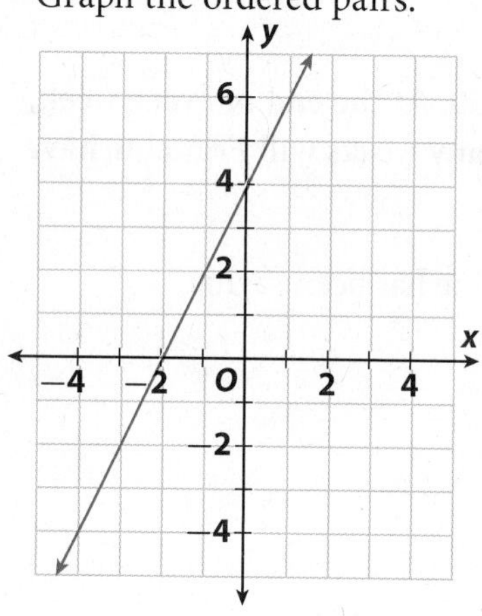

EXAMPLE 2

The functions $f(x)$ and $g(x)$ are defined by the explicit rules $f(x) = 5x + 1$ and $g(x) = 49 - 3x$. Find the value of x for which $f(x) = g(x)$.

Set the functions equal to each other, then solve.

$$f(x) = g(x)$$
$$5x + 1 = 49 - 3x$$
$$\underline{+3x} \qquad \underline{+3x}$$ Add 3x to both sides.
$$8x + 1 = 49$$

$$8x + 1 = 49$$
$$\underline{-1} \quad \underline{-1}$$ Subtract 1 from both sides.
$$8x = 48$$

$$\frac{8x}{8} = \frac{48}{8}$$ Divide both sides by 8.

$$x = 6$$

So, $f(x) = g(x)$ when $x = 6$.

EXAMPLE 3

Find the first 5 terms of the sequence defined by the explicit rule $f(n) = 8n + 6$. Assume that the domain of each function is the set of whole numbers greater than 0.

Use the explicit rule and substitute the values 1 through 5 for n.

$f(1) = 8(1) + 6 = 14$

$f(2) = 8(2) + 6 = 22$

$f(3) = 8(3) + 6 = 30$

$f(4) = 8(4) + 6 = 38$

$f(5) = 8(5) + 6 = 46$

The first five terms are 14, 22, 30, 38, 46.

EXERCISES

3. Does $y = 6x + 5$ represent a function? Explain your answer. (Lesson 5.2)

____

____

4. Given the functions $f(x) = 7x - 2$ and $g(x) = 3x + 6$, find the value of x for which $f(x) = g(x)$. (Lesson 5.2)

____

Consider the function $y = 2x + 8$. Determine if each ordered pair is a solution. (Lesson 5.1)

5. (1, 10) ______________ **6.** (3, 16) ______________

7. (4, 16) ______________ **8.** (5, 20) ______________

Write the first four terms of the sequence. The domain of the function is the set of consecutive integers starting with 1. (Lesson 5.3)

9. $f(n) = 3n(n + 3)$ ______________

10. $f(n) = 2(n + 3)$ ______________

11. $f(1) = 3$ and $f(n) = f(n - 1) - 5$ ______________

12. $f(1) = 4$ and $f(n) = 2 * f(n - 1) + 3$ ______________

MODULE 5 Absolute Value

ESSENTIAL QUESTION

How do you represent absolute value functions and solve absolute value equations and inequalities?

Key Vocabulary

absolute value function *(función de valor absoluto)*

vertex of an absolute-value graph *(vértice de una gráfica de valor absoluto)*

EXAMPLE 1

Graph each function. Compare the graph to the graph of $f(x) = |x|$.

A $g(x) = |x - 2|$

Make a table of values.

x	0	1	2	3	4
$g(x)$	2	1	0	1	2

Graph the function.

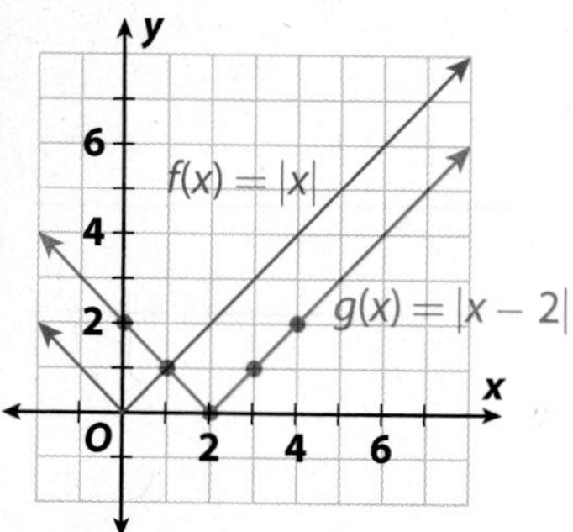

The graph of $g(x)$ is translated 2 units to the right of the graph of $f(x)$.

B $g(x) = |x| - 1$

Make a table of values.

x	−2	−1	0	1	2
$g(x)$	1	0	−1	0	1

Graph the function.

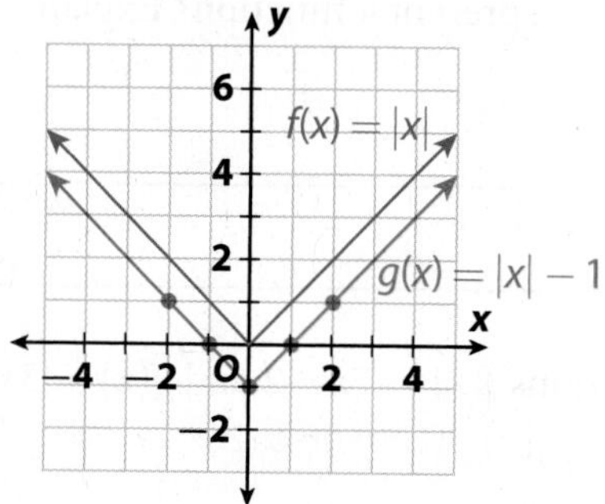

The graph of $g(x)$ is translated 1 unit down from the graph of $f(x)$.

EXAMPLE 2

Solve $3|x + 4| - 6 = 21$.

$3|x + 4| - 6 = 21$ Write original equation.

$3|x + 4| = 27$ Add 6 to both sides.

$|x + 4| = 9$ Divide both sides by 3.

$x + 4 = 9$ OR $x + 4 = -9$ Write as two cases.

$x = 5$ OR $x = -13$ Solve each equation.

The solutions are $x = 5$ or $x = -13$.

EXAMPLE 3

Solve $2|x+5|+3<19$.

$2|x+5|+3<19$	Write original inequality.
$2|x+5|<16$	Subtract 3 from both sides.
$|x+5|<8$	Divide both sides by 2.
$x+5>-8$ AND $x+5<8$	Write as two cases.
$x>-13$ AND $x<3$	Solve each inequality.
$-13<x<3$	

The solutions are all real numbers between -13 and 3.

EXERCISES

1. Graph $g(x)=|x+3|$.
Compare the graph to the graph of $f(x)=|x|$.

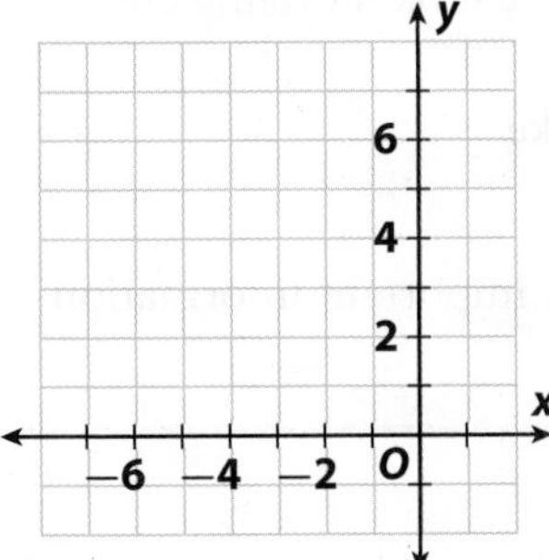

2. Graph $g(x)=|x|-7$.
Compare the graph to the graph of $f(x)=|x|$.

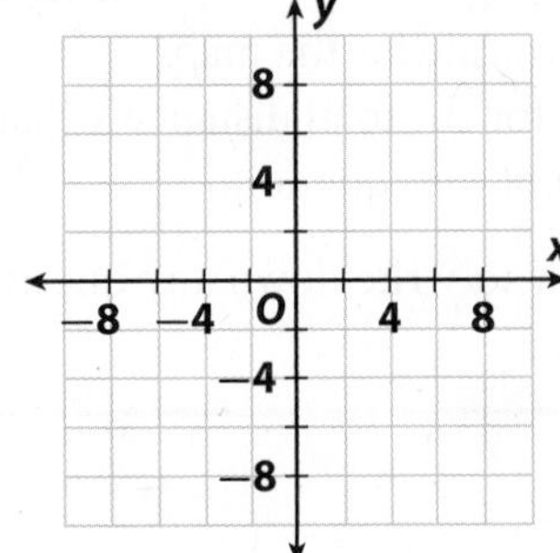

Solve each equation or inequality.

3. $2|x|+3=17$

4. $|x|-5<-2$

5. $4|x-1|-7=17$

6. $|x+4|>3$

7. $|x-1|+5=2$

8. $|2x+3|-4\leq 5$

Unit Project

CA CC A.CED.1, A.REI.1, N.Q.1

Round Trip

Joe rode his bike along Wheeler Road from home to the bike shop. After leaving his bike for a tune-up, he caught a ride home with a friend, a distance one-half mile less than the distance he rode to the shop. Joe spent a total of 30 minutes travelling to and from his house. The table gives his rates on both sections of the trip.

Part of Trip	Rate
Bicycling	15 miles/hour
Riding	3 miles/hour

For this project, create a presentation representing Joe's trip. Your presentation should include the following:

- A map including the bike shop, home, and both routes he took bicycling and riding. Give a scale for the map.
- An equation for the total distance x that Joe rode his bike
- The solution of the equation.

Use the space below to write down any questions you have or important information from your teacher.

MATH IN CAREERS | ACTIVITY

Astronomer Astronomers must sometimes predict the speed of an object. An astronomer discovers an object moving at 2,000 kilometers per minute. The object was spotted at 2,500,000 kilometers from Earth. Assuming constant speed, how long will it take for the object to reach the Moon's orbit, which is 160,000 kilometers away from Earth? Write and solve an equation.

UNIT 2
MIXED REVIEW

Assessment Readiness

1. Consider each equation. Does it have more than one solution?

Select Yes or No.

A. $-4|x-5| = -36$ ○ Yes ○ No

B. $y - 4 = 6(y - 8)$ ○ Yes ○ No

C. $-3|x+2| = 12$ ○ Yes ○ No

2. Consider the inequality $-5(x+1) < 3x + 11$.

Choose True or False for each statement.

A. The graph of the inequality has an open circle at -2. ○ True ○ False

B. The graph of the inequality is shaded to include all values to the left of the endpoint. ○ True ○ False

C. The number 0 is included in the solution set. ○ True ○ False

3. The students in a college marching band are arranged in rows. The recursive rule $f(n) = f(n-1) + 8$ and $f(1) = 13$, gives the number of students in each row, where n is the row number. All of the clarinet players are in row 1, and all of the trumpet players are in row 4. How many more trumpet players than clarinet players are there? Explain your reasoning.

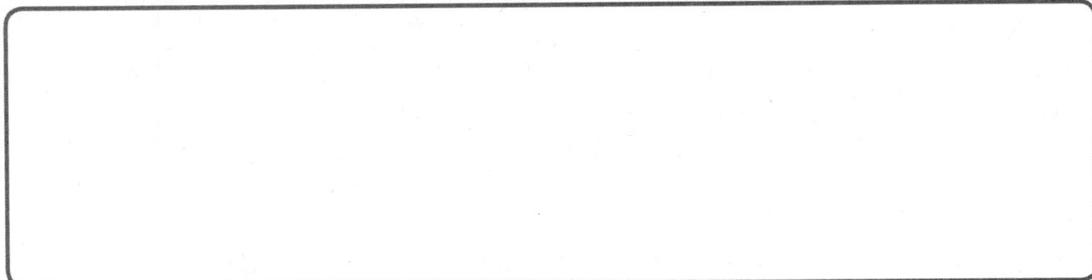

4. A rancher is planning the goat pen shown in the diagram. Determine the value of x, given that the rancher plans to use 100 feet of fencing to enclose the pen. Explain how you solved this problem.

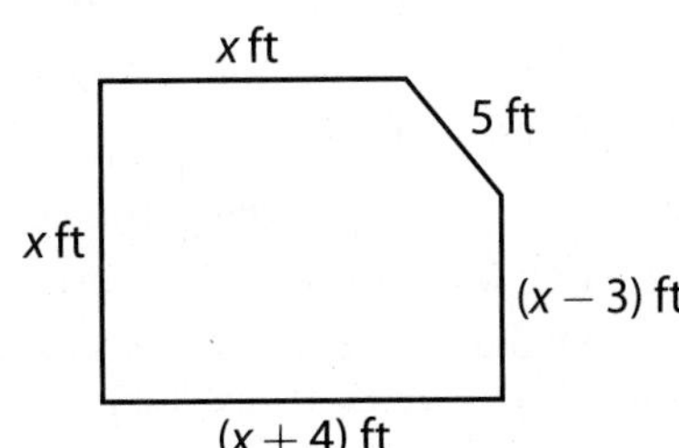

Performance Tasks

★**5.** The equation $a = 0.45(m - 450) + 39.99$ gives the amount a in dollars of Bruce's cell phone bill in a month when he uses m minutes of talk time.

a. Last month, Bruce's bill was \$53.49. How many minutes of talk time did he use?

b. This month, Bruce promises to use no more than half the number of minutes he used last month. He has already used 225 minutes. How many more talk minutes can he use this month without breaking his promise? Use an inequality to explain your reasoning.

★★**6.** A highway rest stop is at mile marker 25. The function $f(x) = |x - 25|$ gives the distance of a car at mile marker x from the rest stop.

a. Graph the function.

b. What is the vertex of the function, and what does it represent in this situation?

c. A hotel on the highway is at mile marker 47. Write a function $g(x)$ that gives the distance in miles of a car at mile marker x from the hotel. Describe $g(x)$ as a transformation of $f(x)$.

d. A car is at mile marker 36. How far is it from the rest stop? How far is it from the hotel? Explain how you know.

★★★**7.** The numbers of seats in the rows of a theater form a sequence. The explicit rule $f(n) = 2n + 4$ defines this sequence, where n is the row number.

a. The theater has a total of 66 seats. How many rows of seats does the theater have? Explain your reasoning.

b. The equation $c = 28 - 3(n - 1)$ gives the cost in dollars of a ticket for a seat in row n of the theater. Mr. Zamora can spend up to \$100 on tickets. Will he be able to buy more tickets if he buys them for the last row of the theater or the first row? Justify your answer.

Linear Relationships

MODULE 6

Linear Functions

CA CC N.Q.1, A.CED.2, F.IF.1, F.IF.2, F.IF.4, F.IF.5, F.IF.6, F.IF.7, F.IF.7a, F.IF.9, F.BF.1, F.BF.3, F.LE.1b, F.LE.2, F.LE.5

MODULE 7

Building Linear Functions

CA CC A.REI.12, F.IF.3, F.BF.1, F.BF.1a, F.BF.1b, F.BF.2, F.LE.2

MODULE 8

Modeling with Linear Functions

CA CC S.ID.6, S.ID.6a, S.ID.6b, S.ID.6c, S.ID.7, S.ID.8, S.ID.9

MODULE 9

Systems of Equations and Inequalities

CA CC A.CED.3, A.REI.5, A.REI.6, A.REI.12

MATH IN CAREERS

Environmental Scientist An environmental scientist uses math to make models to analyze data and understand the effects of human activity on nature.

If you're interested in a career as an environmental scientist, you should study these subjects of math:

- Algebra
- Calculus
- Statistics

Research other careers that involve modeling data with mathematical functions.

ACTIVITY At the end of the unit, check out how an **environmental scientist** uses math.

Unit Project Preview

Changing Flights

The Unit Project at the end of this unit involves designing a new flight of stairs. You will consider the space available and California safety regulations. To successfully complete the Unit Project you'll need to master these skills:

- Take accurate measurements and collect data.
- Represents real-world data with linear equations.
- Graph linear equations on a coordinate plane.

1. A California safety regulation for stairs states that the rise of every step in a stairway cannot be less than 4 inches or greater than $7\frac{1}{2}$ inches. The run cannot be less than 10 inches. Describe in your own words what this regulation means.

____

____

2. According to the safety regulation, what values of rise and run would give the steepest flight of stairs allowed? Explain.

____

____

____

Tracking Your Learning Progression

This unit addresses important California Common Core Standards in the Critical Areas of working with functions, equations, and inequalities.

Domain F.IF Interpreting Functions

Cluster Understand the concept of a function and use function notation.

The unit also supports additional standards.

Domain F.BF Building Functions

Cluster Build a function that models a relationship between two quantities.

Domain A.REI Reasoning with Equations and Inequalities

Cluster Solve equations and inequalities in one variable.

Linear Functions

MODULE  

CALIFORNIA

ESSENTIAL QUESTION

How do equations, graphs, tables, and word descriptions related to linear functions?

CALIFORNIA COMMON CORE

LESSON 6.1
Linear Functions
CA CC F.IF.7, F.IF.7a, F.IF.5

LESSON 6.2
Using Intercepts
CA CC F.IF.7, F.IF.7a, F.IF.4

LESSON 6.3
Using Slope

CA CC F.IF.6, F.IF.4, F.IF.7, F.LE.1b

LESSON 6.4
Slope-Intercept Form
CA CC A.CED.2, F.IF.4, F.IF.6, F.IF.7, F.IF.7a, F.LE.1b

LESSON 6.5
Comparing Linear Functions
CA CC F.IF.9, N.Q.1, F.IF.1, F.IF.2, F.IF.5, F.LE.5

LESSON 6.6
Transforming Linear Functions
CA CC F.BF.3, F.IF.4, F.LE.5

LESSON 6.7
Writing Linear Functions
CA CC F.BF.1, A.CED.2, F.IF.6, F.LE.2

my.hrw.com

Real-World Video

Cyclists adjust their gears to climb up a steep grade or through rocky terrain. Check out how gear ratios, rates of speed, and slope ratios can be used to solve problems involving speed, distance, and time when mountain biking.

GO DIGITAL
my.hrw.com

my.hrw.com

Go digital with your write-in student edition, accessible on any device.

Math On the Spot

Scan with your smart phone to jump directly to the online edition, video tutor, and more.

Animated Math

Interactively explore key concepts to see how math works.

Personal Math Trainer

Get immediate feedback and help as you work through practice sets.

Are YOU Ready?

Complete these exercises to review skills you will need for this chapter.

Personal Math Trainer
Online Practice and Help
my.hrw.com

Solve Multi-Step Equations

EXAMPLE Solve $3x + 4 = 28$.

$$3x + 4 - 4 = 28 - 4 \quad \text{Subtract 4 from both sides.}$$
$$3x = 24$$
$$3x \cdot \frac{1}{3} = 24 \cdot \frac{1}{3} \quad \text{Multiply both sides by } \frac{1}{3}.$$
$$x = 8$$

Solve each equation.

1. $2x + 7 = 19$ __________

2. $0.4y + 8 = -1$ __________

3. $0 = 3z - 6$ __________

Ordered Pairs

EXAMPLE Graph (2, 4) on the coordinate plane.

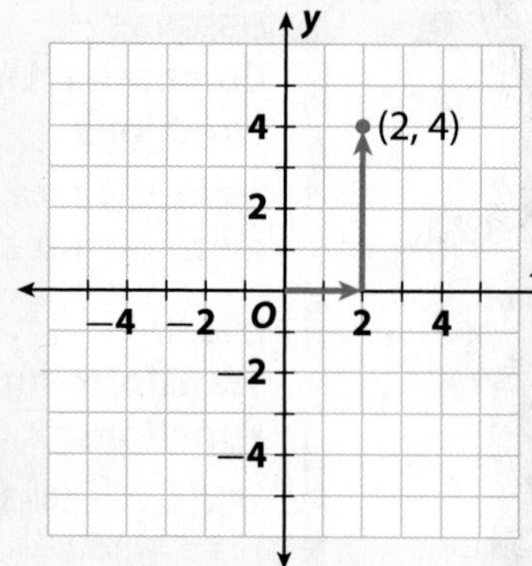

$(2, 4) \rightarrow (x, y)$
The x-coordinate or horizontal coordinate is 2.
Move *right* 2 units.
The y-coordinate or vertical coordinate is 4.
Move *up* 4 units.
Negative coordinates indicate movement to the *left* and *down*.

Graph each point on the coordinate plane provided.

4. (−1, 3)
5. (4, −2)
6. (0, 1)
7. (−2, −3)

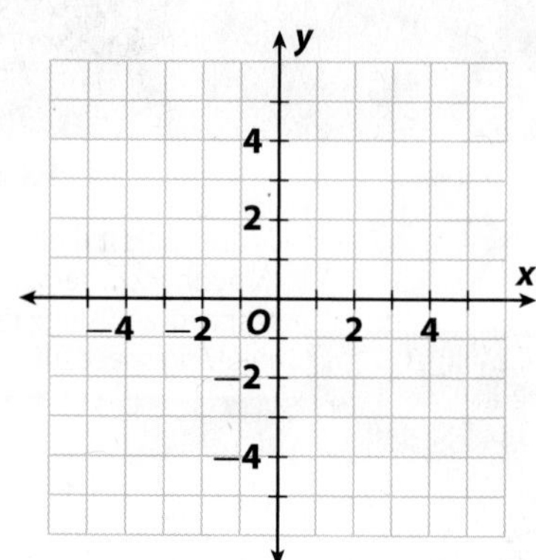

Reading Start-Up

Visualize Vocabulary

Use the Review Words to complete the chart.

Representation	Uses
	To show two expressions are equivalent
	To represent a relationship that has exactly one output for each input
	To visually represent a function on a coordinate plane
	To locate a single point on a coordinate plane

Understand Vocabulary

Complete the sentences using the preview words.

1. An equation written as $Ax + By = C$, where A, B, and C are real numbers is said to be in the

   ____

2. An equation written as $y = mx + b$, where m is the slope and b is the y-intercept is said to be in the

   ____

3. The ____________________ is the y-coordinate of the point where the graph of a line crosses the y-axis.

4. The ____________________ is the x-coordinate of the point where the graph of a line crosses the x-axis.

Vocabulary

Review Words

- ✔ equation *(ecuación)*
- ✔ function *(función)*
- ✔ graph of a function *(gráfica de una función)*
- ordered pair *(línea)*
- ✔ ordered pair *(par ordenado)*

Preview Words

- family of functions
- linear function
- linear equation
- parent function
- parameter
- rate of change
- rise
- run
- slope
- slope formula
- slope-intercept form
- standard form of a linear equation
- *x*-intercept
- *y*-intercept

Active Reading

Key-Term Fold Before beginning the module, create a Key-Term Fold for taking notes as you read the module. Each tab can contain a key term on one side and its definition on the other. As you study each lesson, write important vocabulary and definitions under the appropriate tab.

GETTING READY FOR

Linear Functions

Understanding the standards and the vocabulary terms in the standards will help you know exactly what you are expected to learn in this module.

For a function that models a relationship between two quantities, interpret key features of graphs and tables in terms of the quantities, and sketch graphs showing key features given a verbal description of the relationship.

Key Vocabulary

slope *(pendiente)*
The slope of a line is the ratio of rise to run for any two points on the line.

What It Means to You

Learning to interpret a graph enables a deep visual understanding of all sorts of relationships.

EXAMPLE F.IF.4

A group of friends walked to the town market, did some shopping there, then returned home.

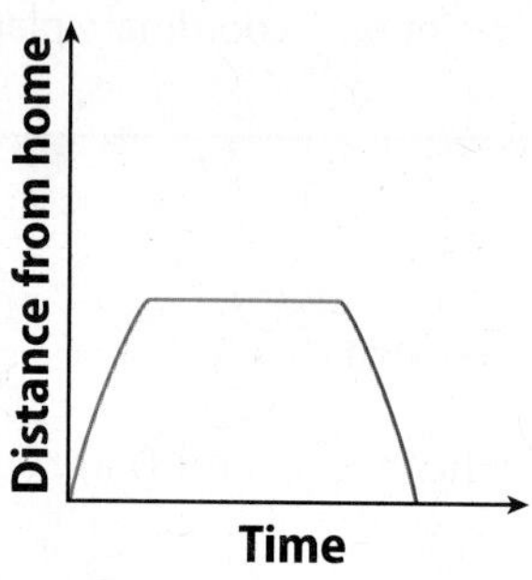

CA CC F.IF.6

Calculate and interpret the average rate of change of a function (presented symbolically or as a table) over a specified interval. Estimate the rate of change from a graph.

Key Vocabulary

rate of change *(tasa de cambio)*
A ratio that compares the amount of change in a dependent variable to the amount of change in an independent variable.

What It Means to You

Average rate of change measures the change in the dependent variable over the change in the independent variable. This helps you understand how quickly the values in a function change.

EXAMPLE F.IF.6

$$\text{Average rate of change} = \frac{180 - 60}{3 - 1} = 60 \text{ mi/h}$$

Time (hours)	1	2	3	4
Distance (miles)	60	120	180	240

Visit **my.hrw.com** to see all **CA Common Core Standards** explained.

my.hrw.com

LESSON

6.1 Linear Functions

CA CC F.IF.7

Graph functions expressed symbolically and show key features of the graph, by hand in simple cases and using technology for more complicated cases. *Also F.IF.5, F.IF.7a*

ESSENTIAL QUESTION

How can you use graphs and equations to identify linear functions?

EXPLORE ACTIVITY  CA CC F.IF.5, F.IF.7, F.IF.7a

Exploring Linear Functions

You get a job planning birthday parties. You are paid a flat fee of \$80 and then \$15 for each hour you work. The function defined by $f(x) = 15x + 80$ represents your earnings in dollars when you work x hours. Assume you get paid for fractions of hours.

A Complete the table to represent the total wages for 0–4 hours worked.

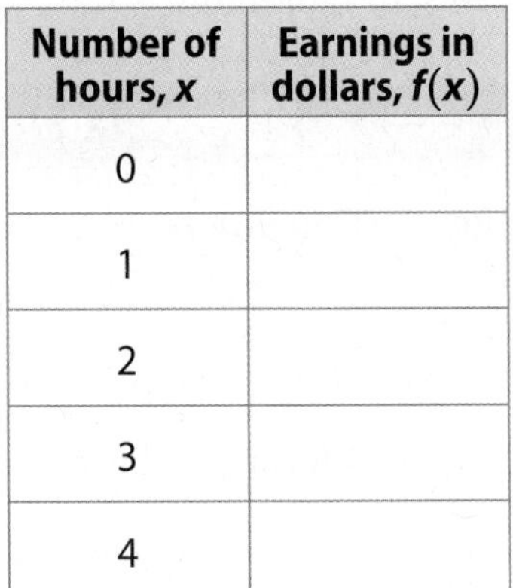

Number of hours, x	Earnings in dollars, $f(x)$
0	
1	
2	
3	
4	

B Graph the function from Part A.

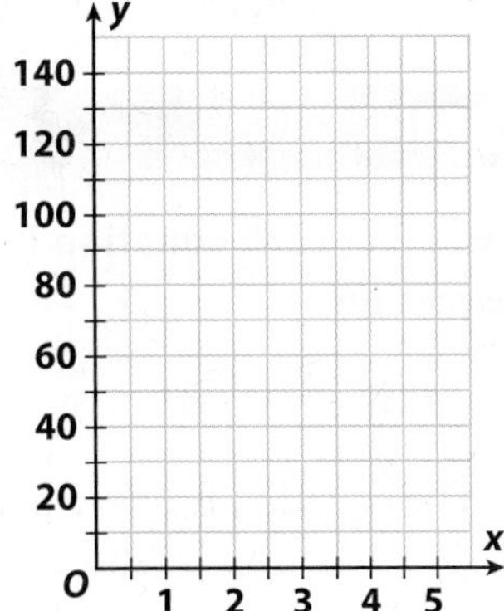

C How do you know that this is a function?

____

REFLECT

1. Identify the domain and range for the function $f(x) = 15x + 80$.

Domain: ______________________________

Range: ______________________________

2. Look for a Pattern Describe the pattern formed by the points in the graph that are from the table.

____

____

Identifying Linear Functions

A **linear function** is a function whose graph forms a line that is not vertical.

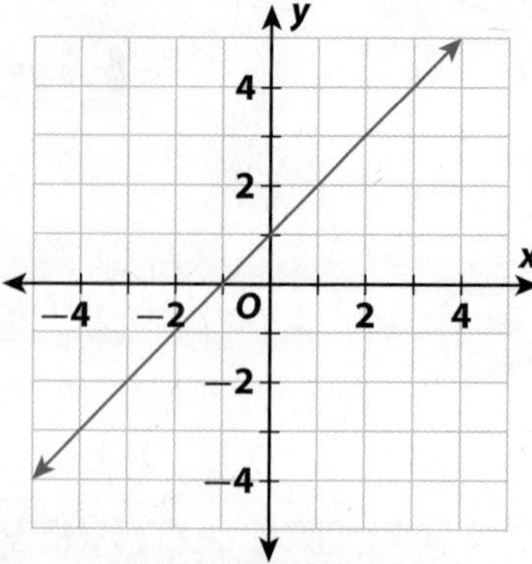

The graph at the right is the graph of a linear function.

Both the domain and the range of the function are the set of all real numbers

If a function is linear, then it can be represented by a *linear equation*. A **linear equation** is any equation that can be written in the *standard form* below.

Standard Form of a Linear Equation

$Ax + By = C$ where A, B, and C are real numbers and A and B are not both 0.

Notice that when a linear equation is written in standard form the following are true.

- x and y both have exponents of 1.
- x and y are not multiplied together.
- x and y do not appear in denominators, exponents, or radicands.

EXAMPLE 1

Tell whether each equation is linear. If so, graph the function represented by the equation.

A $-12x + y = -4$

The equation is linear because it is in the standard form of a linear equation: $A = -12$, $B = 1$, and $C = -4$.

To graph the function, first solve the equation for y.

$$-12x + y = -4$$
$$\underline{+12x} \qquad \underline{+12x}$$
$$y = -4 + 12x$$

Subtraction Property of Equality

Make a table and plot the points. Then connect the points.

x	−2	0	2	4
y	−28	−4	20	44

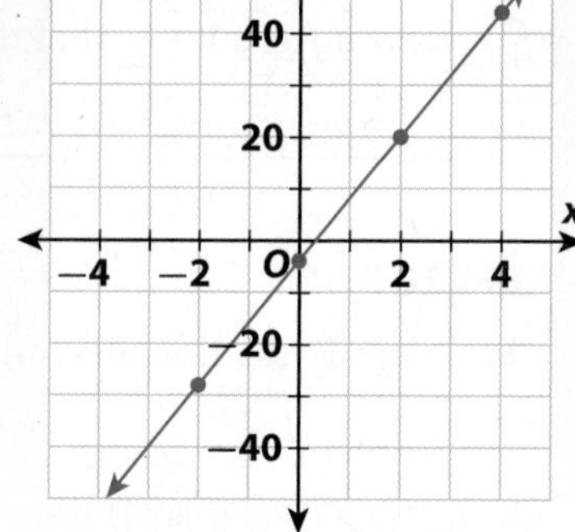

B $y = 12x^2 - 4$

The exponent on x in this equation is not 1, so the function is not linear.

C $xy - 4 = 12$

$xy - 4 = 12$

Since x and y are multiplied together, this function is not linear.

REFLECT

3. **Communicate Mathematical Ideas** Use the bulleted list above Example 1 to write at least two more equations that are not linear. Explain why they are not linear.

---

4. **Make a Conjecture** Why do you think the graph of a linear function has to be a non-vertical line?

My Notes

YOUR TURN

Tell whether each equation is linear. If so, graph the function represented by the equation.

5. $y - 3 = 2x$

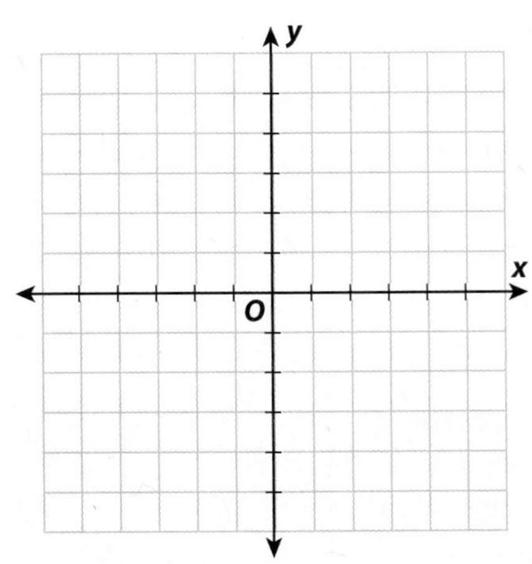

6. $y = \frac{2}{x}$

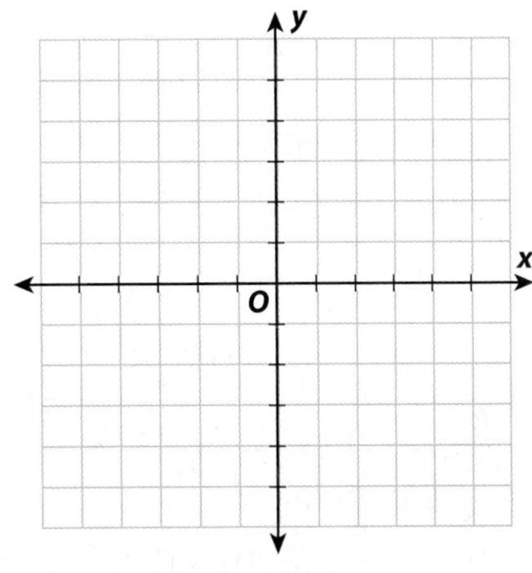

Horizontal and Vertical Lines

As stated earlier in this lesson, a linear equation is in standard form if it is in the form $Ax + Bx = C$, where A, B, and C are real numbers and A and B are not both 0. Notice that in this definition, A and B cannot both be 0, but one or the other can be 0.

EXAMPLE 2

CA CC F.IF.7, F.IF.7a

Graph each line.

A $y = 8$

$0x + 1y = 8$ — This is a linear equation in standard form $A = 0, B = 1, C = 8$.

x	y
0	8
1	8
2	8
3	8
4	8

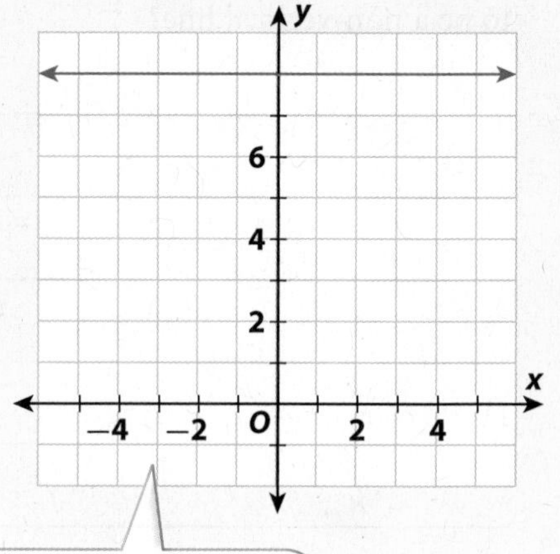

Notice that all ordered pairs have a y-coordinate of 8.

B $x = -1$

$1x + 0y = -1$ — This is a linear equation in standard form $A = 1, B = 0, C = -1$.

x	y
−1	0
−1	1
−1	2
−1	3
−1	4

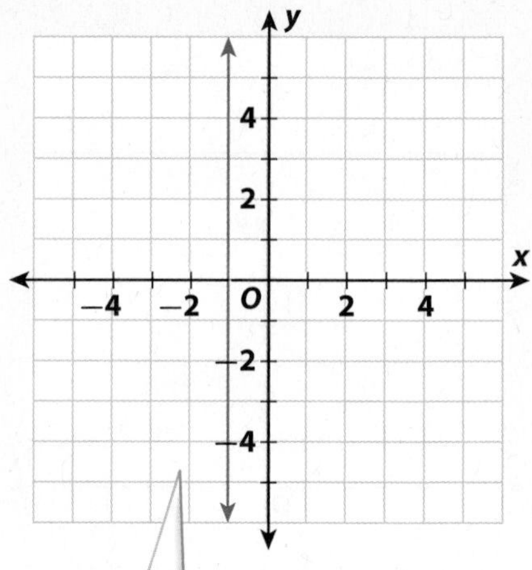

Notice that all ordered pairs have an x-coordinate of −1.

Math Talk

Mathematical Practices

Do all linear equations in two variables represent linear functions?

REFLECT

7. Communicate Mathematical Ideas When the equation of the graph of a horizontal line is written in standard form, the coefficient of x must be 0. Explain why.

____

____

____

Tell whether the equation represents a horizontal line, vertical line, or neither. Graph the equation.

8. $y = 2x$ ______________________

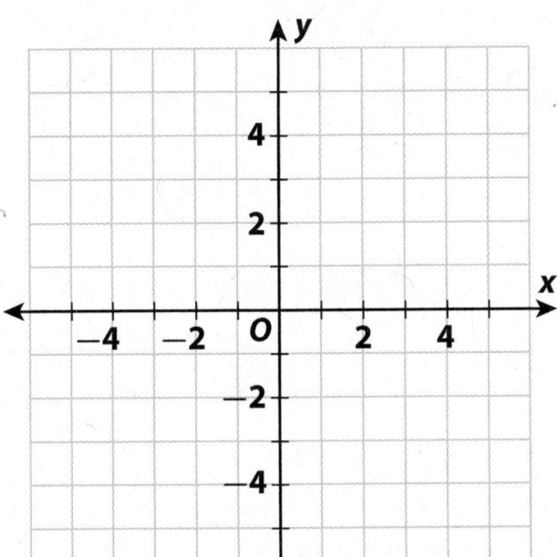

9. $y = -4$ ______________________

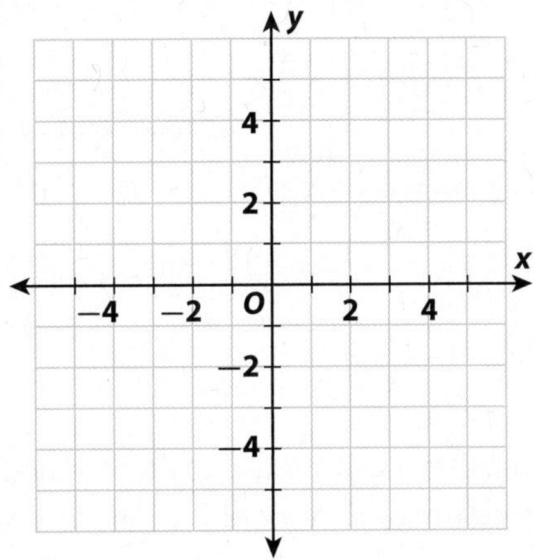

10. $3y = -4$ ______________________

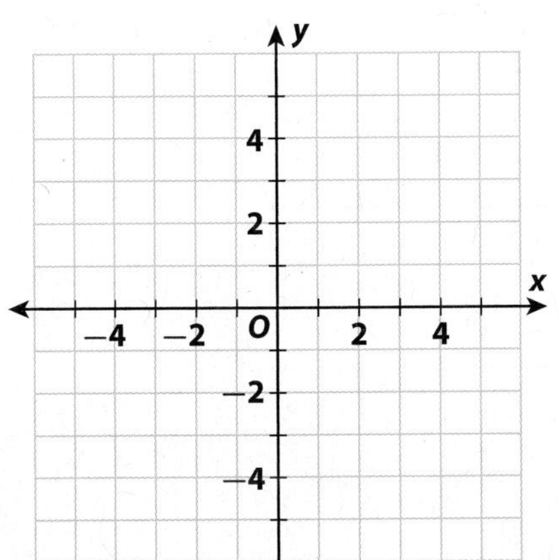

11. $x + 3 = 0$ ______________________

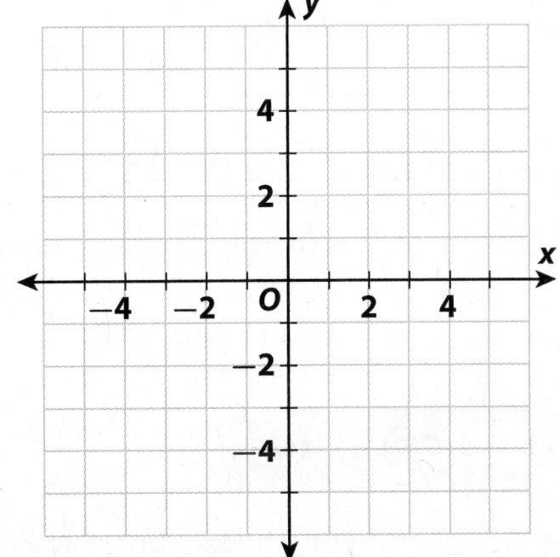

Personal Math Trainer

Online Practice and Help

my.hrw.com

Guided Practice

Write a linear equation in the form $Ax + By = C$ for the given values of A, B, and C. Then simplify the equation. Tell whether the equation represents a horizontal line, vertical line, or neither. (Examples 1 and 2)

1. $A = 0, B = 3, C = 1$

2. $A = 5, B = 0.1, C = 4$

3. $A = -\frac{1}{2}, B = 0, C = 14$

Create a table of values for the function $y = 3x - 4$. Then graph the function, making sure to label the axes to show the scale. (Example 1)

4. $y = 3x - 4$

x	y
0	
1	
2	

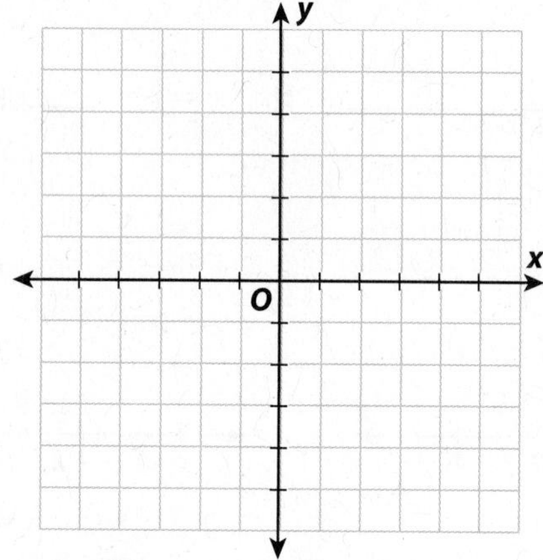

5. Andrea receives a \$40 gift card to use at a town pool. It costs her \$8 per visit to swim. A function relating the value of the gift card, v, to the number of visits, n, is $v(n) = 40 - 8n$. (Explore Activity)

a. Identify a reasonable domain of the function. Explain why you chose that domain.

b. Given that domain, what is the range of the function.

ESSENTIAL QUESTION CHECK-IN

6. How can you use the equation of a linear function to predict what the graph will look like?

Name ______________________ Class ______________________ Date ______________________

6.1 Independent Practice

Personal Math Trainer
Online Practice and Help
my.hrw.com

F.IF.7, F.IF.7a

7. Two friends work at the same company. Friend A gets paid \$50,000 for the year, no matter how many hours she works. Friend B gets paid \$20 an hour. Write an equation for each person that shows the relationship between the annual salary y and the number of hours x that friend works. Fill in each table of values and graph each function.

a. Function for Friend A

____

x	y
0	
1,000	
2,000	

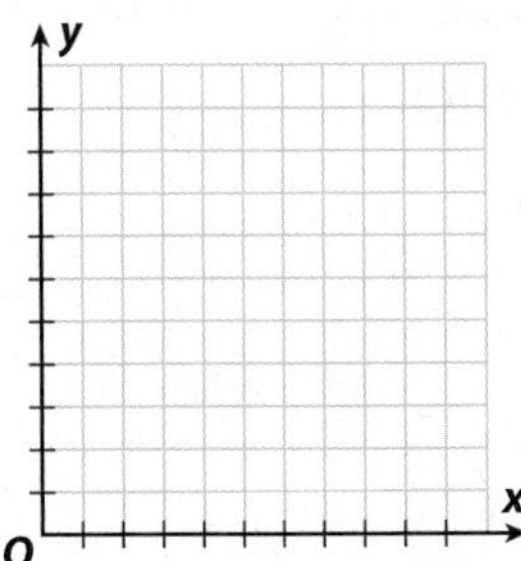

b. Function for Friend B

____

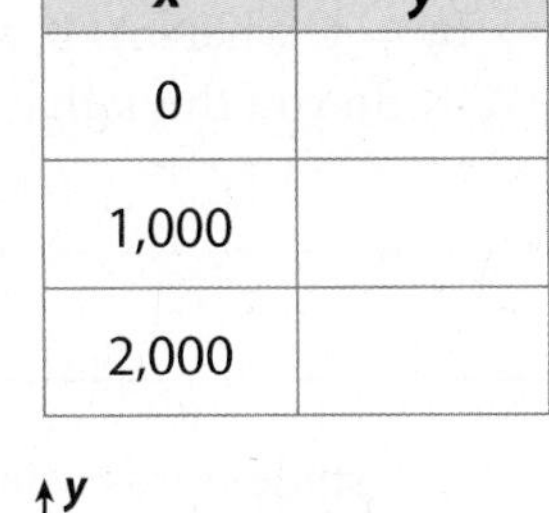

x	y
0	
1,000	
2,000	

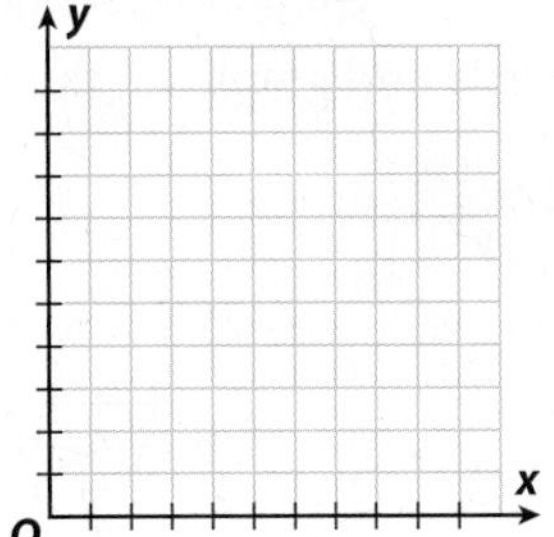

Tell whether each of the following equations represents a linear function.

8. $y = x^2 + 3$ ______________

9. $3x = 4$ ______________

10. $y = 1$ ______________

11. $0.3x + y = 2$ ______________

12. $x^2\left(\frac{1}{y}\right) = 3$ ______________

13. $y = x$ ______________

14. Select a linear equation from Questions 8–13 and create a graph for it.

____

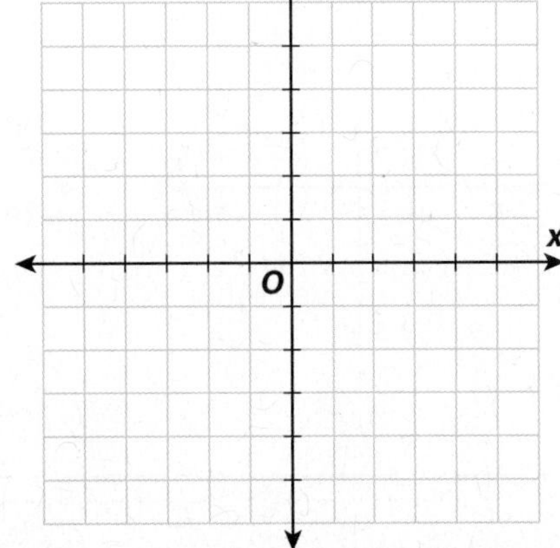

FOCUS ON HIGHER ORDER THINKING

Work Area

15. **Represent Real-World Problems** Write a real-world problem that could represent a function that has a range that includes negative numbers.

16. **Communicate Mathematical Ideas** Recall that the standard form of a linear equation is $Ax + By = C$ where A, B, and C are real numbers and A and B are not both 0. Why do you think that A and B cannot both be zero?

17. **Explain the Error** A student was using a table of values to create a graph of a function. The table and graph are shown below. Explain the student's error.

x	y
0	0
1	3
−1	−3

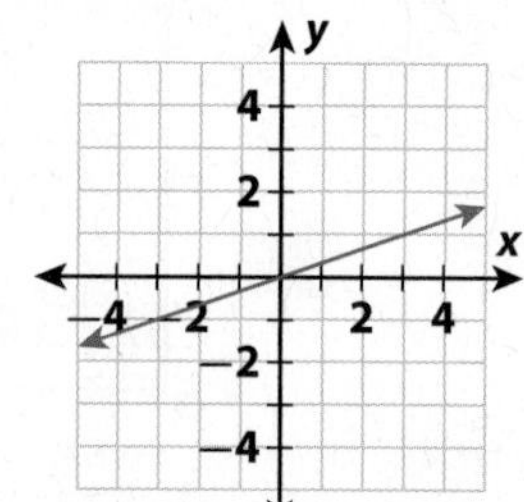

18. **Communicate Mathematical Ideas** Consider the following graphs. They are for the same line. How is this possible?

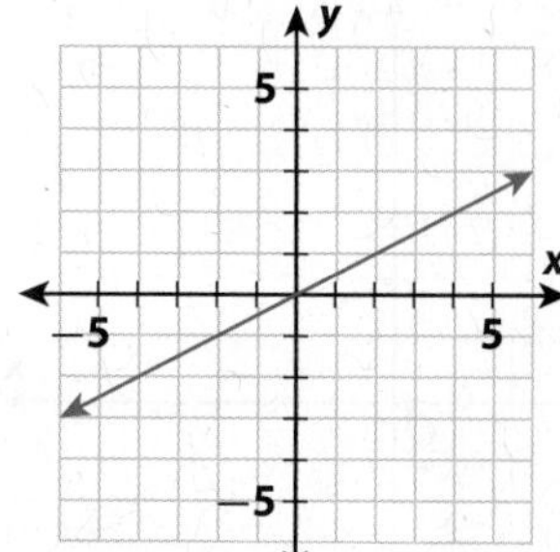

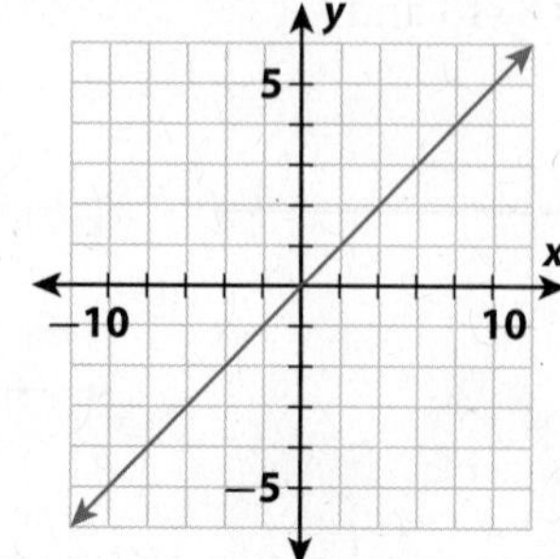

LESSON

6.2 Using Intercepts

CA CC F.IF.7a

Graph linear and quadratic functions and show intercepts, maxima, and minima. *Also* F.IF.4, F.IF.7

ESSENTIAL QUESTION

How can you identify and use intercepts in linear relationships?

EXPLORE ACTIVITY

CA CC F.IF.4, F.IF.7, F.IF.7a

Identifying Intercepts

A diver explored the ocean floor at 120 feet below the surface. The diver then ascended at a constant rate over a period of 4 minutes until he reached the surface.

In the coordinate grid below, the horizontal axis represents the time in minutes from when the diver started ascending and the vertical axis represents the diver's elevation in feet.

A What point represents the diver's elevation at the beginning of the ascent? Graph this point. ____________________

B What point represents the diver's elevation at the end of the ascent? Graph this point. ____________________

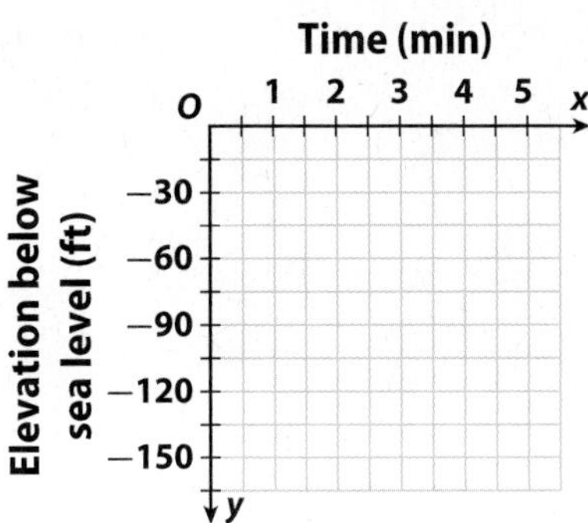

C Connect the points with a line segment. The graph now shows the diver's elevation below sea level during the 4-minute ascent.

Look at points (4, 0) and (0, −120). Notice that these are points where the graph intersects the axes. These points are known as *intercepts*.

REFLECT

1. **Communicate Mathematical Ideas** The diver begins his ascent at the depth represented by the point where a graph intersects the y-axis of the graph. Will the point where a graph intersects the y-axis always be the lowest point of a linear graph? Explain.

____

____

____

____

____

Finding Intercepts of Linear Equations

In the previous Explore Activity, the graph intersected the axes at $(0, -120)$ and $(4, 0)$.

The **y-intercept** is the y-coordinate of the point where the graph intersects the y-axis. The x-coordinate of this point is always 0. This was point $(0, -120)$ in the Explore Activity.

The **x-intercept** is the x-coordinate of the point where the graph intersects the x-axis. The y-coordinate of this point is always 0. This was point $(4, 0)$ in the Explore Activity.

EXAMPLE 1

CA CC F.IF.7, F.IF.7a

My Notes

Find the x- and y-intercepts.

A

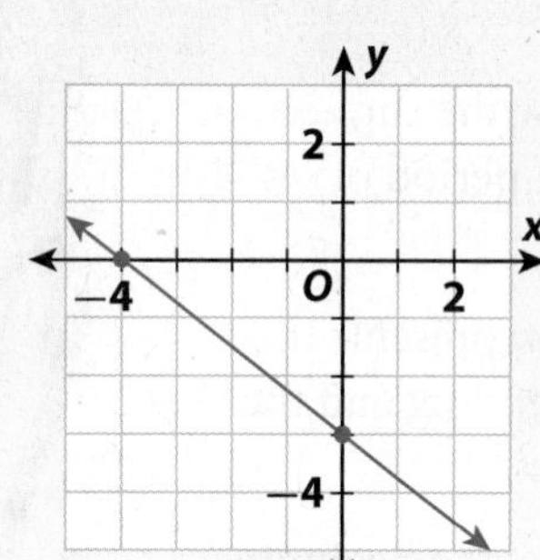

The graph crosses the x-axis at $(-4, 0)$.

The x-intercept is -4.

The graph crosses the y-axis at $(0, -3)$.

The y-intercept is -3.

B $3x - 2y = 12$

To find the x-intercept, replace y with 0 and solve for x.

$$3x - 2y = 12$$
$$3x - 2(0) = 12$$
$$3x - 0 = 12$$
$$3x = 12$$
$$\frac{3x}{3} = \frac{12}{3}$$
$$x = 4$$

The x-intercept is 4.

To find the y-intercept, replace x with 0 and solve for y.

$$3x - 2y = 12$$
$$3(0) - 2y = 12$$
$$0 - 2y = 12$$
$$-2y = 12$$
$$\frac{-2y}{-2} = \frac{12}{-2}$$
$$y = -6$$

The y-intercept is -6.

YOUR TURN

Find the x- and y-intercepts.

2.

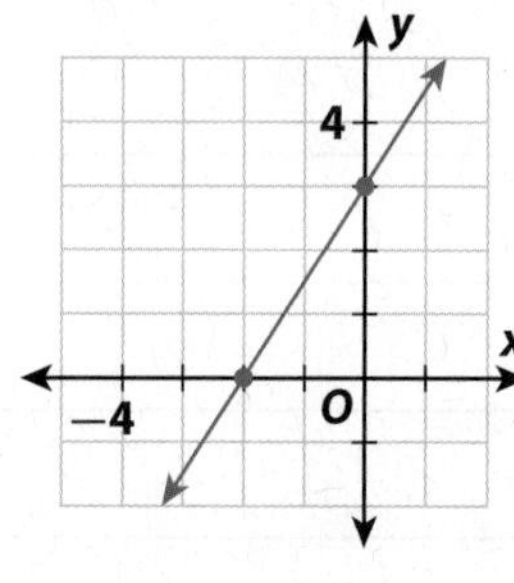

____

3. $-3x + 5y = 30$

____

Interpreting Intercepts of Linear Equations

EXAMPLE 2

CA CC F.IF.4, F.IF.7, F.IF.7a

The Sandia Peak Tramway in Albuquerque, New Mexico, travels a distance of about 4500 meters to the top of Sandia Peak. Its speed is 300 meters per minute. The function $f(x) = 4500 - 300x$ gives the tram's distance in meters from the top of the peak after x minutes.

Graph this function and find the intercepts. What does each intercept represent?

x	$f(x) = 4500 - 300x$
0	4500
2	3900
5	3000

Neither time nor distance can be negative, so choose several nonnegative values for x. Use the function to generate ordered pairs.

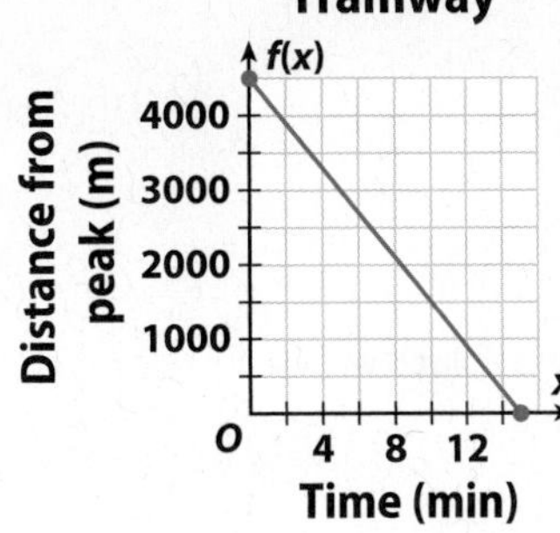

y-intercept: 4500

In the real world, the y-intercept represents the distance from the top at the start (time = 0).

x-intercept: 15

In the real world, the x-intercept represents the time it takes for the tram to reach the top (distance from peak = 0).

Math Talk
Mathematical Practices

A student says that the graph shows the path of the tram. Why is the student incorrect?

YOUR TURN

4. The temperature in an experiment is reduced at a constant rate over a period of time until the temperature reaches 0°C. The equation $y = 20 - \frac{2}{3}x$ gives the temperature y in degrees Celsius x hours after the beginning of the experiment.

a. Graph this function and find the x- and y-intercepts.

____

b. What does each intercept represent?

____

____

____

____

____

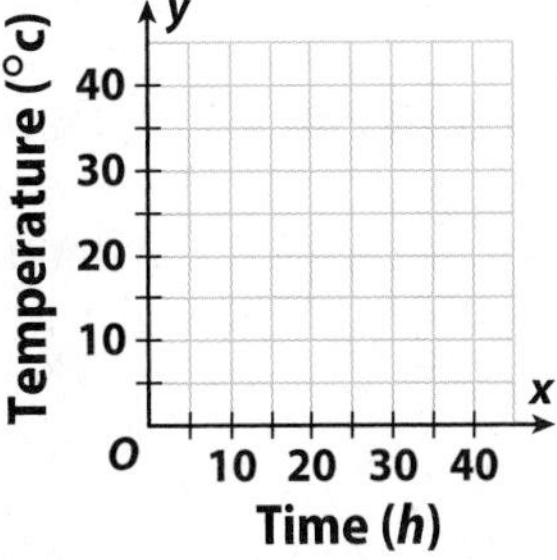

Using Intercepts to Graph Linear Equations

My Notes

EXAMPLE 3

CA CC F.IF.7, F.IF.7a

Use intercepts to graph the line described by each equation.

A $2x - 4y = 8$

STEP 1 Find the intercepts.

x-intercept:

$$2x - 4y = 8$$
$$2x - 4(0) = 8$$
$$2x = 8$$
$$\frac{2x}{2} = \frac{8}{2}$$
$$x = 4$$

y-intercept:

$$2x - 4y = 8$$
$$2(0) - 4y = 8$$
$$-4y = 8$$
$$\frac{-4y}{-4} = \frac{8}{-4}$$
$$y = -2$$

STEP 2 Graph the line.

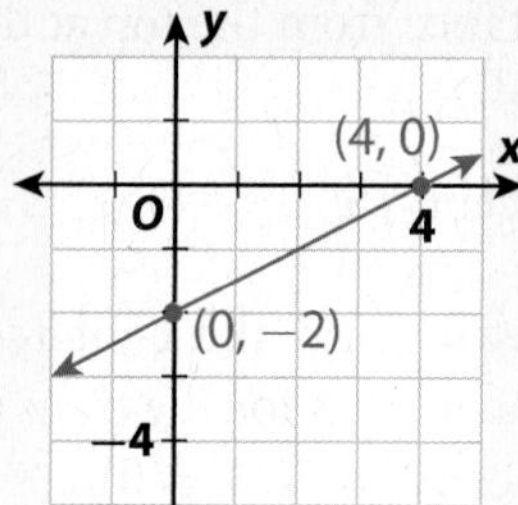

Plot (4, 0) and (0, −2).
Connect the points with a straight line.

B $\frac{2}{3}y = 4 - \frac{1}{2}x$

STEP 1 Write the equation in standard form.

$$\frac{1}{2}x + \frac{2}{3}y = 4 - \frac{1}{2}x + \frac{1}{2}x$$
$$\frac{1}{2}x + \frac{2}{3}y = 4$$

Add $\frac{1}{2}x$ to both sides so both variables are on the same side.

STEP 2 Find the intercepts.

x-intercept:

$$\frac{1}{2}x + \frac{2}{3}y = 4$$
$$\frac{1}{2}x + \frac{2}{3}(0) = 4$$
$$\frac{1}{2}x = 4$$
$$2\left(\frac{1}{2}x\right) = 2(4)$$
$$x = 8$$

y-intercept:

$$\frac{1}{2}x + \frac{2}{3}y = 4$$
$$\frac{1}{2}(0) + \frac{2}{3}y = 4$$
$$\frac{2}{3}y = 4$$
$$\frac{3}{2}\left(\frac{2}{3}y\right) = \frac{3}{2}(4)$$
$$y = 6$$

STEP 3 Graph the line.

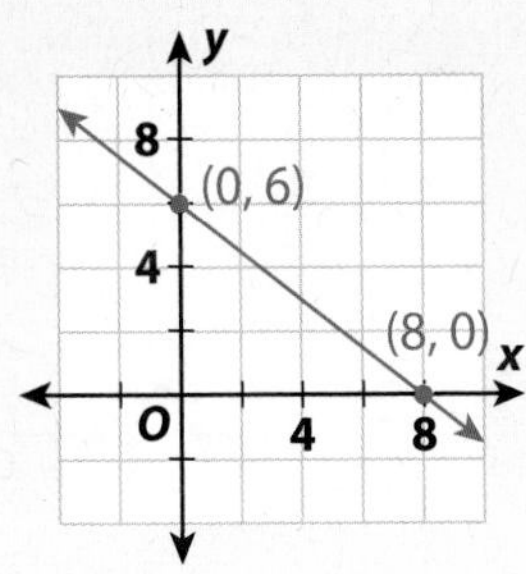

Plot (8, 0) and (0, 6).

Connect the points with a straight line.

REFLECT

5. **Draw Conclusions** Find the intercepts for a linear equation of the form $Ax = C$, where A and C are real numbers and A is not 0.

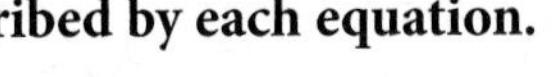

____

____

____

____

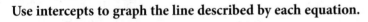

YOUR TURN

Use intercepts to graph the line described by each equation.

6. $-3x + 4y = -12$

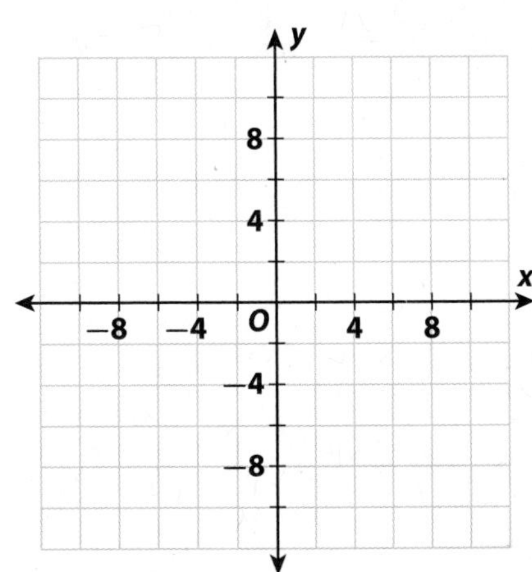

7. $y = \frac{1}{3}x - 2$

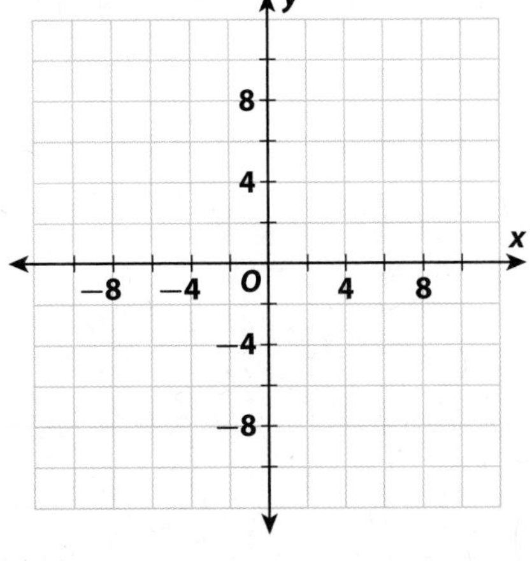

8. A function has x-intercept 4 and y-intercept 2. Name two other points on the graph of this function.

____

Guided Practice

Find the x- and y-intercepts. (Example 1)

1.

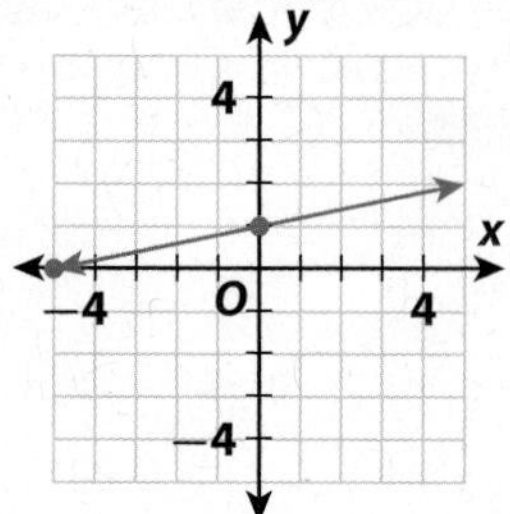

2.

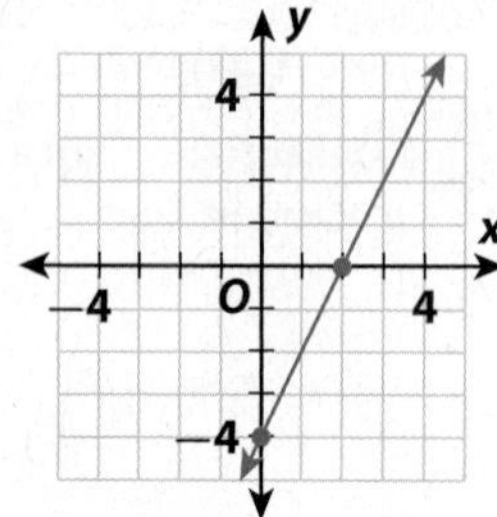

3.

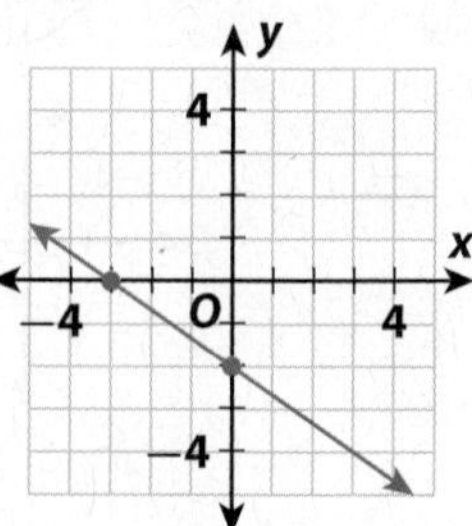

4. $2x - 4y = 4$

5. $-2y = 3x - 6$

6. $4y + 5x = 2y - 3x + 16$

Use intercepts to graph the line described by each equation. (Example 3)

7. $4x - 5y = 20$

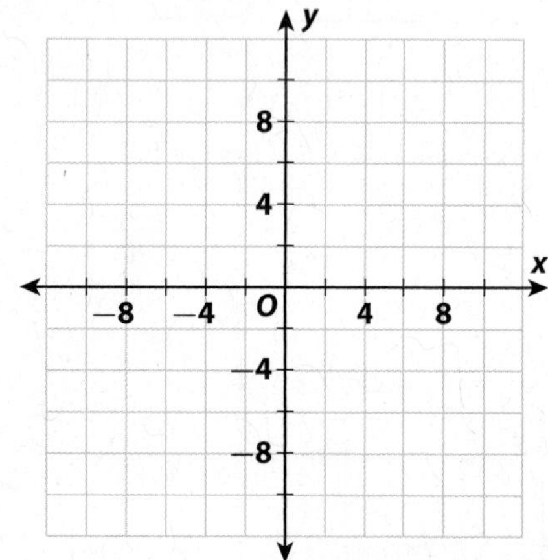

8. $y = \frac{1}{2}x - 4$

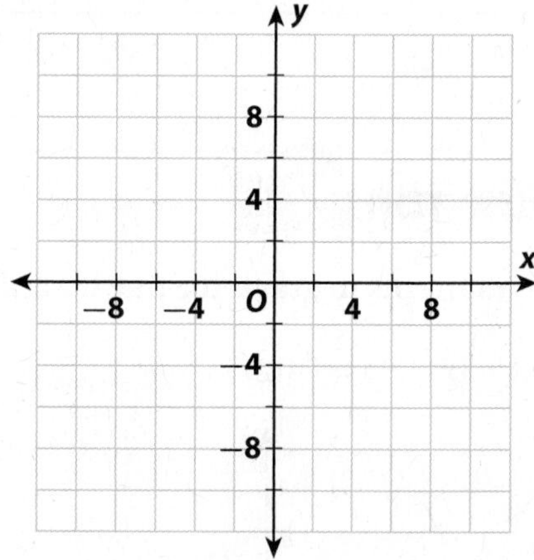

ESSENTIAL QUESTION CHECK-IN

9. What are intercepts and how can they be used?

Name ________________ Class ________________ Date ________________

6.2 Independent Practice

CA CC F.IF.4, F.IF.7, F.IF.7a

10. To thaw a specimen stored at −25 °C, the temperature of a refrigeration tank is raised 5 °C every hour. The temperature in the tank after x hours can be described by the function $f(x) = -25 + 5x$.

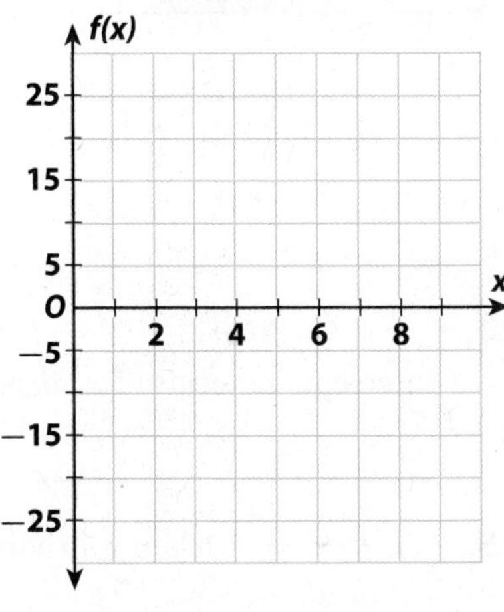

a. Graph the function and find its intercepts.

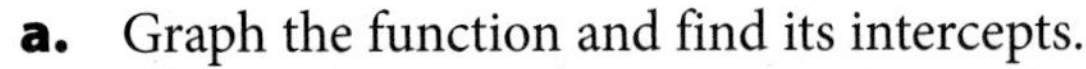

b. What does each intercept represent?

____

____

____

____

____

11. A fishing lake was stocked with 300 bass. Each year, the population decreases by 25. The population of bass in the lake after x years is represented by the function $f(x) = 300 - 25x$.

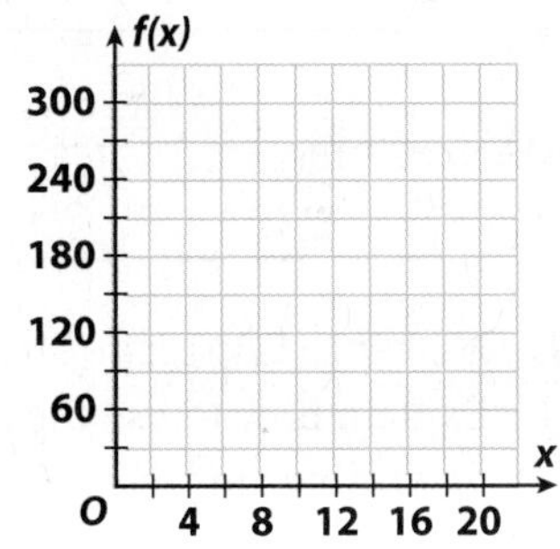

a. Graph the function and find its intercepts.

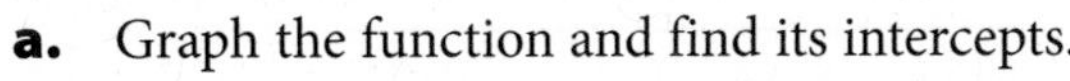

b. What does each intercept represent?

____

____

____

____

12. A bamboo plant is growing 1 foot per day. When first measured, it is 4 feet tall.

a. Write an equation to describe the height, y, in feet, of the bamboo plant x days after you measure it. ______________________________

b. What is the y-intercept? What does the y-intercept represent?

____

____

H.O.T. FOCUS ON HIGHER ORDER THINKING

Work Area

13. Represent Real-World Problems Write a real-world problem that could be modeled by a linear function whose x-intercept is 5 and y-intercept is 60.

____

____

____

____

14. Draw Conclusions For any linear equation $Ax + By = C$, what are the intercepts in terms of A, B, and C?

____

15. Multi-Step Kirsten is driving to a city that is 400 miles away. When Kirsten left home, she had 15 gallons of gas in her car. Assume that her car gets 25 miles per gallon of gas. Define a function f so that $f(x)$ is the amount of gas left in her car after she has driven x miles from home. What are the intercepts for that function? What do they represent?

____

____

____

____

16. Multiple Representations Find the intercepts of $3x + 40y = 1200$. Explain how to use the intercepts to determine appropriate scales for the graph and then create a graph.

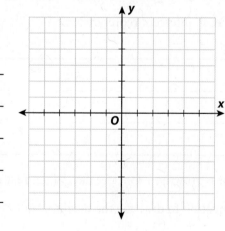

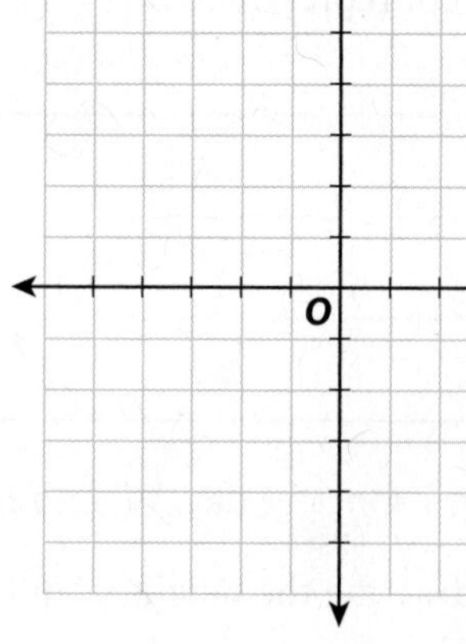

____

____

____

____

____

____

____

____

____

LESSON
6.3 Using Slope

CA CC F.IF.6

Calculate and interpret the average rate of change of a function (presented symbolically or as a table) over a specified interval. Estimate the rate of change from a graph. *Also F.IF.4, F.IF.7, F.LE.1b*

ESSENTIAL QUESTION

How can you relate rate of change and slope in linear relationships?

EXPLORE ACTIVITY 1   F.IF.6

Finding Rates of Change

For a function defined in terms of x and y, the **rate of change** over a part of the domain of the function is a ratio that compares the change in y to the change in x in that part of the domain.

$$\text{rate of change} = \frac{\text{change in } y}{\text{change in } x}$$

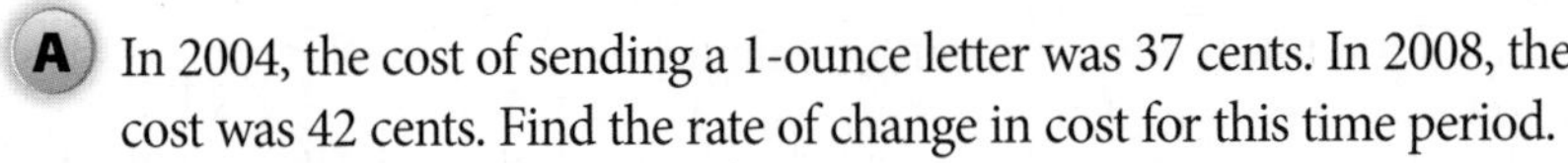

A In 2004, the cost of sending a 1-ounce letter was 37 cents. In 2008, the cost was 42 cents. Find the rate of change in cost for this time period.

$$\text{rate of change} = \frac{\text{change in } y}{\text{change in } x} = \frac{\square - \square}{2008 - 2004} = \frac{\square}{\square} = \square$$

The rate of change was $\square$ cents per year.

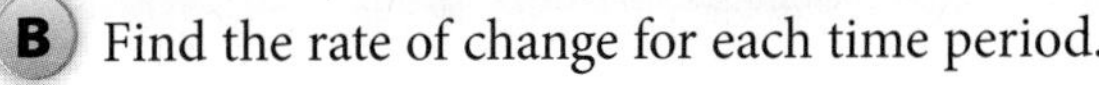

B Find the rate of change for each time period.

Year (x)	1988	1990	1991	2004	2008
Cost in cents (y)	25	25	29	37	42

$$1988 \text{ to } 1990 = \frac{\square - \square}{1990 - 1988} = \square \text{ cents per year}$$

$$1990 \text{ to } 1991 = \frac{\square - \square}{1991 - 1990} = \square \text{ cents per year}$$

Round to the nearest hundredth of a cent.

$$1991 \text{ to } 2004 = \frac{\square - \square}{2004 - 1991} = \square = \square \text{ cents per year}$$

$$2004 \text{ to } 2008 = \frac{\square - \square}{2008 - 2004} = \square = \square \text{ cents per year}$$

EXPLORE ACTIVITY 1 *(cont'd)*

REFLECT

1. **Interpret the Answer** The rate of change for 2004 to 2008 was 1.25 cents per year. Does this mean the actual change in cost each year was 1.25 cents? Explain.

____

____

____

____

Finding Slope of a Line

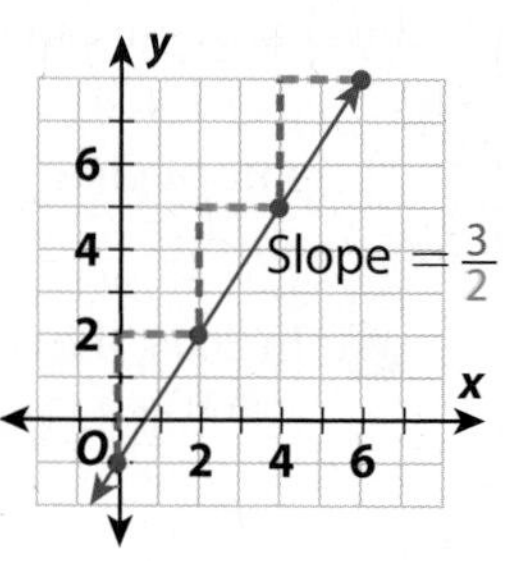

In the previous Explore Activity, the rate of change was not constant. It varied from 0 to 4 cents per year. However, for linear functions, the rate of change is constant.

The rate of change for a linear function can be calculated using the rise and run of the graph of the function. The **rise** is the difference in the y-values of two points on a line. The **run** is the difference in the x-values of two points on a line.

The **slope** of a line is the ratio of rise to run for any two points on the line.

$$\text{slope} = \frac{\text{rise}}{\text{run}} = \frac{\text{difference in } y\text{-values}}{\text{difference in } x\text{-values}}$$

EXAMPLE 1

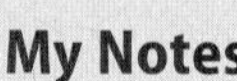

CA CC F.IF.6

Find the slope of each line.

A

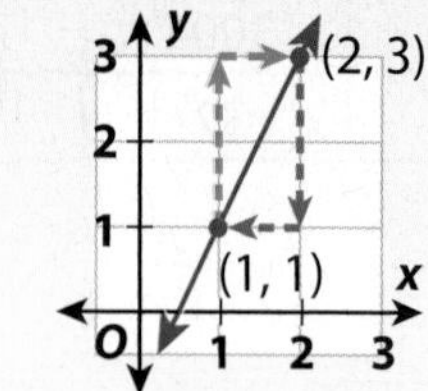

Use (2, 3) as the first point. Subtract y-values to find the change in y or rise. Then subtract x-values to find the change in x or run.

$\text{slope} = \frac{3-1}{2-1} = \frac{2}{1} = 2$

It doesn't matter which point you start with as long as you are consistent. If you start with (1, 1), then

$\text{slope} = \frac{1-3}{1-2} = \frac{-2}{-1} = 2.$

B

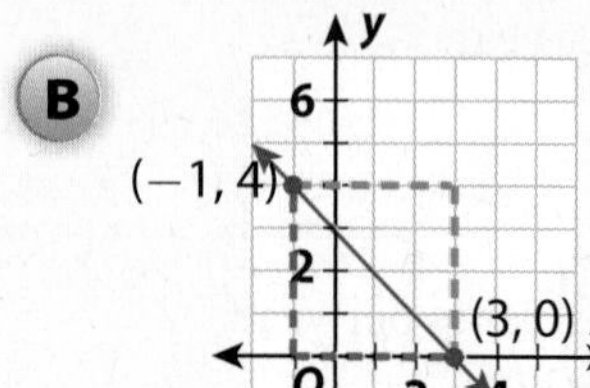

Use (−1, 4) as the first point. Subtract y-values to find the change in y or rise. Then subtract x-values to find the change in x or run.

$\text{slope} = \frac{4-0}{-1-3} = \frac{4}{-4} = -1$

My Notes

YOUR TURN

2. Find the slope of the line in the graph.

____

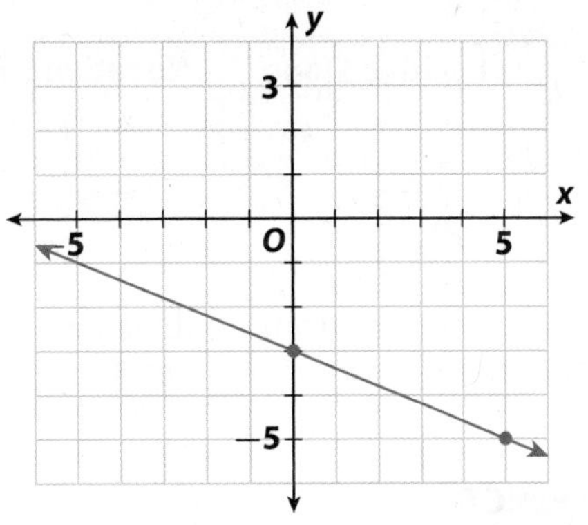

EXPLORE ACTIVITY 2

CA CC F.IF.6

Classifying Slopes

As shown in the previous example, slope can be positive or negative. What about the slope of horizontal and vertical lines?

Find the slope of each line.

A

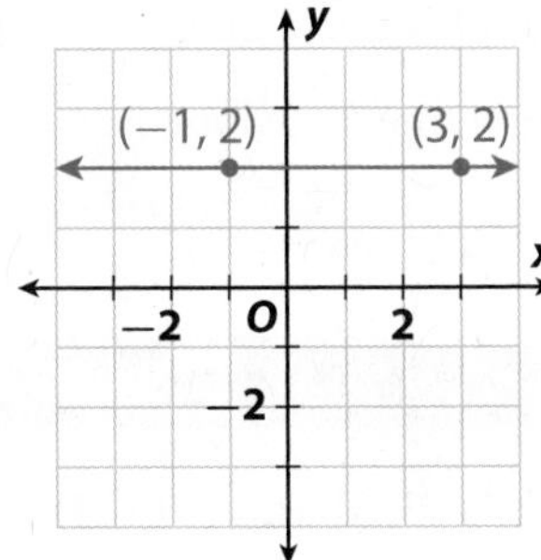

$$\text{slope} = \frac{\text{rise}}{\text{run}} = \frac{\square}{\square} = \frac{\square}{\square} = \square$$

B

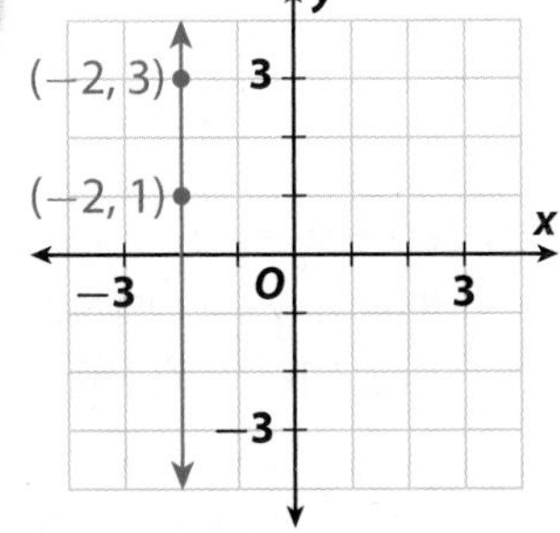

$$\text{slope} = \frac{\text{rise}}{\text{run}} = \frac{\square}{\square} = \frac{\square}{0}$$

Since you cannot divide by 0, the slope is undefined.

EXPLORE ACTIVITY 2 *(cont'd)*

Positive Slope	Negative Slope	Zero Slope	Undefined Slope
Line rises from left to right.	Line falls from left to right.	Horizontal line	Vertical line

REFLECT

3. **Communicate Mathematical Ideas** Explain why the slope of a vertical line is undefined.

____

____

____

Using the Slope Formula

The **slope formula** for the slope of a line is the ratio of the difference in y-values to the difference in x-values between any two different points on the line.

This means if (x_1, y_1) and (x_2, y_2) are any two points on a line, the slope is $m = \frac{y_2 - y_1}{x_2 - x_1}$.

EXAMPLE 2

Find the slope of the line passing through the points (5, 3) and (–1, 15). Describe the slope as positive, negative, zero, or undefined.

STEP 1 Find the rise or difference in y-values.

$y_2 - y_1 = 15 - 3 = 12$

STEP 2 Find the run or difference in x-values.

$x_2 - x_1 = -1 - 5 = -6$

STEP 3 Find the slope.

$\text{slope} = \frac{\text{rise}}{\text{run}} = \frac{12}{-6} = -2$

STEP 4 Describe the slope.

The slope is negative. The line falls from left to right.

YOUR TURN

4. Find the slope of the line passing through the points (9, 1) and $(-1, -4)$. Describe the slope as positive, negative, zero, or undefined.

____

Interpreting Slope

EXAMPLE 3 

CA CC F.IF.4, F.IF.6, F.IF.7, F.LE.1b

The graph shows the relationship between a person's age and his or her estimated maximum heart rate.

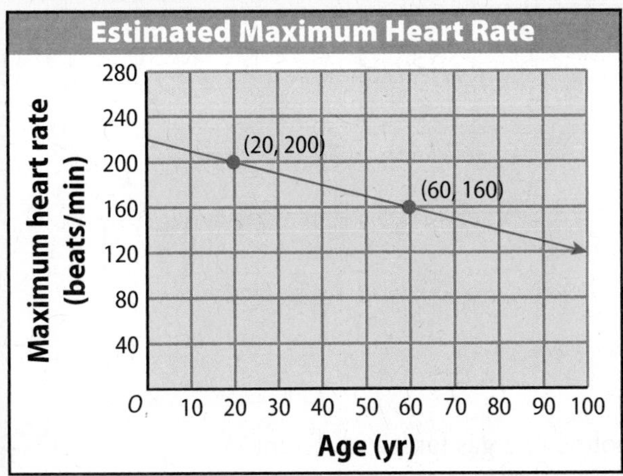

 Find the slope.

Use the two points that are labeled on the graph.

$$\text{slope} = \frac{\text{rise}}{\text{run}} = \frac{160 - 200}{60 - 20} = \frac{-40}{40} = -1$$

 Interpret the slope.

The slope of -1 means that for every year a person's age increases, his or her maximum heart rate decreases by 1 beat per minute.

REFLECT

5. **Multi-Step** Tara and Jade are hiking up a hill together. Each has a different stride. The run for Tara's stride is 32 inches, and the rise is 8 inches. The run for Jade's stride is 36 inches. What is the rise of Jade's stride? What is the slope and what does it mean in this problem?

____

____

Why is it important to know both the formula and the description of what slope is?

YOUR TURN

6. In an experiment, a car began traveling at a constant speed at 1:00 PM. Over a period of 5 hours, the car traveled a total 160 miles A graph shows the relationship between the length of time that the car had been traveling since 1:00 PM and the number of miles that it had traveled. What is the slope of the line? What does the slope mean?

____

____

Personal Math Trainer

Online Practice and Help

my.hrw.com

Guided Practice

Given the linear relationship, find the slope. (Examples 1 and 2)

1. Line passing through the points (2, −1) and (0, 5)

____

2.

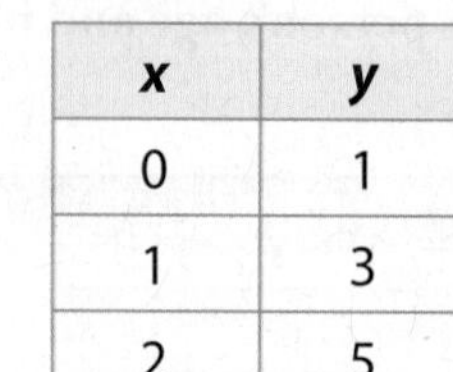

x	y
0	1
1	3
2	5

____

3.

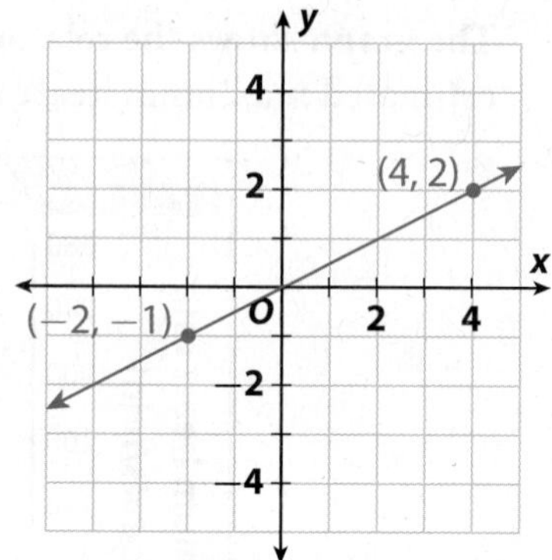

____

4. The table shows the volume of gasoline in a gas tank at different times. (Examples 1 and 3)

Time (h)	Volume (gal)
0	12
1	9
3	5

a. Find the rate of change for each time interval.

____

b. What does the difference in the rates of change mean in this situation?

____

____

____

Tell whether the slope is positive, negative, zero, or undefined. (Explore Activity 2)

5.

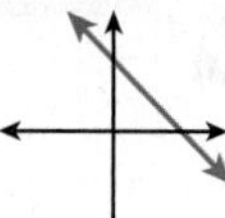

____

6.

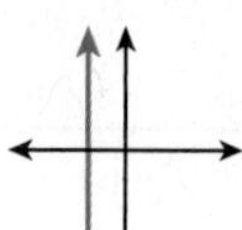

____

7.

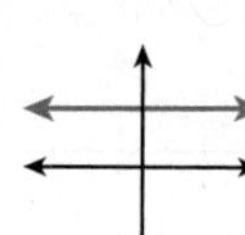

____

8.

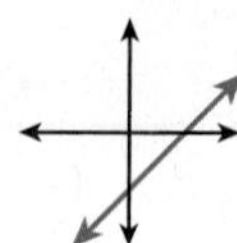

____

ESSENTIAL QUESTION CHECK-IN

9. How are rate of change and slope related for a linear relationship?

____

____

____

____

Name ______________________ Class ______________________ Date ______________________

6.3 Independent Practice

CA CC F.IF.4, F.IF.6, F.IF.7, F.LE.1b

10. At a particular college, a full-time student must take at least 12 credit hours per semester and may take at most 18 credit hours per semester. Tuition costs $200 per credit hour.

Credit Hours	Cost ($)
12	
13	
14	
15	
16	
17	
18	

a. Complete the table by using the information above.

b. What number is added to the cost in each row to get the cost in the next row?

____

c. What does your answer to part b represent?

____

____

d. Graph the ordered pairs from the table.

Full-Time Tuition Cost

Cost ($): 400, 800, 1200, 1600, 2000, 2400, 2800, 3200, 3600, 4000

Credit Hours: 0, 2, 4, 6, 8, 10, 12, 14, 16, 18, 20

e. Describe how the points in the graph are related.

____

____

____

____

11. **Draw Conclusions** The graph shows the number of files scanned by a computer virus detection program over time. Use estimation to find the rate of change between points A and B.

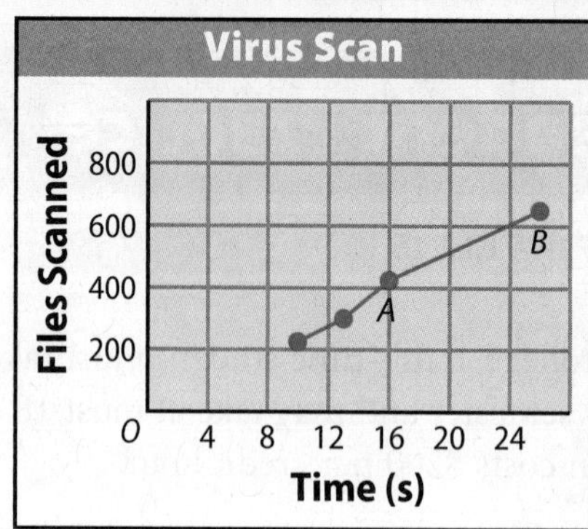

____

____

H.O.T. FOCUS ON HIGHER ORDER THINKING

Work Area

12. **Explain the Error** A student is asked to find the slope of a line containing the points (4, 1) and (−1, 11). He finds the slope the following way: slope $= \frac{\text{rise}}{\text{run}} = \frac{4-(-1)}{1-11} = \frac{5}{-10} = -\frac{1}{2}$. Explain the error.

____

____

____

13. **Critical Thinking** In this lesson, you learned that the slope of a line is constant. Does this mean that all lines with the same slope are the same line? Explain.

____

____

____

14. **Represent Real-World Problems** A ladder is leaned against a building. The bottom of the ladder is 9 feet from the building. The top of the ladder is 16 feet above the ground.

a. What is the slope of the ladder? ______________________

b. What does the slope of the ladder mean in the real world?

____

____

c. If the ladder were set closer to the building, would it be harder or easier to climb? Explain in terms of the slope of the ladder.

____

____

LESSON 6.4

Slope-Intercept Form

CA CC A.CED.2

Create equations in two or more variables to represent relationships between quantities; graph equations on coordinate axes with labels and scales. *Also F.IF.4, F.IF.6, F.IF.7, F.IF.7a, F.LE.1b*

ESSENTIAL QUESTION

How can you use the slope-intercept form of a linear equation to model real-world linear relationships?

Using Slopes and Intercepts

If you know the equation that describes a line, you can find its slope by using any two ordered pairs of numbers that are solutions of the equation. It is often easiest to use the ordered pairs that contain the intercepts.

EXAMPLE 1

CA CC F.IF.6

Find the slope of the line described by $6x - 5y = 30$.

STEP 1 Find the x-intercept.

Substitute 0 for y in the equation and solve for x.

$6x - 5y = 30$

$6x - 5(0) = 30$ Substitute.

$6x - 0 = 30$ Simplify.

$6x = 30$

$x = 5$ Divide both sides by 6.

STEP 2 Find the y-intercept.

Substitute 0 for x in the equation and solve for y.

$6x - 5y = 30$

$6(0) - 5y = 30$ Substitute.

$0 - 5y = 30$ Simplify.

$-5y = 30$

$y = -6$ Divide both sides by -5.

STEP 3 The line contains (5, 0) and (0, −6). Use the slope formula.

$$m = \frac{\text{change in } y\text{-coordinates}}{\text{change in } x\text{-coordinates}}$$

$$= \frac{-6 - 0}{0 - 5}$$

$$= \frac{-6}{-5}$$

$$= \frac{6}{5}$$

The slope of the line is $\frac{6}{5}$.

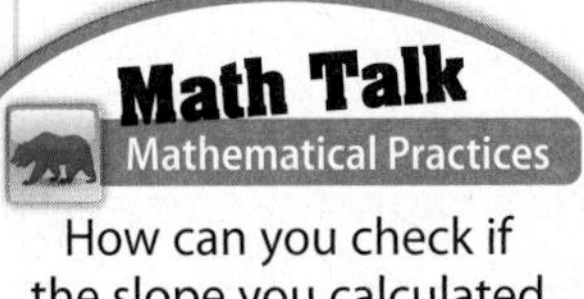

How can you check if the slope you calculated is correct?

YOUR TURN

1. Find the slope of the line described by $3x + 4y = 12$. ________________

Exploring the Slope Formula

If you know the slope of a line and the y-intercept, you can write an equation that describes the line.

EXPLORE ACTIVITY CA CC A.CED.2

Write an equation for the line that has slope 2 and y-intercept 3.

STEP 1 The line has a slope of ☐ and a y-intercept of ☐.

Since ☐ is the y-intercept, (☐, ☐) is a point on the line.

Substitute these values into the slope formula. Since you don't know the coordinates of any other point on the line, use a generic ordered pair (x, y).

$$m = \frac{\text{change in } y\text{-coordinates}}{\text{change in } x\text{-coordinates}} \qquad \square = \frac{y - \square}{x - \square}$$

STEP 2 Solve for y.

$$\square = \frac{y - \square}{x - \square}$$

$$\square = \frac{y - \square}{\square}$$

$$\square = y - \square$$

$$\square + \square = y$$

In this equation, the coefficient of x is equal to the ________________,

and the constant is equal to the ________________.

If a line has slope m and the y-intercept is b, then the line is described by the equation $y = mx + b$. This equation is called the **slope-intercept form** of a linear equation. A linear equation can be written in slope-intercept form by solving for y and simplifying.

My Notes

REFLECT

2. Why can it be helpful to solve a linear equation for y?

______

______

Graphing a Linear Function Using the Slope and y-intercept

You can graph the linear function $f(x) = mx + b$ using only the slope m and y-intercept b. First, locate the point $(0, b)$ on the y-axis. Next, use the rise and run of the slope to locate another point on the line. Draw a line through the two points.

EXAMPLE 2

CA CC F.IF.7a

Graph the function $f(x) = -\frac{2}{3}x + 4$ and determine its domain and range.

STEP 1 The y-intercept is 4. Plot the point (0, 4).

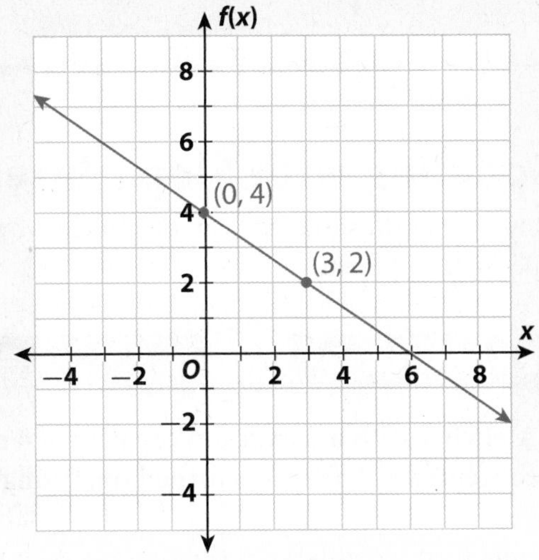

STEP 2 The slope is $-\frac{2}{3}$. If you use -2 as the rise, then the run is 3.

Use the slope to move from the y-intercept to a second point. Begin by moving down 2 units, because the rise is negative. Then move right 3 units because the run is positive. Plot the second point, (3, 2).

STEP 3 Draw a line through the two points.

STEP 4 The domain is the set of real numbers. The range is the set of real numbers.

REFLECT

3. **Multiple Representations** How does the graph of the linear function show that the domain is the set of real numbers and the range is the set of real numbers?

______

______

______

YOUR TURN

Graph each function.

4. $f(x) = -\frac{1}{2}x + 3$

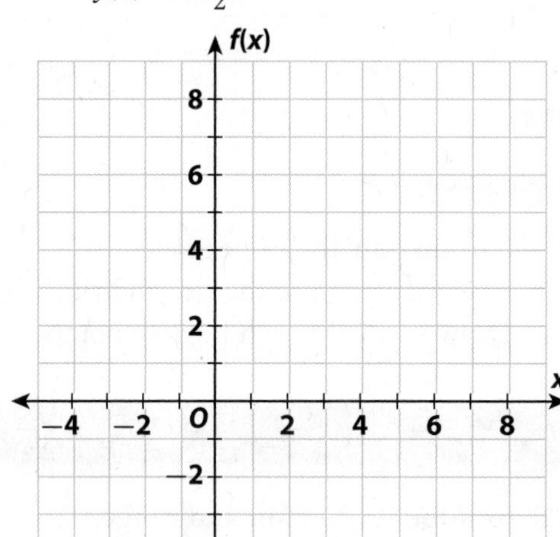

5. $f(x) = 2x - 1$

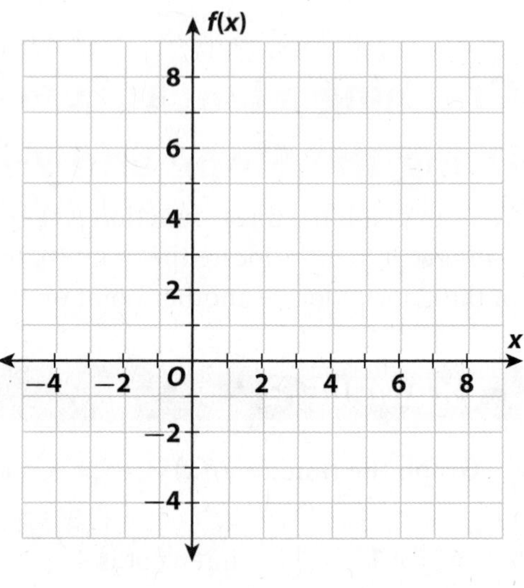

Modeling with Slope-Intercept Form

Many real-world situations can be modeled by linear equations in slope-intercept form.

EXAMPLE 3

A pitcher with a maximum capacity of 4 cups contains 1 cup of apple juice concentrate. A faucet is turned on, filling the pitcher at a rate of 0.25 cup per second. The amount of liquid in the pitcher, $A(t)$, (in cups), is a function of the time t (in seconds) that the water is running. Graph the function $A(t)$, write the rule for the function, and state its domain and range.

STEP 1 The y-intercept is 1 because there is 1 cup in the pitcher at time 0. Plot the point that corresponds to the y-intercept, (0, 1).

STEP 2 The slope is the rate of change: 0.25 cup per second, or 1 cup in 4 seconds. So the rise is 1 and the run is 4.

STEP 3 Use the rise and run to move from the first point to a second point on the line by moving up 1 unit and right 4 units. Plot the second point, (4, 2).

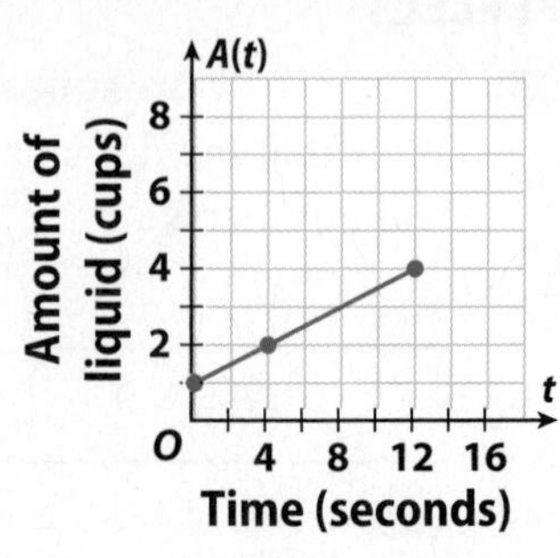

STEP 4 Connect the points and extend the line segment to the maximum value of the function, where $A(t) = 4$ cups.

STEP 5 Use $m = \frac{1}{4}$ and $b = 1$ to write the rule for the function: $A(t) = \frac{1}{4}t + 1$.

STEP 6 The domain is the set of all real numbers t such that $0 \leq t \leq 12$.

The range is the set of all real numbers $A(t)$ such that $1 \leq A(t) \leq 4$.

REFLECT

6. **Critical Thinking** Why are the domain and range restricted in Example 3, rather than each being the set of all real numbers?

____

____

____

____

____

YOUR TURN

7. A pump is set to dispense chlorine from a full 5-gallon container into a swimming pool to sanitize the water. The pump will dispense the chlorine at a rate of 0.5 gallon per minute and will shut off when the container is empty. The amount of chlorine in the container, $A(t)$, (in gallons), is a function of the time t (in minutes) that the pump is running. Graph the function $A(t)$, write the rule for the function, and state its domain and range.

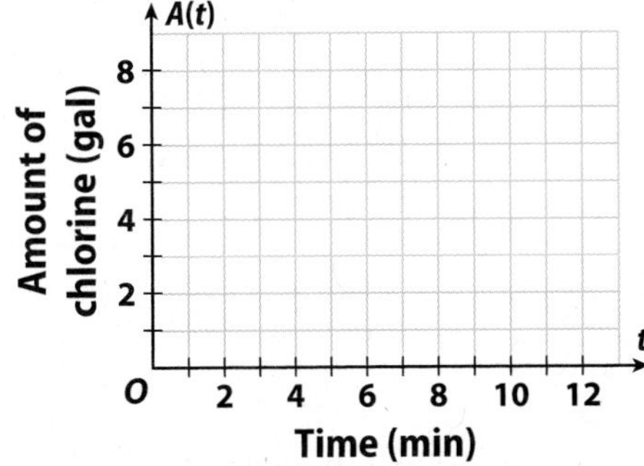

$A(t) =$ _______________

Domain: _______________

Range: _______________

____

Guided Practice

Find the slope of the line described by each equation. (Example 1)

1. $5x - 2y = 10$

$m =$ ______

2. $3y = 4$

$m =$ ______

3. $x - 3y = 6$

$m =$ ______

4. $4x + 2y = 12$

$m =$ ______

5. Graph the function $f(x) = -2x + 3$ and determine its domain and range. (Example 2)

STEP 1 The y-intercept is ☐.

Plot the point (☐, ☐).

STEP 2 The slope is ☐.

Use ☐ as the rise; then the run is ☐.

Use the slope to move from the y-intercept to a second point. Begin by moving ______ unit(s). Then move ______ unit(s).

Plot the second point, (☐, ☐).

STEP 3 Draw a line through the two points.

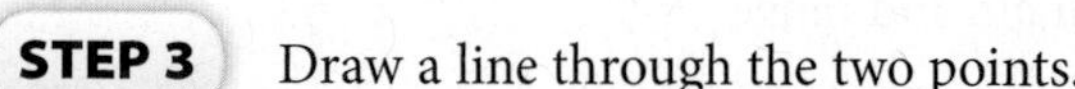

STEP 4 The domain is the set of ______ numbers.

The range is the set of ______ numbers.

ESSENTIAL QUESTION CHECK-IN

6. How is the rate of change in a real-world linear relationship related to the slope-intercept form of the equation that represents the relationship?

______

______

______

______

6.4 Independent Practice

CA CC F.IF.4, F.IF.6, F.IF.7, F.IF.7a, F.LE.1b, A.CED.2

Find the slope of the line described by each equation.

7. $5x + 3y = 0$

$m =$ ______________

8. $3y = 6$

$m =$ ______________

9. $6x - 12y = 36$

$m =$ ______________

10. When graphing a linear function in slope-intercept form, why do you have to plot the y-intercept first? Why can't you use the slope first?

____

____

____

____

Graph each linear function.

11. $f(x) = \frac{1}{4}x - 3$

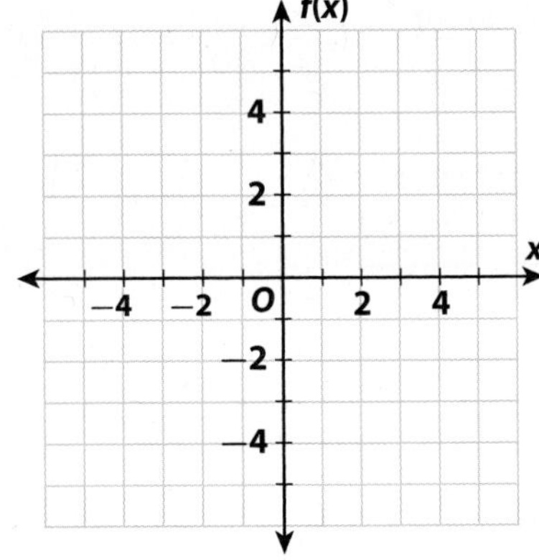

12. $f(x) = -5x + 1$

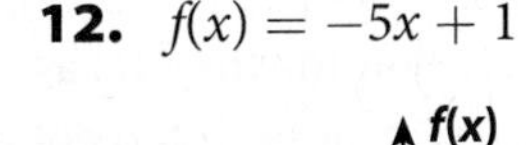

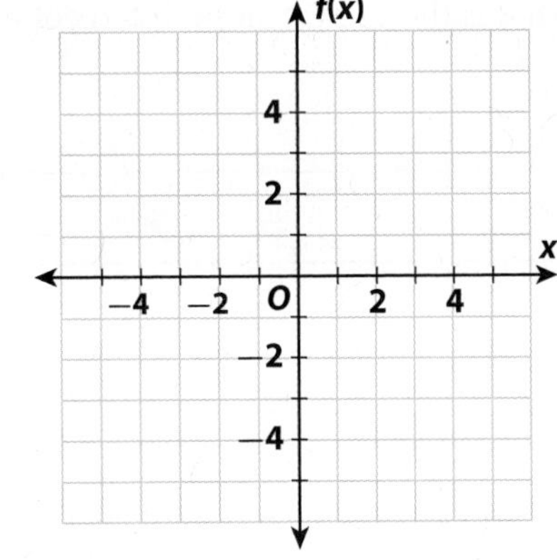

13. $f(x) = -1$

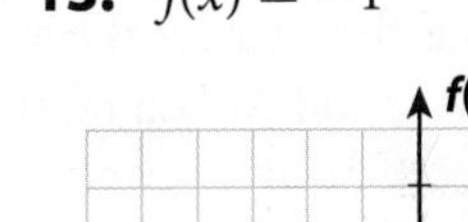

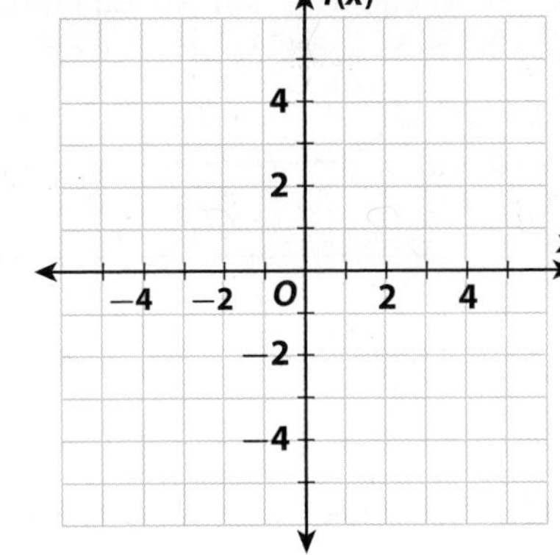

14. A company rents moving vans for a charge of \$30 plus \$0.50 per mile. The company only allows its vans to be used for "in-town" moves, with total mileage limited to 100 miles. The total rental cost, $C(m)$, (in dollars) is a function of the distance m (in miles) that the van is driven. State a rule for the function, graph the function, and state its domain and range.

$C(m) =$ ______________

Domain: ______________

____

Range: ______________

____

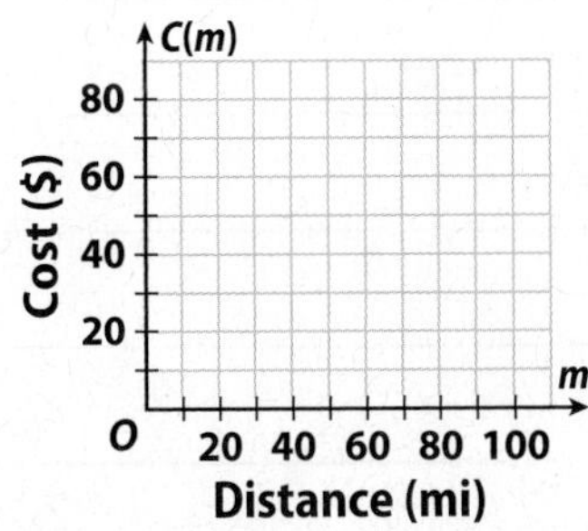

H.O.T. FOCUS ON HIGHER ORDER THINKING

Work Area

15. Draw Conclusions The standard form of a linear equation is $Ax + By = C$. Rewrite this equation in slope-intercept form. What is the slope? What is the y-intercept?

____

____

16. What If? What if the person filling the pitcher in Example 3 gets distracted by a phone call and does not get to turn the faucet off as soon as the pitcher is full? How does this affect the domain and range of the function? How does it affect the graph?

____

____

____

____

____

17. Find the Error Alyssa correctly determines that the graph of a linear equation intersects the x-axis at (6, 0) and intersects the y-axis at (0, 2). She calculates the slope and then writes the slope-intercept equation for the line as $y = -\frac{1}{3}x + 6$. What error did Alyssa make? What is the correct slope-intercept equation for this line?

____

____

____

____

18. Justify Reasoning Is it possible to write the equation of every line in slope-intercept form? Explain your reasoning.

____

____

____

____

____

____

____

LESSON 6.5

Comparing Linear Functions

CA CC F.IF.9

Compare properties of two functions each represented in a different way (algebraically, graphically, numerically in tables, or by verbal descriptions). *Also N.Q.1, F.IF.1, F.IF.2, F.IF.5, F.LE.5*

ESSENTIAL QUESTION

How can you compare linear functions that are represented in different ways?

EXPLORE ACTIVITY  

Comparing Linear Relationships

Comparing linear relationships sometimes involves comparing relationships that are expressed in different ways.

Joe's Plumbing and Mark's Plumbing have different ways of charging their customers. The function defined by $J(t) = 40t$ represents the total amount in dollars that Joe's Plumbing charges for t hours of work. Mark's Plumbing Service charges \$40 per hour plus a \$25 trip charge.

A Define a function $M(t)$ that represents the total amount Mark's Plumbing Service charges for t hours of work and then complete the charts below.

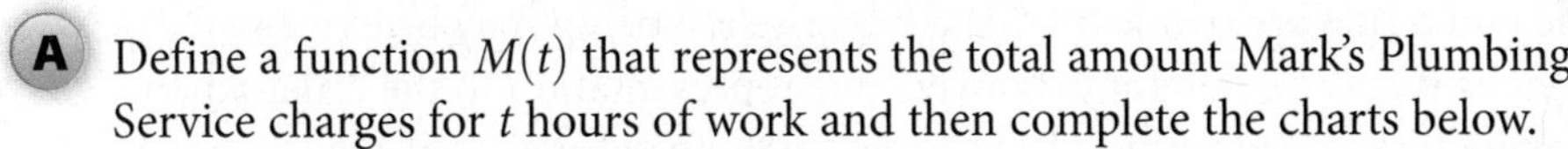

$M(t) = 40t + 25$ represents the total amount in dollars that Mark's Plumbing Service charges for t hours of work.

Cost for Joe's Plumbing

t	$J(t) = 40t$	$(t, J(t))$
0	0	(0, 0)
1		
2		
3		

Cost for Mark's Plumbing Service

t	$M(t) = 40t + 25$	$(t, M(t))$
0	0	(0, 25)
1		
2		
3		

B What domain values for the functions $J(t)$ and for $M(t)$ are reasonable in this context? Explain.

____

____

C Graph the two cost functions for all appropriate domain values.

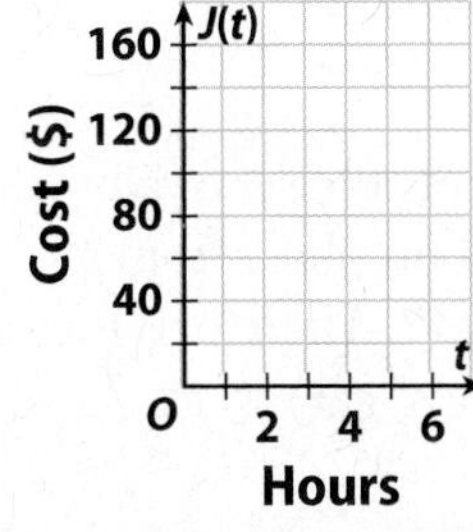

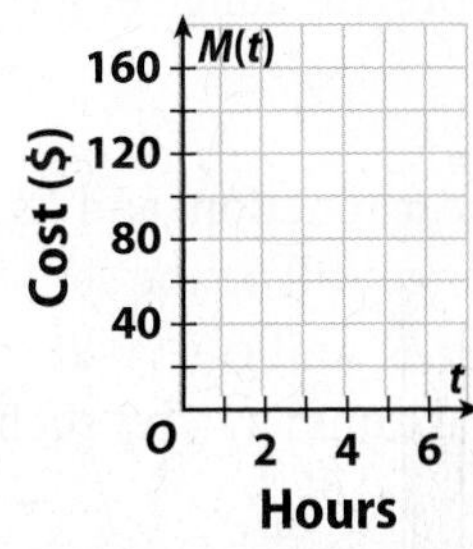

EXPLORE ACTIVITY *(cont'd)*

D Compare the graphs. How are they alike? How are they different?

____

____

REFLECT

1. Describe the range for $J(t)$ and $M(t)$.

____

____

____

Comparing Linear Functions Given a Table and a Rule

A table and a rule are two ways that a linear relationship may be expressed. Sometimes it may be helpful to convert one representation to the other when comparing two relationships. Other times, making comparisons may be possible without converting either representation.

EXAMPLE 1

CA CC F.IF.9

The functions $f(x)$ and $g(x)$ are linear functions. The domain of each function is the set of all real numbers x such that $4 \leq x \leq 7$. The table shows some ordered pairs belonging to $f(x)$. The function $g(x)$ is defined by the rule $g(x) = 2x + 3$. Find the initial value and the range of each function.

x	f(x)
4	8
5	10
6	12
7	14

The initial value is the output that is paired with the least input.

The initial value of $f(x)$ is $f(4) = 8$ The least input for $f(x)$ is 4.

The initial value of $g(x)$ is $g(4) = 2(4) + 3 = 11$.   The least input for $g(x)$ is 4.

Since $f(x)$ is a linear function, and its domain is the set of all real numbers from 4 to 7, its range will be the set of all real numbers from $f(4)$ to $f(7)$. $f(4) = 8$ and $f(7) = 14$. Therefore, the range of $f(x)$ is the set of all real numbers $f(x)$ such that $8 \leq f(x) \leq 14$.

Since $g(x)$ is a linear function, and its domain is the set of all real numbers from 4 to 7, its range will be the set of all real numbers from $g(4)$ to $g(7)$. $g(4) = 2(4) + 3 = 11$ and $g(7) = 2(7) + 3 = 17$. Therefore, the range of $g(x)$ is the set of all real numbers $g(x)$ such that $11 \leq g(x) \leq 17$.

YOUR TURN

2. The rule for $f(x)$ is $f(x) = 2x$. If the domains were extended to all real numbers, how would the slopes and y-intercepts of $f(x)$ and $g(x)$ compare?

Comparing Linear Functions Given a Description and a Graph

Information about a relationship may have to be inferred from the context given in the problem.

EXAMPLE 2

CA CC F.IF.9

Compare the following functions.

- A rainstorm in Atlanta lasted for 2.5 hours, during which time it rained at a steady rate of 0.5 inch per hour. The function $A(t)$ represents the amount of rain that fell in t hours.
- The graph at the right shows the amount of rain that fell during a rainstorm in Knoxville, $K(t)$ (in inches), as a function of time t (in hours).

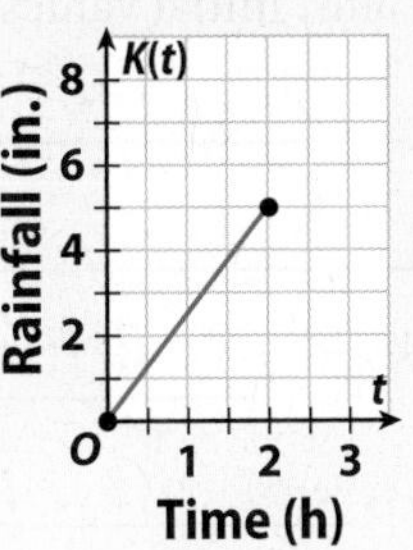

STEP 1 Write a rule for each function.

$A(t) = 0.5t$ for $0 \leq t \leq 2.5$

Since (0, 0) and (2, 5) are the coordinates of points on the line representing $K(t)$, the slope of the line is $\frac{5-0}{2-0} = \frac{5}{2} = 2.5$. The y-intercept is 0, so substituting 2.5 for m and 0 for b in $y = mx + b$ produces $y = 2.5t$, which yields $K(t) = 2.5t$ for $0 \leq t \leq 2$.

STEP 2 Compare the y-intercepts of the graphs of $A(t)$ and $K(t)$.

They are both 0.

What is the meaning of the y-intercepts for the functions $A(t)$ and $K(t)$?

YOUR TURN

3. How do the slopes of the graphs of the functions $A(t)$ and $K(t)$ compare?

Guided Practice

The linear function $f(x)$ is defined by the table below. The linear function $g(x)$ is defined by the graph below. Assume that the domain of $f(x)$ includes all real numbers between the least and greatest values shown in the table. (Examples 1–2)

x	$f(x)$
0	−2
1	1
2	4
3	7
4	10
5	13

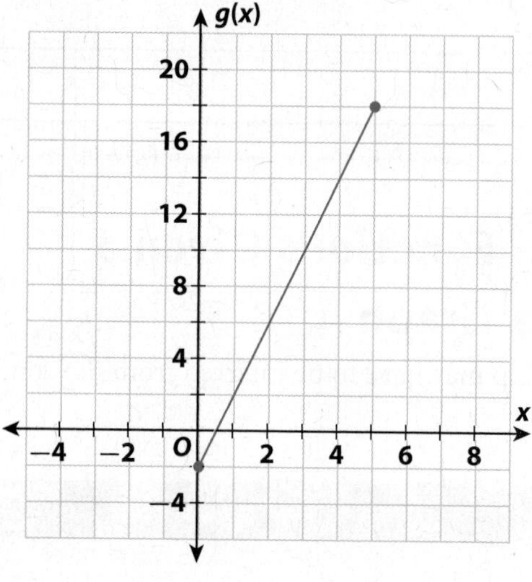

1. Compare the domains, initial values, and ranges of the functions.

Domain of $f(x)$: ______

Domain of $g(x)$: ______

Initial value of $f(x)$: ______

Initial value of $g(x)$: ______

Range of $f(x)$: ______

Range of $g(x)$: ______

2. Calculate how many inches of rain fell per hour during the Knoxville storm in Example 2. How many more inches per hour is this than in the Atlanta storm? (Example 2)

______

ESSENTIAL QUESTION CHECK-IN

3. How can you compare a linear function represented in a table to one represented as a graph?

______

______

______

Name ____________________ Class ____________________ Date ____________________

6.5 Independent Practice

Personal Math Trainer

Online Practice and Help

CA CC F.IF.9

4. Grace works from 10 to 20 hours per week while attending college. She earns \$9.00 per hour. Her roommate Frances also has a job. Her pay for t hours each week is given by the function $f(t) = 10t$, where $5 \leq t \leq 15$.

a. Find the domain and range of each function.

____

____

____

____

____

b. Compare their hourly wages and the amount they each earn per week.

____

____

5. The linear function $f(x)$ is defined by the table below. The linear function $g(x)$ is defined by the graph below. Assume that the domain of $f(x)$ includes all real numbers between the least and greatest values shown in the table.

x	f(x)
−1	7
0	4
1	1
2	−2

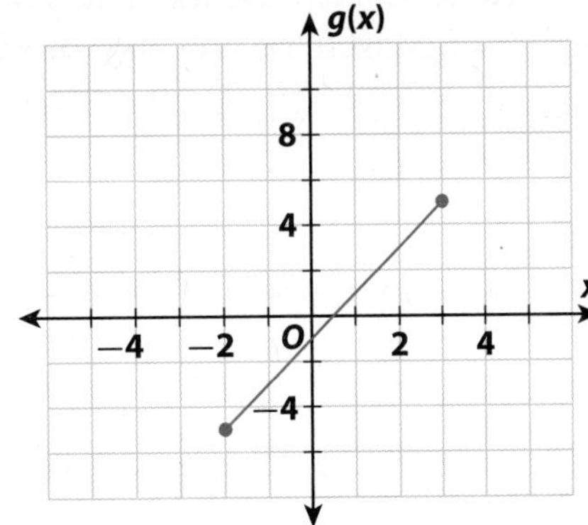

a. Find the domain and range of each function.

____

____

____

____

b. What is the slope of the line represented by each function? What is the y-intercept for each function? ____________________

____

6. Complete the table so that $f(x)$ is a linear function with a slope of 2 and a y-intercept of 5. Assume the domain includes all real numbers between the least and greatest values shown in the table. Compare $f(x)$ to $g(x) = 2x + 5$ if the range of $g(x)$ is $3 \leq g(x) \leq 9$.

x	f(x)
−1	
0	
1	
2	

H.O.T. FOCUS ON HIGHER ORDER THINKING

Work Area

7. **Communicate Mathematical Ideas** Describe a linear function for which the least value in the range does not occur at the least value of the domain, that is, the least value in the range is not the initial value.

8. **Draw Conclusions** Two linear functions have the same slope, same x-intercept, and same y-intercept. Must these functions be identical? Explain your reasoning.

9. **Draw Conclusions** Let $f(x) = 2x$ with domain $\{0, 1, 2, 3, 4\}$ and let $g(x) = \{(0, 0), (1, 1), (2, 4), (3, 9), (4, 16)\}$. Compare the two functions.

LESSON 6.6

Transforming Linear Functions

CA CC F.BF.3

Identify the effect on the graph of replacing $f(x)$ by $f(x) + k$, $k\,f(x)$, $f(kx)$, and $f(x + k)$ for specific values of k (both positive and negative); find the value of k given the graphs. Experiment with cases and illustrate an explanation of the effects on the graph using technology. *Also F.IF.4, F.LE.5*

ESSENTIAL QUESTION

How are changes to the parameters of a linear function reflected in its graph?

EXPLORE ACTIVITY 1

Changing the Parameter b in $f(x) = mx + b$

Changing the value of m or b in $f(x) = mx + b$ causes a change in the graph of that function.

Investigate what happens to the graph of $f(x) = x + b$ when you change the value of b.

A Use a graphing calculator. Start with the standard viewing window, which you can obtain by pressing ZOOM and selecting ZStandard. If the distances between consecutive tick marks on the x-axis and y-axis are not equal, you can make them equal by pressing ZOOM again and selecting ZSquare.

What interval on each axis does the viewing window now show? (Press WINDOW to find out.)

____

B Graph the function $f(x) = x$ by pressing Y= and entering the function's rule next to $Y_1=$. As shown, the graph of the function is a line that makes a 45° angle with each axis.

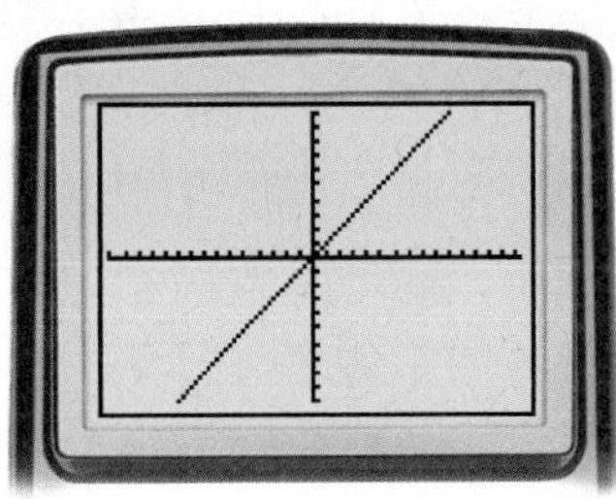

What are the slope and y-intercept of the graph of $f(x) = x$?

____

C Graph other functions of the form $f(x) = x + b$ by entering their rules next to $Y_2=$, $Y_3=$, and so on. Be sure to choose both positive and negative values of b. For instance, graph $f(x) = x + 2$ and $f(x) = x - 3$.

What do the graphs have in common? How are they different?

____

REFLECT

1. A *vertical translation* moves all points on a figure the same distance either up or down. Use the idea of a vertical translation to describe what happens to the graph of $f(x) = x + b$ when you increase the value of b and decrease the value of b.

____

____

EXPLORE ACTIVITY 2

Changing the Parameter m in $f(x) = mx + b$

Investigate what happens to the graph of $f(x) = mx$ when you change the value of m.

A Use a graphing calculator. Press Y= and clear out all but the function $f(x) = x$ from Explore Activity 1. Then graph other functions of the form $f(x) = mx$ by entering their rules next to $Y_2=$, $Y_3=$, and so on. Use only values of m that are greater than 1. For instance, graph $f(x) = 2x$ and $f(x) = 6x$.

What do the graphs have in common? How are they different?

____

____

As the value of m increases from 1, does the graph become steeper or less steep? ____________________

B Again, press Y= and clear out all but the function $f(x) = x$. Then graph other functions of the form $f(x) = mx$ by entering their rules next to $Y_2=$, $Y_3=$, and so on. This time use only values of m that are less than 1 but greater than 0. For instance, graph $f(x) = 0.5x$ and $f(x) = 0.2x$.

As the value of m decreases from 1 to 0, does the graph become steeper or less steep? ____________________

C Again, press Y= and clear out all but the function $f(x) = x$. Then graph the function $f(x) = -x$ by entering its rule next to $Y_2=$.

What are the slope and y-intercept of the graph of $f(x) = -x$?

____

How are the graphs of $f(x) = x$ and $f(x) = -x$ geometrically related?

____

____

D Again, press Y= and clear out all the functions. Graph $f(x) = -x$ by entering its rule next to $Y_1=$. Then graph other functions of the form $f(x) = mx$ where $m < 0$ by entering their rules next to $Y_2=$, $Y_3=$, and so on. Be sure to choose values of m that are less than -1 as well as values of m between -1 and 0.

Describe what happens to the graph of $f(x) = mx$ as the value of m decreases from -1 and as it increases from -1 to 0.

____

____

____

My Notes

REFLECT

2. A function $f(x)$ is called an *increasing function* when the value of $f(x)$ always increases as the value of x increases. For what values of m is the function $f(x) = mx$ an increasing function? How can you tell from the graph of a linear function that it is an increasing function?

---

3. A function $f(x)$ is called a *decreasing function* when the value of $f(x)$ always decreases as the value of x increases. For what values of m is the function $f(x) = mx$ a decreasing function? How can you tell from the graph of a linear function that it is a decreasing function?

---

4. When $m > 0$, increasing the value of m results in an increasing linear function that increases *faster*. What effect does increasing m have on the graph of the function?

---

5. When $m > 0$, decreasing the value of m toward 0 results in an increasing linear function that increases *slower*. What effect does decreasing m have on the graph of the function?

---

6. When $m < 0$, decreasing the value of m results in a decreasing linear function that decreases *faster*. What effect does decreasing m have on the graph of the function?

---

7. When $m < 0$, increasing the value of m toward 0 results in a decreasing linear function that decreases *slower*. What effect does increasing m have on the graph of the function?

---

8. The *steepness* of a line refers to the absolute value of its slope. The greater the absolute value of the slope, the steeper the line. Complete the table to summarize, in terms of steepness, the effect of changing the value of m on the graph of $f(x) = mx$.

How the Value of m Changes	Effect on the Graph of $f(x) = mx$
Increase m when $m > 0$.	
Decrease m toward 0 when $m > 0$.	
Decrease m when $m < 0$.	
Increase m toward 0 when $m < 0$.	

EXPLORE ACTIVITY 3

Families of Linear Functions

A A **family of functions** is a set of functions whose graphs have basic characteristics in common. What do all these variations on the original function $f(x) = x$ have in common?

____

B The most basic function of a family of functions is called the **parent function.** What is the parent function of the family of functions explored in the first two Explore Activities?

____

C A **parameter** is one of the constants in a function or equation that determines which variation of the parent function one is considering. For functions of the form $f(x) = mx + b$, what are the two parameters?

____

For the family of all linear functions, the parent function is $f(x) = x$, where the parameters are $m = 1$ and $b = 0$. Other examples of families of linear functions are shown below. The example on the left shows a family with the same parameter m and differing parameters b. The example on the right shows a family with the same parameter b and differing parameters m.

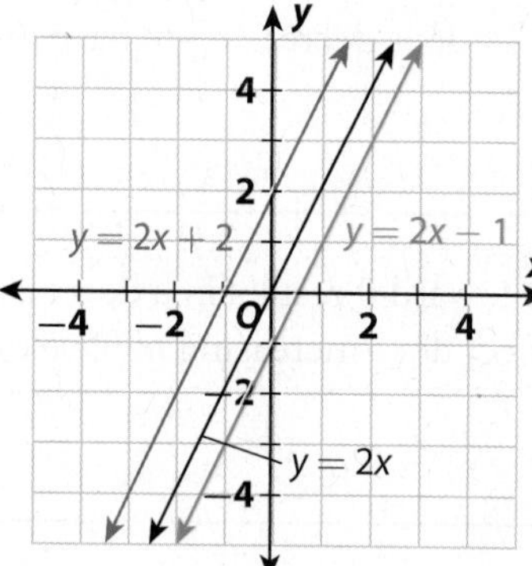

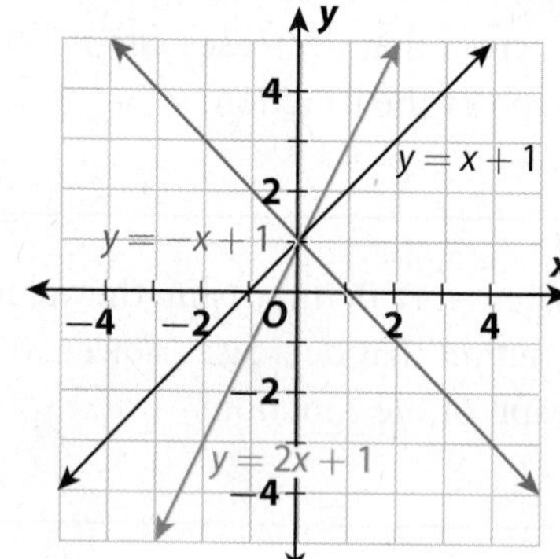

REFLECT

9. Describe the parameter that is left unchanged in the equations of the lines in the graph on the left above.

____

Modeling with Parameter Changes

Real-world scenarios can often be modeled by linear functions. Changes in a particular scenario can be analyzed by making changes in the corresponding parameter of the linear function.

EXAMPLE 1 

CA CC F.IF.4, F.LE.5

A gym charges a one-time joining fee of \$50 and then a monthly membership fee of \$25. The total cost C of being a member of the gym is given by the function $C(t) = 25t + 50$, where t is the time (in months) since joining the gym. For each situation described below, sketch a graph using the given graph of $C(t) = 25t + 50$ as a reference. Describe the impact of the changes on the domain and range of the function.

A The gym decreases its one-time joining fee.

Rather than graphing a specific function for this situation, sketch a representative graph of a function related to the function $C(t) = 25t + 50$ with the appropriate parameter changed.

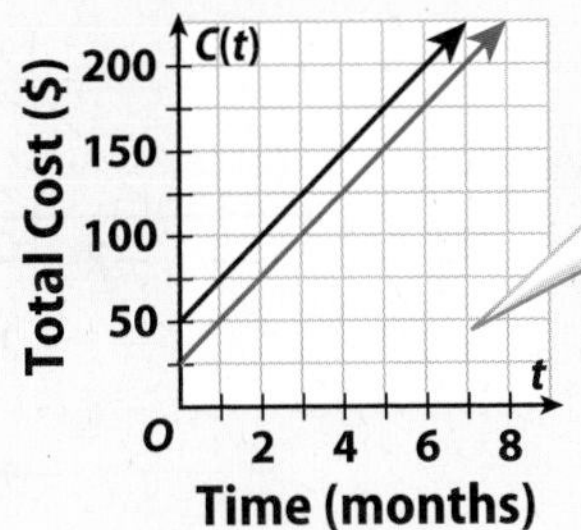

To sketch a graph that represents the new situation, make the y-intercept of the graph lower, but leave the slope the same.

The one-time joining fee is represented by the constant in the equation; the constant represents the y-intercept of the graph.

There is no change in the domain, but the bottom number of the range decreases from $C(t) = 50$ to $C(t)$ equals the new joining fee.

B The gym increases its monthly membership fee.

Rather than graphing a specific function for this situation, sketch a representative graph of a function related to the function $C(t) = 25t + 50$ with the appropriate parameter changed.

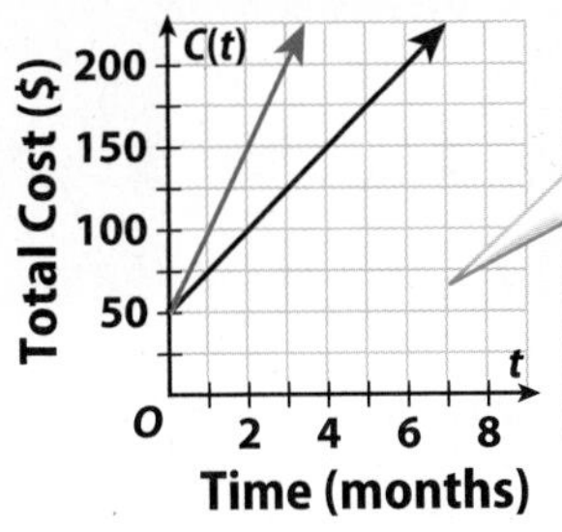

To sketch a graph that represents the new situation, increase the slope of the graph but leave the y-intercept the same.

The monthly membership fee is represented by the coefficient of t in the equation; the coefficient of t represents the slope of the graph.

There is no change in the domain or the range.

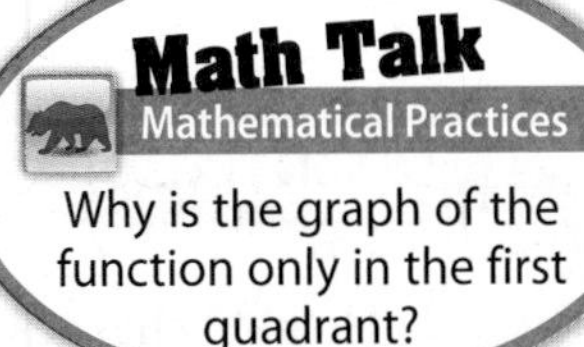

Why is the graph of the function only in the first quadrant?

YOUR TURN

10. Once a year the gym offers a special in which the one-time joining fee is waived for new members. What impact does this special offer have on the graph of the original function $C(t) = 25t + 50$?

____

____

Guided Practice

1. The graph of the function $f(x) = x + 3$ is shown below. Graph two more functions in the same family for which the parameter being changed is the y-intercept. (Example 1)

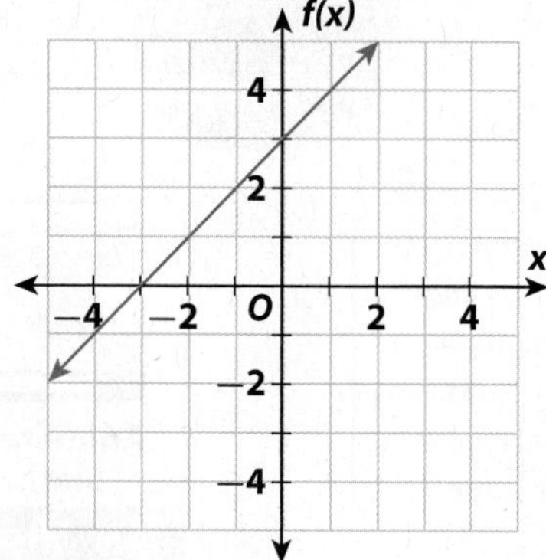

2. The graph of the function $f(x) = x + 3$ is shown below. Graph two more functions in the same family for which the parameter being changed is the slope. (Example 1)

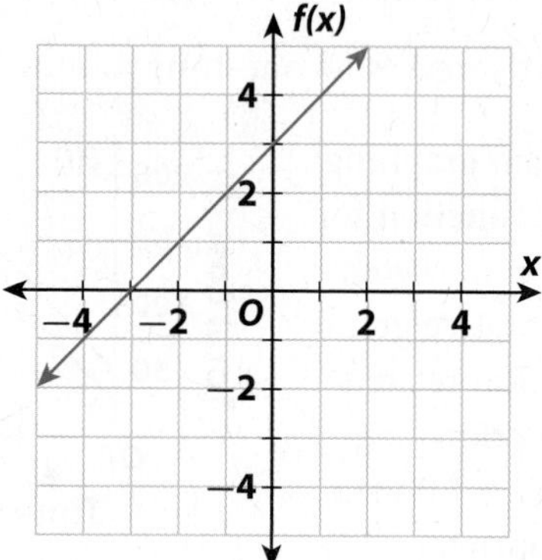

3. For the family of linear functions of the form $f(x) = mx + b$, the parameter that causes the steepness of the graph of the line to change is ______________. (Explore Activities 1 and 2)

4. The graph of the parent linear function $f(x) = x$ is shown in black on the coordinate grid. Write the color of the line that represents this function with the indicated parameter changes. (Explore Activities 1 and 2)

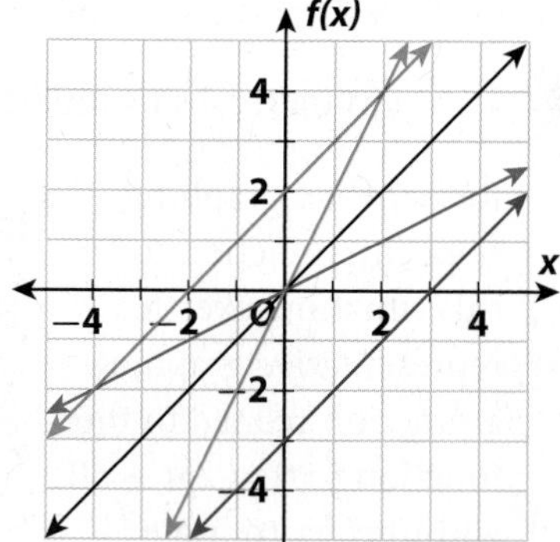

a. m increased, b unchanged ______________

b. m decreased, b unchanged ______________

c. m unchanged, b increased ______________

d. m unchanged, b decreased ______________

ESSENTIAL QUESTION CHECK-IN

5. How do changes in m and b in the equation $y = mx + b$ affect the graph of the equation?

____

____

____

____

____

Name ______________________ Class ______________________ Date ______________________

6.6 Independent Practice

CA CC F.BF.3, F.IF.4, F.LE.5

6. A salesperson earns a base monthly salary of \$2000 plus a 10% commission on sales. The salesperson's monthly income I (in dollars) is given by the function $I(s) = 0.1s + 2000$, where s is the sales (in dollars) that the salesperson makes. Sketch a graph to illustrate each situation using the graph of $I(s) = 0.1s + 2000$ as a reference.

a. The salesperson's base salary is increased.

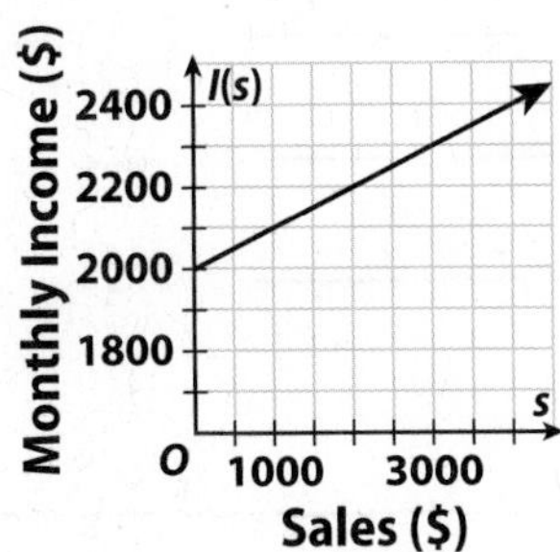

b. The salesperson's commission rate is decreased.

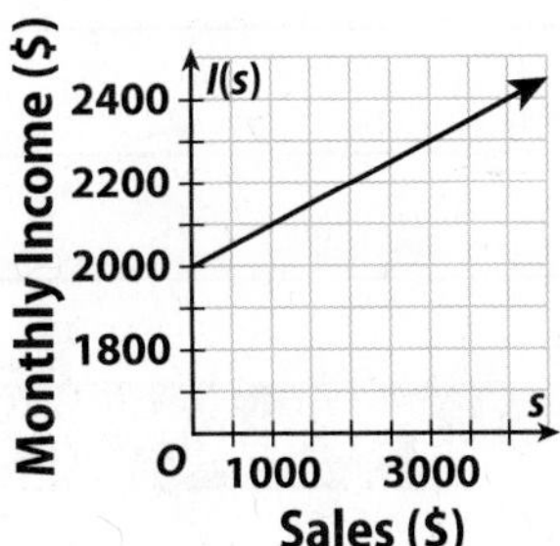

7. Mr. Resnick is driving at a speed of 40 miles per hour to visit relatives who live 100 miles away from his home. His distance d (in miles) from his destination is given by the function $d(t) = 100 - 40t$, where t is the time (in hours) since his trip began. Sketch a graph to illustrate each situation. The graphs shown already represent the function $d(t)$.

a. He increases his speed to get to his destination sooner.

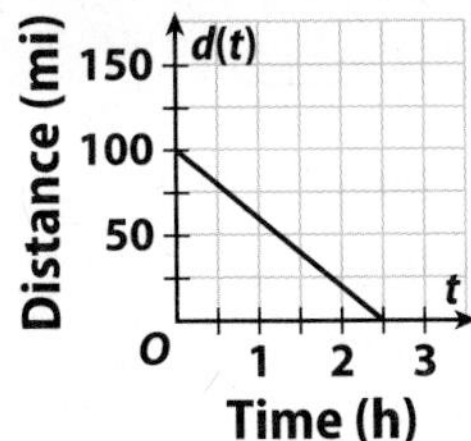

b. He encounters a detour that increases the driving distance.

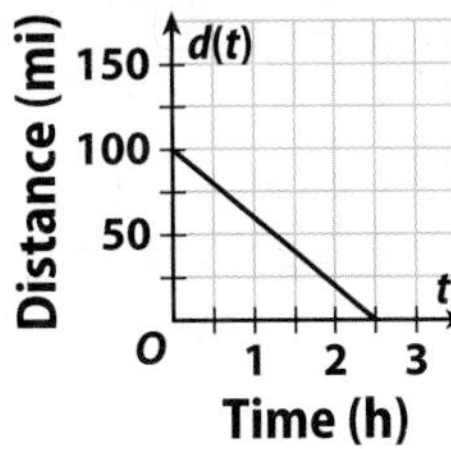

c. Give an example of another linear function within the same family of functions as $d(t) = 100 - 40t$. Explain the meaning of each parameter in your example.

____

____

8. Use the graph of $d(t) = 100 - 40t$ in Exercise 7 to identify the domain and range of the function. Then tell whether the domain, the range, neither, or both are affected by the changes described in each part.

____

____

9. For each linear function graphed on the coordinate grid, state the value of m and the value of b.

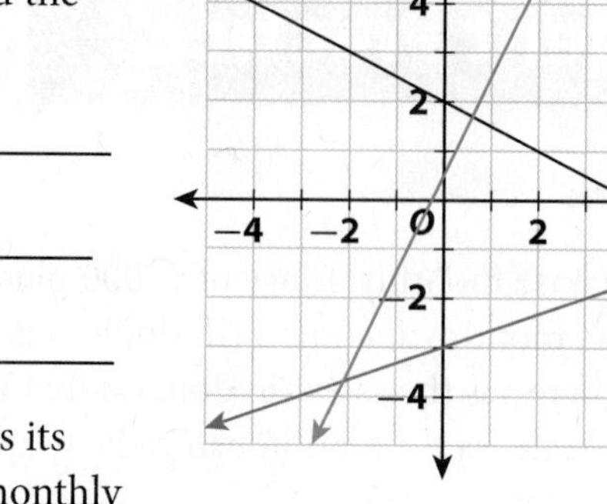

a. black line: $m =$ ________, $b =$ ________

b. blue line: $m =$ ________, $b =$ ________

c. green line: $m =$ ________, $b =$ ________

10. Suppose the gym in Example 1 increases its one-time joining fee and decreases its monthly membership fee. Describe how you would alter the graph of $C(t) = 25t + 50$ to illustrate the new cost function.

____

____

____

H.O.T. FOCUS ON HIGHER ORDER THINKING

Work Area

11. **Critique Reasoning** Geoff says that changing the value of m while leaving b unchanged in $f(x) = mx + b$ has no impact on the intercepts of the graph. Marcus disagrees with this statement. Who is correct? Explain your reasoning.

____

____

____

____

12. **Multiple Representations** The graph of $y = x + 3$ is a vertical translation of the graph of $y = x + 1$, 2 units upward. Examine the intercepts of both lines and state another way that the geometric relationship between the two graphs can be described.

____

____

13. **Critique Reasoning** Stephanie says that the graphs of $y = 3x + 2$ and $y = 3x - 2$ are parallel. Isabella says that the graphs are perpendicular. Who is correct? Explain your reasoning.

____

____

____

LESSON 6.7

Writing Linear Functions

CA CC F.BF.1

Write a function that describes a relationship between two quantities. *Also A.CED.2, F.IF.6, F.LE.2*

ESSENTIAL QUESTION

How can you represent a function symbolically from a graph, verbal description, or table of values?

Using Slope to Write a Linear Function

The information needed to write the equation of a linear function can be provided in different ways, including presented as a graph, given as a description of a relationship, or as input-output pairs. If you know the slope and the y-intercept of a linear function, you can find an equation representing the function.

Math On the Spot

my.hrw.com

EXAMPLE 1

CA CC A.CED.2, F.LE.2

Write an equation for the linear function $f(x)$ whose graph has a slope of 3 and a y-intercept of -1.

A linear function has the form $f(x) = mx + b$ where m is the slope and b is the y-intercept.

$f(x) = mx + b$

$f(x) = 3x + (-1)$ — The slope was given as 3, so substitute 3 for m. The y-intercept was given as -1, so substitute -1 for b.

$f(x) = 3x - 1$

An equation for the function is $f(x) = 3x - 1$.

Math Talk

Mathematical Practices

If you graph the function $f(x)$, how can you use the graph to find more ordered pairs that satisfy the equation $f(x) = 3x - 1$?

REFLECT

1. How can you use the equation $f(x) = 3x - 1$ to find more ordered pairs that are part of the function?

____

____

YOUR TURN

Write an equation for the linear function $f(x)$ whose graph has the given slope and y-intercept.

2. slope of 4, y-intercept of -2

____

3. slope of -3, y-intercept of 5

____

4. slope of 6, y-intercept of 0

____

5. slope of 0, y-intercept of 6

____

Personal Math Trainer

Online Practice and Help

my.hrw.com

My Notes

EXAMPLE 2

CA CC A.CED.2, F.IF.6, F.LE.2

The table shows several ordered pairs for the linear function $f(x)$. Write an equation for $f(x)$.

x	$f(x)$
−1	5
3	−3
7	−11

STEP 1 Calculate the slope using any two ordered pairs from the table. Choose (−1, 5) as the first point and (3, −3) as the second point.

$\text{slope} = \frac{y_2 - y_1}{x_2 - x_1}$ Slope Formula

$m = \frac{-3 - 5}{3 - (-1)}$ Substitute values.

$= \frac{-8}{4}$ Simplify numerator and denominator.

$= -2$ Simplify fraction.

STEP 2 Find the value of b using the fact that $m = -2$ and $f(-1) = 5$.

$f(x) = -2x + b$ Write the function with the known value of m.

$5 = -2(-1) + b$ Substitute −1 for x and 5 for $f(x)$.

$5 = 2 + b$ Simplify the right side of the equation.

$3 = b$ Solve for b.

So, the function is $f(x) = -2x + 3$.

REFLECT

6. How can you check that the equation is correct?

____

____

YOUR TURN

Write an equation of the linear function represented by each table of values.

7.

x	$f(x)$
−1	−4
1	6
3	16

____

8.

x	$f(x)$
−1	1
2	−5
4	−9

____

Writing a Linear Function from a Graph

Writing a linear function from a graph requires the same information and steps as writing a linear function from a table of values. The difference is that the ordered pairs must be determined from the graph. The ordered pairs may or may not be explicitly labeled.

EXAMPLE 3 

CA CC F.LE.2, F.IF.6, F.BF.1

The graph below shows the increase in pressure (measured in pounds per square inch) as a scuba diver descends from a depth of 10 feet to a depth of 30 feet. Pressure is a linear function of depth. At the water's surface, the pressure on the diver is a result of the pressure of the air in the atmosphere. What is the pressure on the diver at the water's surface?

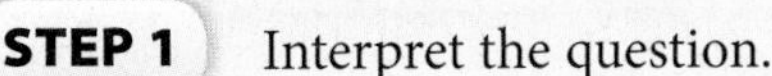

STEP 1 Interpret the question.

Let $P(d)$ represent the pressure in pounds per square inch on the diver at a depth of d feet. At the water's surface, $d = 0$. If the graph below is extended to meet the vertical axis, the value $P(0)$ would represent the pressure on the diver at the water's surface.

STEP 2 Find the value of m in $P(d) = md + b$. Use the fact that $P(10) = 19.1$ and $P(30) = 28.0$.

Scuba Dividing

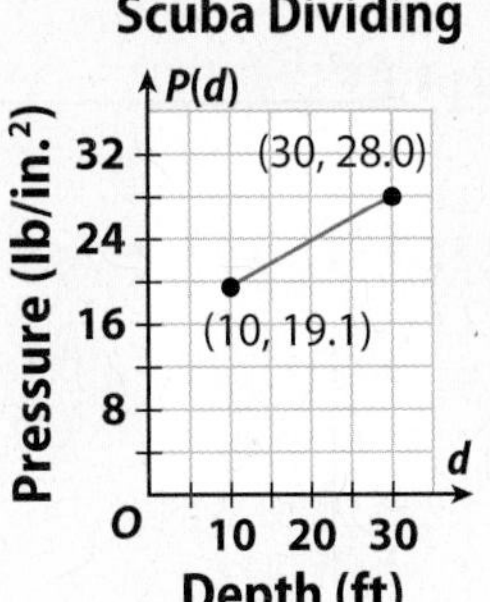

$\text{slope} = \frac{\text{rise}}{\text{run}}$	Definition of slope
$m = \frac{P(30) - P(10)}{30 - 10}$	Write the slope formula.
$= \frac{28.0 - 19.1}{30 - 10}$	Substitute values.
$= \frac{8.9}{20}$	Simplify numerator and denominator.
$= 0.445$	Write in decimal form.

STEP 3 Now that you know the slope, you can find the value of b in $P(d) = md + b$. Use the value of m from Step 2 as well as the fact that $P(10) = 19.1$.

$P(d) = 0.445d + b$	Write the function with the known value of m.
$19.1 = 0.445(10) + b$	Substitute 10 for d and 19.1 for $P(d)$.
$19.1 = 4.45 + b$	Simplify the right side of the equation.
$14.7 \approx b$	Solve for b. Round to the nearest tenth.

An equation for the function is $P(d) = 0.445d + 14.7$.

STEP 4 Find the pressure at the water's surface, where $d = 0$.

$$P(0) = 0.445(0) + 14.7$$
$$= 14.7$$

The pressure on the diver at the water's surface is 14.7 pounds per square inch.

YOUR TURN

9. The graph of the linear function $f(x)$ is shown. Write an equation for the function. Then find $f(0)$.

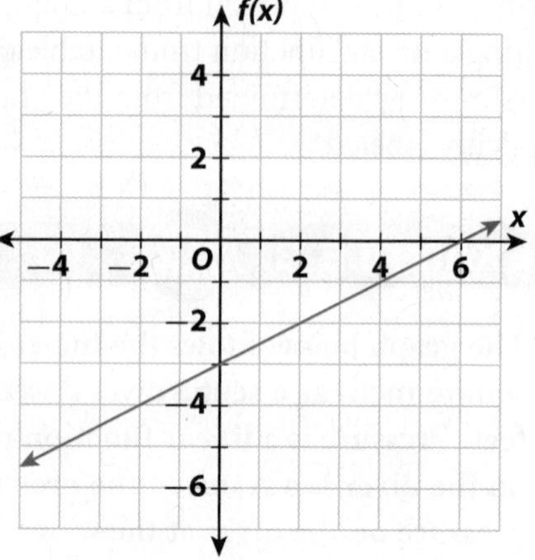

____

Guided Practice

Write an equation for the linear function $f(x)$ using the given information. (Examples 1–3)

1. slope $-\frac{3}{2}$, y-intercept 1 ______________

2.

x	$f(x)$
−4	5
−2	6
4	9

____

3.

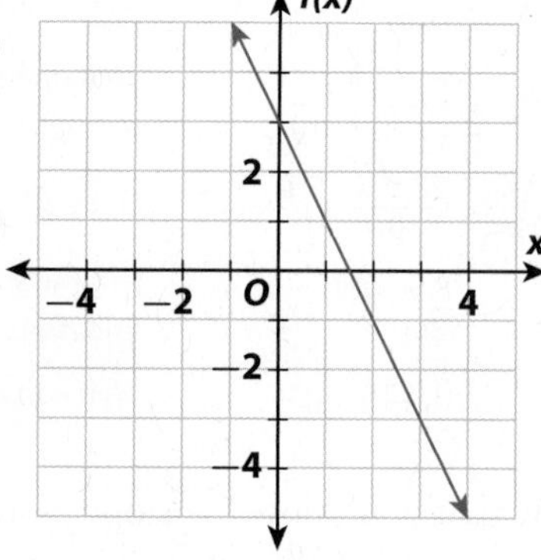

____

ESSENTIAL QUESTION CHECK-IN

4. What information can you use from the graph of a linear function to write the function?

____

____

____

____

Name ____________ Class ____________ Date ____________

6.7 Independent Practice

Personal Math Trainer
Online Practice and Help
my.hrw.com

CA CC F.LE.2, A.CED.2, F.IF.6, F.BF.1

Write an equation for the linear function $f(x)$ using the given information.

5. The graph of the function has a slope of $-\frac{2}{3}$ and a y-intercept of 5.

____

6. The graph of the function has a slope of $\frac{7}{4}$ and a y-intercept of 0.

____

7.

x	f(x)
0	−3
2	0
4	3

____

8.

x	f(x)
5	−2
10	−6
15	−10

____

9.

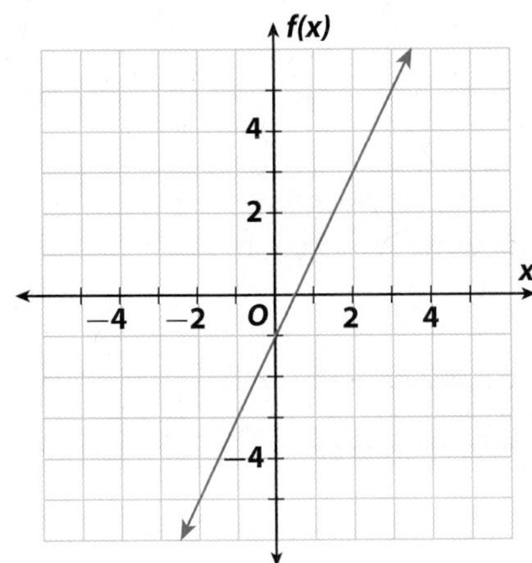

____

10.

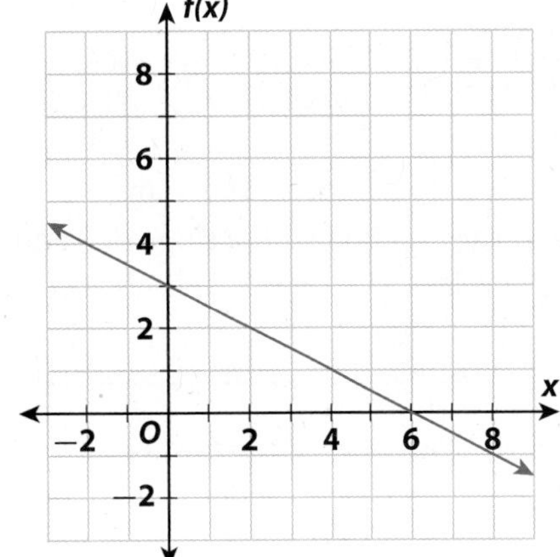

____

11. **Represent Real-World Problems** Javier begins to save for a new bicycle that costs \$415. He already has \$140 and plans to save \$25 per week. Let w represent the number of weeks he has been saving and $s(w)$ represent the total amount in dollars that he has saved. How long does he have to save to buy the bicycle?

a. Give the slope and the y-intercept of the function.

____

b. Write a linear function using the given information. ______________

c. Describe how to use the function to answer the question, and then answer the question.

____

12. The graph shows the amount of gas remaining in the gas tank of Mrs. Liu's car as she drives at a steady speed for 2 hours. How long can she drive before her car runs out of gas?

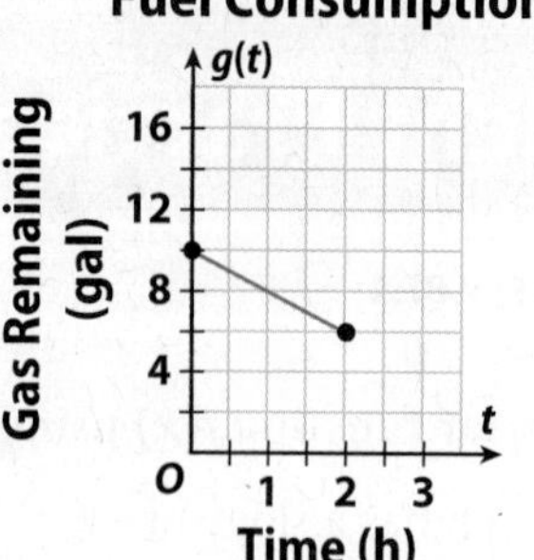

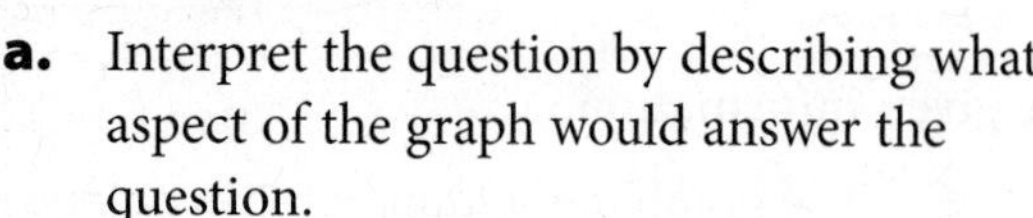

a. Interpret the question by describing what aspect of the graph would answer the question.

____

____

b. Write a linear function whose graph includes the segment shown.

____

c. Describe how to use the function to answer the question, and then answer the question.

____

____

H.O.T. FOCUS ON HIGHER ORDER THINKING

Work Area

13. **Draw Conclusions** Maria and Sam are asked to write an equation representing a linear function with a slope of 2 and y-intercept of -3. Maria writes $y = 2x - 3$. Sam writes $2x - y = 3$. Who is correct? Explain.

____

14. **Communicate Mathematical Ideas** You are given a table of values that represent a function, but you are not told whether the function is linear. How could you use the table to determine whether the function is linear?

____

____

____

____

15. **Explain the Error** Andrew was told that a linear function had a slope of 3 and that $(-2, 0)$ was on the graph. He wrote the function as $f(x) = 3x - 2$. What error did Andrew make? Write the function correctly.

____

____

____

Ready to Go On?

Personal Math Trainer

Online Practice and Help

6.1–6.2 Linear Functions/Using Intercepts

Tell whether each equation is a linear function. If so, give the intercepts.

1. $12x + 3y = 6$ ______

2. $-x^2 + 6y = 24$ ______

3. $6x - \frac{1}{2}y = 3$ ______

6.3–6.4 Using Slope/Slope-Intercept Form

Rewrite in slope-intercept form. Find the slope and y-intercept.

4. $2x + 2y = 8$ ______ ______

5. $8x - 4y = 24$ ______ ______

6. $9 = 3y$ ______ ______

6.5–6.6 Comparing/Transforming Linear Functions

7. Graph each linear function. Compare their domains and ranges. Describe the effect of the parameters on each graph compared to the graph of $y = x$.

a. $f(x) = 3x - 2$

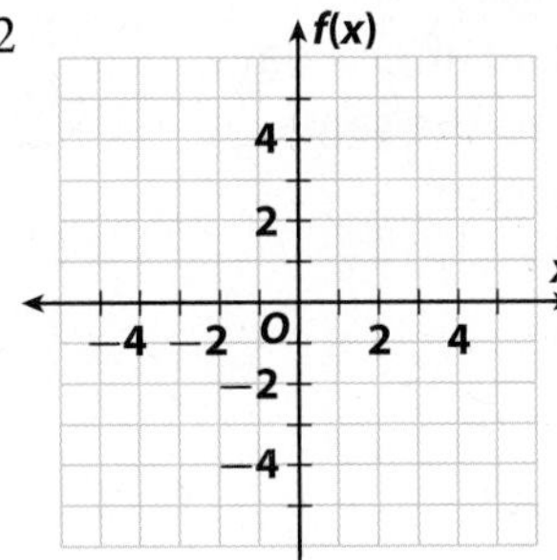

b. $f(x) = \frac{1}{3}x + 2$

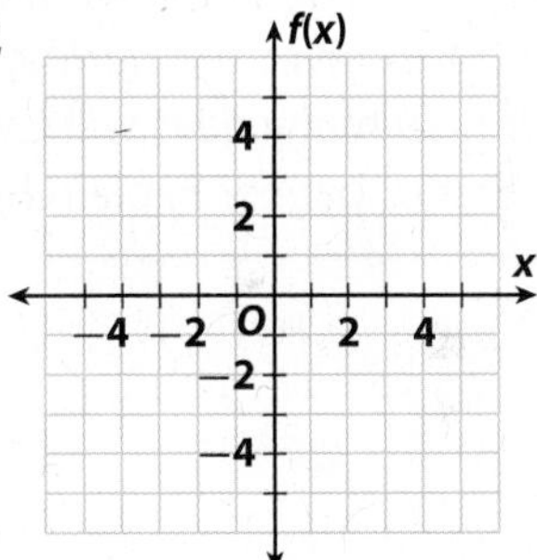

______

______

______

6.7 Writing Linear Functions

8. The graph of the linear function $f(x)$ has a slope of $-\frac{3}{2}$ and a y-intercept of -1. Write an equation for the function. ______

ESSENTIAL QUESTION

9. What are some ways that linear functions can be represented? Give an example of how different representations are related.

______

______

MODULE 6
MIXED REVIEW

Assessment Readiness

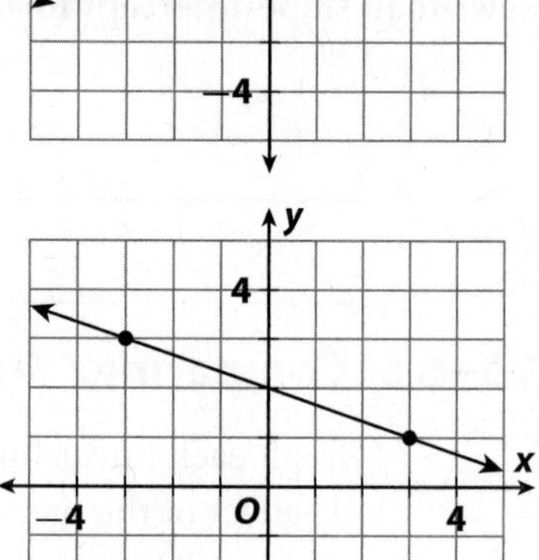

1. Is the graph of each linear function steeper than the one shown at the right?

Select Yes or No for functions A–C.

A. $f(x) = 0.5(x + 2)$ ◯ Yes ◯ No

B. $f(x) = 1 + 2x$ ◯ Yes ◯ No

C. $f(x) = \frac{3}{4}x + 1$ ◯ Yes ◯ No

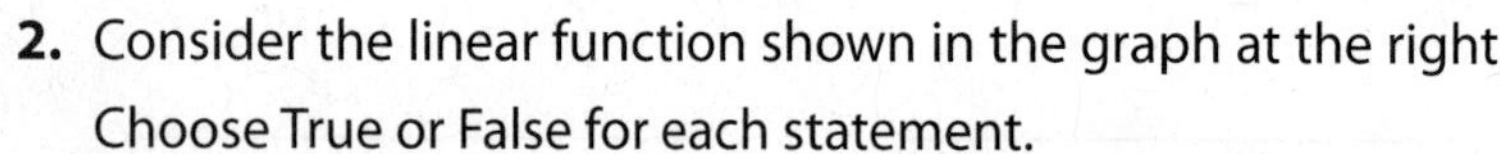

2. Consider the linear function shown in the graph at the right.

Choose True or False for each statement.

A. The slope is $-\frac{1}{3}$. ◯ True ◯ False

B. The function has no x-intercept. ◯ True ◯ False

C. The y-intercept is 2. ◯ True ◯ False

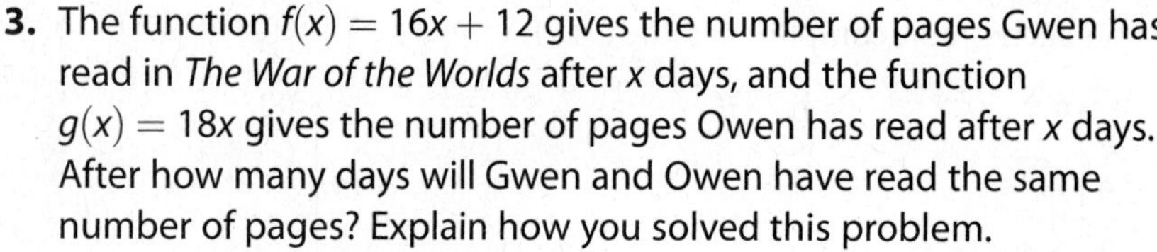

3. The function $f(x) = 16x + 12$ gives the number of pages Gwen has read in *The War of the Worlds* after x days, and the function $g(x) = 18x$ gives the number of pages Owen has read after x days. After how many days will Gwen and Owen have read the same number of pages? Explain how you solved this problem.

4. A truck driver is traveling from Sacramento to Reno. After 1 hour, the driver is 84 miles from Reno. After 2 hours, the driver is 36 miles from Reno. Write the linear function that relates the time x in hours since leaving Sacramento to the driver's distance y in miles from Reno. Explain the meaning of the slope and y-intercept in this situation.

Building Linear Functions

MODULE 7

CALIFORNIA COMMON CORE

LESSON 7.1
Arithmetic Sequences
CA CC F.BF.2, F.IF.3, F.BF.1a, F.LE.2

LESSON 7.2
Operations with Linear Functions
CA CC F.BF.1, F.BF.1b, F.LE.2

LESSON 7.3
Linear Inequalities in Two Variables
CA CC A.REI.12

ESSENTIAL QUESTION

How are mathematical operations related to solving linear equations and inequalities and creating new functions?

Real-World Video

Periodic comets have orbital periods of less than 200 years. Halley's comet is the only short-period comet that is visible to the eye. It returns every 76 years. You can build functions to represent and model predictable occurrences, such the recurrence of Halley's comet.

my.hrw.com

GO DIGITAL
my.hrw.com

my.hrw.com

Go digital with your write-in student edition, accessible on any device.

Math On the Spot

Scan with your smart phone to jump directly to the online edition, video tutor, and more.

Animated Math

Interactively explore key concepts to see how math works.

Personal Math Trainer

Get immediate feedback and help as you work through practice sets.

Are YOU Ready?

Complete these exercises to review skills you will need for this module.

Evaluate Expressions

EXAMPLE Evaluate $3x - 1$ for $x = 2$.

$3(2) - 1$ Substitute 2 for x.

$6 - 1$ Simplify.

5

Evaluate each expression for $x = -3$, 0, and 3.

1. $2x - 3$

2. $\frac{2}{3}x + 1$

3. $-2x + 4$

4. $-x$

5. $x - 5$

6. $\frac{x}{2}$

Solve for a Variable

EXAMPLE Solve $4x - 2y = 10$ for y.

$$4x - 2y = 10$$

$$-2y = -4x + 10 \quad \text{Subtract } 4x \text{ from both sides.}$$

$$y = 2x - 5 \quad \text{Divide both sides by } -2.$$

Solve each equation for y.

7. $y + 2 = 3x$

8. $2x - \frac{3}{4}y = -6$

9. $14 = x + (-2y)$

Solve and Graph Inequalities

EXAMPLE Solve and graph $x - 9 > -10$.

$$x - 9 > -10$$

$$+9 > +9 \quad \text{Add 9 to both sides.}$$

$$x > -1$$

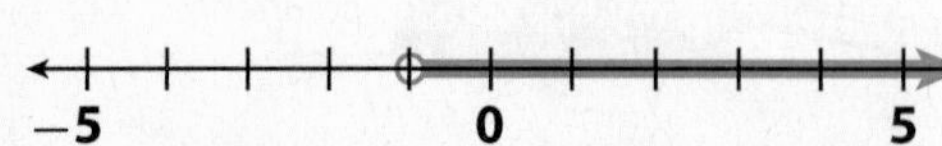

Use an open circle for >.

Solve and graph each inequality.

10. $1 > x - 3$

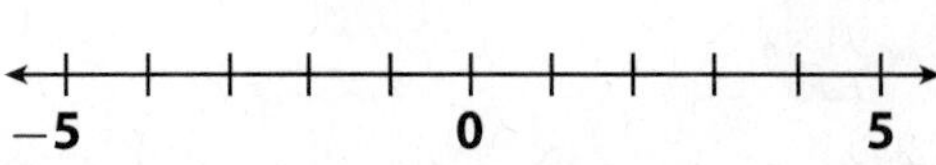

11. $-5x \leq -15$

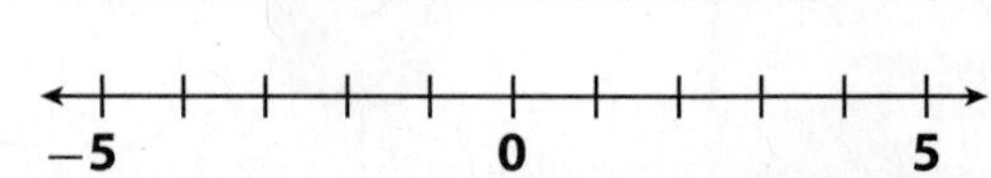

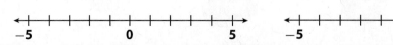

Reading Start-Up

Visualize Vocabulary

Use the Review words to complete the bubble map. You may put more than one word in each bubble. Some words may not be used.

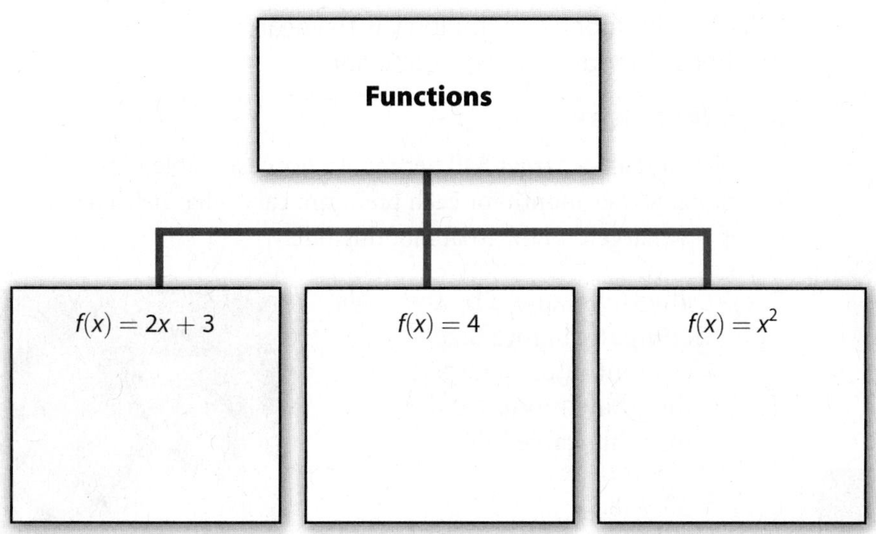

Vocabulary

Review Words

- constant function *(función constante)*
- function *(función)*
- function rule *(fórmula de función)*
- inequality *(desigualdad)*
- linear function *(función lineal)*
- nonlinear function *(función no lineal)*
- rate of change *(tasa de cambio)*

Preview Words

- arithmetic sequence
- boundary line
- common difference
- function of *x*
- half-plane
- linear inequality
- one-to-one function
- solution of an inequality

Understand Vocabulary

To become familiar with some of the vocabulary terms in the module, consider the following. You may refer to the module, the glossary, or a dictionary.

1. Functions in which each *y*-value corresponds to only one *x*-value are called ________________________.

2. The term **boundary line** refers to part of the graph of a linear inequality. What part of the graph do you think **boundary line** refers to?

____

Active Reading

Four-Corner Fold Before beginning the module, create a four-corner fold to help you organize what you learn. As you study this module, note important ideas, vocabulary, properties, and formulas on the flaps. Use one flap for each lesson in the module. You can use your FoldNote later to study for tests and complete assignments.

GETTING READY FOR

Building Linear Functions

Understanding the standards and the vocabulary terms in the standards will help you know exactly what you are expected to learn in this module.

CA CC F.BF.1

Write a function that describes a relationship between two quantities.

Key Vocabulary

function *(función)*
A type of relation that pairs each element in the domain with exactly one element in the range.

What It Means to You

You can add, subtract, or multiply with linear functions to model real-world situations.

EXAMPLE F.BF.1

A cable company charges \$40 per month for basic cable plus an additional \$8 per month for each premium cable channel. There is a tax of 9% charged on the total monthly bill.

$C(c)$ = amount charged by the cable company before taxes
$R(c)$ = amount of tax charged
$T(c)$ = the total amount of the monthly cable bill

$C(c) = 40 + 8c$
$R(c) = 0.09$
$T(c) = C(c) \times R(c) = 3.6 + 0.72c$

CA CC A.REI.12

Graph the solutions to a linear inequality in two variables as a half-plane (excluding the boundary in the case of a strict inequality), and graph the solution set to a system of linear inequalities in two variables as the intersection of the corresponding half-planes.

Key Vocabulary

linear inequality in two variables *(desigualdad lineal en dos variables)*
An inequality that can be written in one of the following forms: $Ax + By < C$, $Ax + By > C$, $Ax + By \leq C$, $Ax + By \geq C$, or $Ax + By \neq C$, where A, B, and C are constants and A and B are not both 0.

What It Means to You

You can graph a linear inequality in a coordinate plane to represent a set of solutions.

EXAMPLE A.REI.12

Graph the solution set for the inequality $-2x + y \leq 3$.

STEP 1 First solve the inequality for y.

$-2x + y \leq 3$

$y \leq 3 + 2x$ — Add $2x$ to both sides.

$y \leq 2x + 3$ — Write in standard form.

STEP 2 Graph the boundary line. The line is solid because the inequality uses the symbol $\leq$.

STEP 3 Because the symbol is $\leq$, shade the part of the plane below the boundary line.

Visit **my.hrw.com** to see all **CA Common Core Standards** explained.

my.hrw.com

LESSON 7.1

Arithmetic Sequences

CA CC F.BF.2

Write arithmetic and geometric sequences both recursively and with an explicit formula, use them to model situations, and translate between the two forms. *Also F.IF.3, F.BF.1a, F.LE.2*

ESSENTIAL QUESTION

How are rules for arithmetic sequences and linear functions alike, and how are they different?

EXPLORE ACTIVITY 

Exploring Arithmetic Sequences

Avocados cost \$1.50 each at the local market. The total cost, in dollars, of a avocados can be found using $C(a) = 1.5a$.

A Complete the table of values for $C(a) = 1.5a$.

Avocados	1	2	3	4
Total Cost (\$)				

B List the consecutive elements of the range. ____________

C What is the difference between any two consecutive elements of the range? ____________

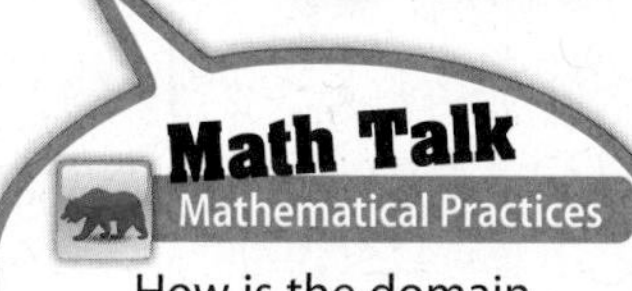

Math Talk
Mathematical Practices
How is the domain limited for this situation?

Writing Rules for an Arithmetic Sequence

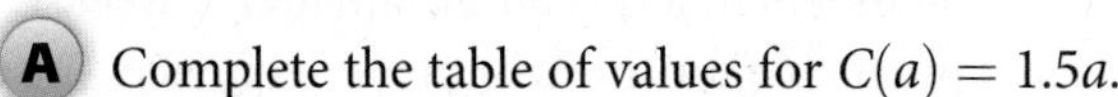

In an **arithmetic sequence**, the difference between consecutive terms is always the same. The constant difference is called the **common difference**, often written as d.

Rules for arithmetic sequences can be *recursive* or *explicit*. A **recursive rule** gives the first term and defines the nth term by relating it to the previous term. An **explicit rule** defines the nth term as a function of n.

EXAMPLE 1 

This table shows the end-of-month balances in a bank account that does not earn interest. Write a recursive rule and an explicit rule for the arithmetic sequence described by the table.

Month	n	1	2	3	4	5
Account Balance (\$)	$f(n)$	60	80	100	120	140

Write the recursive rule.

$f(1) = 60$ — $f(1)$ is the first term.

$f(n) = 20 + f(n-1)$ for $n \geq 2$ — All other terms are the sum of the previous term and the common difference.

Write the explicit rule.

n	$f(n)$	$f(1) + d \cdot x = f(n)$
1	60	$60 + 20(0) = 60$
2	80	$60 + 20(1) = 80$
3	100	$60 + 20(2) = 100$

Remember, d is the difference between two consecutive terms.

Since d is always multiplied by a number equal to $(n - 1)$, we can generalize the results from the table: $f(n) = 60 + 20(n - 1)$.

YOUR TURN

1. The table shows the number of members in a theater group after n weeks. Write a recursive rule and an explicit rule for the arithmetic sequence.

Week	n	1	2	3	4	5
Members	$f(n)$	35	47	59	71	83

____

____

General Rules for Arithmetic Sequences

Arithmetic sequences can be described by general rules. You can substitute values into the general rules to find the recursive rule and explicit rule for a given sequence.

General Recursive Rule	General Explicit Rule
Given $f(1)$, $f(n) = f(n - 1) + d$ for $n \geq 2$	$f(n) = f(1) + d(n - 1)$

EXAMPLE 2

Write a recursive rule and an explicit rule for the sequence 6, 9, 12, 15, 18…

Write the recursive rule.

Given $f(1)$, $f(n) = f(n - 1) + d$ for $n \geq 2$ — Write the general form.

$f(1) = 6$, $f(n) = f(n - 1) + 3$ for $n \geq 2$ — Use $f(1) = 6$. Substitute 3 for d.

The recursive rule is $f(1) = 6$, $f(n) = f(n - 1) + 3$ for $n \geq 2$.

Write the explicit rule.

$$f(n) = f(1) + d(n - 1)$$ Write the general form.

$$f(n) = 6 + 3(n - 1)$$ Substitute 6 for $f(1)$ and 3 for d.

The explicit rule is $f(n) = 6 + 3(n - 1)$.

YOUR TURN

2. Write a recursive rule and an explicit rule for the arithmetic sequence 20, 25, 30, 35, . . .

____

____

Relating Arithmetic Sequences and Linear Functions

The explicit rule for an arithmetic sequence can be expressed as a linear function. You can use the graph of a linear function to help you write an explicit rule.

EXAMPLE 3

CA CC F.BF.2, F.LE.2

The graph shows how the cost of a whitewater rafting trip depends on the number of passengers. Write an explicit rule for the sequence of costs.

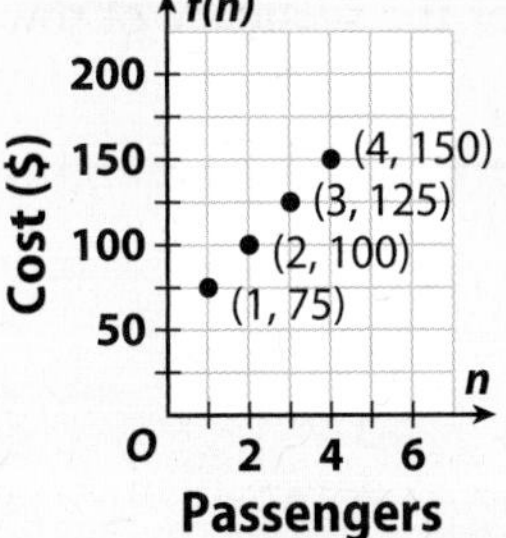

STEP 1 Represent the sequence in a table.

n	1	2	3	4
$f(n)$	75	100	125	150

STEP 2 Find the common difference.

$100 - 75 = 25$ Find the difference between two consecutive terms.

$125 - 100 = 25$

$150 - 125 = 25$ $d = 25$

STEP 3 Write an explicit rule for the sequence.

$$f(n) = f(1) + d(n - 1)$$

$$f(n) = 75 + 25(n - 1)$$

Start with the general rule, then substitute values to find the explicit rule.

YOUR TURN

3. Ed collects autographs. The graph shows the number of autographs that Ed has collected over time. Determine the explicit rule for the sequence.

____

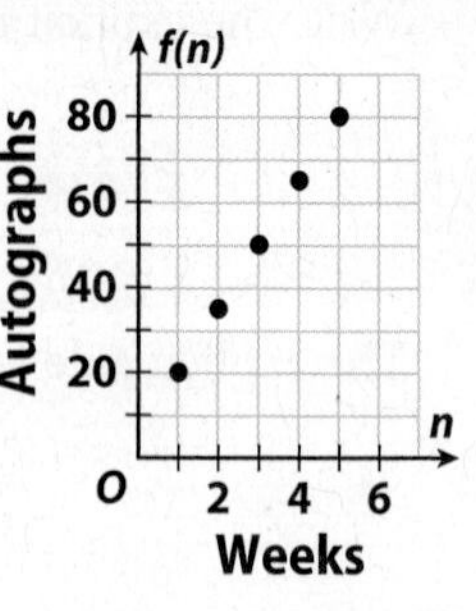

Guided Practice

Write a recursive rule and an explicit rule for the sequence. (Examples 1 and 2)

1.

n	1	2	3	4	5
$f(n)$	6	7	8	9	10

$f(1) = 6,$

$f(n) = f(\square) + \square$ for $n \geq 2;$

$f(n) = \square + \square$

2. 3, 7, 11, 15,. . .

____

____

Write an explicit rule for the sequence. (Example 3)

3. The graph shows the lengths of the rows formed by various numbers of grocery carts when they are nested together. Write an explicit rule for the sequence of row lengths.

____

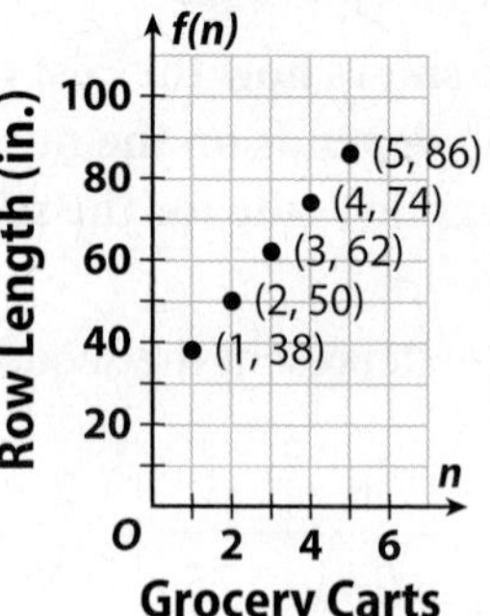

ESSENTIAL QUESTION CHECK-IN

4. What two values do you need to know in order to write a recursive rule and an explicit rule for an arithmetic sequence?

____

____

Name _______________ Class _______________ Date _______________

7.1 Independent Practice

5. Write a recursive rule and an explicit rule for each sequence.

n	1	2	3	4	5
f(n)	27	24	21	18	15

6.

n	1	2	3	4	5
f(n)	3	6	9	12	15

7. Write a recursive rule and an explicit rule for the arithmetic sequence 9, 24, 39, 54,. . .

8. Write a recursive rule and an explicit rule for the arithmetic sequence 19, 9, −1, −11,. . .

9. Write a recursive rule and an explicit rule for the arithmetic sequence 1, 2.5, 4, 5.5, . . .

10. The explicit rule for an arithmetic sequence is $f(n) = 6 + 5(n - 1)$. What are the first three terms? _______________

11. The explicit rule for an arithmetic sequence is $f(n) = 1 + 3(n - 1)$. What are the fourth and fortieth terms? _______________

12. Indicate whether the sequence is arithmetic. If it is, list the common difference. −21, −18, −15, −12,. . .

13. The first term of an arithmetic sequence is 4, and the common difference is 10. How can you find the sixth term of the sequence?

14. Carrie borrowed money interest-free to pay for a car repair. The table shows how much money remains for Carrie to pay back after making *n* monthly payments.

Monthly Payment Number	n	1	2	3	4	5
Loan Balance ($)	f(n)	840	720	600	480	360

a. Explain how you know that the sequence of loan balances is arithmetic.

b. Write recursive and explicit rules for the sequence of loan balances.

c. How many months will it take Carrie to pay off the loan? Explain.

d. How much money did Carrie borrow? Explain.

H.O.T. FOCUS ON HIGHER ORDER THINKING

Work Area

15. Explain the Error The cost of postage for a 1-ounce letter is \$0.46. Each additional ounce costs \$0.20. Cindy wrote this explicit rule to describe the sequence of costs: $f(n) = 0.20 + 0.46(n - 1)$. She then determined the cost of postage for a 6-ounce letter to be \$2.46. Is she correct? If not, identify her error.

16. Communicate Mathematical Ideas What do all arithmetic sequences have in common?

17. Critical Thinking Trevor knows that the 5th term in a sequence is 32, and the 7th term in the same sequence is 48. Explain how he can find the common difference for this sequence.

18. Represent Real-World Problems Describe a situation whose sequence could be represented by the explicit rule $f(n) = 8 + 3(n - 1)$.

LESSON 7.2

Operations with Linear Functions

CA CC F.BF.1b

Combine standard function types using arithmetic operations. *Also F.BF.1, F.LE.2*

ESSENTIAL QUESTION

How can you use operations with linear functions to model real-world situations?

Adding and Subtracting Linear Functions

You can add and subtract linear functions just as you would add and subtract any two expressions. When adding and subtracting functions, be sure to use a different letter to name each function, like $h(x) = f(x) + g(x)$.

EXAMPLE 1

CA CC F.BF.1b

Given the linear functions $f(x) = 2x + 9$ and $g(x) = 6x - 1$, find each new function.

A $h(x) = f(x) + g(x)$

$h(x) = (2x + 9) + (6x - 1)$ Substitute for $f(x)$ and $g(x)$.

$h(x) = (2x + 6x) + (9 - 1)$ Combine like terms.

$h(x) = 8x + 8$ Simplify.

B $j(x) = f(x) - g(x)$

$j(x) = (2x + 9) - (6x - 1)$ Substitute for $f(x)$ and $g(x)$.

$j(x) = (2x + 9) - 6x + 1$ Multiply by -1.

$j(x) = (2x - 6x) + (9 + 1)$ Combine like terms.

$j(x) = -4x + 10$ Simplify.

REFLECT

1. **Critical Thinking** James thinks that $f(x) - g(x)$ and $g(x) - f(x)$ are equal when $f(x) = 3x + 6$ and $g(x) = 5x + 2$. Is he correct? Explain.

____

____

YOUR TURN

2. Given $f(x) = 3x + 4$ and $g(x) = -x + 2$, find the sum $h(x) = f(x) + g(x)$ and the difference $j(x) = f(x) - g(x)$.

____

Multiplying Linear and Constant Functions

Multiplying a linear function by a constant function is similar to using the Distributive Property. When you multiply a linear function by a constant, the result is also a linear function.

My Notes

EXAMPLE 2

Given the linear functions $f(x) = 4$ and $g(x) = -3x + 2$, find the linear function $h(x) = f(x) \times g(x)$.

$h(x) = f(x) \times g(x)$

$h(x) = (4)(-3x + 2)$ Substitute for $f(x)$ and $g(x)$.

$h(x) = -12x + 8$ Multiply using the Distributive Property.

REFLECT

3. **Critical Thinking** Enrique knows that $f(x)$ is a constant function and that $g(x) = 5x + 6$. If $f(x) \times g(x) = 0$, determine $f(x)$.

4. **Explain the Error** Kelly thinks that the product of $f(x) = 6$ and $g(x) = 4x + 8$ is $24x + 8$. Is she correct? If not, explain her error.

YOUR TURN

Given the constant function $f(x)$ and the linear function $g(x)$, find the linear function $h(x) = f(x) \times g(x)$.

5. $f(x) = 7$, $g(x) = 4x - 2$

6. $f(x) = -3$, $g(x) = 2x - 11$

7. $f(x) = \frac{1}{2}$, $g(x) = 14x - 8$

Adding Linear Models

Real-world problems can often be solved by writing linear functions to model the situations, then adding the linear functions as you did in Example 1.

EXAMPLE 3

CA CC F.BF.1b, F.LE.2

Harriet rides from her house to her job using Friendly Taxi Company, which charges \$5 plus \$1.35 per mile. After work, Harriet uses the Great Taxi company to go home. They charge \$2 plus \$1.85 per mile. Find the total amount that Harriet spent on cab rides as a function of x, the distance in miles between her house and her job.

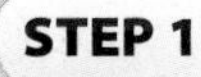

STEP 1 Write $f(x)$, the cost of the Friendly Taxi cab ride, as a function of x.

$f(x) = 5 + 1.35x$

STEP 2 Write $g(x)$, the cost of the Great Taxi cab ride, as a function of x.

$g(x) = 2 + 1.85x$

STEP 3 Write $t(x)$, the total cost of both cab rides, as a function of x. Find the sum of the costs of each taxi ride.

$t(x) = f(x) + g(x)$

$t(x) = (5 + 1.35x) + (2 + 1.85x)$ Substitute for $f(x)$ and $g(x)$.

$t(x) = (1.35x + 1.85x) + (5 + 2)$ Combine like terms.

$t(x) = 3.2x + 7$ Simplify.

The cost of Harriet's rides can be represented by $t(x) = 3.2x + 7$.

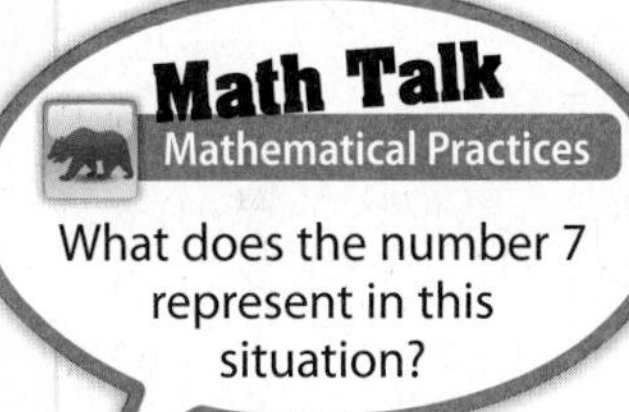

Math Talk
Mathematical Practices
What does the number 7 represent in this situation?

REFLECT

8. What If? Describe the change to $t(x)$ if Harriet used Friendly Taxi to travel to and from her job.

____

YOUR TURN

9. A tennis club is formed for boys and girls. In the first year, 4 boys and 5 girls join the club. Each year after, 2 more boys and 1 more girl join the club. Let t be the number of years since the club was formed. Find a rule for the function $f(t)$, representing the total number of club members.

____

Multiplying Linear and Constant Models

Some real-world situations are modeled by constant functions. To multiply these functions, use the same steps as in Example 2.

EXAMPLE 4 

A phone company charges \$20 a month for service plus \$0.05 per minute for calls. Tax is added to the total charge, and the tax rate is 8%. Find the amount of tax on a monthly bill for *t* minutes of calls.

My Notes

STEP 1 Write $f(t)$, the amount charged by the phone company before taxes for service and t minutes of calls.

$f(t) = 20 + 0.05t$

STEP 2 Write $g(t)$, the tax rate applied to phone company charges.

$g(t) = 0.08$

STEP 3 Write $h(t)$, the tax charged for a monthly bill with t minutes of calls. Find the product of the amount charged by the phone company $f(t)$ and the constant tax rate $g(t)$.

$h(t) = f(t) \times g(t)$

$h(t) = (20 + 0.05t)(0.08)$ Substitute for $f(t)$ and $g(t)$.

$h(t) = 1.6 + 0.004t$ Multiply using the distributive property.

The amount of tax on a monthly bill for t minutes of calls is $h(t) = 1.6 + 0.004t$.

REFLECT

10. **Interpret the Answer** Interpret the number 1.6 in the simplified form of $h(t)$ in Example 4.

____

____

YOUR TURN

11. Sunshine Coffee Shop has 8 employees working, each of whom buy a large coffee. During the day, they sell x large coffees to customers. Each large coffee costs \$1.75. Write a function $c(x)$ that represents the amount of money Sunshine Coffee Shop made selling large coffees.

____

Guided Practice

Given the functions $f(x) = 3x + 9$ and $g(x) = -2x + 5$, find each new function. (Example 1)

1. $h(x) = f(x) + g(x)$

$h(x) = (3x + 9) + (\boxed{})$

$h(x) = (3x + \boxed{}) +$

$(9 + \boxed{})$

$h(x) = \boxed{}$

2. $j(x) = f(x) - g(x)$

$j(x) = (\boxed{}) - (-2x + 5)$

$j(x) = (\boxed{} + 2x)$

$+ (\boxed{} - 5)$

$j(x) = \boxed{}$

Given a constant function $f(x)$ and a linear function $g(x)$, find the function $h(x) = f(x) \times g(x)$. (Example 2)

3. $f(x) = 4$, $g(x) = 2x + 3$

$h(x) = f(x) \times g(x)$

$h(x) = 4(\boxed{})$

$h(x) = \boxed{}$

4. $f(x) = -2$, $g(x) = 4x - 1$

$h(x) = f(x) \times g(x)$

$h(x) = \boxed{}(4x - 1)$

$h(x) = \boxed{}$

5. Colton is making gift bags. He has 120 small prizes, and puts 3 in each gift bag. He also has 75 larger prizes, and puts 2 in each gift bag. Write the function $f(x)$ that represents how many prizes Colton has left after making x gift bags. (Example 3)

____

6. Brenda is buying 6 concert tickets online. Each ticket costs $15, plus a service fee of x dollars. Write the function $g(x)$ that shows the total amount that Brenda will pay for the tickets. (Example 4)

____

ESSENTIAL QUESTION CHECK-IN

7. How is the sum or difference of linear functions related to the equations for the functions?

____

____

____

Name ______________________ Class ______________ Date ______________

7.2 Independent Practice

F.BF.1, F.BF.1b, F.LE.2

Personal Math Trainer

Online Practice and Help

Given the functions $f(x)$ and $g(x)$, find the function $h(x) = f(x) + g(x)$.

8. $f(x) = 2x + 9$, $g(x) = 8x - 3$

____

9. $f(x) = 17x - 1$, $g(x) = 5x + 5$

____

10. $f(x) = -x - 2$, $g(x) = 4x - 3$

____

Given the functions $f(x)$ and $g(x)$, find the function $h(x) = f(x) - g(x)$.

11. $f(x) = 4x + 10$, $g(x) = -2x + 8$

____

12. $f(x) = 3x - 1$, $g(x) = 12x + 2$

____

13. $f(x) = 6x + 7$, $g(x) = x + 6$

____

Given the functions $f(x)$ and $g(x)$, find the function $h(x) = f(x) \times g(x)$.

14. $f(x) = 3$, $g(x) = 7x + 1$

____

15. $f(x) = -2$, $g(x) = 4x - 6$

____

16. $f(x) = \frac{1}{3}$, $g(x) = 9x - 6$

____

17. A school is raising money for new desks. They have collected \$400 in donations, and are hosting a dinner, which costs \$10 to attend. Every person at the dinner buys a \$2 raffle ticket, and the winner of the raffle gets \$500.

a. Write a rule for the function $R(t)$, the profit the school makes on the raffle.

____

b. Write a rule for the function $D(t)$, the earnings made from the donations and dinner.

____

c. Describe how the function $T(t)$, the total amount of money raised by the school for new desks, is related to $R(t)$ and $D(t)$. Then, write a rule for $T(t)$.

____

18. A birthday party is being planned for 20 people at an arcade. It costs \$5 a person to provide food for everyone, and each game costs \$1 per play. Assume that each person at the party plays the same number of games, x.

a. Write a rule for the function $C(x)$, the total cost per person.

____

b. Write a rule for the function $n(x)$, the number of people who attend.

____

c. Describe how the function $T(x)$, the total cost of the party, can be obtained from the functions $C(x)$ and $n(x)$. Then, write a rule for $T(x)$.

____

19. Randy and Heloise both open savings accounts. Randy opens his savings account with \$7 and deposits \$10 every week. Heloise opens her savings account with \$82 and withdraws \$5 every week.

a. Write a function $r(x)$ to represent the amount of money Randy has in his savings account after x weeks.

____

b. Write a function $h(x)$ to represent the amount of money Heloise has in her savings account after x weeks.

____

c. Write a function $b(x)$ to represent the combined total in both savings accounts after x weeks.

____

d. When Randy has \$47 in his savings account, what is the combined total in both accounts?

____

e. When Heloise has \$47 in her savings account, what is the combined total in both accounts?

____

20. A police department issues speeding tickets for \$50 plus an additional dollar for each mile per hour over the speed limit the driver was going. Half of the money from speeding tickets goes toward buying new equipment for the police officers. Write a rule for the function $E(x)$, the amount of money for new equipment generated by a ticket for driving x miles per hour over the speed limit.

____

21. Use the information in the table below to answer the following questions.

x	f(x)	g(x)
0	3	−2
2	−1	4
5	−7	13

a. Use the table to write rules for the functions $f(x)$ and $g(x)$.

____

____

b. Find the sum $h(x) = f(x) + g(x)$ and the difference $j(x) = f(x) - g(x)$.

____

____

c. Compare the functions $h(x)$ and $j(x)$ when $x = 3$.

____

22. A new computer is valued at \$1,000, and its value depreciates by \$150 per year. A new printer is valued at \$100, and its value depreciates by \$5 per year.

a. Write a rule for the combined value of the computer and printer in terms of t, the time in years since the equipment was purchased.

____

b. When will the computer and the printer have a combined value of \$480?

____

c. When the computer is worth \$100, how much will the combined value of the computer and the printer be?

____

H.O.T. FOCUS ON HIGHER ORDER THINKING

Work Area

23. Persevere in Problem Solving Let $f(x) = 3$, $g(x) = -2x + 5$, and $h(x) = x - 4$.

a. Find the function $j(x) = f(x) \times [g(x) + h(x)]$.

b. Find the function $k(x) = [f(x) \times g(x)] + [f(x) \times h(x)]$.

c. Find the function $l(x) = j(x) - k(x)$.

d. Explain how you could find $l(x)$ without finding $j(x)$ or $k(x)$.

24. Interpret the Answer Suppose $B(t)$ is a linear function representing the number of boys who attend a school in year t, and $G(t)$ is a linear function representing the number of girls who attend the same school in year t. What does the function $T(t) = G(t) + B(t)$ represent?

25. Analyze Relationships The function $f(x) = 3x + 3$. Find the function $g(x)$ such that $f(x) + g(x) = 0$ and $f(x) - g(x) = 2 \times f(x)$. What is the relationship between $f(x)$ and $g(x)$? Explain.

26. Analyze Relationships Is it possible for $f(x) - g(x)$ to equal $g(x) - f(x)$? If so, explain how.

LESSON 7.3

Linear Inequalities in Two Variables

CA CC A.REI.12

For the full text of this standard, see the table beginning on page CA2.

ESSENTIAL QUESTION

How do you graph a linear inequality in two variables?

Graphing a Linear Inequality

A **linear inequality** results when you replace the $=$ sign in a linear equation by $<, >, \leq$, or $\geq$. For example, $7x + 14 \leq 28y$ is a linear inequality. A **solution of an inequality** is any ordered pair (x, y) that makes the inequality true.

EXAMPLE 1

CA CC A.REI.12

Graph the solution set for $2x - 3y \geq 6$.

STEP 1 First solve the inequality for y.

$2x - 3y \geq 6$

$-3y \geq 6 - 2x$ Subtract $2x$ from both sides.

$y \leq \frac{6 - 2x}{-3}$ Divide both sides by -3.

$y \leq -2 + \frac{2}{3}x$ Simplify.

$y \leq \frac{2}{3}x - 2$ Write in standard form.

Reverse the inequality sign when dividing both sides of an equation by a negative number.

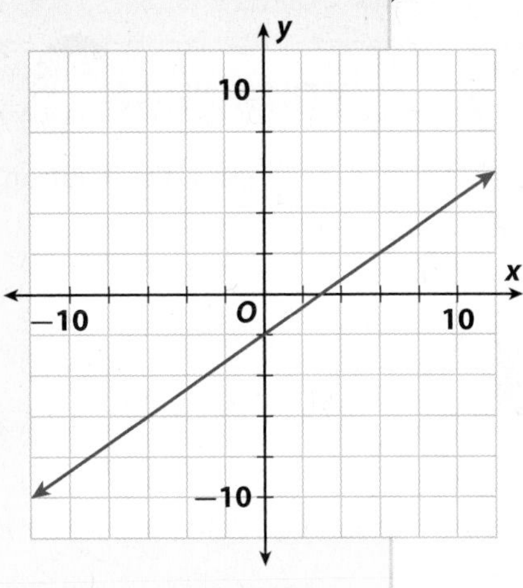

Consider the line where the inequality is replaced by an equal sign: $y = \frac{2}{3}x - 2$. The line is called the **boundary line** of the solution set.

STEP 2 Graph the boundary line. The inequality $y \leq \frac{2}{3}x - 2$ uses the symbol $\leq$, so the line will be solid, to show that the points on the line are part of the solution.

STEP 3 Shade the appropriate part of the graph. The inequality $y \leq \frac{2}{3}x - 2$ uses the symbol $\leq$, so shade below the boundary line.

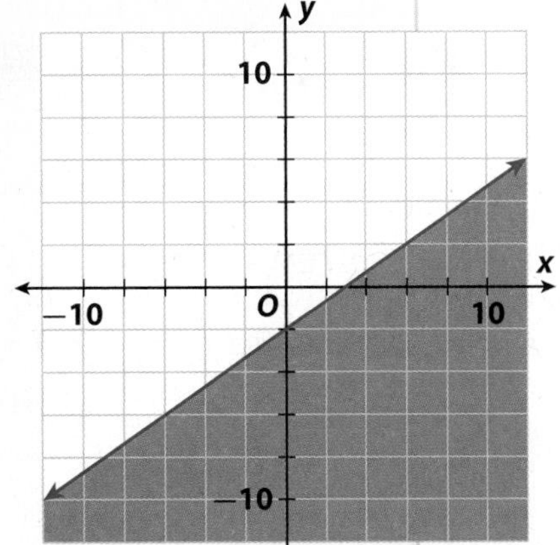

STEP 4 To check your work, choose one point above the boundary line and one point below the boundary line. Substitute both points into the original inequality, and verify that the point below the boundary line makes the inequality true.

Point	Above or Below Line	Inequality	True or False?
(0, 0)	Above	$2(0) - 3(0) \geq 6$	False
(0, −4)	Below	$2(0) - 3(-4) \geq 6$	True

The point below the line makes the inequality true, so the shaded graph is correct.

REFLECT

1. The set of solutions to an inequality is represented on a graph by a shaded region and boundary line. This area is called a **half-plane**. Why is half-plane a good name for this region?

YOUR TURN

2. Graph the solution set for $4x - 8y \geq 32$.

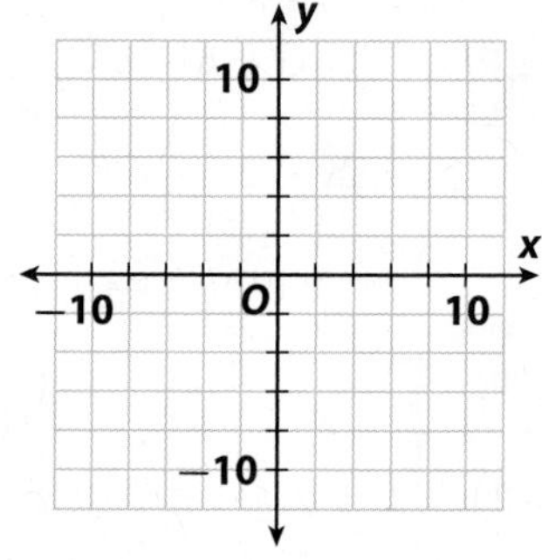

Graphing a Linear Inequality in Two Variables

EXAMPLE 2 CA CC A.REI.12

Graph the solution set for the inequality $26 + 2y > 14x$.

STEP 1 $26 + 2y > 14x$

$2y > 14x - 26$ Subtract 26 from both sides.

$y > \frac{14x - 26}{2}$ Divide both sides by 2.

$y > 7x - 13$ Simplify.

Animated Math
my.hrw.com

STEP 2 Graph the boundary line. The inequality $y > 7x - 13$ uses the symbol $>$, so use a dashed line to show that points on the line are not part of the solution.

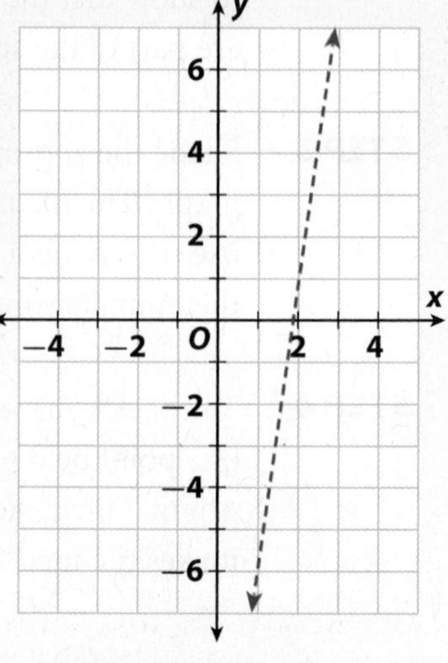

STEP 3 Shade the appropriate part of the graph. The inequality $y > 7x - 13$ uses the symbol $>$, so shade above the boundary line.

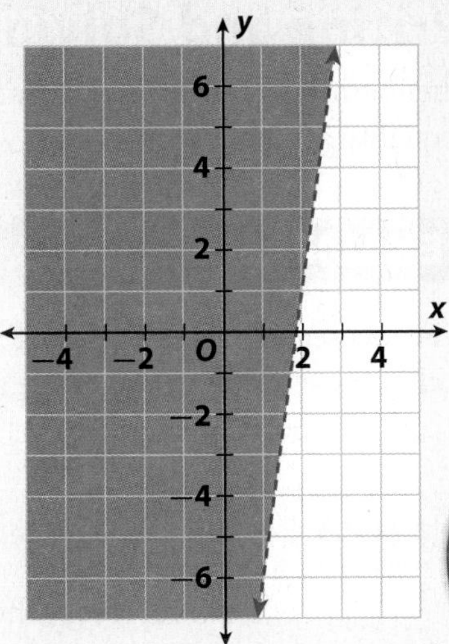

STEP 4 To check your work, choose one point above the boundary line and one point below the boundary line. Substitute both points into the original inequality, and verify that the point above the boundary line makes the inequality true.

Point	Above or Below Line	Inequality	True or False?
(0, 0)	Above	$26 + 2(0) > 14(0)$	True
(4, 0)	Below	$26 + 2(0) > 14(4)$	False

Math Talk
Mathematical Practices
How would the shaded region change if the inequality were $26 + 2y < 14x$?

REFLECT

3. For the linear inequality, $6x - 3y < 24$, which of the following is a solution: $(0, -9)$, $(6, 4)$, or $(4, 1)$?

____

____

4. Is $(4, 0)$ a solution for the inequality $6x - 3y < 24$? Explain.

____

____

____

YOUR TURN

5. Graph $6x + 3y < -12$.

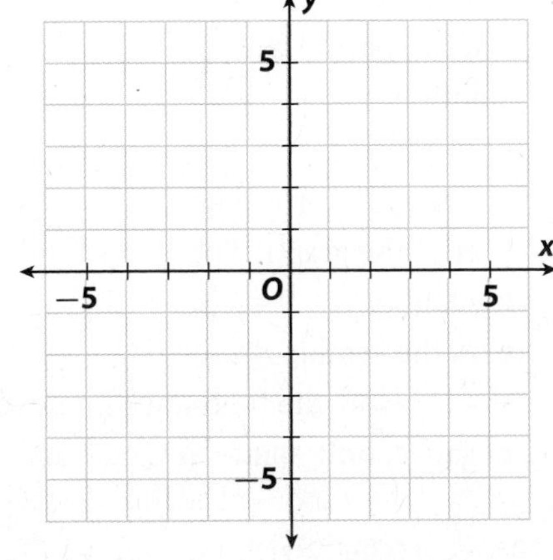

Writing and Solving Linear Inequalities

When writing a linear inequality for a situation, make sure to use the appropriate inequality symbol.

EXAMPLE 3 

Francesca can spend at most \$6.75 on healthy snacks for a party. Veggie chips cost \$1.00 per package and grapes cost \$0.75 per bunch. Find two combinations of veggie chips and grapes that Francesca can buy.

STEP 1 Write a linear inequality to describe the situation.

Let x represent the number of packages of veggie chips and let y represent the number of bunches of grapes.

Write an inequality. Use $\leq$ for "at most."

Total cost of veggie chips	plus	Total cost of grapes	is at most	\$6.75
$1.00x$	$+$	$0.75y$	$\leq$	6.75

Solve the inequality for y.

$$1.00x + 0.75y \leq 6.75$$

$$(100)(1.00x + 0.75y) \leq 100(6.75)$$ Multiply both sides of the equation by 100 to eliminate the decimals.

$$100x + 75y \leq 675$$

$$75y \leq 675 - 100x$$ Subtract $100x$ from both sides.

$$y \leq \frac{675 - 100x}{75}$$ Divide both sides by 75.

$$y \leq 9 - \frac{4}{3}x$$ Simplify.

STEP 2 Graph the boundary line. The inequality $y \leq 9 - \frac{4}{3}x$ uses the symbol $\leq$, so the line will be solid to show that the points on the line are part of the solution.

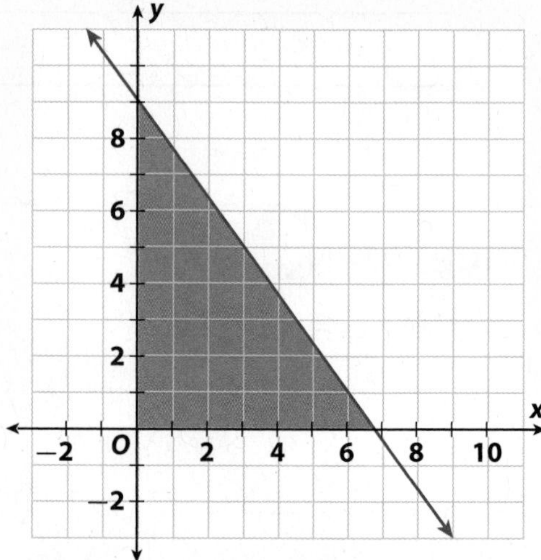

STEP 3 Shade the appropriate part of the graph. The inequality $y \leq 9 - \frac{4}{3}x$ uses the symbol $\leq$, so shade below the boundary line. Since the number of snacks cannot be negative, only shade in Quadrant 1.

STEP 4 Since the line is solid, any point on or underneath the line (in Quadrant 1) will be a solution. Choose two points, and make sure they make the inequality true.

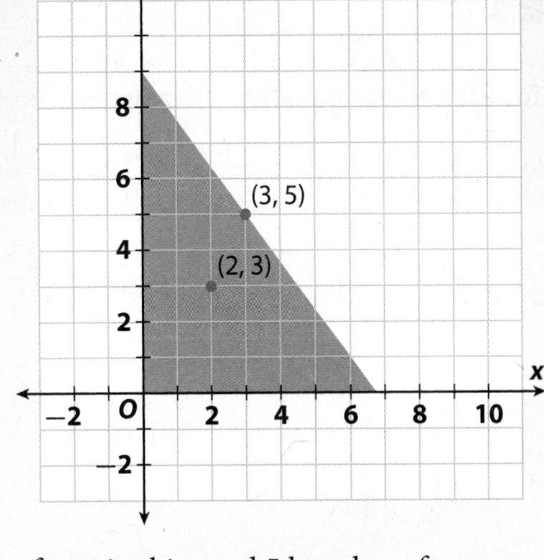

$1.00(3) + 0.75(5) \leq 6.75$
$1.00(2) + 0.75(3) \leq 6.75$

Two different combinations that Francesca could buy for $6.75 or less are 3 packages of veggie chips and 5 bunches of grapes, or 2 packages of veggie chips and 3 bunches of grapes.

REFLECT

6. **What if?** How would the graph of solutions change if grapes were sold at $0.25 per bunch?

____

My Notes

YOUR TURN

7. Lamar has $15.00 that he can spend on food for his cat. Dry cat food costs $4.50 per small bag and wet cat food costs $1.50 per tin can. Write a linear inequality that describes how many bags and cans of cat food Lamar can buy.

____

____

8. Graph the solution set of your linear inequality for Lamar.

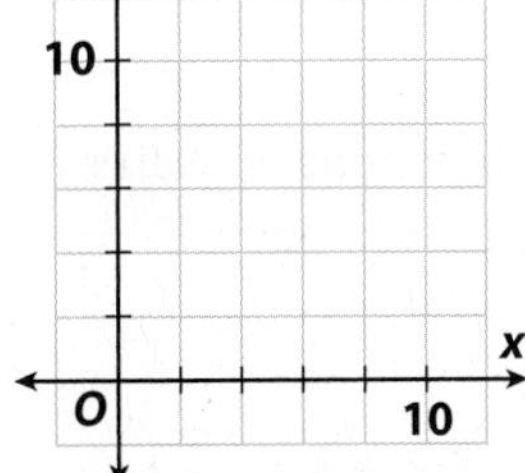

9. Identify two combinations of dry and wet cat food that Lamar can afford.

____

____

____

Guided Practice

Graph the solution set for each linear equality. (Examples 1 and 2)

1. $4y + 3x - y > -6x + 12$

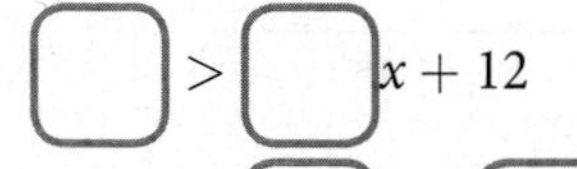

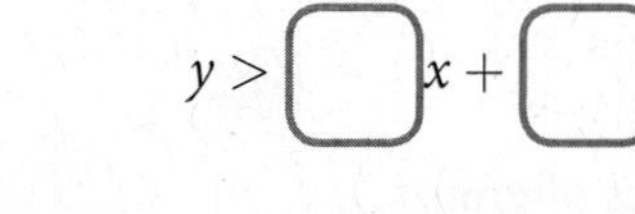

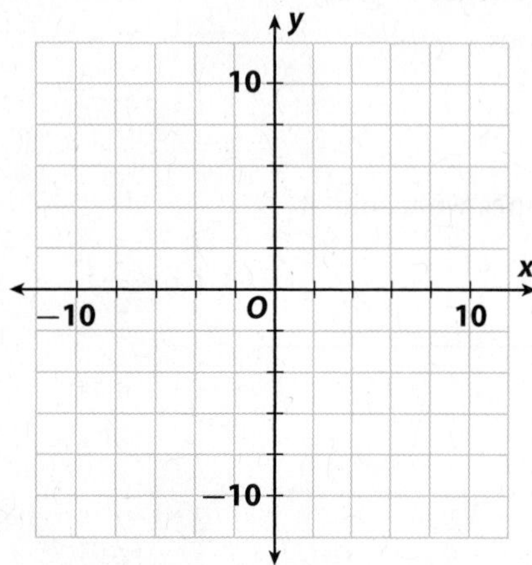

2. $5y + 3 < 2x$

$5y <$ ☐ $- 3$

$y < \frac{2}{5}x - \frac{3}{5}$

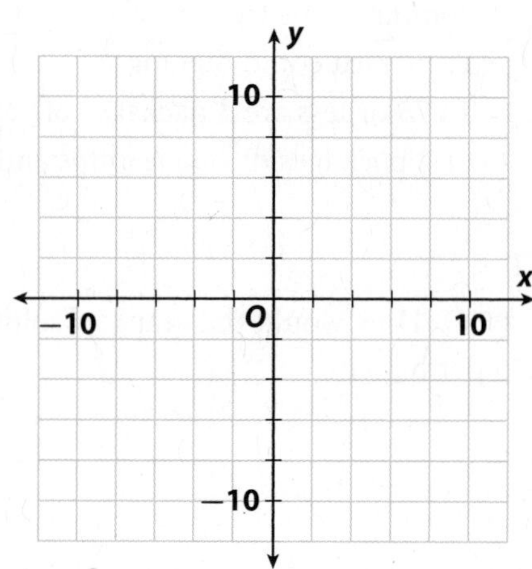

Sam is buying chairs that cost \$15 and tables that cost \$20. He wants to spend no more than \$140. (Example 3)

3. Write a linear inequality to represent the amount Sam can pay for x chairs and y tables. ________________

4. Solve the inequality for y.

____

5. Graph the inequality.

6. What are two combinations of chairs and tables that Sam could buy?

____

ESSENTIAL QUESTION CHECK-IN

7. How do you graph a linear inequality in two variables?

____

____

Name ____________________ Class ____________________ Date ____________________

7.3 Independent Practice

A.REI.12

Graph the inequality.

8. $y \leq 5$

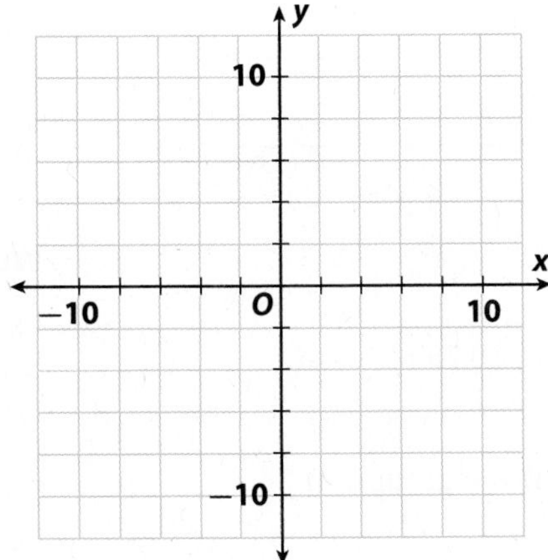

9. $x + 5y < 30$

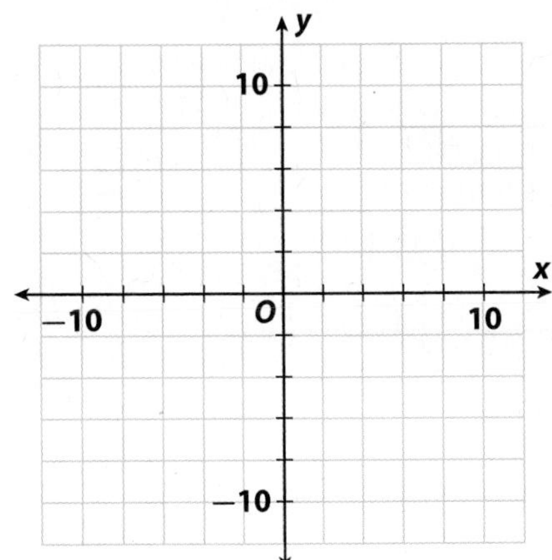

10. $3x - 3y \geq 21$

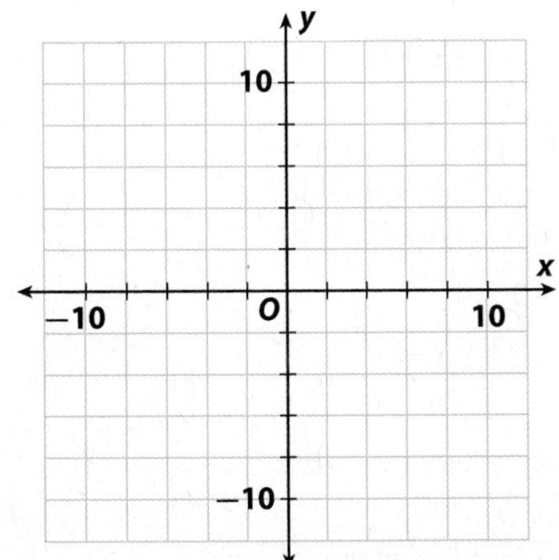

11. Represent Real World Problems Sandra was given a $60.00 gift card to an online music store. She can buy single songs for $1.00 and albums for $12.00.

a. Write the linear inequality that represents how many songs, x, and albums, y, that Sandra can buy with her gift card.

____

b. Explain the steps you would take to solve the linear inequality for y, the number of albums Sandra buys.

____

____

____

c. Complete the table to verify which points make the inequality true.

Point	Inequality	True or False?
(6, 4)		
(8, 5)		

d. Explain the meaning of the point in the table that makes the inequality true.

____

____

e. If you were to shade a graph of this linear inequality, would you shade the point (−3, 4)? Explain.

____

____

____

12. **Communicate Mathematical Ideas** How is graphing a linear inequality on a coordinate plane similar to graphing an inequality on a number line?

____

____

____

____

____

____

H.O.T. FOCUS ON HIGHER ORDER THINKING

Work Area

13. **Multi-step** The fare for a taxi cab is \$2.25 per passenger and \$0.75 for each mile. A group of friends has \$16.00 for cab fare.

a. Write a linear inequality to represent how many miles, y, the group can travel if there are x people in the group. ______________________________

b. If there are 3 people in the group, how far can they travel by taxi? Explain.

____

____

c. If the group wants to travel 10 miles, what is the greatest number of passengers that can travel by taxi? Explain.

____

____

____

14. **Analyze Relationships** For the graph of $x \geq 5$, the boundary line is the vertical line $x = 5$. Would you shade to the left or right of the boundary? Explain.

____

____

15. **Critique Reasoning** Baxter thinks that the inequality $2x - 3y \geq 6$ should be shaded above the boundary line because it uses the $\geq$ inequality symbol. Is he correct? Explain.

____

____

____

Ready to Go On?

Personal Math Trainer

Online Practice and Help

my.hrw.com

7.1 Arithmetic Sequences

Indicate whether each sequence is arithmetic. If so, write an explicit rule for the sequence.

1. 1, 3, 5, 7, …

2. 3, 6, 9, 14, …

3. 25, 20, 15, 10, …

7.2 Operations with Linear Functions

For $f(x) = 5x - 3$ and $g(x) = 2 - x$, compute the following functions.

4. $h(x) = f(x) + g(x)$

5. $j(x) = f(x) - g(x)$

6. $k(x) = 6 \cdot f(x)$

7.3 Linear Inequalities in Two Variables

Graph the following linear inequalities.

7. $3x + 2y \leq 12$

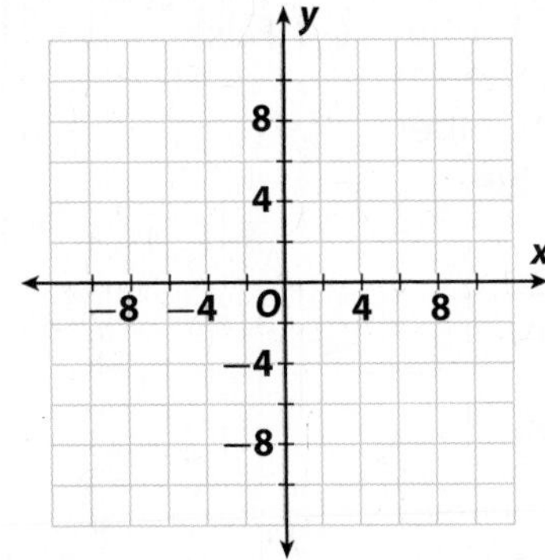

8. $5x - y \geq 10$

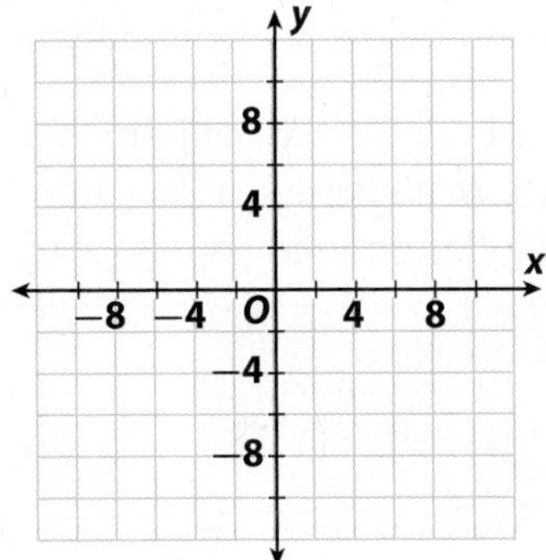

ESSENTIAL QUESTION

9. How are arithmetic sequences similar to linear functions? How are they different?

MODULE 7
MIXED REVIEW

Assessment Readiness

1. The first term of an arithmetic sequence is 7, and the common difference of the sequence is -4.

Select Yes or No if the representation models the sequence.

A. $f(n) = 7 - 4n$ ○ Yes ○ No

B. 7, -4, -15, -26, . . . ○ Yes ○ No

C. $f(1) = 7$, $f(n) = f(n - 1) - 4$, for $n \geq 2$ ○ Yes ○ No

D. ○ Yes ○ No

n	1	2	3	4	. . .
***f*(*n*)**	7	3	-1	-5	. . .

2. Consider the graph of the linear inequality $x - 4y < 8$.

Choose True or False for each statement.

A. The boundary line of the graph is given by $y = \frac{1}{4}x - 2$. ○ True ○ False

B. The boundary line is graphed with a dashed line. ○ True ○ False

C. The half-plane below the boundary line is shaded. ○ True ○ False

3. The table shows how the cost of judo lessons depends on the number of lessons taken. Write the linear function represented in the table. Explain how you determined your answer.

Number of Lessons	1	5	8	10
Cost Including Uniform ($)	48	96	132	156

4. A drill team is raising money by holding a car wash. The team earns $6.00 for each car washed. The team's expenses include $50.00 for advertising plus $0.50 in materials for each car washed. Let $f(x)$ represent the team's total earnings for washing x cars and $g(x)$ represent the team's total expenses for washing x cars. Describe how you can use $f(x)$ and $g(x)$ to obtain a function $p(x)$ that gives the team's profit for washing x cars. Then write a rule for $p(x)$.

Modeling with Linear Functions

ESSENTIAL QUESTION

How can you use statistical methods to find relationships between sets of data?

MODULE

8

CALIFORNIA COMMON CORE

LESSON 8.1

Correlation

CA CC S.ID.6, S.ID.8, S.ID.9

LESSON 8.2

Fitting Lines to Data

CA CC S.ID.6, S.ID.6a, S.ID.6b, S.ID.6c, S.ID.7

LESSON 8.3

Linear Regression

CA CC S.ID.6, S.ID.6a, S.ID.6b, S.ID.6c, S.ID.7, S.ID.8

my.hrw.com

Real-World Video

A fossil is a remnant or trace of an organism of a past geologic age that has been preserved in the earth's crust. Fossils are often dated by using interpolation, a type of calculation that uses an observed pattern to estimate a value between two known values.

GO DIGITAL my.hrw.com

my.hrw.com

Go digital with your write-in student edition, accessible on any device.

Math On the Spot

Scan with your smart phone to jump directly to the online edition, video tutor, and more.

Animated Math

Interactively explore key concepts to see how math works.

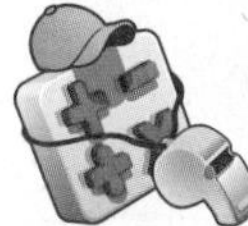

Personal Math Trainer

Get immediate feedback and help as you work through practice sets.

Are YOU Ready?

Complete these exercises to review skills you will need for this module.

Ordered Pairs

EXAMPLE Graph the ordered pairs $A(2, 2)$, $B(-2, 0)$, and $C(-1, -3)$.

The first coordinate refers to position on the x-axis, and the second coordinate refers to position on the y-axis.

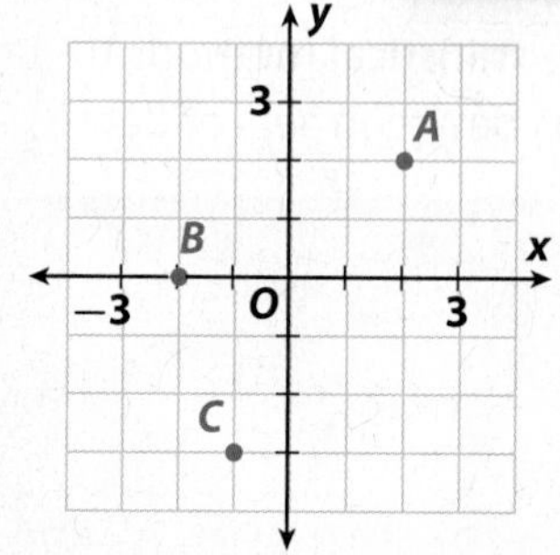

Graph each point on the coordinate plane provided.

1. $A(4, 0)$
2. $B(3, -4)$
3. $C(-1, -2)$
4. $D(-1, 3.5)$
5. $E(0, 5)$
6. $F(4.5, -3)$
7. $G(-2.5, 0.5)$
8. $H(-4, -2.5)$

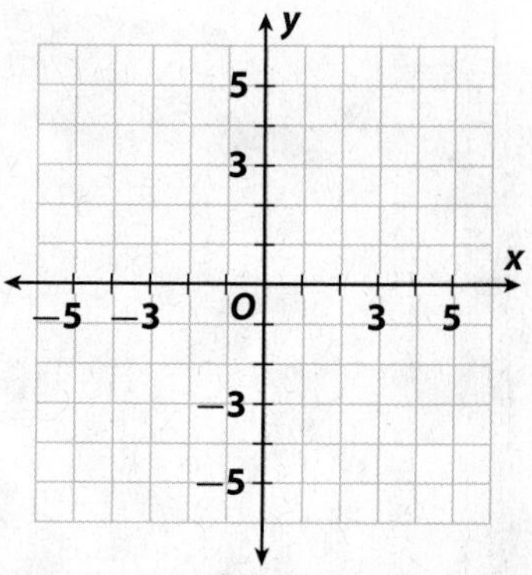

Graph Linear Functions

EXAMPLE Graph $y = -2x + 1$.

Find two points that satisfy the equation. Then connect the points with a straight line.

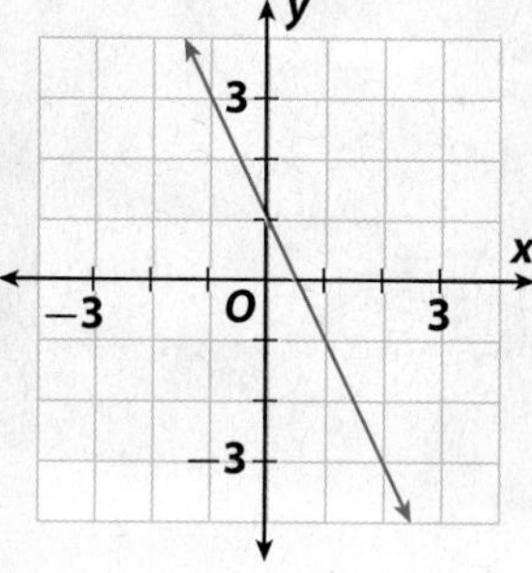

Graph each function.

9. $y = x - 2$

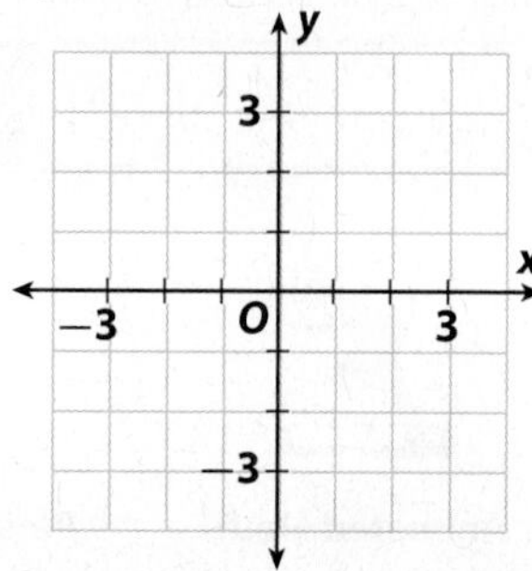

10. $y = -\frac{2}{3}x + 2$

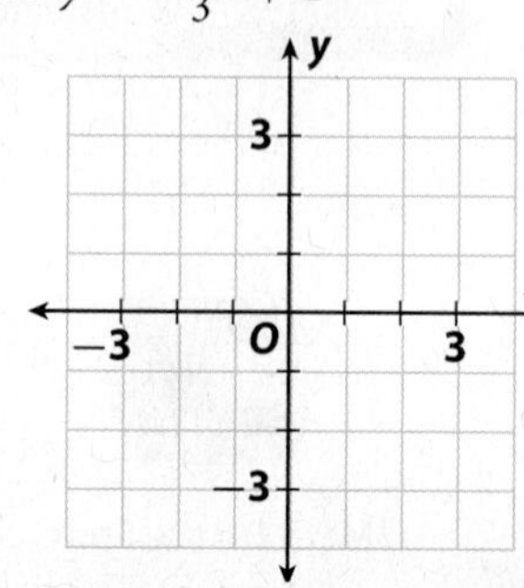

11. $y = \frac{5}{2}x - \frac{1}{2}$

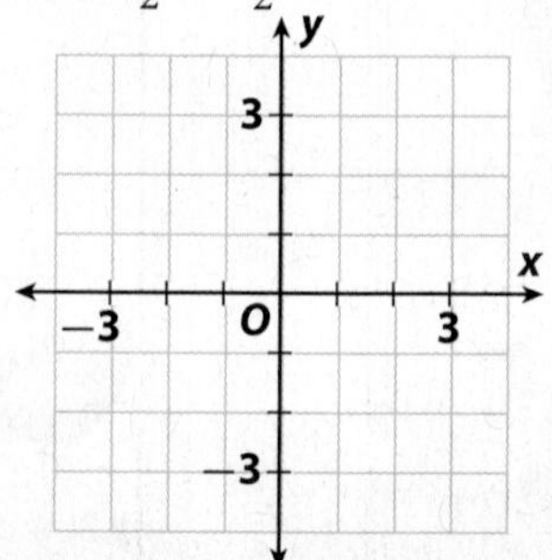

Reading Start-Up

Visualize Vocabulary

Use the review words to complete the sequence diagram. Complete the blanks in each box.

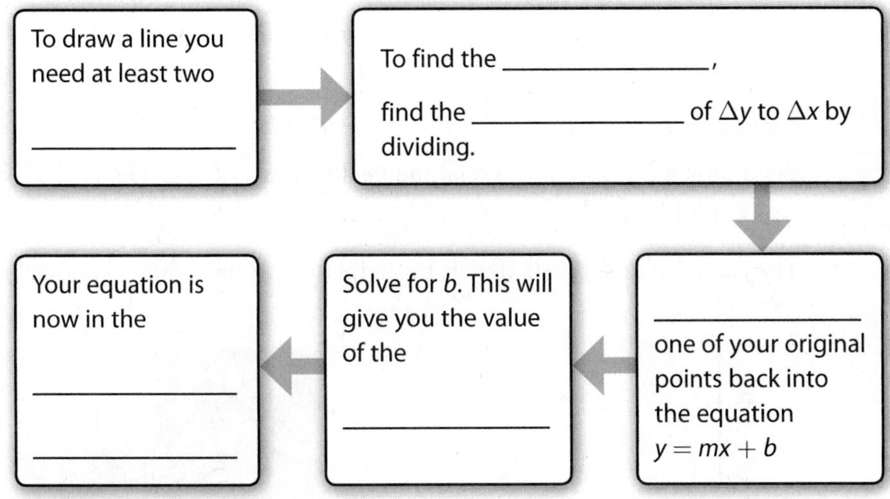

To draw a line you need at least two ______________
To find the ______________,
find the ______________ of Δy to Δx by dividing.
______________ one of your original points back into the equation $y = mx + b$
Solve for b. This will give you the value of the ______________
Your equation is now in the ______________ ______________

Vocabulary

Review Words

- ✔ point *(punto)*
- ✔ ratio *(razón)*
- ✔ slope *(pendiente)*
- ✔ slope-intercept form *(forma de pendiente-intersección)*
- ✔ *y*-intercept *(intersección con el eje y)*

Preview Words

- causation
- correlation
- correlation coefficient
- interpolation
- linear regression
- least squares regression line
- line of best fit
- residual
- residual plot
- scatter plot

Understand Vocabulary

To become familiar with some of the vocabulary terms in the module, consider the following. You may refer to the module, the glossary, or a dictionary.

1. The word *regress* is used when you want to return to a less well-developed state. What do you think an **linear regression** might be?

____

2. The word *residual* refers to what is left over. What do you think a **residual plot** might be?

____

____

Active Reading

Three-Panel Flip Chart Before beginning the module, create a three-panel flip chart to help you organize what you learn. Label each flap with one of the lesson titles from this module. As you study each lesson, write important ideas like vocabulary under the appropriate flap.

GETTING READY FOR

Modeling with Linear Functions

Understanding the standards and the vocabulary terms in the standards will help you know exactly what you are expected to learn in this module.

CA CC S.ID.6

Represent data on two quantitative variables on a scatter plot, and describe how the variables are related.

Key Vocabulary

scatter plot *(diagrama de dispersión)*
A graph with points plotted to show a possible relationship between two variables.

What It Means to You

You can graph real-world data in two variables to see how the variables are related.

EXAMPLE S.ID.6

Reed took a survey about social media attitudes and age. He used a scatter plot to display his data.

The scatter plot suggests that as participants get older they like social media less.

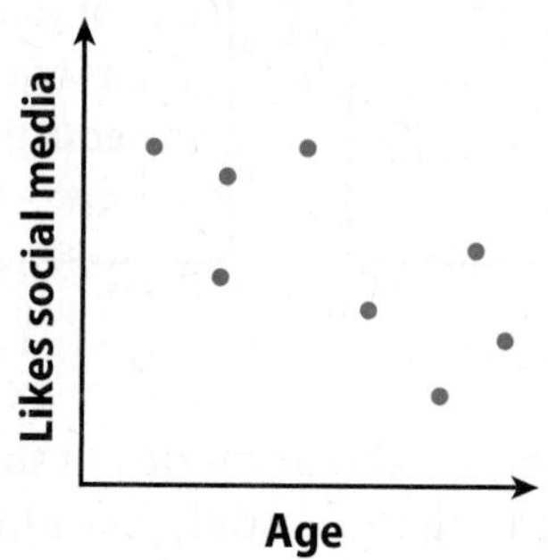

CA CC S.ID.6c

Fit a linear function for a scatter plot that suggests a linear association.

Key Vocabulary

linear function *(función lineal)*
A function whose graph is a straight line.

What It Means to You

In a linear relationship one quantity is directly proportional to another. For example, the greater the altitude, the thinner the air is in the atmosphere.

EXAMPLE S.ID.6C

Reed drew a line in his scatter plot, suggesting a linear correlation between age and how much people like social media.

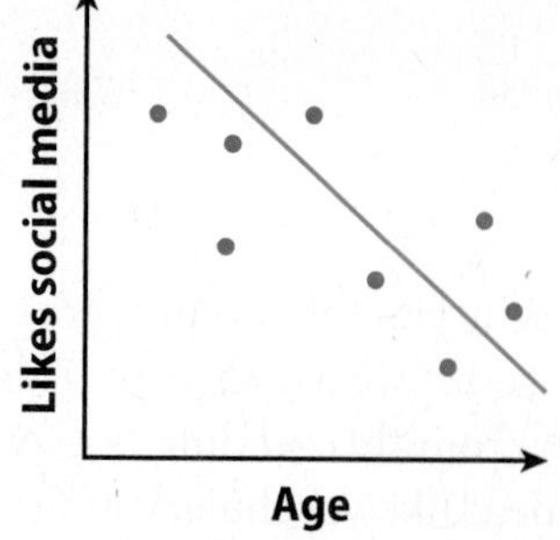

Visit **my.hrw.com** to see all **CA Common Core Standards** explained.

my.hrw.com

LESSON
8.1 Correlation

CA CC S.ID.6

Represent data on two quantitative variables on a scatter plot, and describe how the variables are related. *Also S.ID.8, S.ID.9*

ESSENTIAL QUESTION

How can you describe the relationship between two variables?

EXPLORE ACTIVITY

Graphing Bivariate Data

Bivariate data is data that involves two variables. A **scatter plot** graphs bivariate data as a set of points whose coordinates correspond to the two variables. Scatter plots can help you see relationships between two variables. We say there is a **correlation** between two variables if their values are linked, as shown below.

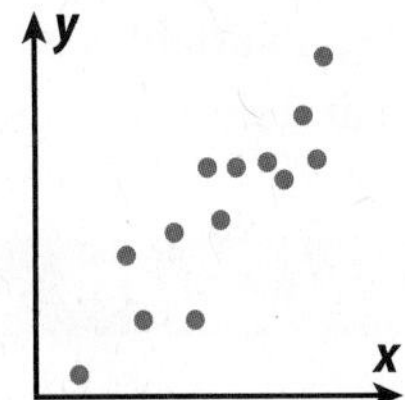

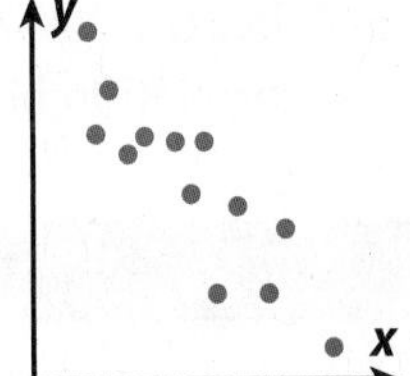

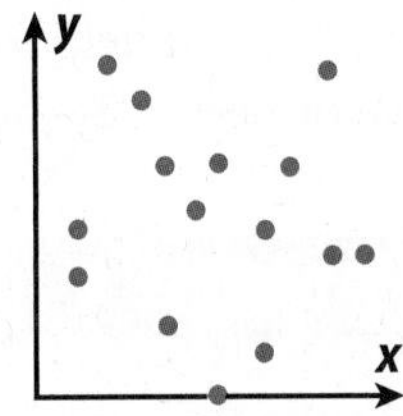

Positive Correlation	Negative Correlation	No Correlation
As the value of one variable increases, the value of the other variable also increases.	As the value of one variable decreases, the value of the other variable increases.	There is no relationship between the two variables.

The table below shows the number of species of mammals on the International Union for the Conservation of Nature's "Red List" of endangered species during the years 2004 to 2012.

IUCN Red List, Number of Endangered Mammal Species							
2004	2006	2007	2008	2009	2010	2011	2012
352	348	349	448	449	450	447	446

Source: *IUCN Red List version 2012*

A Make a scatter plot, using the data in the table as the coordinates of points on the graph. Use the calendar year as the x-value and the number of species as the y-value. One point is plotted for you.

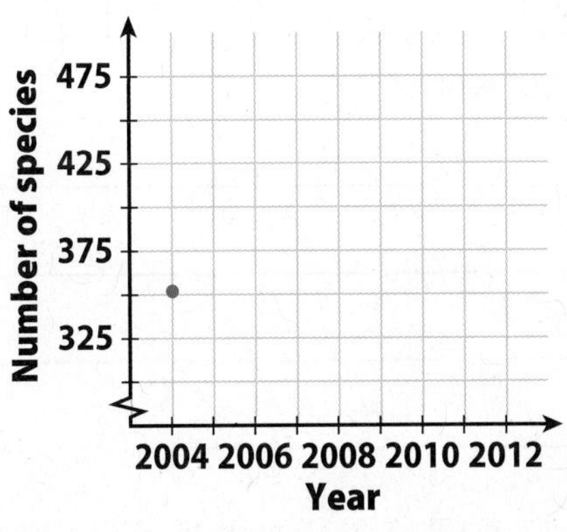

EXPLORE ACTIVITY (cont'd)

REFLECT

1. **Conjecture** Look at the pattern of points. Is there a positive correlation, negative correlation, or no correlation between the number of endangered mammal species and the year? What is the trend? Is the number of endangered species increasing or decreasing over time?

Describing Correlations from Scatter Plots

Scatter plots can help to visualize whether the correlation between variables is positive or negative—or if there is no correlation between the variables.

EXAMPLE 1 

CA CC S.ID.6

Describe the correlation illustrated by the scatter plot.

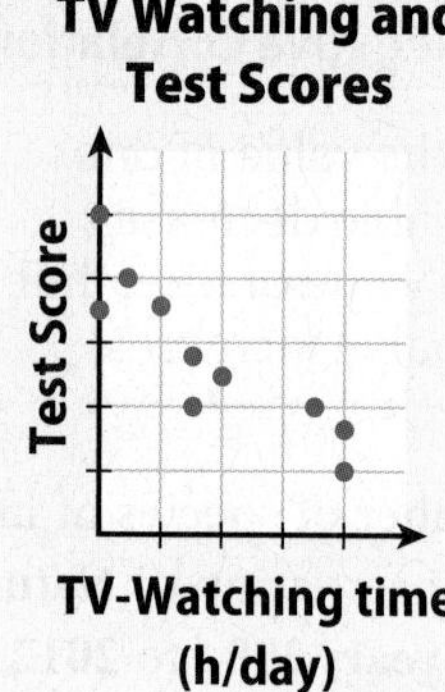

As the number of hours spent watching TV increased, test scores decreased. There is a negative correlation between the two data variables.

REFLECT

2. **What if?** What would you expect to be true of a person from this survey who watches very few hours of TV? Is it possible for that person to have low test scores?

My Notes

YOUR TURN

3. Describe the correlation illustrated by the scatter plot.

____

____

____

____

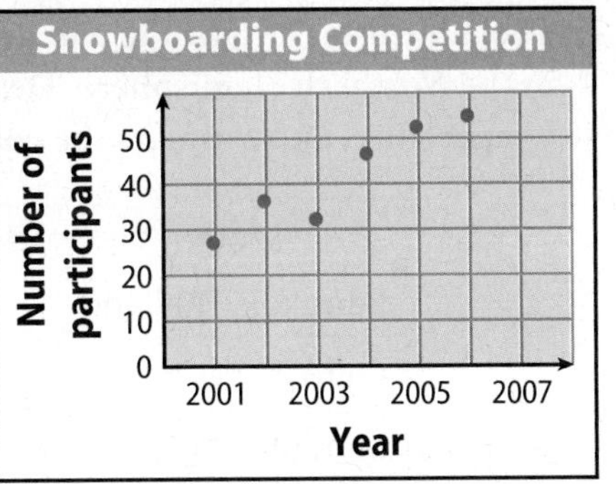

Correlation Coefficients

One measure of the strength and direction of a correlation is the **correlation coefficient**, denoted by r. The value of r ranges from -1 to 1. Although r can be precisely calculated, in this lesson we examine qualitatively how its value describes a correlation.

A positive r value indicates a positive correlation, and a negative r value indicates a negative correlation. The stronger the correlation, the closer the correlation coefficient will be to -1 or 1. The weaker the correlation, the closer r will be to zero.

	Negative	Positive
Strong	Strong negative correlation points lie close to a line with negative slope. r is close to -1.	Strong positive correlation points lie close to a line with positive slope. r is close to 1.
Weak	Weak negative correlation points loosely follow a line with negative slope. r is between 0 and -1.	Weak positive correlation points loosely follow a line with positive slope. r is between 0 and 1.

If there is no correlation between the two variables in a data set, the points in a scatter plot do not lie along a line, and r is close to zero.

EXAMPLE 2 Real World

CA CC S.ID.8

The table lists the latitude and average annual temperature for various cities in the Northern Hemisphere. Describe the correlation between latitude and temperature, and estimate the correlation coefficient.

City	Latitude	Avg. Annual Temperature
Bangkok, Thailand	13.7°N	82.6°F
Cairo, Egypt	30.1°N	71.4°F
London, England	51.5°N	51.8°F
Moscow, Russia	55.8°N	39.4°F
New Delhi, India	28.6°N	77.0°F
Tokyo, Japan	35.7°N	58.1°F
Vancouver, Canada	49.2°N	49.6°F

STEP 1 Make a scatter plot.

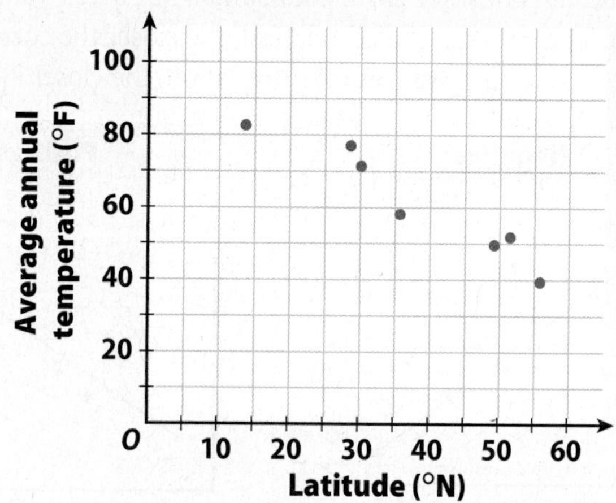

Math Talk
Mathematical Practices

If the point (19.4, 60.8) for Mexico City was added to the scatter plot, how would the correlation coefficient change?

STEP 2 Describe the correlation, and estimate the correlation coefficient.

Because the plotted points appear to lie very close to a line with a **negative** slope, the scatter plot shows a **strong negative** correlation. So the correlation coefficient is close to -1.

YOUR TURN

4. Examine the scatter plot titled Snowboarding Competition in the previous Your Turn. Is the correlation coefficient for the data closer to -1, -0.5, 0, 0.5, or 1? Explain.

____

____

____

Distinguishing Causation from Correlation

A common error when interpreting paired data is confusing correlation and *causation*. If a correlation exists between two variables, this does not necessarily mean that one variable causes the other. When one variable increases, the other variable may increase (or decrease) as a result of other variables that are not being considered. Such variables are sometimes called *lurking variables*.

EXAMPLE 3 

Read the article. Does it describe a positive or negative correlation? Explain whether the correlation is a result of causation.

STEP 1 Identify the two variables.

- size of amygdala
- size of social network

STEP 2 Determine the correlation.

A larger amygdala corresponds to a larger social network, so there is a **positive** correlation.

STEP 3 Explain whether the correlation is a result of causation.

Causation is possible, but it's unknown which variable causes the other. Having a larger amygdala might cause a person to develop a larger social network, or having a large social network might cause a person's amygdala to grow. And it's possible that neither factor causes the other, but that a lurking third variable causes the amygdala to grow and causes the person to develop a large social network.

Brain's Amygdala Connected To Social Behavior

An almond-shaped part of the brain called the amygdala has long been known to play a role in people's emotional states. Now scientists studying the amygdala have discovered a connection between its size and the size of a person's social network. The scientists used a brain scanner to determine the size of the amygdala in the brains of 58 adults. They also gave each person a survey that measured the size of a person's social network. After analyzing the data, they found that people with larger amygdalas tend to have larger social networks.

YOUR TURN

5. A survey found that students who spent more time doing Algebra homework also spent more time doing Biology homework. Identify the two variables, indicate whether they have a positive or negative correlation, and discuss whether the correlation is a result of causation.

Guided Practice

A marine biologist kept a record of the length in inches and mass in kilograms of a newborn dolphin as it grew older. The results are shown in the table below. (Explore Activity and Example 1)

Length (in.)	30	60	90	120	150	180	210
Mass (kg)	28	58	87	117	148	178	205

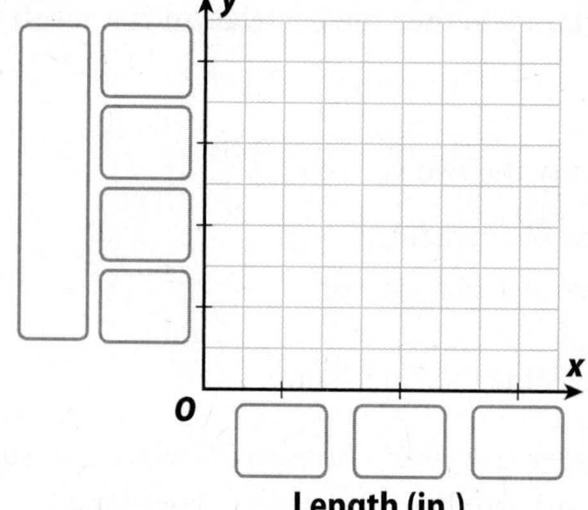

1. Make a scatter plot for this set of data. What does the x value represent? What does the y value represent?

____

____

2. Describe the correlation. Explain.

____

____

____

3. Is the correlation coefficient for the data likely to be closest to -1, -0.5, 0, 0.5, or 1? (Example 2) _______________

4. Suppose the biologist also kept track of the amount of food the dolphin ate and found that the amount of food was positively correlated with the length of the dolphin. Is this correlation due to causation? Explain. (Example 3)

____

____

____

ESSENTIAL QUESTION CHECK-IN

5. How can you describe the relationship between two variables?

____

____

____

____

____

Name_____________________ Class_____________________ Date_____________________

8.1 Independent Practice

Personal Math Trainer

Online Practice and Help

my.hrw.com

The table lists the heights and weights of the six wide receivers that played for a college football team during last year's football season.

Wide Receiver	Height (inches)	Weight (pounds)
Jones	75	192
Walker	76	225
Edwards	71	200
Jefferson	74	210
Tory	69	190
Farmer	72	189

6. Make a scatter plot.

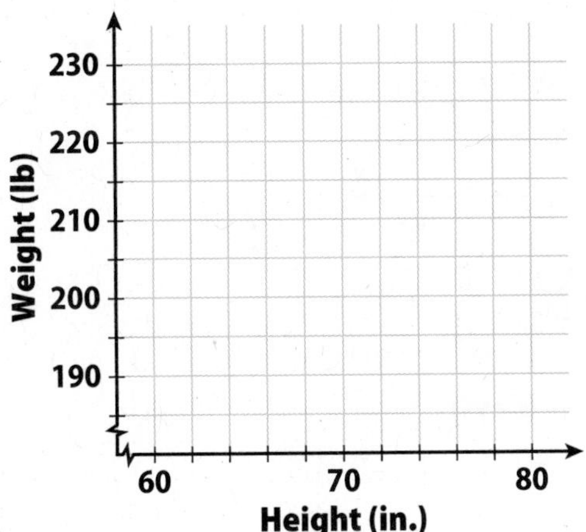

7. Describe the correlation. Is the correlation coefficient likely to be closest to -1, -0.5, 0, 0.5, or 1?.

____

8. Researchers studying senior citizens discovered that an elderly person's walking speed was correlated to that person's chance of living longer. The fastest walkers were more likely to live another 10 years than were the slowest walkers. Describe the correlation, and discuss whether it is due to causation.

____

____

____

____

Identify the correlation you would expect to see between each pair of variables. State whether the correlation coefficient is likely to be closer to -1, 0, or 1.

9. The temperature in Houston and the number of cars sold in Boston.

____

10. The number of members in a family and the size of the family's weekly grocery bill.

____

11. The number of times you sharpen your pencil and the length of the pencil.

____

H.O.T. FOCUS ON HIGHER ORDER THINKING

Work Area

12. Justify Reasoning Choose the scatter plot that best represents the relationship between the number of days since a sunflower seed was planted and the height of the plant. Explain.

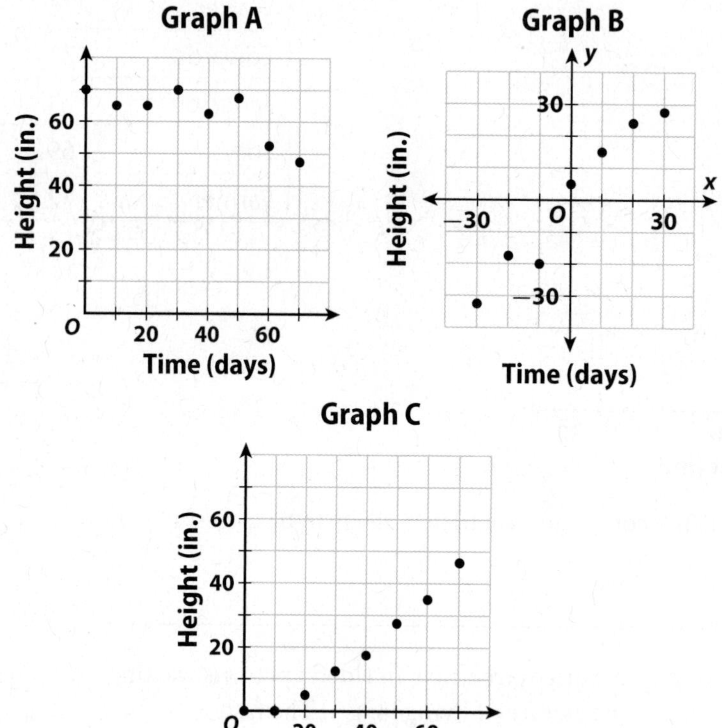

____

____

____

____

____

____

13. Make a Prediction The scatter plot shows the average ocelot population in Laguna Atascosa National Wildlife Refuge near Brownsville, Texas. Based on this information, predict the number of ocelots living at the wildlife refuge in 2014 if conditions do not change.

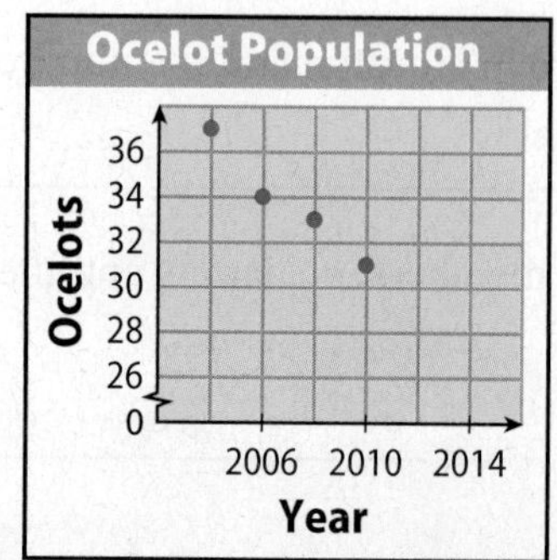

____

LESSON

8.2 Fitting Lines to Data

CA CC S.ID.6c

Fit a linear function for a scatter plot that suggests a linear association. *Also S.ID.6, S.ID.6a, S.ID.6b, and S.ID.7*

ESSENTIAL QUESTION

How do you find a linear model for a bivariate data set, and how do you evaluate the quality of fit?

EXPLORE ACTIVITY 

S.ID.6c

Finding a Line of Fit for Data

When the two variables in a bivariate data set have a strong positive or negative correlation, you can find a linear model for the data. The process is called fitting a line to the data or finding a **line of fit** for the data.

The table lists the median age of females living in the United States, based on the results of the U.S. Census over the past few decades. Determine whether a linear model is reasonable for the data. If so, find a linear model for the data.

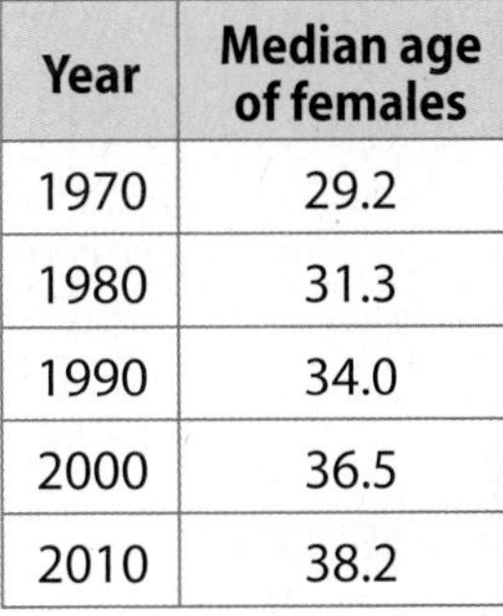

Year	Median age of females
1970	29.2
1980	31.3
1990	34.0
2000	36.5
2010	38.2

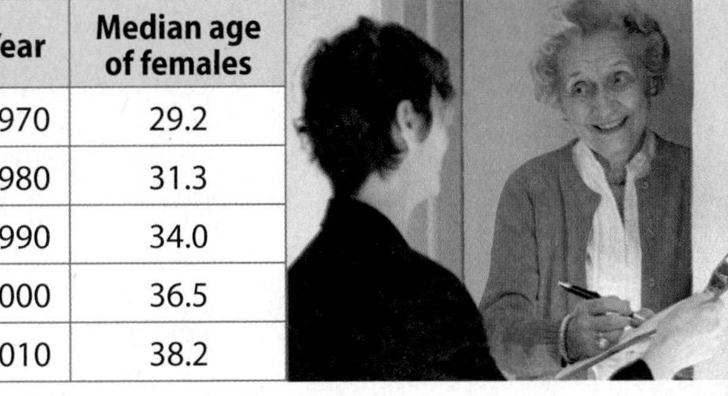

A To simplify calculations with the data, let x represent time in years after 1970.

Let y represent the median age of females.

Make a table of paired values of x and y.

x					
y					

B Make a scatter plot of the data.

If the points fall close to a straight line, then a linear model may provide a good description of the data. Do the points appear to form a line?

____

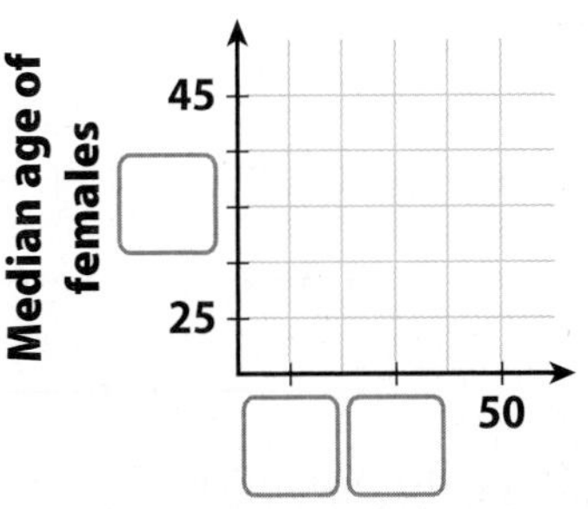

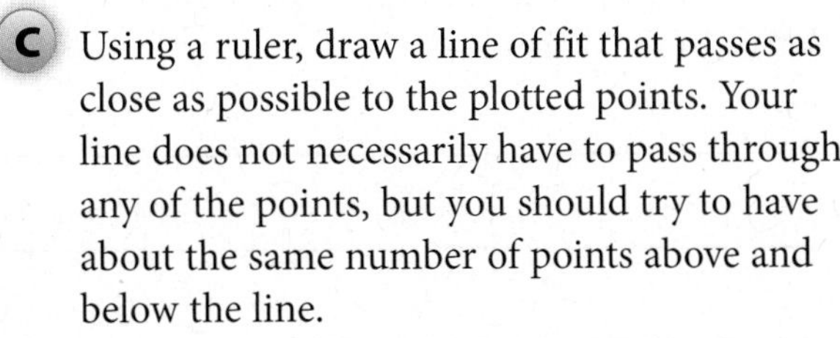

C Using a ruler, draw a line of fit that passes as close as possible to the plotted points. Your line does not necessarily have to pass through any of the points, but you should try to have about the same number of points above and below the line.

EXPLORE ACTIVITY *(cont'd)*

D Find the equation of the line of fit.

We will do the calculation for a line that passes through the points (20, 34) and (40, 38.2).

STEP 1 Find the slope.

$$m = \frac{38.2 - 34}{40 - 20}$$

$$m = \square$$

STEP 2 Find the y-intercept using (20, 34).

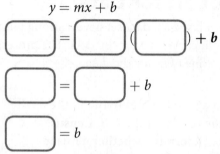

$$y = mx + b$$

$$\square = \square(\square) + b$$

$$\square = \square + b$$

$$\square = b$$

So, in terms of the variables x and y, the equation of the line of fit is

____

REFLECT

1. What does the slope of the line of fit tell you about the data?

____

____

____

2. What does the y-intercept of the line of fit tell you about the data?

____

____

____

3. **Communicate Mathematical Ideas** How does the slope of the line of fit relate to the type of correlation in the data?

____

____

____

Creating a Residual Plot

Some lines will fit a data set better than others. One way to evaluate how well a line fits a data set is to use *residuals*. A **residual** is the signed vertical distance between a data point and a line of fit.

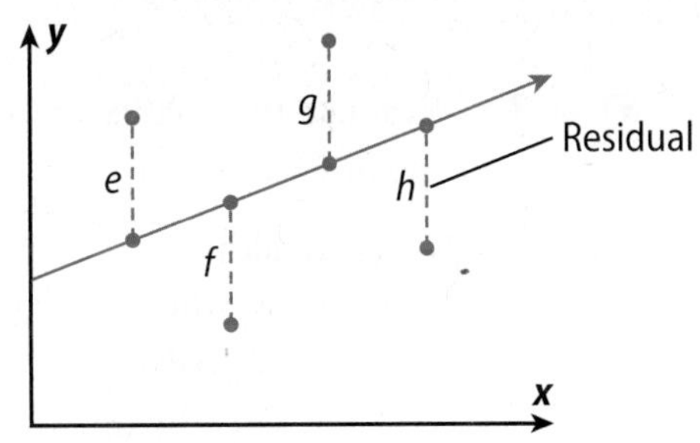

After calculating residuals, you can draw a **residual plot**, which is a graph of points whose x-coordinates are the values of the independent variable and whose y-coordinates are the corresponding residuals.

Looking at the distribution of residuals can help you determine how well a line of fit actually describes the data. The plots below illustrate how the residuals might be distributed for three different data sets and lines of fit.

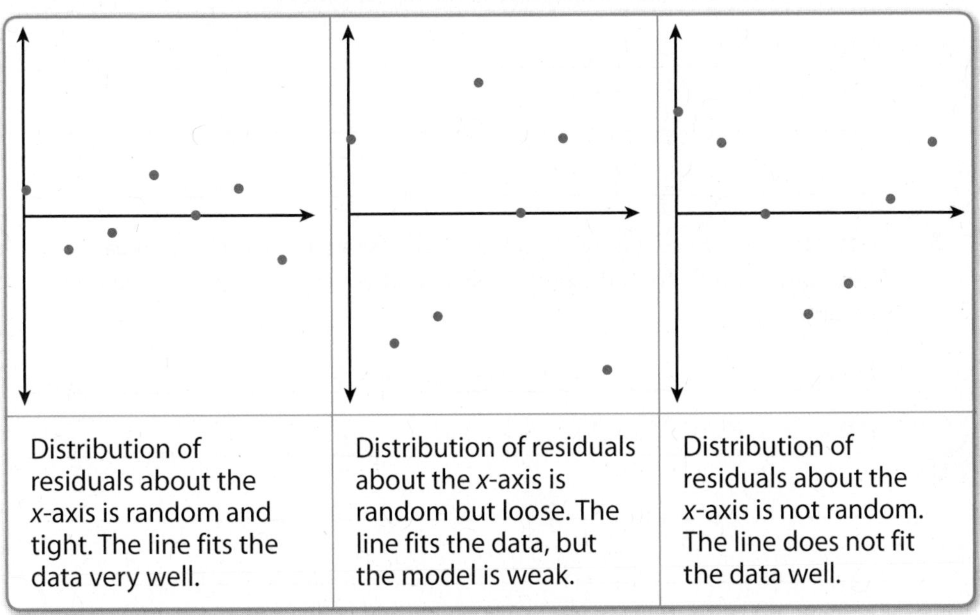

Distribution of residuals about the x-axis is random and tight. The line fits the data very well.	Distribution of residuals about the x-axis is random but loose. The line fits the data, but the model is weak.	Distribution of residuals about the x-axis is not random. The line does not fit the data well.

EXAMPLE 1   CA CC S.ID.6b

Consider the data from the Explore Activity on median ages of females over time. Use residuals to evaluate the quality of fit for the line $y = 0.25x + 29$, where x is years since 1970, and y is median age.

STEP 1 Calculate the residuals.

x	actual y	predicted y, based on $y = 0.25x + 29$	residual Subtract predicted from actual to find the residual
0	29.2	29.0	0.2
10	31.3	31.5	−0.2
20	34.0	34.0	0
30	36.5	36.5	0
40	38.2	39.0	−0.8

STEP 2 Plot the residuals.

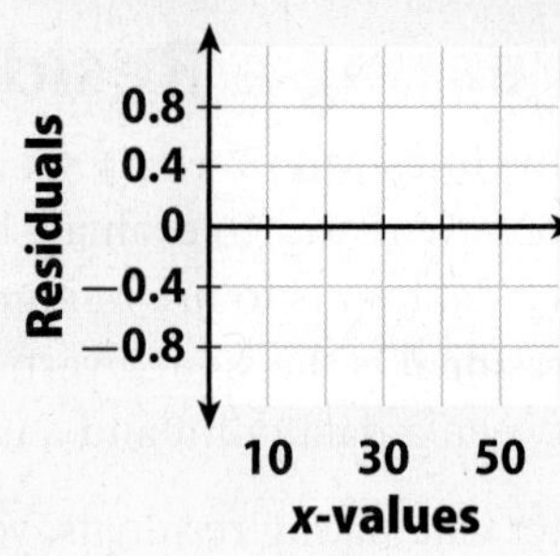

STEP 3 Evaluate the quality of fit to the data for the line $y = 0.25x + 29$.

- The residuals are all small, so the points on the residual plot are tightly distributed around the x-axis.
- Therefore, the line given by $y = 0.25x + 29$ is an appropriate model.

REFLECT

4. If you are comparing two lines of fit for the same data set, how does the size of the residuals indicate which one is the better model?

____

____

____

5. Communicate Mathematical Ideas Suppose you know that a linear model is a good fit for a data set. How would you expect the residual plot to look?

____

____

____

____

Math Talk
Mathematical Practices

How did changing the slope of the line of fit affect the residuals in this example?

YOUR TURN

6. Consider the data used in the Explore Activity and in Example 1 on median ages of females over time. Graph the residuals and evaluate the quality of fit for the line $y = 0.2x + 29.2$.

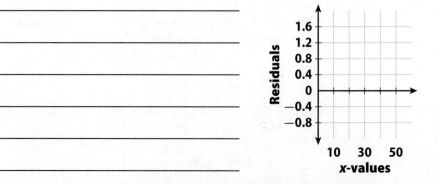

____

____

____

____

____

____

Residuals: 1.6, 1.2, 0.8, 0.4, 0, −0.4, −0.8
x-values: 10, 30, 50

Personal Math Trainer
Online Practice and Help
my.hrw.com

Using a Line of Fit to Make Predictions

Finding a linear model for a data set establishes one variable as a linear function of another variable. The domain of the function is determined by the least and greatest values of the x-values in the actual data.

A linear model can be used to make predictions. Making a prediction based on a value *within* the model's domain is called **interpolation**. Basing a prediction on a value *outside* the domain is called **extrapolation**.

EXAMPLE 2

CA CC S.ID.6a

Suppose you used the data table in the Explore Activity to derive the model $y = 0.25x + 29$, where x is the number of years since 1970 and y is the median age of females in the United States. Use this model to predict the median age of females for the years 1995 and 2015. State whether each prediction is an interpolation or an extrapolation.

A Let $x = 25$ because $1995 - 1970 = 25$.

The predicted value of y is $0.25(25) + 29 \approx 35.3$ years old.
The x-values in the data go from 0 to 40.
The x-value 25 is between 0 and 40, so this prediction is an interpolation.

B Let $x = 45$ because $2015 - 1970 = 45$.

The predicted value of y is $0.25(45) + 29 \approx 40.3$ years old.
The x-values in the data go from 0 to 40.
The x-value 45 is greater than 40, so this prediction is an extrapolation.

My Notes

REFLECT

7. The Census Bureau used interpolation to estimate the median age of females in 1995 and used extrapolation to predict the median age for 2033. They used only the data in the table at the start of this lesson. Which of their predictions is more likely to be accurate? Explain.

____

____

____

____

YOUR TURN

Use the linear model $y = 0.25x + 29$, where x is the number of years since 1970 and y is the median age of females, to predict the median age of females in the years below. State whether each prediction is an interpolation or an extrapolation.

8. 1989 ______________________________

9. 2022 ______________________________

Guided Practice

The table lists the median age of males based on the results of the U.S. Census. (Explore Activity)

Year	1970	1980	1990	2000	2010
Median age of males	26.8	28.8	31.6	34.0	35.5

1. Let x represent time in years after 1970 and let y represent median age. Make a table of paired values of x and y.

x	0		20	30	
y		28.8			35.5

2. Draw a scatter plot and line of fit.

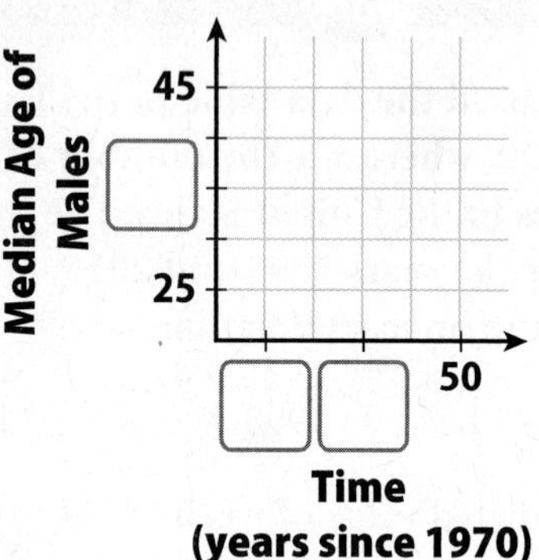

3. Find an equation of the line of fit. (Explore Activity)

___

A student fit the line $y = 0.23x + 27$ to the data above. Use this model for Exercises 4–6.

4. Calculate the residuals. Evaluate the quality of fit. (Example 1)

x	y actual	y predicted	Residual
0		27	
	28.8		−0.5
20			
30		33.9	
	35.5		−0.7

___

5. Predict the median age of males in 1995. (Example 2)

$y + 0.23(\square) + 27 \approx \square$

6. Is the prediction for 1995 an interpolation or extrapolation? (Example 2)

___

ESSENTIAL QUESTION CHECK-IN

7. How do you find a linear model for bivariate data, and how do you evaluate the quality of fit?

___

___

Name ______________________ Class ______________ Date ______________

8.2 Independent Practice

CA CC S.ID.6, S.ID.6a, S.ID.6b, S.ID.6c

The table lists the length (in centimeters) and median weight (in kilograms) of male and female infants in the United States.

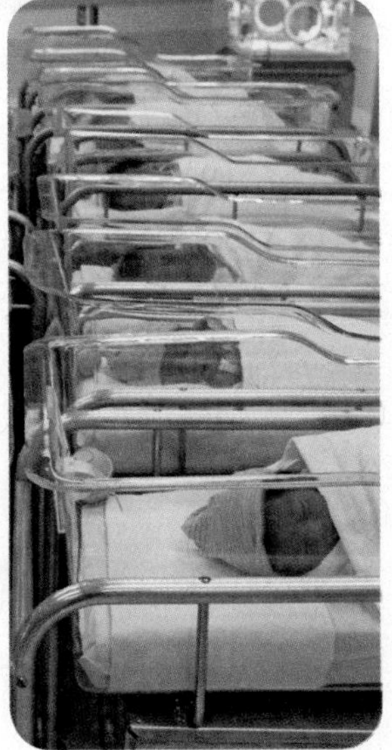

Length (cm)	50	60	70	80	90	100
Median weight (kg) of male infants	3.4	5.9	8.4	10.8	13.0	15.5
Median weight (kg) of female infants	3.4	5.8	8.3	10.6	12.8	15.2

8. Let l represent an infant's length in excess of 50 centimeters (for instance, for an infant whose length is 60 cm, $l = 10$) and let w represent the median weight of female infants. Make a table of paired values of l and w.

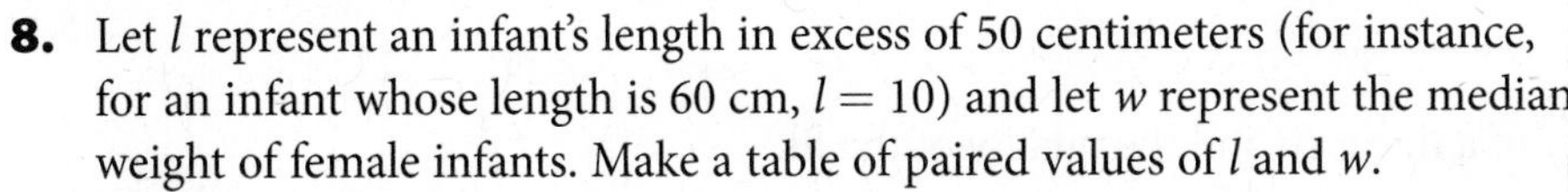

l						
w						

9. Draw a scatter plot of the data for female infants, and draw a line of fit.

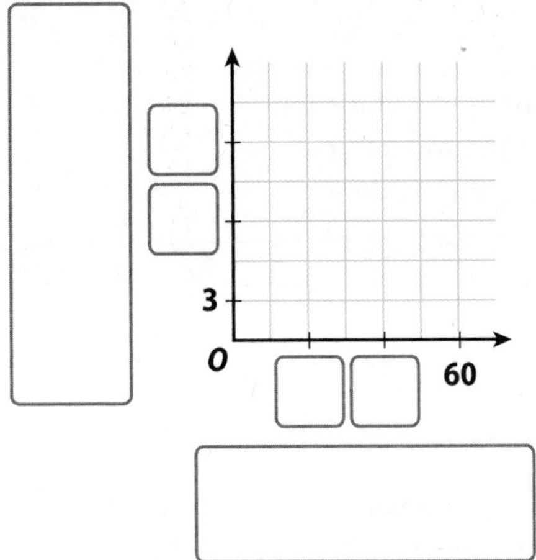

10. **Critical Thinking** Find an equation for the line of fit you drew on the scatter plot. According to your model, at what rate does the weight change as length increases?

____

____

____

____

11. Calculate the residuals, and make a residual plot.

l	w actual	w predicted	Residual
0	3.4		
10	5.8		
20	8.3		
30	10.6		
40	12.8		
50	15.2		

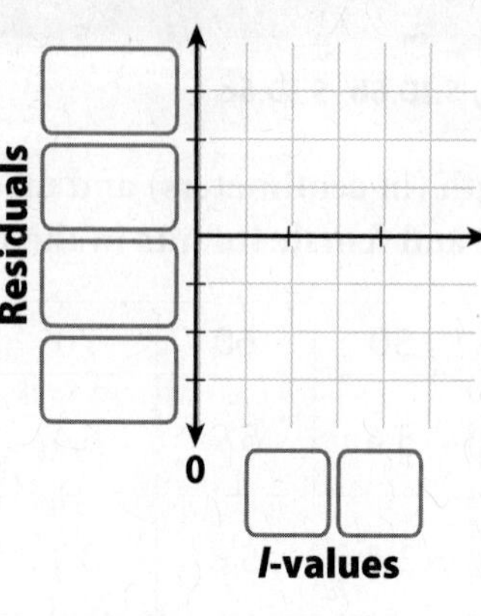

12. Evaluate the suitability of a linear fit and the quality of the fit.

H.O.T. FOCUS ON HIGHER ORDER THINKING

Work Area

13. Critique Reasoning Hector found a linear model based on the data for the length and weight of male infants, and he used it to predict the weight of a boy who is 150 centimeters tall. Is his prediction likely to be reliable? Explain.

14. Analyze Relationships Suppose the line of fit in Example 1 with equation $w = 0.25l + 29$ is changed to $w = 0.25l + 28.8$. What effect does this change have on the residuals? On the residual plot?

15. What If? If the median weight of male infants is 0.2 kg above the median weight of female infants at the same length, how would the line of fit on a scatter plot for male infants' length and weight compare to the one for female infants?

LESSON
8.3 Linear Regression

CA CC S.ID.6b

Informally assess the fit of a function by plotting and analyzing residuals. *Also S.ID.6, S.ID.6a, S.ID.6c, S.ID.7, S.ID.8*

ESSENTIAL QUESTION

How can you use the linear regression function on a graphing calculator to find the line of best fit for a bivariate data set?

EXPLORE ACTIVITY

Calculating Squared Residuals

In a previous lesson, you fit a line to data for the median age of females over time. Because each person in your class fit a line by eye, any two students are likely to have chosen slightly different lines of fit. Suppose one student came up with the equation $y = 0.25x + 29.0$ while another came up with $y = 0.25x + 28.8$ where in each case, x is the time in years since 1970 and y is the median age of females.

A Complete each table below in order to calculate the squares of the residuals for each line of fit.

$y = 0.25x + 29.0$				
x	y (actual)	y (predicted)	Residual	Square of residual
0	29.2	29.0	0.2	0.04
10	31.3			
20	34.0			
30	36.5			
40	38.2			

$y = 0.25x + 28.8$				
x	y (actual)	y (predicted)	Residual	Square of residual
0	29.2	28.8	0.4	0.16
10	31.3			
20	34.0			
30	36.5			
40	38.2			

B Find the sum of squared residuals for each line of fit.

Sum of squared residuals for $y = 0.25x + 29.0$: ____________

Sum of squared residuals for $y = 0.25x + 28.8$: ____________

EXPLORE ACTIVITY *(cont'd)*

C Which line has the smaller sum of squared residuals? ______________

REFLECT

1. **Analyze Relationships** How does squaring a residual affect its value?

____

____

____

____

2. Suppose the residuals for a line of fit for a data set are 2.6, 2.3, −2.3, and −2.5, and the residuals for a second line of fit are 0.6, 0.2, −0.2, and −0.4.

   a. Which line fits the data better? How can you tell?

   ____

   b. Would the sum of the residuals or the sum of the squared residuals be a better measure of the quality of fit? Explain.

   ____

   ____

   ____

   ____

   ____

   ____

Math On the Spot

my.hrw.com

Comparing Squared Residuals

The quality of a line of fit can be evaluated by finding the sum of the squared residuals. The closer the sum of the squared residuals is to 0, the better the line fits the data.

EXAMPLE 1 CA CC S.ID.6b

The data in the table below are graphed at right along with two possible lines of fit. For each line, find the sum of the squares of the residuals. Which line is a better fit?

x	2	4	6	8
y	6	3	7	5

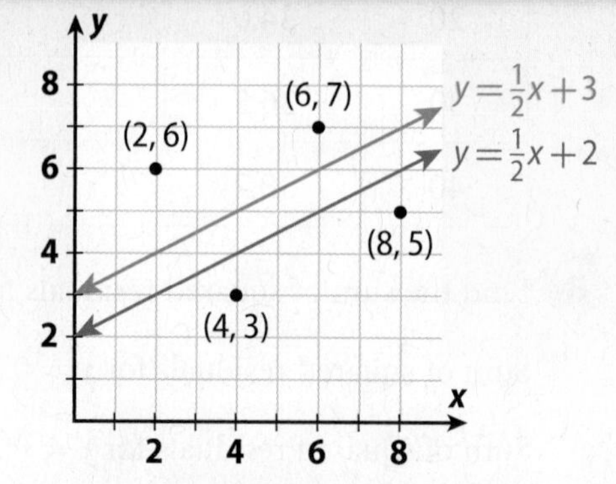

STEP 1 Find the residuals of each line.

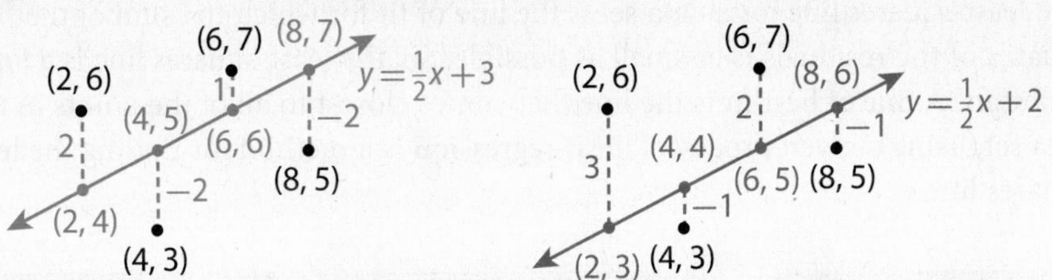

x	y (actual)	y predicted by $y = \frac{1}{2}x + 3$	residual for $y = \frac{1}{2}x + 3$	y predicted by $y = \frac{1}{2}x + 2$	residual for $y = \frac{1}{2}x + 2$
2	6	4	2	3	3
4	3	5	−2	4	−1
6	7	6	1	5	2
8	5	7	−2	6	−1

My Notes

STEP 2 Square the residuals and find their sum.

$y = \frac{1}{2}x + 3$: $(2)^2 + (-2)^2 + (1)^2 + (-2)^2 = 4 + 4 + 1 + 4 = 13$

$y = \frac{1}{2}x + 2$: $(3)^2 + (-1)^2 + (2)^2 + (-1)^2 = 9 + 1 + 4 + 1 = 15$

The sum of the squares for $y = \frac{1}{2}x + 3$ is smaller, so it provides the better fit for the data.

REFLECT

3. **What If?** Suppose the data pair (5, 4) was added to the data set. Which of the two lines would fit the data better now?

___

___

___

YOUR TURN

4. Find the sum of the squares of the residuals for the data above using the line $y = \frac{1}{2}x + 4$. How good is this fit?

___

___

___

___

Performing Linear Regression 

The **least-squares line** for a data set is the line of fit for which the sum of the squares of the residuals is as small as possible. So, the least-squares line is a *line of best fit*. A **line of best fit** is the line that comes closest to all of the points in the data set, using a given process. **Linear regression** is a method for finding the least-squares line.

EXAMPLE 2  

S.ID.6, S.ID.8

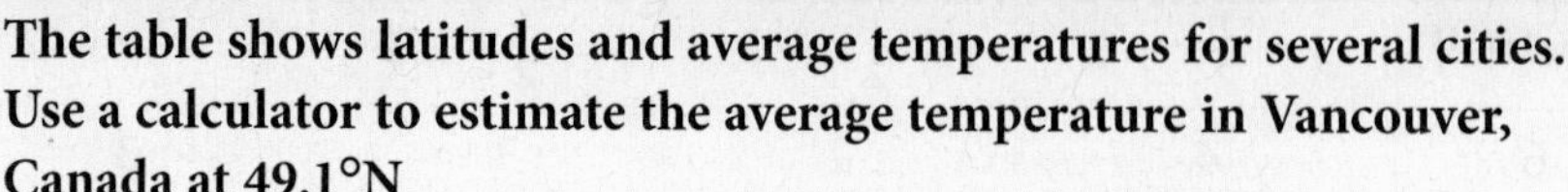

The table shows latitudes and average temperatures for several cities. Use a calculator to estimate the average temperature in Vancouver, Canada at 49.1°N

City	Latitude	Average temperature (°C)
Barrow, Alaska	71.2° N	−12.7
Yakutsk, Russia	62.1° N	−10.1
London, England	51.3° N	10.4
Chicago, Illinois	41.9° N	10.3
San Francisco, California	37.5° N	13.8
Yuma, Arizona	32.7° N	22.8
Tindouf, Algeria	27.7° N	22.8
Dakar, Senegal	14.0° N	24.5
Mangalore, India	12.5° N	27.1

Use your calculator to find an equation for a line of best fit.

STEP 1 Press the STAT key and select **1:Edit**. Enter the latitudes in column **L1** and the average temperatures in column **L2**.

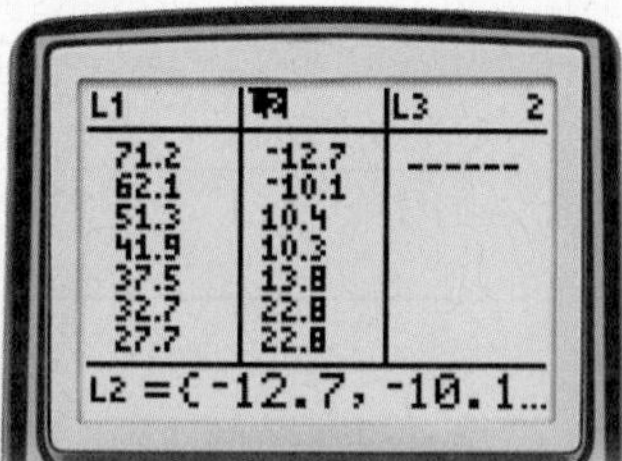

STEP 2 Press STAT PLOT to create a scatter plot of the data.

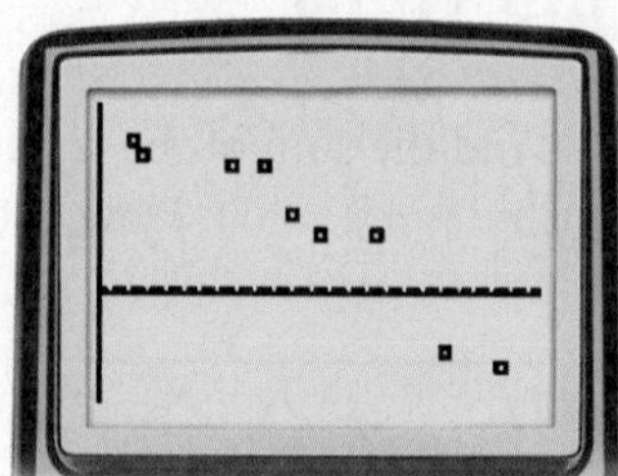

STEP 3 Press STAT again and choose **CALC**. From the menu choose **4:LinReg($ax + b$)**. The calculator will display the slope, a, and the y-intercept, b, of the line of best fit. The screen also displays values for the correlation coefficient r and r^2.

STEP 4 Round the values for a and b and write the equation for the best fit line: $y \approx -0.693x + 39.11$.

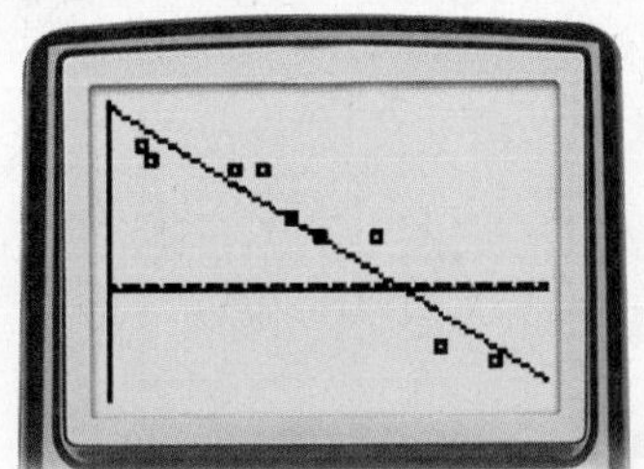

STEP 5 Press Y=, then enter the best fit equation you found in Step 4, then press GRAPH. The calculator graphs the line.

Use the equation to estimate the average temperature in Vancouver, Canada at 49.1° N.

$y \approx -0.693x + 39.11$

$\approx -0.693(49.1) + 39.11$ Substitute the given value for x.

≈ 5.1 Solve.

The average temperature in Vancouver should be near 5.1° C.

Math Talk
Mathematical Practices

Nashville is 5.7° south of Chicago. What estimate would you give for its average temperature?

REFLECT

5. Interpret the slope and y-intercept of the equation from the calculator. For each degree of latitude, how does the temperature change?

____

____

____

____

____

YOUR TURN

6. Use the equation from Example 2 to estimate the average temperature in Munich, Germany at 48.1° N.

____

Guided Practice

Follow the steps to evaluate lines of fit for the data set given in the table. (Explore Activity)

x	1	2	3	6
y (actual)	3	6	4	5
y predicted by $y=\frac{3}{4}x+3$				
Residual				
Squared residual				

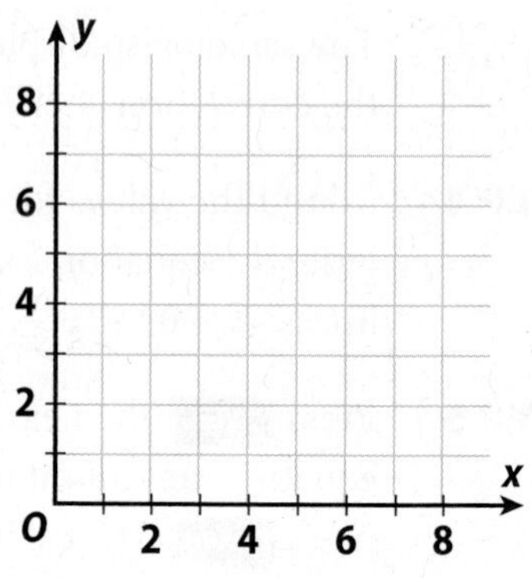

1. Make a scatter plot of the data in the table.
2. Graph the line of fit $y = \frac{3}{4}x + 3$ on the scatter plot.
3. Calculate the y-values predicted by $y = \frac{3}{4}x + 3$, and write them in the table.
4. Calculate the residuals and squared residuals, and write them in the table.
5. What is the sum of the squares of the residuals for the line

   $y = \frac{3}{4}x + 3$? __________

6. Draw the line of fit $y = \frac{3}{4}x + 4$ and calculate the sum of squared residuals for this line. Which line is a better fit? Explain. (Example 1)

   ____

   ____

   ____

7. Use your calculator to find an equation for a line of best fit. (Example 2)

   ____

ESSENTIAL QUESTION CHECK-IN

8. How can you use a graphing calculator to find the line of best fit for a bivariate data set?

   ____

   ____

   ____

Name ______________________ Class ______________________ Date ______________________

8.3 Independent Practice

 CA CC S.ID.6, S.ID.6a, S.ID.6b, S.ID.6c, S.ID.7, S.ID.8

Personal Math Trainer

my.hrw.com

Online Practice and Help

9. The table gives the distance in meters of the gold medal-winning discus throw between 1920 and 1964. When appropriate, use a graphing calculator to solve the problems below.

Olympic Games year	Gold medal discus throw distance (m)
1920	44.685
1924	46.155
1928	47.32
1932	49.49
1936	50.48
1940	No Olympics
1944	No Olympics
1948	52.78
1952	55.03
1956	56.36
1960	59.18
1964	61.00

a. What are the independent variable and dependent variable in this data set?

____

____

b. In which column on the graphing calculator will you represent: years? distance? Write the first 3 entries for each column.

____

____

c. Enter your data. What values does the calculator give for the slope, intercept, and correlation coefficient? Write the best fit equation for the data set.

____

____

____

d. **Draw a Conclusion** How good was the fit of the equation you wrote for this data? Explain.

____

____

e. Suppose the Olympics had been held in 1940 and 1944. What distance would you predict for each year? ______________________

f. **Make a Prediction** In the 2012 London Olympics, Robert Harting of Germany took the Gold Medal with a throw of 68.27 m. Was this distance greater or less than the best fit equation would predict? Explain.

____

____

____

FOCUS ON HIGHER ORDER THINKING

Work Area

10. Represent Real-World Problems The table lists the median heights (in centimeters) of girls and boys from age 2 to age 10.

Age (years)	Median Height (cm) of Girls	Median Height (cm) of Boys
2	84.98	86.45
3	93.92	94.96
4	100.75	102.22
5	107.66	108.90
6	114.71	115.39
7	121.49	121.77
8	127.59	128.88
9	132.92	133.51
10	137.99	138.62

a. Identify the real-world variables that x and y will represent.

b. Find the equation of each line of best fit.

c. Find each correlation coefficient.

d. Evaluate the quality of fit for each line.

e. **Analyze Relationships** Which line is the better line of best fit for its data? Explain.

Ready to Go On?

8.1 Correlation

Estimate the correlation coefficient for each scatter plot.

1. 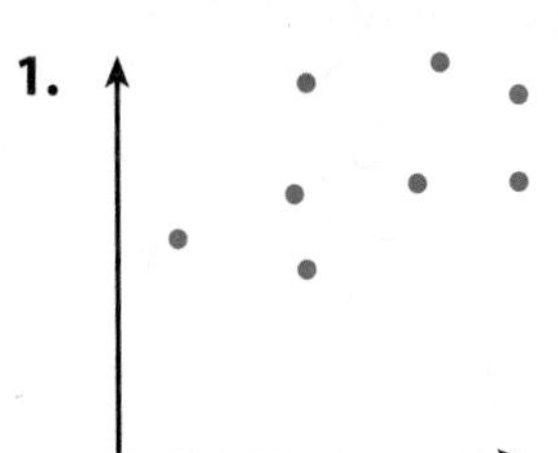

____

2. 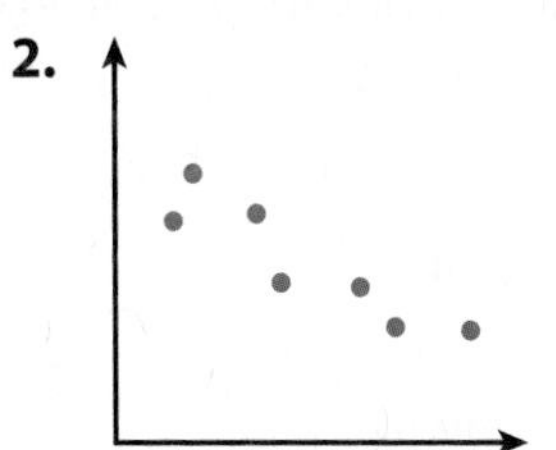

____

3. 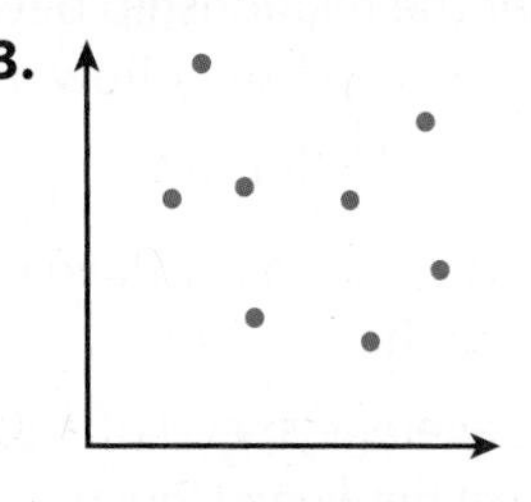

____

8.2 Fitting Lines to Data

The table gives data for the average salary, in millions of dollars, of players on baseball teams and the number of wins each team had last year.

4. Make a scatter plot of the data.

Average Salary	Number of Wins
$2.6	81
$2.7	73
$3.8	83
$4.6	88
$4.6	93
$5.3	89
$6.2	95

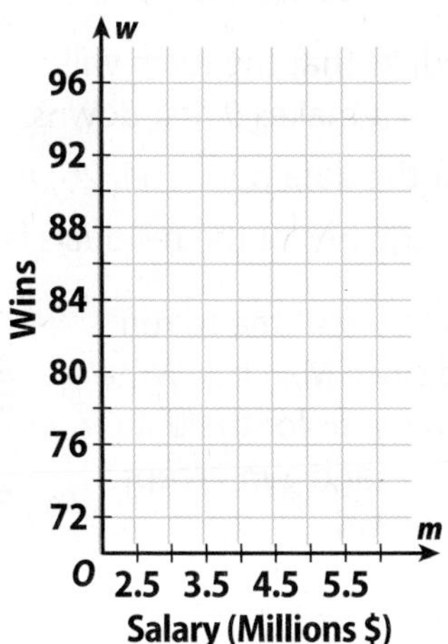

8.3 Linear Regression

5. Use your calculator to find the line of best fit for the data.

Graph the line on the scatter plot. _______________

ESSENTIAL QUESTION

6. How can you use statistical methods to find relationships between variables?

____

____

____

MODULE 8
MIXED REVIEW

Assessment Readiness

1. Consider the relationship between each pair of variables. Would a scatter plot of the relationship likely show a positive correlation?

Select Yes or No for A–C.

A. the distance a car travels and the amount of gas the car uses ○ Yes ○ No

B. the average speed of a car and the time to travel between Houston and Dallas ○ Yes ○ No

C. the age of a car and the number of oil changes the car has had ○ Yes ○ No

2. The table shows the number of first downs and the number of points scored by a football team during its first 4 games. A student wrote the equation $y = 0.3x + 13$ to model the data.

First Downs, x	44	23	9	31
Points, y	26	23	15	19

Choose True or False for each statement.

A. The model predicts that the team will score 15.7 points when it makes 9 first downs. ○ True ○ False

B. The residual for the data point (44, 26) is 5.2. ○ True ○ False

C. The sum of the squares of the residuals is 21.3. ○ True ○ False

3. The graph shows how Ivy's time to run a mile has changed since March 1. Write the equation of a line of fit for the data. Explain what the slope and y-intercept represent in this situation.

Time to run mile (min): 9, 10, 11, 12 (y)

Days since March 1: O, 5, 10, 15, 20 (x)

4. The functions $f(x) = 250x$ and $g(x) = 400x$ model the maximum number of songs that can be stored on an MP3 player with a capacity of x gigabytes. Find the function $h(x) = g(x) - f(x)$. What does the function $h(x)$ represent?

Systems of Equations and Inequalities

MODULE 9

ESSENTIAL QUESTION

How are the graphs of systems of linear equations and inequalities related to their solutions?

Real-World Video

my.hrw.com

A Mars rover is sent into space to land on Mars. This requires planning the trajectory of the rover to intersect with the orbit of Mars. Systems of equations are used to find the intersection of graphs.

GO DIGITAL
my.hrw.com

my.hrw.com

Go digital with your write-in student edition, accessible on any device.

Math On the Spot

Scan with your smart phone to jump directly to the online edition, video tutor, and more.

Animated Math

Interactively explore key concepts to see how math works.

Personal Math Trainer

Get immediate feedback and help as you work through practice sets.

Are YOU Ready?

Complete these exercises to review skills you will need for this module.

Personal Math Trainer

Online Practice and Help

my.hrw.com

Graph Functions

EXAMPLE Graph $y = 2x - 4$.
1. Make a table of values.
2. Plot the ordered pairs.
3. Draw a line through the points.

x	y
0	−4
2	0
−2	−8

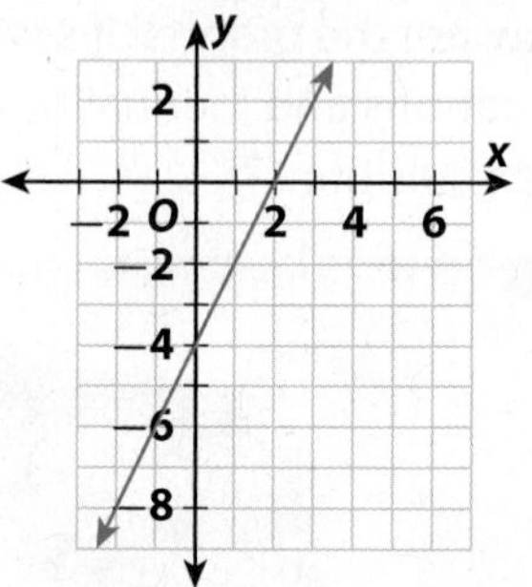

Graph each function.

1. $y = 3x + 6$

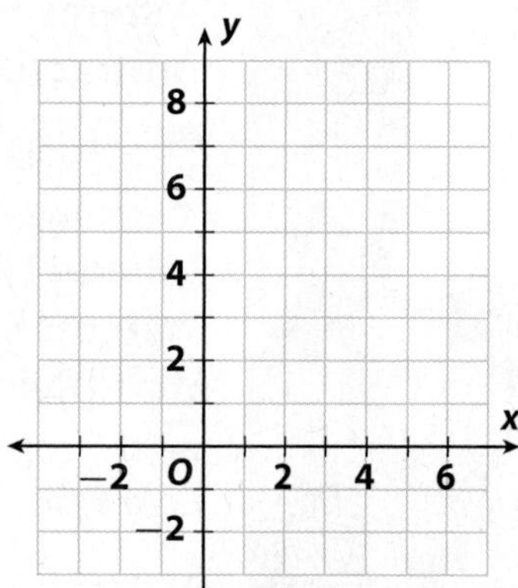

2. $y = -x + 5$

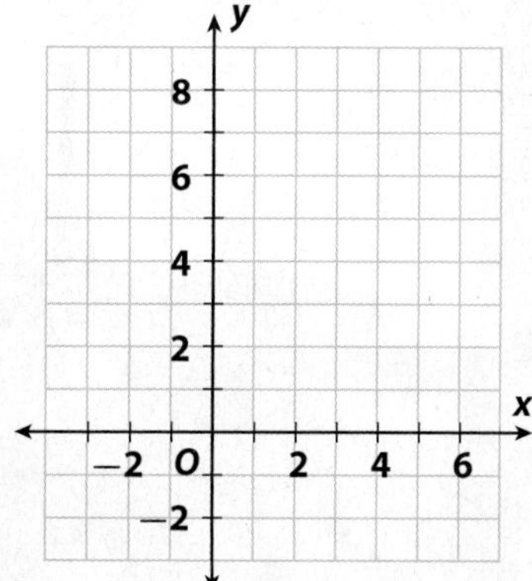

Combine Like Terms

EXAMPLE Simplify $2x + 3 + 3x$.

$2x + 3x + 3$ *Combine like terms.*

$5x + 3$

Simplify each expression.

3. $-4y + (-2y) + 6 - 4$ ________

4. $12x - (-4) - 3x$ ________

5. $9 - 10c + 4c$ ________

6. $9t + (-12t) - 6s + 3s$ ________

7. $-7x - 5y - (-7x) + 2y$ ________

8. $4a + 5b + 3 - (6a + 5b + 8)$ ________

Reading Start-Up

Visualize Vocabulary

Use the ✔ words to complete the chart.

Word	Example
	$y = 2x - 5$
	$y < 2x - 5$
	(x, y)
	$(0, y)$
	$(x, 0)$

Understand Vocabulary

To become familiar with some of the vocabulary terms in the module, read the description and write the term described. You may refer to the module, the glossary, or a dictionary.

1. The word *system* means "a group." How do you think a system of linear equations is different from a linear equation?

____

____

2. What does the word eliminate mean? What might the *elimination* method refer to when solving mathematical equations?

____

____

3. A solution of a linear equation was the ordered pair that made the equation true. Modify this to define solution of a linear inequality.

____

Vocabulary

Review Words

- Distributive Property (*Propiedad distributiva*)
- ✔ linear equation (*ecuación lineal*)
- ✔ linear inequality (*desigualdad lineal*)
- ✔ ordered pair (*par ordenado*)
- solution of a linear equation in two variables (*solución de una ecuación lineal en dos variables*)
- ✔ *x*-intercept (*intersección con el eje x*)
- ✔ *y*-intercept (*intersección con el eje y*)

Preview Words

- elimination method
- solution of a system of linear equations
- solution of a system of linear inequalities
- substitution method
- system of linear equations

Active Reading

Tri-Fold Before beginning the module, create a tri-fold to help you learn the concepts and vocabulary in this module. Fold the paper into three sections. Label the columns "What I Know," "What I Want to Know," and "What I Learned." Complete the first two columns before you read. After studying the module, complete the third column.

GETTING READY FOR

Systems of Equations and Inequalities

Understanding the standards and the vocabulary terms in the standards will help you know exactly what you are expected to learn in this module.

CA CC A.REI.6

Solve systems of linear equations exactly and approximately (e.g., with graphs), focusing on pairs of linear equations in two variables.

Key Vocabulary

system of linear equations *(sistema de ecuaciones lineales)*
A system of equations in which all of the equations are linear.

What It Means to You

You can solve systems of equations to find out when two relationships involving the same variables are true at the same time.

EXAMPLE A.REI.6

Find the solution of the system of equations.

$$\begin{cases} y = 2x - 3 \\ y = -\frac{1}{2}x + 2 \end{cases}$$

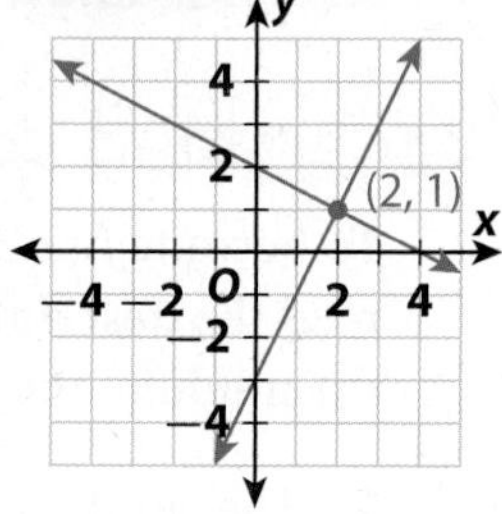

The solution of the system is the point (x, y) that satisfies both equations simultaneously. On a graph, it is the point at which the lines intersect, $(2, 1)$.

CA CC A.CED.3

Represent constraints by equations or inequalities, and by systems of equations and/or inequalities, and interpret solutions as viable or non-viable options in a modeling context.

Key Vocabulary

inequality *(desigualdad)*
A statement that compares two expressions by using one of the following signs: $<, >, \leq, \geq$, or $\neq$.

solution of an inequality in one variable *(solución de una desigualdad en una variable)*
A value or values that make the inequality true.

What It Means to You

You can use inequalities to represent limits on the values in a situation so that the solutions make sense in a real-world context.

EXAMPLE A.CED.3

Anyone riding the large water slide at a the park must be at least 40 inches tall.

Let h represent the heights that are allowed.

Height is at least **40 inches.**

$h \geq 40$

Visit **my.hrw.com** to see all **CA Common Core Standards** explained.

my.hrw.com

LESSON 9.1

Solving Linear Systems by Graphing

A.REI.6

Solve systems of linear equations exactly and approximately (e.g., with graphs), focusing on pairs of linear equations in two variables. *Also A.CED.3*

ESSENTIAL QUESTION

How can you find the solution of a system of linear equations by graphing?

Solving a Linear System by Graphing

Math On the Spot

my.hrw.com

A **system of linear equations,** also called a *linear system*, consists of two or more linear equations that have the same variables. A **solution of a system of linear equations** with two variables is an ordered pair that satisfies all of the equations in the system. The values of the variables in the ordered pair make each equation in the system true.

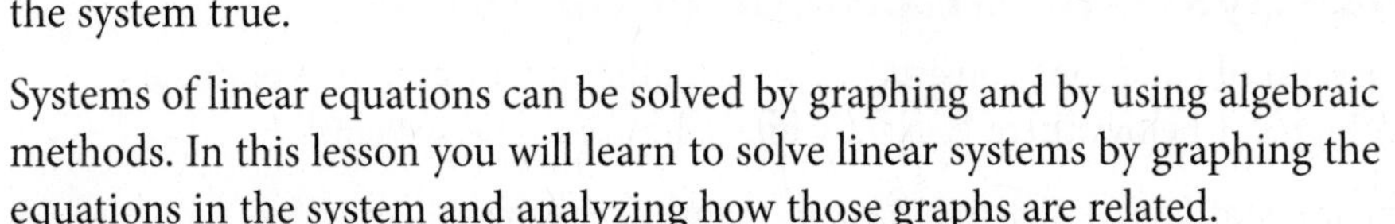

Systems of linear equations can be solved by graphing and by using algebraic methods. In this lesson you will learn to solve linear systems by graphing the equations in the system and analyzing how those graphs are related.

EXAMPLE 1

A.REI.6

Solve the system of linear equations below by graphing. Check your answer.

$$\begin{cases} -x + y = 3 \\ 2x + y = 6 \end{cases}$$

STEP 1 Find the intercepts for each equation, plus a third point for a check. Graph each line.

$-x + y = 3$	$2x + y = 6$
x-intercept: -3	x-intercept: 3
y-intercept: 3	y-intercept: 6
third point: (3, 6)	third point: (−1, 8)

STEP 2 Find the point of intersection.

The two lines appear to intersect at (1, 4).

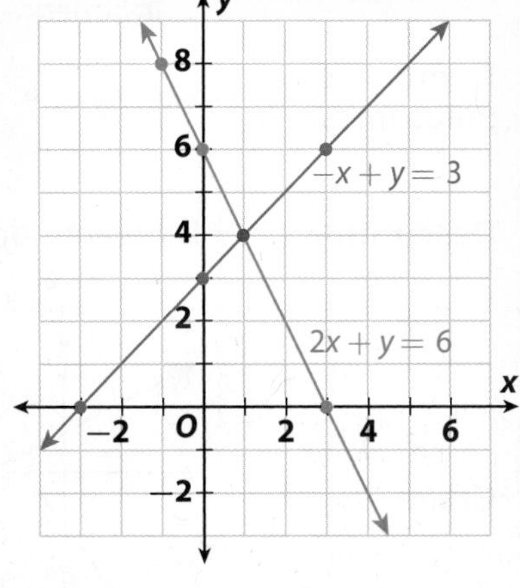

STEP 3 Check to see if (1, 4) makes both equations true.

$-x + y = 3$	$2x + y = 6$
$-(1) + 4 \stackrel{?}{=} 3$	$2(1) + 4 \stackrel{?}{=} 6$
$3 = 3\checkmark$	$6 = 6\checkmark$

The solution is (1, 4).

YOUR TURN

1. Solve the system of linear equations below by graphing. Check your answer.

$$\begin{cases} x + y = 8 \\ x - y = 2 \end{cases}$$

Solution: ______________________

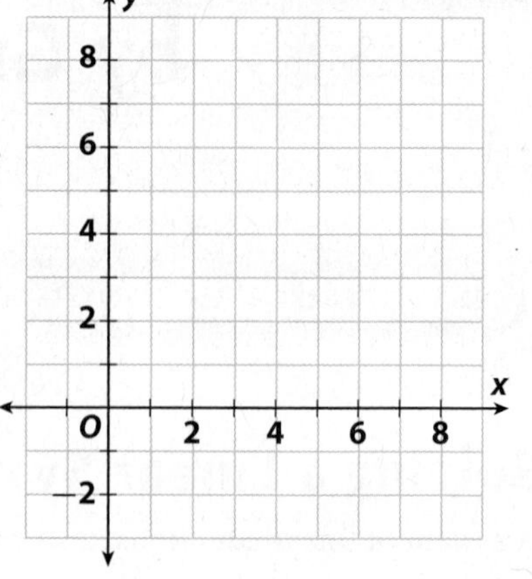

Special Systems of Linear Equations

When a system of equations consists of two lines that intersect in one point, as shown in Figure 1 below, there is exactly one solution to the system.

If two linear equations in a system have the same graph, as shown in Figure 2, the graphs are coincident lines, or the same line. There are infinitely many solutions of the system because every point on the line represents a solution of both equations.

A system with at least one solution is a **consistent system**. Consistent systems can either be independent or dependent.

- An **independent system** has exactly one solution. The graph of an independent system consists of two intersecting lines.
- A **dependent system** has infinitely many solutions. The graph of a dependent system consists of two coincident lines.

When the two lines in a system do not intersect, as shown in Figure 3, they are parallel lines. There are no ordered pairs that satisfy both equations, so there is no solution. A system that has no solution is an **inconsistent system**.

The table below summarizes how systems of linear equations can be classified.

Classification of Systems of Linear Equations

Classification	Consistent and Independent	Consistent and Dependent	Inconsistent
Number of Solutions	Exactly one	Infinitely many	None
Description	Different slopes	Same slope, same *y*-intercept	Same slope, different *y*-intercepts
Graph	Figure 1	Figure 2	Figure 3

EXAMPLE 2

CA CC A.REI.6

Use the graph to solve each system of linear equations. Classify each system.

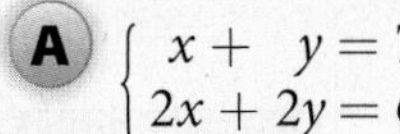

$$\begin{cases} x + y = 7 \\ 2x + 2y = 6 \end{cases}$$

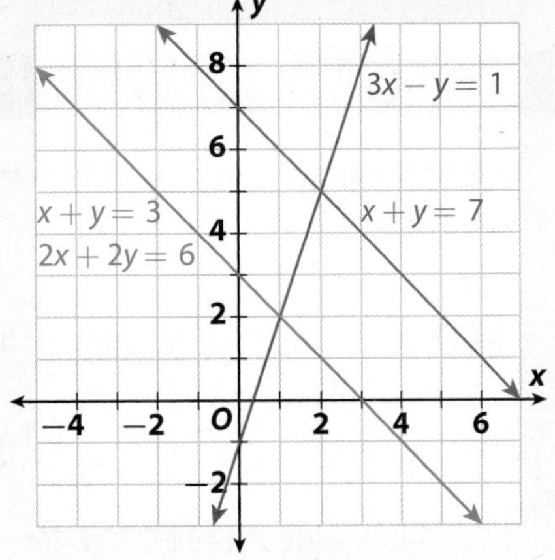

The lines do not intersect and appear to be parallel lines.

This system has no solution. The system is inconsistent.

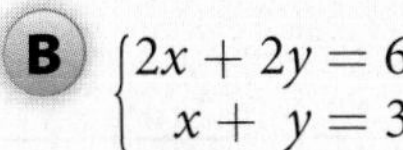

$$\begin{cases} 2x + 2y = 6 \\ x + y = 3 \end{cases}$$

The equations have the same graph, so the graphs are coincident lines.

This system has infinitely many solutions. The system is consistent and dependent.

REFLECT

2. Use the graph above to identify two lines that represent a linear system that is consistent and independent. What are the equations of the lines? Explain your reasoning.

____

____

Math Talk
Mathematical Practices

What is the possible number of solutions for a system of linear equations whose graph shows two distinct lines? Explain.

YOUR TURN

Graph each system of linear equations. Classify each system.

3. $\begin{cases} 2x + 2y = 8 \\ x - y = 4 \end{cases}$

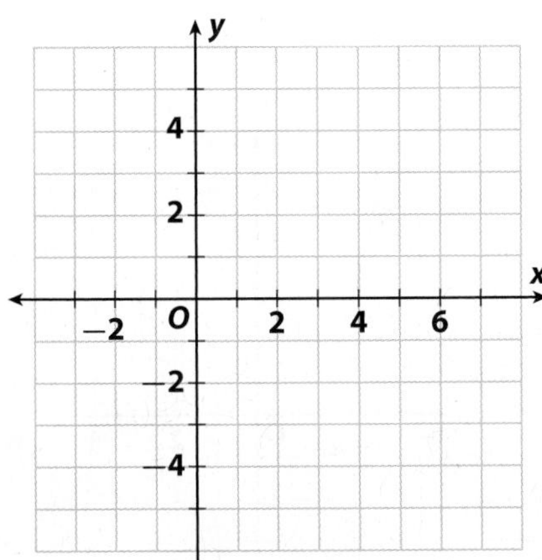

____

____

4. $\begin{cases} y = 2x - 4 \\ y = 2x + 6 \end{cases}$

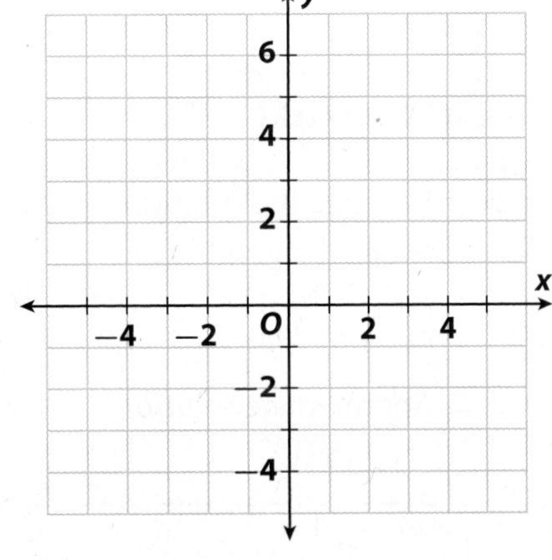

____

____

Personal Math Trainer
Online Practice and Help
my.hrw.com

Estimating a Solution by Graphing

You can estimate a solution for a linear system by graphing and then check your estimate to determine if it is an approximate solution.

EXAMPLE 3

CA CC A.REI.6

Estimate the solution for the linear system by graphing.

$$\begin{cases} x + 2y = 2 \\ 2x - 3y = 12 \end{cases}$$

STEP 1 Graph each equation by finding intercepts.

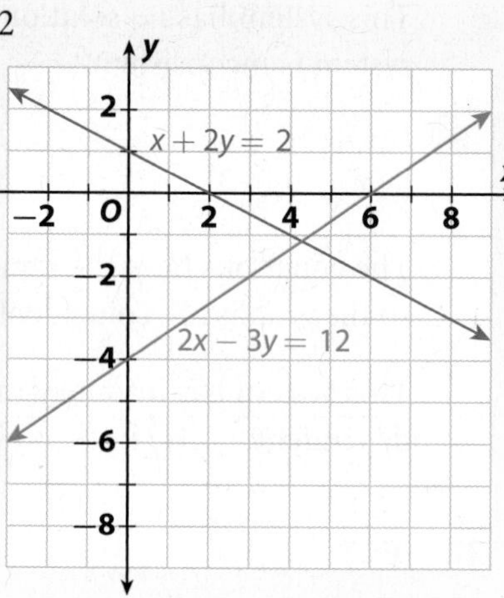

$x + 2y = 2$	$2x - 3y = 12$
x-intercept: 2	x-intercept: 6
y-intercept: 1	y-intercept: -4

STEP 2 Find the point of intersection.

The two lines appear to intersect at about $\left(4\frac{1}{4}, -1\frac{1}{8}\right)$.

STEP 3 Check if $\left(4\frac{1}{4}, -1\frac{1}{8}\right)$ is an approximate solution.

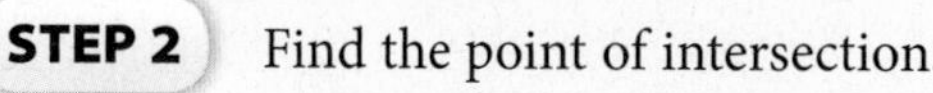

$x + 2y = 2$	$2x - 3y = 12$
$4\frac{1}{4} + 2\left(-1\frac{1}{8}\right) \stackrel{?}{=} 2$	$2\left(4\frac{1}{4}\right) - 3\left(-1\frac{1}{8}\right) \stackrel{?}{=} 12$
$4\frac{1}{4} + \left(-2\frac{1}{4}\right) \stackrel{?}{=} 2$	$8\frac{1}{2} - \left(-3\frac{3}{8}\right) \stackrel{?}{=} 12$
$2 = 2\checkmark$	$11\frac{7}{8} \approx 12\checkmark$

The point $\left(4\frac{1}{4}, -1\frac{1}{8}\right)$ does not make both equations true, but it is acceptable since $11\frac{7}{8}$ is close to 12. So, $\left(4\frac{1}{4}, -1\frac{1}{8}\right)$ is an approximate solution.

YOUR TURN

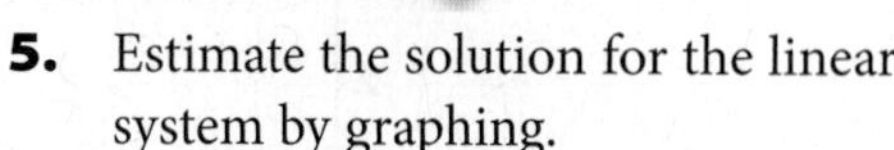

5. Estimate the solution for the linear system by graphing.

$$\begin{cases} x - y = 3 \\ x + 2y = 4 \end{cases}$$

Approximate solution: ______________________

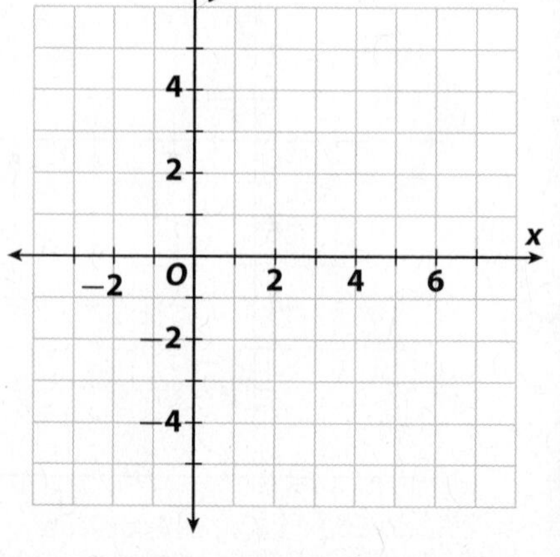

Guided Practice

Solve the system of linear equations by graphing. Check your answer. (Example 1)

1. $\begin{cases} x - y = 7 \\ 2x + y = 2 \end{cases}$

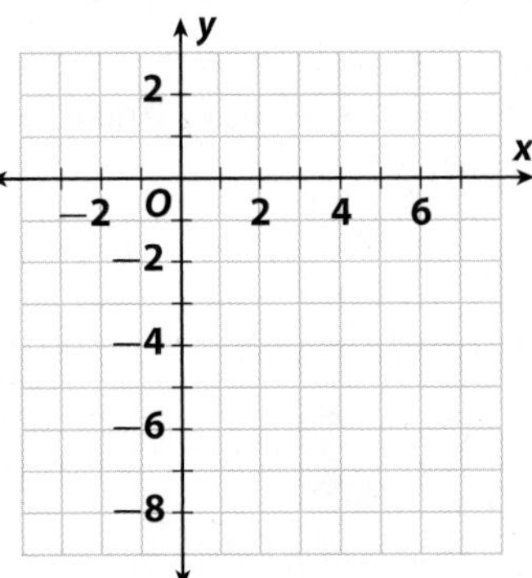

$x - y = 7$	$2x + y = 2$
x-intercept: ________	x-intercept: ________
y-intercept: ________	y-intercept: ________

The solution of the system is ____________________.

Does your solution check in both original equations? ________

Use the graph to solve and classify each system of linear equations. (Example 2)

2. $\begin{cases} x + y = -1 \\ -2x + 2y = -2 \end{cases}$

Is the system consistent?

____

Is the system independent?

____

Solution: ____________

3. $\begin{cases} -x + y = 3 \\ -2x + 2y = -2 \end{cases}$

Is the system consistent?

____

Solution: ____________

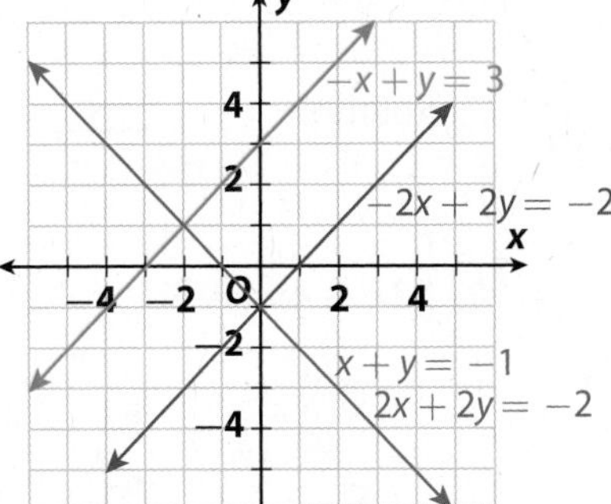

Estimate the solution for the system of linear equations by graphing. (Example 3)

4. $\begin{cases} x + y = -1 \\ 2x - y = 5 \end{cases}$

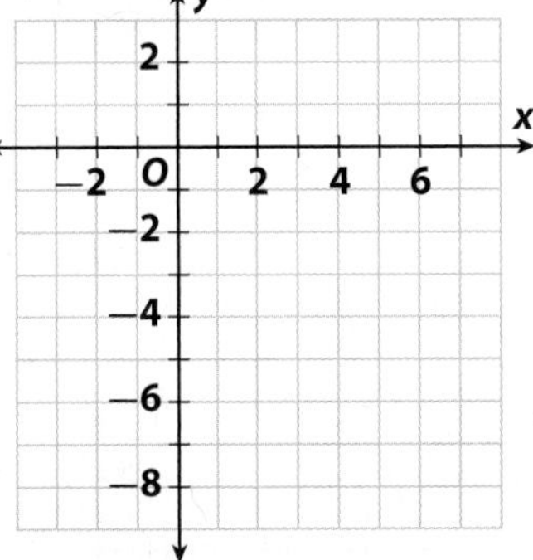

$x + y = -1$	$2x - y = 5$
x-intercept: ________	x-intercept: ________
y-intercept: ________	y-intercept: ________

The two lines appear to intersect at

____________________.

ESSENTIAL QUESTION CHECK-IN

5. How does graphing help you solve a system of linear equations?

____

____

____

Name ________________ Class ________________ Date ________________

9.1 Independent Practice

CA CC A.REI.6, A.CED.3

Solve each system of linear equations by graphing.

6. $\begin{cases} x - y = -2 \\ 2x + y = 8 \end{cases}$

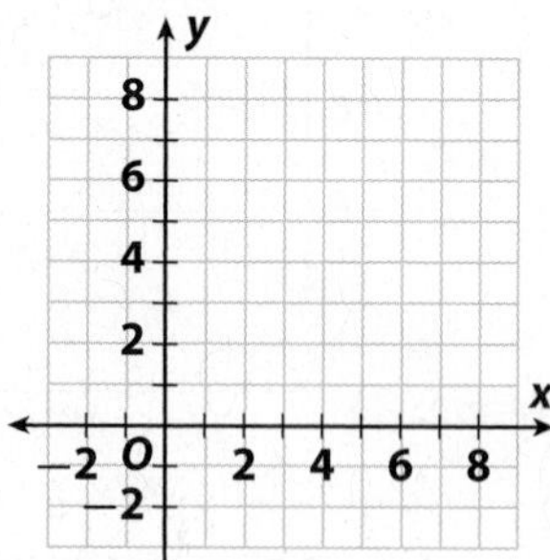

Solution: ________________

7. $\begin{cases} x - y = -5 \\ 2x + 4y = -4 \end{cases}$

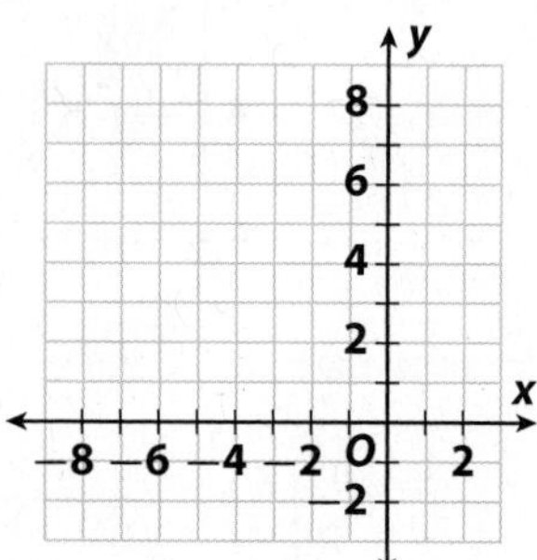

Solution: ________________

8. $\begin{cases} x + 2y = -8 \\ -2x - 4y = 4 \end{cases}$

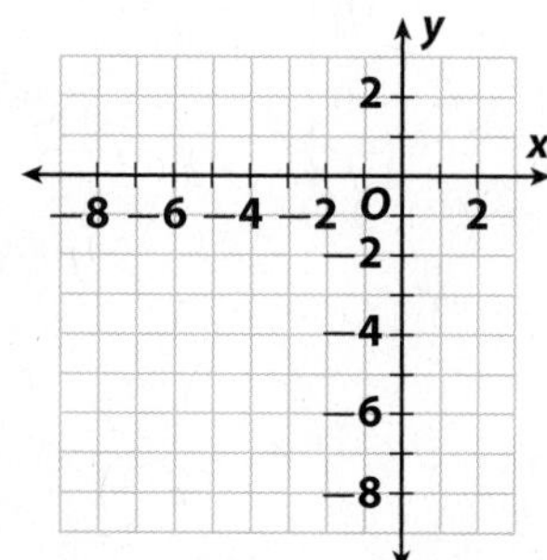

Solution: ________________

Estimate the solution for the linear system by graphing.

9. $\begin{cases} x + y = 5 \\ x - 3y = 3 \end{cases}$

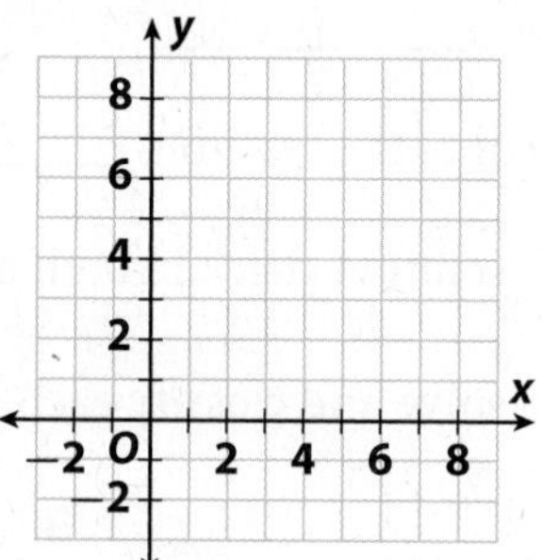

Approximate solution: ________________

Graph each system. Then classify it as *consistent and independent, consistent and dependent,* or *inconsistent.*

10. $\begin{cases} x + 2y = 6 \\ x = 2 \end{cases}$

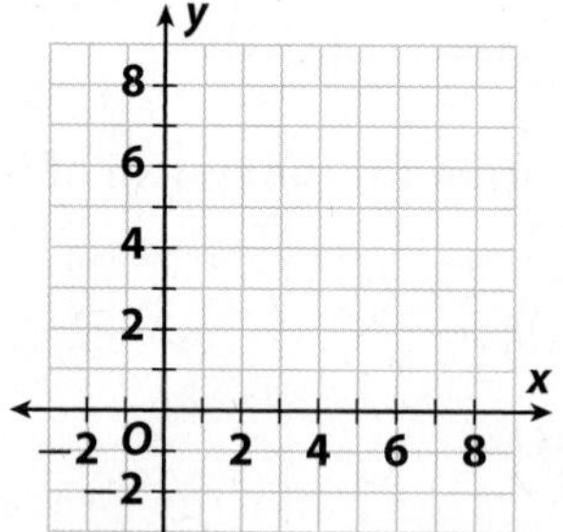

____

11. $\begin{cases} 2x - y = -6 \\ 4x - 2y = -12 \end{cases}$

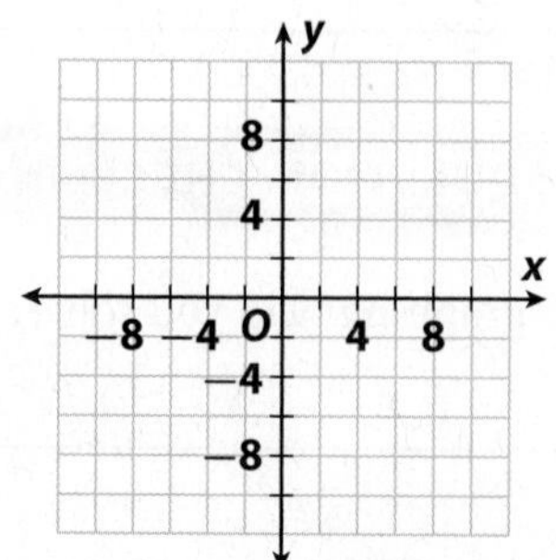

____

12. Use the graphed system below to find an approximate solution. Then write a system of equations that represents the system.

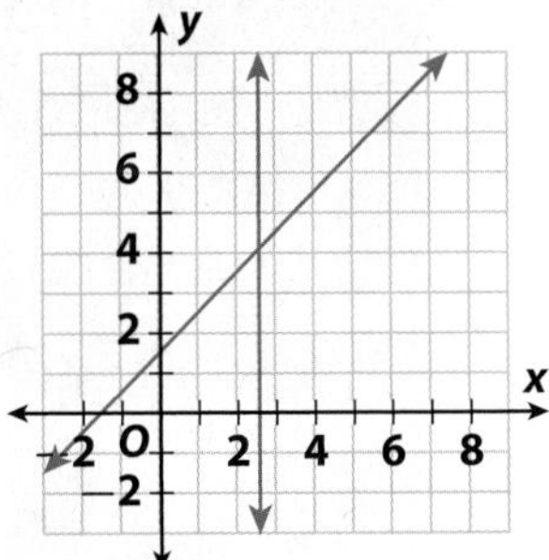

____

____

13. **Communicate Mathematical Ideas** When a system of linear equations is graphed, how is the graph of each equation related to the solutions of that equation?

____

____

____

____

____

____

____

14. **Critical Thinking** Write *sometimes, always,* or *never* to complete the following statement:

If the equations in a system of linear equations have the same slope, there are ________ infinitely many solutions for the system.

____

15. Suppose you use the graph of a system of linear equations to estimate the solution. Explain how you would check your estimate to determine if it is an approximate solution.

____

____

____

____

____

____

____

16. Without graphing, describe the graph of this linear system of equations.

$$\begin{cases} x = 3 \\ y = 4 \end{cases}$$

What is the solution of the linear system?

____

____

____

____

____

____

17. How can you recognize a dependent system of equations by analyzing the equations in the system? ______________________________

____

____

18. How would you classify a system of equations whose graph is composed of two lines with different slopes and the same *y*-intercepts? What is the solution to the system?

____

____

____

19. Sophie and Marcos are each saving for new bicycles. So far, Sophie has $10 saved and can earn $5 per hour walking dogs. Marcos has $4 saved and can earn $8 per hour at his family's plant nursery. After how many hours of work will Sophie and Marcos have saved the same amount? What will that amount be? Use the system of equations below to complete the graph.

Sophie: $y = 5x + 10$

Marcos: $y = 8x + 4$

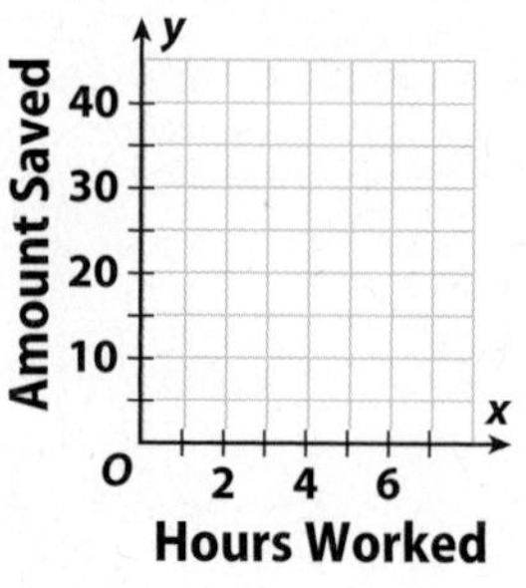

____

H.O.T. FOCUS ON HIGHER ORDER THINKING

Work Area

20. Represent Real-World Problems Cora ran 3 miles last week and will run 7 miles per week from now on. Hana ran 9 miles last week and will run 4 miles per week from now on. The system of linear equations $\begin{cases} y = 7x + 3 \\ y = 4x + 9 \end{cases}$ can be used to represent this situation. Explain what x and y represent in the equations. After how many weeks will Cora and Hana have run the same number of miles? How many miles?

____

____

____

21. Explain the Error Jake classifies the system below as inconsistent because the equations have the same y-intercept. What is his error?

$$\begin{cases} y = 2x - 4 \\ y = x - 4 \end{cases}$$

____

____

____

22. Explain the Error Sara solved the system

$$\begin{cases} 5x + 2y = 6 \\ x - 3y = -4 \end{cases}$$

by graphing and estimated the solution to be about (1.5, 0.6). What is her error? What is the correct answer?

____

____

____

LESSON 9.2

Solving Linear Systems by Substitution

CA CC A.REI.6

Solve systems of linear equations exactly and approximately (e.g., with graphs), focusing on pairs of linear equations in two variables. *Also A.CED.3*

ESSENTIAL QUESTION

How can you solve a system of linear equations by using substitution?

EXPLORE ACTIVITY

Solve by Substituting

In the system of linear equations shown below, the value of y is given. You can use this value of y to find the value of x and the solution of the system.

$$\begin{cases} y = 3 \\ x + y = 5 \end{cases}$$

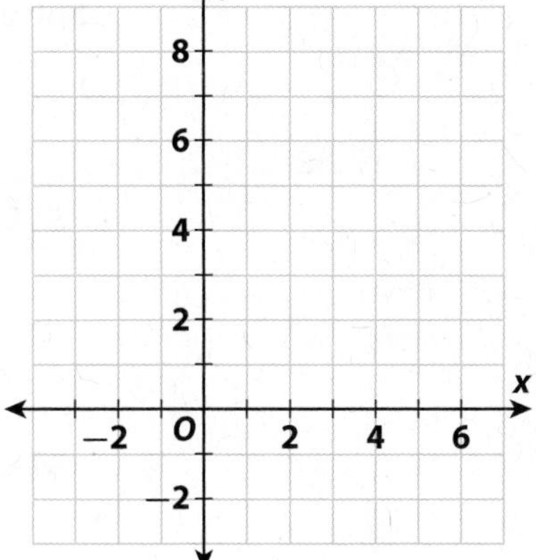

A Substitute the value for y in the second equation and solve for x.

$x + y = 5$

$x + \square = 5$

$x = \square$

B You know the values of x and y. What is the solution of the system?

Solution: $(\square, \square)$

C Graph the system of linear equations. How do your solutions compare?

____

D Use substitution to find the values of x and y in this system of linear equations. Once you find the value for x, substitute it either original equation to find the value for y.

$$\begin{cases} y = 3x \\ 2x + 3y = 55 \end{cases}$$

Solution: $(\square, \square)$

REFLECT

1. For the system in part D, what equation did you get after substituting $3x$ for y in $2x + 3y = 55$ and simplifying?

____

2. How could you check your solution in part D?

____

____

Solve a Linear System by Substitution

The **substitution method** is used to solve systems of linear equations by solving an equation for one variable and then substituting the resulting expression for that variable into the other equation. The steps for this method are as follows:

1. Solve one of the equations for one of its variables.
2. Substitute the expression from Step 1 into the other equation and solve for the other variable.
3. Substitute the value from Step 2 into either original equation and solve to find the value of the variable in Step 1.

EXAMPLE 1

CA CC A.REI.6

My Notes

Solve the system of linear equations by substitution. Check your answer.

$$\begin{cases} -3x + y = 1 \\ 4x + y = 8 \end{cases}$$

STEP 1 Solve an equation for one variable.

$-3x + y = 1$ Select one of the equations.

$y = 3x + 1$ Solve for the variable y. Isolate y on one side.

STEP 2 Substitute the expression for y in the other equation and solve.

$4x + 3x + 1 = 8$ Substitute the expression for the variable y.

$7x + 1 = 8$ Combine like terms.

$7x = 7$ Subtract 1 from each side.

$x = 1$ Divide each side by 7.

STEP 3 Substitute the value of x you found into one of the equations and solve for the other variable, y.

$-3(1) + y = 1$ Substitute the value of x into the first equation.

$-3 + y = 1$ Simplify.

$y = 4$ Add 3 to each side.

So, (1, 4) is the solution of the system.

STEP 4 Check the solution by graphing.

$-3x + y = 1$	$4x + y = 8$
x-intercept: $-\frac{1}{3}$	x-intercept: 2
y-intercept: 1	y-intercept: 8

The point of intersection is (1, 4).

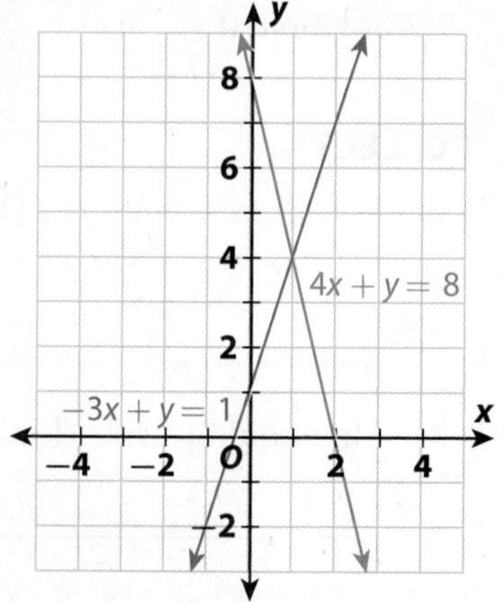

REFLECT

3. **Justify Reasoning** Is it more efficient to solve $-3x + y = 1$ for x? Why or why not?

____

____

4. What is another way to check your solution?

____

____

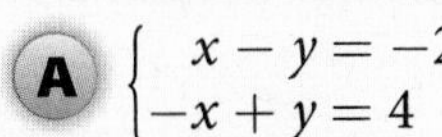

Solve each system of linear equations by substitution. Check your answer.

5. $\begin{cases} 2x + y = 5 \\ y = x - 4 \end{cases}$

Solution: ______________

6. $\begin{cases} x + 3y = 4 \\ -x + 2y = 6 \end{cases}$

Solution: ______________

Solving Special Systems by Substitution

You can use the substitution method for systems of linear equations that have infinitely many solutions and for systems that have no solutions.

EXAMPLE 2 CA CC A.REI.6

Solve each system of linear equations by substitution.

A $\begin{cases} x - y = -2 \\ -x + y = 4 \end{cases}$

STEP 1 Solve $x - y = -2$ for x: $x = y - 2$

STEP 2 Substitute the resulting expression into the other equation and solve.

$-(y - 2) + y = 4$ *Substitute.*

$2 = 4$ *Simplify.*

The resulting equation is false, so the system has no solutions.

STEP 3 Graph the equations to provide more information.

The graph shows that the lines are parallel and do not intersect.

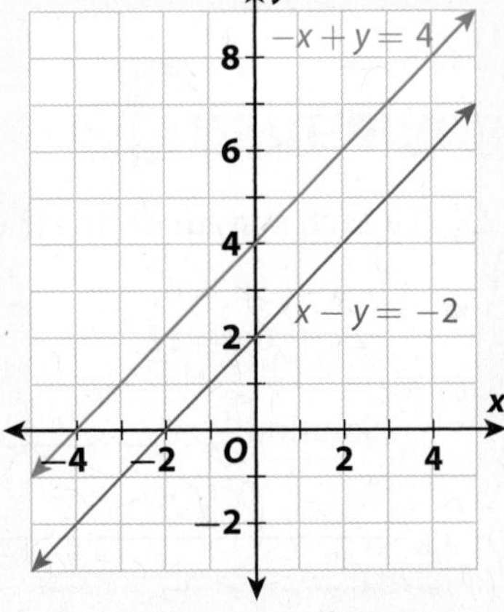

B $\begin{cases} 2x + y = -2 \\ 4x + 2y = -4 \end{cases}$

My Notes

STEP 1 Solve $2x + y = -2$ for y: $y = -2x - 2$

STEP 2 Substitute the resulting expression into the other equation and solve.

$4x + 2(-2x - 2) = -4$ Substitute.

$4x - 4x - 4 = -4$ Use the Distributive Property.

$-4 = -4$ Simplify.

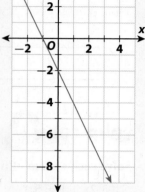

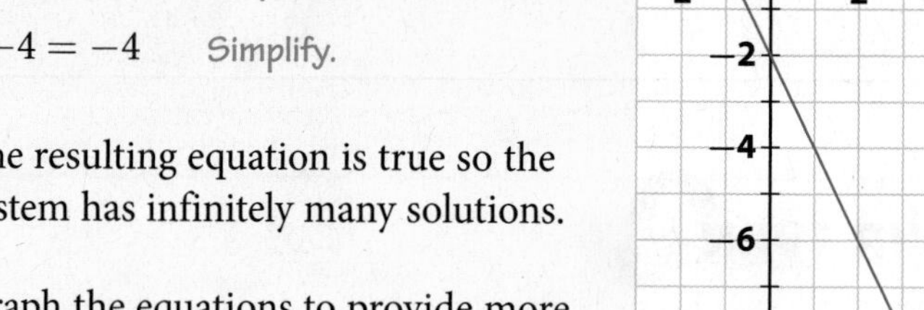

The resulting equation is true so the system has infinitely many solutions.

STEP 3 Graph the equations to provide more information.

The graphs are the same line, so the system has infinitely many solutions.

REFLECT

7. In part B of Example 2, why is it more efficient to solve and substitute for y than to solve and substitute for x?

____

____

____

8. Give two possible solutions of the system in part B of Example 2. How are all the solutions of this system related to one another?

____

____

____

YOUR TURN

Solve each system of linear equations by substitution.

9. $\begin{cases} x + 3y = 6 \\ 2x + 6y = 12 \end{cases}$

Solution: ______________________

10. $\begin{cases} 2x - y = -1 \\ 2x - y = -4 \end{cases}$

Solution: ______________________

Modeling with Linear Systems

You can use a system of linear equations and its graph to model many real-world situations.

EXAMPLE 3  

One family fitness center has a $50 enrollment fee and costs $30 per month. Another center has no enrollment fee and costs $40 per month. Write an equation for each option. Let t represent the total amount paid and m represent the number of months. In how many months will both fitness centers cost the same? What will that cost be?

	Total cost	is	enrollment fee	plus	cost per month	times	months.
Option 1	t	$=$	50	$+$	30	$\cdot$	m
Option 2	t	$=$	0	$+$	40	$\cdot$	m

STEP 1 $t = 50 + 30m$ — Write the system of equations.
$t = 40m$

STEP 2 $50 + 30m = 40m$ — Substitute $50 + 30m$ for t in the second equation.

$\underline{-30m} \quad \underline{-30m}$ — Subtract $30m$ from each side.

$50 = 10m$

$\frac{50}{10} = \frac{10m}{10}$ — Divide each side by 10.

$5 = m$

STEP 3 $t = 40m$ — Write one of the original equations.
$= 40(5)$ — Substitute 5 for m.
$= 200$

STEP 4 $(5, 200)$ — Write the solution as an ordered pair.

In 5 months, the total cost for each option will be the same, $200.

Math Talk

In a graph of the system of equations, why must the values of the variables be greater than or equal to zero?

YOUR TURN

11. One high-speed Internet provider has a $30 setup fee and charges $40 per month. Another provider has a $60 setup fee and charges $30 per month. In how many months will the cost be the same?

____

Personal Math Trainer
Online Practice and Help
my.hrw.com

Guided Practice

Solve each system of linear equations by substitution. Check your answer. (Examples 1 and 2)

1. $\begin{cases} y = x + 5 \\ 4x + y = 20 \end{cases}$

STEP 1 Find the value of x.

$4x + y = 20$

$4x + \square = 20$

$\square x = \square$

$x = \square$

STEP 2 Find the value of y.

$y = x + 5$

$y = \square + 5$

$y = \square$

Solution: ____________

2. $\begin{cases} x + 2y = 6 \\ 2x + 4y = 12 \end{cases}$

STEP 1 Solve $x + 2y = 6$ for x.

$x = \square$

STEP 2 Substitute that expression for x into $2x + 4y = 12$.

$2(\square) + 4y = 12$

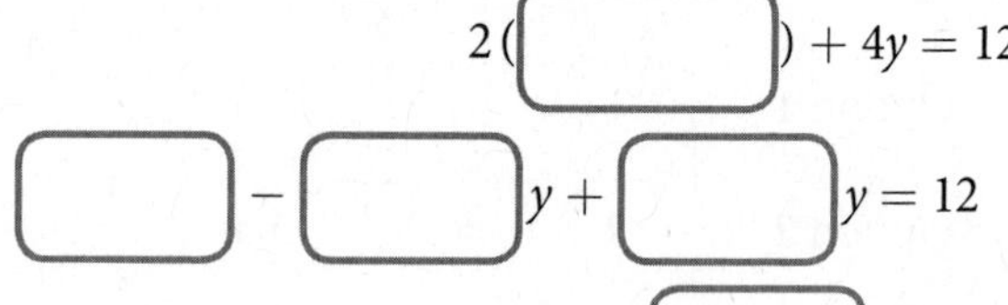

$\square - \square y + \square y = 12$

$\square = 12$

Solution: ____________

____

Solve each system of linear equations by substitution. Check your answer. (Examples 1 and 2)

3. $\begin{cases} x + 2y = 7 \\ 4x + 3y = 3 \end{cases}$

Solution: ____________

4. $\begin{cases} 2x - y = -4 \\ 2x - 2y = -10 \end{cases}$

Solution: ____________

5. $\begin{cases} 2x - 4y = 8 \\ 2y - x = -6 \end{cases}$

Solution: ____________

6. The Blanco family is deciding between two lawn-care services. Evergreen charges a $49 startup fee, plus $29 per month. Great Grass charges a $25 startup fee, plus $37 per month. In how many months will both lawn-care services cost the same? What will that cost be? (Example 3)

____

ESSENTIAL QUESTION CHECK-IN

7. Explain how you can solve a system of linear equations by substitution.

____

____

____

____

Name ______________________ Class ______________________ Date ______________________

9.2 Independent Practice

Personal Math Trainer

Online Practice and Help

CA CC A.REI.6, A.CED.3

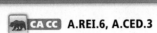

For each linear system, tell whether it is more efficient to solve for x and then substitute for x or to solve for y and then substitute for y. Explain your reasoning. Then solve the system.

8. $\begin{cases} 6x - 3y = 15 \\ x + 3y = -8 \end{cases}$

Solution: ______________________

9. $\begin{cases} 3x - y = -1 \\ 5x - y = 3 \end{cases}$

Solution: ______________________

For each system of linear equations, write the expression you could substitute for x. Then solve the system.

10. $\begin{cases} 2x - y = 6 \\ x + y = -3 \end{cases}$

Solution: ______________________

11. $\begin{cases} x - 2y = 0 \\ 4x - 3y = 15 \end{cases}$

Solution: ______________________

12. **Communicate Mathematical Ideas** The solution of a system of two linear equations yields the equation $0 = 3$. Describe what the graph of the system looks like.

13. Use *one solution, no solutions,* or *infinitely many solutions* to complete this statement.

When the solution of a system of linear equations yields the equation $4 = 6$, the system has ________.

14. **Represent Real-World Problems** Ella buys a book and a pen for $14. The cost of the book is $2 more than twice the cost of the pen. Write a system of linear equations for the situation. Then find the cost of each item. Let x represent the cost of the pen, and let y represent the cost of the book.

15. **Interpret the Answer** The perimeter of a rectangular picture frame is 66 inches. The length is 3 inches greater than the width. The system of linear equations used to represent the situation is shown below.

$\begin{cases} 2x + 2y = 66 \\ x + 3 = y \end{cases}$

Solve the system. Name the dimension represented by each variable.

16. Kim and Leon exercise a total of 20 hours each week. Leon exercises 2 hours less than 3 times the number of hours Kim exercises. How many hours does each exercise?

____

17. Use the receipts below to write and solve a system of linear equations to find the cost of a large fruit bucket and the cost of a small drink.

CINEMA SNAKSHAK
Customer #3598
3 large fruit buckets
2 small drinks
total due: $21.00

CINEMA SNAKSHAK
Customer #3599
2 large fruit buckets
4 small drinks
total due: $22.00

____

____

H.O.T. FOCUS ON HIGHER ORDER THINKING

Work Area

18. Multiple Representations For the first equation in the system of linear equations below, write an equivalent equation without denominators. Then solve the system.

$$\begin{cases} \frac{x}{2} + \frac{y}{3} = 6 \\ x - y = 2 \end{cases}$$

____

19. Critical Thinking Is it possible for a system of three linear equations to have one solution? If so, give an example.

____

____

____

____

20. Draw Conclusions Is it possible to use substitution to solve a system of linear equations if one equation represents a horizontal line and the other equation represents a vertical line? Explain.

____

____

____

LESSON 9.3

Solving Linear Systems by Adding or Subtracting

CA CC A.REI.6 Solve systems of linear equations exactly and approximately (e.g., with graphs), focusing on pairs of linear equations in two variables. Also *A.CED.3*

ESSENTIAL QUESTION

How can you solve a system of linear equations by using addition and subtraction?

EXPLORE ACTIVITY

CA CC A.REI.6

Exploring the Effects: Adding Equations

Remember that the sum of a number and its opposite is zero. You can use that fact to help you solve some systems of linear equations.

A Look at the system of linear equations below.

$$\begin{cases} x - 3y = -15 \\ 5x + 3y = -3 \end{cases}$$

What do you notice about the coefficients of the y-terms.

____

B What is the sum of $-3y$ and $3y$? How do you know?

____

C Find the sum of the two equations by combining like terms.

$$\begin{array}{rrcr} x & -3y & = & -15 \\ +5x & +3y & = & -3 \\ \hline \end{array}$$

$\square + \square = \square$

D Use the resulting equation from part C to find the value of x.

$x = \square$

E Use the value of x to find the value of y. What is the solution of the system?

$y = \square$ Solution: ______________

REFLECT

1. When you add $5x + 3y$ to $x - 3y$ and add -3 to -15, how do you know that the resulting sums are equal?

____

____

____

EXPLORE ACTIVITY *(cont'd)*

2. How could you check your solution in part E?

____

____

Solving a Linear System by Adding or Subtracting

The **elimination method** is another method used to solve a system of linear equations. In this method, one variable is *eliminated* by adding or subtracting the two equations of the system to obtain a single equation in one variable. The steps for this method are as follows:

1. Add or subtract the equations to eliminate one variable, and then solve for the other variable.
2. Substitute the value into either original equation to find the value of the eliminated variable.
3. Write the solution as an ordered pair.

EXAMPLE 1

Solve each system of linear equations using the indicated method. Check your answer.

Solve the system of linear equations below by adding.

$$\begin{cases} 4x - 2y = 12 \\ x + 2y = 8 \end{cases}$$

STEP 1 Add the equations.

$4x - 2y = 12$	Write the equations so that like terms are aligned.
$\underline{+\,x + 2y = 8}$	Notice that the terms $-2y$ and $2y$ are opposites.
$5x + 0 = 20$	Add to eliminate the variable y.
$5x = 20$	Simplify.
$x = 4$	Divide each side by 5.

STEP 2 Substitute the value of x into one of the equations and solve for y.

$x + 2y = 8$	Use the second equation.
$4 + 2y = 8$	Substitute 4 for the variable x.
$2y = 4$	Subtract 4 from each side.
$y = 2$	Divide each side by 2.

STEP 3 Write the solution as an ordered pair.

(4, 2) is the solution of the system.

STEP 4 Check the solution by graphing.

$4x - 2y = 12$	$x + 2y = 8$
x-intercept: 3	x-intercept: 8
y-intercept: −6	y-intercept: 4

The point of intersection is (4, 2).

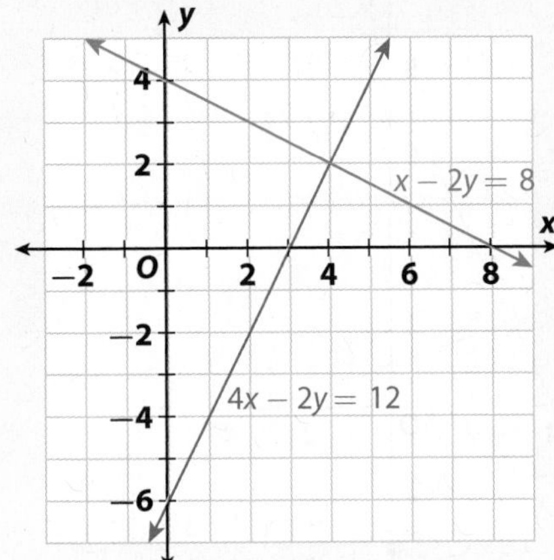

B Solve the system of linear equations below by subtracting.

$$\begin{cases} 2x + 6y = 6 \\ 2x - y = -8 \end{cases}$$

STEP 1 Subtract the equations.

$2x + 6y = 6$	Write the equations so that like terms are aligned.
$\underline{-(2x - y = -8)}$	Notice that both equations contain the term 2x.
$0 + 7y = 14$	Subtract to eliminate the variable x.
$7y = 14$	Simplify.
$\frac{7y}{7} = \frac{14}{7}$	Divide each side by 7.
$y = 2$	Simplify.

STEP 2 Substitute the value of y into one of the equations and solve for x.

$2x - y = -8$	Use the second equation.
$2x - 2 = -8$	Substitute 2 for the variable y.
$2x = -6$	Add 2 to each side.
$x = -3$	Divide each side by 2.

My Notes

STEP 3 Write the solution as an ordered pair.

$(-3, 2)$ is the solution of the system.

My Notes

STEP 4 Check the solution by graphing.

$2x + 6y = 6$	$2x - y = -8$
x-intercept: 3	x-intercept: -4
y-intercept: 1	y-intercept: 8

The point of intersection is $(-3, 2)$.

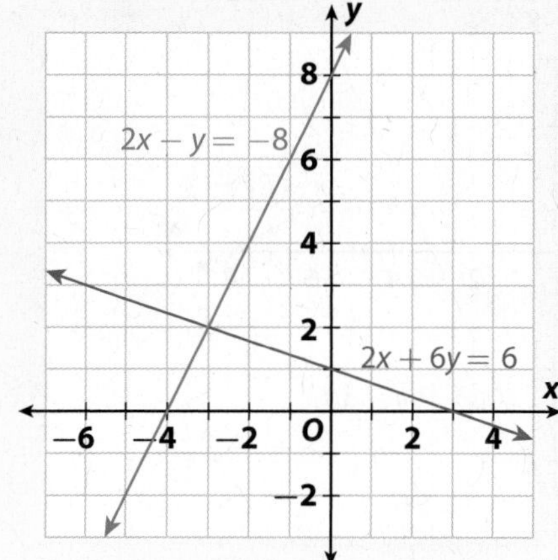

REFLECT

3. **Draw Conclusions** Can the system in part A be solved by subtracting one of the original equations from the other? Why or why not?

4. **What If?** In part B, what would happen if you added the original equations instead of subtracted?

5. **Justify Reasoning** How can you decide whether to add or subtract to eliminate a variable in a linear system? Explain your reasoning.

YOUR TURN

Solve each system of linear equations by adding or subtracting.

6. $\begin{cases} 2x + 5y = -24 \\ 3x - 5y = 14 \end{cases}$

Solution: ________________

7. $\begin{cases} 3x + 2y = 10 \\ 3x - y = 22 \end{cases}$

Solution: ________________

8. $\begin{cases} 3x + 2y = 5 \\ x + 2y = -1 \end{cases}$

Solution: ________________

9. $\begin{cases} 3x - y = -2 \\ -2x + y = 3 \end{cases}$

Solution: ________________

Solving Special Systems

You can use the elimination method for systems of linear equations that have infinitely many solutions and for systems that have no solutions.

Math On the Spot
my.hrw.com

EXAMPLE 2

A.REI.6

Solve each system of linear equations by adding or subtracting.

A $\begin{cases} -4x - 2y = 4 \\ 4x + 2y = -4 \end{cases}$

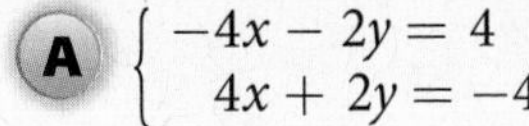

STEP 1 Add the equations.

$$\begin{aligned} -4x - 2y &= 4 \\ +4x + 2y &= -4 \\ \hline 0 + 0 &= 0 \\ 0 &= 0 \end{aligned}$$

Notice that the terms $-4x$ and $4x$ and $-2y$ and $2y$ are opposites.

Add to eliminate the variables.

Simplify.

The resulting equation is true so the system has infinitely many solutions.

STEP 2 Graph the equations to provide more information.

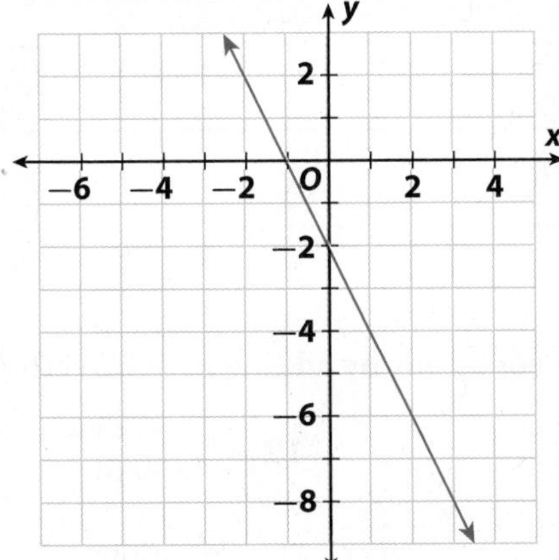

The graphs are the same line, so the system has infinitely many solutions.

B $\begin{cases} x + y = -2 \\ x + y = 4 \end{cases}$

STEP 1 Subtract the equations.

$x + y = -2$	*Write the equations so that like terms are aligned.*
$\underline{-(x + y)} = \underline{-(4)}$	*Notice that both equations contain the terms x and y.*
$0 + 0 = -6$	*Subtract to eliminate the variables.*
$0 = -6$	*Simplify.*

The resulting equation is false, so the system has no solutions.

STEP 2 Graph the equations to provide more information.

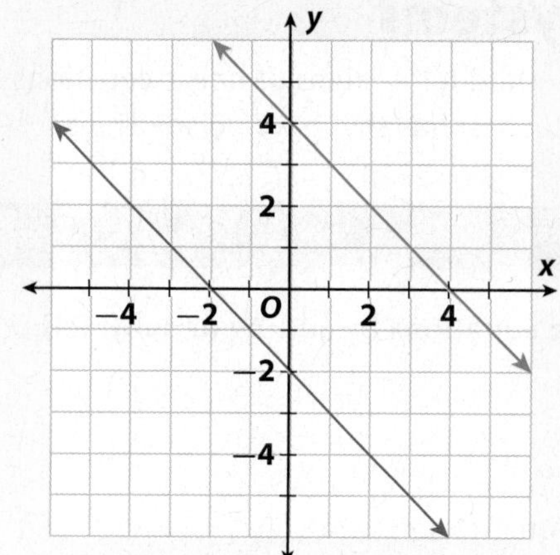

The graph shows that the lines are parallel and do not intersect.

Math Talk
Mathematical Practices

When a linear system has no solution, what happens when you try to solve the system by adding or subtracting?

REFLECT

10. **Communicate Mathematical Ideas** Suppose you solve a system of linear equations in which both variables are eliminated by subtraction. What is the solution of your system?

____

____

____

YOUR TURN

Solve each system of linear equations by adding or subtracting.

11. $\begin{cases} 4x - y = 3 \\ 4x - y = -2 \end{cases}$

Solution: ______________

____

12. $\begin{cases} x - 6y = 7 \\ -x + 6y = -7 \end{cases}$

Solution: ______________

____

Modeling with Linear Systems

Some real-world situations can be modeled with systems of equations that can be solved by the elimination method.

EXAMPLE 3 

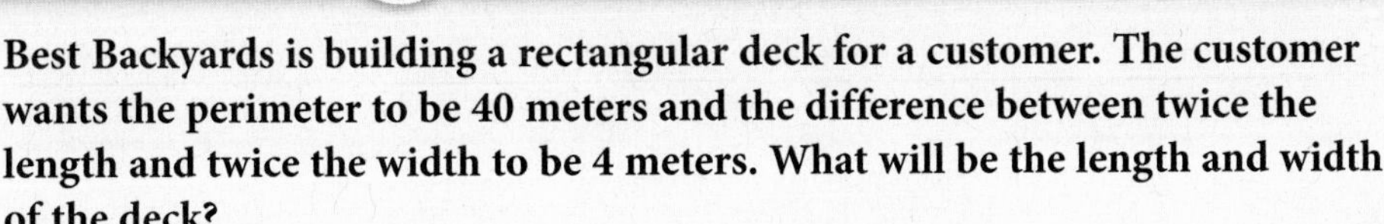

Best Backyards is building a rectangular deck for a customer. The customer wants the perimeter to be 40 meters and the difference between twice the length and twice the width to be 4 meters. What will be the length and width of the deck?

Write an equation for each requirement.

Let l represent the length and w represent the width.

Perimeter:	Twice the length	plus	twice the width	is	40
	$2l$	$+$	$2w$	$=$	40
Difference:	Twice the length	minus	twice the width	is	4
	$2l$	$-$	$2w$	$=$	4

STEP 1 Add the equations.

$2l + 2w = 40$ — Align like terms. Notice that the terms $2w$ and $-2w$ are opposites.

$\underline{2l - 2w = 4}$

$4l + 0 = 44$ — Add to eliminate the variable w.

$4l = 44$ — Simplify.

$l = 11$ — Divide each side by 4.

STEP 2 Substitute the value of l into one of the equations and solve for w.

$2l + 2w = 40$ — Use the first equation.

$2(11) + 2w = 40$ — Substitute 11 for the variable l.

$22 + 2w = 40$ — Simplify.

$2w = 18$ — Subtract 22 from each side.

$w = 9$ — Divide each side by 2.

STEP 3 Write the solution as an ordered pair.

$(l, w) = (11, 9)$ is the solution of the system.

The length of the deck will be 11 meters, and the width will be 9 meters.

YOUR TURN

13. Movies and More is having a one-day sale on certain movie DVDs and video games. You can buy 3 DVDs and 2 video games for \$74. Or you can buy 5 DVDs and 2 video games for \$98. Write and solve a system of equations to find the cost of one DVD and the cost of one video game.

____

Guided Practice

Solve each system of linear equations by adding or subtracting. Check your answer. (Examples 1 and 2)

1. $\begin{cases} -5x + y = -3 \\ 5x - 3y = -1 \end{cases}$

STEP 1 Add the equations. Find the value of y.

$$\begin{array}{r} -5x + y = -3 \\ \underline{+5x - 3y} = \underline{-1} \end{array}$$

$\square + \square = \square$

$y = \square$

STEP 2 Find the value of x.

$-5x + y = -3$

$-5x + \square = -3$

$-5x = \square$

$x = \square$

Solution: _______________

2. $\begin{cases} 2x + y = -6 \\ -5x + y = 8 \end{cases}$

Solution: _______________

3. $\begin{cases} 6x - 3y = 15 \\ 4x - 3y = -5 \end{cases}$

Solution: _______________

4. $\begin{cases} -5x - y = -3 \\ -5x - y = -2 \end{cases}$

Solution: _______________

5. A picture frame has a perimeter of 62 inches. The difference between the length and twice the width is 1 inch. What are the length and width of the frame? (Example 3)

____

ESSENTIAL QUESTION CHECK-IN

6. When you solve a system of linear equations by adding or subtracting, what needs to be true about the variable terms in the equations?

____

____

Name ____________________ Class ____________ Date ____________

9.3 Independent Practice

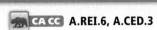

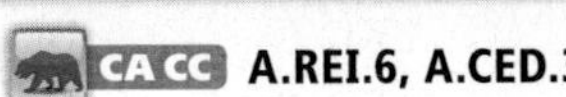

A.REI.6, A.CED.3

7. The sum of two numbers is 65. The difference of the two numbers is 27. Write and solve a system of linear equations to find the two numbers. Let x represent the greater number, and let y represent the lesser number.

System: ____________

Greater number: ____________

Lesser number: ____________

8. The sum of the digits in a two-digit number is 12. The tens digit is 2 more than the ones digit. Write and solve a system of linear equations to find the number. Let x represent the tens digit, and let y represent the ones digit.

System: ____________

Number: ____________

9. **Justify Reasoning** Solve the system of equations below by substitution and by elimination.

$$\begin{cases} x + y = -4 \\ 2x + y = -3 \end{cases}$$

Which method do you prefer? Explain your reasoning.

Solution: ____________

____

____

____

10. Can you solve this system of linear equations by adding or subtracting? Why or why not?

$$\begin{cases} x + 2y = 7 \\ 4x + 3y = 3 \end{cases}$$

____

____

11. **Draw Conclusions** Use addition or subtraction to find the solution of the system below. What does the solution tell you about the graph of the solution of this system?

$$\begin{cases} x + y = 5 \\ x - 3y = 3 \end{cases}$$

Solution: ____________

____

____

____

12. A garden has a perimeter of 120 feet. The difference between the length and twice the width is 24 feet. Write a system of linear equations that represents this situation. Then solve the system to find the length and width of the garden.

System: ____________

Length: ____________

Width: ____________

13. The sum of two angles is 90°. The difference between twice the larger angle and the smaller angle is 105°. Write a system of linear equations that represents this situation. Then solve the system to find the measures of the two angles.

System: ____________

Larger angle: ____________

Smaller angle: ____________

14. Use *one solution, no solutions,* or *infinitely many solutions* to complete this statement.

When the solution of a system of linear equations yields the equation $4 = 4$, the system has ____________.

15. Represent Real-World Problems For a school play, Ricco bought 3 adult tickets and 5 child tickets for \$40. Sasha bought 1 adult ticket and 5 child tickets for \$25. Find the cost of an adult ticket and the cost of a child ticket. Then find how much Julia will pay for 5 adult tickets and 3 child tickets.

____

____

16. Bright Pools is building a rectangular pool at a new house. The perimeter of the pool has to be 94 feet, and the length has to be 2 feet more than twice the width. What will be the length and width of the pool?

____

FOCUS ON HIGHER ORDER THINKING

Work Area

17. Multiple Representations You can use subtraction to solve the system of linear equations shown below.

$$\begin{cases} 2x + 4y = -4 \\ 2x - 2y = -10 \end{cases}$$

Instead of subtracting $2x - 2y = -10$ from $2x + 4y = -4$, what equation can you add to get the same result? Explain.

____

____

18. Explain the Error Liang's solution of a system of linear equations is shown below.

$$\begin{cases} 3x - 2y = 12 \\ -x - 2y = -20 \end{cases}$$

$$\begin{aligned} 3x - 2y &= 12 \\ + \; -x - 2y &= -20 \\ \hline 2x \quad &= -8 \\ x \quad &= -4 \\ 3x + 2y &= 12 \\ 3(-4) + 2y &= 12 \\ 2y &= 24 \\ y &= 12 \end{aligned}$$

Solution: $(-4, 12)$

Explain Liang's error and give the correct solution.

____

____

____

LESSON 9.4

Solving Linear Systems by Multiplying

CA CC **A.REI.5**

Prove that, given a system of two equations in two variables, replacing one equation by the sum of that equation and a multiple of the other produces a system with the same solutions. *Also A.CED.3, A.REI.6*

ESSENTIAL QUESTION

How can you solve a system of linear equations by using multiplication and elimination?

EXPLORE ACTIVITY 1

CA CC A.REI.5, A.REI.6

Understanding Linear Systems and Multiplication

A Graph this system of linear equations. Label each equation and find the solution.

$$\begin{cases} 2x - y = 1 \\ x + y = 2 \end{cases}$$

The solution of the system is ________.

B Use one of the equations in the system to write a new equation.

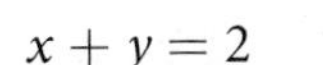

$x + y = 2$	Write the second equation in the system.
$2(x + y = 2)$	Multiply each term in the equation by 2.
$2x + 2y = 4$	Simplify.

C Graph the new equation. How is the graph of this equation related to the graphs of the original two equations?

____

____

REFLECT

1. **Draw Conclusions** What is true about the equations $x + y = 2$ and $2x + 2y = 4$?

____

2. Could you solve the original system by using the elimination method? Explain. Could you solve a new system that contained the new equation and the first equation in the original system? Explain.

____

____

____

EXPLORE ACTIVITY 2 | CA CC A.REI.5

Proving the Elimination Method with Multiplication

If you add the new equation you found in Explore Activity 1 and the first equation in the original system, you get a third equation. The graph of this new equation is shown at the right.

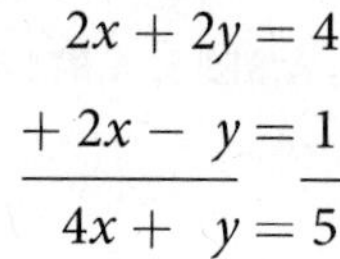

$$\begin{array}{r} 2x + 2y = 4 \\ +\ 2x - \ \ y = 1 \\ \hline 4x + \ \ y = 5 \end{array}$$

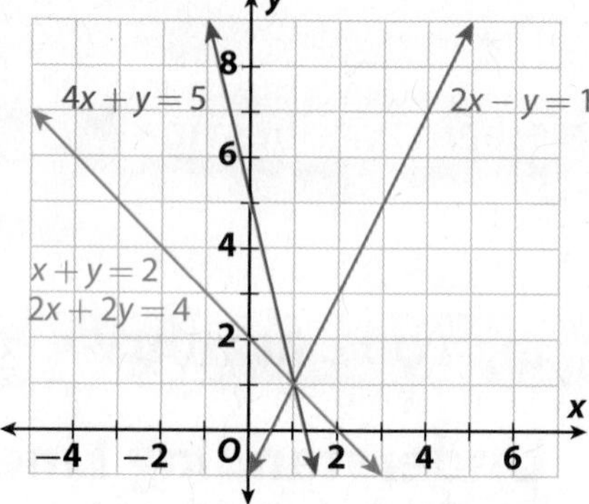

A Is the solution of the original system also a solution of the system formed by the equation $2x - y = 1$ and the third equation? Explain. ______________________

____

B If the original system is $Ax + By = C$ and $Dx + Ey = F$, where A, B, C, D, E, and F are constants, then multiply the second equation by a nonzero constant k to get $kDx + kEy = kF$. Then add this equation to the first equation to get the third equation.

$$\begin{array}{r} Ax + \quad By = C \\ +\ kDx + \quad kEy = \quad kF \\ \hline (A + kD)x + (B + kE)y = C + kF \end{array}$$

C Complete the following proof to show that if (x_1, y_1) is a solution of the original system, then it is also a solution of the new system below.

$$\begin{cases} Ax + By = C \\ (A + kD)x + (B + kE)y = C + kF \end{cases}$$

$Ax_1 + By_1 = C$	(x_1, y_1) is a solution of $Ax + By = C$.
$Dx_1 + Ey_1 = F$	(x_1, y_1) is a solution of $Dx + Ey = F$.
$\square(Dx_1 + Ey_1) = kF$	Multiplication Property of Equality
$kDx_1 + kEy_1 = kF$	Distributive Property
$C + kDx_1 + kEy_1 = \square + kF$	Addition Property of Equality
$Ax_1 + \square + kDx_1 + kEy_1 = C + kF$	Substitute $Ax_1 + By_1$ for C on left.
$Ax_1 + kDx_1 + \square + kEy_1 = C + kF$	Commutative Property of Addition
$(Ax_1 + kDx_1) + (By_1 + kEy_1) = C + kF$	Associative Property of Addition
$(A + kD)x_1 + (\square + kE)y_1 = C + kF$	Distributive Property

Because $(A + kD)x_1 + (B + kE)y_1 = C + kF$, (x_1, y_1) is a solution of the new system.

Solving a Linear System by Multiplying One Equation

In some linear systems, neither variable can be eliminated by adding or subtracting the equations directly. In systems like these, you need to multiply one or both of the equations by a constant so that adding or subtracting the equations will eliminate one or more of the variables. The steps for this method are as follows:

1. Decide which variable to eliminate.
2. Multiply one or both equations by a constant so that adding or subtracting will eliminate that variable.
3. Solve the system using the elimination method.

EXAMPLE 1

Solve the system of linear equations by multiplying. Check your answer.

$$\begin{cases} 3x + 8y = 7 \\ 2x - 2y = -10 \end{cases}$$

STEP 1 Multiply the second equation by a constant and then add the equations.

$4(2x - 2y = -10)$ — Multiply each term in the second equation by 4 to get opposite *y*-coefficients.

$8x - 8y = -40$

$+\ 3x + 8y = 7$ — Add the first equation to the new equation.

$11x + 0y = -33$ — Add the two equations.

$11x = -33$ — Simplify.

$x = -3$ — Divide each side by 11.

STEP 2 Substitute the value of x into one of the original equations and solve for y.

$3x + 8y = 7$ — Use the first equation.

$3(-3) + 8y = 7$ — Substitute -3 for the variable x.

$-9 + 8y = 7$ — Simplify.

$8y = 16$ — Add 9 to each side.

$y = 2$ — Divide each side by 8.

STEP 3 Write the solution as an ordered pair: $(-3, 2)$.

My Notes

STEP 4 Check the solution by graphing.

$3x + 8y = 7$ $\qquad$ $2x - 2y = -10$

x-intercept: $2\frac{1}{3}$ $\qquad$ x-intercept: -5

y-intercept: $\frac{7}{8}$ $\qquad$ y-intercept: 5

The point of intersection is $(-3, 2)$.

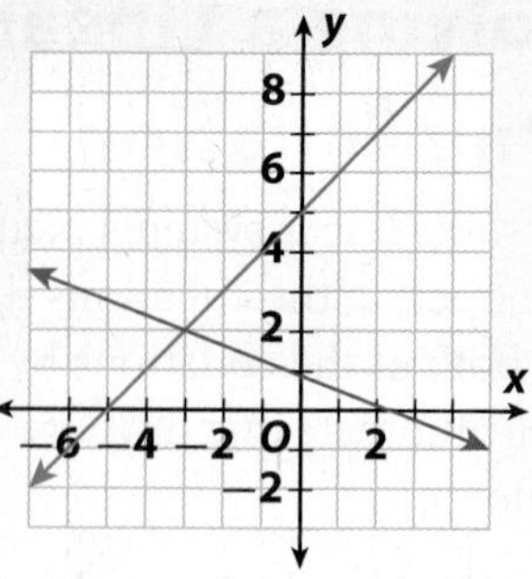

The solution of the system is $(-3, 2)$.

Personal Math Trainer

Online Practice and Help

my.hrw.com

YOUR TURN

3. Solve the system of linear equations by multiplying. Check your answer.

$$\begin{cases} -3x + 4y = 12 \\ 2x + y = -8 \end{cases}$$

Solution: ___________________

Math On the Spot

my.hrw.com

Solving a Linear System by Multiplying Both Equations

You may need to multiply both equations in a system before you can add or subtract.

EXAMPLE 2

Solve the system of linear equations by multiplying.

$$\begin{cases} -3x + 9y = -3 \\ 4x - 13y = 5 \end{cases}$$

STEP 1 Multiply the first equation by 4 and the second equation by 3 to get opposite x-coefficients.

$4(-3x + 9y = -3)$	Multiply the first equation by 4.
$3(4x - 13y = 5)$	Multiply the second equation by 3.
$-12x + 36y = -12$	Simplify the first equation.
$+12x - 39y = 15$	Simplify the second equation.
$-3y = 3$	Add the two equations.
$\frac{-3y}{-3} = \frac{3}{-3}$	Divide each side by -3.
$y = -1$	Simplify.

STEP 2 Substitute the value of y into one of the equations and solve for x.

$4x - 13y = 5$ — Use the second equation.

$4x - 13(-1) = 5$ — Substitute -1 for the variable y.

$4x + 13 = 5$ — Simplify.

$4x = -8$ — Subtract 13 from both sides.

$x = -2$ — Divide each side by 4.

STEP 3 Write the solution as an ordered pair: $(-2, -1)$.

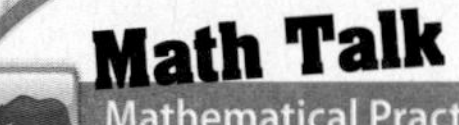

Math Talk
Mathematical Practices

Describe how to find the numbers by which you would multiply both equations to eliminate a variable.

YOUR TURN

Solve each system of linear equations by multiplying. Check your answer.

4. $\begin{cases} 2x + 3y = -1 \\ 5x - 2y = -12 \end{cases}$

Solution: ______________

5. $\begin{cases} 5x - 2y = 11 \\ 3x + 5y = 19 \end{cases}$

Solution: ______________

Personal Math Trainer
Online Practice and Help
my.hrw.com

Applying Linear Systems

EXAMPLE 3   CA CC A.REI.6, A.CED.3

Math On the Spot
my.hrw.com

Jessica spent \$14.85 to buy 13 flowers. The bouquet contained daisies, which cost \$1.25 each, and tulips, which cost \$0.90 each. How many of each type of flower did Jessica buy?

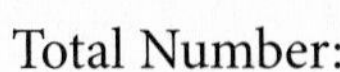

Total Number:	Number of daisies	plus	number of tulips	is	13
	d	$+$	t	$=$	13
Total Cost:	Cost of daisies	plus	cost of tulips	is	14.85
	$1.25d$	$+$	$0.90t$	$=$	14.85

STEP 1 Multiply the first equation by a constant and then subtract the equations.

$$\begin{array}{rcl} 0.90d + 0.90t & = & 11.70 \\ -(1.25d + 0.90t) & = & -(14.85) \\ \hline -0.35d & = & -3.15 \end{array}$$

Multiply the first equation by 0.90.

Subtract the second equation.

$$\frac{-0.35d}{-0.35} = \frac{-3.15}{-0.35}$$ Divide each side by -0.35.

$d = 9$ — Simplify

STEP 2 Substitute the value of d into one of the equations and solve for t.

$d + t = 13$ Use the first equation.

$(9) + t = 13$ Substitute 9 for the variable d.

$t = 4$ Simplify.

Jessica bought 9 daisies and 4 tulips.

YOUR TURN

6. Roses are \$2.50 each and lilies are \$1.75 each. Ellis spent \$24.75 for 12 of the flowers. How many of each type of flower did he buy?

____

Guided Practice

1. Solve the system of linear equations by multiplying. Check your answer. (Example 1)

$$\begin{cases} -2x + 2y = 2 \\ 5x - 6y = -9 \end{cases}$$

$\square x + \square y = 6$

$+5x - 6y = -9$

$-x = \square$

Solution: ______________

Solve each system of linear equations by multiplying. Check your answer. (Examples 1 and 2)

2. $\begin{cases} 3x + 3y = 12 \\ 6x + 11y = 14 \end{cases}$

Solution: ______________

3. $\begin{cases} 4x + 3y = 11 \\ 2x - 2y = -12 \end{cases}$

Solution: ______________

4. $\begin{cases} 3x + 8y = 17 \\ -2x + 9y = 3 \end{cases}$

Solution: ______________

5. The length of a rectangle is 8 inches more than the width. The perimeter of the rectangle is 56 inches. Write and solve a system of linear equations to find the length and width of the rectangle. (Example 3)

____

ESSENTIAL QUESTION CHECK-IN

6. Explain how you can solve a system of linear equations by using multiplication and elimination.

____

____

____

Name ______________________ Class ______________ Date ______________

9.4 Independent Practice

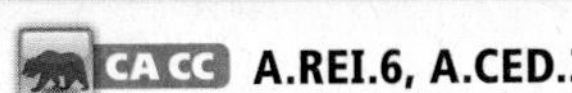

For each linear system, tell whether you would multiply the terms in the first or second equation in order to eliminate one of the variables. Give the number by which you could multiply. Then solve the system.

7. $\begin{cases} x + 3y = -14 \\ 2x + y = -3 \end{cases}$

Equation: ______________

Number: ______________

Solution: ______________

8. $\begin{cases} 9x - 3y = 3 \\ -3x - 8y = 17 \end{cases}$

Equation: ______________

Number: ______________

Solution: ______________

For each linear system, give the number by which you would multiply the terms in each equation in order to eliminate one of the variables. Then solve the system.

9. $\begin{cases} -3x + 2y = 4 \\ 5x - 3y = 1 \end{cases}$

First equation number: ______________

Second equation number:

____

Solution: ______________

10. $\begin{cases} 5x + 2y = -1 \\ 3x + 7y = 11 \end{cases}$

First equation number: ______________

Second equation number:

____

Solution: ______________

11. **Critical Thinking** Suppose you want to eliminate y in this system.

$\begin{cases} 2x + 11y = -3 \\ 3x + 4y = 8 \end{cases}$

What numbers would you need to multiply the two equations by to eliminate y? Why might you choose to eliminate x instead?

____

____

____

____

____

____

12. **Represent Real-World Problems** The Tran family is bringing 12 packages of cheese to the neighborhood picnic. Sliced cheese cost \$2.00 per package. Chunk cheese cost \$1.50 per package. They spent \$20 for the cheese. Write and solve a system of equations that can be used to find the number of packages of each type of cheese they purchased.

System: ______________

Sliced cheese: ______________

Chunk cheese: ______________

13. Conrad drew 2 angles. Three times the measure of angle 1 is 30° more than 5 times the measure of angle 2. The sum of twice the measure of angle 1 and twice the measure of angle 2 is 180°. Find the measure of each angle.

Angle 1: ______________

Angle 2: ______________

14. Represent Real-World Problems The school store is running a promotion on school supplies. Different supplies are placed on two shelves. You can purchase 3 items from shelf A and 2 from shelf B for $16. Or you can purchase 2 items from shelf A and 3 from shelf B for $14. How much more does one item on shelf A cost than an item on shelf B? Explain.

15. A local boys club sold 176 bags of mulch and made a total of $520. They did not sell any of the expensive cocoa mulch. Use the table to determine how many bags of each type of mulch they sold.

	Mulch Prices		
Type of mulch	Cocoa	Hardwood	Pine Bark
Price	$4.75	$3.50	$2.75

FOCUS ON HIGHER ORDER THINKING

Work Area

16. Explain the Error A linear system has two equations, $Ax + By = C$ and $Dx + Ey = F$. A student multiplies the x- and y-coefficients in the second equation by a constant k to get $kDx + kEy = F$. The student then adds the result to $Ax + By = C$ to write a new equation.

a. What is the new equation that the student wrote?

b. If the ordered pair (x_1, y_1) is a solution of the original system and not (0, 0), will it also be a solution of the new equation? Why or why not?

17. Critical Thinking Would you prefer to solve the system in Exercise 7 by using substitution? Explain your reasoning.

LESSON 9.5

Solving Systems of Linear Inequalities

CA CC A.REI.12

Graph the solutions to a linear inequality in two variables as a half-plane (excluding the boundary in the case of a strict inequality), and graph the solution set to a system of linear inequalities in two variables as the intersection of the corresponding half-planes. *Also A.CED.3*

ESSENTIAL QUESTION

How do you solve a system of linear inequalities?

EXPLORE ACTIVITY

Graphing Linear Inequalities on the Same Coordinate Plane

A Graph the inequality $x + y \leq 4$.

Did you shade above or below the boundary line?

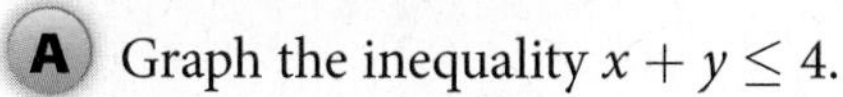

B Graph the inequality $x - y \geq 2$.

Did you shade above or below the boundary line?

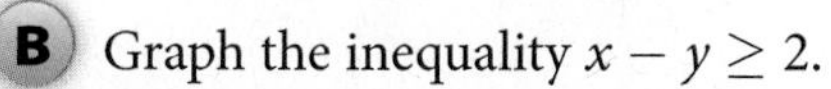

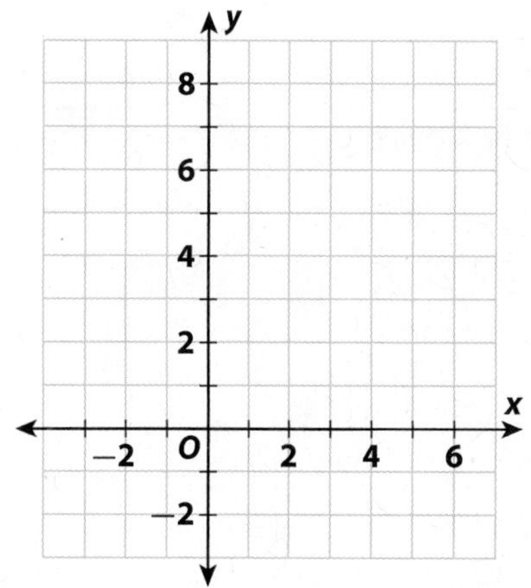

C Look at the region of your graph where the graphs of the two inequalities overlap. Choose three ordered pairs from that region. Test each pair in each inequality.

____

Ordered pair	Satisfies $x + y \leq 4$?	Satisfies $x - y \geq 2$?

REFLECT

1. If you test another ordered pair in the region where the graphs overlap, do you think it will satisfy one, both, or neither of the inequalities? Explain your reasoning.

____

____

____

2. **Draw Conclusions** An ordered pair that makes a linear inequality true is a solution of that linear inequality. What can you conclude about the ordered pairs in the region where the graphs overlap?

____

____

____

Solving a System of Linear Inequalities by Graphing

A **system of linear inequalities** consists of two or more linear inequalities that have the same variables. The **solutions of a system of linear inequalities** are all the ordered pairs that make all the inequalities in the system true.

My Notes

EXAMPLE 1

CA CC A.REI.12

Solve the system of inequalities by graphing. Check your answer.

$$\begin{cases} x + 2y > 2 \\ -x + y \leq 4 \end{cases}$$

STEP 1 Graph $x + 2y > 2$.

The equation of the boundary line is $x + 2y = 2$.

x-intercept: 2 y-intercept: 1

The inequality symbol is $>$, so use a dashed line.

Shade above the boundary line because (0, 0) is *not* a solution of the inequality.

STEP 2 Graph $-x + y \leq 4$.

The equation of the boundary line is $-x + y = 4$.

x-intercept: -4 y-intercept: 4

The inequality symbol is $\leq$, so use a solid line.

Shade below the boundary line because (0, 0) *is* a solution of the inequality.

STEP 3 Identify the solutions.

The solutions are the points in the region where the graphs overlap.

STEP 4 Check your answer by testing a point from each region.

Ordered pair	Satisfies $x + 2y > 2$?	Satisfies $-x + y \leq 4$?	In the region where the graphs overlap?
(0, 0)			
(2, 3)			
(−4, 2)			
(−2, 4)			

REFLECT

3. **Draw Conclusions** How does testing specific ordered pairs tell you that the solution you graphed is correct?

____

____

4. Is $(-2, 2)$ a solution of the system of inequalities? Why or why not?

____

____

____

YOUR TURN

5. Solve the system of inequalities by graphing. Check your answer.

$$\begin{cases} x - y \geq -1 \\ y > 2 \end{cases}$$

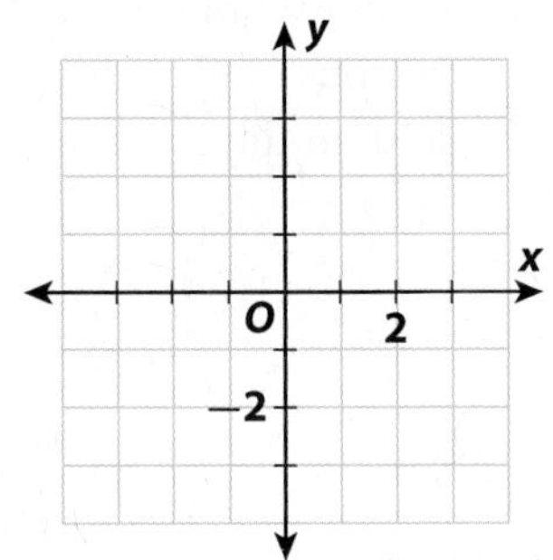

Solving Systems of Inequalities Whose Graphs Have Parallel Boundary Lines

The graphs of linear inequalities in a system can have parallel boundary lines. Unlike in systems of *equations* containing parallel lines, this does not always mean the system of inequalities has no solution.

EXAMPLE 2

CA CC A.REI.12

Graph each system of linear inequalities. Describe the solutions.

A $\begin{cases} -x + y > 3 \\ -x + y \leq -5 \end{cases}$

The two regions do not overlap.

The system has no solution.

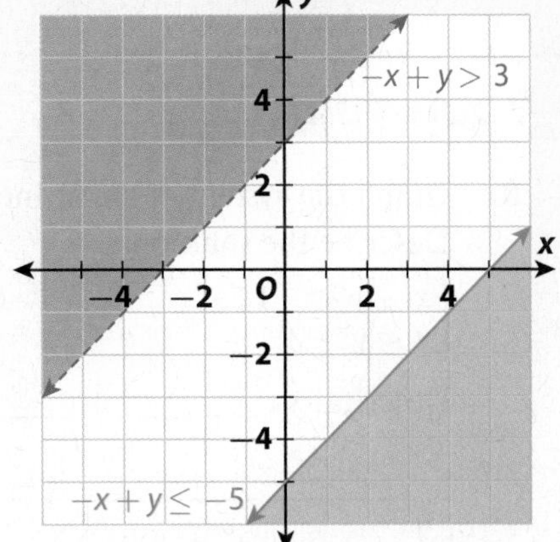

B $\begin{cases} x + y > -4 \\ x + y > -1 \end{cases}$

The solutions are all the points in the region where the graphs overlap. They are all the solutions of $x + y > -1$.

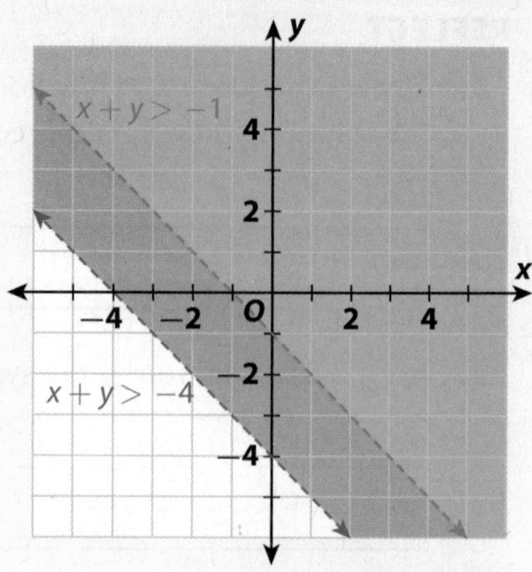

C $\begin{cases} -x + 3y \leq 3 \\ -x + 3y \geq -3 \end{cases}$

The solutions are all the points in the regions between the boundary lines and on the boundary lines.

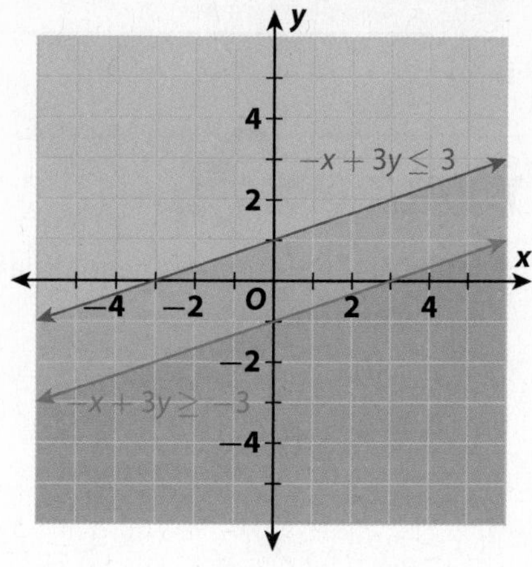

My Notes

REFLECT

6. Can the solution of a system of linear inequalities be a line? If so, give an example.

____

____

7. Does the system $3x - 2y < 4$ and $3x - 2y > 4$ have a solution? Explain.

____

____

____

YOUR TURN

8. Graph the system of linear inequalities. Describe the solutions.

$\begin{cases} x - y < -1 \\ x - y \geq 3 \end{cases}$

Description: ______________________________

____

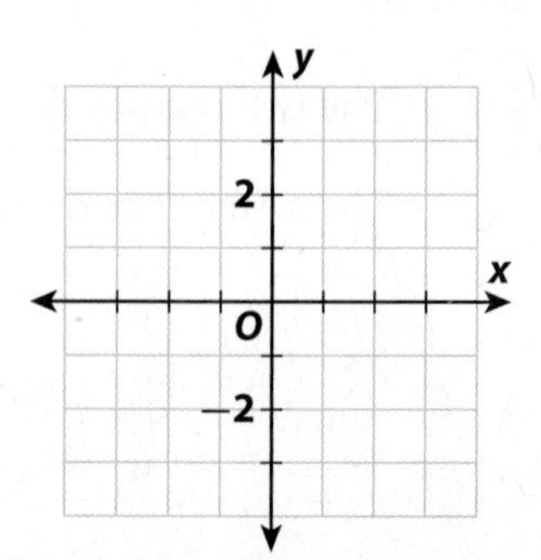

Modeling with Systems of Linear Inequalities

You can use a system of linear inequalities and its graph to model many real-world situations.

Math On the Spot
my.hrw.com

CA CC A.REI.12, A.CED.3

Rosa is buying T-shirts and shorts. T-shirts cost \$12 and shorts cost \$20. She plans to spend no more than \$120 and buy at least 4 items. Show and describe all possible combinations of the number of T-shirts and shorts she could buy. List two possible combinations.

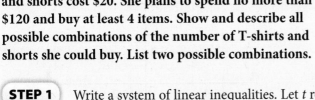

Write a system of linear inequalities. Let t represent the number of T-shirts and s represent the number of shorts.

Total items:	$t + s \geq 4$	She wants to buy at least 4 items.
Total spent:	$12t + 20s \leq 120$	She wants to spend no more than \$120.

STEP 2 Graph the system. The graph should be in only the first quadrant because the numbers of T-shirts and shorts are not negative.

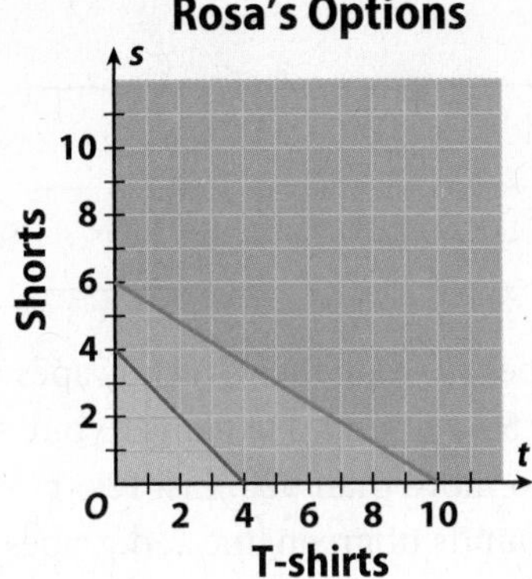

STEP 3 Describe all of the possible combinations. Rosa could buy any combination of T-shirts and shorts represented by a point in the region where the graphs overlap. Answers must be whole numbers because she cannot buy part of a T-shirt or pair of shorts.

STEP 4 List two possible combinations. Two possible combinations: 2 T-shirts and 3 shorts or (2, 3), 1 T-shirt and 5 shorts or (1, 5)

Math Talk
Mathematical Practices
How do you choose which region to select the combinations from?

YOUR TURN

9. Sergio is building a garden. He wants the length to be at least 30 feet and the perimeter to be no more than 100 feet. Graph all possible dimensions of the garden. Is a length of 35 feet and a width of 10 feet a possible combination?

____

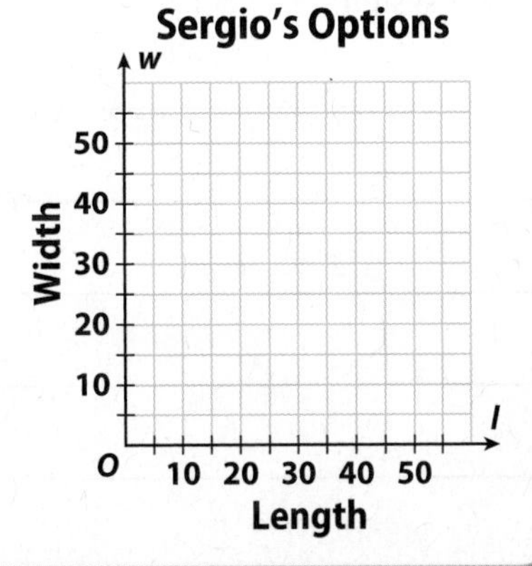

Guided Practice

Solve each system of linear inequalities by graphing. Describe the solutions. (Examples 1 and 2)

1. $\begin{cases} x - y \leq -3 \\ x - y > 3 \end{cases}$

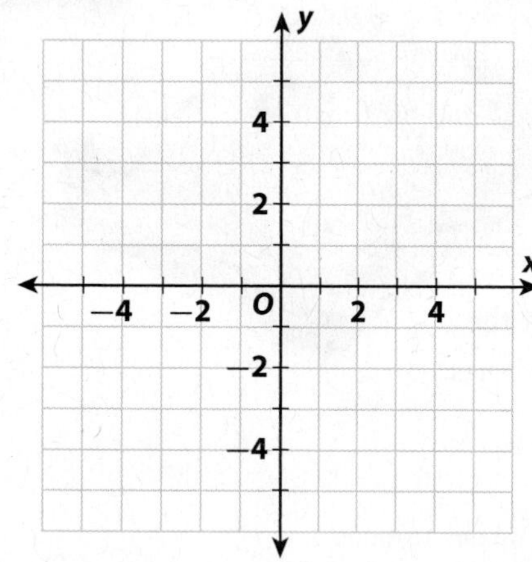

2. $\begin{cases} x + y \leq -2 \\ -x + y > 1 \end{cases}$

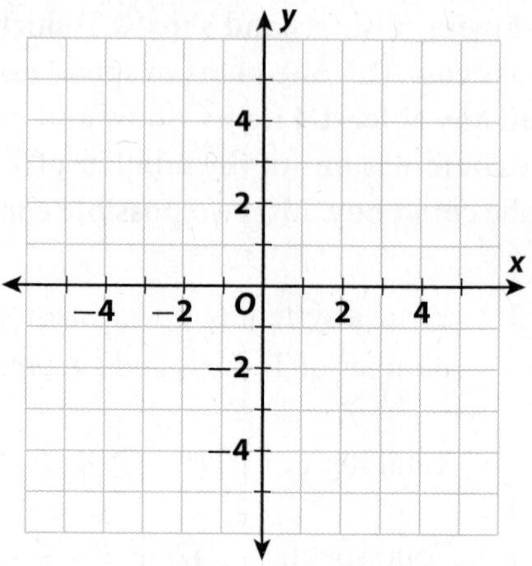

3. Jason is buying grapes for a picnic. Green grapes cost \$2 a pound and red grapes cost \$3 a pound. He plans to buy at least 4 pounds of grapes and spend no more than \$20. List two possible combinations of the number of pounds of green and red grapes he could buy. (Example 3)

Jason's Options

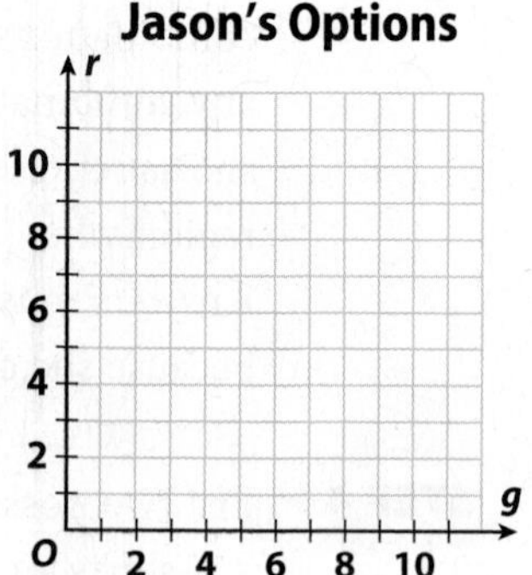

ESSENTIAL QUESTION CHECK-IN

4. How do you solve a system of linear inequalities?

Name ________________ Class ________________ Date ________________

9.5 Independent Practice

CA CC A.REI.12, A.CED.3

Solve each system of linear inequalities by graphing. Name two ordered pairs that are solutions of the system.

5. $\begin{cases} y \geq -2 \\ 4x + y \geq 2 \end{cases}$

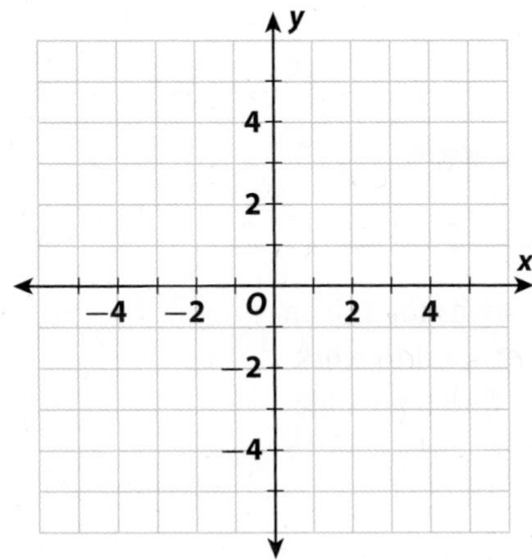

____

6. $\begin{cases} x < 1 \\ 2x + y > 1 \end{cases}$

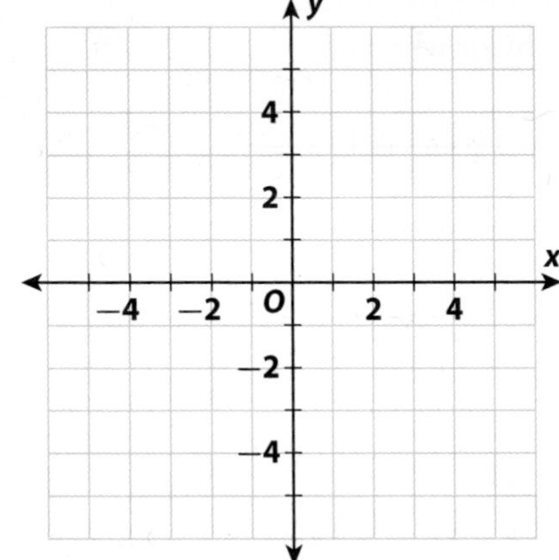

____

7. $\begin{cases} 4x + y \geq 4 \\ 4x + y \geq -4 \end{cases}$

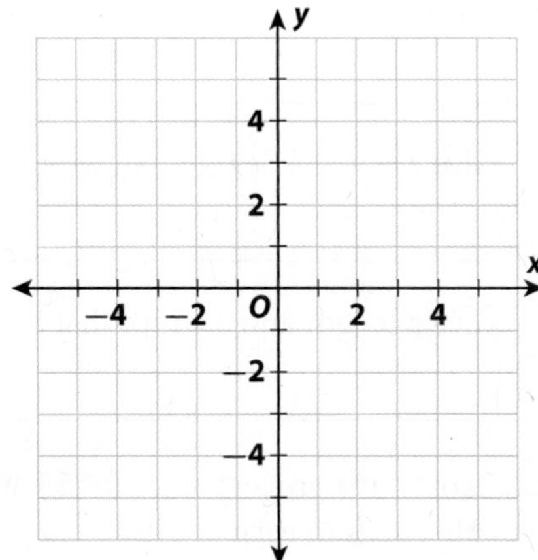

____

8. The system of inequalities below defines the boundaries of a region in the plane. What inequality symbol or symbols could replace "?" to make the solution a triangular region?

$\begin{cases} y \leq -x + 1 \\ y \geq \frac{1}{3}x - 3 \\ x \underline{\ ?\ } -4 \end{cases}$

____

9. Describe the solutions of this system of linear inequalities. Then write a possible system for the graphed inequalities.

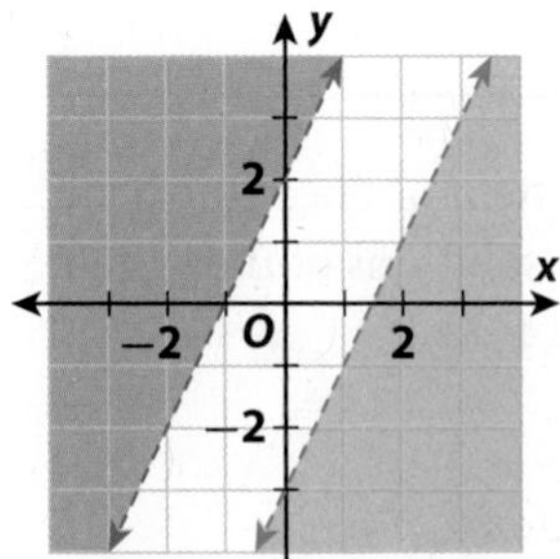

____

____

10. **Critical Thinking** Without graphing, describe the solution of $\begin{cases} x \geq 3 \\ y \leq 4 \end{cases}$.

____

____

11. Natalia is drawing a rectangle. She wants the width to be at least 10 inches and the perimeter to be no more than 72 inches.

a. Write a system of inequalities that can be used to solve this problem.

____

b. Give a possible length and width for the rectangle.

____

c. Give a length and a width that cannot be used for the rectangle.

____

12. Leon works at a grocery store for $8 an hour. He also mows lawns for $10 an hour. He needs to earn at least $120 per week, but he does not want to work more than 20 hours per week. Use a system of inequalities to find a possible combination of hours he can work at the grocery store and mowing lawns in order to meet his goal.

____

FOCUS ON HIGHER ORDER THINKING

Work Area

13. **Communicate Mathematical Ideas** Is it possible for a system of two linear inequalities to have every point in the plane as a solution? Why or why not?

____

____

____

____

14. Graph the system of linear inequalities. Describe the solutions of the system.

$$\begin{cases} x + 4y > -4 \\ x + y \leq 2 \\ x - y \geq 2 \end{cases}$$

____

____

____

____

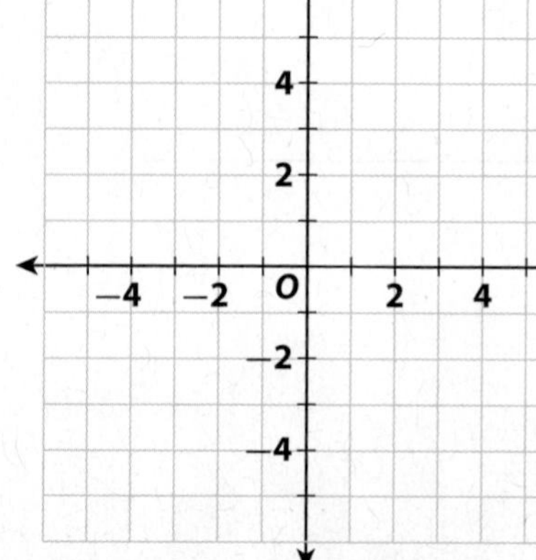

Ready to Go On?

Personal Math Trainer
Online Practice and Help
my.hrw.com

9.1 Solving Linear Systems by Graphing

Solve each system of linear equations by graphing.

1. $\begin{cases} x - y = 5 \\ x + y = 3 \end{cases}$ Solution: ________

2. $\begin{cases} -x + y = 3 \\ -2x + y = 6 \end{cases}$ Solution: ________

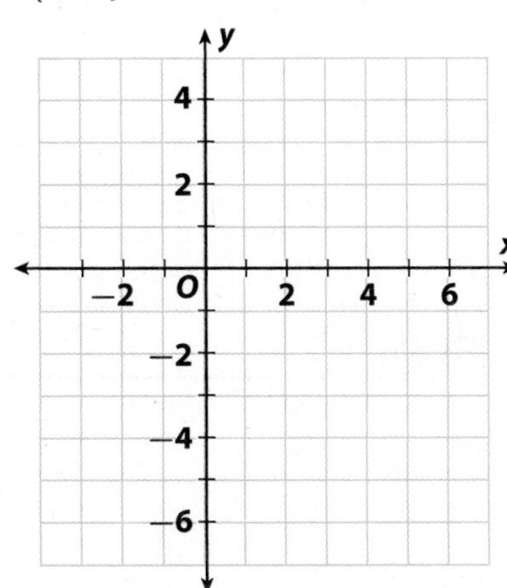

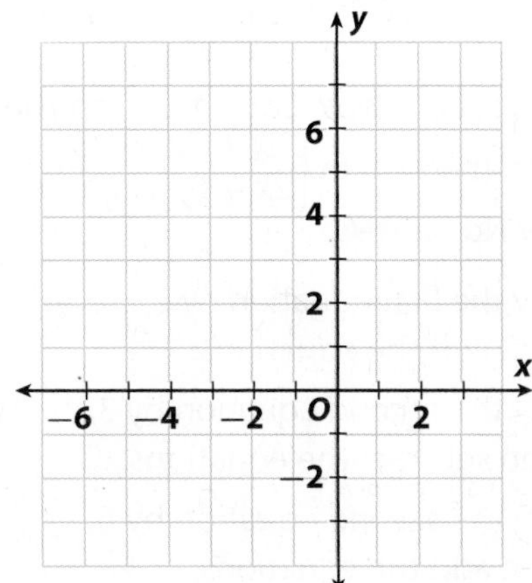

9.2 Solving Linear Systems by Substitution

Solve each system of linear equations by substitution.

3. $\begin{cases} x + \ \ y = -2 \\ 2x - 2y = 8 \end{cases}$ Solution: ________

4. $\begin{cases} x - 2y = -7 \\ 2x - 3y = -10 \end{cases}$ Solution: ________

9.3, 9.4 Solving Linear Systems by Elimination

Solve each system of linear equations by elimination.

5. $\begin{cases} x + 3y = 5 \\ 2x + 3y = 7 \end{cases}$ Solution: ________

6. $\begin{cases} 2x + 5y = 4 \\ 4x + 7y = 2 \end{cases}$ Solution: ________

9.5 Solving Systems of Linear Inequalities

7. Solve the system of linear inequalities by graphing.

$\begin{cases} 2x + y \leq 8 \\ 3x - y < 2 \end{cases}$

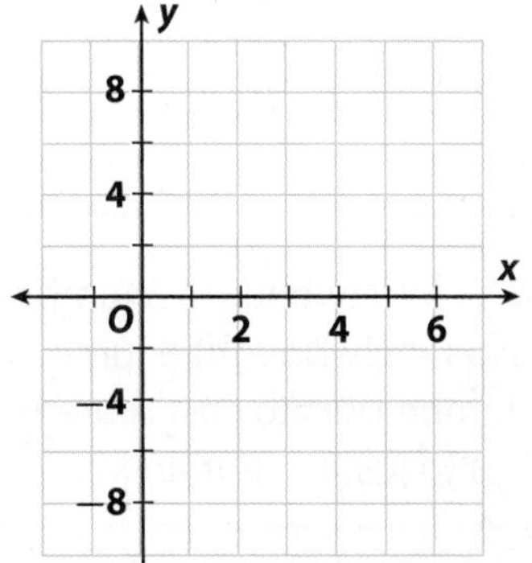

ESSENTIAL QUESTION

8. How are the graphs of systems of linear equations and inequalities related to their solutions?

____

____

MODULE 9
MIXED REVIEW

Assessment Readiness

1. Consider the system of inequalities $\begin{cases} 3x + 2y < 8 \\ x - 2y > -4 \end{cases}$.
Which ordered pair(s) below are solutions of the system? Select all that apply.

○ (−2, −1) ○ (0, 2) ○ (1, 1) ○ (4, −2)

2. Look at each set of steps. Could the steps be used to eliminate a variable from the system $\begin{cases} 6x + 3y = -3 \\ 2x - 6y = 20 \end{cases}$?
Select Yes or No for A–C.

A. Multiply the first equation by 2, and then add the equations. ○ Yes ○ No

B. Multiply the second equation by 3, and then subtract the equations. ○ Yes ○ No

C. Multiply the second equation by 6, and then add the equations. ○ Yes ○ No

3. The table shows data about largemouth bass. Use a calculator to find the equation of the line of best fit for the data. Then predict the weight of a largemouth bass with a length of 12 inches. Explain your reasoning.

Length (in.), *x*	10.0	14.5	17.0	20.0	23.5
Weight (lb), *y*	0.48	1.63	2.74	4.68	7.95

4. The Larsen family bought 3 jumbo burritos and 2 regular burritos for $13.65. The Russo family bought 5 jumbo burritos and 2 regular burritos for $20.23. Does a jumbo burrito cost more than $3.00? Write and solve a system of equations to justify your answer.

Study Guide Review

MODULE 6 Linear Functions

ESSENTIAL QUESTION

How do equations, graphs, tables, and word descriptions relate to linear functions?

Key Vocabulary
linear function *(función lineal)*
linear equation *(ecuación lineal)*
standard form of a linear equation *(forma estándar de una ecuación lineal)*
x-intercept *(intersección con el eje x)*
y-intercept *(intersección con el eje y)*
rate of change *(tasa de cambio)*
rise *(distancia vertical)*
run *(distancia horizontal)*
slope *(pendiente)*
slope formula *(formula de pendiente)*
slope-intercept form *(forma de pendiente-intersección)*
family of functions *(familia de funciones)*
parent function *(función madre)*
parameter *(parámetro)*

EXAMPLE 1

Find the slope and the y-intercept of the line that is graphed below. Then, write the equation of the line in slope-intercept form.

The y-intercept is at 2. Since the line goes through the points (0, 2) and (4, 4), the slope is $m = \frac{(4-2)}{(4-0)} = \frac{1}{2}$. So, the equation for the line in slope-intercept form is $y = \frac{1}{2}x + 2$.

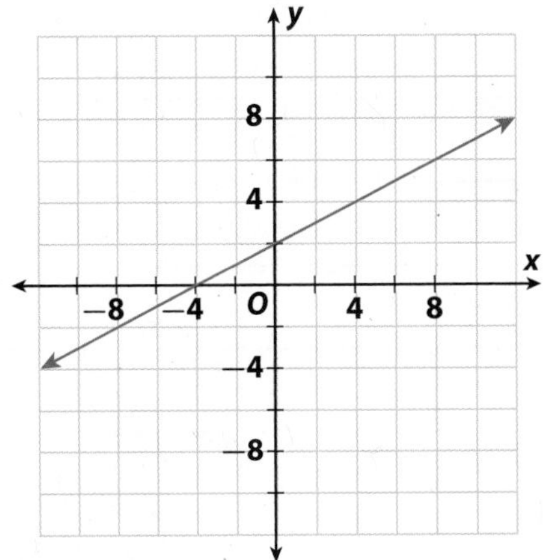

EXAMPLE 2

Find the slope of the line that has its x-intercept at 3 and its y-intercept at 4.

The intercepts give two points on the line, (3, 0) and (0, 4). The slope can be found using these two points in the slope formula: $m = \frac{(4-0)}{(0-3)} = -\frac{4}{3}$.

EXERCISES

1. Tell whether the function given by $y - 3 = 2x$ is linear. Compare it to the linear function represented by the table below. Describe how the functions are alike and how they are different. (Lessons 6.1, 6.5)

x	1	2	3	4
y	1	3	5	7

2. Find the slope and the intercepts of the line from the graph. Then, write the equation of the line in slope-intercept form. (Lessons 6.2, 6.3, 6.7)

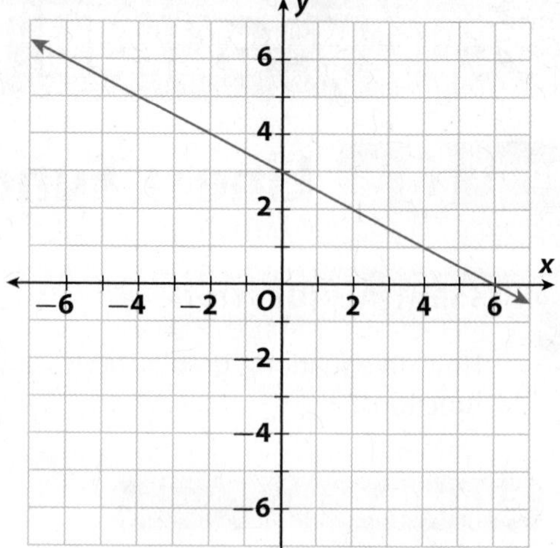

____

____

____

____

3. Find the slope of the line that has its x-intercept at -2 and its y-intercept at 7. (Lesson 6.4)

____

4. Brandon's cell phone bill can be represented by $y = 0.15x + 5$ and Lisa's cell phone bill is given by $y = 0.20x + 25$, where x is the number of text messages each sends in a month. Interpret the meaning of 0.15 and 0.20 in these equations, and describe the difference between the graphs of the functions. (Lesson 6.6)

____

____

____

____

____

MODULE 7 Building Linear Functions

Key Vocabulary

arithmetic sequence *(sucesión aritmética)*

common difference *(diferencia común)*

inverse of a function *(función inversa)*

linear inequality in two variables *(desigualdad lineal en dos variables)*

solution of an inequality *(solución de una desigualdad)*

boundary line *(linea de limite)*

half-plane *(semiplano)*

ESSENTIAL QUESTION

How are mathematical operations related to solving linear equations and inequalities and creating new functions?

EXAMPLE 1

Write a recursive rule and an explicit rule for the sequence.

n	1	2	3	4	5
$f(n)$	5	7.5	10	12.5	15

Recursive rule: $f(1) = 5, f(n) = f(n - 1) + 2.5$ for $n \geq 2$

Explicit rule: $f(n) = 5 + 2.5(n - 1)$

EXAMPLE 2

Add the linear functions $f(x) = 2x - 7$ and $g(x) = 4x + 3$ to get the linear function $h(x) = f(x) + g(x)$.

$f(x) + g(x) = (2x - 7) + (4x + 3)$	Substitute for $f(x)$ and $g(x)$.
$= (2x + 4x) + (-7 + 3)$	Combine like terms.
$= 6x - 4$	Simplify.

EXERCISES

Write a recursive rule and an explicit rule for each arithmetic sequence. (Lesson 7.1)

5. 8, 11, 14, 17, ... ______

6. 10, 5, 0, −5, ... ______

7. The explicit rule for an arithmetic sequence is $f(n) = 60 + 3(n - 1)$. What are the fifth and tenth terms? (Lesson 7.1)

______

8. An employee earns a base salary of \$30,000 plus an additional \$2,000 for each project completed in a year. Her income tax rate is 20%. Write a function $S(x)$ for the salary earned for completing x projects in a year. Then write a function $T(x)$ for the tax owed by the employee for completing x projects in a year. (Lesson 7.2)

______

______

9. Find the sum, $h(x)$, of the function $f(x) = 3x + 7$ and the function

$g(x) = -2x - 5$. (Lesson 7.2) ______

10. Subtract the function $f(x) = 6x - 5$ from the function $g(x) = -2x + 9$.

Denote the difference by $h(x)$. (Lesson 7.2) ______

11. Find the product, $h(x)$, of the function $f(x) = -5x + 7$ and the function $g(x) = 3$. (Lesson 7.2)

______

12. Write the linear inequality $3x - 4y \geq 12$ in standard form. (Lesson 7.3)

______

13. For the linear inequality $-x + 4y > -8$, which of the following is a solution: (2, −4), (−4, 3), or (4, −1)? (Lesson 7.3)

______

14. Graph the solution set for $4x + 2y > 5$. (Lesson 7.3)

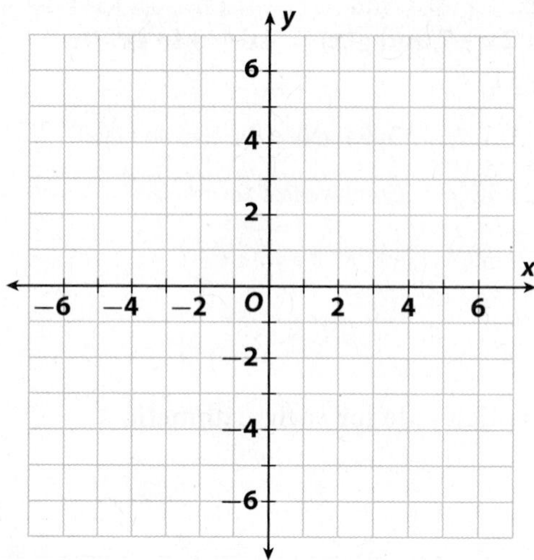

MODULE 8

Modeling with Linear Functions

Key Vocabulary

bivariate data
scatter plot *(diagrama de dispersión)*
correlation *(correlación)*
correlation coefficient *(coeficiente de correlación)*
line of fit *(linea de ajuste)*
residual *(residual)*
residual plot *(parcela residual)*
interpolation *(interpolación)*
extrapolation
linear regression *(regresión lineal)*
least squares regression line *(mínimos cuadrados línea de regresión)*
line of best fit *(linea de major ajuste)*

ESSENTIAL QUESTION

How can you use statistical methods to find relationships between sets of data?

EXAMPLE

Describe the correlation in the scatter plot below, and estimate the correlation coefficient.

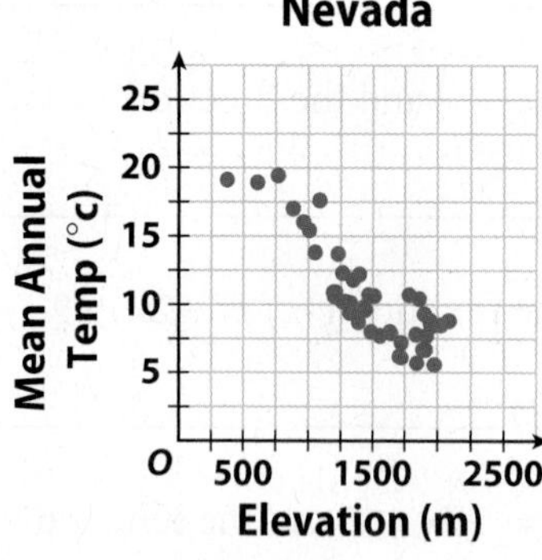

The scatter plot shows a strong negative correlation. Points lie close to a line with a negative slope. The correlation coefficient is close to −1.

EXERCISES

15. The scatter plot shows a relationship between years of experience at a job and income earned. The line of best fit is $I = 1.32x + 25$, where I is income in thousands of dollars per year and x is years of experience. Estimate the correlation coefficient. Then, predict the income earned by someone with 40 years of experience. (Lessons 8.1, 8.2)

16. The table below gives the ages, t, of boys on a middle-school basketball team and their shoe sizes, s. One student estimates that the line of best fit is given by $S_F = 0.8t + 0.5$. Use the table to compute the squares of the residuals for this line. (Lesson 8.3)

$s = 0.8t + 0.5$				
t	s (actual)	s (predicted)	Residuals	Square of Residuals
10	9	8.5	0.5	0.25
11	7			
12	10			
13	12			
13	9.5			

MODULE 9

Systems of Equations and Inequalities

ESSENTIAL QUESTION

How are the graphs of systems of linear equations and inequalities related to their solutions?

Key Vocabulary

system of linear equations *(sistema de ecuaciones lineales)*

solution of a system of linear equations *(solución de un sistema de ecuaciones lineales)*

substitution method *(sustitución)*

elimination method *(eliminación)*

system of linear inequalities *(sistema de desigualdades lineales)*

solution of a system of linear inequalities *(solución de un sistema de desigualdades lineales)*

EXAMPLE

Solve the system of linear equations.

$$\begin{cases} y = 3x + 1 \\ 2y - 3 = 4x \end{cases}$$

$2(3x + 1) - 3 = 4x$ — Substitute the first equation into the second.

$6x - 1 = 4x$ — Distribute.

$2x = 1$ — Combine like terms.

$x = \frac{1}{2}$ — Solve for x.

$y = 3\left(\frac{1}{2}\right) + 1$ — Substitute $\frac{1}{2}$ into the first equation to find y.

$y = \frac{5}{2}$

The solution is $\left(\frac{1}{2}, \frac{5}{2}\right)$.

EXERCISES

17. Solve the system of equations by substitution. (Lesson 9.2)

$$\begin{cases} y - 2 = 4x \\ 5y - 2x = 1 \end{cases}$$

Solve each system of equations by elimination. (Lessons 9.3, 9.4)

18. $\begin{cases} 4x + 6y = 38 \\ 4x - 2y = 14 \end{cases}$

19. $\begin{cases} 3x - 2y = 9 \\ 5x + y = 2 \end{cases}$

Solve each system of equations or inequalities by graphing. (Lessons 9.1, 9.5)

20. $\begin{cases} y = 4x + 9 \\ y = 2x - 1 \end{cases}$

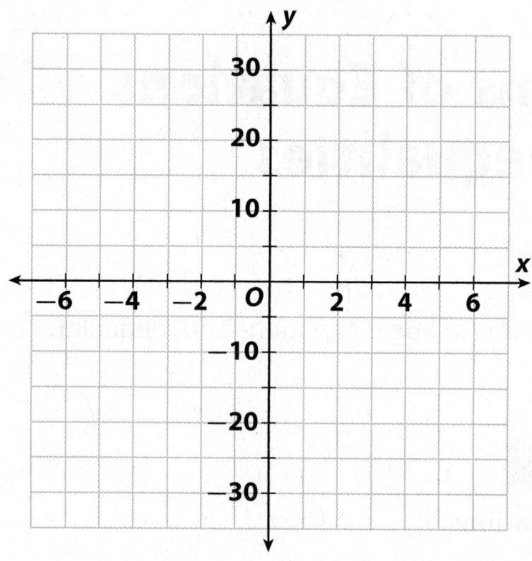

21. $\begin{cases} y = 5x - 6 \\ y = 2x + 3 \end{cases}$

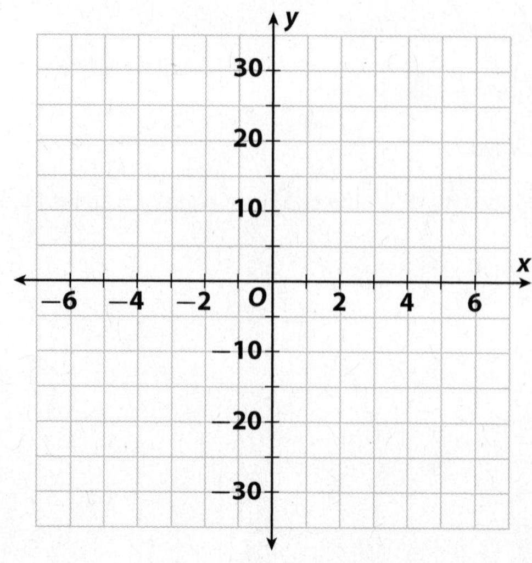

22. $\begin{cases} 3x - y = -4 \\ y = 3x - 5 \end{cases}$ ______________________________

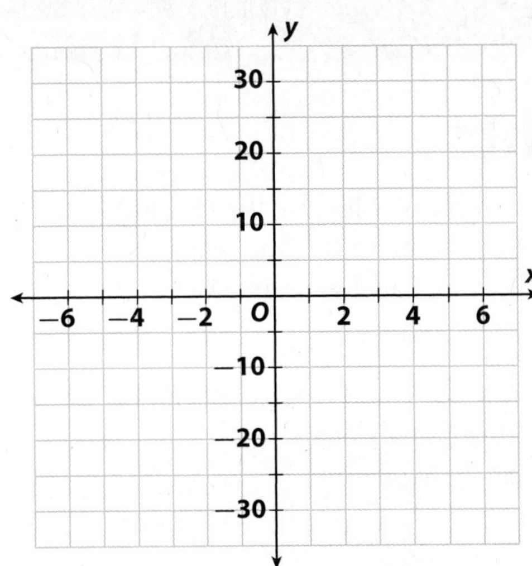

23. $\begin{cases} 2x - y = -5 \\ 3y = 6x + 15 \end{cases}$ ______________________________

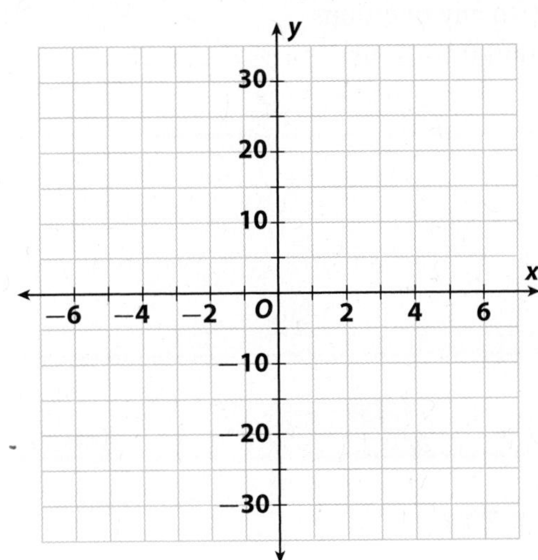

24. $\begin{cases} 4y \leq 15x + 40 \\ 2y + 50 \geq 25x \end{cases}$

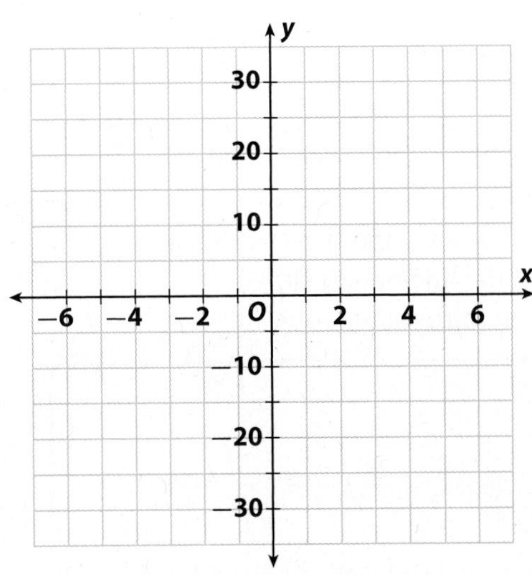

Unit Project CA CC F.IF.4, F.IF.7a, F.BF.1a

Changing Flights

Choose a flight of stairs at home or school. Measure the rise and run of a step. Write and graph an equation for the line that goes from the bottom of the stairs to the top. Label your graph with the number of steps of the flight.

Design two different flights of stairs that could replace this flight. For each plan, include the rise and run of a single step. Be sure to consider the CA safety regulation from the Unit Project Preview.

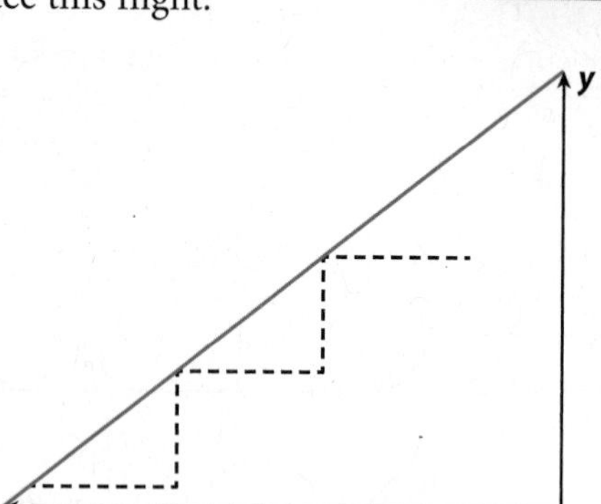

Graph and label equations on the same coordinate plane as the original flight. Write a paragraph that describes which flight you think is best and why.

Use the space below to write down any questions you have or important information from your teacher.

MATH IN CAREERS ACTIVITY

Environmental Scientist To rate the fuel efficiency of a car, the following data were collected comparing the distance traveled to the amount of gasoline used on the trip.

fuel (gal)	1.3	7.5	3.9	2.1	10.8	3.3	6.7
dist. (mi)	42	223	109	58	330	97	188

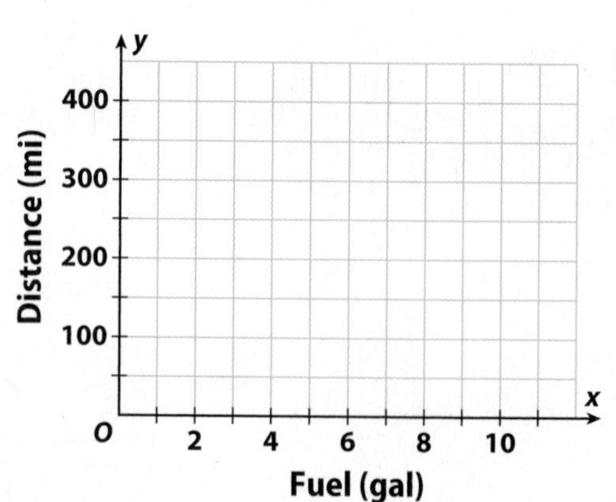

Draw a scatter plot representing this data, and then use linear regression to find the equation of the line of best fit. What does the slope of the line represent in this situation?

UNIT 3A
MIXED REVIEW

Assessment Readiness

1. Consider each linear function. Does the function have a greater y-intercept than the linear function represented in the table?

x	$f(x)$
2	10
4	18
6	26
8	34

Select Yes or No.

A. $g(x) = 2x + 3$ ○ Yes ○ No

B. $g(x) = 1 + 5x$ ○ Yes ○ No

C. $g(x) = -4(x - 1)$ ○ Yes ○ No

2. The table shows how the price of apples at a store has changed over the past 6 months.

Month, x	Price per pound (\$), y
1	1.69
2	1.79
3	1.50
4	1.38
5	1.32
6	1.36

Choose True or False for each statement.

A. A scatter plot of the data shows a negative correlation. ○ True ○ False

B. The correlation coefficient for the data is closer to 1 than to 0. ○ True ○ False

C. The y-intercept of the best line of fit is greater than 1.50. ○ True ○ False

3. Adult tickets to a play cost \$20.50, and student tickets cost \$16.00. Ms. Powers can spend no more than \$120.00 on tickets. If she buys 3 student tickets, how many adult tickets is she able to buy? Use a linear inequality in two variables to explain your reasoning.

4. A hobby pack of baseball cards contains 9 cards, and a jumbo pack contains 35 cards. Ethan bought 7 packs for a total of 141 cards. Write and solve a system of equations to find the number of each type of pack that he bought. State and justify your solution method.

Performance Tasks

★5. A store rents backpacks and sleeping bags. Backpack rental costs \$0.88 per day, plus an initial fee of \$24.84. Sleeping bag rental costs are shown in the table. Write the function $f(x)$ to represent the cost of renting both a backpack and a sleeping bag for x days. Explain how you determined your answer.

Sleeping Bag Rental	
Time (days)	Cost (\$)
3	18.28
6	20.65
9	23.02
12	25.39

★★6. The table shows data for 6 gas-engine cars.

a. Make a scatter plot of the data in the table.

b. Write an equation of a line of fit for the data.

c. Tell what the slope of the line of fit represents.

d. Predict the mileage for a car that weighs 3000 lb. Justify your reasoning.

Weight (lb), x	Gas Mileage (mi/gal), y
3192	28
3427	26
2716	31
3108	31
2907	30
3295	27

★★★7. Rita and Chris are making patterns out of tiles. The first 4 figures in each of their patterns is shown. Continuing these patterns, is there a figure for which the number of tiles in Rita's figure will be the same as the number of tiles in Chris's figure? If so, what is the figure number, and how many tiles will be in each figure? Explain.

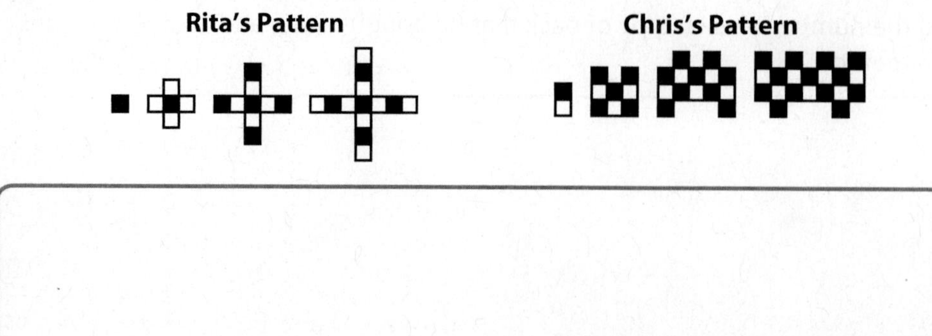

Exponential Relationships

MODULE 10

Exponential Functions and Equations

CA CC A.CED.1, A.CED.2, A.REI.11, F.IF.3, F.IF.4, F.IF.5, F.IF.7, F.IF.7e, F.BF.1, F.BF.1a, F.BF.2, F.BF.3, F.LE.1a, F.LE.1c, F.LE.2, F.LE.5

MODULE 11

Modeling with Exponential Functions

CA CC A.CED.2, F.LE.1, F.LE.1a, F.LE.1b, F.LE.1c, F.LE.3, F.LE.5, S.ID.6a, S.ID.6b

MATH IN CAREERS

Statistician A statistician collects, analyzes, and interprets numerical data of all types. He or she also helps design surveys and experiments. A solid science background is beneficial when helping others design and interpret experiments; for example, monitoring the rise and decline of animal populations. If you're interested in a career as a statistician, you should study these mathematical subjects:

- Algebra
- Trigonometry
- Calculus

Research other careers that require the use of statistics to analyze and interpret data.

ACTIVITY At the end of the unit, check out how **statisticians** use math.

Unit Project Preview

Bank on It

The Unit Project at the end of this unit involves determining the best investment. You will calculate interest rates and create a presentation to a potential investor. To successfully complete the Unit Project you'll need to master these skills:

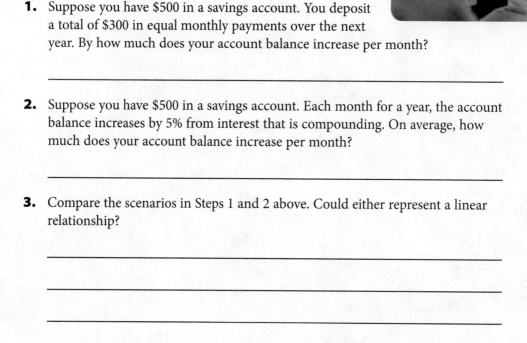

- Calculate with exponential expressions.
- Determine exponential models for given data.
- Graph exponential functions.

1. Suppose you have \$500 in a savings account. You deposit a total of \$300 in equal monthly payments over the next year. By how much does your account balance increase per month?

____

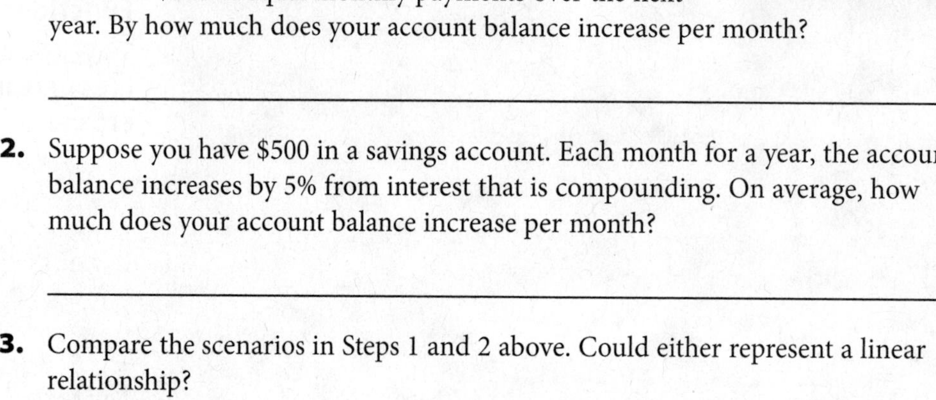

2. Suppose you have \$500 in a savings account. Each month for a year, the account balance increases by 5% from interest that is compounding. On average, how much does your account balance increase per month?

____

3. Compare the scenarios in Steps 1 and 2 above. Could either represent a linear relationship?

____

____

____

____

____

Tracking Your Learning Progression

This unit addresses important California Common Core Standards in the Critical Areas of understanding and modeling linear, quadratic, and exponential functions

Domain F.LE Linear, Quadratic, and Exponential Models

Cluster Construct and compare linear, quadratic, and exponential models and solve problems.

Exponential Functions and Equations

MODULE 10

CALIFORNIA COMMON CORE

LESSON 10.1
Exponential Functions
CA CC F.LE.2, A.CED.2, F.IF.5, F.IF.7e

LESSON 10.2
Exponential Growth and Decay
CA CC F.LE.1c, F.IF.4, F.IF.5, F.IF.7, F.IF.7e, F.LE.2, F.LE.5

LESSON 10.3
Geometric Sequences
CA CC F.BF.2, F.IF.3, F.BF.1, F.BF.1a, F.LE.1a, F.LE.2

LESSON 10.4
Transforming Exponential Functions
CA CC F.BF.3

LESSON 10.5
Equations Involving Exponents
CA CC A.CED.1, A.CED.2, A.REI.11, F.BF.1, F.BF.1a, F.LE.2

ESSENTIAL QUESTION

How can exponential functions be used to represent real-world situations?

my.hrw.com

Real-World Video

Scientists have found many ways to use radioactive elements that decay exponentially over time. Uranium-235 is used to power nuclear reactors, and scientists use Carbon-14 dating to calculate how long ago an organism lived.

GO DIGITAL
my.hrw.com

my.hrw.com

Go digital with your write-in student edition, accessible on any device.

Math On the Spot

Scan with your smart phone to jump directly to the online edition, video tutor, and more.

Animated Math

Interactively explore key concepts to see how math works.

Personal Math Trainer

Get immediate feedback and help as you work through practice sets.

Are YOU Ready?

Complete these exercises to review skills you will need for this module.

Exponents

EXAMPLE Write 10^4 as a multiplication of factors.

$10^4 = 10 \times 10 \times 10 \times 10$ — *10 is the base. It tells you the factor to multiply. 4 is the exponent. It tells you how many times the base is used as a factor. If the exponent is 0, remember that the product is 1.*

Write each expression as a multiplication of factors.

1. 5^1 ______ **2.** 9^0 ______ **3.** 3^5 ______

4. 2^4 ______ **5.** 6^3 ______ **6.** a^2 ______

Evaluate Powers

EXAMPLE Evaluate 4^3.

$4^3 = 4 \times 4 \times 4$ — *Rewrite as repeated multiplication.*

$= 64$ — *Evaluate.*

Evaluate each power.

7. 8^2 ______ **8.** 5^4 ______ **9.** 6^0 ______

Properties of Exponents

EXAMPLE Simplify x^4x^5.

$x^4x^5 = x^{4+5} = x^9$ — *When multiplying numbers with the same base, add exponents.*

Simplify.

10. x^3x ______ **11.** $x^3y^4 \cdot y^3$ ______ **12.** $5a^2b \cdot 6a^3b$ ______

Reading Start-Up

Visualize Vocabulary

Use the ✔ Review Words to complete the bubble map.

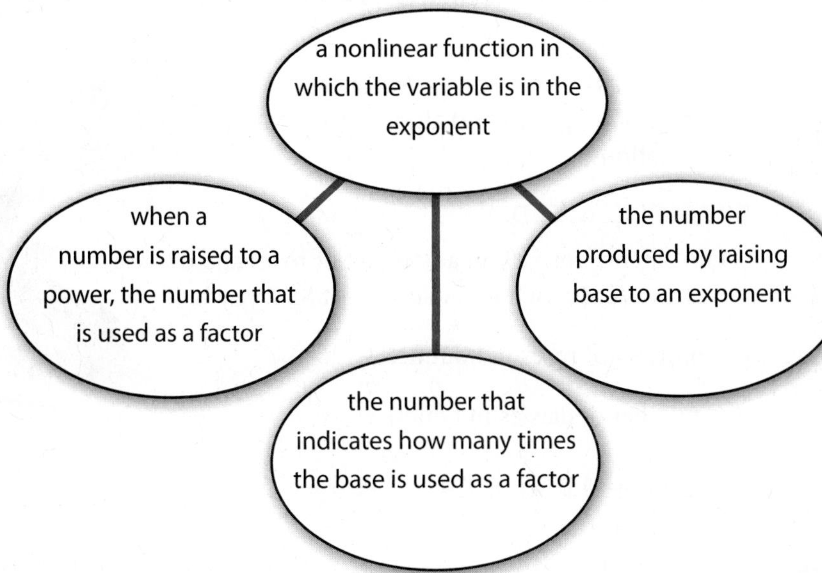
a nonlinear function in which the variable is in the exponent
when a number is raised to a power, the number that is used as a factor
the number produced by raising base to an exponent
the number that indicates how many times the base is used as a factor

Vocabulary

Review Words

- ✔ base *(base)*
- explicit rule *(fórmula explícita)*
- ✔ exponential function *(función exponencial)*
- ✔ exponent *(exponente)*
- family of functions *(familia de funciones)*
- parameter *(parámetro)*
- parent function *(función madre)*
- ✔ power *(potencia)*
- ratio *(razón)*
- recursive rule *(fórmula recurrente)*
- sequence *(sucesión)*
- term *(término)*

Preview Words

- common ratio
- decreasing function
- exponential growth
- exponential decay
- exponential function
- geometric sequence
- increasing function

Understand Vocabulary

To become familiar with some of the vocabulary terms in the module, consider the following. You may refer to the module, the glossary, or a dictionary.

1. Occurs in an exponential function when the output gets smaller as the input gets larger.

____

2. Occurs in an exponential function when the output gets larger as the input gets larger.

____

Active Reading

Booklet Before beginning the module, create a booklet to help you learn the concepts in this module. Write the main idea of each lesson on each page of the booklet. As you study each lesson, write important details that support the main idea, such as vocabulary and formulas. Refer to your finished booklet as you work on assignments and study for tests

GETTING READY FOR

Exponential Functions and Equations

Understanding the standards and the vocabulary terms in the standards will help you know exactly what you are expected to learn in this module.

CA CC A.CED.2

Create equations in two or more variables to represent relationships between quantities; graph equations on coordinate axes with labels and scales.

Key Vocabulary

equation *(ecuación)*
A mathematical statement that two expressions are equivalent.

What It Means to You

Creating equations in two variables to describe relationships gives you access to the tools of graphing and algebra to solve the equations.

EXAMPLE A.CED.2

A customer spent \$29 on a bouquet of roses and daisies. Roses cost \$2.50 each and daisies cost \$1.75 each.

r = number of roses in bouquet

d = number of daisies in bouquet

$$2.5r + 1.75d = 29$$

CA CC F.IF.7e

Graph exponential and logarithmic functions, showing intercepts and end behavior, and trigonometric functions, showing period, midline, and amplitude.

Key Vocabulary

exponential function *(función exponencial)*
A function that can be written in the form $f(x) = ab^x$.

What It Means to You

You will learn to graph a new type of function, called an exponential function, in which successive output values have a constant ratio for each unit increase in the input values.

EXAMPLE F.IF.7E

Graph the function $f(x) = 2^x$.

Find points on the graph using a table, then graph the points and connect them with a smooth curve.

x	$f(x)$
−2	0.25
−1	0.5
0	1
1	2
2	4

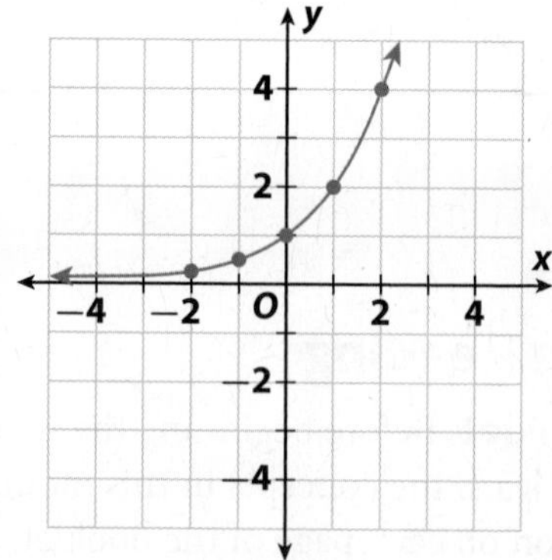

Visit my.hrw.com to see all **CA Common Core Standards** explained.

my.hrw.com

LESSON 10.1

Exponential Functions

CA CC F.LE.2

Construct linear and exponential functions, including arithmetic and geometric sequences, given a graph, a description of a relationship, or two input-output pairs (include reading these from a table). *Also A.CED.2, F.IF.5, F.IF.7e*

ESSENTIAL QUESTION

How can you identify and represent an exponential function?

EXPLORE ACTIVITY

CA CC F.LE.2

Zero and Negative Exponents

Complete the table, and examine the patterns.

Power	5^5	5^4	5^3	5^2	5^1	5^0	5^{-1}	5^{-2}
Values	3125	625	125	25	5			

$\div 5$ $\div 5$ $\div 5$ $\div 5$

A What happens to the value of the power with each decrease of 1 in the exponent?

____

B Show the pattern that you used to find the value for 5^0, 5^{-1}, and 5^{-2}.

____

REFLECT

1. **Communicating Mathematics** Describe how to find the value of 5^{-2} without dividing the value of 5^{-1} by 5.

____

____

The properties of zero and negative exponents are given below.

Zero and Negative Exponents		
Words	**Algebra**	**Example**
Any nonzero number raised to the zero power is 1.	$c^0 = 1, c \neq 0$	$12^0 = 1$
Any nonzero number raised to a negative power is equal to 1 divided by the number raised to the opposite power.	$c^{-n} = \frac{1}{c^n}, c \neq 0$	$2^{-3} = \frac{1}{2^3} = \frac{1}{8}$

Representing an Exponential Function

In an **exponential function**, as the input values increase by 1, the successive output values are related by a constant ratio. An *exponential function* can be represented by an equation of the form $f(x) = ab^x$, where a, b, and x are real numbers, $a \neq 0$, $b > 0$, and $b \neq 1$. The constant ratio is the base b. When evaluating exponential functions, you will need to use the properties of exponents.

EXAMPLE 1

CA CC F.IF.7e

My Notes

Make a table for the function $f(x) = 2\left(\frac{2}{3}\right)^x$ using the input values $x = -2, -1, 0, 1, 2, 3$. Then graph the function using the ordered pairs from the table as a guide.

STEP 1 Make a table of values by calculating the function values for the given values of x.

x	$f(x) = 2\left(\frac{2}{3}\right)^x$	$(x, f(x))$
−2	$2\left(\frac{2}{3}\right)^{-2} = 2\left(\frac{1}{\left(\frac{2}{3}\right)^2}\right) = 2\left(\frac{1}{\frac{4}{9}}\right) = 2\left(\frac{9}{4}\right) = \frac{9}{2}$	$\left(-2, \frac{9}{2}\right)$
−1	$2\left(\frac{2}{3}\right)^{-1} = 2\left(\frac{1}{\left(\frac{2}{3}\right)^1}\right) = 2\left(\frac{1}{\frac{2}{3}}\right) = 2\left(\frac{3}{2}\right) = 3$	$(-1, 3)$
0	$2\left(\frac{2}{3}\right)^0 = 2(1) = 2$	$(0, 2)$
1	$2\left(\frac{2}{3}\right)^1 = 2\left(\frac{2}{3}\right) = \frac{4}{3}$	$\left(1, \frac{4}{3}\right)$
2	$2\left(\frac{2}{3}\right)^2 = 2\left(\frac{4}{9}\right) = \frac{8}{9}$	$\left(2, \frac{8}{9}\right)$
3	$2\left(\frac{2}{3}\right)^3 = 2\left(\frac{8}{27}\right) = \frac{16}{27}$	$\left(3, \frac{16}{27}\right)$

Math Talk
Mathematical Practices

Explain why $f(x)$ is called a decreasing function.

STEP 2 Graph the function.

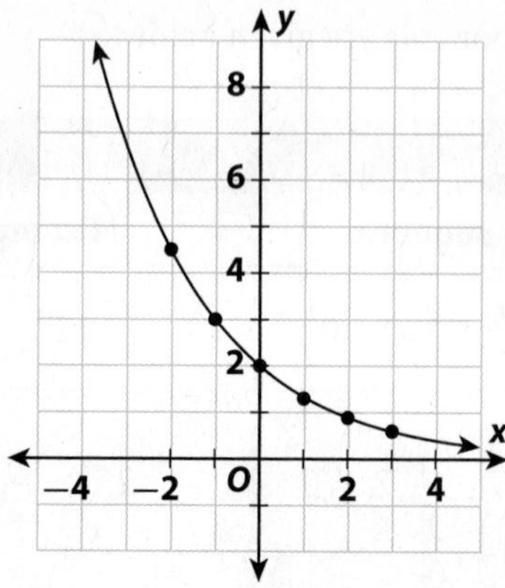

YOUR TURN

2. Find the value of the function $f(x) = 2\left(\frac{2}{3}\right)^x$ when $x = -3$. Graph the corresponding point on the coordinate grid in the example.

____

Writing an Equation from a Verbal Description

You can model a real-world exponential relationship by identifying the values of a and b in the function $f(x) = ab^x$.

EXAMPLE 2  CA CC F.LE.2

When a piece of paper is folded in half, the total thickness doubles. Suppose an unfolded piece of paper is 0.1 millimeter thick. Write an equation for the total thickness $t(n)$ as a function of the number of folds n. Then use the function to determine the thickness of the paper after 5 folds and 8 folds.

STEP 1 Identify the values of a and b, and write the equation in the form $t(n) = ab^n$.

- The value of a is the original thickness of the paper before any folds are made, or 0.1 millimeter.
- Because the thickness doubles with each fold, the value of b (the constant ratio) is 2.
- The equation for the function is $t(n) = 0.1(2)^n$.

STEP 2 To find the thickness after 5 and 8 folds, evaluate the function for $n = 5$ and $n = 8$.

$t(5) = 0.1(2)^5 = 0.1(32) = 3.2$

$t(8) = 0.1(2)^8 = 0.1(256) = 25.6$

After 5 folds the paper is 3.2 millimeters thick.

After 8 folds, the paper is 25.6 millimeters thick.

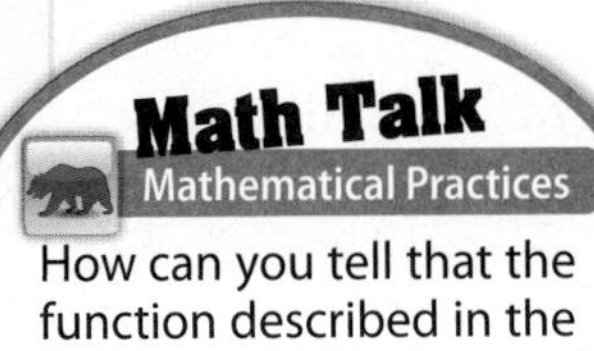

How can you tell that the function described in the example is an exponential function?

YOUR TURN

3. Write a function for the thickness of folding a piece of paper that is 0.2 millimeters thick, and determine the thickness after 3 and 7 folds.

____

Writing an Equation from Input-Output Pairs

Many real-world situations can be modeled by exponential functions. Some of these situations can be easily observed and data from the observations can be used to write the corresponding exponential function.

EXAMPLE 3  

CA CC F.LE.2

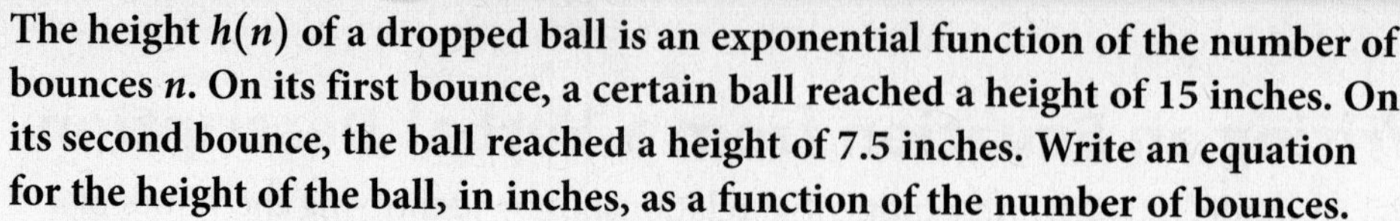

The height $h(n)$ of a dropped ball is an exponential function of the number of bounces n. On its first bounce, a certain ball reached a height of 15 inches. On its second bounce, the ball reached a height of 7.5 inches. Write an equation for the height of the ball, in inches, as a function of the number of bounces.

STEP 1 Divide successive function values, or heights, to find the constant ratio b. $b = 7.5 \div 15 = 0.5$

STEP 2 Use the value of b and a known ordered pair to find the value of a.

$h(n) = ab^n$ Write the general form.

$h(n) = a(0.5)^n$ Substitute the value for b.

$15 = a(0.5)^1$ Substitute the input and output values (1, 15) for the first bounce.

$15 = 0.5a$ Simplify.

$30 = a$ Solve for a.

STEP 3 Write an equation for the function: $h(n) = 30(0.5)^n$.

REFLECT

4. **Justify Reasoning** Use unit analysis to explain why b has no unit of measurement.

____

____

5. **What If?** Show that using the values for the second bounce will give the same result for a.

____

YOUR TURN

6. A pharmaceutical company is testing a new antibiotic. The number of bacteria present in a sample 1 hour after application of the antibiotic is 50,000. After another hour, the number of bacteria present in the sample is 25,000. The number of bacteria remaining $r(n)$ is an exponential function of the number of hours since the antibiotic was applied n. Write an equation for the number of bacteria remaining after n hours. ______________

Guided Practice

1. Make a table of values for the function $f(x) = 2^x$ and graph the function. (Example 1)

x	f(x) = 2^x	(x, f(x))
−3	f( ) = 2 =	
−2	f( ) = 2 =	
−1	f( ) = 2 =	
0	f( ) = 2 =	
1	f( ) = 2 =	
2	f( ) = 2 =	
3	f( ) = 2 =	

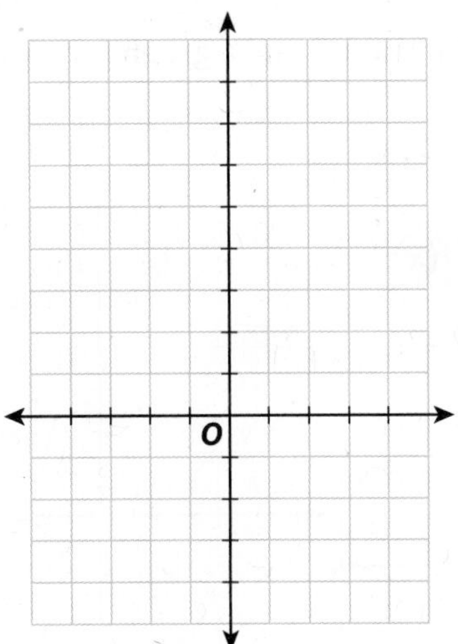

Use two points to write an equation for each function. (Examples 2 and 3)

2.

x	−3	−2	−1	0
f(x)	8	4	2	1

$\frac{f(-1)}{f(-2)} =$ ☐, so $b =$ ☐

$a = f($☐$) =$ ☐

$f(x) =$ ☐

3.

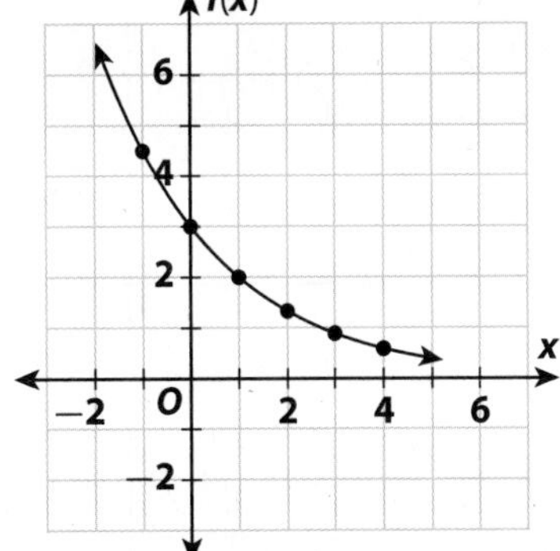

$f(x) =$ ____________

ESSENTIAL QUESTION CHECK-IN

4. How can you determine the values of a and b from a description of an exponential function of the form $f(x) = ab^x$?

____

____

Name ______________________ Class ______________________ Date ______________________

10.1 Independent Practice

CA CC F.LE.2, A.CED.2, F.IF.5, F.IF.7e

Make a table of values and a graph for each function.

5. $f(x) = 2\left(\frac{3}{4}\right)^x$

x	f(x)
−3	
−2	
−1	
0	
1	
2	
3	

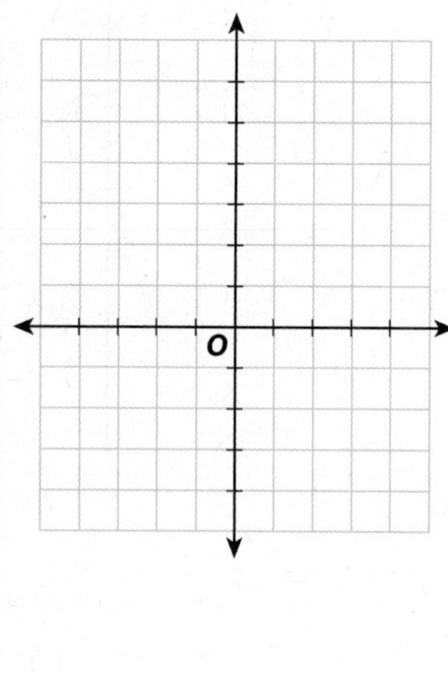

6. $f(x) = 0.9(0.6)^x$

x	f(x)
−3	
−2	
−1	
0	
1	
2	
3	

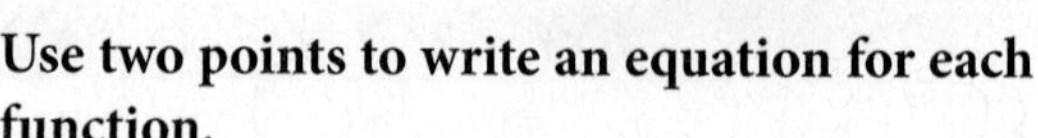

Use two points to write an equation for each function.

7.

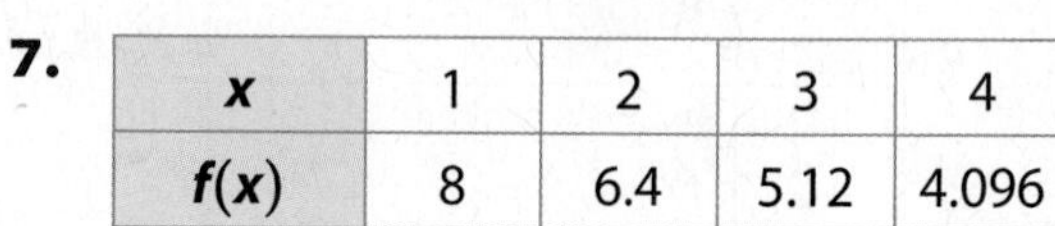

x	1	2	3	4
f(x)	8	6.4	5.12	4.096

____

8.

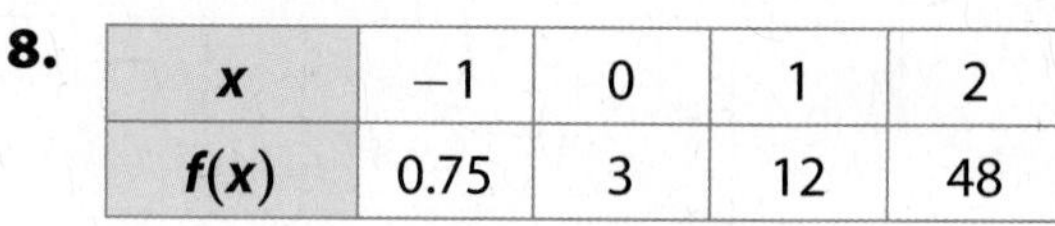

x	−1	0	1	2
f(x)	0.75	3	12	48

____

9.

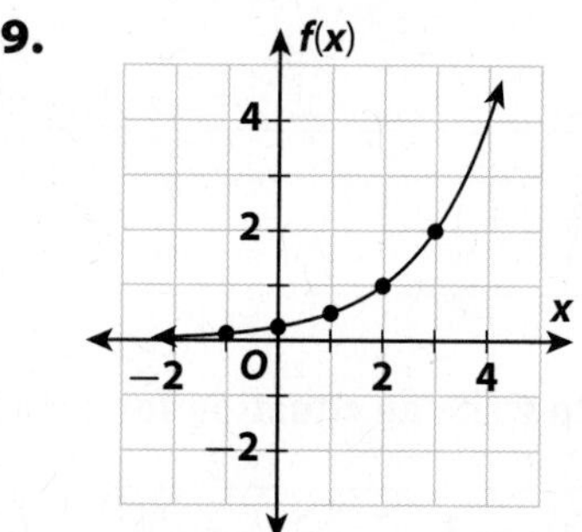

____

10.

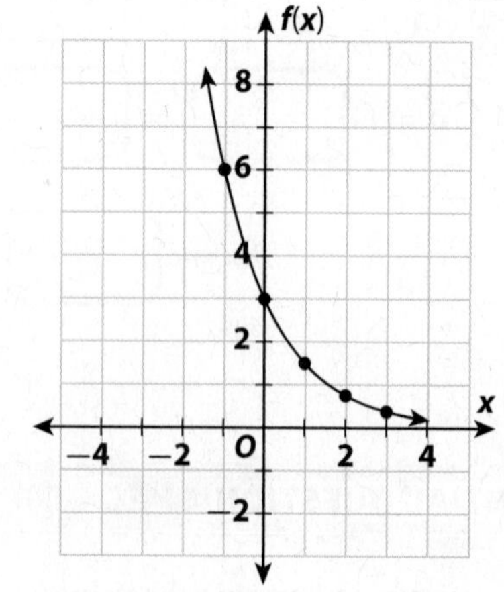

____

11. **Look for a Pattern** As the x-values of an exponential function increase by a constant amount, the values of the function are multiplied by the constant ratio, b. What is the value of b in the function below?

x	f(x)
−1	1.5
0	3
1	6
2	12

____

12. The area of the top surface of an 8.5-inch by 11-inch piece of paper is a function of the number of times it is folded in half.

a. Identify the value of a. What does it represent in this situation?

____

____

____

b. Write an equation for the function that models this situation. Explain why this is an exponential function.

____

____

____

c. What is the area of the top surface after 4 folds? Round to the nearest tenth of a square inch.

____

d. **What if?** What would the equation be if the original piece of paper had dimensions 11 inches by 17 inches? Compare this with the equation in Part b.

____

____

____

13. Suppose you do a favor for 3 people. Then you ask each of them to do a favor for 3 more people, passing along the request that each person who receives a favor does a favor for 3 more people. Suppose you do 3 favors on day 1, each recipient does 3 favors on day 2, and so on.

a. Complete the table for the first five days.

Day (n)	Favors $f(n)$
1	3
2	9
3	
4	
5	

b. Write an equation for the exponential function that models this situation.

____

c. According to the model, how many favors will be done on day 10? Explain your reasoning.

____

____

____

____

____

____

d. What would the equation be if everyone did a favor for 4 people rather than 3 people?

____

14. Write an equation for the function whose graph is shown at the right.

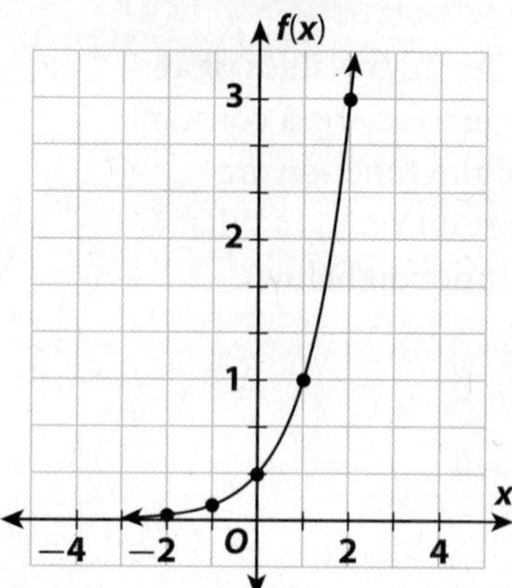

H.O.T. FOCUS ON HIGHER ORDER THINKING

Work Area

15. Draw Conclusions Assume that the domain of the function $f(x) = 3(2)^x$ is the set of all real numbers. What is the range of the function? Explain.

16. Find the Error Kaylee needed to write the equation of an exponential function from points on the graph of the function. To determine the value of b, Kaylee chose the ordered pairs (1, 6) and (3, 54) and divided 54 by 6. She determined that the value of b was 9. What error did Kaylee make?

17. What If? An exponential function can be represented by the equation $f(x) = ab^x$, where a, b, and x are real numbers, $a \neq 0$, $b > 0$, and $b \neq 1$. Why must it be specified that $b \neq 1$? What would the graph of the function look like if $b = 1$?

18. Use properties of exponents to compare the functions $f(x) = 3(4)^{\frac{t}{2}}$ and $g(x) = 3(2)^t$.

LESSON 10.2

Exponential Growth and Decay

CA CC F.LE.1c

Recognize situations in which a quantity grows or decays by a constant percent rate per unit interval relative to another. *Also F.IF.4, F.IF.5, F.IF.7, F.IF.7e, F.LE.2, F.LE.5*

ESSENTIAL QUESTION

How can exponential functions model the increase or decrease of a quantity over time?

Exponential Growth

Exponential growth occurs when a quantity increases by the same rate r in each unit of time t. When this happens, the value of the quantity at any given time can be calculated as a function of the rate and the original amount. Because the function value increases as time increases, exponential growth functions are examples of increasing functions.

Exponential Growth

An exponential growth function has the form $y = a(1 + r)^t$, where $a > 0$.

y represents the final amount.

a represents the original amount.

r represents the rate of growth expressed as a decimal.

t represents time.

The exponential growth form $y = a(1 + r)^t$ is equivalent to the form $y = ab^x$, with $b = 1 + r$, $b > 1$, and $x = t$.

EXAMPLE 1

A painting is sold for \$1400, and its value increases by 9% each year after it is sold. Write an exponential growth function to model this situation. Then find the value of the painting in 25 years. Graph the function. State the domain and range of the function. What does the *y*-intercept represent in the context of the problem?

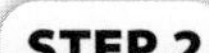

STEP 1 Write the exponential growth function for this situation.

$y = a(1 + r)^t$ — Write the formula.

$= 1400(1 + 0.09)^t$ — Substitute 1400 for *a* and 0.09 for *r*.

$= 1400(1.09)^t$ — Simplify.

STEP 2 Find the value in 25 years.

$y = 1400(1.09)^t$

$= 1400(1.09)^{25}$ — Substitute 25 for *t*.

$\approx 12{,}072.31$ — Use a calculator and round to the nearest hundredth.

After 25 years, the painting will be worth approximately \$12,072.31.

STEP 3 Create a table of values to graph the function.

t	y	(t, y)
0	1400	(0, 1400)
1	1526	(1, 1526)
2	1663.34	(2, 1663.34)
3	1813.04	(3, 1813.04)
4	1976.21	(4, 1976.21)
5	2154.07	(5, 2154.07)
25	12072.31	(25, 12072.31)

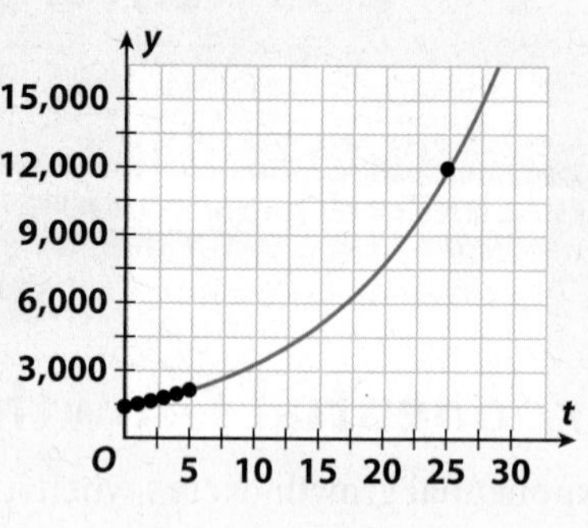

STEP 4 Determine the domain and the range of the function.

The input values represent years after a painting was sold for the first time. The values cannot be negative.

The domain is the set of real numbers t such that $t \geq 0$.

The output values represent the value of the painting in dollars. These values cannot be negative. Also, since this is an increasing function, the values cannot be less than the initial value of the painting.

The range is the set of real numbers y such that $y \geq 1400$.

Math Talk
Mathematical Practices
What is the constant ratio between successive function values when t increases by 1?

STEP 5 The y-intercept is the value of y when $t = 0$. In the context of this problem, $t = 0$ is the time when the painting first sold. Therefore, the y-intercept represents the value of the painting when it was first sold.

YOUR TURN

1. A sculpture is increasing in value at a rate of 8% per year, and its value in 2008 was \$1200. Write an exponential growth function to model this situation. Then find the sculpture's value in 2014. Graph the function.

____

____

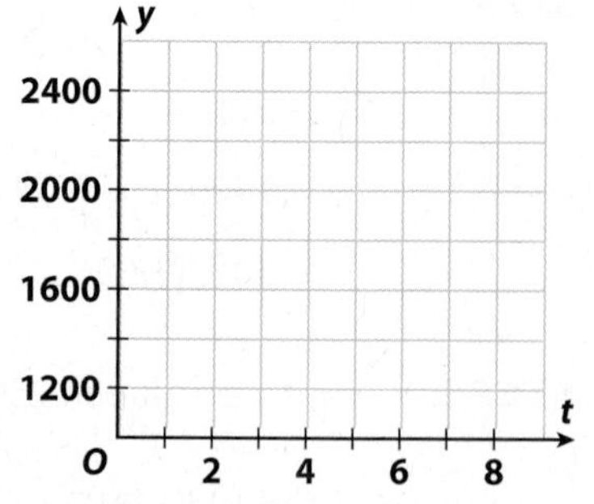

Exponential Decay

Exponential decay occurs when a quantity decreases by the same rate r in each unit of time t. Just like exponential growth, the value of the quantity at any given time can be calculated as a function of the rate and the original amount. Because the function value decreases as time increases, exponential decay functions are examples of decreasing functions.

Exponential Decay

An exponential decay function has the form $y = a(1 - r)^t$, where $a > 0$.

y represents the final amount.

a represents the original amount.

r represents the rate of decay as a decimal.

t represents time.

Notice an important difference between exponential growth functions and exponential decay functions. For exponential growth, the value inside the parentheses will be greater than 1 because r is added to 1 and $r > 0$. For exponential decay, the value inside the parentheses will be less than 1 because r is subtracted from 1 and $r > 0$.

The exponential decay form $y = a(1 - r)^t$ is equivalent to the form $y = ab^x$, with $b = 1 - r$, $0 < b < 1$, and $x = t$.

EXAMPLE 2

The population of a town is decreasing at a rate of 1% per year. In 2005 there were 1300 people. Write an exponential decay function to model this situation. Then find the population in 2013. Graph the function. State the domain and range of the function. What does the y-intercept represent in the context of the problem?

STEP 1 Write the exponential decay function.

$y = a(1 - r)^t$

$= 1300(1 - 0.01)^t$ Substitute 1300 for a and 0.01 for r.

$= 1300(0.99)^t$ Simplify.

STEP 2 Find the population in 2013.

2013 is 8 years after 2005, the year for which the initial value of the population is given. So $t = 8$.

$y = 1300(0.99)^t$

$= 1300(0.99)^8$ Substitute 8 for t.

≈ 1200 Use a calculator.

The population in 2013 is approximately 1200 people.

My Notes

STEP 3 Create a table of values to graph the function.

t	y	(t, y)
0	1300	(0, 1300)
1	1287	(1, 1287)
2	1274	(2, 1274)
3	1261	(3, 1261)
4	1249	(4, 1249)
5	1236	(5, 1236)
8	1200	(8, 1200)

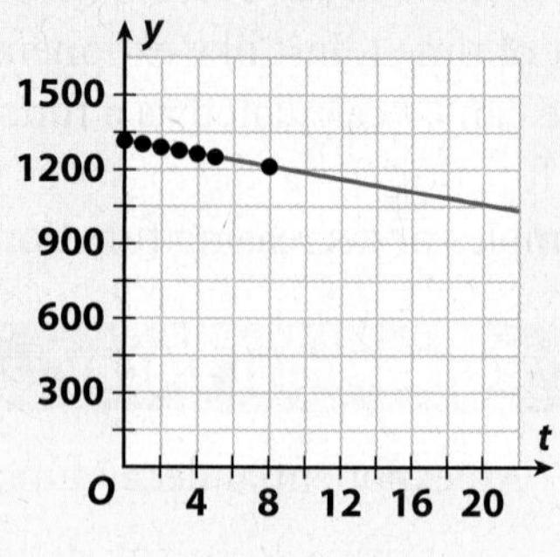

Note that while the graph may appear to be linear, it is not. The graph has this appearance because the population is declining at a slow rate.

STEP 4 Determine the domain and the range of the function.

The input values represent years after the initial population was given. The values cannot be negative.

The domain is the set of real numbers t such that $t \geq 0$.

The output values represent the population of the town. These values cannot be negative. Also, since this is a decreasing function, the values cannot be more than the initial population.

The range is the set of real numbers y such that $0 \leq y \leq 1300$.

STEP 5 The y-intercept is the value of y when $t = 0$. In the context of this problem, $t = 0$ is the year 2005. Therefore, the y-intercept represents the population of the town in 2005.

Math Talk
Mathematical Practices

What would a negative value of t represent in this context?

YOUR TURN

2. The fish population in a local stream is decreasing at a rate of 3% per year. The original population was 48,000. Write an exponential decay function to model this situation. Then find the population after 7 years. Graph the function.

____

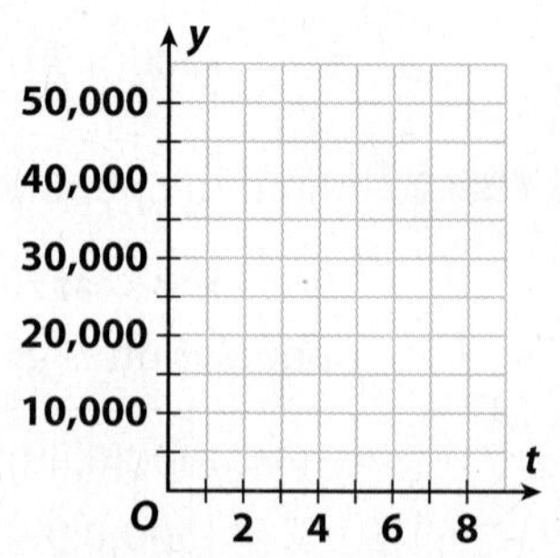

Online Practice and Help

my.hrw.com

Comparing Exponential Growth and Exponential Decay

You can use graphs to describe and compare exponential growth and exponential decay models over time.

EXAMPLE 3 

CA CC F.LE.1c

The graph shows the value of two different shares of stock over the period of four years since they were purchased. The values have been changing exponentially. For each stock write the equation of the function that represents the value of the stock. Describe and compare the behaviors of the two stocks.

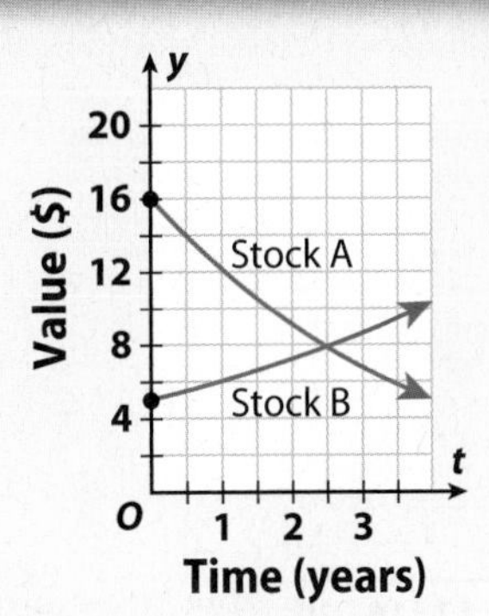

STEP 1 The graph for Stock A shows that the value of the stock is decreasing as time increases.

The initial value, when $t = 0$, is 16. The value when $t = 1$ is 12. Since $12 \div 16 = 0.75$, the function that represents the value of Stock A after t years is $A(t) = 16(0.75)^t$. $A(t)$ is an exponential decay function.

STEP 2 The graph for Stock B shows that the value of the stock is increasing as time increases.

The initial value, when $t = 0$, is 5. The value when $t = 1$ is 6. Since $6 \div 5 = 1.2$, the function that represents the value of Stock B after t years is $B(t) = 5(1.2)^t$. $B(t)$ is an exponential growth function.

STEP 3 The value of Stock A is going down over time. The value of Stock B is going up over time. The initial value of Stock A is greater than the initial value of Stock B. However, after about 2.5 years, the value of Stock B becomes greater than the value of Stock A.

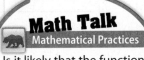

Math Talk
Mathematical Practices

Is it likely that the function representing the value of Stock B can be used to predict its value for 30 years? Explain.

YOUR TURN

3. Two shares of two different stocks changed exponentially over a period of 3 years. For each stock, write the equation and function that represents the value of the stock. For Stock A, the initial value when $t = 0$ is 12. The value when $t = 1$ is 6. For stock B, the initial value when $t = 0$ is 4. The value when $t = 1$ is 6. Describe and compare the two stocks.

____

____

____

____

Guided Practice

Write an exponential growth or decay function to model each situation. Graph each function. Then find the value of the function after the given amount of time.

1. The cost of tuition at a college is $12,000 and is increasing at a rate of 6% per year; 4 years. (Example 1)

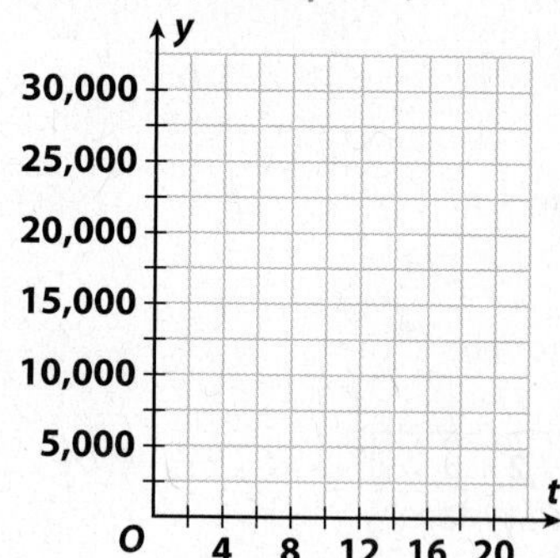

____

2. The value of a car is $18,000 and is depreciating at a rate of 12% per year; 10 years. (Example 2)

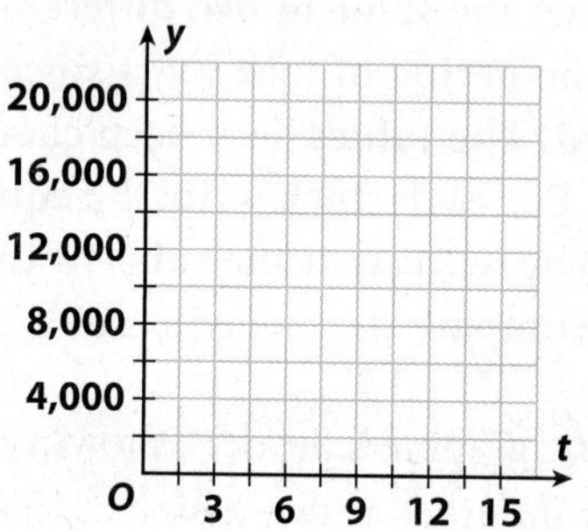

____

3. The value of two parcels of land have been changing exponentially since they were purchased, as shown in the graph. Describe and compare the values of the two parcels of land. (Example 3)

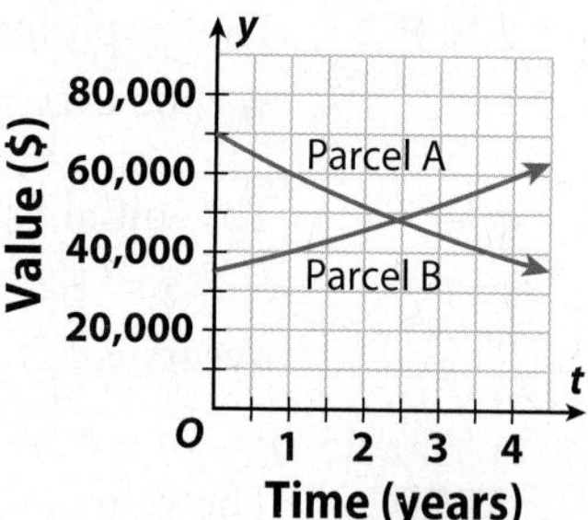

____

____

____

____

____

____

ESSENTIAL QUESTION CHECK-IN

4. How can you tell from its graph whether a function represents exponential growth or exponential decay?

____

____

____

____

____

Name ______________________ Class ______________ Date ______________

10.2 Independent Practice

F.IF.4, F.IF.5, F.IF.7, F.IF.7e, F.LE.1c, F.LE.2, F.LE.5

Write an exponential growth or decay function to model each situation. Graph each function. Then find the value of the function after the given amount of time.

5. The amount (to the nearest hundredth) of a 10-mg dose of a certain antibiotic decreases in your bloodstream at a rate of 16% per hour; 4 hours.

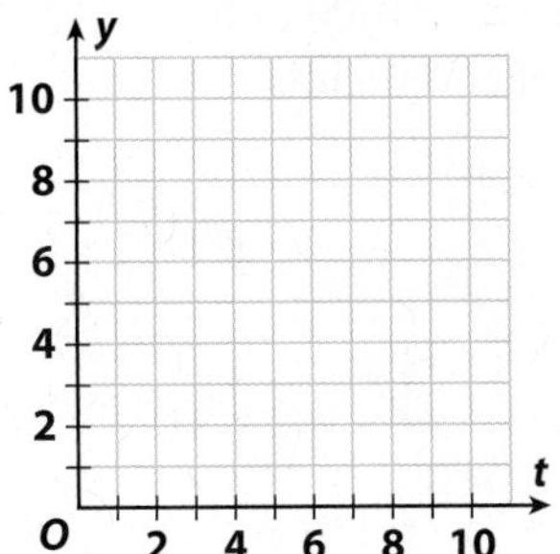

____

6. The number of student-athletes at a local high school is 300 and is increasing at a rate of 8% per year; 5 years.

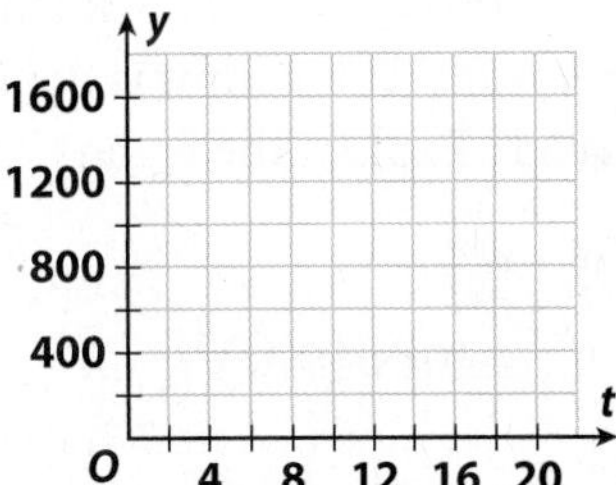

____

Write an exponential growth or decay function to model each situation. Then find the value of the function after the given amount of time.

7. Annual sales for a company are $149,000 and are increasing at a rate of 6% per year; 7 years. ______________________

8. The population of a town is 18,000 and is decreasing at a rate of 2% per year; 6 years. ______________________

9. The population of a small town is 1600 and is increasing at a rate of 3% per year; 10 years. ______________________

10. The value of a book is $58 and decreases at a rate of 10% per year; 8 years.

____

11. A new savings account starts at $700 and increases at 1.2% yearly; 7 years.

____

12. Mr. Nevin buys a car for $18,500. The value of the car depreciates 9% per year; 7 years. ______________________

13. If the domain consists of the set of all nonnegative real numbers, then for the graph of an exponential growth function, the y-intercept represents the ________________ value of the function. For the graph of an exponential decay function, the y-intercept represents the ________________ value of the function. Even though the graph of an exponential decay function is decreasing, if the initial value of the function is positive, the function will never reach the ________________.

H.O.T. FOCUS ON HIGHER ORDER THINKING

Work Area

14. **Explain the Error** Two students were asked to find the value of a $1000 item after 3 years. The item was depreciating at a rate of 40% per year. Which is incorrect? Explain the error.

Student A	Student B
$1000(0.6)^3$	$1000(0.4)^3$
$216	$64

____

____

15. **Make a Conjecture** The value of a certain car can be modeled by the function $y = 20{,}000(0.84)^t$, where t is time in years. Will the value ever be zero? Explain.

____

____

____

16. **Communicate Mathematical Ideas** Lynn says that it is always possible to look at a graph of an exponential function and determine whether it represents growth or decay. Nigel says he thinks it might not be. Who is correct? Explain.

____

____

____

____

____

LESSON
10.3 Geometric Sequences

CA CC F.BF.2

Write arithmetic and geometric sequences both recursively and with an explicit formula, use them to model situations, and translate between the two forms. *Also F.BF.1, F.BF.1a, F.IF.3, F.LE.1a, F.LE.2*

ESSENTIAL QUESTION

How can a geometric sequence be described?

Writing General Rules for Geometric Sequences

In a **geometric sequence**, the ratio of consecutive terms is constant. The constant ratio is called the **common ratio**, often represented by r.

EXAMPLE 1

Makers of Japanese swords in the 1400s repeatedly folded and hammered the metal to form layers. The folding process increased the strength of the sword.

The table shows how the number of layers depends on the number of folds. Write a recursive rule and an explicit rule for the geometric sequence represented by the table.

Number of Folds	n	1	2	3	4	5
Number of Layers	$f(n)$	2	4	8	16	32

STEP 1 Find the common ratio by calculating the ratios of consecutive terms.

$\frac{4}{2} = 2$ $\quad$ $\frac{8}{4} = 2$

$\frac{16}{8} = 2$ $\quad$ $\frac{32}{16} = 2$

The common ratio r is 2.

STEP 2 Write a recursive rule for the sequence.

The first term is 2, so $f(1) = 2$.

All terms after the first term are the product of the previous term and the common ratio: $f(2) = f(1) \cdot 2, f(3) = f(2) \cdot 2, f(4) = f(3) \cdot 2, \ldots$

The recursive rule is stated by providing the first term and the rule for successive terms.

$f(1) = 2$

$f(n) = f(n-1) \cdot 2$ for $n \geq 2$

This can be read as "each term in the sequence after the first term is equal to the previous term times two."

My Notes

STEP 3 Write an explicit rule for the sequence by writing each term as the product of the first term and a power of the common ratio.

n	$f(n)$
1	$2(2)^0 = 2$
2	$2(2)^1 = 4$
3	$2(2)^2 = 8$
4	$2(2)^3 = 16$
5	$2(2)^4 = 32$

Generalize the results from the table: $f(n) = 2 \cdot 2^{n-1}$.

REFLECT

1. **Draw Conclusions** How can you use properties of exponents to simplify the explicit rule found in Example 1?

2. **Justify Reasoning** Explain why the sequence 4, 12, 36, 108, 324, ... appears to be a geometric sequence.

3. **What If?** A geometric sequence has a common ratio of 5. The 6th term of the sequence is 30. What is the 7th term? What is the 5th term? Explain.

4. **Communicate Mathematical Ideas** The first term of a geometric sequence is 81 and the common ratio is $\frac{1}{3}$. Explain how you could find the 4th term of the sequence.

5. What is the recursive rule for the sequence $f(n) = 5(4)^{n-1}$?

YOUR TURN

6. Write a recursive rule and an explicit rule for the geometric sequence represented by the table.

n	1	2	3	4	5
$f(n)$	2	6	18	54	162

____

____

7. Write a recursive rule and an explicit rule for the geometric sequence 128, 32, 8, 2, 0.5, ...

____

____

EXPLORE ACTIVITY

General Rules for Geometric Sequences

Use the geometric sequence 6, 24, 96, 384, 1536, ... to help you write a recursive rule and an explicit rule for any geometric sequence. For the general rules, the values of n are consecutive integers starting with 1.

A Find the common ratio.

Numbers	**Algebra**
6, 24, 96, 384, 1536, ...	$f(1), f(2), f(3), f(4), f(5), \ldots$
Common ratio = 4	Common ratio = r

B Write a recursive rule.

Numbers	**Algebra**
$f(1) = 6$ and	Given $f(1)$,
$f(n) = f(n-1) \cdot 4$ for $n \geq 2$	$f(n) = f(n-1) \cdot r$ for $n \geq 2$

C Write an explicit rule.

Numbers	**Algebra**
$f(n) = 6 \cdot 4^{n-1}$	$f(n) = f(1) \cdot r^{n-1}$

Writing a Geometric Sequence Given Two Terms

The explicit and recursive rules for a geometric sequence can also be written in *subscript notation*. In subscript notation, the subscript indicates the position of the term in the sequence. a_1, a_2, and a_3 are the first, second, and third terms of a sequence, respectively. In general, a_n is the nth term of a sequence.

EXAMPLE 2  

The shutter speed settings on a camera form a geometric sequence where a_n is the shutter speed in seconds and n is the setting number. The fifth setting on the camera is $\frac{1}{60}$ second, and the seventh setting on the camera is $\frac{1}{15}$ second. Write an explicit rule for the sequence using subscript notation.

STEP 1 Identify the given terms in the sequence.

$a_5 = \frac{1}{60}$ — The fifth term of the sequence is $\frac{1}{60}$.

$a_7 = \frac{1}{15}$ — The seventh term of the sequence is $\frac{1}{15}$.

Math Talk Mathematical Practices

When finding the common ratio, why can you ignore the negative square root of 4 when solving $4 = r^2$?

STEP 2 Find the common ratio.

$a_7 = a_6 \cdot r$ — Write the recursive rule for a_7.

$a_6 = a_5 \cdot r$ — Write the recursive rule for a_6.

$a_7 = a_5 \cdot r \cdot r$ — Substitute the expression for a_6 into the rule for a_7.

$\frac{1}{15} = \frac{1}{60} \cdot r^2$ — Substitute $\frac{1}{15}$ for a_7 and $\frac{1}{60}$ for a_5.

$4 = r^2$ — Multiply both sides by 60.

$2 = r$ — Definition of positive square root

STEP 3 Find the first term of the sequence.

$a_n = a_1 \cdot r^{n-1}$ — Write the general explicit rule.

$\frac{1}{60} = a_1 \cdot 2^{5-1}$ — Substitute $\frac{1}{60}$ for a_n, 2 for r, and 5 for n.

$\frac{1}{60} = a_1 \cdot 16$ — Simplify.

$\frac{1}{960} = a_1$ — Divide both sides by 16.

STEP 4 Write the explicit rule.

$a_n = a_1 \cdot r^{n-1}$ — Write the general explicit rule.

$a_n = \frac{1}{960} \cdot 2^{n-1}$ — Substitute $\frac{1}{960}$ for a_1 and 2 for r.

Therefore, $a_n = \frac{1}{960} \cdot 2^{n-1}$.

YOUR TURN

8. The third term of a geometric sequence is $\frac{1}{54}$. The fifth term of the sequence is $\frac{1}{6}$. All terms of the sequence are positive numbers. Write an explicit rule for the sequence using subscript notation. ________________

Relating Geometric Sequences and Exponential Functions

A geometric sequence is equivalent to an exponential function with a domain that is restricted to the positive integers. For an exponential function of the form $f(n) = ab^n$, recall that a represents the initial value and b is the common ratio. Compare this to $f(n) = f(1) \cdot r^{n-1}$, where $f(1)$ represents the initial value and r is the common ratio.

EXAMPLE 3

CA CC F.LE.2

The graph shows the heights to which a ball bounces after it is dropped. Write an explicit rule for the sequence of bounce heights.

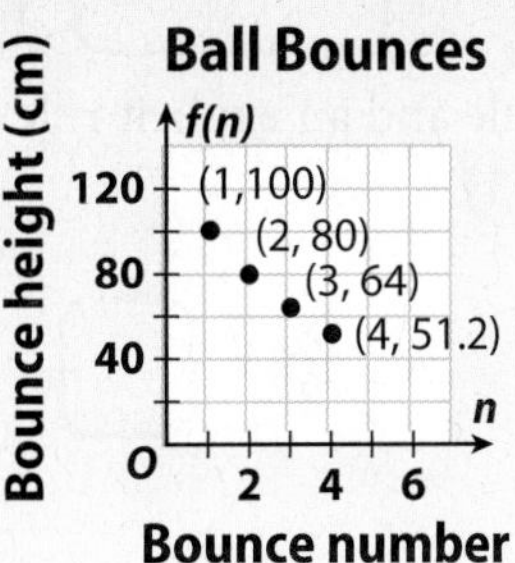

STEP 1 Represent the sequence in a table.

n	1	2	3	4
$f(n)$	100	80	64	51.2

STEP 2 Examine the sequence to determine whether it is geometric. The sequence is geometric because each term is the product of 0.8 and the previous term. The common ratio is 0.8.

STEP 3 Write an explicit rule for the sequence.

$f(n) = f(1) \cdot r^{n-1}$ — *Write the general rule.*

$f(n) = 100 \cdot 0.8^{n-1}$ — *Substitute 100 for f(1) and 0.8 for r.*

The sequence has the rule $f(n) = 100 \cdot 0.8^{n-1}$, where n is the bounce number and $f(n)$ is the bounce height.

YOUR TURN

9. The number of customers $f(n)$ projected to come into a new store in month number n is represented by the following table.

n	1	2	3	4
$f(n)$	1000	1500	2250	3375

Write an explicit rule for the sequence. ________________

Guided Practice

1. The table shows the beginning-of-month balances, rounded to the nearest cent, in Marla's saving account for the first few months after she made an initial deposit in the account. (Example 1)

Month	***n***	1	2	3	4
Account balance ($)	***f(n)***	2000	2010.00	2020.05	2030.15

a. Explain how you know that the sequence of account balances is a geometric sequence.

____

b. Write recursive and explicit rules for the sequences of account balances.

Recursive rule: $f(1) =$ ☐, $f(n) =$ ☐ $\cdot$ ☐ for $n \geq 2$

Explicit rule: $f(n) =$ ☐ $\cdot$ ☐

2. Write a recursive rule and an explicit rule for the geometric sequence 9, 27, 81, 243. (Example 1)

$\frac{27}{9} =$ ☐ $\qquad \frac{81}{27} =$ ☐ $\qquad \frac{243}{81} =$ ☐

Recursive rule: _______________

Explicit rule: _______________

3. Write an explicit rule for the geometric sequence with terms $a_2 = 12$ and $a_4 = 192$. Assume that the common ratio r is positive. (Example 2)

____

4. Write an explicit rule for the geometric sequence with terms $a_3 = 1600$ and $a_5 = 256$. Assume that the common ratio is positive. (Example 2)

____

ESSENTIAL QUESTION CHECK-IN

5. How can you write the explicit rule for a geometric sequence if you know the recursive rule for the sequence?

____

____

____

Name ______________________ Class ______________ Date ______________

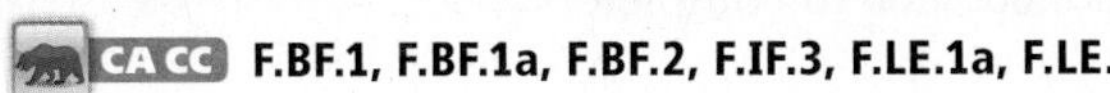

10.3 Independent Practice

CA CC F.BF.1, F.BF.1a, F.BF.2, F.IF.3, F.LE.1a, F.LE.2

6. The graph shows the number of players in the first four rounds of the U.S Open women's singles tennis tournament.

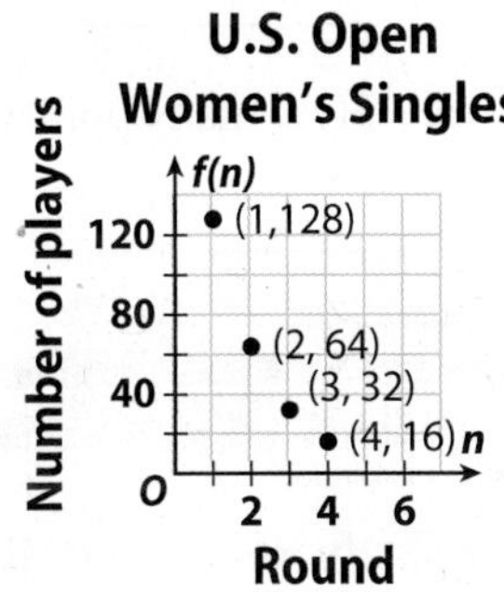

a. Write an explicit rule for the sequence of players in each round.

____

b. How many rounds are there in the tournament? (*Hint:* In the last round, only two players are left.)

____

7. Write a recursive rule and an explicit rule for the geometric sequence $12, 3, \frac{3}{4}, \frac{3}{16}, \ldots$

Recursive rule: ______________________

Explicit rule: ______________________

Each rule represents a geometric sequence. If the given rule is recursive, write it as an explicit rule. If the rule is explicit, write it as a recursive rule. Assume that $f(1)$ is the first term of the sequence.

8. $f(n) = 6(3)^{n-1}$

____

____

9. $f(1) = 10; f(n) = f(n-1) \cdot 8$ for $n \geq 2$

____

____

Write an explicit rule for each geometric sequence based on the given terms from the sequence. Assume that the common ratio r is positive.

10. $a_2 = 50$ and $a_4 = 12.5$

____

11. $a_3 = 24$ and $a_5 = 384$

____

12. An economist predicts that the cost of food will increase by 4% per year for the next several years.

a. Use the economist's prediction to write an explicit rule for a geometric sequence that gives the cost in dollars of a box of cereal in year n that costs \$3.20 in year 1.

____

b. What is the fourth term of the sequence, and what does it represent in this situation?

____

____

13. The numbers of points that a player must accumulate to reach the next level of a video game form a geometric sequence, where $f(n)$ is the number of points needed to complete level n.

a. A player needs 1000 points to complete level 2 and 8,000,000 to complete level 5. Write an explicit rule for the sequence.

____

b. How many points are needed for level 7?

____

H.O.T. FOCUS ON HIGHER ORDER THINKING

Work Area

14. Justify Reasoning If a geometric sequence has a common ratio r that is negative, describe the terms of the sequence. Explain.

____

____

____

____

15. Communicate Mathematical Ideas If you are given the seventh term of a geometric sequence and the common ratio, how can you determine the second term of the sequence without writing an explicit rule or recursive rule? Explain.

____

____

____

____

____

16. Critique Reasoning Miguel writes the following: 5, ___, 5, ___, …

He tells Alicia that what he has written represents a geometric sequence and asks Alicia to fill in the missing terms. Alicia says that the missing terms must both be 5. Miguel says that Alicia is incorrect. Who is right? Explain.

____

____

____

____

____

LESSON 10.4

Transforming Exponential Functions

CA CC F.BF.3

Identify the effect on the graph of replacing $f(x)$ by $f(x) + k$, $k\,f(x)$, $f(kx)$, and $f(x + k)$ for specific values of k (both positive and negative); find the value of k given the graphs. Experiment with cases and illustrate an explanation of the effects on the graph using technology.

ESSENTIAL QUESTION

How does the graph of $f(x) = ab^x$ change when a and b are changed?

EXPLORE ACTIVITY 1

Changing the Value of a in $f(x) = ab^x$

Recall that a family of functions is a set of functions whose graphs have basic characteristics in common. The most basic function of a family of functions is called the parent function. For exponential functions, every different base determines a different parent function for its own family of functions.

You can explore the behavior of an exponential function of the form $f(x) = ab^x$ by examining *parameters* a and b.

A Graph parent function $Y_1 = (1.5)^x$ and functions $Y_2 = 2(1.5)^x$ and $Y_3 = 3(1.5)^x$ on a graphing calculator. Use a viewing window from -5 to 5 for x and from -1 to 6 for y, using a scale of 1. Sketch the curves.

B Use the CALC feature while viewing the graphs to calculate the value of Y_1 when $x = -2$. Then use the up and down arrow keys to jump to the other curves and calculate their values when $x = -2$. Round to the nearest thousandth if necessary. Repeat this process until you have completed the table.

x	Y_1	Y_2	Y_3
-2			
-1			
0			
1			
2			

A **vertical stretch** of a graph is the result of pulling the graph away from the x-axis. Each y-value of an (x, y) pair is multiplied by a factor a such that $a > 1$.

A **vertical compression** of a graph is the result of pushing the graph toward the x-axis. Each y-value of an (x, y) pair is multiplied by a factor a such that $0 < a < 1$.

REFLECT

1. **Communicate Mathematical Ideas** Is the graph of Y_2 a vertical stretch or a vertical compression of the graph of Y_1? By what factor is it multiplied? In the same way, describe the graph of Y_1 compared to the graph of Y_2.

EXPLORE ACTIVITY 2

CA CC F.BF.3

Changing the Value of *b* in $f(x) = b^x$

A Graph the functions $Y_1 = 1.2^x$ and $Y_2 = 1.5^x$ on a graphing calculator. Use a viewing window from -5 to 5 for x and from -2 to 5 for y, with a scale of 1 for both. Sketch the curves.

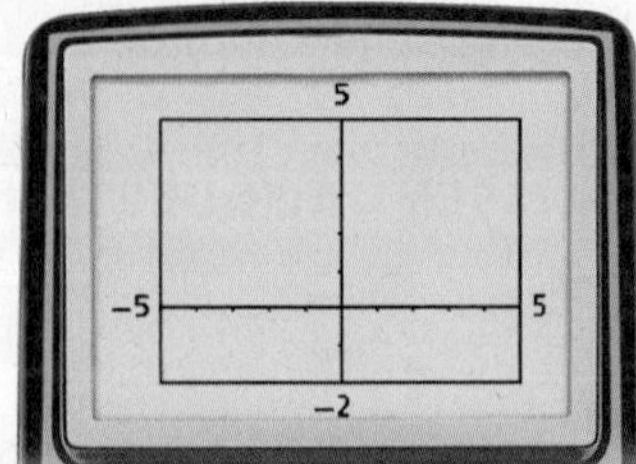

B Use the TBLSET and TABLE features to make a table of values starting at -2 with an increment of 1. Then complete the table. Round to the nearest thousandth if necessary.

x	Y_1	Y_2
-2	0.694	
-1		0.667
0		
1	1.2	1.5
2		

C Which graph rises more quickly as x increases to the right of 0? Which graph falls, or approaches 0, more quickly as x decreases to the left of 0?

____

____

____

____

D Identify the y-intercepts of the graphs of Y_1 and Y_2.

____

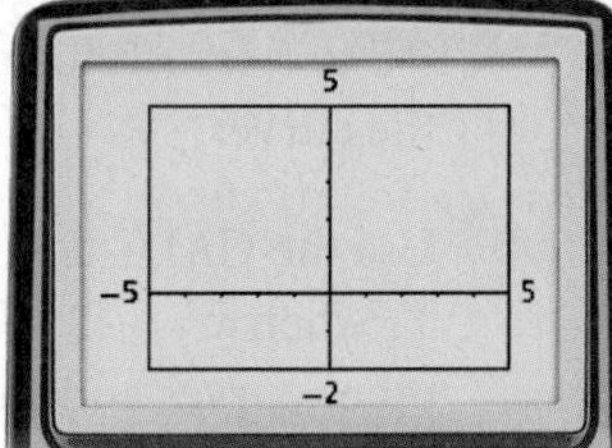

E Using the same window as above, graph the functions $Y_3 = 0.6^x$ and $Y_4 = 0.9^x$. Sketch the curves.

F Make a table of values starting at -2 with an increment of 1. Then complete the table.

x	Y_3	Y_4
-2	2.778	
-1		1.111
0		
1	0.6	0.9
2		

Math Talk
Mathematical Practices

For the graphs of Y_3 and Y_4, which graph rises more quickly as x decreases to the left of 0? Which graph falls more quickly as x increases to the right of 0?

REFLECT

2. **What If?** Consider the function $Y_5 = 1.3^x$. How will its graph compare with the graphs of Y_1 and Y_2? Discuss end behavior and the y-intercept.

____

____

____

____

____

Adding a Constant to an Exponential Function

Adding a constant to an exponential function causes the graph of the function to translate up or down, depending on the constant.

Math On the Spot
my.hrw.com

EXAMPLE 1

CA CC F.BF.3

Describe the effect of transforming the function $f(x) = 1.5^x$ into $g(x) = 1.5^x + 2$.

Make a table of values for the functions and graph them. Round values in the table to the nearest thousandth.

x	f(x)	g(x)
−2	0.444	2.444
−1	0.667	2.667
0	1	3
1	1.5	3.5
2	2.25	4.25

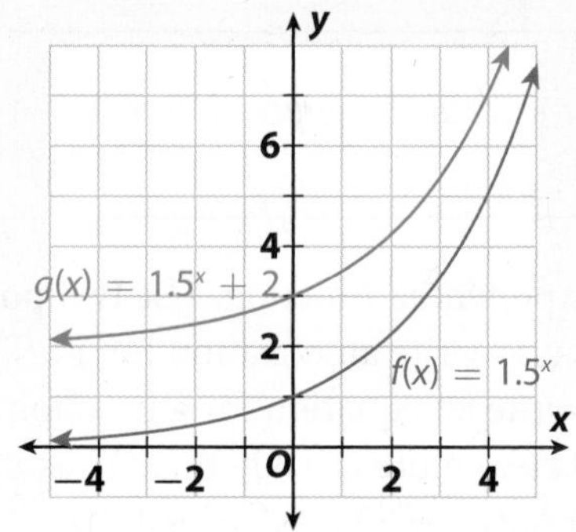

$g(x)$ is a vertical translation of $f(x)$ up 2 units.

YOUR TURN

3. Describe the effect of transforming the function $f(x) = 2^x$ into $g(x) = 2^x - 5$.

____

In general, the constant that is added to an exponential function $f(x)$ determines the size and direction of the translation. For example, if $f(x) = 0.75^x$ and $h(x) = 0.75^x - 3$, then $h(x)$ is a vertical translation of $f(x)$ down 3 units.

The table below summarizes the general shapes of exponential function graphs.

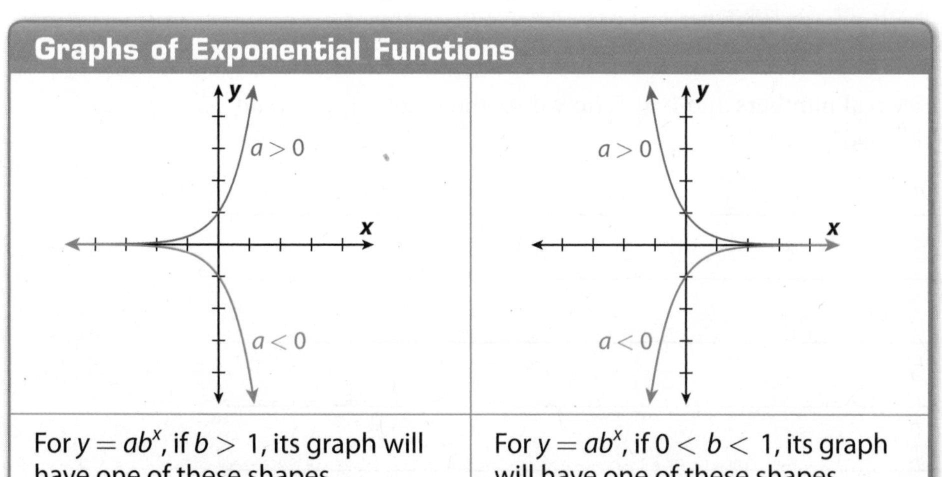

For $y = ab^x$, if $b > 1$, its graph will have one of these shapes.	For $y = ab^x$, if $0 < b < 1$, its graph will have one of these shapes.

Guided Practice

The graphs of the parent function $Y_1 = (0.5)^x$ and the function $Y_2 = 2(0.5)^x$ are shown. Use the graphs for Exercises 1–4. (Explore Activity 1)

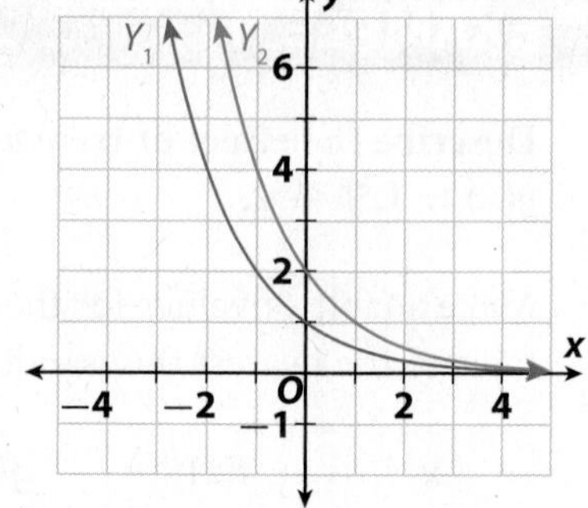

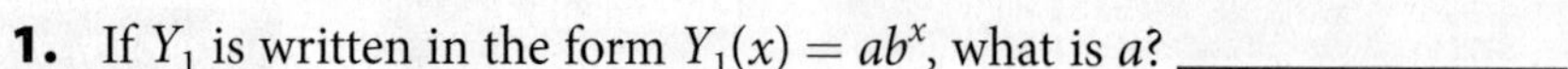

1. If Y_1 is written in the form $Y_1(x) = ab^x$, what is a? ______

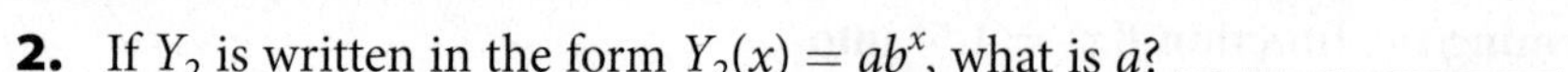

2. If Y_2 is written in the form $Y_2(x) = ab^x$, what is a? ______

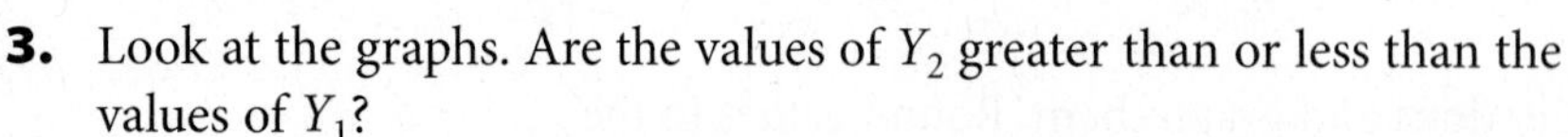

3. Look at the graphs. Are the values of Y_2 greater than or less than the values of Y_1?

______

4. Is Y_2 a *vertical stretch* or a *vertical compression* of Y_1?

______

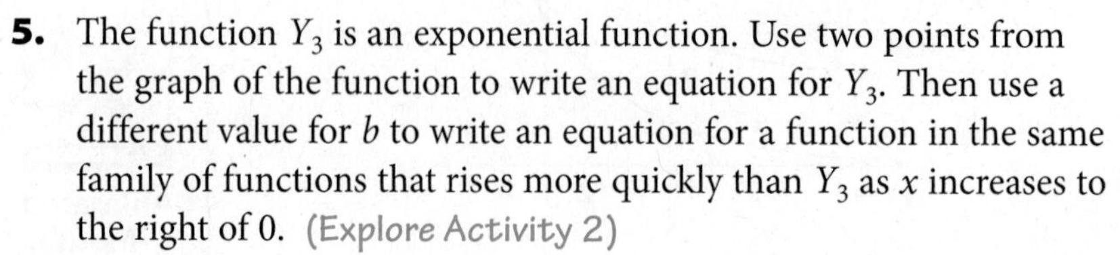

5. The function Y_3 is an exponential function. Use two points from the graph of the function to write an equation for Y_3. Then use a different value for b to write an equation for a function in the same family of functions that rises more quickly than Y_3 as x increases to the right of 0. (Explore Activity 2)

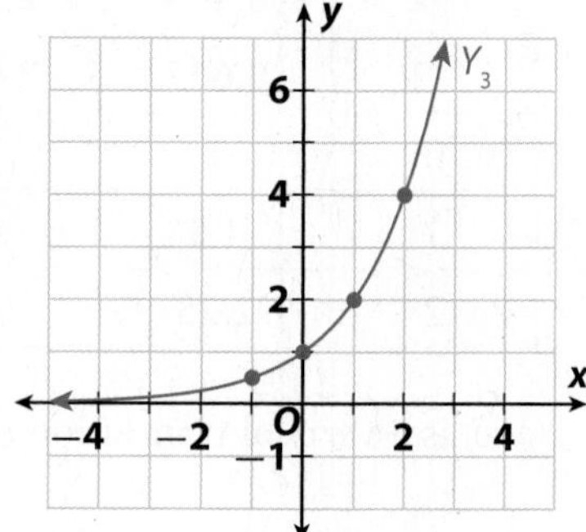

______

The graphs of the function $Y_5 = 1.2^x + 1$ and the function $Y_6 = 1.2^x + 3$ are shown. Use the graphs for Exercises 6–7. (Example 1)

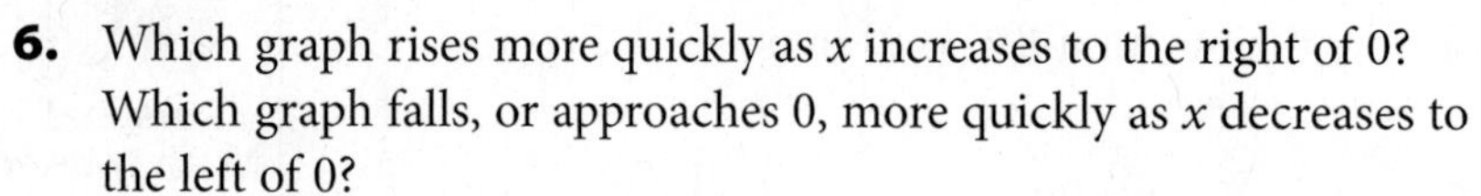

6. Which graph rises more quickly as x increases to the right of 0? Which graph falls, or approaches 0, more quickly as x decreases to the left of 0?

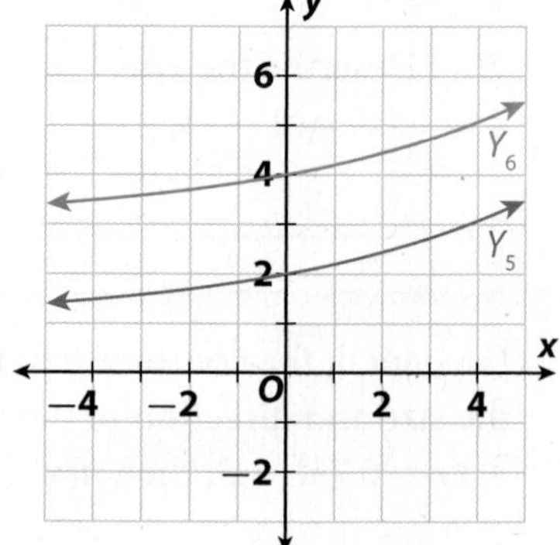

______

7. Y_6 is a vertical translation of Y_5. Tell the number of units Y_5 was translated and the direction of the translation.

______

ESSENTIAL QUESTION CHECK-IN

8. If a and b are positive real numbers and $b \neq 1$, how does the graph of $f(x) = ab^x$ change when b is changed?

______

______

______

______

______

Name ______________________ Class ______________________ Date ______________________

10.4 Independent Practice

CA CC F.BF.3

A parent function and a function in the same family are given. Tell whether the value of *a* or the value of *b* was changed in $f(x) = ab^x$.

9. $f(x) = (0.2)^x$ $\quad$ $f(x) = 2(0.2)^x$ ______

10. $f(x) = 3^x$ $\quad$ $f(x) = 3.5^x$ ______

11. $f(x) = 3^x$ $\quad$ $f(x) = 1.5(3)^x$ ______

Values of the function $Y_1 = (2.5)^x$ and the function $Y_2 = 0.5(2.5)^x$ are shown in the table.

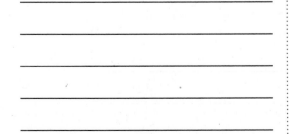

x	Y_1	Y_2
−2	0.16	0.08
−1	0.4	0.2
0	1	0.5
1	2.5	1.25
2	6.25	3.125

12. How do the values in the table for Y_2 compare with the values for Y_1?

____

____

____

____

13. Is Y_2 a *vertical stretch* or a *vertical compression* of Y_1? Explain how you know.

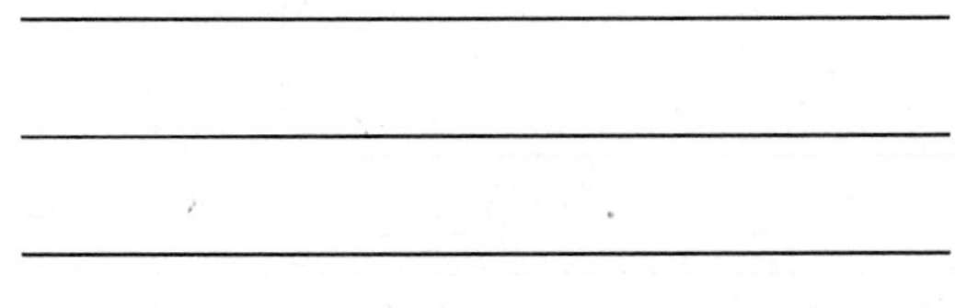

____

____

____

____

____

Values of a parent function are shown below.

x	−2	−1	0	1	2
f(x)	4	2	1	0.5	0.25

14. Write an equation for the parent function.

____

15. Write an equation for a function in the same family of functions whose graph will rise more quickly than the parent function as x decreases to the left of 0.

____

The graphs of the function $Y_3 = 2^x + 4$ and the function $Y_4 = 2^x + 2$ are shown.

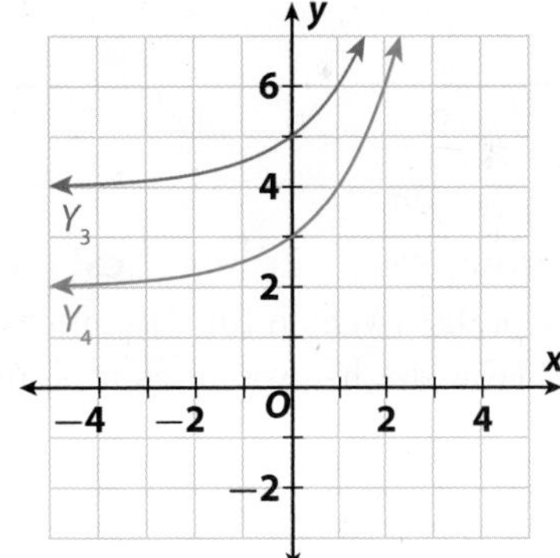

16. Identify the y-intercepts of Y_3 and Y_4.

____

17. **Justify Reasoning** Was Y_4 translated up or down from the graph of Y_3 by the change in the constant? Explain.

____

____

____

____

18. Graph the functions $Y_1 = 0.6^x$ and $Y_2 = 0.3^x$ on a graphing calculator. Use a viewing window from -5 to 5 for x and from -2 to 8 for y, with a scale of 1 for both. Sketch the curves.

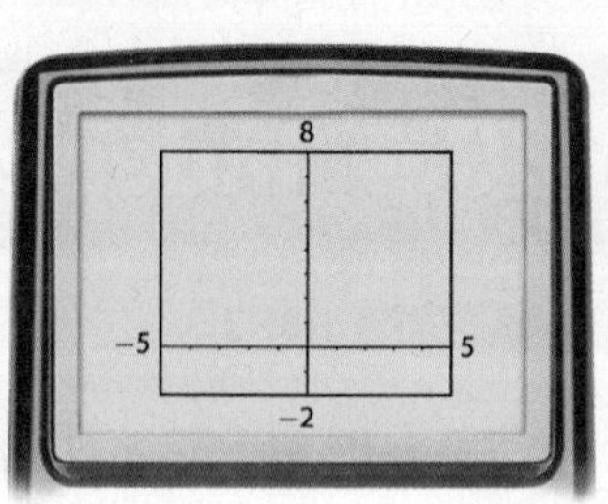

How does the graph of Y_1 compare with the graph of Y_2? Discuss how the graphs rise or fall and the y-intercepts.

____

____

____

____

H.O.T. FOCUS ON HIGHER ORDER THINKING

Work Area

19. Critical Thinking Describe how the graph of $f(x) = ab^x$ changes for a given positive value of a as you increase the value of b when $b > 1$. Discuss the rise and fall of the graph and the y-intercept.

____

____

____

____

____

20. Communicate Mathematical Ideas Consider the functions $Y_1 = (1.02)^x$ and $Y_2 = (1.03)^x$. Which function increases more quickly as x increases to the right of 0? How do the growth factors support your answer?

____

____

____

____

21. Communicate Mathematical Ideas Consider the functions $Y_1 = (0.94)^x$ and $Y_2 = (0.98)^x$. Which function decreases more quickly as x increases to the right of 0? How do the decay factors support your answer?

____

____

____

____

LESSON 10.5

Equations Involving Exponents

CA CC A.CED.1, A.REI.11

For the full text of these standards, see the table beginning on page CA2. *Also A.CED.2, F.BF.1, F.BF.1a, F.LE.2*

ESSENTIAL QUESTION

How can you solve equations involving variable exponents?

EXPLORE ACTIVITY

Exploring Equations Containing Exponents

Some equations have an exponent that is a variable. You can use what you know about powers to find the value of the variable.

A $2^x = 8$

Write 8 as a power of 2.

$$2^x = 8$$

$$2^x = \square \cdot \square \cdot \square$$

$$2^x = \square^{\square}$$

B $2^{\square} = 8 = 2^x$, so $x = \square$

C $3^x = 81$

Write 81 as a power of 3.

$$3^x = 81$$

$$3^x = \square \cdot \square \cdot \square \cdot \square$$

$$3^x = \square^{\square}$$

D $3^{\square} = 81 = 3^x$, so $x = \square$

REFLECT

1. **Communicating Mathematical Ideas** What do you notice about the bases of the expressions 2^x and 2^3? ______________________

Equality of Bases Property

Words	Algebra	Example
Two powers with the same positive base other than 1 are equal if and only if the exponents are equal.	If $b > 0$ and $b \neq 1$, then $b^x = b^y$ if and only if $x = y$.	If $2^x = 2^9$, then $x = 9$. If $x = 9$, then $2^x = 2^9$.

Solving Equations by Equating Exponents

You can apply the properties of equations you already know and the Equality of Bases Property to solve equations involving exponents.

EXAMPLE 1 CA CC A.CED.1

Solve each equation.

A $\frac{5}{2}(2)^x = 80$

$\frac{2}{5} \cdot \frac{5}{2}(2)^x = \frac{2}{5} \cdot 80$ — Multiply by the reciprocal to isolate the power $(2)^x$.

$(2)^x = 32$ — Simplify.

$(2)^x = 2^5$ — Write 32 as a power of 2.

$x = 5$ — $b^x = b^y$ if and only if $x = y$.

B $4\left(\frac{5}{3}\right)^x = \frac{500}{27}$

$\frac{1}{4} \cdot 4\left(\frac{5}{3}\right)^x = \frac{1}{4} \cdot \frac{500}{27}$ — Multiply by the reciprocal to isolate the power.

$\left(\frac{5}{3}\right)^x = \frac{125}{27}$ — Simplify.

$\left(\frac{5}{3}\right)^x = \left(\frac{5}{3}\right)^3$ — Write the fraction as a power of $\frac{5}{3}$.

$x = 3$ — $b^x = b^y$ if and only if $x = y$.

My Notes

REFLECT

2. How can you check a solution?

____

____

3. **Communicate Mathematical Ideas** How can you work backward to write $\frac{125}{27}$ as a power of $\frac{5}{3}$?

____

____

4. **Justify Reasoning** Is it possible to solve the equation $2^x = 96$ using the method in Example 1? Why or why not?

____

____

____

YOUR TURN

Solve each equation.

5. $\frac{2}{3}(3)^x = 54$

$x =$ ________

6. $6\left(\frac{5}{4}\right)^x = \frac{75}{8}$

$x =$ ________

7. $\frac{1}{2}(4)^x = 32$

$x =$ ________

8. $5(3)^x = 405$

$x =$ ________

Writing an Equation and Solving by Graphing

Some equations cannot be solved using the method in Example 1 because it isn't possible to write both sides of the equation as a whole number power of the same base. Instead, you can consider the expressions on either side of the equation as the rules for two different functions. You can then solve the original equation in one variable by graphing the two functions. The solution is the input value for the point where the two graphs intersect.

EXAMPLE 2

A town has 78,918 residents. The population is increasing at a rate of 6% per year. The town council is offering a prize for the best prediction of how long it will take for the population to reach 100,000. Make a prediction.

Write an exponential model to represent the situation.

Let y represent the population and x represent time (in years).

$y = 78{,}918(1 + 0.06)^x$

Write an equation in one variable to represent the time, x, when the population reaches 100,000.

$100{,}000 = 78{,}918(1.06)^x$

Write functions for the expressions on either side of the equation.

$f(x) = 100{,}000$ — *$f(x)$ is a constant function.*

$g(x) = 78{,}918(1.06)^x$ — *$g(x)$ is an exponential growth function.*

STEP 4 Graph the functions on a graphing calculator. Let $Y_1 = f(x)$ and $Y_2 = g(x)$. Use a viewing window from -2 to 8 for x, using a scale of 1, and a viewing window from $-20{,}000$ to $200{,}000$ for y, using a scale of 20,000. Sketch the graphs.

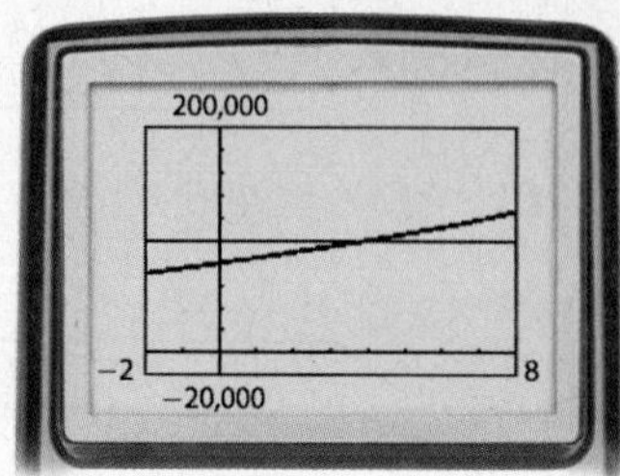

STEP 5 Use the intersect feature on the CALC menu to find the input value where the graphs intersect. (Do not round more than the calculator has already done.)

The input value where the graphs intersect is 4.063245.

STEP 6 Use the input value to make a prediction as to the number of years until the population reaches 100,000.

The population will reach 100,000 in just over 4 years.

Math Talk
Mathematical Practices
Suppose the contest is announced on January 1. Explain how to predict the date on which the population will be 100,000.

REFLECT

9. **Communicate Mathematical Ideas** Why is the input value of the intersection point of $f(x)$ and $g(x)$ the solution?

____

____

____

____

YOUR TURN

There are 250 bass in a lake. The population is increasing at the rate of 20% per year. You want to make a prediction for how long it will take the population to reach 400.

10. Write an equation in one variable to represent the time x when the population reaches 400.

____

11. Make a prediction for how long will it take for the bass population to reach 400. Round the answer to the nearest tenth of a year. ____________

Guided Practice

Solve each equation without graphing. (Example 1)

1. $\frac{3}{4}(6)^x = 162$

   $(6)^x = \square$

   $(6)^x = 6^{\square}$

   $x = \square$

2. $3\left(\frac{5}{6}\right)^x = \frac{75}{36}$

   $\left(\frac{5}{6}\right)^x = \square$

   $\left(\frac{5}{6}\right)^x = \left(\frac{5}{6}\right)^{\square}$

   $x = \square$

3. $7\left(\frac{1}{2}\right)^x = \frac{7}{8}$

   $x =$ ______

4. $\frac{1}{5}(5)^x = 125$

   $x =$ ______

5. $10(4)^x = 640$

   $x =$ ______

Solve each equation by graphing. Round to the nearest hundredth. (Example 2)

6. $6^x = 100$

   $x \approx$ ______

7. $7^x = 400$

   $x \approx$ ______

8. $(2.5)^x = 100$

   $x \approx$ ______

There are 225 wolves in a state park. The population is increasing at the rate of 15% per year. You want to make a prediction for how long it will take the population to reach 500. (Example 2)

9. Write an equation in one variable to represent the time, x, when the population reaches 500. ______

10. Make a prediction for how long will it take for the wolf population to reach 500. Round the answer to the nearest tenth of a year. ______

ESSENTIAL QUESTION CHECK-IN

11. How can you solve equations involving variable exponents?

______

______

______

______

______

______

Name ______ Class ______ Date ______

10.5 Independent Practice

CA CC A.CED.1, A.CED.2, A.REI.11, F.BF.1, F.BF.1a, F.LE.2

Solve each equation without graphing.

12. $8(3)^x = 648$

$x =$ ______

13. $\frac{1}{5}(5)^x = 5$

$x =$ ______

14. $3\left(\frac{3}{10}\right)^x = \frac{27}{100}$

$x =$ ______

15. $6(5)^x = 750$

$x =$ ______

16. $\frac{3}{4}\left(\frac{2}{3}\right)^x = \frac{4}{27}$

$x =$ ______

17. $\frac{1}{2}\left(\frac{1}{5}\right)^x = \frac{1}{50}$

$x =$ ______

18. What would you do first to solve the equation $\frac{1}{25}(5)^x = 5$?

______

For Exercises 19–22, solve each equation by graphing. Round to the nearest hundredth.

19. $6^x = 150$

$x \approx$ ______

20. $5^x = 20$

$x \approx$ ______

21. $3^x = 100$

$x \approx$ ______

22. $(5.5)^x = 40$

$x \approx$ ______

23. Write the constant function and the exponential function you would graph in order to solve the equation $4^x = 20$.

constant function: $f(x) =$ ______

exponential function: $g(x) =$ ______

24. Can you solve the equation $30 = (1.5)^x$ using the method shown in Example 1? Explain.

______

______

Use the equation $2^x = 16$ for Exercises 25–27.

25. Solve the equation using properties of equations and the Equality of Bases Property.

$x =$ ______

26. Solve the equation by graphing a constant function and an exponential function on the coordinate plane below.

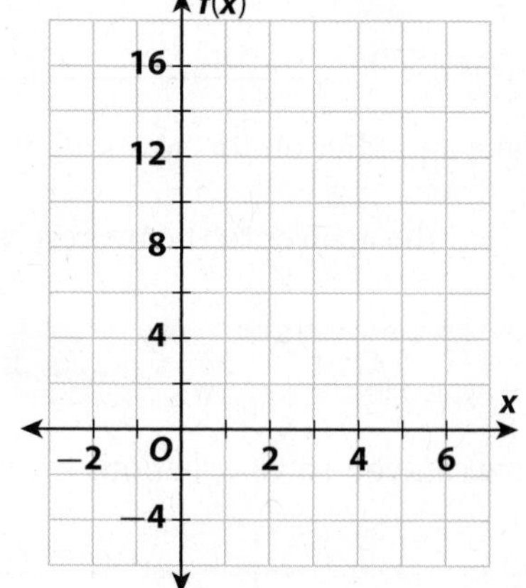

$x =$ ______

27. How do your solutions in Exercises 26 and 25 compare?

______

28. **Justify Reasoning** Which method do you prefer for solving the equation $2^x = 16$? Explain.

____

____

____

____

29. Which method would be better for solving the equation $2^x = 20$? Explain.

____

____

____

Use the following information for 30–34. There are 175 deer in a state park. The population is increasing at the rate of 12% per year. You want to make a prediction for how long it will take the population to reach 300.

30. Write an equation in one variable to represent the time x when the population reaches 300.

____

____

31. Write the constant function and the exponential function you will graph to find the time x when the population reaches 300.

constant function: $f(x) =$ ____________

exponential function: $g(x) =$ ____________

32. Graph the functions from Exercise 31 on a graphing calculator. Sketch the graphs.

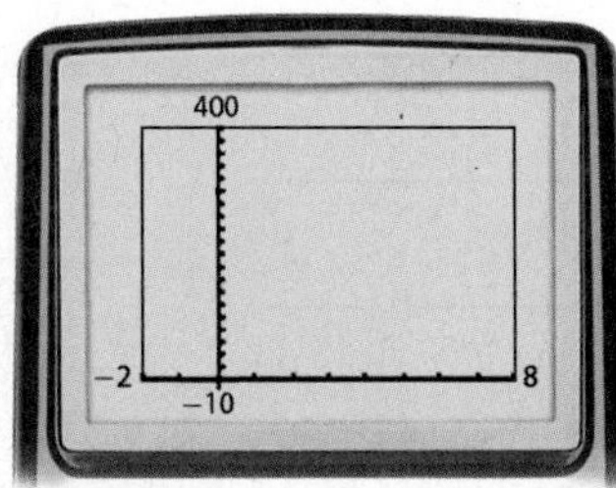

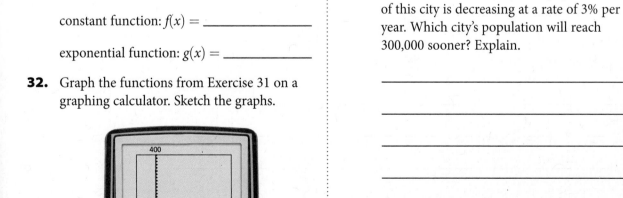

33. Explain how you can use the graphs to find the time when the population reaches 300.

____

____

____

____

34. Make a prediction for how long it will take for the deer population to reach 300. Round the answer to the nearest tenth of a year.

____

Use the following information for 35–37.
A city has 175,000 residents. The population is increasing at the rate of 10% per year. You want to make a prediction for how long it will take the population to reach 300,000.

35. Write an equation in one variable to represent the time, x, when the population reaches 300,000.

____

____

36. Make a prediction for how long will it take for the population to reach 300,000. Round the answer to the nearest tenth of a

year. ______________________________

37. **What If?** Suppose there are 350,000 residents of another city. The population of this city is decreasing at a rate of 3% per year. Which city's population will reach 300,000 sooner? Explain.

____

____

____

____

____

38. Last year a debate club sold 972 fundraiser tickets on their most successful day. This year the 4 club officers plan to match that number on a particular day of ticket sales.

To start off, on Day 0, each of the 4 officers will sell 3 tickets and ask each buyer to sell 3 more tickets the next day. Every time a ticket is sold, the buyer of the ticket will be asked to sell 3 more tickets the next day.

If the plan works, on what day will the number of tickets sold be 972?

a. Write an equation in one variable to model the situation. ______________

b. If the plan works, on what day will the number sold be 972? ____________

FOCUS ON HIGHER ORDER THINKING

Work Area

39. Explain the Error Jean and Marco each solved the equation $9(3)^x = 729$. Which is incorrect? Explain your reasoning.

Jean	Marco
$9(3)^x = 729$	$9(3)^x = 729$
$\frac{1}{9} \cdot 9(3)^x = \frac{1}{9} \cdot 729$	$(3)^x = 9 \cdot 729$
$3^x = 81$	$3^x = 6{,}561$
$3^x = 3^4$	$3^x = 3^8$
$x = 4$	$x = 8$

____

____

____

____

____

40. Critical Thinking Without solving, determine which of the following equations has a greater solution. Explain your reasoning.

$\frac{1}{3}(3)^x = 243$ $\qquad\qquad$ $\frac{1}{3}(9)^x = 243$

____

____

____

____

____

Ready to Go On?

Personal Math Trainer

Online Practice and Help

my.hrw.com

10.1 Exponential Functions

Use two points to write an equation for each function shown.

1.

x	−2	−1	0	1	2
$f(x)$	2.5	5	10	20	40

2.

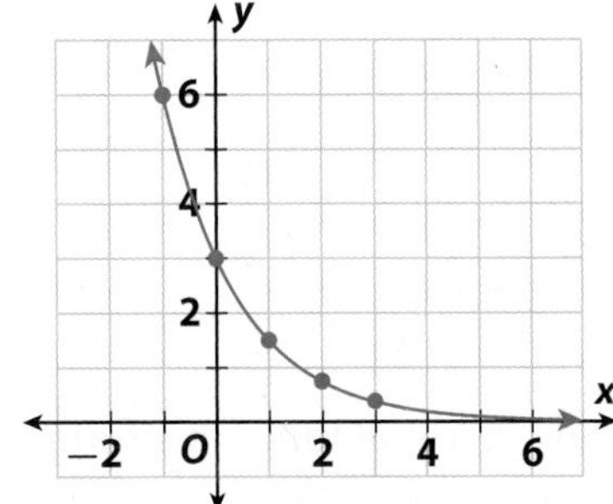

10.2–10.3 Exponential Growth and Decay/Geometric Sequences

Write an exponential growth or decay function to model each situation. Then find the value of the function after the given amount of time.

3. An antique car is worth \$35,000, and its value grows by 6% per year; 8 years.

4. The student enrollment is 980 students and decreases by 1.3% per year; 7 years.

If the given rule is recursive, write it as an explicit rule. If the rule is explicit, write it as a recursive rule. Assume that $f(1)$ is the first term of the sequence.

5. $f(1) = 4.5; f(n) = f(n-1) \cdot 6$ for $n \geq 2$

6. $f(n) = 0.6(7)^{n-1}$

10.4–10.5 Transforming Exponential Functions/Equations Involving Exponents

7. Describe the effect of replacing $f(x) = 4^x$ by $g(x) = 4^x + 1$.

8. Solve $5\left(\frac{1}{3}\right)^x = \frac{5}{27}$ without using a calculator.

ESSENTIAL QUESTION

9. How can exponential functions be used to represent real-world situations?

MODULE 10
MIXED REVIEW

Assessment Readiness

1. Look at each system of equations. Does the system have exactly one solution? Select Yes or No for systems A–C.

A. $\begin{cases} x + y = 16 \\ 3x - 5y = 16 \end{cases}$ ○ Yes ○ No

B. $\begin{cases} 2x + 3y = 4 \\ 6x + 9y = -21 \end{cases}$ ○ Yes ○ No

C. $\begin{cases} 3x - y = 5 \\ 2x - y = 0 \end{cases}$ ○ Yes ○ No

2. Consider the exponential functions $f(x) = 3^x$ and $g(x) = 2(3)^x$. Choose True or False for each statement.

A. The graph of $g(x)$ is a vertical translation of the graph of $f(x)$. ○ True ○ False

B. The y-intercept of $g(x)$ is greater than the y-intercept of $f(x)$. ○ True ○ False

C. For any value of x, the value of $g(x)$ is greater than the value of $f(x)$. ○ True ○ False

3. The table shows how a population of gray seals has changed over time. Write an explicit rule for the geometric sequence represented by the table. In what year will the population first exceed 25,000? Explain your reasoning.

Time (years), n	Population, $f(n)$
1	3000
2	3300
3	3630
4	3993

4. The Kramer family bought a house for \$164,000. The value of the house is expected to increase at a rate of 2.3% per year. Is the house expected to be worth more than \$200,000 after 10 years? Use an exponential function to justify your answer.

Modeling with Exponential Functions

MODULE 11

ESSENTIAL QUESTION

When do you use exponential functions to model real-world data?

CALIFORNIA COMMON CORE

LESSON 11.1

Exponential Regression

CA CC S.ID.6a, S.ID.6b, A.CED.2, F.LE.5

LESSON 11.2

Comparing Linear and Exponential Models

CA CC F.LE.1, F.LE.1a, F.LE.1b, F.LE.1c, F.LE.3, S.ID.6b

Real-World Video

my.hrw.com

Pythons originally kept as pets but later released into the Florida ecosystem find themselves in an environment with no natural predators and prey ill-equipped to evade or defend itself. As a result, the python population can grow exponentially, causing havoc among local wildlife and pets.

GO DIGITAL my.hrw.com

my.hrw.com

Go digital with your write-in student edition, accessible on any device.

Math On the Spot

Scan with your smart phone to jump directly to the online edition, video tutor, and more.

Animated Math

Interactively explore key concepts to see how math works.

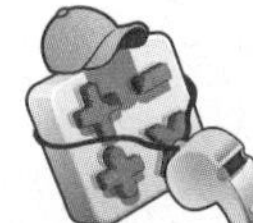

Personal Math Trainer

Get immediate feedback and help as you work through practice sets.

Are YOU Ready?

Complete these exercises to review the skills you will need for this module.

Percent Problems

EXAMPLE What is 108% of \$500?

$$x = 1.08 \times 500 \quad \text{Translate.}$$
$$x = (1.08)(500) \quad \text{Simplify.}$$
$$x = 540$$

Simplify each expression.

1. What is 103% of \$800?

2. What is 95% of 15,000 people?

3. What is 84% of 200 milligrams?

4. What is 105% of 105% of \$30,000?

Function Tables

EXAMPLE Generate ordered pairs for the function $y = 3x + 2$ for $x = 0, 1, 2, 3$.

x	$y = 3x + 2$	y
0	$y = 3(0) + 2 = 2$	2
1	$y = 3(1) + 2 = 5$	5
2	$y = 3(2) + 2 = 8$	8
3	$y = 3(3) + 2 = 11$	11

Generate ordered pairs for each function for $x = 0, 1, 2, 3, 4$.

5. $y = 25{,}000 + 1050x$

x	y
0	
1	
2	
3	
4	

6. $y = 25{,}000(1.04)^x$

x	y
0	
1	
2	
3	
4	

Reading Start-Up

Visualize Vocabulary

Use the Review Words with a check next to them to complete the Venn diagram.

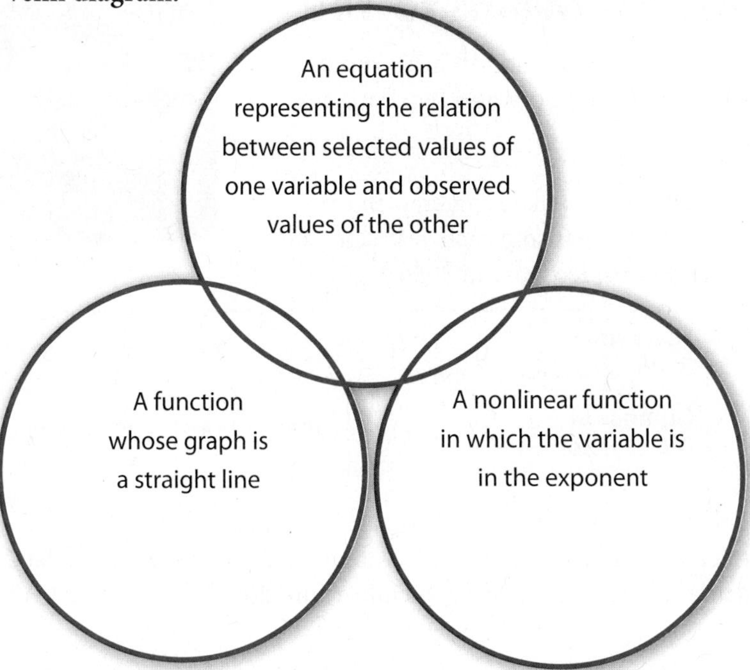
An equation representing the relation between selected values of one variable and observed values of the other
A function whose graph is a straight line
A nonlinear function in which the variable is in the exponent

Vocabulary

Review Words

- correlation coefficient *(coeficiente de correlación)*
- ✔ exponential function *(función exponencial)*
- ✔ linear function *(función lineal)*
- ✔ regression equation *(ecuación de regresión)*
- residual *(residuo)*
- scatter plot *(diagrama de dispersión)*

Understand Vocabulary

Use some of the vocabulary terms in this module to answer the following questions. You may refer to the module, the glossary, or a dictionary.

1. The ______________________________ provides an indication of how well the regression model fits the data.

2. The term scatter plot refers to a type of graph. What do you think a *scatter plot* looks like?

____

Active Reading

Double-Door Fold Create a double-door fold to help you understand the concepts in this module. Label one flap "Exponential Model" and the other flap "Comparing Linear and Exponential Models." As you study the lessons, write important ideas under the appropriate flap.

GETTING READY FOR

Modeling with Exponential Functions

Understanding the standards and the vocabulary terms in the standards will help you know exactly what you are expected to learn in this module.

CA CC S.ID.6a

Fit a function to the data; use functions fitted to data to solve problems in the context of the data. Use given functions or choose a function suggested by the context. Emphasize linear, quadratic, and exponential models.

Key Vocabulary

function *(función)*
An input-output relationship that has exactly one output for each input.

What It Means to You

You can use a function to approximate the relationship between two variables.

EXAMPLE S.ID.6A

This table shows the number of Blu-ray discs Clarissa has sold each year since she opened her video store in 2006.

Years since 2006	0	1	2	3	4	5	6
Number of Blu-rays sold	27	117	252	313	395	423	573

Enter the data from the table on a graphing calculator. Use the calculator's linear regression feature to find the model of the data. This data can be represented by the linear function $f(x) = 85.46x + 43.61$.

CA CC F.LE.1

Distinguish between situations that can be modeled with linear functions and with exponential functions.

Key Vocabulary

exponential function *(función exponencial)*
A non-linear function in which the variable is in the exponent.

linear function *(función lineal)*
A function that has a graph that is a straight line.

What It Means to You

You can determine whether a linear or exponential function is best to model a set of real-world data.

EXAMPLE F.LE.1

The value of a \$15,000 car decreases by \$1000 each year.

The amount of decrease, \$1000, remains constant. The value of the car for the first 3 years is: \$15,000, \$15,000 − \$1000 = \$14,000, and \$14,000 − \$1000 = \$13,000, respectively. This shows a linear function.

The value of a \$15,000 car decreases by 10% each year.

The percent of decrease, 10%, remains constant. But the amount of decrease changes each year based on the value of the car that year. The value of the car for the first 3 years is: \$15,000, \$15,000 × 0.90 = \$13,500, and \$13,500 × 0.9 = \$12,150, respectively. This shows an exponential function.

Visit **my.hrw.com** to see all **CA Common Core Standards** explained.

my.hrw.com

LESSON
11.1 Exponential Regression

CA CC S.ID.6a

Fit a function to the data; use functions fitted to data to solve problems in the context of the data. *Also A.CED.2, F.LE.5, S.ID.6b*

ESSENTIAL QUESTION

How can you use exponential regression to model data?

Fitting an Exponential Function to Data

This lesson will explore data that is best approximated by an exponential function of the form $y = f(x) = ab^x$.

Math On the Spot
my.hrw.com

EXAMPLE 1 

CA CC S.ID.6a

Use a calculator to find an exponential function that models the data.

Number of Internet hosts							
Years since 2001	0	1	2	3	4	5	6
Number (millions)	110	147	172	233	318	395	433

STEP 1 Enter the data from the table on a graphing calculator, with years since 2001 (the x-value) in List 1 and the number of Internet hosts (the y-value) in List 2. Then, graph the data as a scatter plot.

Choose scatter plot with no line

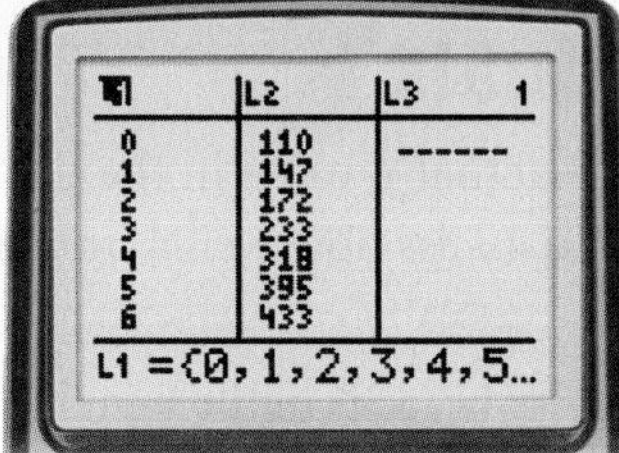

L2
L3
110
147
172
233
318
395
433
L1 ={0,1,2,3,4,5...

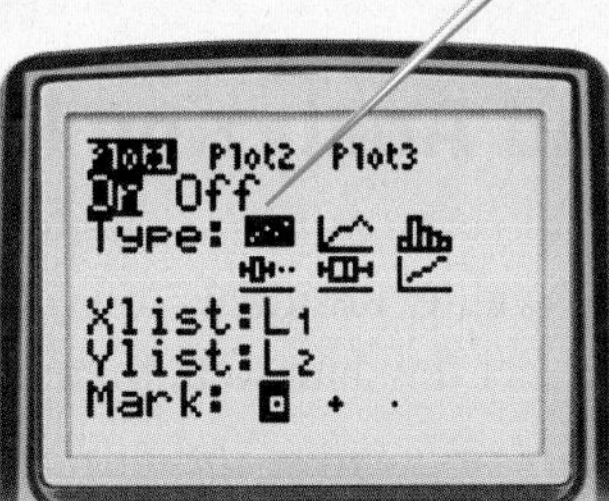

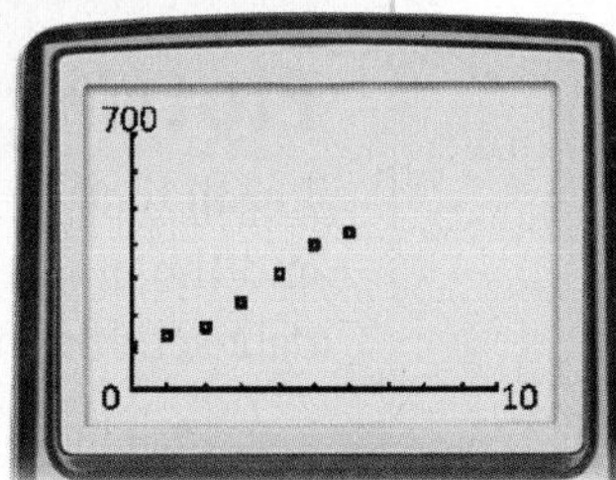

The points in the scatter plot follow an upward curve. An exponential function might fit the data better than a linear model.

STEP 2 Use the exponential regression feature.

Round the values of a and b to write the function $y = 113(1.27)^x$. Because the r value is close to 1, the model is a good fit.

Math Talk
Mathematical Practices

What is the growth rate for the exponential model?

REFLECT

1. **Communicate Mathematical Ideas** Which parameter, a or b, represents the initial value of y? Explain how you know.

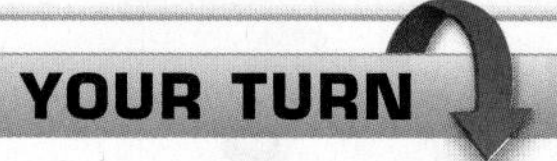

2. Use your calculator to find an exponential function that models the average number of text messages a month shown in the table.

Average Number of Monthly Text Messages							
	2006 (Q4)	**2007 (Q1)**	**2007 (Q2)**	**2007 (Q3)**	**2007 (Q4)**	**2008 (Q1)**	**2008 (Q2)**
Quarter Years	0	1	2	3	4	5	6
Average Number	108	129	172	193	218	288	357

EXPLORE ACTIVITY 

Plotting and Analyzing Residuals 

Recall that a residual is the difference between the actual y-value in the data set and the predicted y-value. Residuals can be used to assess how well a model fits a data set. If a model fits the data well, then:

- The numbers of positive and negative residuals are roughly equal.
- The residuals are randomly distributed about the x-axis on a residual plot.
- The absolute value of the residuals is small relative to the data values.

Analyze the residuals of the exponential model found in Example 1.

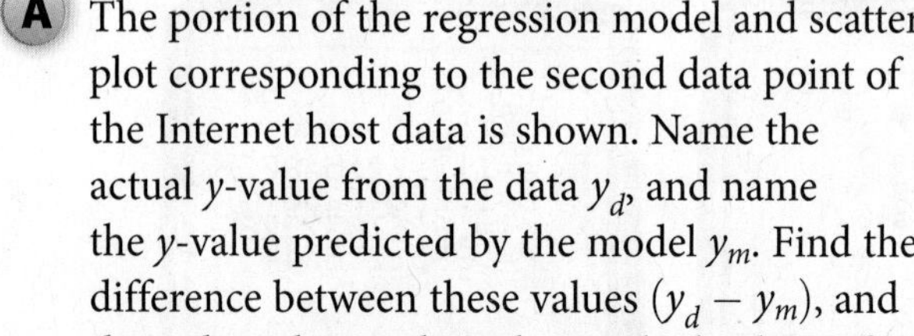

A The portion of the regression model and scatter plot corresponding to the second data point of the Internet host data is shown. Name the actual y-value from the data y_d, and name the y-value predicted by the model y_m. Find the difference between these values $(y_d - y_m)$, and then place the result in the residual column for $x = 1$ in the chart in the next step.

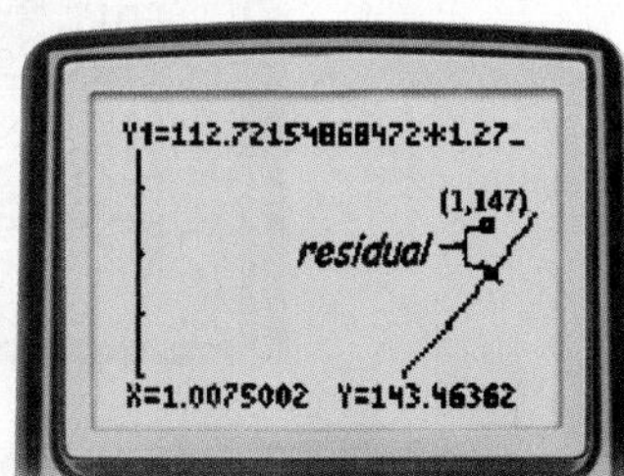

B On your calculator, enter the regression equation as the rule for equation Y_1. Then view the table to find the y-values predicted by model (y_m). Record the results in the table.

C Now complete the residuals column by subtracting the predicted values from the actual values.

D Set up a residual scatter plot of the data and graph it. (The residuals data will automatically be saved as Plot 2. Adjust the viewing window as needed.) Plot the points on the graph provided.

Number of Internet hosts (millions)			
x	Actual value y_d	Predicted value y_m	Residual $y_d - y_m$
0	110	113	−3
1	147	143	
2	172		
3	233		
4	318		
5	395		
6	433		

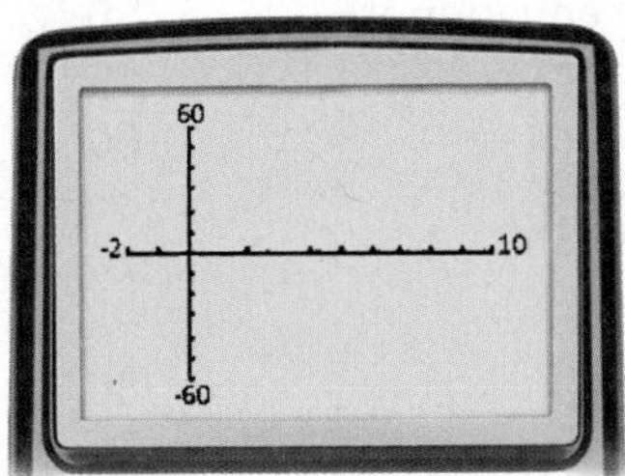

REFLECT

3. Multiple Representations What does the residual plot reveal about the fit of the model? Does this agree with the correlation coefficient?

4. Look for Patterns What can you infer about the accuracy of the model as it moves further away from the initial value? Explain.

Guided Practice

The first two columns of the table show the population of Arizona (in thousands) in each census from 1900–2000. (Example 1 and Explore Activity)

1. Find an exponential function that models the data. Plot the remaining data points on the screen and sketch the regression line.

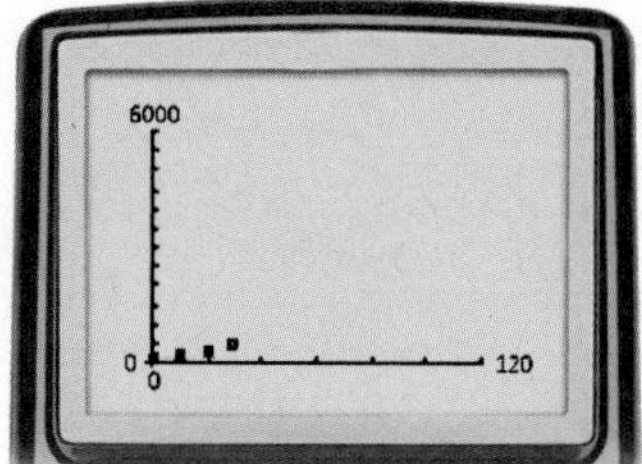

Arizona population in thousands (y)			
Years since 1900 (x)	Actual y_d	Predicted y_m	Residual $y_d - y_m$
0	123		
10	204		8
20	334	283	
30	436		
40	499		−88
50	750	847	
60	1302		
70	1771		
80	2718		178
90	3665		
100	5131	5281	

2. Round the parameters a and b to four significant digits. The regression equation is:

$y = f(x) =$ ☐ × ☐^{x}

The regression equation approximates the Arizona population in 1900 to

be __________ people and the growth rate

to be __________, meaning the population

increases by __________% each year.

3. Round the value of the correlation coefficient to three significant digits.

$r =$ ☐, suggesting the model **is / is not** a good approximation of the population data.

4. Complete the Arizona population table by filling in the remaining y_m and $y_d - y_m$ values. Use the regression model stored in your calculator to obtain the y_m values. Round to the nearest whole number.

5. Complete the residual plot in which five of the residuals have already been plotted.

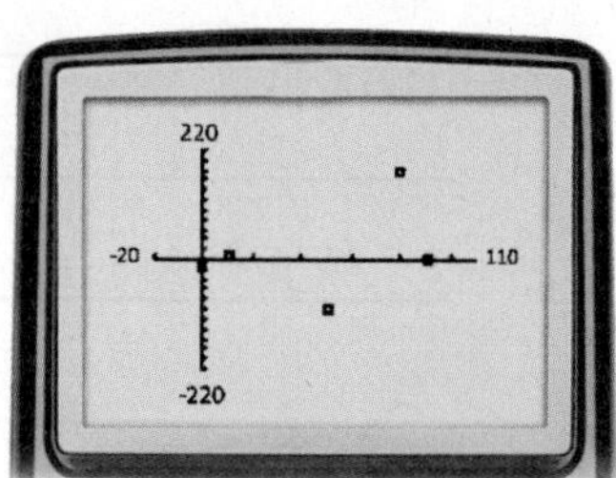

ESSENTIAL QUESTION CHECK-IN

6. How can you use exponential regression to model data?

____

____

____

Name ____________ Class ____________ Date ____________

11.1 Independent Practice

CA CC S.ID.6a, S.ID.6b, A.CED.2, F.LE.5

7. **Multistep** In 2012, the number of Internet hosts was reported to be 888 million.

   a. Based on the model found in Example 1, predict the number of Internet hosts for 2012. Use a graphing calculator to compare the values obtained from reading the table, tracing the graph, and calculating using the regression equation.

   b. Does the residual for 2012 meet the good-fit requirement of being small relative to the data? Explain.

   c. Discuss the likely accuracy of the number of Internet hosts predicted for 2025. Explain your answer.

8. **What if?** Use a graphing calculator to model the Arizona population data in Guided Practice through **linear** regression.

   a. Describe the shape of the residual plot and explain what this suggests about the fit of the model.

   b. Would the correlation coefficient lead you to draw the same conclusion regarding how well the model approximates the data? Explain.

9. **Make a Prediction** Use the exponential regression model of the Arizona population data to predict the year in which the state's population will first exceed 15,000. Explain how you arrived at your answer.

10. Interpret the Answer The concentration of ibuprofen in a person's blood was plotted each hour. An exponential model fit the data with $a = 400$ and $b = 0.71$. Interpret these parameters.

H.O.T. FOCUS ON HIGHER ORDER THINKING

Work Area

11. Critique Reasoning The absolute values of the residuals in Mark's regression model are less than 20. Working on a different data set, Sandy obtained residuals in the hundreds. This led Mark to conclude his data is a better fit than Sandy's. Explain why Mark is wrong to base his critique of their regression models on the values of the residuals.

12. Make a Conjecture When Chris used exponential regression on the Arizona population data in Guided Practice, he obtained the following results: $a = 186$, $b = 1.026$, $r = 0.813$. When he reviewed the data in his lists, he found he had entered a number incorrectly. Is it more likely that his error was in entering the last population value too high or too low? Justify your reasoning.

13. Draw Conclusions Madelyn has recorded the number of bacteria on her growth plate every hour for three hours. She finds that a linear model fits her data better than the expected exponential model. What should she do to improve her model?

LESSON 11.2

Comparing Linear and Exponential Models

CA CC F.LE.1, F.LE.1a, F.LE.1b, F.LE.1c, F.LE.3

For the full text of these standards, see the table beginning on page CA2. *Also S.ID.6b*

ESSENTIAL QUESTION

How can you recognize when to use a linear or exponential model?

EXPLORE ACTIVITY 1

CA CC F.LE.1b, F.LE.1c

Comparing Constant Change and Constant Percent Change

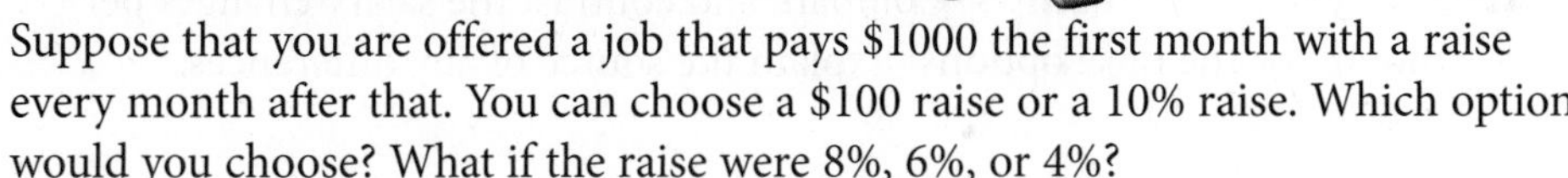

Suppose that you are offered a job that pays $1000 the first month with a raise every month after that. You can choose a $100 raise or a 10% raise. Which option would you choose? What if the raise were 8%, 6%, or 4%?

A Find the monthly salaries for the first three months. Record the results in the table, rounded to the nearest dollar.

- For the $100 raise, enter 1000 into your graphing calculator, press Enter, enter +100, press ENTER, and then press ENTER repeatedly.
- For the 10% raise, enter 1000, press ENTER, enter × 1.10, press ENTER, and then press ENTER repeatedly.
- For the other raises, multiply by 1.08, 1.06, or 1.04.

Monthly Salary After Indicated Monthly Raise					
Month	$100	10%	8%	6%	4%
0	$1000	$1000	$1000	$1000	$1000
1	$1100	$1100	$1080	$1060	$1040
2					
3					

B For each option, find how much the salary changes each month, both in dollars and as a percent of the previous month's salary. Record the values in the table.

Change in Salary per Month for Indicated Monthly Raise										
Interval	$100		10%		8%		6%		4%	
	$	%	$	%	$	%	$	%	$	%
0 – 1	$100	10%	$100	10%	$80	8%	$60	6%	$40	4%
1 – 2	$100			10%		8%		6%		4%
2 – 3	$100			10%		8%		6%		4%

EXPLORE ACTIVITY 1 *(cont'd)*

C Continue the calculations you did in Part A until you find the number of months it takes for each salary with a percent raise to exceed the salary with the $100 raise. Record the number of months in the table below.

Number of Months Until Salary with Percent Raise Exceeds Salary with $100 Raise			
10%	8%	6%	4%
2			

REFLECT

1. **Analyze Relationships** Compare and contrast the salary changes per month for the raise options. Explain the source of any differences.

____

____

____

2. **Justify Reasoning** Which raise option would you choose? What would you consider when deciding? Explain your reasoning.

____

____

____

Comparing Linear and Exponential Functions

When comparing raises, a fixed dollar increase can be modeled by a linear function and a fixed percent increase can be modeled by an exponential function. Using a calculator to graph these functions can help you compare them.

EXAMPLE 1

Compare the two salary plans listed. Will Job B ever have a higher monthly salary than Job A? If so, after how many months will this occur?

- Job A: $1000 for the first month with $100 raise every month thereafter
- Job B: $1000 for the first month with a 1% raise every month thereafter

STEP 1 Write functions that represent the monthly salaries.

Let t represent the number of elapsed months.

Job A: $S_A(t) = 1000 + 100t$ linear function

Job B: $S_B(t) = 1000 \times 1.01^t$ exponential function

STEP 2 Graph the functions on a calculator using Y_1 for Job A and Y_2 for Job B.

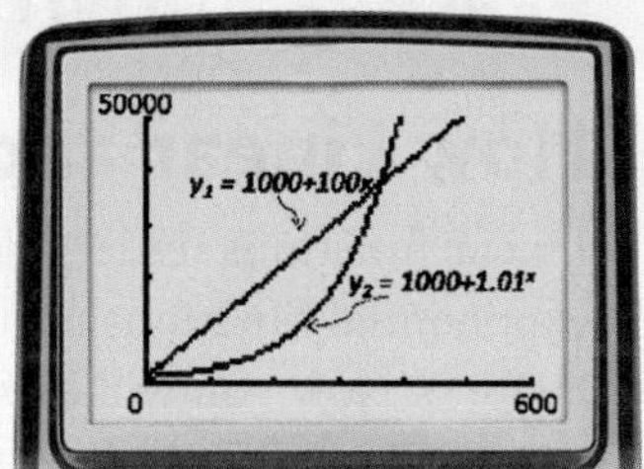

STEP 3 Estimate the number of months it takes for the salaries to become equal using the intersect feature of the calculator.

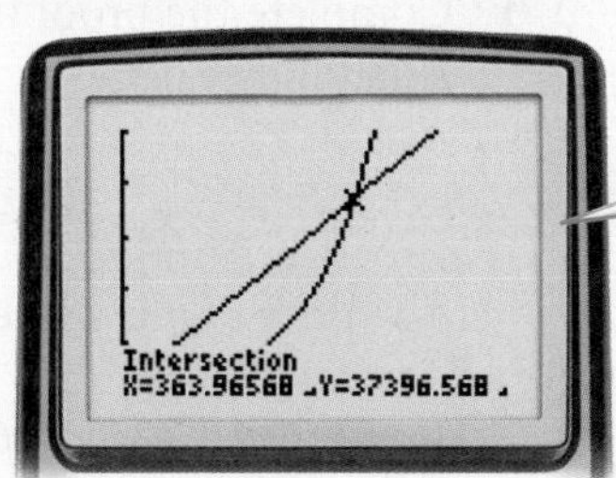

At $x \approx 364$ months, the salaries are equal.

STEP 4 Go to the estimated intersection point in the table feature. Find the first x-value at which Y_2 exceeds Y_1.

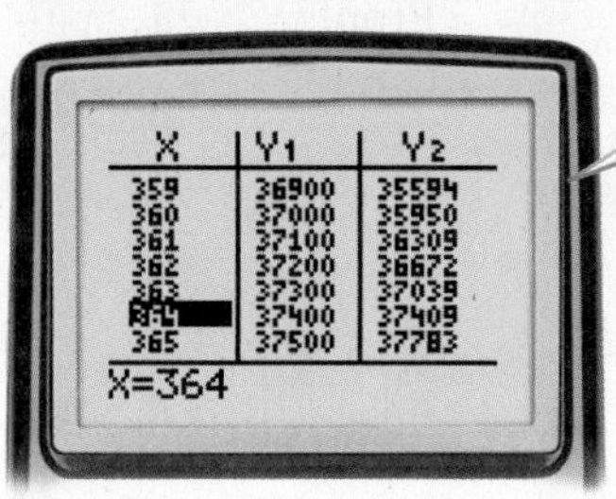

At $x = 364$, $Y_2 > Y_1$

Job B will have a higher monthly salary than Job A at 364 months.

REFLECT

3. **Draw Conclusions** Which job offers a monthly salary that reflects a constant change, and which offers a monthly salary that reflects a constant percent change?

____

____

____

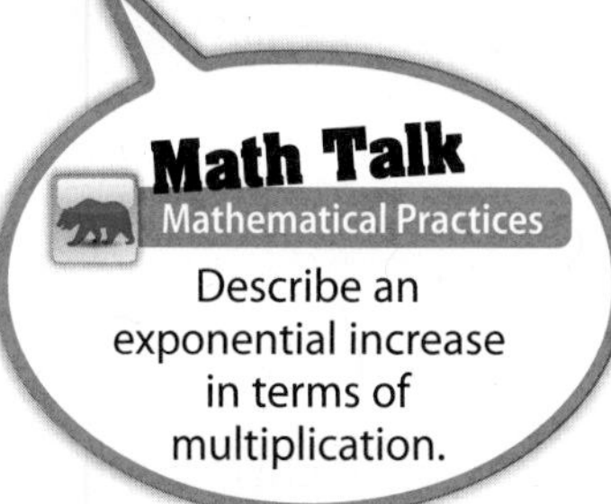

Math Talk
Mathematical Practices
Describe an exponential increase in terms of multiplication.

YOUR TURN

4. Companies A and B each have 50 employees. If Company A increases its workforce by 2 employees per month, and Company B increases its workforce by an average of 2% per month, will Company B ever have more employees than company A? If so, when?

____

____

EXPLORE ACTIVITY 2

CA CC F.LE.1a

How Linear and Exponential Functions Grow

Linear functions undergo a constant change (change by equal differences) while exponential functions undergo a constant percent change (change by equal factors). Now you will explore the proofs of these statements. $x_2 - x_1$ and $x_4 - x_3$ represent two intervals in the x-values of a function.

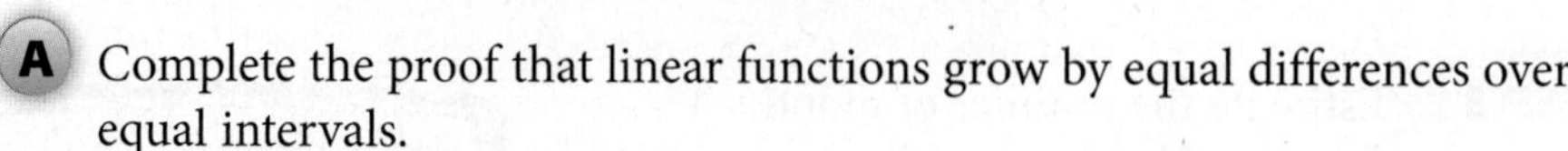

A Complete the proof that linear functions grow by equal differences over equal intervals.

Given: $x_2 - x_1 = x_4 - x_3$

f is a linear function of the form $f(x) = mx + b$

Prove: $f(x_2) - f(x_1) = f(x_4) - f(x_3)$

Proof:

Statement	Reason
1. $x_2 - x_1 = x_4 - x_3$	Given
2. $m(x_2 - x_1) = \square(x_4 - x_3)$	Mult. Prop. of Equality
3. $mx_2 - \square = mx_4 - \square$	Distributive Property
4. $mx_2 + b - mx_1 - b = mx_4 + \square - mx_3 - \square$	Add. & Sub. Prop. of Equality
5. $mx_2 + b - (mx_1 + b) = mx_4 + b - \square$	Distributive Property
6. $f(x_2) - f(x_1) =$ ____________	Definition of $f(x)$

B Complete the proof that exponential functions grow by equal factors over equal intervals.

Given: $x_2 - x_1 = x_4 - x_3$

g is an exponential function of the form $g(x) = ab^x$

Prove: $\frac{g(x_2)}{g(x_1)} = \frac{g(x_4)}{g(x_3)}$

Proof:

Statement	Reason
1. $x_2 - x_1 = x_4 - x_3$	Given
2. $b^{(x_2 - x_1)} = b^{(x_4 - x_3)}$	If $x = y$, then $b^x = b^y$.
3. $\frac{b^{x_2}}{b^{x_1}} = \frac{b^{x_4}}{\square}$	Quotient of Powers Prop.
4. $\frac{ab^{x_2}}{ab^{x_1}} = \frac{ab^{x_4}}{\square}$	Mult. Prop. of Equality
5. $\frac{g(x_2)}{g(x_1)} = \frac{g(x_4)}{\square}$	Definition of $g(x)$

Choosing a Modeling Function 

Both linear equations and exponential equations and their graphs can model real-world situations. Determine whether the dependent variable appears to change by a common difference or a common ratio to select the correct model.

EXAMPLE 2 Real World

CA CC F.LE.1, S.ID.6b

A gas had an initial pressure of 150 torr. Its pressure was then measured every 5 seconds for 25 seconds. Determine whether the change in pressure over time is best described by an increasing or decreasing function, and whether it is a linear or exponential function. Find a regression equation.

STEP 1 Determine whether the dependent variable changes by increasing or decreasing.

Pressure decreases over time.

Pressure over time		Change per interval	
time (s)	pressure (torr)	difference $P(t_n) - P(t_{n-1})$	factor $\frac{P(t_n)}{P(t_{n-1})}$
0	150	—	—
5	117	−33	0.78
10	90	−27	0.77
15	70	−20	0.78
20	56	−14	0.80
25	41	−15	0.73

The factor changes are close to equal while the difference changes are not, suggesting an exponential regression model should be used.

STEP 2 Determine if the dependent variable appears to change by equal differences or by equal factors over equal intervals.

STEP 3 Perform the exponential regression analysis, and evaluate the fit.

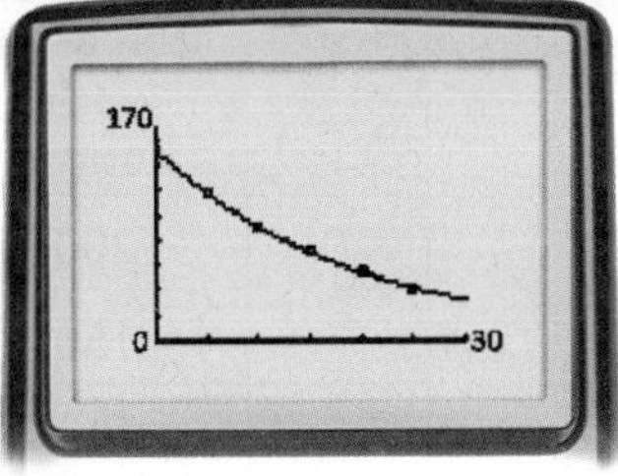

ExpReg
y=a*b^x
a=150.7693765
b=.9501586862
r=-.9992743164

r-value suggests a good fit.

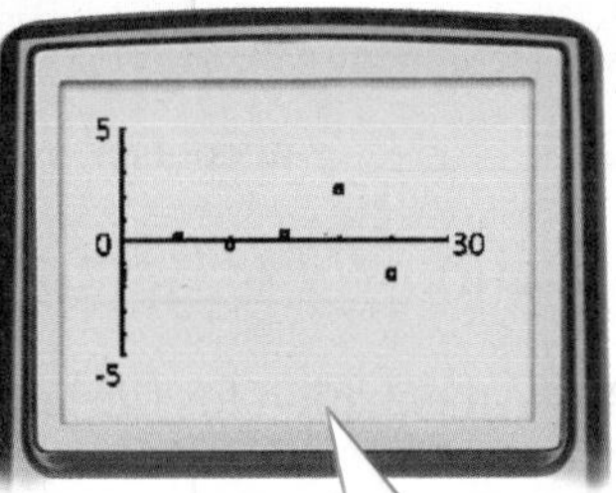

Analysis of residuals suggests a good fit.

A regression equation is $P(t) = 151(0.950)^t$.

YOUR TURN

5. The volume of a gas was measured as the temperature was increased from 173 K to 423 K in 50 K intervals. The gas volumes recorded, starting at 173 K, were 16, 21, 26, 30, 36, and 40 cm^3. Determine whether the data is best described by an increasing or decreasing function, and whether it is linear or exponential. Find a regression equation.

____

Guided Practice

1. Centerville has 2500 residents and Easton has 2000 residents. Centerville's population decreases by 80 people per year and Easton's population decreases by 3% per year. Will Easton ever have a greater population than Centerville? If so, when? (Example 1)

If t is time in years from now, Centerville's population is given by the equation

$P_C(t) = \square - \square t$

and Easton's population is given by the equation

$P_E(t) = \square \times \square^{t}$

Graph both functions on your calculator. The functions intersect at $t \approx$ ______.

Using the table feature on your calculator, find the first x-value at which Easton's population is greater than Centerville's.

Easton's population will exceed Centerville's after ______ years. At this time,

Centerville will have ______ residents, and Easton will have ______ residents.

Complete each statement with the correct function from the table.
(Explore Activity 1, Example 2)

2. ________ decreases by a constant amount per interval, so it is

a(n) ______________________ function.

3. ________ decreases by a constant percent per interval, so it is

a(n) ______________________ function.

4. An equation for the linear function is:

____

5. An equation for the exponential function is:

____

x	$f(x)$ height of ball after each bounce	$g(x)$ number of cookies remaining each day
0	200	300
1	150	288
2	113	276
3	84	264
4	63	252
5	47	240

ESSENTIAL QUESTION CHECK-IN

6. How can you recognize when to use a linear or exponential model?

____

____

____

Name ______________________ Class ______________ Date ______________

11.2 Independent Practice

CA CC F.LE.1, F.LE.1a, F.LE.1b, F.LE.1c, F.LE.3

Personal Math Trainer

Online Practice and Help

For 7–9, without graphing, tell whether the situation involves a quantity that is changing at a constant rate per unit of time, at a constant percent rate per unit of time, or neither. Justify your reasoning.

7. Amy received a $15,000 interest-free loan from her parents and agreed to make monthly payments of $150.

____

____

8. Carla's salary is $50,000 in her first year on a job plus a 1% commission on sales.

____

____

____

9. Enrollment at school is 976 students initially and then increases 2.5% each year thereafter.

____

____

____

____

10. **Draw Conclusions** Maria would like to put $500 in savings for a 5-year period. Should she choose a simple interest account that pays an interest rate of 10% of the principal (initial amount) each year or a compounded interest account that pays 3% of the total account value each month?

____

____

____

____

11. **Critical Thinking** Will an exponential growth function always eventually exceed a linear growth function? Explain.

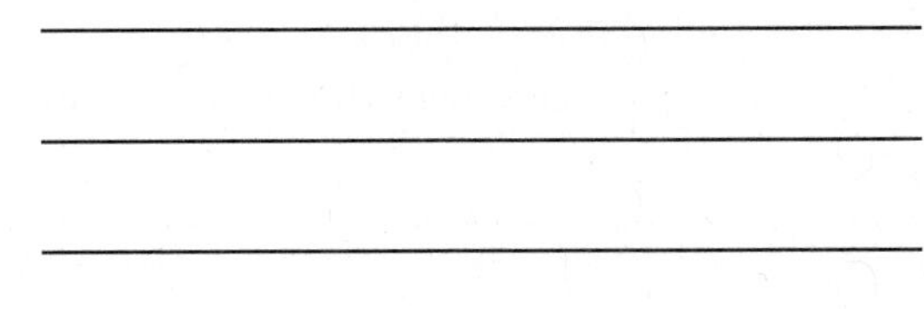

____

____

____

____

12. **Interpret the Answer** Westward and Middleton each have 40,000 residents. Westward's population decreases by 900 people per year and Middleton's population decreases by 2% per year.

a. Write a function for each town's population.

____

____

b. Sketch the functions on the screen provided. Label the functions and include the scale.

c. Will Westward ever have a greater population than Middleton? If so, when? Explain your reasoning.

____

____

____

____

____

FOCUS ON HIGHER ORDER THINKING

Work Area

13. **Critique Reasoning** Jordan analyzed the following data showing the number of cells in a bacteria culture over time.

Time (min)	0	6.9	10.8	13.5	15.7	17.4
Cells	8	16	24	32	40	48

He concluded that since the number of cells showed a constant change and the time did not, neither a linear function nor an exponential function modeled the number of cells over time well. Was he correct? Explain how you know.

14. **Check for Reasonableness** In Example 2, an exponential function was chosen to model the pressure data even though the dependent variable did not change by exactly the same factor in every interval.

a. Do you think this was the best model for the real-world data? Justify your reasoning.

b. Another parameter of the data to consider is the average rate of change (AROC), which is the slope of the line that passes through any two consecutive data points. How does the AROC change for the data in Example 2? Is this more consistent with an exponential or linear function? Explain.

Ready to Go On?

Personal Math Trainer

Online Practice and Help

11.1 Exponential Regression

The first two columns of the table show the population of box turtles in a Tennessee zoo over a period of 5 years.

1. Use a graphing calculator to find an exponential function model for the data. Round to the nearest thousandth.

____

2. Use the model to predict the number of box turtles in the sixth year.

____

____

____

Population of box turtles			
Year (x)	Actual (y_d)	Predicted (y_m)	Residual ($y_d - y_m$)
1	21	22	−1
2	27		
3	33		
4	41		
5	48		

3. Complete the chart using the observed and predicted values for the number of box turtles. Round to the nearest whole number.

11.2 Comparing Linear and Exponential Models

4. Julio is offered jobs with two different companies.

Company A is offering \$2000 a month for the first month with a \$50 raise every month after. Company B is offering \$2000 a month for the first month with a 2% raise every month after.

Write functions that represent the monthly salary at each company, and use the functions to determine which company will have a higher monthly salary after 2 years.

Company A ______________________________

Company B ______________________________

____

ESSENTIAL QUESTION

5. When do you use exponential functions to model real-world data?

____

____

MODULE 11
MIXED REVIEW

Assessment Readiness

1. The recursive rule $f(1) = 20$ and $f(n) = f(n - 1) - 6$ for $n \geq 2$ represents an arithmetic sequence.

Which model(s) below could represent this sequence? Select all that apply.

○ $f(n) = 20 - 6(n - 1)$ for $n \geq 1$

○ 20, 14, 8, 2, −4, ...

○ The first term of the sequence is 20, and the common difference is 6.

○

n	1	2	3	4
$f(n)$	20	26	32	38

2. A dog receives a dose of an antibiotic. The table shows the amount of antibiotic remaining in the dog's bloodstream over time. A student wrote the equation $y = 212(0.39)^x$ to model the data.

Time (h), x	Amount (mg), y
0	200
1	82
2	39
3	11

Choose True or False for each statement.

A. The model predicts that less than 1 milligram of the antibiotic will remain after 5 hours. ○ True ○ False

B. The residual for the data point (1, 82) is −0.68. ○ True ○ False

C. The model predicts that the amount of antibiotic remaining decreases by 61% each hour. ○ True ○ False

3. Maya and Jordan both start blogs in the same month. In the initial month, Maya has 30 page hits, and her number of page hits increases by about 10 per month. Jordan has 18 page hits in the initial month, and his number of page hits increases by about 10% per month. Based on these patterns, how many months after the initial month will Jordan's blog get more page hits than Maya's blog? Explain.

Study Guide Review

MODULE 10 Exponential Functions and Equations

Key Vocabulary

common ratio *(razón común)*

exponential growth *(crecimiento exponencial)*

exponential decay *(disminución exponencial)*

exponential function *(función exponencial)*

geometric sequence *(sucesión geométrica)*

ESSENTIAL QUESTION

How can exponential functions be used to represent real-world situations?

EXAMPLE 1

James bought several shares of two different stocks. The graph below shows the value of Stock A and Stock B over time.

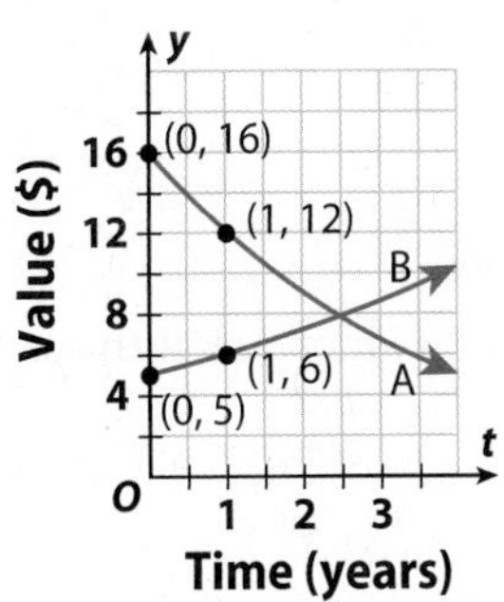

A Write the exponential decay function, $f(t)$, for the price of Stock A.

STEP 1 $b = 12 \div 16 = 0.75$

STEP 2 $f(n) = ab^n$

$f(n) = a(0.75)^n$

$12 = a(0.75)^1$

$12 = 0.75a$

$a = 16$

STEP 3 $f(t) = ab^t$

$f(t) = 16(0.75)^t$

B Write the exponential growth function, $g(t)$, for the price of Stock B.

STEP 1 $b = 6 \div 5 = 1.2$

STEP 2 $g(n) = ab^n$

$g(n) = a(1.2)^n$

$6 = a(1.2)^1$

$6 = 1.2a$

$a = 5$

STEP 3 $f(t) = ab^t$

$f(t) = 5(1.2)^t$

EXAMPLE 2

Write a recursive rule and an explicit rule for the geometric sequence 6, −24, 96, −384.... Determine the sixth term in the sequence.

Identify the first term: 6

Calculate the common ratio: $-24 \div 6 = -4$

Recursive rule: $f(1) = 6, f(n) = f(n-1) \times (-4)$ for $n \geq 2$

Explicit rule: $f(n) = 6 \times (-4)^{n-1}$

Use the explicit rule to find the sixth term: $f(6) = 6 \times (-4)^{6-1} = -6144$

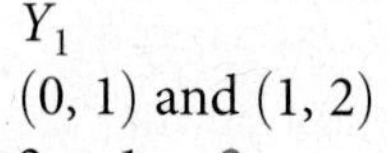

EXAMPLE 3

The graphs of three exponential functions, Y_1, Y_2, and Y_3, are provided. Based on the graphs, identify the parameter changes relative to Y_1 and write the equations of all three functions.

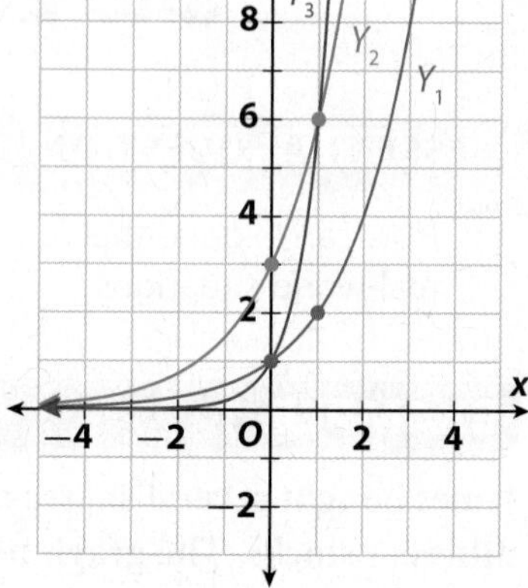

First find the common ratio b for each function.

Y_1	Y_2	Y_3
(0, 1) and (1, 2)	(0, 3) and (1, 6)	(0, 1) and (1, 6)
$2 \div 1 = 2$	$6 \div 3 = 2$	$6 \div 1 = 6$

Use the value of b and a known point to find the value of a.

$Y_1 = ab^x$	$Y_2 = ab^x$	$Y_3 = ab^x$
$Y_1 = a(2)^x$	$Y_2 = a(2)^x$	$Y_3 = a(6)^x$
$2 = a(2)^1$	$6 = a(2)^1$	$6 = a(6)^1$
$2 = 2a$	$6 = 2a$	$6 = 6a$
$1 = a$	$3 = a$	$1 = a$

Write an equation for the function.

$Y_1 = 1(2)^x = 2^x$ $\quad$ $Y_2 = 3(2)^x = 3(2)^x$ $\quad$ $Y_3 = 1(6)^x = 6^x$

Y_2 is a vertical stretch of Y_1. Y_1 and Y_2 increase at the same rate. Y_3 increases more quickly than Y_1.

EXERCISES

An invasive plant species was introduced into a lake in 2002. Two years later, the invasive plant population was recorded at 42 plants; 3 years after the introduction, the plants numbered 55; and after 4 years, their population totaled 72 plants. (Lesson 10.1, 10.2)

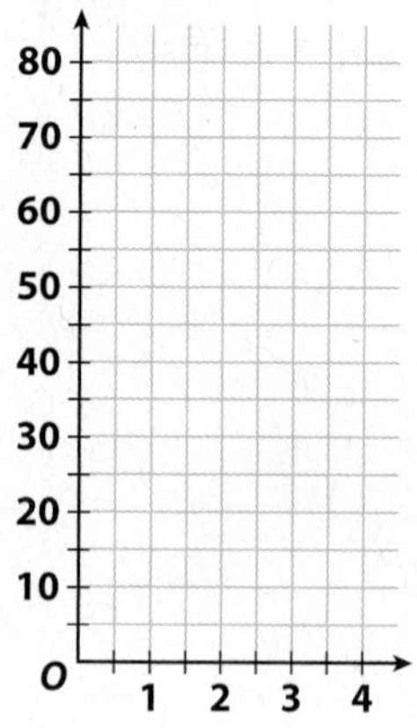

1. Determine the common ratio to the nearest tenth and the initial invasive plant population in 2002 to the nearest tenth. Write the function corresponding to the data described. [Let 2002 correspond to $x = 0$.]

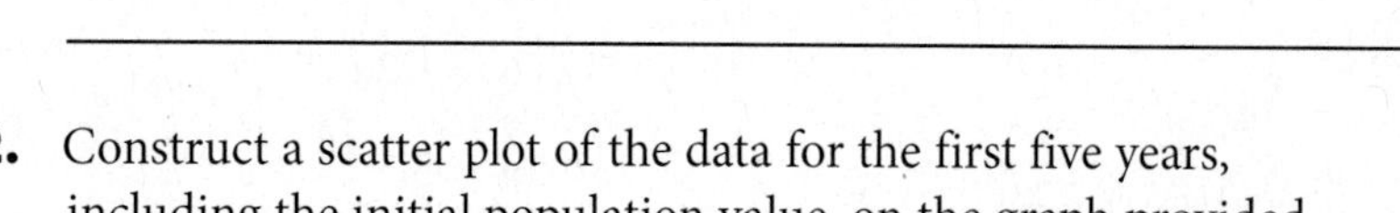

____

2. Construct a scatter plot of the data for the first five years, including the initial population value, on the graph provided.

3. Is the data represented by an exponential growth or exponential decay function? What is the percent rate of change? Explain.

____

____

____

____

4. Based on the model, find the invasive plant population in 2012. Explain.

____

____

The number of players after each round of an online video game tournament is shown in the table. (Lesson 10.3)

Round	Number of Players
1	3840
2	2573
3	1724
4	1155

5. Write the recursive and explicit rules for the geometric sequence.

6. Determine how many players remain after the 11th round.

The graphs of three exponential functions, Y_1, Y_2, and Y_3, are provided. (Lessons 10.4, 10.1)

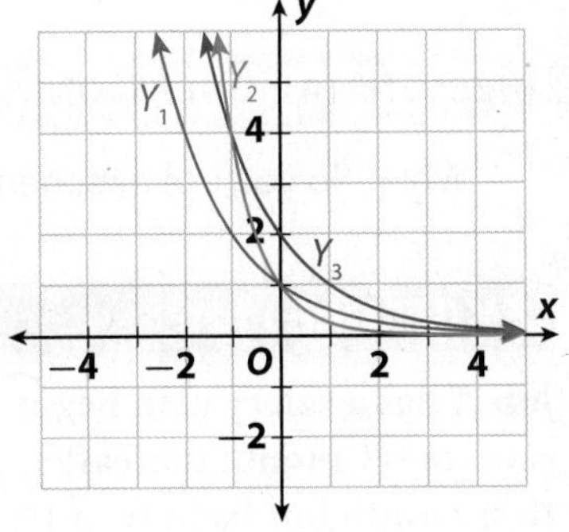

7. Which two functions have the same constant ratio b? Compare the value of a in those two functions.

8. Which two functions have the same y-intercept (value of a)? Compare the value of b in those two functions.

9. Write the equation of each function.

The equation $10 \times 4^x = 640$ can be solved by equating exponents or by graphing each side of the equation as the rule for a function. (Lesson 10.5)

10. Solve by equating exponents. Explain your process.

11. Solve by graphing on a graphing calculator. Sketch your functions on the graph provided and indicate how the value of the exponent is determined from this information.

____

____

____

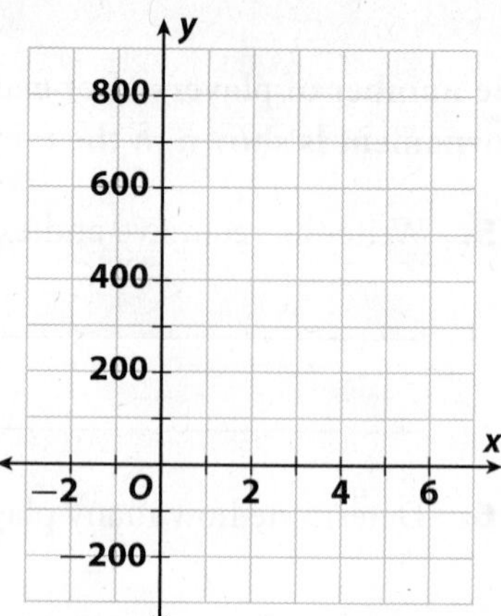

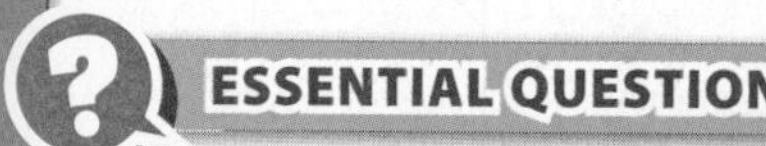

Modeling with Exponential Functions

ESSENTIAL QUESTION

When do you use exponential functions to model real-world data?

EXAMPLE 1

Job A has a salary plan beginning at \$1000 for the first month with a \$50 raise every month thereafter. The salary plan of Job B also starts at \$750 the first month but includes a 1% raise every month thereafter. Determine if a linear or exponential growth function applies to each salary plan and write the corresponding function. Determine how many months it will take for Job B to have a higher monthly salary than Job A.

Let t represent the number of elapsed months.

Job A: The salary increases by a constant amount each month, so the function is linear: $S_A(t) = 1000 + 100t$.

Job B: The salary increases by a constant percent change, so the function is exponential: $S_B(\mathrm{t}) = 750 \times 1.01^t$.

Graph the functions as Y_1 and Y_2. The point of intersection gives an estimate of the month in which the salaries are equal. This information is then used to search the table for a more precise value of x. When $x = 311$, the salary of Job B (\$16558) first exceeds the salary of Job A (\$16550).

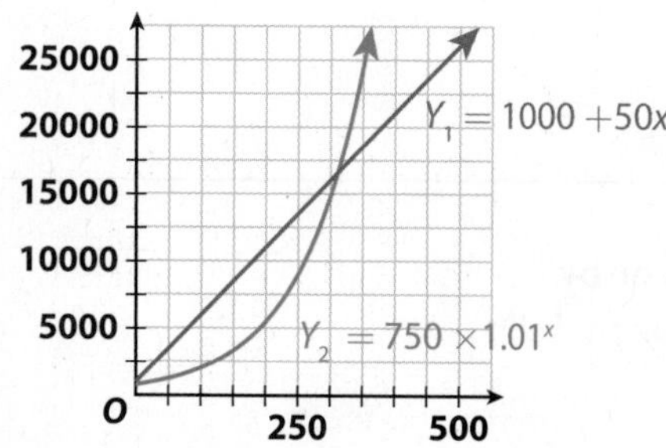

X	Y1	Y2
307	16350	15912
308	16400	16071
309	16450	16232
310	16500	16394
311	16550	16558
312	16600	16724
313	16650	16891

X=311

EXERCISES

12. Jan has \$1200 to start an investment account. Investment plan A will pay 1.3% of the monthly principal. Investment plan B will pay \$24 per month. Write the functions that represent the monthly account balances; let t represent the number of elapsed months. Graph the functions using a calculator. Sketch the functions on the graph provided; include axis labels and the coordinates of intersection. Compare and contrast the benefits of each plan. (Lesson 11.2)

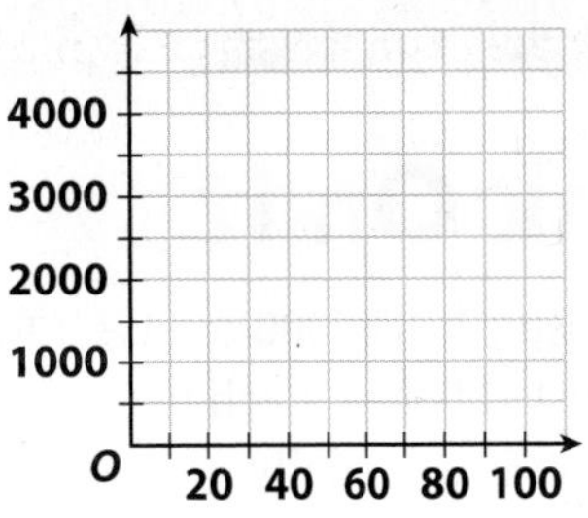

The table shows the temperature of a pizza over three-minute intervals after taking it out of the oven. (Lessons 11.1, 11.2)

Time (min)	0	3	6	9	12	15	18	21
Temperature (°F)	450	350	290	230	190	150	130	110

13. Based on the data, explain why an exponential model is predicted to be a better fit than a linear model.

14. Use technology to find an exponential function model for the data. Report the parameters in the equation to two significant digits. Assess the fit of the model based on the correlation coefficient and the residual plot. Using the regression model, predict how long it will take the pizza to cool down to a room temperature of 70°F.

Unit Project

CA CC F.LE.2, F.BF.1a, F.LE.5

Bank On It

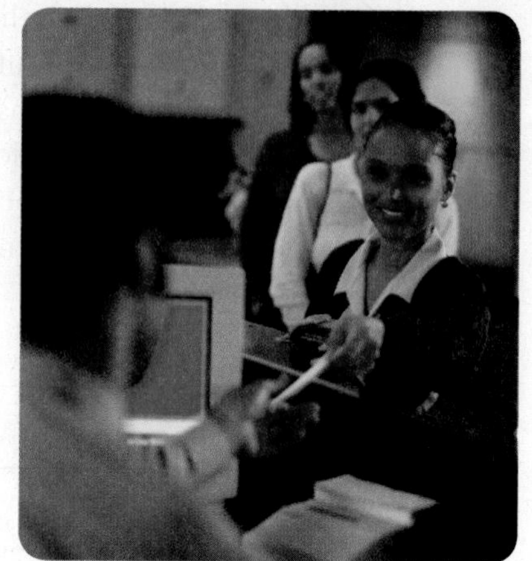

An investor has $5000 to invest for 10 years in one of the banks listed below. Each bank offers an interest rate that is compounded annually.

Bank	Principal	Years	Balance
Super Save	$1000	6	$1173.34
Star Financial	$2500	3	$2684.35
Better Bank	$4000	5	$4525.63

The investor chooses Better Bank because it earned over $100 per year, which is much more than the other banks earned per year.

Create a presentation to the investor explaining which bank is the best choice, based on the given information. Include for each bank

1. a graph showing how the investment would grow over a 10-year period, and
2. the interest rate, including how you found it.

Use the space below to write down any questions you have or important information from your teacher.

MATH IN CAREERS ACTIVITY

Statistician When researching data concerning caribou populations in the Arctic, Lee uncovered some archives of old caribou populations, shown in the first two columns of the table. Use a graphing calculator to find an exponential function that models the data. Complete the table and use the data to make an inference about the accuracy of the model.

Years Since 1972	Actual y_d	Predicted y_m	Residual $y_d - y_m$
0	2812		
1	2880		
2	2970		
3	3130		
4	3281		
5	3437		

UNIT 3B
MIXED REVIEW

Assessment Readiness

1. Consider each ordered pair. Is the ordered pair a solution of the equation $4x - 3y = 12$?

Select Yes or No.

A. $(-3, -8)$ ○ Yes ○ No
B. $(3, 4)$ ○ Yes ○ No
C. $(9, 8)$ ○ Yes ○ No

2. The graph shows two exponential functions.

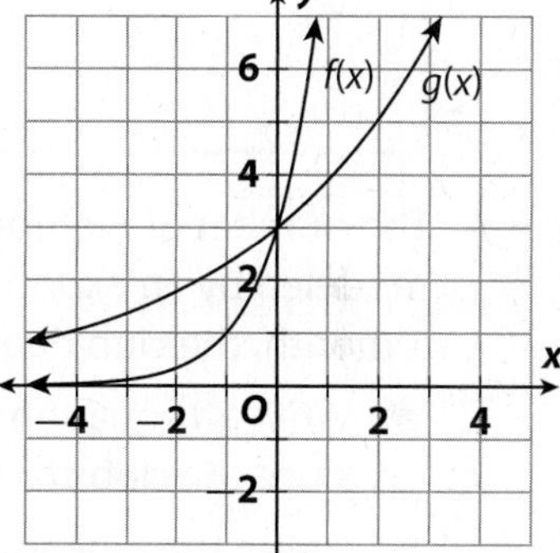

Choose True or False for each statement.

A. The parameter a is greater for $f(x)$ than for $g(x)$. ○ True ○ False
B. The parameter b is greater for $f(x)$ than for $g(x)$. ○ True ○ False
C. For both functions, b is greater than 1. ○ True ○ False

3. A test tube initially holds 25 bacteria. The population of bacteria in the test tube doubles each hour. Without making a graph, determine how many hours it will take for the population of bacteria in the test tube to reach 800. Explain how you solved this problem.

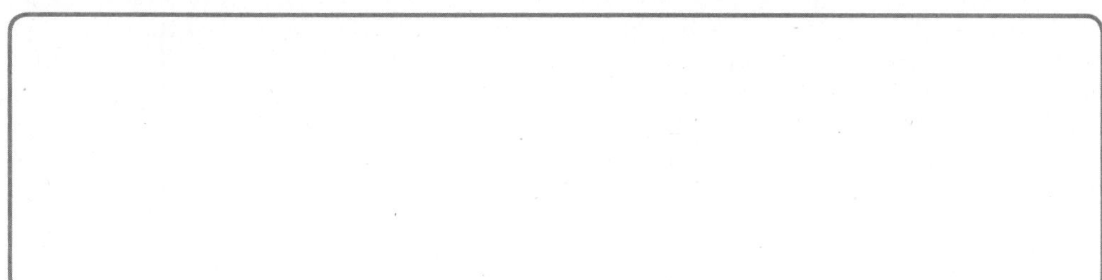

4. The table shows how the price of an item that cost \$10.00 in 1913 has changed over time. Use a calculator to find the exponential function that models the data. Then predict how much an item that cost \$10.00 in 1913 will cost in 2025. Explain how you made your prediction.

Years since 1913 (x)	Cost of item (\$)
0	10.00
20	13.13
40	26.97
60	44.85
80	145.96
100	234.51

Performance Tasks

★ **5.** The number of matches played in each round of a doubles tennis tournament forms a geometric sequence. In the third round, there are 8 matches, and in the fourth round, there are 4 matches.

a. Write an explicit rule for the geometric sequence.

b. How many matches will there be in this tournament? Explain.

★★ **6.** The number of members over time in an online music sharing club can be modeled by an exponential function. The club started with 2100 members. After 1 month, the club had 2142 members.

a. Write an equation for the number of members as a function of time in months since the club started.

b. Graph the function, and label the axes.

c. What is the parameter b in the equation, and what does it represent in this situation?

d. Will the club have more than 5000 members during its first year? Justify your reasoning.

★★★ **7.** The table shows how the number of college degrees earned in the United States has changed over time.

a. Is a linear function or an exponential function a better model for the data? Justify your answer.

b. Predict the number of college degrees earned in the United States in 2050. Is this more likely to be an underestimate or an overestimate? Explain.

Year	College degrees (thousands)
1910	37
1930	122
1950	432
1970	792
1990	1051
2010	1650

UNIT 4

Statistics and Data

MODULE 12

Descriptive Statistics

CA CC S.ID.5

MODULE 13

Data Displays

CA CC S.ID.1, S.ID.2, S.ID.3

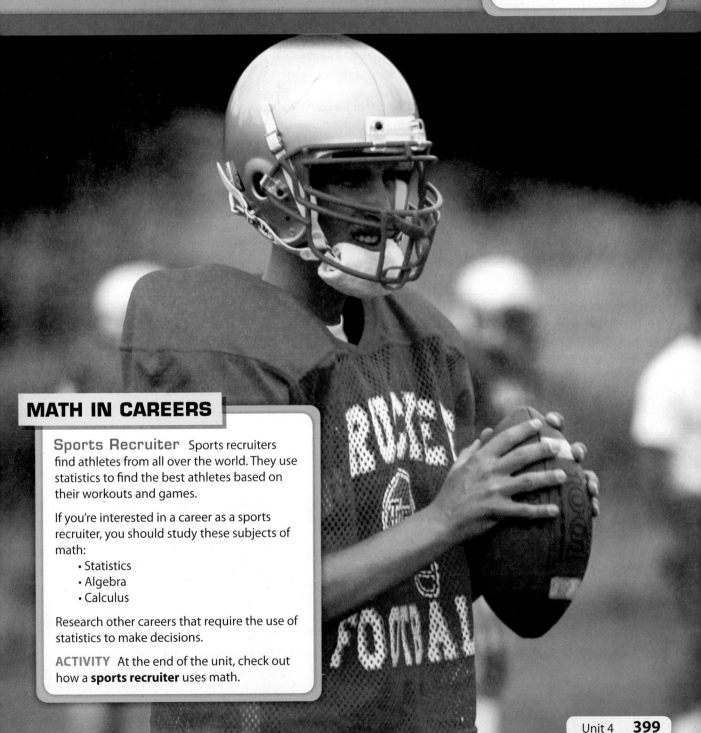

MATH IN CAREERS

Sports Recruiter Sports recruiters find athletes from all over the world. They use statistics to find the best athletes based on their workouts and games.

If you're interested in a career as a sports recruiter, you should study these subjects of math:

- Statistics
- Algebra
- Calculus

Research other careers that require the use of statistics to make decisions.

ACTIVITY At the end of the unit, check out how a **sports recruiter** uses math.

Unit Project Preview

True Story?

The Unit Project at the end of this unit involves analyzing a claim in a current event or advertisement. To successfully complete the Unit Project you'll need to master these skills:

- Research the statistical data behind claims made in a recent news item or advertisement.
- Interpret the statistical data, and consider if the data shows correlation or causation.
- Represent the data using a data display.

Researchers from the Australian National University and the British Antarctic Survey found data taken from an ice core also shows the summer ice melt has been 10 times more intense over the past 50 years compared with 600 years ago.

1. Amy is reading a magazine article about Antarctic ice melt, which begins with the sentence shown above. What statistical or numerical information is given in the statement? What descriptive words require further definition?

____

____

____

____

____

2. What sources would you use to further research this article?

____

Tracking Your Learning Progression

This unit addresses important California Common Core Standards in the Critical Area of working with categorical and quantitative data.

Domain S.ID Interpreting Categorical and Quantitative Data

Cluster Summarize, represent, and interpret data on a single count or measurement variable.

Descriptive Statistics

MODULE 12

ESSENTIAL QUESTION

How can you summarize two categories of categorical data and recognize associations and trends between two categories of categorical data?

CALIFORNIA COMMON CORE

LESSON 12.1

Two-Way Frequency Tables

S.ID.5

LESSON 12.2

Relative Frequency

S.ID.5

Real-World Video

my.hrw.com

With emotions riding high, it can be difficult to evaluate popular opinion concerning personal preferences such as favorite sports teams. Polls and surveys use a methodical, mathematical approach to reduce or eliminate bias.

GO DIGITAL

my.hrw.com

my.hrw.com

Go digital with your write-in student edition, accessible on any device.

Math On the Spot

Scan with your smart phone to jump directly to the online edition, video tutor, and more.

Animated Math

Interactively explore key concepts to see how math works.

Personal Math Trainer

Get immediate feedback and help as you work through practice sets.

Are YOU Ready?

Complete these exercises to review skills you will need for this module.

Fractions, Decimals, and Percents

EXAMPLE Write $\frac{5}{40}$ as a decimal.

$5 \div 40 = 0.125$ *Divide 5 by 40.*

$\frac{5}{40} = 0.125$

Write each fraction as a decimal.

1. $\frac{12}{48}$ ________

2. $\frac{9}{30}$ ________

3. $\frac{25}{40}$ ________

4. $\frac{6}{16}$ ________

Write each decimal as a percent.

5. 0.65 ________

6. 0.07 ________

7. 0.092 ________

8. 0.122 ________

Write each fraction as a percent.

9. $\frac{7}{20}$ ________

10. $\frac{15}{80}$ ________

11. $\frac{2}{25}$ ________

12. $\frac{65}{125}$ ________

Tables and Charts

EXAMPLE Use the table below to find the number of marbles that are blue or red.

$15 + 12 = 27$ *Add the number of blue marbles to the number of red marbles.*

The table shows the colors of all the marbles Arturo owns.

Color	Number of Marbles
Red	15
Blue	12
White	6
Orange	2
Green	10
Purple	5

13. How many of Arturo's marbles are white, orange, or blue?

____

14. How many marbles does Arturo own in all?

____

15. What percent of Arturo's marbles are white, orange, or blue?

____

Reading Start-Up

Visualize Vocabulary

Complete the concept map using the Review Words.

Data that involves two variables describing the same set of items.	→	A group of plotted points that shows the relationship between two variables.	→	The amount of relationship existing between two variables.
______ ______		______ ______		______ ______

Vocabulary

Review Words

- ✔ correlation *(correlación)*
- ✔ scatter plot *(diagrama de dispersión)*
- ✔ two-variable data *(data de dos variables)*

Preview Words

- categorical data
- conditional relative frequency
- frequency table
- joint relative frequency
- marginal relative frequency
- quantitative data
- relative frequency
- two-way frequency table

Understand Vocabulary

Draw a line to match the Preview Word with its definition.

Preview Words	Definitions
1. frequency table	• A relative frequency that is found by dividing a frequency that is not in the Total row or the Total column by the grand total
2. joint relative frequency	• Data that can be expressed with categories such as male/female, analog/digital, citizen/alien and so on
3. relative frequency	• A table that lists the number of times, or frequency, that each data value occurs
	• For a category in a frequency table, the frequency of the category divided by the total of the frequencies

Active Reading

Two-Panel Flip Chart Create a Two-Panel Flip Chart to help you understand the concepts in this module. Label each flap with the title of one of the lessons in the module. As you study each lesson, write important ideas under the appropriate flap. Include any examples that will help you remember the concepts later when you look back at your notes.

GETTING READY FOR

Descriptive Statistics

Understanding the standards and the vocabulary terms in the standards will help you know exactly what you are expected to learn in this module.

CA CC S.ID.5

Summarize categorical data for two categories in two-way frequency tables. Interpret relative frequencies in the context of the data (including joint, marginal, and conditional relative frequencies). Recognize associations and trends in the data.

Key Vocabulary

frequency table *(tabla de frecuencia)*
A table that lists the number of times, or frequency, that each data value occurs

joint relative frequency *(frecuencia relativa conjunta)*
A relative frequency that is found by dividing a frequency that is not in the Total row or the Total column by the grand total

marginal relative frequency *(frecuencia relativa marginal)*
A relative frequency that is found by dividing a row total or column total by the grand total

conditional relative frequency *(frecuencia relativa condicional)*
A relative frequency that is found by dividing a frequency that is not in the Total row or the Total column by the frequency's row total or column total

Visit **my.hrw.com** to see all **CA Common Core Standards** explained.

my.hrw.com

What It Means to You

Two-way frequency tables give you a visual way to organize data categorized by two different variables so that you can more easily identify relationships.

EXAMPLE S.ID.5

The two-way frequency table below shows the numbers of households in a study that own a dog, a cat, or both.

	Owns a Cat		
Owns a Dog	**Yes**	**No**	**Total**
Yes	15	24	39
No	18	43	61
Total	33	67	100

Here are a few conclusions you can draw from the table.

- $\frac{39}{100}$, or 39%, of households own a dog; $\frac{33}{100}$, or 33%, own a cat.
- $\frac{15}{100}$, or 15%, own a dog and a cat; $\frac{43}{100}$, or 43%, own neither.
- Of dog owners, $\frac{15}{39}$, or about 38.5%, also own a cat.
- Of cat owners, $\frac{15}{33}$, or about 45.5%, also own a dog.

You can also show the data in a two-way *relative* frequency table by dividing each number by the grand total and expressing the answer as a percent.

joint relative frequency

	Owns a Cat		
Owns a Dog	**Yes**	**No**	**Total**
Yes	15%	24%	39%
No	18%	43%	61%
Total	33%	67%	100%

marginal relative frequencies

This cell should always be 100% in a two-way relative frequency table.

LESSON 12.1

Two-Way Frequency Tables

CA CC S.ID.5

Summarize categorical data for two categories in two-way frequency tables. Interpret relative frequencies in the context of the data (including joint, marginal, and conditional relative frequencies). Recognize possible associations and trends in the data.

ESSENTIAL QUESTION

How can categorical data for two categories be summarized?

EXPLORE ACTIVITY

Categorical Data and Frequencies

Data that can be expressed with numerical measurements is **quantitative data**. In this lesson you will examine *qualitative data*, or **categorical data**, which cannot be expressed using numbers. Data describing animal type, model of car, or favorite song are examples of categorical data.

A Circle the categorical data variable. Justify your choice.

temperature　　weight　　height　　color

____

____

B Identify whether the given data is categorical or quantitative.

large, medium, small ______________________________

120 ft^2, 130 ft^2, 140 ft^2 ______________________________

C A **frequency table** shows how often each item occurs in a set of categorical data. Use the categorical data listed on the left to complete the frequency table.

Ways Students Get to School
bus car walk car car car bus walk walk walk bus bus car bus bus walk bus car bus car

Way	Frequency
bus	
car	
walk	

REFLECT

1. How did you determine the numbers for each category in the frequency column? ______________________________

____

2. What must be true about the sum of the frequencies in a frequency table?

____

Constructing a Two-Way Frequency Table

If a data set has two categorical variables, you can list the frequencies of the paired values in a **two-way frequency table.**

EXAMPLE 1

CA CC S.ID.5

Jenna asked 40 randomly selected students whether they preferred dogs, cats, or other pets. She also recorded the gender of each student. The results are shown in the two-way frequency table below. Each entry is the frequency of students who prefer a certain pet and are a certain gender. For instance, 8 girls prefer dogs as pets. Complete the table.

	Preferred Pet			
Gender	**Dog**	**Cat**	**Other**	**Total**
Girl	8	7	1	16
Boy	10	5	9	24
Total	18	12	10	40

STEP 1 Find the row totals.

Girl: $8 + 7 + 1 = 16$

Boy: $10 + 5 + 9 = 24$

STEP 2 Find the column totals.

Dog: $8 + 10 = 18$

Cat: $7 + 5 = 12$

Other: $1 + 9 = 10$

STEP 3 Find the grand total.

Sum of row totals $= 16 + 24 = 40$

Sum of column totals $= 18 + 12 + 10 = 40$

Both sums are equal to the grand total. So grand total $= 40$

My Notes

REFLECT

3. Look at the totals for each row. Was Jenna's survey evenly distributed among boys and girls? ______________________

4. Look at the totals for each column. Which pet is preferred most? Justify your answer. ______________________

____

YOUR TURN

5. Complete the two-way frequency table.

	Preferred Fruit			
Grade	**Apple**	**Orange**	**Banana**	**Total**
9th grade	19	12	23	
10th grade	22	9	15	
Total				

Reading a Two-Way Frequency Table

You can extract information about paired categorical variables by reading a two-way frequency table.

Math On the Spot
my.hrw.com

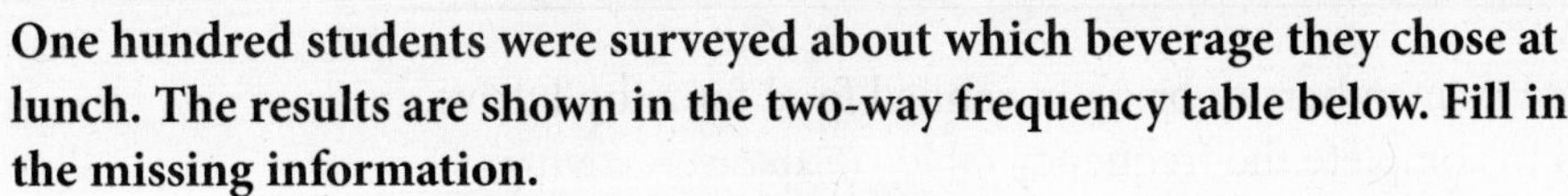

One hundred students were surveyed about which beverage they chose at lunch. The results are shown in the two-way frequency table below. Fill in the missing information.

	Lunch Beverage			
Gender	**Juice**	**Milk**	**Water**	**Total**
Girl	10		17	
Boy	15	24	21	60
Total				

STEP 1 Find the total number of girls.

$100 - 60 = 40$ *Subtract the number of boys from 100.*

There are 40 girls in total.

STEP 2 Find the number of girls who chose milk.

$40 - 10 - 17 = 13$ *Subtract the number of girls who chose juice and the number who chose water from the total number of girls, 40.*

The number of girls who chose milk is 13.

Math Talk
Mathematical Practices
Which lunch beverage is the least preferred? How do you know?

STEP 3 Find the totals for each beverage and check that the grand total equals the total number of students surveyed (100). Complete the table.

	Lunch Beverage			
Gender	**Juice**	**Milk**	**Water**	**Total**
Girl	10	13	17	40
Boy	15	24	21	60
Total	25	37	38	100

YOUR TURN

6. One hundred students were surveyed about whether they played video games. The results are shown in the two-way frequency table. Complete the table.

	Play Video Games		
Gender	**Yes**	**No**	**Total**
Girl	34	19	53
Boy		9	
Total			

Personal Math Trainer
Online Practice and Help
my.hrw.com

Guided Practice

In Exercises 1 and 2, identify whether the data is categorical or quantitative. (Explore Activity)

1. gold medal, silver medal, bronze medal ________________

2. 100 m, 200 m, 400 m ________________

3. A theater company asked its members to bring in canned food for a food drive. Use the categorical data to complete the frequency table. (Explore Activity)

Cans Donated to Food Drive
peas corn peas soup corn corn soup soup corn peas peas corn soup peas corn peas corn peas corn soup corn peas soup corn corn

Cans	Frequency
soup	
peas	
corn	

4. Antonio surveyed 60 of his classmates about their participation in school activities and whether they have a part-time job. The results are shown in the two-way frequency table below. Complete the table. (Example 1)

	Activities				
Have a Job	**Clubs only**	**Sports only**	**Both**	**Neither**	**Total**
Yes	12	13	16	4	
No	3	5	5	2	
Total					

5. Marta surveyed 100 students about whether they like swimming or bicycling. Complete the two-way frequency table. (Example 2)

	Like Swimming		
Like Bicycling	**Yes**	**No**	**Total**
Yes	65	16	81
No		6	
Total			

How many of the students surveyed like swimming but not bicycling? ________________

ESSENTIAL QUESTION CHECK-IN

6. How can categorical data for two categories be summarized?

____

Name ______ Class ______ Date ______

12.1 Independent Practice

S.ID.5

Identify whether the given data is categorical or quantitative.

7. 75°, 79°, 82° ______

8. juice, soda, water ______

Two hundred students were asked to name their favorite science class. The results are shown in the two-way frequency table. Use the table for Exercises 9 and 10.

	Favorite Science Class			
Gender	**Biology**	**Chemistry**	**Physics**	**Total**
Girl	42	39	23	104
Boy		45	32	
Total				

9. How many boys were surveyed? Explain how you found your answer.

______

______

10. Complete the table. How many more girls than boys chose Biology as their favorite science class? Explain how you found your answer.

______

______

______

The results of a survey of 150 students about whether they own an electronic tablet or a laptop are shown in the two-way frequency table. Use the table for Exercises 11 and 12.

	Device				
Gender	**Electronic tablet**	**Laptop**	**Both**	**Neither**	**Total**
Girl	15	54		9	88
Boy		35	8	5	
Total					

11. Complete the table. Do the surveyed students own more laptops or more electronic tablets? ______

12. Which group had more people answer the survey: boys, or students who own an electronic tablet only? Explain.

______

______

13. **Critical Thinking** Teresa surveyed 100 students about whether they like pop music or country music. Out of the 100 students surveyed, 42 like pop only, 34 like country only, 15 like both pop and country, and 9 do not like either pop or country. Use this data to complete the two-way frequency table below.

	Like Pop		
Like Country	**Yes**	**No**	**Total**
Yes			
No			
Total			

14. The table shows the results of a survey about students' preferred frozen yogurt flavor. Complete the table and use it to complete the statement below.

	Preferred Flavor			
Gender	**Vanilla**	**Chocolate**	**Strawberry**	**Total**
Girl		15	18	45
Boy	17	25		
Total				100

Students preferred ______________ the most and ______________ the least.

FOCUS ON HIGHER ORDER THINKING

Work Area

15. **Multiple Representations** Use the data in Exercise 13 to complete the Venn diagram below.

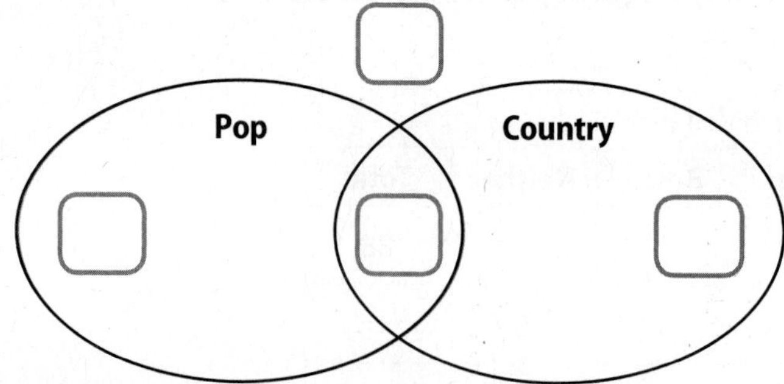

16. **Justify Reasoning** Charles surveyed 100 boys about their favorite color. Of the 100 boys surveyed, 44 preferred blue, 25 preferred green, and 31 preferred red. Can you make a two-way frequency table from the survey results? Explain your reasoning.

____

____

____

LESSON

12.2 Relative Frequency

CA CC S.ID.5

Summarize categorical data for two categories in two-way frequency tables. Interpret relative frequencies in the context of the data (including joint, marginal, and conditional relative frequencies). Recognize possible associations and trends in the data.

ESSENTIAL QUESTION

How can you recognize possible associations and trends between two categories of categorical data?

EXPLORE ACTIVITY

S.ID.5

Relative Frequencies

To show what portion of a data set each category in a frequency table makes up, you can convert the data to *relative frequencies*. The **relative frequency** of a category is the frequency of the category divided by the total of all the frequencies.

The frequency table below shows the results of a survey Kenesha took at school. She asked 80 randomly selected students whether they preferred basketball, football, or soccer.

Preferred Sport	Basketball	Football	Soccer	Total
Frequency	20	32	28	80

A Use the frequencies to make a relative frequency table that uses decimals. Divide each number in the frequency table by the total to obtain the corresponding relative frequency as a decimal. Record the results in the table below.

Preferred Sport	Basketball	Football	Soccer	Total
Relative Frequency	$\frac{20}{80} = 0.25$			

B Make a relative frequency table that uses percents.

Preferred Sport	Basketball	Football	Soccer	Total
Relative Frequency	25%			

REFLECT

1. Explain what the numerator and denominator of the ratio $\frac{20}{80}$ refer to in part A.

____

____

____

2. What types of numbers can you use to write relative frequencies?

____

Two-Way Relative Frequency Tables

You can obtain the following relative frequencies from a two-way frequency table:

- A **marginal relative frequency** is found by dividing a row total or a column total by the grand total. It tells what portion of the total has a specified characteristic.
- A **joint relative frequency** is found by dividing a frequency that is not in the Total row or the Total column by the grand total. It tells what portion of the total has both of two specified characteristics.

EXAMPLE 1

For her survey about sports preferences, Kenesha also recorded the gender of each student. The results are shown in the two-way frequency table below. Create a two-way relative frequency table for Kenesha's data.

	Preferred Sport			
Gender	**Basketball**	**Football**	**Soccer**	**Total**
Girl	6	12	18	36
Boy	14	20	10	44
Total	20	32	28	80

To find the joint relative frequencies and marginal relative frequencies, divide each number in the two-way frequency table by the grand total. Write the quotients as decimals.

joint relative frequency: 7.5% of students surveyed are girls who prefer basketball.

marginal relative frequency: 45% of students surveyed are girls.

	Preferred Sport			
Gender	**Basketball**	**Football**	**Soccer**	**Total**
Girl	$\frac{6}{80} = 0.075$	$\frac{12}{80} = 0.15$	$\frac{18}{80} = 0.225$	$\frac{36}{80} = 0.45$
Boy	$\frac{14}{80} = 0.175$	$\frac{20}{80} = 0.25$	$\frac{10}{80} = 0.125$	$\frac{44}{80} = 0.55$
Total	$\frac{20}{80} = 0.25$	$\frac{32}{80} = 0.4$	$\frac{28}{80} = 0.35$	$\frac{80}{80} = 1$

To check your work, add the joint relative frequencies in each row or column. Verify that the sum equals the row or column's marginal relative frequency.

Girl row:	$0.075 + 0.15 + 0.225 = 0.45$
Boy row:	$0.175 + 0.25 + 0.125 = 0.55$
Basketball column:	$0.075 + 0.175 = 0.25$
Football column:	$0.15 + 0.25 = 0.4$
Soccer column:	$0.225 + 0.125 = 0.35$

My Notes

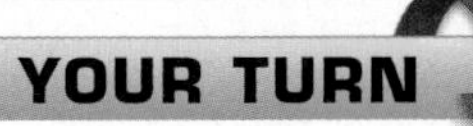

3. Find the joint relative frequency of students surveyed who like jogging and like aerobics. Express your answer as a decimal and as a percent.

____

	Like Aerobics		
Like Jogging	**Yes**	**No**	**Total**
Yes	7	14	21
No	12	7	19
Total	19	21	40

Conditional Relative Frequencies

Conditional relative frequency describes what portion of a group with a given characteristic also has another specified characteristic. A conditional relative frequency is found by dividing a frequency that is not in the Total row or the Total column by the total for that row or column.

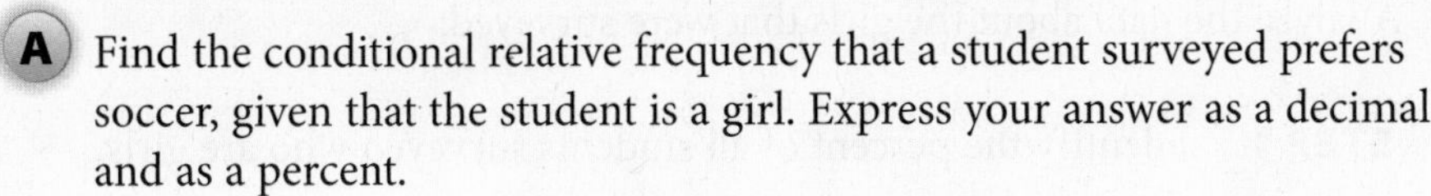

From Kenesha's two-way frequency table about preferred sports, you know that 36 students surveyed were girls and 28 students surveyed prefer soccer. You also know that 18 students surveyed are girls who prefer soccer. Use this information to find each conditional relative frequency.

A Find the conditional relative frequency that a student surveyed prefers soccer, given that the student is a girl. Express your answer as a decimal and as a percent.

$\frac{18}{36} = 0.5$, or 50% — *Divide the number of girls who prefer soccer by the total number of girls.*

The conditional relative frequency is 0.5, or 50%. This means that 50% of girls surveyed prefer soccer.

B Find the conditional relative frequency that a student surveyed is a girl, given that the student prefers soccer. Express your answer as a decimal and as a percent.

$\frac{18}{28} \approx 0.643$, or about 64.3% — *Divide the number of girls who prefer soccer by the number of students who prefer soccer.*

The conditional relative frequency is about 0.643, or 64.3%. This means that about 64.3% of students who prefer soccer are girls.

REFLECT

4. **Communicate Mathematical Ideas** In part A, why was the number of girls who prefer soccer not divided by 80, the grand total?

____

____

____

YOUR TURN

5. From Kenesha's table, you know that 44 students surveyed were boys, 20 students preferred basketball, and 14 students were boys who prefer basketball. Find the conditional relative frequency that a student surveyed is a boy, given that the student prefers basketball. Express your answer as a decimal and as a percent. ______________________

Finding Possible Associations

Two-way frequency tables can be analyzed to locate possible associations or patterns in the data.

EXAMPLE 3

CA CC S.ID.5

Kenesha is interested in the question, "Does gender influence what type of sport people prefer?" If there is no influence, then the distribution of gender within each sport preference will roughly equal the distribution of gender within the whole group. Analyze the results of Kenesha's survey from Example 1. Determine which sport each gender is more likely to prefer.

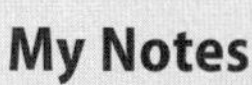

A Analyze the data about the girls that were surveyed.

STEP 1 Identify the percent of all students surveyed who are girls.

$$\frac{36}{80} = 0.45 = 45\%$$

STEP 2 Determine each conditional relative frequency.

Basketball: Of the 20 students who prefer basketball, 6 are girls. Percent who are girls, given a preference for basketball:

$$\frac{6}{20} = 0.3 = 30\%$$

Football: Of the 32 students who prefer football, 12 are girls. Percent who are girls, given a preference for football:

$$\frac{12}{32} = 0.375 = 37.5\%$$

Soccer: Of the 28 students who prefer soccer, 18 are girls. Percent who are girls, given a preference for soccer:

$$\frac{18}{28} \approx 0.643 = 64.3\%$$

STEP 3 Interpret the results by comparing each conditional relative frequency to the percent of all students surveyed who are girls.

Basketball: 30% is less than 45%
Girls are less likely than boys to prefer basketball.

Football: 37.5% is less than 45%
Girls are less likely than boys to prefer football.

Soccer: 64.3% is greater than 45%
Girls are more likely than boys to prefer soccer.

B Analyze the data about boys that were surveyed.

STEP 1 Identify the percent of all students surveyed who are boys. Subtract the percent for girls from 100%.

$$100\% - 45\% = 55\%$$

STEP 2 Determine each conditional relative frequency for boys. Subtract each percent for girls from 100%.

Basketball: $100\% - 30\% = 70\%$
70% of students who prefer basketball are boys.

Football: $100\% - 37.5\% = 62.5\%$
62.5% of students who prefer football are boys.

Soccer: $100\% - 64.3\% = 35.7\%$
35.7% of students who prefer soccer are boys.

STEP 3 Interpret the results by comparing each conditional relative frequency to the percent of all students surveyed who are boys.

Basketball: 70% is more than 55%
Boys are more likely than girls to prefer basketball.

Football: 62.5% is more than 55%
Boys are more likely than girls to prefer football.

Soccer: 35.7% is less than 55%
Boys are less likely than girls to prefer soccer.

Math Talk
Mathematical Practices

If sport preference were completely uninfluenced by gender, about how many girls would prefer each sport? Explain.

YOUR TURN

6. Steven asks 40 students whether they regularly eat breakfast. Of the 25 students who regularly eat breakfast, 9 are boys. Of the 15 who do not regularly eat breakfast, 10 are boys. Which gender is more likely to eat breakfast?

____

____

Guided Practice

The results of a survey of 40 students and the foreign language they are studying are shown in the two-way frequency table. Use the data for Exercises 1 and 2.

	Foreign Language			
Gender	**Chinese**	**French**	**Spanish**	**Total**
Girl	2	8	12	22
Boy	4	1	13	18
Total	6	9	25	40

1. Complete the two-way relative frequency table below using decimals. (Explore Activity and Example 1)

	Foreign Language			
Gender	**Chinese**	**French**	**Spanish**	**Total**
Girl	$\frac{2}{40} = 0.05$	$\frac{8}{40} =$		
Boy				$\frac{18}{40} = 0.45$
Total		$\frac{9}{40} = 0.225$		

2. Give each conditional relative frequency as a percent. (Example 2)

a. The conditional relative frequency that a student surveyed is studying Chinese, given that the student is a boy:

$\frac{\text{number of boys studying Chinese}}{\text{total number of boys surveyed}} = \frac{4}{18} \approx$ ______ ______

b. The conditional relative frequency that a student surveyed is a girl, given that the student is studying Spanish: ______

3. Determine which gender is more likely to study each foreign language. (Example 3)

______

______

ESSENTIAL QUESTION CHECK-IN

4. How can you recognize possible associations and trends between two categories in categorical data?

______

______

______

Name ____________________ Class ____________ Date ____________

12.2 Independent Practice

S.ID.5

Jasmine surveyed 80 students about their after-school activities. She recorded her results in the two-way frequency table below. Use the data for Exercises 5–12.

	Activity			
Gender	**Sports**	**Clubs**	**Other**	**Total**
Girl	9	21	8	38
Boy	22	8	12	42
Total	31	29	20	80

5. Create a two-way relative frequency table for the data using decimals.

	Activity			
Gender	**Sports**	**Clubs**	**Other**	**Total**
Girl				
Boy				
Total				

6. Find the relative frequency, expressed as a percent, of surveyed students who have clubs as their activity.

____

7. Is the relative frequency of surveyed girls that have sports as their activity a joint relative frequency or a marginal relative frequency? Explain.

____

____

____

____

____

____

8. Find the joint relative frequency of surveyed students who are boys and have clubs as their activity. ______________________

9. Find the marginal relative frequency of surveyed students who have sports as their activity. ______________________

10. **What If?** Jasmine surveys 10 more students. Of these, 6 are boys and all 6 boys have sports as their activity. None of the new girls have sports as their activity. How does this new data change the marginal relative frequency of surveyed students who have sports as their activity?

______________________.

11. Find the conditional relative frequency that a surveyed student has clubs as their activity, given that the student is a girl. Express your answer as a decimal and a percent. Explain how you found your answer.

____

____

____

____

12. Find the conditional relative frequency that a surveyed student is a boy, given that the student has an activity other than sports or clubs. Express your answer as a decimal and a percent. Explain how you found your answer.

____

____

____

____

In some states, a driver of a vehicle may not use a handheld cell phone while driving. In one state with this law, 250 randomly selected drivers were surveyed to determine the association between drivers who know the law and drivers who obey the law. The results are shown in the table below.

	Knows Law		
Obeys Law	**Yes**	**No**	**Total**
Yes	160	45	205
No	25	20	45
Total	185	65	250

13. Give each conditional relative frequency as a percent.

a. The conditional relative frequency that a driver surveyed obeys the handheld cell phone law, given that the driver knows the law:

____

b. The conditional relative frequency that a driver surveyed knows the handheld cell phone law, given that the driver obeys the law:

____

c. The conditional relative frequency that a driver surveyed obeys the law, given that the driver does not know the law:

____

14. Is there any association between the drivers who know the handheld cell phone law and drivers who obey the handheld cell phone law? Explain.

____

____

H.O.T. FOCUS ON HIGHER ORDER THINKING

Work Area

15. Analyze Relationships Explain the difference between a relative frequency and a conditional relative frequency in a two-way frequency table.

____

____

____

16. Explain the Error For the data about handheld cell phone laws above, Chelsea found the conditional frequency that a driver surveyed does not know the law, given that the driver obeys the law, by dividing 45 by 250. Explain Chelsea's error.

____

____

Ready to Go On?

Personal Math Trainer

Online Practice and Help

my.hrw.com

12.1 Two-Way Frequency Tables

The results of a survey of 150 students about the type of movie they prefer are shown in the two-way frequency table. Use the table for Exercises 1 and 2.

	Preferred Movie Type			
Gender	**Comedy**	**Drama**	**Science fiction**	**Total**
Girl	24	33		72
Boy		12	36	
Total				

1. Complete the table. How many boys were surveyed? ________

2. How many girls like science fiction movies? ____________

12.2 Relative Frequency

Use the data in the two-way frequency table above for Exercises 3 and 4.

3. Complete the two-way relative frequency table for the data using decimals.

4. Find the conditional relative frequency that a student surveyed is a boy, given that the student prefers comedy.

____

	Preferred Movie Type			
Gender	**Comedy**	**Drama**	**Science fiction**	**Total**
Girl				
Boy				
Total				

5. Use the data to identify which gender is more likely to prefer comedy. Explain.

____

____

____

ESSENTIAL QUESTION

6. How can you recognize possible associations between two categories of categorical data?

____

____

____

MODULE 12
MIXED REVIEW

Assessment Readiness

1. In a survey, 150 randomly selected students were asked whether they are right- or left-handed. The two-way frequency table shows the results. Look at each number below. Does the number belong in the cell that matches the letter?

Select Yes or No for A–C.

A. 135 ◯ Yes ◯ No

B. 6 ◯ Yes ◯ No

C. 73 ◯ Yes ◯ No

	Hand used		
Gender	**Right**	**Left**	**Total**
Boy	78	9	87
Girl	57	**B**	**C**
Total	**A**	15	150

2. A two-way relative frequency table for the data in Item 1 has been partially completed.

Choose True or False for each statement.

A. The joint relative frequency of girls who use their right hands is 0.38.

◯ True ◯ False

B. The marginal relative frequency of girls in the survey is 0.5.

◯ True ◯ False

	Hand used		
Gender	**Right**	**Left**	**Total**
Boy	0.52	0.06	
Girl			
Total			1

3. Use the data from Item 1. Based on the survey, which gender is more likely to be left-handed? Justify your answer.

4. Fatima earns \$8 per hour for the first 40 hours she works in a week and \$12 per hour for each additional hour she works. Fatima always puts 10% of her earnings into her savings account. Write an expression for the amount of money Fatima will put in her savings account for a week in which she works h hours, where $h > 40$. Simplify the expression, and tell which properties you used.

Data Displays

MODULE 13

ESSENTIAL QUESTION

How can data sets be displayed and compared, and what statistics can be gathered using the display?

CALIFORNIA COMMON CORE

LESSON 13.1
Measures of Center and Spread

CA CC S.ID.2

LESSON 13.2
Data Distributions and Outliers
CA CC S.ID.3, S.ID.1, S.ID.2

LESSON 13.3
Histograms

CA CC S.ID.1

LESSON 13.4
Box Plots
CA CC S.ID.1, S.ID.2

my.hrw.com

Real-World Video

In baseball, there are many options for how a team executes a given play. The use of statistics for in-game decision making sometimes reveals surprising strategies that run counter to the common wisdom.

GO DIGITAL
my.hrw.com

my.hrw.com

Go digital with your write-in student edition, accessible on any device.

Math On the Spot

Scan with your smart phone to jump directly to the online edition, video tutor, and more.

Animated Math

Interactively explore key concepts to see how math works.

Personal Math Trainer

Get immediate feedback and help as you work through practice sets.

Are YOU Ready?

Complete these exercises to review skills you will need for this module.

Personal Math Trainer
Online Practice and Help
my.hrw.com

Solve Proportions

EXAMPLE

$\frac{3}{4} = \frac{x}{12}$

$4x = 36$ *Cross-multiply.*

$x = 9$ *Solve for the unknown.*

Solve each proportion.

1. $\frac{15}{9} = \frac{3}{x}$ ________

2. $\frac{10}{20} = \frac{x}{100}$ ________

3. $\frac{250}{1500} = \frac{x}{100}$ ________

4. $\frac{32}{10} = \frac{4}{x}$ ________

5. $\frac{3}{4} = \frac{x}{200}$ ________

6. $\frac{15}{18} = \frac{x}{42}$ ________

Compare and Order Real Numbers

EXAMPLE Compare. Write $<$, $>$, or $=$.

20 ◯ 13 *20 is greater than 13.*

Compare. Write $<$, $>$, or $=$.

7. -18 ◯ -17

8. $\frac{2}{3}$ ◯ $\frac{1}{2}$

9. 0.75 ◯ $\frac{9}{12}$

10. 0.16 ◯ 0.8

Fractions, Decimals, and Percents

EXAMPLE Write the equivalent decimal.

$\frac{1}{2} = 0.5$ *Divide the numerator by the denominator.*

$45\% = 0.45$ *Write the percent over 100 and convert to a decimal.*

Write the equivalent percent.

$\frac{1}{4} = 0.25 \times 100 = 25\%$ *Convert to a decimal and then multiply by 100.*

Write the equivalent decimal.

11. $\frac{3}{5} =$ ________

12. $8\% =$ ________

13. $\frac{3}{4} =$ ________

Write the equivalent percent.

14. $0.2 =$ ________

15. $\frac{1}{10} =$ ________

16. $0.36 =$ ________

Reading Start-Up

Visualize Vocabulary

Use the Review Words to complete the chart.

Word	Definition	Example
	The number of times a data value occurs in a set of data	Henry's goals in each game: 0, 1, 1, 3, 2, 0, 1, 0, 2, 1, 1 Goals / Frequency: 0 – 3; 1 – 5; 2 – 2; 3 – 1
	Numerical measurements gathered from a survey or experiment	Quiz grades: 78, 82, 85, 90, 88, 79
	Data that is qualitative in nature	"liberal," "moderate," or "conservative"

Vocabulary

Review Words

✔ categorical data *(datos categóricos)*
✔ frequency *(frecuencia)*
frequency table *(tabla de frecuencia)*
✔ quantitative data *(datos cuantitativos)*

Preview Words

box plot
dot plot
first quartile (Q_1)
histogram
interquartile range
mean
median
outlier
quartiles
range
skewed to the left
skewed to the right
symmetric
third quartile (Q_3)

Understand Vocabulary

To become familiar with some of the vocabulary terms in the module, consider the following. You may refer to the module, the glossary, or a dictionary.

1. In a ____________ distribution, a vertical line can be drawn and the result is a graph divided in two parts that are approximate mirror images of each other.

2. A ____________ is a bar graph used to display the frequency of data divided into equal intervals.

3. A ____________ is a data representation that uses a number line and x's or dots to show frequency. A ____________ displays a five-number summary of a data set.

Active Reading

Layered Book Before beginning the module, create a Layered Book to help you organize what you learn. Write a vocabulary term or new concept on each page as you proceed. Under each tab, write the definition of the term and an example of the term or concept. See how the concepts build on one another.

GETTING READY FOR

Data Displays

Understanding the standards and the vocabulary terms in the standards will help you know exactly what you are expected to learn in this module.

CA CC S.ID.2

Use statistics appropriate to the shape of the data distribution to compare center (median, mean) and spread (interquartile range, standard deviation) of two or more different data sets.

Key Vocabulary

mean *(media)*
The average of the data values.

median *(mediana)*
The middle value when values are listed in numerical order.

interquartile range *(rango intercuartil)*
A measure of the spread of a data set, obtained by subtracting the first quartile from the third quartile.

What It Means to You

You can use the mean and median of data sets to compare the centers of the data sets. You can use the range, interquartile range, or standard deviation to compare the spreads of the data sets.

EXAMPLE S.ID.2

The lengths in feet of the alligators at a zoo are 9, 7, 12, 6, and 10. The lengths in feet of the crocodiles at the zoo are 13, 10, 8, 19, 18, and 16.

What is the difference between the mean length of the crocodiles and the mean length of the alligators?

Alligators: $\frac{9+7+12+6+10}{5} = 8.8$

Crocodiles: $\frac{13+10+8+19+18+16}{6} = 14$

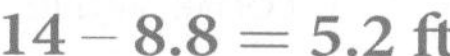

$14 - 8.8 = 5.2$ ft

CA CC S.ID.1

Represent data with plots on the real number line (dot plots, histograms, and box plots).

Key Vocabulary

dot plot *(diagrama de puntos)*
A data representation that uses a number line and x's or dots to show frequency.

What It Means to You

You can represent data sets using various models and use those models to interpret the information.

EXAMPLE S.ID.1

Class Scores on First Test (top) and Second Test (bottom)

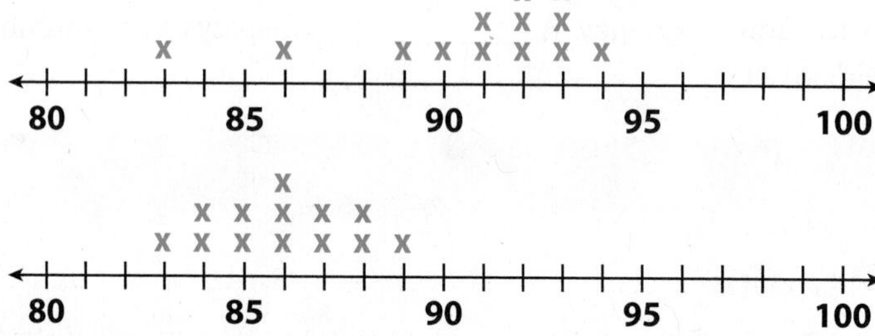

How do the medians of the two sets of test scores compare?

Look at each dot plot and locate the median. The median for the first test (92) is higher than the median for the second test (86).

Visit **my.hrw.com** to see all **CA Common Core Standards** explained.

my.hrw.com

LESSON 13.1

Measures of Center and Spread

S.ID.2

Use statistics appropriate to the shape of the data distribution to compare center (median, mean) and spread (interquartile range, standard deviation) of two or more different data sets.

ESSENTIAL QUESTION

How can you describe and compare data sets?

EXPLORE ACTIVITY

Exploring Data Sets

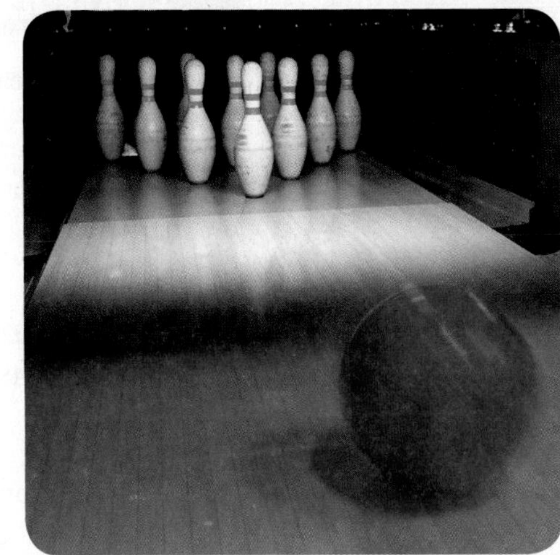

Caleb and Kim have bowled three games. Their scores are shown in the chart below.

Name	Game 1	Game 2	Game 3	Average score
Caleb	151	153	146	
Kim	122	139	189	

A Complete the table by finding each player's average score. How do the average scores compare?

____

B Whose game is more consistent? Explain why.

____

____

C Suppose that in a fourth game, Caleb scores 150 and Kim scores 175. How would that affect your conclusions about the average and consistency of their scores?

____

____

REFLECT

1. **Draw Conclusions** Do you think the average is an accurate representation of the three games that Caleb and Kim played? Why or why not?

____

____

____

____

Measures of Center: Mean and Median

Two commonly used *measures of center* for a set of numerical data are the mean and median. Measures of center represent a central or typical value of a data set.

- The **mean** is the sum of the values in the set divided by the number of values in the set.
- The **median** is the middle value in a set when the values are arranged in numerical order.

EXAMPLE 1

CA CC S.ID.2

Find the mean and the median for each set of values.

A The number of text messages that Isaac received each day for a week is shown.

47, 49, 54, 50, 48, 47, 55

Mean:

$47 + 49 + 54 + 50 + 48 + 47 + 55 = 350$ — Find the sum.

$\frac{350}{7} = 50$ — Divide the sum by the number of data values.

Median:

47, 47, 48, **49**, 50, 54, 55 — Order values, then find the middle value.

Mean: 50 text messages a day;
Median: 49 text messages a day

B The amount of money Elise earns in tips per day for six days is listed below.

\$75, \$97, \$360, \$84, \$119, \$100

Mean:

$75 + 97 + 360 + 84 + 119 + 100 = 835$ — Find the sum of the data values.

$\frac{835}{6} = 139.1\overline{66}$ — Divide the sum by the number of data values.

$\approx \$139.17$

Median:

75, 84, 97, 100, 119, 360 — Order values, then find the mean of the two middle numbers.

$\frac{97 + 100}{2} = 98.5$

Mean: \$139.17 a day; Median: \$98.50 a day

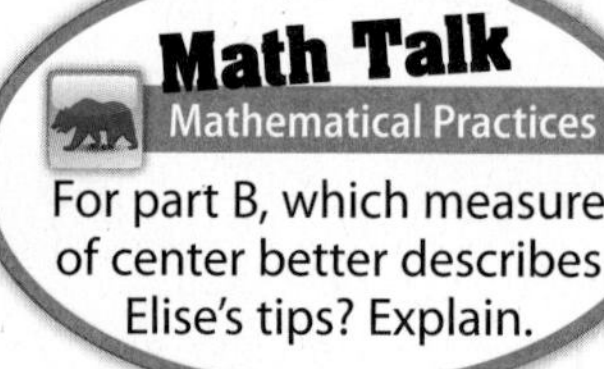

For part B, which measure of center better describes Elise's tips? Explain.

Personal Math Trainer
Online Practice and Help
my.hrw.com

2. Niles scored 70, 74, 72, 71, 73, and 96 on his six geography tests. Find the mean and median of his scores.

____

Measures of Spread: Range and IQR

Measures of spread describe how data values are spread out from the center. Two commonly used *measures of spread* for a set of numerical data are the range and interquartile range.

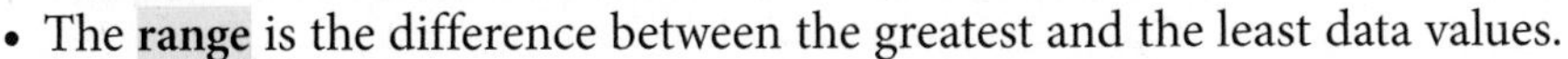

- The **range** is the difference between the greatest and the least data values.
- **Quartiles** are values that divide a data set into four equal parts. The **first quartile** (Q_1) is the median of the lower half of the set, the second quartile is the median of the whole set, and the **third quartile** (Q_3) is the median of the upper half of the set.
- The **interquartile range** (**IQR**) of a data set is the difference between the third and first quartiles. It represents the range of the middle half of the data.

Math On the Spot
my.hrw.com

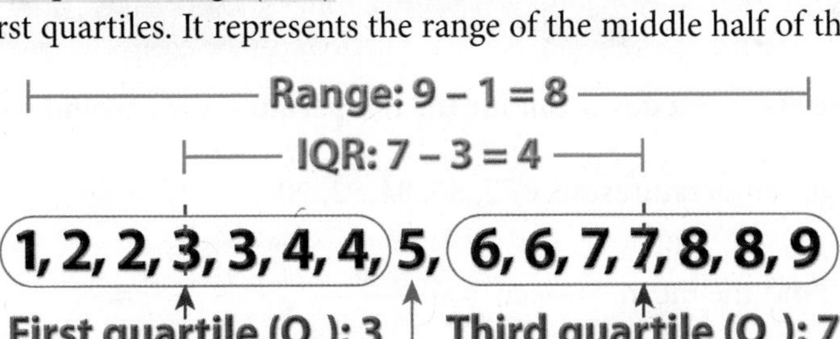

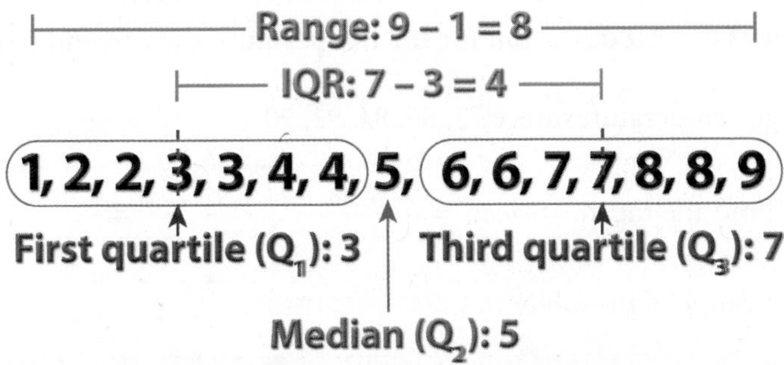

EXAMPLE 2

S.ID.2

The April high temperatures for five years in Boston are 77 °F, 86 °F, 84 °F, 93 °F, and 90 °F. Find the median, range, and IQR for the set.

Find the median.

77, 84, 86, 90, 93 — *Order the values and identify the middle value.*

The median is 86.

Find the range.

Range = 93 − 77 = 16

Find the interquartile range. When finding the quartiles, do not include the median as part of either the lower half or the upper half of the data.

77, 84, 86, 90, 93

This is the lower half. (77, 84)
This is the median. (86)
This is the upper half. (90, 93)

$Q_1 = \frac{77 + 84}{2} = 80.5$ and $Q_3 = \frac{90 + 93}{2} = 91.5$

Find the difference between Q_3 and Q_1: IQR = 91.5 − 80.5 = 11

Math Talk
Mathematical Practices
Why is the IQR less than the range?

YOUR TURN

3. Find the median, range, and interquartile range for this data set.

21, 31, 26, 24, 28, 26 ______________________________

Personal Math Trainer
Online Practice and Help
my.hrw.com

Measures of Spread: Standard Deviation

Standard deviation, another measure of spread, represents the average of the distances between individual data values and the mean.

The formula for finding the standard deviation of the data set $x_1, x_2, \ldots, x_n$ is:

$$\text{standard deviation} = \sqrt{\frac{(x_1 - \overline{x})^2 + (x_2 - \overline{x})^2 + \ldots + (x_n - \overline{x})^2}{n}}$$

where $\overline{x}$ is the mean of the set of data, and n is the number of data values.

EXAMPLE 3  

Calculate the standard deviation for the temperature data from Example 2.

The April high temperatures were 77, 86, 84, 93, 90.

STEP 1 Find the mean. Mean $= \frac{77 + 86 + 84 + 93 + 90}{5} = \frac{430}{5} = 86$

STEP 2 Complete the table.

Data value, x	Deviation from mean, $x - \overline{x}$	Squared deviation, $(x - \overline{x})^2$
77	$77 - 86 = -9$	$(-9)^2 = 81$
86	$86 - 86 = 0$	$0^2 = 0$
84	$84 - 86 = -2$	$(-2)^2 = 4$
93	$93 - 86 = 7$	$7^2 = 49$
90	$90 - 86 = 4$	$4^2 = 16$

STEP 3  Find the mean of the squared deviations.

Mean $= \frac{81 + 0 + 4 + 49 + 16}{5} = \frac{150}{5} = 30$

STEP 4 Take the square root of the mean of the squared deviations. Use a calculator, and round to the nearest tenth.

Square root of mean $= \sqrt{30} \approx 5.5$

The standard deviation is approximately 5.5.

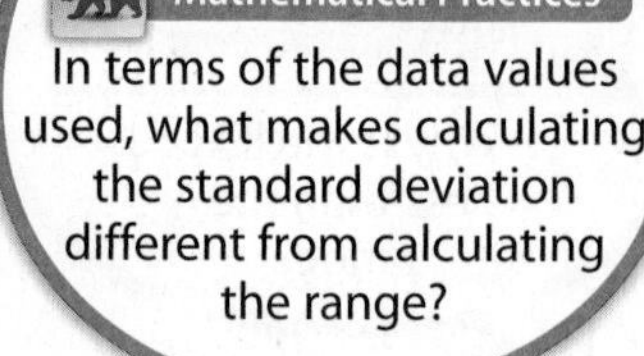

In terms of the data values used, what makes calculating the standard deviation different from calculating the range?

YOUR TURN

4. Find the standard deviation to the nearest tenth for a data set with the following values: 122, 139, 189.

____

Comparing Data Sets 

Numbers that characterize a data set, such as measures of center and spread, are called **statistics**. They are useful when comparing large sets of data.

EXAMPLE 4 

CA CC S.ID.2

The tables list the average ages of players on 15 teams randomly selected from the 2010 teams in the National Football League (NFL) and Major League Baseball (MLB). Calculate the mean, median, interquartile range, and standard deviation for each data set, and describe how the average ages of NFL players compare to those of MLB players.

NFL Players' Average Ages, by Team
25.8, 26.0, 26.3, 25.7, 25.1, 25.2, 26.1, 26.4, 25.9, 26.6, 26.3, 26.2, 26.8, 25.6, 25.7

MLB Players' Average Ages, by Team
28.5, 29.0, 28.0, 27.8, 29.5, 29.1, 26.9, 28.9, 28.6, 28.7, 26.9, 30.5, 28.7, 28.9, 29.3

STEP 1 On a graphing calculator, enter the two sets of data into two lists, L_1 and L_2.

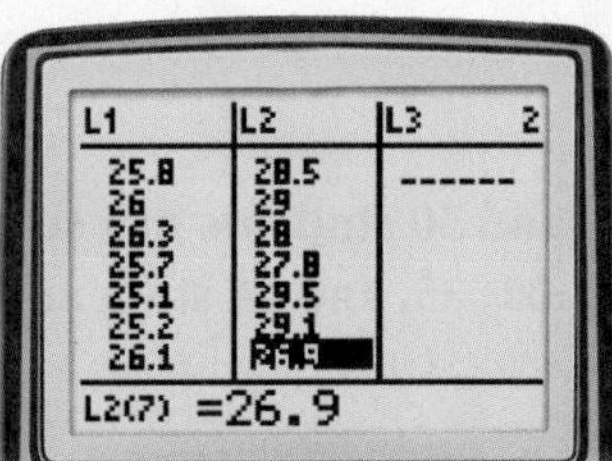

STEP 2 Use the "1-Var Stats" feature to find statistics for the data in lists L_1 and L_2. Your calculator may use the following notations:
Mean: $\bar{x}$
Standard deviation: σx
Scroll down to see the median (Med), Q1, and Q3. Calculate the interquartile range by subtracting Q_1 from Q_3.

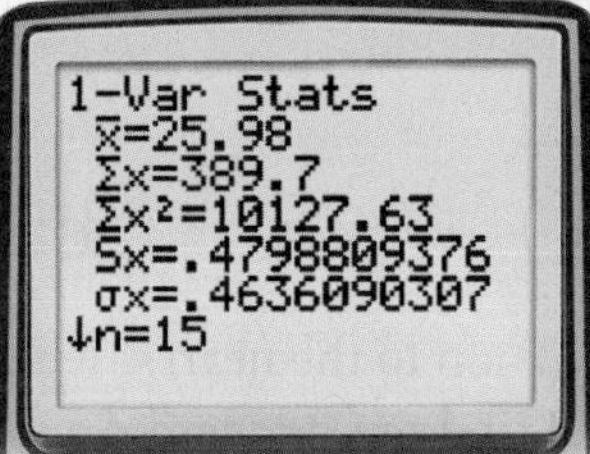
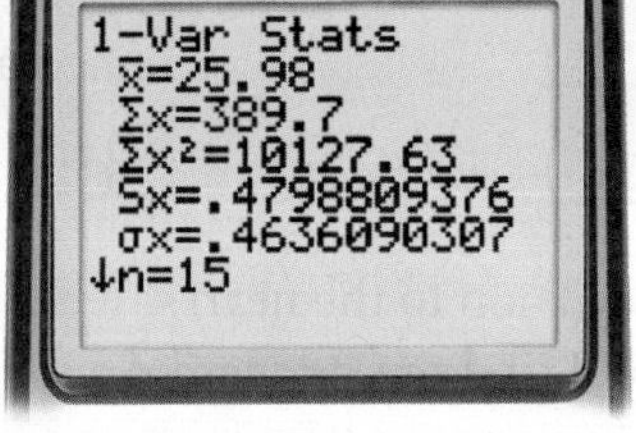

	Mean	Median	IQR ($Q_3 - Q_1$)	Standard Deviation
NFL	25.98	26.00	0.60	0.46
MLB	28.62	28.70	1.10	0.91

STEP 3 Compare the corresponding statistics for the NFL data and the MLB data. The mean and median are lower for the NFL than for the MLB; so we can conclude that NFL players tend to be younger than MLB players.

The IQR and standard deviation are smaller for the NFL; so we know that the ages of NFL players are closer together than those of MLB players.

YOUR TURN

5. a. The average member ages for every gym in Newman County are: 21, 23, 28, 28, 31, 32, 32, 35, 37, 39, 41, 41, 44, 45. Calculate the mean, median, interquartile range, and standard deviation for the data set.

____

b. The following statistics describe the average member ages at gyms in Oldport County: mean = 39, median = 39, IQR = 9, and standard deviation = 6.2. Describe how the ages of gym members in Oldport County compare to those of gym members in Newman County.

____

____

____

Guided Practice

There are 28, 30, 29, 26, 31, and 30 students in a school's six Algebra 1 classes. There are 34, 31, 39, 31, 35, and 34 students in the school's six Spanish classes. (Explore Activity and Examples 1–2)

1. Find the mean, median, range and interquartile range for the number of students in an Algebra 1 class.

mean: _______________ median: _______________

range: _______________ IQR: _______________

2. Find the standard deviation to the nearest tenth for the number of students in an Algebra 1 class, and find the standard deviation to the nearest tenth for the number of students in a Spanish class. (Example 3)

Algebra class: _______________ Spanish class: _______________

3. Draw a conclusion about the typical size of an Algebra 1 class and the typical size of a Spanish class. (Example 4)

____

____

ESSENTIAL QUESTION CHECK-IN

4. How can you describe and compare data sets?

____

____

Name ______________________ Class ______________________ Date ______________________

13.1 Independent Practice

 S.ID.2

Find the mean, median, and range of each data set.

5. 75, 63, 89, 91

____

6. 19, 25, 31, 19, 34, 22, 31, 34

____

Find the mean, median, range, and interquartile range for this data set.

13, 14, 18, 13, 12, 17, 15, 12, 13, 19, 11, 14, 14, 18, 22, 23

7. Mean: ______________________

8. Median: ______________________

9. Range: ______________________

10. Interquartile range: ______________________

The numbers of members in six yoga clubs are: 80, 74, 77, 71, 75, 91. Use this data set for questions 11–13.

11. Explain the steps for finding the standard deviation of the set of membership numbers.

____

12. Find the standard deviation of the number of members to the nearest tenth. ____________

13. **Explain the Error** Suppose a person in the club with 91 members transfers to the club with 71 members. A student claims that the measures of center and the measures of spread will all change. Correct the student's error.

____

14. **Represent Real-World Problems** Lamont's bowling scores were 153, 145, 148, and 166 in four games. For each question, choose the mean, median, or range, and give its value.

a. Which measure gives Lamont's average score? ______________________

b. Which measure should Lamont use to convince his parents that he's skilled enough to join a bowling league? Explain.

____

c. Lamont bowls one more game. Give an example of a score that would convince Lamont to use a different measure of center to persuade his parents. Explain.

____

H.O.T. FOCUS ON HIGHER ORDER THINKING

Work Area

15. Represent Real-World Problems The table lists the heights (in centimeters) of 8 males and 8 females on the U.S. Olympic swim team, all randomly selected from the team that participated in the 2008 Olympic Games in Beijing, China.

Heights of Olympic male swimmers	196	188	196	185	203	183	183	196
Heights of Olympic female swimmers	173	170	178	175	173	180	180	175

a. Use a graphing calculator to complete the table below.

	Center		Spread	
	Mean	**Median**	**IQR ($Q_3 - Q_1$)**	**Standard deviation**
Olympic male swimmers				
Olympic female swimmers				

b. What can you conclude about the heights of Olympic male swimmers and Olympic female swimmers?

____

____

____

16. What If? If all the values in a set are increased by 10, does the range also increase by 10? Explain.

____

____

17. Communicate Mathematical Ideas Jorge has a data set with the following values: 92, 80, 88, 95, and x. If the median value for this set is 88, what must be true about x? Explain.

____

____

18. Critical Thinking If the value for the median of a set is not found in the data set, what must be true about the data set? Explain.

____

____

____

LESSON 13.2

Data Distributions and Outliers

CA CC S.ID.3

Interpret differences in shape, center, and spread in the context of the data sets, accounting for possible effects of extreme data points (outliers). *Also S.ID.1, S.ID.2*

ESSENTIAL QUESTION

Which statistics are most affected by outliers, and what shapes can data distributions have?

Using Dot Plots to Display Data

A **dot plot** is a data representation that uses a number line and x's, dots, or other symbols to show frequency. Dot plots are sometimes called line plots.

CA CC S.ID.1

Twelve employees at a small company make the following annual salaries (in thousands of dollars):

25, 30, 35, 35, 35, 40, 40, 40, 45, 45, 50, 60

Choose an appropriate scale for the number line. Create a dot plot of the data by putting an X above the number line for each time that value appears in the data set.

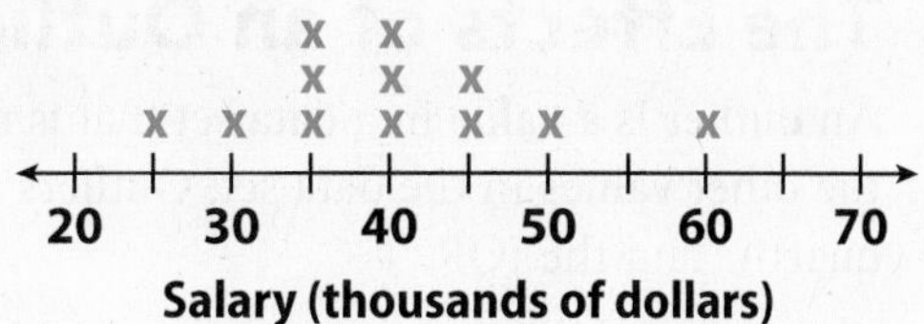

REFLECT

1. Recall that quantitative data can be expressed as a numerical measurement. Categorical, qualitative data is expressed in categories, such as attributes or preferences. Is it appropriate to use a dot plot for displaying quantitative data, qualitative data, or both? Explain.

____

____

2. **Analyze Relationships** How can you use a dot plot to find the median value? What is the median salary at the company?

____

____

____

3. When you examine the dot plot above, which data value appears most unlike the other values? Explain.

____

____

YOUR TURN

4. A cafeteria offers items at seven different prices. John counted how many items were offered at each price one week. Make a dot plot of the data.

Price ($)	1.50	2.00	2.50	3.00	3.50	4.00	4.50
Items	3	3	5	8	6	5	3

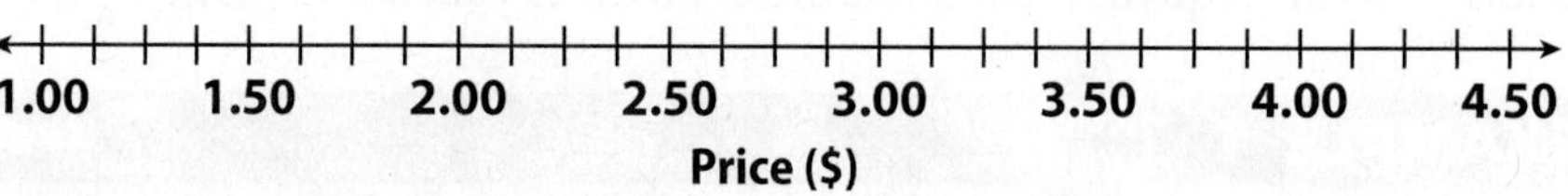

EXPLORE ACTIVITY

The Effects of an Outlier in a Data Set

An **outlier** is a value in a data set that is much greater or much less than most of the other values in the data set. Outliers are determined using the first or third quartile and the IQR.

How to Identify an Outlier
A data value x is an outlier if $x < Q_1 - 1.5(\text{IQR})$ or if $x > Q_3 + 1.5(\text{IQR})$.

Suppose the list of salaries in Example 1 is expanded to include the owner's salary, which is $150,000. Now the list of salaries is: 25, 30, 35, 35, 35, 40, 40, 40, 45, 45, 50, 60, 150.

 Create a dot plot for the revised data set. Choose an appropriate scale for the number line.

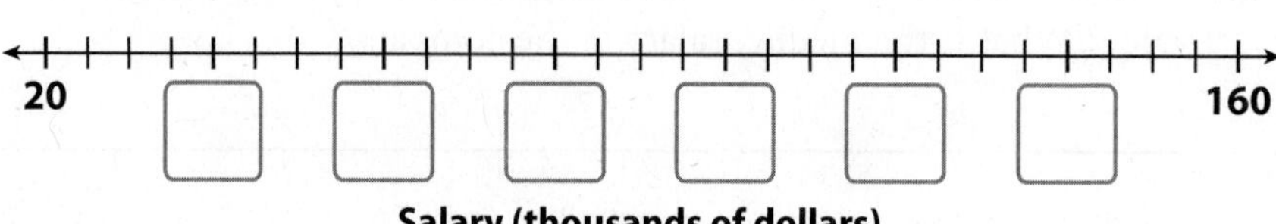

B Is the owner's salary an outlier? Determine if $150 > Q_3 + (1.5)\text{IQR}$.

$Q_3 =$ ______________ $Q_1 =$ ______________

IQR = ______________

$Q_3 + (1.5)\text{IQR} =$ ______________

Is 150 an outlier? ______________

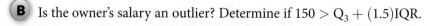

EXPLORE ACTIVITY *(cont'd)*

C Complete the table to see how the owner's salary changes the data set. Use a calculator and round to the nearest hundredth, if necessary.

	Mean	Median	Range	IQR	Standard deviation
Set without 150					
Set with 150					

D Complete each sentence by stating whether the statistic increased, decreased, or stayed the same when the data value 150 was added to the original data set. If the statistic increased or decreased, say by what amount.

The mean ______________________.

The median ______________________.

The range ______________________.

The IQR ______________________.

The standard deviation ______________________.

Math Talk
Mathematical Practices

How does an outlier affect measures of center?

REFLECT

5. **Critical Thinking** Explain why the median was unaffected by the outlier 150.

____

____

____

____

6. Is the value 60 an outlier of the data set including 150? Justify your answer.

____

____

YOUR TURN

Use the following data set to solve each problem: 21, 24, 3, 27, 30, 24

7. Is there an outlier? If so, identify the outlier. ______________________

8. Determine how the outlier affects the mean, median, and range of the data.

____

____

Comparing Data Distributions

A data distribution can be described as **symmetric**, **skewed to the left**, or **skewed to the right**, depending on the general shape of the distribution in a dot plot or other data display.

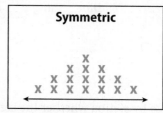

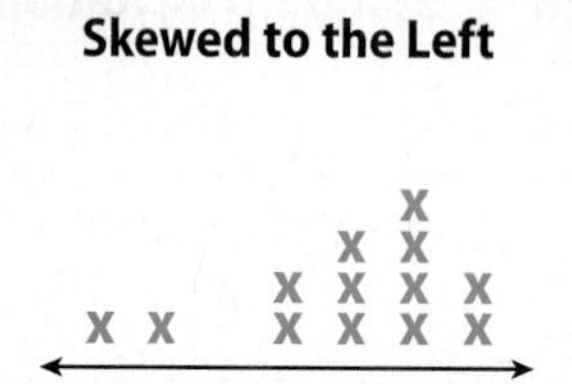

Symmetric

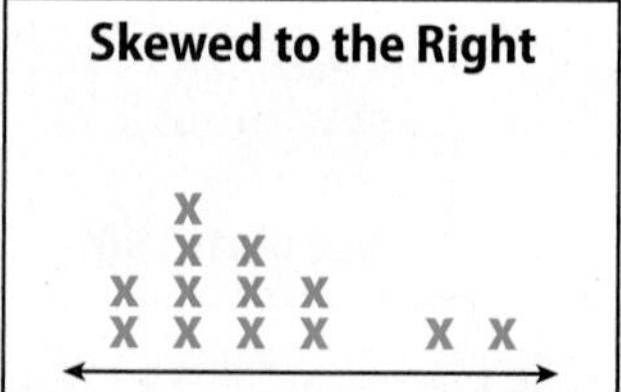

EXAMPLE 2

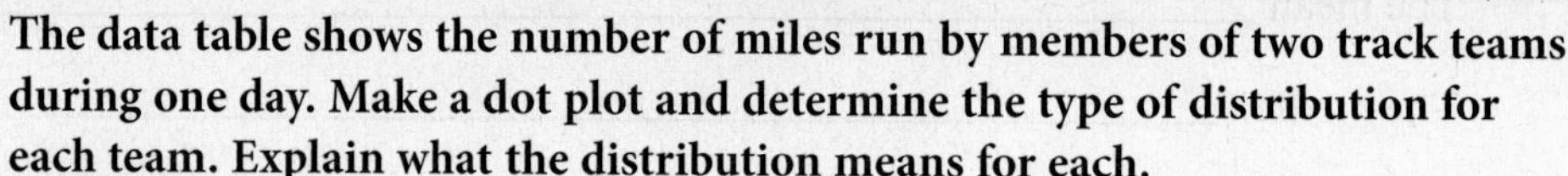

The data table shows the number of miles run by members of two track teams during one day. Make a dot plot and determine the type of distribution for each team. Explain what the distribution means for each.

Miles	3	3.5	4	4.5	5	5.5	6
Members of Team A	2	3	4	4	3	2	0
Members of Team B	1	2	2	3	4	6	5

Make dot plots of the data.

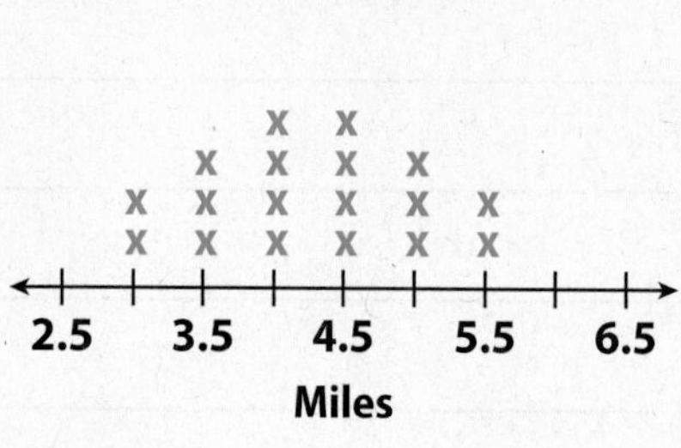

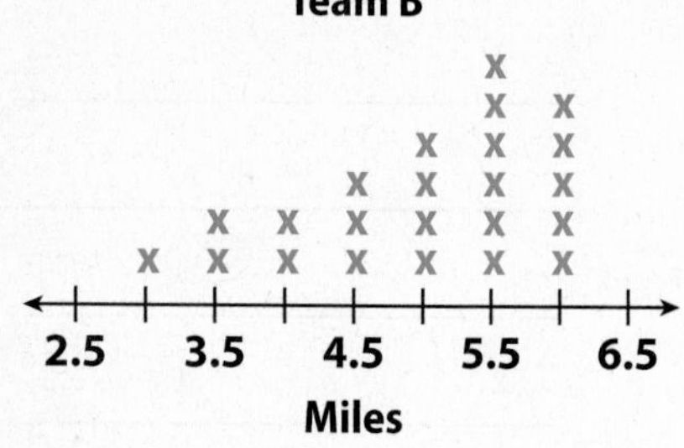

The data for team A show a symmetric distribution. The distances run are evenly distributed about the mean.

The data for team B show a distribution skewed to the left. More than half of the team members ran a distance greater than the mean.

My Notes

REFLECT

9. Will the mean and median in a symmetric distribution always be approximately equal? Explain.

10. Will the mean and median in a skewed distribution always be approximately equal? Explain.

YOUR TURN

11. Create a dot plot for the data. Describe the distribution as skewed to the left, skewed to the right, or symmetric.

Miles	3	3.5	4	4.5	5	5.5	6
Members of Team C	2	2	3	3	3	2	2

Team C

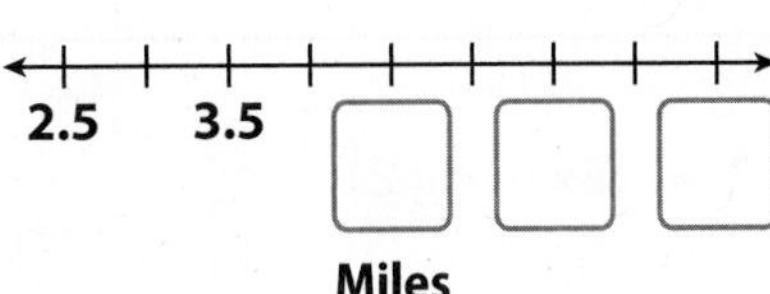

Miles

This distribution is ________________________.

Guided Practice

The list gives the grade level for each member of the marching band at JFK High. (Example 1)

9, 10, 9, 12, 11, 12, 10, 10, 11, 10, 10, 9, 11, 9, 11, 10, 12, 9, 11

1. Make a dot plot of the data.

JFK High Marching Band Member Grade Levels

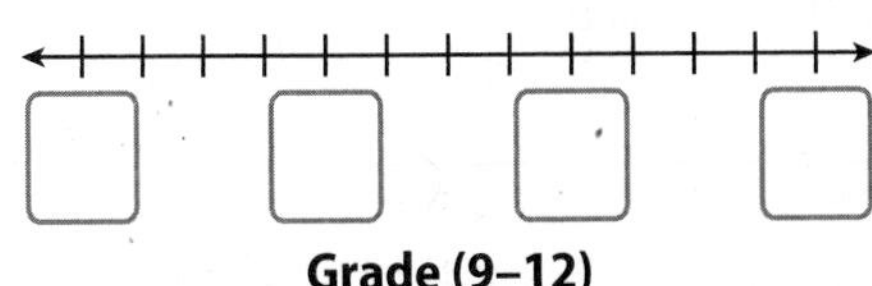

Grade (9–12)

2. Show that the data set {7, 10, 54, 9, 12, 8, 5} has an outlier. Then determine the effect of the outlier. (Explore Activity)

a. Determine if $54 > Q_3 + (1.5)\text{IQR}$.

$Q_3 =$ ________________________ $Q_1 =$ ________________________

IQR = ________________________

$Q_3 + (1.5)\text{IQR} =$ ____________________

Is 54 an outlier? ____________________

b. Complete the table.

	Mean	Median	Range
Set without 54			
Set with 54			

c. How does the outlier affect the mean, the median, and the range?

____

____

Use the dot plots below to answer Exercises 3–6. (Example 2)

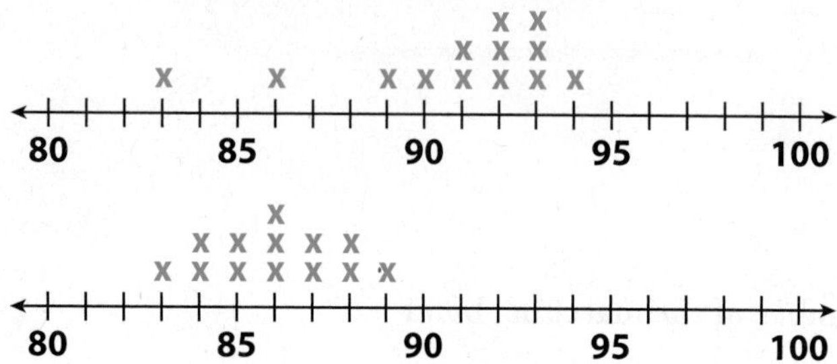

3. How do the medians of the two sets of test scores compare?

____

____

4. For which test is the distribution of scores symmetric? ____________

5. For which test is the median greater than the mean? ____________

6. Which measure of center is appropriate for comparing the two sets of test scores? ____________

ESSENTIAL QUESTION CHECK-IN

7. Which statistics are most affected by outliers, and what shapes can data distributions have?

____

____

____

____

Name ____________ Class ____________ Date ____________

13.2 Independent Practice

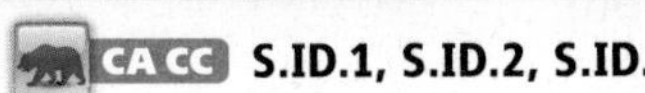

Rounded to the nearest $50,000, the values (in thousands of dollars) of homes sold by a realtor are listed below. Use the data set for Exercises 8–12.

300	**250**	**200**	**250**	**350**
400	**300**	**250**	**400**	**300**

8. Use the number line to create a dot plot for the data set.

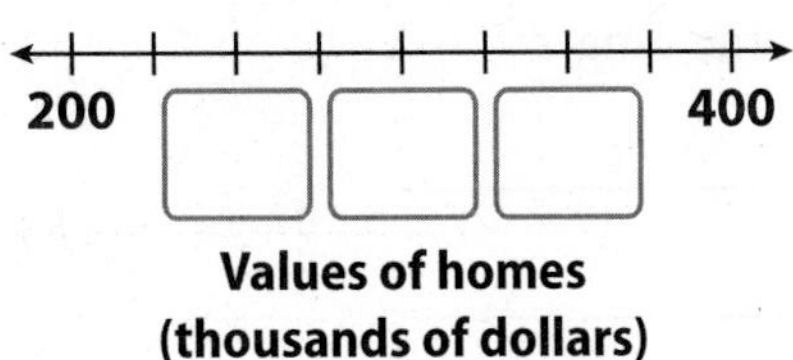

9. Suppose the realtor sells a home with a value of $650,000. Which statistics are affected when 650 is included in the data set?

____

____

10. Would 650 be considered an outlier? Explain.

____

____

____

11. Find the mean and median for the data set with and without the data value 650.

____

____

12. If 650 is included in the data set, why might the realtor want to use the mean instead of the median when advertising the typical value of homes sold?

____

____

13. Represent Real-World Problems The table shows Chloe's scores on math tests in each quarter of the school year.

Chloe's Scores			
I	**II**	**III**	**IV**
74	77	79	74
78	75	76	77
82	80	74	76
76	75	77	78
85	77	87	85

a. Use the number line below to create a dot plot for all of Chloe's scores.

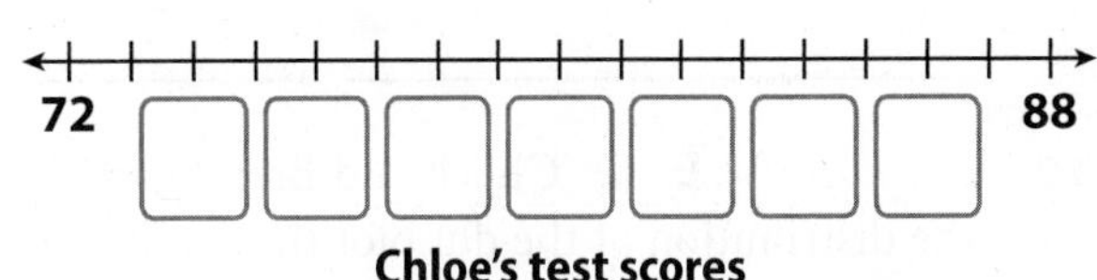

b. Complete the table below for the data set.

Mean	Median	Range	IQR	Standard deviation

c. Identify any outliers in the data set.

____

d. Which of the statistics from the table above would change if the outliers were removed?

____

____

____

e. Describe the shape of the distribution.

____

Work Area

FOCUS ON HIGHER ORDER THINKING

14. Critical Thinking Magdalene and Peter conducted the same experiment. Both of their data sets had the same mean. Both made dot plots of their data that showed symmetric distributions, but Peter's dot plot shows a greater IQR than Magdalene's dot plot. Identify which plot below belongs to Peter and which belongs to Magdalene.

Dot Plot A

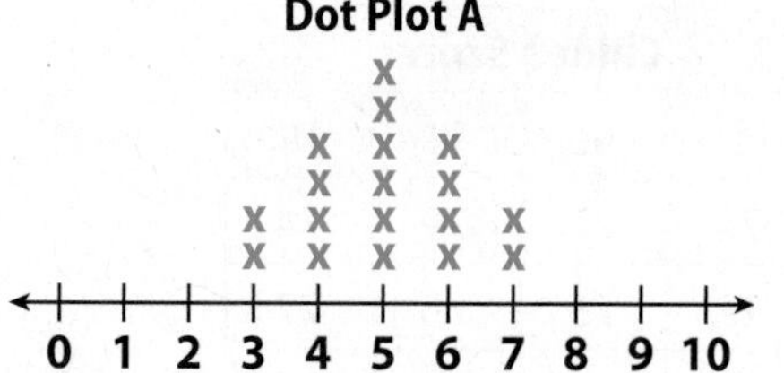

Dot Plot B

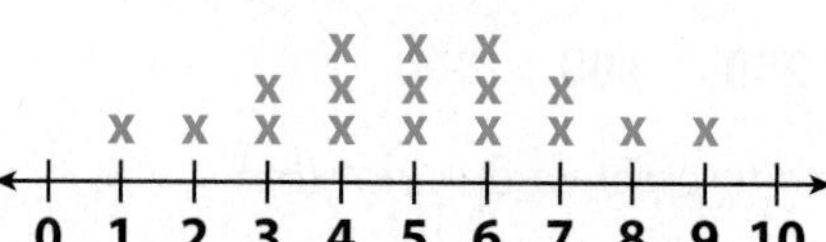

____

15. Justify Reasoning Why will outliers always have an effect on the range?

____

____

____

____

16. Explain the Error Chuck and Brenda are discussing the distribution of the dot plot shown. Brenda says that if you add some families with 5 or 6 siblings then there will be a symmetric distribution. Explain her error.

Number of Siblings

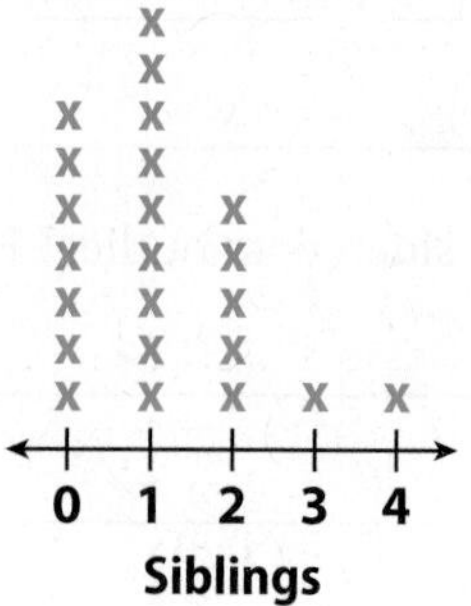

____

____

____

____

____

17. Critique Reasoning Victor thinks that only the greatest and the least values in a data set can be outliers, since an outlier must be much greater or much less than the other values. Is he correct? Explain.

____

____

____

____

LESSON

13.3 Histograms

Represent data with plots on the real number line (dot plots, histograms, and box plots).

ESSENTIAL QUESTION

How can you estimate statistics from data displayed in a histogram?

EXPLORE ACTIVITY

Understanding Histograms

A **histogram** is a bar graph that is used to display the frequency of data divided into equal intervals. The bars must be of equal width and should touch but not overlap. The heights of the bars indicate the frequency of data values within each interval.

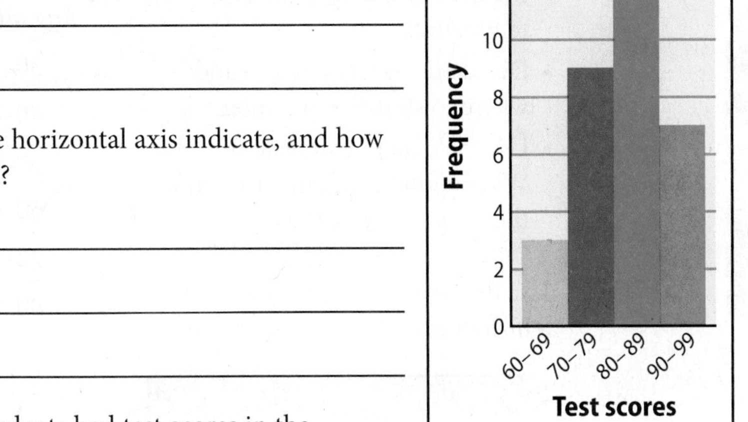

A Look at the histogram of "Scores on a Math Test." Which axis indicates the frequency?

____

____

B What does the horizontal axis indicate, and how is it organized?

____

____

____

C How many students had test scores in the interval 60–69? __________ between 70 and 79? __________

REFLECT

1. What statistical information can you tell about a data set by looking at a histogram? What statistical information cannot be determined by looking at a histogram?

____

____

2. How many test scores were collected? How do you know?

____

____

____

Creating a Histogram

When creating a histogram, make sure that the bars are of equal width and that they touch without overlapping. Create a frequency table to help organize the data before constructing the histogram.

EXAMPLE 1   S.ID.1

Listed below are the ages of the 100 U.S. senators at the start of the 112th Congress on January 3, 2011. Create a histogram for this data set.

39, 39, 42, 44, 46, 47, 47, 47, 48, 49, 49, 49, 50, 50, 51, 51, 52, 52, 53, 53, 54, 54, 55, 55, 55, 55, 55, 55, 56, 56, 57, 57, 57, 58, 58, 58, 58, 58, 59, 59, 59, 59, 60, 60, 60, 60, 60, 60, 60, 61, 61, 62, 62, 62, 63, 63, 63, 63, 64, 64, 64, 64, 66, 66, 66, 67, 67, 67, 67, 67, 67, 67, 68, 68, 68, 68, 69, 69, 69, 70, 70, 70, 71, 71, 73, 73, 74, 74, 74, 75, 76, 76, 76, 76, 77, 77, 78, 86, 86, 86

The data values range from 39 to 86, so use an interval width of 10 and start the first interval at 30.

STEP 1 Create a frequency table.

- It may be helpful to organize the data by listing from least to greatest.
- Decide the interval width and where to start the first interval.
- Use the data to complete the table. When done, check that the sum of the frequencies is 100.

Age interval	Frequency
30–39	2
40–49	10
50–59	30
60–69	37
70–79	18
80–89	3

STEP 2 Use the frequency table to create a histogram.

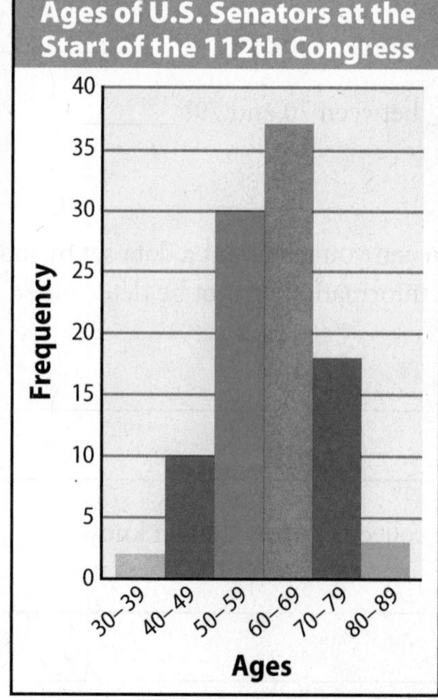

Remember to give the graph a title and label both axes.

REFLECT

3. Describe the shape of the distribution of senators' ages. Explain.

YOUR TURN

4. Listed below are the scores from a golf tournament.

68, 78, 76, 71, 69, 73, 72, 74, 76, 70, 77, 74, 75, 76, 71

a. Complete the frequency table.

Golf scores	Frequency
68 – 70	
71 – 73	
74 – 76	
77 – 79	

b. Complete the histogram.

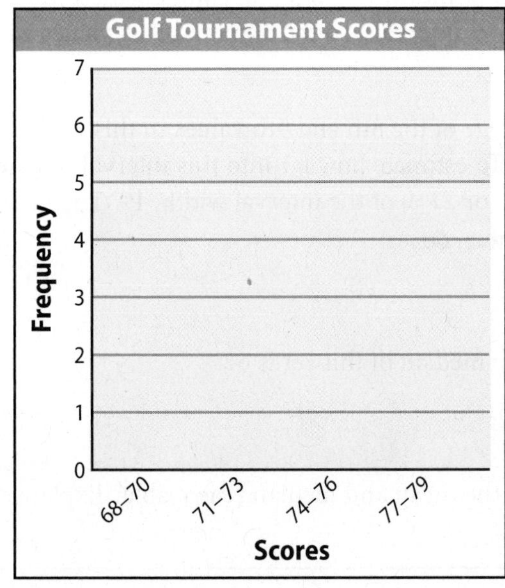

Estimating Statistics from a Histogram

You can estimate statistics by studying a histogram. Reasonable estimates of the mean, median, IQR, and standard deviation can be based on information provided by a histogram.

EXAMPLE 2

CA CC S.ID.1

Look at the histogram from Example 1. Estimate the mean and the median ages from the histogram.

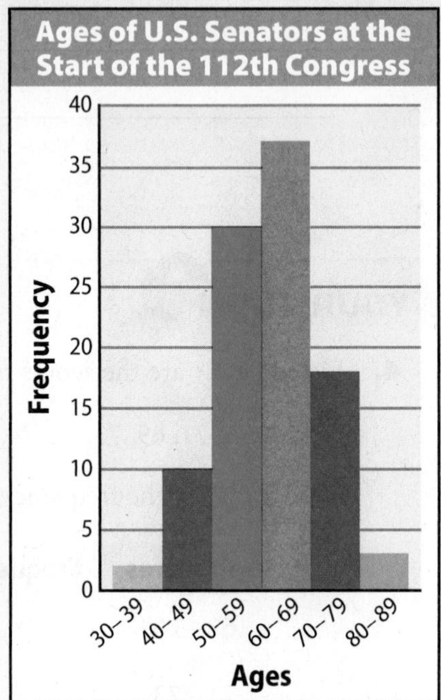

A To estimate the mean, first find the midpoint of each interval and multiply by the frequency. Add the results and divide by the total number of values.

1st interval:	2nd interval:
$(34.5)(2) = 69$	$(44.5)(10) = 445$
3rd interval:	4th interval:
$(54.5)(30) = 1635$	$(64.5)(37) = 2386.5$
5th interval:	6th interval:
$(74.5)(18) = 1341$	$(84.5)(3) = 253.5$

Mean: $\frac{69 + 445 + 1635 + 2386.5 + 1341 + 253.5}{100}$

$= \frac{6130}{100} = 61.3$

A good estimate for the mean of this set is 61.3.

Math Talk
Mathematical Practices
What is represented by the product of the midpoint of an interval and the frequency of that interval?

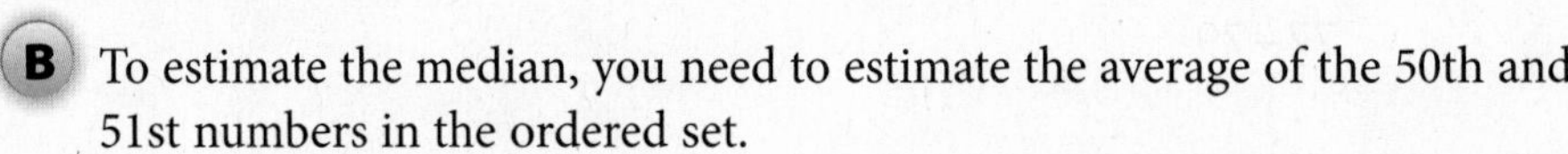

B To estimate the median, you need to estimate the average of the 50th and 51st numbers in the ordered set.

First, use the histogram to find which interval contains these values. There are 42 values in the first 3 intervals, so the 50th and 51st values will be in the interval 60–69.

The median is the average of the 8th and 9th values in this interval. This interval has 37 values. To estimate how far into this interval the median is located, find $\frac{8.5}{37} \approx 0.23$, or 23%, of the interval width, 10. Then add the result to the interval's least value, 60.

$(0.23)10 + 60 \approx 62$

A good estimate for the median of this set is 62.

REFLECT

5. Are these estimates of the mean and median reasonable? Explain.

YOUR TURN

6. The histogram shows the ages of teachers at Plainsville High School. Estimate the teachers' mean and median ages from the histogram.

____

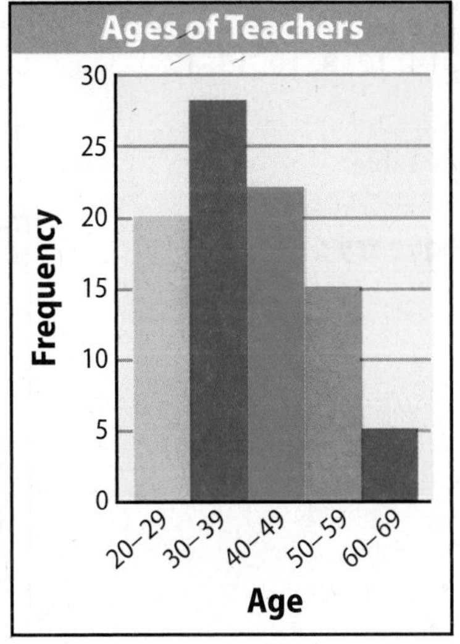

Guided Practice

The histogram shows the 2004 Olympic results for women's weightlifting. Medals were awarded to the three athletes who lifted the most weight. (Explore Activity)

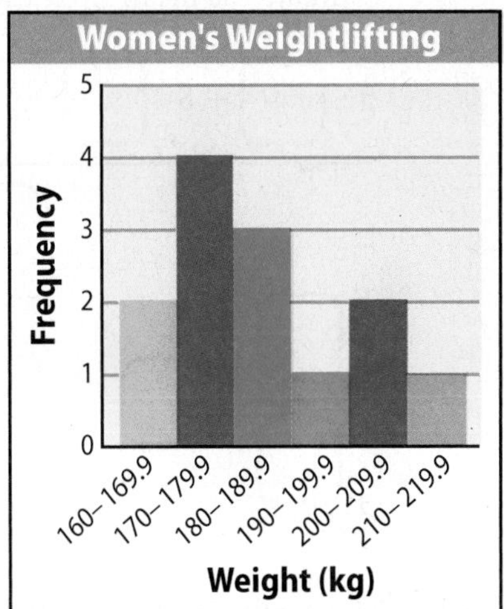

1. How many women lifted between 160 and 169.9 kg?

____

2. How many women lifted between 170 and 209.9 kg?

____

3. Tara Cunningham from the United States lifted 172.5 kg. Did she win a medal for this lift? Explain.

____

4. Can you determine which weight earned the silver medal? Explain.

____

The length (in days) of Maria's last 15 vacations are given.
(Examples 1 and 2)

4, 8, 6, 7, 5, 4, 10, 6, 7, 14, 12, 8, 10, 15, 12

5. Make a frequency table.

Days	Frequency
4–6	
7–9	
10–12	
13–15	

6. Create a histogram using the frequency table.

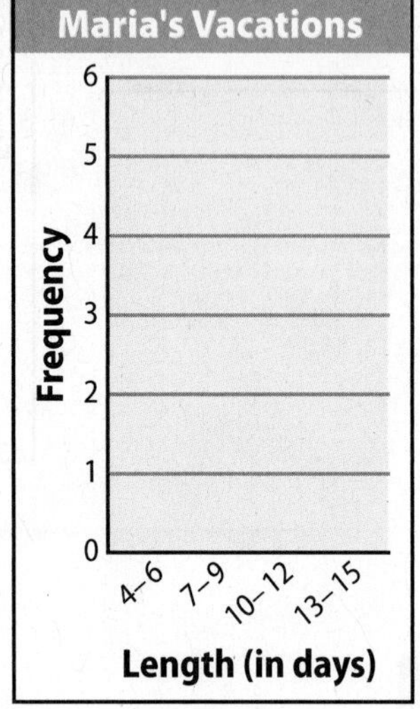

7. Estimate the mean from the histogram.

$$\frac{5 \cdot \square + 8 \cdot \square + \square \cdot \square + \square \cdot \square}{\square}$$

$$= \frac{\square}{\square} = \square$$

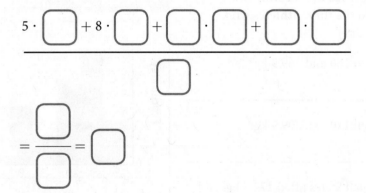

Multiply the midpoint value of each interval by its frequency. Divide the sum of those numbers by the total number of values.

The mean calculated from the data set is about ________,

so the estimate is very close / not very close.

Calculate the mean from the data set and compare the results to your estimate.

ESSENTIAL QUESTION CHECK-IN

8. How can you estimate statistics from data displayed in a histogram?

____

____

____

____

Name ______________________ Class ______________ Date ______________

13.3 Independent Practice

S.ID.1

Use the histogram for Exercises 9 and 10.

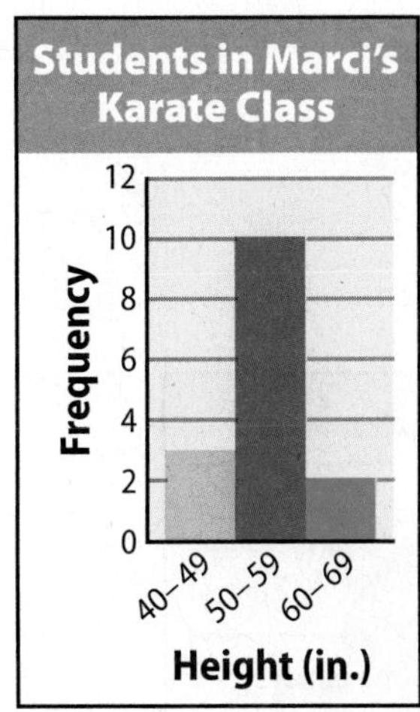

9. How many students are in the class? ______

10. Describe the shape of the distribution.

____

11. The breathing intervals of gray whales are shown. Make a histogram for the data.

Breathing Intervals (min)	
Interval	**Frequency**
5–7	4
8–10	7
11–13	7
14–16	8

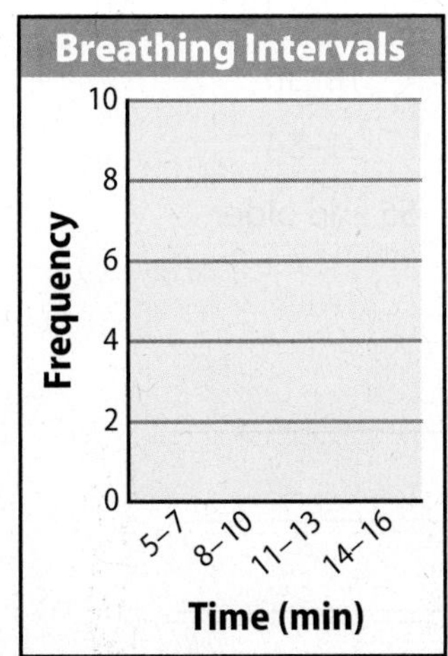

The ages of the first 44 U.S. presidents on the date of their first inauguration are shown in the histogram. Use the histogram for Exercises 12 and 13.

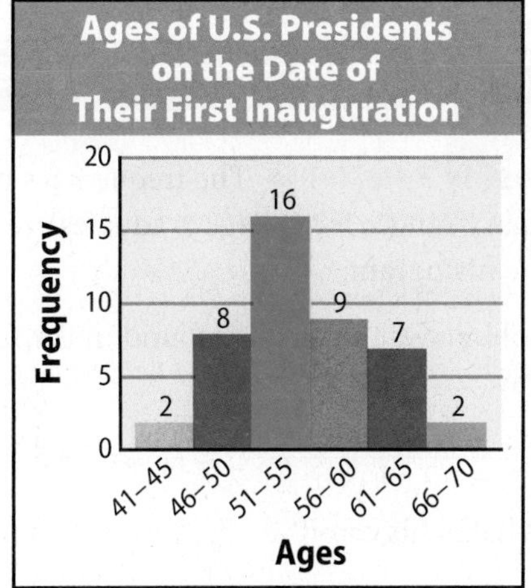

12. **Communicate Mathematical Ideas** Describe the shape of the distribution by telling whether it is approximately symmetric, skewed to the right, or skewed to the left. Explain.

____

____

____

____

____

13. Use the histogram to estimate the mean and median age of presidents at their first inauguration.

a. Mean presidential age at first inauguration: ______________

b. Median presidential age at first inauguration: ______________

14. Communicate Mathematical Ideas Describe how you could estimate the IQR of a data set from a histogram.

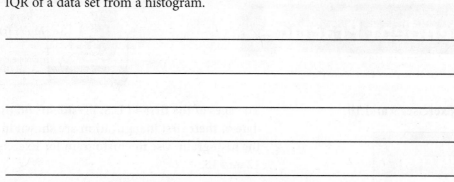

H.O.T. FOCUS ON HIGHER ORDER THINKING

Work Area

15. Justify Reasoning The frequencies of starting salary ranges for college graduates are shown in the histogram.

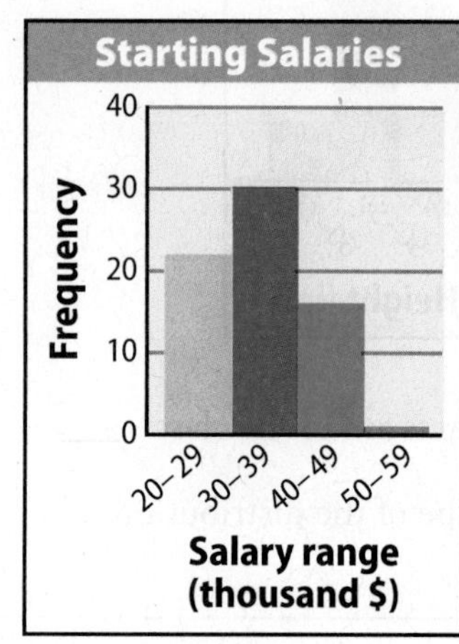

Bobby says the mean is found in the following way:

$$\frac{24.5 + 34.5 + 44.5 + 54.5}{4} = \frac{158}{4} = 39.5$$

What is his error?

16. Critical Thinking Margo's assignment is to make a data display of some data she finds in a newspaper. She found a frequency table with the intervals shown at the right.

Explain why Margo must be careful when drawing the bars of the histogram.

Age
Under 18
18–30
31–54
55 and older

LESSON

13.4 Box Plots

CA CC S.ID.1

Represent data with plots on the real number line (dot plots, histograms, and box plots). *Also S.ID.2*

ESSENTIAL QUESTION

How can you compare data sets using box plots?

Constructing a Box Plot

A **box plot** can be used to show how the values in a data set are distributed. You need five values to make a box plot: the minimum (or least value), first quartile, median, third quartile, and maximum (or greatest value).

EXAMPLE 1 Real World — CA CC S.ID.1

The numbers of runs scored by a softball team in 20 games are given. Use the data to make a box plot.

3, 4, 8, 12, 7, 5, 4, 12, 3, 9, 11, 4, 14, 8, 2, 10, 3, 10, 9, 7

STEP 1 Order the data from least to greatest.

2, 3, 3, 3, 4, 4, 4, 4, 5, 7, 7, 8, 8, 9, 9, 10, 10, 11, 12, 12, 14

STEP 2 Identify the five needed values. Those values are the minimum, first quartile, median, third quartile, and maximum.

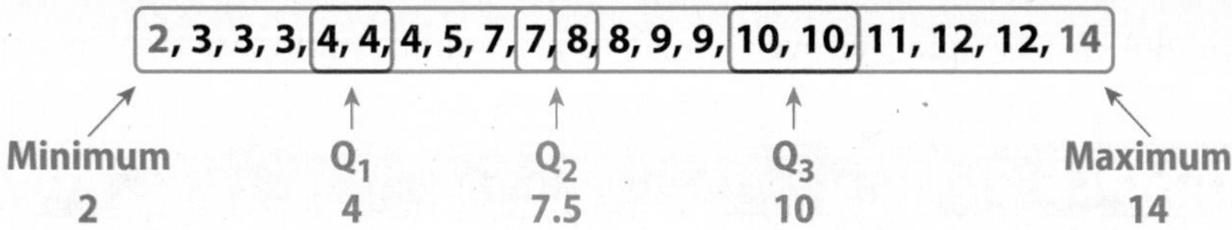

STEP 3 Draw a number line and plot a point above each of the five needed values. Draw a box whose ends go through the first and third quartiles, and draw a vertical line through the median. Draw horizontal lines from the box to the minimum and maximum.

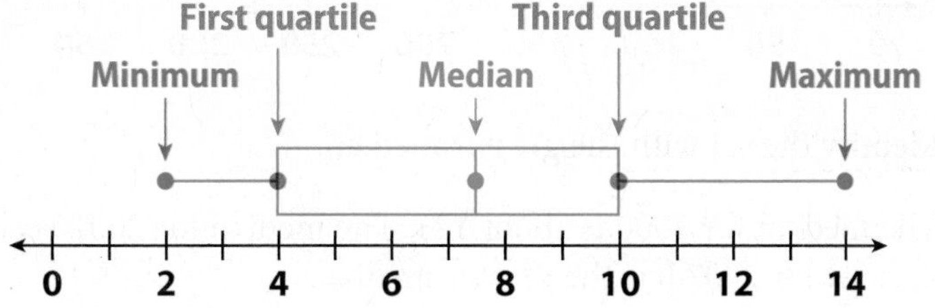

REFLECT

1. The lines that extend from the box in a box plot are sometimes called "whiskers." What part (lower, middle, or upper) and about what percent of the data does the box represent? What part and about what percent does each "whisker" represent?

2. Which measures of spread can be determined from the box plot, and how are they found? Calculate each measure.

YOUR TURN

3. Use the data to make a box plot.

13, 14, 18, 13, 12, 17, 15, 12, 13, 19, 11, 14, 14, 18, 22, 23

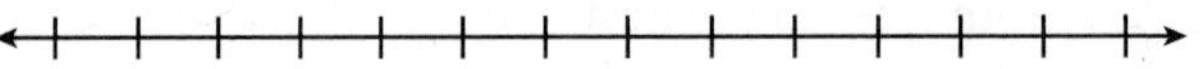

Comparing Data Using Box Plots

You can plot two box plots above a single number line to compare two data sets.

CA CC S.ID.1

The box plots show the ticket sales, in millions of dollars, for the top 25 movies of 2000 and 2007. Use the box plots to compare the data sets.

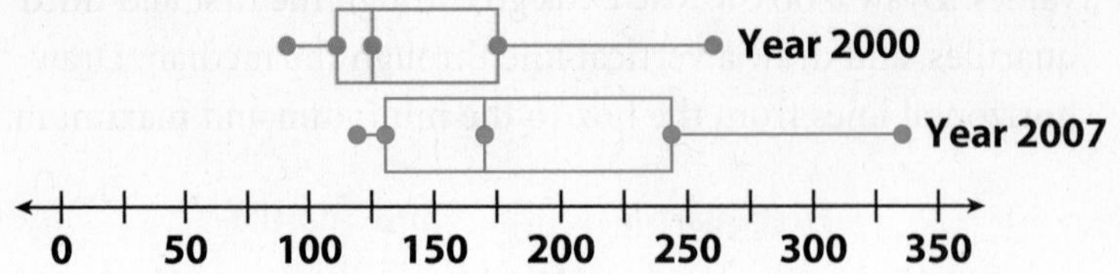

A Identify the set with the greater median.

The median for 2000 is about 125. The median for 2007 is about 170. The data set for 2007 has the greater median.

B Identify the set with the greater interquartile range.

The length of the box for 2007 is greater than the length of the box for 2000. The data set for 2007 has a greater interquartile range.

C About how much greater were the ticket sales for the top movie in 2007 than for the top movie in 2000?

2007 maximum: about $335 million — *Read the maximum values from the box plots.*

2000 maximum: about $260 million

$335 - 260 = 75$ — *Find the difference between the maximum values.*

The ticket sales for the top movie in 2007 were about $75 million more than for the top movie in 2000.

Math Talk
Mathematical Practices
Explain how to find which data set has a smaller range.

REFLECT

4. **Analyze Relationships** Use the box plots to compare the shape of the two data distributions.

____

____

____

____

____

YOUR TURN

The box plots show the scores, in thousands of points, of two players of a video game.

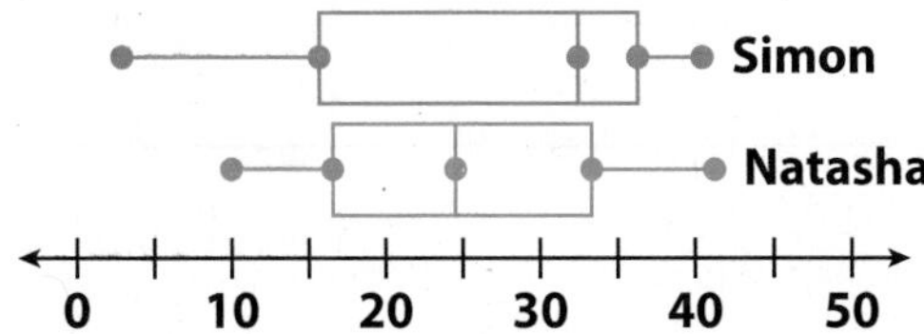

5. Which data set has a greater median? ______________________

6. Which data set has the greater interquartile range? ______________________

7. Which player had a higher top score? About how much higher was it than the other player's top score? ______________________

____

Guided Practice

Use the data to make a box plot. (Example 1)

1. 25, 28, 26, 16, 18, 15, 25, 28, 26, 16

a. Order the data from least to greatest.

____

b. Identify the median and the first and third quartiles.

Median = _______________

First quartile = _______________

Third quartile = _______________

c. Identify the minimum and maximum.

Minimum = _______________

Maximum = _______________

d. Construct the box plot.

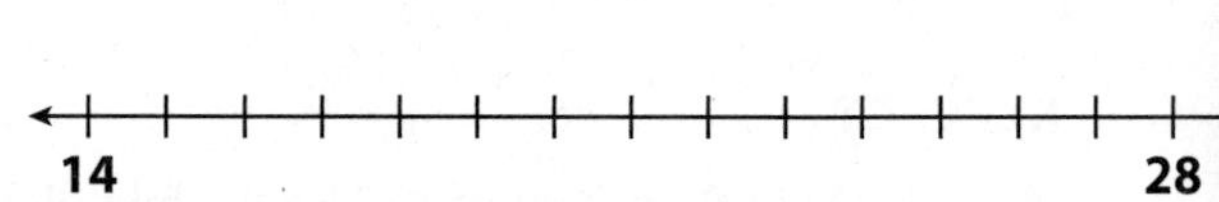

The box plots show the prices, in dollars, of athletic shoes at two sports apparel stores. Use the box plots for Exercises 2 and 3. (Example 2)

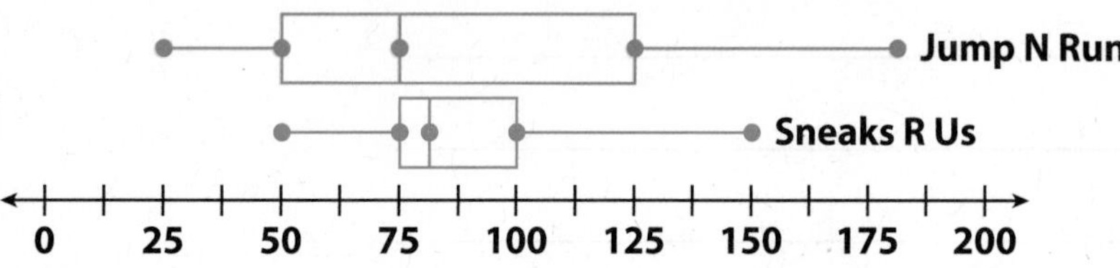

2. Which store has the greater median price? About how much greater?

____

3. Which store has the smaller interquartile range? What does this tell you about the data sets?

____

____

ESSENTIAL QUESTION CHECK-IN

4. How can you compare data sets using box plots?

____

____

____

____

Name ______________________ Class ______________ Date ______________

13.4 Independent Practice

S.ID.1, S.ID.2

The finishing times of two runners for several one-mile races, in minutes, are shown below. Use the box plots for Exercises 5–7.

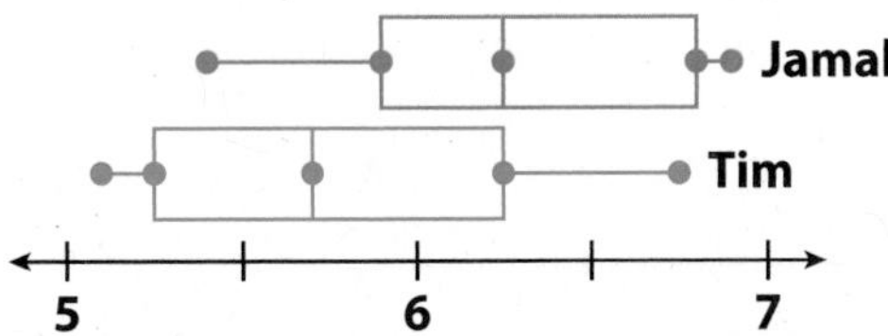

5. Who has the faster median time?

____

6. Who has the slowest time?

____

7. Overall, who is the faster runner? Explain.

____

The table below shows the scores that Gabrielle and Marcus each earned the last 15 times they played a board game together. Use the table to complete Exercises 8–10.

Gabrielle	150, 195, 180, 225, 120, 135, 115, 220, 190, 185, 230, 170, 160, 200, 120
Marcus	170, 155, 175, 200, 190, 165, 170, 180, 160, 175, 155, 170, 160, 180, 175

8. Create a box plot for each data set on the number line below.

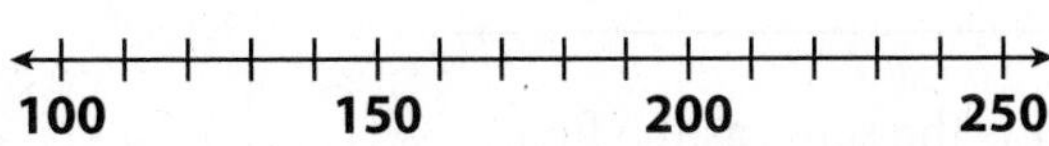

9. Which set has the higher median?

____

10. Which set has more scores that are close to the median? Explain.

____

The number of traffic citations given daily by two police departments over a two-week period is shown. Use the box plots for Exercises 11–13.

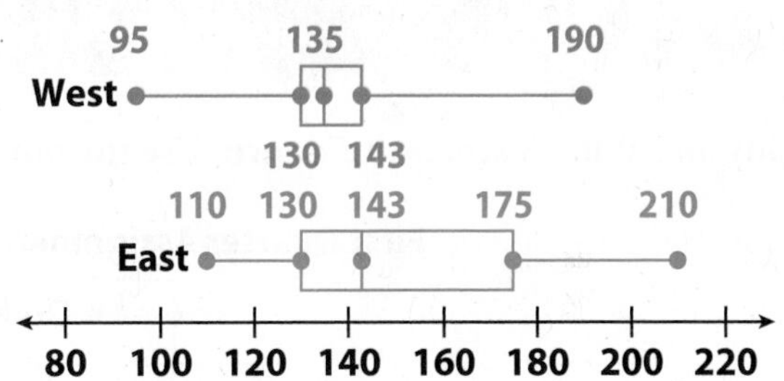

11. Which department gave the greatest number of citations in a day? How much higher was that number than the greatest number given by the other department? ______________________

12. What is the difference in the median number of citations given by the two departments? ______________________

13. Detective Costello says that it looks like the mean numbers of citations per day given by the two departments are about the same because the range looks similar. Is she correct? Explain.

____

The box plots show the prices of vehicles at a used-car dealership.

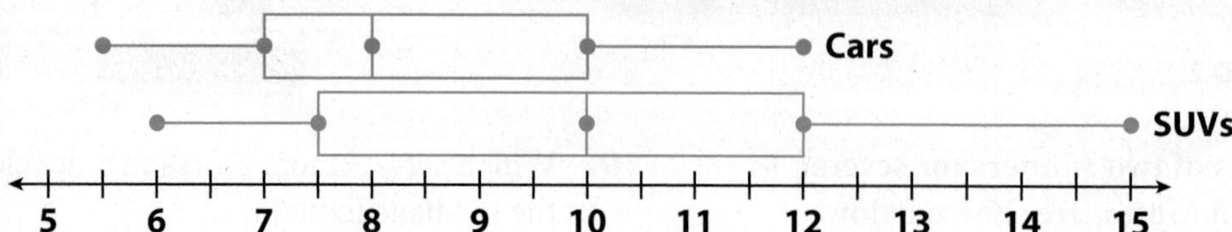

14. Suppose the dealership acquires a used car that it intends to sell for $15,000. Would the price of the car be an outlier? Explain.

____

15. Compare the distribution of SUV prices with the distribution of car prices.

____

____

____

FOCUS ON HIGHER ORDER THINKING

Work Area

Dolly and Willie's scores are shown. Use the box plots for Exercises 16 and 17.

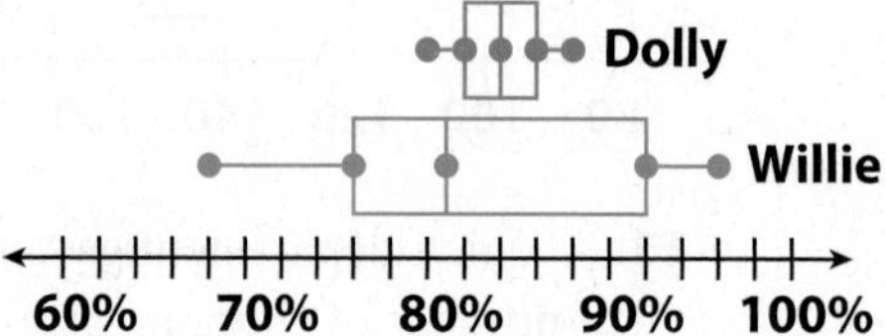

16. Dolly claims that she is the better student. What statistics make Dolly seem like the better student? Explain.

____

____

17. Willie claims that he is the better student. What statistics make Willie seem like the better student? Explain.

____

____

18. **Critical Thinking** Suppose the minimum in a data set is the same as the first quartile. How would this affect a box plot of the data? Explain.

____

____

Ready to Go On?

Personal Math Trainer

Online Practice and Help

13.1 Measures of Center and Spread

1. The high temperatures in degrees Fahrenheit on 11 days were 68, 71, 75, 74, 75, 71, 73, 71, 72, 74, and 79. Find the mean, median, and range.

____

13.2 Data Distributions and Outliers

2. Describe the shape of the distribution. If a data point with a value of 3.0 inches is added, how will the median change?

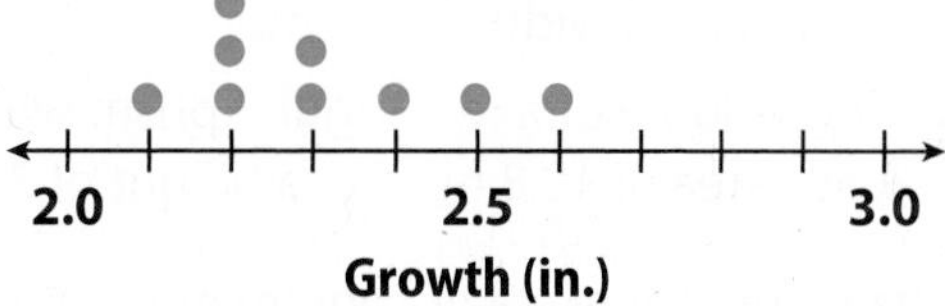

____

13.3 Histograms

3. Use the table showing the average number of hours of sleep for people at different ages to create a histogram.

Age	3–9	10–13	14–18	19–30	31–45	46–50
Sleep (h)	11	10	9	8	7.5	6

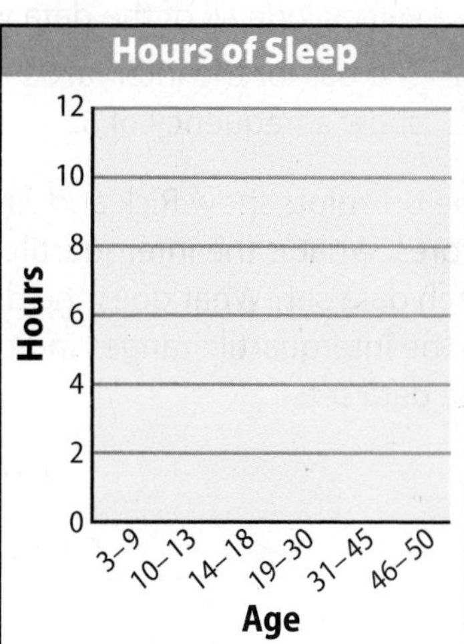

13.4 Box Plots

4. Find the range and the IQR of the data in the box plot.

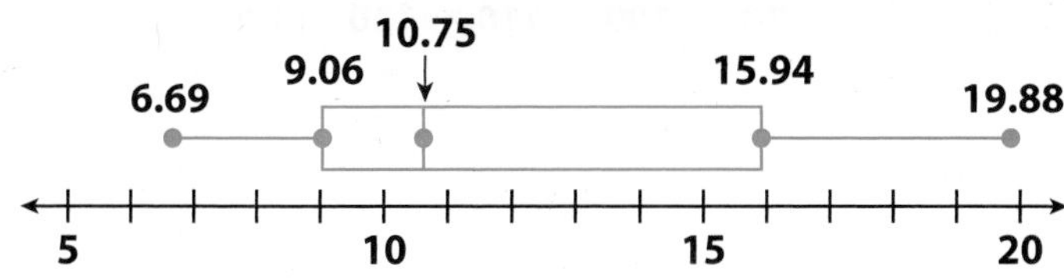

Range = __________ IQR = __________

ESSENTIAL QUESTION

5. How can data sets be displayed and compared, and what statistics can be gathered using the display? _______________

____

____

MODULE 13
MIXED REVIEW

Assessment Readiness

1. Consider each measurement below. Should the measurement be given to 3 significant digits? Select Yes or No for A–C.

   A. The perimeter of a rectangle with a length of 3.6 m and a width of 2.25 m

   ○ Yes ○ No

   B. The area of a rectangle with a length of 4.8 m and a width of 2.2 m

   ○ Yes ○ No

   C. The volume of a rectangular prism with a base area of 10.8 m^2 and a height of 3.45 m ○ Yes ○ No

2. Freya plans to make a histogram of the data set shown in the table.

   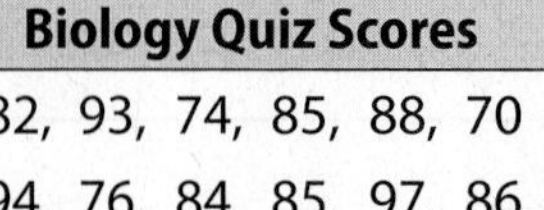

Biology Quiz Scores
82, 93, 74, 85, 88, 70
94, 76, 84, 85, 97, 86

   Choose True or False for each statement.

   A. The intervals 71–80, 81–90, and 91–100 will include all of the data values.

   ○ True ○ False

   B. The bar for the interval 91–100 should show a frequency of 3.

   ○ True ○ False

3. The box plots show Rick and Jin's archery scores. What is the interquartile range of each data set? What does the difference in the interquartile ranges indicate about the data sets?

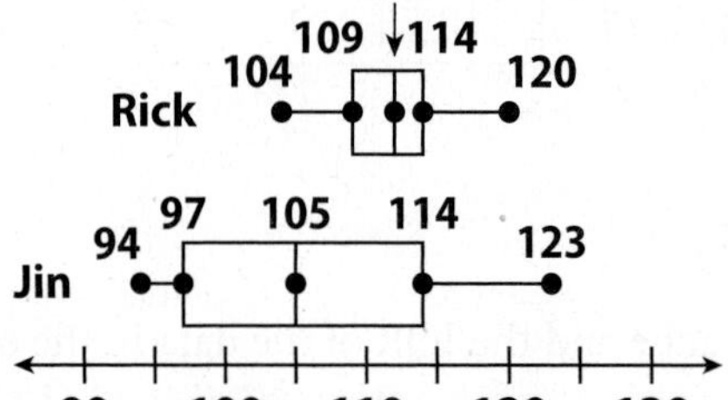

4. Two friends kept track of how much time they spent talking on the phone for seven days. Find the mean and the standard deviation for each friend's data. What do these measures tell you about the data?

   Bob: 35, 15, 12, 5, 40, 10, 2 Kris: 8, 10, 5, 5, 6, 5, 6

UNIT 4

Study Guide Review

MODULE 12 Descriptive Statistics

Key Vocabulary

categorical data *(datos categóricos)*

conditional relative frequency *(frecuencia relativa condicional)*

frequency table *(tabla de frecuencia)*

joint relative frequency *(frecuencia relativa conjunta)*

marginal relative frequency *(frecuencia relativa marginal)*

quantitative data *(datos cuantitativos)*

relative frequency *(frecuencia relativa)*

ESSENTIAL QUESTION

How can you summarize two categories of categorical data and recognize associations and trends between two categories of categorical data?

EXAMPLE 1

Quan asked 100 randomly selected students whether they preferred winter, spring, summer, or fall. He also recorded the gender of each student. The results are shown in the two-way frequency table below. Complete the table.

	Preferred Season				
Gender	**Winter**	**Spring**	**Summer**	**Fall**	**Total**
Girl	8	12	25	5	?
Boy	9	5	30	6	?
Total	?	?	?	?	?

Find the total for each gender by adding the frequencies in each row. Write the row totals in the Total column.

Find the total for each preferred season by adding the frequencies in each column. Write the column totals in the Total row.

Find the grand total, which is the sum of the row totals as well as the sum of the column totals. Write the grand total in the lower-right corner of the table (the intersection of the Total column and the Total row.)

	Preferred Season				
Gender	**Winter**	**Spring**	**Summer**	**Fall**	**Total**
Girl	8	12	25	5	50
Boy	9	5	30	6	50
Total	17	17	55	11	100

EXAMPLE 2

Does gender influence a student's preference for a particular season?

Use the data from Quan's survey to create a two-way relative frequency table. Find the joint relative frequencies and marginal relative frequencies by dividing each number in the frequency table by the grand total. Write the quotients as decimals.

	Preferred Season				
Gender	**Winter**	**Spring**	**Summer**	**Fall**	**Total**
Girl	$\frac{8}{100} = 0.08$	$\frac{12}{100} = 0.12$	$\frac{25}{100} = 0.25$	$\frac{5}{100} = 0.05$	$\frac{50}{100} = 0.5$
Boy	$\frac{9}{100} = 0.09$	$\frac{5}{100} = 0.05$	$\frac{30}{100} = 0.3$	$\frac{6}{100} = 0.06$	$\frac{50}{100} = 0.5$
Total	$\frac{17}{100} = 0.17$	$\frac{17}{100} = 0.17$	$\frac{55}{100} = 0.55$	$\frac{11}{100} = 0.11$	$\frac{100}{100} = 1$

Determine each conditional relative frequency to find what percent of the students who prefer each season are girls. Compare each percentage to the percent of surveyed students who are girls (50%).

Winter: $\frac{8}{17} \approx 0.47 = 47\%$ 8 out of 17 people who prefer winter are girls.

Spring: $\frac{12}{17} \approx 0.71 = 71\%$ 12 out of 17 people who prefer spring are girls.

Summer: $\frac{25}{55} \approx 0.45 = 45\%$ 25 out of 55 people who prefer Summer are girls.

Fall: $\frac{5}{11} \approx 0.45 = 45\%$ 5 out of 11 people who prefer Fall are girls.

All of the percentages are close to 50% except spring. According to the survey, girls are more likely than boys to prefer spring.

EXERCISES

The results of a survey asking 40 students the number of siblings they have are shown in the two-way relative frequency table below. (Lessons 16.1, 16.2)

1. Complete the table.

	Siblings				
Gender	**0**	**1**	**2**	**3+**	**Total**
Freshman	$\frac{6}{40} =$ ____	$\frac{7}{40} =$ ____	$\frac{6}{40} =$ ____	$\frac{3}{40} =$ ____	$\frac{\_\_}{40} =$ ____
Seniors	$\frac{4}{40} =$ ____	$\frac{8}{40} =$ ____	$\frac{4}{40} =$ ____	$\frac{2}{40} =$ ____	$\frac{\_\_}{40} =$ ____
Total	$\frac{\_\_}{40} =$ ____	$\frac{\_\_}{40} =$ ____	$\frac{\_\_}{40} =$ ____	$\frac{\_\_}{40} =$ ____	$\frac{\_\_}{40} =$ ____

2. Analyze the data to decide if freshman are more likely or less likely than seniors to have zero siblings. Explain.

____

____

____

____

____

MODULE 13 Data Displays

ESSENTIAL QUESTION

How can data sets be displayed and compared, and what statistics can be gathered using the display?

Key Vocabulary
- box plot *(gráfica de mediana y rango)*
- dot plot *(diagrama de acumulación)*
- histogram *(histograma)*
- interquartile range *(rango entre cuartiles)*
- mean *(media)*
- median *(mediana)*
- outlier *(valor extremo)*
- quartiles *(cuartil)*
- range *(rango)*
- symmetric *(simétrico)*

EXAMPLE 1

Estimate the mean, median, and standard deviation of the heights from the histogram.

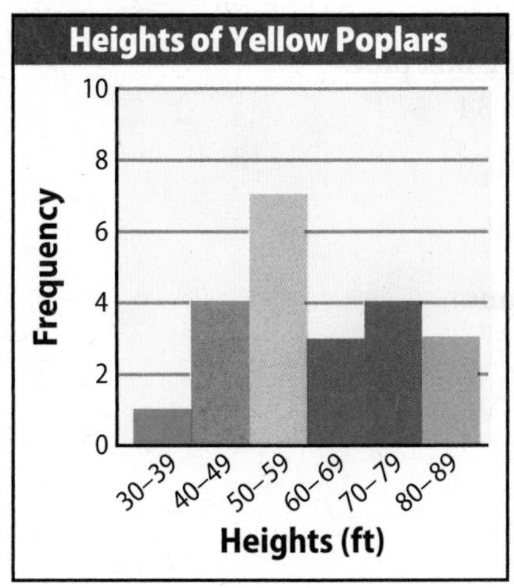

Find the estimated mean.

30–39: 34.5; 1 — Find the midpoint of each range.

40–49: 44.5; 4 — Find the frequency of each range.

50–59: 54.5; 7

60–69: 64.5; 3

70–79: 74.5; 4

80–89: 84.5; 3

$$\frac{34.5 \times 1 + 44.5 \times 4 + 54.5 \times 7 + 64.5 \times 3 + 74.5 \times 4 + 84.5 \times 3}{22} \approx 61$$

Multiply each midpoint by the frequency for that interval, and then find the mean of those values.

Find the estimated standard deviation.

30–39: $(34.5 - 61)^2 = 702.25$ — Subtract the estimated mean from the midpoint of each range and square it.

40–49: $(44.5 - 61)^2 = 272.25$

50–59: $(54.5 - 61)^2 = 42.25$

60–69: $(64.5 - 61)^2 = 12.25$

70–79: $(74.5 - 61)^2 = 182.25$

80–89: $(84.5 - 61)^2 = 552.25$

$$\sqrt{\frac{702.25 \times 1 + 272.25 \times 4 + 42.25 \times 7 + 12.25 \times 3 + 182.25 \times 4 + 552.25 \times 3}{22}} \approx 14$$

Multiply each square by the frequency for the corresponding interval, and then find the mean of the products. Take the square root of the result.

Find the estimated median.

The median value will be the mean of the 11th value and the 12th value in the ordered set. This falls in the 50–59 range.

This interval has seven values. Since the previous intervals together contain five values, the median will be the mean of the 6th and 7th values in the interval 50–59. Estimate the median as the sum of the interval's least value, 50, and $\frac{1}{7}$ of the interval width, 10, multiplied by the mean of 6 and 7

$50 + \left(\frac{1}{7} \times 10 \times \frac{6+7}{2}\right) \approx 59.3$, so 59 is a good estimate for the median.

EXAMPLE 2

The heights of pine trees in a forest are given. Use the data to make a box plot.
18, 13, 22, 25, 27, 32, 35, 60, 36, 16, 26, 24, 31, 46, 38, 29, 23, 19, 42, 34

Order the data from least to greatest.
13, 16, 18, 19, 22, 23, 24, 25, 26, 27, 29, 31, 32, 34, 35, 36, 38, 42, 46, 60

Find the minimum, first quartile, median, third quartile, and maximum.

Remember, you may have to calculate the mean of two numbers when finding the median and the first and third quartiles.

median $= \frac{27 + 29}{2} = 28$

first quartile $= \frac{22 + 23}{2} = 22.5$

third quartile $= \frac{35 + 36}{2} = 35.5$

Plot these points above a number line and draw the box plot.

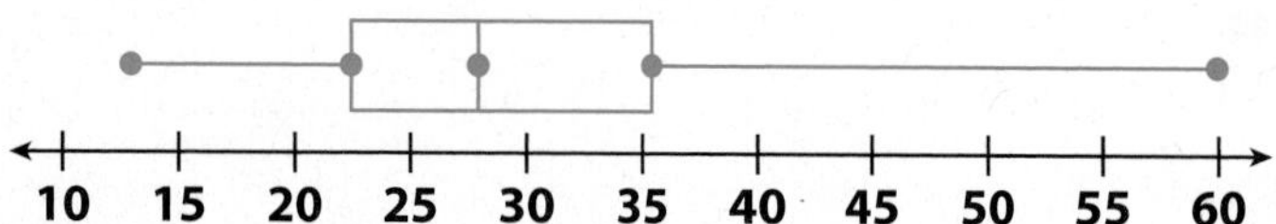

EXAMPLE 3

The frequency table shows the ages of contestants in a spelling bee. Use the data to make a dot plot. Determine the type of distribution and explain what the distribution means.

Make a dot plot.

Age	Number of contestants
11	1
12	2
13	2
14	3
15	4
16	6
17	5

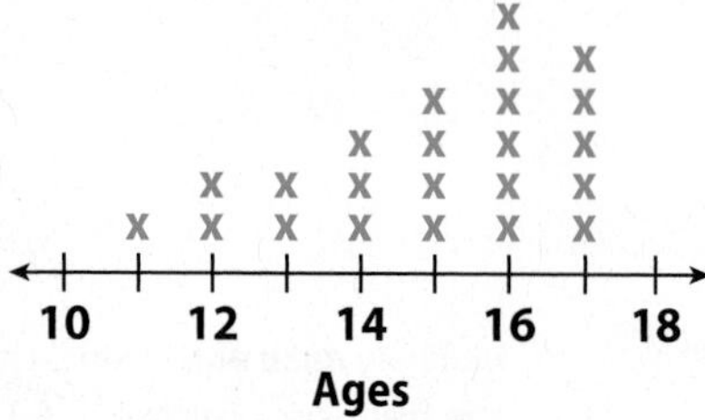

The data distribution is skewed to the left. The median of the data is 15, and the mean is about 15. More than half the contestants are the median age or older.

EXERCISES

The histogram represents the test scores in two different math classes. (Lesson 13.3)

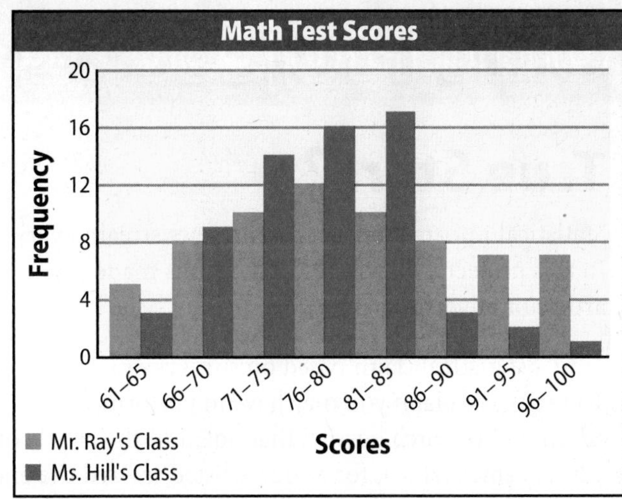

3. Which class has a greater median?

____

4. Which class has a greater standard deviation?

____

The following box plot represents the amount people spend at two different movie theaters. (Lessons 13.1, 13.2, 13.4)

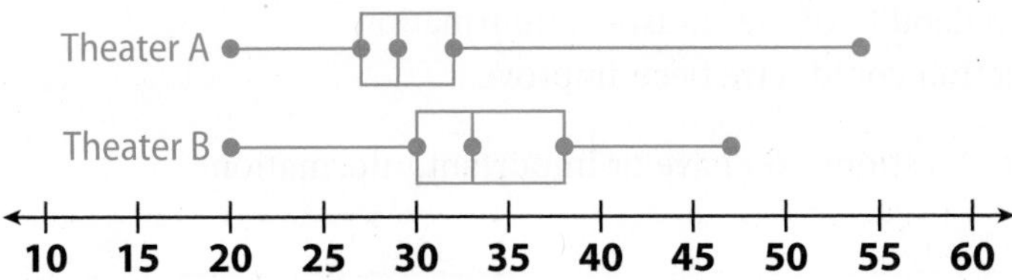

5. Which set has a greater median? ______________________________

6. Which set has a greater interquartile range? ______________________________

7. Is the maximum value for Theater A, 54, an outlier? Explain.

____

____

8. Mr. Hanson made a dot plot of the quiz scores of the 18 students in his history class. Two students received scores of 91, which was the lowest score anybody received. Two students received 96, which was the highest score anybody received. The data distribution was symmetric. Draw a dot plot that could represent the scores. (Lesson 13.2)

Quiz Scores

Unit Project

CA CC S.ID.1, S.ID.5

True Story?

Statistical information floods our news stream every day. In this project, you will research claims made in a recent article or advertisement.

Find a statistical claim based on surveys or experiments. To verify the claim you may have to perform additional research beyond that noted in the article or advertisement. Look for a source listed toward the end of the article or a footnote in the advertisement.

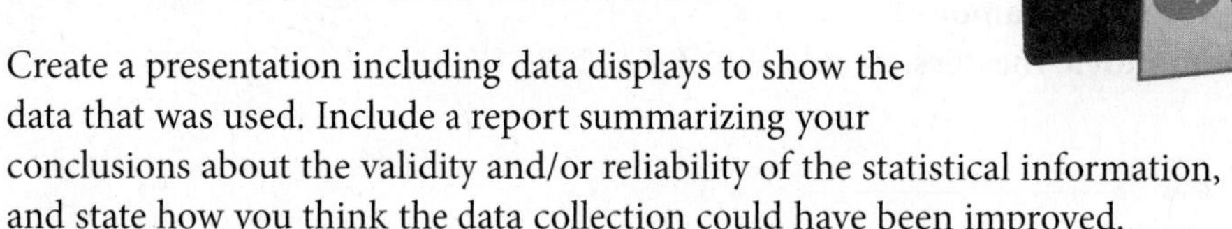

Create a presentation including data displays to show the data that was used. Include a report summarizing your conclusions about the validity and/or reliability of the statistical information, and state how you think the data collection could have been improved.

Use the space below to write down any questions you have or important information from your teacher.

MATH IN CAREERS ACTIVITY

Sports Recruiter The data table shows the 40-yard dash times of two running backs over a week. Find the mean, median, range, and standard deviation for both athletes' times. Which athlete would you choose to be your team's running back? Explain.

	1	2	3	4	5	6	7
Athlete A	4.21	4.18	4.28	4.15	4.19	4.18	4.25
Athlete B	4.15	4.31	4.24	4.41	4.26	4.24	4.31

UNIT 4

MIXED REVIEW

Assessment Readiness

Personal Math Trainer

Online Practice and Help

1. Consider each function. Is it an exponential growth function?

Select Yes or No.

A. $y = 0.3(1 + 0.5)^t$ ○ Yes ○ No

B. $y = 28(0.85)^t$ ○ Yes ○ No

C. $y = \frac{1}{2}(2)^t$ ○ Yes ○ No

2. The two-way frequency table shows the results of a survey of a group of randomly selected students about whether they own a cat or a dog.

	Has a Dog		
Has a Cat	**Yes**	**No**	**Total**
Yes	10	16	26
No	21	33	54
Total	31	49	80

Choose True or False for each statement.

A. Ten students in the survey own both pets. ○ True ○ False

B. The marginal relative frequency of students surveyed who own a cat is 32.5%. ○ True ○ False

C. The joint relative frequency of students surveyed who own a dog but not a cat is about 67.7%. ○ True ○ False

3. The weights of 5 lion cubs in pounds are 19, 22, 21, 23, and 21. Is the standard deviation of the weights more than 1 lb? Explain.

4. Give an example of a set of data that would show a distribution skewed to the right if plotted on a dot plot. Then give an example of a set of data that would show a symmetric distribution. Explain your reasoning.

Performance Tasks

★**5.** The dot plot shows the number of actors in each scene of an episode of a television show. Identify the outlier in the data and determine how it affects the mean and median of the data.

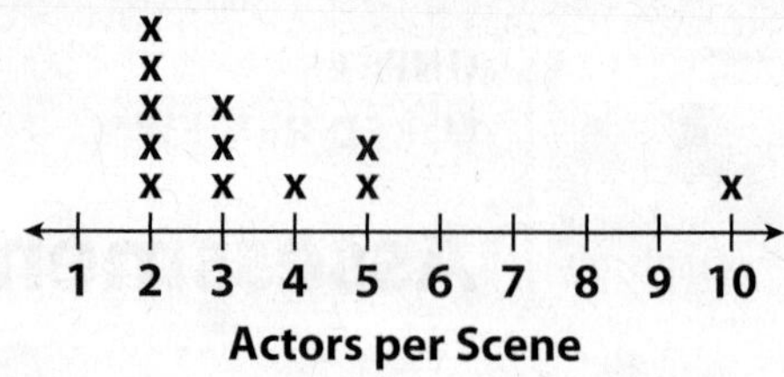

★★**6.** Last month, a car dealership sold 96 cars. Of the 2-door cars, 2 were hybrids and 21 were not hybrids. Of the 4-door cars, 5 were hybrids, and 68 were not hybrids.

a. Complete the two-way frequency table for the data.

b. Create a two-way relative frequency table for the data.

c. For the cars sold at the dealership, is there any association between the number of car doors and whether the car is a hybrid? Justify your reasoning.

	Hybrid		
Doors	**Yes**	**No**	**Total**
2			
4			
Total			

★★★**7.** A college baseball coach is deciding between two pitchers to add to the team. In general, a better pitcher throws more strikes. The table shows the percent of strikes thrown per game by the two pitchers in their last high school baseball season. Which pitcher should the coach add to the team? Justify your answer by using both data displays and statistics.

Acevedo	59, 62, 71, 67, 64, 58, 68, 63, 65, 64, 59, 69
Forbes	54, 67, 51, 61, 52, 54, 52, 60, 64, 51, 60, 62

Transformations, Congruence, and Constructions

MODULE 14
Geometric Terms and Transformations
CA CC G.CO.1, G.CO.2, G.CO.3, G.CO.4, G.CO.5, G.CO.6, G.CO.12

MODULE 15
Transformations and Congruence
CA CC G.CO.5, G.CO.6, G.CO.7, G.CO.8, G.CO.12

MODULE 16
Geometric Constructions
CA CC G.CO.5, G.CO.12, G.CO.13

MATH IN CAREERS

Fashion Designer Fashion designers design a wide variety of items, including clothing, textiles, and accessories. In many cases, they use transformations of geometric shapes to create new designs to use on the textiles. Fashion designers may have degrees in art or fine arts, or they may have done an apprenticeship with another designer.

If you're interested in a career in fashion design, you should study these mathematical subjects:

- Algebra
- Geometry

Research other careers that require the use of algebra and geometry.

ACTIVITY At the end of the unit, check out how **fashion designers** use math.

Unit Project Preview

Loco for Logos

The Unit Project at the end of this unit involves creating a company logo using symmetry, constructions, and transformations. To successfully complete the Unit Project you'll need to master these skills:

- Construct lines and circles with certain properties.
- Recognize translations, reflections, and rotations.
- Describe the symmetry of a figure.

1. Describe any transformations you see in the figure.

2. Could you draw a line through the figure so that each half is a mirror image of the other? Explain.

3. The petal shapes are not circles, but circles were used to create them. How might this have been accomplished?

Tracking Your Learning Progression

This unit addresses important California Common Core Standards related to analyzing using distance, angle, and congruence, and recognizing and applying transformations in the plane.

Domain **G.CO** Congruence
Cluster Experiment with transformations in the plane.

Domain **G.CO** Congruence
Cluster Understand congruence in terms of rigid motions.

Domain **G.CO** Congruence
Cluster Make geometric constructions.

Geometric Terms and Transformations

MODULE 14

ESSENTIAL QUESTION

What are the similarities and differences among transformations that are rigid motions?

CALIFORNIA COMMON CORE

LESSON 14.1
Geometric Terms

CA CC G.CO.1, G.CO.12

LESSON 14.2
Introduction to Transformations

CA CC G.CO.2, G.CO.5

LESSON 14.3
Translations

CA CC G.CO.4, G.CO.2, G.CO.5

LESSON 14.4
Reflections

CA CC G.CO.4, G.CO.2, G.CO.3, G.CO.5

LESSON 14.5
Rotations

CA CC G.CO.4, G.CO.2, G.CO.3, G.CO.5

LESSON 14.6
Combining Transformations

CA CC G.CO.6, G.CO.2, G.CO.5

my.hrw.com

Real-World Video

People who sew clothes cut out many separate pieces to make a garment. They have to be careful about rotating or flipping pattern pieces when using printed fabric or fabric with a nap, like corduroy. Otherwise, the pieces may not match.

GO DIGITAL
my.hrw.com

my.hrw.com

Go digital with your write-in student edition, accessible on any device.

Math On the Spot

Scan with your smart phone to jump directly to the online edition, video tutor, and more.

Animated Math

Interactively explore key concepts to see how math works.

Personal Math Trainer

Get immediate feedback and help as you work through practice sets.

Are YOU Ready?

Complete these exercises to review skills you will need for this module.

Function Tables

EXAMPLE Generate ordered pairs for the function $f(x) = -x + 5$ for $x = -2, -1, 0, 1$ and 2.

x	$f(x) = -x + 5$	$f(x)$
−2	$f(x) = -(-2) + 5 = 2 + 5 = 7$	7
−1	$f(x) = -(-1) + 5 = 1 + 5 = 6$	6
0	$f(x) = -(0) + 5 = 0 + 5 = 5$	5
1	$f(x) = -(1) + 5 = -1 + 5 = 4$	4
2	$f(x) = -(2) + 5 = -2 + 5 = 3$	3

x	$f(x)$
−2	7
−1	6
0	5
1	4
2	3

Generate ordered pairs for each function for $x = -2, -1, 0, 1$ and 2.

1. $f(x) = x - 8$

x	$f(x)$
−2	
−1	
0	
1	
2	

2. $f(x) = -x - 1$

x	$f(x)$
−2	
−1	
0	
1	
2	

3. $f(x) = 4x - 6$

x	$f(x)$
−2	
−1	
0	
1	
2	

4. $f(x) = -2x + 3$

x	$f(x)$
−2	
−1	
0	
1	
2	

Ordered Pairs

EXAMPLE Graph the point $A(-2, -6)$ on the coordinate plane.

$A(-2, -6)$
Start at (0, 0).
Move 2 units to the left. *The x-coordinate is −2.*
Move 6 units down. *The y-coordinate is −6.*

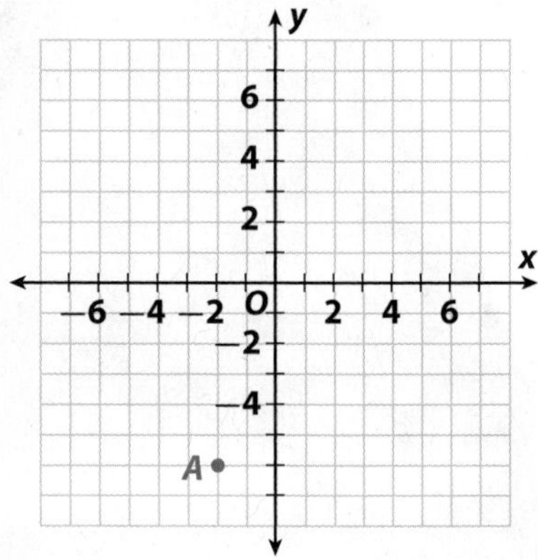

Graph each point on the coordinate plane.

5. $B(3, 4)$

6. $C(1, -5)$

7. $D(-6, -2)$

8. $E(-3, 4)$

9. $F(-5, 1)$

10. $G(4, -3)$

Reading Start-Up

Visualize Vocabulary

Use the Review words to complete the summary triangle.

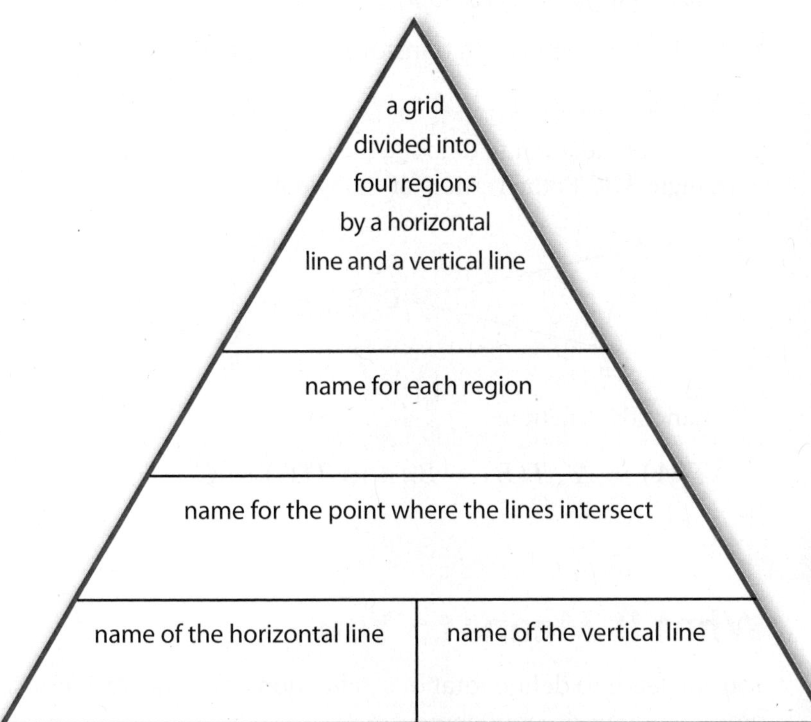

Vocabulary

Review Words

✔ coordinate plane *(plano cartesiano)*
✔ origin *(origen)*
✔ quadrant *(cuadrante)*
✔ *x*-axis *(eje x)*
✔ *y*-axis *(eje y)*

Preview Words

angle
endpoint
image
line
plane
point
postulate
preimage
reflection
rigid motion
rotation
segment
symmetry
transformation
translation
vertex
vector

Understand Vocabulary

To become familiar with some of the vocabulary terms in the module, consider the following. You may refer to the module or the glossary.

1. In geometry, a transformation is a function for which inputs are ______________ in the plane and outputs are other ______________ in the plane.

2. A ______________ produces a mirror image of the original figure.

Active Reading

Key-Term Fold Before beginning the module, create a Key-Term Fold to help you organize what you learn. Write a vocabulary term on each tab. Write its definition and an example underneath.

GETTING READY FOR

Geometric Terms and Transformations

Understanding the standards and the vocabulary terms in the standards will help you know exactly what you are expected to learn in this module.

G.CO.2

Represent transformations in the plane using, e.g., transparencies and geometry software; describe transformations as functions that take points in the plane as inputs and give other points as outputs. Compare transformations that preserve distance and angle to those that do not (e.g., translation versus horizontal stretch).

What It Means to You

You will learn to think of a transformation as a function.

EXAMPLE G.CO.2

Use function notation to describe the translation that maps the vertices of triangle ABC to the vertices of triangle $A'B'C'$.

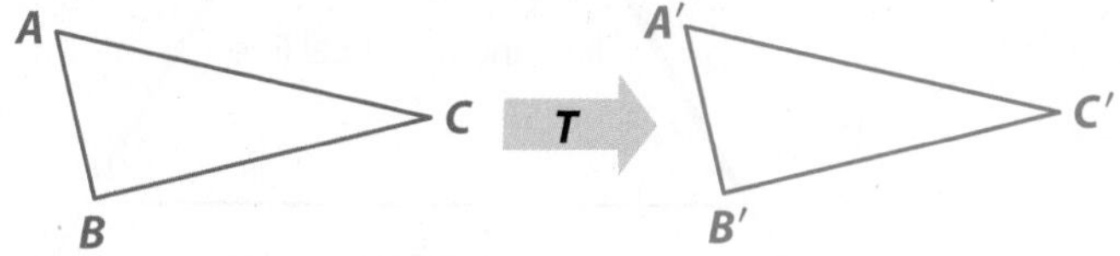

Function notation:

$T(A) = A'$, $T(B) = B'$, and $T(C) = C'$

CA CC G.CO.4

Develop definitions of rotations, reflections, and translations in terms of angles, circles, perpendicular lines, parallel lines, and line segments.

Key Vocabulary

rotation *(rotación)*
A transformation that turns a figure by a specified angle about a point called the center of rotation.

reflection *(reflexión)*
A transformation that flips a figure across a line, called the line of reflection, to create a mirror image.

translation *(traslación)*
A transformation that slides every point of a figure along a given vector.

What It Means to You

You will learn to define rotations, reflections, and translations using precise geometric language.

EXAMPLE G.CO.4

These images illustrate the key features of each transformation.

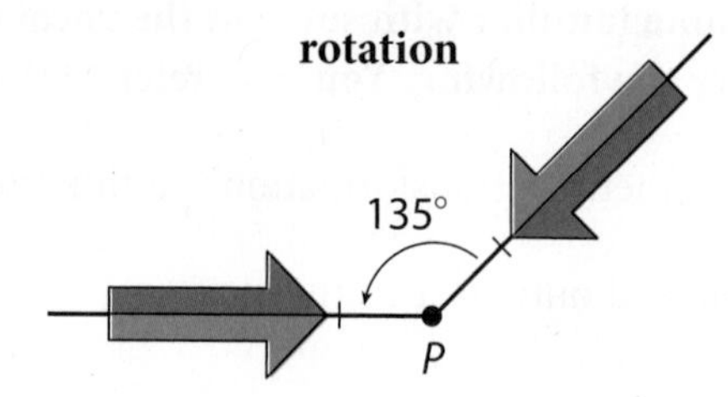

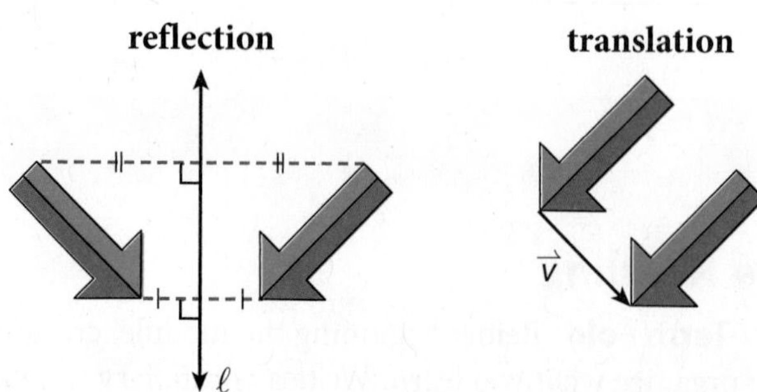

Visit my.hrw.com to see all CA Common Core Standards explained.

my.hrw.com

LESSON

14.1 Geometric Terms

CA CC G.CO.1

Know precise definitions of angle, circle, perpendicular line, parallel line, and line segment, based on undefined notions of point, line, distance along a line, and distance around a circular arc. *Also G.CO.12*

ESSENTIAL QUESTION

How do you describe basic geometric figures and relationships?

EXPLORE ACTIVITY

Relationships Between Lines and Planes

In geometry, the terms *point, line,* and *plane* are undefined terms. Although they do not have formal definitions, they can be described as shown in the table.

Undefined Term	Geometric Figure	Ways to Name the Figure
A **point** is a specific location. It has no dimension and is represented by a dot.	• *P*	point *P*
A **line** is a connected straight path. It has no thickness and it continues forever in both directions.	*A* *B* ℓ	line ℓ, line *AB*, line *BA*, $\overleftrightarrow{AB}$, or $\overleftrightarrow{BA}$
A **plane** is a flat surface. It has no thickness and it extends forever.	*X* • *Z* • $\Re$ *Y* •	plane $\Re$ or plane *XYZ*

Think about the relationships that exist between points, lines, and planes in your classroom. Tell which figure fits each description.

A Through any two points there is a unique __________, and the points are *collinear*. Another way to say this is that two points *determine* a __________.

B Through any three points that are not all on the same line there is a unique __________. Another way to say this is that three non-collinear points *determine* a __________.

C **Parallel lines** are lines in the same plane that do not intersect. The intersection of two lines in the same plane that are *not* parallel is a __________.

D **Parallel planes** are planes that do not intersect. The intersection of two planes that are *not* parallel is a __________.

EXPLORE ACTIVITY *(cont'd)*

REFLECT

1. What are the three possible relationships between a line and a plane?

____

____

2. Counterexamples A student stated that three points always determine three lines, with each line passing through two of the points. Give a counterexample to show that the student's statement is incorrect.

____

____

3. Communicate Mathematical Ideas Are any two lines either parallel lines or intersecting lines? Explain.

____

____

____

Constructing Line Segments

In geometry, the word *between* is an undefined term, but its meaning is understood from its use in everyday language. You can use undefined terms as building blocks to write definitions, as shown in the table.

Definition	Geometric Figure	Ways to Name the Figure
A **line segment** (or *segment*) is a portion of a line consisting of two points (called **endpoints**) and all points between them.	C •———• D	segment *CD*, segment *DC*, $\overline{CD}$, or $\overline{DC}$

A **distance along a line** is undefined until a linear unit, such as 1 inch or 1 centimeter, is chosen. You can use a ruler to find the distance between two points on a line. The distance is the absolute value of the difference of the numbers on the ruler that correspond to the two points. This distance is the **length** of the segment determined by the points.

In the figure, the length of $\overline{RS}$, written RS, is the distance between R and S.

$RS = |4 - 1| = |3| = 3$ cm

In the Explore Activity, you observed that two points determine a unique line. This fact is taken to be true without proof. A statement that is accepted as true without proof is a **postulate** (or *axiom*). The following postulate ties together the ideas of betweenness, distance, and line segments.

Segment Addition Postulate

If B is between A and C, then $AB + BC = AC$.

EXAMPLE 1

CA CC G.CO.12

Use a compass and straightedge to construct a segment whose length is $AB + CD$.

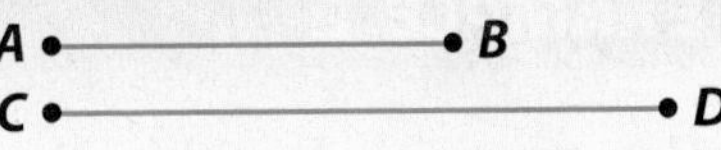

STEP 1 Use the straightedge to draw a line segment that is longer than $AB + CD$. Choose an endpoint of the segment and label it X.

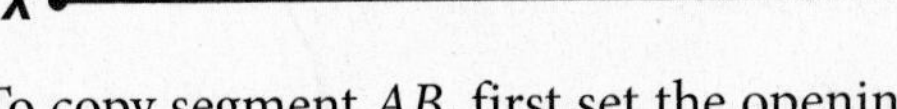

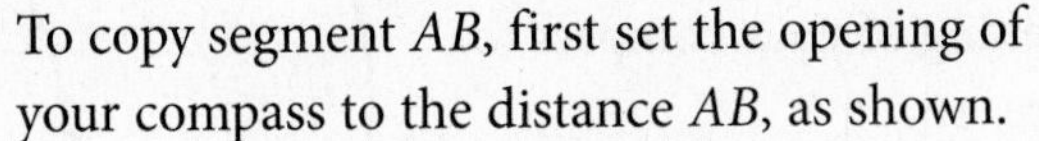

STEP 2 To copy segment AB, first set the opening of your compass to the distance AB, as shown.

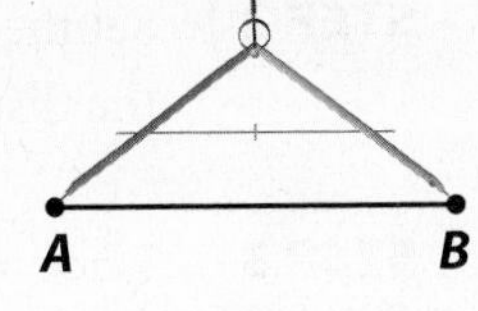

STEP 3 Place the point of the compass on X. Make a small arc that intersects the line segment. Label the point Y where the arc intersects the segment.

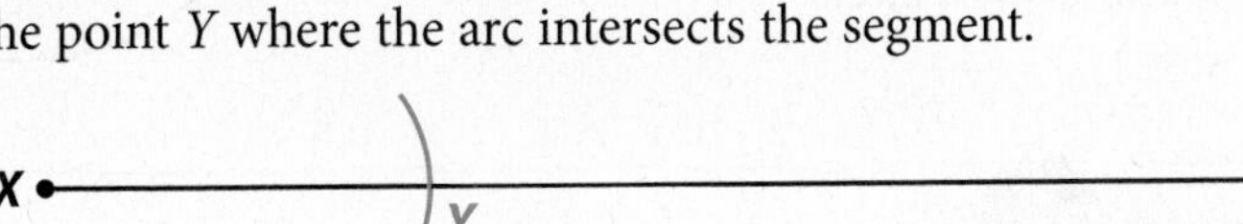

Math Talk
Mathematical Practices
How do you know $\overline{XZ}$ has the required length?

STEP 4 To copy segment CD, set the opening of your compass to the distance CD. Place the point of the compass on Y. Make a small arc that intersects the line segment. Label the point Z where the arc intersects the segment.

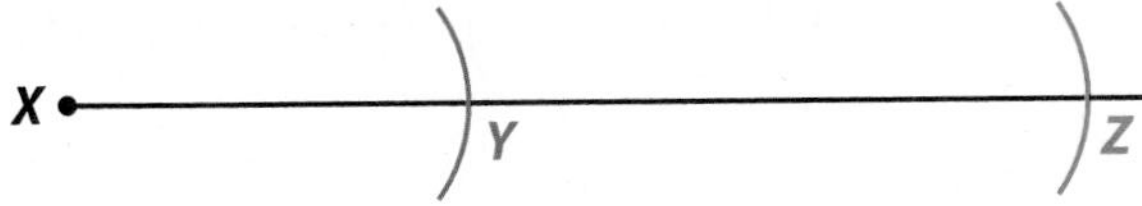

$\overline{XZ}$ is the required line segment.

YOUR TURN

4. Use a compass and straightedge to construct a segment whose length is $CD - AB$.

Constructing Circles

A **circle** is the set of all points in a plane that are a fixed distance from a point called the **center** of the circle.

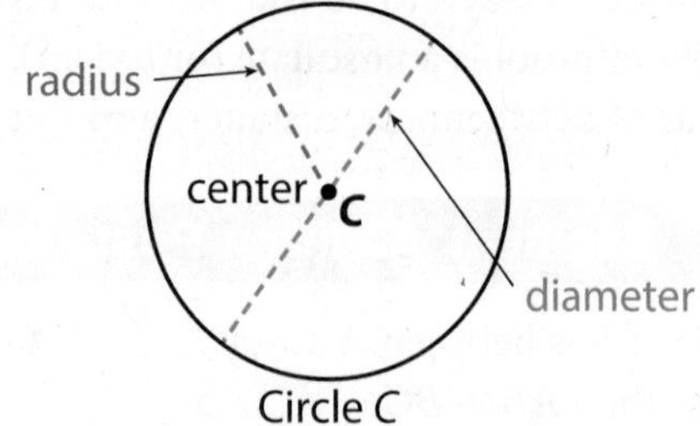

A **radius** is a line segment whose endpoints are the center of the circle and a point on the circle. The length of such a segment is also called the radius.

A **diameter** is a line segment that has endpoints on the circle and that passes through the center. The length of such a segment is also called the diameter.

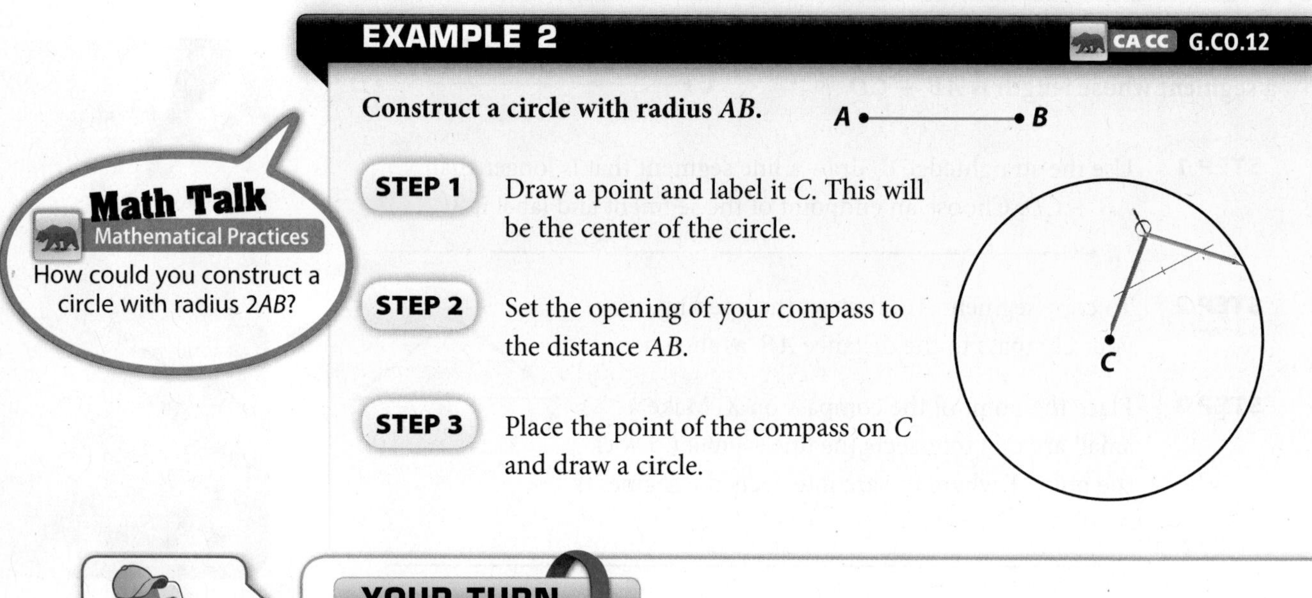

Construct a circle with radius *AB*.

STEP 1 Draw a point and label it *C*. This will be the center of the circle.

STEP 2 Set the opening of your compass to the distance *AB*.

STEP 3 Place the point of the compass on *C* and draw a circle.

YOUR TURN

5. Construct a circle with radius *MN*.

Angle Measures

A **ray** is a portion of a line that starts at a point (the *endpoint*) and continues forever in one direction.

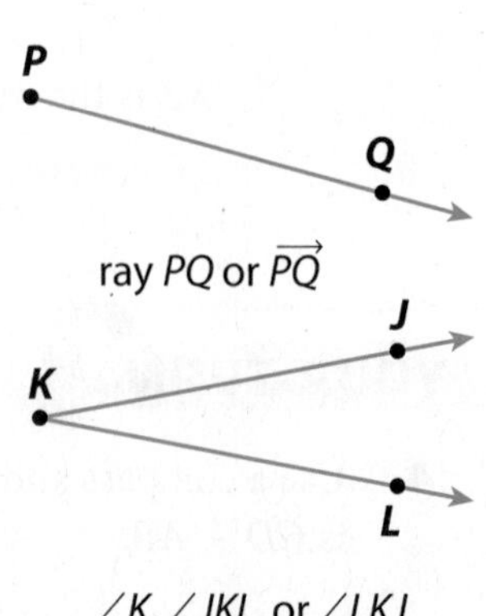

An **angle** is a figure formed by two rays with the same endpoint. The common endpoint is the **vertex** of the angle. The rays are the **sides** of the angle.

Angles are often measured in *degrees*. There are 360° in a circle, so one **degree** is $\frac{1}{360}$ of a circle. You write $m\angle A$ for the measure of $\angle A$. An angle can have a measure from 0° to 180°. The table that follows shows some useful angle measures.

Right Angle	Straight Angle	A Complete Rotation
m∠A = 90°	m∠A = 180°	m∠A = 360°

Perpendicular lines are lines that intersect at right angles.

Adjacent angles are angles in the same plane that have a common vertex and a common side but no common interior points. The Angle Addition Postulate describes an important fact about adjacent angles.

Angle Addition Postulate

If D is in the interior of $\angle ABC$, then $m\angle ABD + m\angle DBC = m\angle ABC$.

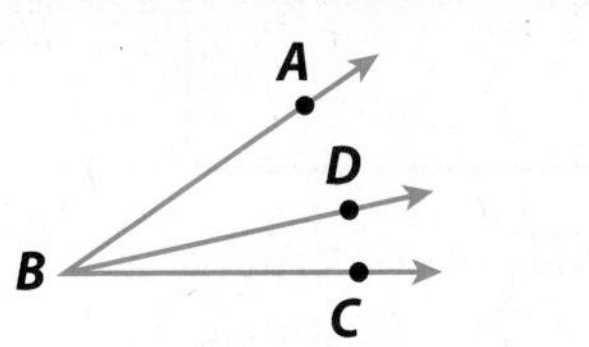

EXAMPLE 3

CA CC G.CO.1

Use the figure to solve each problem.

A Find the measure of $\angle SZU$.

By the Angle Addition Postulate,

$m\angle SZU = m\angle SZT + m\angle TZU$

$= 62° + 28°$

$= 90°$

$m\angle SZU = 90°$

B Find a pair of perpendicular lines.

Since $m\angle SZU = 90°$, $\overleftrightarrow{SW}$ and $\overleftrightarrow{YU}$ intersect at right angles.

The perpendicular lines in the figure are $\overleftrightarrow{SW}$ and $\overleftrightarrow{YU}$.

In diagrams, assume that points that appear collinear are collinear unless labeled otherwise.

YOUR TURN

Use the above figure to solve each problem.

6. The straight angles in the figure are ________, ________, and ________.

7. $m\angle VZU =$ ____________

8. $\angle RZX$ **is / is not** a right angle.

Personal Math Trainer
Online Practice and Help
my.hrw.com

Guided Practice

Complete each statement. (Explore Activity)

1. Two intersecting lines determine a unique [line / plane].

2. Two parallel lines determine a unique [line / plane].

3. Use a compass and straightedge to construct a segment whose length is $RS + TU$. (Example 1)

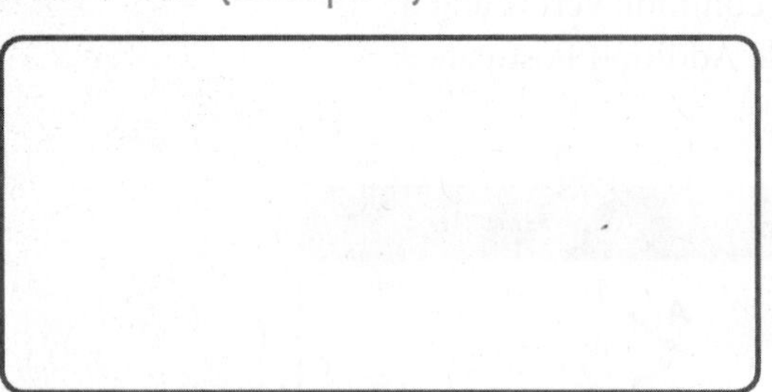

4. Use a compass and straightedge to construct a segment whose length is $RS - TU$. (Example 1)

5. Construct a circle with radius TU. (Example 2)

Use the figure to complete each statement. (Example 3)

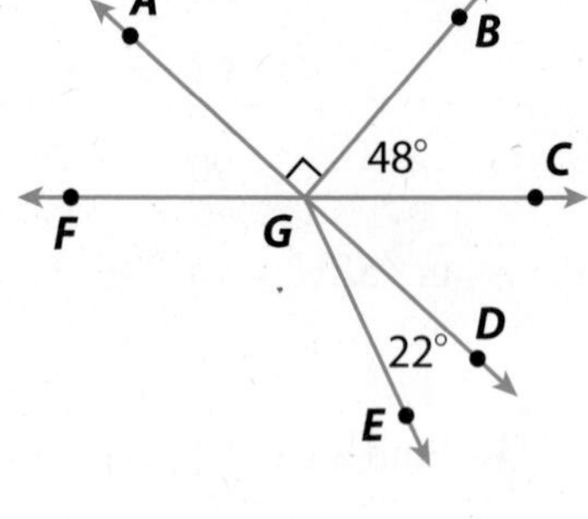

6. $m\angle AGC =$ ________

$m\angle AGC =$ [ ] + [ ] Angle Addition Postulate

$=$ [ ] + [ ] Substitute angle measures.

$=$ [ ] Add.

7. The right angles in the figure are __________ and __________.

ESSENTIAL QUESTION CHECK-IN

8. When you use a point to divide a segment into two shorter segments or a ray to divide an angle into two adjacent angles, how are the parts related to the whole?

____

____

____

Name ______________________ Class ______________________ Date ______________________

14.1 Independent Practice

9. Lines ℓ and m are parallel. Line p intersects line ℓ. Can you conclude that line p also intersects line m? Explain your reasoning and provide one or more sketches in the space below to illustrate your answer.

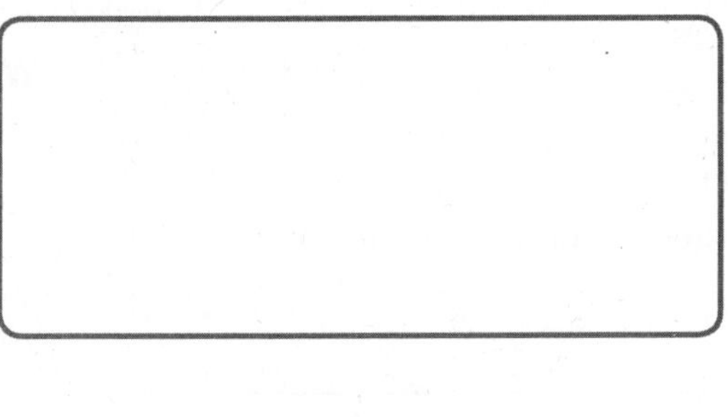

____

____

____

____

10. **Look for a Pattern** Two points determine one line segment. Three collinear points determine three line segments.

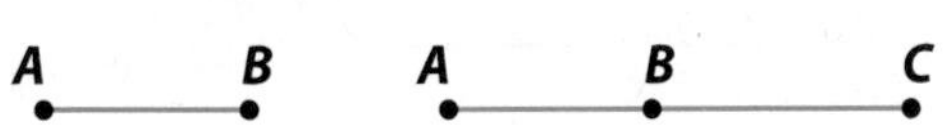

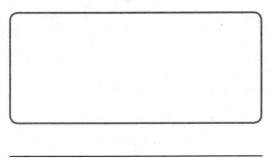

1 segment: $\overline{AB}$ 3 segments: $\overline{AB}$, $\overline{BC}$, $\overline{AC}$

a. Complete the table.

Collinear Points	2	3	4	5
Line Segments	1	3		

b. Describe any patterns in the table.

____

____

____

c. Predict the number of segments that are determined by 8 collinear points.

____

11. Construct two circles that intersect at exactly one point so that one circle has radius PQ and the other circle has radius RS.

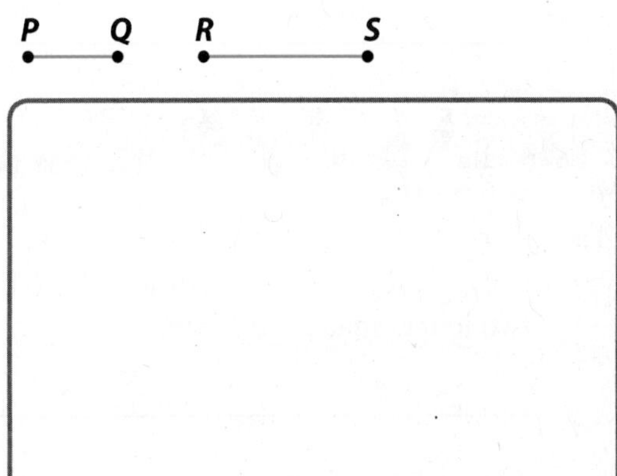

12. The distance from Belleville to Canton is 2 km more than twice the distance from Canton to Donner. What is the distance from Belleville to Donner? Explain.

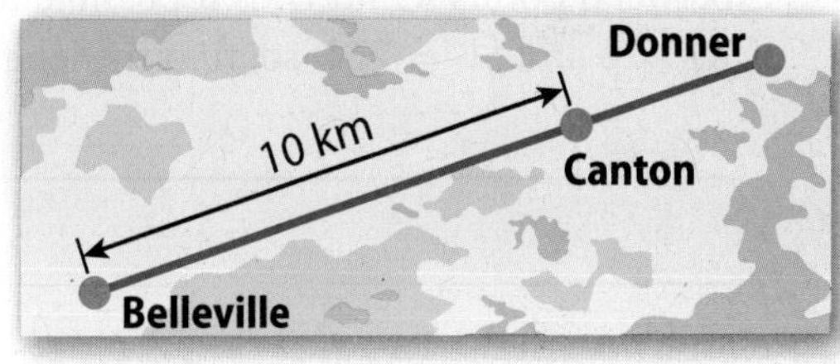

____

____

13. In the figure, $m\angle JKL = 120°$. Find the measure of each of the adjacent angles. Is either angle a right angle? Why or why not?

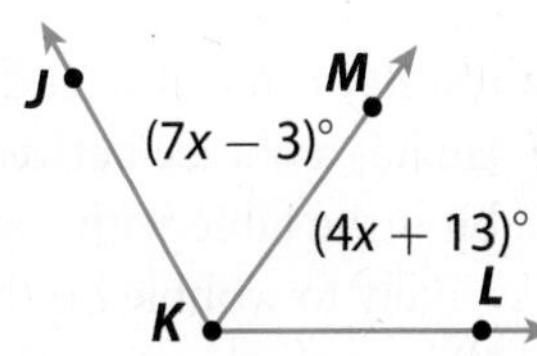

____

____

14. What is the measure of the angle formed by the hands of a clock when it is 12:20? Explain how you found your answer.

H.O.T. **FOCUS ON HIGHER ORDER THINKING**

Work Area

15. Communicate Mathematical Ideas You can use two letters to name a line ($\overleftrightarrow{AB}$), a segment ($\overline{AB}$), or a ray ($\overrightarrow{AB}$). Does the order in which you write the two letters matter? Explain.

16. Critical Thinking Points *R*, *S*, *T*, and *U* are collinear, and points *S* and *T* lie between points *R* and *U*. Is it possible to find the length of $\overline{RU}$ if you know that $RT = 6$ and $SU = 7$? If so, find the length. If not, explain why not.

17. Draw Conclusions Given that $\angle ABC$ and $\angle CBD$ are both right angles and given that the angles are adjacent, what must be true about $\angle ABD$? Explain your reasoning.

18. Critique Reasoning Xavier is buying a table for a patio with an uneven surface. He has a choice between a table with three legs and a table with four legs. He buys the table with four legs and states that the extra leg will make the table less likely to wobble on the patio. Do you agree? Explain.

LESSON 14.2

Introduction to Transformations

CA CC G.CO.2

For the full text of this standard, see the table beginning on page CA2. *Also G.CO.5*

ESSENTIAL QUESTION

How can you recognize a transformation that is a rigid motion?

EXPLORE ACTIVITY

Exploring Transformations

A **transformation** is a change in the position, shape, or size of a figure. The original figure is the **preimage**. The transformed figure is the **image**.

Images are labeled using the *prime symbol*. You read A' as *A prime*, A'' as *A double prime*, and so on.

Use tracing paper or a transparency to help you draw each transformation. Label the image $A'B'C'D'$. Include E and its image.

A A *slide*, or *translation*, moves points of a figure the same distance in the same direction.

Translate *ABCD* 2 units right and 5 units down.

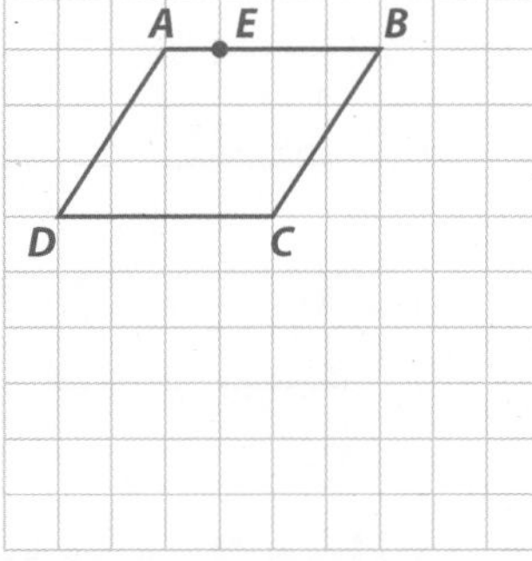

B A *flip*, or *reflection*, moves points of a figure by flipping them over a line called the *line of reflection* to create a mirror image.

Reflect *ABCD* across line *m*.

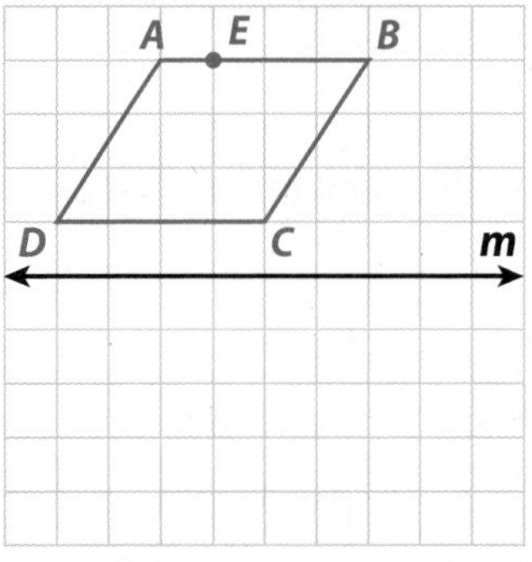

C A *turn*, or *rotation*, turns points of a figure around a point called the *center of rotation*.

Rotate *ABCD* 90° clockwise around point *P*.

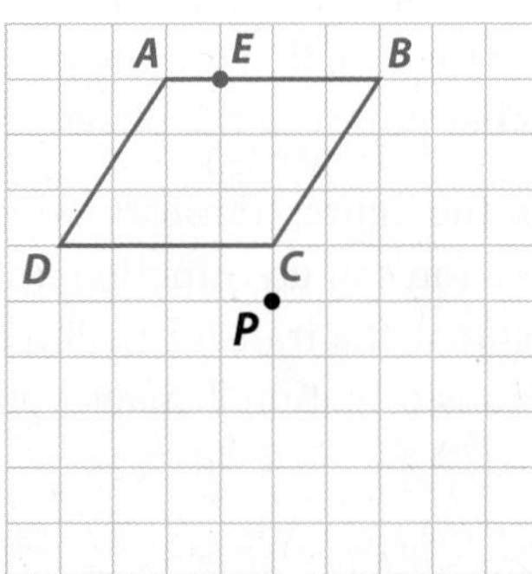

EXPLORE ACTIVITY *(cont'd)*

REFLECT

1. **Make a Conjecture** For each transformation in the Explore Activity, use a ruler to measure the length of $\overline{AB}$ and the length of $\overline{A'B'}$. Use a protractor to measure $\angle D$ and $\angle D'$. What does this suggest about translations, reflections, and rotations?

2. If two lines or line segments are parallel, do they remain parallel after a translation, reflection, or rotation? Justify your response.

3. **Communicate Mathematical Ideas** In each preimage, how are points A, E, and B related? Is this relationship preserved by the transformation? Justify your response.

Drawing Transformations in a Coordinate Plane

A **rigid motion** is a transformation that changes the position of a figure without changing the size or shape of the figure.

Properties of Rigid Motions

Rigid motions preserve the following characteristics of a figure.

- length
- angle measure
- parallel lines
- betweenness
- collinearity

You can think of a transformation as a function. The inputs for the function are the points in the plane; the outputs are other points in the plane.

In the figure, transformation T moves point A to point A'. You can use function notation to write $T(A) = A'$. Note that a transformation is sometimes called a *mapping*. Transformation T maps point A to point A'.

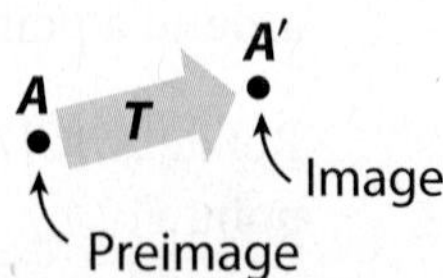

Transformations in a coordinate plane are sometimes represented using coordinates. For example, a translation 2 units right and 5 units down might be written as $(x, y) \rightarrow (x + 2, y - 5)$.

EXAMPLE 1

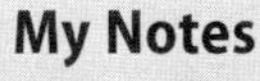

G.CO.2, G.CO.5

Draw the image of $\triangle ABC$ under the given transformation. Tell whether the transformation is a rigid motion. If so, identify the transformation. If not, explain why not.

A $(x, y) \rightarrow (x + 4, y - 1)$

STEP 1 Use the rule to find the coordinates of the vertices of the image.

$$A(-3, 3) \rightarrow A'(-3 + 4, 3 - 1) = A'(1, 2)$$

$$B(-3, -3) \rightarrow B'(-3 + 4, -3 - 1) = B'(1, -4)$$

$$C(-1, -3) \rightarrow C'(-1 + 4, -3 - 1) = C'(3, -4)$$

STEP 2 Draw the image.

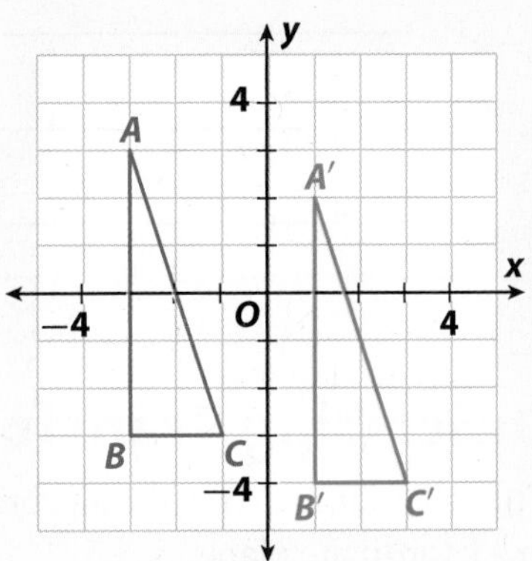

STEP 3 Compare the preimage and the image.

The transformation preserves lengths and angle measures, so it is a rigid motion. The transformation is a translation.

B $(x, y) \rightarrow (2x, 4y)$

STEP 1 Use the rule to find the coordinates of the vertices of the image.

$$A(0, 1) \rightarrow A'(2 \cdot 0, 4 \cdot 1) = A'(0, 4)$$

$$B(-1, -1) \rightarrow B'(2 \cdot (-1), 4 \cdot (-1)) = B'(-2, -4)$$

$$C(1, -1) \rightarrow C'(2 \cdot 1, 4 \cdot (-1)) = C'(2, -4)$$

STEP 2 Draw the image.

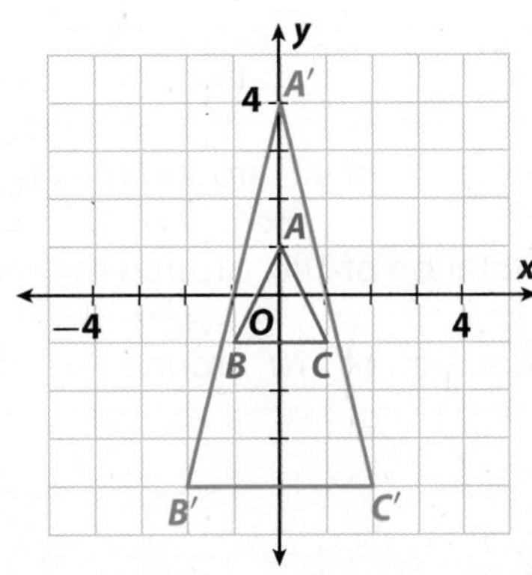

STEP 3 Compare the preimage and the image.

The transformation is not a rigid motion because it does not preserve length or angle measure.

My Notes

Describe the transformation $(x, y) \rightarrow (0, 0)$. Is it a rigid motion? Why or why not?

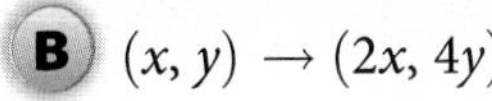

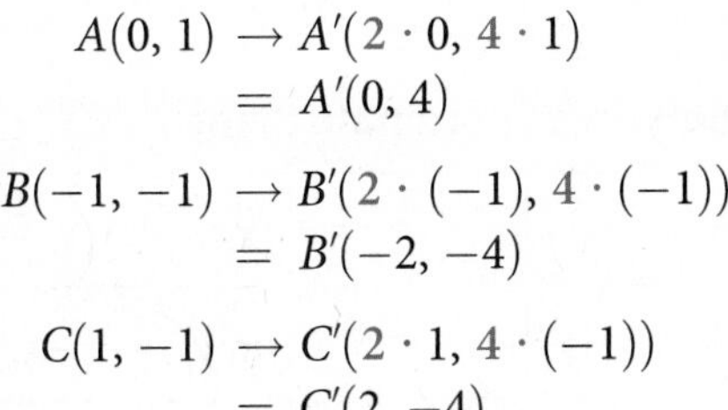

YOUR TURN

Draw the image of $\triangle ABC$ under the given transformation. Tell whether the transformation is a rigid motion. If so, identify the transformation. If not, explain why not.

4. $(x, y) \rightarrow (-x, y)$

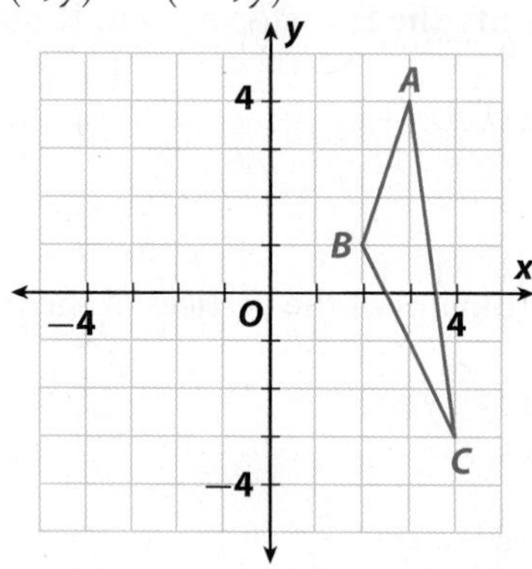

5. $(x, y) \rightarrow (x + 2, 3y)$

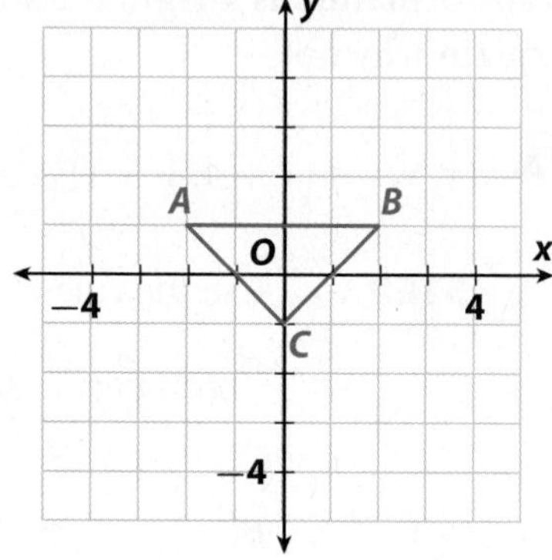

Describing Transformations Using Coordinates

The table summarizes the algebraic rules for translations, reflections, and rotations in a coordinate plane.

Translations in a Coordinate Plane	
Translation by a units horizontally and b units vertically	$(x, y) \rightarrow (x + a, y + b)$
Reflections in a Coordinate Plane	
Reflection across the x-axis	$(x, y) \rightarrow (x, -y)$
Reflection across the y-axis	$(x, y) \rightarrow (-x, y)$
Rotations in a Coordinate Plane (Counterclockwise)	
Rotation of 90° around the origin	$(x, y) \rightarrow (-y, x)$
Rotation of 180° around the origin	$(x, y) \rightarrow (-x, -y)$
Rotation of 270° around the origin	$(x, y) \rightarrow (y, -x)$

Unless otherwise specified, you should assume all rotations are in the counterclockwise direction.

EXAMPLE 2

CA CC G.CO.5

Identify the transformation that maps each figure to its image. Then give an algebraic rule for the transformation.

A

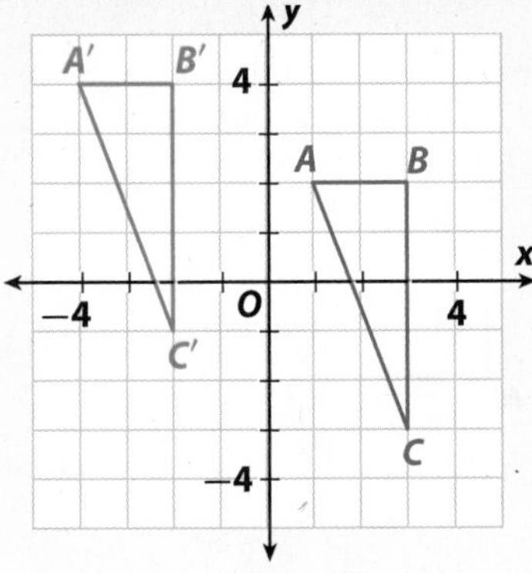

All points of the figure move the same distance in the same direction, so the transformation is a translation.

The figure is translated 5 units left, so $a = -5$.

The figure is also translated 2 units up, so $b = 2$.

The rule for the translation is $(x, y) \rightarrow (x - 5, y + 2)$.

Math Talk

Mathematical Practices

How do you know the transformation in Example 2A is not a reflection?

B

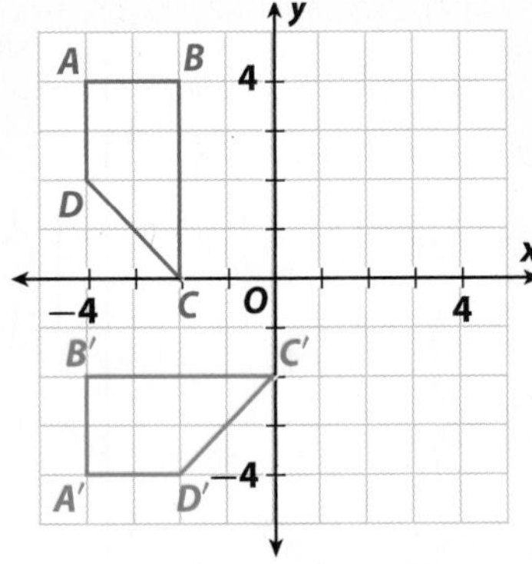

All points of the figure turn around a point, so the transformation is a rotation.

The figure is rotated 90° counterclockwise around the origin.

The rule for the rotation is $(x, y) \rightarrow (-y, x)$.

YOUR TURN

Identify the transformation that maps each figure to its image. Then give an algebraic rule for the transformation.

6.

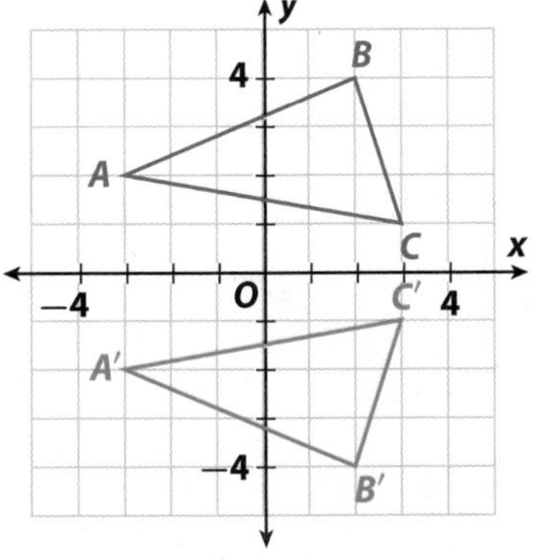

____

____

____

7.

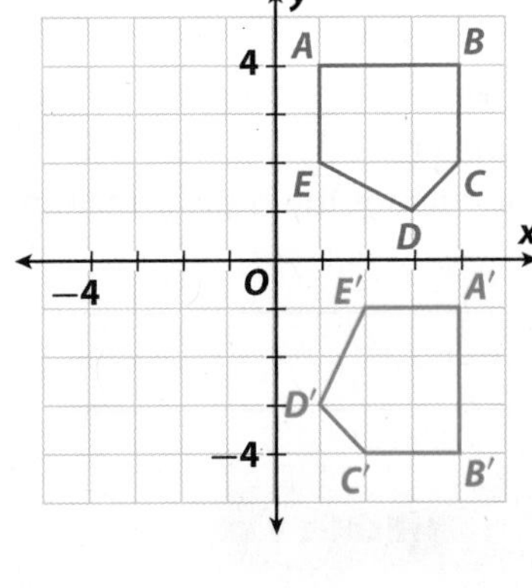

____

____

____

Personal Math Trainer

Online Practice and Help

my.hrw.com

Guided Practice

Use tracing paper or a transparency to help you draw each transformation. Label the image *J′K′L′M′*. (Explore Activity)

1. Reflect *JKLM* across line *n*.

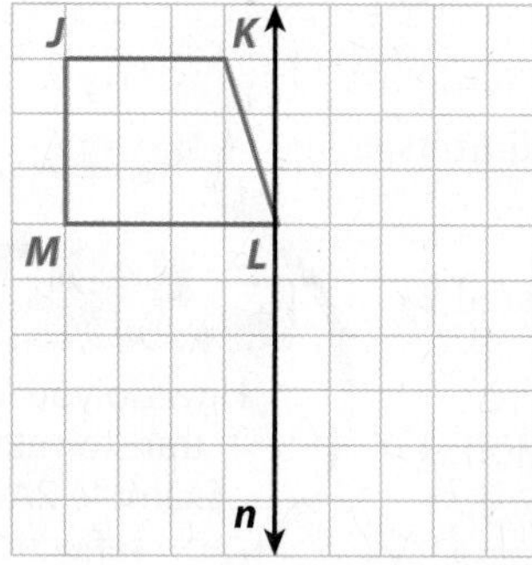

2. Rotate *JKLM* 180° around point *P*.

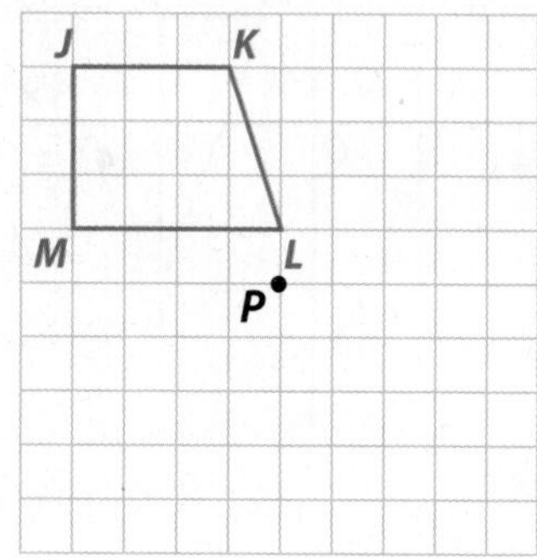

3. Draw the image of $\triangle ABC$ under the transformation $(x, y) \rightarrow (x - 4, y - 4)$. Tell whether the transformation is a rigid motion. If so, identify the transformation. If not, explain why not. (Example 1)

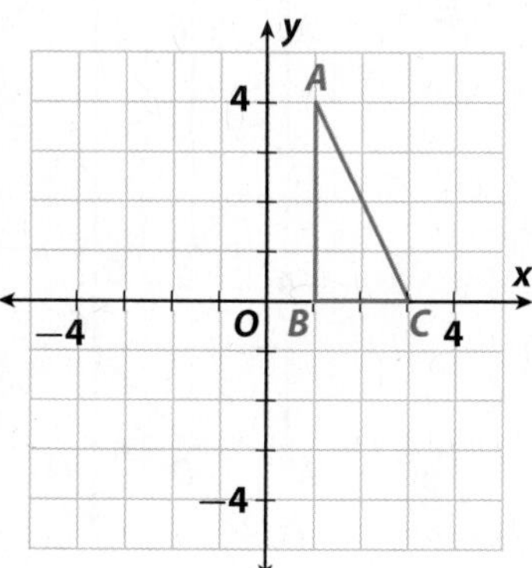

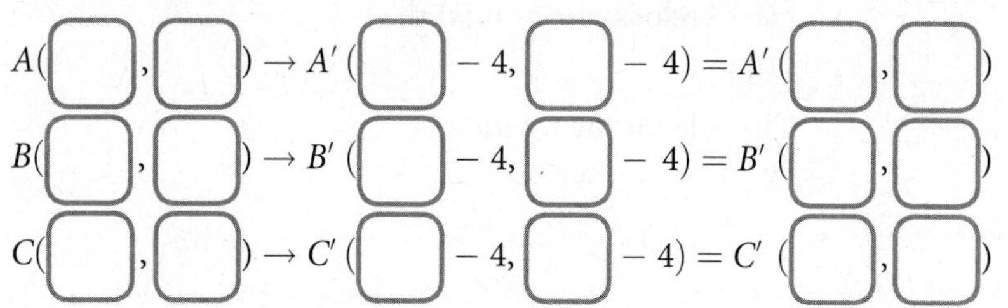

A(___ , ___) → A′ (___ − 4, ___ − 4) = A′ (___ , ___)

B(___ , ___) → B′ (___ − 4, ___ − 4) = B′ (___ , ___)

C(___ , ___) → C′ (___ − 4, ___ − 4) = C′ (___ , ___)

The transformation is ______________________.

4. Identify the transformation that maps the figure to its image. Then give an algebraic rule for the transformation. (Example 2)

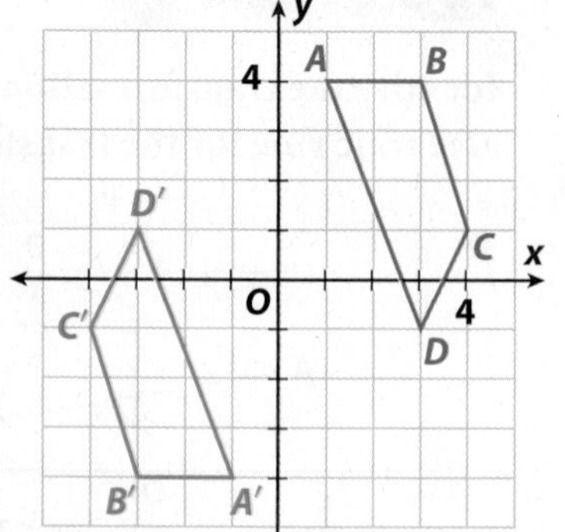

____

5. Identify the transformation that maps *ABCD* from Exercise 4 to a figure with vertices $A'(-4, 1)$, $B'(-4, 3)$, $C'(-1, 4)$, and $D'(1, 3)$. Then give an algebraic rule for the transformation. (Example 2)

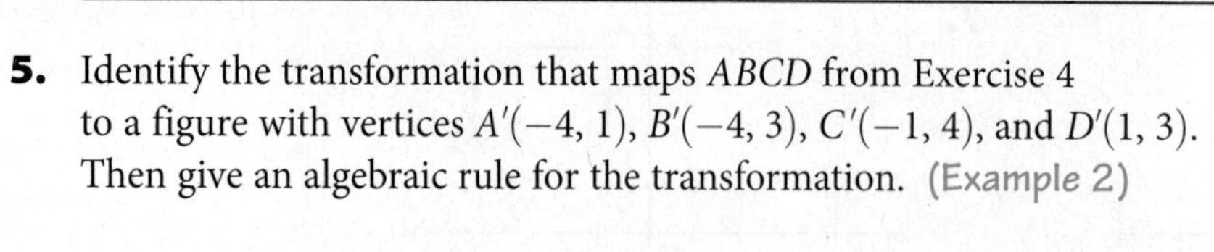

____

____

ESSENTIAL QUESTION CHECK-IN

6. Describe the properties of a rigid motion.

____

____

____

Name ____________________ Class ____________________ Date ____________________

14.2 Independent Practice

CA CC G.CO.2, G.CO.5

7. Use tracing paper or a transparency to help you draw the image of *PQRS* when it is reflected across line *m*.

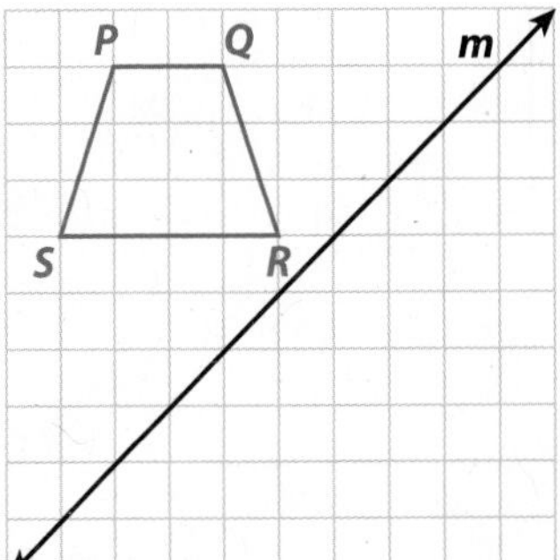

8. Explain the Error Aiden was asked to draw the image of $\triangle JKL$ under the transformation $(x, y) \rightarrow (-x, y)$. His drawing is shown below. Explain Aiden's error.

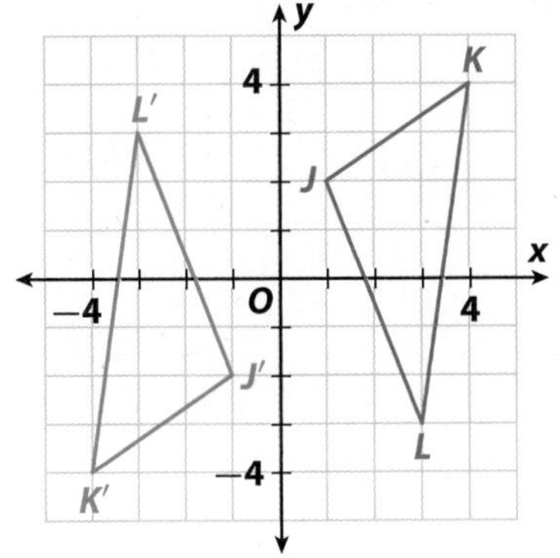

____

____

____

____

9. Transformation *T* maps $\triangle ABC$ to $\triangle A'B'C'$. Can you conclude that $AB = A'B'$? Explain.

____

____

____

____

10. In the table of algebraic rules for rotations given earlier in the lesson, a rotation of 360° around the origin is not listed. Why do you think this rotation is not listed? What rule would be given if this rotation were listed?

____

____

____

____

11. Represent Real-World Problems A graphic designer created the logo shown below for a company that makes antivirus software.

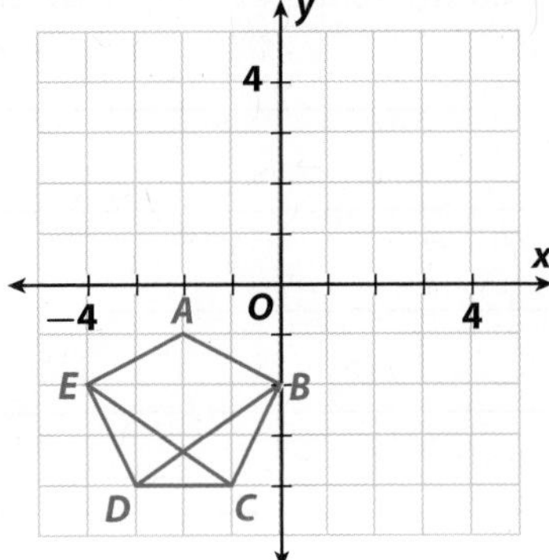

a. The designer translates the logo so that the image of point *A* is at (2, 4). Draw and label the image of the logo.

b. What are the coordinates of the image of point *E*? ____________________

c. Give an algebraic rule for the translation. ____________________

d. Will an enlargement of the logo to show on a sign be a rigid motion? Explain your reasoning.

____

____

H.O.T. FOCUS ON HIGHER ORDER THINKING

Work Area

12. **Critical Thinking** The figure shows the image of $\triangle ABC$ after the translation $(x, y) \rightarrow (x - 1, y + 4)$. What are the coordinates of the vertices of $\triangle ABC$?

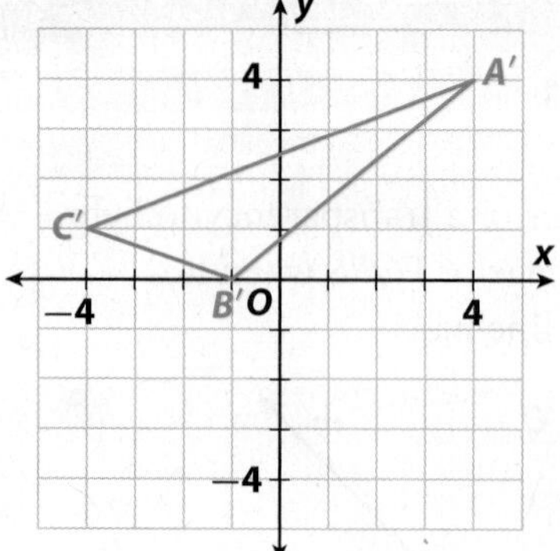

13. **Analyze Relationships** Compare transformations that are rigid motions and transformations that are not rigid motions. Describe similarities and differences.

14. **Communicate Mathematical ideas** In the translation $(x, y) \rightarrow (x + a, y + b)$, how do the values of a and b determine the direction of the translation?

15. **Justify Reasoning** Do rigid motions preserve the perimeter of a figure? Justify your answer.

16. **Make a Conjecture** Which points in the plane remain fixed under a reflection across the x-axis? That is, which points have a preimage and image in the same location? Explain.

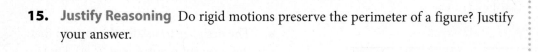

LESSON
14.3 Translations

CA CC G.CO.4

Develop definitions of rotations, reflections, and translations in terms of angles, circles, perpendicular lines, parallel lines, and line segments. *Also G.CO.2, G.CO.5*

ESSENTIAL QUESTION

How do you draw the image of a figure under a translation?

EXPLORE ACTIVITY

Exploring Translations

Use geometry software.

A Draw a triangle and label the vertices *A*, *B*, and *C*.

Then draw a segment and label the endpoints *X* and *Y*.

Select $\overline{XY}$, go to the Transform menu, and choose Mark Vector to show that you want to translate figures the distance from *X* to *Y* in the direction of *X* to *Y*.

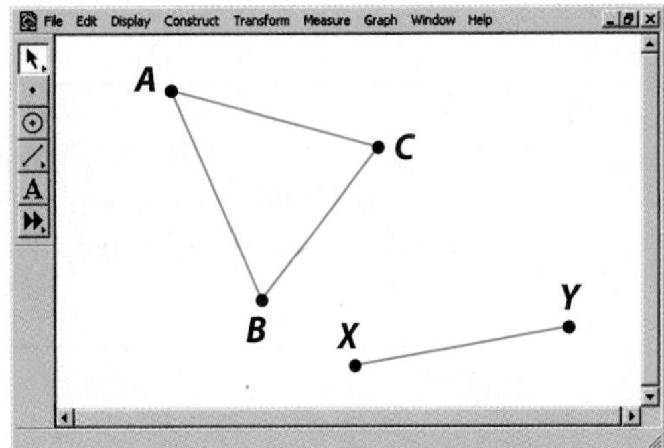

B Select $\triangle ABC$, go to the Transform menu, and choose Translate.

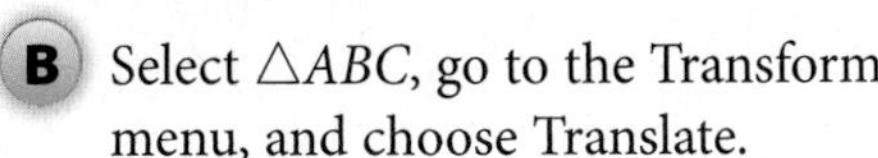

Label the image of $\triangle ABC$ as $\triangle A'B'C'$.

Drag point *Y* to change the length or direction of the translation. Notice how the location of $\triangle A'B'C'$ changes.

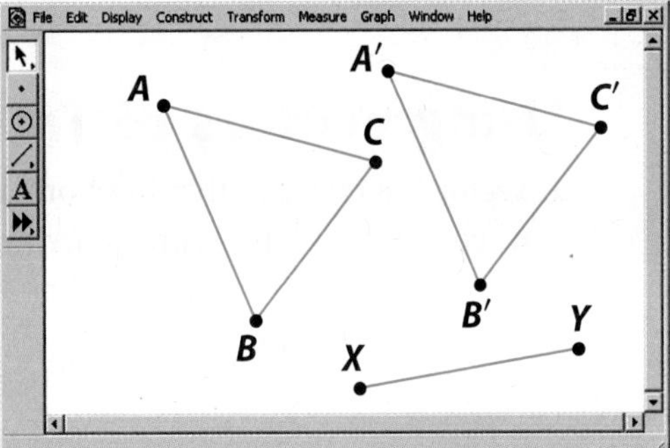

C Use the software to measure the length of $\overline{XY}$. Then measure the distance between each vertex of $\triangle ABC$ and its image. What do you notice? Does this relationship remain true as you change the position of *Y*?

____

____

____

D Use the software to draw $\overline{AA'}$, $\overline{BB'}$, and $\overline{CC'}$. How do these segments appear to be related to $\overline{XY}$?

____

EXPLORE ACTIVITY *(cont'd)*

REFLECT

1. When you drag $\overline{XY}$ to a new location without changing its length or its direction, what happens to $\triangle ABC$ and its image? What does this tell you about translations?

____

____

____

2. **Make a Prediction** Predict what will happen if you drag $\overline{XY}$ so that X coincides with vertex B of $\triangle ABC$. Then use the geometry software to check your prediction.

____

3. **Critique Reasoning** A student used geometry software to draw a triangle $\triangle ABC$ with a right angle at $\angle A$. The student claimed that $\angle A'$ in the translation image must also be a right angle. Do you agree? Explain.

____

____

____

Using Vectors to Translate Figures

A **vector** is a quantity that has both a direction and a magnitude (or *length*). You can represent a vector with an arrow. The **initial point** of a vector is the starting point of the arrow. The **terminal point** of a vector is the ending point. The vector shown may be named $\overrightarrow{EF}$ or $\vec{v}$.

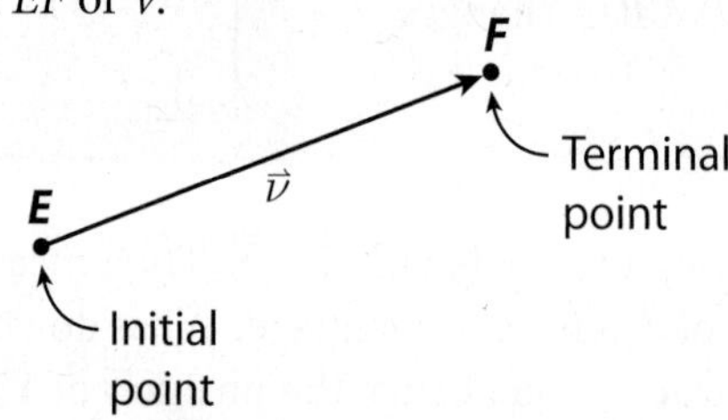

A vector can be named in **component form**, $\langle a, b\rangle$, which specifies the horizontal change a and the vertical change b from the initial point to the terminal point. The component form for $\overrightarrow{PQ}$ is $\langle 5, 3\rangle$.

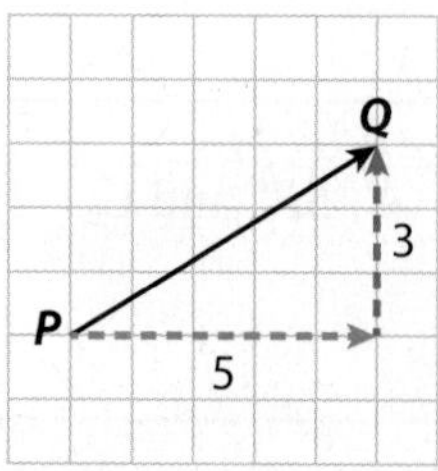

You can use vectors to give a formal definition of a translation.

A **translation** is a transformation along a vector such that the segment joining a point and its image has the same length as the vector and is parallel to the vector.

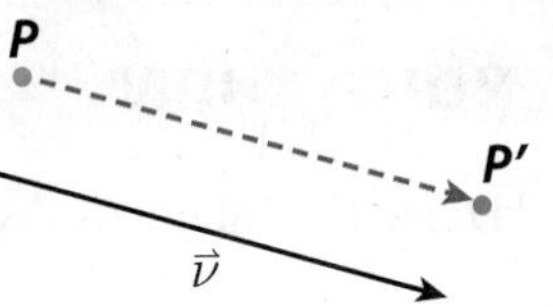

The function notation $T_{\vec{v}}(P) = P'$ says that the image of point P under a translation along vector $\vec{v}$ is P'.

EXAMPLE 1

CA CC G.CO.2, G.CO.5

Draw the image of $\triangle ABC$ after a translation along $\vec{v}$.

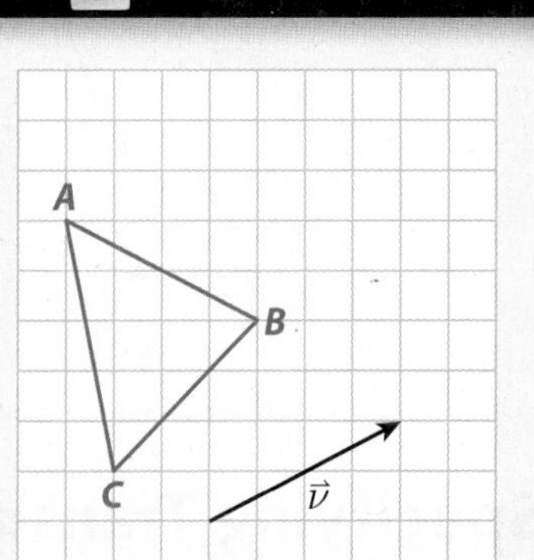

STEP 1 Draw a copy of $\vec{v}$ with its initial point at vertex A of $\triangle ABC$.

Be sure the copy has the same length as $\vec{v}$ and is parallel to it.

Repeat the process at vertices B and C.

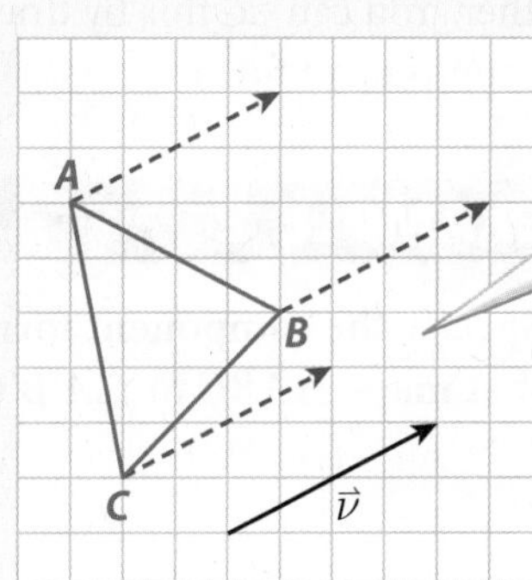

Drawing vectors with the same components as $\vec{v}$ results in vectors that are parallel to $\vec{v}$

STEP 2 Draw segments to connect the terminal points of the vectors. Label the points A', B', and C'.

$\triangle A'B'C'$ is the image of $\triangle ABC$.

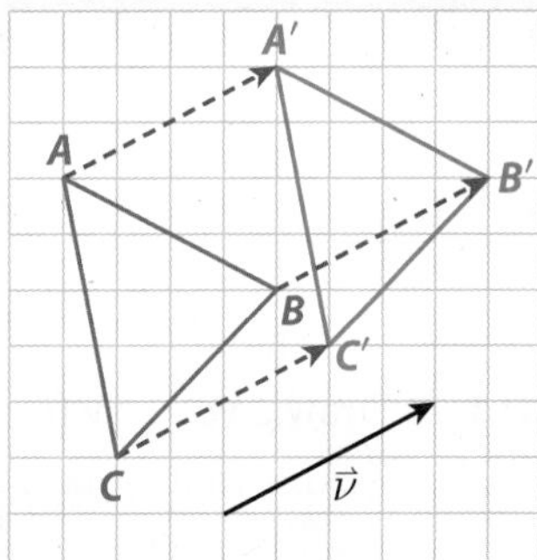

Math Talk
Mathematical Practices

How can you be sure that all copies of the vector are the same length?

REFLECT

4. What is the relationship between the lines through the vectors? How can you find the slopes of those lines and how are the slopes related?

____

____

____

____

YOUR TURN

Draw the image of $\triangle ABC$ after a translation along $\vec{v}$.

5.

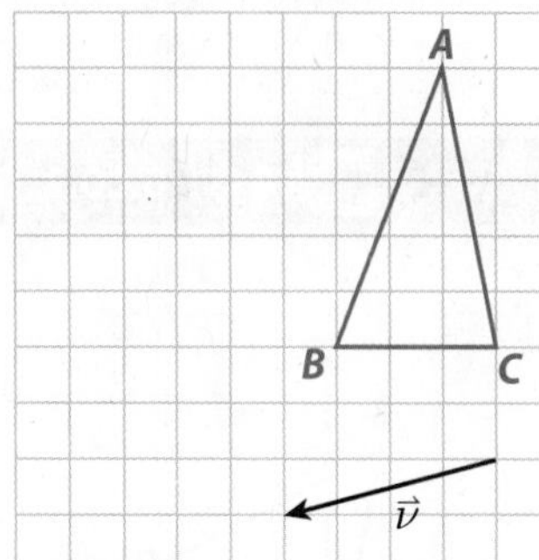

6.

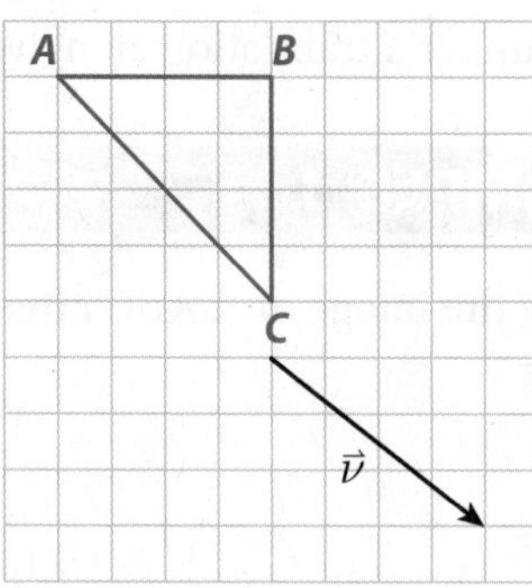

Specifying Translation Vectors

You may be asked to specify a translation that carries one given figure onto another. You can do this by drawing the translation vector and then writing it in component form.

EXAMPLE 2

CA CC G.CO.5

Specify the component form of the vector that maps $\triangle ABC$ to $\triangle A'B'C'$.

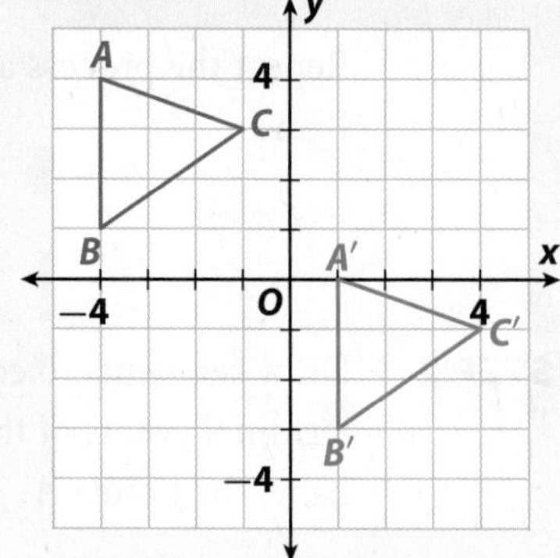

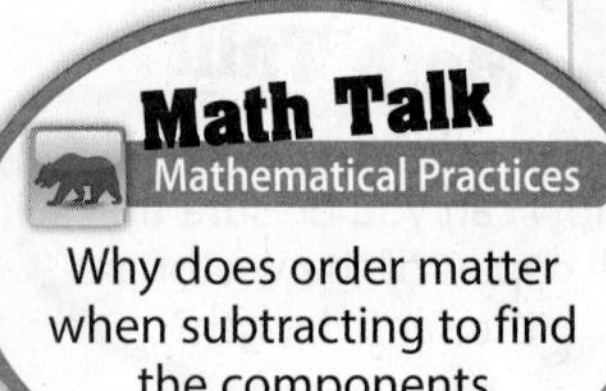

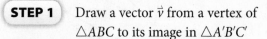

STEP 1 Draw a vector $\vec{v}$ from a vertex of $\triangle ABC$ to its image in $\triangle A'B'C'$

STEP 2 Determine the components of $\vec{v}$.

The horizontal change from the initial point $(-4, 1)$ to the terminal point $(1, -3)$ is $1 - (-4) = 5$.

The vertical change from the initial point $(-4, 1)$ to the terminal point $(1, -3)$ is $-3 - 1 = -4$.

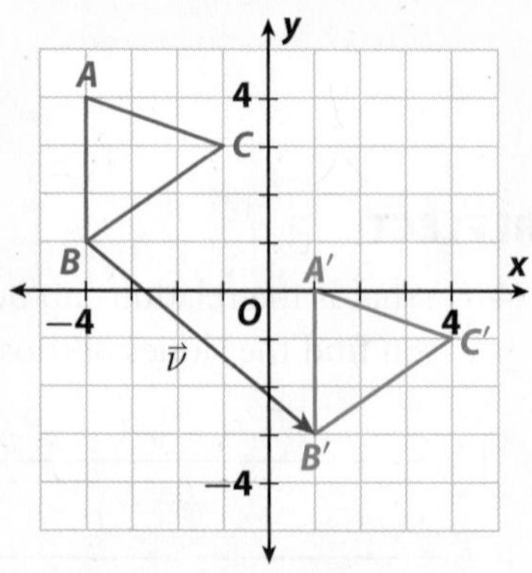

STEP 3 Write the vector in component form.
$\vec{v} = \langle 5, -4 \rangle$

REFLECT

7. Analyze Relationships What is the algebraic rule for the translation in Example 2? How is the algebraic rule related to the component form of the translation vector?

8. What If? In Example 2, suppose $\triangle A'B'C'$ is the preimage and $\triangle ABC$ is the image after a translation. What is the component form of the translation vector in this case? How is this vector related to the vector you wrote in Example 2?

9. Critical Thinking What is the component form of a vector that translates figures horizontally? Explain.

My Notes

YOUR TURN

Specify the component form of the vector that maps each figure to its image.

10.

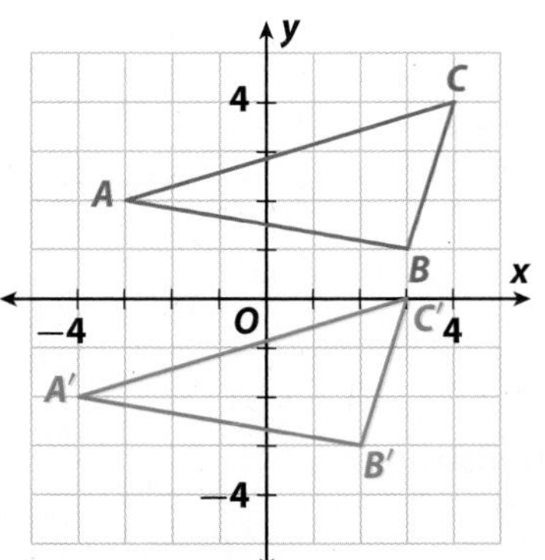

11.

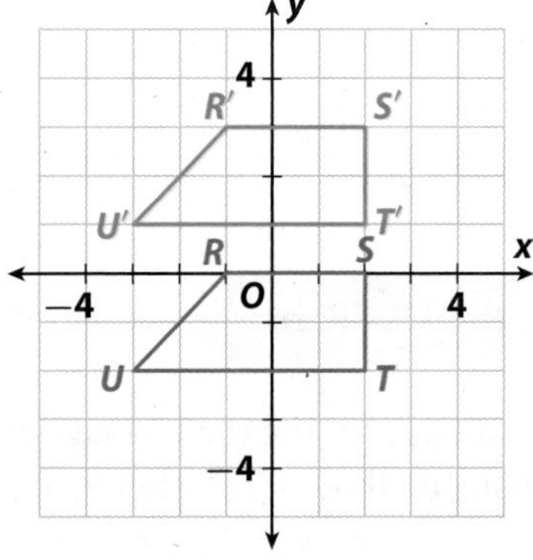

Guided Practice

Draw the image of $\triangle ABC$ after a translation along $\vec{v}$. (Example 1)

1.

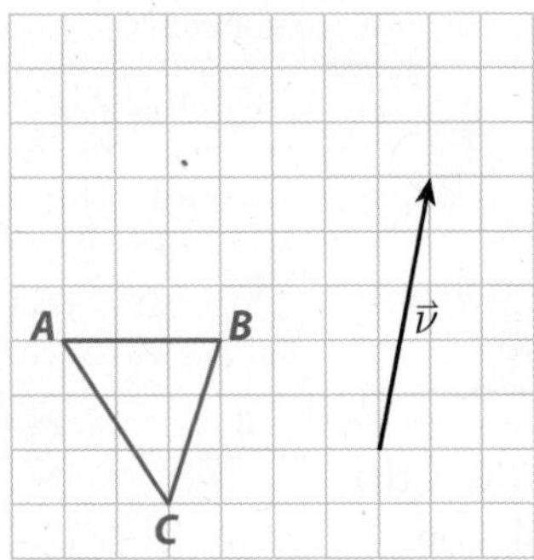

2.

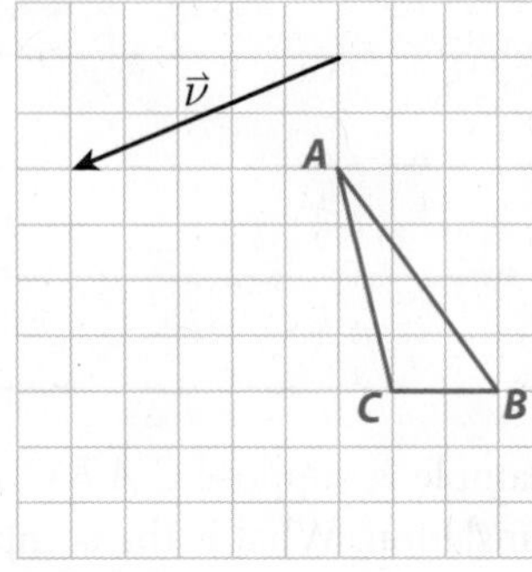

3. Specify the vector that maps $\triangle ABC$ to $\triangle A'B'C'$. (Example 2)

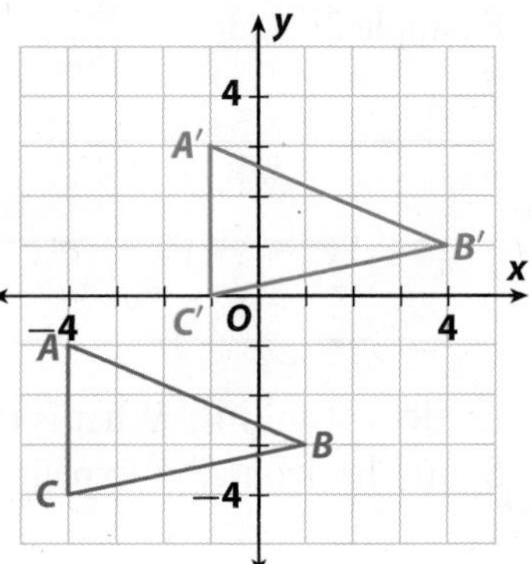

Use the vector with initial point $A(-4, -1)$ and terminal point $A'(-1, 3)$.

The horizontal change is ☐ − ☐ = ☐.

The vertical change is ☐ − ☐ = ☐.

The component form of the vector is ___________

Specify the component form of the vector that maps each figure to its image. (Example 2)

4.

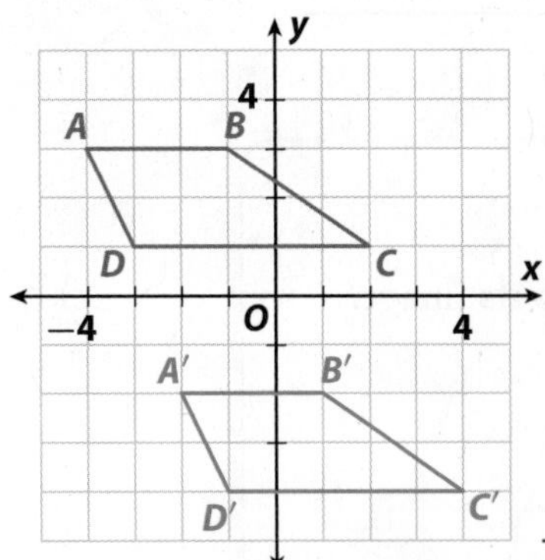

____

5.

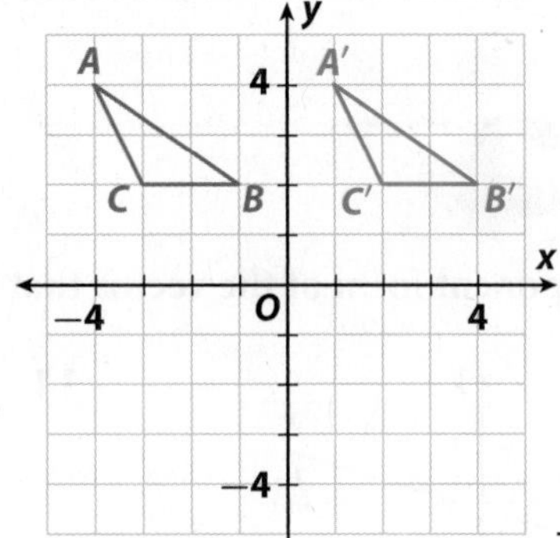

____

ESSENTIAL QUESTION CHECK-IN

6. How does translating a figure using the formal definition of a translation compare to the previous method of translating a figure?

____

____

____

Name ____________________ Class ____________ Date ____________

14.3 Independent Practice

Personal Math Trainer
my.hrw.com
Online Practice and Help

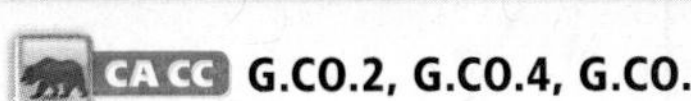

G.CO.2, G.CO.4, G.CO.5

7. Explore multiple translations.

a. Draw the image of $\triangle ABC$ after a translation along $\vec{v}$ followed by a translation along $\vec{w}$.

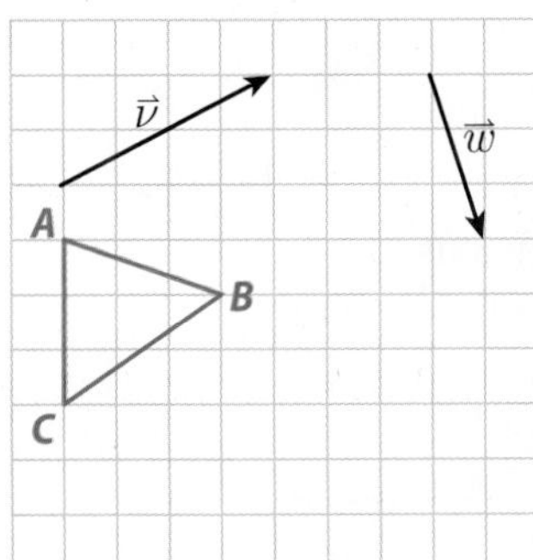

b. Now draw the image of $\triangle ABC$ after a translation along $\vec{w}$ followed by a translation along $\vec{v}$. Compare the results.

____

____

c. Can the sequence of translations be represented by one translation? If so, write an algebraic rule for the single translation. If not, explain why not.

____

8. Draw the image of $\triangle RST$ after a translation along the vector $\langle -3, 2 \rangle$.

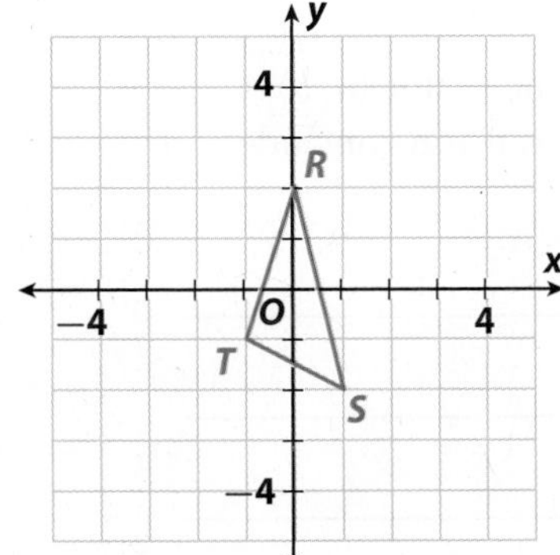

In Exercises 9–12, use the figure to complete the statements.

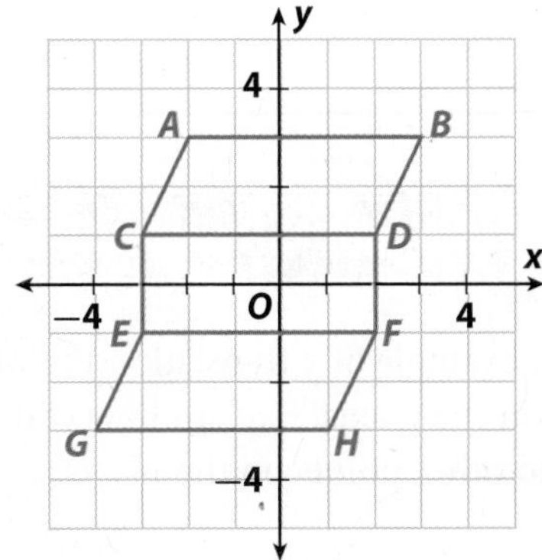

9. $T_{\langle -1, -4 \rangle}(\overline{AB}) =$ ______________

10. $T_{\langle -5, 0 \rangle}(\overline{DF}) =$ ______________

11. $T_{\langle 6, 4 \rangle}(\overline{EG}) =$ ______________

12. $T_{\langle 1, 4 \rangle}(\overline{GH}) =$ ______________

13. **Multi-Step** A cartographer is making a city map. Line m represents Murphy Street. The cartographer translates points on line m along the vector $\langle 2, -2 \rangle$ to draw Nolan Street.

Draw the line for Nolan Street on the coordinate plane and write its equation. What is the image of the point (0, 3) in this situation?

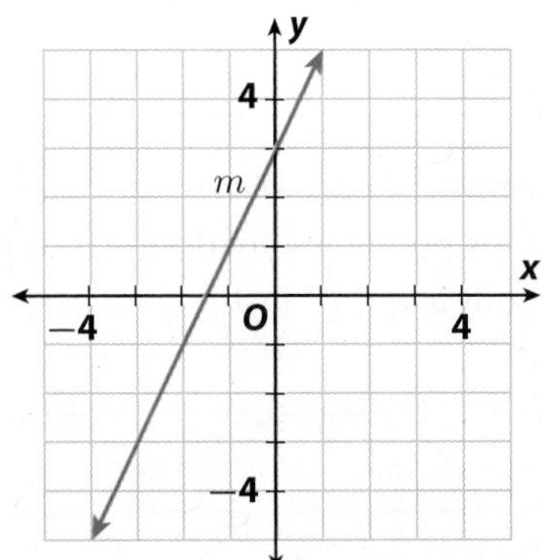

____

14. Explain the Error Emmanuel was asked to identify the vector that maps $\triangle DEF$ to $\triangle D'E'F'$. He drew a vector as shown and determined that the component form of the vector is $\langle 3, 1 \rangle$. Explain his error.

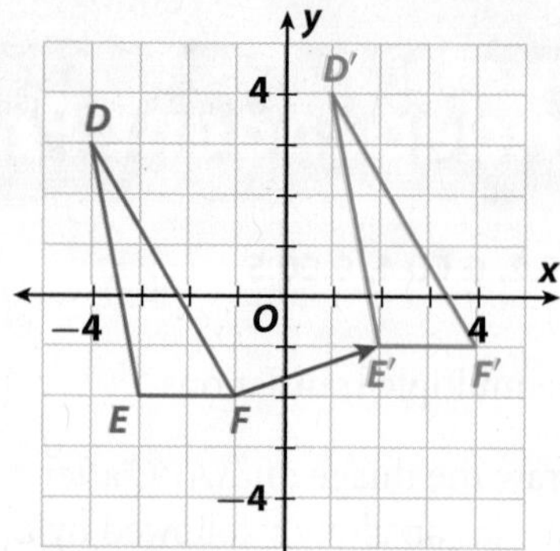

H.O.T. FOCUS ON HIGHER ORDER THINKING

Work Area

15. Give an example of a translation vector that maps points on the *y*-axis to other points on the *y*-axis. Explain how you know the translation maps points on the *y*-axis to other points on the *y*-axis.

16. Analyze Relationships How are translations along the vectors $\langle a, b \rangle$ and $\langle -a, -b \rangle$ similar and how are they different?

17. Critical Thinking A translation along the vector $\langle -2, 7 \rangle$ maps point *P* to point Q. The coordinates of point Q are $(4, -1)$. What are the coordinates of point *P*? Explain your reasoning.

18. Communicate Mathematical Ideas A translation along the vector $\langle a, b \rangle$ maps points in Quadrant III to points in Quadrant I. What can you conclude about *a* and *b*? Justify your response.

LESSON

14.4 Reflections

CA CC G.CO.4

Develop definitions of rotations, reflections, and translations in terms of angles, circles, perpendicular lines, parallel lines, and line segments. *Also G.CO.2, G.CO.3, G.CO.5*

ESSENTIAL QUESTION

How do you draw the image of a figure under a reflection?

EXPLORE ACTIVITY

Exploring Reflections

Use tracing paper to explore reflections.

A Draw and label a line ℓ on tracing paper. Then draw and label a quadrilateral $ABCD$ with vertex C on line ℓ.

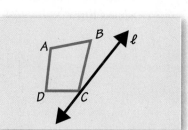

B Fold the tracing paper along line ℓ as shown. Trace the quadrilateral and press firmly to make an impression on the paper below. Then unfold the paper and draw the image of the quadrilateral. Label it $A'B'C'D'$.

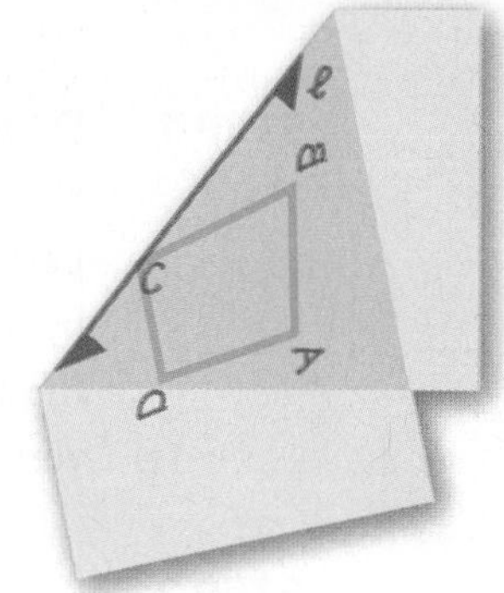

C Draw segments to connect each vertex of quadrilateral $ABCD$ with its image. How are these segments related to the line of reflection, line ℓ?

____

____

____

____

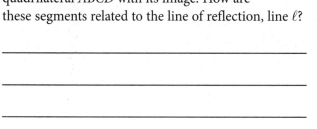

D What do you notice about the location of point C' in the image of the quadrilateral?

____

REFLECT

1. A student claims that a figure and its reflected image always lie on opposite sides of the line of reflection. Do you agree? Why or why not?

____

____

____

____

Drawing Reflected Figures

A **reflection** across line ℓ maps a point P to its image P' as follows.

If P is not on line ℓ, then ℓ is the perpendicular bisector of $\overline{PP'}$.

If P is on line ℓ, then $P = P'$.

The function notation $r_\ell(P) = P'$ says that the image of point P under a reflection across line ℓ is P'.

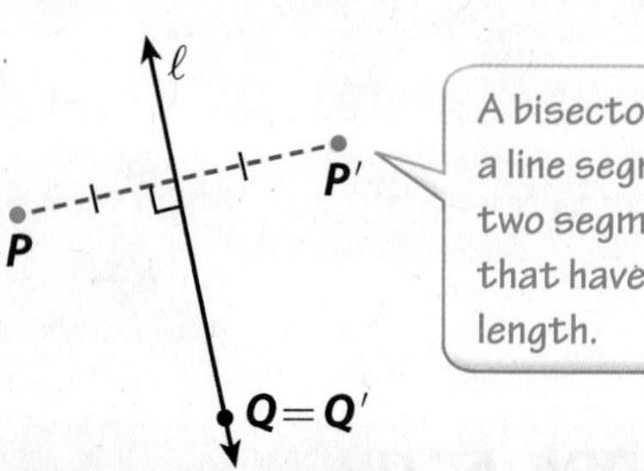

A bisector divides a line segment into two segments that have the same length.

EXAMPLE 1

CA CC G.CO.5

My Notes

Draw the image of $\triangle ABC$ after a reflection across line ℓ.

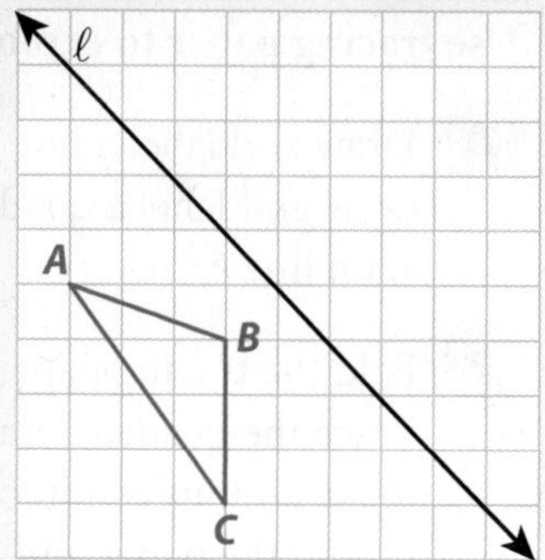

STEP 1 Draw a segment with an endpoint at vertex A so that the segment is perpendicular to line ℓ and is bisected by line ℓ. Label the other endpoint of the segment A'. Repeat the process at vertices B and C.

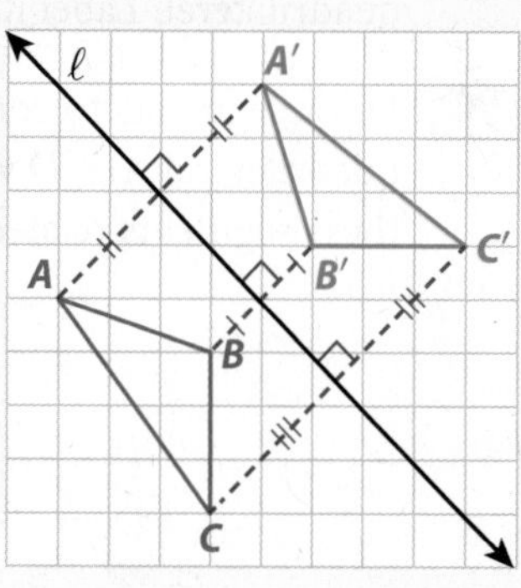

STEP 2 Connect points A', B', and C'. $\triangle A'B'C'$ is the image of $\triangle ABC$.

REFLECT

2. **Check for Reasonableness** How can you check that you drew the image of the triangle correctly?

____

____

____

3. How can you tell that $\overline{AA'}$ is perpendicular to line ℓ?

____

____

____

YOUR TURN

Draw the image of $\triangle ABC$ after a reflection across line ℓ.

4.

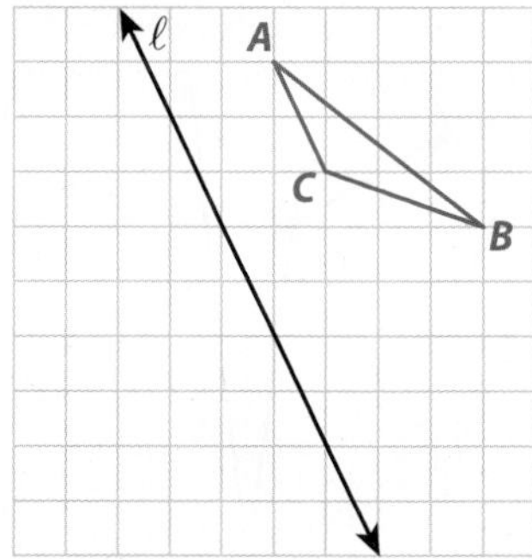

5.

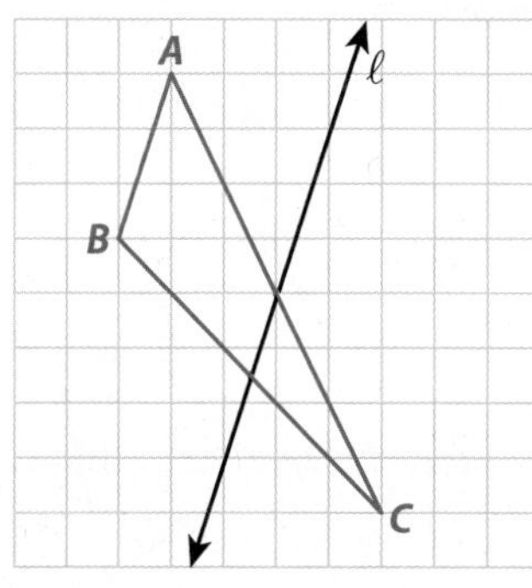

Specifying Lines of Reflection

You may be asked to specify a reflection that carries one given figure onto another. You can do this by connecting corresponding points and drawing the perpendicular bisector of the segments.

EXAMPLE 2

CA CC G.CO.5

Draw the line of reflection for the reflection that maps $\triangle ABC$ onto $\triangle A'B'C'$.

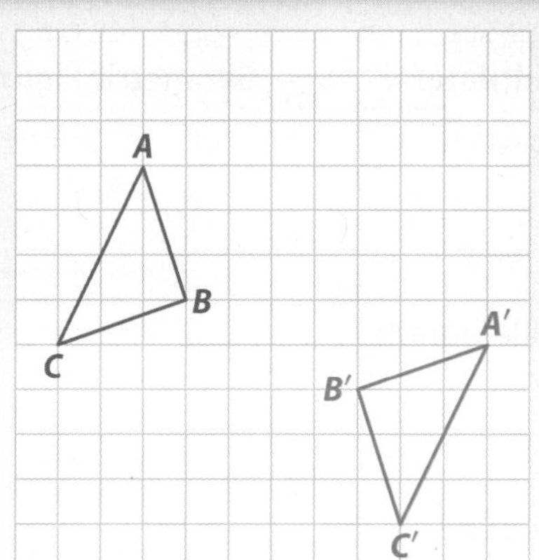

STEP 1 Draw the segments $\overline{AA'}$, $\overline{BB'}$, and $\overline{CC'}$.

STEP 2 Locate and mark the midpoint of each segment.

STEP 3 Draw and label line ℓ through the midpoints. Line ℓ is the line of reflection.

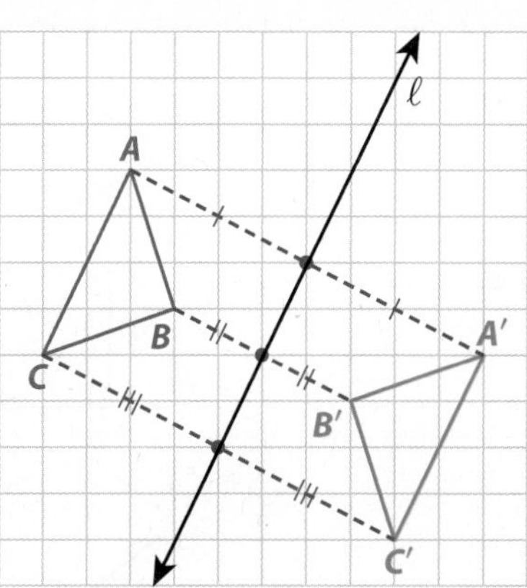

Math Talk
Mathematical Practices

How could you use paper folding to find the line of reflection?

YOUR TURN

Draw the line of reflection for the reflection that maps each figure onto its image.

6.

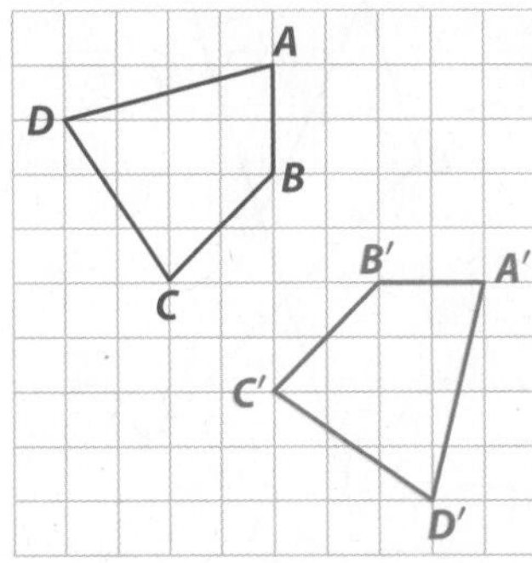

7.

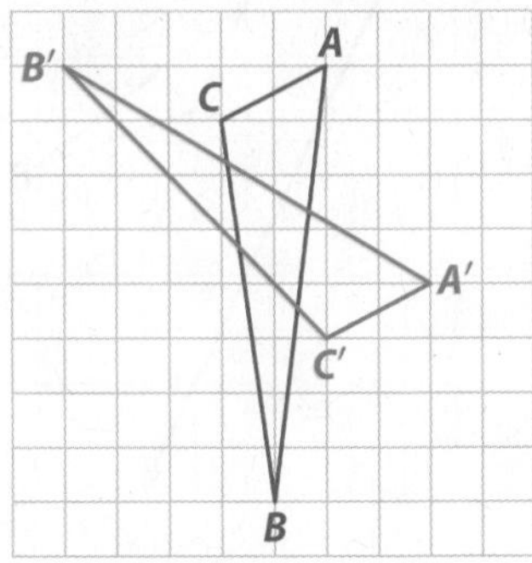

Reflecting Figures onto Themselves

A **polygon** is a closed plane figure formed by three or more segments such that each segment intersects exactly two other segments only at their endpoints and no two segments with a common endpoint are collinear. In a **regular polygon**, all sides are of equal length and all angles are of equal measure.

A **quadrilateral** is a polygon with four sides. In the following definitions of some special quadrilaterals, the term *congruent* means *of equal measure.*

Quadrilateral	Geometric Figure	Definition
Trapezoid		A **trapezoid** is a quadrilateral with at least one pair of parallel sides.
Parallelogram		A **parallelogram** is a quadrilateral with two pairs of parallel sides.
Rectangle		A **rectangle** is a quadrilateral with four right angles.
Rhombus		A **rhombus** is a quadrilateral with four congruent sides.
Square		A **square** is a quadrilateral with four right angles and four congruent sides.
Kite		A **kite** is a quadrilateral with two distinct pairs of congruent consecutive sides.

A figure has **line symmetry** if it can be reflected across a line so that the image coincides with the preimage. A line of reflection for a reflection that maps a figure onto itself is a **line of symmetry**.

EXAMPLE 3

Draw all possible lines of symmetry for the rectangle.

STEP 1 Trace the figure on a piece of tracing paper.

STEP 2 Check to see if the figure can be folded along a straight line so that one half of the figure coincides with the other half. If so, the fold line is one of the lines of symmetry.

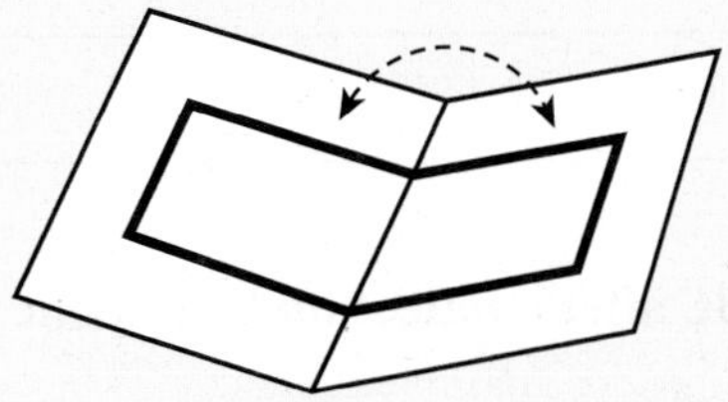

STEP 3 Draw the lines of symmetry on the figure.

There are two lines of symmetry.

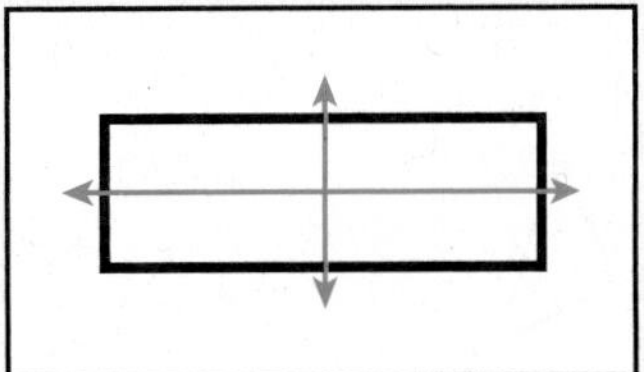

My Notes

REFLECT

8. How many lines of symmetry does a circle have? Explain.

9. **Draw Conclusions** What must be true about a rectangle that has four lines of symmetry? Describe the lines of symmetry.

Draw all possible lines of symmetry for each figure.

10. isosceles trapezoid

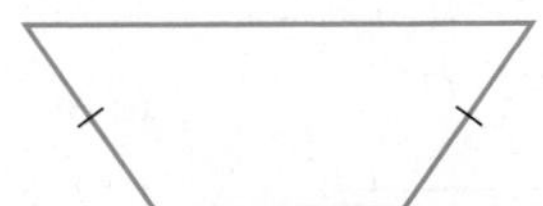

11. parallelogram

Guided Practice

1. Copy the figure onto tracing paper, flip the tracing paper across line *m*, and place it so that the copy of line *m* coincides with the original. What is the image of point *S*? Explain. (Explore Activity)

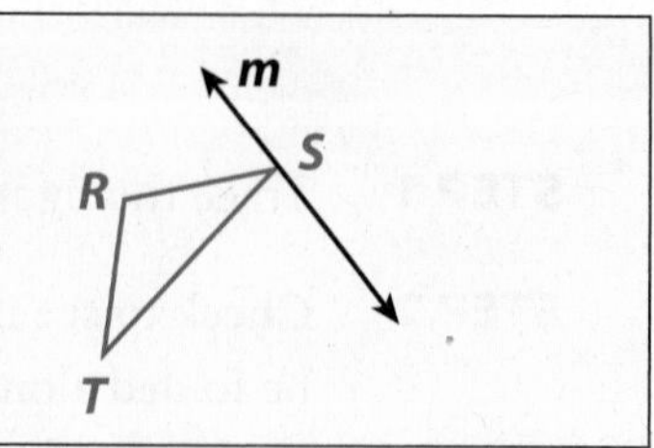

____

____

Draw the image of $\triangle ABC$ after a reflection across line ℓ. (Example 1)

2.

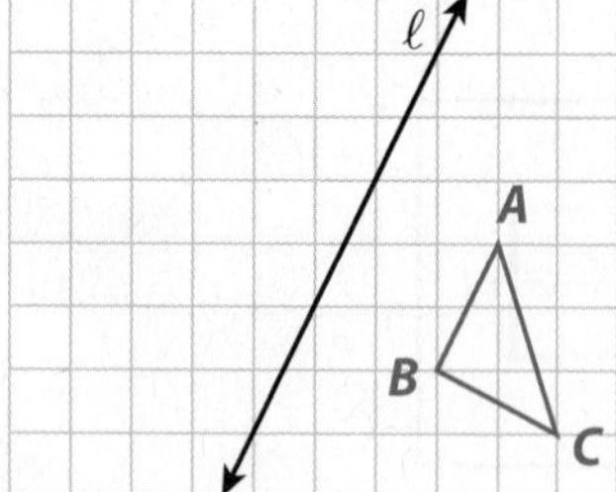

3.

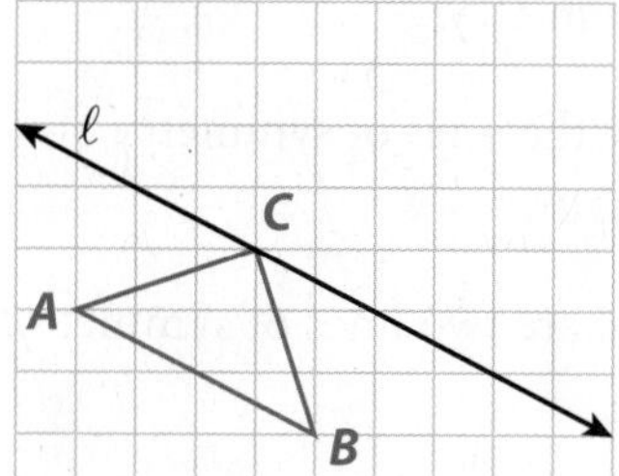

Draw the line of reflection for the reflection that maps each figure onto its image. (Example 2)

4.

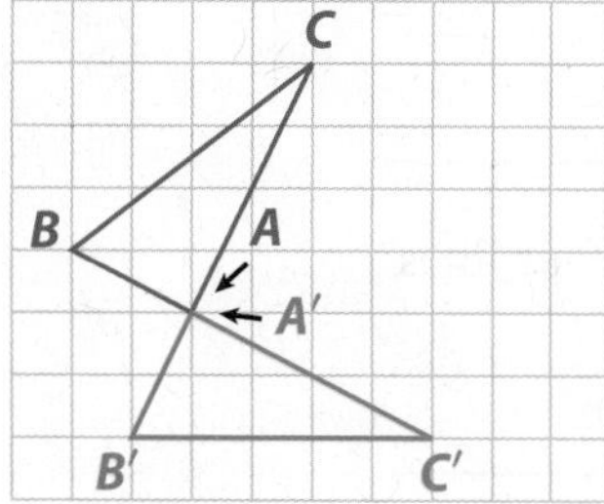

5.

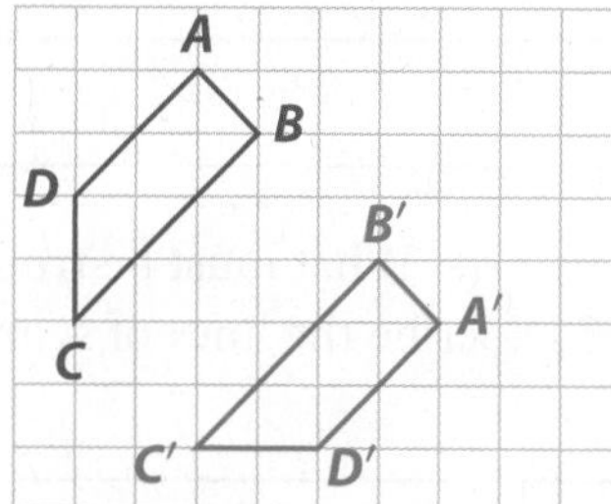

Draw all possible lines of symmetry for each figure. (Example 3)

6. regular hexagon

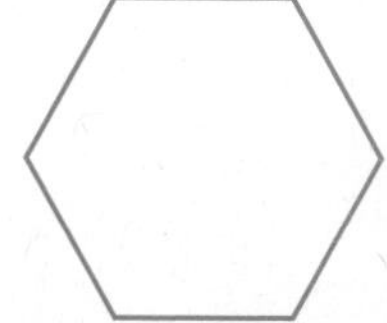

7. kite

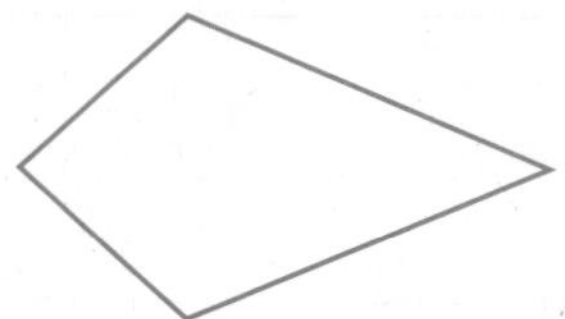

ESSENTIAL QUESTION CHECK-IN

8. How can you use the formal definition of a reflection to help you to draw the image of a figure under a reflection?

____

____

Name ______ Class ______ Date ______

14.4 Independent Practice

CA CC G.CO.2, G.CO.3, G.CO.4, G.CO.5

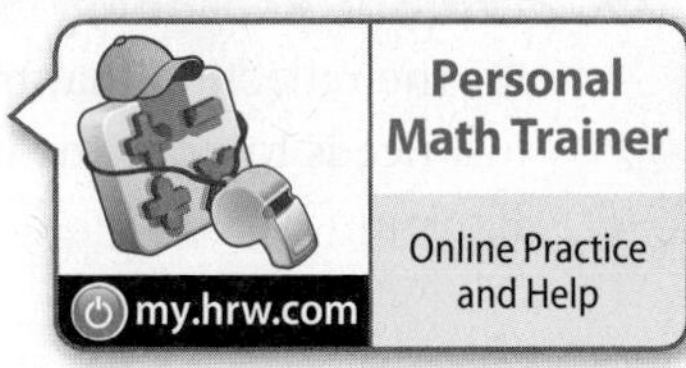

In the figure, $\triangle MNP$ is the image of $\triangle JKL$ after a reflection across line ℓ. Complete each statement in Exercises 9–13.

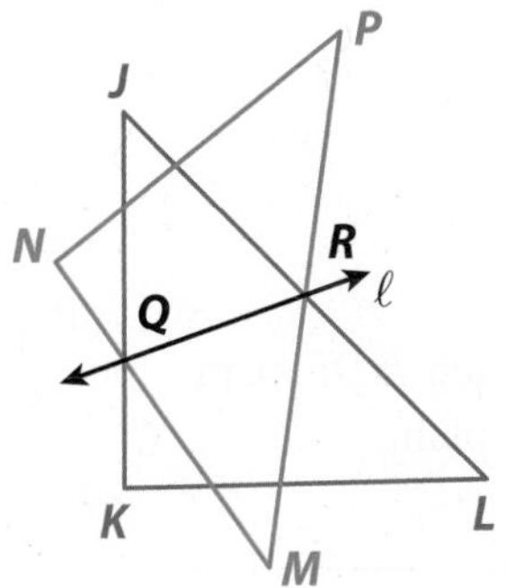

9. $r_\ell(\overline{JK}) =$ ______

10. $r_\ell(P) =$ ______

11. $r_\ell(\overline{QR}) =$ ______

12. $r_\ell($______$) = \overline{MR}$

13. $r_\ell($______$) = \overline{JL}$

14. A hiker wants to find the shortest path from her tent (T) to the river (line r) and then to the cave (C). Given that C' is the reflection image of C, explain why the path shown from T to R to C is the shortest path.

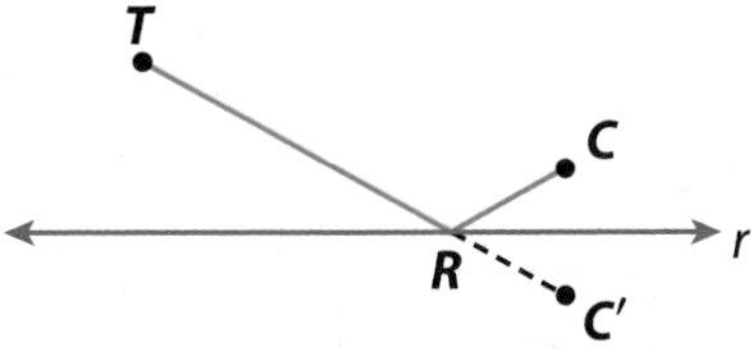

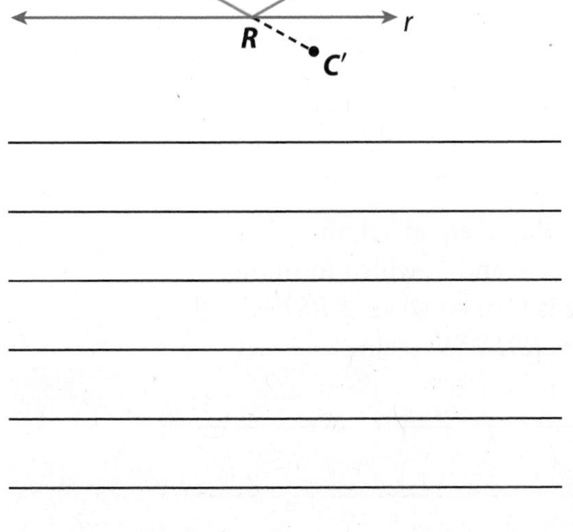

15. How many lines of symmetry does each octagon in the photo have? Explain.

______

______

16. **Multi-Step** Write the equation of the line of reflection for the reflection that maps figure $ABCD$ onto figure $A'B'C'D'$.

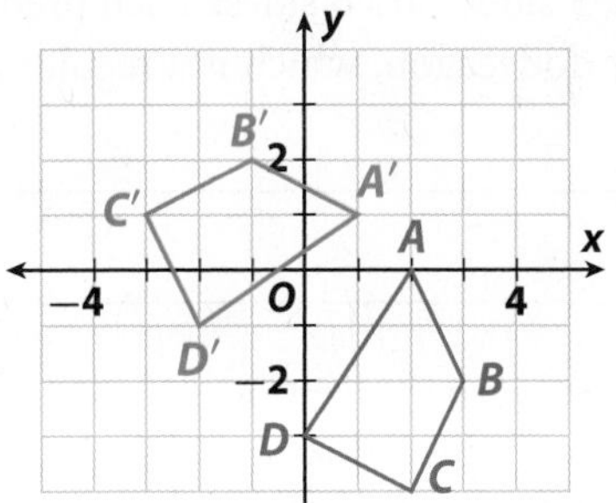

______

17. **Explain the Error** Jamar was asked to draw the line of reflection for the reflection of $\triangle ABC$ onto $\triangle A'B'C'$. He drew line ℓ as shown. Explain his error. Draw the correct line.

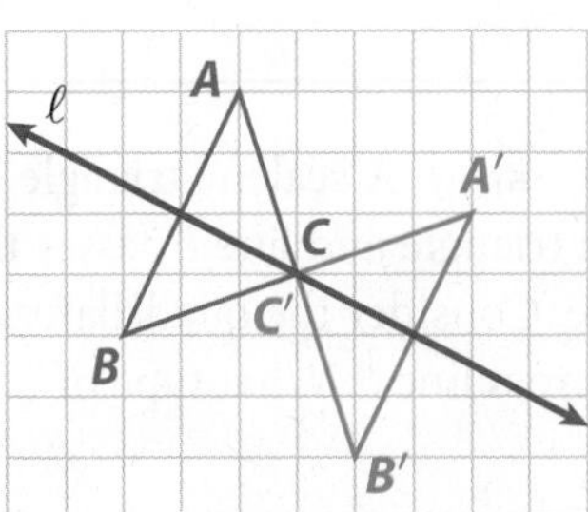

______

______

18. Critique Reasoning Mayumi wants to draw the line of reflection for the reflection that maps $\triangle ABC$ to $\triangle A'B'C'$. She claims that she just needs to draw the line through points X and Y. Do you agree? Explain.

A' A X Y C B B' C'

H.O.T. FOCUS ON HIGHER ORDER THINKING

Work Area

19. Draw Conclusions There are three lines of reflection across which $\triangle DEF$ can be reflected onto itself. What can you conclude about $\triangle DEF$? Explain.

20. Make a Prediction A regular polygon has sides of equal length and angles of equal measure. Find the number of lines of symmetry for a regular polygon with 4 sides, 5 sides, and 6 sides. Then predict the number of lines of symmetry for a regular dodecagon, which is a regular polygon with 12 sides. Justify your answer.

21. Communicate Mathematical Ideas When you reflect point P across line ℓ, the location of point P does not change. When you reflect point P across line m, the location of point P does not change. Explain why lines ℓ and m must intersect.

22. Critical Thinking A scalene triangle has no two sides of equal length. $\triangle RST$ is a scalene triangle and line ℓ passes through points R and T, which form the longest side. Consider the quadrilateral $RSTS'$ that is formed when $\triangle RST$ is reflected across line ℓ. What type of quadrilateral is $RSTS'$? Explain.

LESSON

14.5 Rotations

CA CC G.CO.4

Develop definitions of rotations, reflections, and translations in terms of angles, circles, perpendicular lines, parallel lines, and line segments. *Also G.CO.2, G.CO.3, G.CO.5*

ESSENTIAL QUESTION

How do you draw the image of a figure under a rotation?

EXPLORE ACTIVITY CA CC G.CO.4, G.CO.2

Exploring Rotations

Use geometry software to explore rotations.

A Draw a triangle and label the vertices A, B, and C. Then draw a point P.

Select point P, go to the Transform menu, and choose Mark Center. This will allow you to rotate figures around point P.

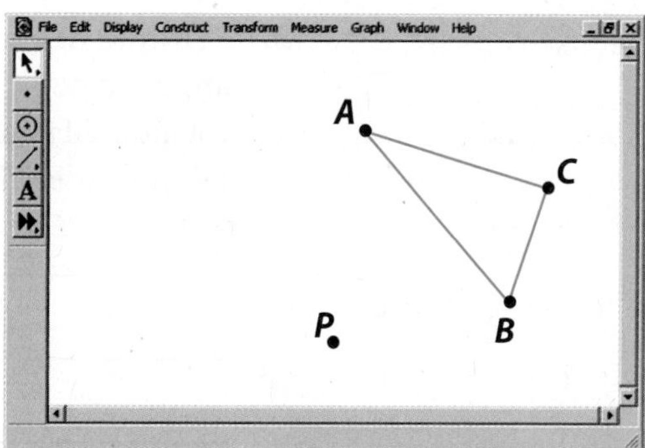

B Select $\triangle ABC$, go to the Transform menu, and choose Rotate.

Rotate $\triangle ABC$ 90° around point P.

Label the image of $\triangle ABC$ as $\triangle A'B'C'$.

Change the shape, size, or location of $\triangle ABC$ and notice how $\triangle A'B'C'$ changes.

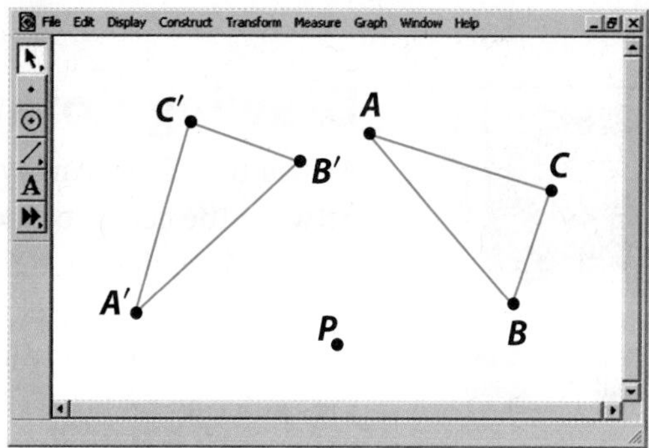

C Draw $\angle APA'$, $\angle BPB'$, and $\angle CPC'$. Then use the software to measure these angles. What do you notice? Does this relationship remain true as you move point P and as you change the size and shape of $\triangle ABC$?

____

____

D Use the software to measure the distance from A to P and the distance from A' to P. What do you notice? Does this relationship remain true as you move point P and as you change the size and shape of $\triangle ABC$?

____

____

EXPLORE ACTIVITY (cont'd)

REFLECT

1. **Draw Conclusions** What can you conclude about the distance of a point and its image from the center of rotation?

____

____

2. **Communicate Mathematical Ideas** Describe what happens when the center of rotation is on the figure that is being rotated.

____

____

3. **Critique Reasoning** Jacob used software to draw a point X and rotate it around a point Y. He observed that point X was its own image after the rotation. Marcello said that point X must be at the center of the rotation. Do you agree? Explain.

____

____

____

Drawing Rotated Figures

As you turn a steering wheel, the distance between the center of the wheel and a point on the wheel does not change. Also, as you turn the steering wheel through an angle of $m°$, all points on the wheel move around the center by $m°$. These two ideas are the basis of the definition of a rotation.

A **rotation** is a transformation around point P such that the following are true.

- Every point and its image are the same distance from P.
- All angles with vertex P formed by a point and its image have the same measure.

The function notation $R_{P,\,m°}(A) = A'$ says that the image of point A under a rotation of $m°$ around point P is A'.

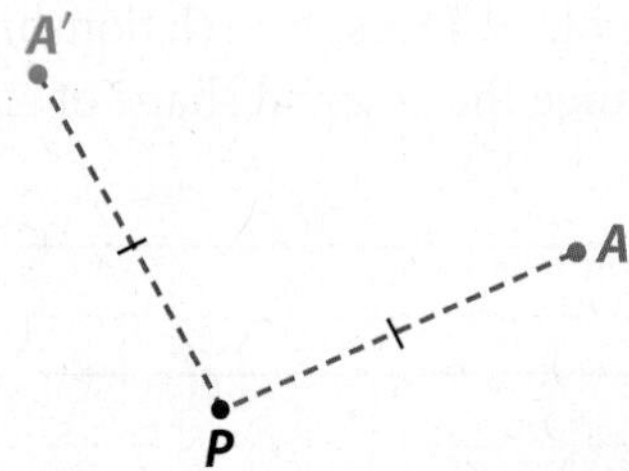

EXAMPLE 1

CA CC G.CO.5

Draw the image of $\triangle ABC$ after a 150° rotation around point P.

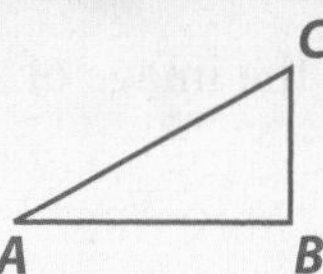

STEP 1 Draw $\overline{PA}$. Then use a protractor to draw a ray that forms a 150° angle with $\overline{PA}$.

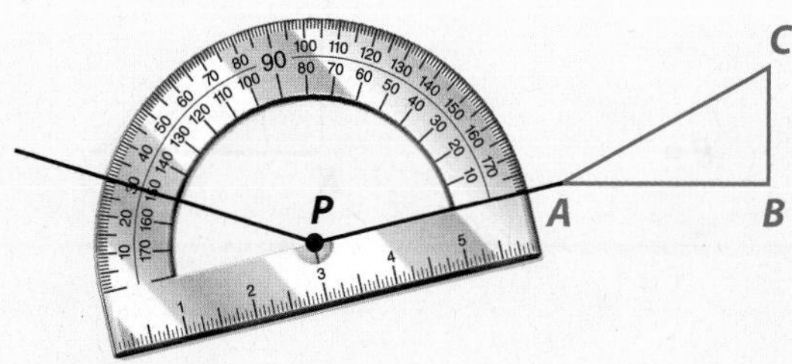

STEP 2 Use a ruler to mark point A' along the ray so that $PA' = PA$.

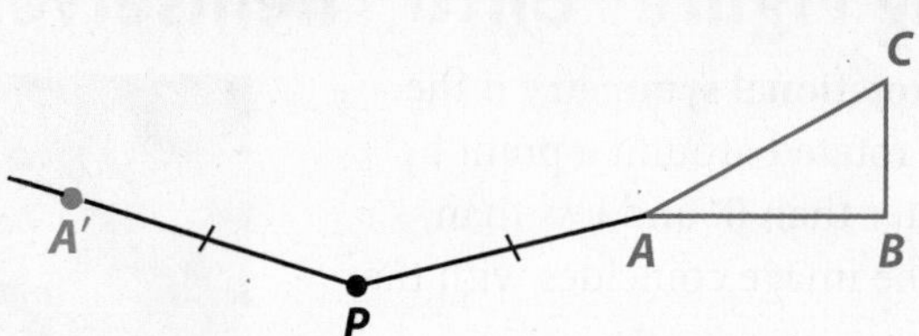

STEP 3 Repeat the process for points B and C to locate points B' and C'. Connect points A', B', and C' to draw $\triangle A'B'C'$.

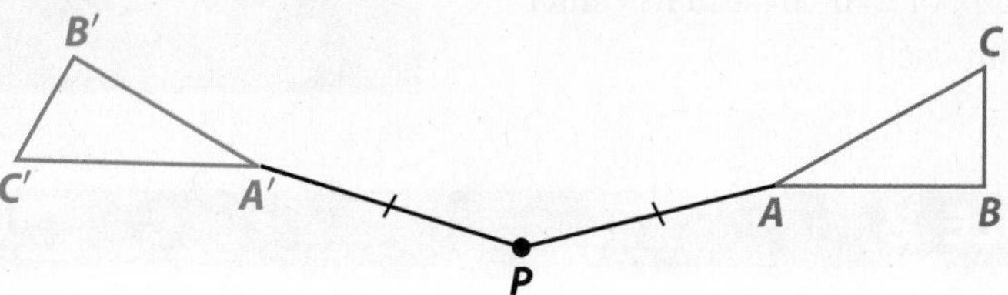

Math Talk
Mathematical Practices
How could you use a compass to locate point A' on the ray so that $PA' = PA$?

REFLECT

4. **What If?** Would the process be different if you were asked to draw the image of $\triangle ABC$ after a 210° rotation around point P? If so, what would you need to do differently?

____

____

5. How could you use tracing paper to draw the image of $\triangle ABC$?

____

____

____

____

____

YOUR TURN

6. Draw the image of $\triangle JKL$ after a 40° rotation around point P.

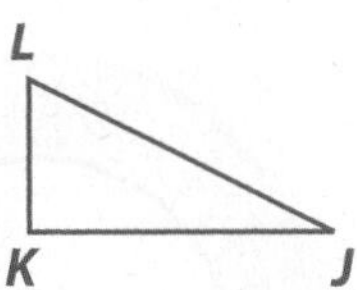

Rotating Figures onto Themselves

A figure has **rotational symmetry** if the figure can be rotated around a point by an angle greater than 0° and less than 360° so that the image coincides with the preimage.

The architectural element at the right has rotational symmetry, because it can be rotated 90°, 180°, or 270° around its center to coincide with itself.

EXAMPLE 2

CA CC G.CO.3

Describe all rotations of less than 360°, if any, that map the parallelogram onto itself.

STEP 1 Trace the figure on a piece of tracing paper.

STEP 2 Without moving the tracing paper, firmly place the point of your pencil on the center point of the figure. Rotate the tracing paper. Check to see if the figure coincides with itself after a rotation of less than 360°.

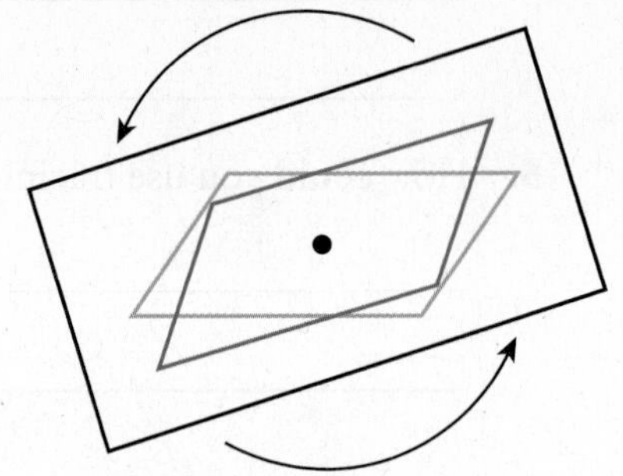

STEP 3 Identify and list all such angles. A rotation of 180° maps the parallelogram onto itself.

REFLECT

7. **Communicate Mathematical Ideas** In Example 2, why do you think it is specified that the rotations must be less than 360°?

8. Describe all rotations of less than 360° that map a circle onto itself.

9. **Critique Reasoning** Amelia claimed that every line segment has rotational symmetry. Do you agree or disagree? Explain.

My Notes

YOUR TURN

Describe all rotations of less than 360°, if any, that map the figure onto itself.

10. square

11. rectangle

Personal Math Trainer
Online Practice and Help
my.hrw.com

Guided Practice

1. Jenrick draws $\triangle RST$ and point Q. He traces $\triangle RST$ on a piece of tracing paper and rotates it around point Q, as shown. He finds that $m\angle T'QT = 63°$. Which other angles must measure 63°? How is this related to the definition of a rotation? (Explore Activity)

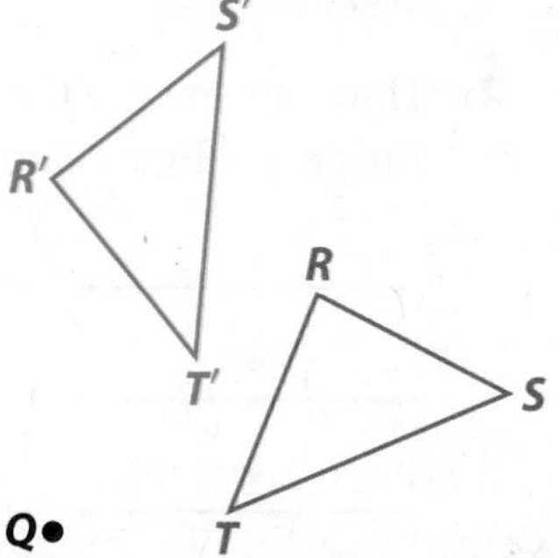

2. Draw the image of $\triangle DEF$ after a 165° rotation around point P. (Example 1)

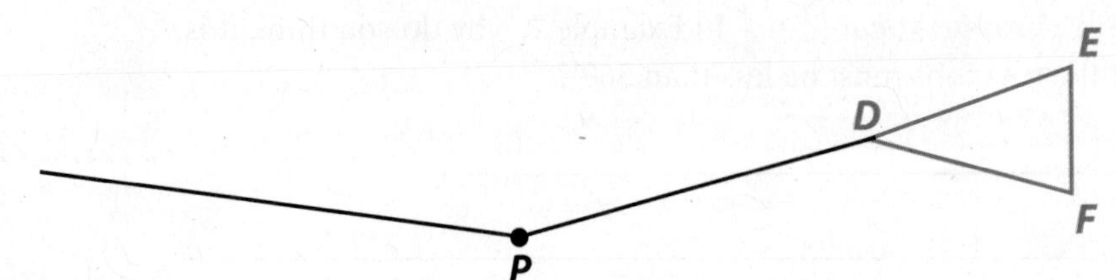

STEP 1 Draw $\overline{PD}$. Then use a protractor to draw a ray that forms an angle of ________ with $\overline{PD}$. The segment and ray have been drawn above.

STEP 2 Use a ruler to mark point D' along the ray so that $PD' =$ ________.

STEP 3 Repeat the process for points E and F to locate points E' and F'. Connect points D', E', and F' to draw $\triangle D'E'F'$.

Draw the image of $\triangle ABC$ after a rotation around point P by the given number of degrees. (Example 1)

3. 30°

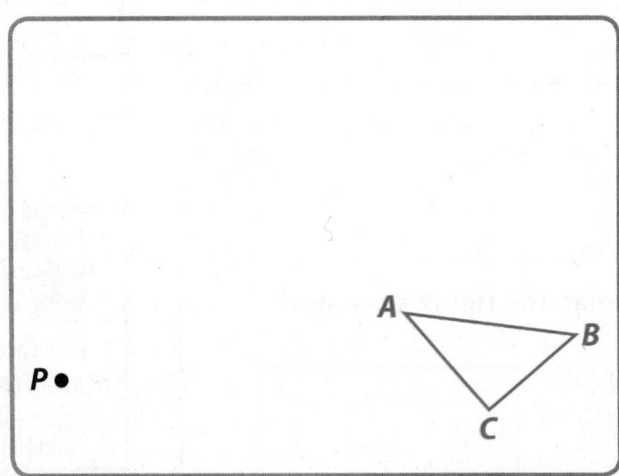

4. 90°

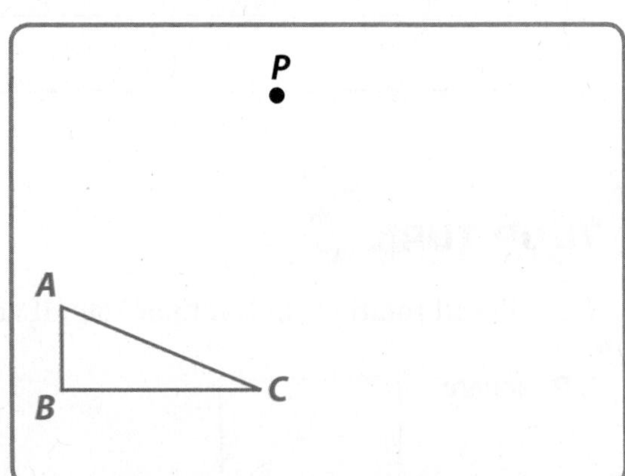

Describe all rotations of less than 360°, if any, that map the figure onto itself. (Example 2)

5. isosceles trapezoid

____

6. equilateral triangle

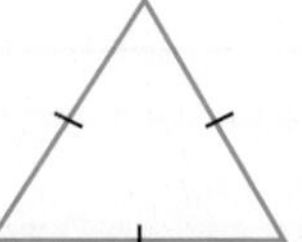

____

ESSENTIAL QUESTION CHECK-IN

7. How can you use the formal definition of a rotation to help you to draw the image of a figure under a rotation?

____

____

____

Name ______________________ Class ______________ Date ______________

14.5 Independent Practice

CA CC G.CO.2, G.CO.3, G.CO.4, G.CO.5

Trapezoid *WXYZ* is the image of trapezoid *JKLM* after a rotation around point *P* by 32°. Use the figure to complete the statements.

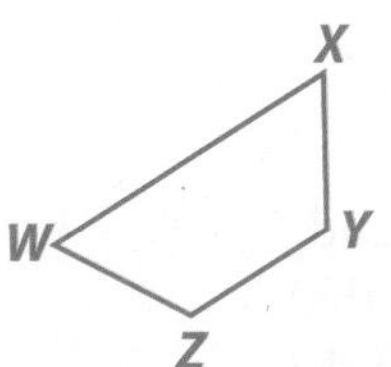

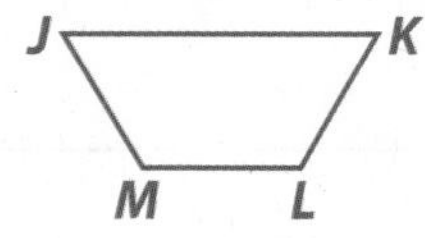

8. $m\angle WPJ =$ ________

9. $R_{P,\,32°}(\overline{KL}) =$ ________

10. $R_{P,\,32°}($ ________ $) = Z$

11. ________ $= PW$

12. **Explain the Error** Marisol drew the image of $\triangle ABC$ after a rotation of 85° around point *P*. Her work is shown below. Explain how you can tell from the figure that she made an error. Describe the error.

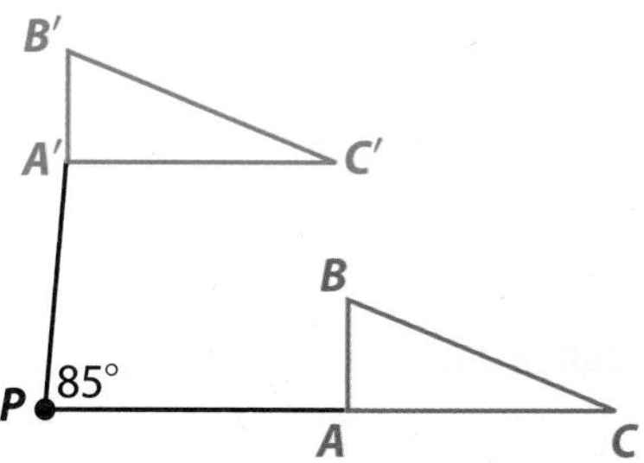

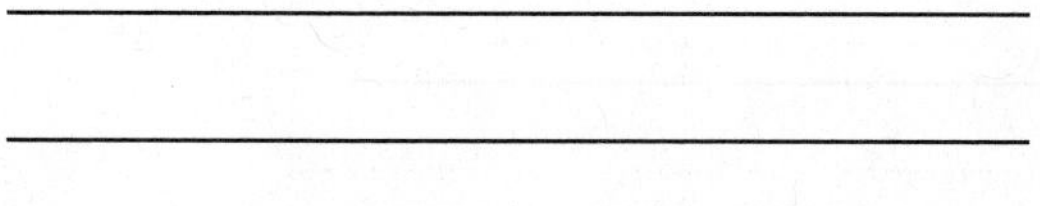

13. **Critical Thinking** What is the greatest rotation of less than 360° that maps the regular octagon onto itself?

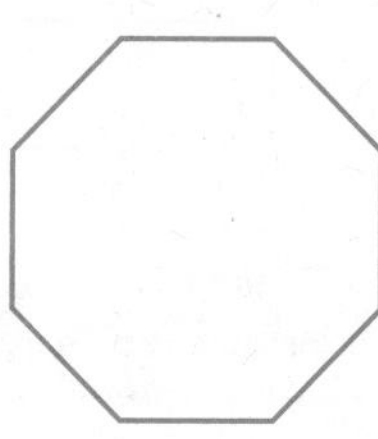

____

14. A Ferris wheel has 20 cars equally spaced around the circumference of the wheel. The wheel rotates so that the car at the bottom of the ride is replaced by the next car. By how many degrees does the wheel rotate? Explain.

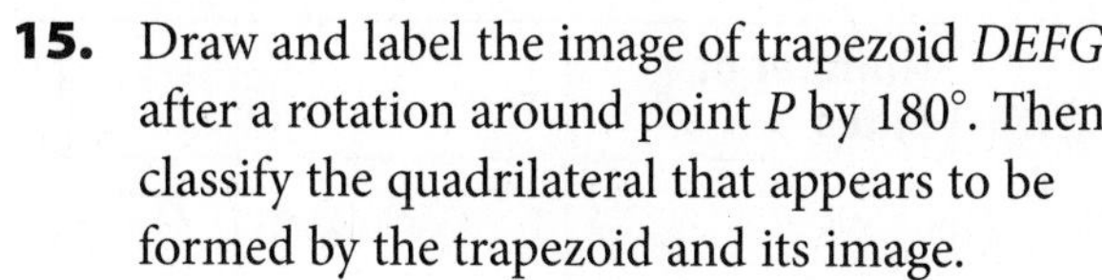

15. Draw and label the image of trapezoid *DEFG* after a rotation around point *P* by 180°. Then classify the quadrilateral that appears to be formed by the trapezoid and its image.

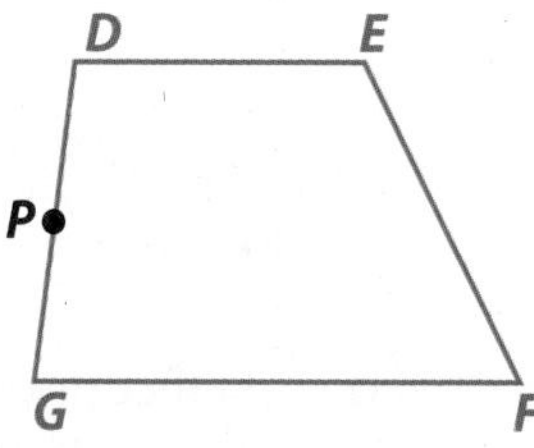

____

16. The smallest rotation that maps quadrilateral *ABCD* onto itself is a rotation of 180°. The quadrilateral has no lines of symmetry. Draw quadrilateral *ABCD*.

17. Square $A'B'C'D'$ is the image of square $ABCD$ under a rotation around point P. Use a ruler, protractor, or other tools to determine the angle of the rotation. Explain your method.

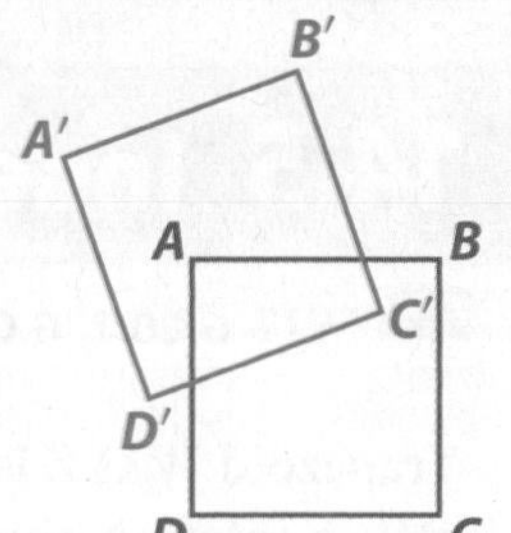

P•

H.O.T. FOCUS ON HIGHER ORDER THINKING

Work Area

18. **Communicate Mathematical Ideas** Naomi rotated $\triangle ABC$ by $m°$ around point P. Now she wants to rotate the image, $\triangle A'B'C'$, around point P so that the triangle returns to its original location. By how many degrees should she rotate $\triangle A'B'C'$? Explain.

19. **Look for a Pattern** A polygon is a *regular polygon* if all the sides are the same length and all the angles have the same measure.

a. Complete the table by finding the smallest angle of rotation that maps each regular polygon onto itself.

Number of Sides	3	4	5	6
Figure				
Smallest Angle of Rotation				

b. Predict the smallest angle of rotation that maps a 16-sided regular polygon onto itself. Justify your answer.

20. **Critique Reasoning** Rajan said that all points turn around the center of rotation by the same angle, so all points move the same distance under a rotation. Do you agree with Rajan's statement? Explain.

LESSON 14.6 Combining Transformations

CA CC G.CO.6

Use geometric descriptions of rigid motions to transform figures and to predict the effect of a given rigid motion on a given figure; given two figures, use the definition of congruence in terms of rigid motions to decide if they are congruent. *Also G.CO.2, G.CO.5*

ESSENTIAL QUESTION

How can you predict the effect of a combination of transformations?

EXPLORE ACTIVITY

Combine Transformations

Use geometry software to explore combinations of transformations.

A Draw a triangle and label the vertices A, B, and C. Then draw a point P.

Rotate $\triangle ABC$ by 70° around point P. Label the image as $\triangle A'B'C'$. Then rotate $\triangle A'B'C'$ by 60° around point P. Label the image as $\triangle A''B''C''$.

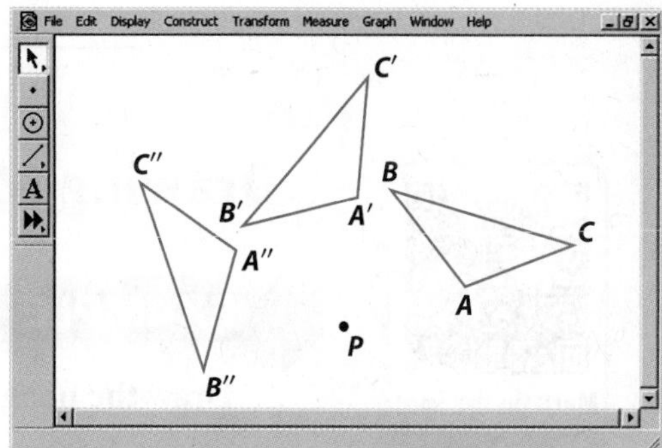

B Consider the relationship between $\triangle ABC$ and $\triangle A''B''C''$. Is there a single transformation that maps $\triangle ABC$ to $\triangle A''B''C''$? Explain.

____

____

C Draw a triangle and label the vertices D, E, and F. Then draw a pair of parallel lines and label them line j and line k.

Reflect $\triangle DEF$ across line j and label the image as $\triangle D'E'F'$. Then reflect $\triangle D'E'F'$ across line k and label the image as $\triangle D''E''F''$.

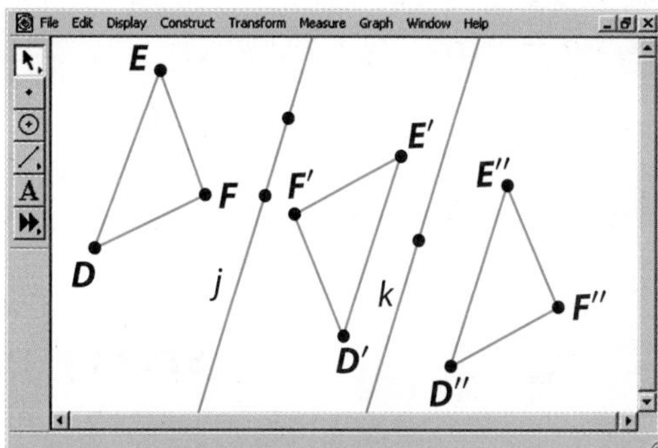

D Consider the relationship between $\triangle DEF$ and $\triangle D''E''F''$. What type of transformation maps $\triangle DEF$ to $\triangle D''E''F''$? How do you know?

____

____

E Experiment to determine whether your findings from part D are true for a combination of reflections across intersecting lines. Describe your results.

____

____

____

EXPLORE ACTIVITY *(cont'd)*

REFLECT

1. **Make a Conjecture** What single transformation is equivalent to a rotation of $m°$ around point P followed by a rotation of $n°$ around point P?

____

2. **Communicate Mathematical Ideas** Consider a reflection across line m followed by a reflection across line n. Assuming line m is parallel to line n, are there any fixed points under this combination of transformations? Justify your response.

____

____

____

Drawing Multiple Transformations in a Plane

EXAMPLE 1

CA CC G.CO.2, G.CO.5

Draw the image of $\triangle ABC$ after the given combination of transformations.

A reflection across line ℓ then translation along $\vec{v}$

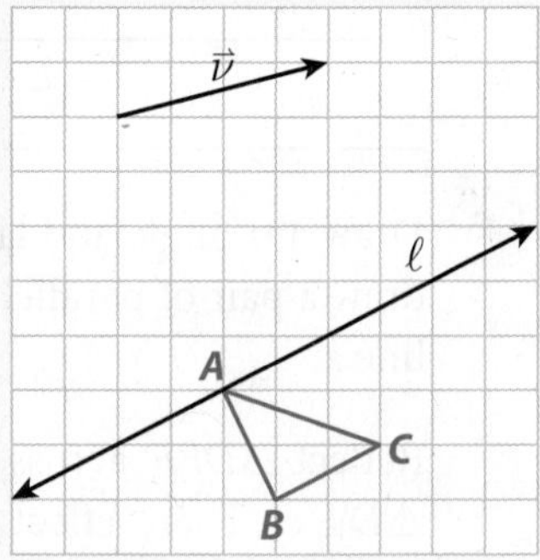

STEP 1 Draw the image of $\triangle ABC$ after a reflection across line ℓ.

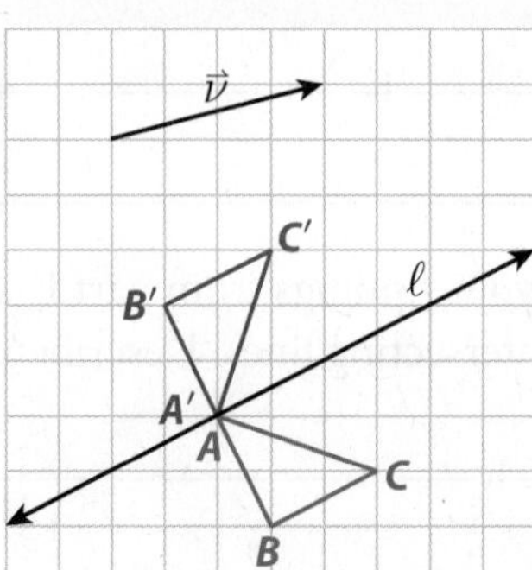

STEP 2 Draw the image of $\triangle A'B'C'$ after a translation along $\vec{v}$.

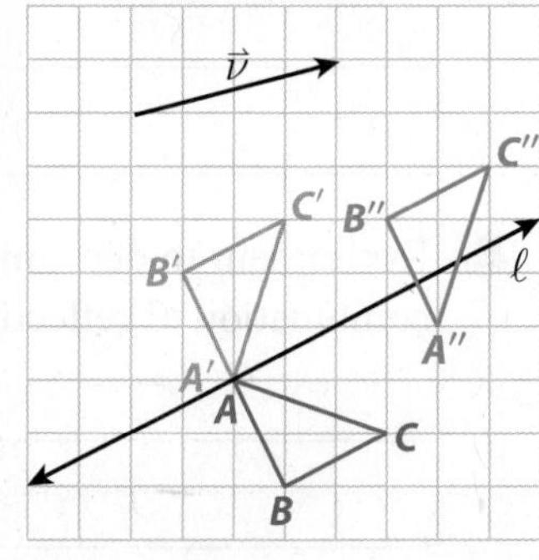

B 180° rotation around point P then translation along $\vec{v}$ then reflection across line ℓ

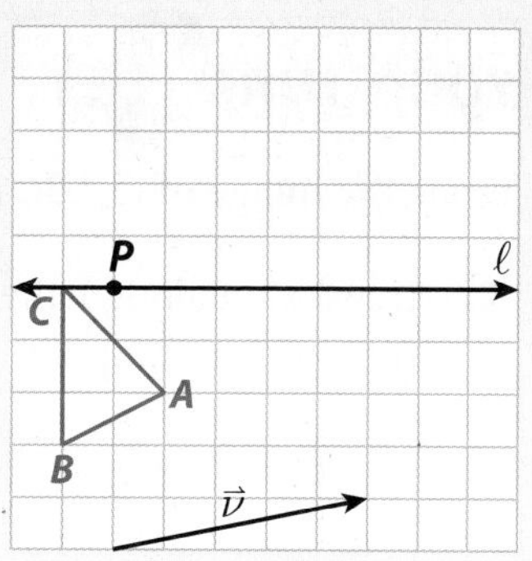

STEP 1 Draw the image of $\triangle ABC$ after a 180° rotation around point P.

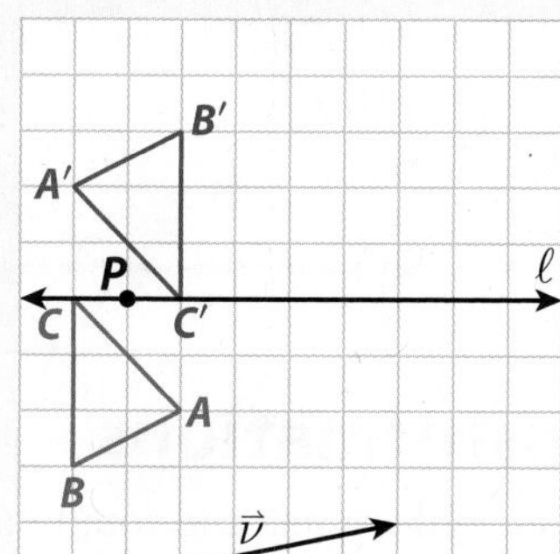

STEP 2 Draw the image of $\triangle A'B'C'$ after a translation along $\vec{v}$.

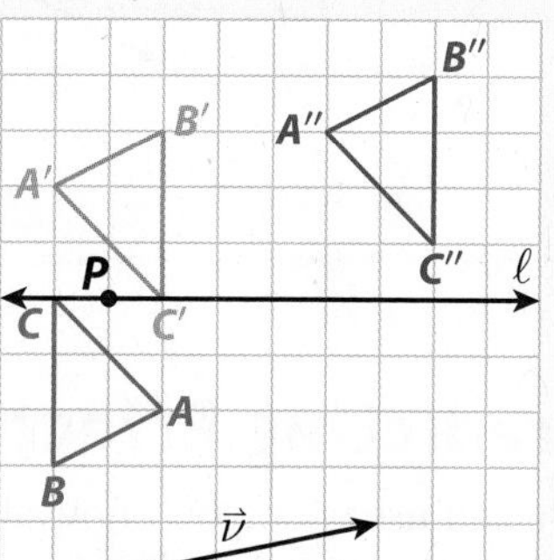

STEP 3 Draw the image of $\triangle A''B''C''$ after a reflection across line ℓ

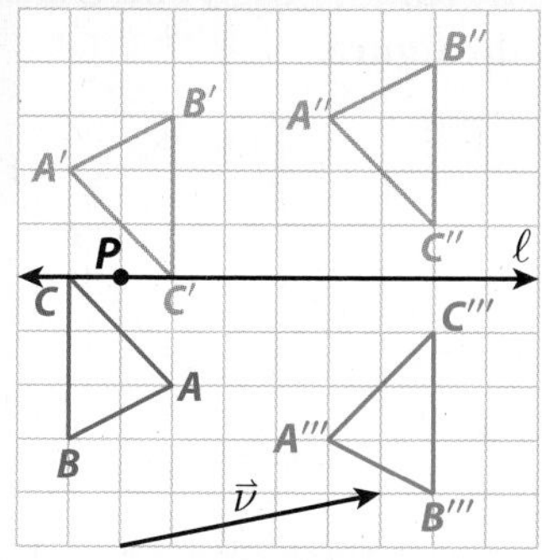

My Notes

Math Talk
Mathematical Practices

What must be true about the size and shape of $\triangle ABC$ and $\triangle A'''B'''C'''$? Why?

REFLECT

3. **Justify Reasoning** In part A of Example 1, does the order in which you perform the transformations matter? Justify your response.

YOUR TURN

Draw the image of $\triangle ABC$ after the given combination of transformations.

4. translation along $\vec{v}$ then 270° rotation around point P

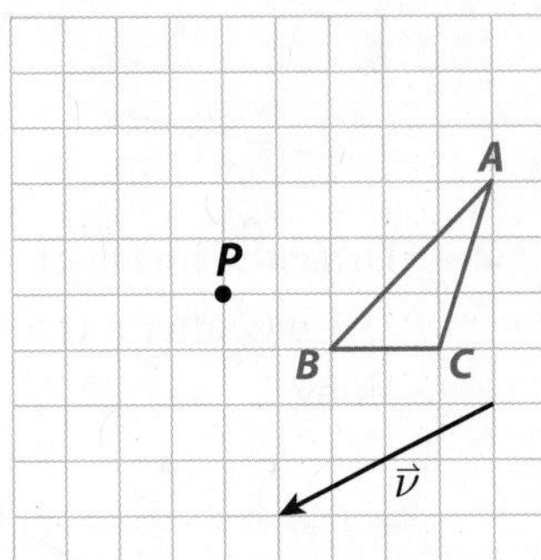

5. 90° rotation around point P then 180° rotation around point Q then translation along $\vec{v}$

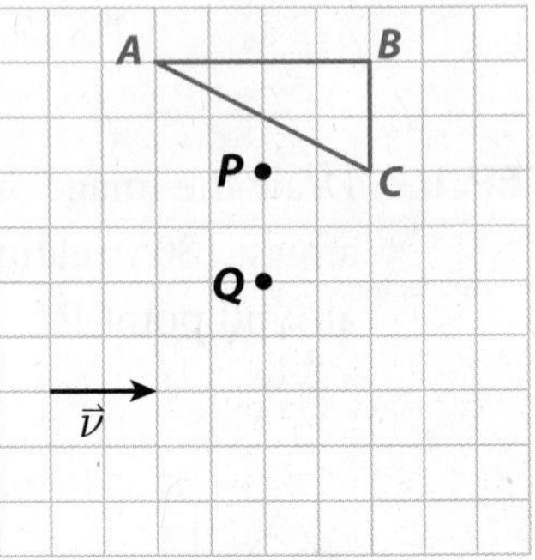

Predicting Effects of Transformations

You can use what you know about translations, reflections, and rotations to predict how the location of a figure will be affected by one or more transformations.

EXAMPLE 2

CA CC G.CO.6

Square *JKLM* is reflected across the *x*-axis, rotated 180°, and translated along the vector $\langle 3, 2 \rangle$. Describe the effect on the figure.

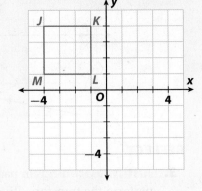

STEP 1 Predict the effect of the first transformation.

Since *JKLM* is in Quadrant II, a reflection across the *x*-axis maps the square to Quadrant III.

STEP 2 Predict the effect of the second transformation.

A rotation of 180° maps a square in Quadrant III to Quadrant I.

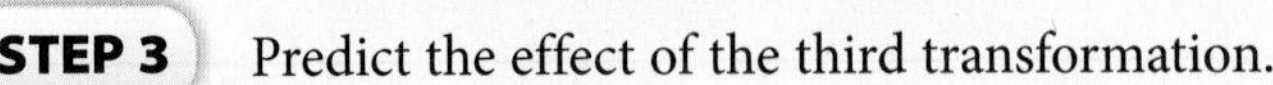

STEP 3 Predict the effect of the third transformation.

A translation along the vector $\langle 3, 2 \rangle$ moves a figure 3 units right and 2 units up. For a figure in Quadrant I, this moves the figure away from both the *x*- and *y*-axis.

The final image of *JKLM* is a square in Quadrant I that is farther from the axes than the original square was.

REFLECT

6. How do you know that the final image of *JKLM* must be a square?

7. **What If?** Would the overall effect on the figure be different if the final transformation were a translation along the vector $\langle 2, 3\rangle$? Explain.

8. **Communicate Mathematical Ideas** Describe a sequence of three different transformations that maps square *JKLM* to a square in Quadrant III that is farther from the axes than the original figure was.

My Notes

YOUR TURN

Describe the effect of the transformations on the figure.

9. $\triangle ABC$ is reflected across the line $y = x$.

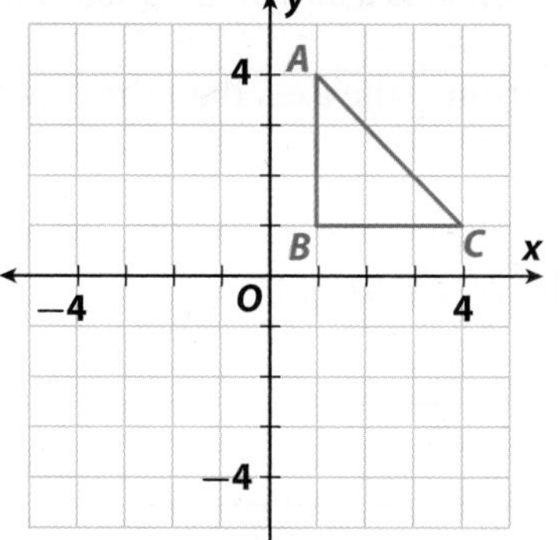

10. Rectangle *PQRS* is reflected across the *y*-axis, translated along the vector $\langle 2, -2\rangle$, and rotated 90°.

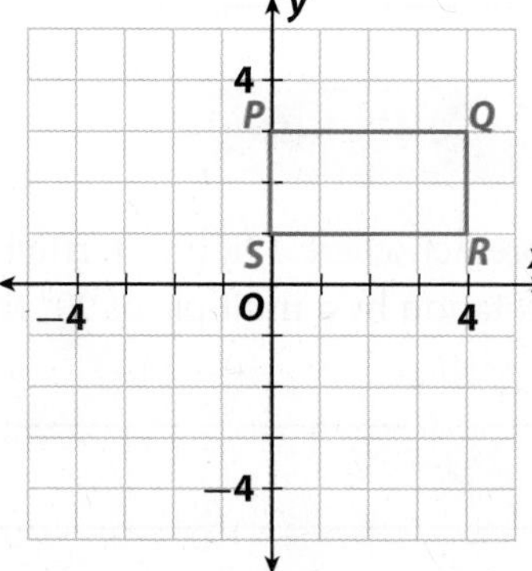

Guided Practice

Draw the image of $\triangle ABC$ after the given combination of transformations. (Example 1)

1. reflection across line ℓ then reflection across line m

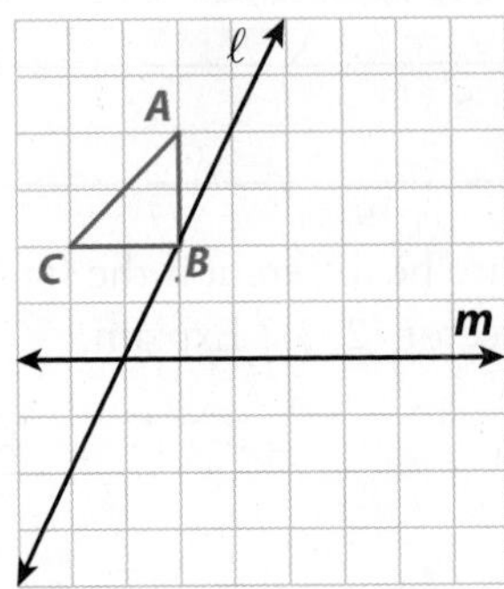

2. translation along $\vec{v}$ then reflection across line ℓ then 180° rotation around point P

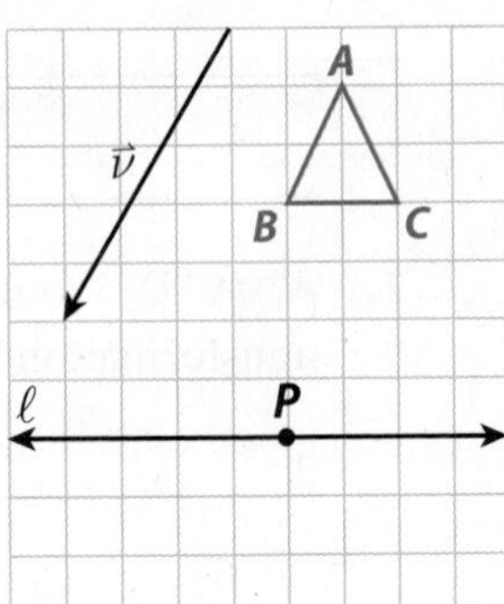

Describe the effect of the transformations on the figure. (Example 2)

3. Square $DEFG$ is translated along the vector $\langle -5, -5 \rangle$, reflected across the x-axis, and rotated 270°.

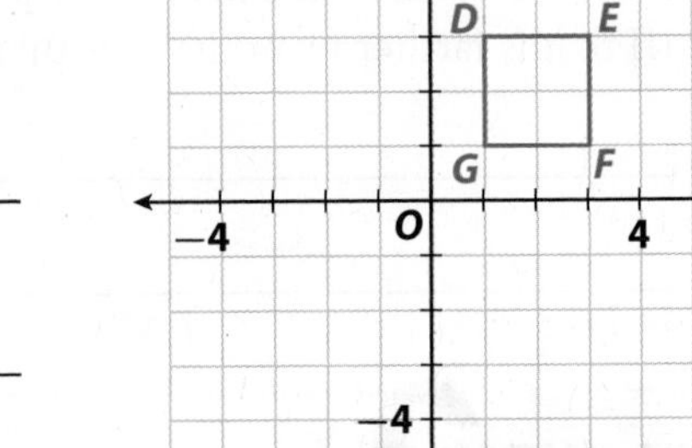

(1) The translation along $\langle -5, -5 \rangle$ maps the square to which quadrant? __________

(2) The reflection across the x-axis maps the square to which quadrant? __________

(3) The 270° rotation maps the square to which quadrant? __________

The final image of $DEFG$ is a square in Quadrant __________ that is **closer to/farther from** the axes than the original square was.

4. $\triangle JKL$ is rotated 180°, translated along the vector $\langle 4, 0 \rangle$, and translated along the vector $\langle 0, -4 \rangle$.

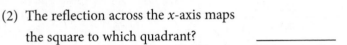

____

____

____

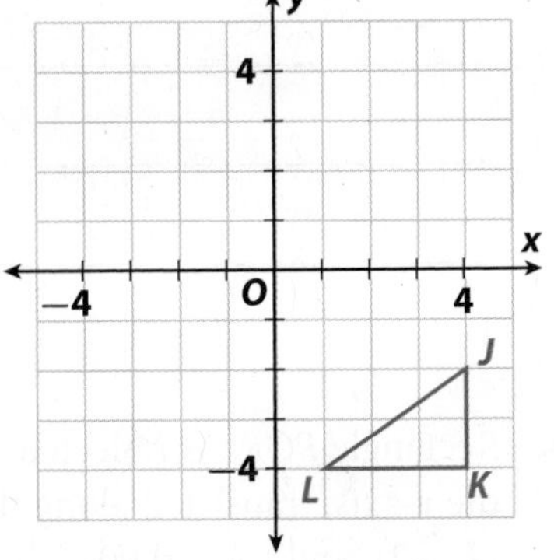

5. Why is it easier to predict where a figure starting in Quadrant I will be after a reflection across an axis or a rotation by a multiple of 90° than after a translation?

____

____

____

Name ________________ Class ________________ Date ________________

14.6 Independent Practice

CA CC G.CO.2, G.CO.5, G.CO.6

6. Draw the image of line m after a reflection across the y-axis followed by a translation along the vector $\langle 0, 3 \rangle$. (*Hint*: Consider the effect on two points on line m.)

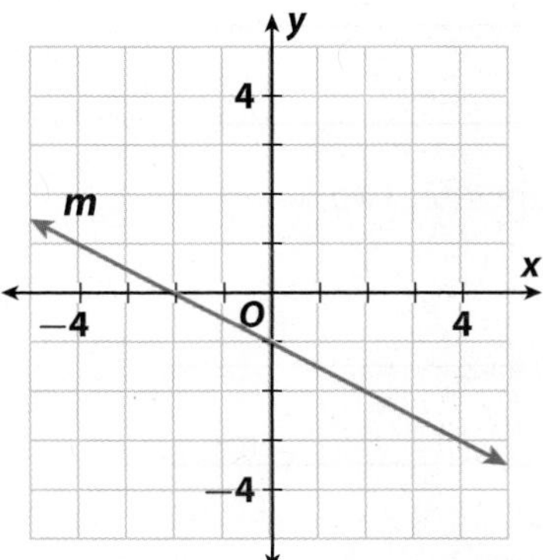

7. Sometimes a combination of transformations is equivalent to a single transformation.

   a. Draw the image of $\triangle ABC$ after a reflection across the x-axis followed by a reflection across the y-axis.

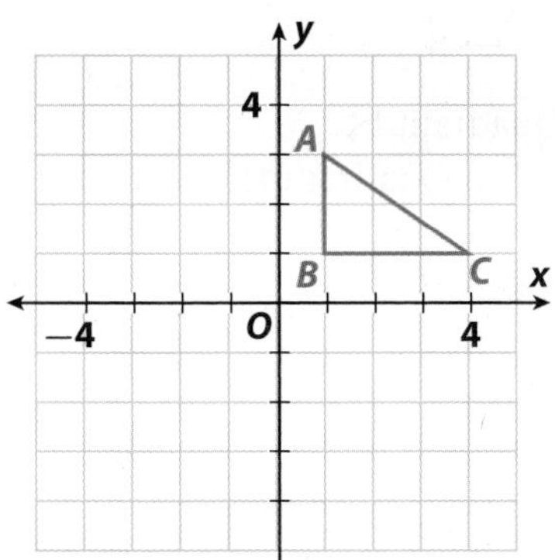

   b. Draw and label your own figure in Quadrant II. Then draw the image of the figure after a reflection across the x-axis followed by a reflection across the y-axis.

   c. **Make a Conjecture** What single transformation is equivalent to a reflection across the x-axis followed by a reflection across the y-axis?

   ____

8. Square $ABCD$ is rotated by 90° around its center point and then reflected across the vertical line shown.

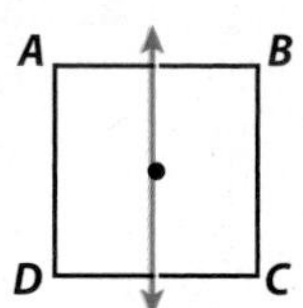

   a. Draw and label the image of the square after the two transformations.

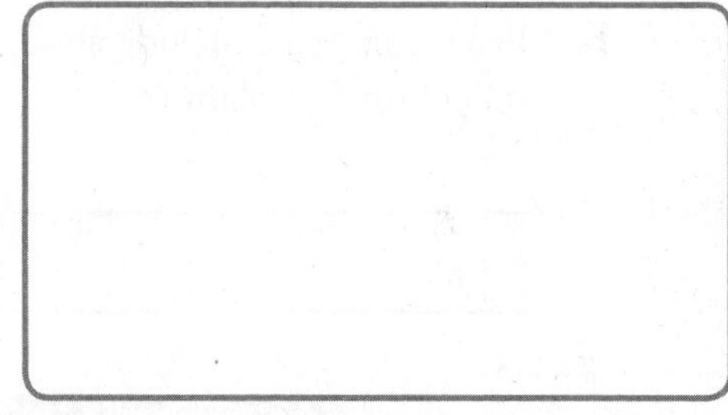

   b. Does the order of the transformations matter? Explain.

   ____

   ____

   ____

9. Jamilla is creating an animation. She wants the moon to face in the opposite direction and lie across Quadrants II and III. Describe a sequence of transformations she can use.

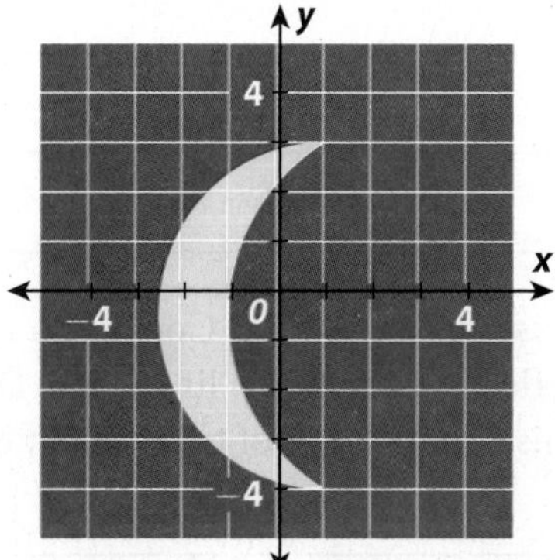

____

____

____

10. To examine the *orientation* of a figure, label consecutive vertices as *A*, *B*, *C*, and so on. As you do so, note whether you move around the figure in a clockwise or counterclockwise direction. After a transformation, label the corresponding vertices as A', B', C', and so on. As you do so, note the direction in which you move around the figure.

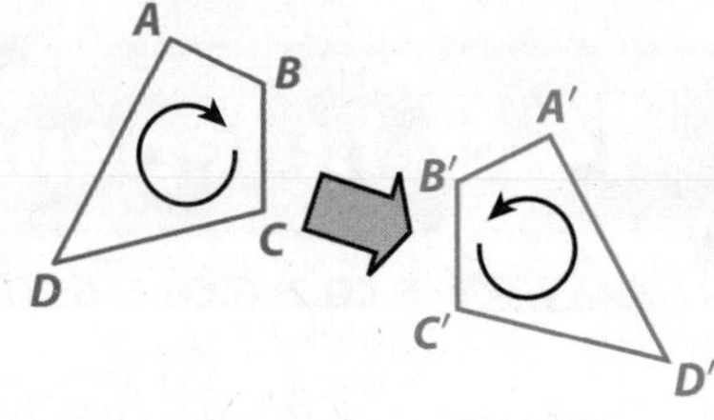

The orientation of *ABCD* is reversed.

a. Sketch and label a figure and its image after a translation. Examine the orientation. Repeat the process for a reflection and a rotation. Which transformations preserve the orientation of a figure? Which transformations reverse the orientation?

____

____

b. What can you conclude about the orientation of a figure after two reflections? Explain.

____

____

FOCUS ON HIGHER ORDER THINKING

Work Area

11. Draw Conclusions Caitlyn plotted a point on a coordinate plane. She reflected it across the *x*-axis, reflected it across the *y*-axis, and then rotated it 90°. The final image of the point was in Quadrant IV. What can you conclude about the location of the point that Caitlyn plotted?

____

12. Look for a Pattern One 90° rotation maps a triangle in Quadrant I to Quadrant II. Two 90° rotations map a triangle in Quadrant I to Quadrant III. Suppose you perform a sequence of fifty 90° rotations on a triangle in Quadrant I. In which quadrant does the final image lie? Explain.

____

____

____

13. Justify Reasoning Consider a reflection across the line $x = a$ followed by a reflection across the line $y = b$. Do any points of the plane remain fixed under this combination of transformations? Justify your answer.

____

____

____

____

____

Ready to Go On?

Personal Math Trainer

Online Practice and Help

14.1 Geometric Terms

Use the figure to complete each statement.

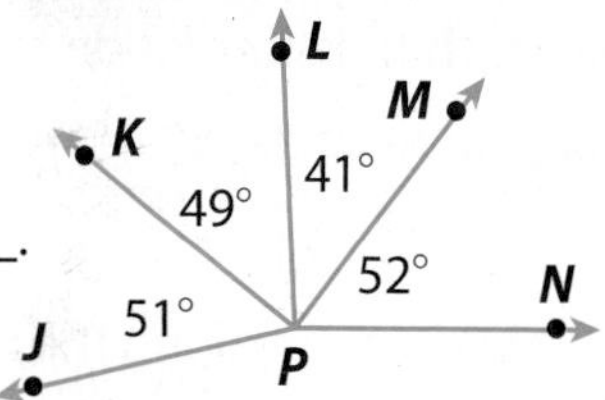

1. $m\angle LPN =$ ____________________

2. The perpendicular rays in the figure are ________ and ________.

14.2–14.4 Introduction to Transformations/ Translations/Reflections

Draw the image of $\triangle ABC$ under the given transformation.

3. $(x, y) \rightarrow (-x, y)$

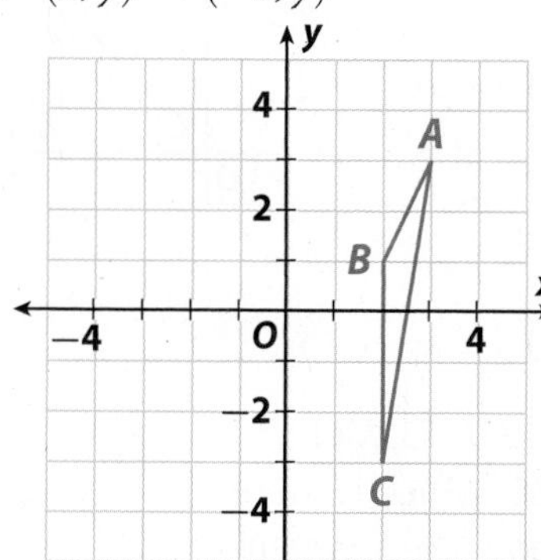

4. translation along $\vec{v}$

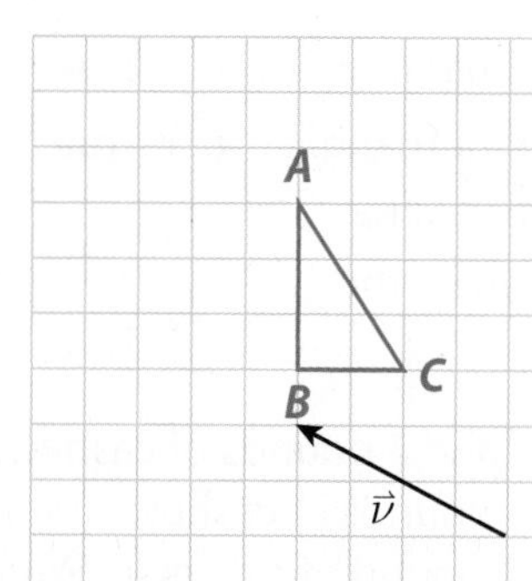

5. reflection across line ℓ

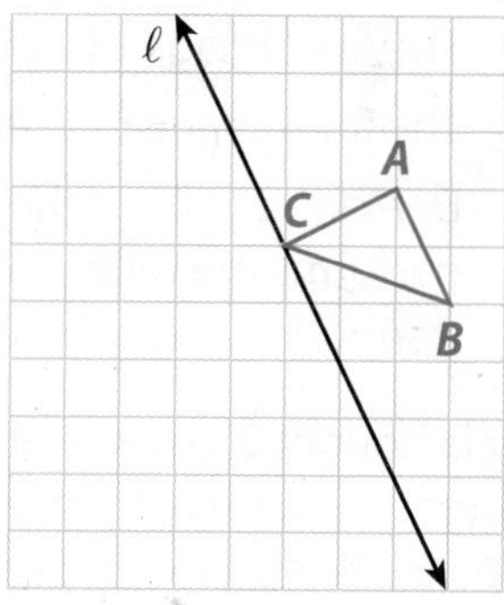

14.5 Rotations

Describe all rotations of less than 360°, if any, that map the figure onto itself.

6. kite

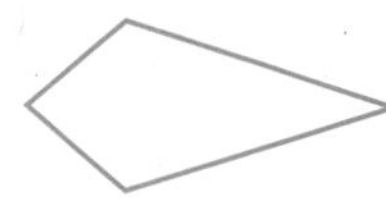

____

7. regular hexagon

____

14.6 Combining Transformations

8. Draw the image of $\triangle ABC$ after a 90° rotation around point P followed by a translation along $\vec{v}$.

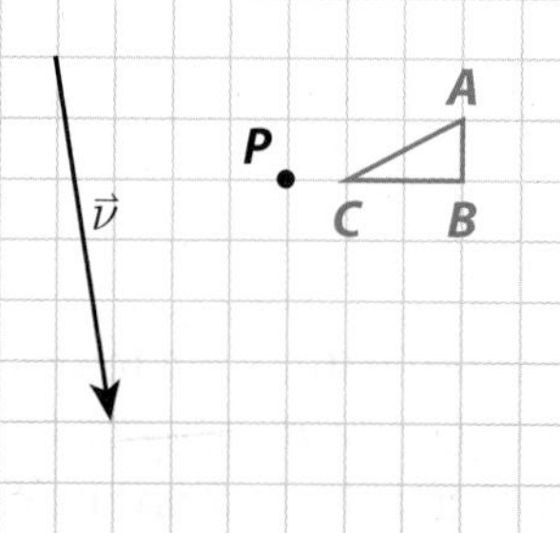

ESSENTIAL QUESTION

9. What do translations, reflections, and rotations have in common?

____

____

MODULE 14
MIXED REVIEW

Assessment Readiness

1. Does each transformation map a triangle in Quadrant II to Quadrant I?

Select Yes or No for A–C.

A. A rotation of 270° ○ Yes ○ No

B. A translation along the vector $\langle -2, -2 \rangle$ ○ Yes ○ No

C. A reflection across the *y*-axis ○ Yes ○ No

2. DeMarcus draws $\triangle ABC$. Then he translates it along the vector $\langle -4, -3 \rangle$, rotates it 180°, and reflects it across the *x*-axis.

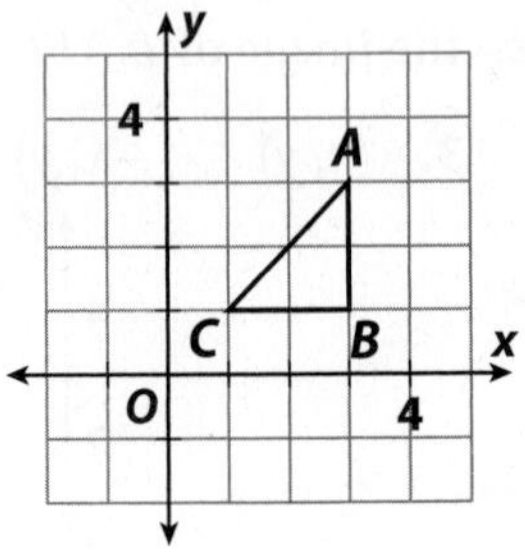

Choose True or False for each statement.

A. The final image of $\triangle ABC$ is in Quadrant IV. ○ True ○ False

B. The final image of $\triangle ABC$ is a right triangle. ○ True ○ False

C. DeMarcus will get the same result if he performs the reflection followed by the translation and rotation. ○ True ○ False

3. Alicia bought 2 pounds of peanuts and 3 pounds of cashews for \$10.15. Mei bought 2 pounds of peanuts and 4 pounds of cashews for \$12.30. Which is more expensive: 1 pound of peanuts or 1 pound of cashews? Write and solve a system of equations to justify your answer.

4. Chase is using a coordinate plane to design a video game. In the game, a golf ball moves from $A(3, 3)$ to $B(-3, -3)$. Describe three different transformations or combinations of transformations he can use to move the golf ball. Give an algebraic rule for each transformation.

Transformations and Congruence

MODULE 15

CALIFORNIA

? **ESSENTIAL QUESTION**

How are transformations related to the ASA, SAS, and SSS triangle congruence theorems?

CALIFORNIA COMMON CORE

LESSON 15.1
Congruent Figures

CA CC G.CO.6, G.CO.5

LESSON 15.2
Triangle Congruence

CA CC G.CO.7

LESSON 15.3
Triangle Congruence Criteria: ASA

CA CC G.CO.8

LESSON 15.4
Triangle Congruence Criteria: SAS
CA CC G.CO.8

LESSON 15.5
Triangle Congruence Criteria: SSS
CA CC G.CO.8, G.CO.12

Real-World Video

When designing a landscape, whether for a private home or public park, a landscape architect transforms geometric shapes to produce an attractive design. In the process, the architect may use congruent shapes in repeating patterns.

my.hrw.com

GO DIGITAL
my.hrw.com

my.hrw.com

Go digital with your write-in student edition, accessible on any device.

Math On the Spot

Scan with your smart phone to jump directly to the online edition, video tutor, and more.

Animated Math

Interactively explore key concepts to see how math works.

Personal Math Trainer

Get immediate feedback and help as you work through practice sets.

Are YOU Ready?

Complete these exercises to review skills you will need for this module.

Points, Lines, and Planes

EXAMPLE **Use the diagram to name a point, a segment, a ray, a line, and a plane (if possible).**

All of the following are points: *M*, *N*, *O*, or *P*.
There are two segments: $\overline{MN}$ and $\overline{NP}$.
There are three rays: $\overrightarrow{MN}$, $\overrightarrow{NM}$, and $\overrightarrow{NP}$.
There is one line: $\overleftrightarrow{MN}$.
There is one plane: $\mathfrak{R}$.

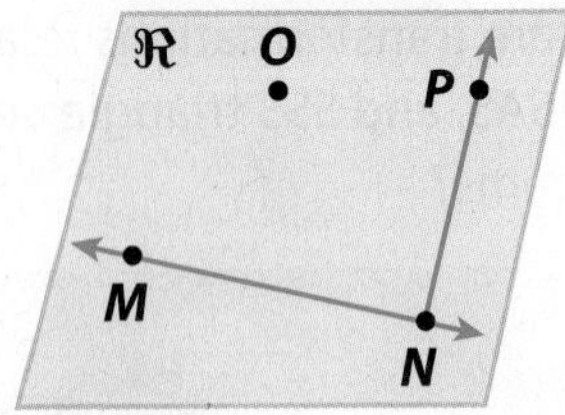

Use the diagram on the right to name each of the following.

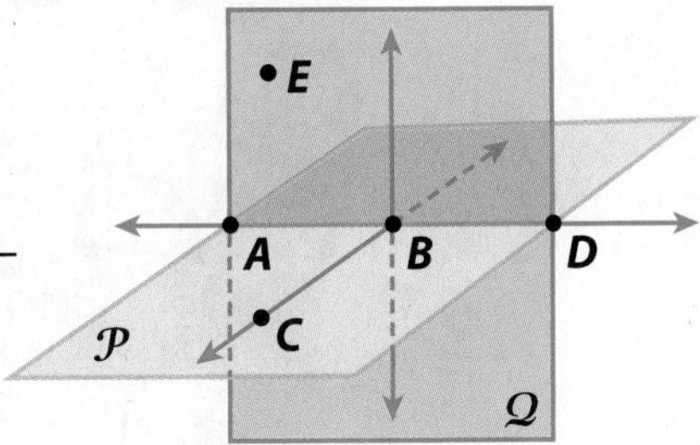

1. a point ____________

2. a ray with endpoint *C* ____________

3. a plane that contains the point *E* ____________

4. a segment with one endpoint at point *A*

____

5. a line that passes through point *D* ____________

Measure Angles

EXAMPLE **Find the measure of the angle shown.**

One ray of the angle is lined up with the zero along the outer set of degree measures, so read the number where the other ray of the angle intersects the protractor on this same set of degree measures.
The measure of the angle is 55°.

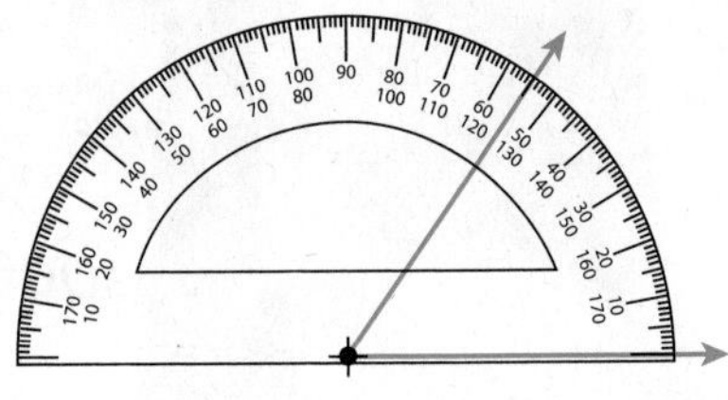

Use a protractor to measure each angle.

6. ____________ **7.** ____________ **8.** ____________

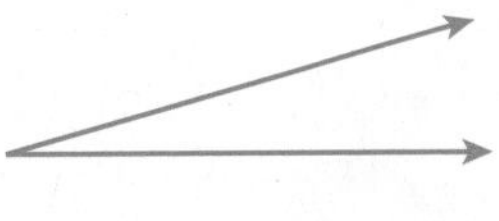

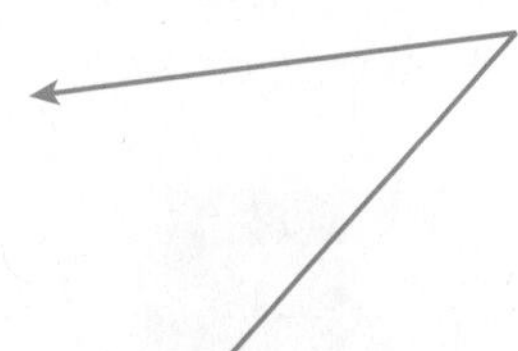

Reading Start-Up

Visualize Vocabulary

Use the review words to complete the bubble map.

a transformation that changes the position of a figure without changing its size or shape

moves points of a figure the same distance in the same direction

turns points of a figure around a point

moves points of a figure by flipping them over a line to create a mirror image

Vocabulary

Review Words

✔ reflection *(reflexión)*
✔ rigid motion *(movimiento rígido)*
✔ rotation *(rotación)*
transformation *(transformación)*
✔ translation *(traslación)*

Preview Words

congruent
theorem

Understand Vocabulary

To become familiar with some of the vocabulary terms in the module, consider the following. You may refer to the module or the glossary.

1. Have you heard the term **congruent** before? How do you think this term may be related to geometric transformations?

____

____

2. You have learned what a postulate is. How do you think a postulate is different from a **theorem**?

____

____

Active Reading

Layered Book Before beginning the module, create a Layered Book to help you organize what you learn. Use a separate flap for each lesson from this module. As you study each lesson, write vocabulary, theorems, and summaries of important ideas under the appropriate flap.

GETTING READY FOR

Transformations and Congruence

Understanding the standards and the vocabulary terms in the standards will help you know exactly what you are expected to learn in this module.

G.CO.7

Use the definition of congruence in terms of rigid motions to show that two triangles are congruent if and only if corresponding pairs of sides and corresponding pairs of angles are congruent.

Key Vocabulary

congruent *(congruente)*
Two plane figures are congruent if one can be obtained from the other by rigid motion (a sequence of rotations, reflections, and translations). The symbol for congruent is ≅.

What It Means to You

You will learn to use rigid motions to show that triangles are congruent.

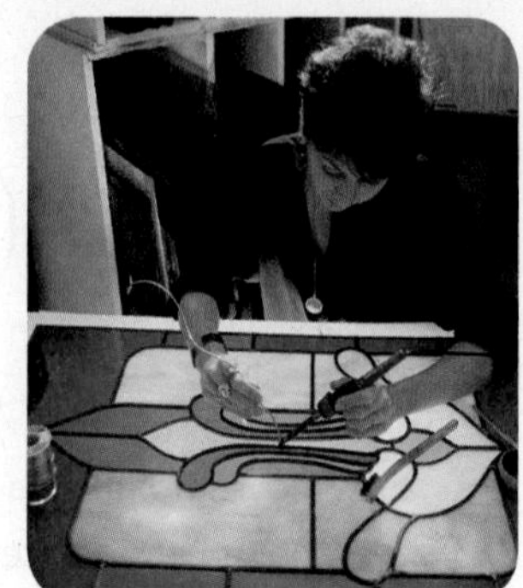

EXAMPLE G.CO.7

Two pieces of colored glass have corresponding pairs of angles and sides that are congruent. How can you show that the triangles are congruent?

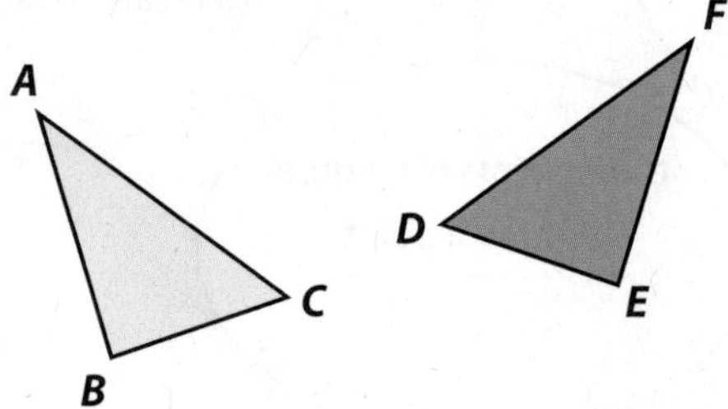

Use a translation to map point C to point D. Then, because corresponding pairs of sides and angles are congruent, you can reflect $\triangle ABC$ across a line through C and D so that point A maps to point F and point B maps to point E. The triangles are congruent because a sequence of rigid motions (translation, reflection) maps one triangle onto the other.

CA CC G.CO.8

Explain how the criteria for triangle congruence (ASA, SAS, and SSS) follow from the definition of congruence in terms of rigid motions.

Key Vocabulary

theorem *(teorema)*
A conjecture that can be proved using a logical sequence of definitions, postulates, and already-proven theorems.

What It Means to You

You will use rigid motions to justify some minimum criteria for deciding whether two triangles are congruent.

EXAMPLE G.CO.8

How can you show that $\triangle PQS$ and $\triangle RQS$ are congruent?

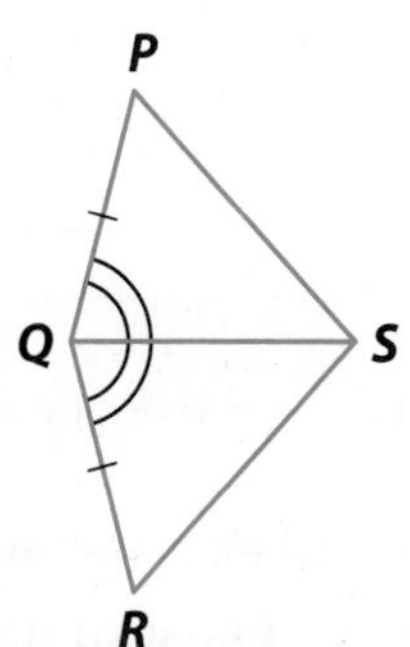

Because $\overline{QS} \cong \overline{QS}$, $\angle PQS \cong \angle RQS$, and $\overline{PQ} \cong \overline{RQ}$, you can reflect $\triangle PQS$ across $\overline{QS}$ so that it maps onto $\triangle RQS$. Knowing that two pairs of corresponding sides are congruent and their included angles are congruent is enough to show that the triangles are congruent. This is the basis of the ASA Triangle Congruence Theorem.

Visit my.hrw.com to see all CA Common Core Standards explained.

my.hrw.com

LESSON

15.1 Congruent Figures

CA CC G.CO.6

Use geometric descriptions of rigid motions to transform figures and to predict the effect of a given rigid motion on a given figure; given two figures, use the definition of congruence in terms of rigid motions to decide if they are congruent. *Also G.CO.5*

ESSENTIAL QUESTION

How can you determine whether two figures are congruent?

EXPLORE ACTIVITY 1

Confirming Congruence

Two figures in a plane are **congruent** if one can be obtained from the other by rigid motion: that is, by a sequence of one or more translations, reflections, or rotations.

A landscape architect uses a grid to design a landscape. Use tracing paper to confirm that the landscape elements are congruent.

A Trace flower bed *ABCD* on tracing paper.

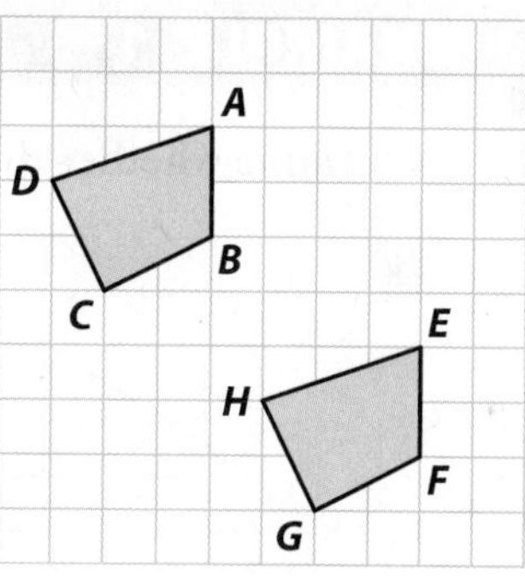

What type of transformation can you use to move the tracing paper so that flower bed *ABCD* is mapped onto flower bed *EFGH*?

____

What does this confirm about the flower beds?

____

B Trace pools *JKLM* and *NPQR* on tracing paper.

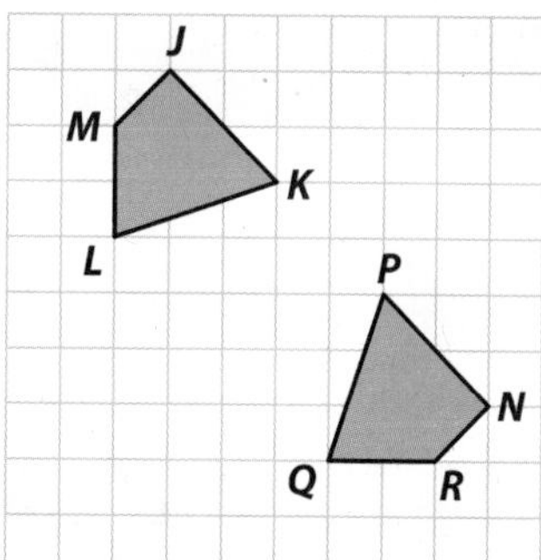

Fold the paper so that pool *JKLM* is mapped onto pool *NPQR*. What type of transformation is this?

____

What does this confirm about the pools?

____

C Trace lawn *STUV* on tracing paper.

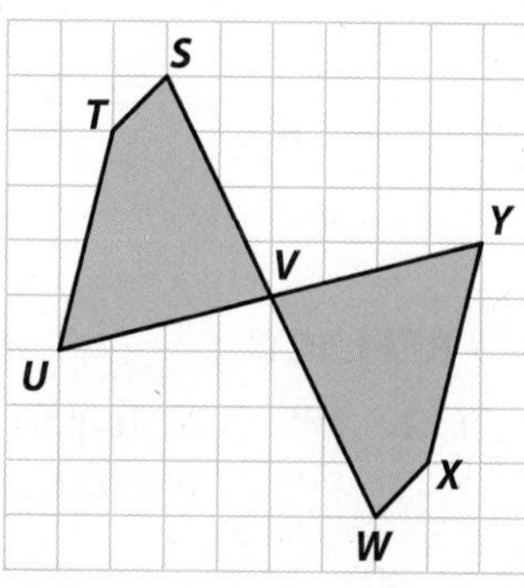

What type of transformation can you use to move the tracing paper so that lawn *STUV* is mapped onto lawn *WXYV*?

____

What does this confirm about the lawns?

____

EXPLORE ACTIVITY 1 *(cont'd)*

REFLECT

1. Describe the transformations that you used to map the figures onto one another.

____

____

____

____

Deciding If Figures Are Congruent

You can use the definition of congruence to determine whether two figures are congruent.

EXAMPLE 1

CA CC G.CO.6

Determine whether the two figures are congruent. Explain your answer.

A

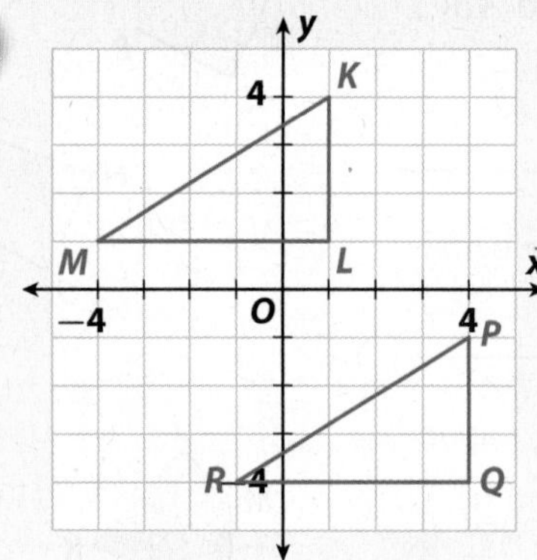

You can map $\triangle KLM$ onto $\triangle PQR$ by a translation.

The translation has the algebraic rule $(x, y) \rightarrow (x + 3, y - 5)$.

Since a translation is a rigid motion, $\triangle KLM$ is congruent onto $\triangle PQR$.

Math Talk
Mathematical Practices
What is another way to describe the translation in Example 1A?

B

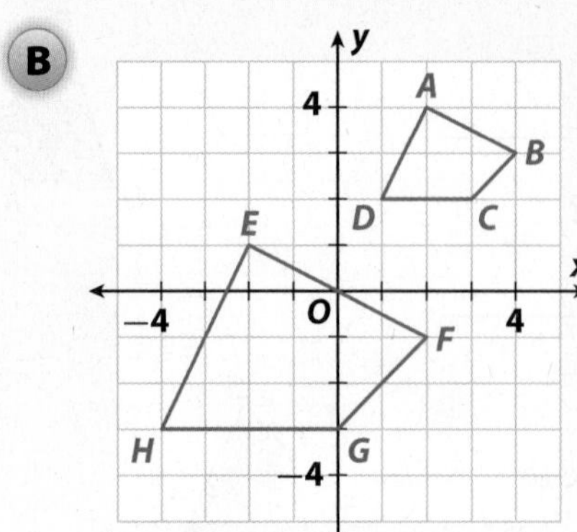

Quadrilaterals *ABCD* and *EFGH* have different sizes.

Since rigid motions preserve length, there is no rigid motion that maps quadrilateral *ABCD* onto quadrilateral *EFGH*.

The quadrilaterals are not congruent.

REFLECT

2. **What If?** In part A of Example 1, suppose you reflect $\triangle PQR$ across the y-axis. Will $\triangle KLM$ be congruent to $\triangle P'Q'R'$? Why or why not?

____

____

YOUR TURN

Determine whether the two figures are congruent. Explain your answer.

3.

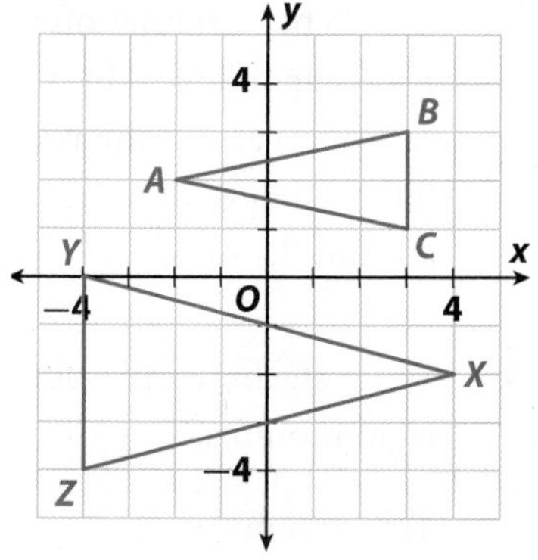

4.

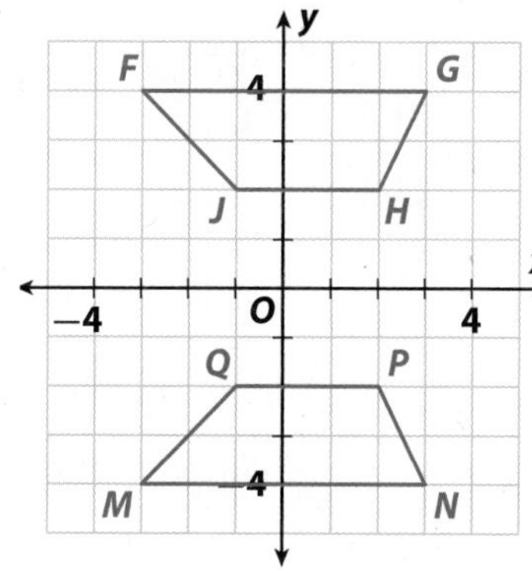

Specifying Sequences of Rigid Motions

When two figures are congruent, you can be certain that there is a sequence of rigid motions that maps one figure onto the other. When you specify this sequence, be sure to list the vertices in the order in which they correspond.

Math On the Spot
my.hrw.com

EXAMPLE 2

For each pair of congruent figures, specify a sequence of rigid motions that maps one figure onto the other.

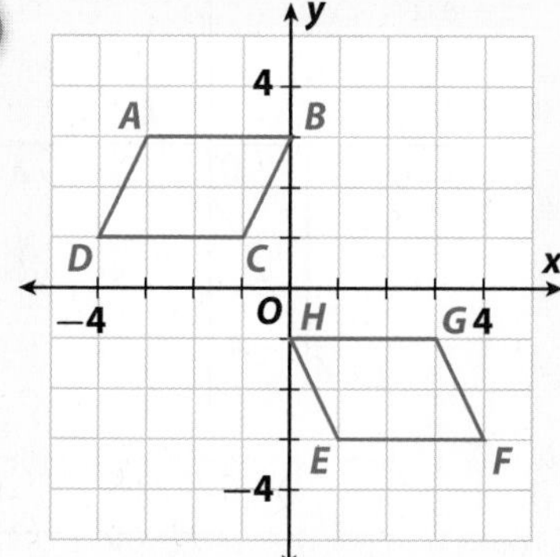

STEP 1 Determine a sequence of rigid motions.

Notice that you have to both slide and flip *ABCD*. You can map *ABCD* onto *EFGH* by a translation of 4 units right followed by a reflection across the *x*-axis.

Write algebraic rules for the rigid motions.

Translation: $(x, y) \rightarrow (x + 4, y)$
Reflection: $(x, y) \rightarrow (x, -y)$

B

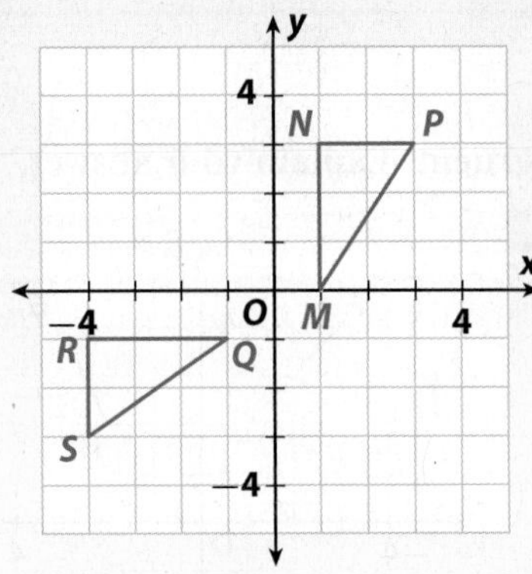

STEP 1 Determine a sequence of rigid motions.

You can map $\triangle MNP$ onto $\triangle QRS$ by a translation of 1 unit up followed by a reflection across the y-axis followed by a 90° rotation around the origin.

STEP 2 Write algebraic rules for the rigid motions.

Translation: $(x, y) \rightarrow (x, y + 1)$
Reflection: $(x, y) \rightarrow (-x, y)$
Rotation: $(x, y) \rightarrow (-y, x)$

Math Talk
Mathematical Practices

How can you tell that $\triangle MNP$ has to at least be rotated or flipped?

REFLECT

5. **Critique Reasoning** Miguel said that it is possible to use a different translation and reflection to map one figure onto the other in Example 2A so that the vertices are paired in a different way. Do you agree or disagree? Justify your reasoning.

____

____

YOUR TURN

For each pair of congruent figures, specify a sequence of rigid motions that maps one figure onto the other.

6.

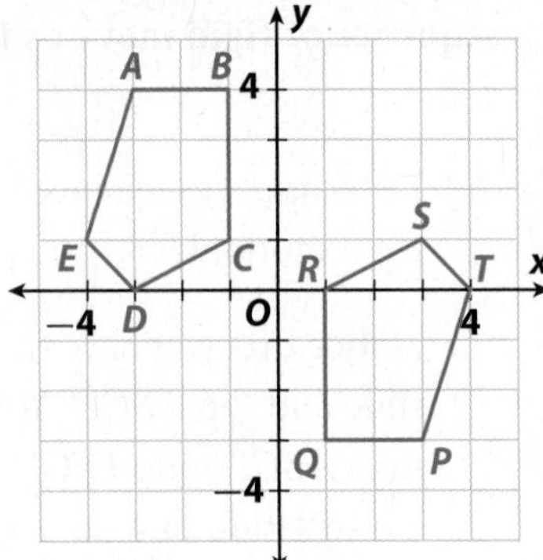

____

____

____

____

7.

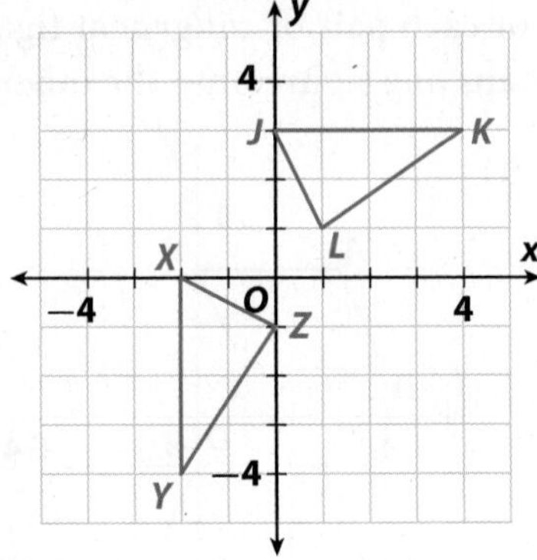

____

____

____

____

Personal Math Trainer
Online Practice and Help
my.hrw.com

EXPLORE ACTIVITY 2

Congruent Segments and Angles

A Use a straightedge to trace $\overline{AB}$ on a piece of tracing paper. Then slide, flip, and/or turn the tracing paper to determine if there is a sequence of rigid motions that maps $\overline{AB}$ onto one of the other segments.

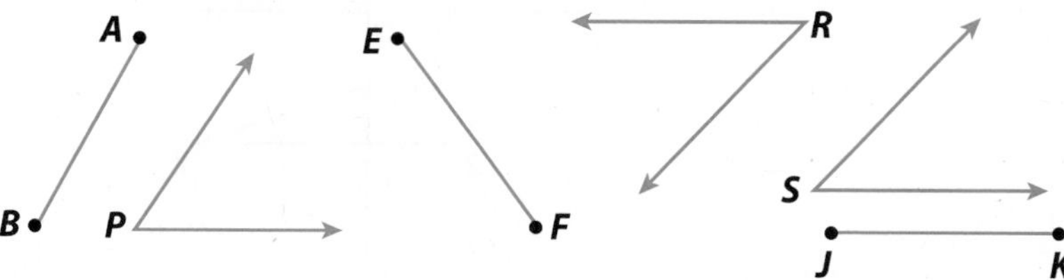

B Repeat the process with the other segments and angles. Tell which pairs of segments and which pairs of angles are congruent.

Congruent segments: ________________________________

Congruent angles: ________________________________

C Check your results by measuring the segments and angles.

REFLECT

8. **Draw Conclusions** Will two line segments that are the same length always be congruent? Justify your answer.

____

____

9. **Make a Conjecture** Make a conjecture about the relationship between two angles that have the same measure. Justify your answer.

____

____

Guided Practice

1. Rimah and Aaron each draw a triangle on a transparency. Rimah flips her transparency over and slides it so that her triangle coincides with Aaron's triangle. What can you conclude about the two triangles? Explain. (Explore Activity 1)

____

____

____

Determine whether the two figures are congruent. Explain your answer. (Example 1)

2.

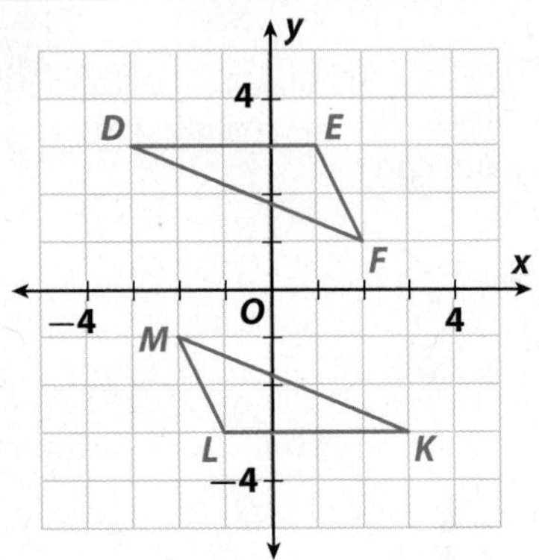

3.

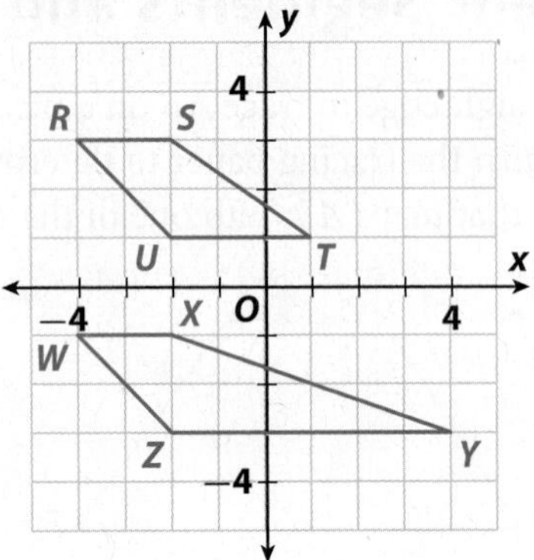

4. For the pair of congruent figures, specify a sequence of rigid motions that maps one figure onto the other. (Example 2)

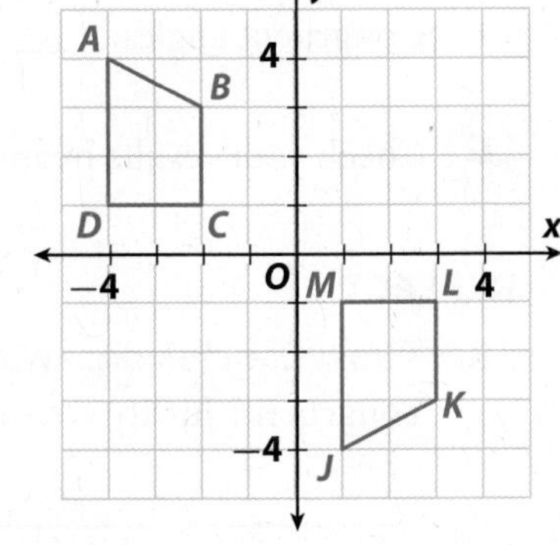

STEP 1 Determine the sequence of rigid motions.

You can map *ABCD* onto *JKLM* by a reflection across the ________-axis followed by a translation of ________ units **left/right**.

STEP 2 Write algebraic rules for the rigid motions.

Reflection: $(x, y) \rightarrow (\square, \square)$ Translation: $(x, y) \rightarrow (x + \square, y)$

5. Identify all pairs of congruent segments and congruent angles in the figure. (Explore Activity 2)

Q
R
4.2 m
45°
3.8 m
45°
P 3.8 m T 4.2 m S

ESSENTIAL QUESTION CHECK-IN

6. What two things can you conclude about the relationship between two figures using the definition of the word *congruent* in terms of rigid motions?

Name ____________________ Class ____________ Date ____________

15.1 Independent Practice

CA CC G.CO.5, G.CO.6

7. Give algebraic rules for a sequence of rigid motions a textile designer can use to map figure *ABC* onto figure *DEF*.

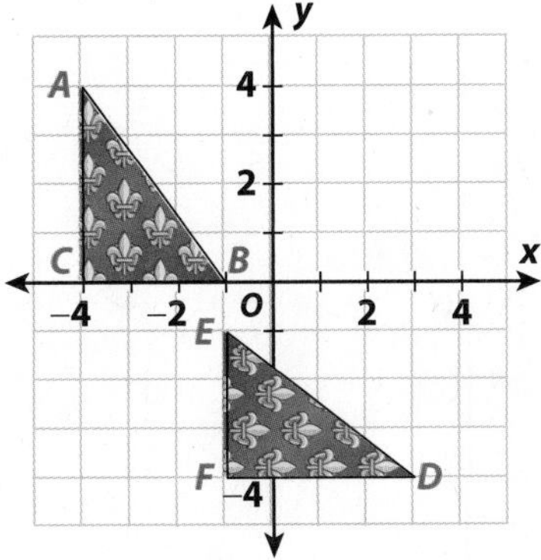

____

____

8. Explain why a line of symmetry divides a figure into two congruent halves.

____

____

9. Draw a pair of congruent quadrilaterals on the coordinate plane. Then explain how you know they are congruent.

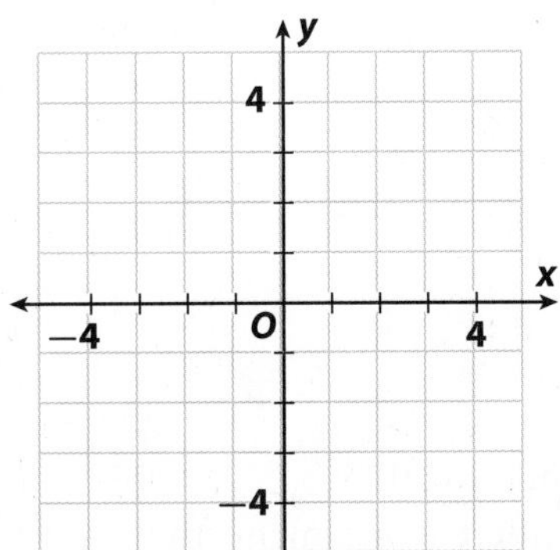

____

____

____

10. The figure shows a map of the first-aid stations in a 10-kilometer race.

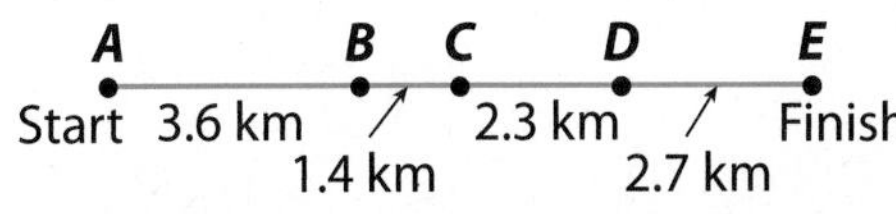

a. Determine which two segments are congruent and justify your answer. Name any properties that you use.

____

____

____

____

b. **What If?** Does your answer change if first-aid station *D* is moved 0.1 km closer to the finish line? Explain.

____

____

11. **Critique Reasoning** Gabriel says that quadrilateral *JKLM* and quadrilateral *NPQR* are congruent because the transformation $(x, y) \rightarrow (2x, 2y)$ maps *JKLM* to *NPQR*. Do you agree with Gabriel? Explain.

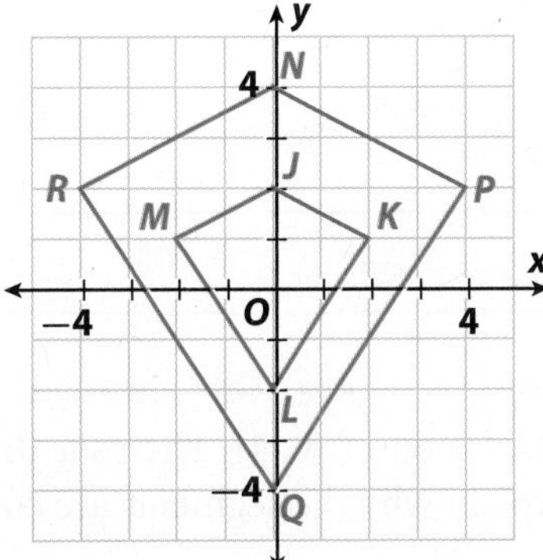

____

____

____

12. Wei drew two congruent triangles on a coordinate plane. She said that the rigid motions that map one triangle onto the other are $(x, y) \rightarrow (-y, x)$ followed by $(x, y) \rightarrow (x + 1, y - 3)$. Draw a pair of triangles that could be Wei's triangles.

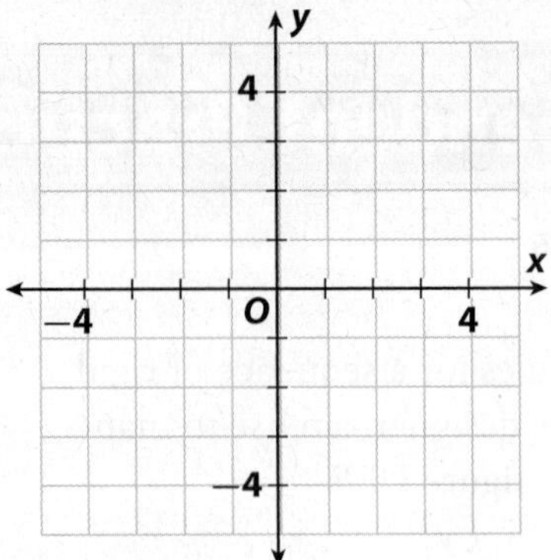

FOCUS ON HIGHER ORDER THINKING

Work Area

13. Look for a Pattern Assume the pattern of congruent squares shown in the figure continues forever.

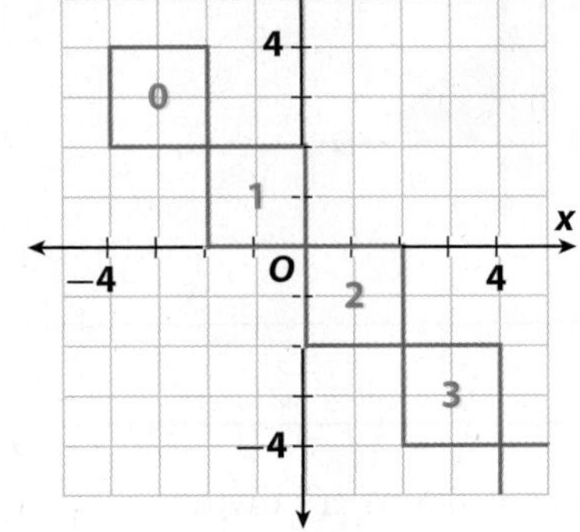

a. Write rules for rigid motions that map square 0 onto square 1, square 0 onto square 2, and square 0 onto square 3.

____

____

____

b. Write a rule for a rigid motion that maps square 0 onto square n.

____

14. Analyze Relationships Suppose you know that $\triangle ABC$ is congruent to $\triangle DEF$ and that $\triangle DEF$ is congruent to $\triangle GHJ$. Can you conclude that $\triangle ABC$ is congruent to $\triangle GHJ$? Explain.

____

____

____

____

15. Communicate Mathematical Ideas Ella plotted the points $A(0, 0)$, $B(4, 0)$, and $C(0, 4)$. Then she drew $\overline{AB}$ and $\overline{AC}$. Give two different arguments to explain why the segments are congruent.

____

____

____

____

LESSON

15.2 Triangle Congruence

Use the definition of congruence in terms of rigid motions to show that two triangles are congruent if and only if corresponding pairs of sides and corresponding pairs of angles are congruent.

ESSENTIAL QUESTION

What can you conclude about congruent triangles?

EXPLORE ACTIVITY 1

Exploring Congruent Triangles

The symbol for congruence is ≅. When you write a congruence statement like $\triangle ABC \cong \triangle DEF$, it means there is a sequence of rigid motions that maps $\triangle ABC$ to $\triangle DEF$ and that vertex A maps to vertex D, vertex B maps to vertex E, and vertex C maps to vertex F. The parts that match up when you perform a transformation are called *corresponding parts*.

The two triangles in the figure are congruent.

Q J Z H M D

A Trace $\triangle JZQ$ on a piece of tracing paper or on a transparency. Then slide, flip, and/or turn the tracing so that $\triangle JZQ$ coincides with the other triangle. Compare your sequence of transformations with those of your classmates.

B Complete the following to show how the vertices correspond.

Vertex $J \rightarrow$ ________________

Vertex $Z \rightarrow$ ________________

Vertex $Q \rightarrow$ ________________

C Write a congruence statement for the triangles. ________________________

D When you use a sequence of rigid motions to map $\triangle JZQ$ onto $\triangle MDH$, what is the image of $\overline{JZ}$? ________________

What does this tell you about the two segments? Why?

____

____

What can you conclude about their lengths? ________________________

E What can you say about the relationship between $\angle Q$ and $\angle H$? Explain.

____

____

EXPLORE ACTIVITY 1 *(cont'd)*

REFLECT

1. **Draw Conclusions** What six congruence statements about segments and angles can you write for the two triangles in Explore Activity 1? Why?

____

____

____

____

Finding Unknown Measures in Triangles

A **theorem** is a conjecture that can be proved using a logical sequence of definitions, postulates, and already-proven theorems. Your findings in Explore Activity 1 can be stated as a theorem.

Corresponding Parts of Congruent Triangles Theorem (CPCTC)

If two triangles are congruent, then corresponding sides are congruent and corresponding angles are congruent.

Math Talk
Mathematical Practices

How can you identify corresponding parts from a congruence statement like $\triangle ABC \cong \triangle DEF$?

EXAMPLE 1

CA CC G.CO.7

A $\triangle ABC \cong \triangle DEF$. **Find** BC.

STEP 1 Find the side that corresponds to $\overline{BC}$.

Since $\triangle ABC \cong \triangle DEF$, $\overline{BC} \cong \overline{EF}$.

STEP 2 Find the unknown length.

$BC = EF$, and $EF = 3.7$ cm, so $BC = 3.7$ cm.

B $\triangle ABC \cong \triangle DEF$. **Find** $m\angle B$.

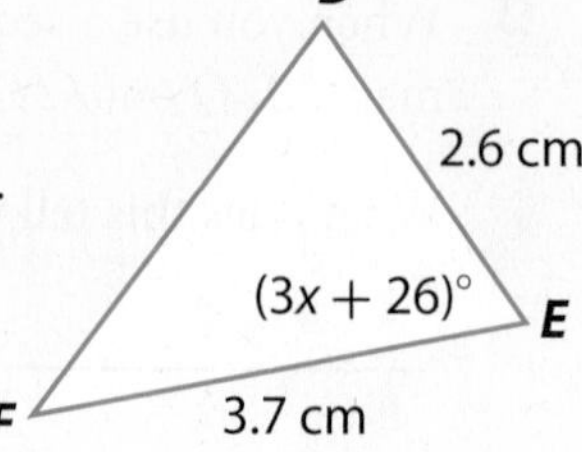

STEP 1 Find the angle that corresponds to $\angle B$.

Since $\triangle ABC \cong \triangle DEF$, $\angle B \cong \angle E$.

STEP 2 Find the unknown angle measure.

$5x = 3x + 26$ $m\angle B = m\angle E$

$2x = 26$ Subtract $3x$ from each side.

$x = 13$ Divide each side by 2.

So, $m\angle B = (5x)^\circ = (5 \cdot 13)^\circ = 65^\circ$.

REFLECT

2. What other side lengths or angle measures of $\triangle ABC$ can you determine based on the fact that $\triangle ABC \cong \triangle DEF$? Explain.

____

____

YOUR TURN

$\triangle RST \cong \triangle XYZ$. Find each given side length or angle measure.

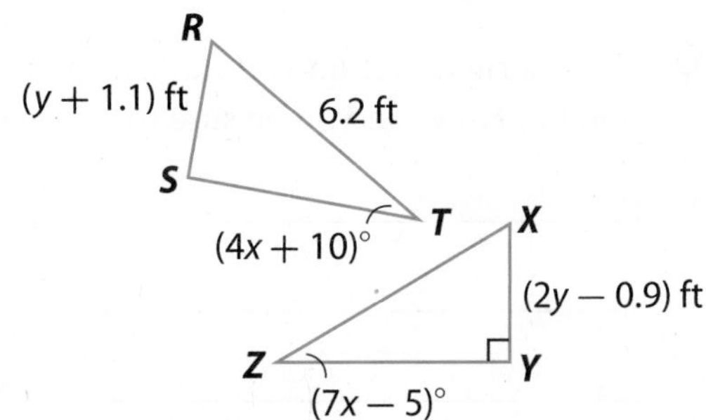

3. m∠S ____________

4. ZX ____________

5. m∠Z ____________

6. RS ____________

EXPLORE ACTIVITY 2

G.CO.7

Exploring What Makes Triangles Congruent

You form the **converse** of an if-then statement "if p, then q" by swapping p and q.

CPCTC Theorem	Converse of CPCTC Theorem
If two triangles are congruent, then they have congruent corresponding parts.	If two triangles have congruent corresponding parts, then the triangles are congruent.

Use a straightedge and tracing paper to explore the converse of the CPCTC Theorem.

A Trace the angles and segments shown to draw $\triangle ABC$. Repeat the process to draw $\triangle DEF$ on a separate piece of tracing paper. Label the triangles.

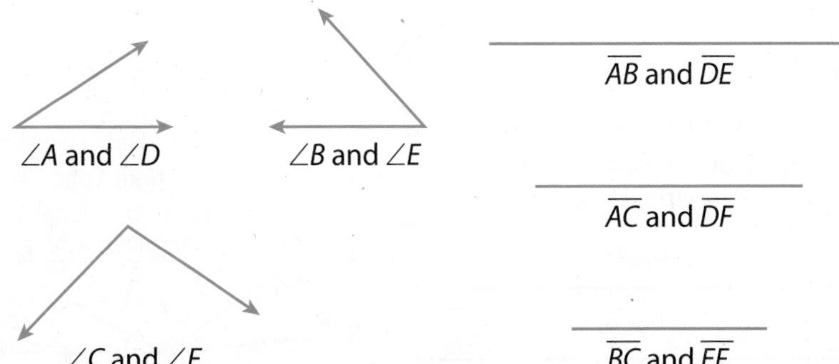

B What must you do to show that the triangles are congruent?

____

____

EXPLORE ACTIVITY 2 *(cont'd)*

My Notes

C Flip the piece of tracing paper with $\triangle ABC$ over and arrange the two triangles on a desk as shown at the right. Then move the tracing paper with $\triangle ABC$ so that point A maps to point D. Name the rigid motion you used.

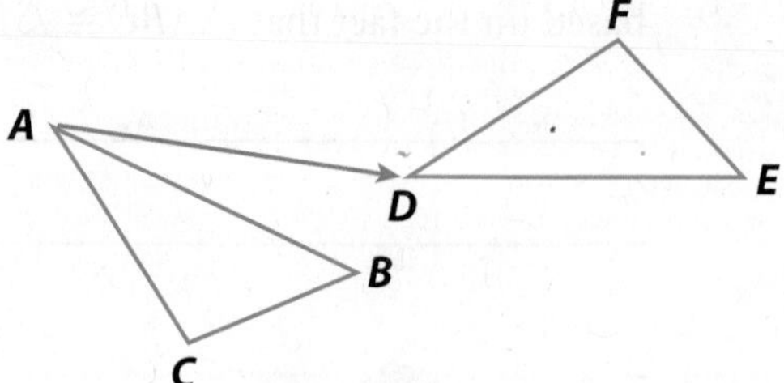

____

D Name a rigid motion you can use to map point B to point E. How can you be sure the image of B is E?

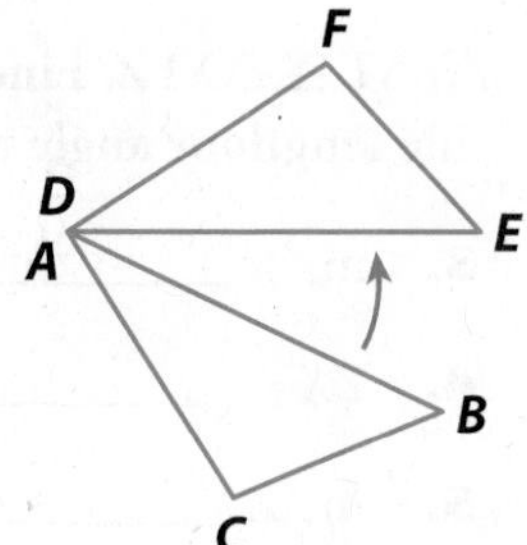

____

____

____

E Name a rigid motion you can use to map point C to point F.

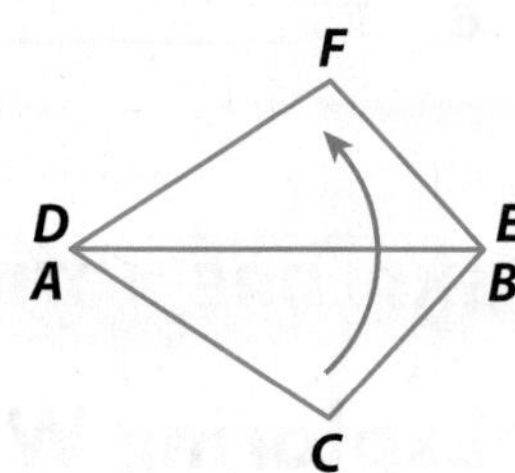

____

To show that the image of point C is point F, complete the following.

$\angle A$ is reflected across $\overleftrightarrow{DE}$, so the measure of the angle is preserved. Since $\angle A \cong \angle D$, you can conclude that the image of $\overrightarrow{AC}$ lies on ______________. It is given that $\overline{AC} \cong \overline{DF}$. So, the image of point C must be ______________.

F What sequence of rigid motions maps $\triangle ABC$ onto $\triangle DEF$?

____

____

REFLECT

7. Describe a sequence of rigid motions that maps $\triangle MNP$ onto $\triangle MQR$ to show that $\triangle MNP \cong \triangle MQR$.

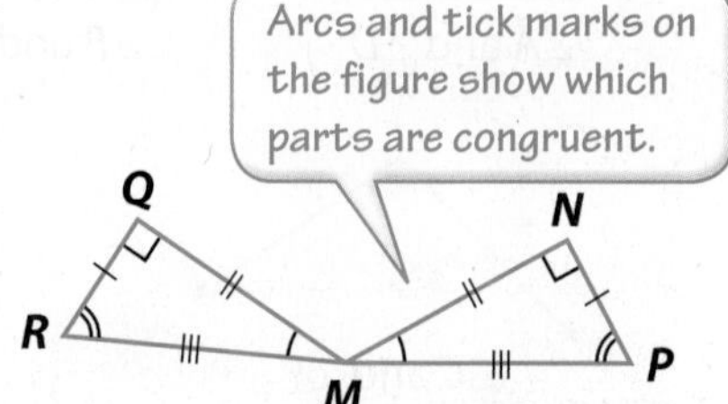

____

____

____

Deciding If Triangles Are Congruent

Your findings in Explore Activity 2 can be stated as a theorem.

Congruent Triangles Theorem

If the corresponding sides and the corresponding angles of two triangles are congruent, then the triangles are congruent.

EXAMPLE 2

CA CC G.CO.7

Determine whether the given triangles are congruent. Explain your answer.

A Look for three pairs of congruent corresponding sides.

$\overline{GH} \cong \overline{KL}$, $\overline{HJ} \cong \overline{LM}$, and $\overline{GJ} \cong \overline{KM}$

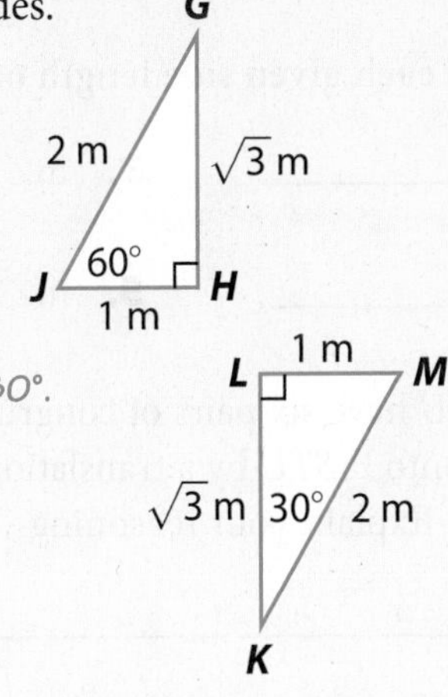

Look for three pairs of congruent corresponding angles. First find m∠G.

$m\angle G + 60° + 90° = 180°$ *The angle measures of a triangle add up to 180°.*

$m\angle G + 150° = 180°$

$m\angle G = 30°$

By similar reasoning, $m\angle M = 60°$.

$\angle G \cong \angle K$, $\angle H \cong \angle L$, and $\angle J \cong \angle M$

$\triangle GHJ \cong \triangle KLM$, because there are three pairs of congruent corresponding sides and three pairs of congruent corresponding angles.

B Look for three pairs of congruent corresponding sides.

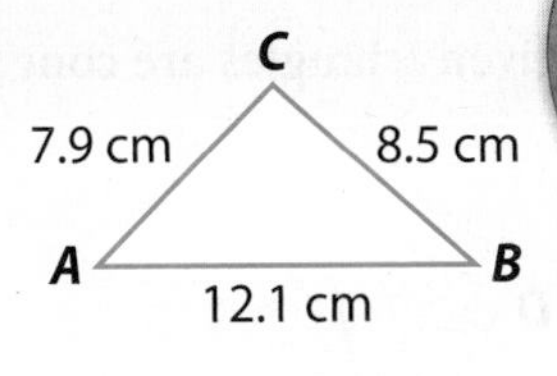

$\overline{AB} \cong \overline{DE}$ and $\overline{AC} \cong \overline{DF}$

Since $BC \neq EF$, $\overline{BC}$ is not congruent to $\overline{EF}$.

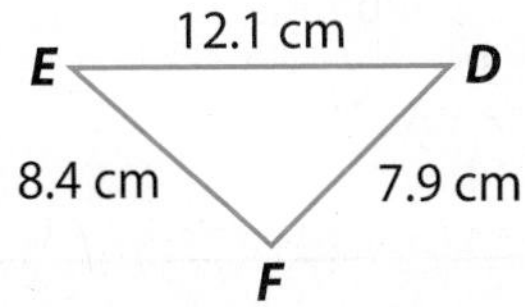

Two corresponding sides are not congruent, so the triangles are not congruent because there are not six pairs of congruent corresponding parts.

Math Talk
Mathematical Practices

Which of the theorems in this lesson do you use in Example 2B? Explain.

YOUR TURN

8. Determine whether the triangles are congruent. Explain your answer.

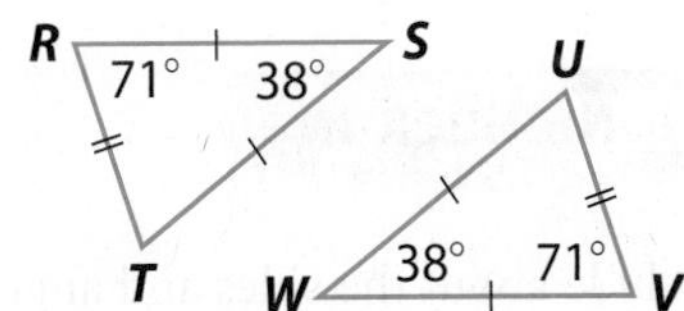
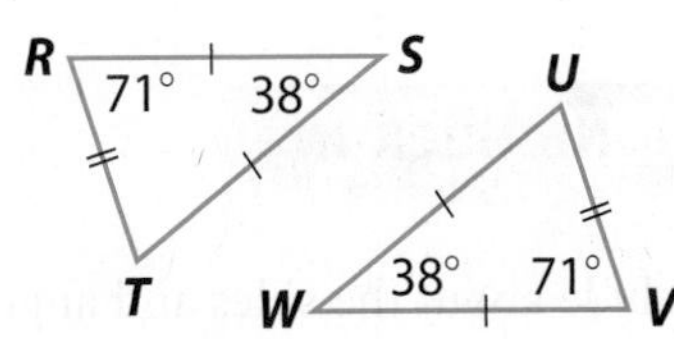

____

____

____

Personal Math Trainer
Online Practice and Help
my.hrw.com

Guided Practice

1. Tyrell uses a reflection and a translation to map $\triangle XQW$ to $\triangle VRH$ so that X maps to V, Q maps to R, and W maps to H. What conclusions can Tyrell draw about the triangles and their sides and angles? Explain. (Explore Activity 1)

____

____

____

____

$\triangle ABC \cong \triangle DBC$. Find each given side length or angle measure. (Example 1)

B
4.5 ft
A
$(6y - 1)^\circ$ C $(3y + 20)^\circ$
D

2. AB ______________ **3.** $m\angle D$ ______________

4. $m\angle ACB$ ______________ **5.** $m\angle ACB$ ______________

6. $\triangle PQR$ and $\triangle STU$ have six pairs of congruent corresponding parts and $\triangle PQR$ can be mapped onto $\triangle STU$ by a translation followed by a rotation. How are the triangles related? Explain your reasoning. (Explore Activity 2)

____

____

____

Determine whether the given triangles are congruent. Explain your answer. (Example 2)

7.

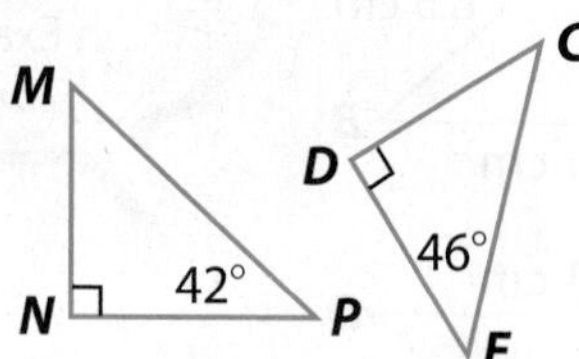

____

____

____

8.

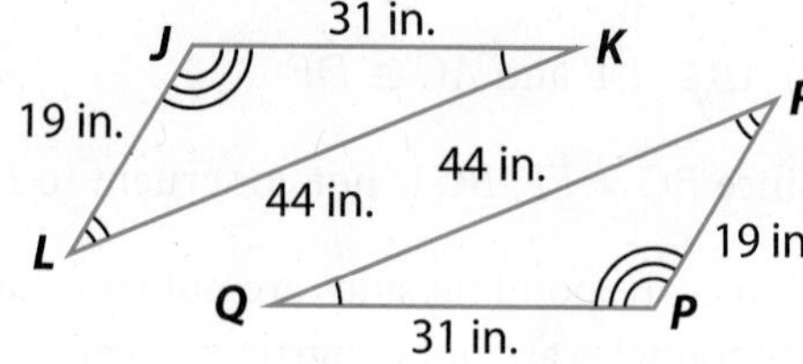

____

____

____

ESSENTIAL QUESTION CHECK-IN

9. What can you conclude about the sides and angles of congruent triangles?

____

____

Name ______________________ Class ______________________ Date ______________________

15.2 Independent Practice

G.CO.7

10. Tenaya designed the earrings shown. She wants to be sure they are congruent. She knows that the three pairs of corresponding angles are congruent. What additional measurements should she make? Explain.

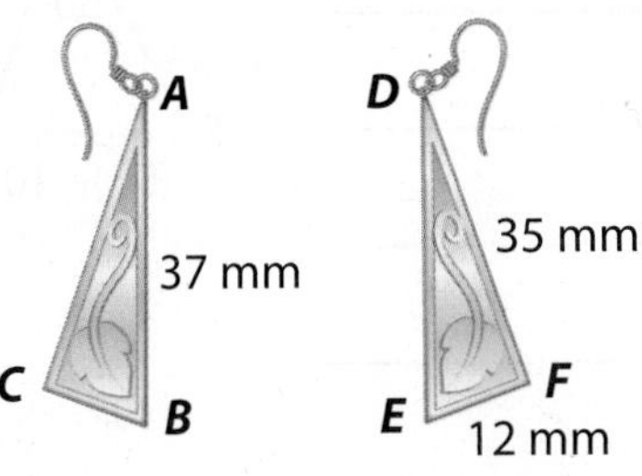

____

____

____

11. Adam drew two triangles, $\triangle MNP$ and $\triangle RST$, that have six pairs of congruent corresponding parts. He wants to use transformations to show that the triangles are congruent. He has already used a translation to map point P to point T, as shown. What should he do next? Explain.

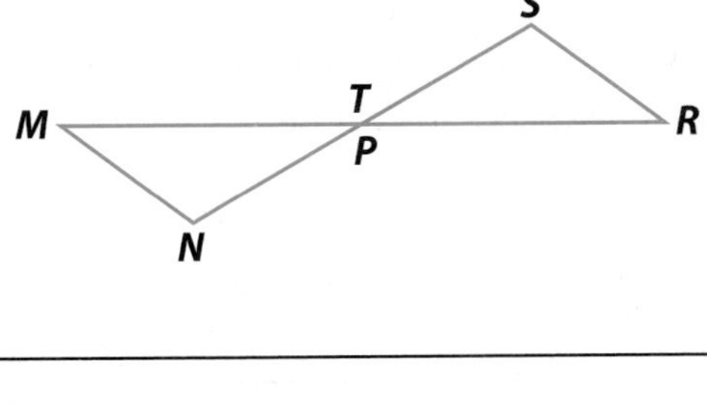

____

____

____

____

____

____

____

12. Given that $\triangle ABC \cong \triangle DEF$, $AB = 2.7$ ft, and $AC = 3.4$ ft, is it possible to determine the length of $\overline{EF}$? If so, find the length. If not, explain why not.

____

____

____

13. Keiko used a sequence of transformations to map $\triangle ABC$ to $\triangle DEF$. She noticed that the transformations mapped $\overline{AC}$ to $\overline{DF}$ and she concluded that these segments are the same length. What must be true about the transformations in order for Keiko to be correct? Explain.

____

____

____

____

14. **Counterexamples** Isaiah says it is not necessary to check all six pairs of congruent corresponding parts to decide whether two triangles are congruent. He says it is enough to check that the corresponding angles are congruent. Sketch a counterexample. Explain your counterexample.

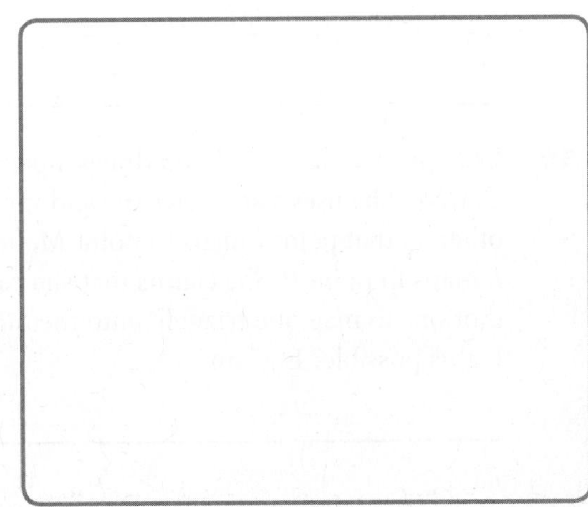

15. Critical Thinking In $\triangle ABC$, $m\angle A = 55°$ and $m\angle B = 50°$. In $\triangle DEF$, $m\angle E = 50°$ and $m\angle F = 65°$. Is it possible for the triangles to be congruent? Explain.

____

____

____

16. In the figure, $\triangle RST \cong \triangle UVW$. What is the value of x? Explain.

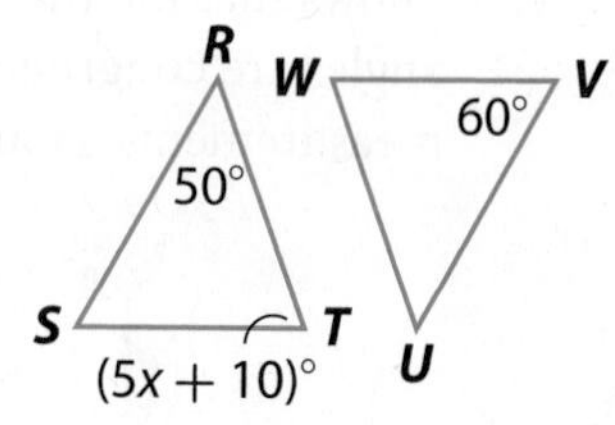

____

____

____

____

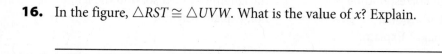

H.O.T. FOCUS ON HIGHER ORDER THINKING

Work Area

17. Analyze Relationships Sara draws and labels two congruent triangles. She uses a sequence of rigid motions to map one triangle onto the other, and she finds that the image of vertex D is vertex L, the image of vertex V is vertex C, and the image of vertex W is vertex Y. In how many different ways can Sara write a congruence statement for the triangles? Explain.

____

____

____

18. Justify Reasoning Tyler's garden has two congruent triangular flowerbeds, $\triangle ABC$ and $\triangle DEF$. He knows that $\overline{AB}$ is 5 feet long, $\overline{EF}$ is 3 feet long, and $\overline{DF}$ is 4 feet long. If possible, determine how much fencing Tyler needs to enclose both flowerbeds. Explain your reasoning.

____

____

____

19. Critique Reasoning Luisa draws a pair of congruent triangles, $\triangle JKL$ and $\triangle MNP$. She uses a sequence of rigid motions to map one triangle onto the other so that point J maps to point M, point K maps to point N, and point L maps to point P. She claims that she can use a different sequence of rigid motions to map one triangle onto the other so that point J maps to point N. Is this possible? Explain.

____

____

LESSON

15.3 Triangle Congruence Criteria: ASA

CA CC G.CO.8

Explain how the criteria for triangle congruence (ASA, SAS, and SSS) follow from the definition of congruence in terms of rigid motions.

ESSENTIAL QUESTION

How can you explain the ASA Triangle Congruence Theorem?

EXPLORE ACTIVITY 1 

G.CO.8

Drawing Triangles Given Two Angles and a Side

In a polygon, the side that connects two consecutive angles is the *included side* of those two angles. Follow the instructions below to draw a triangle with a 30° angle, a 40° angle, and an *included side* that is 4 inches long.

Use a ruler, a protractor, and either tracing paper or a transparency.

A Draw a segment that is 4 inches long. Label the endpoints A and B.

B Use a protractor to draw a 30° angle so that one side is $\overline{AB}$ and its vertex is point A.

C Use a protractor to draw a 40° angle so that one side is $\overline{AB}$ and its vertex is point B. Label the point where the sides of the angles intersect as point C.

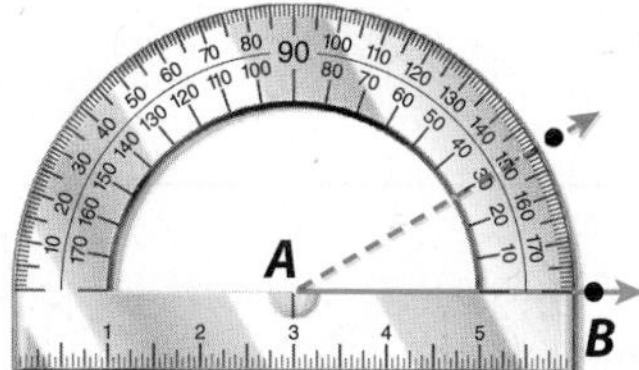

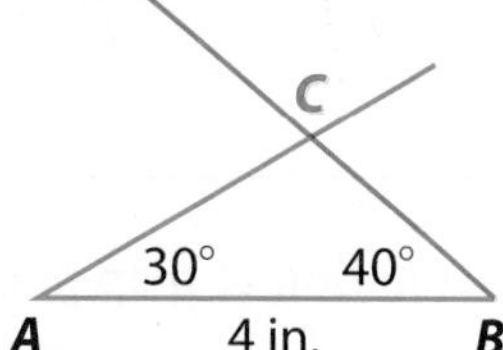

D Put your triangle and a classmate's triangle beside each other on the same surface. Is there a sequence of rigid motions that maps one onto the other? What does this tell you about the triangles?

___

REFLECT

1. **Make a Conjecture** Based on your results, how can you decide whether two triangles are congruent without checking that all six pairs of corresponding sides and corresponding angles are congruent?

___

___

___

___

EXPLORE ACTIVITY 2

CA CC G.CO.8

ASA Triangle Congruence

You can explain the results of Explore Activity 1 using transformations.

My Notes

A Use tracing paper to make two copies of the triangle from Explore Activity 1. Identify and mark the following angles and sides you know to be congruent.

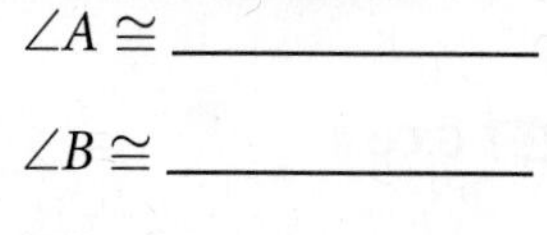

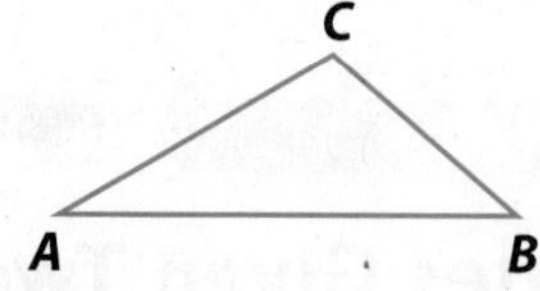

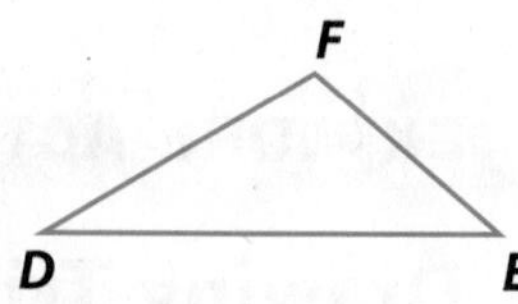

B What can you do to show that these triangles are congruent?

C Position the triangles as shown. You will have to flip your copy of $\triangle ABC$ over. Translate $\triangle ABC$ so that point A maps to point D. What translation vector did you use?

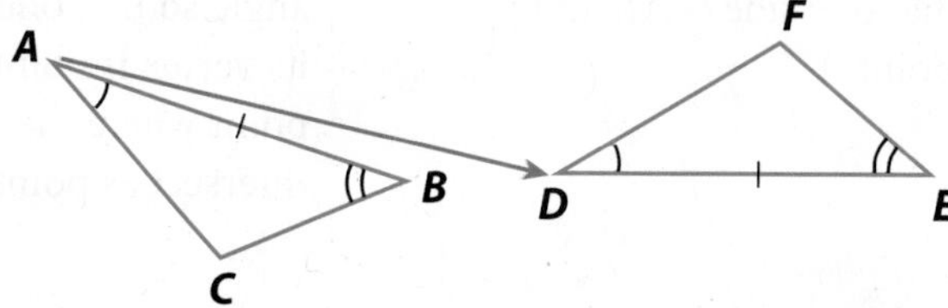

D Use a rotation to map point B to point E. What is the center of the rotation? What is the angle of the rotation?

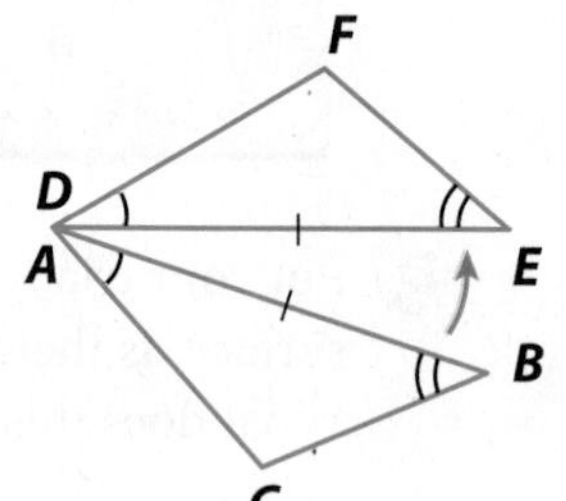

E How do you know the image of point B is point E?

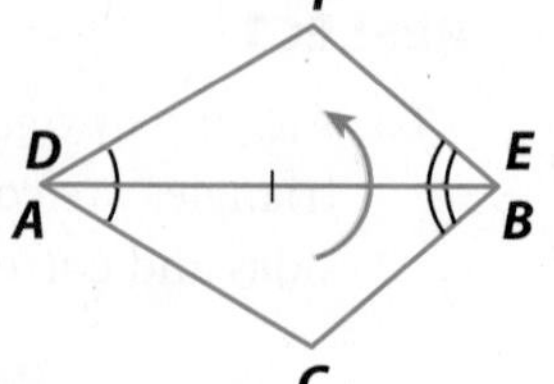

F What rigid motion do you think will map point C to point F?

G To show that the image of point C is point F, notice that $\angle A$ is reflected across $\overleftrightarrow{DE}$, so the measure of the angle is preserved. Since $\angle A \cong \angle D$, you can conclude that the image of $\overrightarrow{AC}$ lies on __________. In particular, the image of point C must lie on __________. By similar reasoning, the image of $\overrightarrow{BC}$ lies on __________ and the image of point C must lie on __________. The only point that lies on both $\overrightarrow{DF}$ and $\overrightarrow{EF}$ is __________.

H Describe the sequence of rigid motions used to map $\triangle ABC$ to $\triangle DEF$.

____

REFLECT

2. **Critique Reasoning** Arturo said the argument in Explore Activity 2 works for any triangles with two pairs of congruent corresponding angles, and it is not necessary for the included sides to be congruent. Do you agree? Explain.

____

____

Applying ASA Triangle Congruence

What you learned in Explore Activities 1 and 2 may be stated as a theorem.

ASA Triangle Congruence Theorem

If two angles and the included side of one triangle are congruent to two angles and the included side of another triangle, then the triangles are congruent.

EXAMPLE 1

CA CC G.CO.8

Determine whether the triangles are congruent. Explain your reasoning.

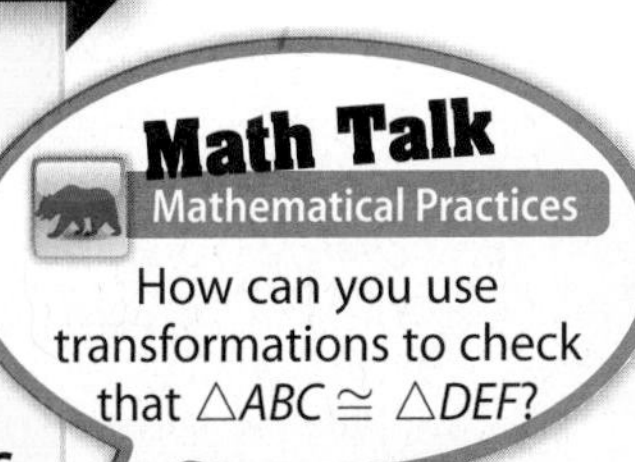

Math Talk
Mathematical Practices
How can you use transformations to check that △ABC ≅ △DEF?

STEP 1 Find $m\angle D$.

$$m\angle D + m\angle E + m\angle F = 180°$$

$$m\angle D + 74° + 61° = 180°$$

$$m\angle D + 135° = 180°$$

$$m\angle D = 45°$$

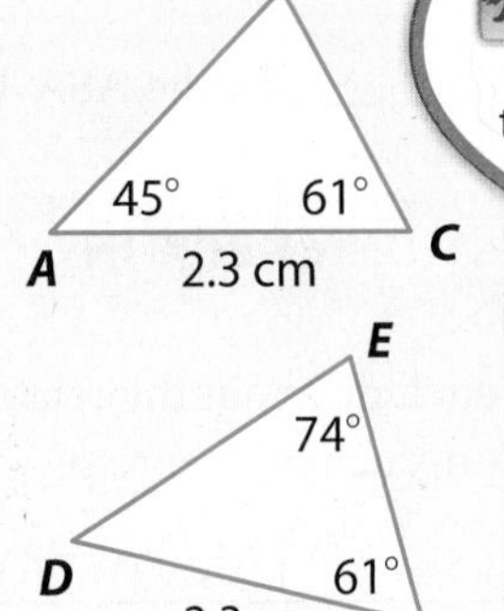

STEP 2 Compare the angle measures and side lengths.

$m\angle A = m\angle D = 45°$, $AC = DF = 2.3$ cm, and $m\angle C = m\angle F = 61°$

$\triangle ABC \cong \triangle DEF$ by the ASA Triangle Congruence Theorem.

YOUR TURN

Determine whether the triangles are congruent. Explain your reasoning.

3.

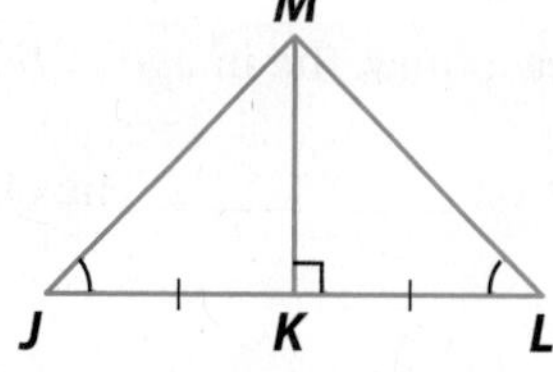

____

____

____

4.

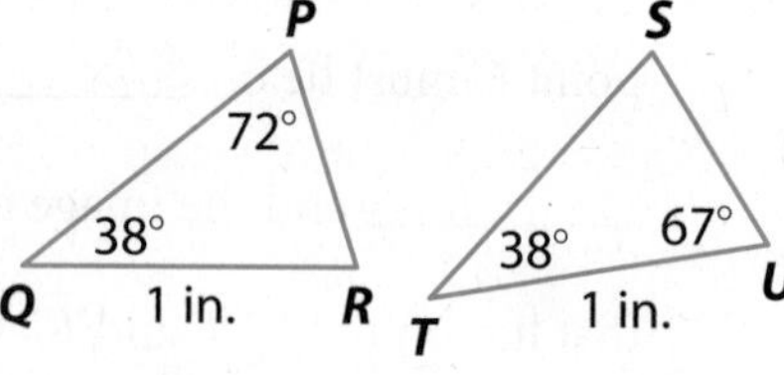

____

____

____

Guided Practice

1. Explain how you can use rigid motions to show that $\triangle ABC \cong \triangle DEC$. Justify your reasoning. (Explore Activities 1 and 2)

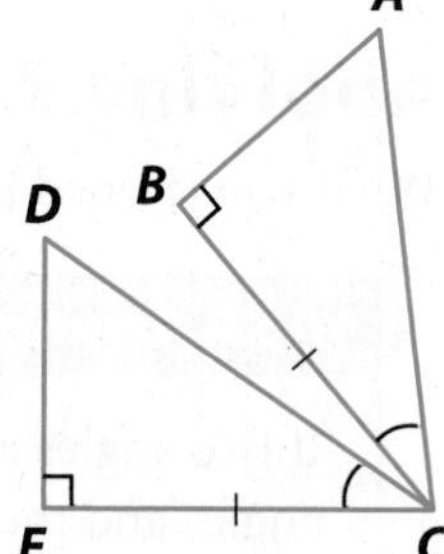

$\overline{BC} \cong \overline{EC}$, so rotate around point C to map point B to ______________________.

The angle of rotation is ______________________.

Since $\angle ABC \cong \angle DEC$, the image of $\overrightarrow{BA}$ lies on ______________________.

Since $\angle ACB \cong \angle DCE$, the image of $\overrightarrow{CA}$ lies on ______________________.

The image of point A lies on both $\overrightarrow{ED}$ and $\overrightarrow{CD}$, so it must be ______________.

2. Determine whether the triangles are congruent. Explain your reasoning. (Example 1)

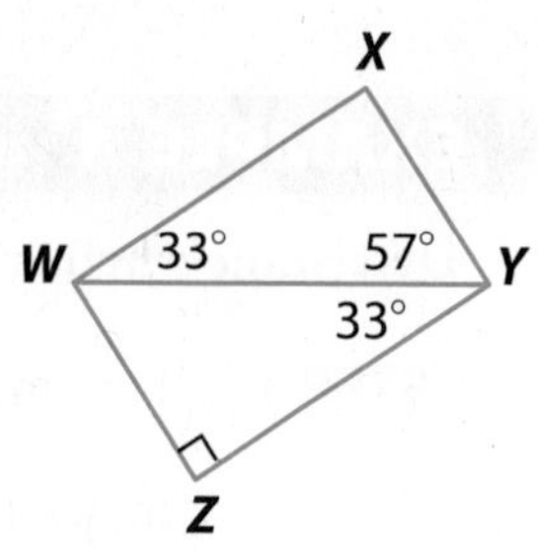

$m\angle ZWY = 180° - (90° + 33°) =$ ______________________

$\angle ZWY \cong$ ____________, $\angle XWY \cong$ ____________, $\overline{WY} \cong$ ____________

$\triangle ZWY \cong$ ____________ by the ASA Triangle Congruence Theorem.

ESSENTIAL QUESTION CHECK-IN

3. What can you conclude about the relationship between two triangles using the ASA Triangle Congruence Theorem?

____

____

____

Name ______________________ Class ______________ Date ______________

15.3 Independent Practice

G.CO.8

4. Represent Real-World Problems Rob is making the kite shown in the figure.

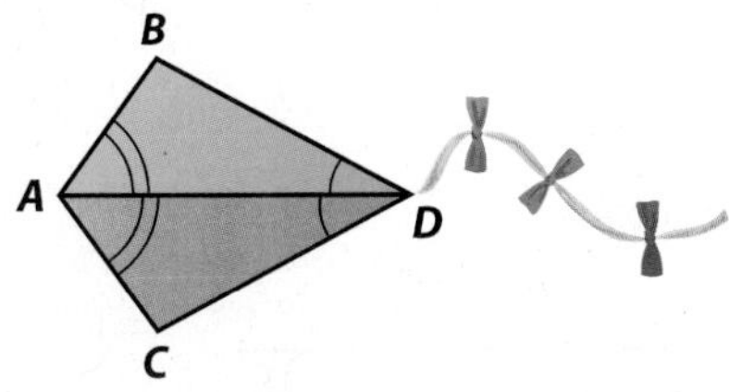

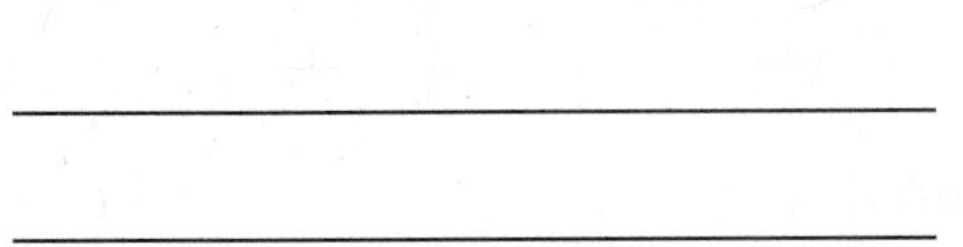

a. Explain why $\triangle ABD \cong \triangle ACD$.

____

____

____

____

b. Rob says that $AB = AC$ and $BD = CD$. Do you agree? Explain.

____

____

____

c. Given that $BD = x + 15$ cm and $AB = x$ cm, write an expression for the distance around the kite in centimeters.

____

5. The figure shows quadrilateral *PQRS*. What additional information do you need in order to conclude that $\triangle SPR \cong \triangle QRP$ by the ASA Triangle Congruence Theorem? Explain.

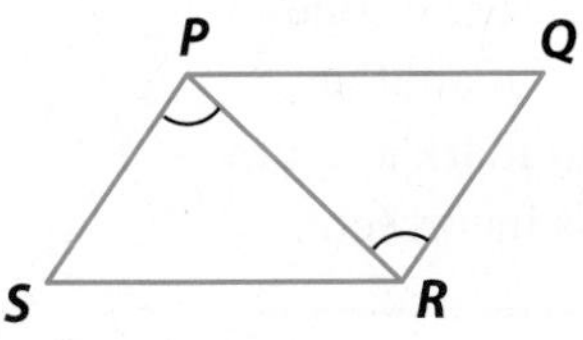

____

____

____

6. In $\triangle ABC$, $m\angle A = 72°$, $m\angle C = 18°$, and $AC = 4$ inches. In $\triangle DEF$, $m\angle D = 72°$ and $m\angle F = 18°$. What else must you know to conclude that $\triangle ABC \cong \triangle DEF$ by the ASA Triangle Congruence Theorem? Explain.

____

____

7. Communicate Mathematical Ideas In the figure, $\overline{WX}$ is parallel to $\overline{LM}$.

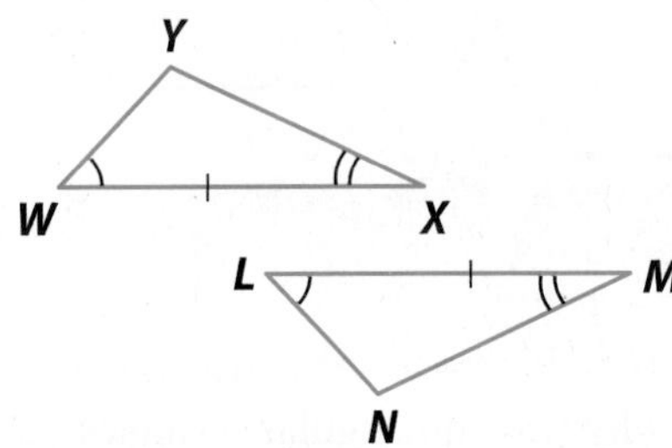

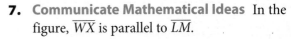

a. Describe a sequence of two rigid motions that maps $\triangle LMN$ to $\triangle WXY$.

____

____

b. How can you be sure that point *N* maps to point *Y*?

____

____

____

____

____

8. Critical Thinking In $\triangle ABC$ and $\triangle DEF$, $\angle A \cong \angle D$, $\angle C \cong \angle F$, and $\overline{AC} \cong \overline{DE}$. Is it possible to tell whether the triangles are congruent? Why or why not?

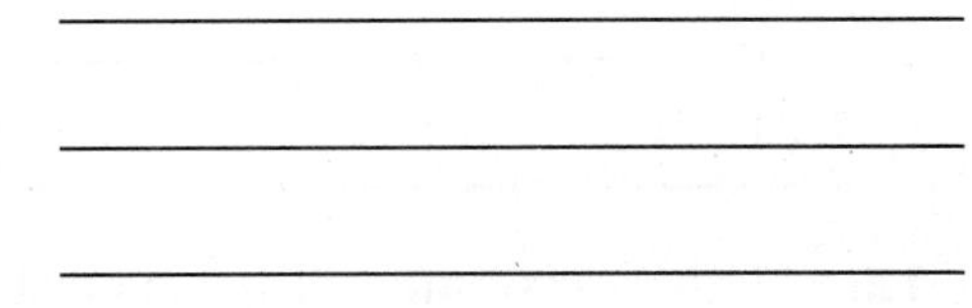

____

____

9. The figure shows $\triangle GHJ$ and $\triangle PQR$ on a coordinate plane.

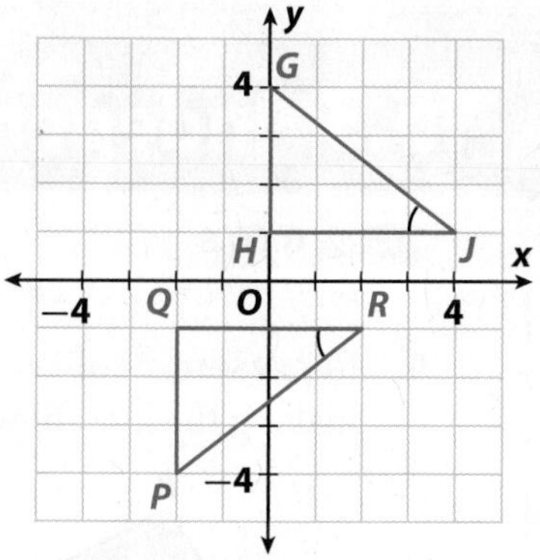

a. Explain why the triangles are congruent using the ASA Triangle Congruence Theorem.

b. Explain why the triangles are congruent using rigid motions.

H.O.T. FOCUS ON HIGHER ORDER THINKING

Work Area

10. **Justify Reasoning** An equiangular triangle has three 60° angles. Explain why two equiangular triangles that each have a side 5 inches long must be congruent.

11. **Critique Reasoning** $\triangle ABC$ and $\triangle DEF$ are both right triangles and both triangles contain a 30° angle. Both triangles have a side that is 9.5 mm long. Yoshio claims that he can use the ASA Congruence Theorem to show that the triangles are congruent. Do you agree? Explain.

12. **Counterexamples** Elena said that the ASA Triangle Congruence Theorem works for quadrilaterals. That is, if two angles and the included side of one quadrilateral are congruent to two angles and the included side of another quadrilateral, then the quadrilaterals are congruent. Sketch and mark a figure of two quadrilaterals as a counterexample to show that Elena is incorrect.

LESSON 15.4

Triangle Congruence Criteria: SAS

CA CC G.CO.8

Explain how the criteria for triangle congruence (ASA, SAS, and SSS) follow from the definition of congruence in terms of rigid motions.

ESSENTIAL QUESTION

How do you explain the SAS Triangle Congruence Theorem?

EXPLORE ACTIVITY 1

Drawing Triangles Given Two Sides and an Angle

Follow these instructions to draw different triangles with a 3-inch side, a 2.5-inch side, and a 45° angle. Make each triangle on a separate piece of tracing paper or separate transparency.

A Use a protractor to draw a 45° angle, $\angle A$. Mark point B on one of the rays so that $\overline{AB}$ is 3 inches long.

B Place the end of your ruler on point B and locate a point C on the other ray of $\angle A$ so that $\overline{BC}$ is 2.5 inches long. Draw $\overline{BC}$.

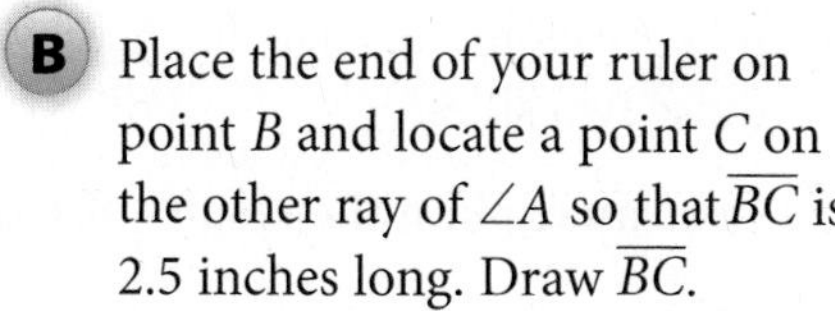

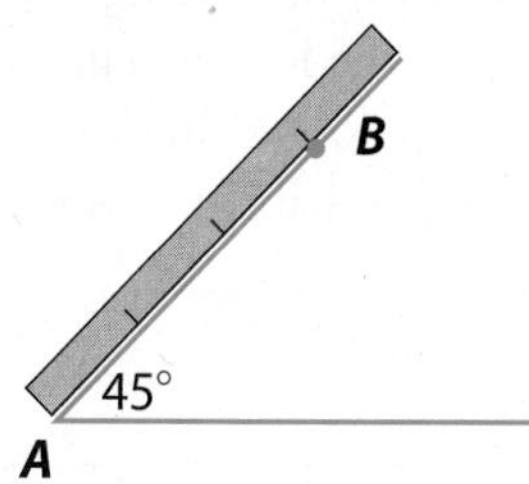

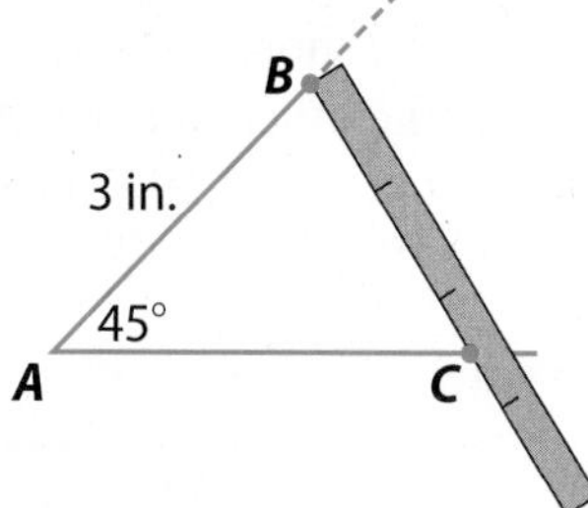

C Compare your triangle to those made by other students. Is there more than one possible result? Explain.

___

D Now use the ruler to draw $\overline{AB}$ that is 3 inches long. Then use a protractor to draw a 45° angle at point A.

E Use the ruler to locate a point C on the ray you just drew so that the length of $\overline{AC}$ is 2.5 inches. Then draw $\overline{BC}$.

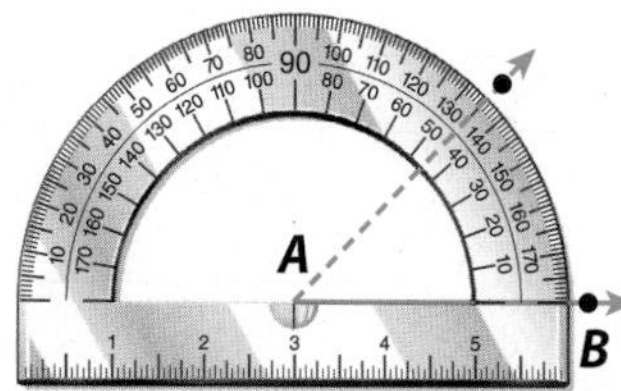

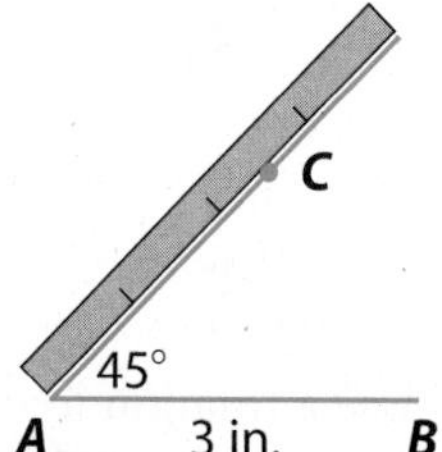

F Compare your triangle to those made by other students. Is there more than one possible result? Explain.

___

___

EXPLORE ACTIVITY 1 *(cont'd)*

REFLECT

1. **Make a Conjecture** If two sides and an angle of one triangle are congruent to two sides and an angle of another triangle, can you conclude that the triangles are congruent? Are there any restrictions on the location of the angle? Explain.

____

____

EXPLORE ACTIVITY 2

CA CC G.CO.8

SAS Triangle Congruence

In a polygon, the angle formed by two consecutive sides is the *included angle* of those two sides.

You can explain the results of Explore Activity 1 using transformations.

A Using a straightedge, trace the angle shown below on tracing paper. Copy the shorter segment $\overline{AC}$ on one side of $\angle A$ and the longer segment $\overline{AB}$ on the other side of $\angle A$. Connect B and C to form $\triangle ABC$. Repeat the process to draw $\triangle DEF$ on another piece of tracing paper. Label the vertices.

$\overline{AC}$ and $\overline{DF}$

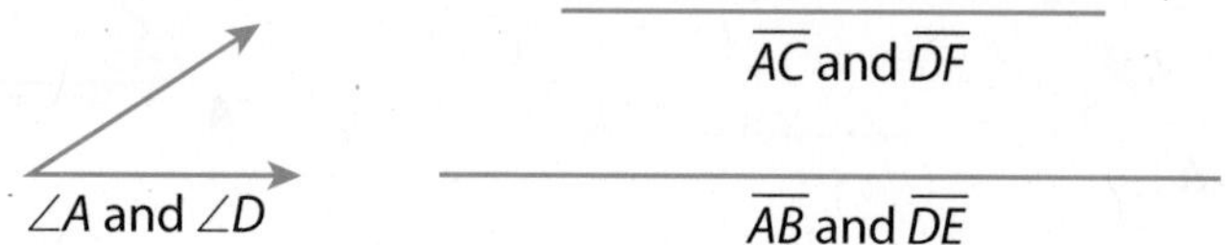

B Complete each congruence statement based on your two triangles. Then mark these congruent corresponding parts on your triangles.

$\overline{AB} \cong$ ________ $\overline{AC} \cong$ ________ $\angle A \cong$ ________

C Position the triangles as shown. (Flip over one or both triangles if necessary.) Translate $\triangle ABC$ so that point A maps to point D. What translation vector did you use?

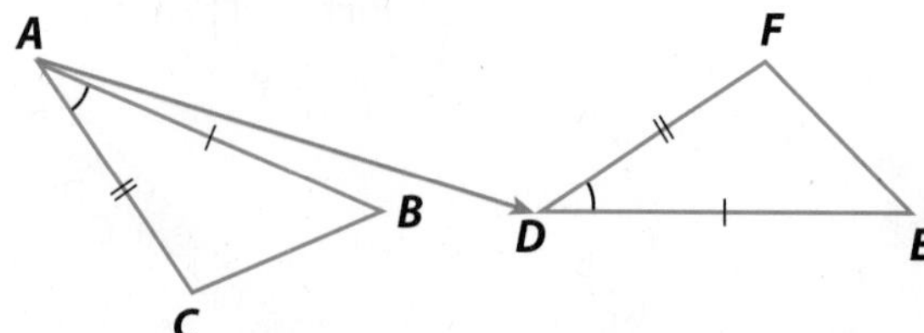

____

D Use a rotation to map point B to point E. Identify the center and the angle of rotation.

____

E How do you know the image of point B is point E?

____

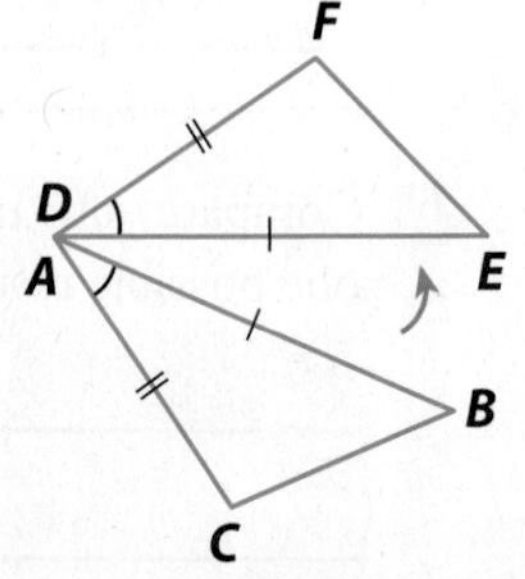

F What rigid motion do you think will map point C to point F?

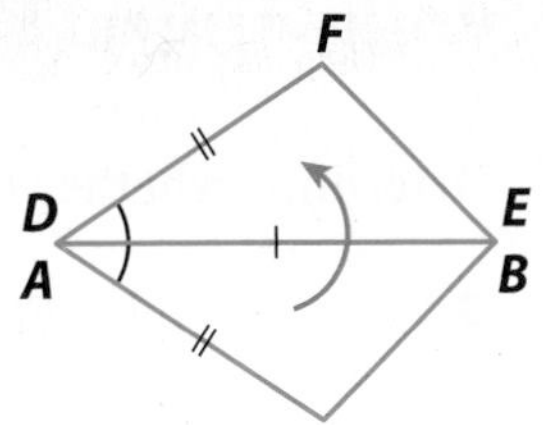

____

To show that the image of point C is point F, notice that $\angle A$ is reflected across $\overleftrightarrow{DE}$, so the measure of the angle is preserved.

Since $\angle A \cong \angle D$, you can conclude that the image of $\overrightarrow{AC}$ lies on __________ and the image of point C also lies on __________. Since the reflection preserves distance, the image of point C is at a distance of AC from point D. But $AC =$ __________, so the image of point C must be __________.

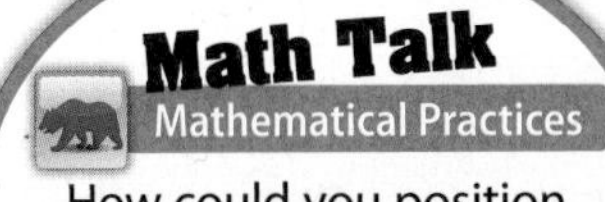

How could you position the triangles in step B so that you could map one to the other using only a rotation?

Describe the sequence of rigid motions used to map $\triangle ABC$ to $\triangle DEF$.

____

Applying SAS Triangle Congruence

What you learned in Explore Activities 1 and 2 may be stated as a theorem.

If two sides and the included angle of one triangle are congruent to two sides and the included angle of another triangle, then the triangles are congruent.

EXAMPLE 1

G.CO.8

Determine whether the triangles are congruent. Explain your reasoning.

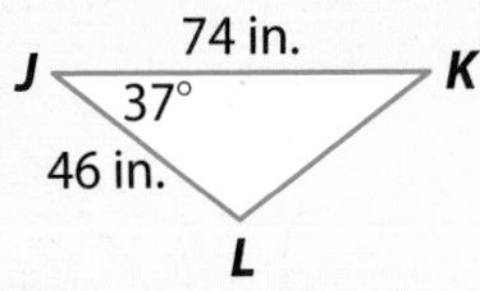

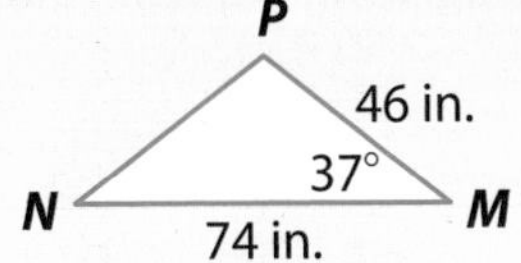

$\angle M$ is the included angle between $\overline{PM}$ and $\overline{NM}$.

$JK = MN = 74$ in., so $\overline{JK} \cong \overline{MN}$.

$JL = MP = 46$ in., so $\overline{JL} \cong \overline{MP}$.

$m\angle J = m\angle M = 37°$, so $\angle J \cong \angle M$.

Two sides and the included angle of $\triangle JKL$ are congruent to two sides and the included angle of $\triangle MNP$.

$\triangle JKL \cong \triangle MNP$ by the SAS Triangle Congruence Theorem.

YOUR TURN

Determine whether the triangles are congruent. Explain your reasoning.

2. $\triangle BAC$ and $\triangle EDF$

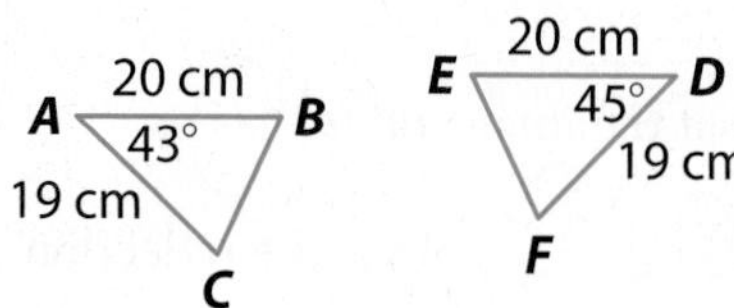

____

____

____

3. $\triangle UTV$ and $\triangle UTW$

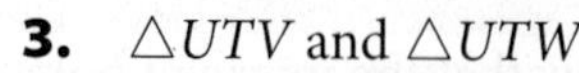

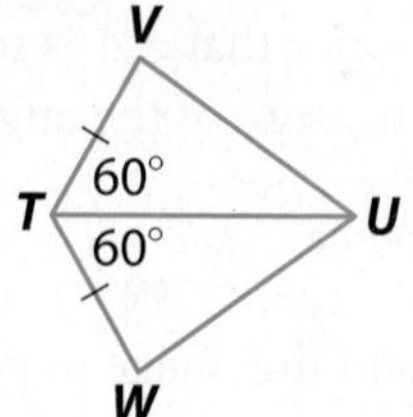

____

____

____

Guided Practice

1. Jeffrey draws $\triangle PQR$ and $\triangle TUV$. He uses a translation to map point P to point T and point R to point V as shown. What should be his next step in showing $\triangle PQR \cong \triangle TUV$? Why? (Explore Activities 1 and 2)

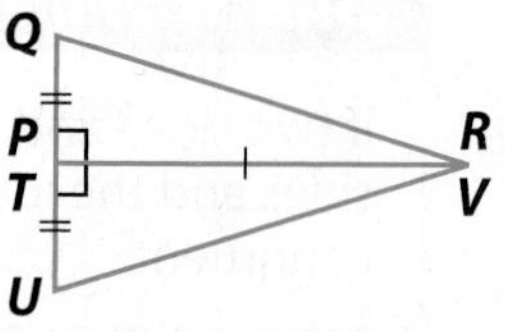

____

____

____

2. Determine whether the triangles are congruent. Explain your reasoning. (Example 1)

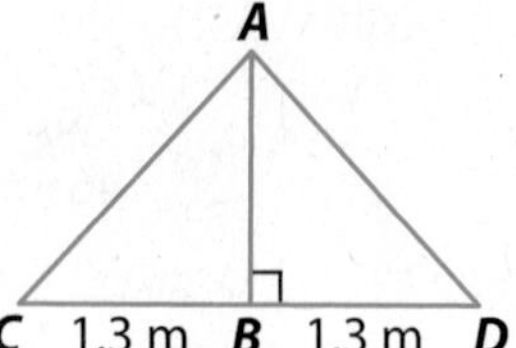

____

____

ESSENTIAL QUESTION CHECK-IN

3. What can you conclude about the relationship between two triangles using the SAS Triangle Congruence Theorem?

____

____

____

____

Name ____________________ Class ____________ Date ____________

15.4 Independent Practice

CA CC G.CO.8

Tell if the triangles are congruent by the ASA or SAS Triangle Congruence Theorem, or if they are not congruent.

4.

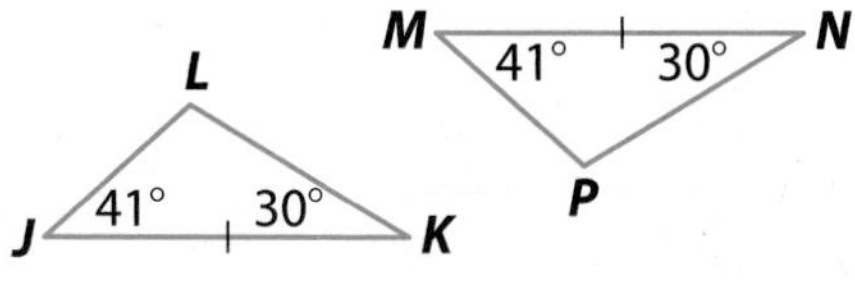

$\triangle MNP$ and $\triangle JKL$ ____________

5.

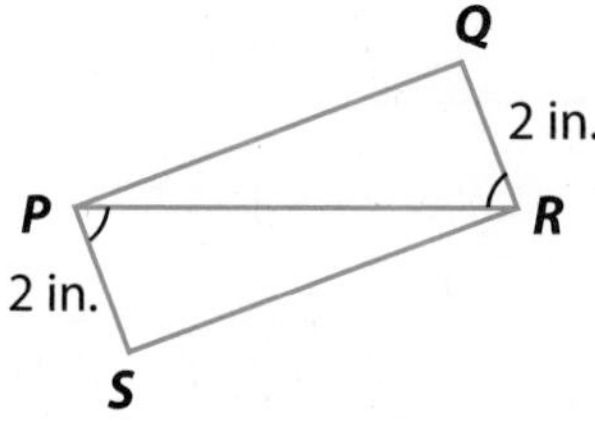

$\triangle RPS$ and $\triangle RPQ$ ____________

6.

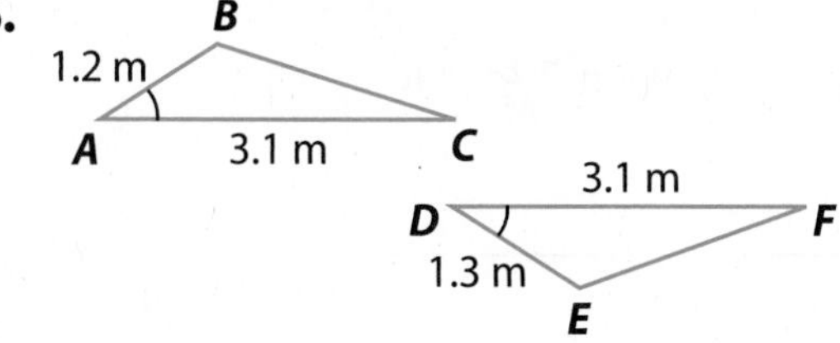

$\triangle BAC$ and $\triangle EDF$ ____________

7. Sarah performs rigid motions mapping point A to point D and point B to point E, as shown. Does she have enough information to confirm that the triangles are congruent? Explain your reasoning.

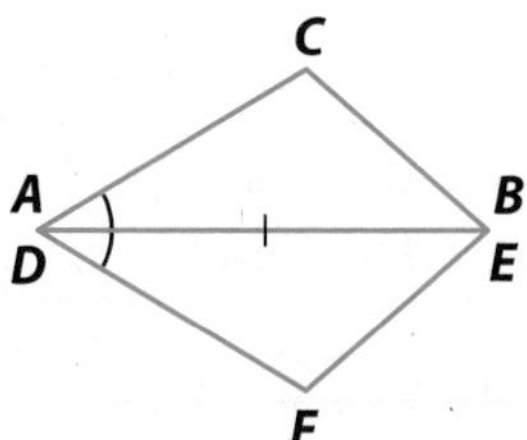

____

____

____

8. Communicate Mathematical Ideas The figure shows a side panel of a skateboard ramp. Kalim wants to confirm that the right triangles in the panel are congruent.

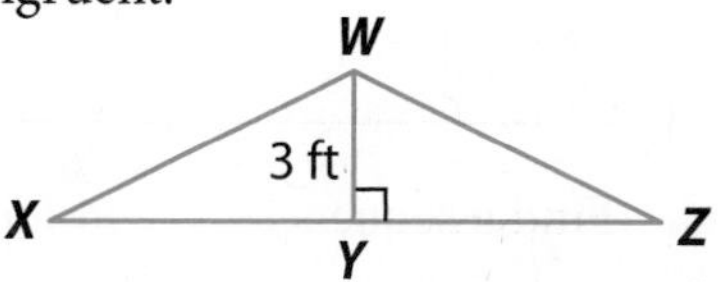

a. What measurements should Kalim take if he wants to confirm that the triangles are congruent by SAS? Explain.

____

____

____

____

b. What measurements should Kalim take if he wants to confirm that the triangles are congruent by ASA? Explain.

____

____

____

____

9. Is it possible to determine the length of $\overline{HJ}$ in the figure? If so, explain how. If not, explain why not.

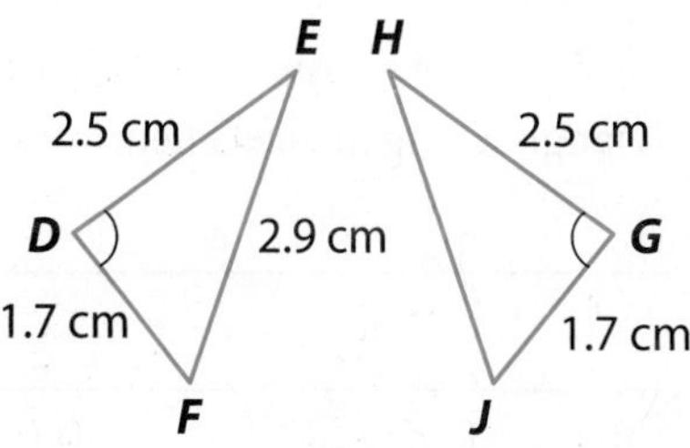

____

____

10. The figure shows $\triangle ABC$ and $\triangle DEF$ on a coordinate plane.

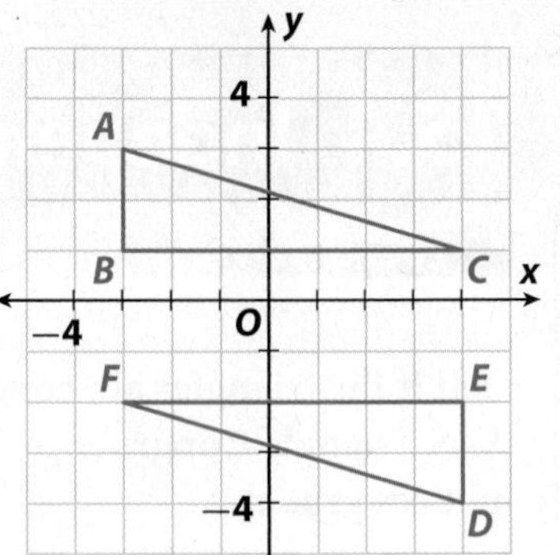

a. 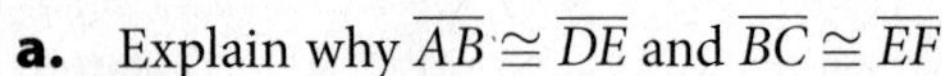Explain why $\overline{AB} \cong \overline{DE}$ and $\overline{BC} \cong \overline{EF}$.

____

____

b. Explain why $\angle B \cong \angle E$.

____

c. What can you conclude about the triangles? Why?

____

d. Find a sequence of rigid motions that maps $\triangle ABC$ to $\triangle DEF$.

____

____

H.O.T. FOCUS ON HIGHER ORDER THINKING

Work Area

11. Explain the Error Marc was asked if it is possible to use the information in the figure to show that $\triangle JLM \cong \triangle KLM$. He said that it is possible, since $\overline{LM} \cong \overline{LM}$, $\angle JLM \cong \angle KLM$, and $\overline{JM} \cong \overline{KM}$. He concluded that the triangles are congruent by the SAS Triangle Congruence Theorem. Explain his error.

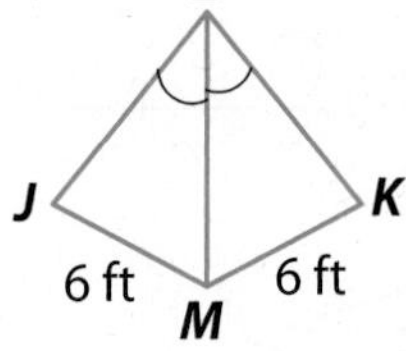

____

____

12. Justify Reasoning The opposite sides of a rectangle are congruent. Can you conclude that a diagonal of a rectangle divides the rectangle into two congruent triangles? Justify your response.

____

____

____

13. Analyze Relationships Describe similarities and differences between the ASA Triangle Congruence Theorem and the SAS Triangle Congruence Theorem.

____

____

____

____

LESSON 15.5

Triangle Congruence Criteria: SSS

CA CC G.CO.8

Explain how the criteria for triangle congruence (ASA, SAS, and SSS) follow from the definition of congruence in terms of rigid motions. *Also G.CO.12*

ESSENTIAL QUESTION

How do you explain the SSS Triangle Congruence Theorem?

EXPLORE ACTIVITY 1

Constructing Triangles Given Side Lengths

Follow these instructions to draw a triangle with sides of length 4 cm, 5 cm, and 6 cm. Make your drawing on a piece of tracing paper or on a transparency.

A Use a ruler to draw a segment that is 6 cm long. Label the endpoints A and B as shown.

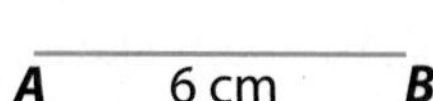

B Open your compass to 4 cm, place the point of the compass on point A, and draw an arc as shown.

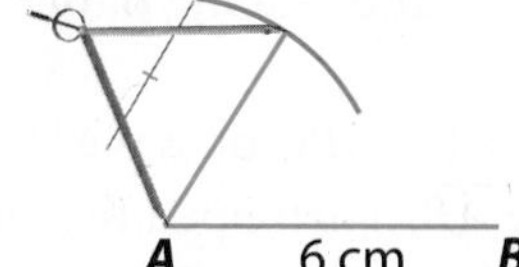

C Open your compass to 5 cm, place the point of the compass on point B, and draw an arc as shown.

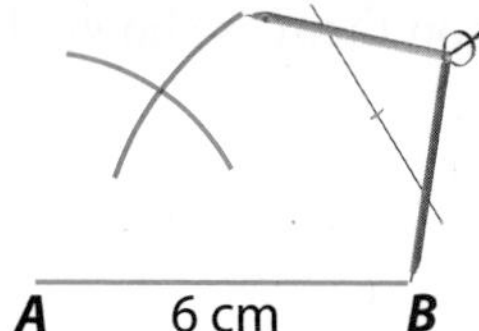

D Label the point where the arcs intersect as point C. Draw $\overline{AC}$ and $\overline{BC}$. Label the side lengths on the figure.

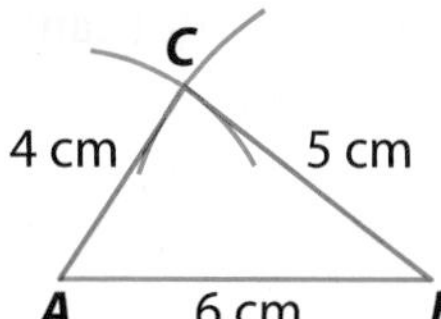

E Compare your triangle to those made by other students. Are all of the triangles congruent? If so, how do you know?

____

____

F Repeat the process to make a triangle with sides of length 4.5 cm, 6 cm, and 7 cm. Compare your triangle to those made by other students. Are all of the triangles congruent? Explain.

____

____

EXPLORE ACTIVITY 1 *(cont'd)*

REFLECT

1. **Make a Conjecture** Make a conjecture about the results of Activity 1.

____

____

EXPLORE ACTIVITY 2

CA CC G.CO.8, G.CO.12

SSS Triangle Congruence

The following theorem can help you explain the results of Explore Activity 1.

Perpendicular Bisector Theorem

A point is on the perpendicular bisector of a segment if and only if it is equidistant from the endpoints of the segment.

Use a compass and tracing paper or a transparency.

A Construct $\triangle ABC$ on a piece of tracing paper as follows. Use a compass to copy $\overline{AB}$. Then open the compass to the length of $\overline{AC}$ and make an arc centered at point A. Open the compass to the length of $\overline{BC}$ and draw an arc centered at point B that intersects the previous arc. The intersection of the arcs is point C. Repeat the process to draw $\triangle DEF$ on a separate piece of tracing paper.

$\overline{AB}$ and $\overline{DE}$ ____________ $\overline{AC}$ and $\overline{DF}$ ____________ $\overline{BC}$ and $\overline{EF}$ ____________

B Flip over one or both triangles as needed to position them as shown. Identify and mark the following sides you know to be congruent.

$\overline{AB} \cong$ ________

$\overline{AC} \cong$ ________

$\overline{BC} \cong$ ________

A B C D E F

C As in previous lessons, you can use a sequence of two rigid motions to transform $\triangle ABC$ so that the triangles are positioned as shown. Describe the rigid motions.

____

____

____

F D E A B C

D What rigid motion do you think will map point C to point F?

____

To show that the image of point C is point F, notice that $DC =$ ________.

This means point D is equidistant from point ________ and point ________.

Therefore, point D lies on the perpendicular bisector of ________ by the Perpendicular Bisector Theorem.

Similarly, $EC =$ ________. So, point E is equidistant from points ________.

Therefore, point E lies on the perpendicular bisector of ________ by the Perpendicular Bisector Theorem.

Point D and point E both lie on the perpendicular bisector of $\overline{CF}$,

so ________ is the perpendicular bisector of $\overline{CF}$. By the definition of

reflection, the image of point C must be ________.

Math Talk
Mathematical Practices
Can you conclude that two triangles are congruent if two pairs of corresponding sides are congruent? Explain.

E Describe the sequence of rigid motions that maps $\triangle ABC$ onto $\triangle DEF$.

____

REFLECT

2. **Analyze Relationships** How is the justification of SSS congruence similar to and different from the justifications of ASA and SAS congruence?

____

____

____

Applying SSS Triangle Congruence

What you learned in Explore Activities 1 and 2 may be stated as a theorem.

SSS Triangle Congruence Theorem

If three sides of one triangle are congruent to three sides of another triangle, then the triangles are congruent.

EXAMPLE 1 — CA CC G.CO.8

Determine whether the triangles are congruent. Explain your reasoning.

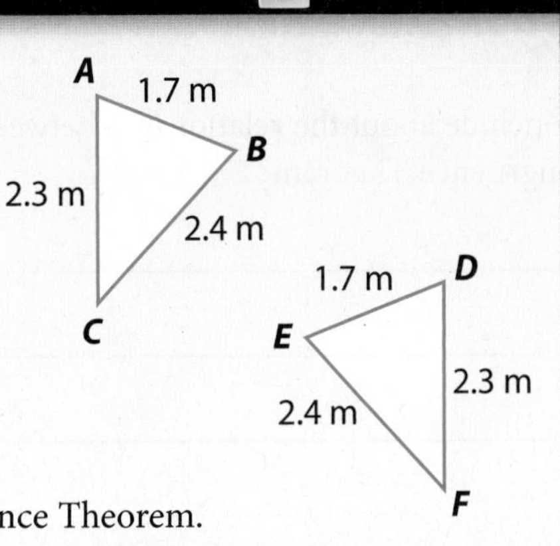

$AB = DE = 1.7$ m, so $\overline{AB} \cong \overline{DE}$.

$BC = EF = 2.4$ m, so $\overline{BC} \cong \overline{EF}$.

$AC = DF = 2.3$ m, so $\overline{AC} \cong \overline{DF}$.

Three sides of $\triangle ABC$ are congruent to three sides of $\triangle DEF$.

$\triangle ABC \cong \triangle DEF$ by the SSS Triangle Congruence Theorem.

YOUR TURN

Determine whether the triangles are congruent. Explain your reasoning.

3.

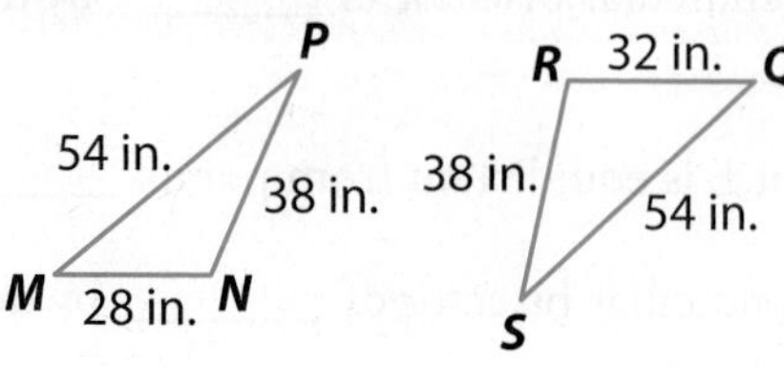

4.

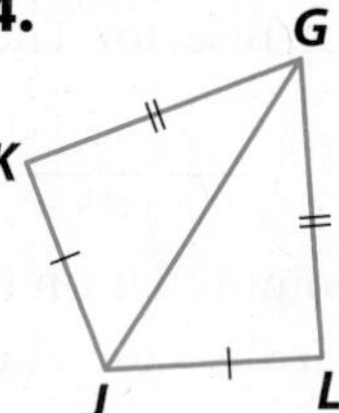

Guided Practice

1. A sequence of rigid motions maps $\overline{JL}$ onto $\overline{RT}$, as shown. How can you use the Perpendicular Bisector Theorem to confirm that a reflection across $\overleftrightarrow{RT}$ will map point K to point S? (Explore Activities 1 and 2)

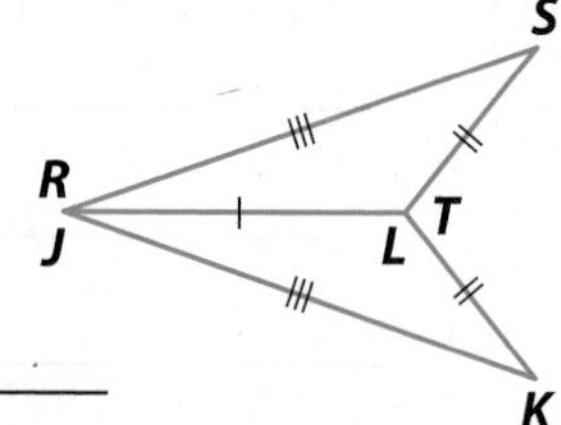

2. Determine whether the triangles are congruent. Explain your reasoning. (Example 1)

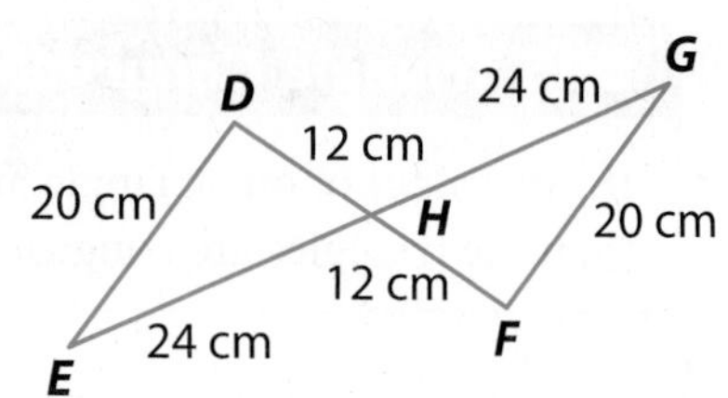

ESSENTIAL QUESTION CHECK-IN

3. What can you conclude about the relationship between two triangles using the SSS Triangle Congruence Theorem?

Name ______________________ Class ______________________ Date ______________________

15.5 Independent Practice

G.CO.8

Tell if the triangles are congruent by the ASA, SAS, or SSS Triangle Congruence Theorem, or if they are not congruent.

4.

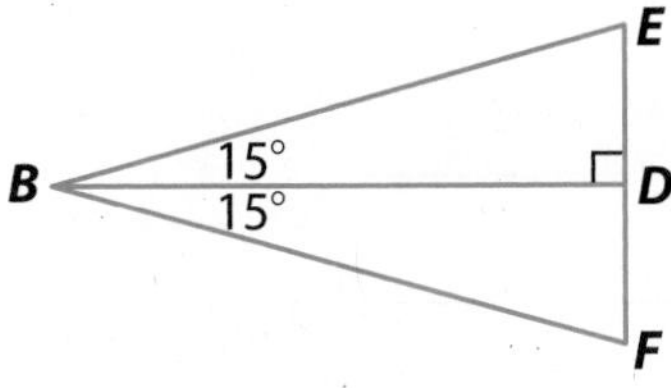

$\triangle EBD$ and $\triangle FBD$ ______________________

5.

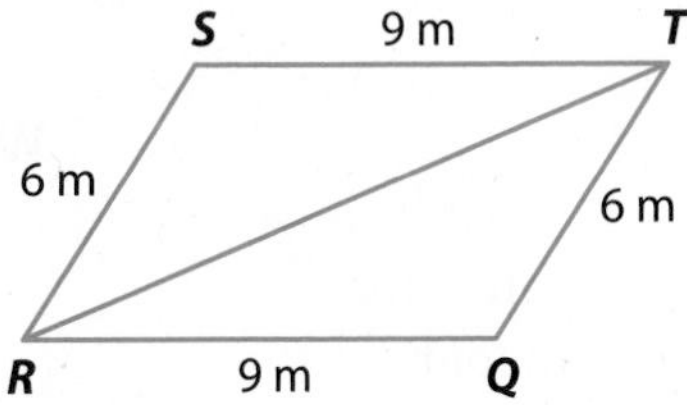

$\triangle RST$ and $\triangle TQR$ ______________________

6.

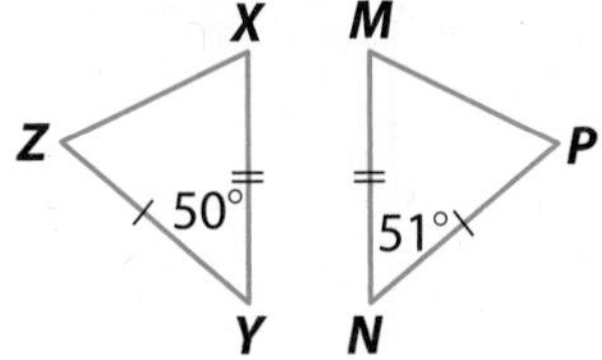

$\triangle XYZ$ and $\triangle MNP$ ______________________

7. Colin wants to map point C to point F in such a way that he can then use a reflection and the Perpendicular Bisector Theorem to show that point B maps to point E. Describe rigid motions he can use to do this.

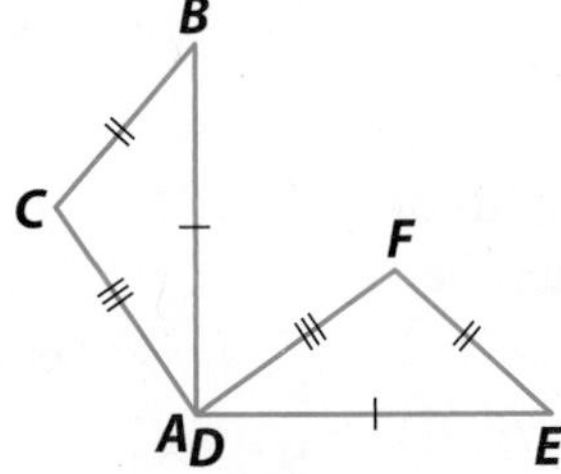

____

____

____

8. Explain the Error Ava wants to know the distance JK across a pond. She locates points as shown. She says that the distance across the pond must be 160 ft by the SSS Triangle Congruence Theorem. Explain her error.

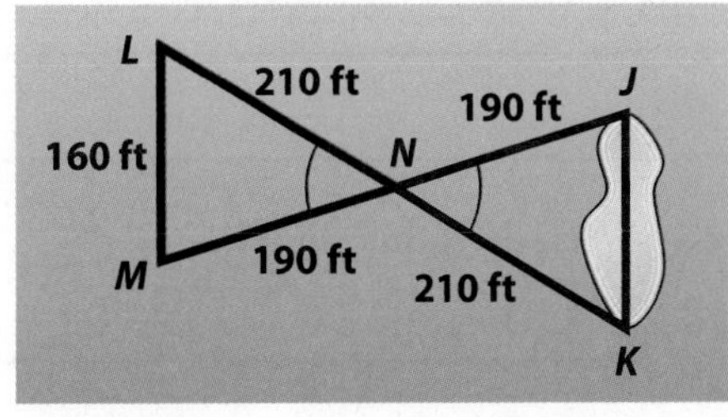

____

____

____

____

____

9. Critical Thinking In the figure, $\overline{AB}$ is perpendicular to $\overline{CD}$ and $\overline{CB} \cong \overline{BD}$.

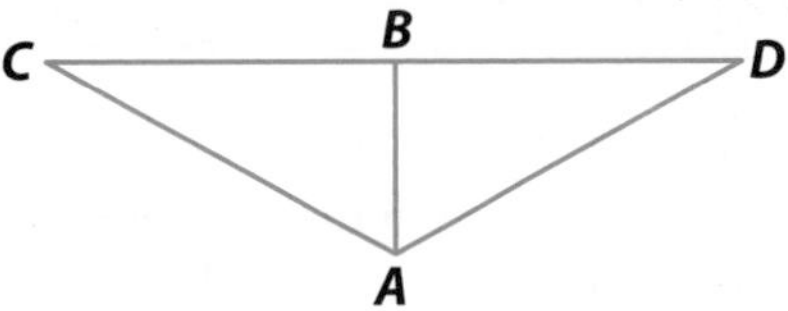

a. What additional information, if any, do you need to show $\triangle CAB \cong \triangle DAB$ by SSS?

____

b. What additional information, if any, do you need to show $\triangle CAB \cong \triangle DAB$ by SAS?

____

c. What additional information, if any, do you need to show $\triangle CAB \cong \triangle DAB$ by ASA?

____

10. Complete this exercise to show that if a point is on the perpendicular bisector of a segment, then it is equidistant from the endpoints of the segment, as is stated in the Perpendicular Bisector Theorem.

a. Suppose point P is on the perpendicular bisector ℓ of $\overline{AB}$. Consider the reflection across line ℓ. What is the image of point A? Why?

b. Explain why $PA = PB$.

c. What does this show?

H.O.T. FOCUS ON HIGHER ORDER THINKING

Work Area

11. Counterexamples Emmet said that there is an SSSS Congruence Theorem for quadrilaterals. That is, if four sides of one quadrilateral are congruent to four sides of another quadrilateral, then the quadrilaterals are congruent. Sketch and mark a figure as a counterexample to Emmet's statement.

12. Draw Conclusions Lee and Hannah each have a wire that is 12 inches long. Lee bends the wire 3 inches from one end and 4 inches from the other end to form a triangle. Hannah makes a triangle in the same way. Can you conclude that their triangles are congruent? Explain.

13. Critical Thinking Suppose you are given two triangles with no side lengths or angle measures marked. Is it possible to use only a ruler to check whether the triangles are congruent? Is it possible to use only a protractor? Explain.

Ready to Go On?

Personal Math Trainer

Online Practice and Help

15.1 Congruent Figures

Determine whether the figures are congruent. Explain.

1.

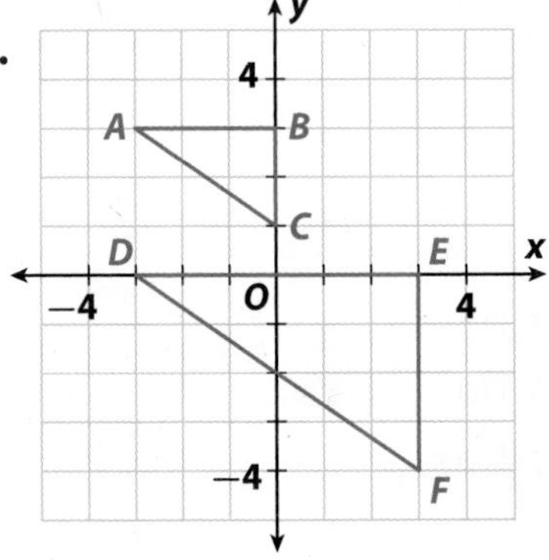

2.

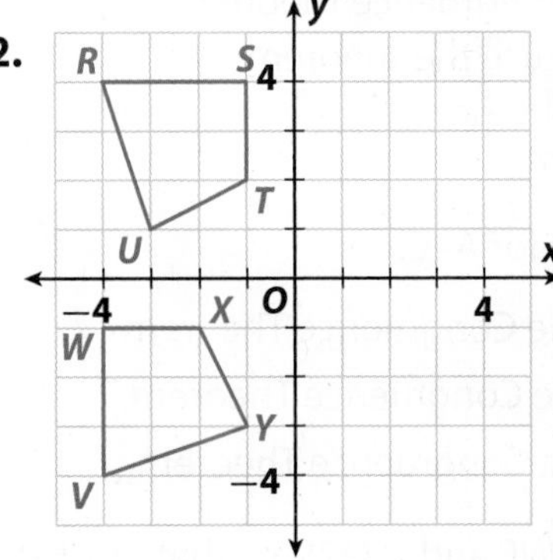

______________________ ______________________

______________________ ______________________

15.2 Triangle Congruence

$\triangle JKL \cong \triangle MNP$. Find the given side length or angle measure.

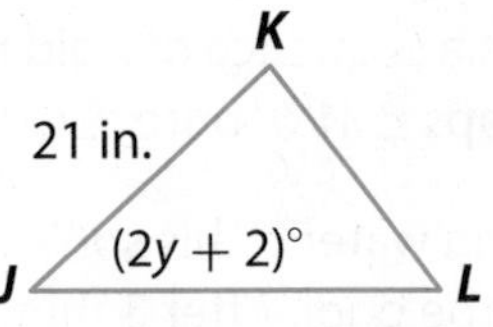

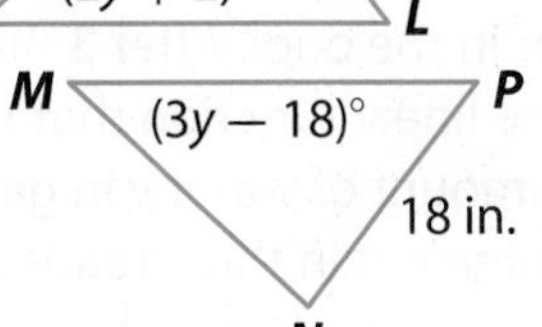

3. KL ______________

4. MN ______________

5. $m\angle J$ ______________

6. $m\angle M$ ______________

15.3–15.5 Triangle Congruence Criteria: ASA/SAS/SSS

Determine whether the triangles are congruent. Explain your reasoning.

7.

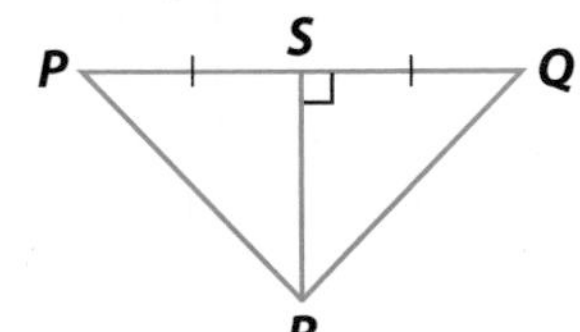

8.

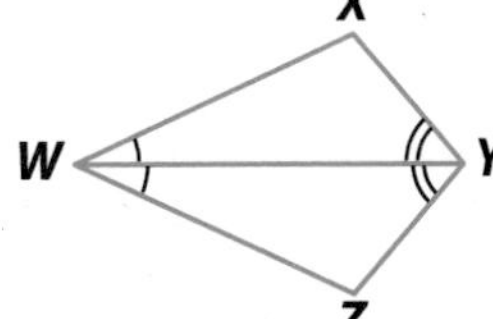

9.

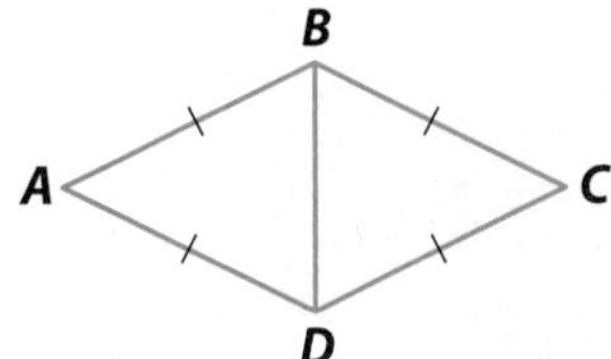

______________ ______________ ______________

ESSENTIAL QUESTION

10. Explain how you can show that two plane figures are congruent, in the general case and then in the special case of triangles.

____

____

____

MODULE 15
MIXED REVIEW

Assessment Readiness

1. Consider each congruence theorem below. Can you use the theorem to determine whether $\triangle ABC \cong \triangle ABD$?

A, 40°, 40°, C, B, D

Select Yes or No for A–C.

A. ASA Triangle Congruence Theorem ○ Yes ○ No
B. SAS Triangle Congruence Theorem ○ Yes ○ No
C. SSS Triangle Congruence Theorem ○ Yes ○ No

2. Kylie draws $\triangle MNP$ and $\triangle QRS$, so that $\triangle MNP \cong \triangle QRS$.

Choose True or False for each statement.

A. $\overline{MN}$ must be congruent to $\overline{QR}$. ○ True ○ False
B. $\angle M$ must be congruent to $\angle S$. ○ True ○ False
C. There is a sequence of rigid motions that maps $\triangle MNP$ onto $\triangle QRS$. ○ True ○ False

3. Yun is adding water to his son's wading pool. After 1 minute, there are 43 gallons of water in the pool. After 3 minutes, there are 49 gallons of water in the pool. Write the linear function that relates the time x since Yun started filling the pool to the amount of water y in gallons in the pool. Explain the meaning of the slope and y-intercept in this situation.

4. Rebecca is designing a logo for an airline. She starts by making a figure with angle measures as shown. She measures $\overline{AB}$ and finds that the length of the segment is 5 inches. Can she determine the length of $\overline{DB}$ without measuring? If so, explain how. If not, explain why not.

A, 17°, 110°, B, C, 110°, 17°, D

Geometric Constructions

ESSENTIAL QUESTION

How can you explain why a geometric construction works?

MODULE

16

CALIFORNIA COMMON CORE

LESSON 16.1

Segments and Angles

 G.CO.12

LESSON 16.2

Parallel and Perpendicular Lines

 G.CO.12, G.CO.5

LESSON 16.3

Polygons

 G.CO.13, G.CO.12

my.hrw.com

Real-World Video

A draftsperson uses software to draw lines, circles, and arcs in order to construct precise diagrams and plans for everything from medical devices to the plans for a city.

GO DIGITAL

my.hrw.com

my.hrw.com

Go digital with your write-in student edition, accessible on any device.

Math On the Spot

Scan with your smart phone to jump directly to the online edition, video tutor, and more.

Animated Math

Interactively explore key concepts to see how math works.

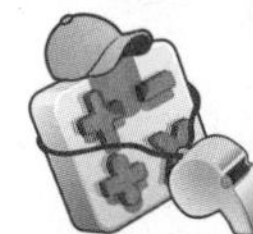

Personal Math Trainer

Get immediate feedback and help as you work through practice sets.

Are YOU Ready?

Complete these exercises to review skills you will need for this module.

Parallel Lines and Transversals

EXAMPLE If the measure of $\angle 6$ is 68°, what is the measure of $\angle 2$? $\angle 4$? $\angle 3$? $\angle 8$? $\angle 7$?

If two parallel lines are cut by a transversal, then:

- Corresponding angles are congruent. So, $m\angle 2 = 68°$.
- Alternate interior angles are congruent. So, $m\angle 4 = 68°$.
- Same-side interior angles are supplementary. So, $m\angle 3 = 112°$.
- Vertical angles are congruent. So, $m\angle 8 = 68°$.
- Straight angles have measures of 180°. So, $m\angle 7 = 112°$.

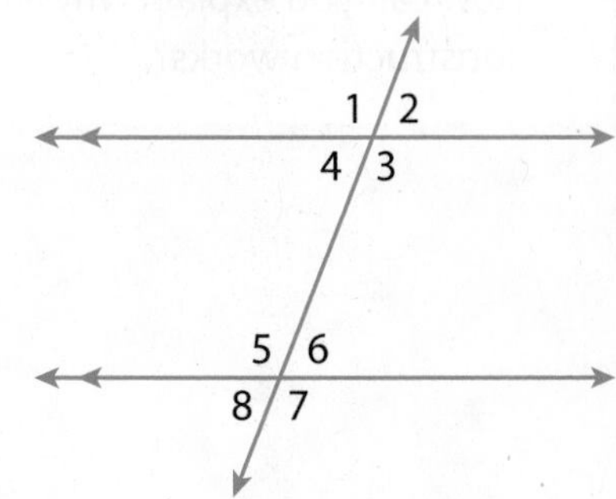

Find the measure of each numbered angle.

$p \parallel q$

p q
1 2 5 6
4 3 7 125°

1. $m\angle 1 =$ ________
2. $m\angle 2 =$ ________
3. $m\angle 3 =$ ________
4. $m\angle 4 =$ ________
5. $m\angle 5 =$ ________
6. $m\angle 6 =$ ________
7. $m\angle 7 =$ ________

Triangle Sum Theorem

Triangle Sum Theorem: The sum of the measures of the angles of a triangle is 180°.

EXAMPLE Find the value of x.

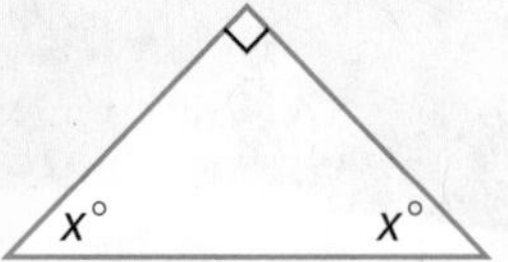

$$90° + x° + x° = 180°$$
$$90° + 2x° = 180°$$
$$2x° = 180° - 90°$$
$$2x° = 90°$$
$$x° = 45°$$

Find the value of x.

8. 18°, x° ________
9. 2x°, 2x°, x° ________
10. 44°, 45°, x° ________
11. ________

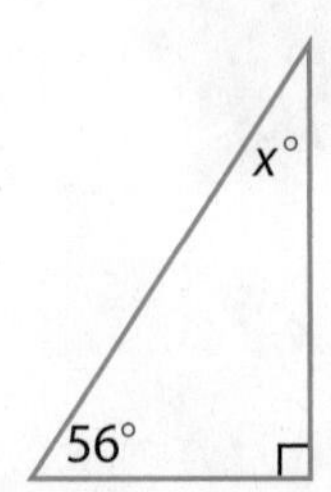

Reading Start-Up

Visualize Vocabulary

Use the review words to complete the information wheel.

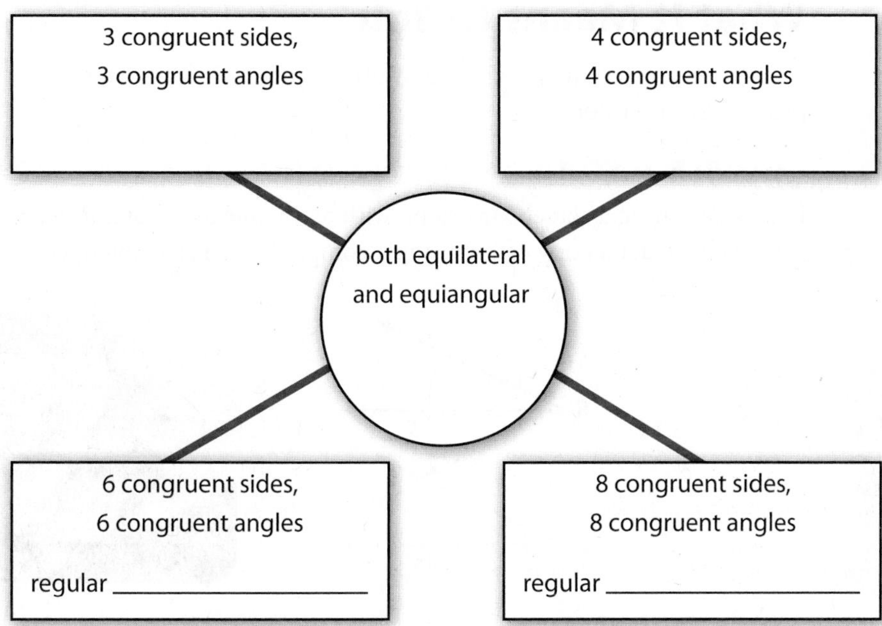

Vocabulary

Review Words

congruent *(congruente)*
✔ equilateral triangle *(triángulo equilátero)*
✔ hexagon *(hexágono)*
✔ octagon *(octágono)*
✔ regular polygon *(polígono regular)*
✔ square *(cuadrado)*

Preview Words

angle bisector
construction
inscribed

Understand Vocabulary

To become familiar with some of the vocabulary terms in the module, consider the following. You may refer to the module, the glossary, or a dictionary.

1. The word *bisect* means to divide something into two equal parts. How do you think this definition relates to an **angle bisector**?

   ____

2. Hammers and saws are tools that are used to construct buildings. What are some tools that may be used for a geometric **construction**?

   ____

Active Reading

Three-Panel Flip Chart Before beginning the module, create a Three-Panel Flip Chart to help you organize your notes about the constructions in each lesson of the module and compare them.

GETTING READY FOR

Geometric Constructions

Understanding the standards and the vocabulary terms in the standards will help you know exactly what you are expected to learn in this module.

CA CC G.CO.12

Make formal geometric constructions with a variety of tools and methods (compass and straightedge, string, reflective devices, paper folding, dynamic geometric software, etc.).

Key Vocabulary

construction *(construcción)*
A method of creating a figure that is said to be geometrically precise. Figures may be constructed by using a compass and straightedge, geometry software, or paper folding.

What It Means to You

You will learn to draw precise geometric figures without using a protractor or a ruler.

EXAMPLE G.CO.12

Pete is designing a skateboard ramp with an incline angle of $\angle R$. How can he construct a copy of $\angle R$ using a compass and a straightedge?

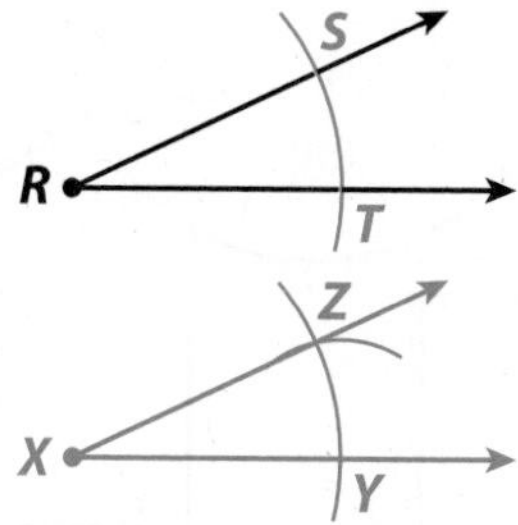

- Use a straightedge to draw a ray with endpoint X.
- Draw an arc centered at R, labeling the intersections S and T.
- With the same compass width, draw an arc centered at X and intersecting the ray. Label the intersection Y.
- Using compass width ST, draw an arc centered at Y and intersecting the previous arc. Label the intersection Z.
- Use a straightedge to draw a ray from X through Z.

CA CC G.CO.13

Construct an equilateral triangle, a square, and a regular hexagon inscribed in a circle.

Key Vocabulary

Inscribed polygon *(polígono inscrito)*
A polygon in which every vertex of the polygon lies on the circle.

Visit **my.hrw.com** to see all **CA Common Core Standards** explained.

my.hrw.com

What It Means to You

You will learn to construct polygons inscribed in circles.

EXAMPLE G.CO.13

A polygon is inscribed in a circle if all of the polygon's vertices lie on the circle.

In the figure, the quadrilateral is inscribed in the circle, because all 4 vertices lie on the circle.

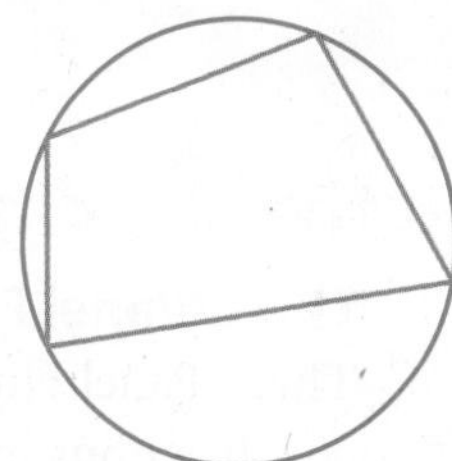

Every regular polygon can be inscribed in a circle. You can draw some of them using geometric constructions.

LESSON

16.1 Segments and Angles

CA CC G.CO.12

Make formal geometric constructions with a variety of tools and methods (compass and straightedge, string, reflective devices, paper folding, dynamic geometric software, etc.).

ESSENTIAL QUESTION

How are geometric constructions different from sketches or drawings?

EXPLORE ACTIVITY

G.CO.12

Using Paper Folding to Construct a Perpendicular Bisector

The steps for making an origami animal may include folding a piece of paper to construct a perpendicular bisector.

Follow these instructions to construct the perpendicular bisector of a line segment.

A Use a straightedge to draw a segment on a piece of tracing paper. Label the endpoints A and B.

A • ———— • B

B Fold the paper so that point A meets point B.

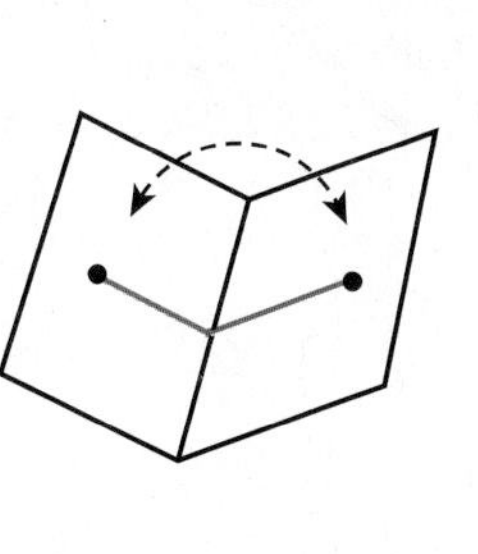

C Unfold the paper and draw a line ℓ along the crease. Line ℓ is the perpendicular bisector of $\overline{AB}$.

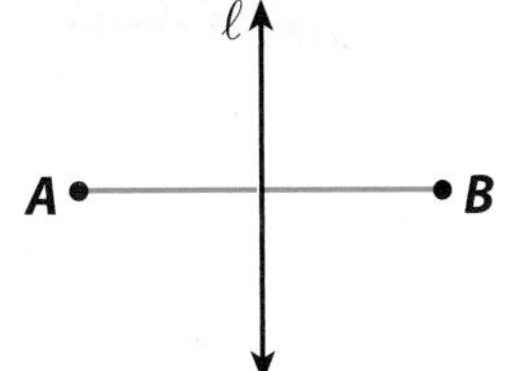

D Mark a point on line ℓ. Use a ruler to measure the distance to point A and the distance to point B. Record the distances and then repeat the process with two more points on line ℓ.

REFLECT

1. How do you know the crease is the perpendicular bisector of $\overline{AB}$? Use a rigid motion in your explanation.

____

____

____

____

2. **Look for a Pattern** What did you notice about each of the points you chose on line ℓ?

____

Bisecting a Segment

When you make a **construction**, you create a mathematically precise figure using geometric relationships rather than measurement tools such as a ruler or protractor. Tools for constructions include compass and straightedge, string, reflective devices, paper folding, and geometry software. Unless you are told otherwise, use a compass and straightedge for constructions.

EXAMPLE 1

CA CC G.CO.12

Construct the perpendicular bisector of $\overline{AB}$.

STEP 1 Place the point of the compass at point A. Using a compass setting that is greater than half the length of $\overline{AB}$, draw an arc.

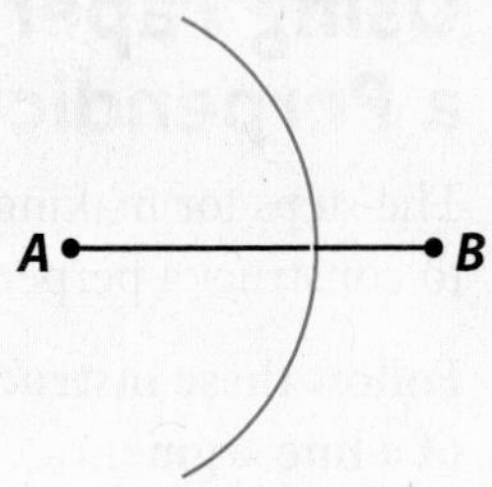

Math Talk
Mathematical Practices
In Step 1, why do you open the compass to a setting that is greater than half the length of $\overline{AB}$?

STEP 2 Without adjusting the compass, place the point of the compass at point B and draw an arc intersecting the first arc. Label the points of intersection C and D.

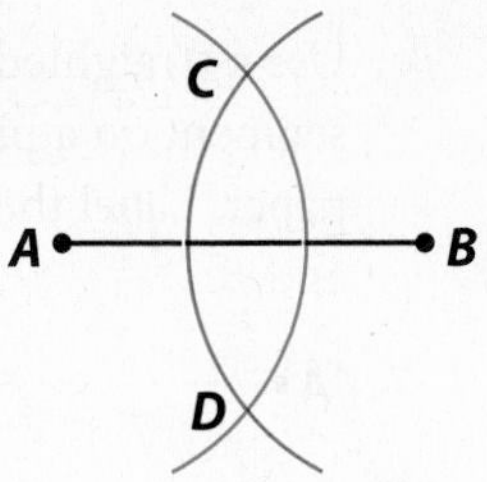

STEP 3 Use a straightedge to draw $\overleftrightarrow{CD}$, which is the perpendicular bisector of $\overleftrightarrow{AB}$.

The final step in a construction shows all of the compass and straightedge marks.

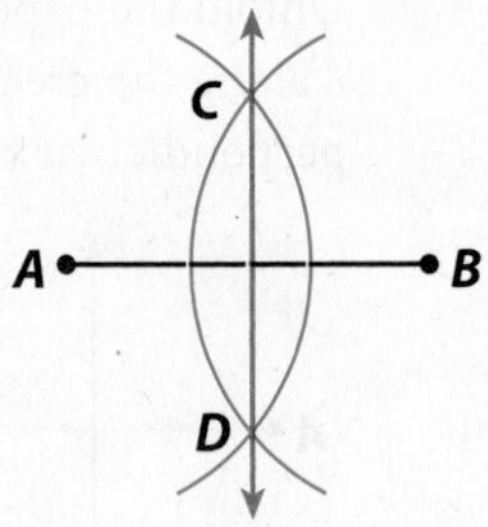

My Notes

REFLECT

3. **Communicate Mathematical Ideas** Explain why this construction produces the perpendicular bisector of the segment.

4. **Check for Reasonableness** How can you use a ruler and protractor to check the construction?

YOUR TURN

Construct the perpendicular bisector of each segment.

5.

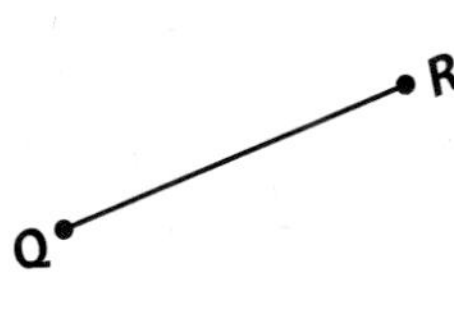

6.

Copying an Angle

You can use construction tools rather than a protractor to copy a given angle.

EXAMPLE 2

CA CC G.CO.12

Construct an angle with the same measure as ∠S.

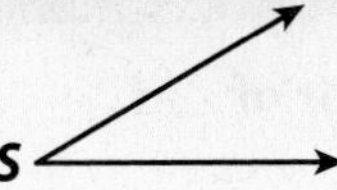

STEP 1 Use a straightedge to draw a ray. Label the endpoint X.

X

STEP 2 Place the point of the compass on S and draw an arc. Label the two points of intersection T and U.

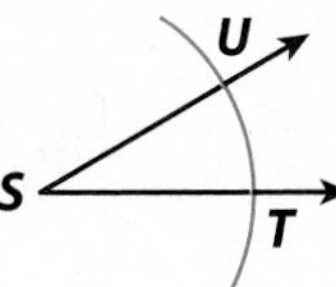

STEP 3 Without adjusting the compass, place the point of the compass on X and draw an arc. Label the point of intersection Y.

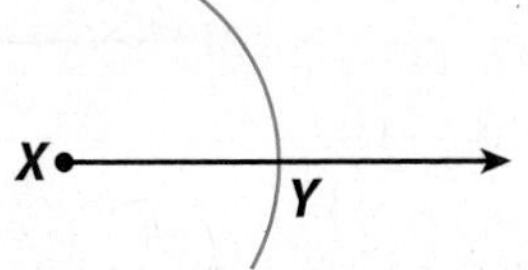

STEP 4 Place the point of the compass on T and open it to the distance TU.

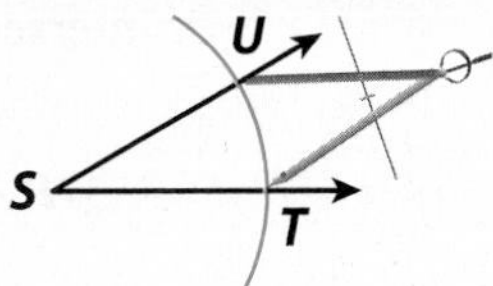

STEP 5 Without adjusting the compass, place its point on Y and draw an arc. Label the intersection with the first arc Z. Use a straightedge to draw $\overrightarrow{XZ}$.

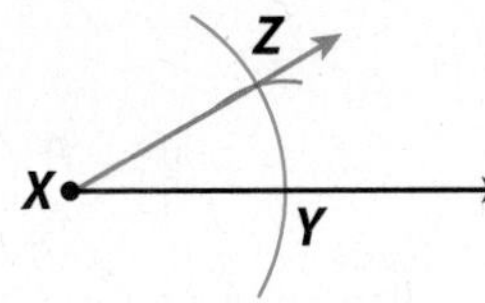

Math Talk
Mathematical Practices

How does a triangle congruence theorem help explain why this construction works?

YOUR TURN

7. In the space provided, construct an angle with the same measure as $\angle A$.

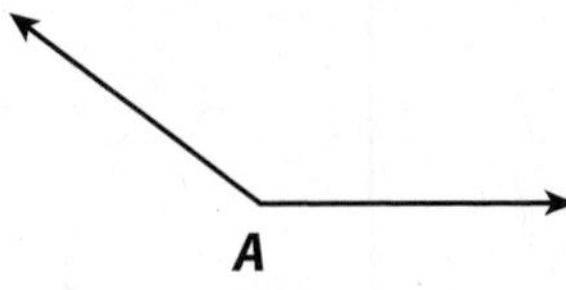

Bisecting an Angle

An **angle bisector** is a ray that divides an angle into two congruent angles. In the figure, $\overrightarrow{EG}$ is the bisector of $\angle DEF$.

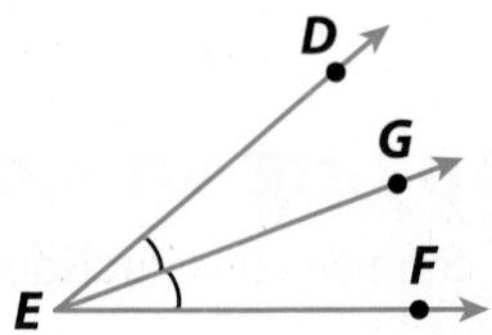

EXAMPLE 3

CA CC G.CO.12

Construct the angle bisector of $\angle M$.

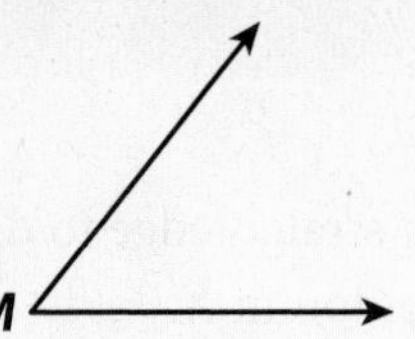
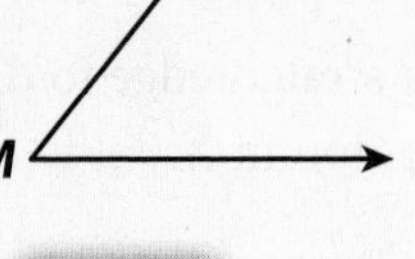

My Notes

STEP 1 Place the point of the compass on M and draw an arc that intersects both sides of the angle. Label the points of intersection P and Q.

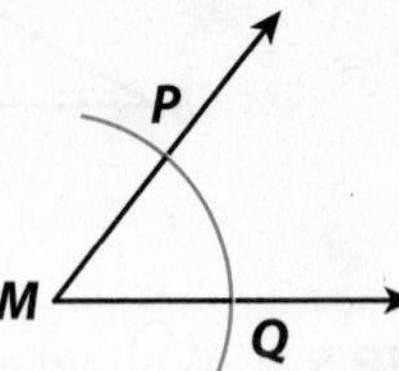

STEP 2 Place the point of the compass on P and draw an arc in the interior of the angle.

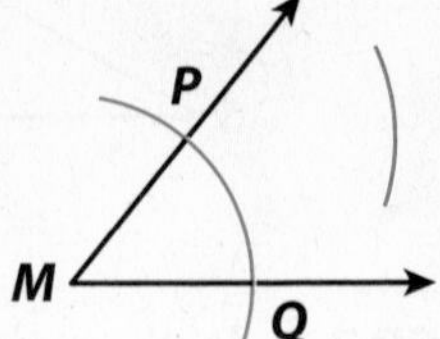
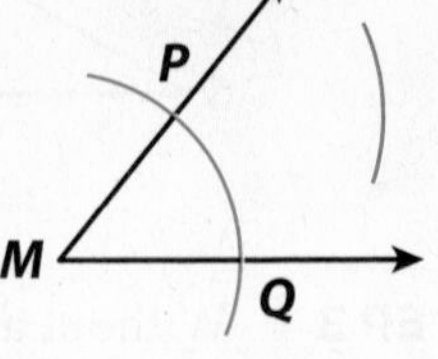

STEP 3 Without adjusting the compass, place the point of the compass on Q and draw an arc that intersects the arc from Step 2. Label the intersection of the arcs R.

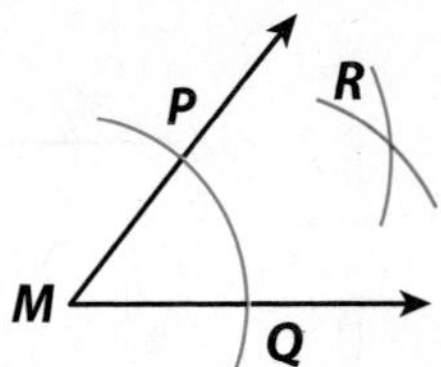

STEP 4 Use a straightedge to draw $\overrightarrow{MR}$.

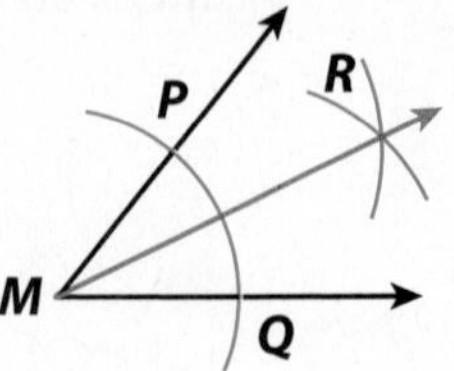

REFLECT

8. **Communicate Mathematical Ideas** How does a triangle congruence theorem help explain why this construction works?

____

____

9. **What If?** Suppose you do not have a compass. How could you use paper folding to construct the bisector of an angle?

____

____

YOUR TURN

Construct the angle bisector of each angle.

10.

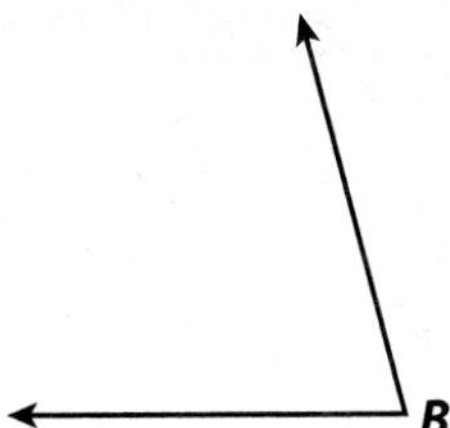

11.

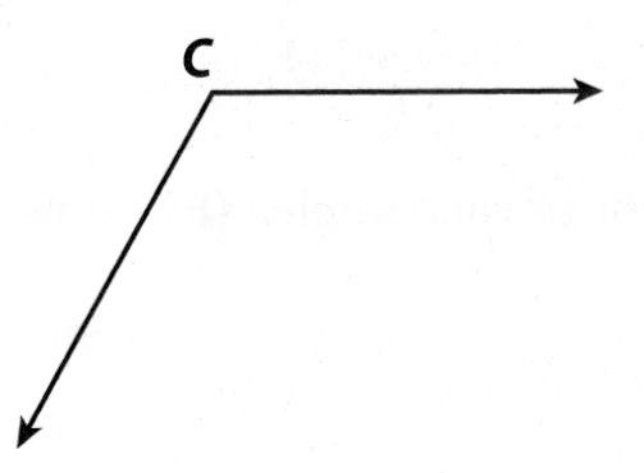

Guided Practice

Construct the perpendicular bisector of each segment.
(Explore Activity and Example 1)

1.

2.

3.

4.

In the space provided, construct an angle with the same measure as the given angle. (Example 2)

5.

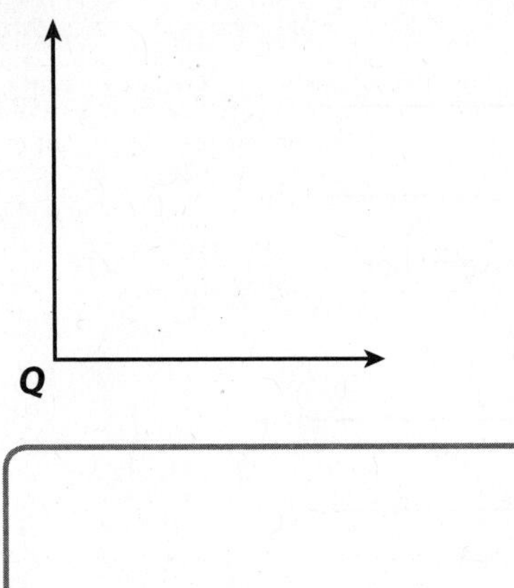

6.

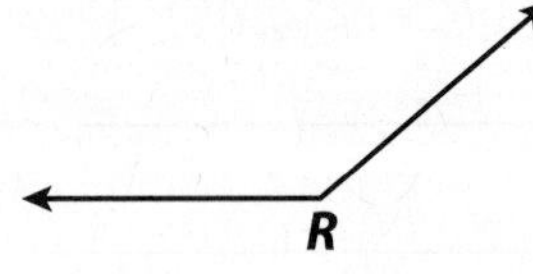

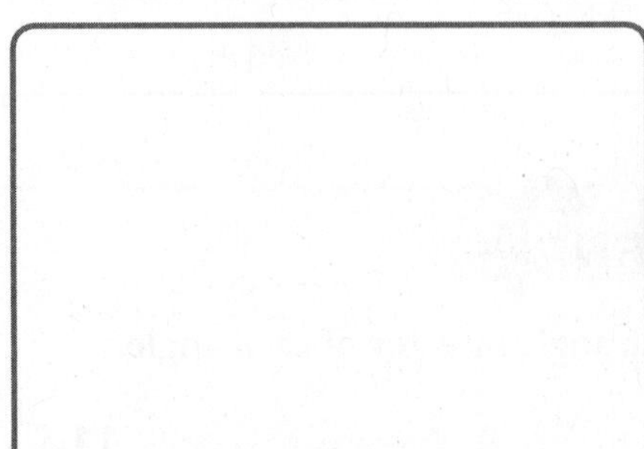

Construct the angle bisector of each angle. (Example 3)

7.

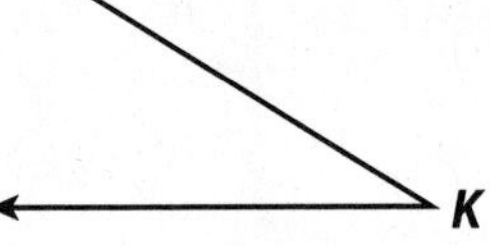

8.

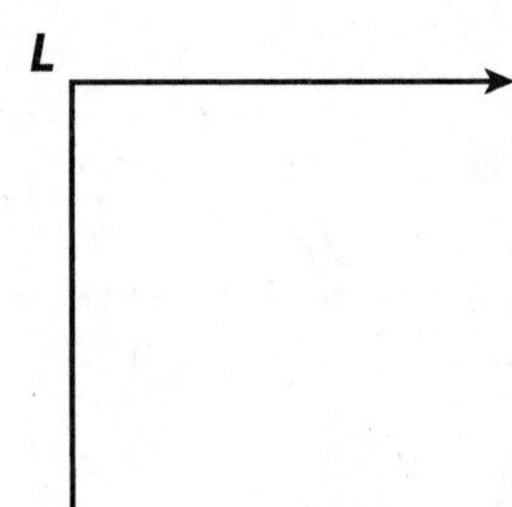

9.

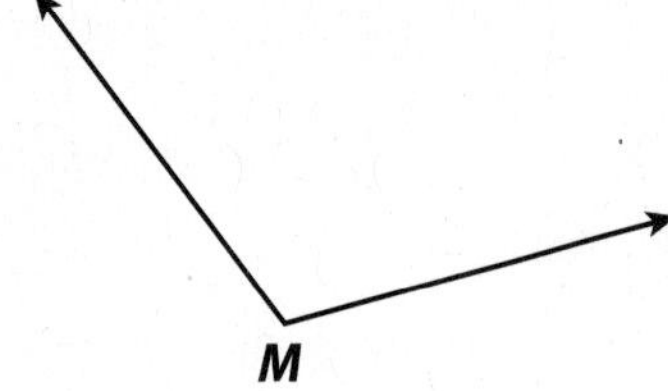

10.

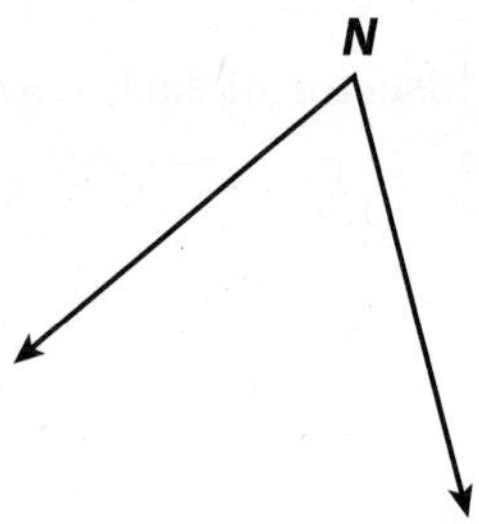

ESSENTIAL QUESTION CHECK-IN

11. How is using a compass like using a ruler? How is it different?

____

____

____

____

Name ________________ Class ________________ Date ________________

16.1 Independent Practice

CA CC G.CO.12

12. Use $\angle J$ for the following.

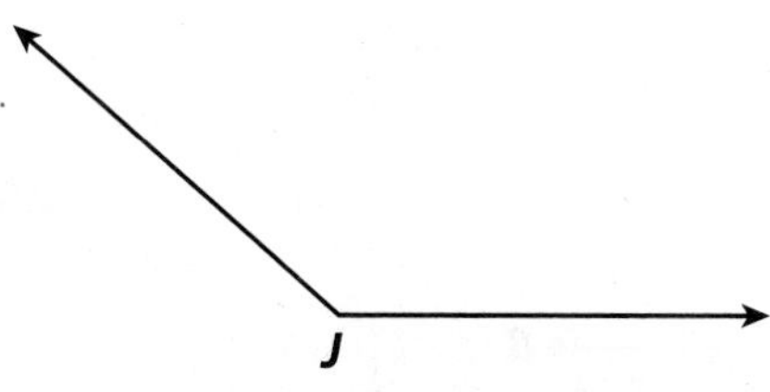

a. Use a compass and straightedge to copy $\angle J$ on a separate piece of paper.

b. Use paper folding to construct the bisector of the angle.

c. Use a protractor to find the measure of the two angles formed by the angle bisector.

____

13. Explain the Error Matt was asked to copy $\angle P$. His work is shown in red. Explain Matt's error.

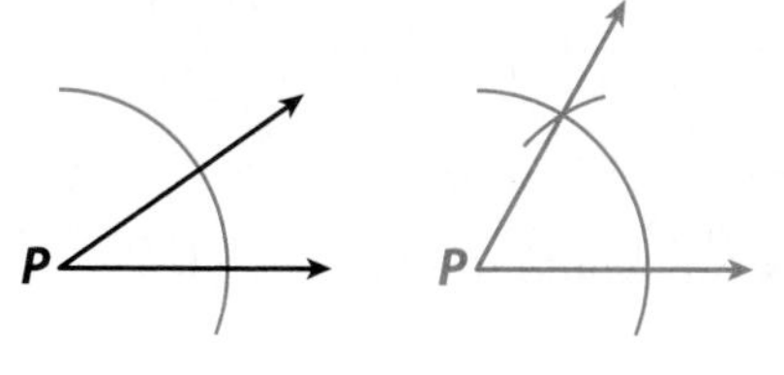

____

____

____

____

14. Critical Thinking Construct a 45° angle whose vertex is the midpoint of $\overline{AB}$. (*Hint*: How does a 45° angle relate to a 90° angle?)

15. Represent Real-World Problems A field of soybeans is watered by a rotating irrigation system. The watering arm, $\overline{CD}$, rotates around its center point. To show the area of the crop of soybeans that will be watered, construct a circle with diameter CD.

16. Construct an angle whose measure is $\frac{1}{4}$ the measure of $\angle Z$. Justify the construction.

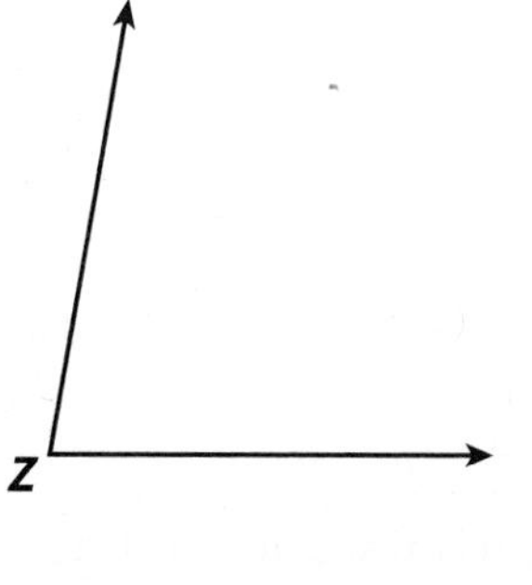

____

____

____

____

17. Sonia draws a segment on a piece of paper. She wants to find three points that are equidistant from the endpoints of the segment. Explain how she can use paper folding to help her locate the three points.

______

______

______

H.O.T. FOCUS ON HIGHER ORDER THINKING

Work Area

18. **Justify Reasoning** Use the segments shown at the right.

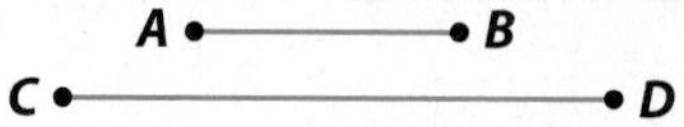

A • ——— • B

C • ————— • D

a. In the space at the right, construct and label a segment, $\overline{XY}$, whose length is the average of the lengths of $\overline{AB}$ and $\overline{CD}$.

b. Justify the method you used in part **a**.

______

______

______

19. **Communicate Mathematical Ideas** Explain the steps you would use to construct an angle whose measure is 22.5°.

______

______

______

______

20. **What If?** Mikayla wants to construct the perpendicular bisector of a segment. She has a straightedge, but she finds that her compass has rusted and is stuck in the open position. Will she be able to do the construction? Explain.

______

______

______

______

LESSON
16.2 Parallel and Perpendicular Lines

CA CC G.CO.12

Make formal geometric constructions with a variety of tools and methods (compass and straightedge, string, reflective devices, paper folding, dynamic geometric software, etc.). *Also G.CO.5*

ESSENTIAL QUESTION

How do you use basic constructions to do more complex constructions?

EXPLORE ACTIVITY 1

Using Reflective Devices to Construct Perpendicular Lines

In this activity, you will use a reflective device to construct lines perpendicular to the given lines below through the given points.

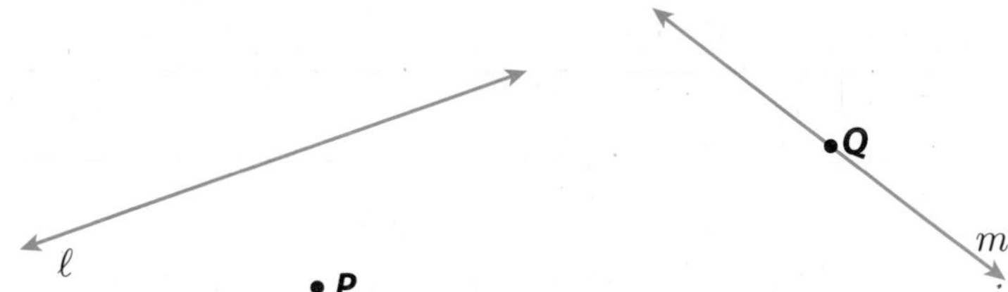

A Place the reflective device along line ℓ. Look through the device to locate the image of point P on the opposite side of line ℓ. Draw the image of point P and label it P'.

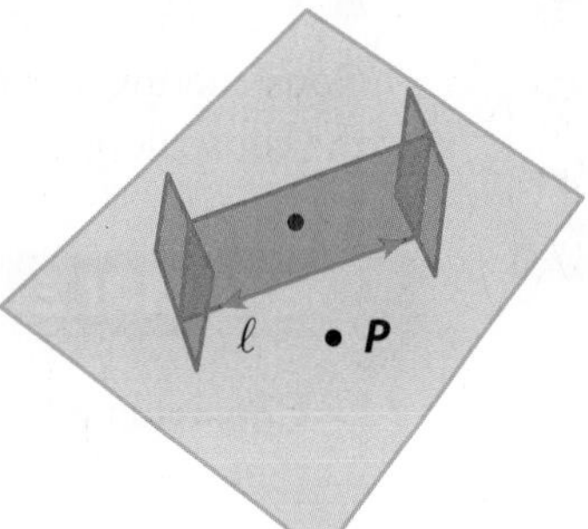

B Use a straightedge to draw $\overleftrightarrow{PP'}$.

C Explain why $\overleftrightarrow{PP'}$ is perpendicular to line ℓ.

____

____

D Place the reflective device so that it passes through point Q and is approximately perpendicular to line m. Adjust the angle of the device until the image of line m coincides with line m.

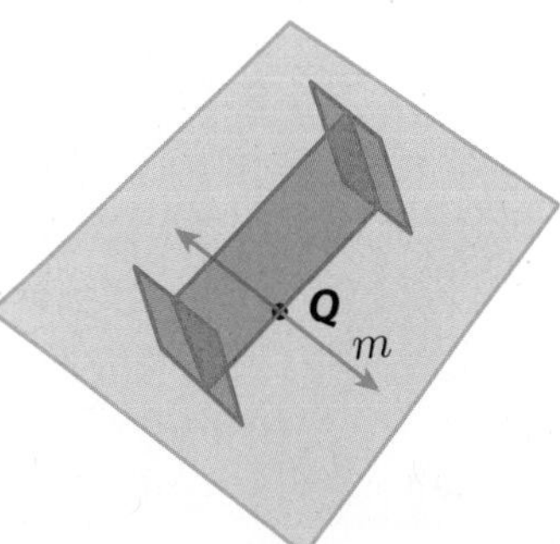

E Draw a line along the reflective device and label it line n.

F Explain why line n is perpendicular to line m.

____

____

____

____

EXPLORE ACTIVITY 1 *(cont'd)*

REFLECT

1. **Check for Reasonableness** How can you check that the lines you drew are perpendicular to lines ℓ and m?

2. **Make a Prediction** Use the reflective device to draw two points on line ℓ that are reflections of each other. Label the points X and X'. What prediction can you make about PX and PX'? Why? Use a ruler to check your prediction.

Constructing a Perpendicular to a Line Through a Point Not on the Line

Constructing a perpendicular to a line through a point not on the line is related to the construction of a perpendicular bisector of a segment.

EXAMPLE 1

CA CC G.CO.12

Construct a line perpendicular to line ℓ that passes through point P.

STEP 1 Place the point of the compass at P. Draw an arc that intersects line ℓ at two points, A and B.

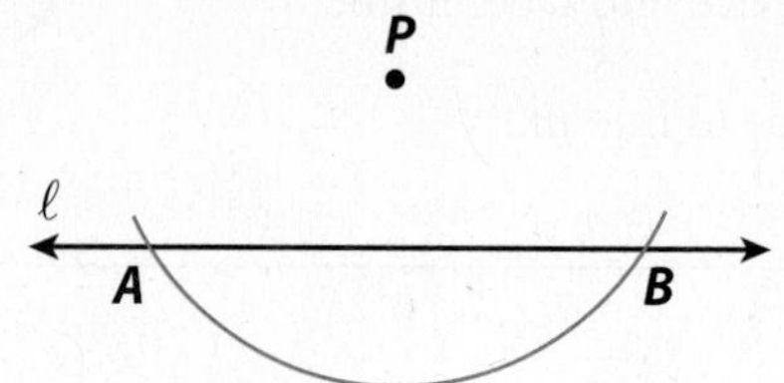

STEP 2 Construct the perpendicular bisector of $\overline{AB}$.

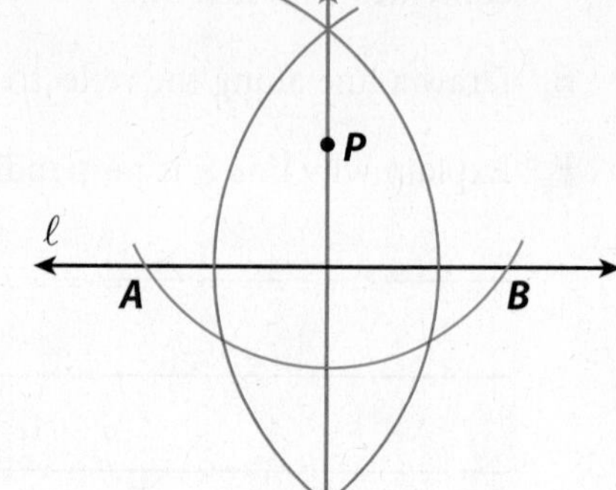

Math Talk
Mathematical Practices

How do you know the perpendicular bisector of $\overline{AB}$ will pass through point P?

REFLECT

3. How can you do this construction using paper folding?

____

____

YOUR TURN

Construct a line perpendicular to line ℓ that passes through point *P*.

4.

5.

Personal Math Trainer

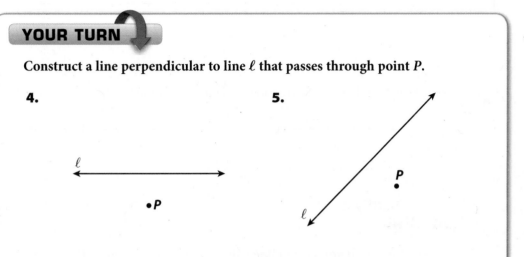

Online Practice and Help

my.hrw.com

Constructing a Perpendicular to a Line Through a Point on the Line

As in Example 1, the first step in constructing a perpendicular to a line through a given point on the line is constructing two points on the line that are equidistant from the given point.

EXAMPLE 2 CA CC G.CO.12

Construct a line perpendicular to line ℓ that passes through point *P*.

STEP 1 Place the point of the compass at *P*. Draw arcs on either side of point *P*. Label the points of intersection *A* and *B*.

STEP 2 Construct the perpendicular bisector of $\overline{AB}$.

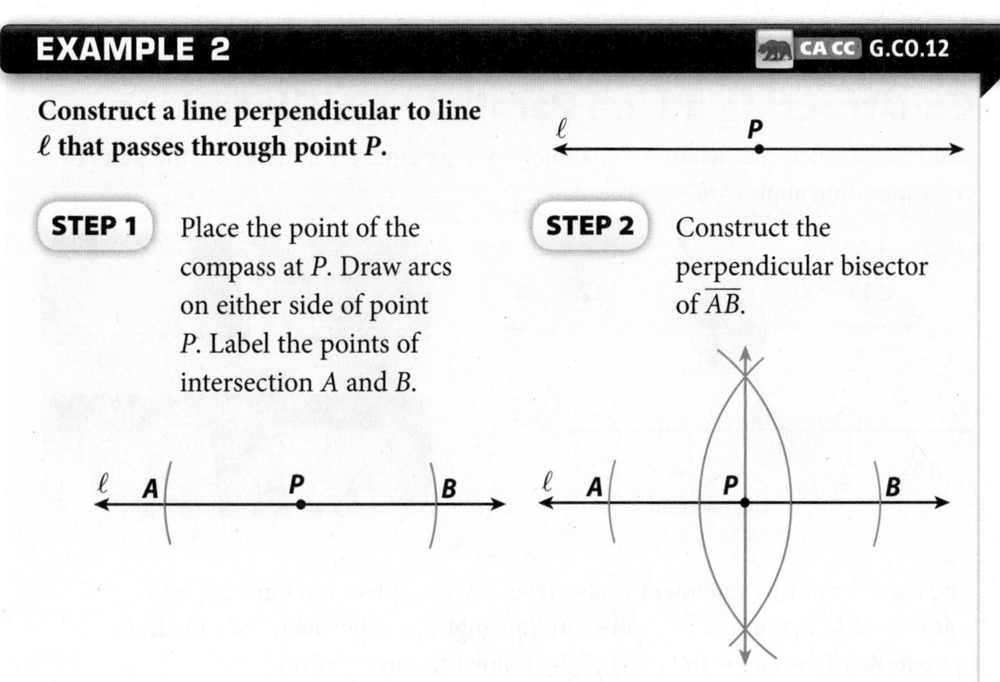

REFLECT

6. **Communicate Mathematical Ideas** Explain how you know that this construction produces a line that is perpendicular to line ℓ and that passes through point P.

7. How can you do this construction using paper folding?

Construct a line perpendicular to line ℓ that passes through point P.

8.

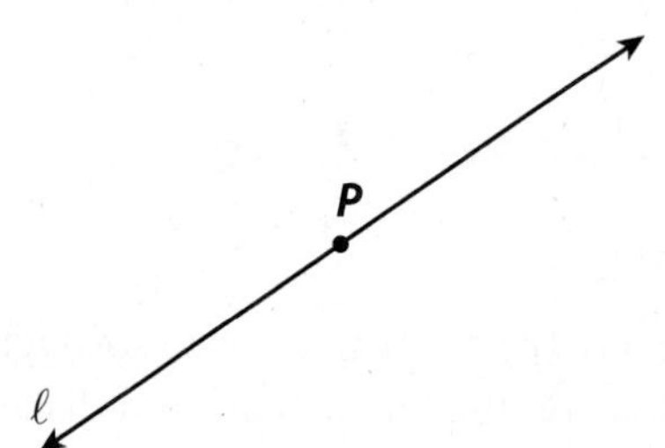

9.

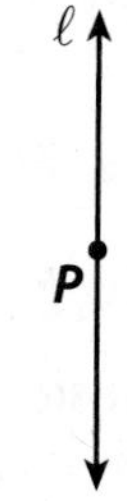

Constructing a Line Parallel to a Given Line

You have learned that when two parallel lines are cut by a transversal, the pairs of corresponding angles are congruent.

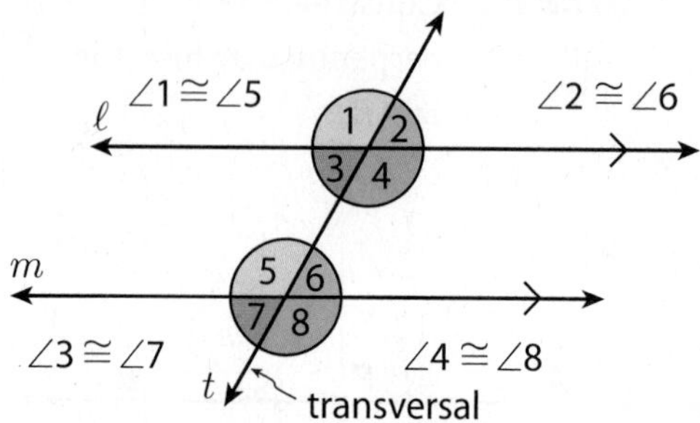

The *converse* of this statement is also true. That is, if two lines are cut by a transversal so that a pair of corresponding angles is congruent, then the lines are parallel. This fact is the basis of the following construction.

EXAMPLE 3

CA CC G.CO.12

Construct a line parallel to line ℓ that passes through point *P*.

STEP 1 Choose two points on line ℓ and label them *Q* and *R*. Use a straightedge to draw $\overleftrightarrow{PQ}$.

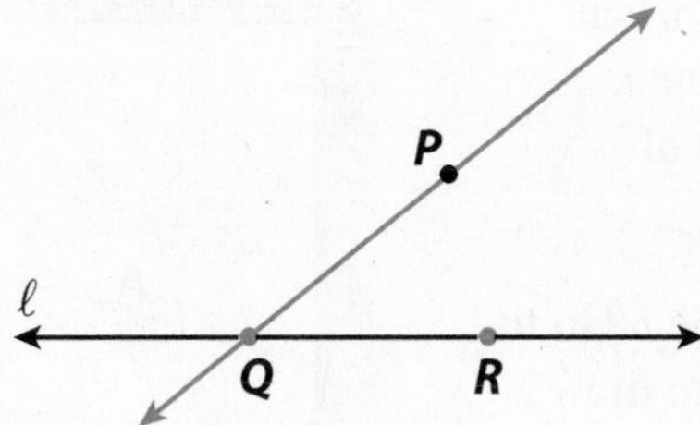

STEP 2 Copy ∠*PQR* at point *P*, as shown, to construct line *m*. Line *m* is parallel to line ℓ.

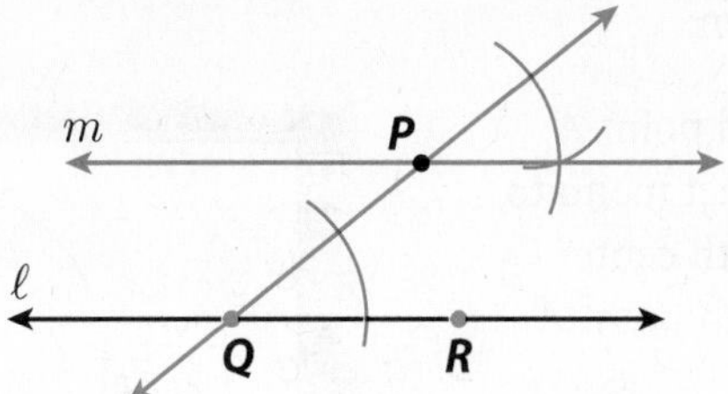

REFLECT

10. **Communicate Mathematical Ideas** Explain how you know that this construction produces a line that is parallel to line ℓ and that passes through point *P*.

____

____

____

YOUR TURN

Construct a line parallel to line ℓ that passes through point *P*.

11.

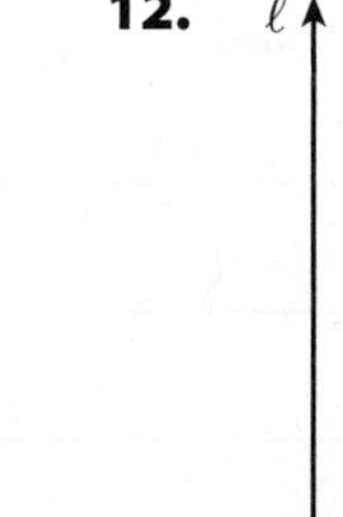

12.

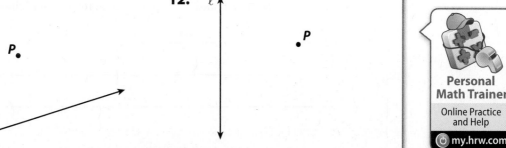

EXPLORE ACTIVITY 2 CA CC G.CO.5, G.CO.12

Using Constructions to Transform Figures

My Notes

Geometry software has built-in functions for transformations. You can also use geometry software to perform transformations using constructions.

Follow these instructions to construct the image of a segment under a reflection.

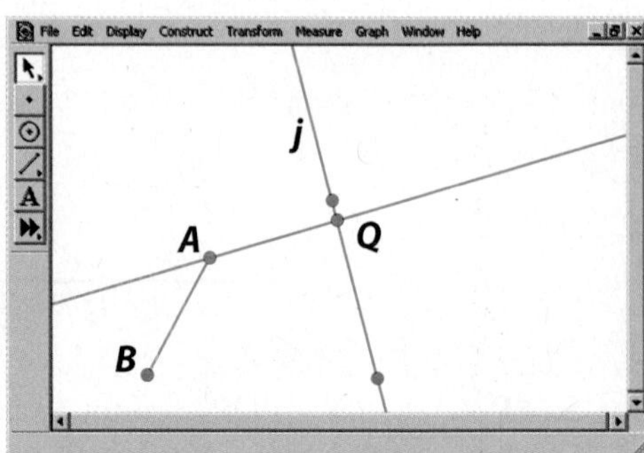

A Use the software to draw a segment, $\overline{AB}$, and a line j, which will be the line of reflection.

B Select point A and line j. Go to the Construct menu to draw a perpendicular to line j through point A. Construct the point at the intersection of the lines and label it Q, as shown.

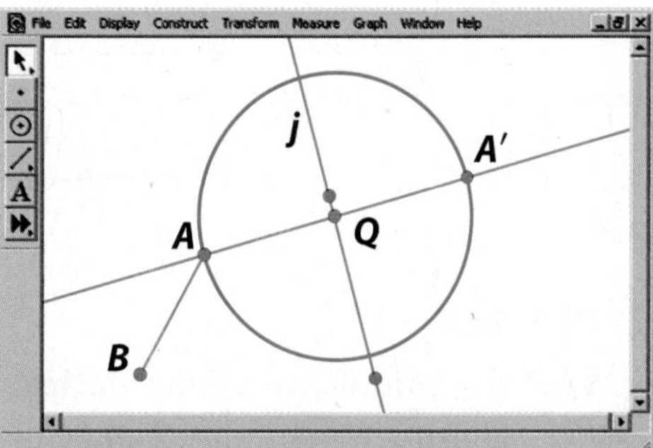

C Select point Q and point A. Go to the Construct menu to draw the circle with center Q that passes through point A.

D Construct the point at the intersection of the circle and the line you drew that was perpendicular to line j. Label it A', as shown.

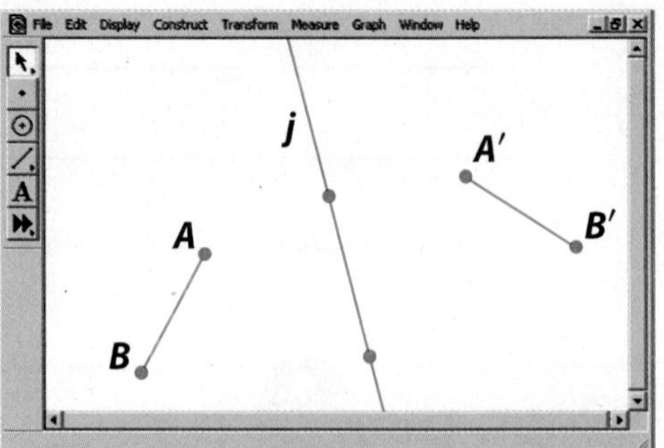

E Hide the line that is perpendicular to line j, hide point Q, and hide the circle.

F Construct point B' by starting with point B and repeating Steps B through E.

G Draw the segment $\overline{A'B'}$.

H Change the size and location of $\overline{AB}$ and notice how the size and location of $\overline{A'B'}$ change. Change the position of line j and notice the effect on $\overline{AB}$ and $\overline{A'B'}$. How do $\overline{AB}$ and $\overline{A'B'}$ appear to be related to each other?

____

____

____

REFLECT

13. Why do you draw a line through point A that is perpendicular to line j?

14. Why do you draw a circle with center Q that passes through point A?

15. **Make a Prediction** What will happen if you move point A so that it lies on line j? Describe your prediction and then use the software to check whether you are correct.

Guided Practice

1. Julia is given a line ℓ and a point P not on line ℓ. She is asked to use a reflective device to construct a line through P that is perpendicular to line ℓ. She places the device as shown in the figure. What should she do next to draw the required line? (Explore Activity 1)

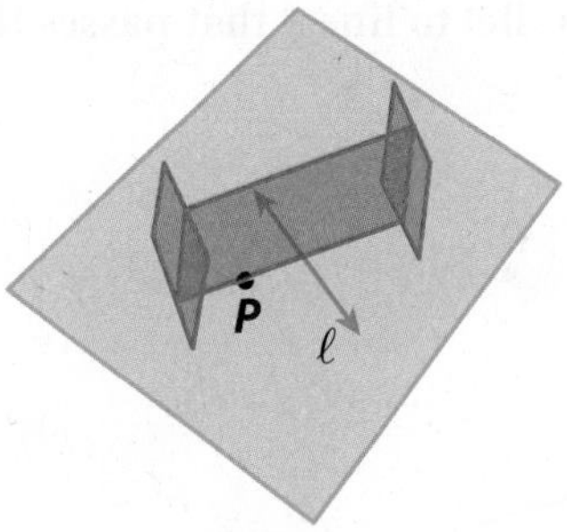

2. How can you use a reflective device to draw the perpendicular bisector of a segment? (Explore Activity 1)

3. Construct a line perpendicular to line ℓ that passes through point P. (Example 1)

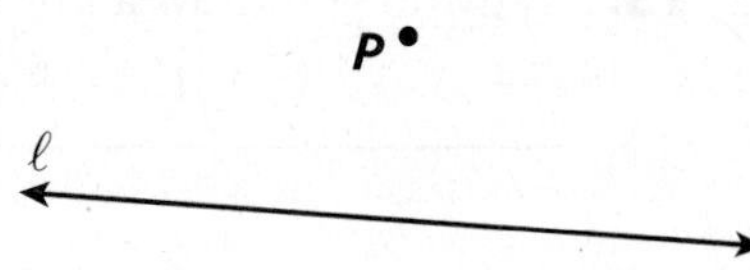

STEP 1 Place the point of the compass at P. Draw an arc that intersects line ℓ at two points, A and B.

STEP 2 Construct the perpendicular bisector of $\overline{AB}$.

Construct a line perpendicular to line ℓ that passes through point P. (Examples 1 and 2)

4.

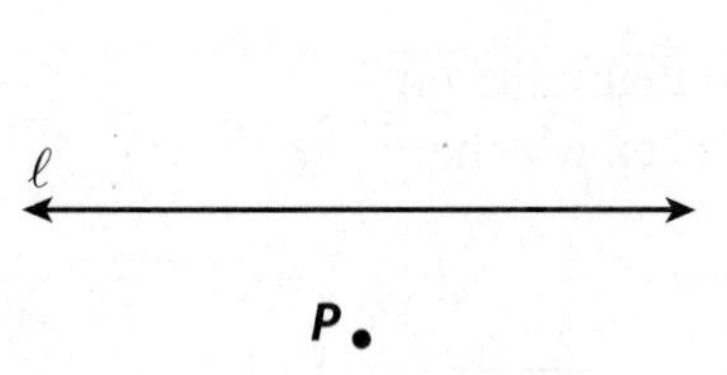

5.

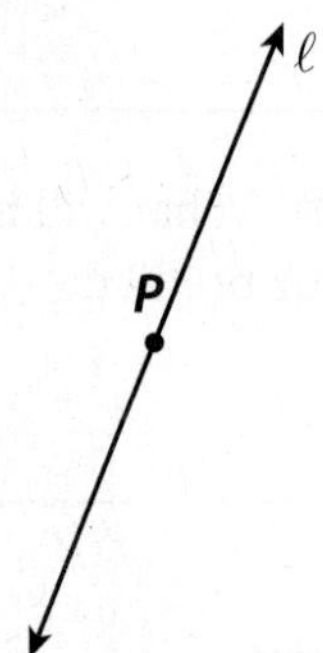

Construct a line parallel to line ℓ that passes through point P. (Example 3)

6.

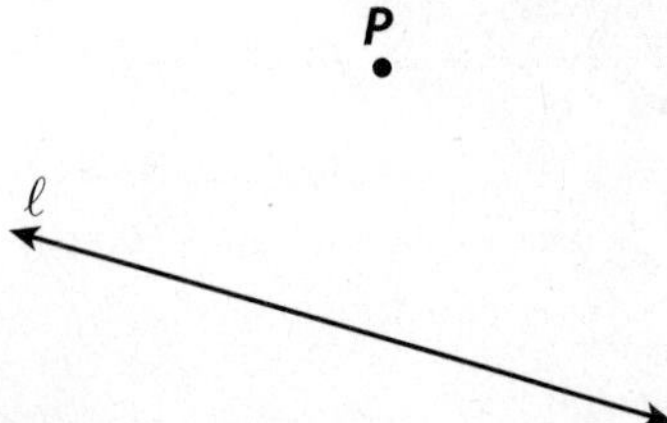

7.

8. DeMarcus is using geometry software to translate a segment. He draws $\overline{AB}$ and another segment, $\overline{XY}$, that he will use as his translation vector. He then constructs line j through point A parallel to $\overline{XY}$, as shown. What should his next step be? Explain. (Explore Activity 2)

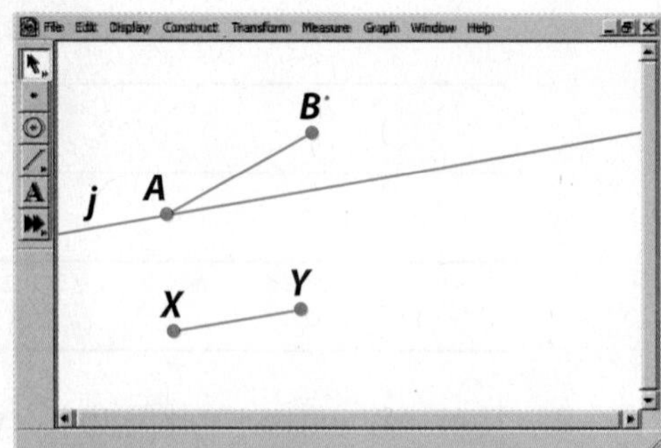

____

____

____

ESSENTIAL QUESTION CHECK-IN

9. What basic constructions are used to construct parallel and perpendicular lines?

____

____

Name _______________ Class _______________ Date _______________

16.2 Independent Practice

CA CC G.CO.5, G.CO.12

10. **Represent Real-World Problems** A regional planner is designing two new roads. One of the roads must be perpendicular to Highway 1 and pass through Albertville (point A). The other road must be parallel to Highway 5 and pass through Belleview (point B). The regional planner needs to know where the new roads will intersect. Construct this point below and label it C.

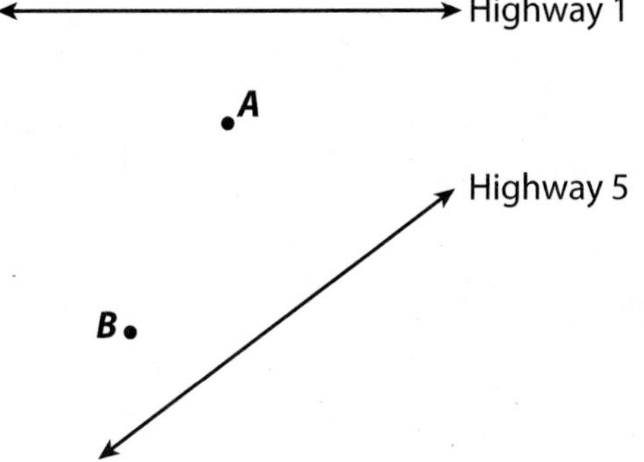

11. The figure below consists of eight congruent segments. It is the top half of a geometric design on a sweatshirt.

a. Use a reflective device to complete the design.

b. What type of quadrilaterals appear in the completed design? Explain.

____

____

____

12. **Critique Reasoning** Maya has a sheet of paper that shows line m. She wants to construct a line perpendicular to line m. She folds the paper along line m and then uses a pin to make a hole through the folded paper. Then she opens the paper and uses a straightedge to draw a line through the two pinholes. She claims that this is the required line. Does Maya's method work? Explain.

____

____

____

____

____

13. Recall that a trapezoid is a quadrilateral with at least one pair of parallel sides.

a. Construct and label a trapezoid $ABCD$ so that one of its sides lies along line ℓ and one of its vertices is point A.

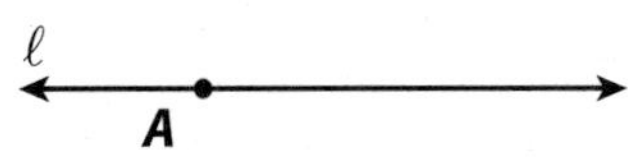

b. **Justify Reasoning** Explain how you know your construction works.

____

____

____

____

____

H.O.T. FOCUS ON HIGHER ORDER THINKING

Work Area

14. Draw Conclusions Mariano constructed a line m that passes through point P and is perpendicular to line ℓ. Then he constructed a line n that passes through point Q (not on line m) and is perpendicular to line ℓ. What can you conclude about lines m and n? Explain.

______

______

______

15. Critical Thinking A rectangle is a quadrilateral with four right angles.

a. Construct and label a rectangle $ABCD$ so that one side of the rectangle lies along line ℓ and one vertex of the rectangle is point A.

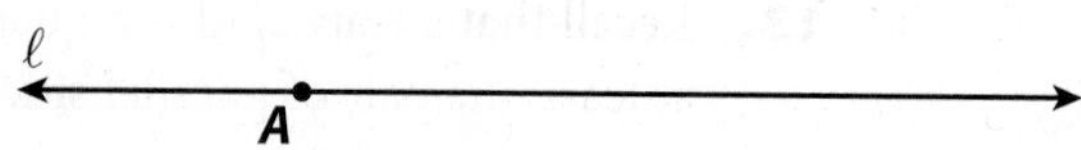

b. Explain the method you used to construct the rectangle.

______

______

______

______

______

______

c. Explain how you know that the angles at D are right angles.

______

______

______

______

LESSON

16.3 Polygons

CA CC G.CO.13

Construct an equilateral triangle, a square, and a regular hexagon inscribed in a circle. *Also G.CO.12*

ESSENTIAL QUESTION

How are the constructions of different types of inscribed polygons related to each other?

EXPLORE ACTIVITY 1

Constructing a Square Inscribed in a Circle

A polygon is **inscribed** in a circle if all of the polygon's vertices lie on the circle. In the figure, $\triangle XYZ$ is inscribed in circle O.

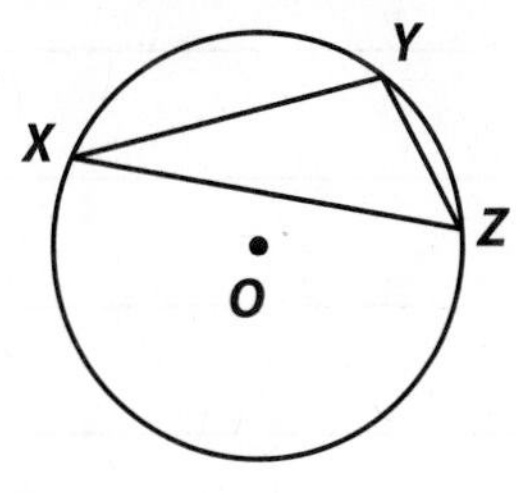

Follow these instructions to construct a square inscribed in a circle. Make your construction in the space provided at the right below.

A Use your compass to draw a circle. Mark the center. Draw a diameter, $\overline{AB}$, using a straightedge.

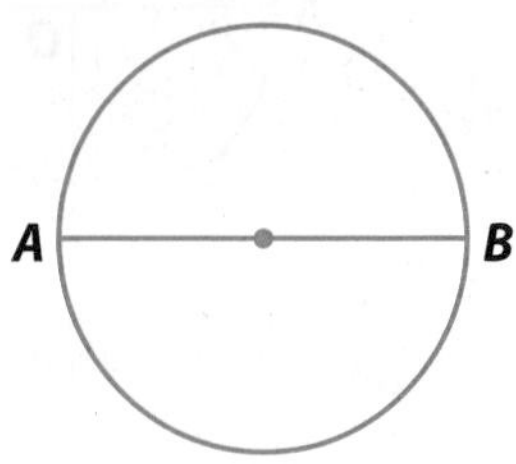

B Construct the perpendicular bisector of $\overline{AB}$. Label the points where the perpendicular bisector intersects the circle as C and D.

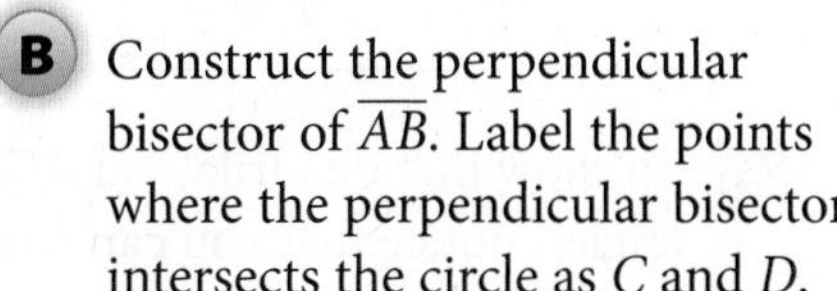

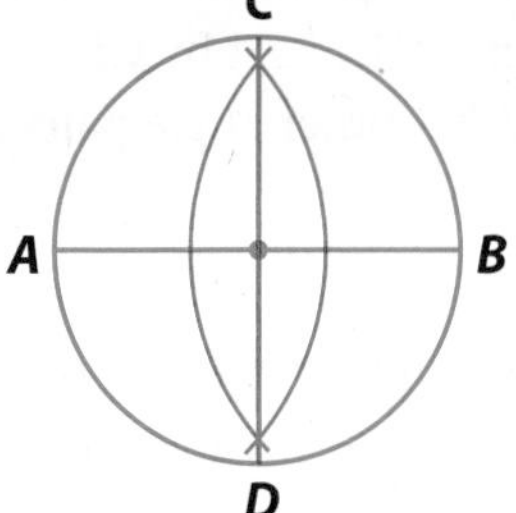

C Use the straightedge to draw $\overline{AC}$, $\overline{CB}$, $\overline{BD}$, and $\overline{DA}$.

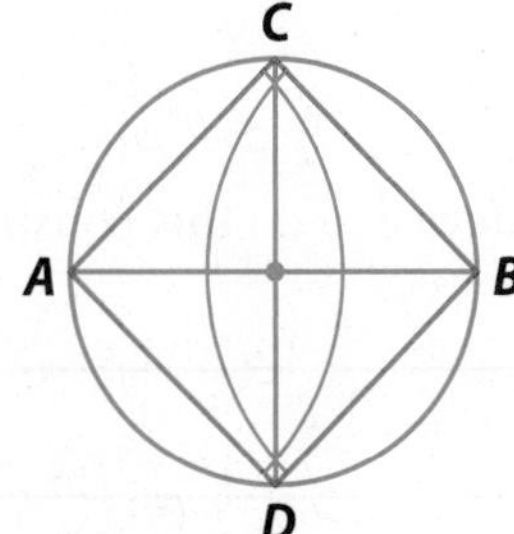

EXPLORE ACTIVITY 1 *(cont'd)*

D To explain why the construction works, you must show that quadrilateral *ACBD* is a square. What do you need to do to show that *ACBD* is a square?

E To show that quadrilateral *ACBD* has four congruent sides, let the center of the circle be *O*. Consider $\triangle AOC$, $\triangle COB$, $\triangle BOD$, and $\triangle DOA$. Explain why these triangles are all congruent.

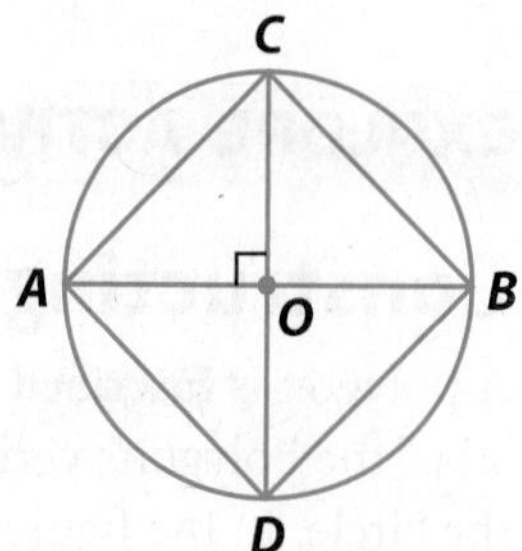

F What can you conclude about $\overline{AC}$, $\overline{CB}$, $\overline{BD}$, and $\overline{DA}$. Why?

G To show that quadrilateral *ACBD* has four right angles, notice that you can write $\triangle AOC \cong \triangle COB$, so that $\angle 1 \cong \angle 3$ by CPCTC. You can also write the congruence statement as $\triangle AOC \cong \triangle BOC$, so that $\angle 1 \cong \angle 4$ by CPCTC. This means $\angle 3 \cong \angle 4$. What other angle pairs are congruent in this way?

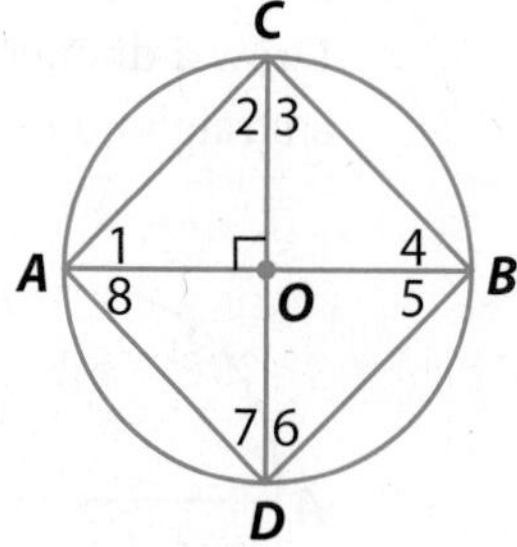

Math Talk
Mathematical Practices

Is the transformation in part G that maps $\triangle AOC$ onto $\triangle COB$ the same as the one that maps $\triangle AOC$ onto $\triangle BOC$? Explain.

H Recall that the sum of the angle measures in a triangle is 180°. What can you say about the measures of the eight numbered angles?

I What are the measures of the four angles of quadrilateral *ACBD*? Why?

REFLECT

1. What If? How could you use a reflective device to do this construction?

EXPLORE ACTIVITY 2 

G.CO.13

Animated Math
my.hrw.com

Constructing a Regular Hexagon in a Circle

You can use a straightedge and piece of string to do constructions. To begin, tie a pencil to one end of the string.

Follow these instructions to construct a regular hexagon inscribed in a circle. Make your construction in the space provided at the right below.

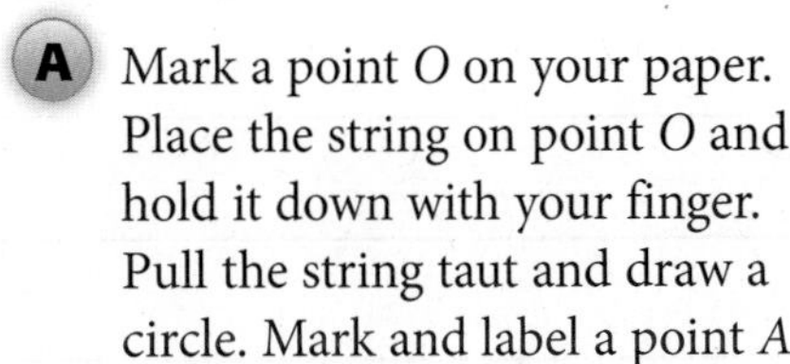

A Mark a point *O* on your paper. Place the string on point *O* and hold it down with your finger. Pull the string taut and draw a circle. Mark and label a point *A*.

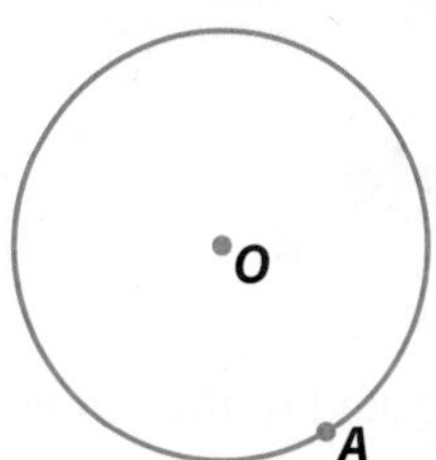

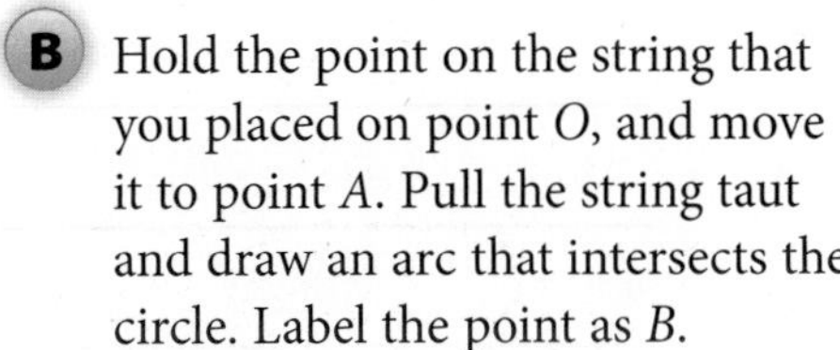

B Hold the point on the string that you placed on point *O*, and move it to point *A*. Pull the string taut and draw an arc that intersects the circle. Label the point as *B*.

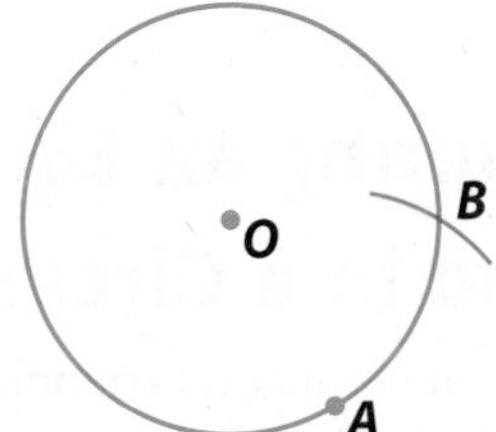

C Hold the point on the string that you placed on point *A*, and move it to point *B*. Draw an arc to locate point *C* on the circle. Repeat to locate points *D*, *E*, and *F*. Use your straightedge to draw *ABCDEF*.

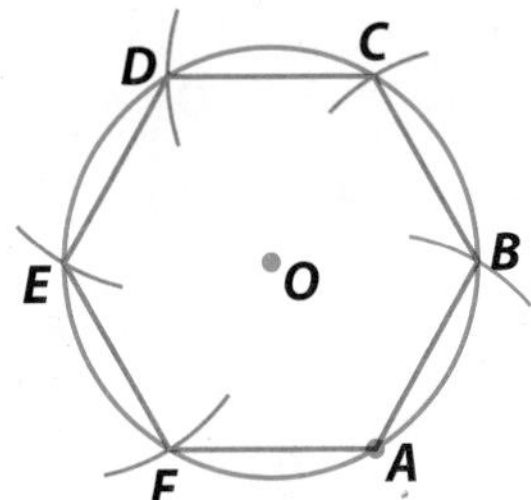

D Consider $\triangle AOB$, $\triangle BOC$, $\triangle DOC$, $\triangle EOD$, and $\triangle FEO$. Explain why the triangles are congruent when mapped this way. Then find their angle measures. Explain your reasoning.

____

____

____

E Use the fact that there are 360° in a full circle to find $m\angle FOA$. Show your work. Then use $\angle FOA$ to explain why $\triangle FOA \cong \triangle AOB$ and $\overline{FA} \cong \overline{AB}$.

____

____

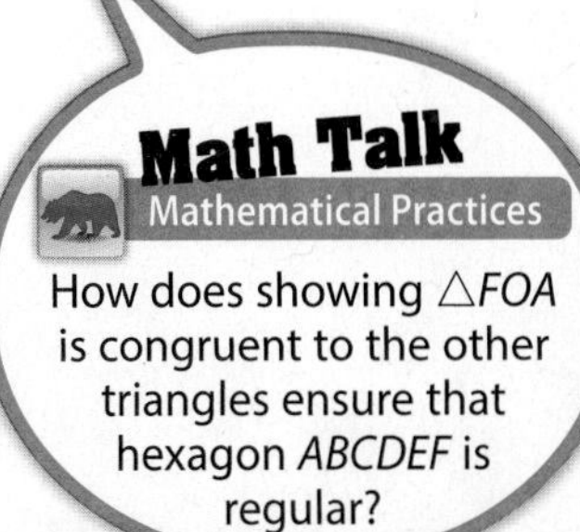

Math Talk
Mathematical Practices
How does showing △FOA is congruent to the other triangles ensure that hexagon ABCDEF is regular?

EXPLORE ACTIVITY 2 *(cont'd)*

REFLECT

2. Communicate Mathematical Ideas What must be true about the string as you move it from point to point in the construction? Why?

____

____

____

____

____

Constructing an Equilateral Triangle Inscribed in a Circle

Constructing an equilateral triangle inscribed in a circle is related to the hexagon construction in Explore Activity 2.

EXAMPLE 1

CA CC G.CO.13

My Notes

Construct an equilateral triangle inscribed in a circle.

STEP 1 Use a compass to draw a circle O. Mark a point A on the circle.

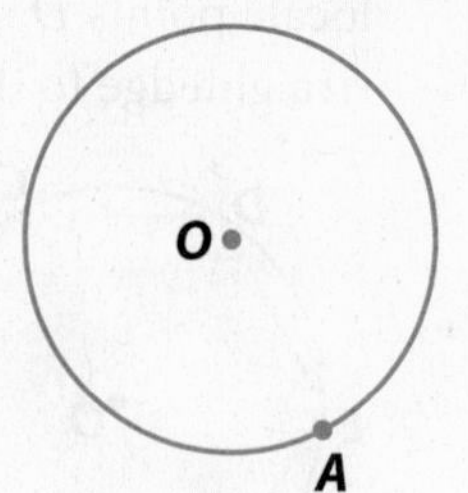

STEP 2 Without adjusting the compass, place the point of the compass at point A and make an arc that intersects the circle at point B. Continue to make arcs as you would to construct a regular hexagon.

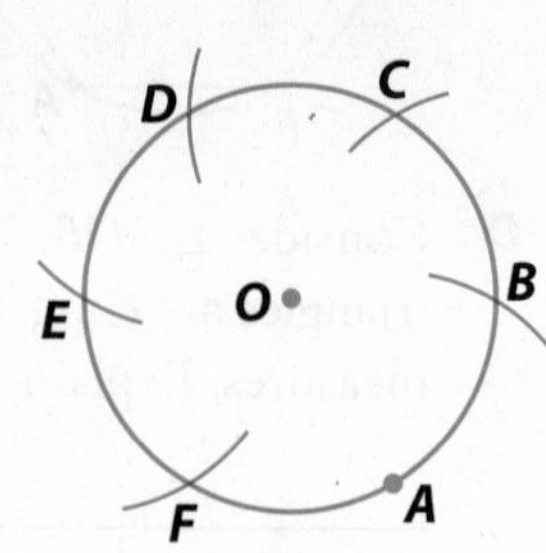

STEP 3 Use a straightedge to connect every other point around the circle.

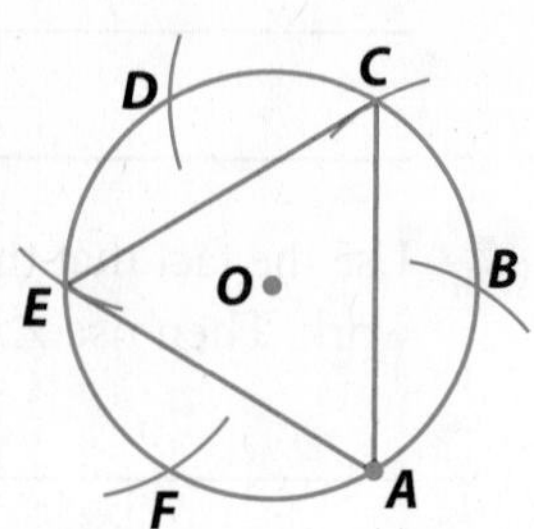

REFLECT

3. **Check for Reasonableness** Explain how you can use one or more measurement tools to check that your construction produced an equilateral triangle.

4. How can you use the fact that *ABCDEF* is a regular hexagon and CPCTC to explain why the construction produces an equilateral triangle?

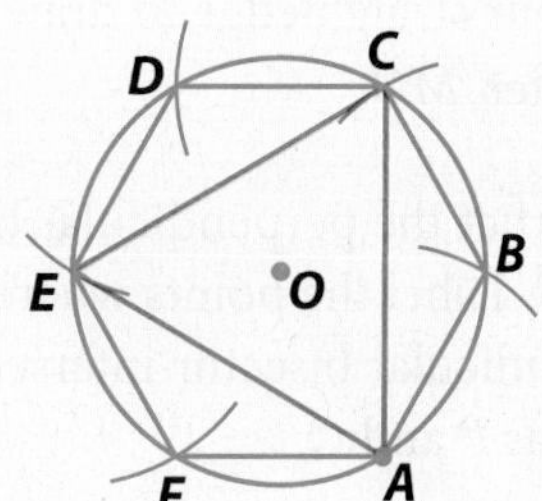

5. When would a string be more appropriate than a compass for constructing an equilateral triangle? Give an example.

YOUR TURN

6. Construct an equilateral triangle inscribed in a circle. Make your construction in the space provided below.

Guided Practice

1. Construct a square inscribed in a circle. Make your construction in the space provided at the right. (Explore Activity 1)

STEP 1 Use your compass to draw a circle. Use your straightedge to draw a diameter, $\overline{MN}$.

STEP 2 Construct the perpendicular bisector of $\overline{MN}$. Label the points where the perpendicular bisector intersects the circle as P and Q.

STEP 3 Use the straightedge to draw $\overline{MP}$, $\overline{PN}$, $\overline{NQ}$, and $\overline{QM}$.

2. Construct a regular hexagon inscribed in a circle. Make your construction in the space provided below. (Explore Activity 2)

3. Construct an equilateral triangle inscribed in a circle. Make your construction in the space provided below. (Example 1)

ESSENTIAL QUESTION CHECK-IN

4. How is the construction of an equilateral triangle related to the construction of a regular hexagon?

Name ______ Class ______ Date ______

16.3 Independent Practice

CA CC G.CO.12, G.CO.13

5. Rafael was asked to construct a square inscribed in a circle. The figure shows the work he did before he was interrupted. Complete his construction.

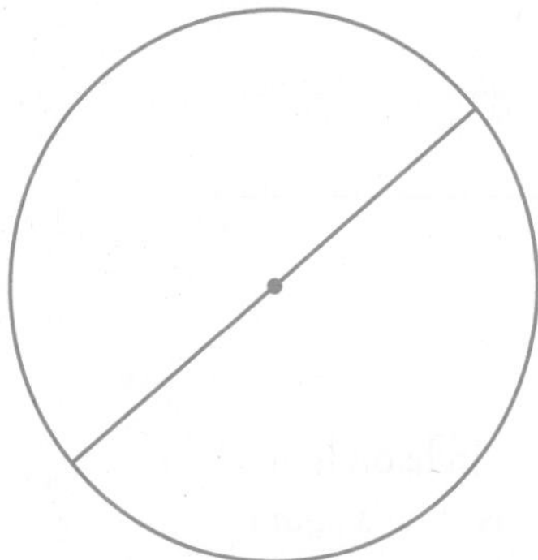

6. Construct a regular hexagon *PQRSTU* inscribed in circle *C*.

7. Construct a regular hexagon whose sides are congruent to $\overline{JK}$. Make your construction in the space provided below.

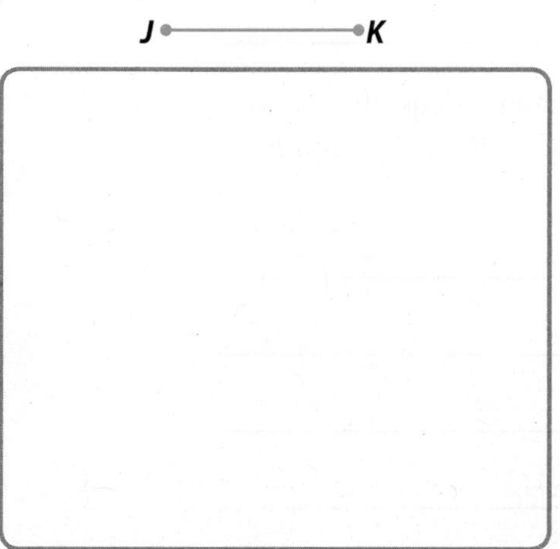

8. **Critical Thinking** Jessika has a flowerbed in the shape of a regular hexagon, as shown below. Construct a circle that passes through all of the vertices. Explain your method.

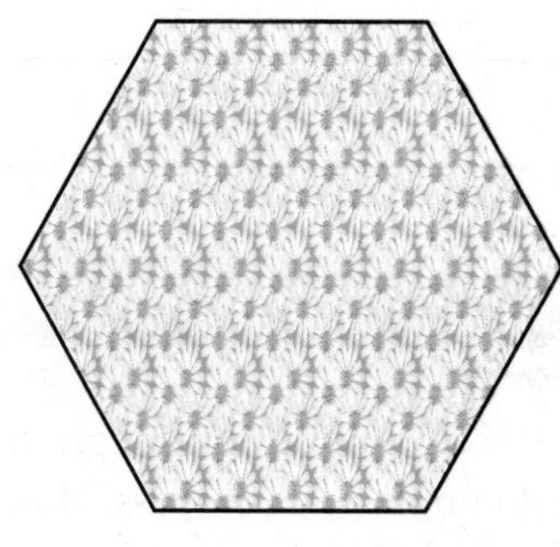

______

______

______

______

______

______

9. **Explain the Error** Malik was asked to construct an equilateral triangle inscribed in a circle. He began as shown. Explain and correct his error.

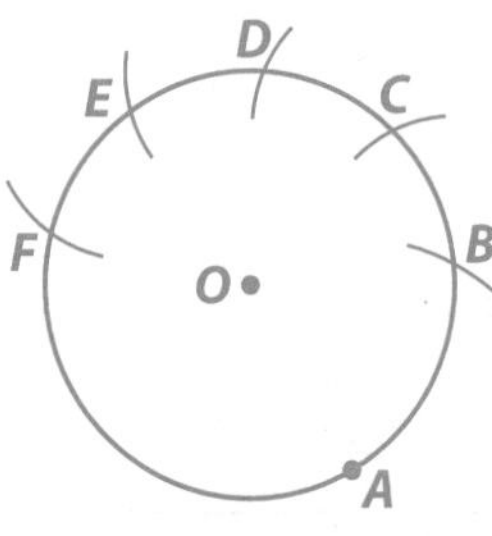

______

______

______

______

______

______

10. **Justify Reasoning** Use a straightedge and a piece of string to construct an equilateral triangle that has $\overline{AB}$ as one of its sides. Then explain how you know your construction works. (*Hint*: Consider an arc centered at *A* with radius *AB* and an arc centered at *B* with radius *AB*.)

A —— B

H.O.T. FOCUS ON HIGHER ORDER THINKING

Work Area

11. **What If?** Suppose you are given a piece of tracing paper with a circle on it and you do not have a compass. How can you use paper folding to inscribe a square in the circle?

12. **Critical Thinking** Explain how you can use one of the constructions you learned as the starting point for constructing a regular octagon inscribed in a circle.

13. **Draw Conclusions** Martina constructs a circle and locates six equally spaced points around the circle. She labels consecutive points as *A*, *B*, *C*, *D*, *E*, and *F*. What type of quadrilateral is *ACDE*? Explain.

Ready to Go On?

16.1 Segments and Angles

1. Construct the perpendicular bisector of the line segment.

2. Construct the bisector of the angle.

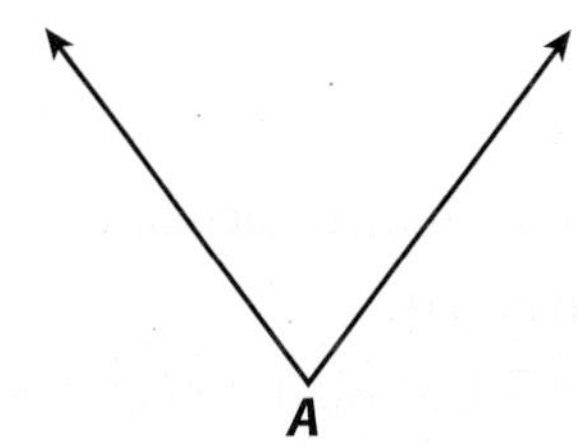

16.2 Parallel and Perpendicular Lines

3. Use a reflective device. Construct a line through point *P* perpendicular to line ℓ.

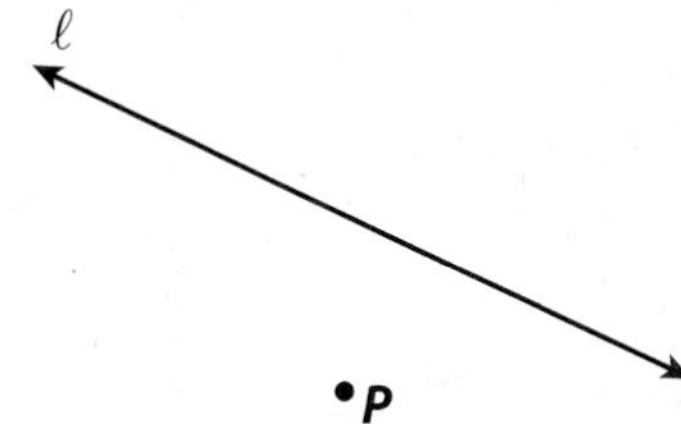

4. Construct a line parallel to line ℓ that passes through point *P*.

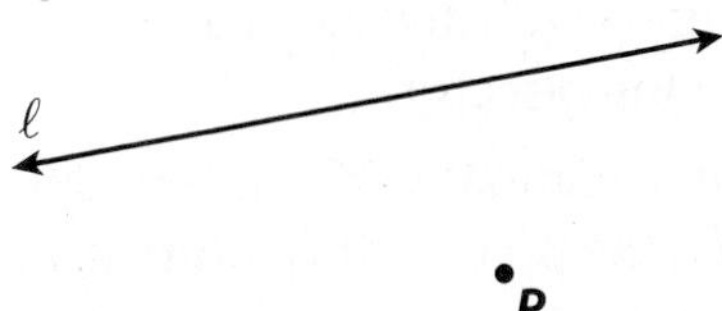

16.3 Polygons

5. Construct a square inscribed in a circle.

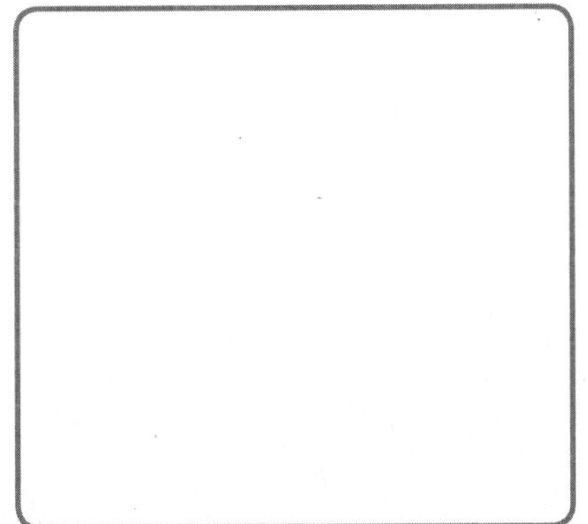

6. Construct a regular hexagon inscribed in a circle.

ESSENTIAL QUESTION

7. What is a geometric construction?

____

MODULE 16
MIXED REVIEW

Assessment Readiness

1. Consider each construction below. Do you use the construction as one of the steps when you construct a line through point P parallel to line ℓ?

Select Yes or No for A–C.

A. Constructing a perpendicular bisector ○ Yes ○ No

B. Copying an angle ○ Yes ○ No

C. Constructing the bisector of an angle ○ Yes ○ No

2. Michelle is constructing the angle bisector of a given angle.

Choose True or False for each statement.

A. She can use paper folding to construct the bisector. ○ True ○ False

B. She can use a reflective device to construct the bisector. ○ True ○ False

C. If she uses a compass, she must begin by placing the point of the compass in the interior of the angle. ○ True ○ False

3. Franco collects shells at the beach once each week. The sequence 7, 15, 23, 31, 39, … represents the number of shells in his collection each week. Write an explicit rule and a recursive rule for the sequence. Then determine how many weeks it will take for Franco to have 95 shells in his collection. Explain.

4. Haruki is designing a fountain that consists of a square pool inscribed in a circular base represented by circle O. He wants to construct the square so that one of its vertices is point X. Construct the square and then explain your method.

UNIT 5

Study Guide Review

MODULE 14 Geometric Terms and Transformations

ESSENTIAL QUESTION

What are the similarities and differences among transformations that are rigid motions?

Key Vocabulary

point *(punto)*
line *(línea)*
plane *(plano)*
line segment *(segmento de una línea)*
circle *(círculo)*
ray *(rayo)*
angle *(ángulo)*
transformation *(transformación)*
rigid motion *(movimiento rígido)*
vector *(vector)*
translation *(traslación)*
reflection *(reflexión)*
line of symmetry *(eje de simetría)*
rotation *(rotación)*

EXAMPLE 1

What type of angle is $\angle PTR$? Find the value of x.

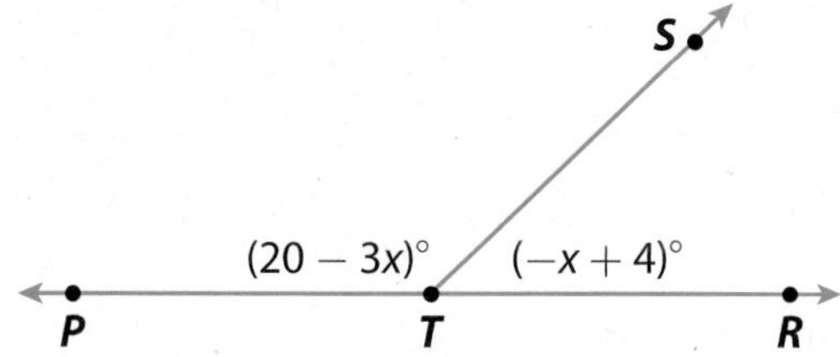

$\angle PTR$ is a straight angle. $m\angle PTR = 180°$

$m\angle PTS + m\angle STR = 180°$ by the Angle Addition Postulate.

$(20 - 3x) + (-x + 4) = 180$

$-4x + 24 = 180$ Combine like terms.

$-4x = 156$ Simplify.

$x = -39$

EXAMPLE 2

Draw the image of $\triangle ABC$ after a translation along $\vec{v}$, a reflection across line m, and a 90° rotation around point P.

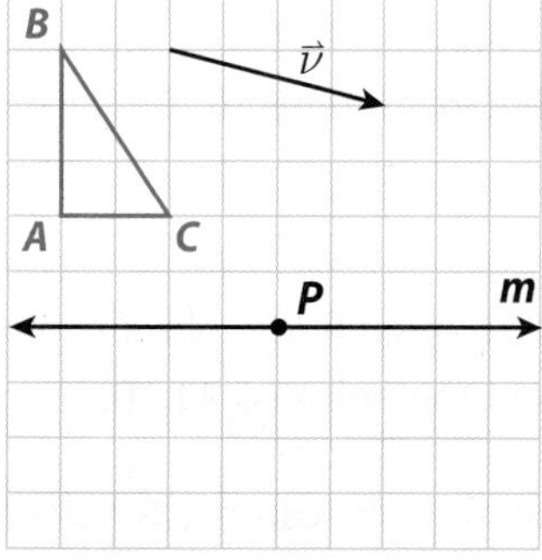

STEP 1 Draw the image of $\triangle ABC$ after a translation along $\vec{v}$.

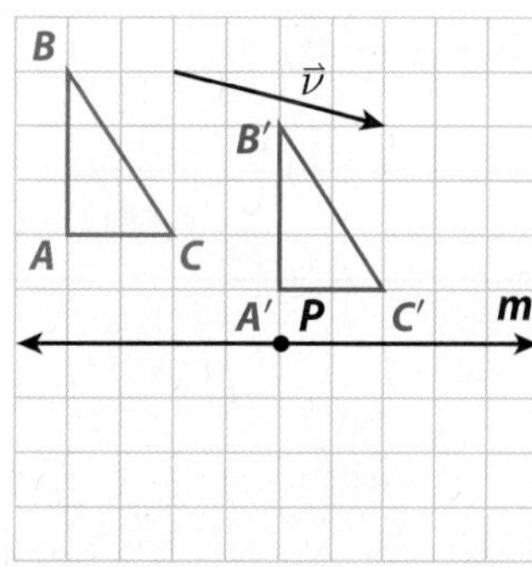

STEP 2 Draw the image of $\triangle A'B'C'$ after a reflection across line m.

STEP 3 Draw the image of $\triangle A''B''C''$ after a 90° rotation around point P.

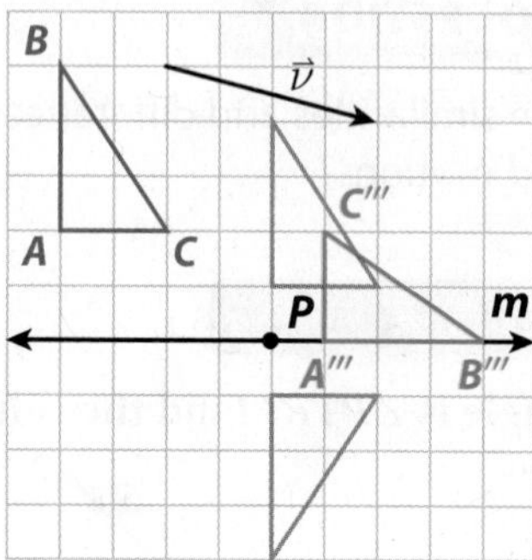

EXERCISES

1. **Draw Conclusions** Points A, B, and C are collinear in that order. AC is 3 times AB. How does BC compare to AB? (Lesson 14.1)

____

Use the figure for Exercises 2–5.

2. Identify the transformation that maps figure $DEFG$ to its image $D'E'F'G'$. Then give an algebraic rule for the transformation. (Lessons 14.2, 14.3)

____

3. The original figure is reflected such that the image of point E is point D. What is the line of reflection? (Lesson 14.4)

____

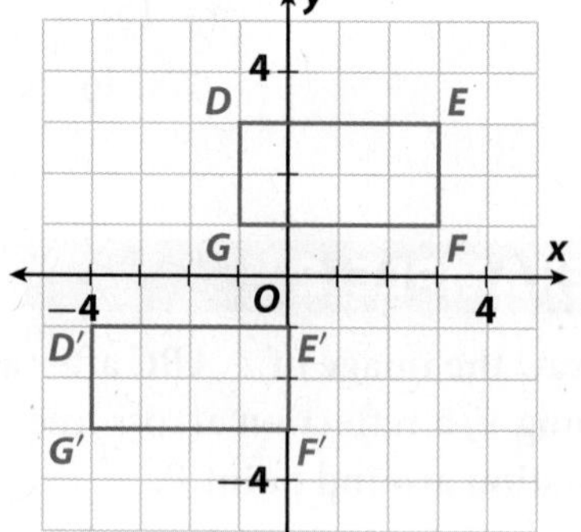

4. Draw the image if the original figure is rotated 90° counterclockwise about the point (4, 1). (Lesson 14.5)

5. **Explain the Error** Ha says she can use a reflection across an axis followed by a translation to get the rotation image from Exercise 4. Explain her error. (Lesson 14.6)

____

____

MODULE 15 Transformations and Congruence

Key Vocabulary
congruent *(congruente)*
theorem *(teorema)*

ESSENTIAL QUESTION

How are transformations related to the ASA, SAS, and SSS triangle congruence theorems?

EXAMPLE 1

Determine whether the given triangles are congruent. Explain.

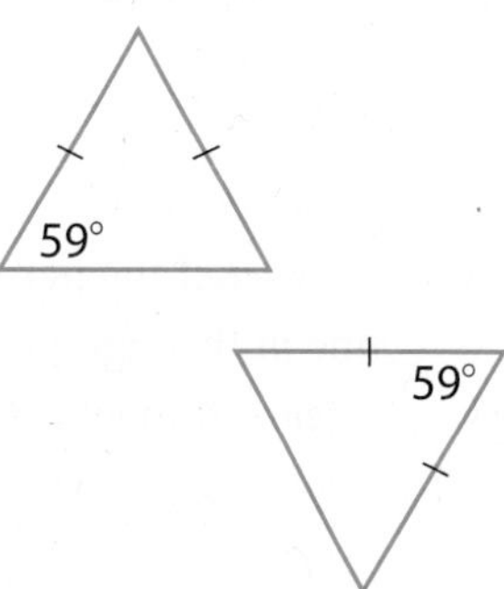

Both triangles are isosceles, so they have line symmetry. So, in the top triangle, the angles opposite the congruent sides measure 59°. The third angle measures 62°. The other triangle has a vertex angle of 59°. Each of the other two angles measures $\frac{180-59}{2}$, or 60.5°. Since the angle measures are different, there is no transformation that will map one triangle onto the other. The triangles are not congruent.

EXAMPLE 2

Tell if the triangles are congruent by the ASA, SAS, or SSS Triangle Congruence Theorem, or if they are not congruent.

A $\triangle DFG$ and $\triangle FDE$

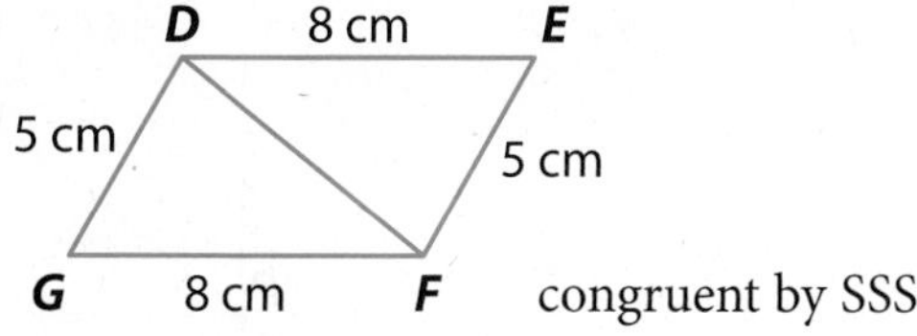

congruent by SSS

B $\triangle BAD$ and $\triangle BAC$

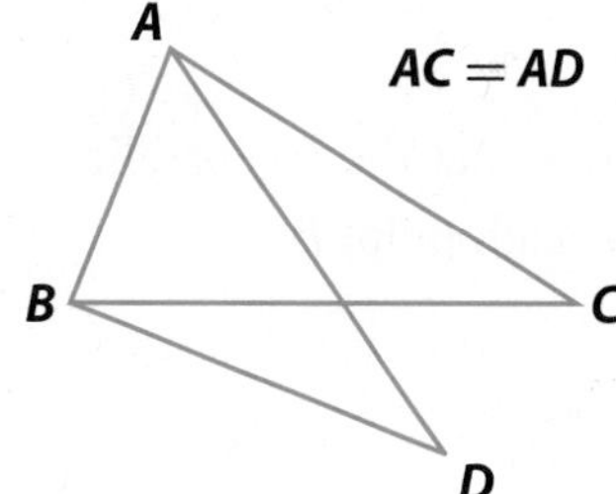

not congruent

EXERCISES

6. Specify a sequence of rigid motions that maps $\triangle ABC$ onto $\triangle A'B'C'$. (Lessons15.1and 15.2)

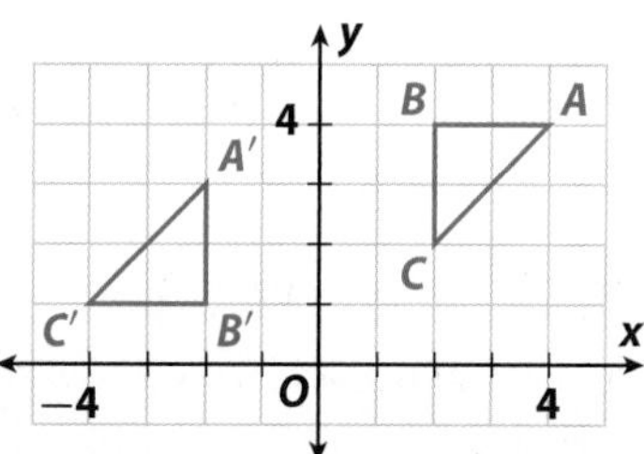

____

____

7. **Jusitify Reasoning** Explain why the triangles are congruent by either ASA or SAS. Justify your choice. (Lessons15.3 and 15.4)

____

____

8. Explain why two equilateral triangles with equal perimeters are congruent. (Lesson 15.5)

____

____

MODULE 16

Geometric Constructions

ESSENTIAL QUESTION

How can you explain why a geometric construction works?

Key Vocabulary

construction *(construcción)*

angle bisector *(bisectriz de un ángulo)*

inscribed polygon *(polígono inscrito)*

EXAMPLE 1

Construct a line perpendicular to line *m* through point *P*, a line parallel to line *m* through point *P*, and a 45° angle *APB*, where point *B* lies on line *m*.

P

m

STEP 1 Construct the perpendicular to line *m* through point *P*. Label its intersection with line *m* as point *A*.

P

m A

STEP 2 Construct the line parallel to line *m* through point *P*.

P

m A

STEP 3 Bisect a right angle at *P* so that the bisector intersects line *m*. Label the point where the bisector intersects line *m* as point *B*. Angle *APB* is a 45° angle.

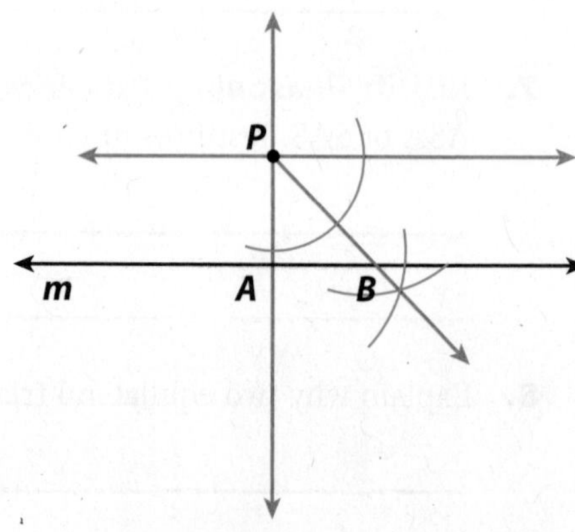

EXAMPLE 2

The construction shows an equilateral triangle inscribed in a circle. If possible, list the points that can be connected to form the given figure. Justify your answer.

A Regular hexagon
The construction of an equilateral triangle uses six evenly spaced arcs about the circle. So, connecting consecutive points *A, B, C, D, E, F,* and *A* with line segments forms a regular hexagon.

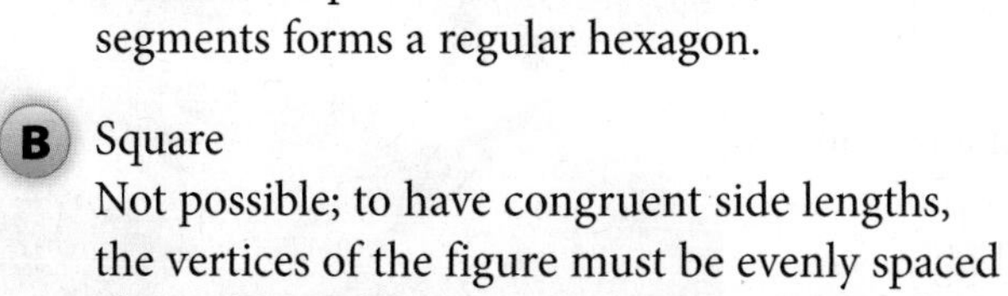

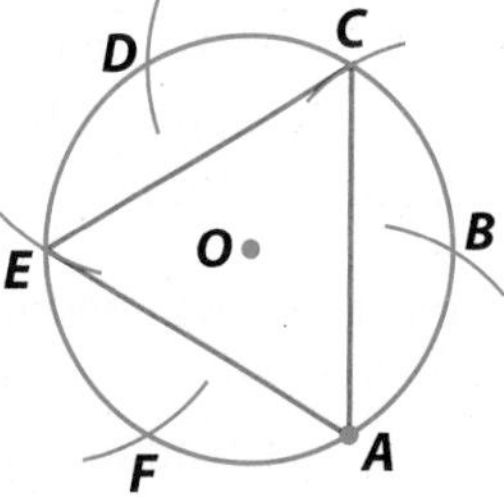

B Square
Not possible; to have congruent side lengths, the vertices of the figure must be evenly spaced about the circle. Since 4 is not a multiple of 6, a square cannot be formed.

EXERCISES

Use the figure below for Exercises 9–11. (Lessons 16.1 and 16.2)

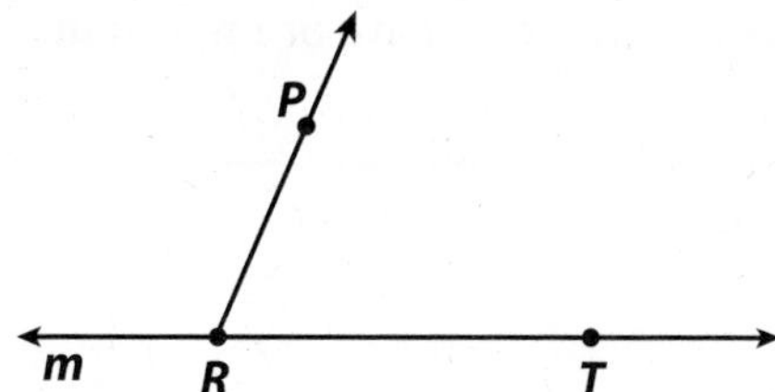

9. Construct a line through point *P*, parallel to line *m*.

10. Construct the perpendicular bisector of $\overline{RT}$.

11. **Analyze Relationships** What name can you give the quadrilateral formed by the original lines and the lines constructed in Exercises 9 and 10? Justify your answer.

____

12. Example 2 shows an equilateral triangle. Can an equilateral triangle be formed if two consecutive points on the circle are connected to form one side? Explain. (Lesson 16.3)

____

____

____

____

Unit Project

CA CC G.CO.2, G.CO.3, G.CO.5, G.CO.12

Loco for Logos

Companies use a logo to establish recognition of their brand with consumers. Often these designs can become so familiar that the name of the company is not needed to recognize the company.

For this project, you will design a logo for a company. You will draw the logo on a poster board to display to your class. You should use constructions to create the initial figures for your logo. These shapes could include equilateral, isosceles, or right triangles, squares, or hexagons. In presenting your logo, you will describe the following:

- How you were able to draw the logo accurately, including any constructions
- Ways that you used translations, reflections, or rotations in the logo design
- Any symmetry in the logo

Use the space below to write down any questions you may have or important information from your teacher.

MATH IN CAREERS | **ACTIVITY**

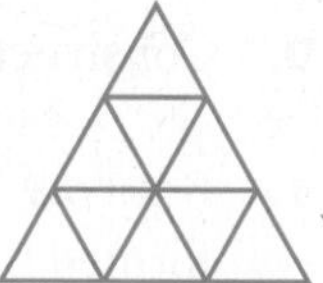

Fashion Designer A fashion designer will weave together equilateral triangles to form a larger triangle. She uses a computer program to first draw the top triangle.

a. Can the designer use translations to generate any of the other triangles? If so, how many of them? If she can do this, explain how to do it.

b. Describe how the designer can use a rotation to generate the first triangle in the middle row, using the top triangle.

c. Describe how the designer can use a reflection to generate the middle triangle in the middle row, using the top triangle. Then describe how she could use rotations of that triangle to generate the second and fourth triangles in the bottom row.

UNIT 5
MIXED REVIEW

Assessment Readiness

1. Do the solutions of the following inequalities include negative values of x? Select Yes or No.

A. $x - 3 > 5$ ○ Yes ○ No

B. $3x + 1 \leq 2(4 - x)$ ○ Yes ○ No

C. $-x < -10$ ○ Yes ○ No

2. The transformation $(x, y) \rightarrow (x + 1, y - 2)$ is applied to $\triangle JKL$. Choose True or False for each statement.

A. The transformation is a reflection. ○ True ○ False

B. The area of $\triangle J'K'L'$ is the same as the area of $\triangle JKL$. ○ True ○ False

C. The distance from J to J' is equal to the distance from K to K'. ○ True ○ False

3. A trapezoid with only one pair of parallel sides can be mapped onto itself by a reflection in only one way. Draw a possible figure to represent the trapezoid. Justify your drawing.

4. Line m is in plane R, and line n is in plane Z. Plane R and plane Z are parallel planes. Claire says that line m and line n must be parallel lines. Do you agree with Claire? Justify your response.

Performance Tasks

★**5.** Triangle *ABC* has vertices at $A(-2, 2)$, $B(3, 2)$, and $C(3, -1)$.

a. Draw the triangle on the coordinate plane. Then draw its image after a 90° rotation about the origin, followed by a reflection over the *x*-axis.

b. Specify the algebraic rules for this sequence of rigid motions.

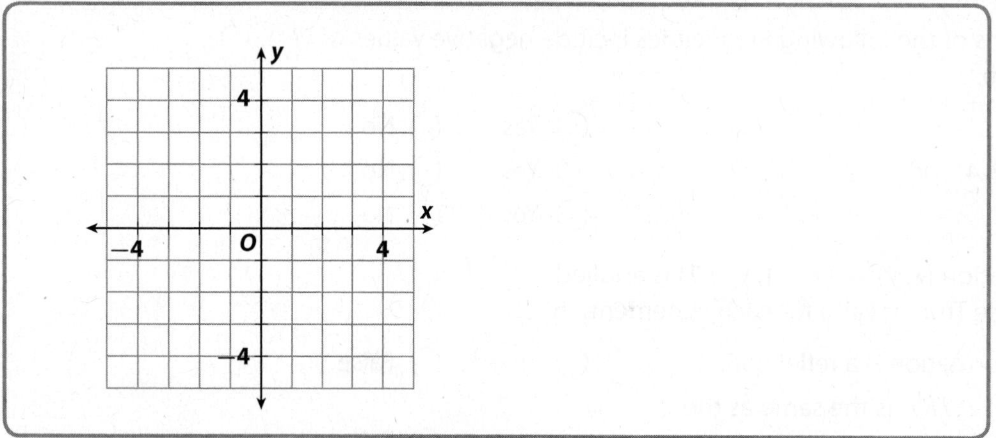

★★**6.** Najib wants to go to the store, then return home. He can use his bike on 1st Avenue and Main Street, but not on the trail. If he uses the trail, he needs to walk.

a. Compare the distances from Najib's home to the store using either 1st Avenue and Main Street or the trail.

b. Describe why each route might be preferable in comparison to the other.

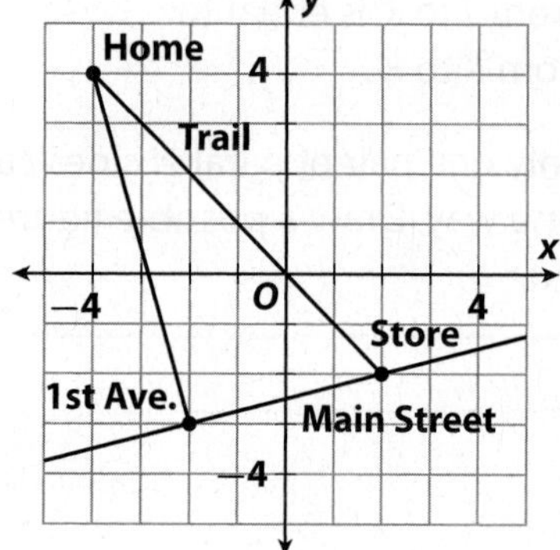

★★★**7.** Troy constructs equilateral triangle *XYZ*. He then constructs the perpendicular bisector of $\overline{XZ}$. He labels the point of intersection of the perpendicular bisector and $\overline{XZ}$ as point *P*.

a. Mandy says that the perpendicular bisector could have been drawn by constructing the line perpendicular to $\overline{XZ}$ through point *Y*. Explain why this is so.

b. Explain why $\triangle XYP \cong \triangle ZYP$ in terms of rigid motions.

c. Explain why $\triangle XYP \cong \triangle ZYP$ by using a triangle congruence theorem.

UNIT 6

Coordinate Geometry

MODULE 17

Coordinate Proofs and Applications

CA CC G.GPE.4, G.GPE.5, G.GPE.7

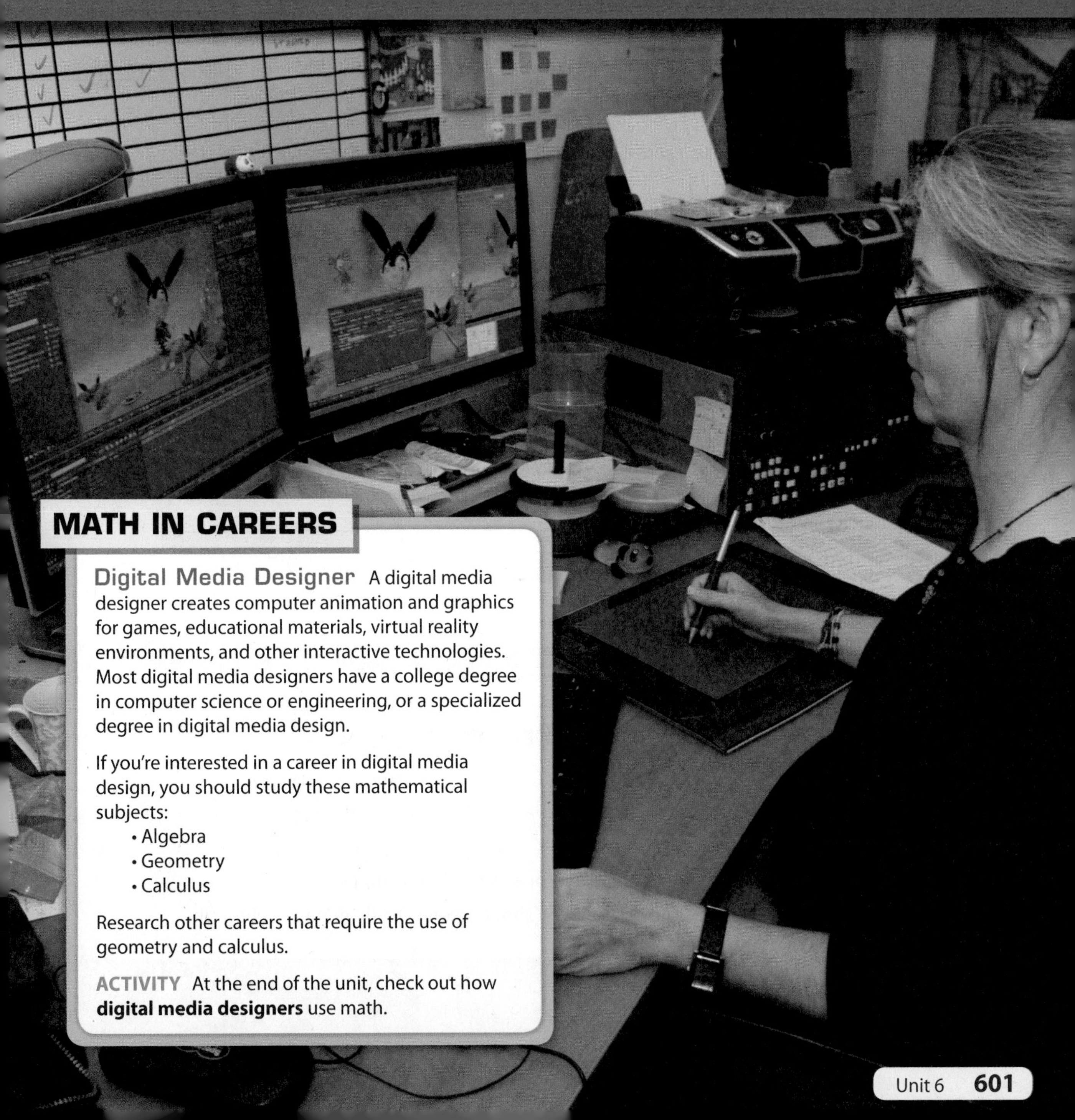

MATH IN CAREERS

Digital Media Designer A digital media designer creates computer animation and graphics for games, educational materials, virtual reality environments, and other interactive technologies. Most digital media designers have a college degree in computer science or engineering, or a specialized degree in digital media design.

If you're interested in a career in digital media design, you should study these mathematical subjects:

- Algebra
- Geometry
- Calculus

Research other careers that require the use of geometry and calculus.

ACTIVITY At the end of the unit, check out how **digital media designers** use math.

Unit Project Preview

Knight Moves

The Unit Project at the end of this unit involves devising your own board game. To successfully complete the Unit Project you'll need to master these skills:

- Use coordinates to describe lines and figures in the plane.
- Relate slope to parallel and perpendicular lines.
- Apply the distance formula.

1. A chessboard is a square made up of 64 smaller squares. If you think of it as a grid with one corner square representing the origin, what are the coordinates of the opposite corner?

____

2. A bishop is a chess piece. It can move diagonally any number of squares in one move. How would you describe this in terms of slope and distance?

____

____

____

3. A knight can move two squares horizontally or vertically, followed by one square in a perpendicular direction, all in one move. If a knight is at (3, 4), list three points that represent where the knight could move to in one move.

____

____

Tracking Your Learning Progression

This unit addresses important California Common Core Standards related to slopes of lines and geometric figures, and understanding and applying the Pythagorean Theorem as it relates to the distance formula.

Domain G.GPE Expressing Geometric Properties with Equations

Cluster Use coordinates to prove simple geometric theorems algebraically.

Coordinate Proofs and Applications

MODULE 17

ESSENTIAL QUESTION

How can you write proofs involving figures on the coordinate plane?

CALIFORNIA COMMON CORE

Real-World Video

Surveyors use specialized tools to map points and boundaries and to measure distances, angles, and areas for construction projects. You can calculate real-world distances and areas using coordinate geometry.

my.hrw.com

GO DIGITAL

my.hrw.com

my.hrw.com

Go digital with your write-in student edition, accessible on any device.

Math On the Spot

Scan with your smart phone to jump directly to the online edition, video tutor, and more.

Animated Math

Interactively explore key concepts to see how math works.

Personal Math Trainer

Get immediate feedback and help as you work through practice sets.

Are YOU Ready?

Complete these exercises to review skills you will need for this module.

Graph Linear Functions

EXAMPLE Graph the function $y = -\frac{3}{2}x + 2$.

Step 1: The y-intercept is 2. Plot the point (0, 2).

Step 2: Move down 3 units and then move 2 units to the right. Plot a second point at the new location.

Step 3: Draw a line through the two points.

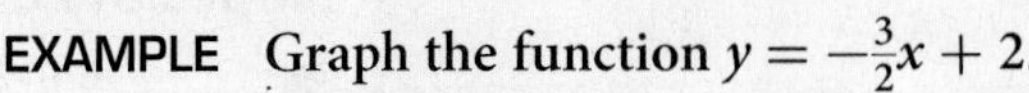

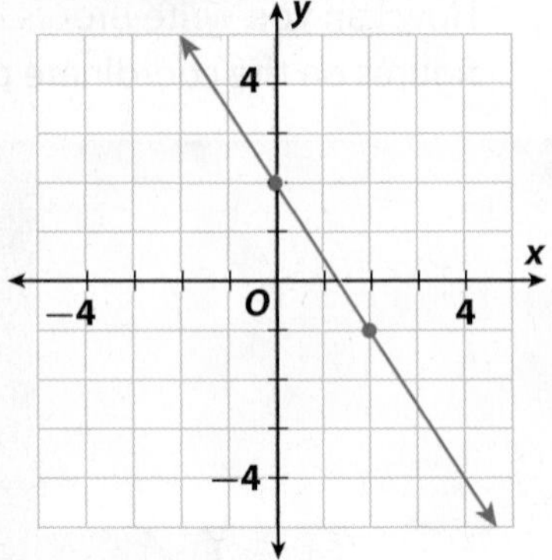

Graph each function.

1. $y = \frac{1}{4}x - 1$

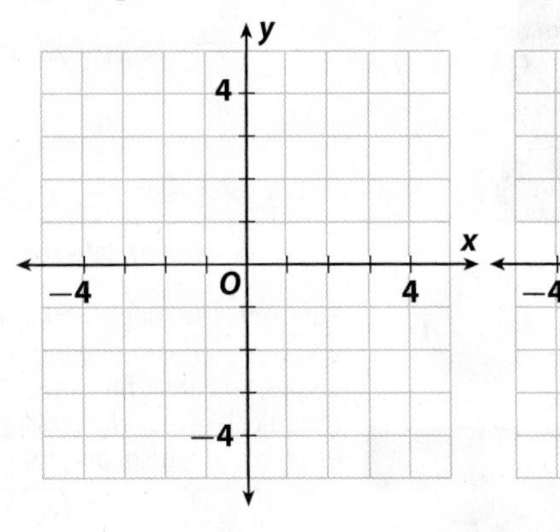

2. $y = 3$

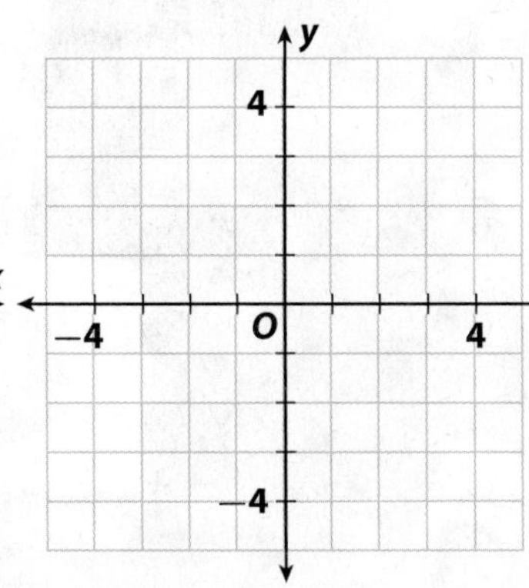

3. $y = 3x$

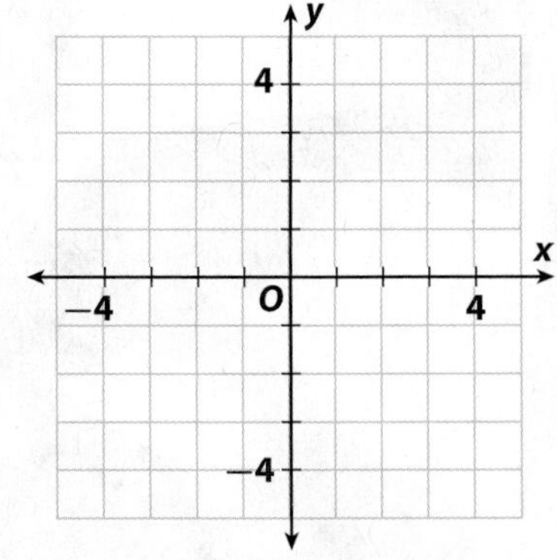

Area of Polygons

EXAMPLE Find the area of the triangle.

$A = \frac{1}{2}bh$

$A = \frac{1}{2}(12)(9) = \frac{1}{2}(108) = 54 \text{ cm}^2$

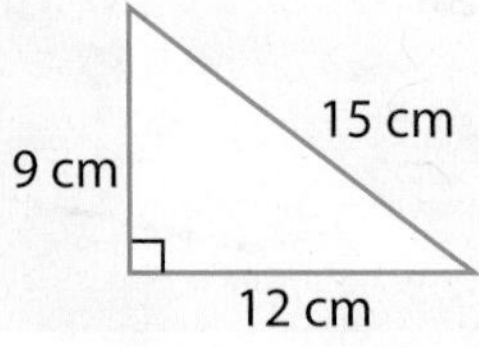

Find the area of each figure.

4.

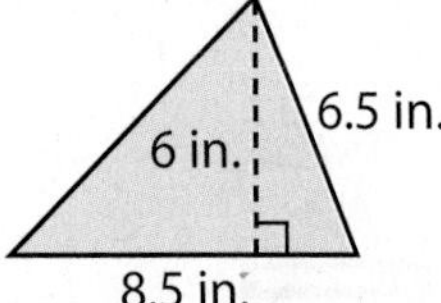

$A =$ ________

5.

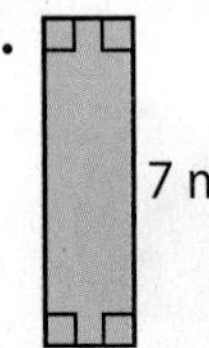

$A =$ ________

6.

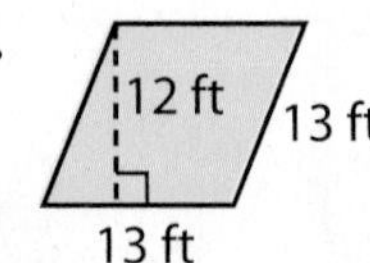

$A =$ ________

Reading Start-Up

Visualize Vocabulary

Complete the main idea web using the checked review words. Words may only be used once.

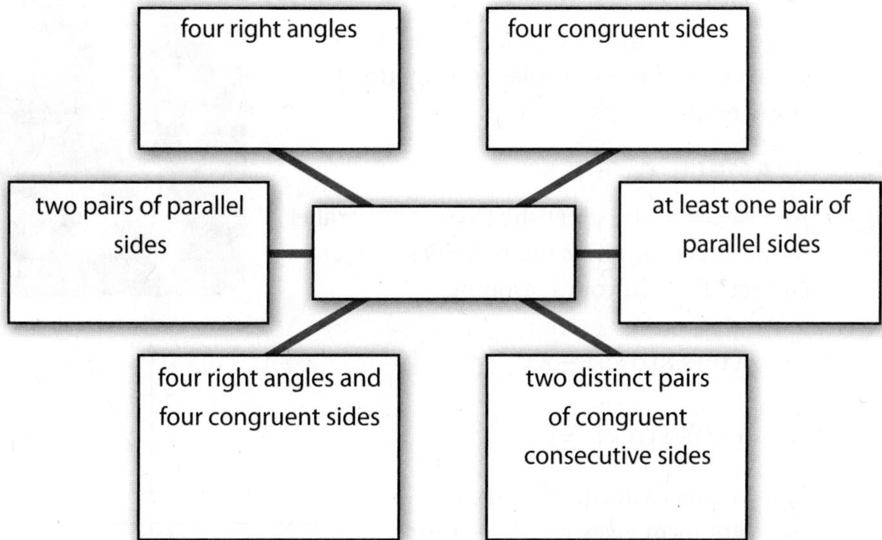

Vocabulary

Review Words

- ✔ kite *(cometa o papalote)*
- midpoint *(punto medio)*
- distance formula *(fórmula de distancia)*
- parallel lines *(líneas paralelas)*
- ✔ parallelogram *(paralelogramo)*
- perpendicular lines *(líneas perpendiculares)*
- ✔ quadrilateral *(cuadrilátero)*
- ✔ rectangle *(rectángulo)*
- ✔ rhombus *(rombo)*
- ✔ square *(cuadrado)*
- ✔ trapezoid *(trapecio)*

Understand Vocabulary

Complete the sentences using the remaining review words. You may refer to the module, the glossary, or a dictionary.

1. If the slopes of two lines are the same, the lines are ____________________.

2. If the slopes of two lines have a product of -1, the lines are ____________________.

3. To find the distance d between points (x_1, y_1) and (x_2, y_2) in the coordinate plane, use the ____________________: $d = \sqrt{(x_2 - x_1)^2 + (y_2 - y_1)^2}$.

4. In the coordinate plane, the ____________________ of a segment with endpoints (x_1, y_1) and (x_2, y_2) is $M\left(\frac{x_1 + x_2}{2}, \frac{y_1 + y_2}{2}\right)$.

Active Reading

Double-Door Fold Create a Double-Door Fold to help you understand some of the concepts in this module. Label one flap "Slopes of Parallel Lines" and the other flap "Slopes of Perpendicular Lines." As you study the lessons, write important ideas under the appropriate flap. How are these concepts the same? How are they different?

GETTING READY FOR

Coordinate Proofs and Applications

Understanding the standards and the vocabulary terms in the standards will help you know exactly what you are expected to learn in this module.

G.GPE.5

Prove the slope criteria for parallel and perpendicular lines and use them to solve geometric problems (e.g., find the equation of a line parallel or perpendicular to a given line that passes through a given point).

Key Vocabulary

parallel lines *(líneas paralelas)*
Lines in the same plane that do not intersect. Parallel lines have the same slope.

perpendicular lines *(líneas perpendiculares)* Lines that intersect to form right angles. If two lines are perpendicular, the product of their slopes is −1.

What It Means to You

You will learn to solve problems involving parallel and perpendicular lines by using slope relationships.

EXAMPLE G.GPE.5

Ana says that the street she lives on is parallel to the street Josh lives on. Is Ana's statement correct? Explain your reasoning.

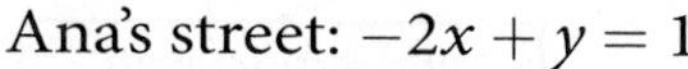

Ana's street: $-2x + y = 1$

Josh's street: $\frac{1}{2}y + \frac{3}{2} = x$

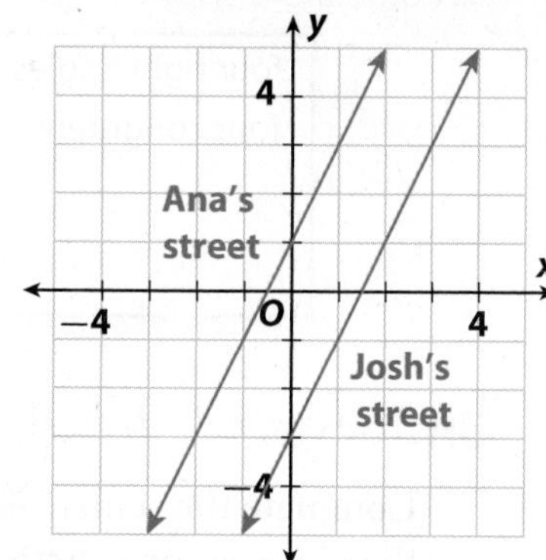

Yes; writing each equation in slope-intercept form gives $y = 2x + 1$ for Ana's street and $y = 2x - 3$ for Josh's street. The slopes are the same, so the streets are parallel. You can check Ana's statement by graphing the two lines.

CA CC

G.GPE.7

Use coordinates to compute perimeters of polygons and areas of triangles and rectangles, e.g., using the distance formula.

Key Vocabulary

distance formula *(fórmula de distancia)* In a coordinate plane, the distance d from (x_1, y_1) to (x_2, y_2) is $d = \sqrt{(x_2 - x_1)^2 + (y_2 - y_1)^2}$.

What It Means to You

You will learn to use the distance formula to find perimeters and areas.

EXAMPLE G.GPE.7

Find the perimeter of the triangle.

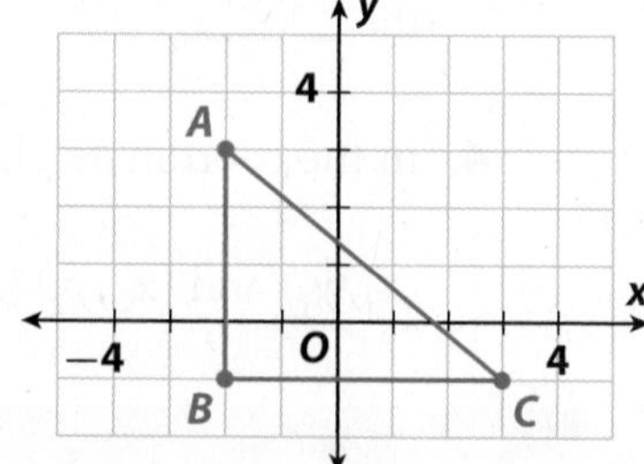

Find the length of each side. Then add.

$\overline{AB}$ is vertical, so $AB = 4$ units.

$\overline{BC}$ is horizontal, so $BC = 5$ units.

Use the distance formula to find AC.

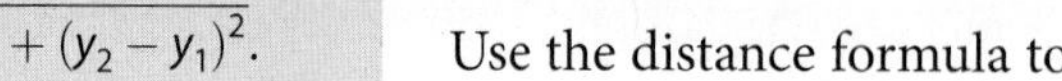

$$AC = \sqrt{(3 - (-2))^2 + ((-1) - 3)^2} = \sqrt{25 + 16} = \sqrt{41}$$

$$AB + BC + AC = 4 + 5 + \sqrt{41} \text{ units.}$$

Use a calculator to evaluate the expression and round to the nearest tenth. So, the perimeter is about 15.4 units.

Visit **my.hrw.com** to see all **CA Common Core Standards** explained.

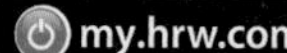

LESSON

17.1 Slopes of Parallel Lines

CA CC G.GPE.5

Prove the slope criteria for parallel and perpendicular lines and use them to solve geometric problems (e.g., find the equation of a line parallel or perpendicular to a given line that passes through a given point). *Also G.GPE.4*

ESSENTIAL QUESTION

How can you use slope to solve problems involving parallel lines?

EXPLORE ACTIVITY 1

Proving the Slope Criteria for Parallel Lines

There is an important connection between slope and parallel lines.

When a theorem is stated in "if and only if" form, the proof has two parts, one for each "direction" of the theorem.

Theorem: Slope Criteria for Parallel Lines

Two nonvertical lines are parallel if and only if they have the same slope.

Follow these instructions to prove the criteria.

A First prove that if two lines are parallel, then they have the same slope.

Suppose lines m and n are parallel lines that are neither vertical nor horizontal.

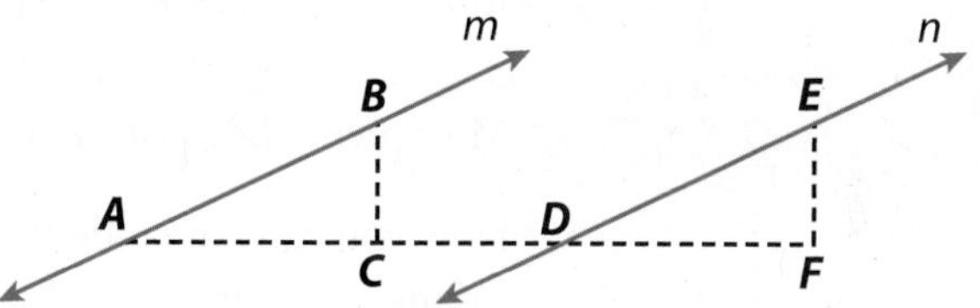

Let A and B be two points on line m, as shown. You can draw a horizontal line through A and a vertical line through B to create the "slope triangle," $\triangle ABC$.

You can extend $\overline{AC}$ to intersect line n at point D and then extend it to point F so that $AC = DF$. Finally, you can draw a vertical line through F intersecting line n at point E.

Mark the figure to show parallel lines, right angles, and congruent segments.

B When parallel lines are cut by a transversal, corresponding angles are congruent,

so $\angle BAC \cong$ ____________.

$\triangle BAC \cong$ ____________ by the ____________ Triangle Congruence Theorem.

By CPCTC, $\overline{BC} \cong$ ____________ and $BC =$ ____________.

The slope of line $m = \frac{\square}{AC}$, and the slope of line $n = \frac{\square}{DF}$.

The slopes of the lines are equal because ____________

____

____

EXPLORE ACTIVITY 1 *(cont'd)*

C Now prove that if two lines have the same slope, then they are parallel.

Suppose lines m and n are two lines with the same nonzero slope. You can set up a figure in the same way as before.

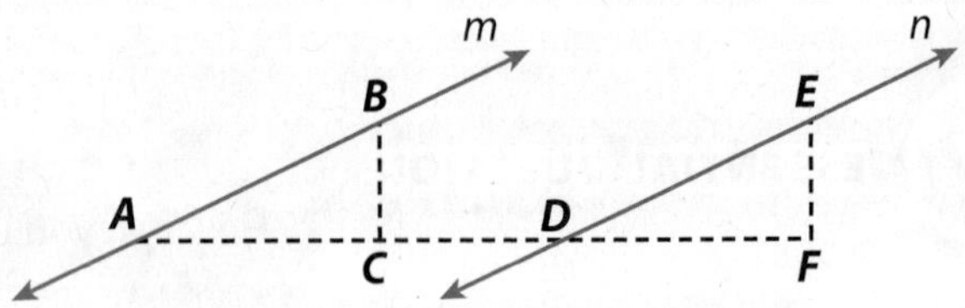

Let A and B be two points on line m, as shown. You can draw a horizontal line through A and a vertical line through B to create the "slope triangle," $\triangle ABC$.

You can extend $\overline{AC}$ to intersect line n at point D and then extend it to point F so that $AC = DF$. Finally, you can draw a vertical line through F intersecting line n at point E.

Mark the figure to show right angles and congruent segments.

D Since line m and line n have the same slope, $\frac{\square}{AC} = \frac{\square}{DF}$.

But $DF = AC$, so by substitution, $\frac{\square}{AC} = \frac{\square}{AC}$.

Multiplying both sides by AC shows that $BC =$ ____________.

Now you can conclude that $\triangle BAC \cong$ ____________ by the ____________ Triangle Congruence Theorem.

By CPCTC, $\angle BAC \cong$ ____________.

Line m and line n are two lines that are cut by a transversal so that a pair of corresponding angles are congruent.

You can conclude that ______________________________.

REFLECT

1. **What If?** Explain why the slope criteria can be applied to horizontal lines.

____

____

____

2. **What If?** Explain why the slope criteria cannot be applied to vertical lines even though all vertical lines are parallel.

____

____

____

Proving Sides of Figures Are Parallel

You can use the slope criteria for parallel lines to analyze figures in the coordinate plane.

EXAMPLE 1

 CA CC G.GPE.4

Prove that quadrilateral *ABCD* is a trapezoid.

STEP 1 Find the coordinates of the vertices of quadrilateral *ABCD*.

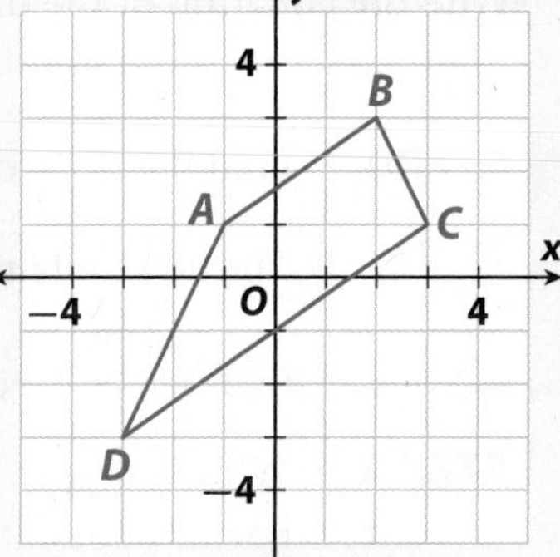

$A(-1, 1)$, $B(2, 3)$, $C(3, 1)$, $D(-3, -3)$

STEP 2 Use the slope formula to find the slope of $\overline{AB}$ and the slope of $\overline{DC}$.

$$\text{slope of } \overline{AB} = \frac{y_2 - y_1}{x_2 - x_1} = \frac{3 - 1}{2 - (-1)} = \frac{2}{3}$$

$$\text{slope of } \overline{DC} = \frac{y_2 - y_1}{x_2 - x_1} = \frac{1 - (-3)}{3 - (-3)} = \frac{4}{6} = \frac{2}{3}$$

STEP 3 Compare the slopes.

Since the slopes are the same, $\overline{AB}$ is parallel to $\overline{DC}$.

Quadrilateral *ABCD* is a trapezoid because it is a quadrilateral with at least one pair of parallel sides.

My Notes

REFLECT

3. **Justify Reasoning** A parallelogram is a quadrilateral with two pairs of parallel sides. Is quadrilateral *ABCD* a parallelogram? Justify your answer.

______

______

______

YOUR TURN

4. Quadrilateral *PQRS* has vertices $P(-3, 3)$, $Q(3, 0)$, $R(2, -3)$, and $S(-4, 0)$. Prove that quadrilateral *PQRS* is a parallelogram.

______

______

______

______

Writing Equations of Parallel Lines

Given a line ℓ and a point P not on the line, you have seen how to construct a line through point P that is parallel to line ℓ. Now you will see how to write the equation of the required line.

EXAMPLE 2

CA CC G.GPE.5

Write the equation of the line parallel to line ℓ that passes through point P.

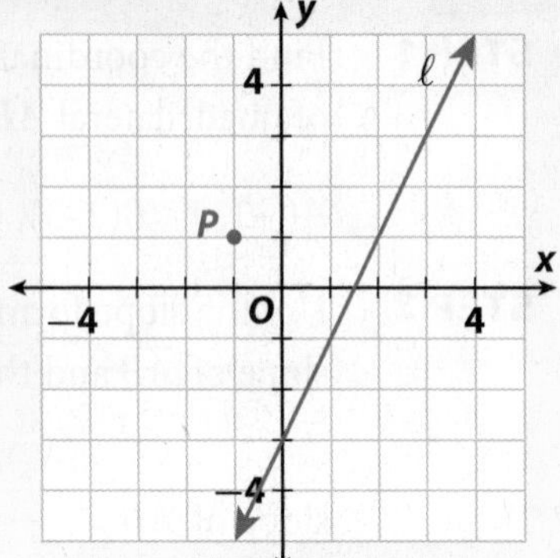

STEP 1 Find the slope of line ℓ.

The line contains (3, 3) and (2, 1).

$m = \frac{y_2 - y_1}{x_2 - x_1} = \frac{3 - 1}{3 - 2} = \frac{2}{1} = 2$

STEP 2 Write the equation of the required line in slope-intercept form. The slope of the line must also be 2.

$y = mx + b$ — Write slope-intercept form.

$y = 2x + b$ — Substitute the slope of the line for m.

STEP 3 The coordinates of P are $(-1, 1)$. Substitute the coordinates of P to find the value of b.

$1 = 2(-1) + b$ — Substitute -1 for x and 1 for y.

$1 = -2 + b$ — Simplify.

$3 = b$ — Solve for b.

So, the equation of the required line is $y = 2x + 3$.

Math Talk — Mathematical Practices

In Example 2, what is the equation of the line through point P that is parallel to the x-axis. Why?

REFLECT

5. **Check for Reasonableness** How can you check that the equation of the required line is correct?

______

______

______

YOUR TURN

6. Write the equation of the line parallel to $y = -3x - 2$ that passes through the point $(-2, 7)$.

______

EXPLORE ACTIVITY 2  CA CC G.GPE.4

Slope and Systems of Equations

You can use slope to help you analyze a system of equations. A city park is a quadrilateral bounded by the four streets shown in the table.

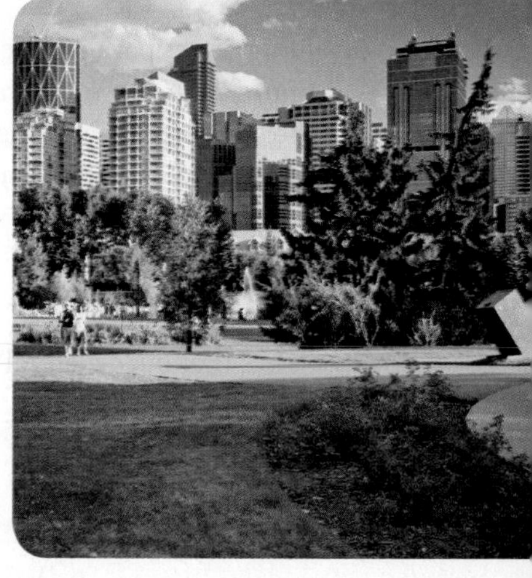

A Write the equation for each street in slope-intercept form.

Street	Equation	Slope-Intercept Form
Valley Avenue	$-3x + y = 4$	
Powell Street	$y = x$	
Ortega Road	$y = 3x - 2$	
Broadway	$y - 2 = x$	

B Which pairs of streets, if any, are parallel? Explain.

____

____

C What type of quadrilateral is formed by the intersections of the streets? Why?

____

D For each pair of streets below, solve a system of equations to find the point of intersection of the streets or state that the streets do not intersect.

Valley and Powell	Valley and Ortega	Valley and Broadway
________	________	________
Powell and Ortega	**Powell and Broadway**	**Ortega and Broadway**
________	________	________

E Graph and label the streets to check whether you correctly identified the quadrilateral formed by the intersections of the streets.

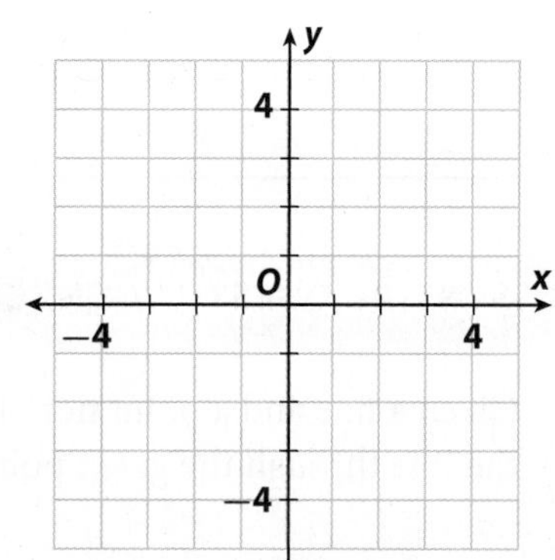

REFLECT

7. Critique Reasoning DeShawn said the streets intersect to form both a parellelogram and a trapezoid. Do you agree? Explain.

____

____

____

Guided Practice

1. Jodie draws parallel lines p and q. She sets up a figure as shown to prove that the lines must have the same slope. First she proves $\triangle JKL \cong \triangle RST$ by the SAS Triangle Congruence Theorem. What should she do next? (Explore Activity 1)

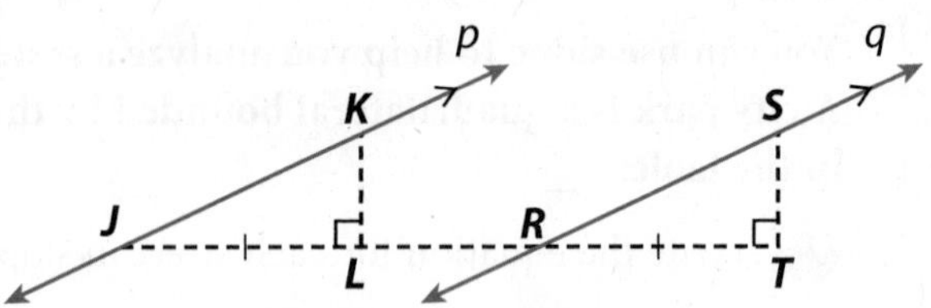

____

2. Prove that quadrilateral $ABCD$ is a trapezoid. (Example 1)

Coordinates of the vertices:

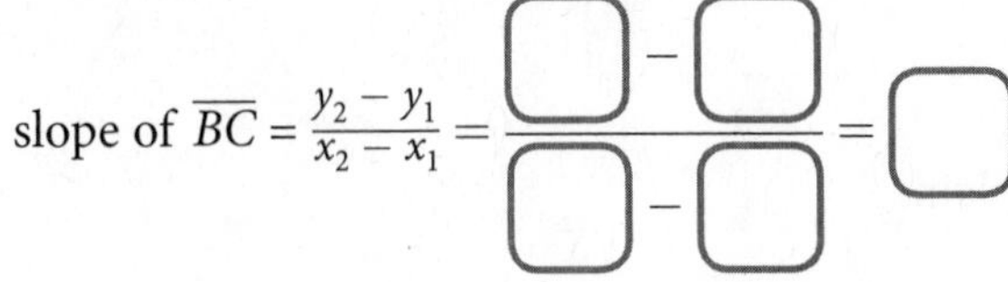

slope of $\overline{BC} = \frac{y_2 - y_1}{x_2 - x_1} = \frac{\square - \square}{\square - \square} = \square$

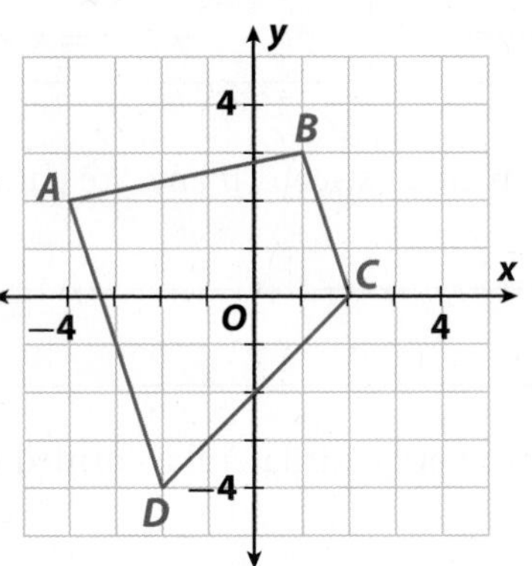

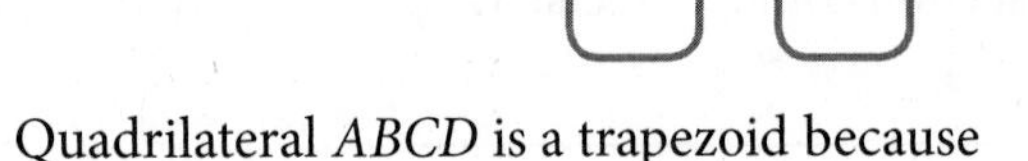

slope of $\overline{AD} = \frac{y_2 - y_1}{x_2 - x_1} = \frac{\square - \square}{\square - \square} = \square$

Quadrilateral $ABCD$ is a trapezoid because

____

Write the equation of the line that is parallel to the given line and passes through the given point. (Example 2)

3. $y = \frac{2}{3}x + 7$; $(6, -1)$ ______________

4. $2x + y = 1$; $\left(\frac{1}{2}, -\frac{5}{2}\right)$ ______________

5. What type of quadrilateral is formed by the intersections of the four lines in the table? Explain. (Explore Activity 2)

Line	Equation
Line ℓ	$2y = x + 4$
Line m	$x = 2$
Line n	$y = -2x - 8$
Line p	$y = \frac{1}{2}x - 3$

____

____

ESSENTIAL QUESTION CHECK-IN

6. Given a line and a point not on the line, how do you find the equation of the line through the given point that is parallel to the given line?

____

____

____

Name ______ Class ______ Date ______

17.1 Independent Practice

 G.GPE.4, G.GPE.5

7. Prove *ABCD* is *not* a trapezoid.

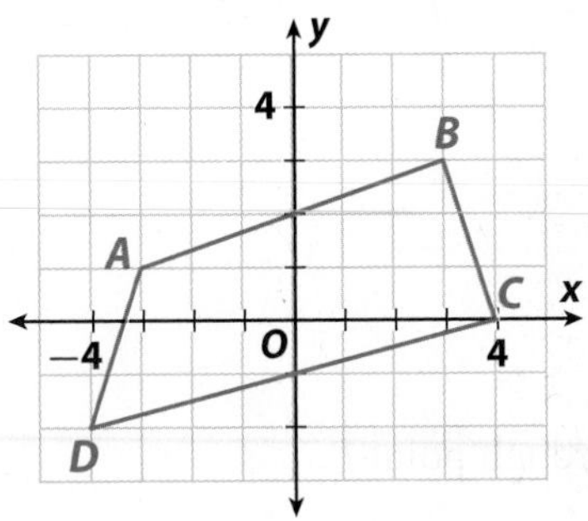

8. **Represent Real-World Problems** In a video game, an asteroid moves along a path parallel to line ℓ. The asteroid eventually crashes into a planet at point *P*.

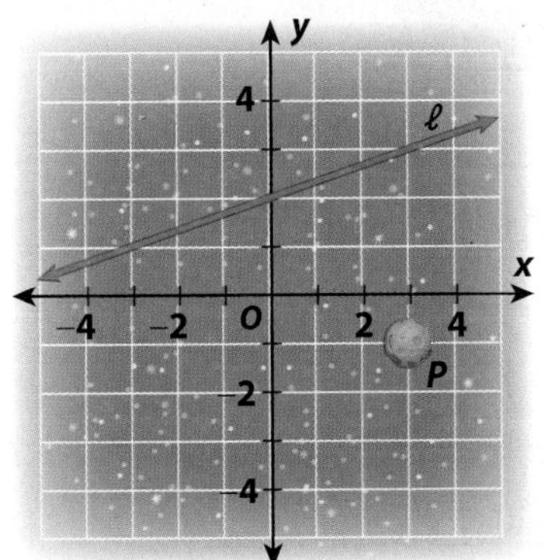

a. Write an equation of the line that represents the path of the asteroid.

b. Will the asteroid crash into a star at $(-1, -3)$? Explain.

Explain whether the quadrilateral determined by the intersections of the given lines is a trapezoid, a parallelogram, both, or neither.

9.

Line	Equation
Line ℓ	$y = 2x + 3$
Line *m*	$2y = -x + 6$
Line *n*	$y = x - 3$
Line *p*	$x + y = -3$

10.

Line	Equation
Line ℓ	$y = x + 3$
Line *m*	$y - x = 0$
Line *n*	$x + 2y = 6$
Line *p*	$y = -0.5x - 3$

11. **Explain the Error** Tariq was given the points $P(0, 3)$, $Q(3, -3)$, $R(0, -4)$, and $S(-2, -1)$ and was asked to decide whether *PQRS* is a trapezoid. Explain his error.

Slope of $\overline{SP} = \frac{3 - (-1)}{0 - (-2)} = \frac{4}{2} = 2$

Slope of $\overline{QP} = \frac{3 - (-3)}{3 - 0} = \frac{6}{3} = 2$

Since at least two sides are parallel, the quadrilateral is a trapezoid.

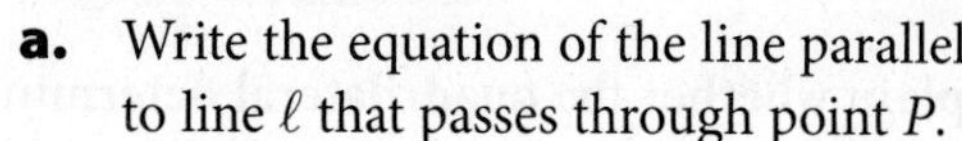

FOCUS ON HIGHER ORDER THINKING

Work Area

12. Analyze Relationships Explore how a translation of a given line affects the equation of a line parallel to the given line.

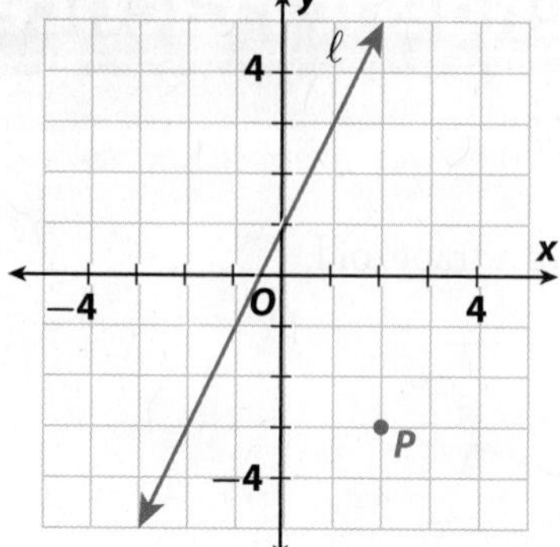

a. Write the equation of the line parallel to line ℓ that passes through point P.

____

b. Draw the image of line ℓ after the translation $(x, y) \rightarrow (x + 2, y - 1)$. (*Hint*: Plot the image of two points on line ℓ.) Label the image line m.

c. Write the equation of the line parallel to line m that passes through point P. What do you notice?

____

13. Justify Reasoning You can use algebra to prove that parallel lines have the same slope. Suppose lines p and q are parallel lines that are neither vertical nor horizontal. Then you can write their equations as follows.

Line p: $y = m_1x + b_1$ Line q: $y = m_2x + b_2$ with $m_1 \neq 0$, $m_2 \neq 0$

a. Assume the slopes are different. Solve a system of equations to find the x-coordinate of the intersection point of the lines.

____

b. How do you use the assumption that the slopes are different to ensure that this value of x exists?

____

____

c. Explain how this proves that parallel lines have the same slope.

____

____

____

14. Critical Thinking Quadrilateral $ABCD$ is a parallelogram. Three of the vertices of the parallelogram are $A(-1, 2)$, $C(2, -1)$, and $D(-2, -2)$. What are the coordinates of vertex B? Explain how you know your answer is correct.

____

____

____

____

LESSON 17.2

Slopes of Perpendicular Lines

CA CC G.GPE.5

Prove the slope criteria for parallel and perpendicular lines and use them to solve geometric problems (e.g., find the equation of a line parallel or perpendicular to a given line that passes through a given point). *Also G.GPE.4*

ESSENTIAL QUESTION

How can you use slope to solve problems involving perpendicular lines?

EXPLORE ACTIVITY 1

Proving the Slope Criteria for Perpendicular Lines

The following theorem describes the connection between slope and perpendicular lines.

Theorem: Slope Criteria for Perpendicular Lines

Two nonvertical lines are perpendicular if and only if the product of their slopes is -1.

Follow these instructions to prove the criteria.

A First prove that if two lines are perpendicular, then the product of their slopes is -1.

Suppose lines m and n are perpendicular lines that intersect at point P, and that neither line is vertical. Assume the slope of line m is positive. (You can write a similar proof if the slope of line m is negative.)

Mark the figure to show the perpendicular lines.

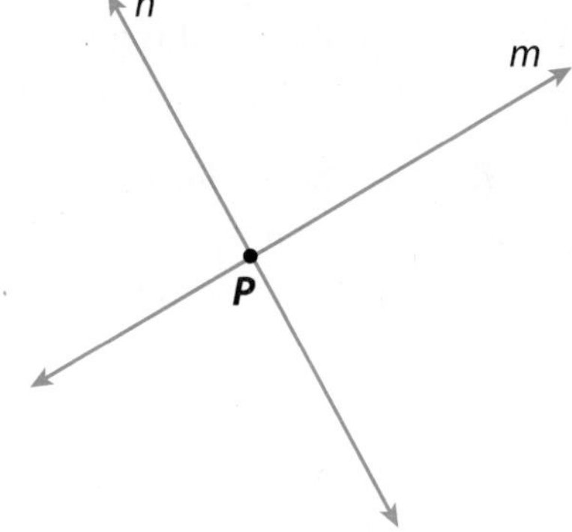

B Let Q be a point on line m, and draw a right triangle, $\triangle PQR$, as shown. Which line is this a "slope triangle" for?

____

Mark the figure to show the perpendicular segments.

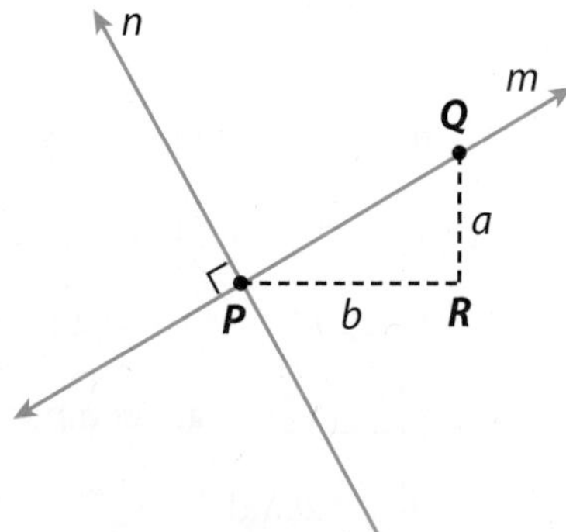

C Assume that a and b are both positive.

The slope of line m is $\frac{\square}{\square}$.

Animated Math

my.hrw.com

EXPLORE ACTIVITY 1 *(cont'd)*

D Rotate $\triangle PQR$ 90° around point P. The image is $\triangle PQ'R'$, as shown.

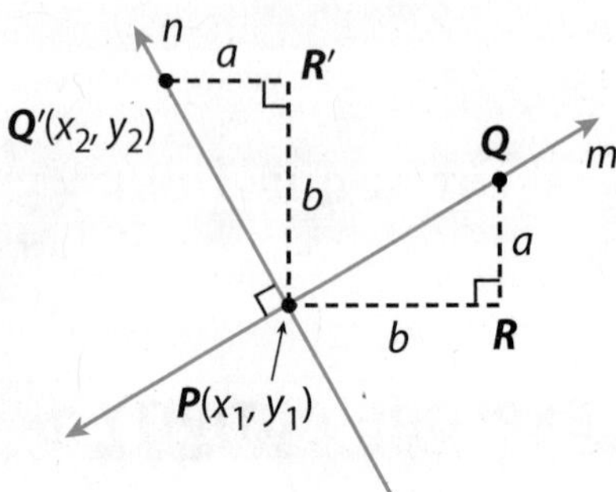

Which line is $\triangle PQ'R'$ a slope triangle for?

____

Let the coordinates of P be (x_1, y_1) and let the coordinates of Q' be (x_2, y_2).

Then the slope of line n is

$$\frac{y_2 - y_1}{x_2 - x_1} = \frac{b}{\square} = -\frac{\square}{\square}.$$

E Now find the product of the slopes.

$$(\text{slope of line } m) \cdot (\text{slope of line } n) = \frac{\square}{\square} \cdot \left(-\frac{\square}{\square}\right) = \square$$

F Now prove that if the product of the slopes of two lines is -1, then the lines are perpendicular.

Let the slope of line m be $\frac{a}{b}$, where a and b are both positive. Let line n have slope z. It is given that $z \cdot \frac{a}{b} = -1$. Solving for z gives the slope of line n.

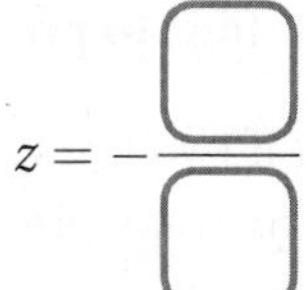

$$z = -\frac{\square}{\square}$$

G Assume the lines intersect at P. Since the slope of m is positive and the slope of n is negative, you can set up slope triangles.

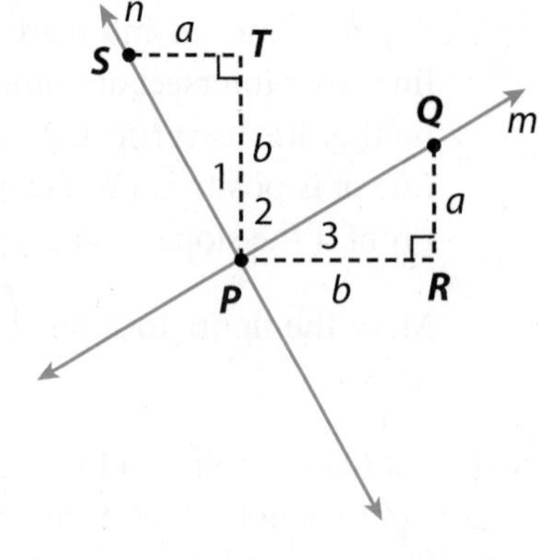

Based on the figure, $\overline{ST} \cong$ __________

and $\overline{PT} \cong$ __________.

Also, $\angle T \cong$ ________ because all right angles are congruent.

Therefore, __________ $\cong$ __________ by the SAS Triangle Congruence Theorem.

H By CPCTC, $\angle 1 \cong$ __________.

Since $\overline{TP}$ is vertical and $\overline{PR}$ is horizontal, $\angle TPR$ is a right angle. So $\angle 2$ and __________ are complementary angles. You can conclude by substitution that $\angle 2$ and __________ are complementary angles.

By the Angle Addition Postulate, $m\angle 1 + m\angle 2 = m\angle SPQ$, so $\angle SPQ$ must measure __________ and therefore line m is perpendicular to line n.

REFLECT

1. **Communicate Mathematical Ideas** Suppose line ℓ has slope $\frac{a}{b}$ where $a \neq 0$ and $b \neq 0$, and suppose lines m and n are both perpendicular to line ℓ. Explain how you can use the slope criteria to show that line m must be parallel to line n.

____

____

____

____

Proving Angles in Figures Are Right Angles

Recall that a rectangle is a quadrilateral that has four right angles.

EXAMPLE 1 CA CC G.GPE.4

Prove that quadrilateral *JKLM* is a rectangle.

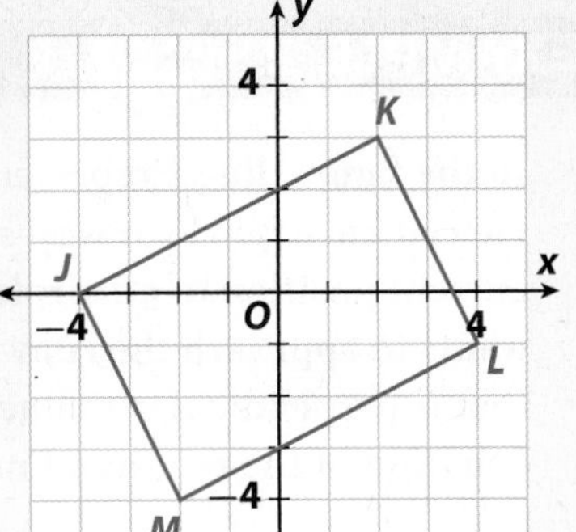

STEP 1 Find the coordinates of the vertices of quadrilateral *JKLM*.

$J(-4, 0), K(2, 3), L(4, -1), M(-2, -4)$

STEP 2 Find the slope of each side of the quadrilateral.

$$\text{slope of } \overline{JK} = \frac{y_2 - y_1}{x_2 - x_1} = \frac{3 - 0}{2 - (-4)} = \frac{3}{6} = \frac{1}{2}$$

$$\text{slope of } \overline{KL} = \frac{y_2 - y_1}{x_2 - x_1} = \frac{-1 - 3}{4 - 2} = \frac{-4}{2} = -2$$

$$\text{slope of } \overline{ML} = \frac{y_2 - y_1}{x_2 - x_1} = \frac{-1 - (-4)}{4 - (-2)} = \frac{3}{6} = \frac{1}{2}$$

$$\text{slope of } \overline{JM} = \frac{y_2 - y_1}{x_2 - x_1} = \frac{-4 - 0}{-2 - (-4)} = \frac{-4}{2} = -2$$

STEP 3 Find the products of the slopes of consecutive sides.

$$(\text{slope of } \overline{JK}) \cdot (\text{slope of } \overline{KL}) = \frac{1}{2} \cdot (-2) = -1$$

$$(\text{slope of } \overline{KL}) \cdot (\text{slope of } \overline{ML}) = -2 \cdot \frac{1}{2} = -1$$

$$(\text{slope of } \overline{ML}) \cdot (\text{slope of } \overline{JM}) = \frac{1}{2} \cdot (-2) = -1$$

$$(\text{slope of } \overline{JM}) \cdot (\text{slope of } \overline{JK}) = -2 \cdot \frac{1}{2} = -1$$

Since the products of the slopes of consecutive sides are -1, consecutive sides are perpendicular. Quadrilateral *JKLM* has four right angles, so it is a rectangle.

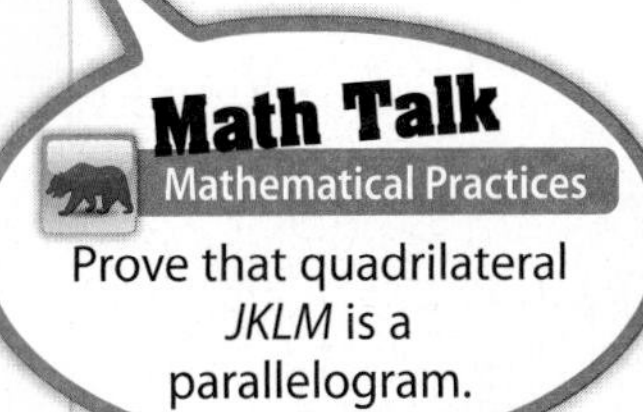

Math Talk
Mathematical Practices
Prove that quadrilateral JKLM is a parallelogram.

YOUR TURN

2. $\triangle ABC$ has vertices $A(-2, -2)$, $B(2, 4)$, and $C(5, 2)$. Prove that $\triangle ABC$ is a right triangle.

____

____

____

____

Writing Equations of Perpendicular Lines

Given a line ℓ and a point P, you have seen how to construct a line through point P that is perpendicular to line ℓ. Now you will see how to write the equation of the required line.

EXAMPLE 2  CA CC G.GPE.5

In the figure, line ℓ represents an overhead view of an airport runway, and point P is the current position of an airplane. The pilot wants to approach the runway along a line that is perpendicular to line ℓ. Write the equation of the required line.

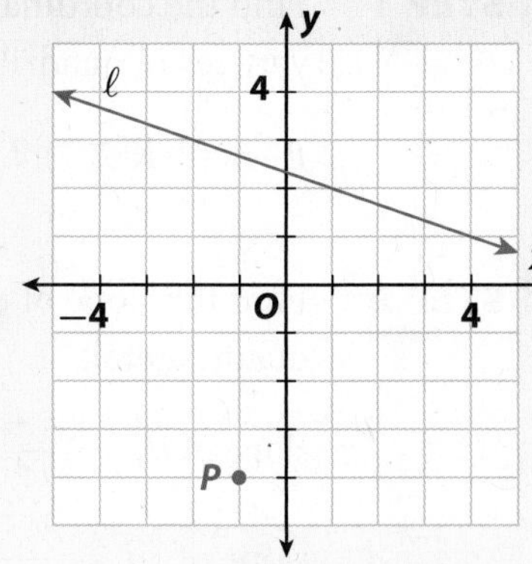

STEP 1 Find the slope of line ℓ.

The line contains (1, 2) and (4, 1).

$$m = \frac{y_2 - y_1}{x_2 - x_1} = \frac{1-2}{4-1} = \frac{-1}{3} = -\frac{1}{3}$$

STEP 2 Write the equation of the required line in slope-intercept form. Let the slope of the required line be z. Then $z \cdot \left(-\frac{1}{3}\right) = -1$. Solving for z shows that $z = 3$, which is the opposite of the reciprocal of m.

$y = mx + b$ Write slope-intercept form.

$y = 3x + b$ Substitute the slope of the required line.

STEP 3 The coordinates of P are $(-1, -4)$. Substitute the coordinates of P to find the value of b.

$-4 = 3(-1) + b$ Substitute −1 for x and −4 for y.

$-4 = -3 + b$ Simplify.

$-1 = b$ Solve for b.

So, the equation of the required line is $y = 3x - 1$.

REFLECT

3. Check for Reasonableness How can you use graphing to check that the equation of the required line is reasonable?

____

YOUR TURN

Write the equation of the line that is perpendicular to the given line and that passes through the given point.

4.

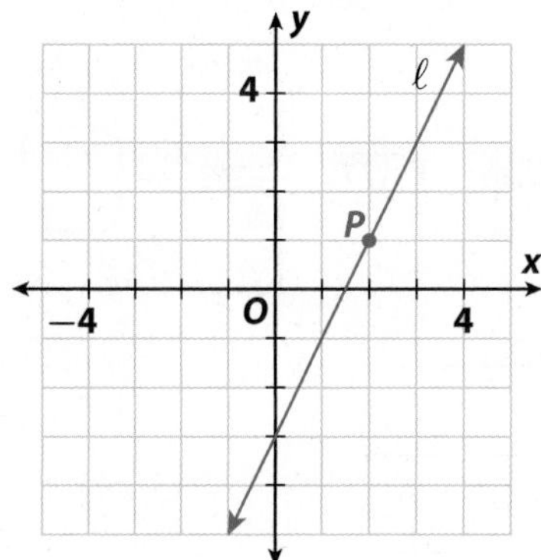

5.

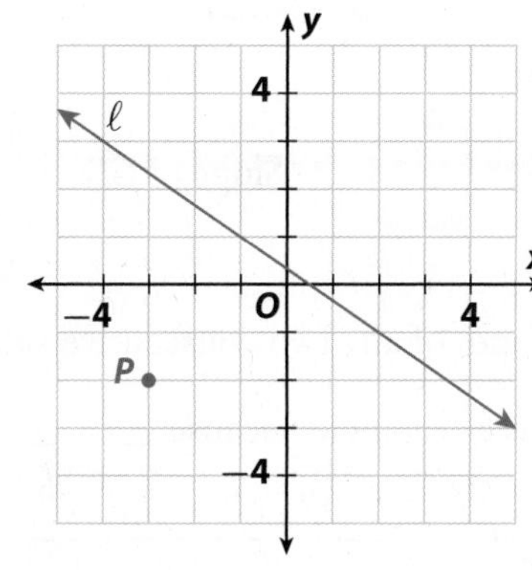

______________________ ______________________

Guided Practice

1. In Explore Activity 1, you proved that if two lines are perpendicular, then the product of their slopes is −1. You assumed that the slope of line m was positive. Complete the following proof starting with the assumption that the slope of line m is negative. (Explore Activity 1)

a. Suppose lines m and n are nonvertical, perpendicular lines that intersect at point P. Let Q be a point on line m and draw a slope triangle as shown.

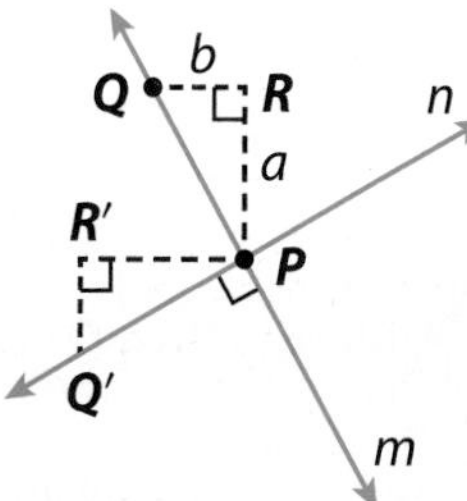

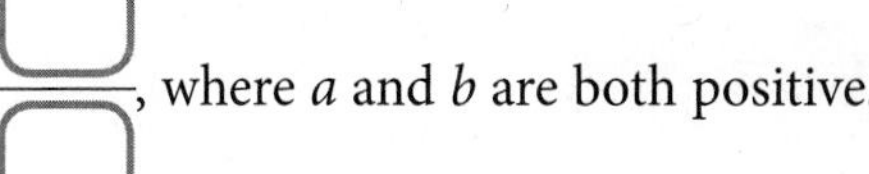
The slope of line m is $-\frac{\square}{\square}$, where a and b are both positive.

b. Rotate $\triangle PQR$ 90° around point P. The image is $\triangle PQ'R'$, as shown.

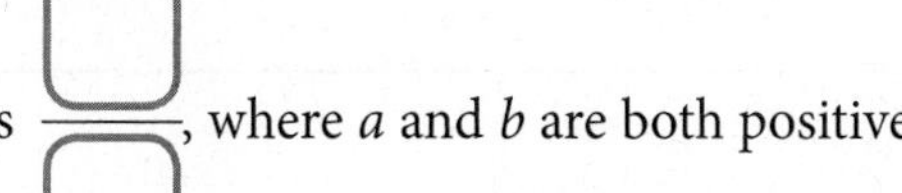
Using $\triangle PQ'R'$, the slope of line n is $\frac{\square}{\square}$, where a and b are both positive.

c. Explain how to complete the proof.

____

2. Prove that quadrilateral *ABCD* is a rectangle. (Example 1)

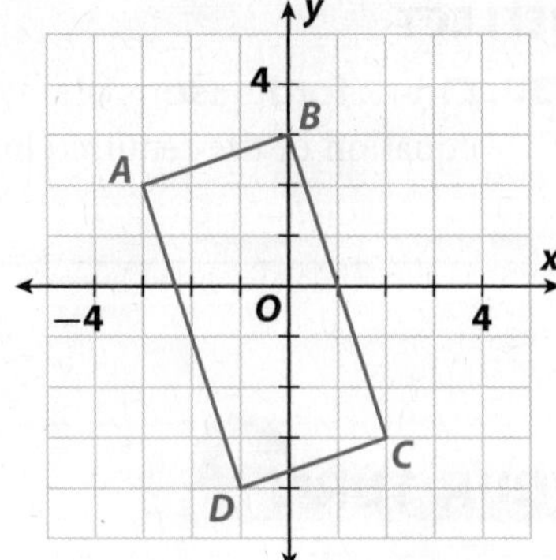

Coordinates of the vertices:

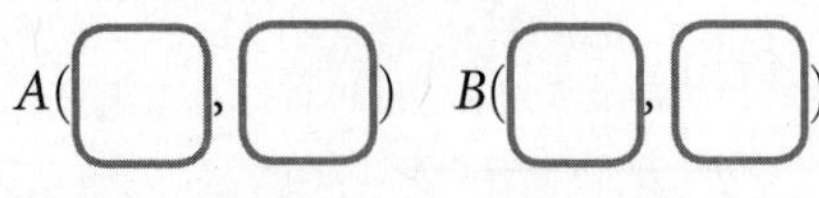

C(___ , ___) D(___ , ___)

Slope of $\overline{AB} = \frac{y_2 - y_1}{x_2 - x_1} = \frac{\square - \square}{\square - \square} = \frac{\square}{\square}$

Slope of $\overline{BC} = \frac{\square}{\square} = \square$ Slope of $\overline{CD} = \frac{\square}{\square}$ Slope of $\overline{AD} = \frac{\square}{\square} = \square$

The product of the slopes of any two consecutive sides is ______________.

Quadrilateral *ABCD* is a rectangle because ______________________________

____.

Write the equation of the line that is perpendicular to the given line and that passes through the given point. (Example 2)

3.

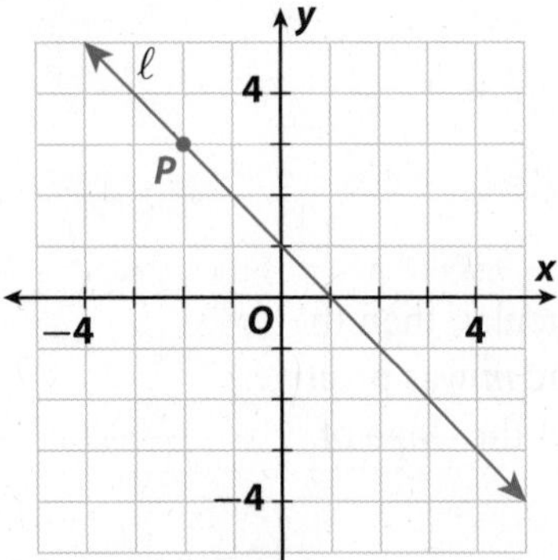

____

4.

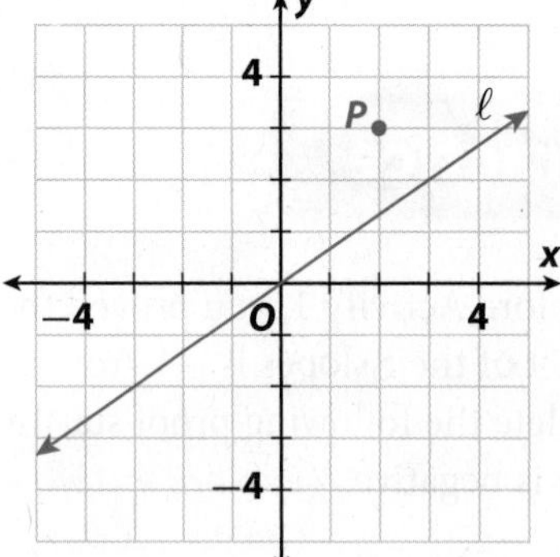

____

ESSENTIAL QUESTION CHECK-IN

5. Given a line and a point not on the line, how do you find the equation of the line through the given point that is perpendicular to the given line?

____

____

____

____

Name________________________ Class________________ Date________________

17.2 Independent Practice

G.GPE.4, G.GPE.5

6. **Represent Real-World Problems** Line ℓ represents an existing subway line with stations at points P (Park) and B (Beach).

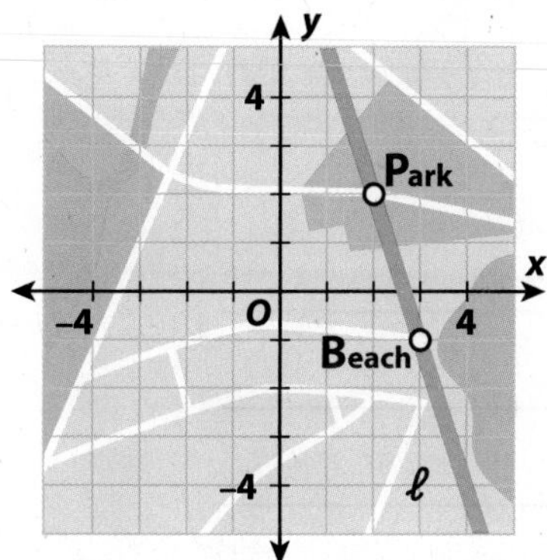

a. Two new subway lines, lines m and n, will intersect line ℓ at points P and B, respectively, and both lines will be perpendicular to line ℓ. Write equations for the new lines.

____

____

b. What can you conclude about the two new subway lines based on their equations? Explain.

____

____

____

c. Line h in the subway system is represented by the equation $y = 3x - \frac{1}{3}$. Is this line parallel or perpendicular to any of the three lines described above? Explain.

____

____

____

____

Classify the quadrilateral determined by the intersections of the given lines as a rectangle, parallelogram, or trapezoid, using the most specific term possible. Explain your answer.

7.

Line	Equation
Line ℓ	$y = -\frac{1}{2}x - 3$
Line m	$2x - y = -2$
Line n	$2y = -x + 4$
Line p	$y = 2x - 3$

____

____

8.

Line	Equation
Line ℓ	$y = 3x + 4$
Line m	$x - y = 0$
Line n	$x + 2 = y$
Line p	$\frac{1}{3}y = x - \frac{2}{3}$

____

____

9. **Critique Reasoning** Malia says $\triangle ABC$ is a right triangle. Do you agree? Explain.

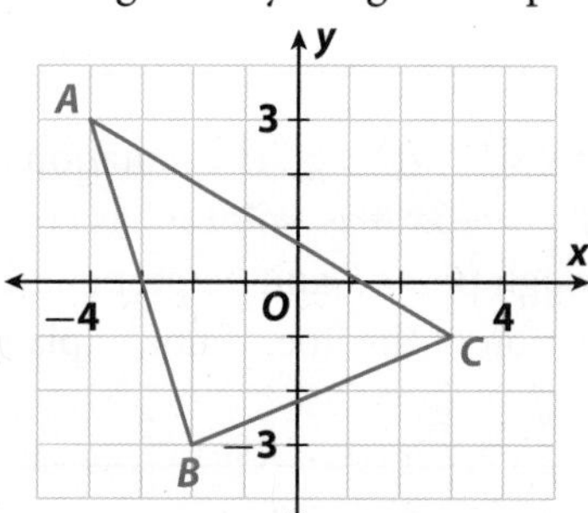

____

____

____

H.O.T. FOCUS ON HIGHER ORDER THINKING

Work Area

10. Check for Reasonableness Alex was asked to find the equation of the line through point P that is perpendicular to line ℓ. He said the equation of the required line is $y = 0.4x - 0.5$. Natalie looked at the equation he wrote and quickly said that his answer was not reasonable. Explain how Natalie was able to determine this without doing any calculations.

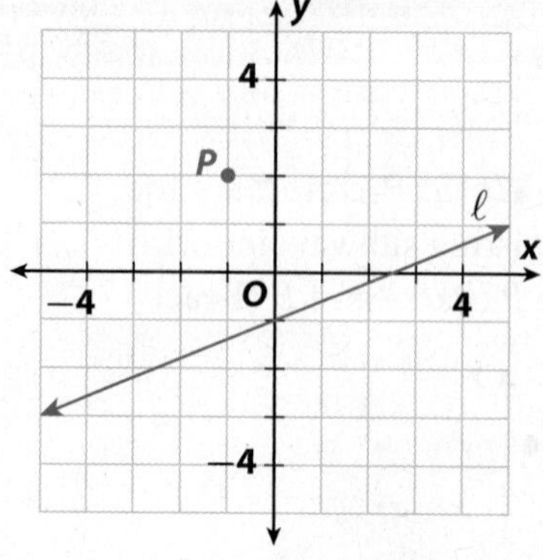

11. Justify Reasoning In the figure, points A and C are two vertices of a right triangle, $\triangle ABC$. The triangle's right angle, at vertex B, lies on line ℓ. Determine the coordinates of vertex B. Then explain how you know you have identified the coordinates correctly.

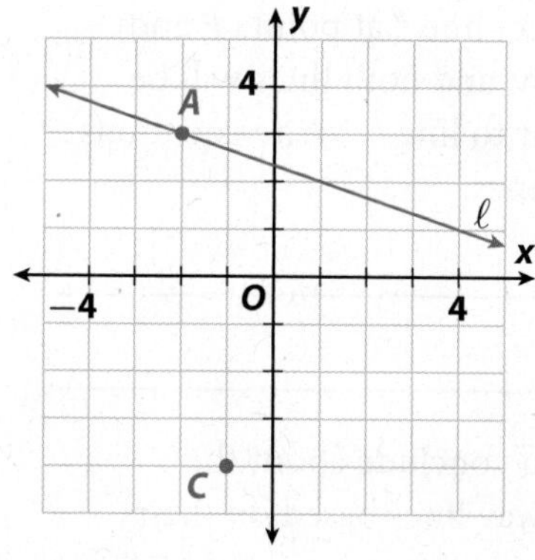

12. Critical Thinking The equation of line m is $y = \frac{1}{2}x - 4$. The equation of line n is $y = -3x + \frac{1}{2}$. Point P has coordinates $(1, 4)$. Is it possible for a line to pass through point P and be perpendicular to both line m and line n? If so, find the equation of the line. If not, explain why not.

LESSON

17.3 The Distance Formula

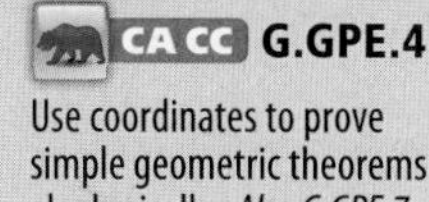

Use coordinates to prove simple geometric theorems algebraically. *Also G.GPE.7*

ESSENTIAL QUESTION

How do you find the distance between two points in the coordinate plane?

EXPLORE ACTIVITY

Deriving the Distance Formula

In this Explore Activity you will derive a formula for the distance between two points in the coordinate plane. Along the way, you will use the Pythagorean Theorem. Recall that if a right triangle has legs of length *a* and *b* and a hypotenuse of length *c*, then the Pythagorean Theorem states that $c^2 = a^2 + b^2$.

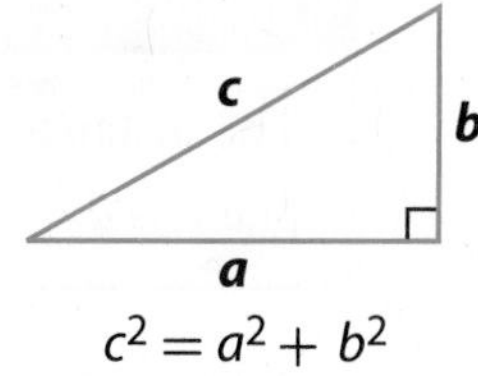

Complete the following to derive the distance formula.

A Let *A* and *B* be points in the coordinate plane with coordinates as shown in the figure.

Draw $\overline{AB}$ in the figure. The goal is to find the length of $\overline{AB}$.

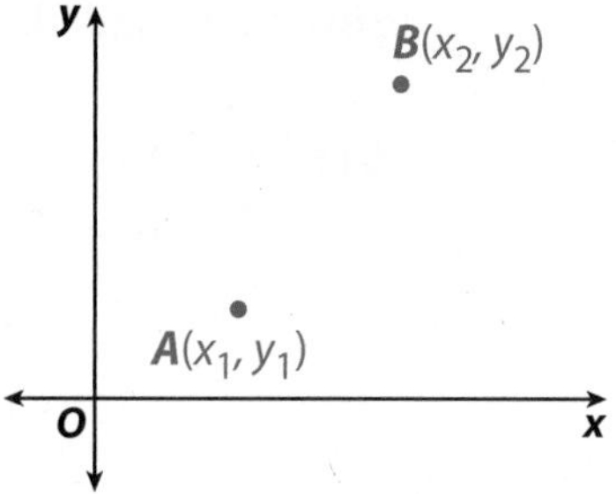

B Draw a horizontal segment with left endpoint *A* and a vertical segment with endpoint *B* to create a right triangle. Label the intersection of the vertical segment and horizontal segment as point *C*.

C What are the coordinates of point *C*? ________________

D Write the lengths of $\overline{AC}$ and $\overline{BC}$ in terms of the coordinates of the points.

$AC =$ ________________ $BC =$ ________________

E Use the Pythagorean Theorem and the lengths from part D to complete the following.

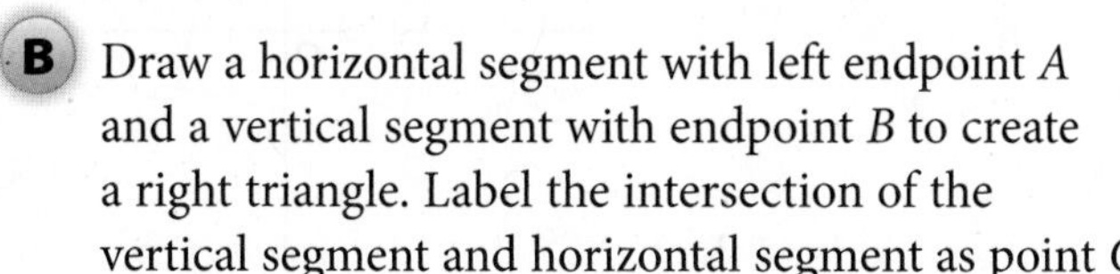

F Solve for *AB* to write a formula for the length of $\overline{AB}$.

$AB =$ ______________________________

REFLECT

1. In the figure with the Explore Activity, points *A* and *B* are shown in Quadrant I, with point *B* above and to the right of point *A*. Does your formula depend upon the location and position of the points? Explain.

____

EXPLORE ACTIVITY *(cont'd)*

2. What If? Suppose $\overline{AB}$ is a horizontal or vertical segment. Does your formula still work? If so, is it possible to simplify the formula? Explain your reasoning.

____

____

Proving Sides of Figures Are Congruent

You can use the distance formula to prove theorems about figures.

Theorem: The Distance Formula

The distance d between two points (x_1, y_1) and (x_2, y_2) in a coordinate plane is $d = \sqrt{(x_2 - x_1)^2 + (y_2 - y_1)^2}$.

EXAMPLE 1

CA CC G.GPE.4

Prove that quadrilateral $ABCD$ is a rhombus.

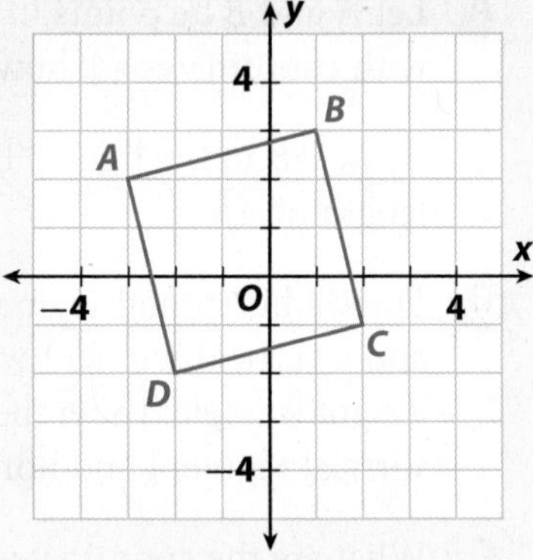

STEP 1 Find the coordinates of the vertices of quadrilateral $ABCD$.

$A(-3, 2)$ $B(1, 3)$
$C(2, -1)$ $D(-2, -2)$

STEP 2 Find the length of each side of the quadrilateral.

$$AB = \sqrt{(x_2 - x_1)^2 + (y_2 - y_1)^2} = \sqrt{(1 - (-3))^2 + (3 - 2)^2}$$
$$= \sqrt{4^2 + 1^2} = \sqrt{17}$$

$$BC = \sqrt{(x_2 - x_1)^2 + (y_2 - y_1)^2} = \sqrt{(2 - 1)^2 + (-1 - 3)^2}$$
$$= \sqrt{1^2 + (-4)^2} = \sqrt{17}$$

$$CD = \sqrt{(x_2 - x_1)^2 + (y_2 - y_1)^2} = \sqrt{(-2 - 2)^2 + (-2 - (-1))^2}$$
$$= \sqrt{(-4)^2 + (-1)^2} = \sqrt{17}$$

$$AD = \sqrt{(x_2 - x_1)^2 + (y_2 - y_1)^2} = \sqrt{(-2 - (-3))^2 + (-2 - 2)^2}$$
$$= \sqrt{1^2 + (-4)^2} = \sqrt{17}$$

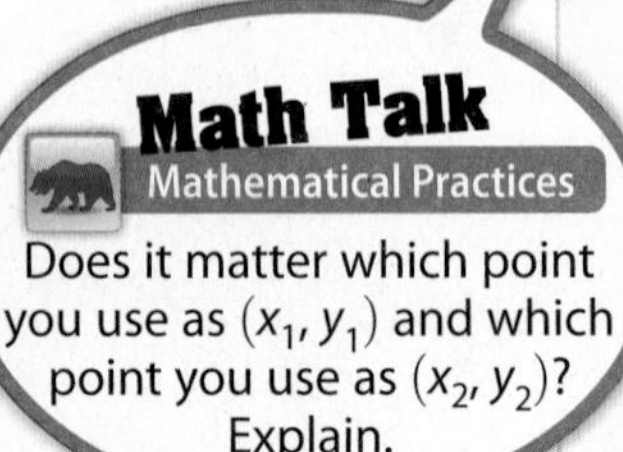

Math Talk
Mathematical Practices
Does it matter which point you use as (x_1, y_1) and which point you use as (x_2, y_2)? Explain.

STEP 3 Compare the side lengths.

$AB = BC = CD = AD$, so the sides are congruent.

Quadrilateral $ABCD$ is a rhombus since it has four congruent sides.

REFLECT

3. **Justify Reasoning** In Example 1, can you conclude that quadrilateral *ABCD* is a square? Explain why or why not.

____

____

____

____

____

____

YOUR TURN

4. Prove that quadrilateral *JKLM* is a kite.

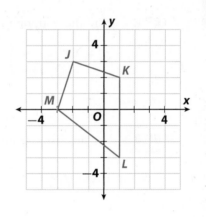

____

____

____

____

____

____

____

The Midpoint Formula

Recall that when you construct the perpendicular bisector of a segment you also locate the midpoint of the segment. The midpoint formula gives you a way to find the midpoint of a segment on the coordinate plane.

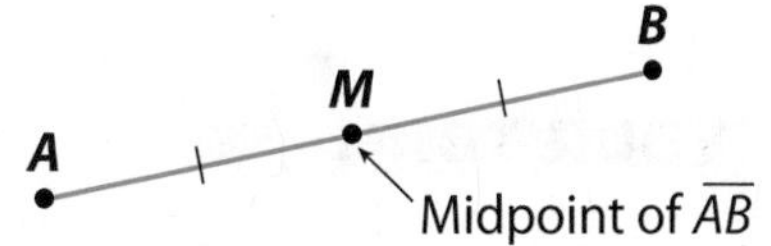

Theorem: The Midpoint Formula

The midpoint M of $\overline{AB}$ with endpoints $A(x_1, y_1)$ and $B(x_2, y_2)$ is given by $M\left(\frac{x_1 + x_2}{2}, \frac{y_1 + y_2}{2}\right)$.

EXAMPLE 2 Real World

CA CC G.GPE.7

The figure shows the route for a hike at a state park, where each unit of the coordinate plane represents one kilometer. Trail planners are creating a shorter trail. The new trail will be a straight shortcut that connects the midpoint of $\overline{AB}$ and the midpoint of $\overline{BC}$. What is the length of the shortcut to the nearest tenth of a kilometer?

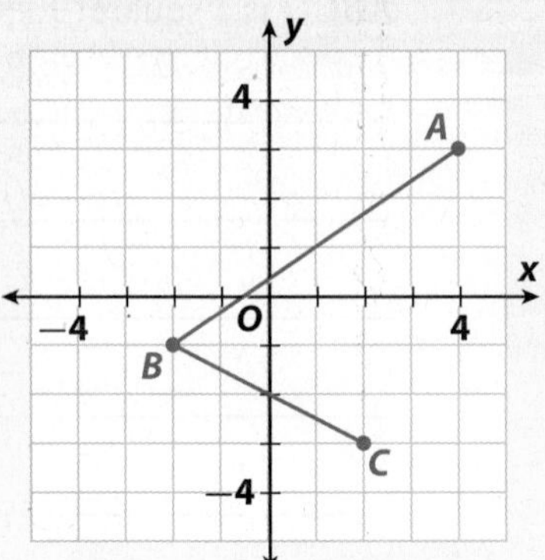

STEP 1 Find the midpoint M of $\overline{AB}$. Use the coordinates $A(4, 3)$ and $B(-2, -1)$.

$$M\left(\frac{x_1 + x_2}{2}, \frac{y_1 + y_2}{2}\right) = M\left(\frac{4 + (-2)}{2}, \frac{3 + (-1)}{2}\right)$$

$$= M\left(\frac{2}{2}, \frac{2}{2}\right) = M(1, 1)$$

STEP 2 Find the midpoint N of $\overline{BC}$. Use $B(-2, -1)$ and $C(2, -3)$.

$$N\left(\frac{x_1 + x_2}{2}, \frac{y_1 + y_2}{2}\right) = N\left(\frac{-2 + 2}{2}, \frac{-1 + (-3)}{2}\right)$$

$$= N\left(\frac{0}{2}, \frac{-4}{2}\right) = N(0, -2)$$

STEP 3 Use the distance formula to find the length of $\overline{MN}$.

$$MN = \sqrt{(x_2 - x_1)^2 + (y_2 - y_1)^2} = \sqrt{(0 - 1)^2 + (-2 - 1)^2}$$

$$= \sqrt{(-1)^2 + (-3)^2}$$

$$= \sqrt{10} \approx 3.2$$

So, the length of the shortcut is approximately 3.2 km.

YOUR TURN

5. Quadrilateral $PQRS$ represents a garden plot at a botanical garden. Each unit of the coordinate plane represents one meter. A gardener plans to create a straight path from the midpoint of $\overline{PQ}$ to the midpoint of $\overline{QR}$. What is the length of the path to the nearest tenth of a meter?

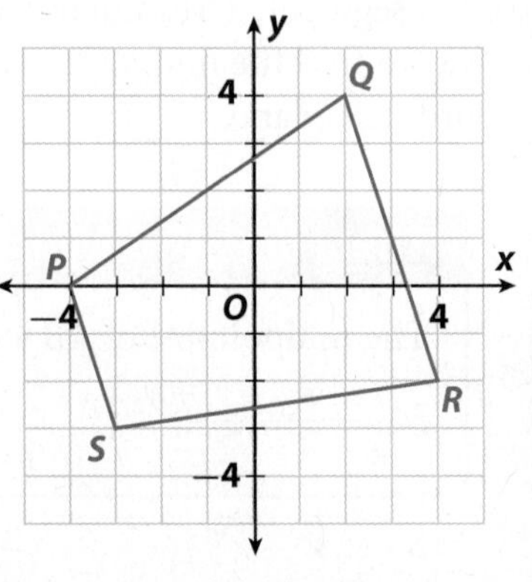

____

Guided Practice

1. You can derive the distance formula by setting up a figure as shown here. (Explore Activity 1)

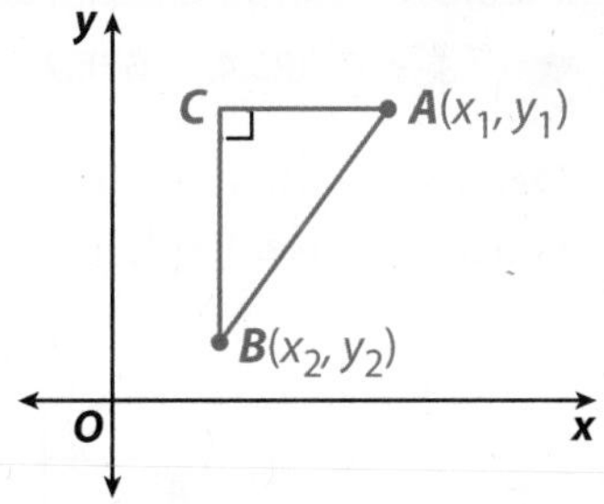

a. What are the coordinates of point C? ______________

b. Write the lengths of $\overline{AC}$ and $\overline{BC}$ in terms of the coordinates of the points.

$AC =$ ______________ $BC =$ ______________

c. Explain how to complete the derivation of the distance formula.

____

____

____

2. Prove that quadrilateral $PQRS$ is a rhombus. (Example 1)

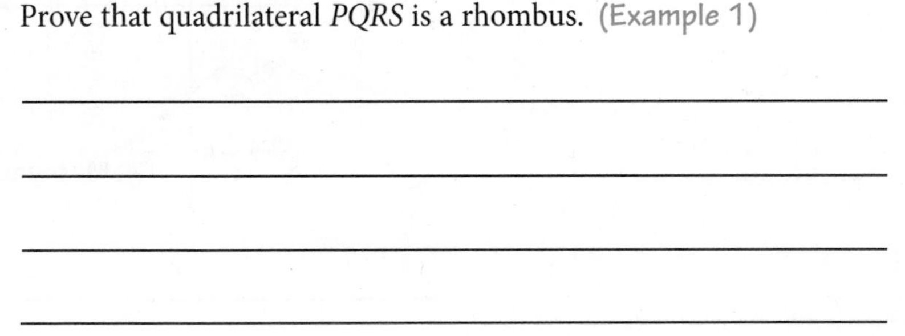

____

____

____

____

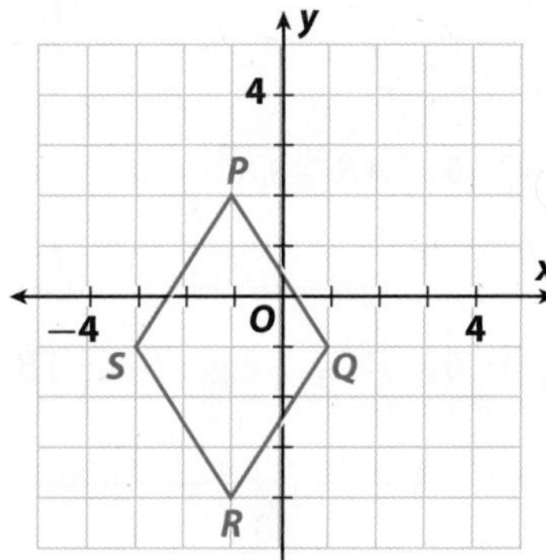

3. Find the distance from the midpoint of $\overline{AB}$ to point C. (Example 2)

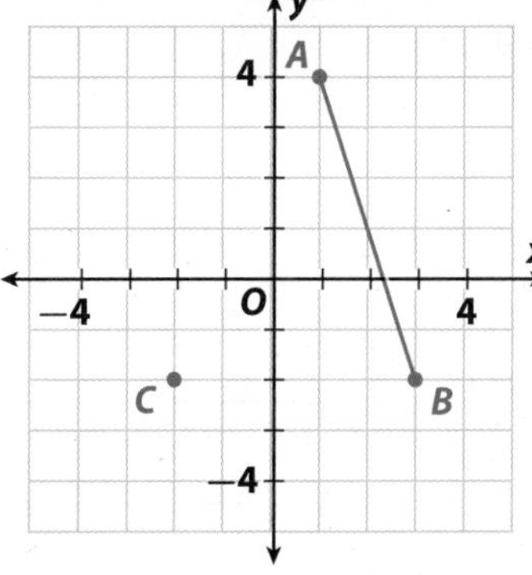

The midpoint M of $\overline{AB}$ is $M\left(\frac{x_1 + x_2}{2}, \frac{y_1 + y_2}{2}\right)$.

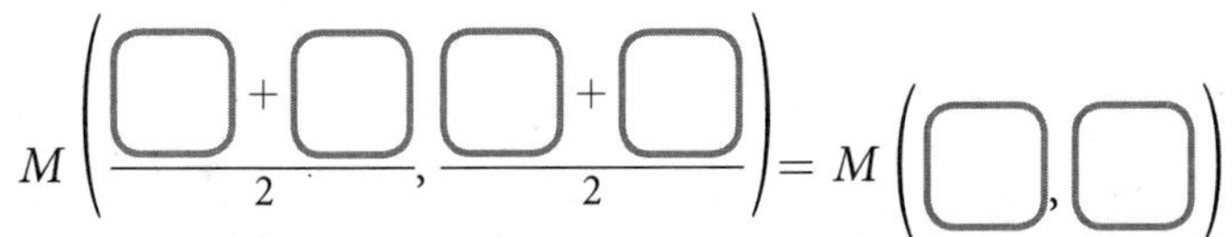

$M\left(\frac{\square + \square}{2}, \frac{\square + \square}{2}\right) = M(\square, \square)$

The distance from C to M is $\sqrt{(x_2 - x_1)^2 + (y_2 - y_1)^2}$.

$\sqrt{(\square - \square)^2 + (\square - \square)^2} = \sqrt{\square^2 + \square^2} = \square$

ESSENTIAL QUESTION CHECK-IN

4. How do you use the distance formula?

____

____

Name________________________ Class________________ Date________________

17.3 Independent Practice

Determine whether each statement about *ABCD* is true or false. Explain your answers.

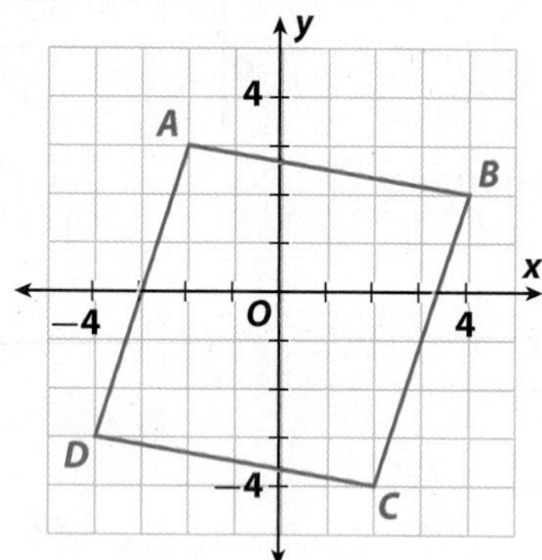

5. $\overline{AB} \cong \overline{DC}$

____

6. $\overline{BC}$ is longer than $\overline{AB}$.

____

____

7. Quadrilateral *ABCD* is a rhombus.

____

____

8. The midpoint of $\overline{BC}$ is in Quadrant IV.

____

____

9. The distance from the midpoint of $\overline{AD}$ to the midpoint of $\overline{BC}$ is less than 6.

____

____

____

10. The distance from point *D* to the origin is 5.

____

11. Critique Reasoning The figure shows a map in which each unit of the coordinate plane represents one mile. Grace says it is shorter to travel from the library to the museum along Main Street and Waller Road than along Green Street and Forest Avenue. Do you agree? Explain.

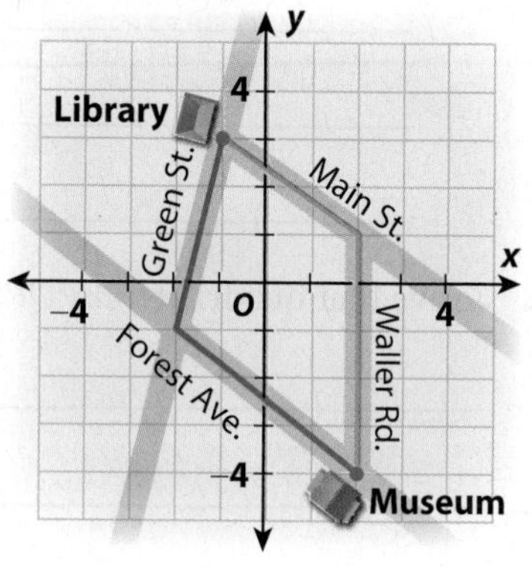

____

____

____

____

____

____

____

____

12. Critical Thinking The midpoint *M* of $\overline{PQ}$ has coordinates $M(2, -1)$. The coordinates of point *P* are $P(-2, -3)$. What are the coordinates of point *Q*? Explain.

____

____

____

____

13. Prove that quadrilateral *PQRS* is an isosceles trapezoid.

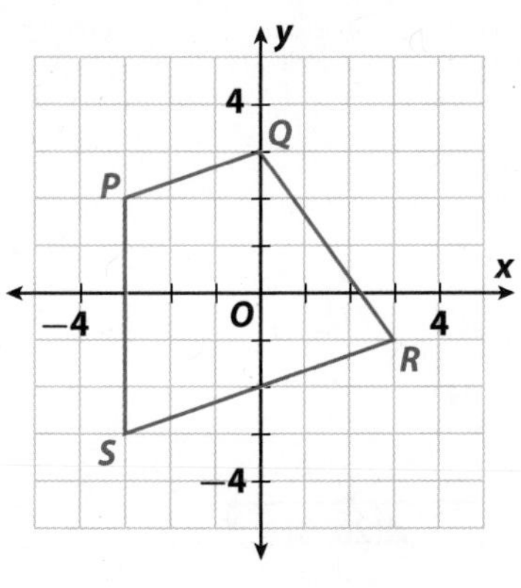

14. Prove $\triangle ABC \cong \triangle DEF$.

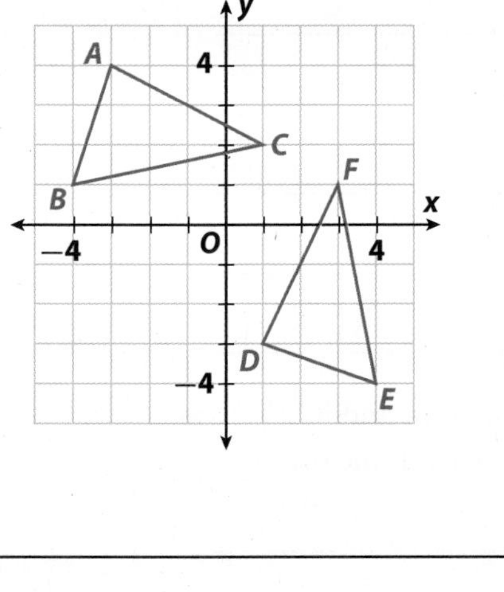

15. Multi-Step $\overline{AB}$ and $\overline{CD}$ are two paths in a community garden, where each unit of the coordinate plane represents one meter. Isaac wants to place a straight fence from the midpoint of $\overline{AB}$ to the midpoint of $\overline{CD}$. The fence costs \$12 per meter. Will Isaac be able to buy the fence for less than \$60? Explain.

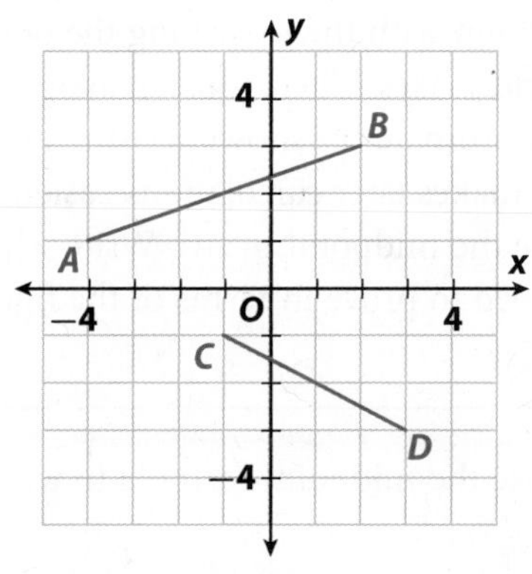

16. Explain how you can use the SAS Triangle Congruence Theorem to prove $\triangle RST \cong \triangle UVW$.

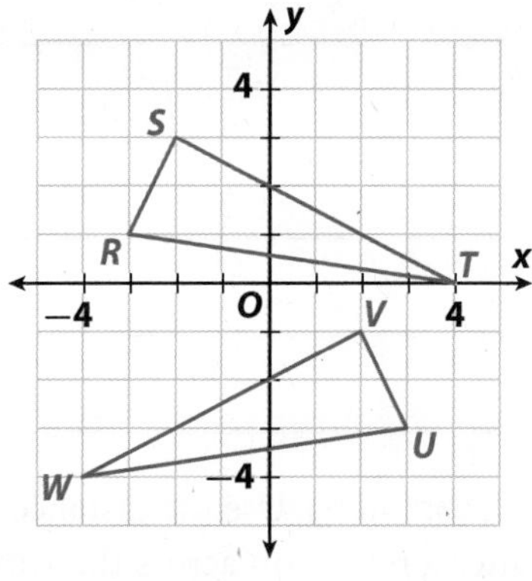

H.O.T. FOCUS ON HIGHER ORDER THINKING

Work Area

17. Communicate Mathematical Ideas Follow these steps to prove that in a right triangle, the midpoint of the hypotenuse is equidistant from all three vertices.

a. You can place any right triangle at the origin with the legs along the positive x- and y-axes. Then you can assign general coordinates as shown. (Using multiples of 2 makes later calculations easier.) Let M be the midpoint of $\overline{AC}$. Write what you need to prove in terms of the figure.

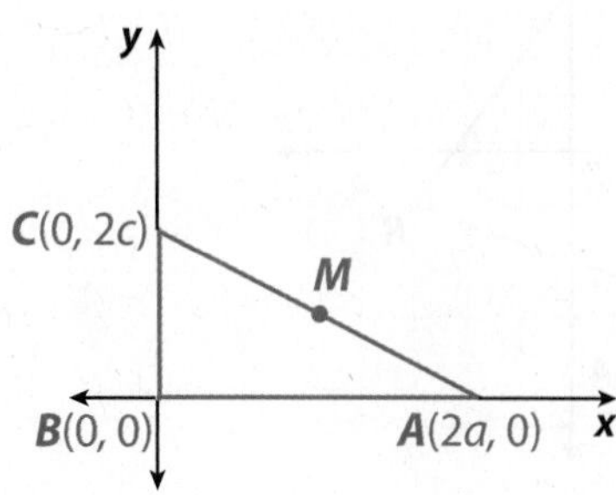

____

b. Use the midpoint formula to write the coordinates of point M.

____

c. Use the distance formula to find MA, MB, and MC.

____

18. Analyze Relationships The midpoint of $\overline{PQ}$ is the origin. How are the coordinates of point P and the coordinates of point Q related? Justify your answer.

____

____

____

____

____

____

____

19. Justify Reasoning Use the distance formula to prove that a point and its image after a reflection across the y-axis are the same distance from the origin.

____

____

____

____

____

____

LESSON 17.4

Perimeter and Area in the Coordinate Plane

Use coordinates to compute perimeters of polygons and areas of triangles and rectangles, e.g., using the distance formula. *Also G.GPE.4*

ESSENTIAL QUESTION

How do you calculate perimeter and area in the coordinate plane?

Finding the Perimeter of a Polygon

The perimeter of a polygon is the sum of the lengths of all of its sides. You can find the perimeter of a polygon in the coordinate plane by using the distance formula to find the length of each side.

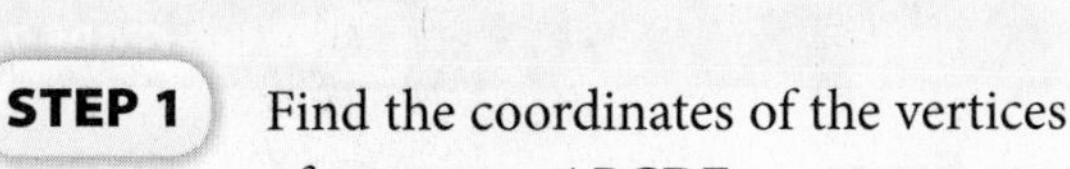

CA CC G.GPE.7

Pentagon *ABCDE* shows the path of an obstacle course, where each unit of the coordinate plane represents ten meters. Find the length of the course to the nearest meter.

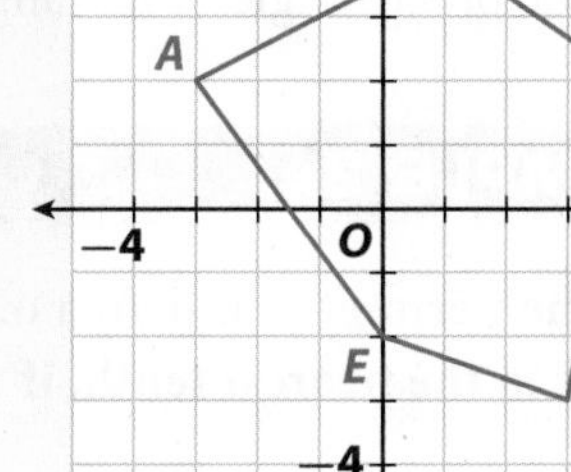

STEP 1 Find the coordinates of the vertices of pentagon *ABCDE*.

$A(-3, 2)$ $B(1, 4)$ $C(4, 2)$

$D(3, -3)$ $E(0, -2)$

STEP 2 Use the distance formula to find the length of each side.

$$d = \sqrt{(x_2 - x_1)^2 + (y_2 - y_1)^2}$$

$$AB = \sqrt{(1 - (-3))^2 + (4 - 2)^2} = \sqrt{4^2 + 2^2} = \sqrt{20}$$

$$BC = \sqrt{(4 - 1)^2 + (2 - 4)^2} = \sqrt{3^2 + (-2)^2} = \sqrt{13}$$

$$CD = \sqrt{(3 - 4)^2 + (-3 - 2)^2} = \sqrt{(-1)^2 + (-5)^2} = \sqrt{26}$$

$$DE = \sqrt{(0 - 3)^2 + (-2 - (-3))^2} = \sqrt{(-3)^2 + 1^2} = \sqrt{10}$$

$$EA = \sqrt{(-3 - 0)^2 + (2 - (-2))^2} = \sqrt{(-3)^2 + 4^2} = \sqrt{25} = 5$$

STEP 3 Use a calculator to add the side lengths. Then multiply to find the actual distance.

$\sqrt{20} + \sqrt{13} + \sqrt{26} + \sqrt{10} + 5 \approx 21.3$ units

21.3 units $\times$ 10 meters per unit $= 213$ meters

The length of the course is approximately 213 meters.

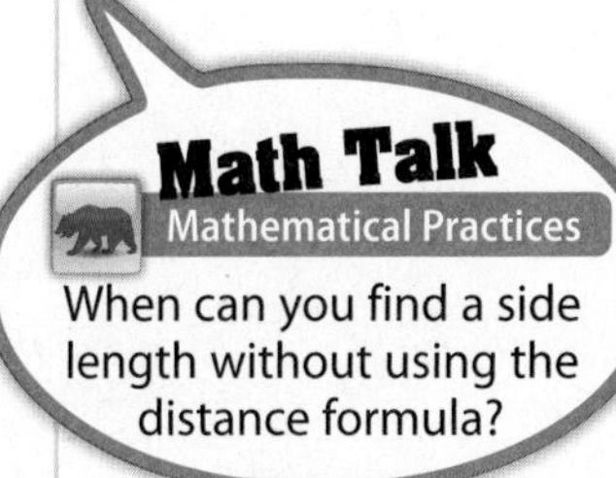

Math Talk
Mathematical Practices
When can you find a side length without using the distance formula?

YOUR TURN

1. Hexagon *MNPQRS* shows the boundary of a farm, where each unit of the coordinate plane represents one kilometer. The farm's owner wants to put a new fence along the boundary of the farm. Find the length of the fence to the nearest tenth of a kilometer.

____

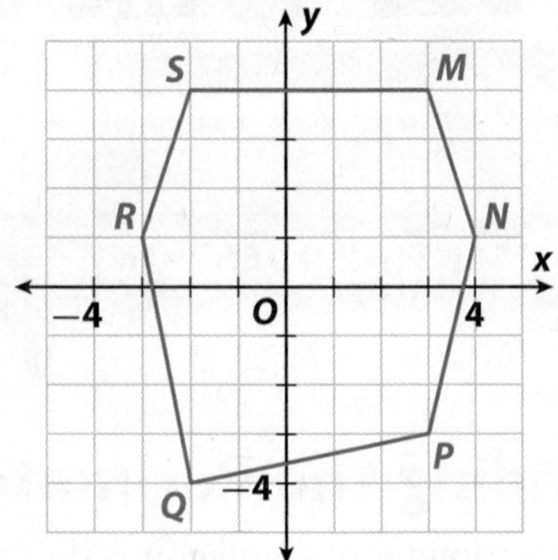

Finding Perimeter and Area of Right Triangles and Rectangles

You can use what you know about slopes of perpendicular lines to determine when a side of a triangle or rectangle may be used as the height.

EXAMPLE 2 CA CC G.GPE.7

Find the perimeter and area of each figure. Round to the nearest tenth, if necessary.

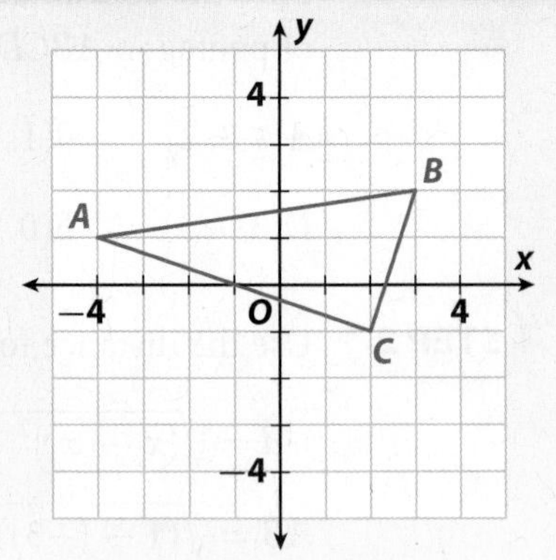

 **A** $\triangle ABC$

STEP 1 Find the coordinates of the vertices of $\triangle ABC$.

$A(-4, 1)$ $B(3, 2)$ $C(2, -1)$

STEP 2 Find the perimeter of $\triangle ABC$.

$AB = \sqrt{(3-(-4))^2 + (2-1)^2} = \sqrt{7^2 + 1^2} = \sqrt{50}$

$BC = \sqrt{(2-3)^2 + (-1-2)^2} = \sqrt{(-1)^2 + (-3)^2} = \sqrt{10}$

$CA = \sqrt{(-4-2)^2 + (1-(-1))^2} = \sqrt{(-6)^2 + 2^2} = \sqrt{40}$

Perimeter of $\triangle ABC = \sqrt{50} + \sqrt{10} + \sqrt{40} \approx 16.6$ units

> When you use a calculator to find a perimeter or area, you should round only at the final step.

STEP 3 Confirm that $\triangle ABC$ is a right triangle.

The slope of $\overline{CA} = -\frac{1}{3}$. The slope of $\overline{BC} = 3$. Since $-\frac{1}{3} \cdot 3 = -1$, $\overline{CA}$ is perpendicular to $\overline{BC}$, so $\overline{CA}$ can be the base and BC can be the height.

STEP 4 Determine the area of $\triangle ABC$.

Area $= \frac{1}{2}bh = \frac{1}{2}(CA)(BC) = \frac{1}{2} \cdot \sqrt{40} \cdot \sqrt{10} = 10$ square units

B Quadrilateral *JKLM*

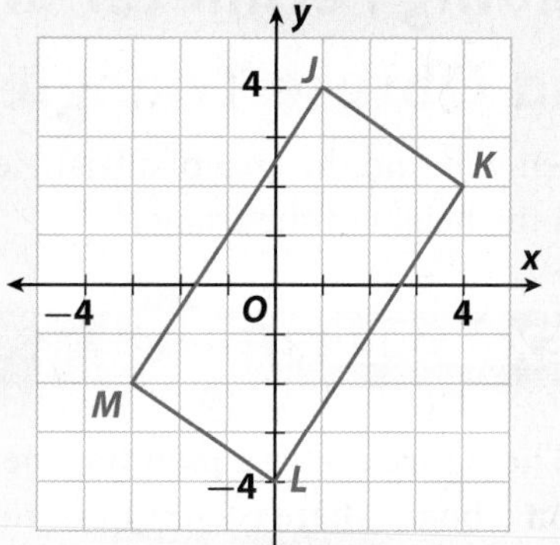

STEP 1 Find the coordinates of the vertices of quadrilateral *JKLM*.

$J(1, 4)$ $K(4, 2)$

$L(0, -4)$ $M(-3, -2)$

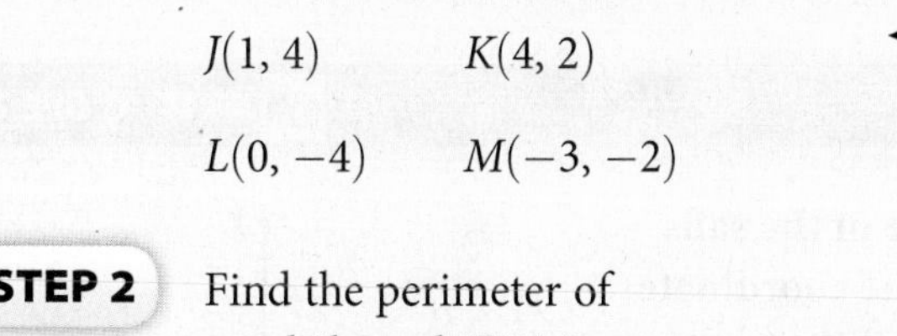

STEP 2 Find the perimeter of quadrilateral *JKLM*.

$$JK = \sqrt{(4-1)^2 + (2-4)^2} = \sqrt{3^2 + (-2)^2} = \sqrt{13}$$

$$KL = \sqrt{(0-4)^2 + (-4-2)^2} = \sqrt{(-4)^2 + (-6)^2} = \sqrt{52}$$

$$LM = \sqrt{(-3-0)^2 + (-2-(-4))^2} = \sqrt{(-3)^2 + 2^2} = \sqrt{13}$$

$$MJ = \sqrt{(1-(-3))^2 + (4-(-2))^2} = \sqrt{4^2 + 6^2} = \sqrt{52}$$

Perimeter of $JKLM = \sqrt{13} + \sqrt{52} + \sqrt{13} + \sqrt{52} \approx 21.6$ units

STEP 3 Confirm that quadrilateral *JKLM* is a rectangle.

$\overline{JK}$ and $\overline{ML}$ both have slope $-\frac{2}{3}$. $\overline{JM}$ and $\overline{KL}$ both have slope $\frac{3}{2}$. Since $-\frac{2}{3} \cdot \frac{3}{2} = -1$, both $\overline{JK}$ and $\overline{ML}$ are perpendicular to both $\overline{JM}$ and $\overline{KL}$. So, *JKLM* is a rectangle. *KL* and *JK* can be its base and height.

STEP 4 Determine the area of quadrilateral *JKLM*.

Area $= bh = (KL)(JK) = \sqrt{52} \cdot \sqrt{13} = 26$ square units

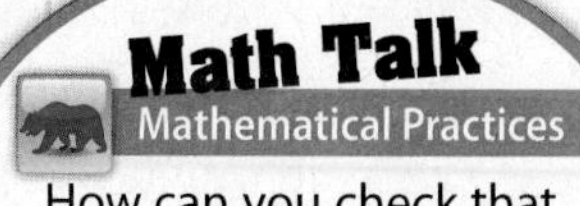

How can you check that an area of 26 square units is a reasonable answer in part B

YOUR TURN

Find the perimeter and area of each figure. Round to the nearest tenth.

2. $\triangle XYZ$

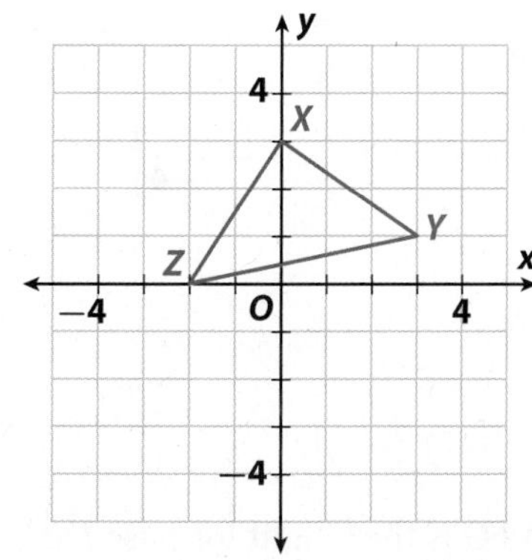

3. Quadrilateral *ABCD*

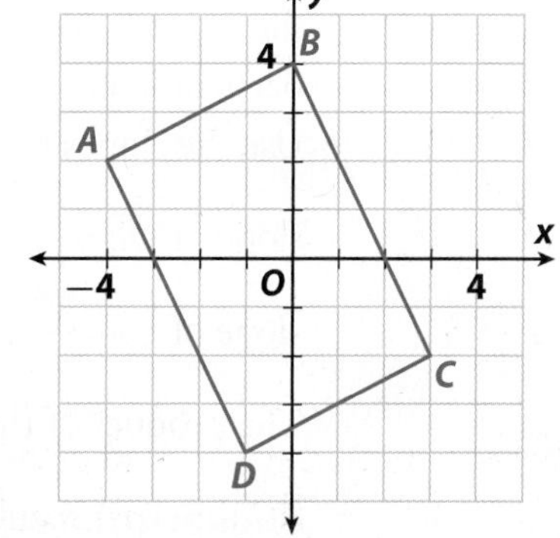

Personal Math Trainer

Online Practice and Help

my.hrw.com

Finding Perimeter and Area of Acute and Obtuse Triangles

When you find the area of a triangle that is a not a right triangle, you must first find the height of the triangle.

EXAMPLE 3

CA CC G.GPE.7

The figure shows a plan for one of the sails on a boat, where each unit of the coordinate plane represents one meter. Find the perimeter and area of the sail. Round to the nearest tenth, if necessary.

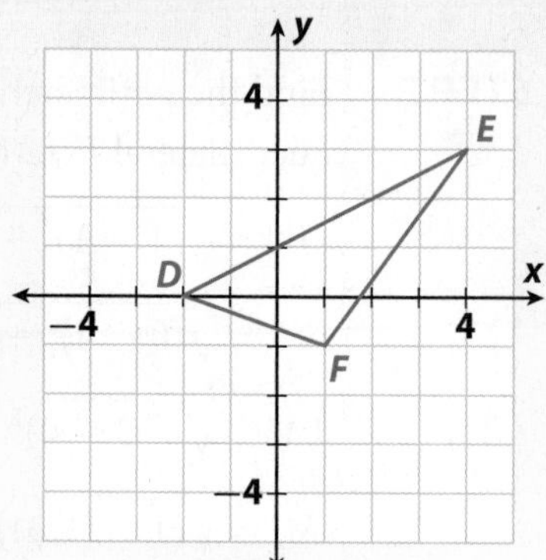

STEP 1 Find the coordinates of the vertices of $\triangle DEF$.

$D(-2, 0) \quad E(4, 3) \quad F(1, -1)$

STEP 2 Use the distance formula to find the length of each side of the triangle.

$$DE = \sqrt{(4-(-2))^2 + (3-0)^2} = \sqrt{6^2 + 3^2} = \sqrt{45}$$

$$EF = \sqrt{(1-4)^2 + (-1-3)^2} = \sqrt{(-3)^2 + (-4)^2} = \sqrt{25} = 5$$

$$FD = \sqrt{(-2-1)^2 + (0-(-1))^2} = \sqrt{(-3)^2 + 1^2} = \sqrt{10}$$

Perimeter of $\triangle DEF = \sqrt{45} + 5 + \sqrt{10} \approx 14.9$ meters

STEP 3 Choose a base for which you can easily find the height of the triangle.

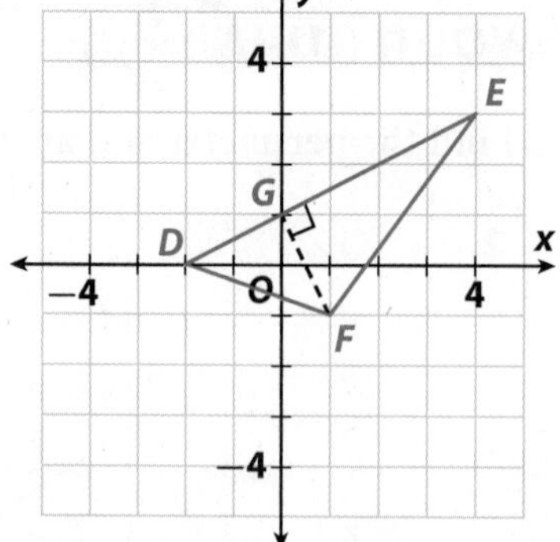

Let the base be $\overline{DE}$. A segment from the opposite vertex, F, to the point $G(0, 1)$ appears to be perpendicular to the base $\overline{DE}$. Use the slopes to check.

slope of $\overline{DE} = \frac{1}{2}$

slope of $\overline{FG} = -2$

The product of the slopes is $\frac{1}{2} \cdot (-2) = -1$.

$\overline{FG}$ is perpendicular to $\overline{DE}$, so FG is the height for base $\overline{DE}$.

$$FG = \sqrt{(0-1)^2 + (1-(-1))^2} = \sqrt{(-1)^2 + 2^2} = \sqrt{5}$$

STEP 4 Determine the area of $\triangle DEF$.

Area $= \frac{1}{2}bh = \frac{1}{2}(DE)(FG) = \frac{1}{2} \cdot \sqrt{45} \cdot \sqrt{5} = 7.5$ square meters

REFLECT

4. **Communicate Mathematical Ideas** Is it possible to use another side of $\triangle DEF$ as the base? If so, what length represents the height of the triangle?

____

____

____

____

____

____

5. **What If?** Suppose you reflect $\triangle DEF$ across the y-axis. Does the image of $\triangle DEF$ have the same perimeter and area as $\triangle DEF$? Explain.

____

____

____

YOUR TURN

6. The figure shows a pen for small animals at a children's petting zoo. Each unit of the coordinate plane represents one foot. Find the perimeter and area of the pen. Round to the nearest tenth, if necessary.

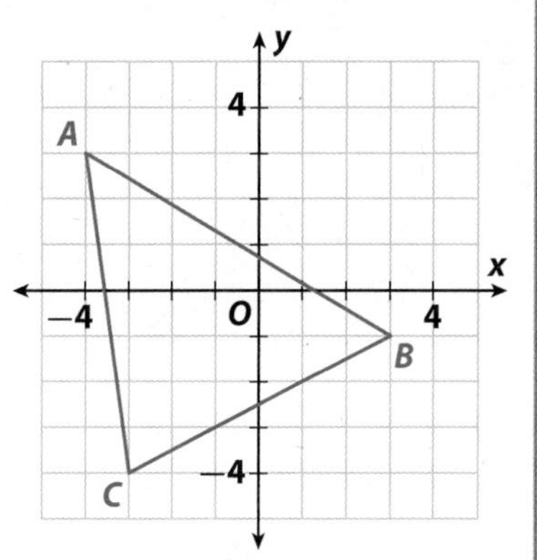

____

____

Guided Practice

1. Pentagon $JKLMN$ shows the boundary of a city's historic district, where each unit of the coordinate plane represents one mile. Find the length of the district's boundary to the nearest tenth of a mile. (Example 1)

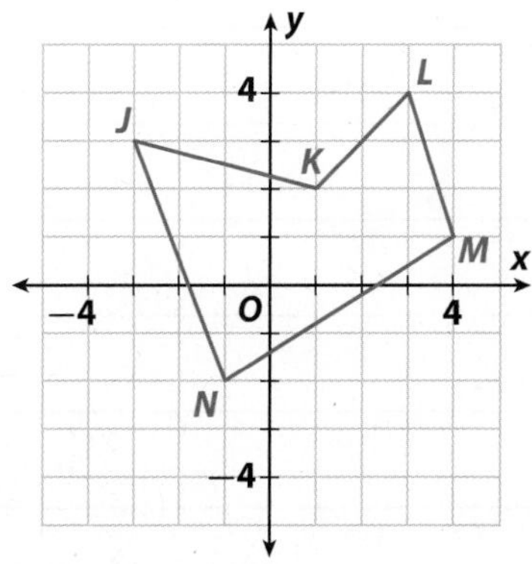

____

Find the perimeter and area of each figure. Round to the nearest tenth, if necessary. (Examples 2 and 3)

2. $\triangle ABC$

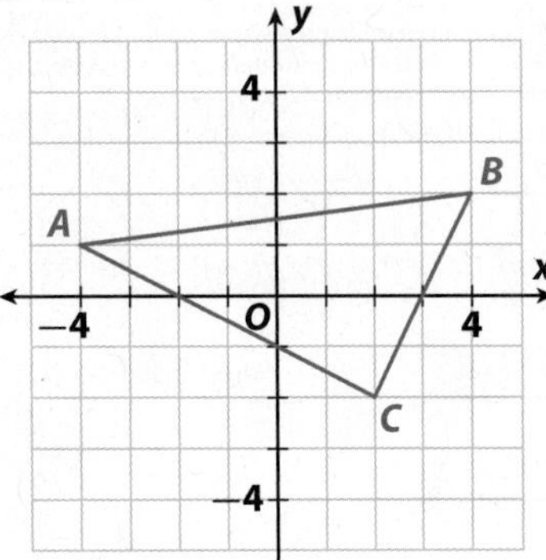

3. Quadrilateral $EFGH$

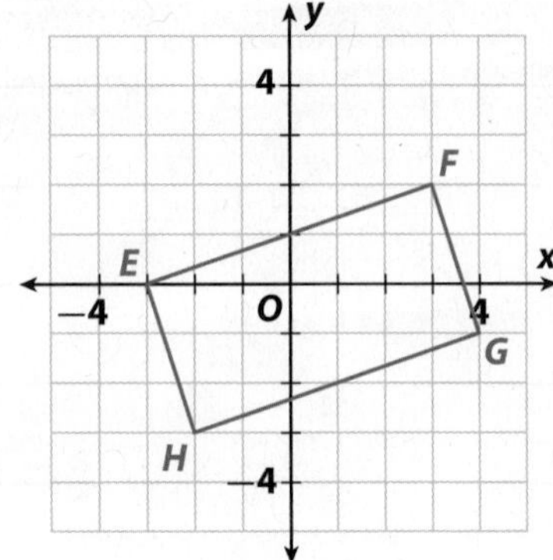

4. $\triangle XYZ$

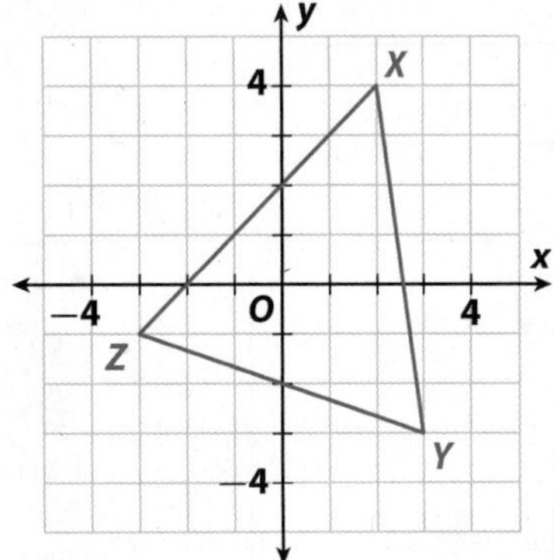

5. $\triangle PQR$

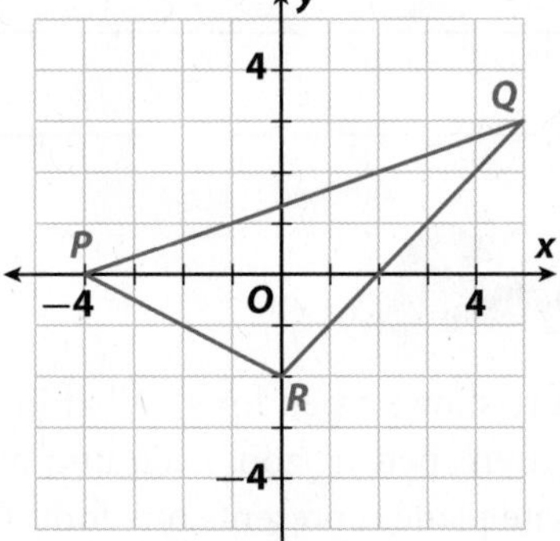

ESSENTIAL QUESTION CHECK-IN

6. How do you calculate the perimeter and area of a right triangle in the coordinate plane?

Name ________________ Class ________________ Date ________________

17.4 Independent Practice

CA CC G.GPE.4, G.GPE.7

7. The figure shows a ceramic tile in the shape of an octagon. Each unit of the coordinate plane represents one inch.

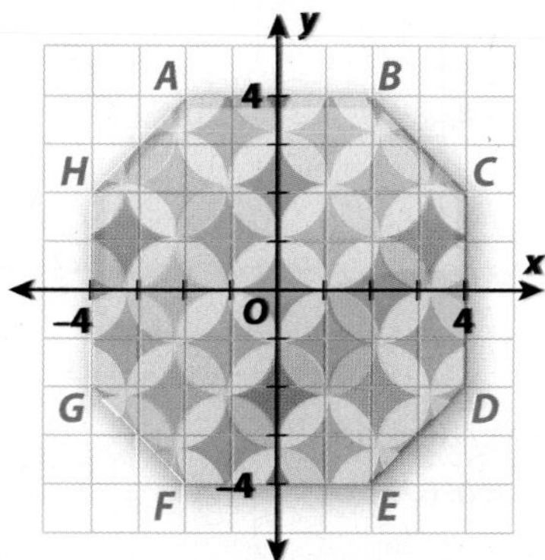

a. Find the perimeter of the tile to the nearest tenth of an inch.

____

b. Is the tile a regular octagon? Explain.

____

____

____

____

c. Draw lines on the figure to divide it into rectangles and triangles that you can use to find the area of the tile. Then explain how to find the area.

____

____

____

____

8. Find the perimeter and area of $\triangle PQR$ with vertices $P(-5, -2)$, $Q(3, 2)$, and $R(6, -4)$. Round to the nearest tenth, if necessary.

____

9. **Represent Real-World Problems** The intersections of three straight streets determine a triangular plot of land. The equations of the streets are $y = \frac{1}{2}x + 1$, $y = x - 1$, and $y = -x - 5$.

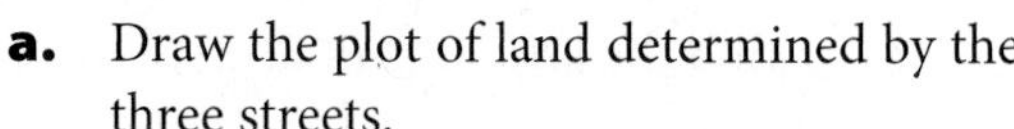

a. Draw the plot of land determined by the three streets.

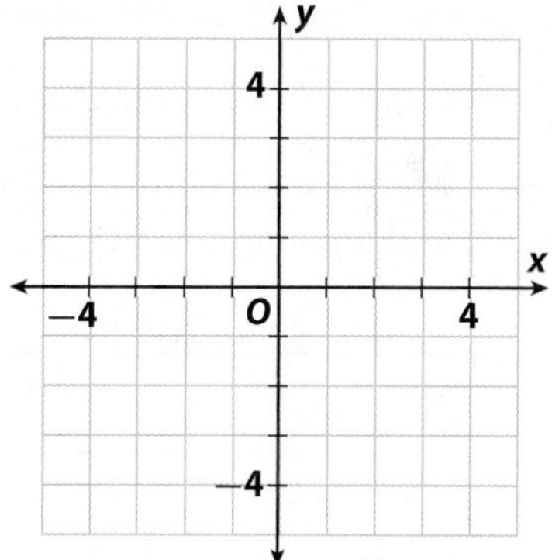

b. Each unit of the coordinate plane represents one kilometer. Find the perimeter and area of the plot of land. Round to the nearest tenth, if necessary.

____

10. Kayla cuts a hole in a wood board to create a target for a beanbag toss, as shown. Each unit of the coordinate plane represents one inch. Find the area of the wood that remains after she cuts the hole.

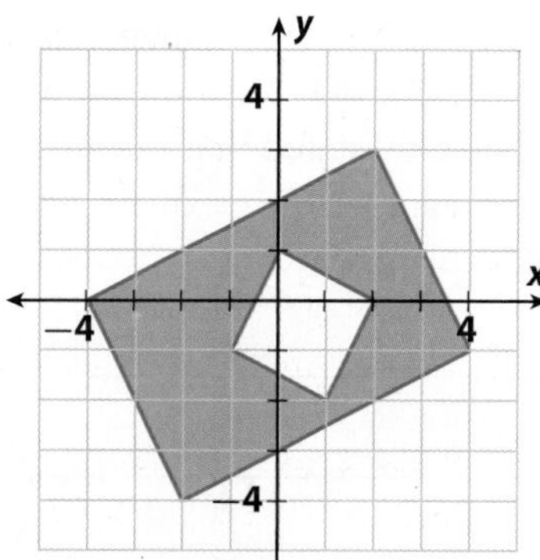

____

FOCUS ON HIGHER ORDER THINKING

Work Area

11. Make a Conjecture In the figure, $PQRS$ is a quadrilateral and point A lies on $\overline{QR}$.

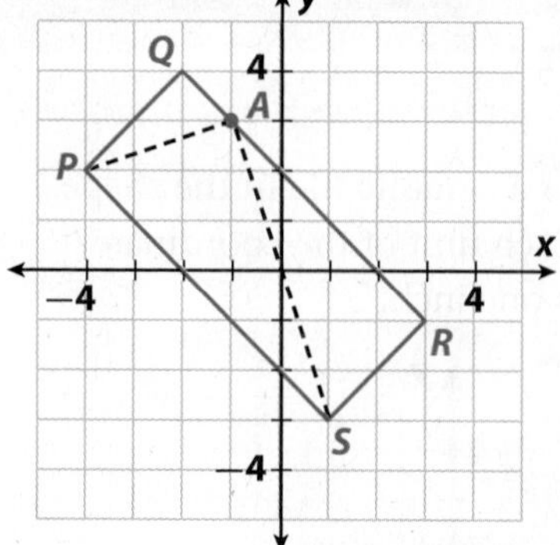

a. Find the area of $\triangle PAS$.

____

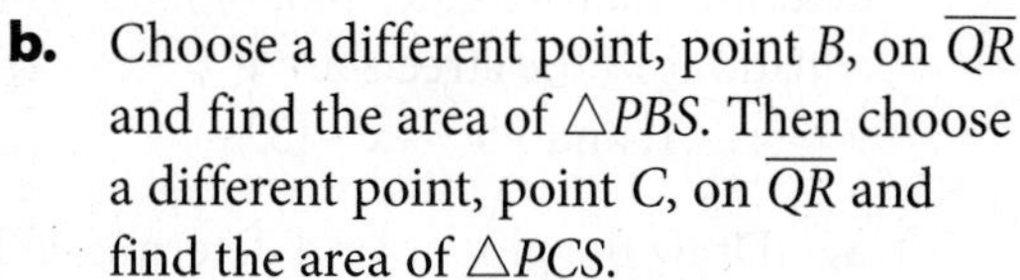

b. Choose a different point, point B, on $\overline{QR}$ and find the area of $\triangle PBS$. Then choose a different point, point C, on $\overline{QR}$ and find the area of $\triangle PCS$.

____

____

c. Make a conjecture about the area of any triangle whose vertices are P, S, and a point on $\overline{QR}$. Explain why your conjecture makes sense.

____

____

____

12. Look for a Pattern Two of the vertices of $\triangle JKL$ are $J(-2, 1)$ and $K(0, 0)$.

a. Different coordinates for vertex L are given in the table. Complete the table by finding the area of $\triangle JKL$ in each case.

Coordinates of Vertex *L*	(1, 2)	(2, 4)	(3, 6)
Area of $\triangle JKL$ (square units)			

b. Predict the area of $\triangle JKL$ when the coordinates of vertex L are $(10, 20)$. Explain.

____

13. Justify Reasoning Jamar was asked to find the area of $\triangle ABC$ with vertices $A(-2, -3)$, $B(1, 3)$, and $C(3, 0)$. He sketched the triangle on a coordinate plane and quickly stated that the area of the triangle must be less than 30 square units. Do you agree? If so, explain how Jamar could have made this quick estimate. If not, explain why not.

____

____

____

____

Ready to Go On?

Personal Math Trainer
my.hrw.com
Online Practice and Help

17.1–17.2 Slopes of Parallel/Perpendicular Lines

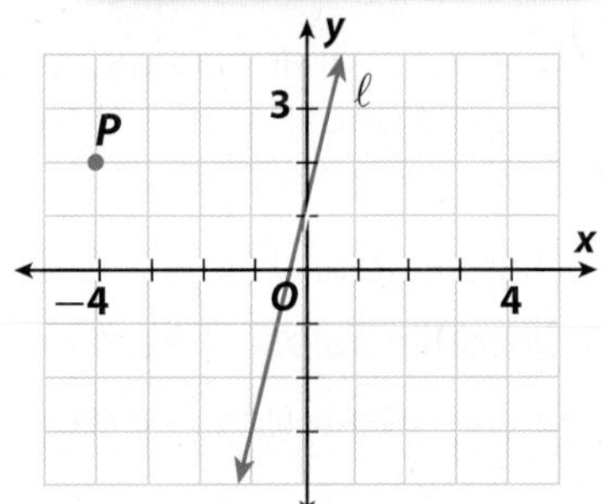

1. Write the equation of the line parallel to line ℓ that passes through point P.

______

2. Write the equation of the line perpendicular to line ℓ that passes through point P.

______

17.3 The Distance Formula

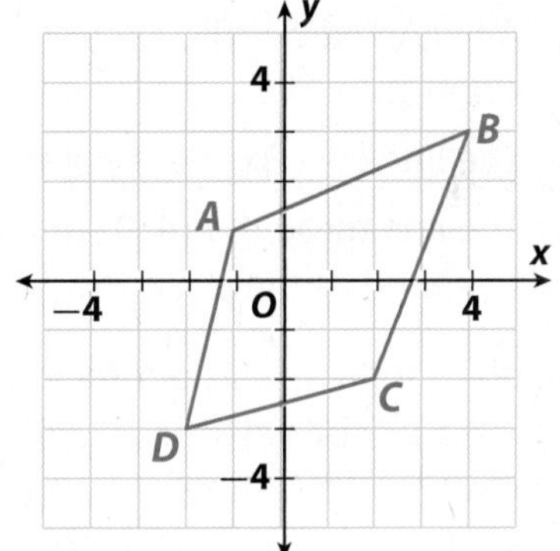

3. Prove that quadrilateral $ABCD$ is a kite.

______

______

17.4 Perimeter and Area in the Coordinate Plane

Find the perimeter and area. Round to the nearest tenth, if necessary.

4. $PQRS$

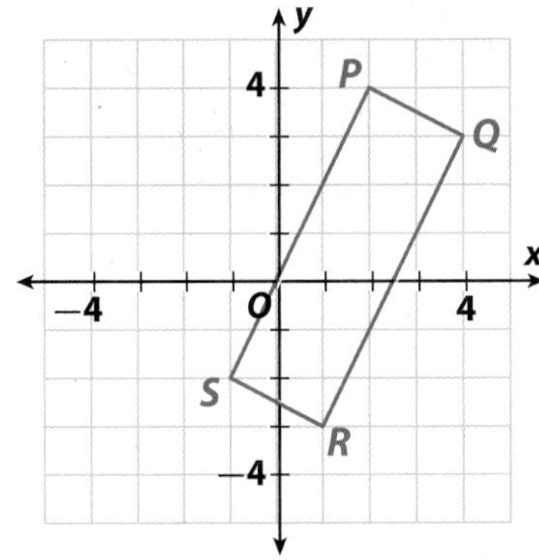

______

______

5. $\triangle GHJ$

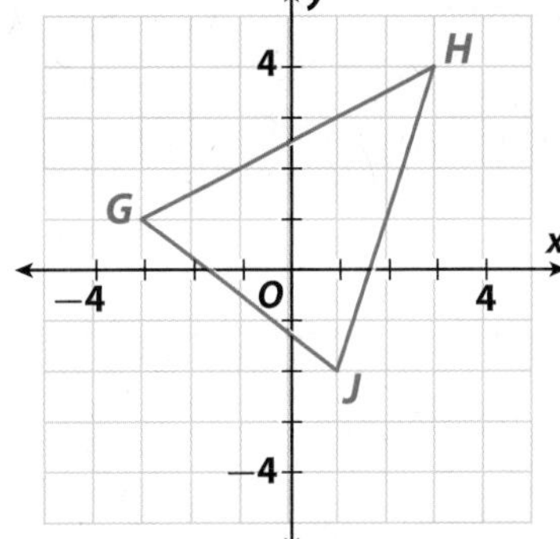

______

______

ESSENTIAL QUESTION

6. What theorems can you use to do proofs and calculations in a coordinate plane?

______

______

MODULE 17
MIXED REVIEW

Assessment Readiness

1. The vertices of quadrilateral *JKLM* are $J(-2, 0)$, $K(-1, 2)$, $L(1, 3)$, and $M(0, 1)$. Can you use slopes and/or the distance formula to prove each statement? Select Yes or No for A–C.

A. Quadrilateral *JKLM* is a parallelogram. ○ Yes ○ No

B. Quadrilateral *JKLM* is a rhombus. ○ Yes ○ No

C. Quadrilateral *JKLM* is a rectangle. ○ Yes ○ No

2. The equation of line ℓ is $y = \frac{3}{2}x - 2$. Choose True or False for each statement.

A. Any line perpendicular to line ℓ has slope $\frac{2}{3}$. ○ True ○ False

B. The line $2y - 3x = 6$ is parallel to line ℓ. ○ True ○ False

C. The line through $P(4, 0)$ that is parallel to line ℓ has the equation $y = \frac{3}{2}x - 6$. ○ True ○ False

3. The plans for a new house include a wall with two triangular windows, $\triangle ABC$ and $\triangle A'B'C'$. The vertices of $\triangle ABC$ are $A(-4, 1)$, $B(-1, 1)$, and $C(-1, 5)$. The vertices of $\triangle A'B'C'$ are $A'(-1, -5)$, $B'(-1, -2)$, and $C'(-5, -2)$. The architect wants to give a sequence of rigid motions that maps $\triangle ABC$ to $\triangle A'B'C'$. Provide verbal descriptions and algebraic rules for the appropriate sequence of rigid motions.

4. The figure shows the floor of a storage space in Nick's apartment. Each unit of the coordinate plane represents one foot. Nick wants to carpet the floor of the storage space using carpet that costs \$3.50 per square foot. Can Nick purchase the carpet and stay within his budget of \$50? Explain.

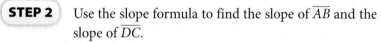

UNIT 6

Study Guide Review

MODULE 17 Coordinate Proofs and Applications

ESSENTIAL QUESTION

How can you write proofs involving figures on the coordinate plane?

EXAMPLE 1

Prove that quadrilateral *ABCD* is a parallelogram.

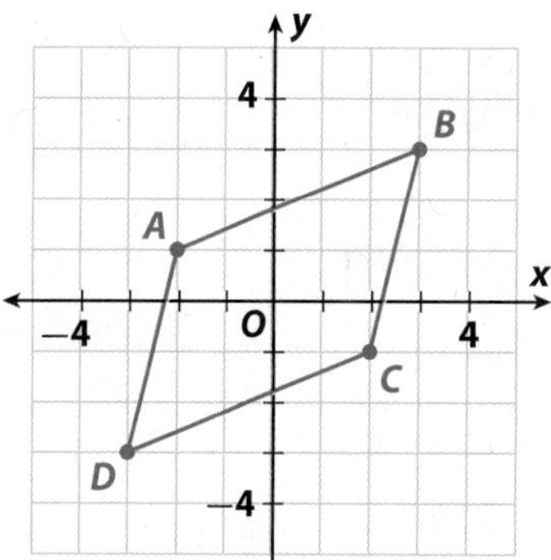

STEP 1 Find the coordinates of the vertices of quadrilateral *ABCD*.

$A(-2, 1)$ $B(3, 3)$ $C(2, -1)$ $D(-3, -3)$

STEP 2 Use the slope formula to find the slope of $\overline{AB}$ and the slope of $\overline{DC}$.

slope of $\overline{AB} = \frac{y_2 - y_1}{x_2 - x_1} = \frac{3 - 1}{3 - (-2)} = \frac{2}{5}$

slope of $\overline{DC} = \frac{y_2 - y_1}{x_2 - x_1} = \frac{-1 - (-3)}{2 - (-3)} = \frac{2}{5}$

Similarly, the slopes of $\overline{AD}$ and $\overline{BC}$ are both equal to 4.

Quadrilateral *ABCD* is a parallelogram because it has two pairs of parallel sides.

EXAMPLE 2

Refer to parallelogram *ABCD* from Example 1. Find the equation of the line perpendicular to $\overline{CD}$ from vertex *A*.

STEP 1 Write the equation of the perpendicular line in slope-intercept form. The line perpendicular to $\overline{CD}$ will have a slope that is the opposite reciprocal of the slope of $\overline{CD}$, so that the product of the slopes will be −1. So, the slope of that perpendicular line is $-\frac{5}{2}$.

$y = mx + b$ Write slope-intercept form.

$y = -\frac{5}{2}x + b$ Substitute the slope of the perpendicular line.

STEP 2 The coordinates of *A* are $(-2, 1)$. Substitute the coordinates of *A* to find the value of *b*.

$1 = -\frac{5}{2}(-2) + b$ Substitute −2 for *x* and 1 for *y*.

$1 = 5 + b$ Simplify.

$-4 = b$ Solve for *b*.

The equation of the perpendicular line is $y = -\frac{5}{2}x - 4$.

EXAMPLE 3

Prove that $\triangle XYZ$ is isosceles.

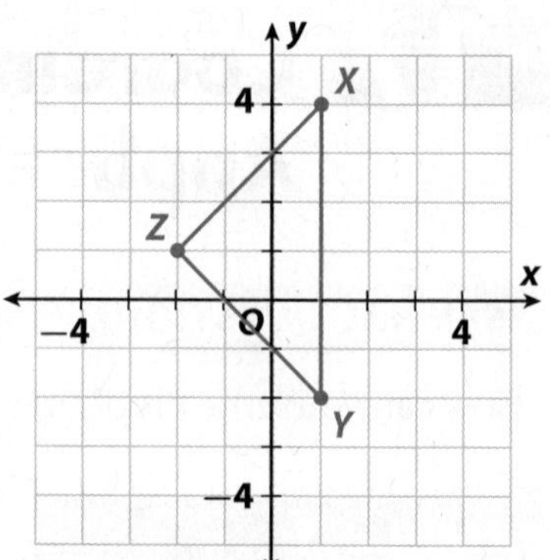

STEP 1 Find the coordinates of the vertices of triangle XYZ.

$X(1, 4)$ $Y(1, -2)$ $Z(-2, 1)$

STEP 2 Find the length of each side of the triangle.
The length of $\overline{XY}$ is $|4 - (-2)| = |6| = 6$.

$$\begin{aligned} XZ &= \sqrt{(x_2 - x_1)^2 + (y_2 - y_1)^2} \\ &= \sqrt{(-2 - 1)^2 + (1 - 4)^2} \\ &= \sqrt{(-3)^2 + (-3)^2} \\ &= \sqrt{18} \end{aligned}$$

$$\begin{aligned} YZ &= \sqrt{(x_2 - x_1)^2 + (y_2 - y_1)^2} \\ &= \sqrt{(-2 - 1)^2 + (1 - (-2))^2} \\ &= \sqrt{(-3)^2 + 3^2} \\ &= \sqrt{18} \end{aligned}$$

STEP 3 Compare the side lengths.

$\overline{XY}$ is longer than the other two sides, but $\overline{XZ} \cong \overline{YZ}$.

$\triangle XYZ$ is isosceles since it has two congruent sides.

EXAMPLE 4

Find the perimeter and area of $\triangle XYZ$ from Example 3. Round to the nearest tenth, if necessary.

STEP 1 Find the perimeter of $\triangle XYZ$.

Perimeter $= XY + XZ + YZ = 6 + \sqrt{18} + \sqrt{18} \approx 14.5$ units

STEP 2 Determine the height of $\triangle XYZ$ relative to the base $\overline{YZ}$.

slope of $\overline{XZ} = 1$

slope of $\overline{YZ} = -1$

Since $1 \cdot (-1) = -1$, $\overline{XZ}$ is perpendicular to $\overline{YZ}$, so XZ may be used as the height.

STEP 3 Determine the area of $\triangle XYZ$.

$$\begin{aligned} \text{Area} &= \frac{1}{2}bh \\ &= \frac{1}{2}(YZ)(XZ) \\ &= \frac{1}{2} \cdot \sqrt{18} \cdot \sqrt{18} \\ &= 3 \text{ square units} \end{aligned}$$

EXERCISES

1. Mr. Hernandez plots the points $(-1, 2)$, $(3, 4)$, and $(3, 0)$ on a coordinate plane. He asks his students to find a fourth point so that the points form a parallelogram. The table shows the points that some students chose.

Student	Point
Kamil	$(-1, 6)$
Jane	$(7, 2)$
Edgar	$(-2, -2)$

a. Show that both Kamil and Jane chose correct points. (Lesson 17.1)

b. **Explain the Error** Edgar was slightly off with his point. Change one of the coordinates of his point so that the points form a parallelogram. (Lesson 17.1)

c. Which student chose a point that forms a rhombus? Find the perimeter of the rhombus. Round to the nearest tenth of a unit. (Lessons 17.3, 17.4)

Use the figure for Exercises 2–4. The line represents Mill Road. A farmer wants to make a direct path from the well to the road.

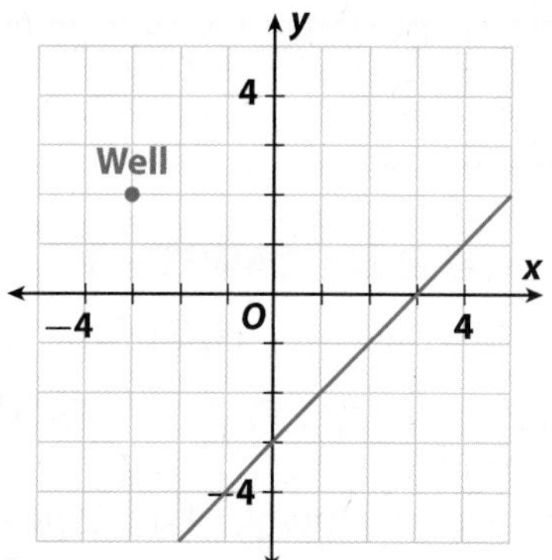

2. **Communicate Mathematical Ideas** What should the slope of the path be? Explain your reasoning. (Lesson 17.2)

3. Find the equation of the line containing the path. (Lesson 17.2)

4. **Interpret the Answer** Each square in the grid represents 9 square yards. To the nearest yard, how far is the well from the road? (Lesson 17.3)

Unit Project

G.GPE.4, G.GPE.5, G.GPE.7

Knight Moves

In the project preview, you learned about the game of chess, and how certain pieces can be moved. You may also be familiar with the game checkers, played on the same board.

For this project, you will invent your own board game. Create a grid for the board, and then define at least three different pieces. Define how each piece can be moved in one of the following ways:

- The piece must move with a certain slope
- The piece must move a specific distance
- Any combination of the moves above

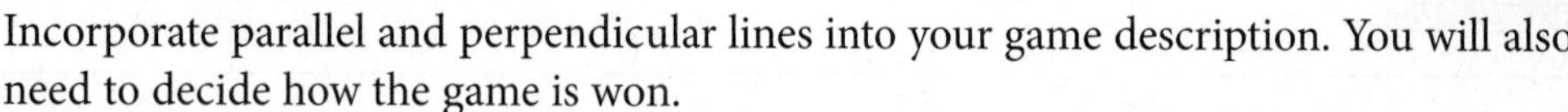

Incorporate parallel and perpendicular lines into your game description. You will also need to decide how the game is won.

Meet with a partner and take turns playing each other's game. Discuss ways to improve each game.

Use the space below to write down any questions you have or important information from your teacher.

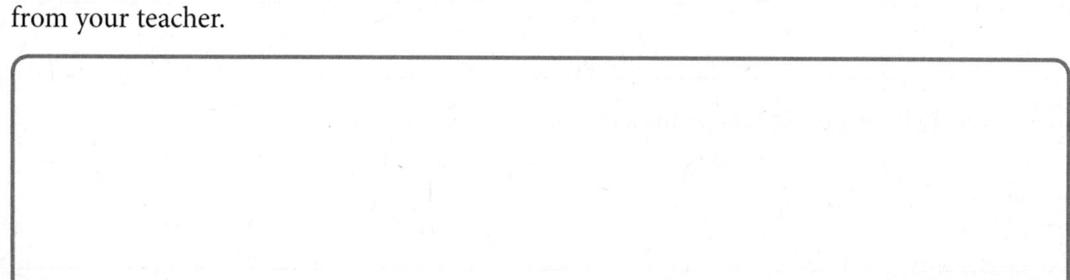

MATH IN CAREERS | **ACTIVITY**

Digital Media Designer A digital media designer is working on a geometry applet for a website. In the applet, the user clicks on a point on a coordinate grid. When the mouse is dragged to a second point, a right triangle is created with the two points as endpoints of the hypotenuse.

a. Suppose the user clicks on $(3, 5)$ and drags to $(-2, 4)$. What is the area of the resulting triangle?

b. The designer wrote the applet so that the x-coordinate of the vertex at the right angle is the same as the x-coordinate of the second point. What are the coordinates of the vertex at the right angle for the triangle from part **a**?

UNIT 6
MIXED REVIEW

Assessment Readiness

1. Is the sequence shown an arithmetic sequence? Select Yes or No for sequences A–C.

A. 2, 4, 8, 16, 32,... ◯ Yes ◯ No
B. 5, 10, 15, 20,... ◯ Yes ◯ No
C. $a_1 = -3, a_{n+1} = 2 + a_n$ ◯ Yes ◯ No

2. Which values of *x* are solutions of the inequality $|x + 4| \geq 2$? Select all that apply.

◯ $x = 2, 6$
◯ $x \geq -2$
◯ $x \leq -6$
◯ $-6 < x < -2$

3. The following points are graphed on the coordinate plane: $A(-3, 5)$, $B(4, 1)$, and $C(-1, 1)$. Does the given point make *ABCD* a trapezoid? Select Yes or No for ordered pairs A–C.

A. $D(-2, 3)$ ◯ Yes ◯ No
B. $D(3, 3)$ ◯ Yes ◯ No
C. $D(-3, 6)$ ◯ Yes ◯ No

4. Find the perimeter of parallelogram *JKLM*. Round your answer to the nearest tenth. Show your work or explain how you got your answer.

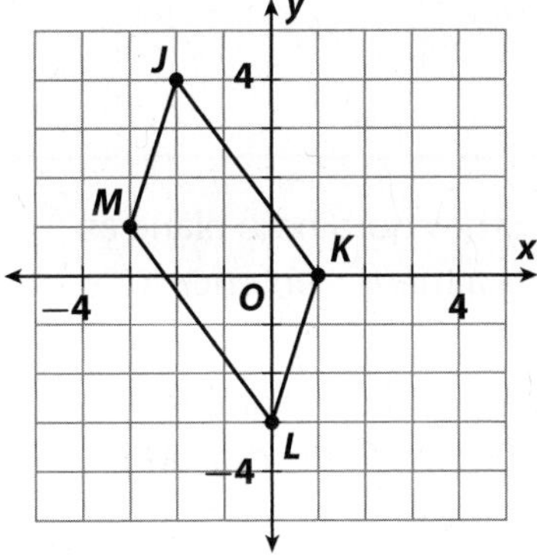

Performance Tasks

★ **5.** Quadrilateral *MNPQ* has coordinates $M(2, 1)$, $N(7, 1)$, $P(6, -3)$, and $Q(-1, -2)$. Determine whether *MNPQ* is a trapezoid. Explain your reasoning.

★★ **6.** Sandy is using a geometry program. She draws Triangle 1 and transforms it to make Triangle 2. She forgets what steps she used to make the image.

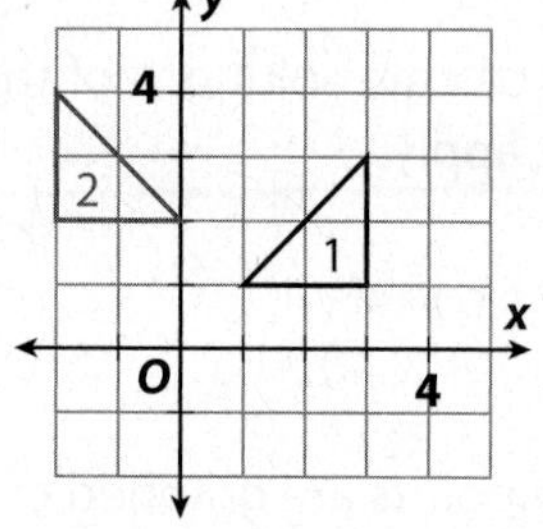

a. Describe a reflection followed by a translation that would result in Triangle 2.

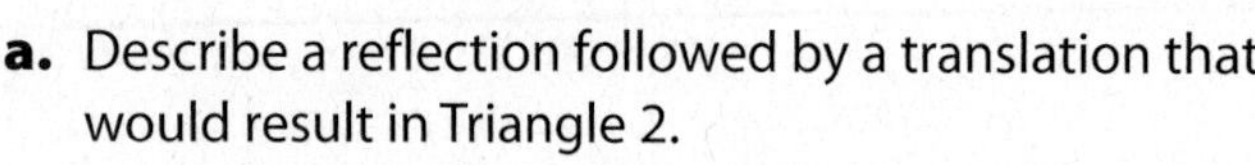

b. Sandy recalls that she first rotated Triangle 1 90° clockwise about the vertex at the right angle. What translation would then result in the image?

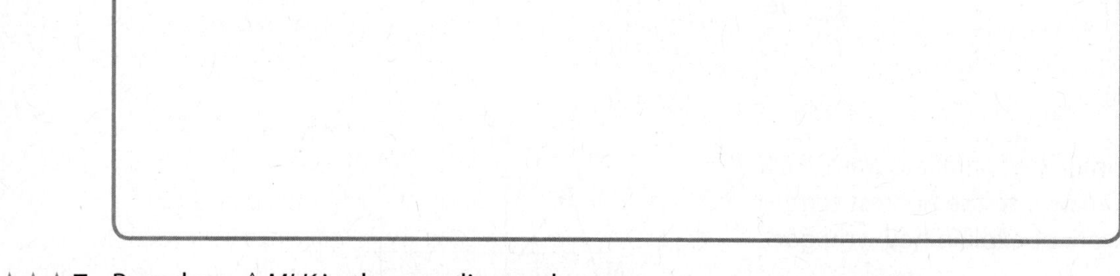

★★★ **7.** Pam drew $\triangle MLK$ in the coordinate plane as shown. It represents a triangular fence for a garden.

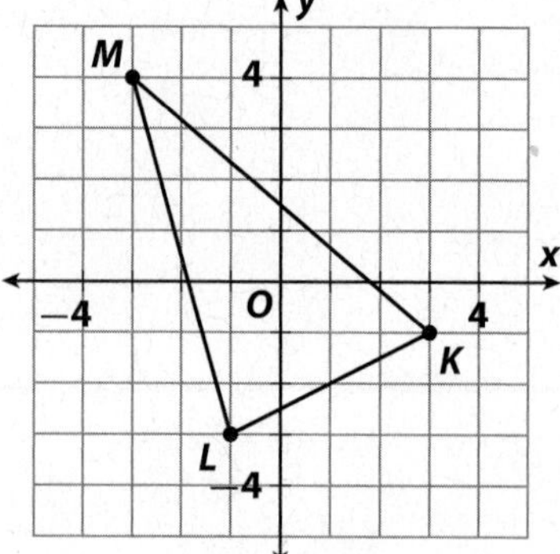

a. The fence should meet at a right angle at point *L*. Explain why Pam's drawing doesn't illustrate this.

b. Pam was off by 1 unit or less plotting point *M*. Find the correct coordinates for this point.

c. There is a gate in the fence at the midpoint of $\overline{KL}$. At the origin, there is a fountain. How far is the fountain from the gate?

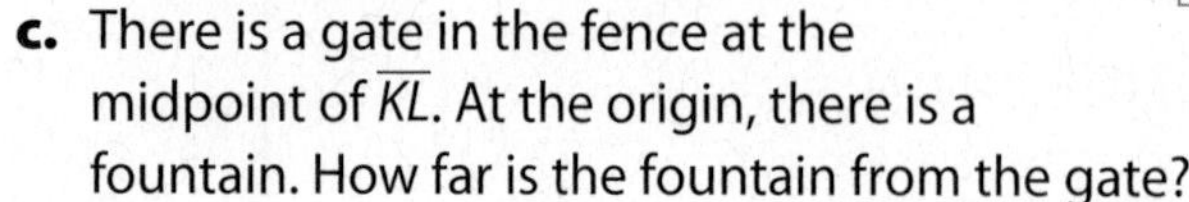

UNIT 1 Selected Answers

MODULE 1

LESSON 1.1

Your Turn

2. 31 oz **3.** 4 in. **4.** 676.5 cm **5.** 5280 ft **7.** 2 **8.** 1 **9.** 3 **12.** perimeter: 15.9 ft; area: 16 ft^2 **13.** 11 g/mL

Guided Practice

1. 177 mm; 176.5 mm and <177.5 mm **2.** 10 ft; 9.5 ft and <10.5 ft **3.** 71 cm; 70.5 cm and <71.5 cm **4.** 19 in.; 18.5 in. and <19.5 in. **5.** 4 **6.** 1 **7.** 5 **8.** 238.8; 38; ones; ones; 239 **9.** 3093.2; 38; 2; 2; 3100 **10.** 125.3; 4.71; 1.253; 4.71; 5.963; 4.71; hundredths place: 5.96 m; speed $= \frac{\text{total distance}}{\text{time}}$ $= \frac{5.96 \text{ m}}{2.4 \text{ s}} = 2.48333\ldots$ m/s; 2.4; two; two; 2.5; 2.5 m/s **11.** When performing calculations using measurements, your answer cannot be more precise than any of the measurements provided.

Independent Practice

13. 8.5 lb **15.** millimeter, centimeter, meter, decameter, kilometer **17.** cups, pints, quarts, gallons **19.** 57.2 **21.** 2.37 **23.** 1980 m **25.** Yes, he should buy more paint. The actual dimensions could be slightly greater than 4 m by 20 m depending upon the level of precision Yoshi used in his measurements. For example, if the actual dimensions are 4.1 m by 20.1 m, the area would be 82.41 m^2, and more paint would be needed. **27.** The 0 in 1.30 is a significant digit, so the answer should be given to 3 significant digits, not 2. The area is 1.69 m^2.

LESSON 1.2

Your Turn

3. 0.9 **4.** 0.1 **5.** 26 **6.** 10 **8.** 2.8 lb/ft **9.** 1848 ft/min **10.** 10.4 in./min **11.** 132 ft/s **12.** 34.7 m^2 **13.** 188 cm^2 **14.** 11,664 in^2

Guided Practice

1. multiply; 16.4 **2.** divide; 2.9 **3.** 3.28 ft/1 m **4.** 1 L/0.26 gal **5.** 1 kg/2.2 lb **6.** 1 L = 1000 mL

1 wk = 7 days   1 day = 24 hr

1 hr = 60 min   1 min = 60 s

$\frac{0.5 \text{ mL}}{1 \text{ s}} \cdot \frac{1\text{L}}{1000 \text{ mL}} \cdot \frac{60 \text{ s}}{1 \text{ min}} \cdot \frac{60 \text{ min}}{1 \text{ hr}} \cdot \frac{24 \text{ h}}{1 \text{ day}} \cdot \frac{7 \text{ d}}{1 \text{ wk}} = 302.4$ L/wk

1 significant digit(s); 300 L/wk

7. $\frac{3100 \text{ cm}^2}{1 \text{ min}} \cdot \left(\frac{0.39 \text{ in.}}{1 \text{ cm}}\right)^2 \cdot \frac{60 \text{ min}}{1 \text{ hr}}$

$= \frac{3100 \cancel{\text{cm}^2}}{1 \cancel{\text{min}}} \cdot \frac{0.1521 \text{ in}^2}{1 \cancel{\text{cm}^2}} \cdot \frac{60 \cancel{\text{min}}}{1 \text{ hr}}$

$= \frac{3100 \cdot 0.1521 \cdot 60 \text{ in}^2}{1 \text{ hr}}$

$= 28{,}290.6 \text{ in}^2\text{/hr}$

2; 28,000 **8.** Dimensional analysis can be used to convert between different units and different measurement systems. This allows you to work with measurements in different units.

Independent Practice

9. F **11.** D **13.** C **15.** 17 feet **17.** 31 mi/hr **19.** $3180.00. **21.** Sample answer: A juice company wanted to sell one of its juices in a country that uses the metric system. If the bottle contains 12 fluid ounces of the juice, how many liters should be indicated on the label? Answer: 0.36 liter. **23.** The student used the conversion factor 3.28 ft/m instead of its square. When converting areas, you must account for the fact that area is measured in square units. Area: 23 ft^2.

MODULE 2

LESSON 2.1

Your Turn

5. 37 **6.** 200 **7.** About 16.7 mi/h

Guided Practice

1. terms: 7, $8p$, $2r^3$; coefficients: 8, −2 **2.** terms: g^2, $-14h$, 10; coefficients: 1, −14

3. $(4x + y)^2 - 3z = (4 \cdot 2 + -1)^2 - 3(5)$

$= (8 - 1)^2 - 15$

$= (49) - 15$

$= 34$

4a. the amount she earns in t hours **b.** The terms are 60, $9t$. The coefficient is 9. **c.** \$60 + \$9(5) **d.** \$105

5. To evaluate an algebraic expression, substitute the value(s) of the variable(s) into the expression and simplify using the order of operations. To interpret an algebraic expression, identify the terms and coefficients and what they represent.

Independent Practice

7. 18 **9.** 18 **11.** 10 **13.** −1 **15a.** Substitute 5 for x and −3 for y. $(x + y)^2 = 4$; $(x - y)^2 = 64$. $(x - y)^2$ is greater. **b.** Substitute −5 for x and −3 for y. $(x + y)^2 = 64$; $(x - y)^2 = 4$. $(x + y)^2$ is greater. **17.** The rate is 25 miles per hour. 15 minutes = 0.25 hour.

$d = rt$

$= 25 \frac{\text{miles}}{\text{hour}} \cdot 0.25 \text{ hour}$

$= 6.25$ miles

19. Nita found that $(a + 1)^2$ is greater than $(a + 1)^3$ for any negative value of a except −1.

UNIT 1 Selected Answers *(cont'd)*

LESSON 2.2

Your Turn

4. $10x$ **5.** $25y$ **6.** $12r$ **7.** $3z$
8. $2x + 9y^2$ **9.** $2n^3 + 3n^2$
10. $y^4 - 2y^2$ **11.** $-m^3 + m^2 + 4n^2$
15. $20t$ dollars **16.** \$160
17. $9t + 10.50$ dollars

Guided Practice

1. The expressions $3(k - 3)$ and $3k - 9$; $9k - 9$ and $9(k - 1)$; and $3k + 3$ and $3 + 3k$ are equivalent.
2. $7x$ **3.** $8b + 4c$ **4.** $-8r$ **5.** $7g$
6. $15x$ **7.** $4z$ **8.** $6m - 3n$
9. $3x + 3y$ **10.** $4z$ **11.** $8r^3 - r^2$
12. $8 + 3h^2$ **13.** $3a + 3b^2$
14. $4(m) - 4(7) + 15$
$4m - 13$
15. $10g + 7g - 8h$
$17g - 8h$
16. $4(m) - 4(2) + 3m$
$7m - 8$
17. $4x + 15x + 4y - x$
$18x + 4y$
18. $12 - 3(4) + 3(t) + 4t$
$7t$
19. $3g + 3(2) - 3(g) + 4(g) + 4(1)$
$4g + 10$
20.

$3b + 2(4b) + 7$	Commutative Property.
$3b + 8b + 7$	Simplify.
$11b + 7$	Combine like terms.

21. Sample answer:
$2w + 2(w + 2)$; $4w + 4$
22. You can simplify algebraic expressions by using the properties of real numbers and combining like terms.

Independent Practice

23. Distributive Property
25. Commutative Property of Addition **27.** $8a + 7$
29. $2n - 48$ **31.** $14b + 3c - 3$
33a. $15 \frac{\text{calories}}{\text{minute}} \cdot r$ minutes = number of calories burned when running. **b.** $60 - r$ represents the number of minutes she spends walking; $6(60 - r)$ is the number of calories burned during walking. **c.** $9r + 360$; calories
d. When $r = 20$, it is 540; when $r = 30$, it is 630; when $r = 40$, it is 720; The greater the value of r, the greater the number of calories that are burned. **35.** $7.5c - 10$; dollars **37.** 3.5 cups; when $c = 4$, the expression gives 31 cups; when $c = 3$, it yields 23 cups. Because 27 is halfway between 23 and 31, c is 3.5.
39. Rectangle: $n(n + 2)$, or $n^2 + 2n$; Square: $(n + 1)(n + 1)$, or $n^2 + 2n + 1$; So the square is larger in area by 1 unit.

LESSON 2.3

Your Turn

8. $1.075p$ **9.** $500 + 0.105s$
10. $0.80c$ **11.** $1.33p + \$16.50$
14. $20 + 8w$ **15.** $120 + 100d$
16a. $800 - 30w$ dollars. **b.** \$560
17a. $50{,}000 - 2000m$ miles
b. 25 months

Guided Practice

1. $30 - 0.10t$
$30 - 0.1t$
2. total cost = hourly cost × number of hours + rental cost; $20h + 3$; dollars **3.** $175 + 5h$; dollars **4.** $21 + 4(y - 2)$ where y represents dog years and $y \geq 2$
5a. dollars + $\frac{\text{dollars}}{\text{week}}$ × weeks; dollars **b.** $35 + 10w$ **c.** $355 - 10w$
6. First look for descriptive words that indicate which arithmetic operations are involved. Then create a verbal model relating the quantities. Finally, choose a variable to represent the unknown quantity, and write the expression.

Independent Practice

7a. $4(t + 7) + 2$ **b.** $4t + 30$
c. 42 degrees **9a.** $\frac{t + t(0.08) + 10}{3}$; $\frac{1.08t + 10}{3}$ **b.** The variable t represents the total cost of the tickets. Units: dollars per person.
11. meters per second squared; Since velocity = $\frac{\text{meters}}{\text{second}}$,

$$\text{accel.} = \frac{\text{meters}}{\text{second}} \div \text{time} = \frac{\text{meters}}{\text{second}} \cdot \frac{1}{\text{seconds}} = \frac{\text{meters}}{\text{second}^2}$$

13. Sunil is correct. For a right triangle, the base and height must be the two smaller sides with the hypotenuse being the largest side. Monica incorrectly used the two larger sides for her formula.

UNIT 2 Selected Answers

MODULE 3

LESSON 3.1

Your Turn

1. $k = -1$ **2.** $m = 3$ **3.** $z = -1.5$ **4.** $m = -17$ **5.** $b = 2.25$ **6.** $n = -3$ **7.** $p = 1.5$ **8.** $t = 6$ **9.** infinitely many solutions **10.** no solution **11.** $p - 0.2p = 28.76$; \$35.95

Guided Practice

1. Subtraction Property of Equality, Division Property of Equality; $x = -2$. **2.** Combine like terms, Addition Property of Equality, Division Property of Equality; $y = 3$. **3.** $x = 5.5$ **4.** $b = 4$ **5.** $k = 9$ **6.** $n = -0.2$ **7.** $z = -8$ **8.** $r = 2$ **9.** no solution; the statement is false **10.** infinitely many solutions; the equation is an identity **11.** no solution; the statement is false **12.** $12 - 2t = -4$; 8 P.M. **13.** $7.50(20) - (7.50)(20)r = (6.75)(20)$; The rate is 0.10, or 10%. **14.** To undo any operation, use the opposite property of equality. For example, you can undo addition by using the Subtraction Property of Equality.

Independent Practice

15. $y = 6$ **17.** $m = -2$ **19.** $z = \frac{9}{2}$, or 4.5 **21.** $a = -1$ **23.** $d = 4$ **25.** $s + (3a - 5) = 215$; Aaron's score is 55, and David's score is 160. **27.** $s + (2s + 4) = 28$; One group has 8 students, and the other group has 20 students. **29.** $p + 0.08p = 37.80$; The jeans cost \$35. **31.** $2x + 9 = 25$; The dimensions are 8 ft by 9 ft. **33a.** length and width of the garden; write an equation for the perimeter of the garden and then solve to find the length and the width. **b.** Let w represent the width of the garden. Then $w + 6$ represents the length of the garden.

$P = 2l + 2w$
$160 = 2(w + 6) + 2w$
$160 = 4w + 12$
$148 = 4w$
$37 = w$

$A = 43(37) = 1591$. The area is 1591 square feet.

LESSON 3.2

Your Turn

1. $n > \frac{1}{2}$

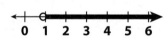

−2 −1 0 1 2 3 4

2. $h \leq -2$

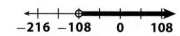

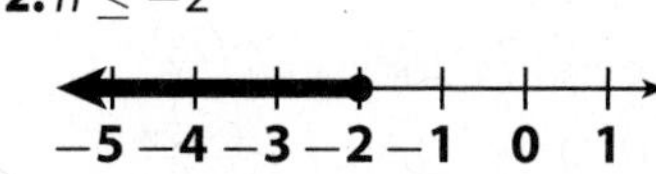

3. $m \geq 4$

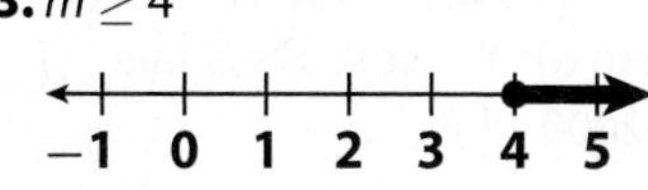

4. $s < 3$

−1 0 1 2 3 4 5

6. $t \leq -0.7$

−2 −1 0 1

7. $y > \frac{9}{10}$

0 1 2 3 4 5 6

8. $x > -2$

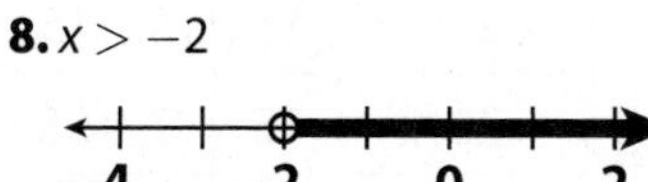

9. $y > -108$

−216 −108 0 108

10. $k < 3$

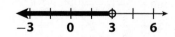

−3 0 3 6

11. $a \geq -5$

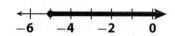

−6 −4 −2 0

12. No solution

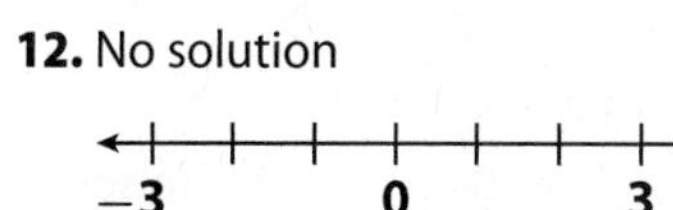

13. All real numbers are solutions.

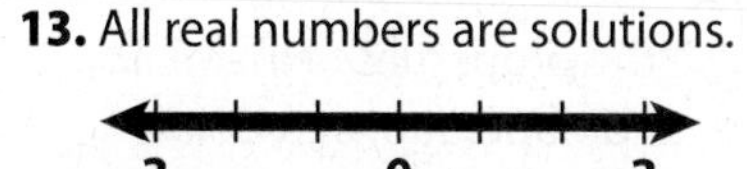

15. Ammon: 13 hours; Nakia: 16 hours

Guided Practice

1.

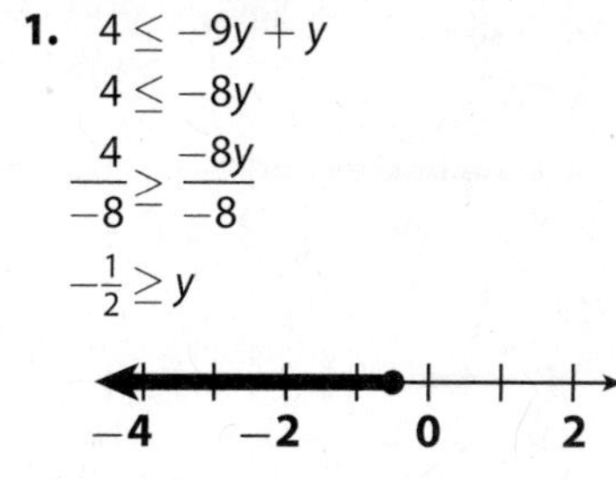

$4 \leq -9y + y$
$4 \leq -8y$
$\frac{4}{-8} \geq \frac{-8y}{-8}$
$-\frac{1}{2} \geq y$

2. $7 - 4x < -1$

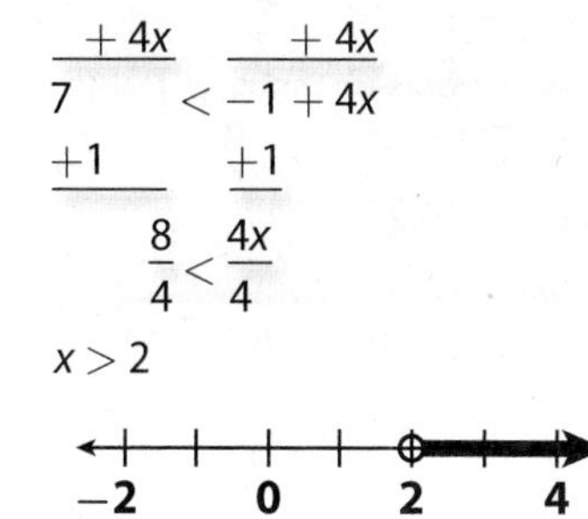

$\underline{+4x} \quad \underline{+4x}$
$7 < -1 + 4x$
$\underline{+1} \quad \underline{+1}$
$\frac{8}{4} < \frac{4x}{4}$
$x > 2$

3. $d > -3$

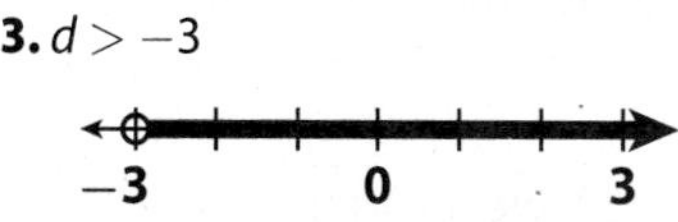

4. $k < -47$

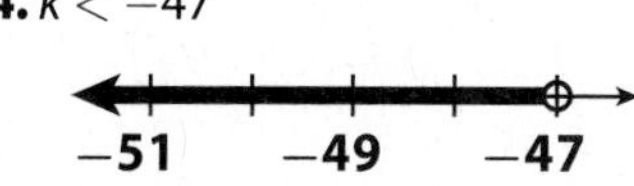

5. $m \geq 2$

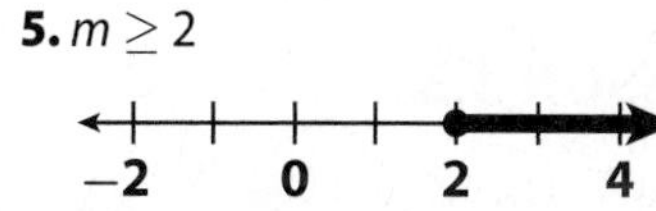

6. $a < -5$

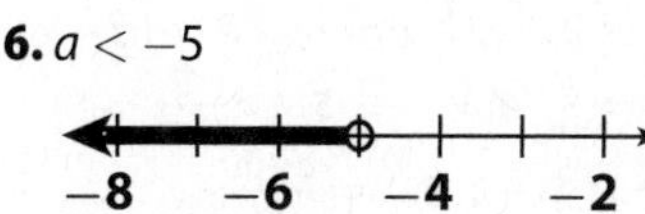

7. no solution

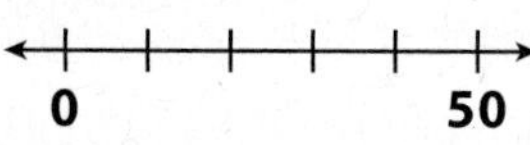

8. $y \geq -2$

9. 20.5 hours.

10. at least 94 points **11.** To solve an inequality in one variable, use the properties of inequality to undo operations to isolate the variable. When multiplying or dividing both sides of an inequality by a negative number, reverse the inequality symbol.

Independent Practice

13. $k < 0$

15. $m \leq 11$

17. $q \leq \frac{1}{2}$

19. $x > -10.25$

21. sometimes **23.** Fewer than 87 copies **25.** 18 gallons **27.** when the job takes 4 or more hours **29.** when the job takes 4 or more hours.

31. Sample answer:

$-\frac{1}{3}x < -12$

$(-3)(-\frac{1}{3}x) < (-3)(-12)$

$x > 36$

LESSON 3.3

Your Turn

1. $b = P - a - c$ or $b = P - (a + c)$

2. $h = \frac{V}{\pi r^2}$ **4.** $V = \frac{m}{D}$ **5.** $r = \frac{S}{2\pi h}$

7. $m = \frac{5}{2} - k$ **8.** $x = \frac{c+b}{a}$

9. $y = \frac{2x+14}{5}$ **10.** $s = \frac{3w}{4}$

Guided Practice

1. $t = \frac{d}{r}$ **2.** $l = \frac{V}{H}$ **3.** $h = \frac{SA - 2\pi r^2}{2\pi r}$

4. $h = \frac{2A}{a+b}$ **5.** $c = 3A - a - b$

6. $F = \frac{9}{5}C + 32$

7. You know the total cost and the item price and want to find the sales tax rate;

$s = \frac{T-p}{p}$ **8.** $x = \frac{c}{b}$ **9.** $p = \frac{q - kn}{m}$

10. $r = \frac{a-b}{b}$ **11.** $t = \frac{A-P}{Pr}$

12. $y = mx + b$ **13.** $p = \frac{mq}{n}$

14. You use the properties of equality to undo operations to isolate the variable.

Independent Practice

15. $h = \frac{V}{\pi r^2}$ **17.** $n = \frac{S}{180} + 2$

19. $w = \frac{3V}{lh}$ **21.** $C = \frac{5}{9}(F - 32)$

23. $m = \frac{2p}{2k-1}$ **25.** $s = \frac{v+t}{r-u}$

27. $h = \frac{1}{g} - \frac{2}{3}$

29. $A = \left(x \cdot \frac{1}{2}x\right) + (x \cdot x)$

$= \frac{3}{2}x^2$

Solve $A = \frac{3}{2}x^2$ for x; $x = \sqrt{\frac{2}{3}A}$.

31. 10 inches **33a.** $l = \frac{P - 2w}{2}$

b. 18 cm **35a.** $s = 0.07c + 600$, where c is the cost of his sales.

b. \$2000

MODULE 4

LESSON 4.1

Your Turn

1. No **2.** Yes **3.** No **4.** No

6.

x	$y = 20x + 15$	(x, y)
3	$y = 20(3) + 15$	(3, 75)
5	$y = 20(5) + 15$	(5, 115)
7	$y = 20(7) + 15$	(7, 155)
9	$y = 20(8) + 15$	(8, 175)

Cost of Party

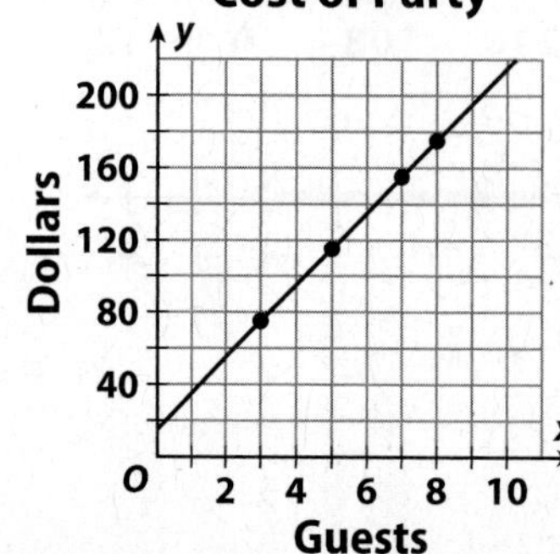

Guided Practice

1. $6(5) - 3(1) \stackrel{?}{=} 24$

$30 - 3 \stackrel{?}{=} 24$

$27 \stackrel{?}{=} 24$

(5, 1) is not a solution.

2. $6(0) - 3(-8) \stackrel{?}{=} 24$

$0 + 24 \stackrel{?}{=} 24$

$24 \stackrel{?}{=} 24$

(0, −8) is a solution.

3. Yes **4.** No **5.** No

6.

x	$4x - 6 = y$	(x, y)
−1	$4(-1) - 6 = y$	(−1, −10)
$-\frac{1}{2}$	$4\left(-\frac{1}{2}\right) - 6 = y$	$\left(-\frac{1}{2}, -8\right)$
0	$4(0) - 6 = y$	(0, −6)
2	$4(2) - 6 = y$	(2, 2)
4	$4(4) - 6 = y$	(4, 10)

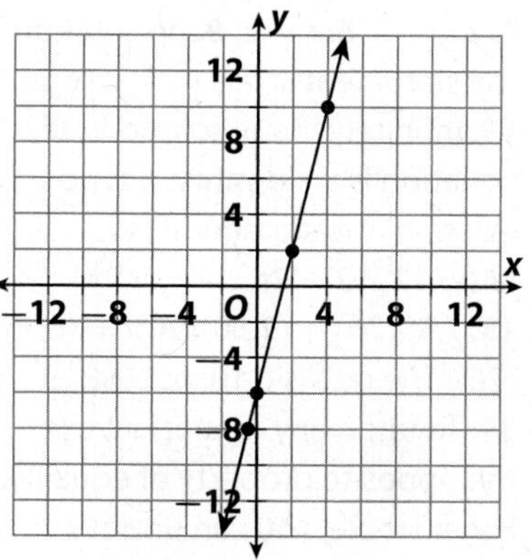

7.

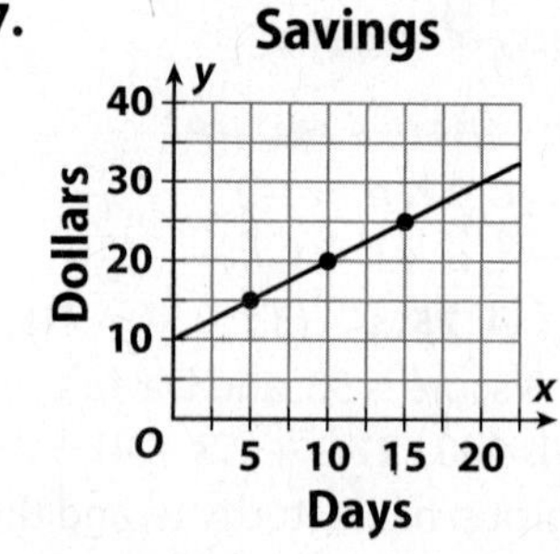

8. Every point on the graph is a solution of the linear equation.

Independent Practice

9. No;

$-5(4) + 2(8) \stackrel{?}{=} 4$

$-20 + 16 \stackrel{?}{=} 4$

$-4 \neq 4$

11. Yes;

$\frac{1}{3}(9) - 2(-2) \stackrel{?}{=} 7$

$3 + 4 \stackrel{?}{=} 7$

$7 = 7$

13a. Sample answer: (0, 200), (10, 120), (25, 0) **b.** Sample answer: (10, 120); this means that 10 seconds after the start of the race, Trish still has 120 meters left to run.

c. Sample answer: (10, 120);

$$8(10) + 120 \stackrel{?}{=} 200$$
$$200 = 200$$

d. Sample answer: (0, 0);

$$8(0) + 0 \stackrel{?}{=} 200$$
$$0 \neq 200$$

15. Sample answer: (100, 42); after 100 days, the pool has 42 m^3 of water left. **17.** He can plot a few points so that he can draw the line. He can then find other solutions by identifying the coordinates of other points on the line.

LESSON 4.2

Your Turn

2.

Ranking	Prize, in Dollars
1	60
2	40
3	20
4	10

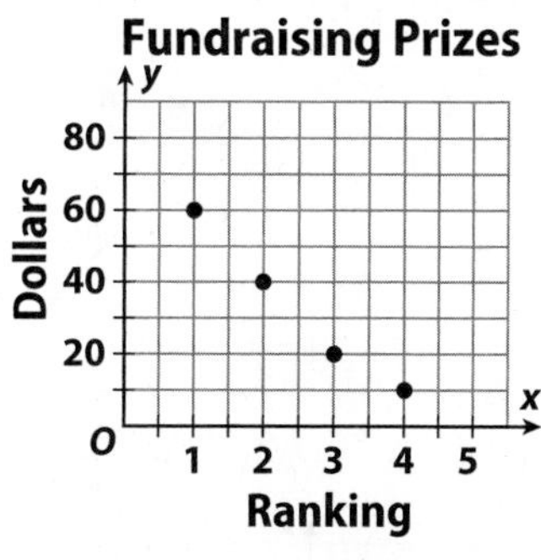

Ranking	Prize, in Dollars
1	→ 60
2	→ 40
3	→ 20
4	→ 10

4.

x	$f(x) = 4x + 6$	(x, y)
0	$f(0) = 6$	(0, 6)
2	$f(2) = 14$	(2, 14)
3	$f(3) = 18$	(3, 18)
5	$f(5) = 26$	(5, 26)

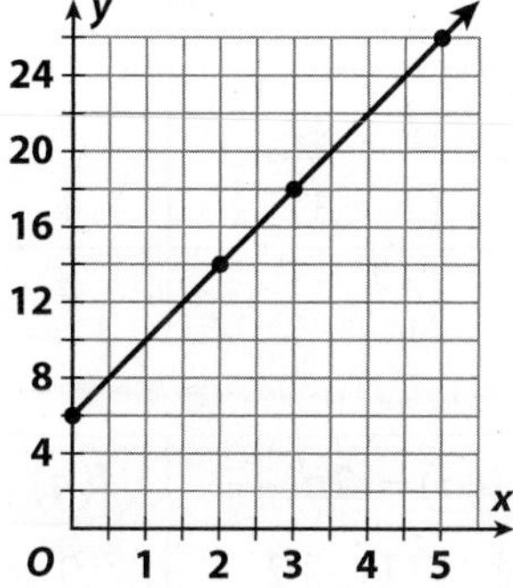

8. $x = 3$ **9.** $x = -1$

Guided Practice

1.

Domain	Range
0	−1
1	1
3	5

2.

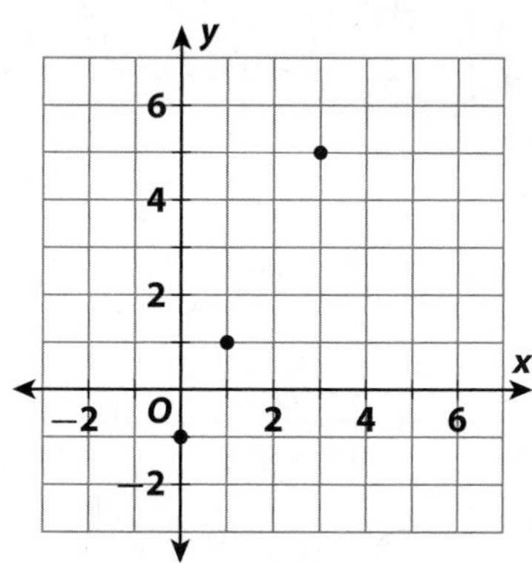

3. Domain Range

Domain	Range
0	→ −1
1	→ 1
3	→ 5

4.

x	$f(x) = 2x - 4$	(x, y)
−2	$f(-2) = 2(-2) - 4 = -8$	(−2, −8)
0	$f(0) = 2(0) - 4 = -4$	(0, −4)
2	$f(2) = 2(2) - 4 = 0$	(2, 0)
4	$f(4) = 2(4) - 4 = 4$	(4, 4)

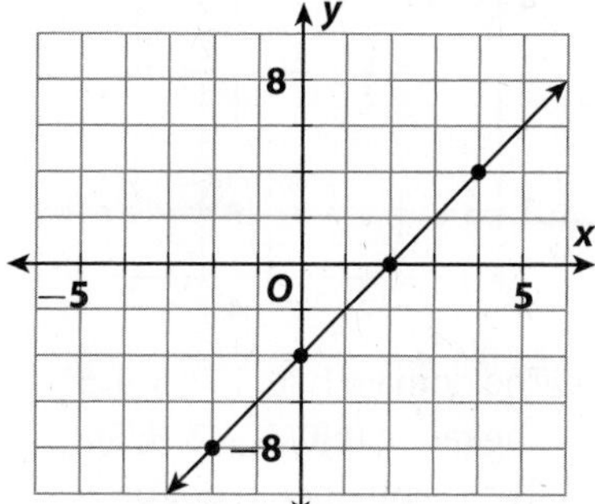

5. Step 1:

$$-2x + 4 = 2x - 8$$
$$\underline{+2x \quad = +2x}$$
$$4 = 4x - 8$$

Step 2:

$$4 = 4x - 8$$
$$\underline{+8 = \quad +8}$$
$$12 = 4x$$

Step 3:

$$\frac{12}{4} = \frac{4x}{4}$$
$$3 = x$$

The x-coordinate at the point of intersection is 3. So, $f(x) = g(x)$ when $x = 3$.

6.

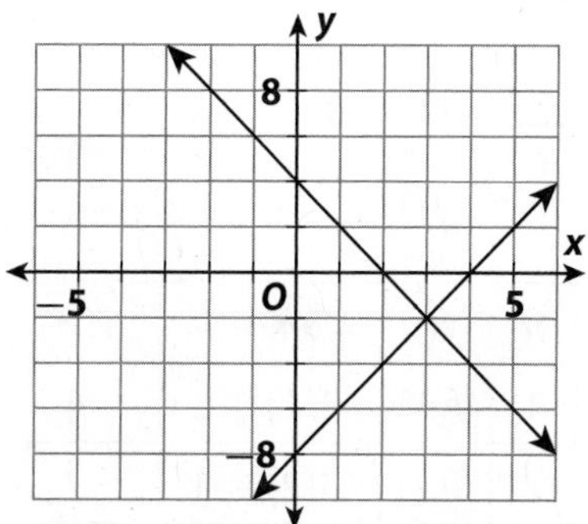

7. Functions can be represented by ordered pairs, mapping diagrams, tables, graphs, and equations.

Selected Answers

Independent Practice

9. No; each input is paired with two outputs.

11a.

x	0	1	2	3	4	5
$f(x)$	5	4	3	2	1	0

b.

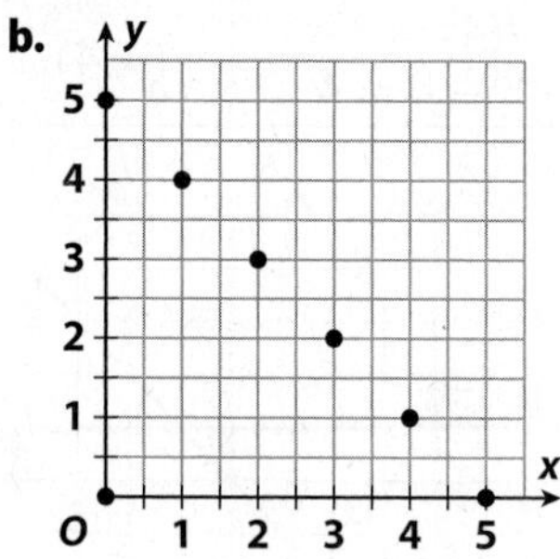

c. The domain is {0, 1, 2, 3, 4, 5}. The range is {0, 1, 2, 3, 4, 5}.
d. The points should not be connected because the x-values represent the number of downloaded songs, which will always be a whole number.
13a. $x = 15$; 15 months.
b. Find $f(15)$ and $g(15)$ and verify that they are equal. **c.** The graph of the two functions would look like two lines that intersect at (15, 52.5). **15.** No, Fred is not correct; $f(3) = 45(3) - 40$
$= 135 - 40 = \$95$
$g(3) = 85(3) - 110$
$= 255 - 110 = \$145$.
After 3 weeks, Fred has earned \$95, while George has earned \$145.

LESSON 4.3

Your Turn

6.

n	$f(n) = 3n + 1$	$f(n)$
1	$f(1) = 3(1) + 1$	4
2	$f(2) = 3(2) + 1$	7
3	$f(3) = 3(3) + 1$	10
4	$f(4) = 3(4) + 1$	13

4, 7, 10, and 13.

7. 240 **8.** 134
10. 37, 34, 31, 28, 25, 22, 19, 16

Guided Practice

1. $f(4) = 14$ **2.** $f(7) = 23$
3.

n	$f(n) = (n-1)^2$	$f(n)$
1	$(1-1)^2$	0
2	$(2-1)^2$	1
3	$(3-1)^2$	4
4	$(4-1)^2$	9

4.

n	$f(n) = 2n - 2$	$f(n)$
1	$2(1) - 2$	0
2	$4 - 2$	2
3	$6 - 2$	4
4	$8 - 2$	6

5.

n	$f(n)$
1	$3\frac{1}{2}$
2	4
3	$4\frac{1}{2}$
4	5

6. $f(25) = \frac{1}{2}25 + 3 = 15.5$
7. $f(25) = \frac{25-3}{11} = 2$
8. The first 4 terms are 2, 8, 14, and 20.

n	$f(n) = f(n-1)_6$	$f(n)$
1	1st term	2
2	$f(2-1) + 6 =$ $f(1) + 6$ $2 + 6 = 8$	8
3	$f(2) + 6 = 8 + 6$	14
4	$f(3) + 6 = 14 + 6$	20

9. Each position number n from the domain is associated with exactly one term $f(n)$ from the range.

Independent Practice

11. 4, 12, 24, 40 **13.** 1, 3, 7, 15
15. 6.2, 7.6, 4.8, 10.4
17. −6 **19.** 2048
21a. $f(1) = 185$, $f(n) = f(n-1) + 35$ for each positive whole number **b.** \$360
23. Explicit rule: $f(n) = -3(n-1) + 37$
Recursive rule: $f(1) = 37$, $f(n) = f(n-1) - 3$
25a. \$240 **b.** 8 months
29. Explicit rule: $f(n) = 2n$; Recursive rule: $f(1) = 2$ and $f(n) = f(n-1) + 2$ for each whole number greater than 1.
31. Sample answer: $f(1) = 5$ and $f(n) = f(n-1)$ for each whole number greater than 1.

MODULE 5

LESSON 5.1

Your Turn

4.

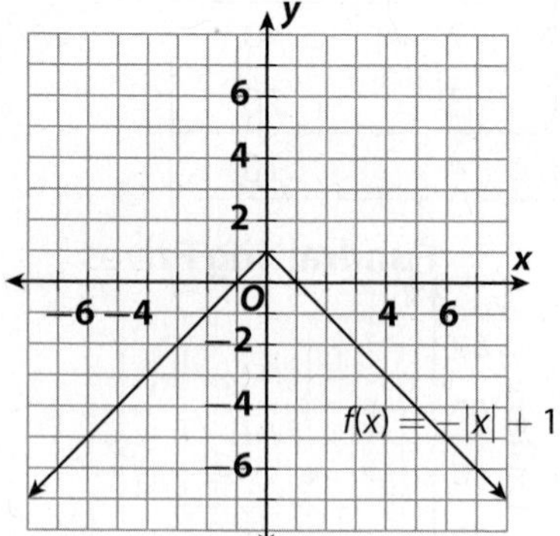

8.

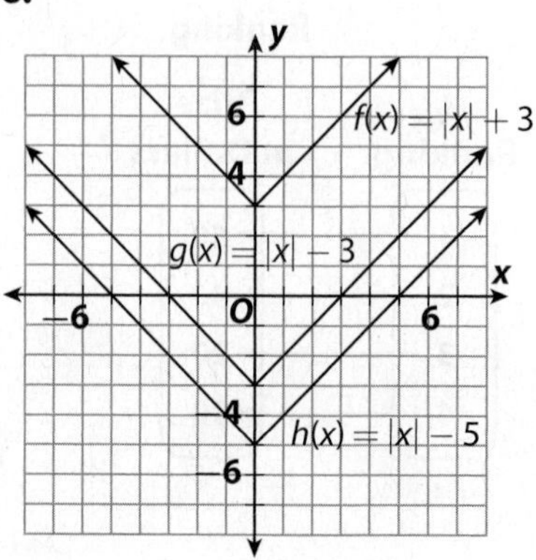

9.

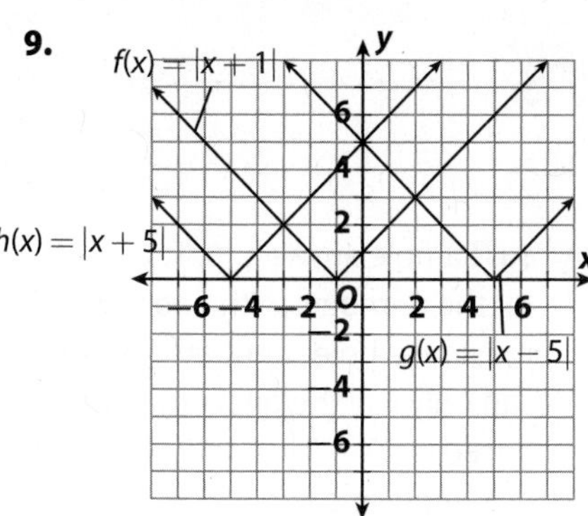

Guided Practice

1. and **2.**

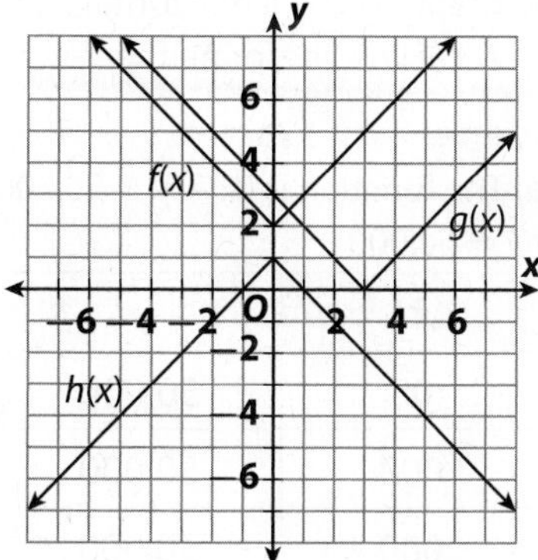

3. (0, 2), the set of all real numbers, $y \geq 2$

4. (3, 0), the set of all real numbers, $y \geq 0$

5. The graph of an absolute value function is composed of two rays that meet at a vertex. The graph is V-shaped and symmetrical about a vertical line passing through the vertex.

Independent Practice

7. $(-3, 0)$, the set of all real numbers y such that $y \geq 0$

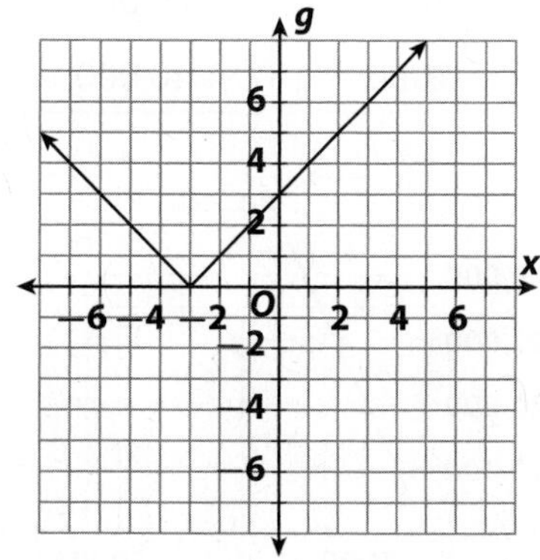

9.

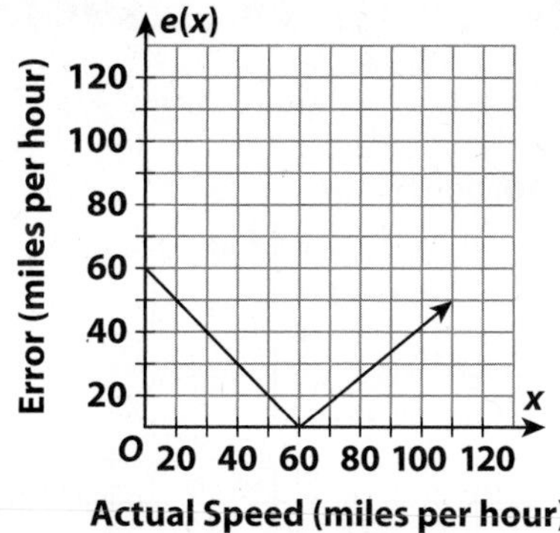

11. Sample answer: $a(x) = -|x| - 2$. Since the absolute value of x is nonnegative, $-|x| \leq 0$. So, $-|x| - 2 \leq -2$.

LESSON 5.2

Your Turn

4. $-7, 7$ **5.** $-5.5, 10.5$ **6.** no solution **7.** 4 **8.** $-3 \leq x \leq 3$
9. $x < -2$ or $x > 2$ **10.** $|x - 134| = 0.18$ min. height: 133.82 m; max. height: 134.18 m

Guided Practice

1. 3

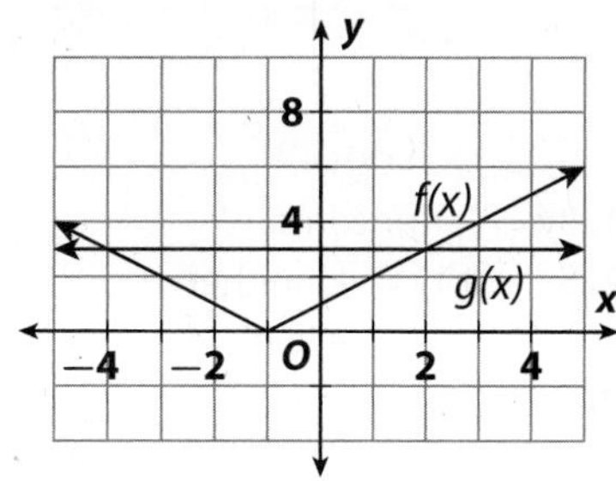

$-4, 2$

2. $2|x|$; 4

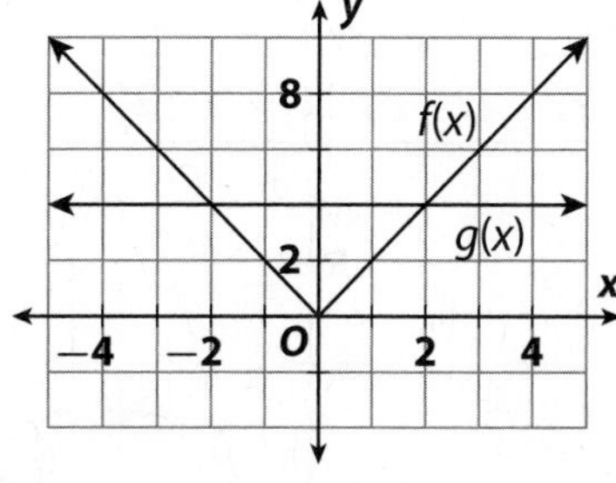

$-2, 2$

3. $-14, 4$ **4.** $-2, 2$ **5.** $-5, 11$
6. no solution **7.** -3
8. no solution **9.** $-2 \leq x \leq 2$
10. $x < -9$ or $x > 5$
11. $x \leq 1$ or $x \geq 5$
12. $|x - 207| = 2$; mile markers 205 and 209 **13.** Use inverse operations to isolate the absolute-value expression. Rewrite as zero, one, or two cases without absolute value expressions. Solve each case.

Independent Practice

15. $-5, 7$ **17.** 0 **19.** 1
21. $-15 \leq x \leq 13$ **23.** 8, -2
25. $|x - 1500| = 75$; 1575 bricks; 1425 bricks **27.** No; the acceptable range is from 64.9 inches to 65.3 inches
29. $|x - 175| \leq 12$; the actual temperature range is from 163 °F to 187 °F.

UNIT 3A Selected Answers

LESSON 6.1

Your Turn

5. linear

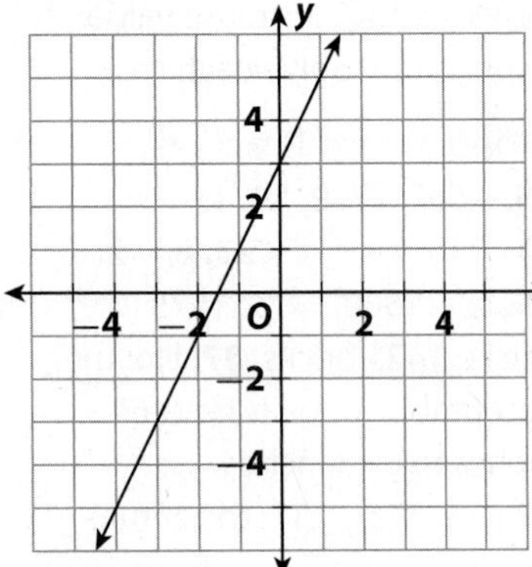

6. not linear

8. neither

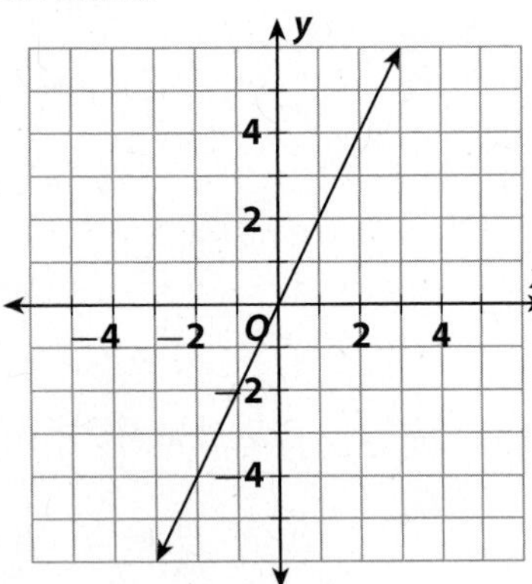

9. horizontal

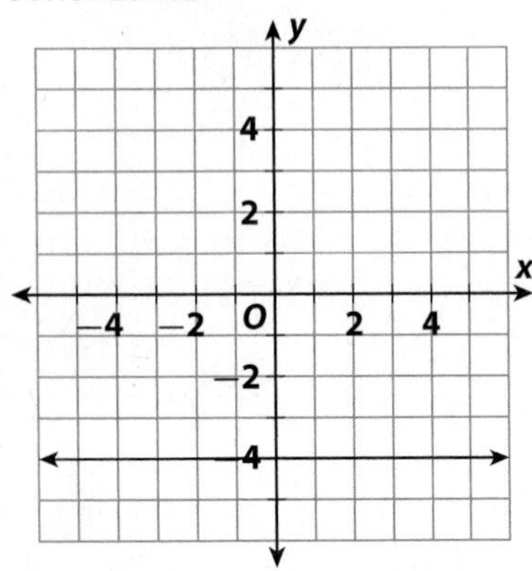

10. horizontal

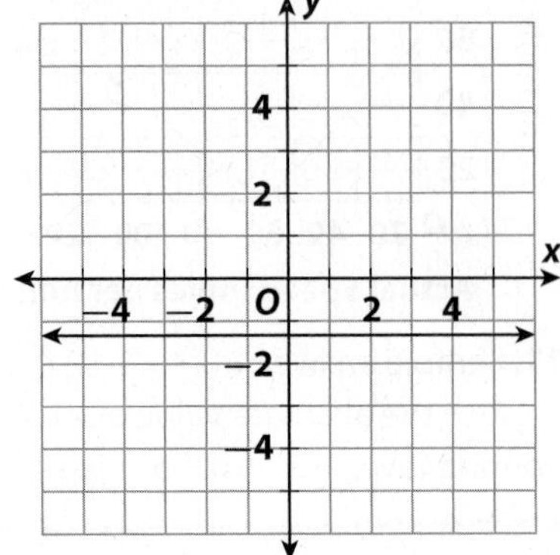

11. vertical

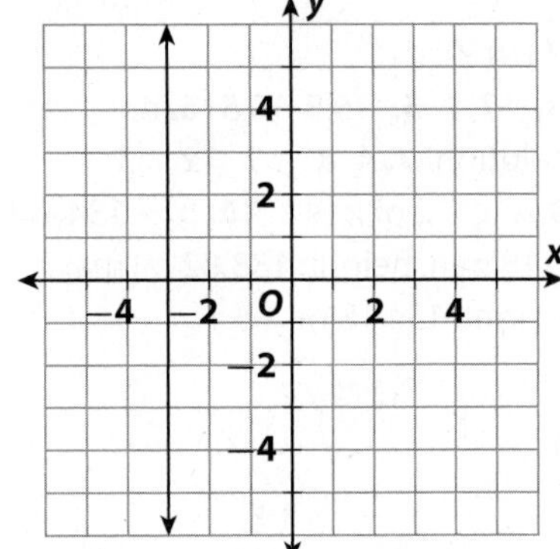

Guided Practice

1. $3y = 1$; horizontal

2. $5x + 0.1y = 4$; neither

3. $-\frac{1}{2}x = 14$; vertical

4.

x	y
0	−4
1	−1
2	2

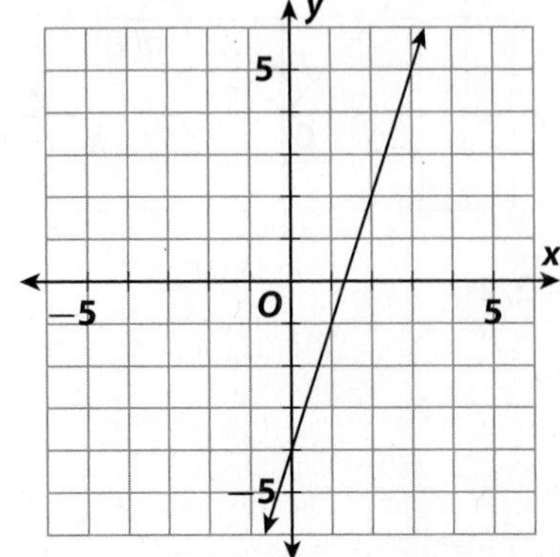

5a. Sample answer: {0, 1, 2, 3, 4, 5}; the numbers in the domain must be whole numbers. Andrea can only use the gift card 5 times, because $40 - 8(5) = 40 - 40 = 0$. **b.** Sample answer: {40, 32, 24, 16, 8, 0} **6.** If the equation is in standard form, then the coefficients can indicate whether the graph will be a horizontal line, a vertical line line, or neither.

Independent Practice

7a. The function is $0x + y = 50{,}000$ or $y = 50{,}000$.

x	y
0	50,000
1000	50,000
2000	50,000

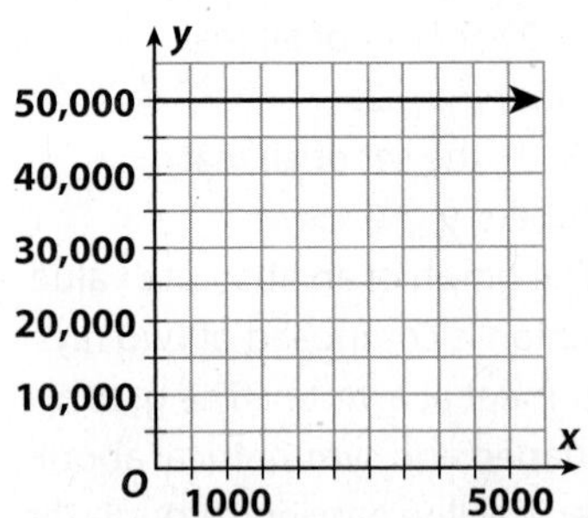

b. The function is $y = 20x$.

x	y
0	0
1000	20,000
2000	40,000

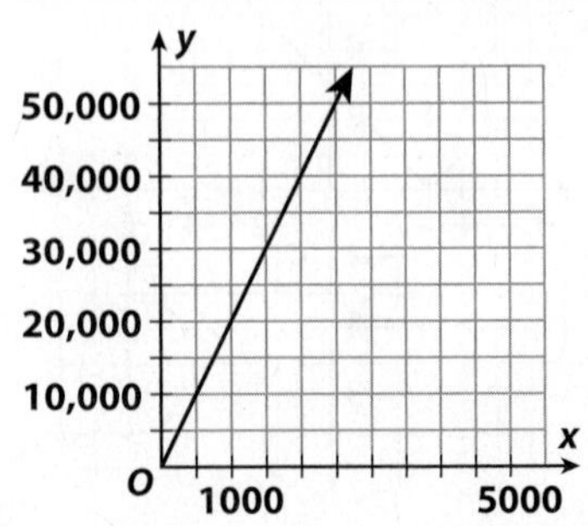

9. not a linear function **11.** linear function **13.** linear function **15.** Sample answer: The Johnsons have a $300,000 mortgage on their house. If they pay $1500 per month, the function representing their balance can be written as $M(n) = -300{,}000 + 1500n$, where n is the number of payments they have made. **17.** The student plotted the points incorrectly, interchanging the x- and y-coordinates.

LESSON 6.2

Your Turn

2. The x-intercept is -2. The y-intercept is 3.
3. The x-intercept is -10. The y-intercept is 6.
4a.

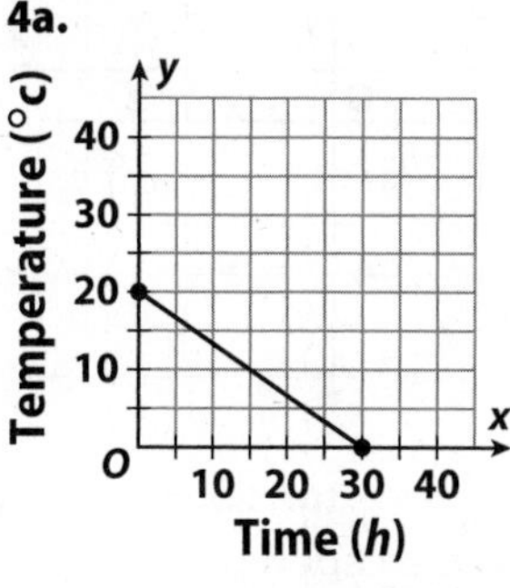

The x-intercept is 30. The y-intercept is 20. **b.** The x-intercept represents the number of hours that have elapsed when the temperature reaches 0 °C; the y-intercept, the temperature at the beginning of the experiment.
6.

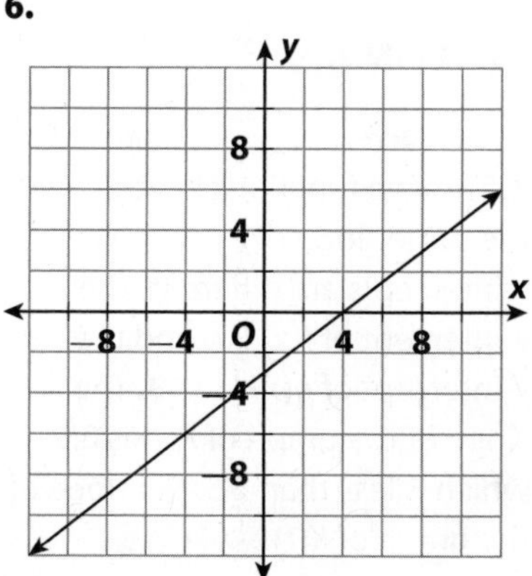

7.

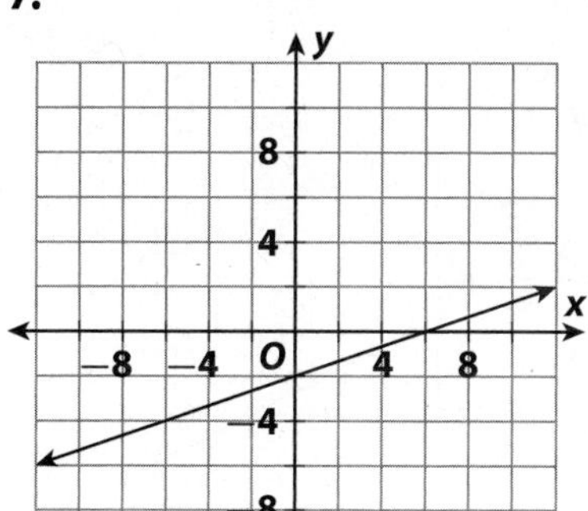

8. Sample answer: (2, 1) and (6, −1)

Guided Practice

1. The x-intercept is -5. The y-intercept is 1. **2.** The x-intercept is 2. The y-intercept is -4. **3.** The x-intercept is -3. The y-intercept is -2. **4.** The x-intercept is 2. The y-intercept is -1. **5.** The x-intercept is 2. The y-intercept is 3. **6.** The x-intercept is 2. The y-intercept is 8.
7.

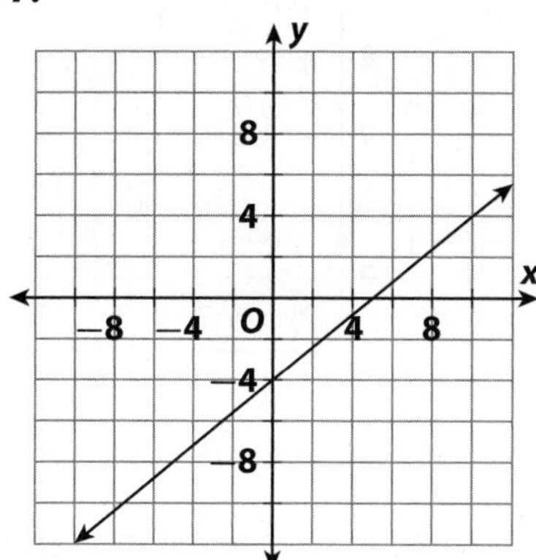

8.

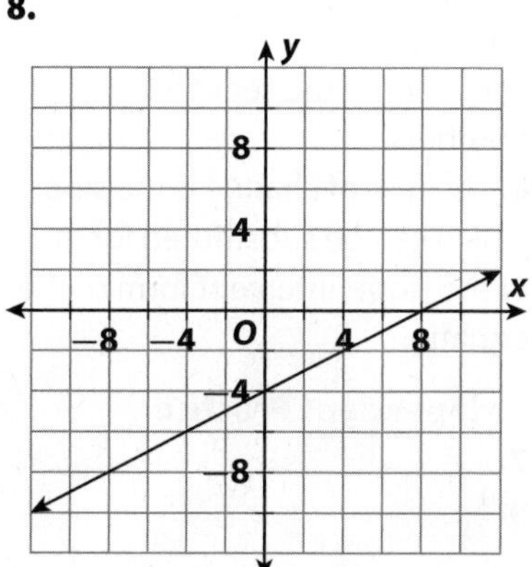

9. The x-intercept is the x-coordinate of the point where the graph crosses the x-axis. The y-intercept is the y-coordinate of the point where the graph crosses the y-axis. They can be used to graph linear equations.

Independent Practice

11a.

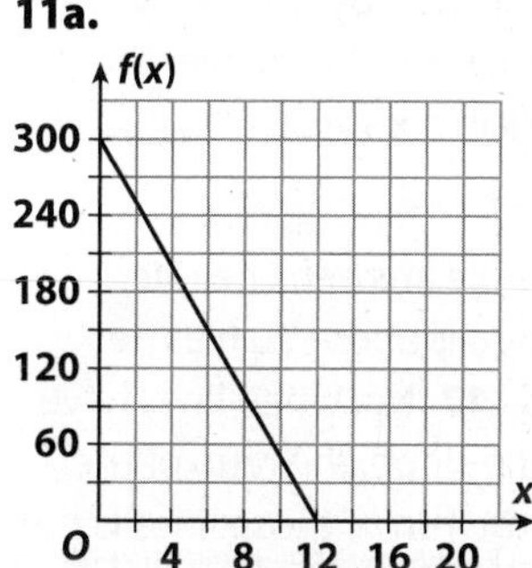

The x-intercept is 12. The y-intercept is 300. **b.** The x-intercept represents the amount of time it takes for the population to reach 0 fish; the y-intercept represents the population at the beginning of the stocking process, when time was 0 years.
13. Sample answer: Bridget jogs across a field that is 60 yards wide. It takes her 5 seconds to reach the other side of the field. The distance from the other side of the field after x seconds is represented by y. **15.** $f(x) = 15 - 0.04x$; the x-intercept is 375 and it represents the distance that Kirsten can drive on 15 gallons of gas; the y-intercept is 15 and it represents the number of gallons of gas in the car when Kirsten left home.

LESSON 6.3

Your Turn

2. $-\frac{2}{5}$ **4.** $\frac{1}{2}$; positive **6.** 32; the slope of 32 means that the car was traveling at the rate 32 miles per hour.

Guided Practice

1. −3 **2.** 2 **3.** $\frac{1}{2}$ **4a.** −3 gallons per hour; −2 gallons per hour **b.** The difference in the rates of change shows that on average, the fuel was used more slowly between hours 1 and 3 than between hours 0 and 1. **5.** negative **6.** undefined **7.** zero **8.** positive **9.** For a linear relationship, rate of change and slope are the same. Both are given by the ratio of the difference in *y*-values over the difference in *x*-values.

Independent Practice

11. Sample answer: The rate of change is about 20 files per second. **13.** No; when lines have the same slope, the ratio of the rise to the run of those lines is the same. The lines are not necessarily in the same location.

LESSON 6.4

Your Turn

1. $-\frac{3}{4}$

4.

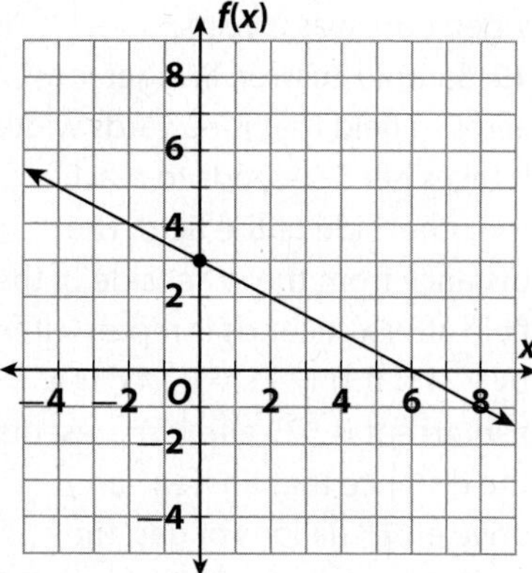

5.

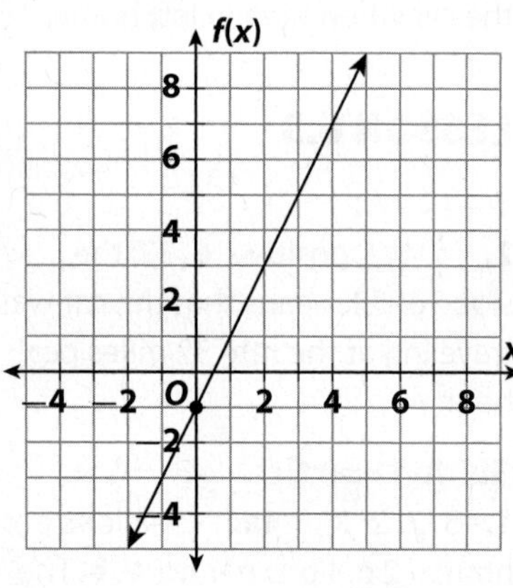

7.

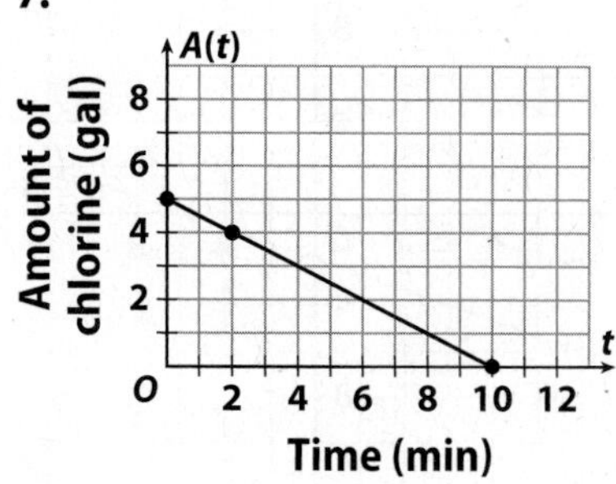

$A(t) = -\frac{1}{2}t + 5$

Domain: the set of all real numbers t such that $0 \leq t \leq 10$

Range: the set of all real numbers $A(t)$ such that $0 \leq A(t) \leq 5$

Guided Practice

1. $\frac{5}{2}$ **2.** 0 **3.** $\frac{1}{3}$ **4.** -2 **5.** The *y*-intercept is 3. Plot the point (0, 3). The slope is -2. Use -2 as the rise; then the run is 1. Begin by moving down 2 units. Then move right 1 unit. Plot the second point, (1, 1).

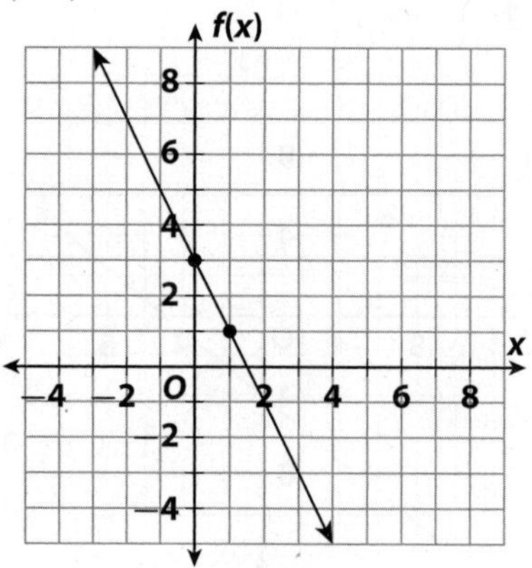

The domain is the set of real numbers.

The range is the set of real numbers.

6. The rate of change is the slope, which can be substituted for *m* in the slope-intercept form of the equation.

Independent Practice

7. $-\frac{5}{3}$

9. $\frac{1}{2}$

11.

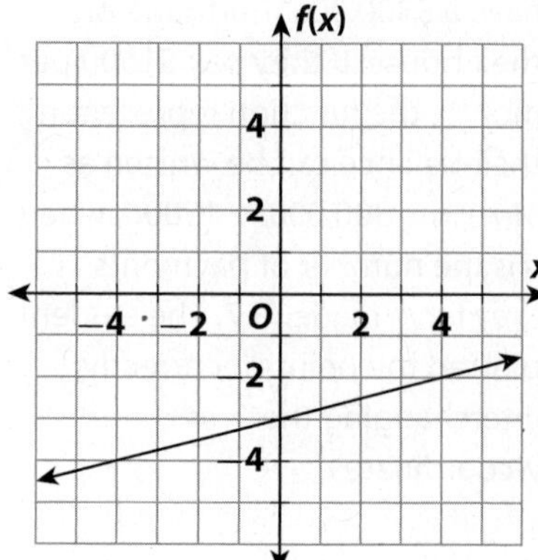

13.

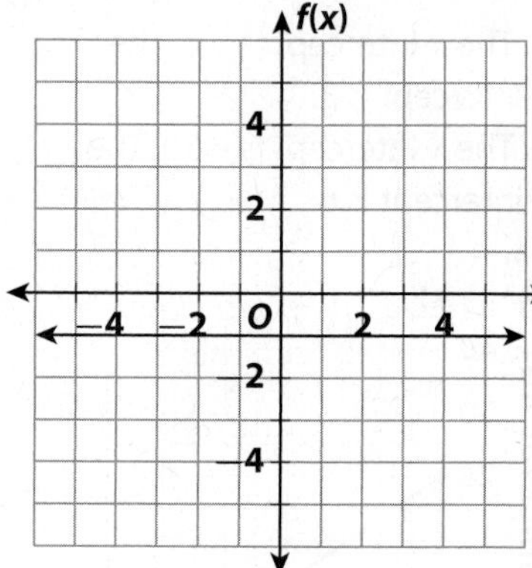

15. $y = -\frac{A}{B}x + \frac{C}{B}$; the slope is $-\frac{A}{B}$; the *y*-intercept is $\frac{C}{B}$.

17. Sample answer: Alyssa found the correct slope and substituted it for *m* in the equation $y = mx + b$. However, she substituted the *x*-intercept, 6, for *b* instead of the *y*-intercept, 2. The correct equation is $y = -\frac{1}{3}x + 2$.

LESSON 6.5

Your Turn

2. The two functions have the same slope (2), but their *y*-intercepts are different. The *y*-intercept of $f(x)$ is 0 and the *y*-intercept of $g(x)$ is 3. **3.** The slope of the graph of $A(t)$ is 0.5, which is less than 2.5, the slope of the graph of $K(t)$.

Guided Practice

1. Domain of $f(x)$: the set of all real numbers from 0 to 5

Domain of $g(x)$: the set of all real numbers from 0 to 5
Initial value of $f(x)$: -2
Initial value of $g(x)$: -2
Range of $f(x)$: the set of all real numbers from -2 to 13
Range of $g(x)$: the set of all real numbers from -2 to 18
2. 2.5 inches per hour; 2 more inches per hour **3.** Plot the ordered pairs in the table to convert the representation to a graph. Then you can compare the slopes and intercepts of the two graphs.

Independent Practice

5a. Domain of $f(x)$: the set of all real numbers x such that $-1 \leq x \leq 2$
Range of $f(x)$: the set of all real numbers $f(x)$ such that $-2 \leq f(x) \leq 7$
Domain of $g(x)$: the set of all real numbers x such that $-2 \leq x \leq 3$
Range of $g(x)$: the set of all real numbers $g(x)$ such that $-5 \leq g(x) \leq 5$ **b.** For $f(x)$, the slope is -3, and the y-intercept is 4. For $g(x)$, the slope is 2, and the y-intercept is -1. **7.** For a line segment with a negative slope, the initial value wil! be the greatest value in the range. The least value in the range will be paired with the greatest value in the domain.

LESSON 6.6

Your Turn

10. The graph will have the same slope, but it will intersect the vertical axis at $(0, 0)$.

Guided Practice

1. Sample answer:

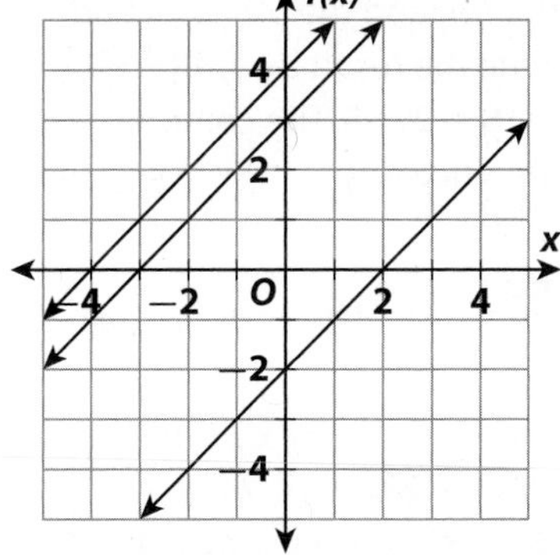

2. Sample answer:

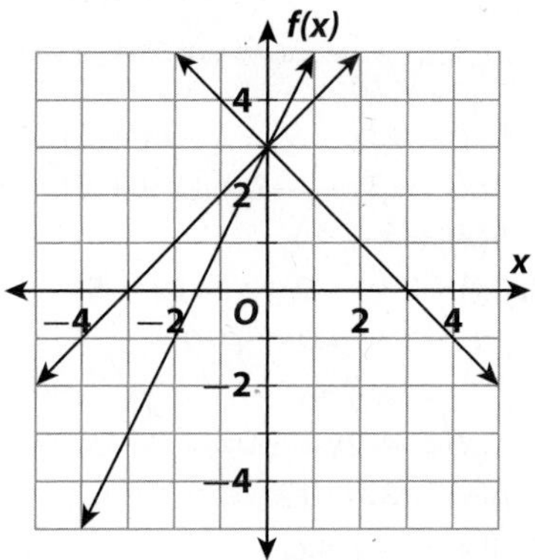

3. m. **4a.** green **b.** blue **c.** red **d.** purple **5.** As b increases or decreases, the y-intercept of the graph increases or decreases. As $|m|$ increases, the graph gets steeper, as $|m|$ decreases, the graph gets less steep.

Independent Practice

7a. Sample answer:

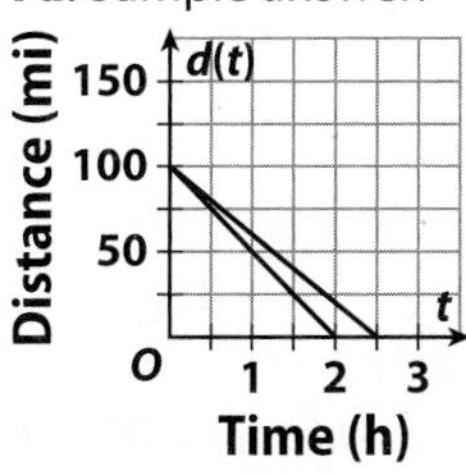

b. Sample answer:

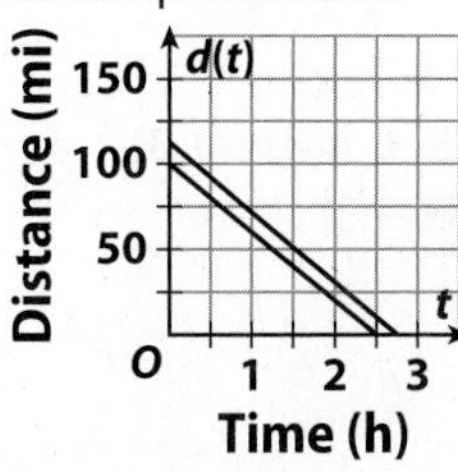

c. Sample answer: $d(t) = 150 - 40t$; In this function, 150 represents the initial distance he has to travel, and -40 means that the distance from his destination is decreasing at 40 miles per hour.
9a. black line: $m = -\frac{1}{2}, b = 2$
b. blue line: $m = \frac{1}{3}, b = -3$
c. green line: $m = 2, b = \frac{1}{2}$
11. Marcus is correct. Unless the y-intercept is the same as the x-intercept, which can only happen when both are 0, changing the value of m while leaving b unchanged will cause the x-intercept to change.
13. Stephanie is correct. The graph of $y = 3x + 2$ is a vertical translation up 4 units of the graph of $y = 3x - 2$, so the two graphs are parallel.

LESSON 6.7

Your Turn

2. $f(x) = 4x - 2$ **3.** $f(x) = -3x + 5$
4. $f(x) = 6x$ **5.** $f(x) = 6$
7. $f(x) = 5x + 1$ **8.** $f(x) = -2x - 1$
9. $f(x) = \frac{1}{2}x - 3$ and $f(0) = -3$

Guided Practice

1. $f(x) = -\frac{3}{2}x + 1$ **2.** $f(x) = \frac{1}{2}x + 7$
3. $f(x) = -2x + 3$ **4.** You can use two points to determine the slope and then solve for the y-intercept to write the function. If the slope and the y-intercept are clear from the graph, you can write the function directly from them.

Independent Practice

5. $f(x) = -\frac{2}{3}x + 5$ **7.** $f(x) = \frac{3}{2}x - 3$
9. $f(x) = 2x - 1$ **11a.** The slope is 25. The y-intercept is 140.
b. $s(w) = 25w + 140$ **c.** Substitute 415 for $s(w)$ and solve for w; It will take 11 weeks. **13.** Both are; $y = 2x - 3$ can be rewritten as $2x - y = 3$ **15.** Andrew substituted the value of the x-intercept instead of the value of the y-intercept. He needs to find the value of the y-intercept. The function is $f(x) = 3x + 6$.

UNIT 3A Selected Answers *(cont'd)*

MODULE 7

LESSON 7.1

Your Turn

1. recursive rule: $f(1) = 35$, $f(n) = f(n-1) + 12$ for $n \geq 2$; explicit rule: $f(n) = 35 + 12(n-1)$.
2. recursive rule: $f(1) = 20$, $f(n) = f(n-1) + 5$, for $n \geq 2$; explicit rule: $f(n) = 20 + 5(n-1)$
3. $f(n) = 20 + 15(n-1)$

Guided Practice

1. $f(1) = 6$,
$f(n) = f(n-1) + 1$ for $n \geq 2$
$f(n) = 6 + n - 1$
2. $f(1) = 3$, $f(n) = f(n-1) + 4$, for $n \geq 2$; $f(n) = 3 + 4(n-1)$.
3. $f(n) = 38 + 12(n-1)$ **4.** You need to know the first term, $f(1)$, and the common difference, d.

Independent Practice

5. recursive rule: $f(1) = 27$, $f(n) = f(n-1) - 3$, for $n \geq 2$; explicit rule: $f(n) = 27 - 3(n-1)$.
7. recursive rule: $f(1) = 9$, $f(n) = f(n-1) + 15$, for $n \geq 2$; explicit rule: $f(n) = 9 + 15(n-1)$.
9. recursive rule: $f(1) = 1$, $f(n) = f(n-1) + 1.5$, for $n \geq 2$; explicit rule: $f(n) = 1 + 1.5(n-1)$.
11. The fourth term is 10; the fortieth term is 118.
13. Write the general rule as $f(n) = f(1) + d(n-1)$. Substitute 4 for $f(1)$ and 10 for d to solve: $f(6) = 4 + 10(6-1)$ so $f(6) = 54$.
15. No; Cindy wrote an incorrect explicit rule. The correct rule is $f(n) = 0.46 + 0.20(n-1)$, and the cost of a 6-ounce letter is \$1.46. **17.** The difference between the 7th term and the 5th term will be twice the common difference. Find the difference between the 7th term and the 5th term and divide the result by 2. $48 - 32 = 16$; $16 \div 2 = 8$. The common difference is 8.

LESSON 7.2

Your Turn

2. $h(x) = 2x + 6$; $j(x) = 4x + 2$
5. $h(x) = 28x - 14$ **6.** $h(x) = -6x + 33$ **7.** $h(x) = 7x - 4$
9. $f(t) = 9 + 3t$ **11.** $c(x) = 14 + 1.75x$

Guided Practice

1. $h(x) = (3x + 9) + (-2x + 5)$
$h(x) = (3x + -2x) + (9 + 5)$
$h(x) = x + 14$
2. $j(x) = (3x + 9) - (-2x + 5)$
$j(x) = (3x + 2x) + (9 - 5)$
$j(x) = 5x + 4$
3. $h(x) = 4(2x + 3)$
$h(x) = 8x + 12$
4. $h(x) = -2(4x - 1)$
$h(x) = -8x + 2$
5. $f(x) = 195 - 5x$
6. $g(x) = 90 + 6x$ **7.** The equation for the sum or difference of the functions is the sum or difference of the equations for the original functions.

Independent Practice

9. $h(x) = 22x + 4$ **11.** $h(x) = 6x + 2$
13. $h(x) = 5x + 1$
15. $h(x) = -8x + 12$
17a. $R(t) = 2t - 500$
b. $D(t) = 10t + 400$ **c.** $T(t) = R(t) + D(t)$, $T(t) = 12t - 100$
19a. $r(x) = 7 + 10x$
b. $h(x) = 82 - 5x$ **c.** $b(x) = 89 + 5x$
d. \$109 **e.** \$124
21a. $f(x) = -2x + 3$, $g(x) = 3x - 2$ **b.** $h(x) = x + 1$, $j(x) = -5x + 5$ **c.** $h(3) > j(3)$
25. $g(x) = -3x - 3$

LESSON 7.3

Your Turn

2.

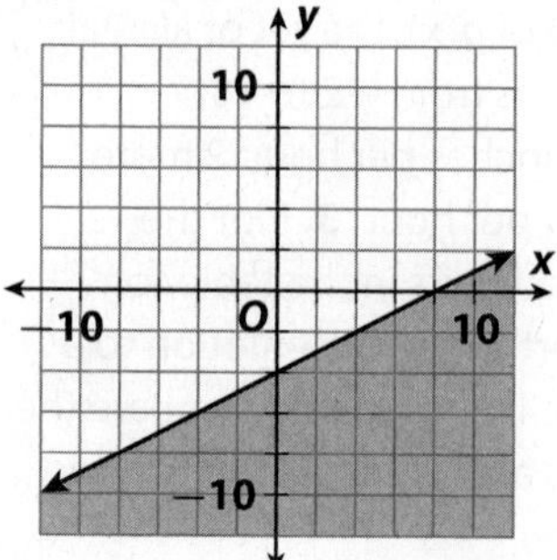

5.

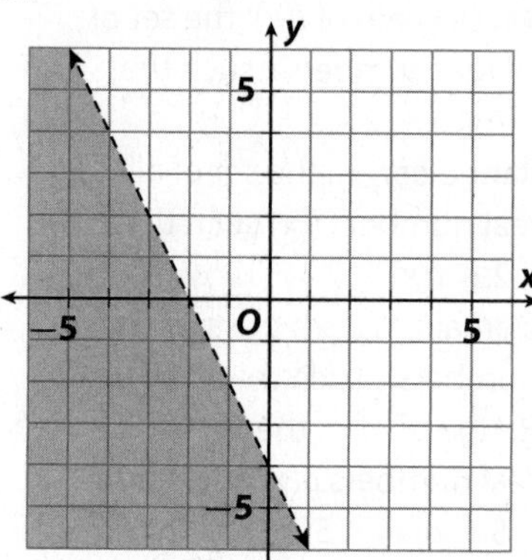

7. Let the amount of dry food equal x and the amount of wet food equal y. This gives us $4.50x + 1.50y \leq 15.00$.
8.

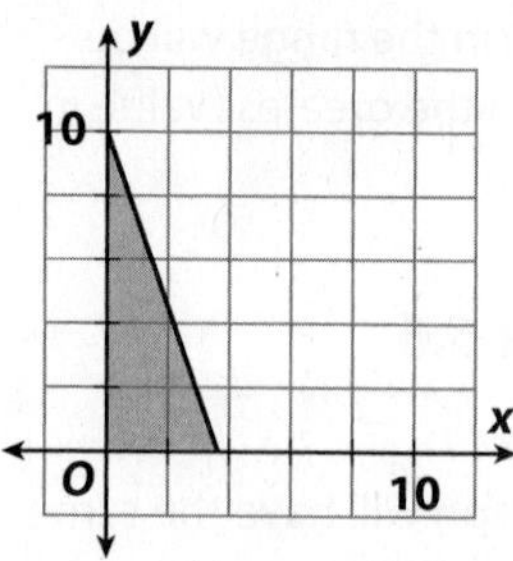

9. Sample answer: 1 bag of dry food and 6 cans of wet food; 2 bags of dry food and 4 cans of wet food

Guided Practice

1. $4y + 3x - y > -6x + 12$

$\underline{-3x} \quad \underline{-3x}$

$4y - y > -9x + 12$

$3y > -9x + 12$

$y > -3x + 4$

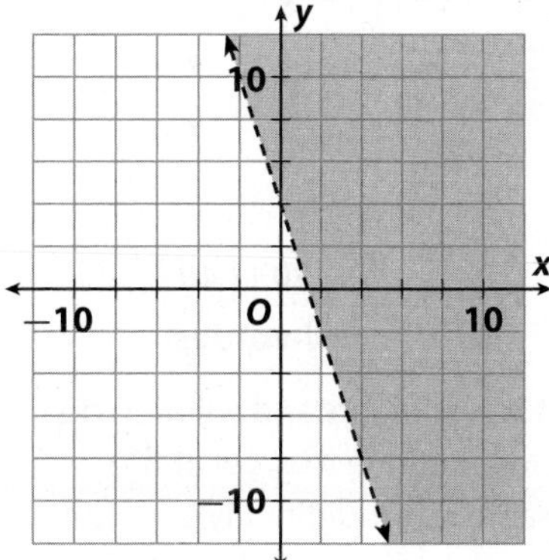

2. $5y + 3 < 2x$

$\underline{-3} \quad \underline{-3}$

$5y < 2x - 3$

$y < \frac{2}{5}x - \frac{3}{5}$

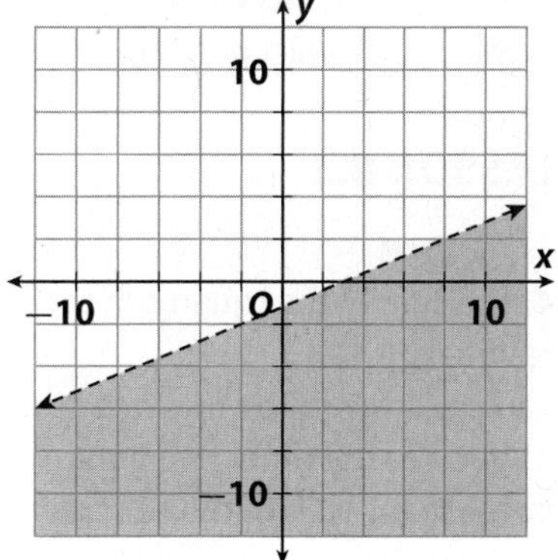

3. $15x + 20y \leq 140$ **4.** $y \leq 7 - \frac{3}{4}x$

5.

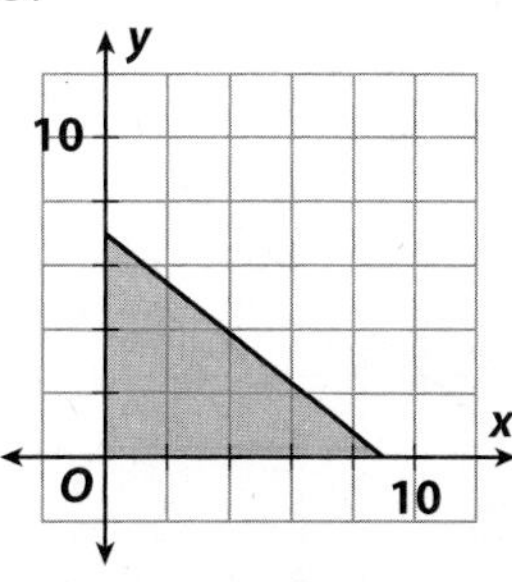

6. Sample answer: 4 chairs and 2 tables, or 2 chairs and 4 tables

7. Graph the related linear equation as a dashed or solid boundary line, and shade the appropriate half-plane containing solutions.

Independent Practice

9.

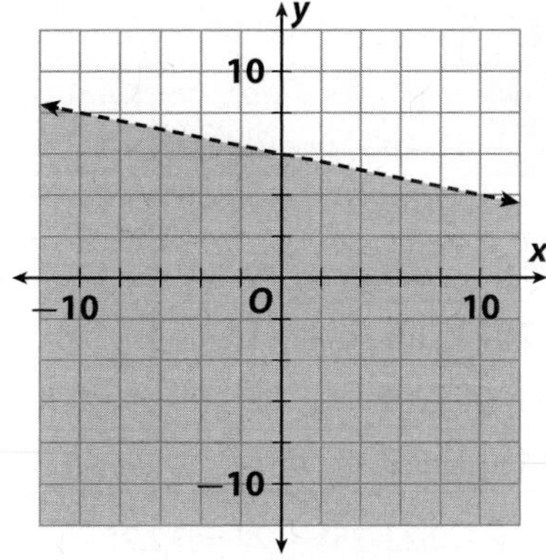

11a. $x + 12y \leq 60$ **b.** Subtract x from both sides. Then divide both sides by 12.

$y \leq 5 - \frac{1}{12}x$

c.

Point	Inequality	True? False?
(6, 4)	$(6) + 12(4) = 54 \leq 60$	True
(8, 5)	$(8) + 12(5) = 68 \leq 60$	False

d. Sandra can purchase 6 songs and 4 albums. **e.** No, because Sandra cannot buy a negative number of songs.

13a. $2.25x + 0.75y \leq 16.00$

b. They can travel $12\frac{1}{3}$ miles; substitute 3 for x in the inequality and solve for y to get $y \leq 12\frac{1}{3}$.

c. 3 passengers; substituting 10 for y in the inequality gives $x \leq 3\frac{7}{9}$. Since the number of passengers has to be a whole number, at most 3 friends can ride in the taxi.

15. No; when you solve this equation for y, you must divide both sides of the equation by a negative number, which reverses the inequality symbol.

$y \leq -2 + \left(\frac{2}{3}\right)x$, so you must shade below the line.

LESSON 8.1

Your Turn

3. Positive correlation: the number of participants is increasing over time. **4.** Close to 1; the data shown a strong positive correlation between year and number of participants.

5. Variables: time spent on Algebra homework and time spent on Biology homework; positive correlation. It is unlikely that one variable causes the other. The time spent on both subjects might be influenced by other common factors.

Guided Practice

1.

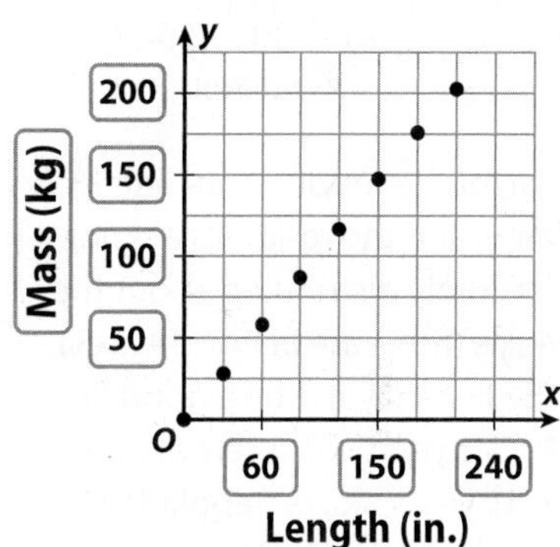

x value: length in inches, y value: mass in kg **2.** strong positive correlation; as the length increased the mass increased

3. 1 **4.** It could be. As the dolphin got bigger, it most likely required more food. However, there may be a lurking variable that caused this effect as well. **5.** You can decide whether two variables have positive, negative, or no correlation by making a scatter plot. You can describe the strength of the correlation with a correlation coefficient.

UNIT 3A Selected Answers *(cont'd)*

Independent Practice

7. weak positive correlation; 0.5
9. no correlation, 0 **11.** negative correlation, −1 **13.** The number of ocelots in 2014 will probably be somewhere between 26 and 28.

LESSON 8.2

Your Turn

6.

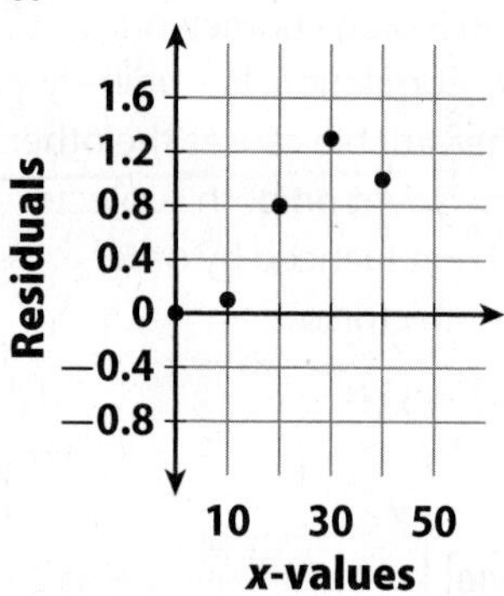

Two of the residuals are relatively large, and the residuals are not randomly distributed about the x-axis (none are below the axis). The line may not be a good fit.
8. 33.8 years old; interpolation
9. 42 years old; extrapolation

Guided Practice

1.

x	0	10	20	30	40
y	26.8	28.8	31.6	34.0	35.5

2.

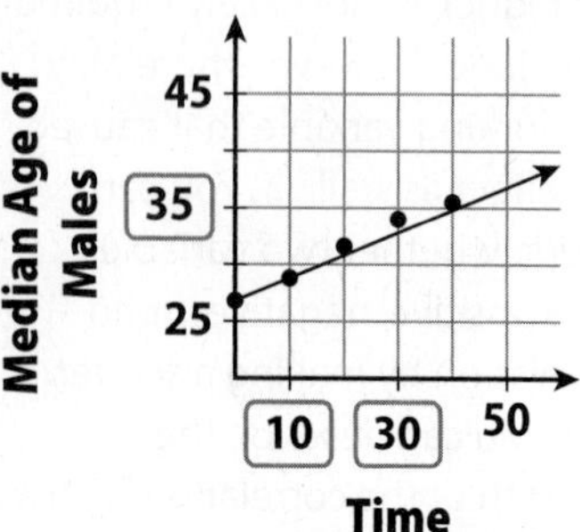

3. Sample answer: $y = 0.17x + 28.3$

4.

x	y actual	y predicted	Residual
0	26.8	27.0	−0.2
10	28.8	29.3	−0.5
20	31.6	31.6	0
30	34.0	33.9	0.1
40	35.5	36.2	−0.7

5. $y + 0.23(25) + 27 \approx 32.75$
6. interpolation **7.** Make a scatter plot of the data, find the equation of a line of fit, and use residuals to evaluate the quality of fit.

Independent Practice

9.

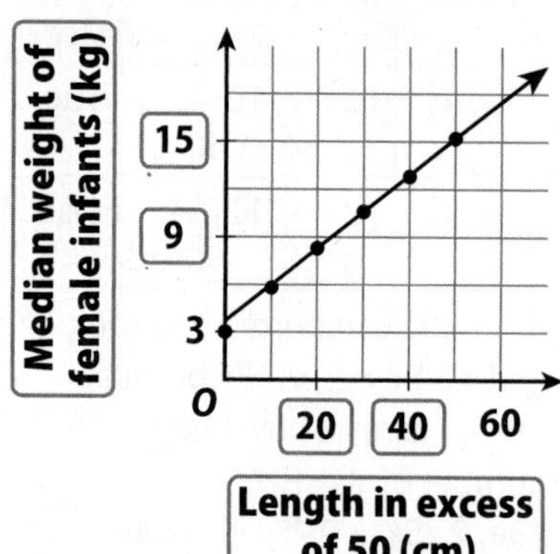

11. Sample answer: The residuals for $w = 0.238l + 3.4$:

w predicted	Residual
3.4	0
5.78	0.02
8.16	0.14
10.54	0.06
12.92	−0.12
15.3	−0.1

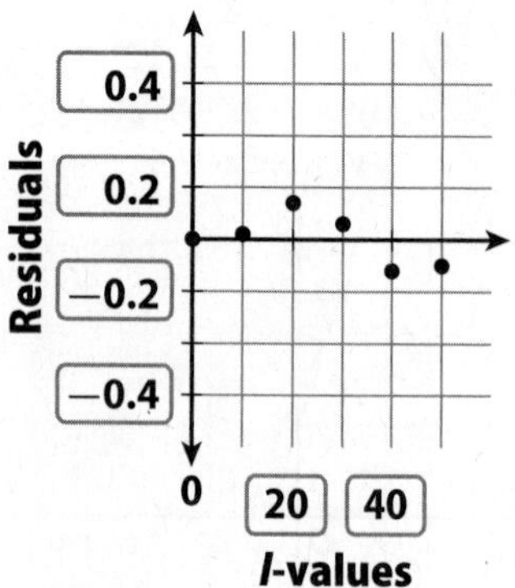

13. No. Infants and children do not continue to grow at the same rate indefinitely, so it is not reasonable to use the data for infants to predict the weight of a much larger child.
15. The line of fit would be shifted up by 0.2 kg; it would have the same slope, but its y-intercept would be 0.2 units greater.

LESSON 8.3

Your Turn

4. The sum of the squares of the residuals = 19.
Sample answer: The fit is not as good as the other two lines because the sum of the squares of the residuals is greater than the sums for those lines. **6.** $\approx 5.8°C$

Guided Practice

1.

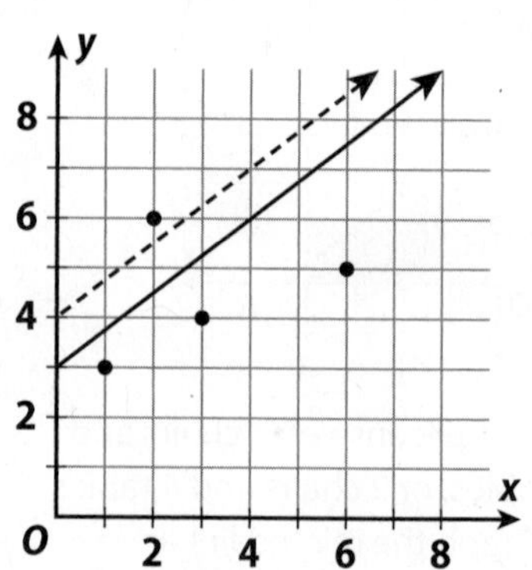

x	1	2	3	6
y	3	6	4	5
y predicted by $y = \frac{3}{4}x + 3$	3.75	4.5	5.25	7.5
Residual	−0.75	1.5	−1.25	−2.5
Squared residual	0.56	2.25	1.56	6.25

5. 10.62 **6.** Sum = 20.62. The original line was a better fit. The sum of its squared residuals was 10.62 compared to 20.62 for the new line. **7.** $y = 0.2143x + 3.857$ **8.** Enter the numerical data as lists using the STAT function and perform a linear regression on the data using the LinReg function.

Independent Practice

9a. The independent variable is year, and the dependent variable is distance. **b.** years: L1, 0, 4, 8; distance: L2, 44.685, 46.155, 47.32 **c.** The calculator expresses the slope as 0.34611403508772, the y-intercept as 44.63349122807, and the correlation coefficient (r) as 0.98956637439792. The best fit equation for the data set is $y \approx 0.346x + 44.63$. **d.** The equation written for this data was a very good fit. The value of r was close to 1, meaning that the data points are very close to the line. **e.** 1940: 51.6 meters; 1944: 52.9 meters **f.** Less; The best fit line predicts that the 2012 winner would have a distance of 76.5 meters. Harting was considerably below this mark.

MODULE 9

LESSON 9.1

Your Turn

1. (5, 3)

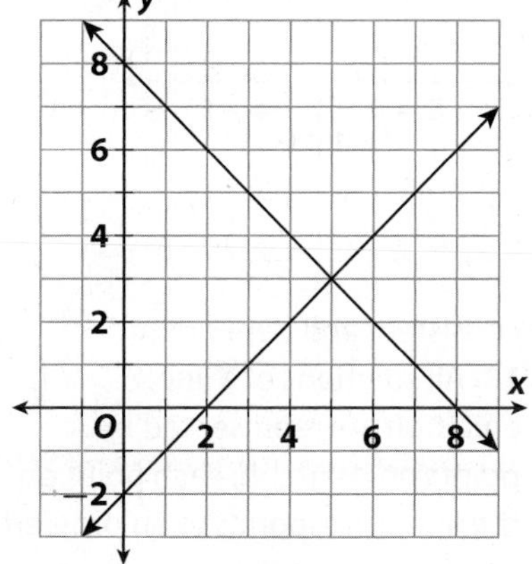

3.

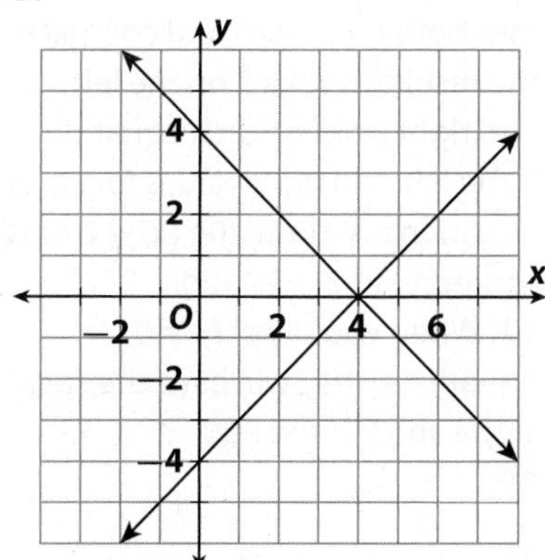

The system is consistent and independent.

4.

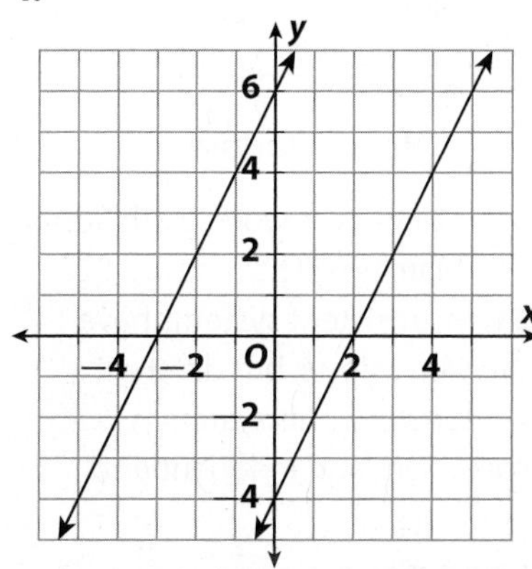

The system is inconsistent.

5. $\left(3\frac{1}{3}, \frac{1}{3}\right)$

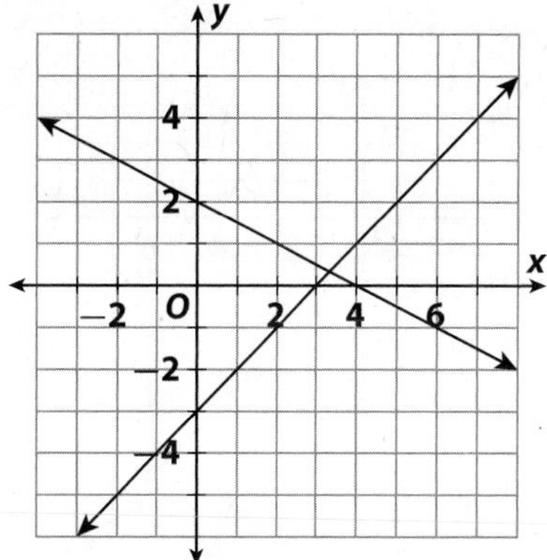

Guided Practice

1. $x - y = 7$
x-int: 7;
y-int: −7;
$2x + y = 2$
x-int: 1;
y-int: 2;
(3, −4); Yes

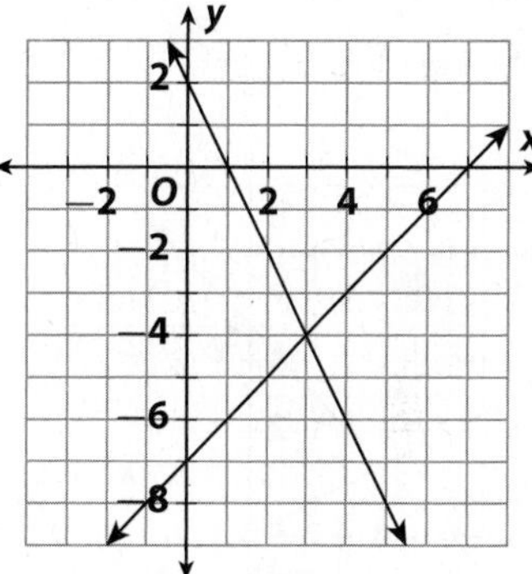

2. System consistent? Yes;
System independent? Yes;
(0, −1)
3. System consistent? No;
no solution
4. $x + y = -1$
x-intercept is −1;
y-intercept is −1;
$2x - y = 5$
x-intercept is 2.5;
y-intercept is −5;
$\left(1\frac{1}{3}, -2\frac{1}{3}\right)$

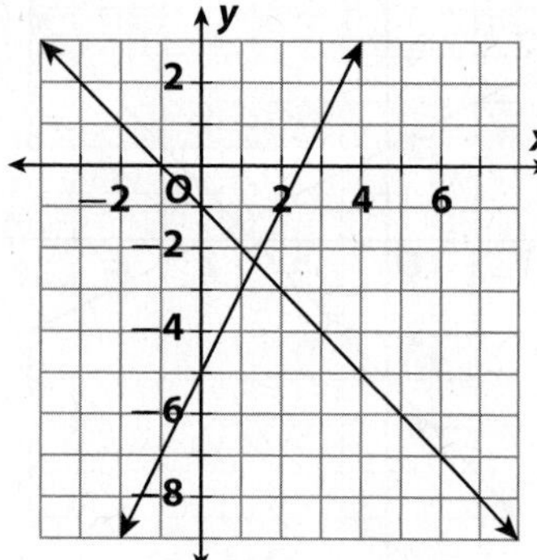

5. If the lines intersect in one point, you can solve the system by finding the coordinates of the point of intersection. If not, you can see that the system has either infinitely many solutions (coincident lines) or no solutions (parallel lines).

Independent Practice

7.

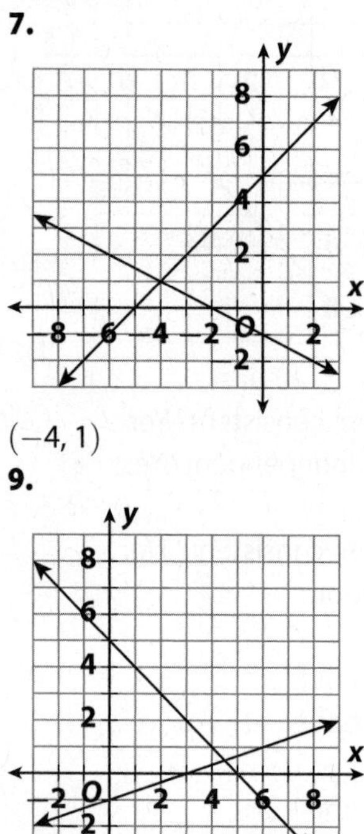

$(-4, 1)$

9.

$\left(4\frac{1}{2}, \frac{1}{2}\right)$

11.

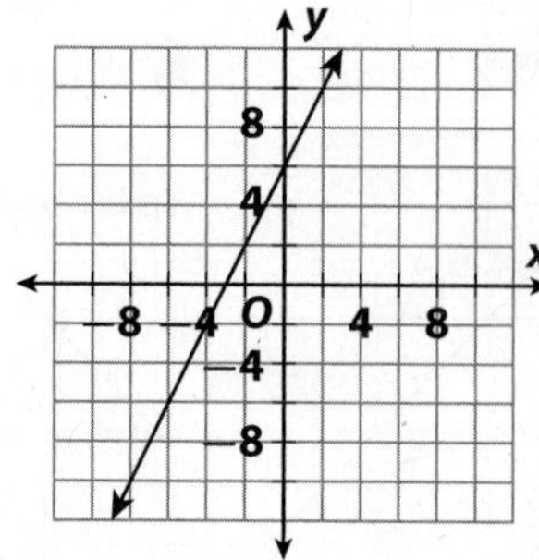

consistent and dependent

13. All solutions of a linear equation are represented by points on its graph; each point on the line corresponds to an ordered pair that makes the equation true.

15. Substitute the x- and y-values into both equations and compare the resulting values on the left and right sides of each equation. If the left and right values for each equation are close, the (x, y) pair is an approximate solution.

17. When you simplify the equations, they will have the same slope and y-intercept.

19.

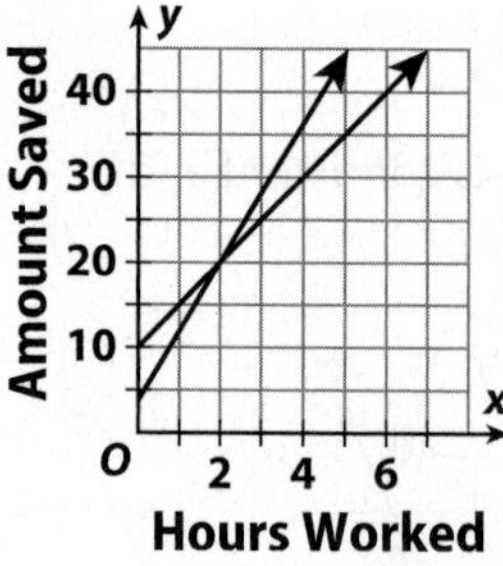

After 2 hours of work, both Sophie and Marcos will have saved \$20.

21. Inconsistent systems have the same slope, but different y-intercepts. This system is consistent and independent.

LESSON 9.2

Your Turn

5. $(3, -1)$ **6.** $(-2, 2)$ **9.** infinitely many solutions **10.** no solutions **11.** 3 months.

Guided Practice

1. $4x + x + 5 = 20$

$5x = 15$

$x = 3;$

$y = 3 + 5$

$y = 8$

The solution is $(3, 8)$.

2. $x = -2y + 6;$

$2(-2y + 6) + 4y = 12$

$12 - 4y + 4y = 12$

$12 = 12$

There are infinitely many solutions.

3. $(-3, 5)$ **4.** $(1, 6)$ **5.** no solution **6.** The cost will be the same in 3 months; The cost will be \$136. **7.** Solve one equation for one variable and use the result to substitute into the other equation. Solve for the value of the other variable, then substitute that value into either equation to find the value of the first variable.

Independent Practice

9. Solve for y first; if solving for x first, each side would have to be divided by a constant after isolating the x-term. The solution is $(2, 7)$.

11. Sample answer: $x = 2y$ The solution is $(6, 3)$.

13. no solutions. **15.** $(15, 18)$; x represents the width, and y represents the length. **17.** Sample answer: $3x + 2y = 21$ and $2x + 4y = 22$; cost of large fruit bucket: \$5; cost of small drink: \$3

19. Yes; The solution will be a single ordered pair that is a solution of each of the equations. For example, the solution of the system containing the equations $2x - y = 4$, $x + y = -1$; and $y = -2x$, is $(1, -2)$.

LESSON 9.3

Your Turn

6. $(-2, -4)$ **7.** $(6, -4)$ **8.** $(3, -2)$
9. $(1, 5)$ **11.** no solution
12. infinitely many solutions
13. $3x + 2y = 74$; $5x + 2y = 98$; A DVD costs \$12. A video game costs \$19.

Guided Practice

1. $0 + -2y = -4$

$$y = 2;$$
$$-5x + 2 = -3$$
$$-5x = -5$$
$$x = 1$$

The solution is $(1, 2)$.
2. $(-2, -2)$ **3.** $(10, 15)$
4. no solution **5.** The length is 21 inches. The width is 10 inches.
6. The equations must have at least one pair of variable terms that are the same or opposites.

Independent Practice

7. The system of equations is $\begin{cases} x + y = 65 \\ x - y = 27 \end{cases}$; The greater number is 46; The lesser number is 19.
9. Solution: $(1, -5)$ Sample answer: elimination; the elimination method requires fewer steps than the substitution method. **11.** Solution: $\left(4\frac{1}{2}, \frac{1}{2}\right)$; The solution tells me that the two lines in the graph intersect at $(4.5, 0.5)$.
13. The system of equations is $\begin{cases} x + y = 90 \\ 2x - y = 105 \end{cases}$; The larger angle measures 65°; The smaller angle measures 25°. **15.** An adult ticket costs \$7.50. A child ticket costs \$3.50; Julia will pay \$48.00
17. $-2x + 2y = 10$; Subtracting is the same as adding the opposite.

LESSON 9.4

Your Turn

3. $(-4, 0)$ **4.** $(-2, 1)$ **5.** $(3, 2)$
6. 5 roses and 7 lilies

Guided Practice

1.
$$\begin{array}{r} -6x + 6y = 6 \\ + 5x - 6y = -9 \\ \hline -x = -3 \end{array}$$

Solution: $(3, 4)$
2. $(6, -2)$ **3.** $(-1, 5)$ **4.** $(3, 1)$
5. $2l + 2w = 56$, $l - w = 8$; The length is 18 inches. The width is 10 inches. **6.** Multiply one or both equations so that one variable can be eliminated by using addition or subtraction, and then solve the system by elimination.

Independent Practice

7. Equation: Sample answer: first Number: -2
Solution: $(1, -5)$
9. First equation number: Sample answer: 3 Second equation number: Sample answer: 2
Solution: $(14, 23)$
11. Sample answer: To eliminate y, you would multiply the first equation by 4 and the second by -11. To eliminate x, you could use 3 and -2 which are smaller numbers and easier to work with.
13. Angle 1: 60° Angle 2: 30°
15. They sold 48 bags of hardwood mulch and 128 bags of pine bark mulch. **17.** Sample answer: Yes, because it seems easier for me to solve $x + 3y = -14$ for x and substitute the expression for x in $2x + y = -3$ to find the value of y. Then I would substitute that value of y into either equation to find the value of x.

LESSON 9.5

Your Turn

5.

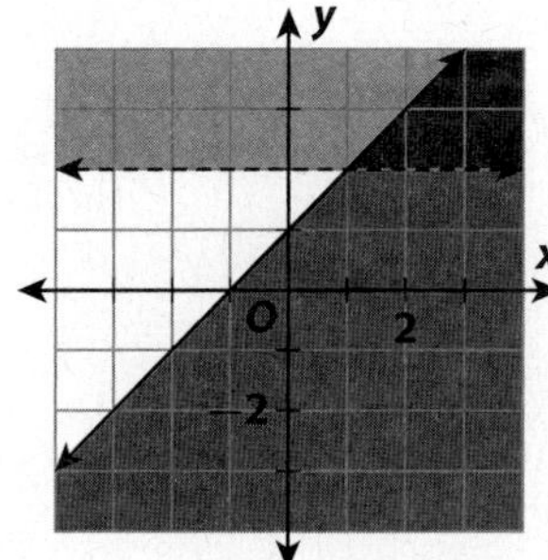

8.

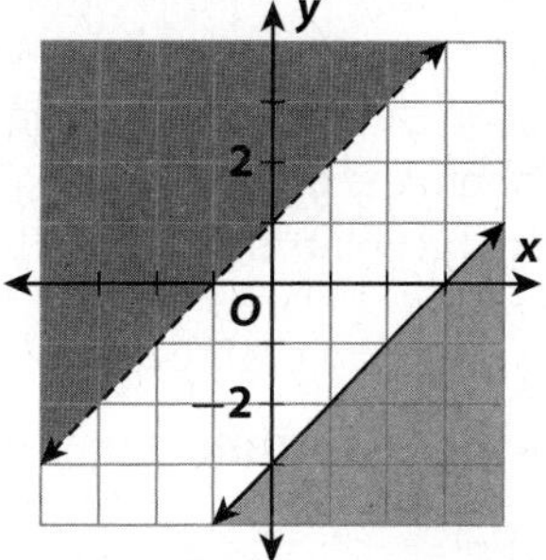

The two regions do not overlap, so the system has no solution.

9.

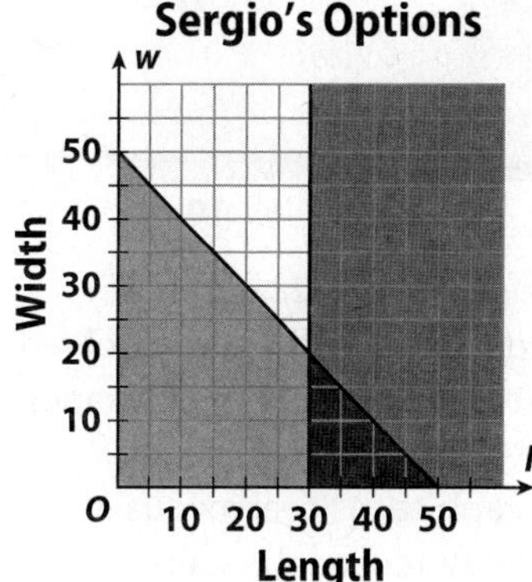

yes

Guided Practice

1.

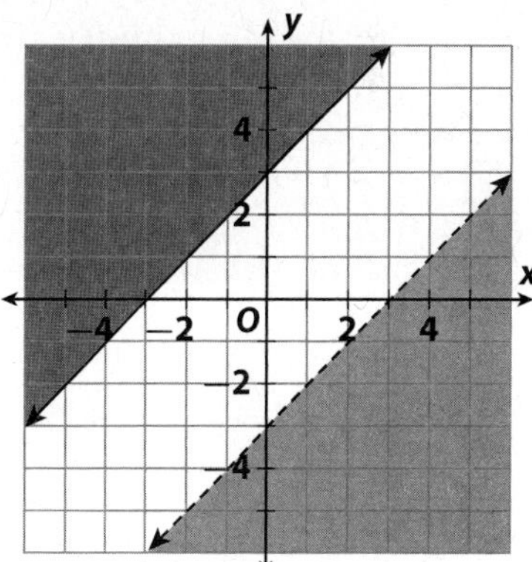

The system has no solutions.

2.

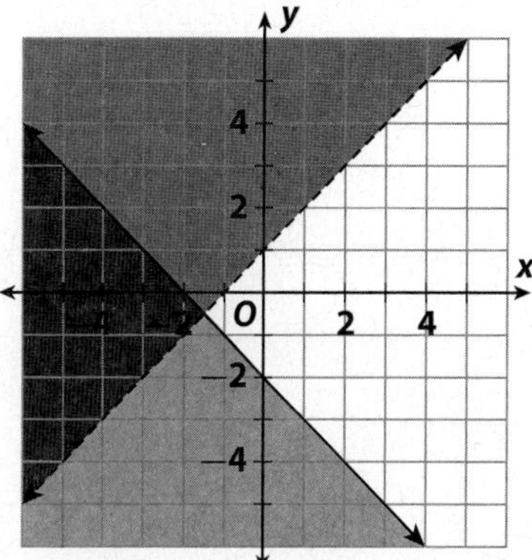

Selected Answers

UNIT 3A Selected Answers *(cont'd)*

The solutions are the points in the region where the graphs overlap, including the points on the solid boundary line.

3.

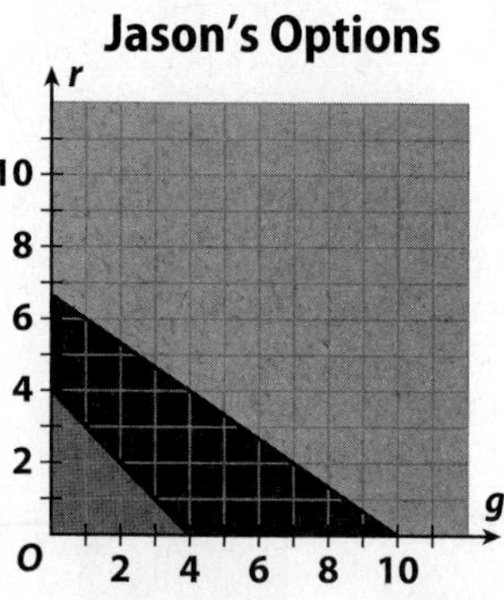

Sample answer: 2 pounds of green grapes and 4 pounds of red grapes; 4 pounds of green grapes and 3 pounds of red grapes.

4. Graph each linear inequality in the system on the same coordinate plane. The solution of the system is represented by the region where the graphs overlap.

Independent Practice

5.

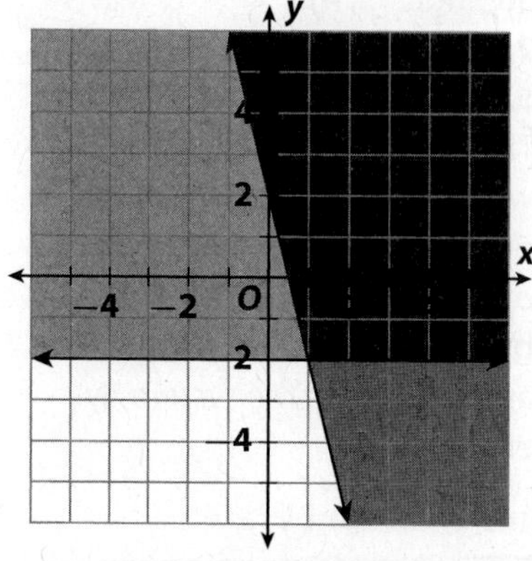

Sample pairs: (2, 2) and (4, −2)

7.

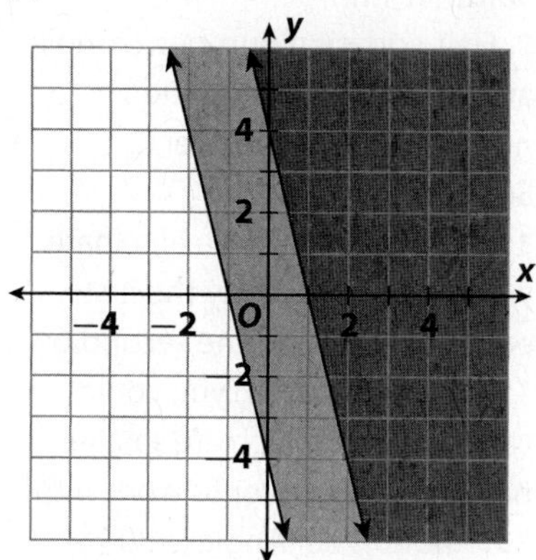

Sample pairs: (1, 1) and (4, 4)

9. The graphs do not overlap, so the system has no solution; Possible answer: $\begin{cases} 2x - y < -2 \\ 2x - y > 3 \end{cases}$

11a. $\begin{cases} x > 10 \\ 2x + 2y \leq 72 \end{cases}$ **b.** Sample answer: length: 15 inches; width 10 inches **c.** Sample answer: length: 25 inches; width 15 inches

13. No; each boundary line divides the plane into two half-planes, each the solution of one of the inequalities. It is not possible for the two half-planes to overlap and completely cover the plane.

UNIT 3B Selected Answers

MODULE 10

LESSON 10.1

Your Turn

2. $f(-3) = 6.75$

3. $t(n) = 0.2(2)^n$;
1.6 mm; 25.6 mm

6. $r(n) = 100{,}000(0.5)^n$

Guided Practice

1.

x	$f(x) = 2^x$	$(x, f(x))$
-3	$f(-3) = 2^{-3} = \frac{1}{8}$	$\left(-3, \frac{1}{8}\right)$
-2	$f(-2) = 2^{-2} = \frac{1}{4}$	$\left(-2, \frac{1}{4}\right)$
-1	$f(-1) = 2^{-1} = \frac{1}{2}$	$\left(-1, \frac{1}{2}\right)$
0	$f(0) = 2^0 = 1$	$(0, 1)$
1	$f(1) = 2^1 = 2$	$(1, 2)$
2	$f(2) = 2^2 = 4$	$(2, 4)$
3	$f(3) = 2^3 = 8$	$(3, 8)$

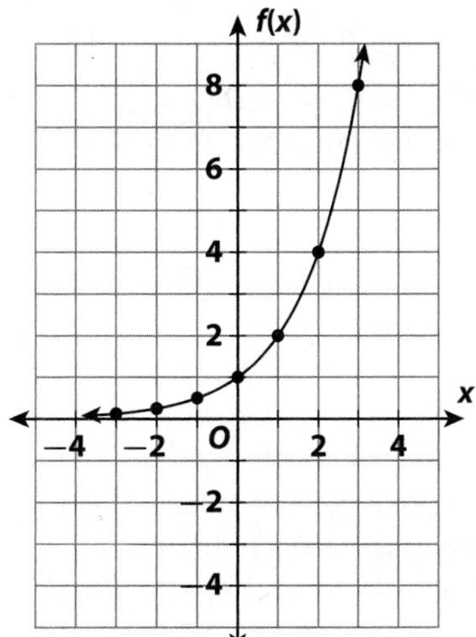

2. $\frac{f(-1)}{f(-2)} = 0.5$, so $b = 0.5$
$a = f(0) = 1$
$f(x) = (0.5)^x$

3. $f(x) = 3\left(\frac{2}{3}\right)^x$

4. a is the initial value of the function, when the input value is 0. b is the ratio of output values whose input values differ by 1.

Independent Practice

5.

x	$f(x)$
-3	$\frac{128}{27}$
-2	$\frac{32}{9}$
-1	$\frac{8}{3}$
0	2
1	$\frac{3}{2}$
2	$\frac{9}{8}$
3	$\frac{27}{32}$

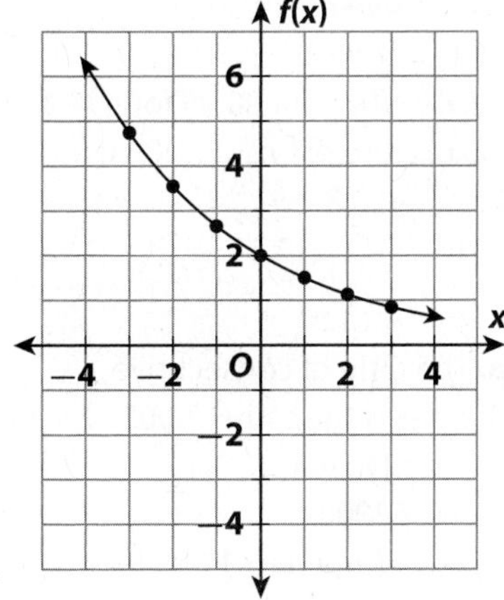

7. $f(x) = 10(0.8)^x$ **9.** $f(x) = \frac{1}{4}(2)^x$

11. 2

13a.

Day (n)	Favors $f(n)$
1	3
2	9
3	27
4	81
5	243

b. $f(n) = 3^n$. **c.** 59,049 favors; the number of favors done on Day 10 is 3^{10}. **d.** $f(n) = 4^n$

15. The range is the set of positive real numbers. Even for negative values of x, $f(x)$ is always positive.

17. If $b = 1$, then $f(x) = ab^x$ would be $f(x) = a(1)^x$. Raising 1 to any power that is a real number results in a value of 1. So the equation would become $f(x) = a(1) = a$, a constant. The graph of $f(x) = a$ is a horizontal line.

LESSON 10.2

Your Turn

1. $y = 1200(1.08)^t$;
$1,904.25

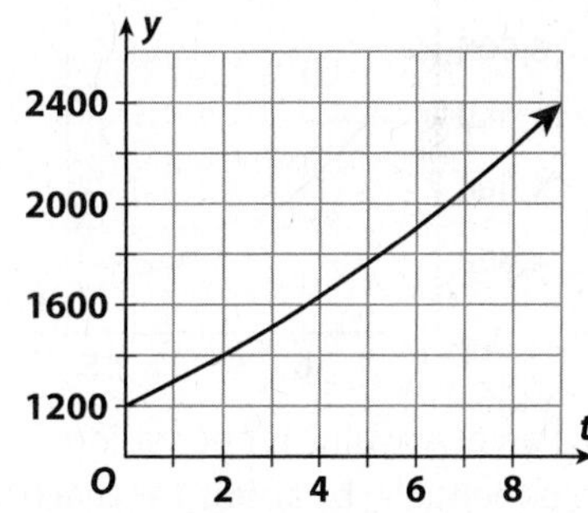

2. $y = 48{,}000(0.97)^t$;
The population after 7 years is 38,783.

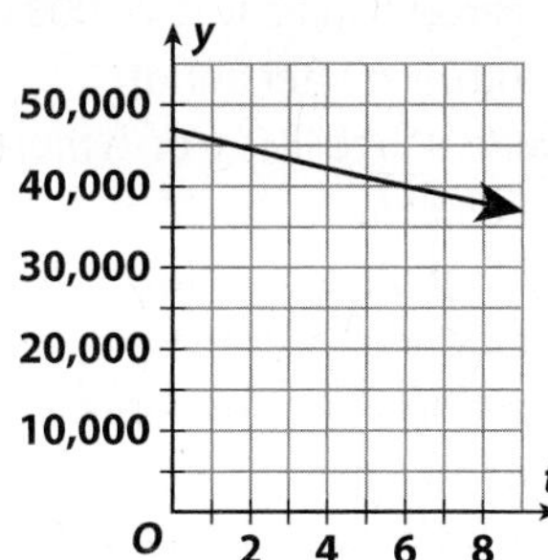

3. Stock A is $A(t) = 16(0.75)^t$ and Stock B is $B(t) = 4(1.5)^t$. The value of Stock A is decreasing and the value of Stock B is increasing. The initial value of Stock A is greater than the initial value of Stock B but eventually, the value of Stock B will be greater.

Selected Answers

UNIT 3B Selected Answers *(cont'd)*

Guided Practice

1. $y = 12{,}000(1.06)^t$; \$15,149.72

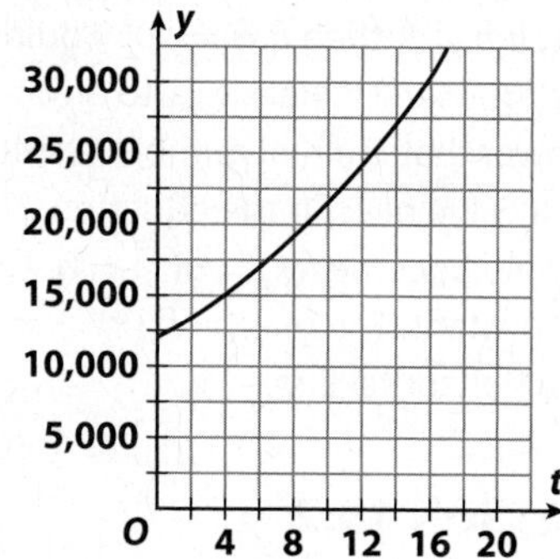

2. $y = 18{,}000(0.88)^t$; \$5,013.02

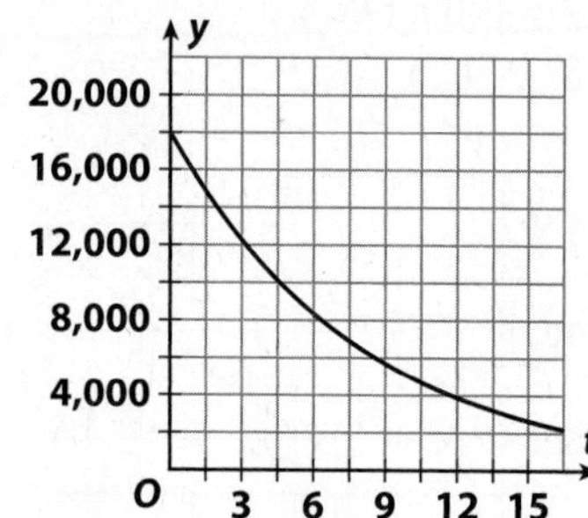

3. Parcel A's value is decreasing exponentially by about 14% each year. Parcel B's value is increasing exponentially by about 14% each year. Parcel A was worth more than Parcel B initially (\$70,000 vs. \$35,000), but after about 2.5 years, Parcel B is worth more than Parcel A.

4. If the graph slopes upward as the values on the horizontal axis increase, the function represents exponential growth. If the graph slopes downward as the values on the horizontal axis increase, the function represents exponential decay.

Independent Practice

5. $y = 10(0.84)^t$; 4.98 mg

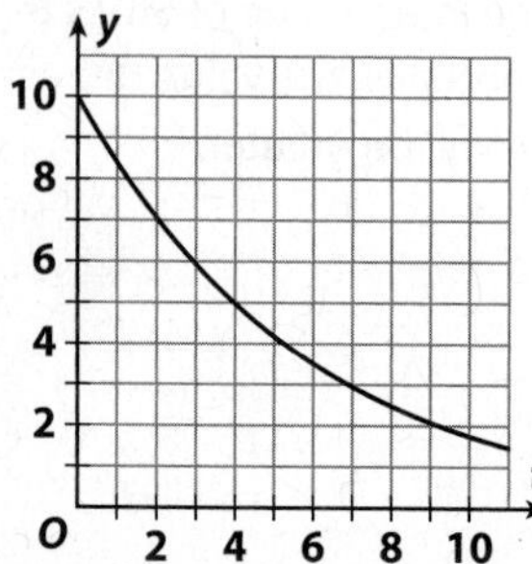

7. $y = 149{,}000(1.06)^t$; \$224,040.91
9. $y = 1600(1.03)^t$; 2150
11. $y = 700(1.012)^t$; \$760.96
13. least; greatest; horizontal axis **15.** Based on the function, the value will never be 0. The right side of the function equation is a product of positive numbers. So, the value can be close to 0, but not equal to 0.

LESSON 10.3

Your Turn

6. Recursive rule:
$f(1) = 2$,
$f(n) = f(n-1) \cdot 3$ for $n \geq 2$
Explicit rule: $f(n) = 2 \cdot 3^{n-1}$
7. Recursive rule:
$f(1) = 128$,
$f(n) = f(n-1) \cdot 0.25$ for $n \geq 2$
Explicit rule: $f(n) = 128 \cdot 0.25^{n-1}$
8. $a_n = \frac{1}{486} \cdot 3^{n-1}$
9. $f(n) = 1000 \cdot 1.5^{n-1}$

Guided Practice

1a. The ratio of consecutive balances is the same, 1.005.
b. Recursive rule:
$f(1) = 2000$,
$f(n) = f(n-1) \cdot 1.005$ for $n \geq 2$
Explicit rule:
$f(n) = 2000 \cdot 1.005^{n-1}$
2. $\frac{27}{9} = 3 \quad \frac{81}{27} = 3 \quad \frac{243}{81} = 3$
Recursive rule: $f(1) = 9$,
$f(n) = f(n-1) \cdot 3$ for $n \geq 2$
Explicit rule: $f(n) = 9 \cdot 3^{n-1}$
3. $a_n = 3 \cdot 4^{n-1}$
4. $a_n = 10{,}000 \cdot (0.4)^{n-1}$
5. Use the first term of the sequence and the common ratio as given in the recursive rule. Use these values in the form $f(n) = f(1) \cdot r^{n-1}$

Independent Practice

7. Recursive rule: $f(1) = 12$,
$f(n) = f(n-1) \cdot \frac{1}{4}$ for $n \geq 2$
Explicit rule: $f(n) = 12 \cdot \left(\frac{1}{4}\right)^{n-1}$
9. $f(n) = 10 \cdot 8^{n-1}$
11. $a_n = 1.5 \cdot 4^{n-1}$
13a. $f(n) = 50 \cdot 20^{n-1}$
b. 3,200,000,000 points
15. Divide the 7th term by the common ratio 5 times. If given the 2nd term, you would multiply by the common ratio 5 times to get the 7th term, so perform the inverse operation.

LESSON 10.4

Your Turn

3. $g(x)$ is a vertical translation of $f(x)$ down 5 units.

Guided Practice

1. 1 **2.** 2 **3.** greater than
4. vertical stretch **5.** $Y_3 = 2^x$; Sample answer: $f(x) = 2.5^x$
6. Y_5 and Y_6 rise and fall at exactly the same rate. **7.** Y_5 was translated 2 units up.
8. If $b > 1$, increasing the b-value makes the graph rise more quickly as x increases. If $0 < b < 1$, increasing the b-value makes the graph fall more gradually as x increases.

Independent Practice

9. *a* **11.** *a* **13.** Vertical compression: for a given x-value, the graph of $Y_2(x)$ is half of $Y_1(x)$.
15. Sample answer: $f(x) = 0.25^x$
17. Down; the values of Y_4 are less than the values of Y_3.
19. The y-intercept equals a for all values of $b > 1$ because $ab^0 = a$. As the value of b increases, the graph rises more quickly as x increases to the right of 0 and it falls more quickly as x decreases to the left of 0. **21.** Y_1; Y_1 has the greater decay rate (6% rather than 2%); you would expect Y_1 to decrease more quickly as x increases to the right of 0.

LESSON 10.5

Your Turn

5. $x = 4$ **6.** $x = 2$ **7.** $x = 3$ **8.** $x = 4$
10. $400 = 250(1 + 0.2)^x$ or $400 = 250(1.2)^x$ **11.** 2.6 years

Guided Practice

1.
$$\frac{3}{4}(6)^x = 162$$
$$(6)^x = 216$$
$$(6)^x = 6^3$$
$$x = 3$$

2.
$$3\left(\frac{5}{6}\right)^x = \frac{75}{36}$$
$$\left(\frac{5}{6}\right)^x = \frac{25}{36}$$
$$\left(\frac{5}{6}\right)^x = \left(\frac{5}{6}\right)^2$$
$$x = 2$$

3. $x = 3$ **4.** $x = 4$ **5.** $x = 3$ **6.** 2.57
7. $x \approx 3.08$ **8.** $x \approx 5.03$
9. $500 = 225(1.15)^x$
10. 5.7 years **11.** When the bases are equal, use the Equality of Bases Property. When the bases are not equal, graph each side of the equation as its own function and find the intersection.

Independent Practice

13. $x = 2$ **15.** $x = 3$ **17.** $x = 2$
19. $x \approx 2.80$ **21.** $x \approx 4.19$
23. constant function: $f(x) = 20$
exponential function: $g(x) = 4^x$
25. $x = 4$ **27.** They are the same.
29. Sample answer: Graphing, because 20 is not a whole number power of 2.
31. constant function: $f(x) = 300$
exponential function:
$g(x) = 175(1.12)^x$
33. You can find the intersection of the graphs to find the time when the population reaches 300.
35. $300{,}000 = 175{,}000(1 + 0.1)^x$ or
$300{,}000 = 175{,}000(1.1)^x$
37. The second city's population will reach 300,000 sooner, in about 5.1 years compared to 5.7 years.
39. Marco is incorrect. He did not multiply each side by $\frac{1}{9}$ to isolate the power $(3)^x$. He moved the 9 from the left side of the equation to the right side and multiplied.

MODULE 11

LESSON 11.1

Your Turn

2. $y = 108.5(1.21)^x$

Guided Practice

1.

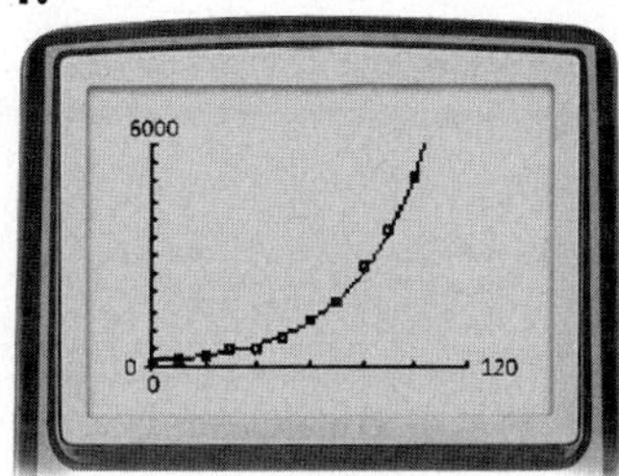

2. $y = f(x) = 135.9 \times 1.037^x$;
135,900; 1.037; 3.7%
3. $r = 0.997$; is
4.

y_m	$y_d - y_m$
136	−13
196	8
283	51
407	29
587	−88
847	−97
1221	81
1761	10
2540	178
3662	3
5281	−150

5.

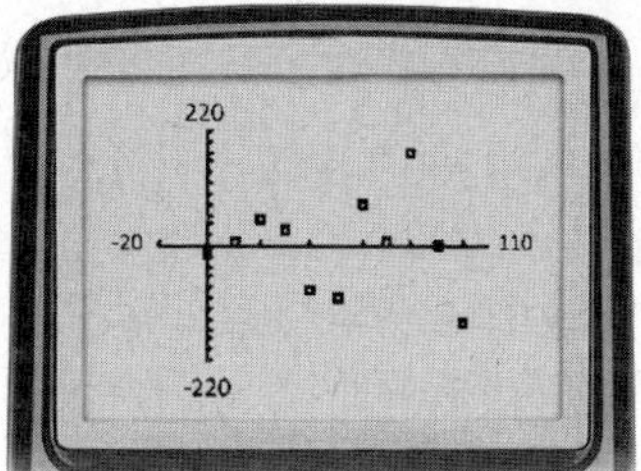

6. You can use an exponential regression program to generate an equation, and then analyze the residuals.

Independent Practice

7a. For $x = 11$, the table and rounded regression equation, $f(x) = 113 \times 1.27^{11}$, predict very similar results: 1.569 versus 1.566 billion. The trace predicts a result of 1.561 billion, which is also very close. **b.** No, using the equation, $y_d - y_m = 678$ which is about 76% of the actual value.
c. The value predicted (35 billion) is likely to be very inaccurate. The accuracy of an exponential model decreases significantly the further from the origin it gets.
9. The year 2029. If the regression table is viewed in 1-year increments, the first y-value $>$ 15,000 (15,264) occurs for $x = 129$.
11. It is the size of the residual relative to that of the data that is important. Sandy's data values may have been quite large relative to the data values Mark was using. **13.** She needs to gather data for longer than three hours. Exponential functions can appear linear, especially in the beginning.

LESSON 11.2

Your Turn

4. At $x = 65$ months, Company B will have more employees: 181 employees compared to Company A's 180 employees. **5.** increasing; linear; $f(x) = -0.61 + 0.097x$

UNIT 3B Selected Answers *(cont'd)*

Guided Practice

1. $P_C(t) = 2500 - 80t$;
$P_E(t) = 2000 \times 0.97^t$;
$t \approx 16$; 16 years;
Centerville: 1220;
Easton: 1229
2. $g(x)$; linear **3.** $f(x)$; exponential
4. $g(x) = 300 - 12x$
5. $f(x) = 200 \times (0.75)^x$
6. A linear model should be used when the amount of increase or decrease in each interval is constant. An exponential model is appropriate when the amount of increase or decrease in each interval changes by a constant ratio.

Independent Practice

7. Constant rate; She's paying a fixed dollar amount. **9.** Constant percent rate. The number of students grows by the same 2.5% each year. **11.** Yes, the exponential growth function eventually curves upward while a linear growth function continues in a line with a positive slope. **13.** No, an exponential function is a good model. Graphing the data reveals an upward curve. Exponential regression gives an equation with $r = 0.9999$.

UNIT 4 Selected Answers

LESSON 12.1

Your Turn

5.

Preferred Fruit			
Apple	**Orange**	**Banana**	**Total**
19	12	23	54
22	9	15	46
41	21	38	100

6.

Play Video Games		
Yes	**No**	**Total**
34	19	53
38	9	47
72	28	100

Guided Practice

1. categorical **2.** quantitative

3.

Cans	Frequency
soup	6
peas	8
corn	11

4.

Activities				
Clubs only	**Sports only**	**Both**	**Neither**	**Total**
12	13	16	4	45
3	5	5	2	15
15	18	21	6	60

5. 13

Like Swimming		
Yes	**No**	**Total**
65	16	81
13	6	19
78	22	100

6. You can summarize categorical data for two categories in two-way frequency tables.

Independent Practice

7. quantitative **9.** 96 boys; 104 of the 200 students were girls, so $200 - 104 = 96$ of them were boys. **11.** laptops

13.

Like Pop		
Yes	**No**	**Total**
15	34	49
42	9	51
57	43	100

15.

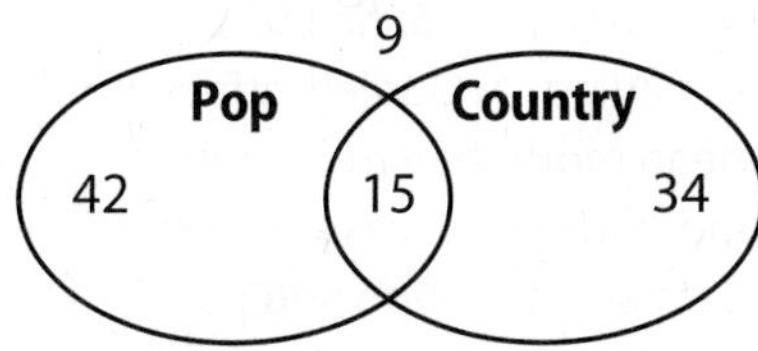

LESSON 12.2

Your Turn

3. 0.175, or 17.5% **5.** 0.7, or 70%
6. girls

Guided Practice

1.

Foreign Language			
Chinese	**French**	**Spanish**	**Total**
$\frac{2}{40} = 0.05$	$\frac{8}{40} = 0.2$	$\frac{12}{40} = 0.3$	$\frac{22}{40} = 0.55$
$\frac{4}{40} = 0.1$	$\frac{1}{40} = 0.025$	$\frac{13}{40} = 0.325$	$\frac{18}{40} = 0.45$
$\frac{6}{40} = 0.15$	$\frac{9}{40} = 0.225$	$\frac{25}{40} = 0.625$	$\frac{40}{40} = 1$

2a. 0.222; about 22.2% **b.** 48%
3. Boys are more likely than girls to study Chinese and Spanish, and girls are more likely than boys to study French. **4.** You can use relative frequencies to find associations and trends by comparing conditional relative frequencies to marginal relative frequencies.

Independent Practice

5.

Activity			
Sports	**Clubs**	**Other**	**Total**
0.1125	0.2625	0.1	0.475
0.275	0.1	0.15	0.525
0.3875	0.3625	0.25	1

7. A joint relative frequency; it comes from dividing a frequency that is not in the Total row or the Total column by the grand total.
9. 0.3875, or 38.75%
11. About 0.553, or 55.3%; divide the number of girls who have clubs as their activity by the total number of girls.
13a. about 86.5% **b.** about 78% **c.** about 69%
15. A relative frequency is a frequency divided by the grand total. A conditional relative frequency is a frequency divided by the column or row total.

MODULE 13

LESSON 13.1

Your Turn

2. The mean is 76. The median is 72.5. **3.** median: 26; range: 10; IQR: 4 **4.** 28.4 **5a.** mean: 34.1; median: 33.5; IQR: 13; standard deviation: 7.2 **b.** Members of Oldport County gyms tend to be older than members of Newman County gyms, and the average ages at Oldport County gyms are less spread out.

Guided Practice

1. mean: 29; median: 29.5; range: 5; IQR: 2 **2.** Algebra class: 1.6; Spanish class: 2.7
3. A typical Spanish class has more students than a typical Algebra 1 class.

UNIT 4 Selected Answers *(cont'd)*

4. Use measures of center (mean and median) and measures of spread (range, IQR, and standard deviation) to compare data sets.

Independent Practice

5. mean: 79.5; median: 82; range: 28 **7.** 15.5 **9.** 12 **11.** Find the mean value. Then find the difference between the mean and each number. Next, square each deviation. Finally, find the mean of the six squared deviations and take the square root. **13.** The mean, median, and IQR will not change, but the range decreases from 20 to 18, and the standard deviation decreases from 6.4 to 5.9.

15a.

Center		Spread	
Mean	Median	IQR $(Q_3 - Q_1)$	Standard deviation
191.3	192	12	7.0
175.5	175	6	3.4

b. The typical height of a male is greater than the typical height of a female. The heights of the females are more tightly clustered. **17.** $x \leq 88$; for 5 ordered values, the median is the 3rd. Since 95 and 92 are > 88, they must be 4th and 5th; so x must be $\leq$ to the median.

LESSON 13.2

Your Turn

4.

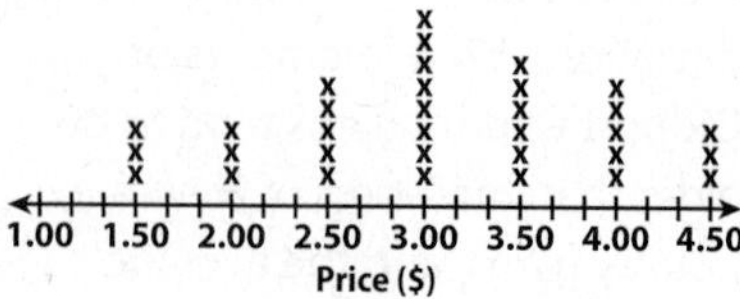

7. Yes; 3 **8.** The outlier decreases the mean from 25.2 to 21.5 and increases the range from 9 to 27. It has no effect on the median.
11. symmetric

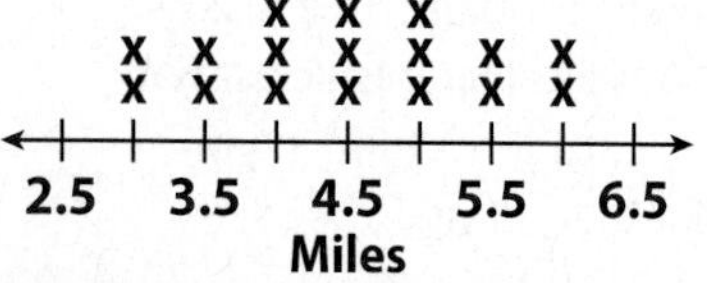

Guided Practice

1.

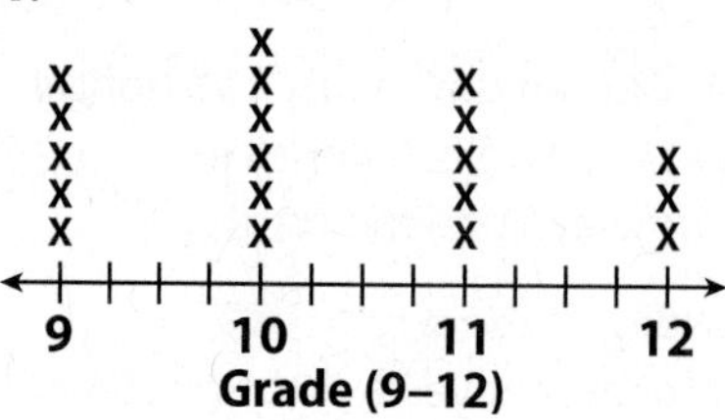

2a. 12; 7; 5; 19.5; yes
b.

Mean	Median	Range
8.5	8.5	7
15	9	49

c. The outlier increases the mean by 6.5, the median by 0.5, and the range by 42. **3.** The median for the first test, 92, is greater than the median for the second test, 86. **4.** second test **5.** first test **6.** median **7.** Outliers affect the mean more than the median, and outliers increase both the standard deviation and the IQR. Distributions can be symmetric, skewed to the left, or skewed to the right.

Independent Practice

9. the mean, range, IQR, and standard deviation **11.** Without: mean = median = 300; With: mean ≈ 332, median = 300
13a.

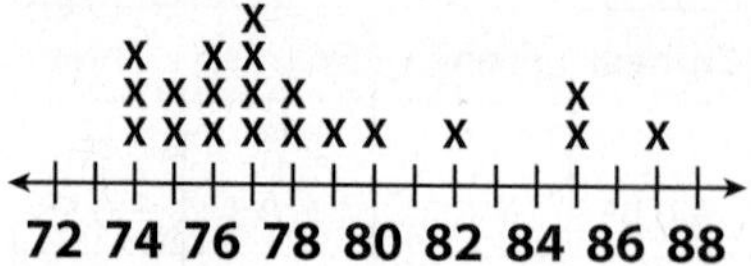

b.

Mean	78.1
Median	77
Range	13
IQR	4
Standard deviation	3.75

c. 87 **d.** The mean, range, and standard deviation would change. **e.** Skewed to the right

15. Because one of the outliers will be either the highest or the lowest number in the data set, and the range is found by finding the difference between the highest and lowest numbers. **17.** No; if a data set has two outliers that are much greater than the other values, then the greatest and the second greatest values would both be outliers.

LESSON 13.3

Your Turn

4a.

Golf scores	Frequency
68–70	3
71–73	4
74–76	6
77–79	2

b.

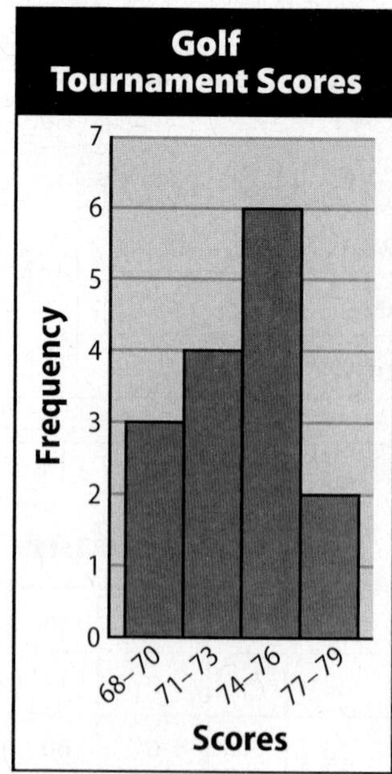

6. mean: 40; median: 39

Guided Practice

1. two **2.** ten **3.** No; only the three heaviest lifts get a medal, and 172.5 is not among the top three heaviest lifts. **4.** No; the silver medal was awarded for a lift between 200 and 209.9 kg, but there is no way to know the exact weight.

5.

Days	Frequency
4–6	5
7–9	4
10–12	4
13–15	2

6.

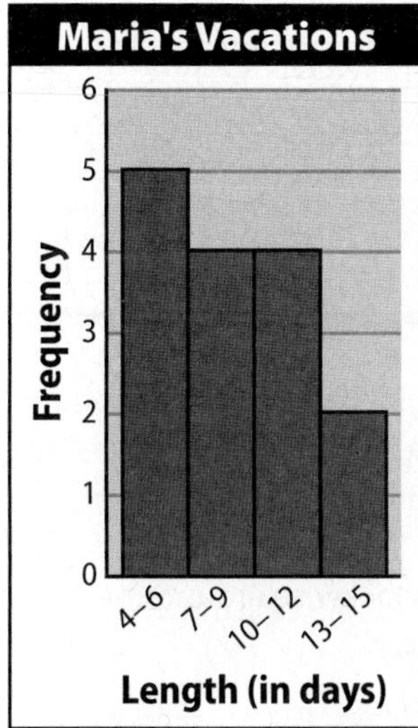

7. $\frac{5 \cdot 5 + 8 \cdot 4 + 11 \cdot 4 + 14 \cdot 2}{15} = \frac{129}{15} = 8.6$; very close

8. Use the midpoint value and frequency for each interval to estimate the mean. To estimate the median, first identify the correct interval, then estimate where the value will be in the interval.

Independent Practice

9. 15

11.

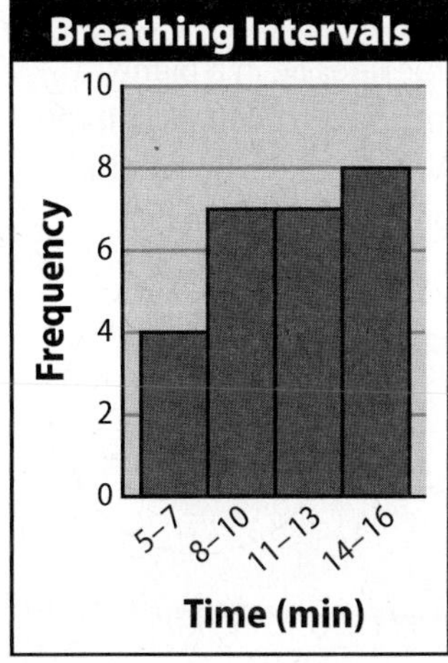

13a. 55 **b.** 55 **15.** He found the midpoint of each interval and divided their sum by the number of intervals instead of multiplying the frequency by the midpoint for each interval and then dividing the sum of these products by the total number of data values.

LESSON 13.4

Your Turn

3.

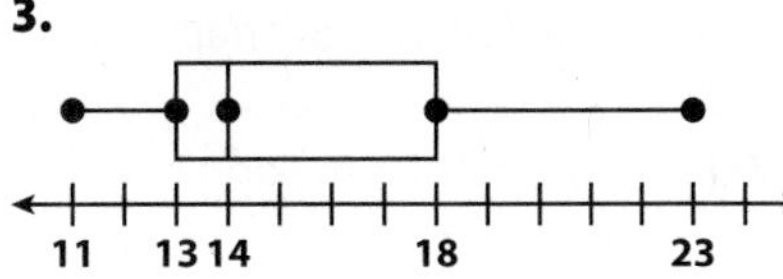

5. Simon's **6.** Simon's **7.** Natasha; about 1000 points

Guided Practice

1a. 15, 16, 16, 18, 25, 25, 26, 26, 28, 28 **b.** Median = 25; First quartile = 16; Third quartile = 26 **c.** Minimum = 15; Maximum = 28

d.

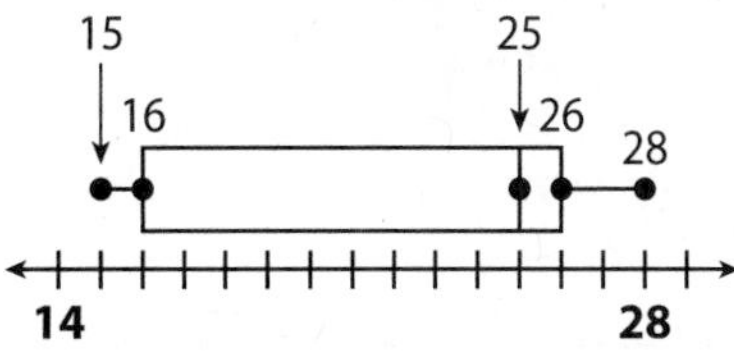

2. Sneaks R Us; about \$6 greater

3. Sneaks R Us; the middle 50% of prices don't vary as much at Sneaks R Us as at Jump N Run.

4. By plotting two box plots on the same number line, you can compare the center, spread, and shape of the distributions.

Independent Practice

5. Tim **7.** Tim; his box plot is more toward the left than Jamal's.

9. Gabrielle's **11.** East; 20 **13.** No; the range does not affect the mean of a set of data. **15.** The distribution of SUV prices is more symmetric than the distribution of car prices. The SUV prices have a greater median and are more spread out than the car prices.

17. Willie's set has the higher third quartile and maximum; his greatest 25% of scores are all higher than Dolly's highest score.

Selected Answers

UNIT 5 Selected Answers

LESSON 14.1

Your Turn

4.

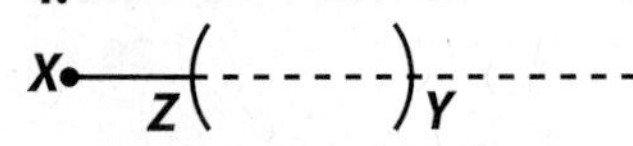

$\overline{XZ}$ is the required segment.

6. $\angle SZW$, $\angle YZU$, and $\angle XZT$

7. 49° **8.** is not

Guided Practice

1. plane **2.** plane

3.

$\overline{XZ}$ is the required segment.

4.

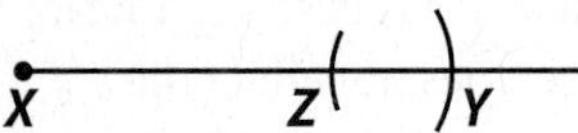

$\overline{XZ}$ is the required segment.

6. $m\angle AGC = 138°$

$$m\angle AGC = m\angle AGB + m\angle BGC$$
$$= 90° + 48°$$
$$= 138°$$

7. $\angle AGB$, $\angle BGD$

8. The length of the original segment is equal to the sum of the lengths of the two shorter segments. The measure of the original angle is equal to the sum of the measures of the adjacent angles.

Independent Practice

9.

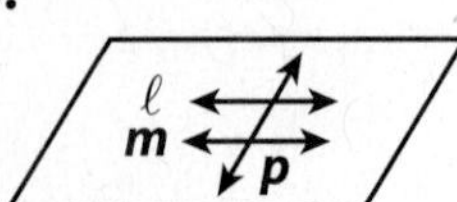

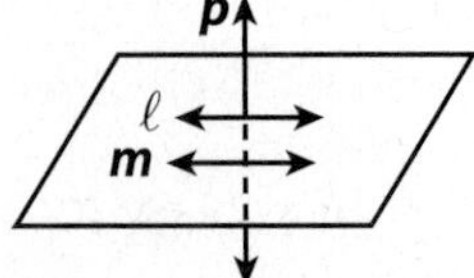

If all three lines lie in a plane, line *p* must intersect line *m*. If the lines do not all lie in a plane, line *p* may not intersect line *m*.

11.

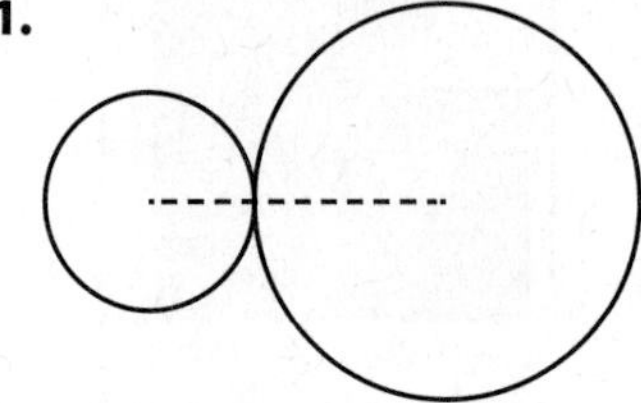

13. $m\angle JKM = 67°$; $m\angle MKL = 53°$; No; neither angle measures 90°.

15. For a line and a segment, the order does not matter since $\overleftrightarrow{AB}$ and $\overleftrightarrow{BA}$ represent the same line and $\overline{AB}$ and $\overline{BA}$ represent the same segment. For a ray, the order matters since $\overrightarrow{AB}$ and $\overrightarrow{BA}$ have different endpoints and the rays continue in opposite directions.

17. $\angle ABD$ must be a straight angle; Sample answer: The two angles share a common side, ray *BC*. Because they are adjacent angles, they do not overlap. So, $m\angle ABC + m\angle CBD = 90° + 90° = 180°$, making $\angle ABD$ a straight angle.

LESSON 14.2

Your Turn

4.

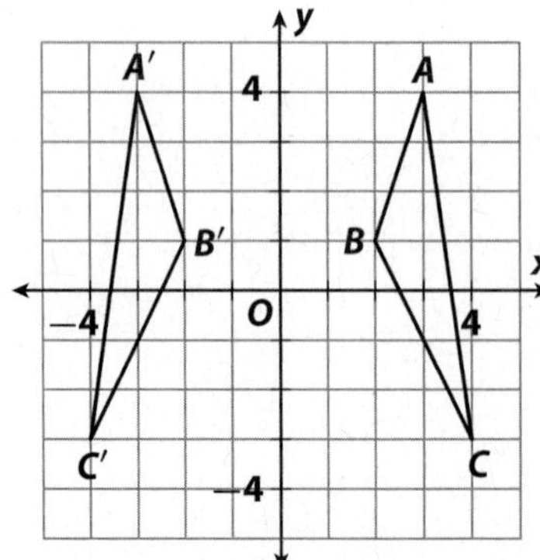

Rigid motion; reflection

5.

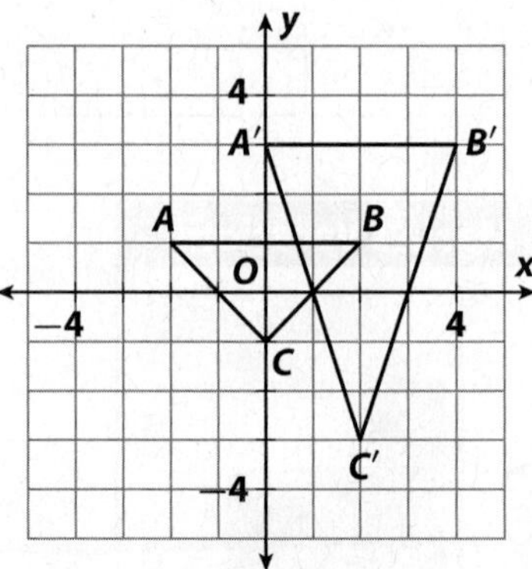

Not a rigid motion; it does not preserve length or angle measure.

6. reflection across the *x*-axis; $(x, y) \rightarrow (x, -y)$ **7.** rotation of 270° counterclockwise around the origin; $(x, y) \rightarrow (y, -x)$

Guided Practice

1.

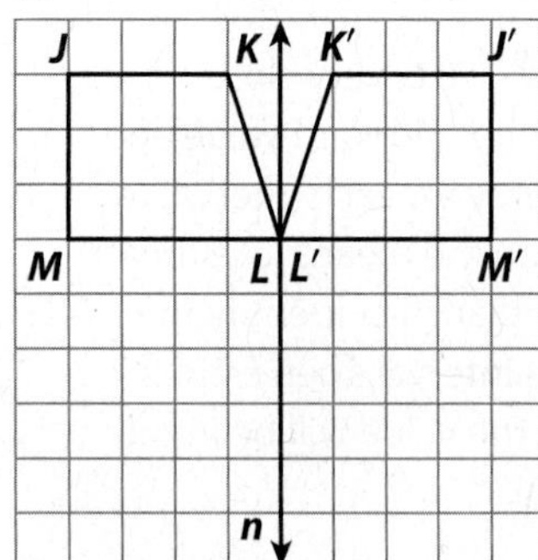

2.

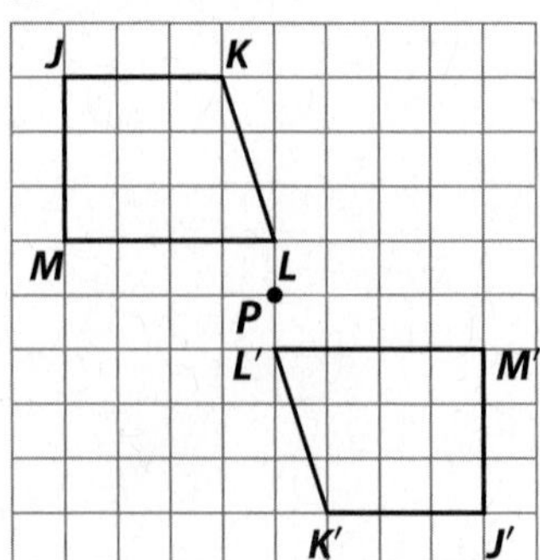

3.

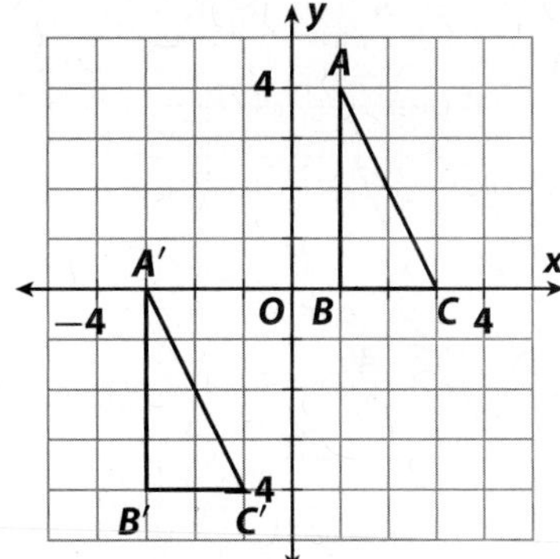

$A(1, 4) \rightarrow A'(1 - 4, 4 - 4) =$
$A'(-3, 0)$
$B(1, 0) \rightarrow B'(1 - 4, 0 - 4) =$
$B'(-3, -4)$
$C(3, 0) \rightarrow C'(3 - 4, 0 - 4) =$
$C'(-1, -4)$
The transformation is a rigid motion. It is a translation.
4. rotation of 180° around the origin; $(x, y) \rightarrow (-x, -y)$
5. rotation of 90° counter-clockwise around the origin; $(x, y) \rightarrow (-y, x)$
6. A rigid motion is a transformation that does not change the lengths or angle measures in the figure. In addition, parallel lines remain parallel and points on the figure keep their positions relative to one another.

Independent Practice

7.

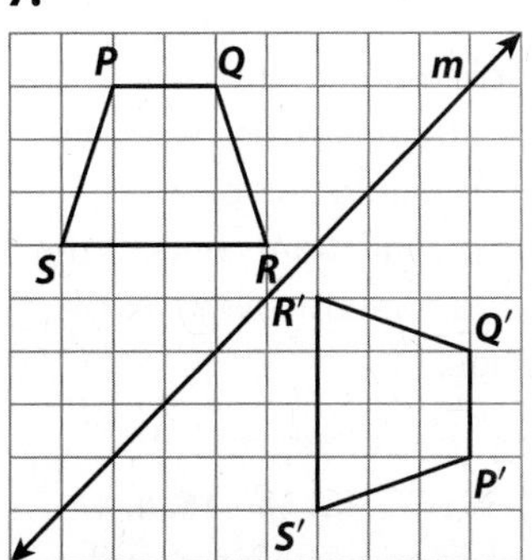

9. No; you can only conclude that these lengths are the same if you know that the transformation is a rigid motion.

11a.

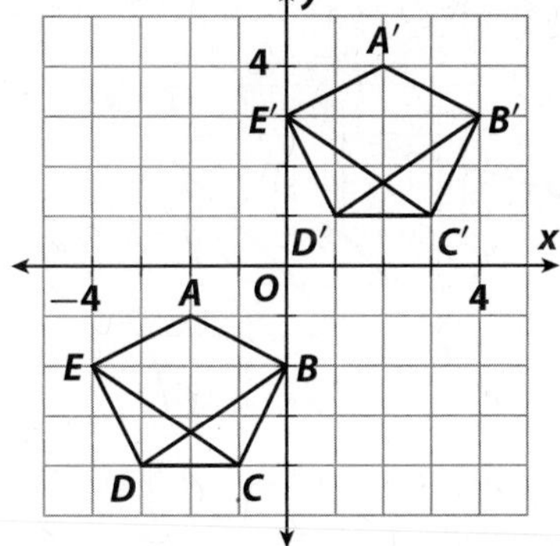

b. $(0, 3)$ **c.** $(x, y) \rightarrow (x + 4, y + 5)$
d. No; an enlargement is not a rigid motion, because it does not preserve length. **13.** Similarities: Both types are functions that map points in a plane to other points in the plane. Differences: Transformations that are not rigid motions change the size and/or the shape of a figure. Rigid motions do not. **15.** Yes; Rigid motions preserve length. Therefore, the length of each side of the image is the same as the length of each side of the preimage. This means the perimeter of the image is the same as the perimeter of the preimage.

LESSON 14.3

Your Turn

5.

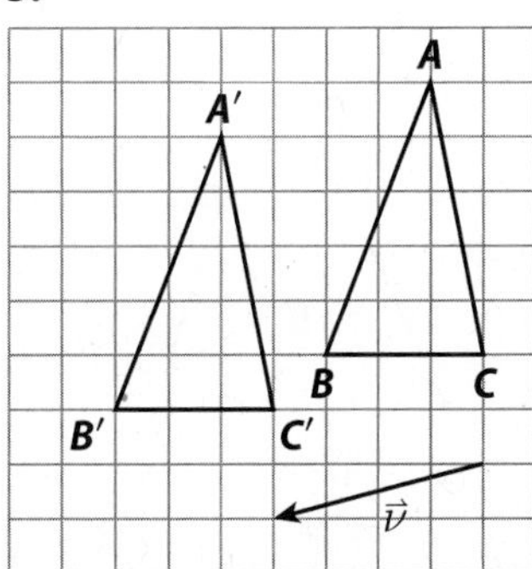

6.

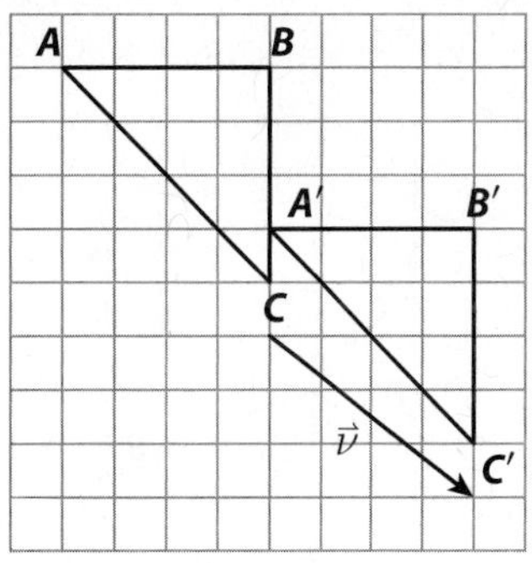

10. $\langle -1, -4 \rangle$
11. $\langle 0, 3 \rangle$

Guided Practice

1.

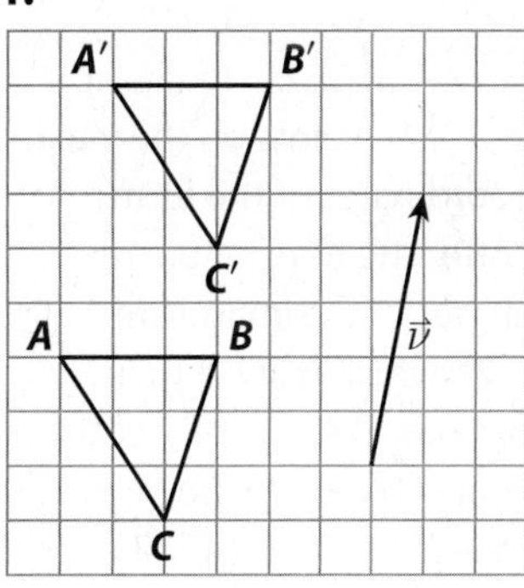

2.

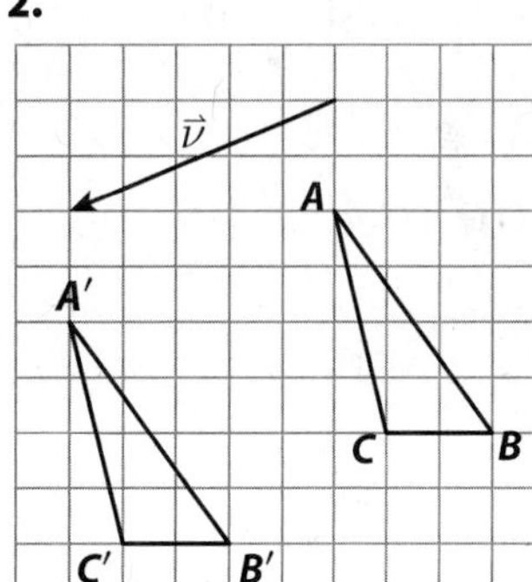

3. The horizontal change is $-1 - (-4) = 3$.
The vertical change is $3 - (-1) = 4$.
The component form of the vector is $\langle 3, 4 \rangle$.
4. $\langle 2, -5 \rangle$ **5.** $\langle 5, 0 \rangle$ **6.** Sample answer: Rather than sliding a figure left or right and then up or down to translate it, you slide it parallel to a given vector a distance equal to the length of the vector.

UNIT 5 Selected Answers *(cont'd)*

7a.

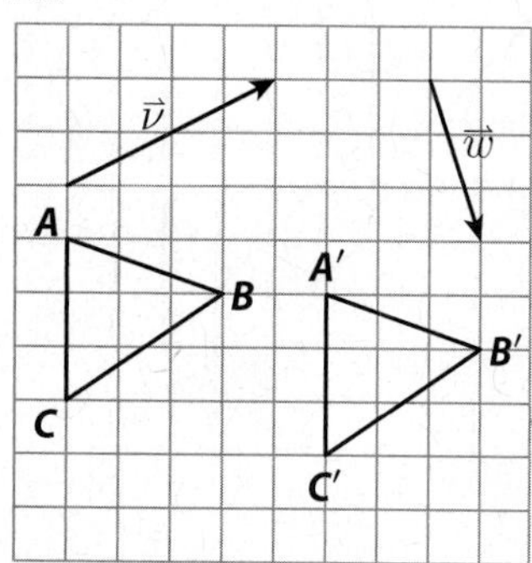

b. The images are the same in both cases. **c.** yes; $(x, y) \rightarrow (x + 5, y - 1)$ **9.** $\overline{EF}$ **11.** $\overline{BD}$ **13.** $y = 2x - 3$; (2, 1) **15.** Sample answer: $\langle 0, 2 \rangle$. Points on the *y*-axis have coordinates of the form $(0, b)$. After the translation, the coordinates of the image are $(0, b + 2)$, which is still a point on the *y*-axis. **17.** $(6, -8)$; let the coordinates of point *P* be (x, y). Then $(x - 2, y + 7) = (4, -1)$. Solving the equations $x - 2 = 4$ and $y + 7 = -1$ shows that $x = 6$ and $y = -8$.

LESSON 14.4

Your Turn

4.

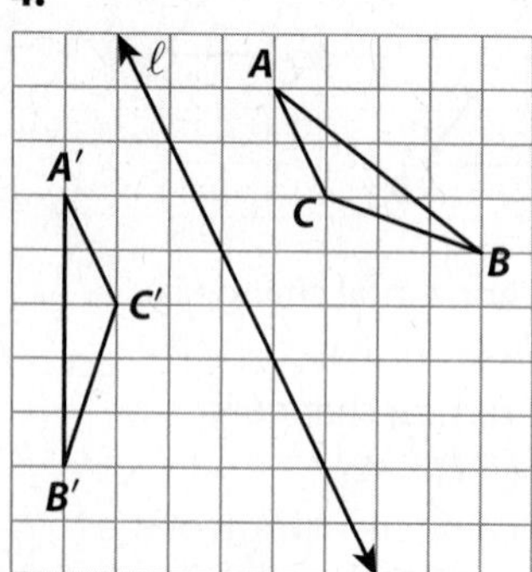

5.

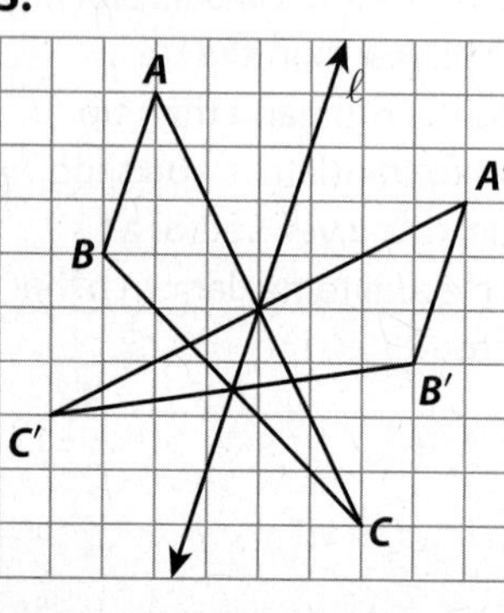

6.

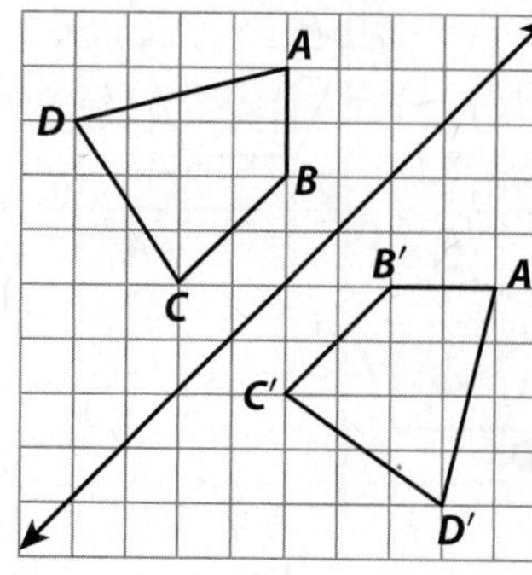

7.

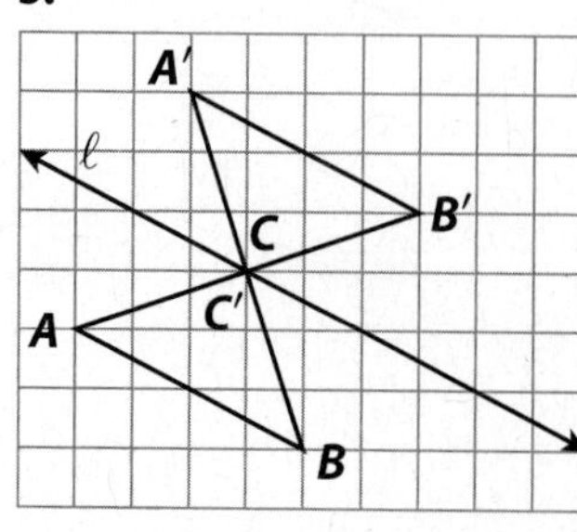

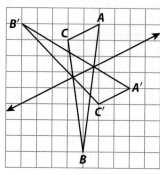

10.

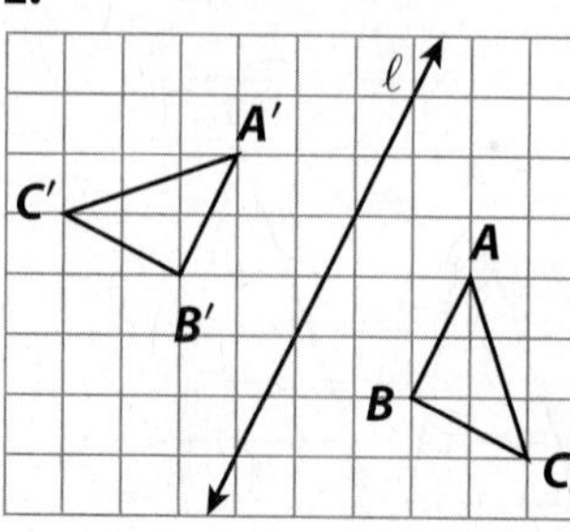

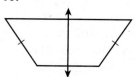

11. no lines of symmetry

Guided Practice

1. *S*; points on the line of reflection remain fixed.

2.

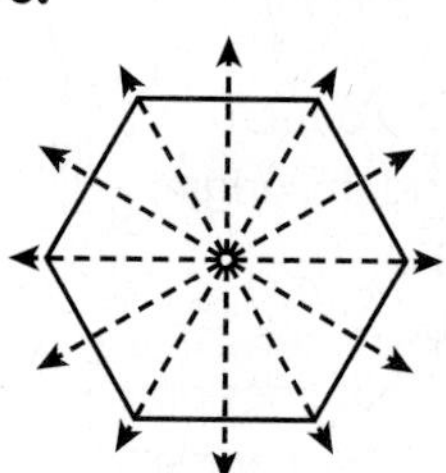

3.

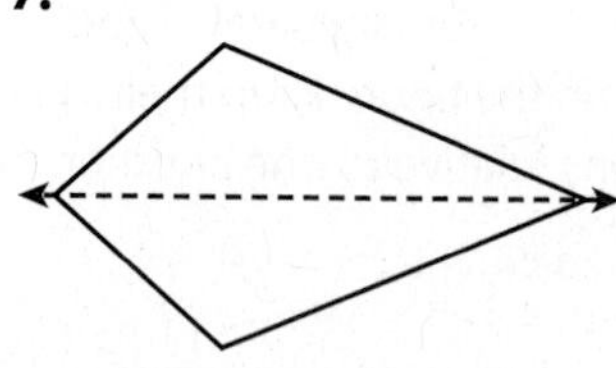

4.

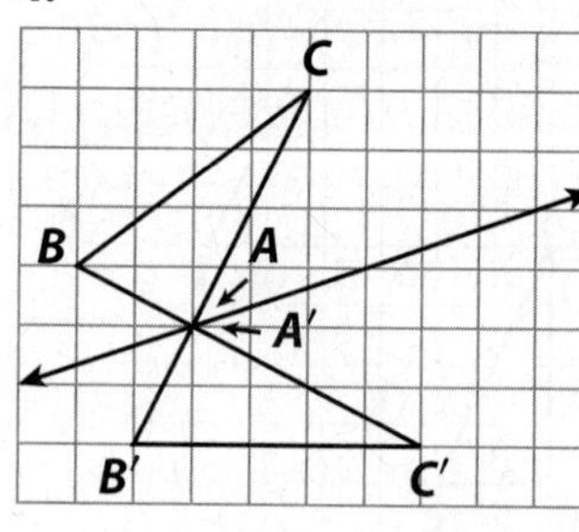

5.

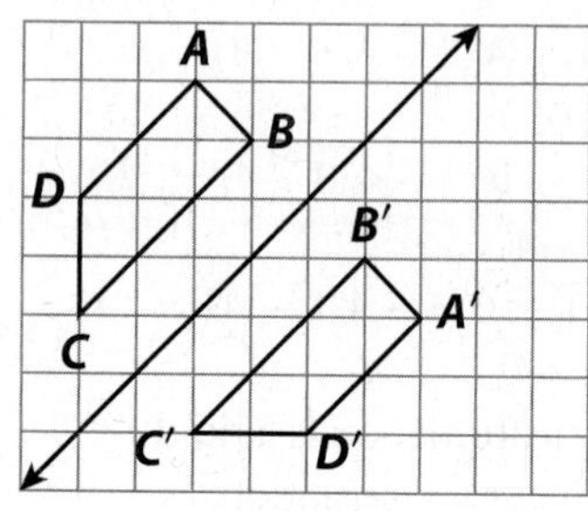

6.

7.

8. Sample answer: Draw a segment from each vertex that is perpendicular to and bisected by the line of reflection. Connect the other endpoints, the vertices of the image.

Independent Practice

9. $\overline{MN}$ **11.** $\overline{QR}$ **13.** $\overline{MP}$ **15.** 8; 4 that bisect opposite sides, and 4 through opposite vertices **17.** He drew a line of symmetry rather than a line of reflection. **19.** The triangle is equilateral. Each side is mapped to another side. Since reflections preserve length, all three sides must have the same length.

21. Since the location of point *P* does not change under a reflection across line ℓ, point *P* must lie on line ℓ. Similarly, point *P* must lie on line *m*. Since point *P* is on both of the lines, lines ℓ and *m* intersect at point *P*.

LESSON 14.5

Your Turn

6.

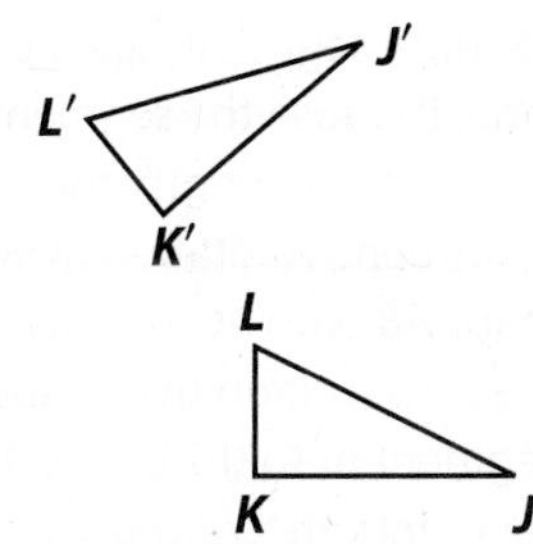

P•

10. 90°, 180°, 270° **11.** 180°

Guided Practice

1. $\angle R'QR$ and $\angle S'QS$; under a rotation, all angles with vertex *Q* formed by a point and its image have the same measure.

2.

Step 1: 165°

Step 2: *PD*

Step 3:

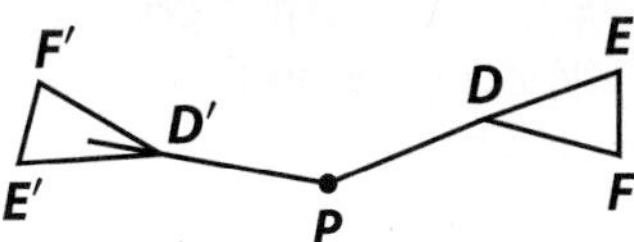

3.

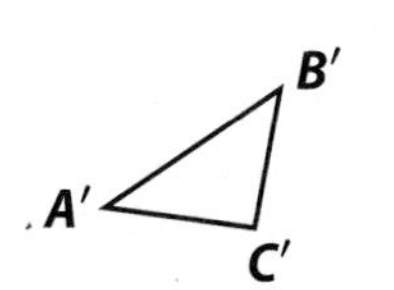

P•

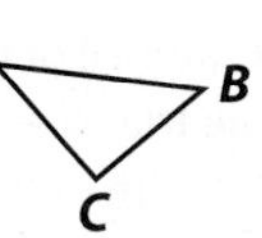

4.

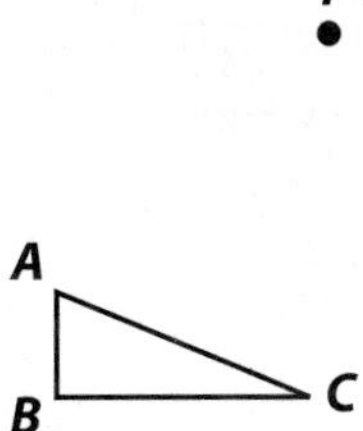

5. none **6.** 120°, 240° **7.** Draw a segment from the center of rotation to a point on the figure. Draw a ray that forms the required angle with this segment. Locate the image point on the ray. Repeat for other points to complete the figure.

Independent Practice

9. $\overline{XY}$ **11.** *PJ* **13.** 315°

15.

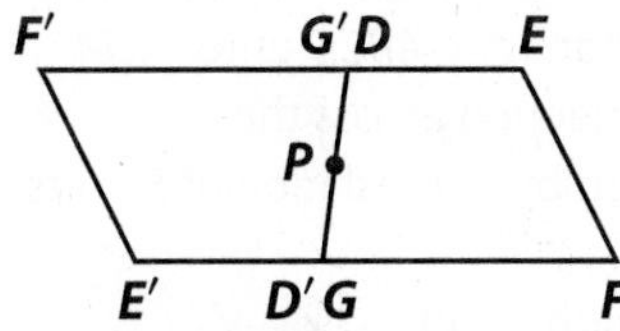

parallelogram

17. 20°; draw $\overline{PD}$ and $\overline{PD'}$. Then use a protractor to measure $\angle D'PD$.

19a. 3 sides: 120°, 4 sides: 90°, 5 sides: 72°, 6 sides: 60°

b. 22.5°; rotating by the smallest angle of rotation maps one vertex to the next. So divide 360° by the number of sides: 360° ÷ 16 = 22.5°.

LESSON 14.6

Your Turn

4.

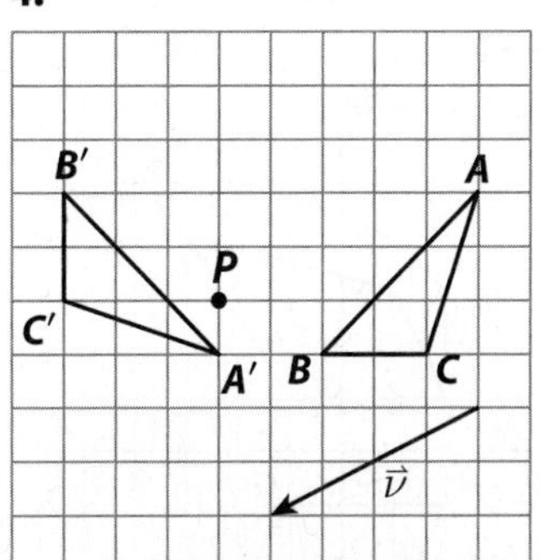

5.

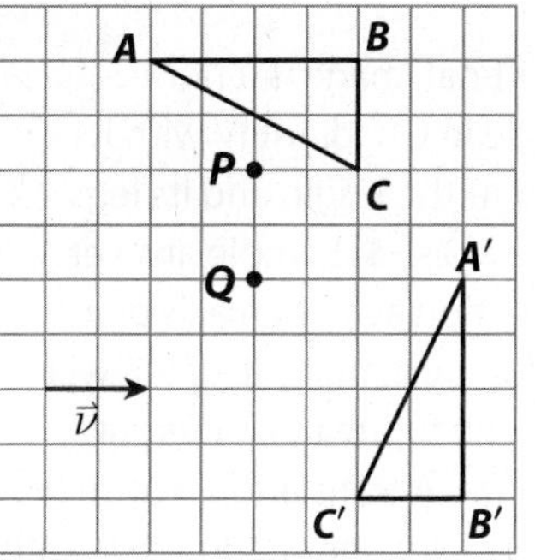

9. The triangle is mapped onto itself, with *A* and *C* mapping to one another and *B* mapping to itself. **10.** The final image is a rectangle centered at the origin. It is oriented so that the longer sides are vertical and the shorter sides are horizontal.

Guided Practice

1.

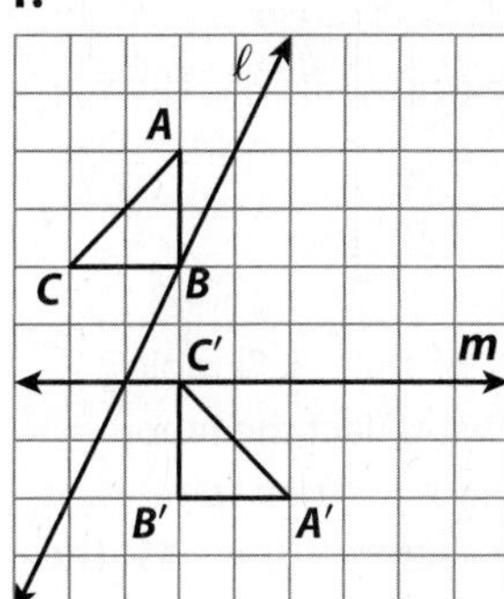

2.

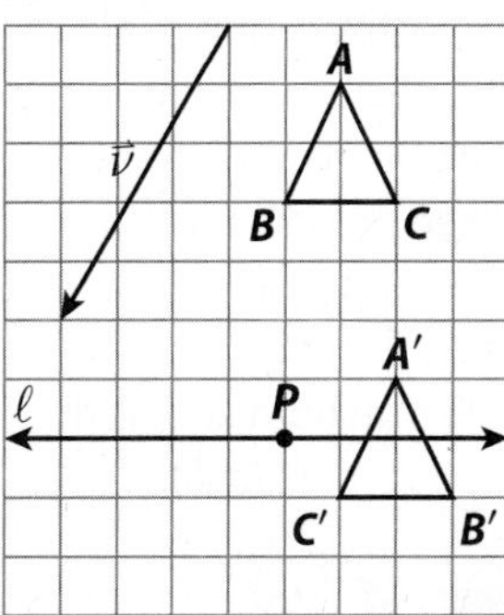

3.

(1) Quadrant III

(2) Quadrant II

(3) Quadrant I

The final image of *DEFG* is a square in Quadrant I that is farther from the axes than the original square was.

Selected Answers

UNIT 5 Selected Answers *(cont'd)*

4. The final image is a right triangle in Quadrant IV with its vertex at the origin and its legs on the axes. **5.** Sample answer: A reflection across an axis or a rotation by a multiple of 90° will move the figure to a different quadrant. A translation may or may not, depending on the length and direction of the translation vector.

Independent Practice

7a.

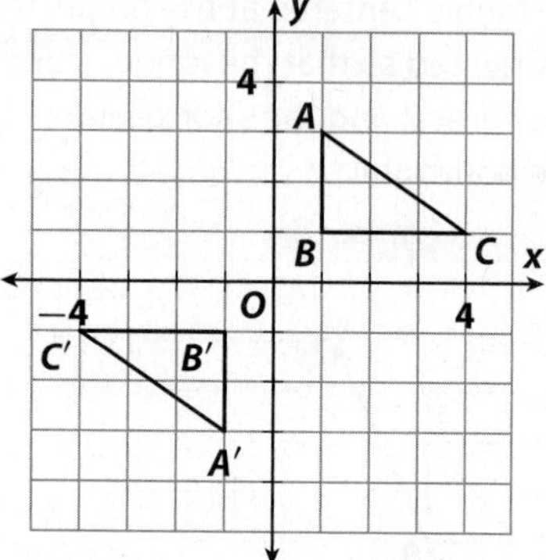

c. rotation of 180° **9.** Sample answer: First reflect the moon across the y-axis. Then translate it along the vector $\langle -3, 1 \rangle$. **11.** The point was located in Quadrant I. **13.** The point (a, b) remains fixed. The only fixed points under the reflection across the line $x = a$ are the points on the line. The only fixed points under the reflection across the line $y = b$ are the points on the line. The only point that lies on both lines is the point of intersection, (a, b).

LESSON 15.1

Your Turn

3. Not congruent; the figures are different sizes, so there is no rigid motion that maps one onto the other. **4.** Congruent; a rigid motion (a reflection across the x-axis) maps one figure onto the other.

6. *ABCDE* maps onto *PQRST*.
rotation: $(x, y) \rightarrow (-x, -y)$
translation: $(x, y) \rightarrow (x, y + 1)$
7. *JKL* maps onto *XYZ*.
reflection: $(x, y) \rightarrow (-x, y)$
rotation: $(x, y) \rightarrow (-y, x)$
translation: $(x, y) \rightarrow (x + 1, y)$

Guided Practice

1. The triangles are congruent by definition. That is, there is a sequence of rigid motions (a reflection followed by a translation) that maps one triangle onto the other. **2.** Congruent; a rigid motion (a rotation of 180°) maps one figure onto the other. **3.** Not congruent; lengths and angle measures are not preserved. **4.** You can map *ABCD* onto *JKLM* by a reflection across the x-axis followed by a translation of 5 units right.
Reflection: $(x, y) \rightarrow (x, -y)$
Translation: $(x, y) \rightarrow (x + 5, y)$
5. $\overline{PT}$ and $\overline{TR}$; $\overline{QT}$ and $\overline{TS}$; $\angle QTR$ and $\angle RTS$; $\angle PTQ$ and $\angle QTS$
6. If there is a series of rigid motions mapping one figure onto the other, you can conclude that the figures are congruent. If the two figures are congruent, there exists a sequence of rigid motions that maps one onto the other.

Independent Practice

7. Sample answer: $(x, y) \rightarrow (-y, x)$, $(x, y) \rightarrow (-x, y)$, $(x, y) \rightarrow (x - 1, y)$
9. Sample drawing:

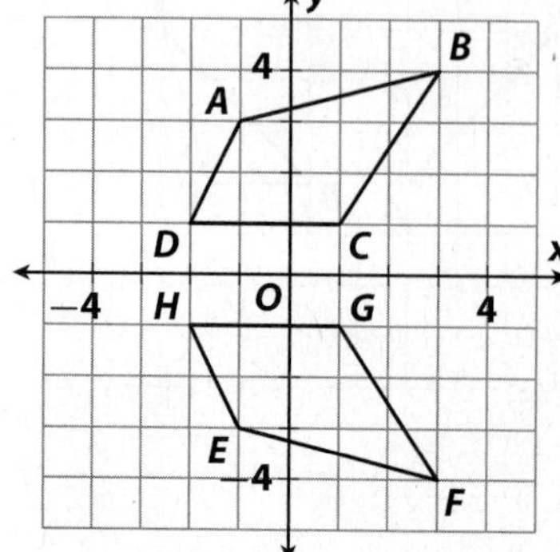

Sample answer: A reflection across the x-axis maps one quadrilateral onto the other. **11.** No; the transformation is not a rigid motion so the figures are not congruent.
13a. $(x, y) \rightarrow (x + 2, y - 2)$;
$(x, y) \rightarrow (x + 4, y - 4)$;
$(x, y) \rightarrow (x + 6, y - 6)$
b. $(x, y) \rightarrow (x + 2n, y - 2n)$
15. Both segments are 4 units long. Because the segments are the same length, they are congruent. A rotation of 90° maps $\overline{AB}$ onto $\overline{AC}$. Because there is a rigid motion that maps one segment onto the other, the segments are congruent.

LESSON 15.2

Your Turn

3. 90° **4.** 6.2 ft **5.** 30° **6.** 3.1 ft
8. Yes; $m\angle T = m\angle U = 71°$, so six pairs of corresponding parts are congruent.

Guided Practice

1. The triangles are congruent; $\overline{XQ} \cong \overline{VR}$, $\overline{QW} \cong \overline{RH}$, $\overline{XW} \cong \overline{VH}$, $\angle X \cong \angle V$, $\angle Q \cong \angle R$, and $\angle W \cong \angle H$, because a reflection and a translation are rigid motions, and rigid motions preserve length and angle measure. **2.** 4.5 ft **3.** 41° **4.** 90° **5.** 49° **6.** The triangles are congruent by the Congruent Triangles Theorem and because a sequence of rigid motions maps one triangle onto the other.
7. No; $m\angle M = 48°$ and $m\angle C = 44°$ so there are not six pairs of congruent corresponding parts.
8. Yes; there are six pairs of congruent corresponding parts.
9. Their corresponding sides and corresponding angles are congruent.

Independent Practice

11. Rotate $\triangle MNP$ around point P so that point M maps to point R and point N maps to point S. This will show that a sequence of rigid motions (translation and rotation) maps one triangle to the other triangle. **13.** The transformations must be rigid motions. In that case, the segments will be congruent and will have the same length. **15.** No; the angles of $\triangle ABC$ measure 55°, 50°, and 75°; the angles of $\triangle DEF$ measure 65°, 50°, and 65°. Corresponding angles are not congruent, so the triangles cannot be congruent. **17.** 12 ways; $\triangle DVW \cong \triangle LCY$, $\triangle DWV \cong \triangle LYC$, $\triangle VDW \cong \triangle CLY$, $\triangle VWD \cong \triangle CYL$, $\triangle WDV \cong \triangle YLC$, or $\triangle WVD \cong \triangle YCL$, and 6 more with the order of the triangles reversed. **19.** Yes; Sample answer: if J maps to N, then K will map to M. This is possible if these four angles are congruent.

LESSON 15.3

Your Turn

3. congruent by the ASA Thm.: $\angle J \cong \angle L$, $\overline{JK} \cong \overline{KL}$, and $\angle JKM \cong \angle LKM$
4. Not congruent; $m\angle R = 70°$ and $m\angle S = 75°$, so not all pairs of corresponding parts are $\cong$.

Guided Practice

1. point E; $m\angle BCE$; $\overrightarrow{ED}$; $\overrightarrow{CD}$; point D
2. 57°; $\angle XYW$; $\angle ZYW$; $\overline{YW}$; $\triangle XYW$
3. If two angles and the included side of one triangle are congruent to two angles and the included side of another triangle, you can conclude that the triangles are congruent.

Independent Practice

5. $\angle SRP \cong \angle QPR$; you need to have two pairs of congruent angles with $\overline{PR}$ as the included side.
7a. Translate $\overline{LM}$ to $\overline{WX}$, then reflect $\triangle LMN$ across $\overleftrightarrow{WX}$. **b.** The images of $\overrightarrow{LN}$ and $\overrightarrow{MN}$ lie on $\overrightarrow{WY}$ and $\overrightarrow{XY}$, respectively. The image of N must lie on both rays, so the image is the intersection point Y. **9a.** $\angle J \cong \angle R$, $\angle H \cong \angle Q$ (both are right angles), and $\overline{HJ} \cong \overline{QR}$ (both are 4 units long). Two pairs of angles and their included sides are congruent, so the triangles are congruent by the ASA Theorem. **b.** Sample answer: You can map $\triangle GHJ$ onto $\triangle PQR$ by a translation 2 units left followed by a reflection across the x-axis. By the definition of congruence in terms of rigid motion, the triangles must be congruent.
11. No; the triangles are congruent only if the sides that are 9.5 mm long are corresponding sides.

LESSON 15.4

Your Turn

2. Not congruent; no sequence of rigid motions will map $\triangle BAC$ onto $\triangle EDF$. **3.** congruent by the SAS Theorem: $\overline{VT} \cong \overline{WT}$, $\overline{TU} \cong \overline{TU}$, $\angle VTU \cong \angle WTU$

Guided Practice

1. Reflect $\triangle PQR$ across $\overleftrightarrow{TV}$; this will map point Q to point U and show that there is a sequence of rigid motions that maps $\triangle PQR$ to $\triangle TUV$. **2.** congruent by the SAS Theorem: $\overline{CB} \cong \overline{DB}$, $\overline{AB} \cong \overline{AB}$, $\angle ABC \cong \angle ABD$ **3.** If two sides and the included angle of one triangle are congruent to two sides and the included angle of another triangle, you can conclude that the triangles are congruent.

Independent Practice

5. SAS **7.** No; she can map $\overrightarrow{AC}$ to $\overrightarrow{DF}$ by a reflection across $\overleftrightarrow{DE}$, but C will map to F only if $AC = DF$.
9. Yes; the triangles are congruent by SAS, so $HJ = 2.9$ cm by CPCTC.
11. In the figure, the congruent angles are not included angles, so SAS does not apply. **13.** Sample answer: In both theorems, you use three pairs of congruent corresponding parts to conclude that two triangles are congruent. In the ASA Theorem, the side is included between two angles; in the SAS Theorem, the angle is included between two sides.

LESSON 15.5

Your Turn

3. Not congruent; no sequence of rigid motions maps one triangle onto the other because $MN \neq QR$.
4. congruent by the SSS Theorem: $\overline{GJ} \cong \overline{GJ}$, $\overline{GK} \cong \overline{GL}$, $\overline{KJ} \cong \overline{LJ}$

Guided Practice

1. R and T are both equidistant from S and K. So $\overleftrightarrow{RT}$ is the perpendicular bisector of $\overline{SK}$, and a reflection across $\overleftrightarrow{RT}$ maps point K to point S. **2.** Sample answer: congruent by the SSS Theorem: $\overline{HD} \cong \overline{HF}$, $\overline{HE} \cong \overline{HG}$, $\overline{DE} \cong \overline{FG}$
3. If three sides of one triangle are congruent to three sides of another triangle, you can conclude that the triangles are congruent.

Independent Practice

5. SSS **7.** Sample answer: reflect $\triangle ABC$ across $\overleftrightarrow{AB}$, then rotate the image around point D by $m\angle CAF$.
9a. $\overline{AC} \cong \overline{AD}$ **b.** none **c.** $\angle C \cong \angle D$ or $\angle CAB \cong \angle DAB$
11. Sample sketch

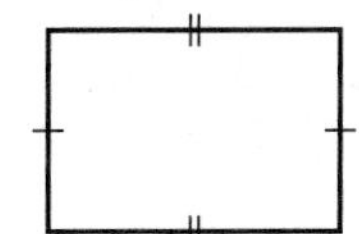

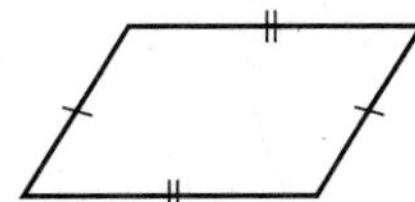

13. Yes; no; you can use a ruler to check for congruence by SSS. You can use a protractor to check whether all pairs of corresponding angles are congruent. However, the triangles still might not be congruent, because one might be an enlargement of the other.

UNIT 5 Selected Answers *(cont'd)*

LESSON 16.1

Your Turn

5.

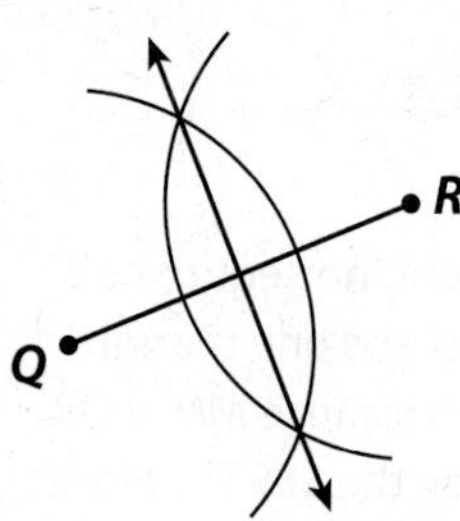

6.

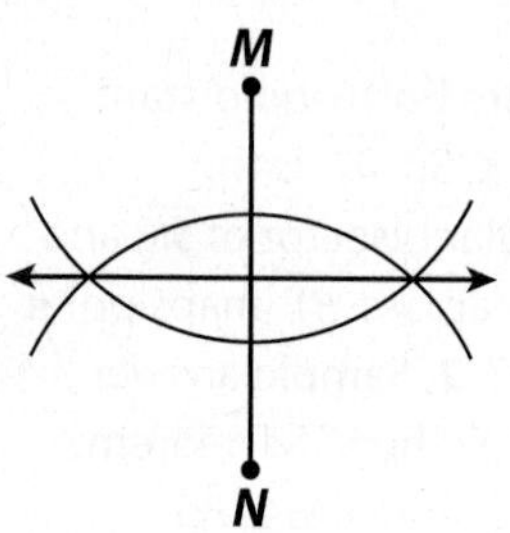

7.

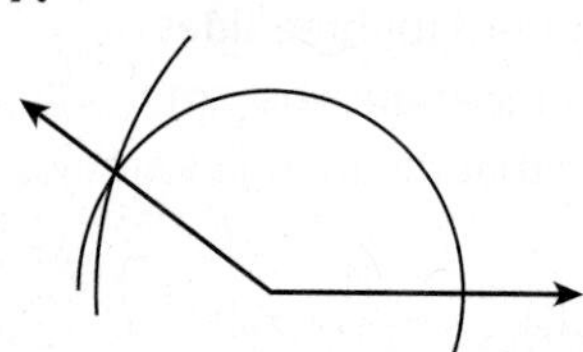

10.

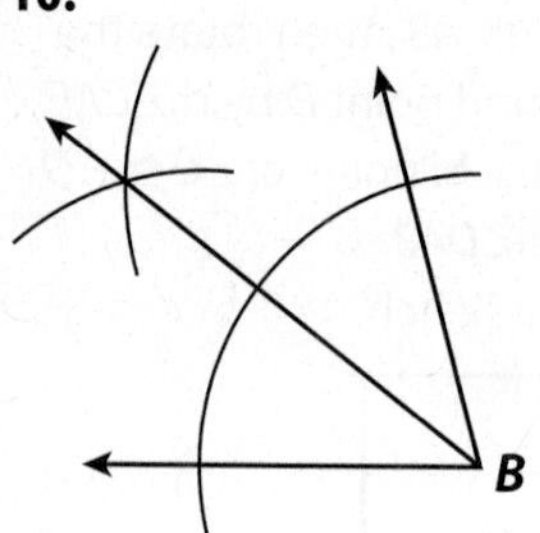

11.

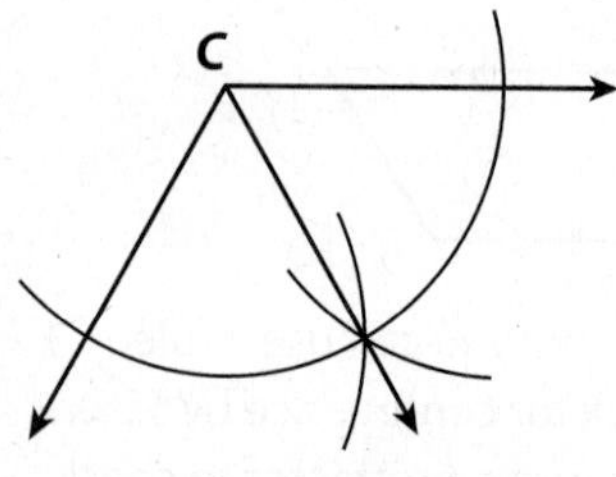

Guided Practice

1.

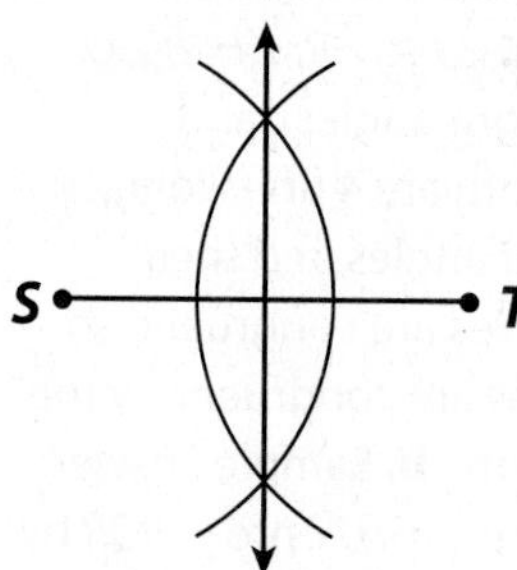

2.

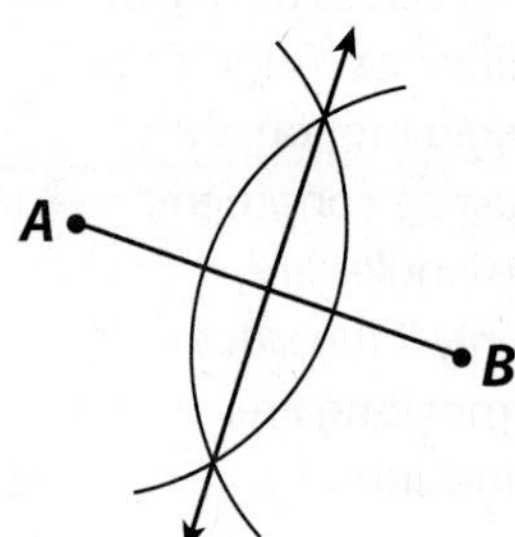

3.

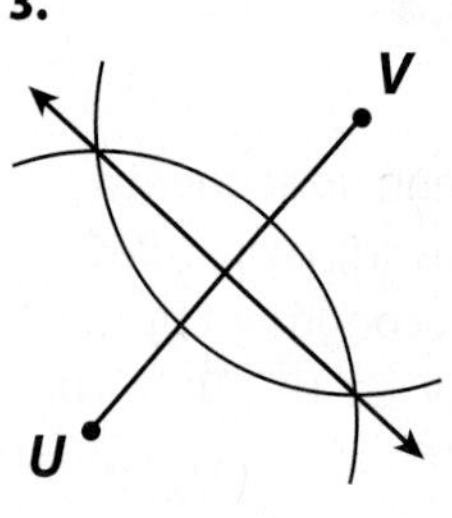

4.

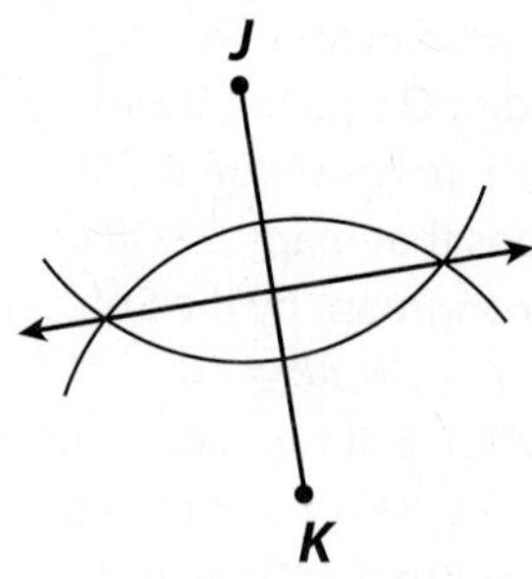

5.

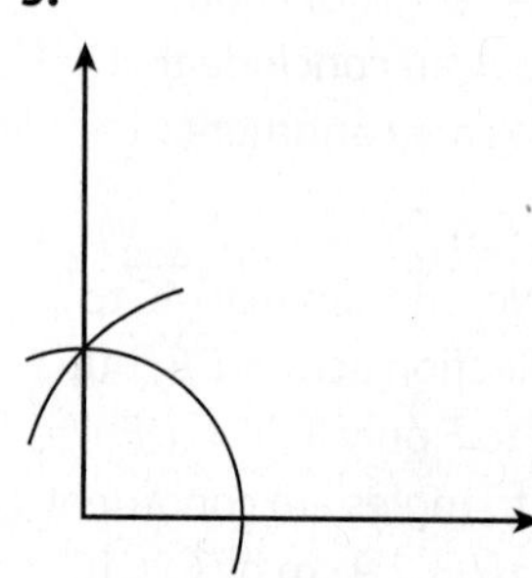

6.

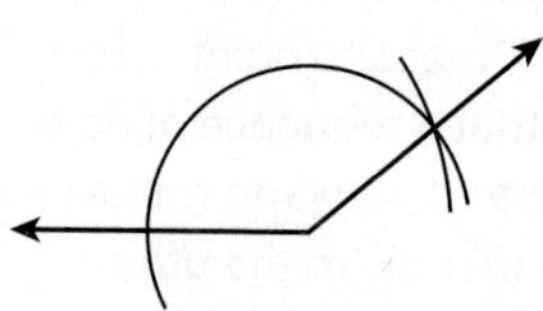

7.

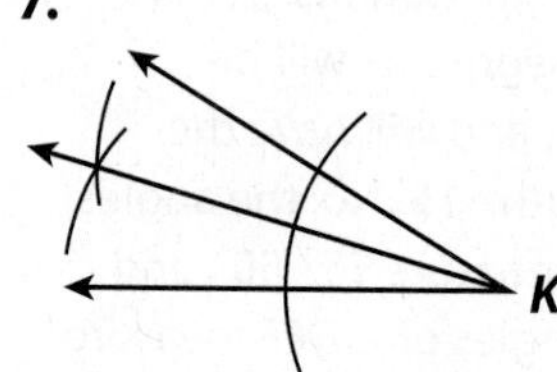

8.

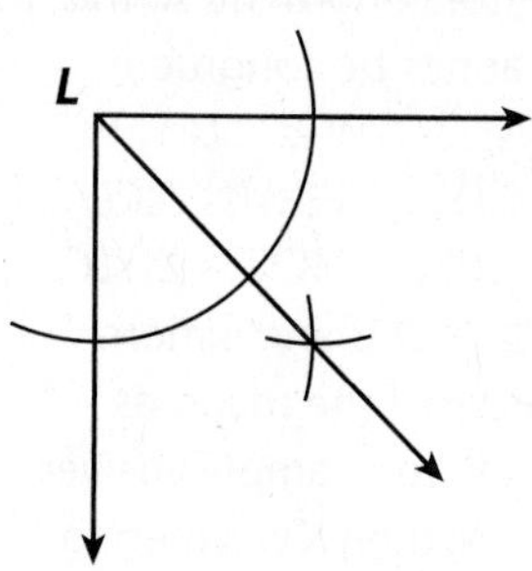

9.

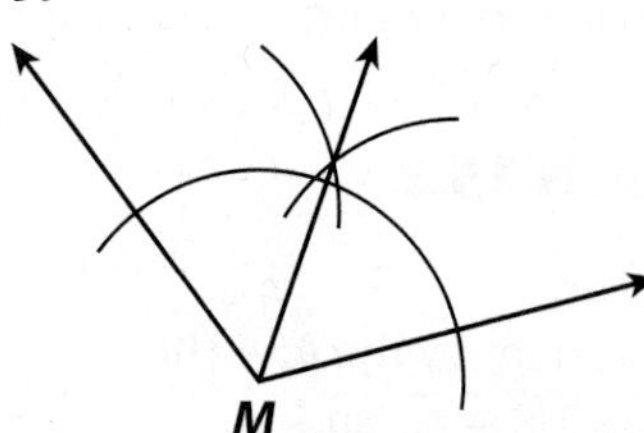

10.

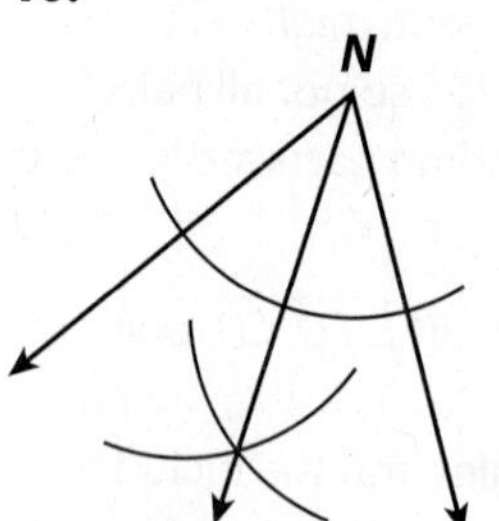

11. When you use a compass to copy a segment, you are measuring and marking a distance, as you would with a ruler. Unlike a ruler, a compass doesn't have defined units of measurement. Also, you make arcs with a compass, but you make straight lines with a ruler.

Independent Practice

13. Matt used the radius of his first arc, not the distance between the points of intersection, to draw the second arc.

15.

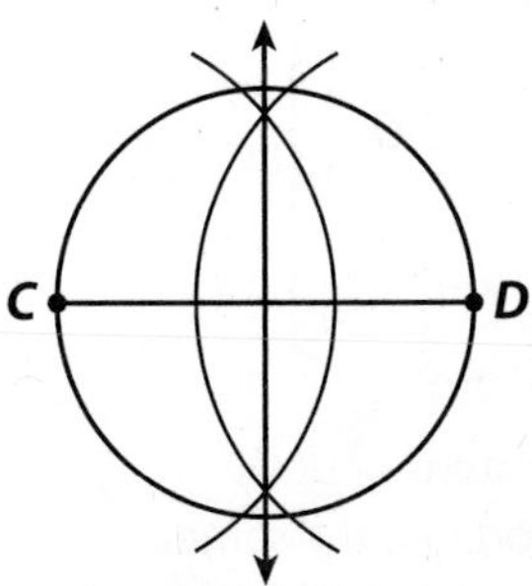

17. Fold the paper so that the segment's endpoints coincide. The fold line is the segment's perpendicular bisector, so any three points on the fold line will be equidistant from the endpoints. **19.** Draw a segment and construct its perpendicular bisector. Then construct the angle bisector of one of the right angles. This creates two 45° angles. Finally, construct the angle bisector of one of the 45° angles to form two 22.5° angles.

LESSON 16.2

Your Turn

4.

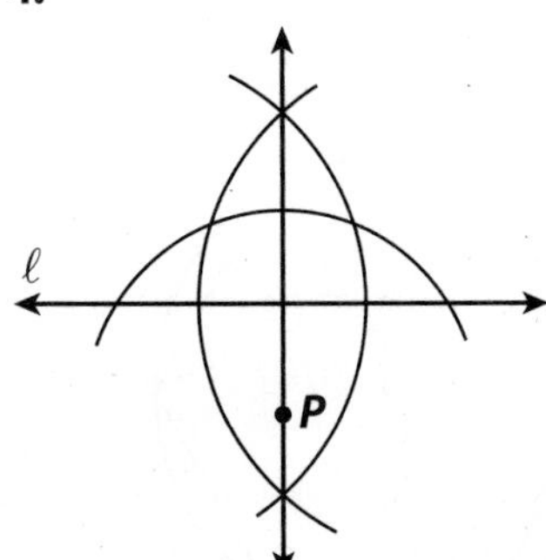

5.

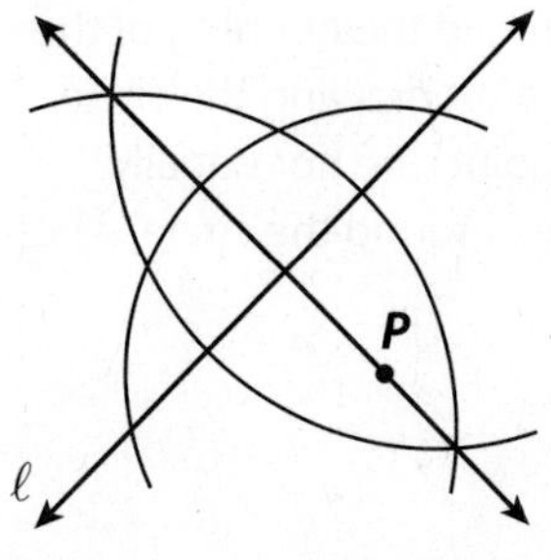

8.

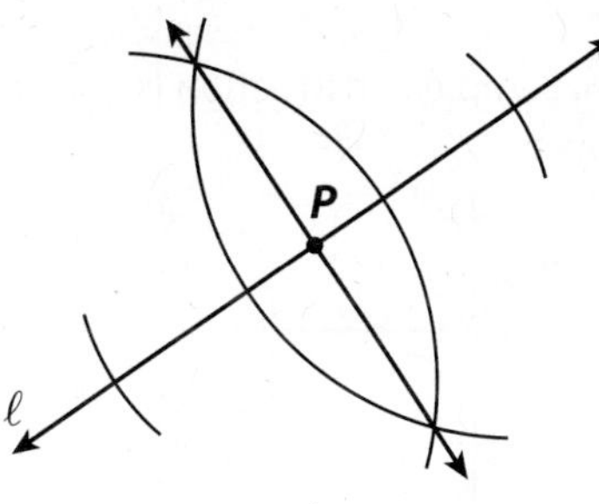

9.

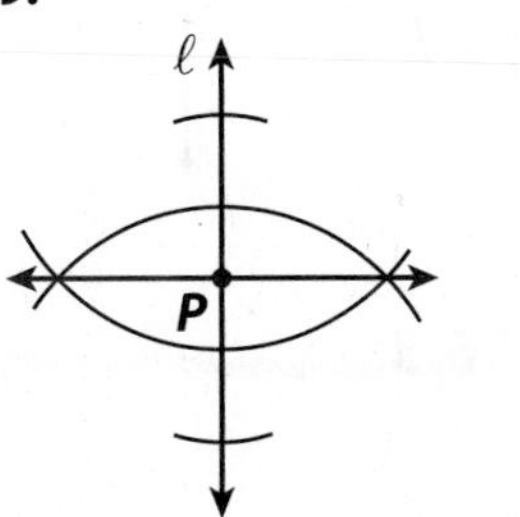

11.

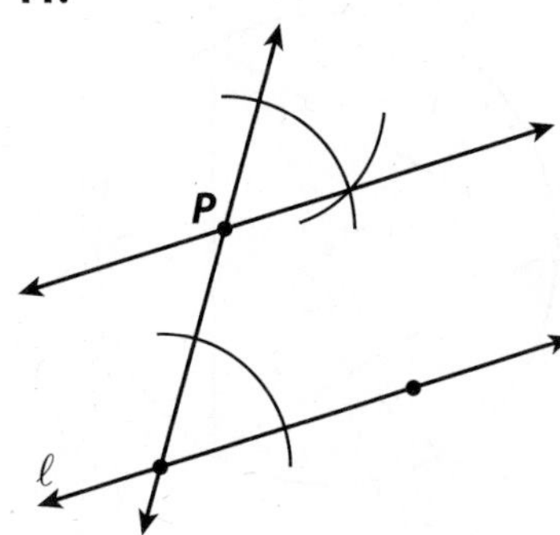

12.

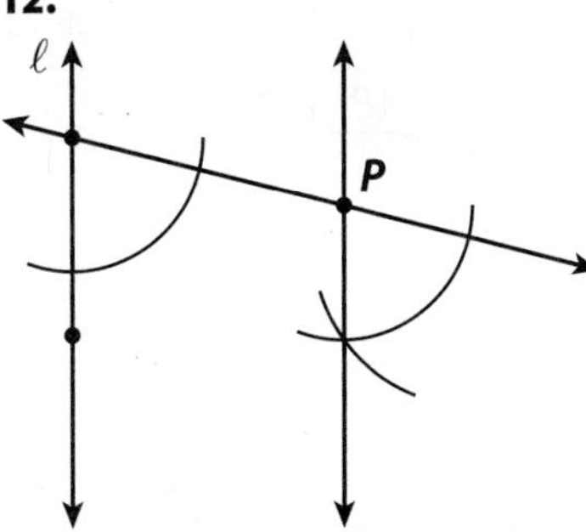

Guided Practice

1. She should adjust the angle of the reflective device until the image of line ℓ coincides with line ℓ. Then she should draw a line along the edge of the reflective device. This is the required line.

2. Place the device at the approximate midpoint and at an approximate right angle to the segment. Adjust the device until the image of one endpoint coincides with the other endpoint. Draw a line along the device. The line is the perpendicular bisector of the segment.

3.

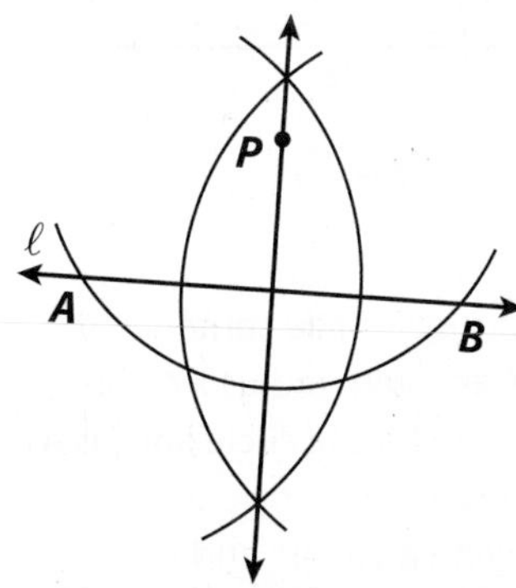

4.

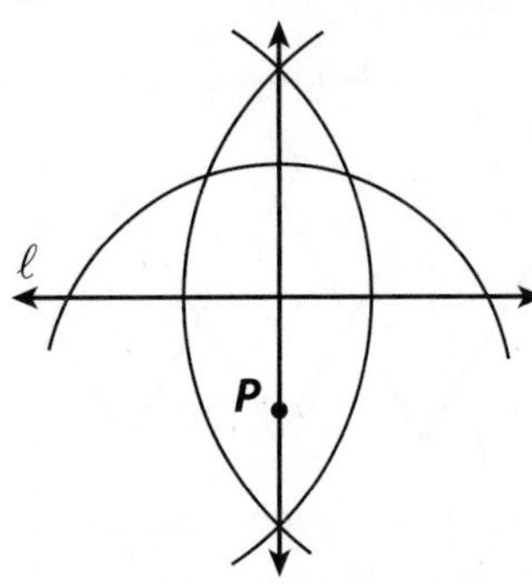

5.

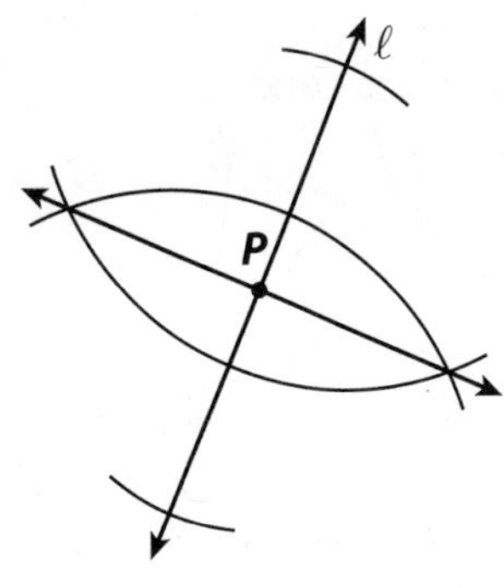

6.

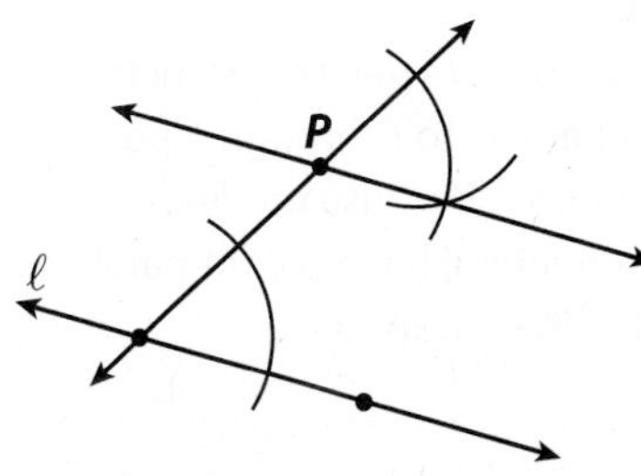

UNIT 5 Selected Answers *(cont'd)*

7.

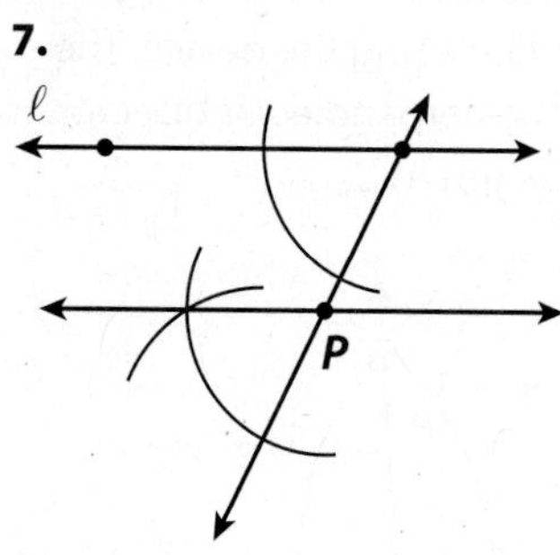

8. Construct a circle centered at point A and with radius XY. The intersection of the circle and j is A'.

9. You use the construction for copying an angle and the construction for making a perpendicular bisector.

Independent Practice

11.

Rhombuses; the given segments are all congruent, so each quadrilateral has four congruent sides.

13a. Sample construction:

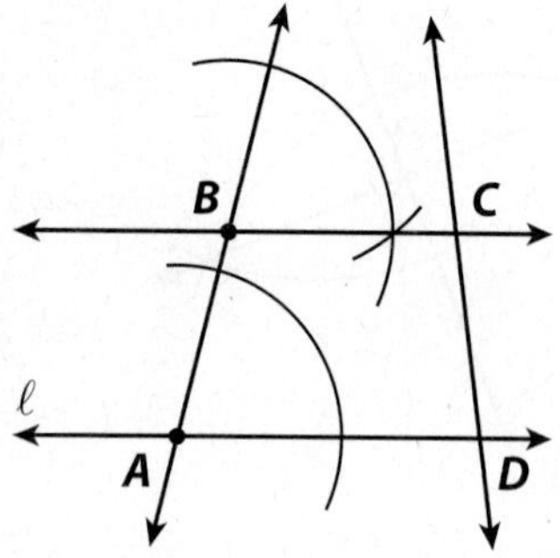

b. Sample answer: I constructed a line parallel to ℓ through a point B not on ℓ. Because the final quadrilateral has a pair of parallel sides, it is a trapezoid.

15a. Sample construction is shown.

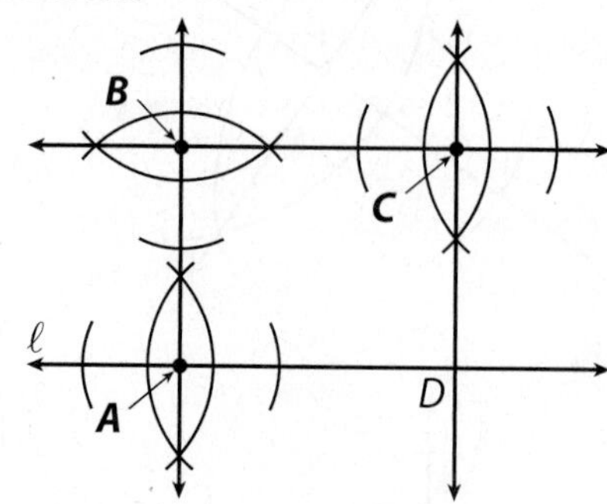

LESSON 16.3

Your Turn

6.

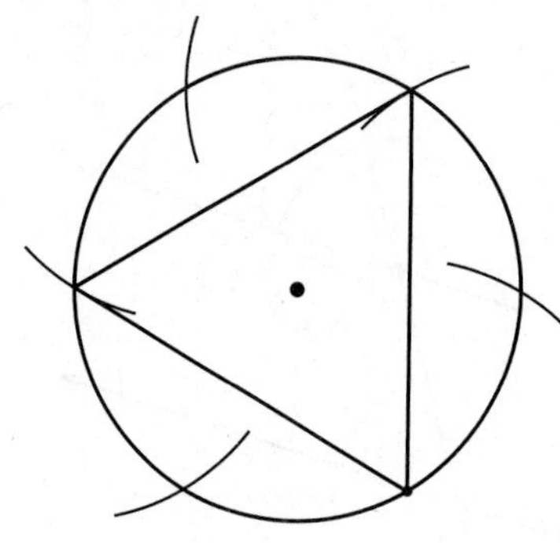

Guided Practice

1.

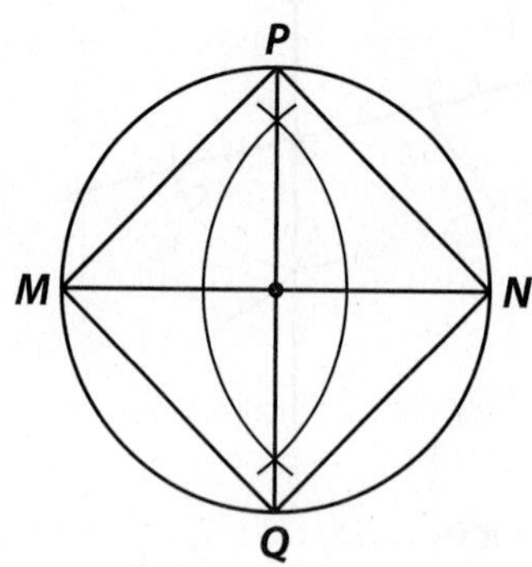

2.

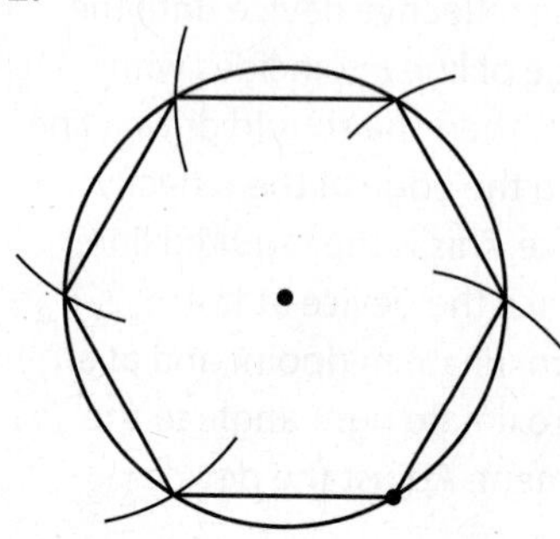

3.

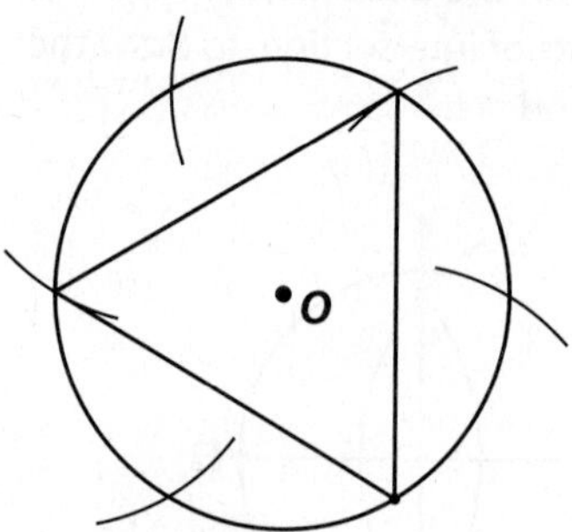

4. The first steps of both constructions are the same. You draw a circle and locate six equally spaced points around the circle. For the hexagon, you connect consecutive points with a straightedge; for the equilateral triangle, you connect every other point.

Independent Practice

5.

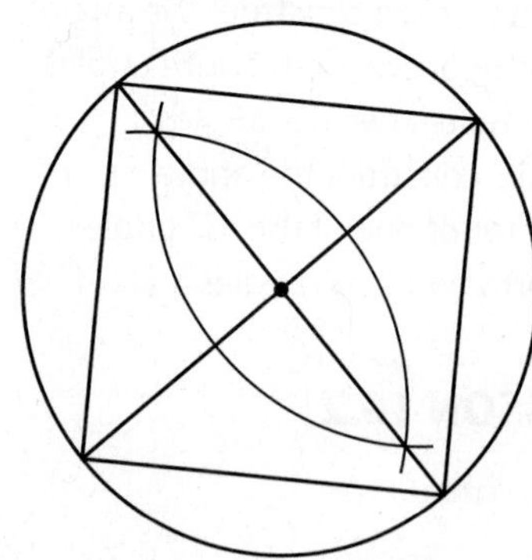

7.

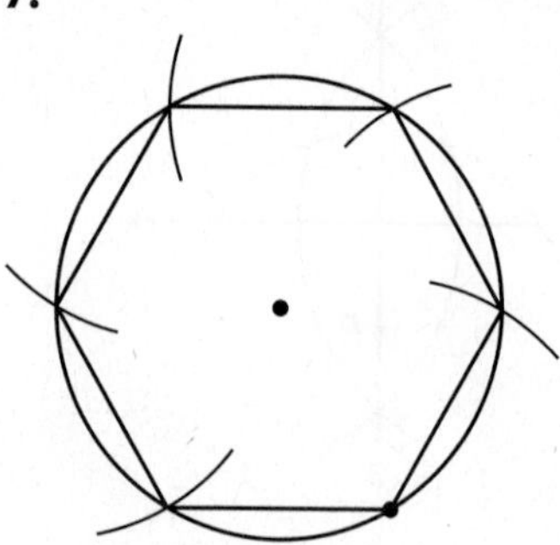

9. He changed the opening of the compass after drawing the circle, so the 6 points are not equally distributed around the circle.

11. Fold the circle so that one half coincides with the other. The crease is a diameter. Then fold the diameter onto itself to make another crease that is the perpendicular bisector of the diameter. The two creases determine the four vertices of the square on the circle.

13. A kite; the consecutive sides $\overline{EA}$ and $\overline{AC}$ are two sides of an equilateral triangle, so they are congruent; the consecutive sides $\overline{CD}$ and $\overline{DE}$ are two sides of a regular hexagon, so they are congruent. Since the quadrilateral has two distinct pairs of congruent consecutive sides, it is a kite.

Selected Answers

UNIT 6 Selected Answers

MODULE 17

LESSON 17.1

Your Turn

4. $\overline{PQ}$ and $\overline{SR}$ both have a slope of $-\frac{1}{2}$, so they are parallel. $\overline{QR}$ and $\overline{PS}$ both have a slope of 3, so they are parallel. Quadrilateral *PQRS* is a parallelogram because it is a quadrilateral with two pairs of parallel sides. **6.** $y = -3x + 1$

Guided Practice

1. Use CPCTC to show that $\frac{KL}{JL} = \frac{ST}{RT}$. **2.** $A(-4, 2), B(1, 3), C(2, 0), D(-2, -4)$

$$\text{slope of } \overline{BC} = \frac{0-3}{2-1} = -3$$
$$\text{slope of } \overline{AD} = \frac{-4-2}{-2-(-4)} = -3$$

Quadrilateral *ABCD* is a trapezoid because it is a quadrilateral with at least one pair of parallel sides. **3.** $y = \frac{2}{3}x - 5$ **4.** $y = -2x - \frac{3}{2}$ **5.** Trapezoid; lines ℓ and p are parallel, so the quadrilateral has at least one pair of parallel sides. **6.** Determine the slope of the given line. The required line has the same slope. Use this slope, the given point, and the slope-intercept form to find the equation of the required line.

Independent Practice

7. Sample answer: Slope of $\overline{AB} = \frac{1}{3}$, slope of $\overline{BC} = -3$, slope of $\overline{DC} = \frac{1}{4}$, slope of $\overline{AD} = 3$. Since no two sides have the same slope, no two sides are parallel, so *ABCD* is not a trapezoid. **9.** Neither; no two lines are parallel. **11.** The slope of $\overline{PQ}$ is incorrect. No sides are parallel, so *PQRS* is not a trapezoid. **13a.** $x - \frac{b_2 - b_1}{m_1 - m_2}$ **b.** Since $m_1 \neq m_2$, $m_1 - m_2 \neq 0$, so the value of the fraction $\frac{b_2 - b_1}{m_1 - m_2}$ exists. **c.** If the slopes are different, you can determine a point of intersection, but parallel lines do not intersect, so the slopes must be the same.

LESSON 17.2

Your Turn

2. The slope of $\overline{AB}$ is $\frac{3}{2}$; the slope of $\overline{BC}$ is $-\frac{2}{3}$. Since the product of the slopes is -1, these sides are perpendicular and form a right angle. Therefore, $\triangle ABC$ contains a right angle and is a right triangle. **4.** $y = -\frac{1}{2}x + 2$ **5.** $y = \frac{3}{2}x + \frac{5}{2}$

Guided Practice

1a. The slope of line *m* is $-\frac{a}{b}$, where *a* and *b* are both positive. **b.** Using $\triangle PQ'R'$, the slope of line *n* is $\frac{b}{a}$, where *a* and *b* are both positive. **c.** The product of the slopes of the lines is $-\frac{a}{b} \cdot \frac{b}{a} = -1$. **2.** $A(-3, 2), B(0, 3), C(2, -3), D(-1, -4)$

$$\text{slope of } \overline{AB} = \frac{3-2}{0-(-3)} = \frac{1}{3}$$
$$\text{slope of } \overline{BC} = \frac{-6}{2} = -3$$
$$\text{slope of } \overline{CD} = \frac{1}{3}$$
$$\text{slope of } \overline{AD} = \frac{-6}{2} = -3$$

The product of the slopes of any two consecutive sides is -1. Quadrilateral *ABCD* is a rectangle because consecutive sides are perpendicular, so the quadrilateral has four right angles. **3.** $y = x + 5$ **4.** $y = -\frac{3}{2}x + 6$ **5.** Determine the slope of the given line. Use the Slope Criteria for Perpendicular Lines Theorem to find the slope of the required line. Use the slope, the given point, and the slope-intercept form to find the equation of the required line.

Independent Practice

7. Rectangle; the quadrilateral has four right angles. **9.** No; slope of $\overline{AB} = -3$, slope of $\overline{BC} = \frac{2}{5}$, slope of $\overline{AC} = -\frac{4}{7}$. No two slopes have the product -1. No two sides are perpendicular. **11.** $B(1, 2)$; Point *B* lies on line ℓ. The slope of $\overline{AB}$ is $-\frac{1}{3}$ and the slope of $\overline{BC}$ is 3. Since $-\frac{1}{3} \cdot 3 = -1$, these sides of the triangle are perpendicular. This means there is a right angle at vertex *B*.

LESSON 17.3

Your Turn

4. By the distance formula, $JK = \sqrt{10}$, $KL = 5$, $ML = 5$, and $JM = \sqrt{10}$. Therefore, $\overline{JK} \cong \overline{JM}$ and $\overline{KL} \cong \overline{ML}$, so quadrilateral *JKLM* is a kite since it has two distinct pairs of congruent consecutive sides. **5.** 4.1 m

Guided Practice

1a. $C(x_2, y_1)$ **b.** $AC = x_1 - x_2$, $BC = y_1 - y_2$ **c.** By the Pythagorean Theorem, $AB^2 = (x_1 - x_2)^2 + (y_1 - y_2)^2$, and solving for *AB* gives $AB = \sqrt{(x_1 - x_2)^2 + (y_1 - y_2)^2}$, which is equivalent to $AB = \sqrt{(x_2 - x_1)^2 + (y_2 - y_1)^2}$. **2.** By the distance formula, $PQ = \sqrt{13}$, $QR = \sqrt{13}$, $RS = \sqrt{13}$, and $SP = \sqrt{13}$, so all sides are congruent. Quadrilateral *PQRS* is a rhombus since it has four congruent sides. **3.** midpoint: $M\left(\frac{1+3}{2}, \frac{4+(-2)}{2}\right) = M(2, 1)$;

distance:

$$\sqrt{(2-(-2))^2 + (1-(-2))^2}$$
$$= \sqrt{4^2 + 3^2} = 5$$

4. To find the distance between $A(x_1, y_1)$ and $B(x_2, y_2)$, substitute the coordinates into the distance formula, $\sqrt{(x_2 - x_1)^2 + (y_2 - y_1)^2}$.

Independent Practice

5. True; $AB = DC = \sqrt{37}$, so $\overline{AB} \cong \overline{DC}$. **7.** False; the four sides are not congruent to each other.

9. False; the distance between $(-3, 0)$ and $(3, -1)$ is $\sqrt{37}$, and $\sqrt{37} > 6$. **11.** Yes; the distance from the library to the museum along Main St. and Waller Rd. is $(\sqrt{13} + 5)$ mi and the distance along Green St. and Forest Ave. is $(\sqrt{17} + 5)$ mi. Since $\sqrt{13} < \sqrt{17}$, the distance along Main St. and Waller Rd. is shorter. **13.** The slope of $\overline{PQ}$ is $\frac{1}{3}$ and the slope of $\overline{RS}$ is $\frac{1}{3}$, so $\overline{PQ}$ and $\overline{RS}$ are parallel. By the distance formula, $PS = QR = 5$, so $\overline{PS} \cong \overline{QR}$. Quadrilateral $PQRS$ is an isosceles trapezoid since it has at least one pair of parallel sides and a pair of congruent nonparallel sides. **15.** Yes; midpoints are $M(-1, 2)$ and $N(1, -2)$. $MN = \sqrt{20} \approx 4.47$ m. Since $4.47 \times 12 = \$53.64$, Isaac can buy the fence for less than \$60.
17a. Prove that $MA = MB = MC$. **b.** $M(a, c)$ **c.** $MA = MB = MC = \sqrt{a^2 + c^2}$
19. Let the point have coordinates $P(x_1, y_1)$. Then the coordinates of its image are $P'(-x_1, y_1)$. By the distance formula, the distance from P to the origin is $\sqrt{(x_1 - 0)^2 + (y_1 - 0)^2} = \sqrt{{x_1}^2 + {y_1}^2}$. The distance from P' to the origin is $\sqrt{(-x_1 - 0)^2 + (y_1 - 0)^2} = \sqrt{(-x_1)^2 + {y_1}^2} = \sqrt{{x_1}^2 + {y_1}^2}$. So both points are the same distance from the origin.

LESSON 17.4

Your Turn

1. 25.6 km **2.** perimeter: 12.3 units; area: 6.5 square units **3.** perimeter: 22.4 units; area: 30 square units **6.** perimeter: 21.8 ft; area: 22.5 ft^2

Guided Practice

1. 21.3 mi **2.** perimeter: 19.2 units; area: 15 square units **3.** perimeter: 19.0 units; area: 20 square units **4.** perimeter: 20.5 units; area: 20 square units **5.** perimeter: 21.0 units; area: 15 square units **6.** Use the distance formula to find the length of each side, and then add the lengths to find the perimeter. Use slopes to confirm that two sides are perpendicular. Then find the lengths of these sides, and use them in the formula $A = \frac{1}{2}bh$ to find the area.

Independent Practice

7a. 27.3 in. **b.** No; the horizontal and vertical sides are 4 in. long; the other sides are $\sqrt{8}$ in. long. Not all sides are congruent, so the tile is not a regular octagon. **c.** Sample answer: There are 4 triangles with area 2 in^2, 2 rectangles with area 8 in^2, and 1 rectangle with area 32 in^2. The total area is 56 in^2.

9a.

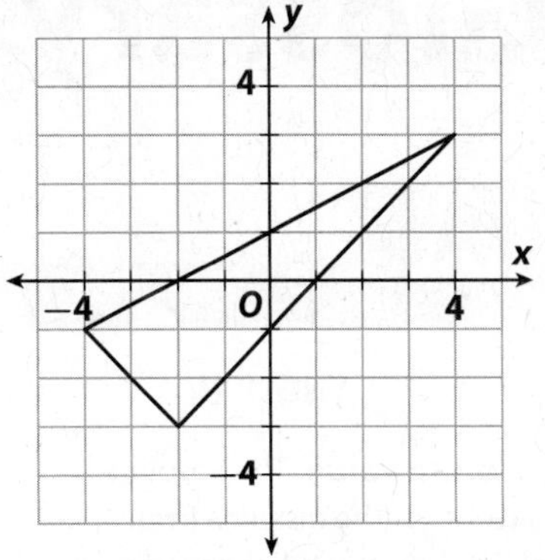

b. perimeter: 20.3 km; area: 12 km^2
11a. 10 square units **b.** Both triangles have an area of 10 square units. **c.** The area is always 10 square units; this makes sense because all of these triangles have the same base ($\overline{PS}$) and a height that is equal to PQ. **13.** Agree; the triangle fits inside a rectangle with vertices $(-2, 3)$, $(3, 3)$, $(3, -3)$, and $(-2, -3)$. The area of the rectangle is $5 \cdot 6 = 30$ square units, so the area of the triangle must be less than 30 square units.

Selected Answers

Glossary/Glosario

A

ENGLISH	SPANISH	EXAMPLES
absolute value The absolute value of x is the distance from zero to x on a number line, denoted $\|x\|$. $\|x\| = \begin{cases} x & \text{if } x \geq 0 \\ -x & \text{if } x < 0 \end{cases}$	**valor absoluto** El valor absoluto de x es la distancia de cero a x en una recta numérica, y se expresa $\|x\|$. $\|x\| = \begin{cases} x & \text{si } x \geq 0 \\ -x & \text{si } x < 0 \end{cases}$	$\|3\| = 3$ $\|-3\| = 3$
absolute-value equation An equation that contains absolute-value expressions.	**ecuación de valor absoluto** Ecuación que contiene expresiones de valor absoluto.	$\|x + 4\| = 7$
absolute-value function A function whose rule contains absolute-value expressions.	**función de valor absoluto** Función cuya regla contiene expresiones de valor absoluto.	$y = \|x + 4\|$
absolute-value inequality An inequality that contains absolute-value expressions.	**desigualdad de valor absoluto** Desigualdad que contiene expresiones de valor absoluto.	$\|x + 4\| > 7$
accuracy The closeness of a given measurement or value to the actual measurement or value.	**exactitud** Cercanía de una medida o un valor a la medida o el valor real.	
acute angle An angle that measures greater than 0° and less than 90°.	**ángulo agudo** Ángulo que mide más de 0° y menos de 90°.	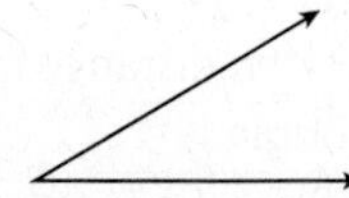
acute triangle A triangle with three acute angles.	**triángulo acutángulo** Triángulo con tres ángulos agudos.	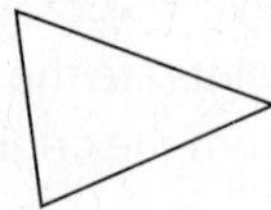
Addition Property of Equality For real numbers a, b, and c, if $a = b$, then $a + c = b + c$.	**Propiedad de igualdad de la suma** Dados los números reales a, b y c, si $a = b$, entonces $a + c = b + c$.	$x - 6 = 8$ $\underline{\;+6 \quad +6}$ $x \quad = 14$
Addition Property of Inequality For real numbers a, b, and c, if $a < b$, then $a + c < b + c$. Also holds true for $>$, $\leq$, $\geq$, and $\neq$.	**Propiedad de desigualdad de la suma** Dados los números reales a, b y c, si $a < b$, entonces $a + c < b + c$. Es válido también para $>$, $\leq$, $\geq$ y $\neq$.	$x - 6 < 8$ $\underline{\;+6 \quad +6}$ $x \quad < 14$
additive inverse The opposite of a number. Two numbers are additive inverses if their sum is zero.	**inverso aditivo** El opuesto de un número. Dos números son inversos aditivos si su suma es cero.	The additive inverse of 5 is −5. The additive inverse of −5 is 5.

ENGLISH	SPANISH	EXAMPLES

adjacent angles Two angles in the same plane with a common vertex and a common side, but no common interior points.

ángulos adyacentes Dos ángulos en el mismo plano que tienen un vértice y un lado común pero no comparten puntos internos.

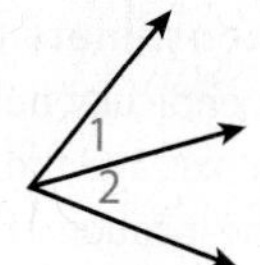

$\angle 1$ and $\angle 2$ are adjacent angles.

---

algebraic expression An expression that contains at least one variable.

expresión algebraica Expresión que contiene por lo menos una variable.

AND A logical operator representing the intersection of two sets.

Y Operador lógico que representa la intersección de dos conjuntos.

$A = \{2, 3, 4, 5\}$ $B = \{1, 3, 5, 7\}$
The set of values that are in A AND B is $A \cap B = \{3, 5\}$.

---

angle A figure formed by two rays with a common endpoint.

ángulo Figura formada por dos rayos con un extremo común.

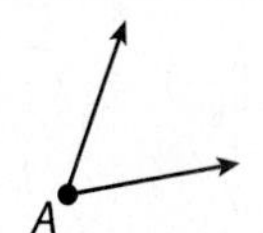

---

angle bisector A ray that divides an angle into two congruent angles.

bisectriz de un ángulo Rayo que divide un ángulo en dos ángulos congruentes.

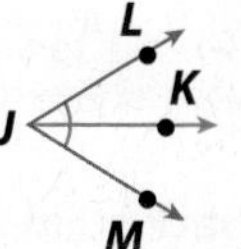

$\overrightarrow{JK}$ is an angle bisector of $\angle LJM$.

---

area The number of nonoverlapping unit squares of a given size that will exactly cover the interior of a plane figure.

área Cantidad de cuadrados unitarios de un determinado tamaño no superpuestos que cubren exactamente el interior de una figura plana.

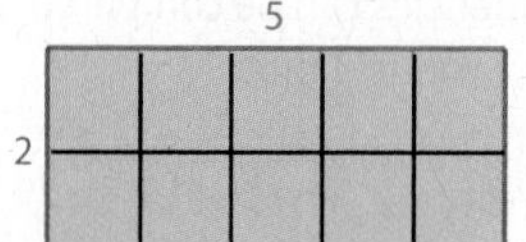

The area is 10 square units.

---

arithmetic sequence A sequence whose successive terms differ by the same nonzero number d, called the *common difference.*

sucesión aritmética Sucesión cuyos términos sucesivos difieren en el mismo número distinto de cero d, denominado *diferencia común.*

4, 7, 10, 13, 16, …
+3 +3 +3 +3
$d = 3$

Associative Property of Addition For all numbers a, b, and c, $(a + b) + c = a + (b + c)$.

Propiedad asociativa de la suma Dados tres números cualesquiera a, b y c, $(a + b) + c = a + (b + c)$.

$(5 + 3) + 7 = 5 + (3 + 7)$

Associative Property of Multiplication For all numbers a, b, and c, $(a \cdot b) \cdot c = a \cdot (b \cdot c)$.

Propiedad asociativa de la multiplicación Dados tres números cualesquiera a, b y c, $(a \cdot b) \cdot c = a \cdot (b \cdot c)$.

$(5 \cdot 3) \cdot 7 = 5 \cdot (3 \cdot 7)$

---

asymptote A line that a graph gets closer to as the value of a variable becomes extremely large or small.

asíntota Línea recta a la cual se aproxima una gráfica a medida que el valor de una variable se hace sumamente grande o pequeño.

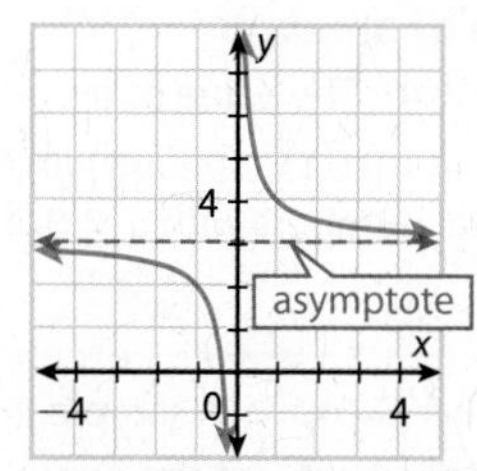

---

average *See* mean.

promedio *Ver* media.

ENGLISH	SPANISH	EXAMPLES

axis of a coordinate plane One of two perpendicular number lines, called the x-axis and the y-axis, used to define the location of a point in a coordinate plane.

eje de un plano cartesiano Una de las dos rectas numéricas perpendiculares, denominadas eje x y eje y, utilizadas para definir la ubicación de un punto en un plano cartesiano.

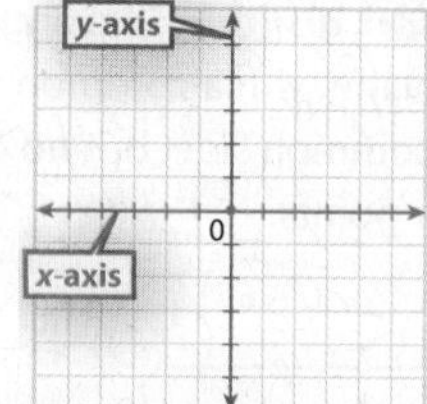

---

axis of symmetry A line that divides a plane figure or a graph into two congruent reflected halves.

eje de simetría Línea que divide una figura plana o una gráfica en dos mitades reflejadas congruentes.

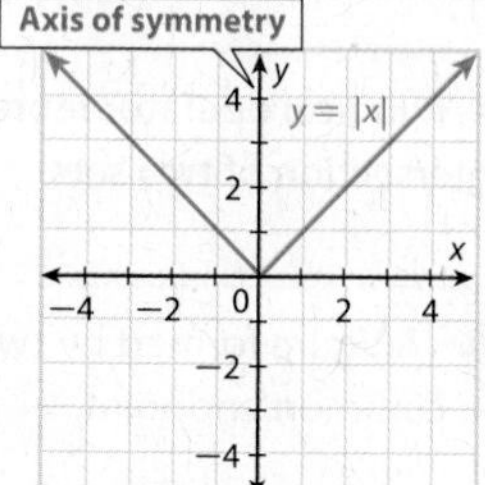

back-to-back stem-and-leaf plot (A graph used to organize and compare two sets of data so that the frequencies can be compared. *See also* stem-and-leaf plot.

diagrama doble de tallo y hojas Gráfica utilizada para organizar y comparar dos conjuntos de datos para poder comparar las frecuencias. *Ver también* diagrama de tallo y hojas.

Data set A: 9, 12, 14, 16, 23, 27
Data set B: 6, 8, 10, 13, 15, 16, 21

Set A		Set B
9	0	6 8
6 4 2	1	0 3 5 6
7 3	2	1

Key: |2| 1 means 21
7 |2| means 27

---

bar graph A graph that uses vertical or horizontal bars to display data.

gráfica de barras Gráfica con barras horizontales o verticales para mostrar datos.

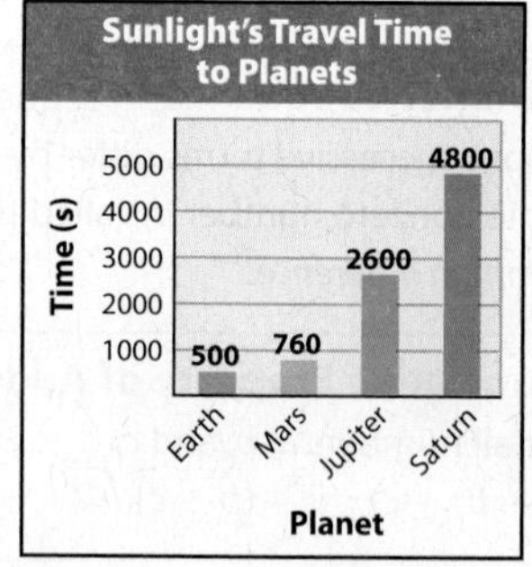

---

base of a power The number in a power that is used as a factor.

base de una potencia Número de una potencia que se utiliza como factor.

$3^4 = 3 \cdot 3 \cdot 3 \cdot 3 = 81$
3 is the base.

---

base of an exponential function The value of b in a function of the form $f(x) = ab^x$, where a and b are real numbers with $a \neq 0$, $b > 0$, and $b \neq 1$.

base de una función exponencial Valor de b en una función del tipo $f(x) = ab^x$, donde a y b son números reales con $a \neq 0$, $b > 0$ y $b \neq 1$.

In the function $f(x) = 5(2)^x$, the base is 2.

---

biased sample A sample that does not fairly represent the population.

muestra no representativa Muestra que no representa adecuadamente una población.

To find out about the exercise habits of average Americans, a fitness magazine surveyed its readers about how often they exercise. The population is all Americans and the sample is readers of the fitness magazine. This sample will likely be biased because readers of fitness magazines may exercise more often than other people do.

ENGLISH	SPANISH	EXAMPLES

binomial A polynomial with two terms.

binomio Polinomio con dos términos.

$x + y$
$2a^2 + 3$
$4m^3n^2 + 6mn^4$

---

boundary line A line that divides a coordinate plane into two half-planes.

línea de límite Línea que divide un plano cartesiano en dos semiplanos.

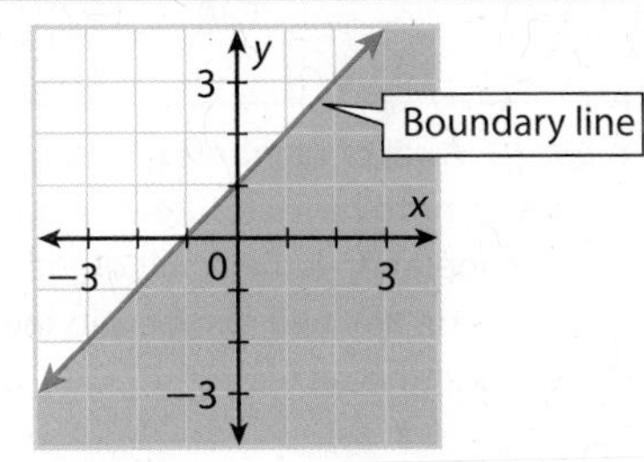

---

box-and-whisker plot A method of showing how data are distributed by using the median, quartiles, and minimum and maximum values; also called a *box plot*.

gráfica de mediana y rango Método para mostrar la distribución de datos utilizando la mediana, los cuartiles y los valores mínimo y máximo; también llamado *gráfica de caja*.

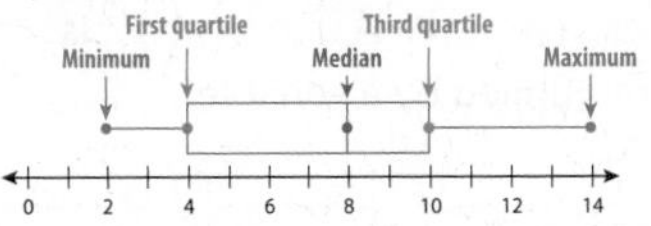

C

Cartesian coordinate system *See* coordinate plane.

sistema de coordenadas cartesianas *Ver* plano cartesiano.

---

categorical data Data that are qualitative in nature, such as "liberal," "moderate," and "conservative."

datos categóricos Datos de índole cualitativa, como "liberal", "moderado" y "conservador".

---

center of a circle The point inside a circle that is the same distance from every point on the circle.

centro de un círculo Punto dentro de un círculo que se encuentra a la misma distancia de todos los puntos del círculo.

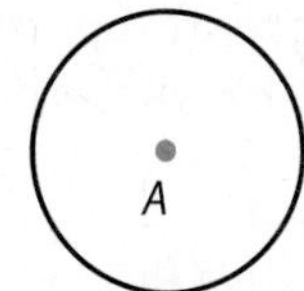

---

central angle of a circle An angle whose vertex is the center of a circle.

ángulo central de un círculo Ángulo cuyo vértice es el centro de un círculo.

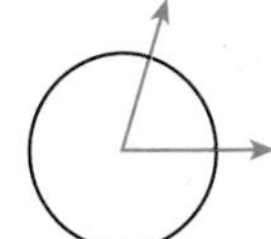

---

circle The set of points in a plane that are a fixed distance from a given point called the center of the circle.

círculo Conjunto de puntos en un plano que se encuentran a una distancia fija de un punto determinado denominado centro del círculo.

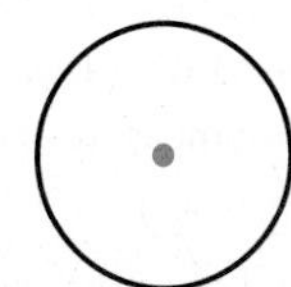

---

circle graph A way to display data by using a circle divided into non-overlapping sectors.

gráfica circular Forma de mostrar datos mediante un círculo dividido en sectores no superpuestos.

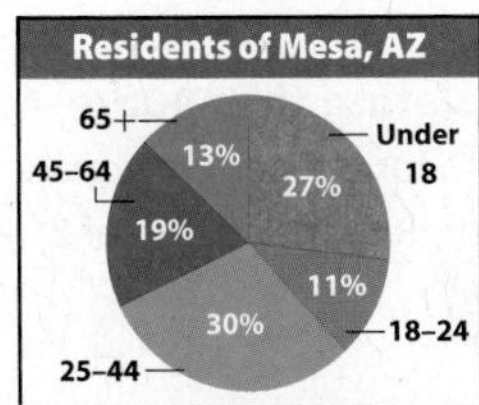

ENGLISH	SPANISH	EXAMPLES
circumference The distance around a circle.	**circunferencia** Distancia alrededor de un círculo.	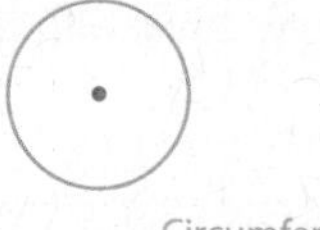
closure A set of numbers is said to be closed, or to have closure, under a given operation if the result of the operation on any two numbers in the set is also in the set.	**cerradura** Se dice que un conjunto de números es cerrado, o tiene cerradura, respecto de una operación determinada, si el resultado de la operación entre dos números cualesquiera del conjunto también está en el conjunto.	The natural numbers are closed under addition because the sum of two natural numbers is always a natural number.
coefficient A number that is multiplied by a variable.	**coeficiente** Número que se multiplica por una variable.	In the expression $2x + 3y$, 2 is the coefficient of x and 3 is the coefficient of y.
common difference In an arithmetic sequence, the nonzero constant difference of any term and the previous term.	**diferencia común** En una sucesión aritmética, diferencia constante distinta de cero entre cualquier término y el término anterior.	In the arithmetic sequence 3, 5, 7, 9, 11, …, the common difference is 2.
common factor A factor that is common to all terms of an expression or to two or more expressions.	**factor común** Factor que es común a todos los términos de una expresión o a dos o más expresiones.	Expression: $4x^2 + 16x^3 - 8x$ Common factor: $4x$ Expressions: 12 and 18 Common factors: 2, 3, and 6
common ratio In a geometric sequence, the constant ratio of any term and the previous term.	**razón común** En una sucesión geométrica, la razón constante entre cualquier término y el término anterior.	In the geometric sequence 32, 16, 8, 4, 2, . . ., the common ratio is $\frac{1}{2}$.
Commutative Property of Addition For any two numbers a and b, $a + b = b + a$.	**Propiedad conmutativa de la suma** Dados dos números cualesquiera a y b, $a + b = b + a$.	$3 + 4 = 4 + 3 = 7$
Commutative Property of Multiplication For any two numbers a and b, $a \cdot b = b \cdot a$.	**Propiedad conmutativa de la multiplicación** Dados dos números cualesquiera a y b, $a \cdot b = b \cdot a$.	$3 \cdot 4 = 4 \cdot 3 = 12$
complement of an event The set of all outcomes that are not the event.	**complemento de un suceso** Todos los resultados que no están en el suceso.	In the experiment of rolling a number cube, the complement of rolling a 3 is rolling a 1, 2, 4, 5, or 6.
complementary angles Two angles whose measures have a sum of 90°.	**ángulos complementarios** Dos ángulos cuyas medidas suman 90°.	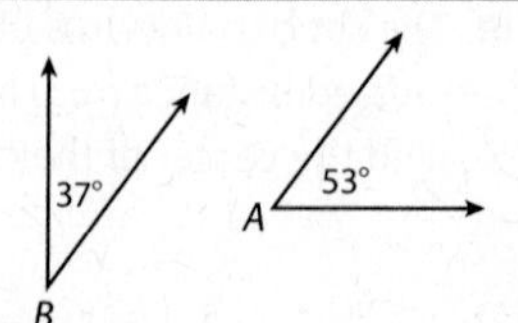
completing the square A process used to form a perfect-square trinomial. To complete the square of $x^2 + bx$, add $\left(\frac{b}{2}\right)^2$.	**completar el cuadrado** Proceso utilizado para formar un trinomio cuadrado perfecto. Para completar el cuadrado de $x^2 + bx$, hay que sumar $\left(\frac{b}{2}\right)^2$.	$x^2 + 6x + \blacksquare$ Add $\left(\frac{6}{2}\right)^2 = 9$. $x^2 + 6x + 9$
complex fraction A fraction that contains one or more fractions in the numerator, the denominator, or both.	**fracción compleja** Fracción que contiene una o más fracciones en el numerador, en el denominador, o en ambos.	$\dfrac{\frac{1}{2}}{1 + \frac{2}{3}}$

ENGLISH	SPANISH	EXAMPLES
component form The form of a vector that lists the vertical and horizontal change from the initial point to the terminal point.	**forma de componente** Forma de un vector que muestra el cambio horizontal y vertical desde el punto inicial hasta el punto terminal.	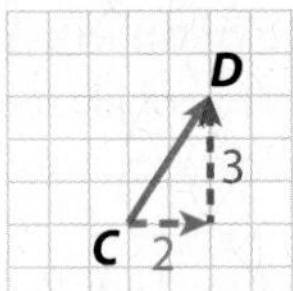 The component form of $\overrightarrow{CD}$ is $\langle 2, 3 \rangle$.
composite figure A plane figure made up of triangles, rectangles, trapezoids, circles, and other simple shapes, or a three-dimensional figure made up of prisms, cones, pyramids, cylinders, and other simple three-dimensional figures.	**figura compuesta** Figura plana compuesta por triángulos, rectángulos, trapecios, círculos y otras figuras simples, o figura tridimensional compuesta por prismas, conos, pirámides, cilindros y otras figuras tridimensionales simples.	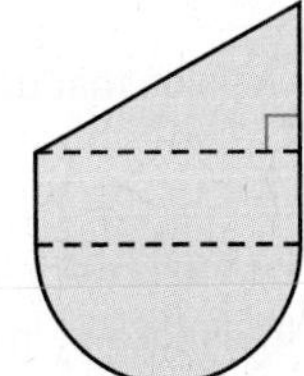
compound event An event made up of two or more simple events.	**suceso compuesto** Suceso formado por dos o más sucesos simples.	In the experiment of tossing a coin and rolling a number cube, the event of the coin landing heads and the number cube landing on 3.
compound inequality Two inequalities that are combined into one statement by the word *and* or *or*.	**desigualdad compuesta** Dos desigualdades unidas en un enunciado por la palabra *y* u *o*.	$x \geq 2$ AND $x < 7$ (also written $2 \leq x < 7$) $x < 2$ OR $x > 6$ 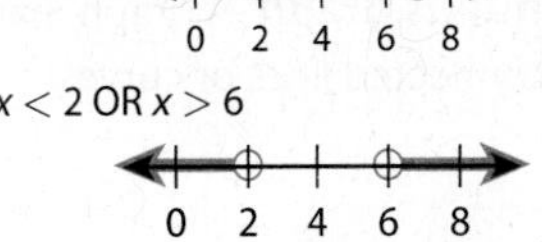
compound interest Interest earned or paid on both the principal and previously earned interest. The formula for compound interest is $A = P\left(1 + \frac{r}{n}\right)^{nt}$, where A is the final amount, P is the principal, r is the interest rate expressed as a decimal, n is the number of times interest is compounded, and t is the time.	**interés compuesto** Intereses ganados o pagados sobre el capital y los intereses ya devengados. La fórmula de interés compuesto es $A = P\left(1 + \frac{r}{n}\right)^{nt}$, donde A es la cantidad final, P es el capital, r es la tasa de interés expresada como un decimal, n es la cantidad de veces que se capitaliza el interés y t es el tiempo.	If \$100 is put into an account with an interest rate of 5% compounded monthly, then after 2 years, the account will have $100\left(1 + \frac{0.05}{12}\right)^{12 \cdot 2} = \$110.49$.
compound statement Two statements that are connected by the word *and* or *or*.	**enunciado compuesto** Dos enunciados unidos por la palabra *y* u *o*.	The sky is blue and the grass is green. I will drive to school or I will take the bus.
conditional relative frequency The ratio of a joint relative frequency to a related marginal relative frequency in a two-way table.	**frecuencia relativa condicional** Razón de una frecuencia relativa conjunta a una frecuencia relativa marginal en una tabla de doble entrada.	
cone A three-dimensional figure with a circular base and a curved surface that connects the base to a point called the vertex.	**cono** Figura tridimensional con una base circular y una superficie lateral curva que conecta la base con un punto denominado vértice.	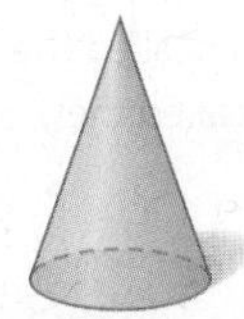
congruent Two plane figures are congruent if one can be obtained from the other by rigid motion (a sequence of translations, reflections, and/or rotations).	**congruente** Dos figuras planas son congruentes si una figura se obtiene de la otra por movimiento rígido (una secuencia de traslaciones, reflexiones, y/o rotaciones).	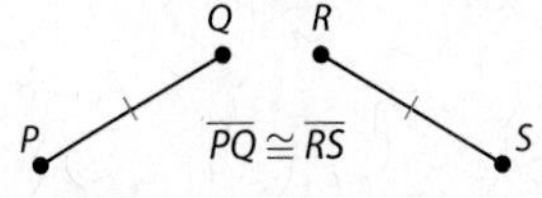

ENGLISH	SPANISH	EXAMPLES
conjugate of an irrational number The conjugate of a number in the form $a + \sqrt{b}$ is $a - \sqrt{b}$.	**conjugado de un número irracional** El conjugado de un número en la forma $a + \sqrt{b}$ es $a - \sqrt{b}$.	The conjugate of $1 + \sqrt{2}$ is $1 - \sqrt{2}$.
consistent system A system of equations or inequalities that has at least one solution.	**sistema consistente** Sistema de ecuaciones o desigualdades que tiene por lo menos una solución.	$\begin{cases} x + y = 6 \\ x - y = 4 \end{cases}$ solution: $(5, 1)$
constant A value that does not change.	**constante** Valor que no cambia.	$3, 0, \pi$
constant of variation The constant k in direct and inverse variation equations.	**constante de variación** La constante k en ecuaciones de variación directa e inversa.	$y = 5x$ (5: constant of variation)
construction A method of creating a figure that is considered to be mathematically precise. Figures may be constructed by using a compass and straightedge, geometry software, or paper folding.	**construcción** Método para crear una figura que es considerado matemáticamente preciso. Se pueden construir figuras utilizando un compás y una regla, un programa de computación de geometría o plegando papeles.	
continuous graph A graph made up of connected lines or curves.	**gráfica continua** Gráfica compuesta por líneas rectas o curvas conectadas.	
convenience sample A sample based on members of the population that are readily available.	**muestra de conveniencia** Una muestra basada en miembros de la población que están fácilmente disponibles.	A reporter surveys people he personally knows.
converse For an if-then statement "if p, then q," the statement formed by exchanging p and q.	**recíproco** Para un enunciado si-entonces "si p, entonces q", el enunciado que se forma al intercambiar p y q.	Statement: If $n + 1 = 3$, then $n = 2$. Converse: If $n = 2$, then $n + 1 = 3$.
conversion factor The ratio of two equal quantities, each measured in different units.	**factor de conversión** Razón entre dos cantidades iguales, cada una medida en unidades diferentes.	$\frac{12 \text{ inches}}{1 \text{ foot}}$
coordinate plane A plane that is divided into four regions by a horizontal line called the x-axis and a vertical line called the y-axis.	**plano cartesiano** Plano dividido en cuatro regiones por una línea horizontal denominada eje x y una línea vertical denominada eje y.	

ENGLISH	SPANISH	EXAMPLES
correlation A measure of the strength and direction of the relationship between two variables or data sets.	**correlación** Medida de la fuerza y dirección de la relación entre dos variables o conjuntos de datos.	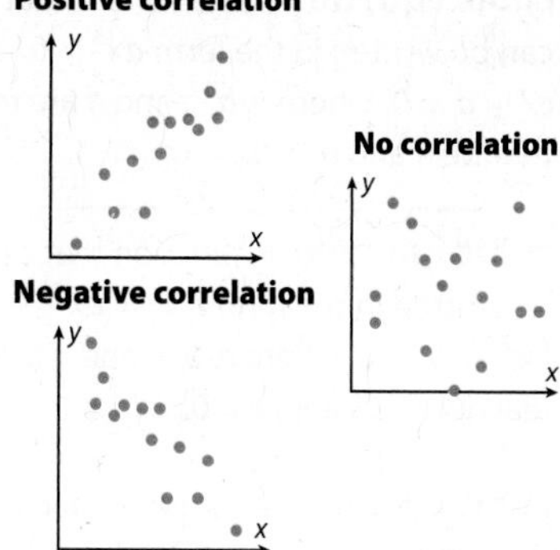
correlation coefficient A number r, where $-1 \leq r \leq 1$, that describes how closely the points in a scatter plot cluster around the least-squares line.	**coeficiente de correlación** Número r, donde $-1 \leq r \leq 1$, que describe a qué distancia de la recta de mínimos cuadrados se agrupan los puntos de un diagrama de dispersión.	An r-value close to 1 describes a strong positive correlation. An r-value close to 0 describes a weak correlation or no correlation. An r-value close to -1 describes a strong negative correlation.
corresponding angles of polygons Angles in the same relative position in polygons with an equal number of angles.	**ángulos correspondientes de los polígonos** Ángulos que se ubican en la misma posición relativa en polígonos que tienen el mismo número de ángulos.	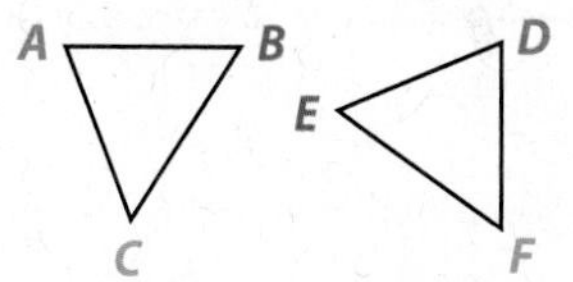 $\angle A$ and $\angle D$ are corresponding angles.
corresponding sides of polygons Sides in the same relative position in polygons with an equal number of sides.	**lados correspondientes de los polígonos** Lados que se ubican en la misma posición relativa en polígonos que tienen el mismo número de lados.	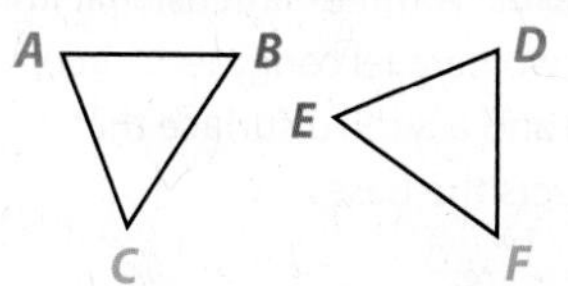 $\overline{AB}$ and $\overline{DE}$ are corresponding sides.
cosine In a right triangle, the cosine of angle A is the ratio of the length of the leg adjacent to angle A to the length of the hypotenuse.	**coseno** En un triángulo rectángulo, el coseno del ángulo A es la razón entre la longitud del cateto adyacente al ángulo A y la longitud de la hipotenusa.	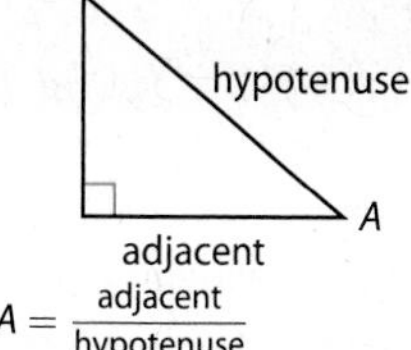 $\cos A = \frac{\text{adjacent}}{\text{hypotenuse}}$
cross products In the statement $\frac{a}{b} = \frac{c}{d}$, bc and ad are the cross products.	**productos cruzados** En el enunciado $\frac{a}{b} = \frac{c}{d}$, bc y ad son productos cruzados.	$\frac{1}{2} = \frac{3}{6}$ Cross products: $2 \cdot 3 = 6$ and $1 \cdot 6 = 6$
Cross Product Property For any real numbers a, b, c, and d, where $b \neq 0$ and $d \neq 0$, if $\frac{a}{b} = \frac{c}{d}$, then $ad = bc$.	**Propiedad de productos cruzados** Dados los números reales a, b, c y d, donde $b \neq 0$ y $d \neq 0$, si $\frac{a}{b} = \frac{c}{d}$, entonces $ad = bc$.	If $\frac{4}{6} = \frac{10}{x}$, then $4x = 60$, so $x = 15$.
cube A prism with six square faces.	**cubo** Prisma con seis caras cuadradas.	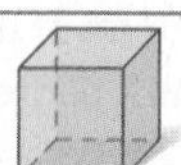
cube in numeration The third power of a number.	**cubo en numeración** Tercera potencia de un número.	8 is the cube of 2.
cube root A number, written as $\sqrt[3]{x}$, whose cube is x.	**raíz cúbica** Número, expresado como $\sqrt[3]{x}$, cuyo cubo es x.	$\sqrt[3]{64} = 4$, because $4^3 = 64$; 4 is the cube root of 64.

Glossary/Glosario

ENGLISH	SPANISH	EXAMPLES

cubic equation An equation that can be written in the form $ax^3 + bx^2 + cx + d = 0$, where a, b, c, and d are real numbers and $a \neq 0$.

ecuación cúbica Ecuación que se puede expresar como $ax^3 + bx^2 + cx + d = 0$, donde a, b, c, y d son números reales y $a \neq 0$.

$4x^3 + x^2 - 3x - 1 = 0$

---

cubic function A function that can be written in the form $f(x) = ax^3 + bx^2 + cx + d$, where a, b, c, and d are real numbers and $a \neq 0$.

función cúbica Función que se puede expresar como $f(x) = ax^3 + bx^2 + cx + d$, donde a, b, c, y d son números reales y $a \neq 0$.

$f(x) = x^3 + 2x^2 - 6x + 8$

---

cubic polynomial A polynomial of degree 3.

polinomio cúbico Polinomio de grado 3.

$x^3 + 4x^2 - 6x + 2$

---

cumulative frequency The frequency of all data values that are less than or equal to a given value.

frecuencia acumulativa Frecuencia de todos los valores de los datos que son menores que o iguales a un valor dado.

For the data set 2, 2, 3, 5, 5, 6, 7, 7, 8, 8, 8, 9, the cumulative frequency table is shown below.

Data	Frequency	Cumulative Frequency
2	2	2
3	1	3
5	2	5
6	1	6
7	2	8
8	3	11
9	1	12

---

cylinder A three-dimensional figure with two parallel congruent circular bases and a curved surface that connects the bases.

cilindro Figura tridimensional con dos bases circulares congruentes paralelas y una superficie lateral curva que conecta las bases.

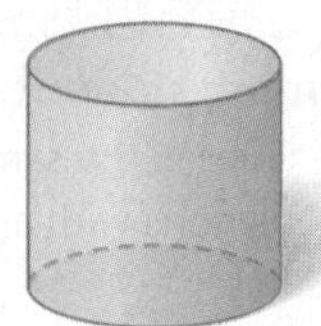

D

data Information gathered from a survey or experiment.

datos Información reunida en una encuesta o experimento.

---

degree measure of an angle A unit of angle measure; one degree is $\frac{1}{360}$ of a circle.

medida en grados de un ángulo Unidad de medida de los ángulos; un grado es $\frac{1}{360}$ de un círculo.

---

degree of a monomial The sum of the exponents of the variables in the monomial.

grado de un monomio Suma de los exponentes de las variables del monomio.

$4x^2y^5z^3$ Degree: $2 + 5 + 3 = 10$

$5 = 5x^0$ Degree: 0

---

degree of a polynomial The degree of the term of the polynomial with the greatest degree.

grado de un polinomio Grado del término del polinomio con el grado máximo.

$3x^2y^2 + 4xy^5 - 12x^3y^2$

Degree 4 Degree 6 Degree 5

Degree 6

---

dependent events Events for which the occurrence or nonoccurrence of one event affects the probability of the other event.

sucesos dependientes Dos sucesos son dependientes si el hecho de que uno de ellos ocurra o no afecta la probabilidad del otro suceso.

From a bag containing 3 red marbles and 2 blue marbles, draw a red marble, and then draw a blue marble without replacing the first marble.

ENGLISH	SPANISH	EXAMPLES
dependent system A system of equations that has infinitely many solutions.	**sistema dependiente** Sistema de ecuaciones que tiene infinitamente muchas soluciones.	$\begin{cases} x + y = 2 \\ 2x + 2y = 4 \end{cases}$
dependent variable The output of a function; a variable whose value depends on the value of the input, or independent variable.	**variable dependiente** Salida de una función; variable cuyo valor depende del valor de la entrada, o variable independiente.	For $y = 2x + 1$, y is the dependent variable. input: x output: y
diameter A segment that has endpoints on the circle and that passes through the center of the circle; also the length of that segment.	**diámetro** Segmento que atraviesa el centro de un círculo y cuyos extremos están sobre la circunferencia; longitud de dicho segmento.	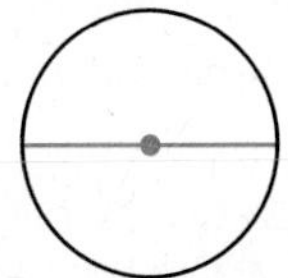
difference of two cubes A polynomial of the form $a^3 - b^3$, which may be written as the product $(a - b)(a^2 + ab + b^2)$.	**diferencia de dos cubos** Polinomio del tipo $a^3 - b^3$, que se puede expresar como el producto $(a - b)(a^2 + ab + b^2)$.	$x^3 - 8 = (x - 2)(x^2 + 2x + 4)$
difference of two squares A polynomial of the form $a^2 - b^2$, which may be written as the product $(a + b)(a - b)$.	**diferencia de dos cuadrados** Polinomio del tipo $a^2 - b^2$, que se puede expresar como el producto $(a + b)(a - b)$.	$x^2 - 4 = (x + 2)(x - 2)$
dimensional analysis A process that uses rates to convert measurements from one unit to another.	**análisis dimensional** Un proceso que utiliza tasas para convertir medidas de unidad a otra.	$\mathbf{12\ pt \cdot \frac{1\ qt}{2\ pt} = 6\ qt}$
direct variation A linear relationship between two variables, x and y, that can be written in the form $y = kx$, where k is a nonzero constant.	**variación directa** Relación lineal entre dos variables, x e y, que puede expresarse en la forma $y = kx$, donde k es una constante distinta de cero.	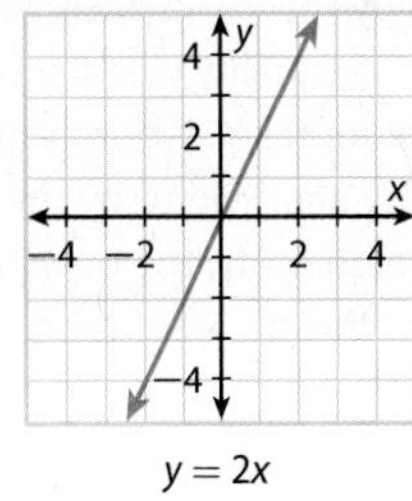 $y = 2x$
discontinuous function A function whose graph has one or more jumps, breaks, or holes.	**función discontinua** Función cuya gráfica tiene uno o más saltos, interrupciones u hoyos.	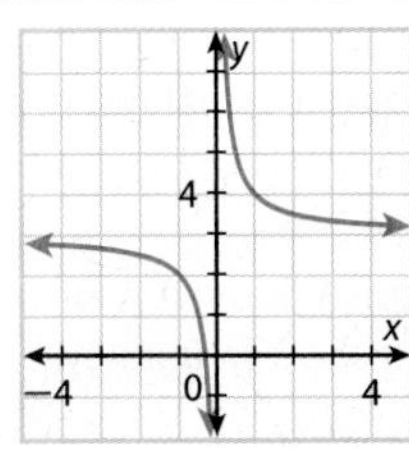
discount An amount by which an original price is reduced.	**descuento** Cantidad por la que se reduce un precio original.	
discrete graph A graph made up of unconnected points.	**gráfica discreta** Gráfica compuesta de puntos no conectados.	**Theme Park Attendance** 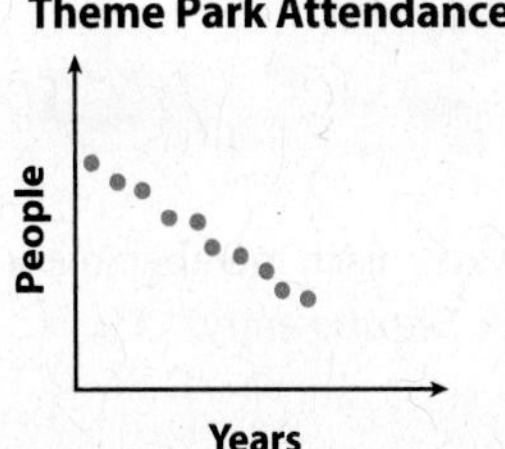

ENGLISH	SPANISH	EXAMPLES
discriminant The discriminant of the quadratic equation $ax^2 + bx + c = 0$ is $b^2 - 4ac$.	**discriminante** El discriminante de la ecuación cuadrática $ax^2 + bx + c = 0$ es $b^2 - 4ac$.	The discriminant of $2x^2 - 5x - 3 = 0$ is $(-5)^2 - 4(2)(-3)$ or 49.
distance along a line The length of the segment determined by two points on the line.	**distancia a lo largo de una línea** Longitud del segmento determinado por dos puntos en la línea.	A B a b $AB = \|a - b\| = \|b - a\|$
Distance Formula In a coordinate plane, the distance d from (x_1, y_1) to (x_2, y_2) is $d = \sqrt{(x_2 - x_1)^2 + (y_2 - y_1)^2}$.	**Fórmula de distancia** En un plano cartesiano, la distancia d desde (x_1, y_1) hasta (x_2, y_2) es $d = \sqrt{(x_2 - x_1)^2 + (y_2 - y_1)^2}$.	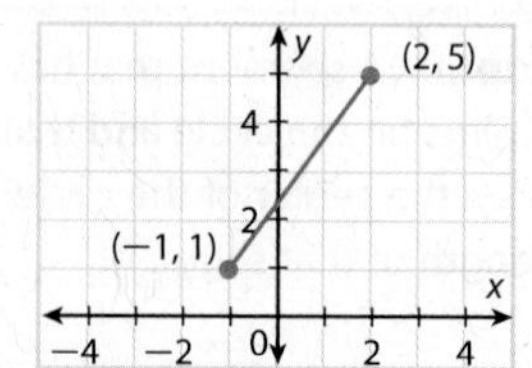 The distance from (2, 5) to (−1, 1) is $d = \sqrt{(-1 - 2)^2 + (1 - 5)^2}$ $= \sqrt{(-3)^2 + (-4)^2}$ $= \sqrt{9 + 16} = \sqrt{25} = 5$.
Distributive Property For all real numbers a, b, and c, $a(b + c) = ab + ac$, and $(b + c)a = ba + ca$.	**Propiedad distributiva** Dados los números reales a, b y c, $a(b + c) = ab + ac$, y $(b + c)a = ba + ca$.	$3(4 + 5) = 3 \cdot 4 + 3 \cdot 5$ $(4 + 5)3 = 4 \cdot 3 + 5 \cdot 3$
Division Property of Equality For real numbers a, b, and c, where $c \neq 0$, if $a = b$, then $\frac{a}{c} = \frac{b}{c}$.	**Propiedad de igualdad de la división** Dados los números reales a, b y c, donde $c \neq 0$, si $a = b$, entonces $\frac{a}{c} = \frac{b}{c}$.	$4x = 12$ $\frac{4x}{4} = \frac{12}{4}$ $x = 3$
Division Property of Inequality If both sides of an inequality are divided by the same positive quantity, the new inequality will have the same solution set. If both sides of an inequality are divided by the same negative quantity, the new inequality will have the same solution set if the inequality symbol is reversed.	**Propiedad de desigualdad de la división** Cuando ambos lados de una desigualdad se dividen entre el mismo número positivo, la nueva desigualdad tiene el mismo conjunto solución. Cuando ambos lados de una desigualdad se dividen entra el mismo número negativo, la nueva desigualdad tiene el mismo conjunto solución si se invierte el símbolo de desigualdad.	$4x \geq 12$ $\frac{4x}{4} \geq \frac{12}{4}$ $x \geq 3$ $-4x \geq 12$ $\frac{-4x}{-4} \leq \frac{12}{-4}$ $x \leq -3$
domain The set of all first coordinates (or x-values) of a relation or function.	**dominio** Conjunto de todos los valores de la primera coordenada (o valores de x) de una función o relación.	The domain of the function $\{(-5, 3), (-3, -2), (-1, -1), (1, 0)\}$ is $\{-5, -3, -1, 1\}$.
dot plot A number line with marks or dots that show frequency.	**diagrama de puntos** Recta numérica con marcas o puntos que indican la frecuencia.	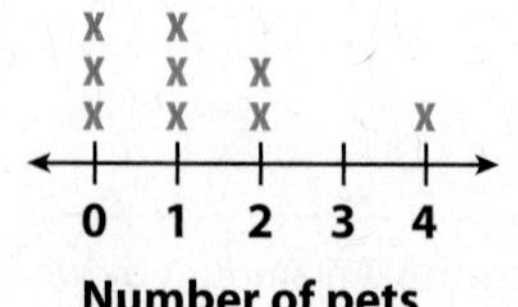

E

ENGLISH	SPANISH	EXAMPLES
element Each member in a set or matrix. *See also* entry.	**elemento** Cada miembro en un conjunto o matriz. *Ver también* entrada.	

ENGLISH	SPANISH	EXAMPLES
elimination method A method used to solve systems of equations in which one variable is eliminated by adding or subtracting two equations of the system.	**eliminación** Método utilizado para resolver sistemas de ecuaciones por el cual se elimina una variable sumando o restando dos ecuaciones del sistema.	
empty set A set with no elements.	**conjunto vacío** Conjunto sin elementos.	The solution set of $\|x\| < 0$ is the empty set, $\{\}$, or $\varnothing$.
end behavior The trends in the *y*-values of a function as the *x*-values approach positive and negative infinity.	**comportamiento extremo** Tendencia de los valores de *y* de una función a medida que los valores de *x* se aproximan al infinito positivo y negativo.	
endpoint A point at an end of a segment or the starting point of a ray.	**extremo** Punto en el final de un segmento o punto de inicio de un rayo.	A B D
entry Each value in a matrix; also called an element.	**entrada** Cada valor de una matriz, también denominado elemento.	3 is the entry in the first row and second column of $A = \begin{bmatrix} 2 & 3 \\ 0 & 1 \end{bmatrix}$, denoted a_{12}.
equally likely outcomes Outcomes are equally likely if they have the same probability of occurring. If an experiment has *n* equally likely outcomes, then the probability of each outcome is $\frac{1}{n}$.	**resultados igualmente probables** Los resultados son igualmente probables si tienen la misma probabilidad de ocurrir. Si un experimento tiene *n* resultados igualmente probables, entonces la probabilidad de cada resultado es $\frac{1}{n}$.	If a fair coin is tossed, then $P(\text{heads}) = P(\text{tails}) = \frac{1}{2}$. So the outcome "heads" and the outcome "tails" are equally likely.
equation A mathematical statement that two expressions are equivalent.	**ecuación** Enunciado matemático que indica que dos expresiones son equivalentes.	$x + 4 = 7$ $2 + 3 = 6 - 1$ $(x - 1)^2 + (y + 2)^2 = 4$
equilateral triangle A triangle with three congruent sides.	**triángulo equilátero** Triángulo con tres lados congruentes.	
equivalent ratios Ratios that name the same comparison.	**razones equivalentes** Razones que expresan la misma comparación.	$\frac{1}{2}$ and $\frac{2}{4}$ are equivalent ratios.
evaluate To find the value of an algebraic expression by substituting a number for each variable and simplifying by using the order of operations.	**evaluar** Calcular el valor de una expresión algebraica sustituyendo cada variable por un número y simplificando mediante el orden de las operaciones.	Evaluate $2x + 7$ for $x = 3$. $2x + 7$ $2(3) + 7$ $6 + 7$ 13
event An outcome or set of outcomes of an experiment.	**suceso** Resultado o conjunto de resultados en un experimento.	In the experiment of rolling a number cube, the event "an odd number" consists of the outcomes 1, 3, and 5.
excluded values Values of *x* for which a function or expression is not defined.	**valores excluidos** Valores de *x* para los cuales no está definida una función o expresión.	The excluded values of $\frac{(x+2)}{(x-1)(x+4)}$ are $x = 1$ and $x = -4$, which would make the denominator equal to 0.

ENGLISH	SPANISH	EXAMPLES
experiment An operation, process, or activity in which outcomes can be used to estimate probability.	**experimento** Una operación, proceso o actividad en la que se usan los resultados para estimar una probabilidad.	Tossing a coin 10 times and noting the number of heads
experimental probability The ratio of the number of times an event occurs to the number of trials, or times, that an activity is performed.	**probabilidad experimental** Razón entre la cantidad de veces que ocurre un suceso y la cantidad de pruebas, o veces, que se realiza una actividad.	Kendra attempted 27 free throws and made 16 of them. The experimental probability that she will make her next free throw is $P(\text{free throw}) = \frac{\text{number made}}{\text{number attempted}} = \frac{16}{27} \approx 0.59$.
explicit rule for *n*th term of a sequence A rule that defines the *n*th term a_n, or a general term, of a sequence as a function of *n*.	**fórmula explícita** Fórmula que define el enésimo término a_n, o término general, de una sucesión como una función de *n*.	
exponent The number that indicates how many times the base in a power is used as a factor.	**exponente** Número que indica la cantidad de veces que la base de una potencia se utiliza como factor.	$3^4 = 3 \cdot 3 \cdot 3 \cdot 3 = 81$ 4 is the exponent.
exponential decay An exponential function of the form $f(x) = ab^x$ in which $0 < b < 1$. If *r* is the rate of decay, then the function can be written $y = a(1 - r)^t$, where *a* is the initial amount and *t* is the time.	**decremento exponencial** Función exponencial del tipo $f(x) = ab^x$ en la cual $0 < b < 1$. Si *r* es la tasa decremental, entonces la función se puede expresar como $y = a(1 - r)^t$, donde *a* es la cantidad inicial y *t* es el tiempo.	$f(x) = 3\left(\frac{1}{2}\right)^x$ 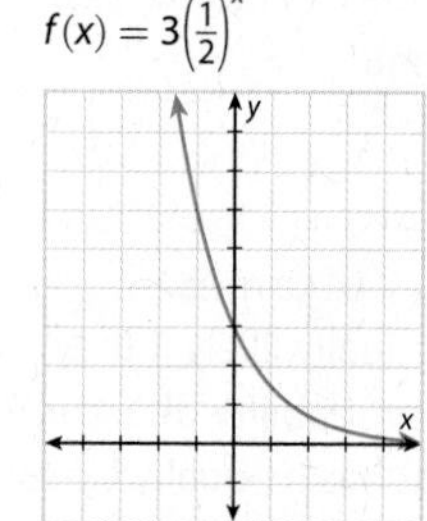
exponential expression An algebraic expression in which the variable is in an exponent with a fixed number as the base.	**expresión exponencial** Expresión algebraica en la que la variable está en un exponente y que tiene un número fijo como base.	2^{x+1}
exponential function A function of the form $f(x) = ab^x$, where *a* and *b* are real numbers with $a \neq 0$, $b > 0$, and $b \neq 1$.	**función exponencial** Función del tipo $f(x) = ab^x$, donde *a* y *b* son números reales con $a \neq 0$, $b > 0$ y $b \neq 1$.	$f(x) = 3 \cdot 4^x$ 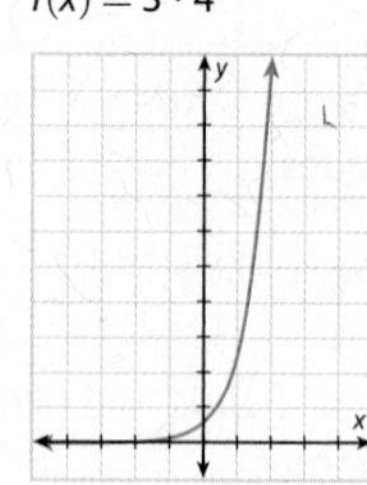
exponential growth An exponential function of the form $f(x) = ab^x$ in which $b > 1$. If *r* is the rate of growth, then the function can be written $y = a(1 + r)^t$, where *a* is the initial amount and *t* is the time.	**crecimiento exponencial** Función exponencial del tipo $f(x) = ab^x$ en la que $b > 1$. Si r es la tasa de crecimiento, entonces la función se puede expresar como $y = a(1 + r)^t$, donde *a* es la cantidad inicial y *t* es el tiempo.	$f(x) = 2^x$ 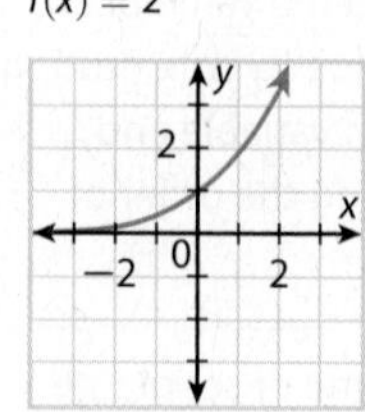
expression A mathematical phrase that contains operations, numbers, and/or variables.	**expresión** Frase matemática que contiene operaciones, números y/o variables.	$6x + 1$

ENGLISH	SPANISH	EXAMPLES
extraneous solution A solution of a derived equation that is not a solution of the original equation.	**solución extraña** Solución de una ecuación derivada que no es una solución de la ecuación original.	To solve $\sqrt{x} = -2$, square both sides; $x = 4$. ***Check*** $\sqrt{4} = -2$ is false; so 4 is an extraneous solution.

ENGLISH	SPANISH	EXAMPLES
factor A number or expression that is multiplied by another number or expression to get a product. *See also factoring.*	**factor** Número o expresión que se multiplica por otro número o expresión para obtener un producto. *Ver también* factoreo.	$12 = 3 \cdot 4$ 3 and 4 are factors of 12. $x^2 - 1 = (x - 1)(x + 1)$ $(x - 1)$ and $(x + 1)$ are factors of $x^2 - 1$.
factorial If n is a positive integer, then n factorial, written $n!$, is $n \cdot (n - 1) \cdot (n - 2) \cdot \ldots \cdot 2 \cdot 1$. The factorial of 0 is defined to be 1.	**factorial** Si n es un entero positivo, entonces el factorial de n, expresado como $n!$, es $n \cdot (n - 1) \cdot (n - 2) \cdot \ldots \cdot 2 \cdot 1$. Por definición, el factorial de 0 será 1.	$7! = 7 \cdot 6 \cdot 5 \cdot 4 \cdot 3 \cdot 2 \cdot 1 = 5040$
factoring The process of writing a number or algebraic expression as a product.	**factorización** Proceso por el que se expresa un número o expresión algebraica como un producto.	$x^2 - 4x - 21 = (x - 7)(x + 3)$
fair When all outcomes of an experiment are equally likely.	**justo** Cuando todos los resultados de un experimento son igualmente probables.	When tossing a fair coin, heads and tails are equally likely. Each has a probability of $\frac{1}{2}$.
family of functions A set of functions whose graphs have basic characteristics in common. Functions in the same family are transformations of their parent function.	**familia de funciones** Conjunto de funciones cuyas gráficas tienen características básicas en común. Las funciones de la misma familia son transformaciones de su función madre.	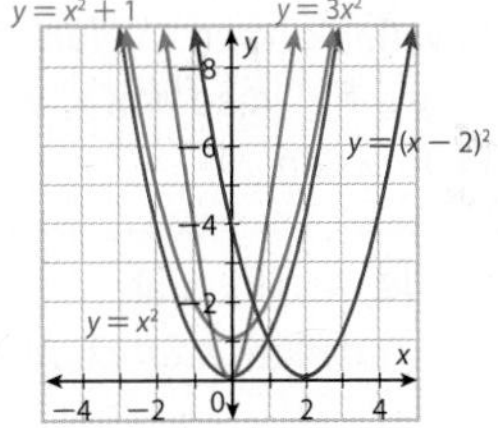
first differences The differences between y-values of a function for evenly spaced x-values.	**primeras diferencias** Diferencias entre los valores de y de una función para valores de x espaciados uniformemente.	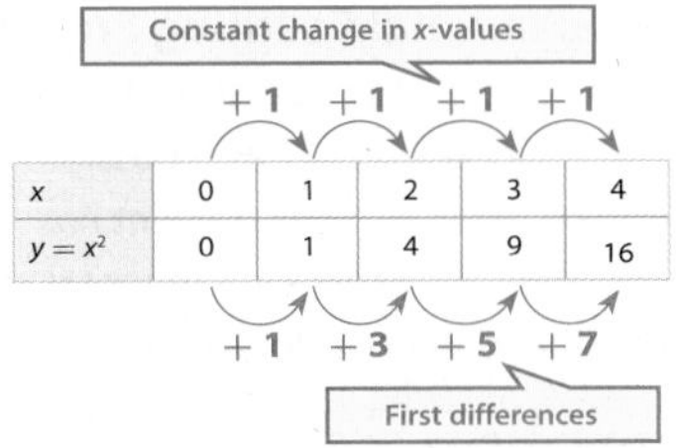
first quartile The median of the lower half of a data set, denoted Q_1. Also called *lower quartile.*	**primer cuartil** Mediana de la mitad inferior de un conjunto de datos, expresada como Q_1. También se llama *cuartil inferior.*	**Lower half** **Upper half** 18, 23, 28, 29, 36, 42 **First quartile**
FOIL A mnemonic (memory) device for a method of multiplying two binomials: Multiply the **First** terms. Multiply the **Outer** terms. Multiply the **Inner** terms. Multiply the **Last** terms.	**FOIL** Regla mnemotécnica para recordar el método de multiplicación de dos binomios: Multiplicar los términos **Primeros** (*First*). Multiplicar los términos **Externos** (*Outer*). Multiplicar los términos **Internos** (*Inner*). Multiplicar los términos **Últimos** (*Last*).	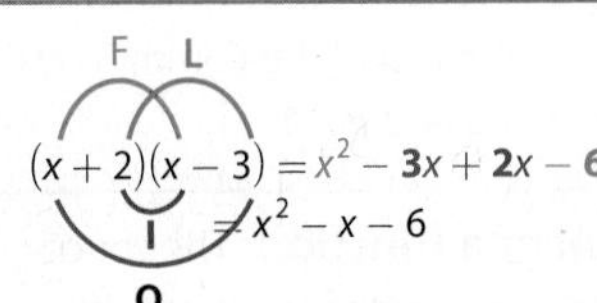

ENGLISH	SPANISH	EXAMPLES
formula A literal equation that states a rule for a relationship among quantities.	**fórmula** Ecuación literal que establece una regla para una relación entre cantidades.	$A = \pi r^2$
fractional exponent *See* rational exponent.	**exponente fraccionario** *Ver* exponente racional.	
frequency The number of times the value appears in the data set.	**frecuencia** Cantidad de veces que aparece el valor en un conjunto de datos.	In the data set 5, 6, 6, 7, 8, 9, the data value 6 has a frequency of 2.
frequency table A table that lists the number of times, or frequency, that each data value occurs.	**tabla de frecuencia** Tabla que enumera la cantidad de veces que ocurre cada valor de datos, o la frecuencia.	Data set: 1, 1, 2, 2, 3, 4, 5, 5, 5, 6, 6, 6, 6 Frequency table: (see below)

Data	Frequency
1	2
2	2
3	1
4	1
5	3
6	4

function A relation in which every domain value is paired with exactly one range value.

función Relación en la que a cada valor de dominio corresponde exactamente un valor de rango.

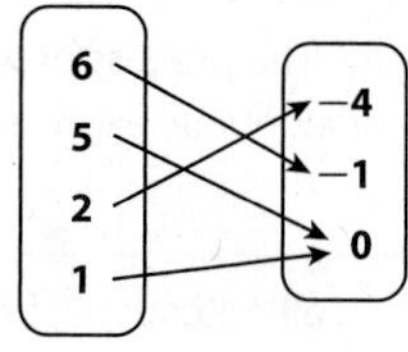

ENGLISH	SPANISH	EXAMPLES
function notation If x is the independent variable and y is the dependent variable, then the function notation for y is $f(x)$, read "f of x," where f names the function.	**notación de función** Si x es la variable independiente e y es la variable dependiente, entonces la notación de función para y es $f(x)$, que se lee "f de x," donde f nombra la función.	equation: $y = 2x$ function notation: $f(x) = 2x$
function rule An algebraic expression that defines a function.	**regla de función** Expresión algebraica que define una función.	$f(x) = \underline{2x^2 + 3x - 7}$ ↑ **function rule**
Fundamental Counting Principle If one event has m possible outcomes and a second event has n possible outcomes after the first event has occurred, then there are mn total possible outcomes for the two events.	**Principio fundamental de conteo** Si un suceso tiene m resultados posibles y otro suceso tiene n resultados posibles después de ocurrido el primer suceso, entonces hay mn resultados posibles en total para los dos sucesos.	If there are 4 colors of shirts, 3 colors of pants, and 2 colors of shoes, then there are $4 \cdot 3 \cdot 2 = 24$ possible outfits.

G

ENGLISH	SPANISH	EXAMPLES
geometric sequence A sequence in which the ratio of successive terms is a constant r, called the common ratio, where $r \neq 0$ and $r \neq 1$.	**sucesión geométrica** Sucesión en la que la razón de los términos sucesivos es una constante r, denominada razón común, donde $r \neq 0$ y $r \neq 1$.	1, 2, 4, 8, 16, ... $\cdot 2 \quad \cdot 2 \quad \cdot 2 \quad \cdot 2 \qquad r = 2$
graph of a function The set of points in a coordinate plane with coordinates (x, y), where x is in the domain of the function f and $y = fx$).	**gráfica de una función** Conjunto de los puntos de un plano cartesiano con coordenadas (x, y), donde x está en el dominio de la función f e $y = f(x)$.	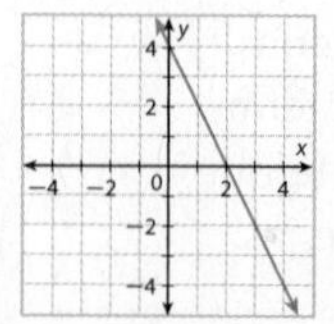 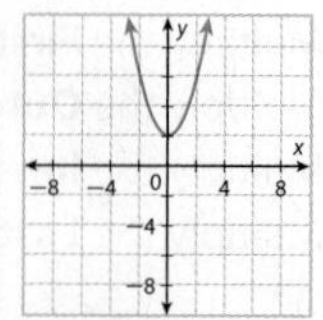

ENGLISH	SPANISH	EXAMPLES
graph of a system of linear inequalities The region in a coordinate plane consisting of points whose coordinates are solutions to all of the inequalities in the system.	**gráfica de un sistema de desigualdades lineales** Región de un plano cartesiano que consta de puntos cuyas coordenadas son soluciones de todas las desigualdades del sistema.	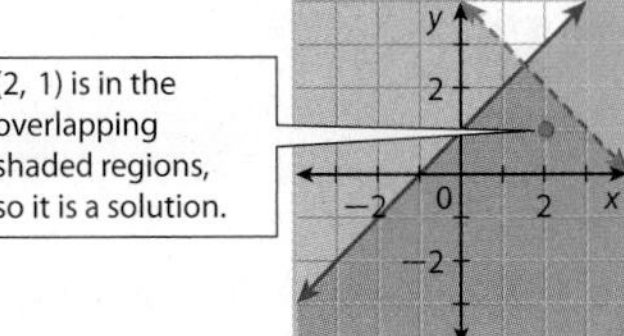
graph of an inequality in one variable The set of points on a number line that are solutions of the inequality.	**gráfica de una desigualdad en una variable** Conjunto de los puntos de una recta numérica que representan soluciones de la desigualdad.	$x \geq 2$ 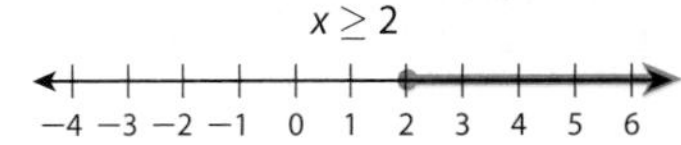
graph of an inequality in two variables The set of points in a coordinate plane whose coordinates (x, y) are solutions of the inequality.	**gráfica de una desigualdad en dos variables** Conjunto de los puntos de un plano cartesiano cuyas coordenadas (x, y) son soluciones de la desigualdad.	$y \leq x + 1$ 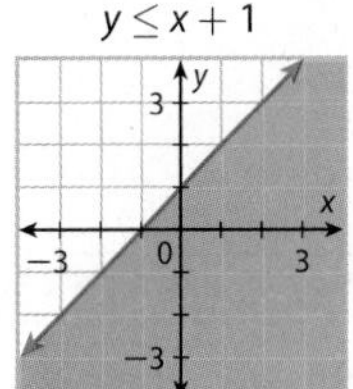
graph of an ordered pair For the ordered pair (x, y), the point in a coordinate plane that is a horizontal distance of x units from the origin and a vertical distance of y units from the origin.	**gráfica de un par ordenado** Dado el par ordenado (x, y), punto en un plano cartesiano que está a una distancia horizontal de x unidades desde el origen y a una distancia vertical de y unidades desde el origen.	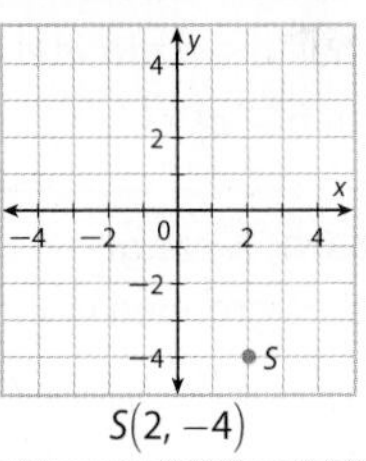 $S(2, -4)$
greatest common factor (monomials) (GCF) The product of the greatest integer and the greatest power of each variable that divide evenly into each monomial.	**máximo común divisor (monomios) (MCD)** Producto del entero mayor y la potencia mayor de cada variable que divide exactamente cada monomio.	The GCF of $4x^3y$ and $6x^2y$ is $2x^2y$.
greatest common factor (numbers) (GCF) The largest common factor of two or more given numbers.	**máximo común divisor (números) (MCD)** El mayor de los factores comunes compartidos por dos o más números dados.	The GCF of 27 and 45 is 9.
greatest integer function A function denoted by $f(x) = [x]$ in which the number x is rounded down to the greatest integer that is less than or equal to x.	**función de entero mayor** Función expresada como $f(x) = [x]$ en la cual el número x se redondea hacia abajo hasta el entero mayor que sea menor o igual a x.	
grouping symbols Symbols such as parentheses ( ), brackets [ ], and braces { } that separate part of an expression. A fraction bar, absolute-value symbols, and radical symbols may also be used as grouping symbols.	**símbolos de agrupación** Símbolos tales como paréntesis ( ), corchetes [ ] y llaves { } que separan parte de una expresión. La barra de fracciones, los símbolos de valor absoluto y los símbolos de radical también se pueden utilizar como símbolos de agrupación.	$6 + \{3 - [(4 - 3) + 2] + 1\} - 5$ $6 + \{3 - [1 + 2] + 1\} - 5$ $6 + \{3 - 3 + 1\} - 5$ $6 + 1 - 5$ 2

ENGLISH	SPANISH	EXAMPLES

half-life The half-life of a substance is the time it takes for one-half of the substance to decay into another substance.

vida media La vida media de una sustancia es el tiempo que tarda la mitad de la sustancia en desintegrarse y transformarse en otra sustancia.

Carbon-14 has a half-life of 5730 years, so 5 g of an initial amount of 10 g will remain after 5730 years.

half-plane The part of the coordinate plane on one side of a line, which may include the line.

semiplano La parte del plano cartesiano de un lado de una línea, que puede incluir la línea.

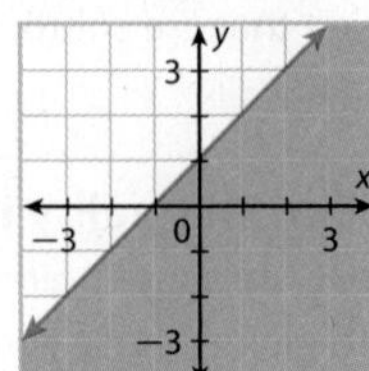

Heron's Formula A triangle with side lengths a, b, and c has area $A = \sqrt{s(s-a)(s-b)(s-c)}$, where s is one-half the perimeter, or $s = \frac{1}{2}(a+b+c)$.

fórmula de Herón Un triángulo con longitudes de lado a, b y c tiene un área $A = \sqrt{s(s-a)(s-b)(s-c)}$, donde s es la mitad del perímetro ó $s = \frac{1}{2}(a+b+c)$.

histogram A bar graph used to display data grouped in intervals.

histograma Gráfica de barras utilizada para mostrar datos agrupados en intervalos de clases.

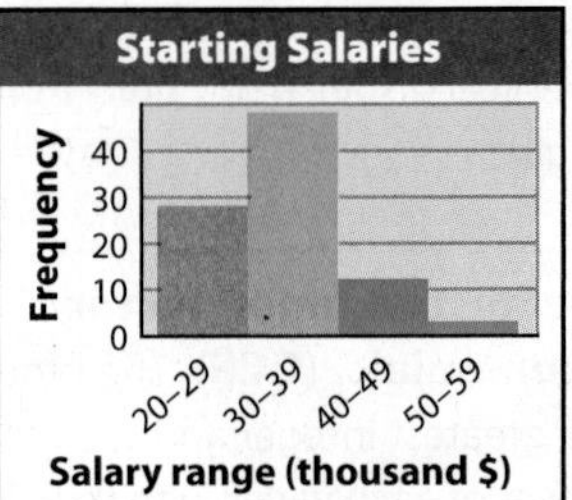

horizontal line A line described by the equation $y = b$, where b is the y-intercept.

línea horizontal Línea descrita por la ecuación $y = b$, donde b es la intersección con el eje y.

$y = 4$

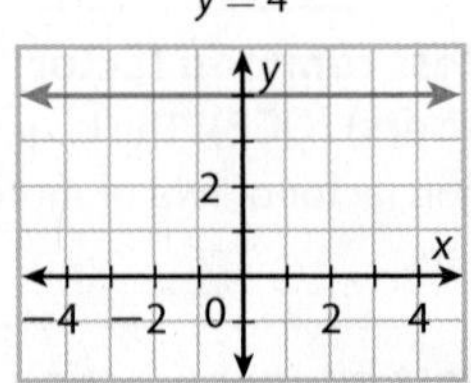

hypotenuse The side opposite the right angle in a right triangle.

hipotenusa Lado opuesto al ángulo recto de un triángulo rectángulo.

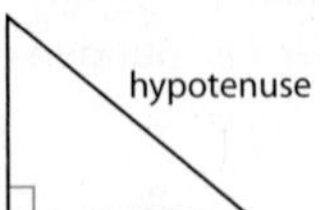

identity An equation that is true for all values of the variables.

identidad Ecuación verdadera para todos los valores de las variables.

$3 = 3$
$2(x-1) = 2x - 2$

image A shape that results from a transformation of a figure known as the preimage.

imagen Forma resultante de la transformación de una figura conocida como imagen original.

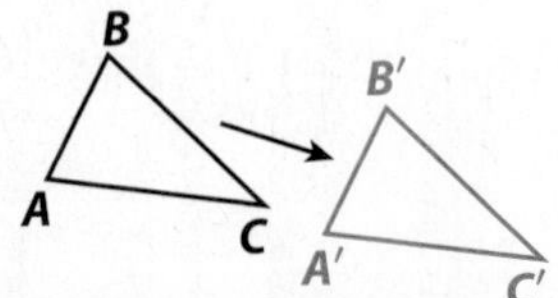

ENGLISH	SPANISH	EXAMPLES
inclusive events Events that have one or more outcomes in common.	**sucesos inclusivos** Sucesos que tienen uno o más resultados en común.	In the experiment of rolling a number cube, rolling an even number and rolling a number less than 3 are inclusive events because both contain the outcome 2.
inconsistent system A system of equations or inequalities that has no solution.	**sistema inconsistente** Sistema de ecuaciones o desigualdades que no tiene solución.	$\begin{cases} x+y=0 \\ x+y=1 \end{cases}$
independent events Events for which the occurrence or nonoccurrence of one event does not affect the probability of the other event.	**sucesos independientes** Dos sucesos son independientes si el hecho de que se produzca o no uno de ellos no afecta la probabilidad del otro suceso.	From a bag containing 3 red marbles and 2 blue marbles, draw a red marble, replace it, and then draw a blue marble.
independent system A system of equations that has exactly one solution.	**sistema independiente** Sistema de ecuaciones que tiene sólo una solución.	$\begin{cases} x+y=7 \\ x-y=1 \end{cases}$ Solution: $(4, 3)$
independent variable The input of a function; a variable whose value determines the value of the output, or dependent variable.	**variable independiente** Entrada de una función; variable cuyo valor determina el valor de la salida, o variable dependiente.	For $y = 2x + 1$, x is the independent variable.
index In the radical $\sqrt[n]{x}$, which represents the nth root of x, n is the index. In the radical $\sqrt{x}$, the index is understood to be 2.	**índice** En el radical $\sqrt[n]{x}$, que representa la enésima raíz de x, n es el índice. En el radical $\sqrt{x}$, se da por sentado que el índice es 2.	The radical $\sqrt[3]{8}$ has an index of 3.
indirect measurement A method of measurement that uses formulas, similar figures, and/or proportions.	**medición indirecta** Método de medición en el que se usan fórmulas, figuras semejantes y/o proporciones.	
inequality A statement that compares two expressions by using one of the following signs: $<, >, \leq, \geq$, or $\neq$.	**desigualdad** Enunciado que compara dos expresiones utilizando uno de los siguientes signos: $<, >, \leq, \geq$, o $\neq$.	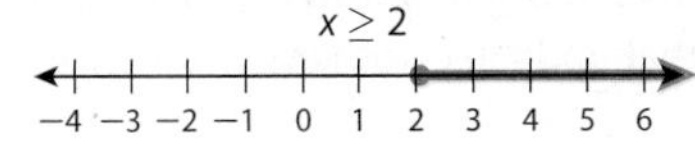
initial point of a vector The starting point of a vector.	**punto inicial de un vector** Punto donde comienza un vector.	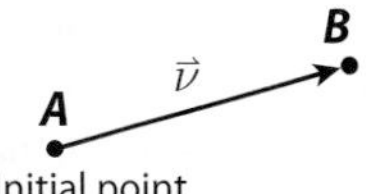
input A value that is substituted for the independent variable in a relation or function.	**entrada** Valor que sustituye a la variable independiente en una relación o función.	For the function $f(x) = x + 5$, the input 3 produces an output of 8.
input-output table A table that displays input values of a function or expression together with the corresponding outputs.	**tabla de entrada y salida** Tabla que muestra los valores de entrada de una función o expresión junto con las correspondientes salidas.	Input: **x** 1, 2, 3, 4 Output: **y** 4, 7, 10, 13
inscribed polygon A polygon in which every vertex of the polygon lies on the circle.	**polígono inscrito** Polígono cuyos vértices se encuentran sobre el círculo.	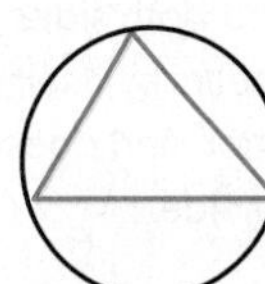

Glossary/Glosario

ENGLISH	SPANISH	EXAMPLES
integer A member of the set of whole numbers and their opposites.	**entero** Miembro del conjunto de números cabales y sus opuestos.	$\ldots, -3, -2, -1, 0, 1, 2, 3, \ldots$
intercept *See* x-intercept and y-intercept.	**intersección** *Ver* intersección con el eje x e intersección con el eje y.	
interest The amount of money charged for borrowing money or the amount of money earned when saving or investing money. *See also* compound interest, simple interest.	**interés** Cantidad de dinero que se cobra por prestar dinero o cantidad de dinero que se gana cuando se ahorra o invierte dinero. *Ver también* interés compuesto, interés simple.	
interpolation Making a prediction using a value of the independent variable from within a model's domain.	**interpolación** Hacer una predicción con un valor de la variable independiente a partir del dominio de un modelo.	
interquartile range (IQR) The difference of the third (upper) and first (lower) quartiles in a data set, representing the middle half of the data.	**rango entre cuartiles** Diferencia entre el tercer cuartil (superior) y el primer cuartil (inferior) de un conjunto de datos, que representa la mitad central de los datos.	**Lower half** **Upper half** 18, (23), 28, | 29, (36), 42 **First quartile** **Third quartile** Interquartile range: $36 - 23 = 13$
intersection The intersection of two sets is the set of all elements that are common to both sets, denoted by $\cap$.	**intersección de conjuntos** La intersección de dos conjuntos es el conjunto de todos los elementos que son comunes a ambos conjuntos, expresado por $\cap$.	$A = \{1, 2, 3, 4\}$ $B = \{1, 3, 5, 7, 9\}$ $A \cap B = \{1, 3\}$
inverse of a function The relation that results from exchanging the input and output values of a function.	**inverso de una función** La relación que se genera al intercambiar los valores de entrada y de salida de una función.	
inverse operations Operations that undo each other.	**operaciones inversas** Operaciones que se anulan entre sí.	Addition and subtraction of the same quantity are inverse operations: $5 + 3 = 8$, $8 - 3 = 5$ Multiplication and division by the same quantity are inverse operations: $2 \cdot 3 = 6$, $6 \div 3 = 2$
inverse variation A relationship between two variables, x and y, that can be written in the form $y = \frac{k}{x}$, where k is a nonzero constant and $x \neq 0$.	**variación inversa** Relación entre dos variables, x e y, que puede expresarse en la forma $y = \frac{k}{x}$, donde k es una constante distinta de cero y $x \neq 0$.	$y = \frac{8}{x}$
irrational number A real number that cannot be expressed as the ratio of two integers.	**número irracional** Número real que no se puede expresar como una razón de enteros.	$\sqrt{2}, \pi, e$
isolate the variable To isolate a variable in an equation, use inverse operations on both sides until the variable appears by itself on one side of the equation and does not appear on the other side.	**despejar la variable** Para despejar la variable de una ecuación, utiliza operaciones inversas en ambos lados hasta que la variable aparezca sola en uno de los lados de la ecuación y no aparezca en el otro lado.	$10 = 6 - 2x$ $\underline{-6 \quad -6}$ $4 = -2x$ $\frac{4}{-2} = \frac{-2x}{-2}$ $-2 = x$

ENGLISH	SPANISH	EXAMPLES
isosceles triangle A triangle with at least two congruent sides.	**triángulo isósceles** Triángulo que tiene al menos dos lados congruentes.	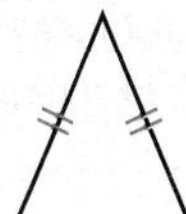

ENGLISH	SPANISH	EXAMPLES
joint relative frequency The ratio of the frequency in a particular category divided by the total number of data values.	**frecuencia relativa conjunta** La línea de ajuste en que la suma de cuadrados de los residuos es la menor.	

ENGLISH	SPANISH	EXAMPLES
kite A quadrilateral with two distinct pairs of congruent consecutive sides.	**cometa o papalote** Cuadrilátero con dos pares distintos de lados congruentes consecutivos.	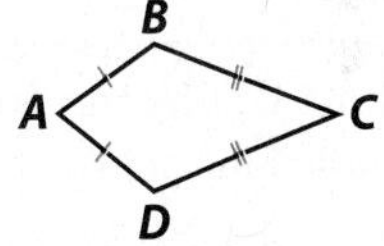 Kite *ABCD*

ENGLISH	SPANISH	EXAMPLES
leading coefficient The coefficient of the first term of a polynomial in standard form.	**coeficiente principal** Coeficiente del primer término de un polinomio en forma estándar.	$3x^2 + 7x - 2$ Leading coefficient: 3
least common denominator (LCD) The least common multiple of the denominators of two or more given fractions or rational expressions.	**mínimo común denominador (MCD)** Mínimo común múltiplo de los denominadores de dos o más fracciones dadas o expresionnes racionales.	The LCD of $\frac{3}{4}$ and $\frac{5}{6}$ is 12.
least common multiple (monomials) (LCM) The product of the smallest positive number and the lowest power of each variable that divide evenly into each monomial.	**mínimo común múltiplo (monomios) (MCM)** El producto del número positivo más pequeño y la menor potencia de cada variable que divide exactamente cada monomio.	The LCM of $6x^2$ and $4x$ is $12x^2$.
least common multiple (numbers) (LCM) The smallest whole number, other than zero, that is a multiple of two or more given numbers.	**mínimo común múltiplo (números) (MCM)** El menor de los números cabales, distinto de cero, que es múltiplo de dos o más números dados.	The LCM of 10 and 18 is 90.
least-squares regression line The line of fit for which the sum of the squares of the residuals is as small as possible	**línea de regresión de mínimos cuadrados** La línea de ajuste en que la suma de cuadrados de los residuos es la menor.	

Glossary/Glosario

ENGLISH	SPANISH	EXAMPLES
length The distance between the two endpoints of a segment.	**longitud** Distancia entre los dos extremos de un segmento.	A B a b $AB = \|a - b\| = \|b - a\|$
like terms Terms with the same variables raised to the same exponents.	**términos semejantes** Términos con las mismas variables elevadas a los mismos exponentes.	
line An undefined term in geometry, a line is a straight path that has no thickness and extends forever.	**línea** Término indefinido en geometría; una línea es un trazo recto que no tiene grosor y se extiende infinitamente.	ℓ
line graph A graph that uses line segments to show how data changes.	**gráfica lineal** Gráfica que se vale de segmentos de recta para mostrar cambios en los datos.	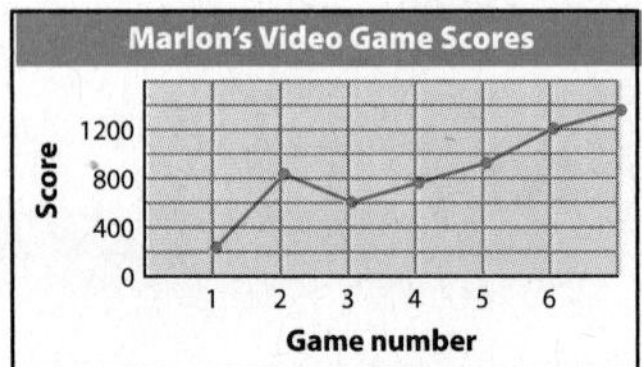
line of best fit The line that comes closest to all of the points in a data set.	**línea de mejor ajuste** Línea que más se acerca a todos los puntos de un conjunto de datos.	
line of fit *See trend line.*	**línea de ajuste** *Ver línea de tendencia.*	
line of symmetry A line of reflection for a reflection that maps a figure onto itself.	**eje de simetría** Línea de reflexión que sirve para definir la reflexión de una figura.	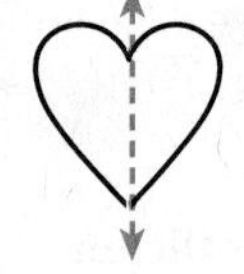
line plot A number line with marks or dots that show frequency.	**diagrama de acumulación** Recta numérica con marcas o puntos que indican la frecuencia.	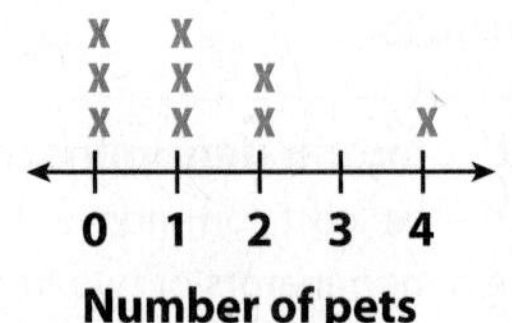
line segment A part of a line consisting of two endpoints and all points between them.	**segmento de una línea** Parte de una línea que consiste en dos extremos y todos los puntos entre éstos.	A B
line symmetry A figure that can be reflected across a line so that the image coincides with the preimage has line symmetry.	**simetría axial** Figura que puede reflejarse sobre una línea de forma tal que la imagen coincida con la imagen original tiene simetría axial.	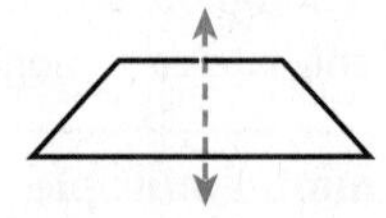
linear equation in one variable An equation that can be written in the form $ax = b$ where a and b are constants and $a \neq 0$.	**ecuación lineal en una variable** Ecuación que puede expresarse en la forma $ax = b$ donde a y b son constantes y $a \neq 0$.	$x + 1 = 7$
linear equation in two variables An equation that can be written in the form $Ax + By = C$ where A, B, and C are constants and A and B are not both 0.	**ecuación lineal en dos variables** Ecuación que puede expresarse en la forma $Ax + By = C$ donde A, B y C son constantes y A y B no son ambas 0.	$2x + 3y = 6$

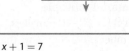

ENGLISH	SPANISH	EXAMPLES
linear function A function that can be written in the form $y = mx + b$, where x is the independent variable and m and b are real numbers. Its graph is a line.	**función lineal** Función que puede expresarse en la forma $y = mx + b$, donde x es la variable independiente y m y b son números reales. Su gráfica es una línea.	$y = x - 1$ 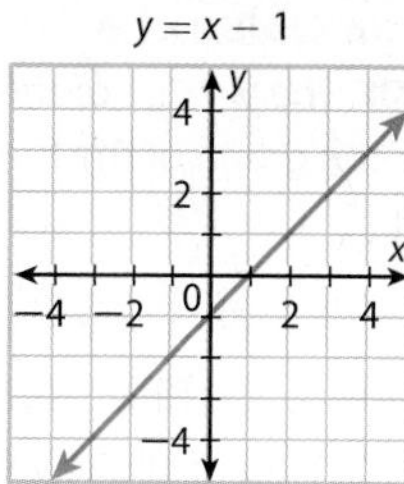
linear inequality in one variable An inequality that can be written in one of the following forms: $ax < b$, $ax > b$, $ax \leq b$, $ax \geq b$, or $ax \neq b$, where a and b are constants and $a \neq 0$.	**desigualdad lineal en una variable** Desigualdad que puede expresarse de una de las siguientes formas: $ax < b$, $ax > b$, $ax \leq b$, $ax \geq b$ o $ax \neq b$, donde a y b son constantes y $a \neq 0$.	$3x - 5 \leq 2(x + 4)$
linear inequality in two variables An inequality that can be written in one of the following forms: $Ax + By < C$, $Ax + By > C$, $Ax + By \leq C$, $Ax + By \geq C$, or $Ax + By \neq C$, where A, B, and C are constants and A and B are not both 0.	**desigualdad lineal en dos variables** Desigualdad que puede expresarse de una de las siguientes formas: $Ax + By < C$, $Ax + By > C$, $Ax + By \leq C$, $Ax + By \geq C$ o $Ax + By \neq C$, donde A, B y C son constantes y A y B no son ambas 0.	$2x + 3y > 6$
linear regression A statistical method used to fit a linear model to a given data set.	**regresión lineal** Método estadístico utilizado para ajustar un modelo lineal a un conjunto de datos determinado.	
literal equation An equation that contains two or more variables.	**ecuación literal** Ecuación que contiene dos o más variables.	$d = rt$ $A = \frac{1}{2}h(b_1 + b_2)$
lower quartile *See* first quartile.	**cuartil inferior** *Ver* primer cuartil.	

M

ENGLISH	SPANISH	EXAMPLES
mapping diagram A diagram that shows the relationship of elements in the domain to elements in the range of a relation or function.	**diagrama de correspondencia** Diagrama que muestra la relación entre los elementos del dominio y los elementos del rango de una función.	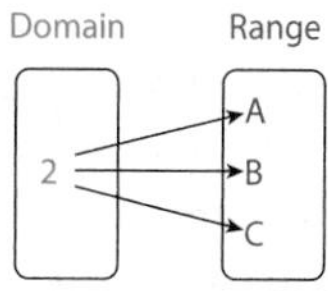
marginal relative frequency The sum of the joint relative frequencies in a row or column of a two-way table.	**frecuencia relativa marginal** La suma de las frecuencias relativas conjuntas en una fila o columna de una tabla de doble entrada.	
markup The amount by which a wholesale cost is increased.	**margen de ganancia** Cantidad que se agrega a un costo mayorista.	
matrix A rectangular array of numbers.	**matriz** Arreglo rectangular de números.	$\begin{bmatrix} 1 & 0 & 3 \\ -2 & 2 & -5 \\ 7 & -6 & 3 \end{bmatrix}$

Glossary/Glosario

ENGLISH	SPANISH	EXAMPLES
maximum value of a function The y-value of the highest point on the graph of the function.	**máximo de una función** Valor de y del punto más alto en la gráfica de la función.	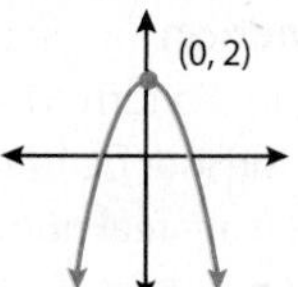 The maximum of the function is 2.
mean The sum of all the values in a data set divided by the number of data values. Also called the *average*.	**media** Suma de todos los valores de un conjunto de datos dividida entre el número de valores de datos. También llamada *promedio*.	Data set: 4, 6, 7, 8, 10 Mean: $\frac{4+6+7+8+10}{5}$ $=\frac{35}{5}=7$
measure of an angle Angles are measured in degrees. A degree is $\frac{1}{360}$ of a complete circle.	**medida de un ángulo** Los ángulos se miden en grados. Un grado es $\frac{1}{360}$ de un círculo completo.	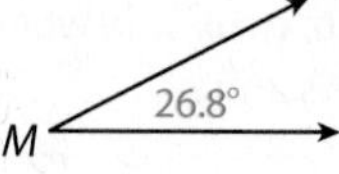
measure of central tendency A measure that describes the center of a data set.	**medida de tendencia dominante** Medida que describe el centro de un conjunto de datos.	mean, median, or mode
median For an ordered data set with an odd number of values, the median is the middle value. For an ordered data set with an even number of values, the median is the average of the two middle values.	**mediana** Dado un conjunto de datos ordenado con un número impar de valores, la mediana es el valor medio. Dado un conjunto de datos con un número par de valores, la mediana es el promedio de los dos valores medios.	8, 9, (9,) 12, 15 Median: 9 4, 6, (7, 10,) 10, 12 Median: $\frac{7+10}{2}=8.5$
midpoint The point that divides a segment into two congruent segments.	**punto medio** Punto que divide un segmento en dos segmentos congruentes.	A B C Point B is the midpoint of $\overline{AC}$.
minimum value of a function The y-value of the lowest point on the graph of the function.	**mínimo de una función** Valor de y del punto más bajo en la gráfica de la función.	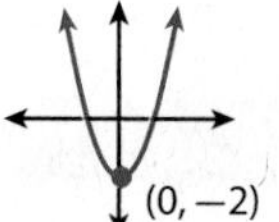 The minimum of the function is −2.
mode The value or values that occur most frequently in a data set; if all values occur with the same frequency, the data set is said to have no mode.	**moda** El valor o los valores que se presentan con mayor frecuencia en un conjunto de datos. Si todos los valores se presentan con la misma frecuencia, se dice que el conjunto de datos no tiene moda.	Data set: 3, 6, 8, 8, 10 Mode: 8 Data set: 2, 5, 5, 7, 7 Modes: 5 and 7 Data set: 2, 3, 6, 9, 11 No mode
monomial A number or a product of numbers and variables with whole-number exponents, or a polynomial with one term.	**monomio** Número o producto de números y variables con exponentes de números cabales, o polinomio con un término.	$3x^2y^4$
Multiplication Property of Equality If a, b, and c are real numbers and $a=b$, then $ac=bc$.	**Propiedad de igualdad de la multiplicación** Si a, b y c son números reales y $a=b$, entonces $ac=bc$.	$\frac{1}{3}x=7$ $(3)\left(\frac{1}{3}x\right)=(3)(7)$ $x=21$

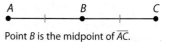

ENGLISH	SPANISH	EXAMPLES
Multiplication Property of Inequality If both sides of an inequality are multiplied by the same positive quantity, the new inequality will have the same solution set. If both sides of an inequality are multiplied by the same negative quantity, the new inequality will have the same solution set if the inequality symbol is reversed.	**Propiedad de desigualdad de la multiplicación** Si ambos lados de una desigualdad se multiplican por el mismo número positivo, la nueva desigualdad tendrá el mismo conjunto solución. Si ambos lados de una desigualdad se multiplican por el mismo número negativo, la nueva desigualdad tendrá el mismo conjunto solución si se invierte el símbolo de desigualdad.	$\frac{1}{3}x > 7$ $(3)\left(\frac{1}{3}x\right) > (3)(7)$ $x > 21$ $-x \leq 2$ $(-1)(-x) \geq (-1)(2)$ $x \geq -2$
multiplicative inverse The reciprocal of the number.	**inverso multiplicativo** Recíproco de un número.	The multiplicative inverse of 5 is $\frac{1}{5}$.
mutually exclusive events Two events are mutually exclusive if they cannot both occur in the same trial of an experiment.	**sucesos mutuamente excluyentes** Dos sucesos son mutuamente excluyentes si ambos no pueden ocurrir en la misma prueba de un experimento.	In the experiment of rolling a number cube, rolling a 3 and rolling an even number are mutually exclusive events.

N

ENGLISH	SPANISH	EXAMPLES
natural number A counting number.	**número natural** Número que se utiliza para contar.	1, 2, 3, 4, 5, 6, …
negative correlation Two data sets have a negative correlation if one set of data values increases as the other set decreases.	**correlación negativa** Dos conjuntos de datos tienen una correlación negativa si un conjunto de valores de datos aumenta a medida que el otro conjunto disminuye.	
negative exponent For any nonzero real number x and any integer n, $x^{-n} = \frac{1}{x^n}$.	**exponente negativo** Para cualquier número real distinto de cero x y cualquier entero n, $x^{-n} = \frac{1}{x^n}$.	$x^{-2} = \frac{1}{x^2}$; $3^{-2} = \frac{1}{3^2}$
negative number A number that is less than zero. Negative numbers lie to the left of zero on a number line.	**número negativo** Número menor que cero. Los números negativos se ubican a la izquierda del cero en una recta numérica.	-2 is a negative number. −4 −3 −2 −1 0 1 2 3 4
net A diagram of the faces of a three-dimensional figure arranged in such a way that the diagram can be folded to form the three-dimensional figure.	**plantilla** Diagrama de las caras de una figura tridimensional que se puede plegar para formar la figura tridimensional.	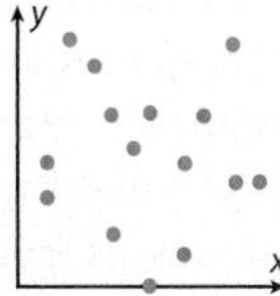 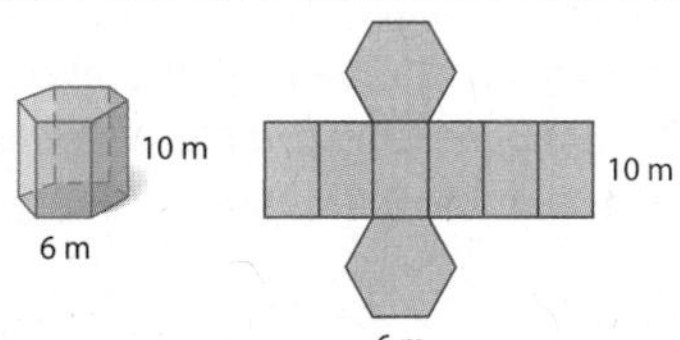 10 m, 6 m, 10 m, 6 m
no correlation Two data sets have no correlation if there is no relationship between the sets of values.	**sin correlación** Dos conjuntos de datos no tienen correlación si no existe una relación entre los conjuntos de valores.	
nonlinear system of equations A system in which at least one of the equations is not linear.	**sistema no lineal de ecuaciones** Sistema en el cual por lo menos una de las ecuaciones no es lineal.	A system that contains one quadratic equation and one linear equation is a nonlinear system.

ENGLISH	SPANISH	EXAMPLES
normal curve The graph of a probability density function that corresponds to a normal distribution; bell-shaped and symmetric about the mean, with the *x*-axis as a horizontal asymptote.	**curva normal** La gráfica de una función de densidad de probabilidad que corresponde a la distribución normal; con forma de campana y simétrica con relación a la media, el eje *x* es una asíntota horizontal.	
normal distribution A distribution of data that varies about the mean in such a way that the graph of its probability density function is a normal curve.	**distribución normal** Distribución de datos que varía respecto de la media de tal manera que la gráfica de su función de densidad de probabilidad es una curva normal.	
***n*th root** The *n*th root of a number *a*, written as $\sqrt[n]{a}$ or $a^{\frac{1}{n}}$, is a number that is equal to *a* when it is raised to the *n*th power.	**enésima raíz** La enésima raíz de un número *a*, que se escribe $\sqrt[n]{a}$ o $a^{\frac{1}{n}}$, es un número igual a *a* cuando se eleva a la enésima potencia.	$\sqrt[5]{32} = 2$, because $2^5 = 32$.
number line A line used to represent the real numbers.	**recta numérica** Línea utilizada para representar los números reales.	−4 −3 −2 −1 0 1 2 3 4 5 6
numerical expression An expression that contains only numbers and operations.	**expresión numérica** Expresión que contiene únicamente números y operaciones.	

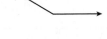

ENGLISH	SPANISH	EXAMPLES
obtuse angle An angle that measures greater than 90° and less than 180°.	**ángulo obtuso** Ángulo que mide más de 90° y menos de 180°.	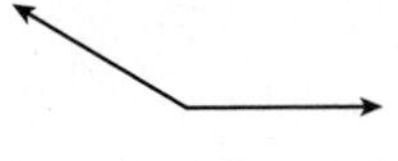
obtuse triangle A triangle with one obtuse angle.	**triángulo obtusángulo** Triángulo con un ángulo obtuso.	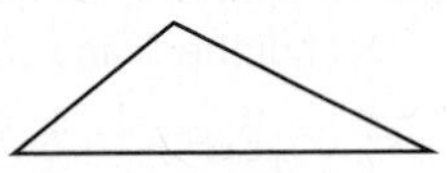
odds A comparison of favorable and unfavorable outcomes. The odds in favor of an event are the ratio of the number of favorable outcomes to the number of unfavorable outcomes. The odds against an event are the ratio of the number of unfavorable outcomes to the number of favorable outcomes.	**probabilidades a favor y en contra** Comparación de los resultados favorables y desfavorables. Las probabilidades a favor de un suceso son la razón entre la cantidad de resultados favorables y la cantidad de resultados desfavorables. Las probabilidades en contra de un suceso son la razón entre la cantidad de resultados desfavorables y la cantidad de resultados favorables.	The odds in favor of rolling a 3 on a number cube are 1:5. The odds against rolling a 3 on a number cube are 5:1.
opposite The opposite of a number *a*, denoted −*a*, is the number that is the same distance from zero as *a*, on the opposite side of the number line. The sum of opposites is 0.	**opuesto** El opuesto de un número *a*, expresado −*a*, es el número que se encuentra a la misma distancia de cero que *a*, del lado opuesto de la recta numérica. La suma de los opuestos es 0.	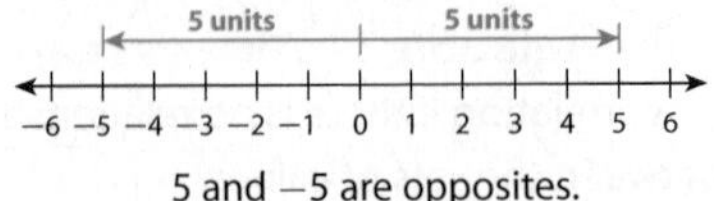 5 and −5 are opposites.

ENGLISH	SPANISH	EXAMPLES
opposite reciprocal The opposite of the reciprocal of a number. The opposite reciprocal of any nonzero number a is $-\frac{1}{a}$.	**recíproco opuesto** Opuesto del recíproco de un número. El recíproco opuesto de a es $-\frac{1}{a}$.	The opposite reciprocal of $\frac{2}{3}$ is $-\frac{3}{2}$.
OR A logical operator representing the union of two sets.	**O** Operador lógico que representa la unión de dos conjuntos.	$A = \{2, 3, 4, 5\}$ $B = \{1, 3, 5, 7\}$ The set of values that are in A OR B is $A \cup B = \{1, 2, 3, 4, 5, 7\}$.
order of operations A process for evaluating expressions: First, perform operations in parentheses or other grouping symbols. Second, simplify powers and roots. Third, perform all multiplication and division from left to right. Fourth, perform all addition and subtraction from left to right.	**orden de las operaciones** Regla para evaluar las expresiones: Primero, realizar las operaciones entre paréntesis u otros símbolos de agrupación. Segundo, simplificar las potencias y las raíces. Tercero, realizar todas las multiplicaciones y divisiones de izquierda a derecha. Cuarto, realizar todas las sumas y restas de izquierda a derecha.	$2 + 3^2 - (7 + 5) \div 4 \cdot 3$ $2 + 3^2 - 12 \div 4 \cdot 3$ Add inside parentheses. $2 + 9 - 12 \div 4 \cdot 3$ Simplify the power. $2 + 9 - 3 \cdot 3$ Divide. $2 + 9 - 9$ Multiply. $11 - 9$ Add. 2 Subtract.
ordered pair A pair of numbers (x, y) that can be used to locate a point on a coordinate plane. The first number x indicates the distance to the left or right of the origin, and the second number y indicates the distance above or below the origin.	**par ordenado** Par de números (x, y) que se pueden utilizar para ubicar un punto en un plano cartesiano. El primer número, x, indica la distancia a la izquierda o derecha del origen y el segundo número, y, indica la distancia hacia arriba o hacia abajo del origen.	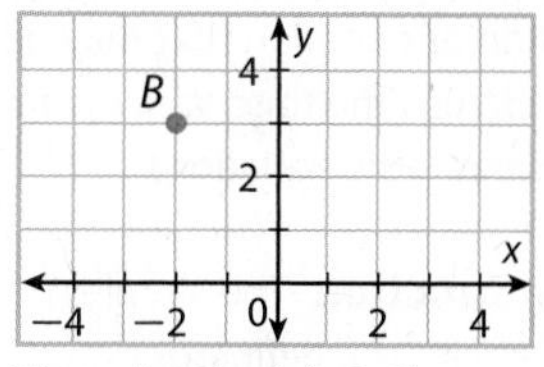 The ordered pair $(-2, 3)$ can be used to locate B.
origin The intersection of the x- and y-axes in a coordinate plane. The coordinates of the origin are $(0, 0)$.	**origen** Intersección de los ejes x e y en un plano cartesiano. Las coordenadas de origen son $(0, 0)$.	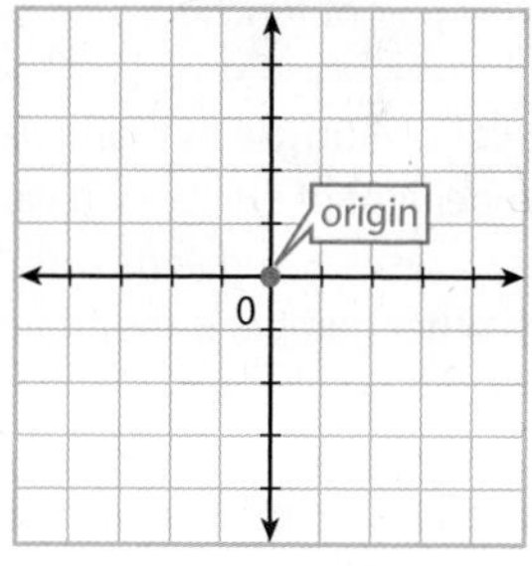
outcome A possible result of a probability experiment.	**resultado** Resultado posible de un experimento de probabilidad.	In the experiment of rolling a number cube, the possible outcomes are 1, 2, 3, 4, 5, and 6.
outlier A data value that is far removed from the rest of the data.	**valor extremo** Valor de datos que está muy alejado del resto de los datos.	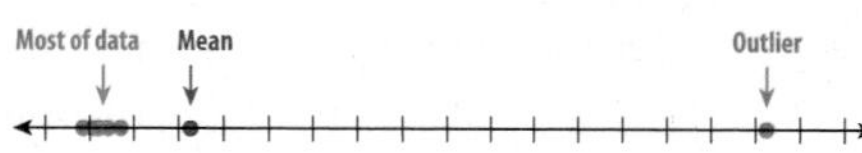
output The result of substituting a value for a variable in a function.	**salida** Resultado de la sustitución de una variable por un valor en una función.	For the function $f(x) = x^2 + 1$, the input 3 produces an output of 10.

ENGLISH	SPANISH	EXAMPLES

parabola The shape of the graph of a quadratic function.	**parábola** Forma de la gráfica de una función cuadrática.	
parallel lines Lines in the same plane that do not intersect.	**líneas paralelas** Líneas en el mismo plano que no se cruzan.	r s
parallel planes Two planes that do not intersect.	**planos paralelos** Planos que no se cruzan.	
parallelogram A quadrilateral with two pairs of parallel sides.	**paralelogramo** Cuadrilátero con dos pares de lados paralelos.	
parameter One of the constants in a function or equation that may be changed. Also the third variable in a set of parametric equations.	**parámetro** Una de las constantes en una función o ecuación que se puede cambiar. También es la tercera variable en un conjunto de ecuaciones paramétricas.	
parent function The simplest function with the defining characteristics of the family. Functions in the same family are transformations of their parent function.	**función madre** La función más básica que tiene las características distintivas de una familia. Las funciones de la misma familia son transformaciones de su función madre.	$f(x) = x^2$ is the parent function for $g(x) = x^2 + 4$ and $h(x) = (5x + 2)^2 - 3$.
Pascal's triangle A triangular arrangement of numbers in which every rowstarts and ends with 1 and each other number is the sum of the two numbers above it.	**triángulo de Pascal** Arreglo triangular de números en el cual cada fila comienza y termina con 1 y los demás números son la suma de los dos valores que están arriba de cada uno.	1 1 1 1 2 1 1 3 3 1 1 4 6 4 1
percent A ratio that compares a number to 100.	**porcentaje** Razón que compara un número con 100.	$\frac{17}{100} = 17\%$
percent change An increase or decrease given as a percent of the original amount. *See also* percent decrease, percent increase.	**porcentaje de cambio** Incremento o disminución dada como un porcentaje de la cantidad original. *Ver también* porcentaje de disminución, porcentaje de incremento.	
percent decrease A decrease given as a percent of the original amount.	**porcentaje de disminución** Disminución dada como un porcentaje de la cantidad original.	If an item that costs \$8.00 is marked down to \$6.00, the amount of the decrease is \$2.00, so the percent decrease is $\frac{2.00}{8.00} = 0.25 = 25\%$.
percent increase An increase given as a percent of the original amount.	**porcentaje de incremento** Incremento dado como un porcentaje de la cantidad original.	If an item's wholesale cost of \$8.00 is marked up to \$12.00, the amount of the increase is \$4.00, so the percent increase is $\frac{4.00}{8.00} = 0.5 = 50\%$.

ENGLISH	SPANISH	EXAMPLES
perfect square A number whose positive square root is a whole number.	**cuadrado perfecto** Número cuya raíz cuadrada positiva es un número cabal.	36 is a perfect square because $\sqrt{36} = 6$.
perfect-square trinomial A trinomial whose factored form is the square of a binomial. A perfect-square trinomial has the form $a^2 - 2ab + b^2 = (a - b)^2$ or $a^2 + 2ab + b^2 = (a + b)^2$.	**trinomio cuadrado perfecto** Trinomio cuya forma factorizada es el cuadrado de un binomio. Un trinomio cuadrado perfecto tiene la forma $a^2 - 2ab + b^2 = (a - b)^2$ o $a^2 + 2ab + b^2 = (a + b)^2$.	$x^2 + 6x + 9$ is a perfect-square trinomial, because $x^2 + 6x + 9 = (x + 3)^2$.
perimeter The sum of the side lengths of a closed plane figure.	**perímetro** Suma de las longitudes de los lados de una figura plana cerrada.	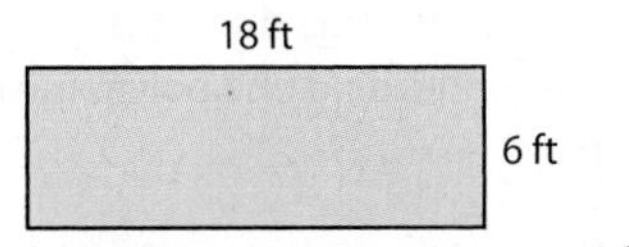 Perimeter $= 18 + 6 + 18 + 6 = 48$ ft
permutation An arrangement of a group of objects in which order is important.	**permutación** Arreglo de un grupo de objetos en el cual el orden es importante.	For objects *A*, *B*, *C*, and *D*, there are 12 different permutations of 2 objects. *AB*, *AC*, *AD*, *BC*, *BD*, *CD* *BA*, *CA*, *DA*, *CB*, *DB*, *DC*
perpendicular Intersecting to form 90° angles.	**perpendicular** Que se cruza para formar ángulos de 90°.	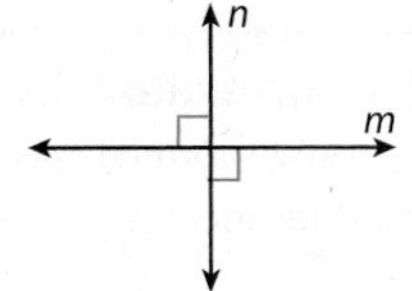
perpendicular lines Lines that intersect at 90° angles.	**líneas perpendiculares** Líneas que se cruzan en ángulos de 90°.	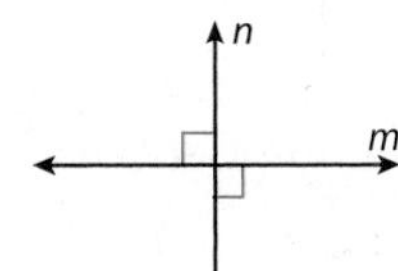
piecewise function A function that is a combination of one or more functions.	**función a trozos** Función que es una combinación de una o más funciones.	
plane An undefined term in geometry, a plane is a flat surface that has no thickness and extends forever.	**plano** Término indefinido en geometría; un plano es una superficie plana que no tiene grosor y se extiende infinitamente.	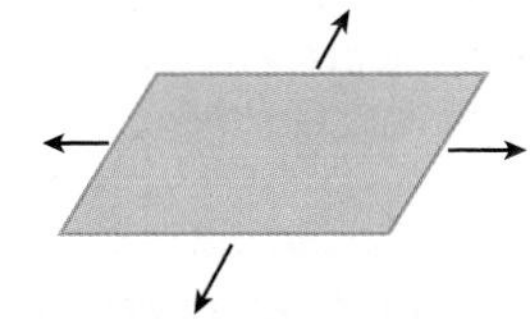
point An undefined term in geometry, a point is a specific location and has no size.	**punto** Término indefinido de la geometría que denomina una ubicación y no tiene tamaño.	*P* • point *P*
point-slope form The point-slope form of a linear equation is $y - y_1 = m(x - x_1)$, where *m* is the slope and (x_1, y_1) is a point on the line.	**forma de punto y pendiente** La forma de punto y pendiente de una ecuación lineal es $y - y_1 = m(x - x_1)$, donde *m* es la pendiente y (x_1, y_1) es un punto en la línea.	$y - 3 = 2(x - 3)$

ENGLISH	SPANISH	EXAMPLES
polygon A closed plane figure formed by three or more segments such that each segment intersects exactly two other segments only at their endpoints and no two segments with a common endpoint are collinear.	**polígono** Figura plana cerrada formada por tres o más segmentos tal que cada segmento se cruza únicamente con otros dos segmentos sólo en sus extremos y ningún segmento con un extremo común a otro es colineal con éste.	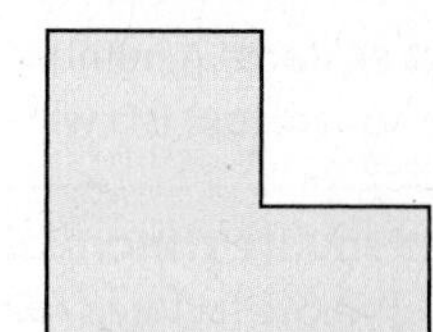
polynomial A monomial or a sum or difference of monomials.	**polinomio** Monomio o suma o diferencia de monomios.	$2x^2 + 3xy - 7y^2$
polynomial long division A method of dividing one polynomial by another.	**división larga polinomial** Método por el que se divide un polinomio entre otro.	$\begin{array}{r} x+1 \\ x+2\overline{)\ x^2+3x+5} \\ \underline{-(x^2+2x)} \\ x+5 \\ \underline{-(x+2)} \\ 3 \end{array}$ $\frac{x^2+3x+5}{x+2} = x+1+\frac{3}{x+2}$
population The entire group of objects or individuals considered for a survey.	**población** Grupo completo de objetos o individuos que se desea estudiar.	In a survey about the study habits of high school students, the population is all high school students.
positive correlation Two data sets have a positive correlation if both sets of data values increase.	**correlación positiva** Dos conjuntos de datos tienen correlación positiva si los valores de ambos conjuntos de datos aumentan.	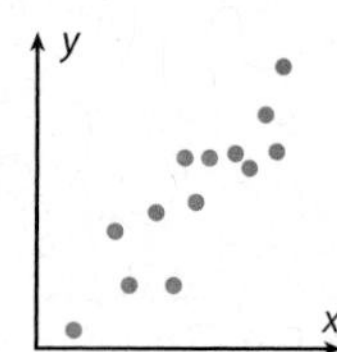
positive number A number greater than zero.	**número positivo** Número mayor que cero.	2 is a positive number. −4 −3 −2 −1 0 1 2 3 4
postulate A statement that is accepted as true without proof. Also called an *axiom*.	**postulado** Enunciado que se acepta como verdadero sin demostración. También denominado *axioma*.	
Power of a Power Property If a is any nonzero real number and m and n are integers, then $(a^m)^n = a^{mn}$.	**Propiedad de la potencia de una potencia** Dado un número real a distinto de cero y los números enteros m y n, entonces $(a^m)^n = a^{mn}$.	$(6^7)^4 = 6^{7\cdot 4}$ $= 6^{28}$
Power of a Product Property If a and b are any nonzero real numbers and n is any integer, then $(ab)^n = a^n b^n$.	**Propiedad de la potencia de un producto** Dados los números reales a y b distintos de cero y un número entero n, entonces $(ab)^n = a^n b^n$.	$(2 \cdot 4)^3 = 2^3 \cdot 4^3$ $= 8 \cdot 64$ $= 512$
Power of a Quotient Property If a and b are any nonzero real numbers and n is an integer, then $\left(\frac{a}{b}\right)^n = \frac{a^n}{b^n}$.	**Propiedad de la potencia de un cociente** Dados los números reales a y b distintos de cero y un número entero n, entonces $\left(\frac{a}{b}\right)^n = \frac{a^n}{b^n}$.	$\left(\frac{3}{5}\right)^4 = \frac{3}{5}\cdot\frac{3}{5}\cdot\frac{3}{5}\cdot\frac{3}{5}$ $= \frac{3\cdot 3\cdot 3\cdot 3}{5\cdot 5\cdot 5\cdot 5}$ $= \frac{3^4}{5^4}$
precision The level of detail of a measurement, determined by the unit of measure.	**precisión** Detalle de una medición, determinado por la unidad de medida.	A ruler marked in millimeters has a greater level of precision than a ruler marked in centimeters.
prediction An estimate or guess about something that has not yet happened.	**predicción** Estimación o suposición sobre algo que todavía no ha sucedido.	

ENGLISH	SPANISH	EXAMPLES

preimage The original figure in a transformation.

imagen original Figura original en una transformación.

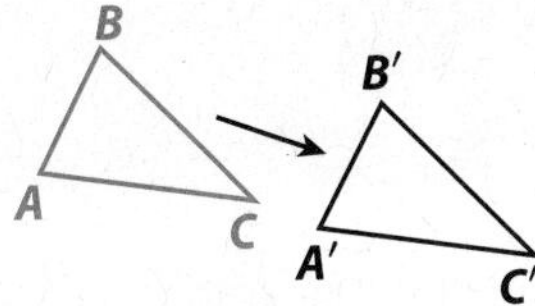

---

prime factorization A representation of a number or a polynomial as a product of primes.

factorización prima Representación de un número o de un polinomio como producto de números primos.

The prime factorization of 60 is $2 \cdot 2 \cdot 3 \cdot 5$.

---

prime number A whole number greater than 1 that has exactly two positive factors, itself and 1.

número primo Número cabal mayor que 1 que es divisible únicamente entre sí mismo y entre 1.

5 is prime because its only positive factors are 5 and 1.

---

principal An amount of money borrowed or invested.

capital Cantidad de dinero que se pide prestado o se invierte.

---

prism A polyhedron formed by two parallel congruent polygonal bases connected by faces that are parallelograms.

prisma Poliedro formado por dos bases poligonales congruentes y paralelas conectadas por caras laterales que son paralelogramos.

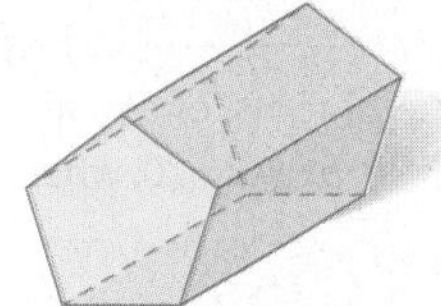

---

probability A number from 0 to 1 (or 0% to 100%) that is the measure of how likely an event is to occur.

probabilidad Número entre 0 y 1 (o entre 0% y 100%) que describe cuán probable es que ocurra un suceso.

A bag contains 3 red marbles and 4 blue marbles. The probability of randomly choosing a red marble is $\frac{3}{7}$.

Product of Powers Property If a is any nonzero real number and m and n are integers, then $a^m \cdot a^n = a^{m+n}$.

Propiedad del producto de potencias Dado un número real a distinto de cero y los números enteros m y n, entonces $a^m \cdot a^n = a^{m+n}$.

$$6^7 \cdot 6^4 = 6^{7+4} = 6^{11}$$

Product Property of Square Roots For $a \geq 0$ and $b \geq 0$, $\sqrt{ab} = \sqrt{a} \cdot \sqrt{b}$.

Propiedad del producto de raíces cuadradas Dados $a \geq 0$ y $b \geq 0$, $\sqrt{ab} = \sqrt{a} \cdot \sqrt{b}$.

$$\sqrt{9 \cdot 25} = \sqrt{9} \cdot \sqrt{25} = 3 \cdot 5 = 15$$

---

proportion A statement that two ratios are equal; $\frac{a}{b} = \frac{c}{d}$.

proporción Ecuación que establece que dos razones son iguales; $\frac{a}{b} = \frac{c}{d}$.

$$\frac{2}{3} = \frac{4}{6}$$

---

pyramid A polyhedron formed by a polygonal base and triangular lateral faces that meet at a common vertex.

pirámide Poliedro formado por una base poligonal y caras laterales triangulares que se encuentran en un vértice común.

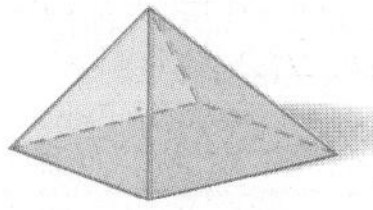

Pythagorean Theorem If a right triangle has legs of lengths a and b and a hypotenuse of length c, then $a^2 + b^2 = c^2$.

Teorema de Pitágoras Dado un triángulo rectángulo con catetos de longitudes a y b y una hipotenusa de longitud c, entonces $a^2 + b^2 = c^2$.

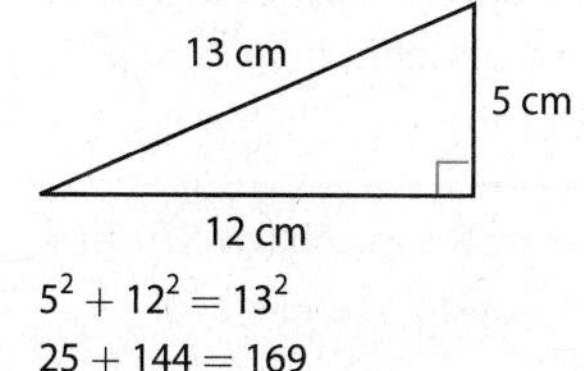

$5^2 + 12^2 = 13^2$
$25 + 144 = 169$

Pythagorean triple A set of three positive integers a, b, and c such that $a^2 + b^2 = c^2$.

Tripleta de Pitágoras Conjunto de tres enteros positivos a, b y c tal que $a^2 + b^2 = c^2$.

The numbers 3, 4, and 5 form a Pythagorean triple because $3^2 + 4^2 = 5^2$.

ENGLISH	SPANISH	EXAMPLES

quadrant One of the four regions into which the x- and y-axes divide the coordinate plane.

cuadrante Una de las cuatro regiones en las que los ejes x e y dividen el plano cartesiano.

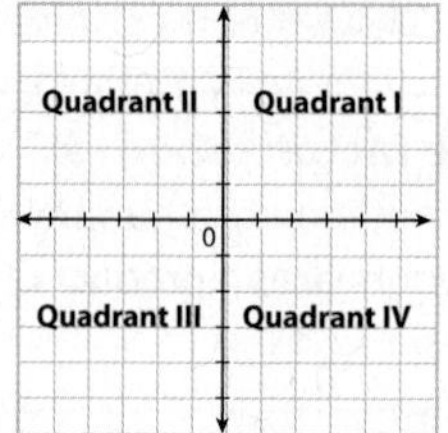

---

quadratic equation An equation that can be written in the form $ax^2 + bx + c = 0$, where a, b, and c are real numbers and $a \neq 0$.

ecuación cuadrática Ecuación que se puede expresar como $ax^2 + bx + c = 0$, donde a, b y c son números reales y $a \neq 0$.

$x^2 + 3x - 4 = 0$
$x^2 - 9 = 0$

Quadratic Formula The formula $x = \frac{-b \pm \sqrt{b^2 - 4ac}}{2a}$, which gives solutions, or roots, of equations in the form $ax^2 + bx + c = 0$, where $a \neq 0$.

fórmula cuadrática La fórmula $x = \frac{-b \pm \sqrt{b^2 - 4ac}}{2a}$, que da soluciones, o raíces, para las ecuaciones del tipo $ax^2 + bx + c = 0$, donde $a \neq 0$.

The solutions of $2x^2 - 5x - 3 = 0$ are given by

$$x = \frac{-(-5) \pm \sqrt{-(5^2) - 4(2)(-3)}}{2(2)}$$
$$= \frac{5 \pm \sqrt{25 + 24}}{4} = \frac{5 \pm 7}{4}$$
$$x = 3 \text{ or } x = -\frac{1}{2}$$

---

quadratic function A function that can be written in the form $f(x) = ax^2 + bx + c$, where a, b, and c are real numbers and $a \neq 0$.

función cuadrática Función que se puede expresar como $f(x) = ax^2 + bx + c$, donde a, b y c son números reales y $a \neq 0$.

$f(x) = x^2 - 6x + 8$

---

quadratic polynomial A polynomial of degree 2.

polinomio cuadrático Polinomio de grado 2.

$x^2 - 6x + 8$

---

quadrilateral A four-sided polygon.

cuadrilátero Polígono de cuatro lados.

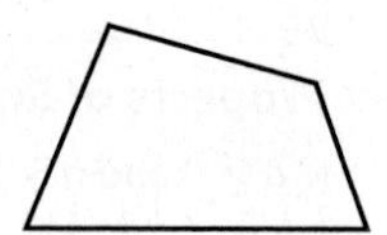

---

quantitative data Numerical data.

datos cuantitativos Datos numéricos.

---

quartile The median of the upper or lower half of a data set. *See also* first quartile, third quartile.

cuartil La mediana de la mitad superior o inferior de un conjunto de datos. *Ver también* primer cuartil, tercer cuartil.

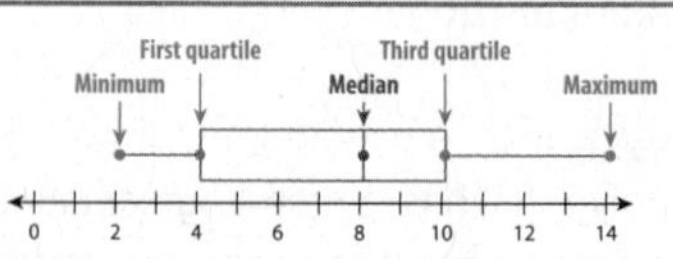

Quotient of Powers Property If a is a nonzero real number and m and n are integers, then $\frac{a^m}{a^n} = a^{m-n}$.

Propiedad del cociente de potencias Dado un número real a distinto de cero y los números enteros m y n, entonces $\frac{a^m}{a^n} = a^{m-n}$.

$\frac{6^7}{6^4} = 6^{7-4} = 6^3$

Quotient Property of Square Roots For $a \geq 0$ and $b > 0$, $\sqrt{\frac{a}{b}} = \frac{\sqrt{a}}{\sqrt{b}}$.

Propiedad del cociente de raíces cuadradas Dados $a \geq 0$ y $b > 0$, $\sqrt{\frac{a}{b}} = \frac{\sqrt{a}}{\sqrt{b}}$.

$\sqrt{\frac{9}{25}} = \frac{\sqrt{9}}{\sqrt{25}} = \frac{3}{5}$

ENGLISH	SPANISH	EXAMPLES
radical equation An equation that contains a variable within a radical.	**ecuación radical** Ecuación que contiene una variable dentro de un radical.	$\sqrt{x+3} + 4 = 7$
radical expression An expression that contains a radical sign.	**expresión radical** Expresión que contiene un signo de radical.	$\sqrt{x+3} + 4$
radical symbol The symbol $\sqrt{\ }$ used to denote a root. The symbol is used alone to indicate a square root or with an index, $\sqrt[n]{\ }$, to indicate the *n*th root.	**símbolo de radical** Símbolo $\sqrt{\ }$ que se utiliza para expresar una raíz. Puede utilizarse solo para indicar una raíz cuadrada, o con un índice, $\sqrt[n]{\ }$, para indicar la enésima raíz.	$\sqrt{36} = 6$ $\sqrt[3]{27} = 3$
radicand The expression under a radical sign.	**radicando** Número o expresión debajo del signo de radical.	Expression: $\sqrt{x+3}$ Radicand: $x + 3$
radius A segment whose endpoints are the center of a circle and a point on the circle; the distance from the center of a circle to any point on the circle.	**radio** Segmento cuyos extremos son el centro de un círculo y un punto de la circunferencia; distancia desde el centro de un círculo hasta cualquier punto de la circunferencia.	Radius
random sample A sample selected from a population so that each member of the population has an equal chance of being selected.	**muestra aleatoria** Muestra seleccionada de una población tal que cada miembro de ésta tenga igual probabilidad de ser seleccionada.	Mr. Hansen chose a random sample of the class by writing each student's name on a slip of paper, mixing up the slips, and drawing five slips without looking.
range of a data set The difference of the greatest and least values in the data set.	**rango de un conjunto de datos** La diferencia del mayor y menor valor en un conjunto de datos.	The data set $\{3, 3, 5, 7, 8, 10, 11, 11, 12\}$ has a range of $12 - 3 = 9$.
range of a function or relation The set of all second coordinates (or *y*-values) of a function or relation.	**rango de una función o relación** Conjunto de todos los valores de la segunda coordenada (o valores de *y*) de una función o relación.	The range of the function $\{(-5, 3), (-3, -2), (-1, -1), (1, 0)\}$ is $\{-2, -1, 0, 3\}$.
rate A ratio that compares two quantities measured in different units.	**tasa** Razón que compara dos cantidades medidas en diferentes unidades.	$\frac{55 \text{ miles}}{1 \text{ hour}} = 55$ mi/h
rate of change A ratio that compares the amount of change in a dependent variable to the amount of change in an independent variable.	**tasa de cambio** Razón que compara la cantidad de cambio de la variable dependiente con la cantidad de cambio de la variable independiente.	The cost of mailing a letter increased from 22 cents in 1985 to 25 cents in 1988. During this period, the rate of change was $\frac{\text{change in cost}}{\text{change in year}} = \frac{25 - 22}{1988 - 1985} = \frac{3}{3}$ $= 1$ cent per year.
ratio A comparison of two quantities by division.	**razón** Comparación de dos cantidades mediante una división.	$\frac{1}{2}$ or $1:2$
rational equation An equation that contains one or more rational expressions.	**ecuación racional** Ecuación que contiene una o más expresiones racionales.	$\frac{x+2}{x^2 + 3x - 1} = 6$

ENGLISH | **SPANISH** | **EXAMPLES**

rational exponent An exponent that can be expressed as $\frac{m}{n}$ such that if m and n are integers, then $b^{\frac{m}{n}} = \sqrt[n]{b^m} = (\sqrt[n]{b})^m$.

exponente racional Exponente que se puede expresar como $\frac{m}{n}$ tal que si m y n son números enteros, entonces $b^{\frac{m}{n}} = \sqrt[n]{b^m} = (\sqrt[n]{b})^m$.

$64^{\frac{1}{6}} = \sqrt[6]{64}$

---

rational expression An algebraic expression whose numerator and denominator are polynomials and whose denominator has a degree ≥ 1.

expresión racional Expresión algebraica cuyo numerador y denominador son polinomios y cuyo denominador tiene un grado ≥ 1.

$\frac{x+2}{x^2+3x-1}$

---

rational function A function whose rule can be written as a rational expression.

función racional Función cuya regla se puede expresar como una expresión racional.

$f(x) = \frac{x+2}{x^2+3x-1}$

---

rational number A number that can be written in the form $\frac{a}{b}$, where a and b are integers and $b \neq 0$.

número racional Número que se puede expresar como $\frac{a}{b}$, donde a y b son números enteros y $b \neq 0$.

$3, 1.75, 0.\overline{3}, -\frac{2}{3}, 0$

---

rationalizing the denominator A method of rewriting a fraction by multiplying by another fraction that is equivalent to 1 in order to remove radical terms from the denominator.

racionalizar el denominador Método que consiste en escribir nuevamente una fracción multiplicándola por otra fracción equivalente a 1 a fin de eliminar los términos radicales del denominador.

$\frac{1}{\sqrt{2}} \cdot \frac{\sqrt{2}}{\sqrt{2}} = \frac{\sqrt{2}}{2}$

---

ray A part of a line that starts at an endpoint and extends forever in one direction.

rayo Parte de una recta que comienza en un extremo y se extiende infinitamente en una dirección.

D

real number A rational or irrational number. Every point on the number line represents a real number.

número real Número racional o irracional. Cada punto de la recta numérica representa un número real.

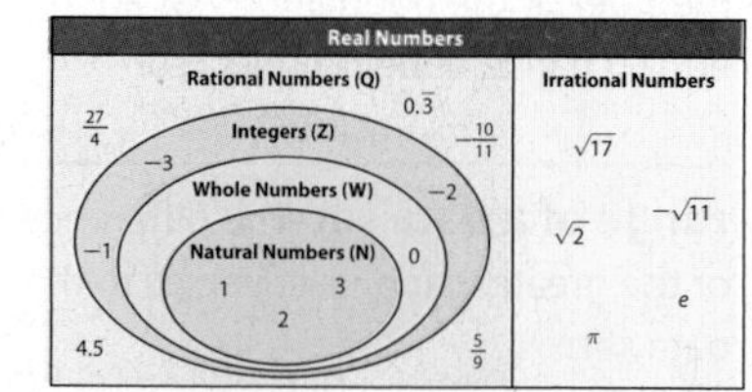

---

reciprocal For a real number $a \neq 0$, the reciprocal of a is $\frac{1}{a}$. The product of reciprocals is 1.

recíproco Dado el número real $a \neq 0$, el recíproco de a es $\frac{1}{a}$. El producto de los recíprocos es 1.

Number	Reciprocal
2	$\frac{1}{2}$
1	1
−1	−1
0	No reciprocal

---

rectangle A quadrilateral with four right angles.

rectángulo Cuadrilátero con cuatro ángulos rectos.

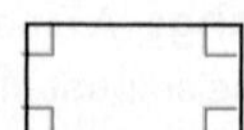

---

rectangular prism A prism whose bases are rectangles.

prisma rectangular Prisma cuyas bases son rectángulos.

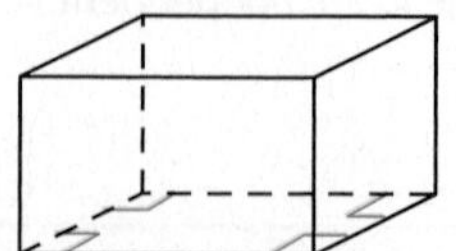

---

rectangular pyramid A pyramid whose base is a rectangle.

pirámide rectangular Pirámide cuya base es un rectángulo.

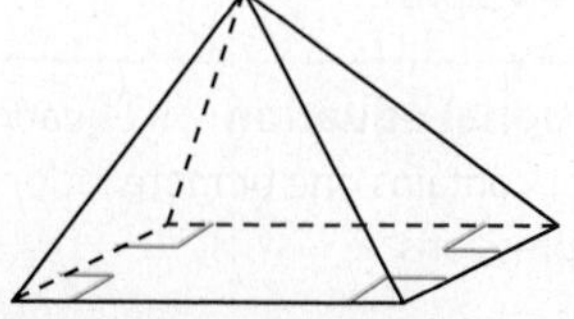

ENGLISH	SPANISH	EXAMPLES
recursive rule for *n*th term of a sequence A rule for a sequence in which one or more previous terms are used to generate the next term.	**fórmula recurrente para hallar el enésimo término de una sucesión** Fórmula para una sucesión en la cual uno o más términos anteriores se usan para generar el término siguiente.	
reflection A mapping of a point P to its image P' as follows: If P is not on line ℓ, then ℓ is the perpendicular bisector of $\overline{PP'}$; if P is on line ℓ, then $P = P'$.	**reflexión** Aplicación de un punto P a su imagen P' como sigue: Si P no está en la línea ℓ, entonces ℓ es la mediatriz de $\overline{PP'}$; si P está en la línea ℓ, entonces $P = P'$.	ℓ, P, P', $Q = Q'$
regular polygon A polygon for which all sides are of equal length and all angles are of equal measure.	**polígono regular** Polígono que tiene todos los lados de la misma longitud y todos los ángulos de la misma medida.	
relation A set of ordered pairs.	**relación** Conjunto de pares ordenados.	$\{(0, 5), (0, 4), (2, 3), (4, 0)\}$
repeating decimal A rational number in decimal form that has a nonzero block of one or more digits that repeat continuously.	**decimal periódico** Número racional en forma decimal que tiene un bloque de uno o más dígitos que se repite continuamente.	$1.\overline{3}$, $0.\overline{6}$, $2.\overline{14}$, $6.77\overline{3}$
replacement set A set of numbers that can be substituted for a variable.	**conjunto de reemplazo** Conjunto de números que pueden sustituir una variable.	
residual The signed vertical distance between a data point and a line of fit.	**residuo** La diferencia vertical entre un dato y una línea de ajuste.	
residual plot A scatter plot of points whose x-coordinates are the values of the independent variable and whose y-coordinates are the corresponding residuals.	**diagrama de residuos** Diagrama de dispersión de puntos en el que la coordenada x representa los valores de la variable independiente y la coordenada y representa los residuos correspondientes.	
rhombus A quadrilateral with four congruent sides.	**rombo** Cuadrilátero con cuatro lados congruentes.	
right angle An angle that measures 90°.	**ángulo recto** Ángulo que mide 90°.	
rigid motion A transformation that does not change the size or shape of a figure.	**movimiento rígido** Transformación que no cambia el tamaño ni la forma de una figura.	Reflections, translations, and rotations are all examples of rigid motion.

Glossary/Glosario

ENGLISH	SPANISH	EXAMPLES
rise The difference in the y-values of two points on a line.	**distancia vertical** Diferencia entre los valores de y de dos puntos de una línea.	For the points $(3, -1)$ and $(6, 5)$, the rise is $5 - (-1) = 6$.
rotation A transformation around point P such that the following are true. • Every point and its image are the same distance from P. • All angles with vertex P formed by a point and its image have the same measure.	**rotación** Transformación alrededor del punto P de tal manera que los siguientes puntos son verdaderos: • Cada punto y su imagen están a la misma distancia de P. • Todos los ángulos con vértice P que son formados por un punto y su imagen tienen la misma medida.	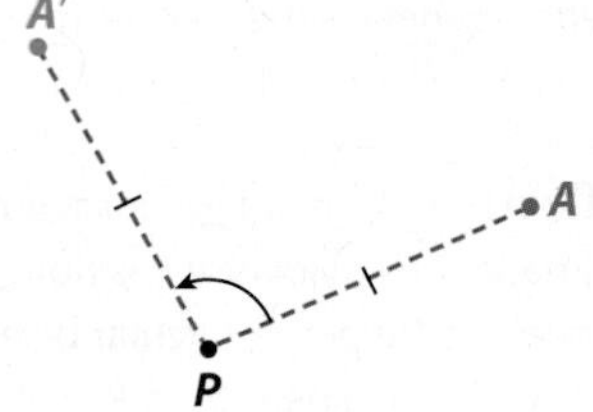
rotational symmetry A figure that can be rotated about a point by an angle less than 360° so that the image coincides with the preimage has rotational symmetry.	**simetría de rotación** Una figura que puede rotarse alrededor de un punto en un ángulo menor de 360° de forma tal que la imagen coincide con la imagen original tiene simetría de rotación.	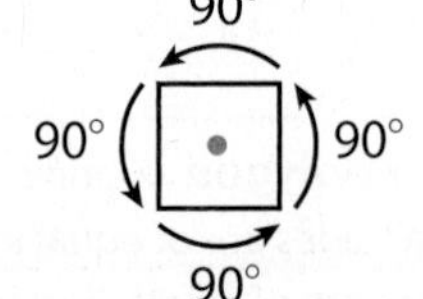 Order of rotational symmetry: 4
run The difference in the x-values of two points on a line.	**distancia horizontal** Diferencia entre los valores de x de dos puntos de una línea.	For the points $(3, -1)$ and $(6, 5)$, the run is $6 - 3 = 3$.

S

ENGLISH	SPANISH	EXAMPLES
sample A part of the population.	**muestra** Una parte de la población.	In a survey about the study habits of high school students, a sample is a survey of 100 students.
sample space The set of all possible outcomes of a probability experiment.	**espacio muestral** Conjunto de todos los resultados posibles de un experimento de probabilidad.	In the experiment of rolling a number cube, the sample space is $\{1, 2, 3, 4, 5, 6\}$.
scale The ratio between two corresponding measurements.	**escala** Razón entre dos medidas correspondientes.	1 cm : 5 mi
scale drawing A drawing that uses a scale to represent an object as smaller or larger than the actual object.	**dibujo a escala** Dibujo que utiliza una escala para representar un objeto como más pequeño o más grande que el objeto original.	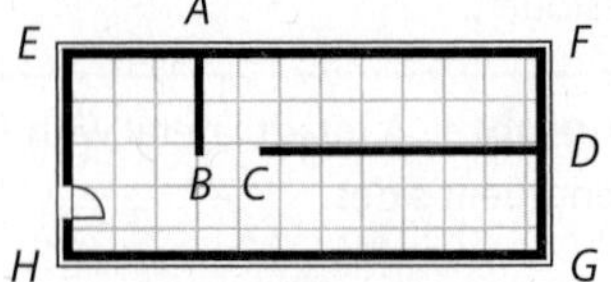 A blueprint is an example of a scale drawing.
scale factor The multiplier used on each dimension to change one figure into a similar figure.	**factor de escala** El multiplicador utilizado en cada dimensión para transformar una figura en una figura semejante.	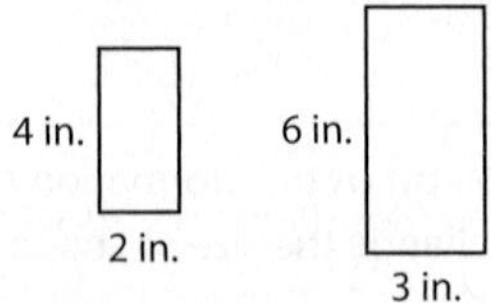 Scale factor: $\frac{3}{2} = 1.5$
scale model A three-dimensional model that uses a scale to represent an object as smaller or larger than the actual object.	**modelo a escala** Modelo tridimensional que utiliza una escala para representar un objeto como más pequeño o más grande que el objeto real.	

ENGLISH	SPANISH	EXAMPLES
scalene triangle A triangle with no congruent sides.	**triángulo escaleno** Triángulo sin lados congruentes.	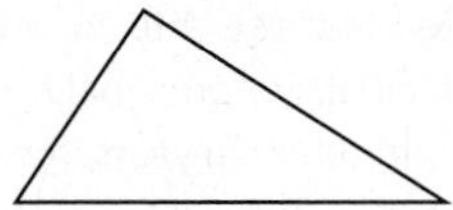
scatter plot A graph with points plotted to show a possible relationship between two sets of data.	**diagrama de dispersión** Gráfica con puntos que se usa para demostrar una relación posible entre dos conjuntos de datos.	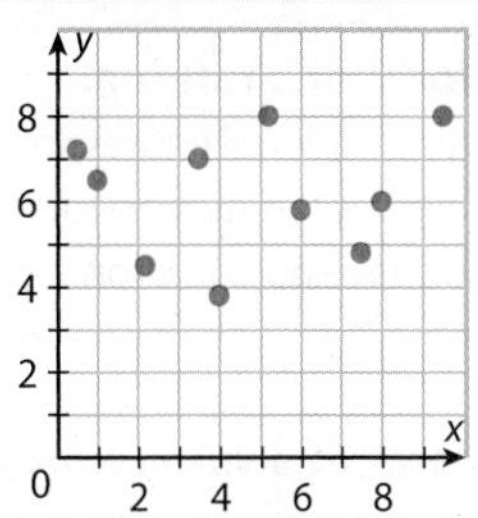
second differences Differences between first differences of a function.	**segundas diferencias** Diferencias entre las primeras diferencias de una función.	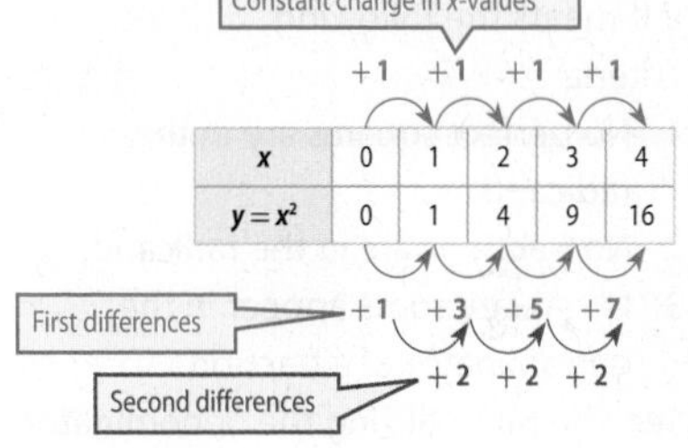
sequence A list of numbers that often form a pattern.	**sucesión** Lista de números que generalmente forman un patrón.	1, 2, 4, 8, 16, …
set A collection of items called elements.	**conjunto** Grupo de componentes denominados elementos.	{1, 2, 3}
set-builder notation A notation for a set that uses a rule to describe the properties of the elements of the set.	**notación de conjuntos** Notación para un conjunto que se vale de una regla para describir las propiedades de los elementos del conjunto.	$\{x \mid x > 3\}$ is read "The set of all x such that x is greater than 3."
side of an angle One of the two rays that form an angle.	**lado de un ángulo** Uno de los dos rayos que forman un ángulo.	C A B $\overrightarrow{AB}$ and $\overrightarrow{AC}$ are the sides
significant digits The digits used to express the precision of a measurement.	**dígitos significativos** Dígitos usados para expresar la precisión de una medida.	
similar Two figures are similar if they have the same shape but not necessarily the same size.	**semejantes** Dos figuras con la misma forma pero no necesariamente del mismo tamaño.	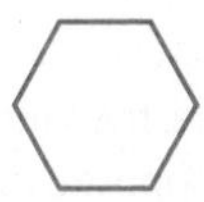 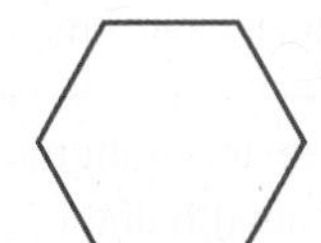
simple event An event consisting of only one outcome.	**suceso simple** Suceso que tiene sólo un resultado.	In the experiment of rolling a number cube, the event consisting of the outcome 3 is a simple event.

ENGLISH	SPANISH	EXAMPLES
simple interest A fixed percent of the principal. For principal P, interest rate r, and time t in years, the simple interest is $I = Prt$.	**interés simple** Porcentaje fijo del capital. Dado el capital P, la tasa de interés r y el tiempo t expresado en años, el interés simple es $I = Prt$.	If \$100 is put into an account with a simple interest rate of 5%, then after 2 years, the account will have earned $I = 100 \cdot 0.05 \cdot 2 = \$10$ in interest.
simplest form of a rational expression A rational expression is in simplest form if the numerator and denominator have no common factors.	**forma simplificada de una expresión racional** Una expresión racional está en forma simplificada cuando el numerador y el denominador no tienen factores comunes.	$\frac{x^2-1}{x^2+x-2} = \frac{(x-1)(x+1)}{(x-1)(x+2)} = \frac{x+1}{x+2}$ ← Simplest form
simplest form of a square root expression A square root expression is in simplest form if it meets the following criteria: 1. No perfect squares are in the radicand. 2. No fractions are in the radicand. 3. No square roots appear in the denominator of a fraction. *See also* rationalizing the denominator.	**forma simplificada de una expresión de raíz cuadrada** Una expresión de raíz cuadrada está en forma simplificada si reúne los siguientes requisitos: 1. No hay cuadrados perfectos en el radicando. 2. No hay fracciones en el radicando. 3. No aparecen raíces cuadradas en el denominador de una fracción. *Ver también* racionalizar el denominador.	Not Simplest Form → Simplest Form: $\sqrt{180}$ → $6\sqrt{5}$ $\sqrt{216a^2b^2}$ → $6ab\sqrt{6}$ $\frac{\sqrt{7}}{\sqrt{2}}$ → $\frac{\sqrt{14}}{2}$
simplest form of an exponential expression An exponential expression is in simplest form if it meets the following criteria: 1. There are no negative exponents. 2. The same base does not appear more than once in a product or quotient. 3. No powers, products, or quotients are raised to powers. 4. Numerical coefficients in a quotient do not have any common factor other than 1.	**forma simplificada de una expresión exponencial** Una expresión exponencial está en forma simplificada si reúne los siguientes requisitos: 1. No hay exponentes negativos. 2. La misma base no aparece más de una vez en un producto o cociente. 3. No se elevan a potencias productos, cocientes ni potencias. 4. Los coeficientes numéricos en un cociente no tienen ningún factor común que no sea 1.	Not Simplest Form → Simplest Form: $7^8 \cdot 7^4$ → 7^{12} $(x^2)^{-4} \cdot x^5$ → $\frac{1}{x^3}$ $\frac{a^5b^9}{(ab)^4}$ → ab^5
simplify To perform all indicated operations.	**simplificar** Realizar todas las operaciones indicadas.	$13 - 20 + 8$ $-7 + 8$ 1
simulation A model of an experiment, often one that would be too difficult or time-consuming to actually perform.	**simulación** Modelo de un experimento; generalmente se recurre a la simulación cuando realizar dicho experimento sería demasiado difícil o llevaría mucho tiempo.	
sine In a right triangle, the ratio of the length of the leg opposite $\angle A$ to the length of the hypotenuse.	**seno** En un triángulo rectángulo, razón entre la longitud del cateto opuesto a $\angle A$ y la longitud de la hipotenusa.	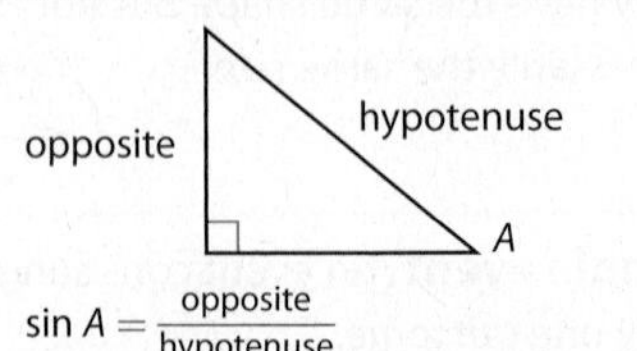 $\sin A = \frac{\text{opposite}}{\text{hypotenuse}}$
skewed distribution A type of distribution in which the right or left side of its display indicates frequencies that are much greater than those of the other side.	**distribución sesgada** Tipo de distribución en la que el lado derecho o izquierdo muestra frecuencias mucho mayores que las del otro lado.	

ENGLISH	SPANISH	EXAMPLES
slope A measure of the steepness of a line. If (x_1, y_1) and (x_2, y_2) are any two points on the line, the slope of the line, known as m, is represented by the equation $m = \frac{y_2 - y_1}{x_2 - x_1}$.	**pendiente** Medida de la inclinación de una línea. Dados dos puntos (x_1, y_1) y (x_2, y_2) en una línea, la pendiente de la línea, denominada m, se representa con la ecuación $m = \frac{y_2 - y_1}{x_2 - x_1}$.	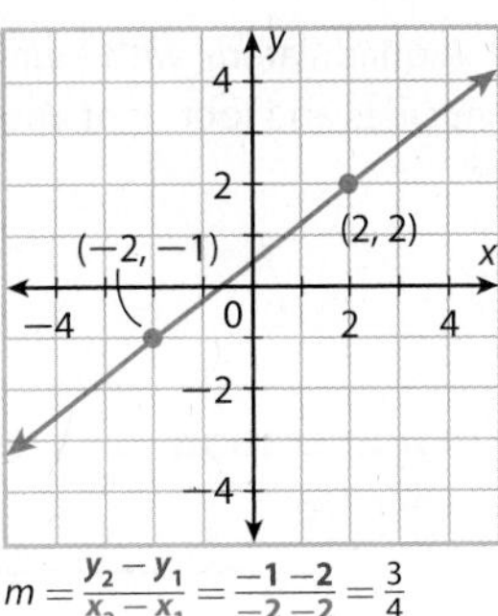 $m = \frac{y_2 - y_1}{x_2 - x_1} = \frac{-1-2}{-2-2} = \frac{3}{4}$
slope-intercept form The slope-intercept form of a linear equation is $y = mx + b$, where m is the slope and b is the y-intercept.	**forma de pendiente-intersección** La forma de pendiente-intersección de una ecuación lineal es $y = mx + b$, donde m es la pendiente y b es la intersección con el eje y.	$y = -2x + 4$ The slope is -2. The y-intercept is 4.
solution of a system of equations Any ordered pair that satisfies all the equations in a system.	**solución de un sistema de ecuaciones** Cualquier par ordenado que resuelva todas las ecuaciones de un sistema.	$\begin{cases} x + y = -1 \\ -x + y = -3 \end{cases}$ Solution: $(1, -2)$
solution of a system of inequalities Any ordered pair that satisfies all the inequalities in a system.	**solución de un sistema de desigualdades** Cualquier par ordenado que resuelva todas las desigualdades de un sistema.	$\begin{cases} y \leq x + 1 \\ y < -x + 4 \end{cases}$ 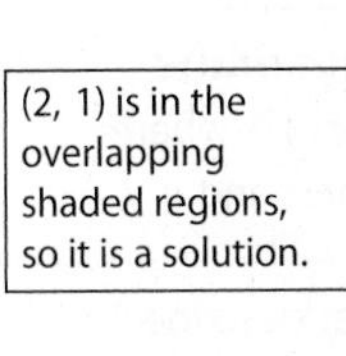 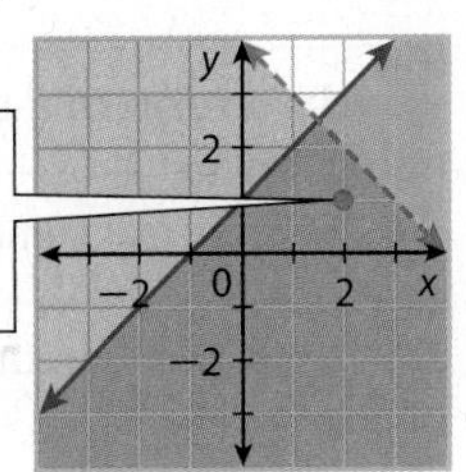
solution of an equation in one variable A value or values that make the equation true.	**solución de una ecuación en una variable** Valor o valores que hacen que la ecuación sea verdadera.	Equation: $x + 2 = 6$ Solution: $x = 4$
solution of an inequality in one variable A value or values that make the inequality true.	**solución de una desigualdad en una variable** Valor o valores que hacen que la desigualdad sea verdadera.	Inequality: $x + 2 < 6$ Solution: $x < 4$
solution of an equation in two variables An ordered pair or ordered pairs that make the equation true.	**solución de una ecuación en dos variables** Un par ordenado o pares ordenados que hacen que la ecuación sea verdadera.	$(4, 2)$ is a solution of $x + y = 6$.
solution of an inequality in two variables An ordered pair or ordered pairs that make the inequality true.	**solución de una desigualdad en dos variables** Un par ordenado o pares ordenados que hacen que la desigualdad sea verdadera.	$(3, 1)$ is a solution of $x + y < 6$.
solution set The set of values that make a statement true.	**conjunto solución** Conjunto de valores que hacen verdadero un enunciado.	Inequality: $x + 3 \geq 5$ Solution set: $\{x \mid x \geq 2\}$ −4 −3 −2 −1 0 1 2 3 4 5 6

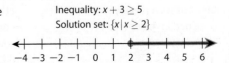

ENGLISH	SPANISH	EXAMPLES
square A quadrilateral with four congruent sides and four right angles.	**cuadrado** Cuadrilátero con cuatro lados congruentes y cuatro ángulos rectos.	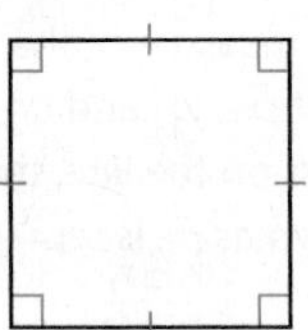
square in numeration The second power of a number.	**cuadrado en numeración** La segunda potencia de un número.	16 is the square of 4.
square root function A function whose rule contains a variable under a square root sign.	**función de raíz cuadrada** Función cuya regla contiene una variable bajo un signo de raíz cuadrada.	
standard form of a linear equation $Ax + By = C$, where A, B, and C are real numbers and A and B are not both 0.	**forma estándar de una ecuación lineal** $Ax + By = C$, donde A, B y C son números reales y A y B no son ambos cero.	$2x + 3y = 6$
standard form of a polynomial A polynomial in one variable is written in standard form when the terms are in order from greatest degree to least degree.	**forma estándar de un polinomio** Un polinomio de una variable se expresa en forma estándar cuando los términos se ordenan de mayor a menor grado.	$4x^5 - 2x^4 + x^2 - x + 1$
standard form of a quadratic equation $ax^2 + bx + c = 0$, where a, b, and c are real numbers and $a \neq 0$.	**forma estándar de una ecuación cuadrática** $ax^2 + bx + c = 0$, donde a, b y c son números reales y $a \neq 0$.	$2x^2 + 3x - 1 = 0$
statistics Numbers that describe a sample or samples.	**estadísticas** Números que describen una o varias muestras.	
stem-and-leaf plot A graph used to organize and display data by dividing each data value into two parts, a stem and a leaf.	**diagrama de tallo y hojas** Gráfica utilizada para organizar y mostrar datos dividiendo cada valor de datos en dos partes, un tallo y una hoja.	**Stem** | **Leaves** 3 | 2 3 4 4 7 9 4 | 0 1 5 7 7 7 8 5 | 1 2 2 3 *Key: 3|2 means 3.2*
step function A piecewise function that is constant over each interval in its domain.	**función escalón** Función a trozos que es constante en cada intervalo en su dominio.	
stratified random sample A sample in which a population is divided into distinct groups and members are selected at random from each group.	**muestra aleatoria estratificada** Muestra en la que la población está dividida en grupos diferenciados y los miembros de cada grupo se seleccionan al azar.	Ms. Carter chose a stratified random sample of her school's student population by randomly selecting 30 students from each grade level.
subset A set that is contained entirely within another set. Set B is a subset of set A if every element of B is contained in A, denoted $B \subset A$.	**subconjunto** Conjunto que se encuentra dentro de otro conjunto. El conjunto B es un subconjunto del conjunto A si todos los elementos de B son elementos de A; se expresa $B \subset A$.	The set of integers is a subset of the set of rational numbers.

ENGLISH	SPANISH	EXAMPLES
substitution method A method used to solve systems of equations by solving an equation for one variable and substituting the resulting expression into the other equation(s).	**sustitución** Método utilizado para resolver sistemas de ecuaciones resolviendo una ecuación para una variable y sustituyendo la expresión resultante en las demás ecuaciones.	
Subtraction Property of Equality If a, b, and c are real numbers and $a = b$, then $a - c = b - c$.	**Propiedad de igualdad de la resta** Si a, b y c son números reales y $a = b$, entonces $a - c = b - c$.	$\begin{array}{rcr} x + 6 & = & 8 \\ -6 & & -6 \\ \hline x & = & 2 \end{array}$
Subtraction Property of Inequality For real numbers a, b, and c, if $a < b$, then $a - c < b - c$. Also holds true for $>$, $\leq$, $\geq$, and $\neq$.	**Propiedad de desigualdad de la resta** Dados los números reales a, b y c, si $a < b$, entonces $a - c < b - c$. Es válido también para $>$, $\leq$, $\geq$ y $\neq$.	$\begin{array}{rcr} x + 6 & < & 8 \\ -6 & & -6 \\ \hline x & < & 2 \end{array}$
supplementary angles Two angles whose measures have a sum of 180°.	**ángulos suplementarios** Dos ángulos cuyas medidas suman 180°.	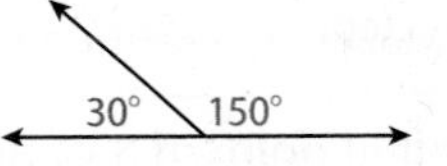
surface area The total area of all faces and curved surfaces of a three-dimensional figure.	**área total** Área total de todas las caras y superficies curvas de una figura tridimensional.	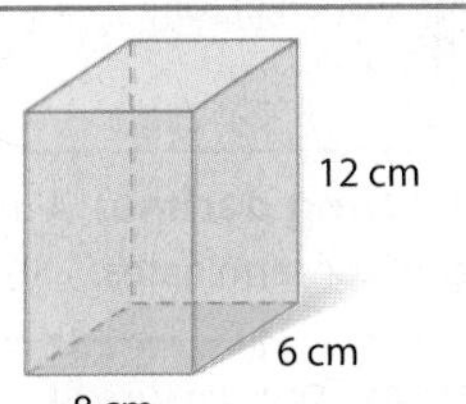 Surface area $= 2(8)(12) + 2(8)(6) + 2(12)(6)$ $= 432 \text{ cm}^2$
symmetric distribution A type of distribution in which the right and left sides of its display indicate frequencies that are mirror images of each other.	**distribución simétrica** Tipo de distribución en la que los lados derecho e izquierdo muestran frecuencias que son idénticas.	
system of linear equations A system of equations in which all of the equations are linear.	**sistema de ecuaciones lineales** Sistema de ecuaciones en el que todas las ecuaciones son lineales.	$\begin{cases} 2x + 3y = -1 \\ x - 3y = 4 \end{cases}$
system of linear inequalities A system of inequalities in which all of the inequalities are linear.	**sistema de desigualdades lineales** Sistema de desigualdades en el que todas las desigualdades son lineales.	$\begin{cases} 2x + 3y > -1 \\ x - 3y \leq 4 \end{cases}$
systematic random sample A sample based on selecting one member of the population at random and then selecting other members by using a pattern.	**muestra sistemática** Muestra en la que se elige a un miembro de la población al azar y luego se elige a otros miembros mediante un patrón.	Mr. Martin chose a systematic random sample of customers visiting a store by selecting one customer at random and then selecting every tenth customer after that.

ENGLISH	SPANISH	EXAMPLES

ENGLISH	SPANISH	EXAMPLES
tangent In a right triangle, the ratio of the length of the leg opposite $\angle A$ to the length of the leg adjacent to $\angle A$.	**tangente** En un triángulo rectángulo, razón entre la longitud del cateto opuesto a $\angle A$ y la longitud del cateto adyacente a $\angle A$.	opposite; adjacent; A $\tan A = \frac{\text{opposite}}{\text{adjacent}}$
term of a sequence An element or number in the sequence.	**término de una sucesión** Elemento o número de una sucesión.	5 is the third term in the sequence 1, 3, 5, 7, …
term of an expression The parts of the expression that are added or subtracted.	**término de una expresión** Parte de una expresión que debe sumarse o restarse.	$3x^2 + 6x - 8$ Term Term Term
terminal point of a vector The endpoint of a vector.	**punto terminal de un vector** Extremo de un vector.	A; $\vec{v}$; B; Terminal point
terminating decimal A decimal that ends, or terminates.	**decimal finito** Decimal con un número determinados de posiciones decimales.	1.5, 2.75, 4.0
theorem A conjecture that can be proved using a logical sequence of definitions, postulates, and already-proven theorems.	**teorema** Conjetura que se puede demostrar por una secuencia lógica de definiciones, postulados y teoremas que han sido demostrados.	
theoretical probability The ratio of the number of equally likely outcomes in an event to the total number of possible outcomes.	**probabilidad teórica** Razón entre el número de resultados igualmente probables de un suceso y el número total de resultados posibles.	In the experiment of rolling a number cube, the theoretical probability of rolling an odd number is $\frac{3}{6} = \frac{1}{2}$.
third quartile The median of the upper half of a data set. Also called *upper quartile*.	**tercer cuartil** La mediana de la mitad superior de un conjunto de datos. También se llama *cuartil superior*.	**Lower half** **Upper half** 18, 23, 28, 29, (36,) 42 **Third quartile**
tolerance The amount by which a measurement is permitted to vary from a specified value.	**tolerancia** La cantidad por que una medida se permite variar de un valor especificado.	
transformation A change in the position, size, or shape of a figure or graph.	**transformación** Cambio en la posición, tamaño o forma de una figura o gráfica.	Preimage; A, B, C; Image; A′, B′, C′ $\triangle ABC \rightarrow \triangle A'B'C'$

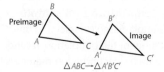

ENGLISH	SPANISH	EXAMPLES
translation A transformation along a vector such that the segment joining a point and its image has the same length as the vector and is parallel to the vector.	**traslación** Transformación a lo largo de un vector de tal manera que el segmento que conecte con un punto y su imagen tiene la misma longitud del vector y es paralelo al vector.	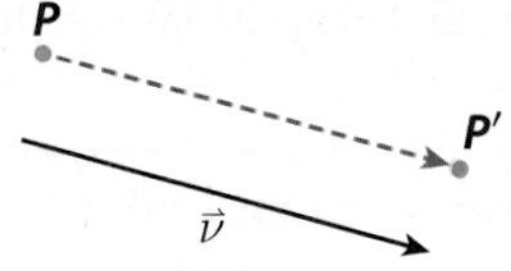
trapezoid A quadrilateral with at least one pair of parallel sides.	**trapecio** Cuadrilátero con por lo menos un par de lados paralelos.	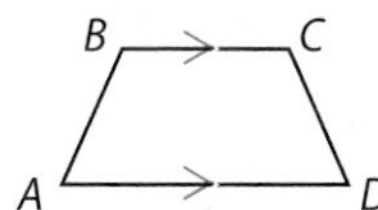
tree diagram A branching diagram that shows all possible combinations or outcomes of an experiment.	**diagrama de árbol** Diagrama con ramificaciones que muestra todas las combinaciones o resultados posibles de un experimento.	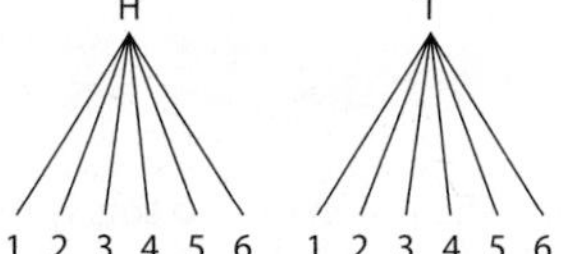The tree diagram shows the possible outcomes when tossing a coin and rolling a number cube.
trend line A line on a scatter plot that helps show the correlation between data sets more clearly.	**línea de tendencia** Línea en un diagrama de dispersión que sirve para mostrar la correlación entre conjuntos de datos más claramente.	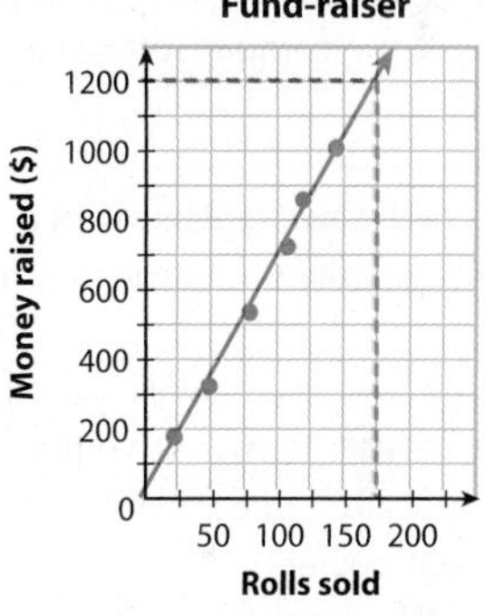
trial Each repetition or observation of an experiment.	**prueba** Una sola repetición u observación de un experimento.	In the experiment of rolling a number cube, each roll is one trial.
triangle A three-sided polygon.	**triángulo** Polígono de tres lados.	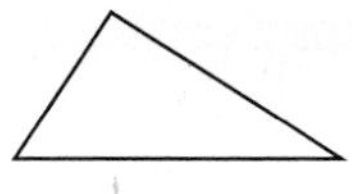
triangular prism A prism whose bases are triangles.	**prisma triangular** Prisma cuyas bases son triángulos.	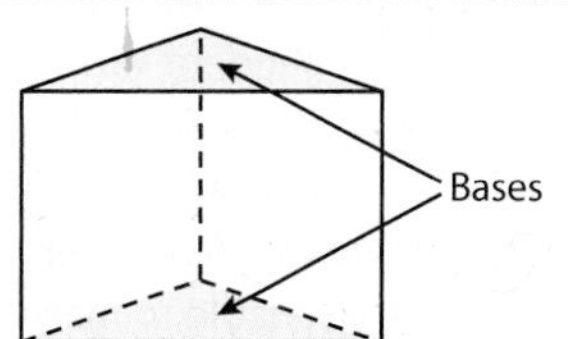
triangular pyramid A pyramid whose base is a triangle.	**pirámide triangular** Pirámide cuya base es un triángulo.	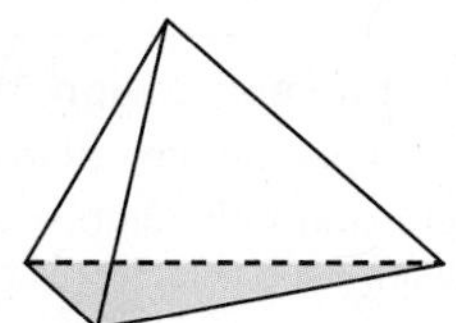
trigonometric ratio Ratio of the lengths of two sides of a right triangle.	**razón trigonométrica** Razón entre dos lados de un triángulo rectángulo.	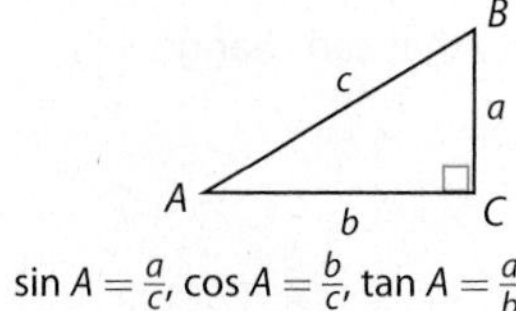$\sin A = \frac{a}{c}$, $\cos A = \frac{b}{c}$, $\tan A = \frac{a}{b}$

Glossary/Glosario

ENGLISH	SPANISH	EXAMPLES
trinomial A polynomial with three terms.	**trinomio** Polinomio con tres términos.	$4x^2 + 3xy - 5y^2$
two-way frequency table A frequency table that displays two-variable data in rows and columns.	**table de frecuencia de doble entrada** Una tabla de frecuencia que muestra los datos de dos variables organizados en filas y columnas.	(see table below)

Pet	Preference: inside	Outside	*Total*
Cats	35	15	50
Dogs	20	30	50
Total	55	45	100

U

ENGLISH	SPANISH	EXAMPLES
union The union of two sets is the set of all elements that are in either set, denoted by ∪.	**unión** La unión de dos conjuntos es el conjunto de todos los elementos que se encuentran en ambos conjuntos, expresado por ∪.	$A = \{1, 2, 3, 4\}$ $B = \{1, 3, 5, 7, 9\}$ $A \cup B = \{1, 2, 3, 4, 5, 7, 9\}$
unit rate A rate in which the second quantity in the comparison is one unit.	**tasa unitaria** Tasa en la que la segunda cantidad de la comparación es una unidad.	$\frac{30 \text{ mi}}{1 \text{ h}} = 30 \text{ mi/h}$
unlike radicals Radicals with a different quantity under the radical.	**radicales distintos** Radicales con cantidades diferentes debajo del signo de radical.	$2\sqrt{2}$ and $2\sqrt{3}$
unlike terms Terms with different variables or the same variables raised to different powers.	**términos distintos** Términos con variables diferentes o las mismas variables elevadas a potencias diferentes.	$4xy^2$ and $6x^2y$
upper quartile *See* third quartile.	**cuartil superior** *Ver* tercer cuartil.	

V

ENGLISH	SPANISH	EXAMPLES
value of a function The result of replacing the independent variable with a number and simplifying.	**valor de una función** Resultado de reemplazar la variable independiente por un número y luego simplificar.	The value of the function $f(x) = x + 1$ for $x = 3$ is 4.
value of a variable A number used to replace a variable to make an equation true.	**valor de una variable** Número utilizado para reemplazar una variable y hacer que una ecuación sea verdadera.	In the equation $x + 1 = 4$, the value of x is 3.
value of an expression The result of replacing the variables in an expression with numbers and simplifying.	**valor de una expresión** Resultado de reemplazar las variables de una expresión por un número y luego simplificar.	The value of the expression $x + 1$ for $x = 3$ is 4.
variable A symbol used to represent a quantity that can change.	**variable** Símbolo utilizado para representar una cantidad que puede cambiar.	In the expression $2x + 3$, x is the variable.

ENGLISH	SPANISH	EXAMPLES
vector A quantity that has both magnitude and direction.	**vector** Cantidad que tiene magnitude y dirección.	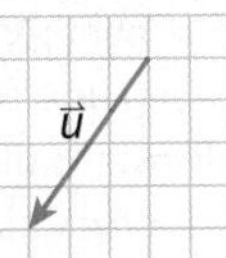
Venn diagram A diagram used to show relationships between sets.	**diagrama de Venn** Diagrama utilizado para mostrar la relación entre conjuntos.	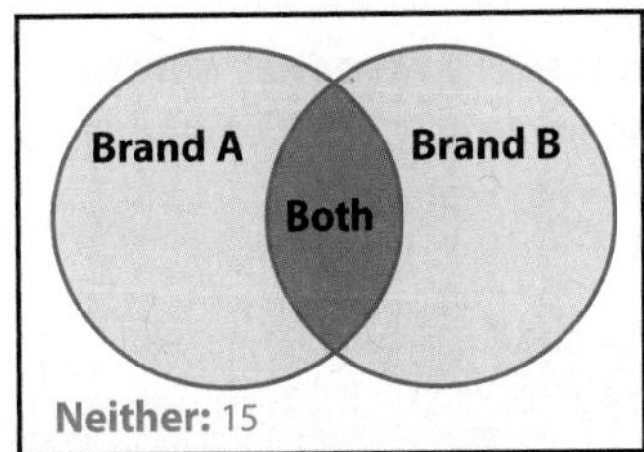
vertex of a parabola The highest or lowest point on the parabola.	**vértice de una parábola** Punto más alto o más bajo de una parábola.	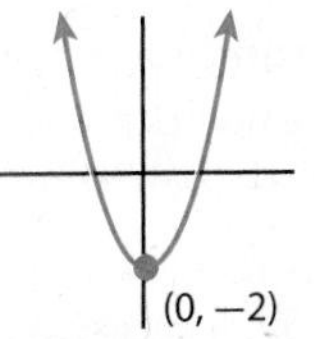 The vertex is $(0, -2)$.
vertex of an absolute-value graph The point on the axis of symmetry of the graph.	**vértice de una gráfica de valor absoluto** Punto en el eje de simetría de la gráfica.	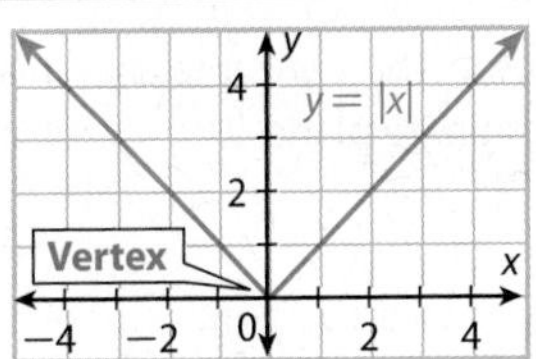
vertex of an angle The common endpoint of the sides of the angle.	**vértice de un ángulo** Extremo común de los lados del ángulo.	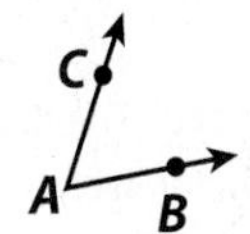 A is the vertex of $\angle CAB$.
vertical angles The nonadjacent angles formed by two intersecting lines.	**ángulos opuestos por el vértice** Ángulos no adyacentes formados por dos líneas que se cruzan.	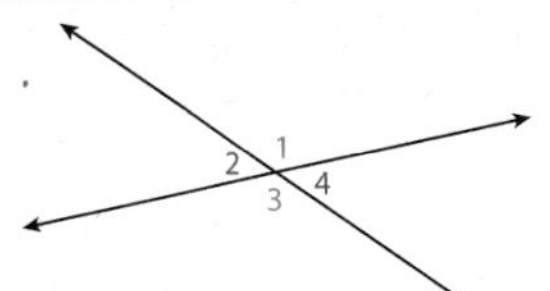 $\angle$**1** and $\angle$**3** are vertical angles. $\angle$**2** and $\angle$**4** are vertical angles.
vertical line A line whose equation is $x = a$, where a is the x-intercept.	**línea vertical** Línea cuya ecuación es $x = a$, donde a es la intersección con el eje x.	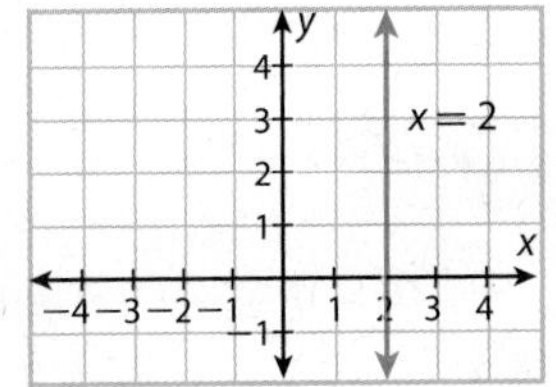
vertical-line test A test used to determine whether a relation is a function. If any vertical line crosses the graph of a relation more than once, the relation is not a function.	**prueba de la línea vertical** Prueba utilizada para determinar si una relación es una función. Si una línea vertical corta la gráfica de una relación más de una vez, la relación no es una función.	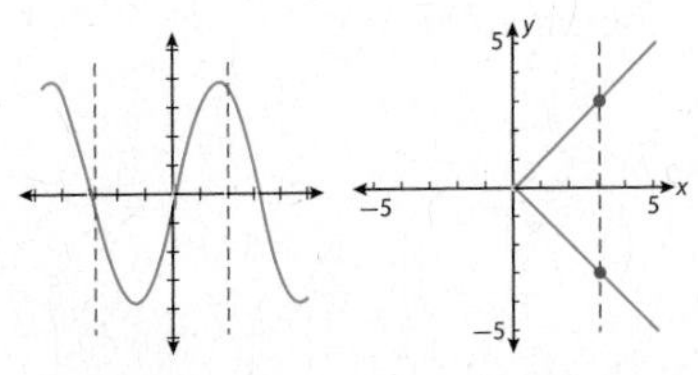 Function Not a function

ENGLISH	SPANISH	EXAMPLES

volume The number of nonoverlapping unit cubes of a given size that will exactly fill the interior of a three-dimensional figure.

volumen Cantidad de cubos unitarios no superpuestos de un determinado tamaño que llenan exactamente el interior de una figura tridimensional.

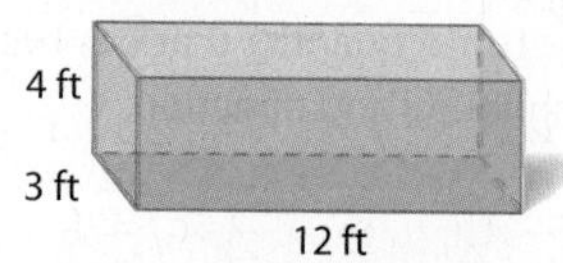

Volume $= (3)(4)(12) = 144$ ft^3

---

voluntary response sample A sample in which members choose to be in the sample.

muestra de respuesta voluntaria Una muestra en la que los miembros eligen participar.

A store provides survey cards for customers who wish to fill them out.

whole number A member of the set of natural numbers and zero.

número cabal Miembro del conjunto de los números naturales y cero.

0, 1, 2, 3, 4, 5, …

***x*-axis** The horizontal axis in a coordinate plane.

eje *x* Eje horizontal en un plano cartesiano.

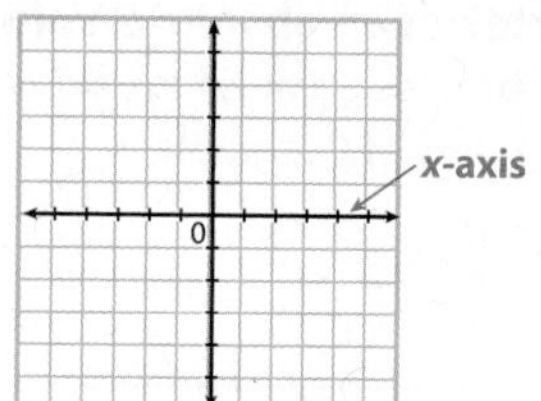

***x*-coordinate** The first number in an ordered pair, which indicates the horizontal distance of a point from the origin on the coordinate plane.

coordenada *x* Primer número de un par ordenado, que indica la distancia horizontal de un punto desde el origen en un plano cartesiano.

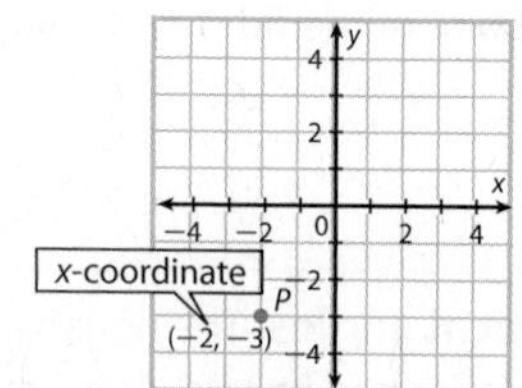

***x*-intercept** The *x*-coordinate(s) of the point(s) where a graph intersects the *x*-axis.

intersección con el eje *x* Coordenada(s) *x* de uno o más puntos donde una gráfica corta el eje *x*.

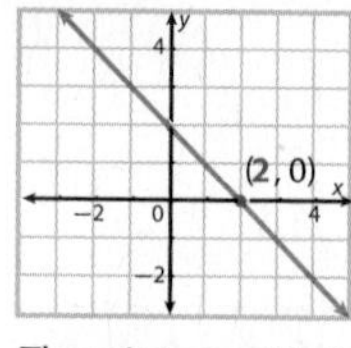

The *x*-intercept is 2.

***y*-axis** The vertical axis in a coordinate plane.

eje *y* Eje vertical en un plano cartesiano.

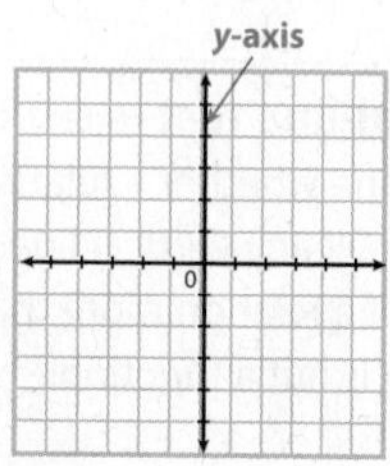

ENGLISH	SPANISH	EXAMPLES
y-coordinate The second number in an ordered pair, which indicates the vertical distance of a point from the origin on the coordinate plane.	**coordenada *y*** Segundo número de un par ordenado, que indica la distancia vertical de un punto desde el origen en un plano cartesiano.	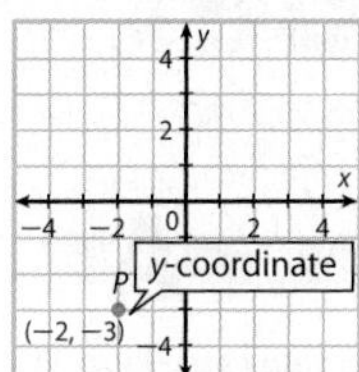
y-intercept The *y*-coordinate(s) of the point(s) where a graph intersects the *y*-axis.	**intersección con el eje *y*** Coordenada(s) *y* de uno o más puntos donde una gráfica corta el eje *y*.	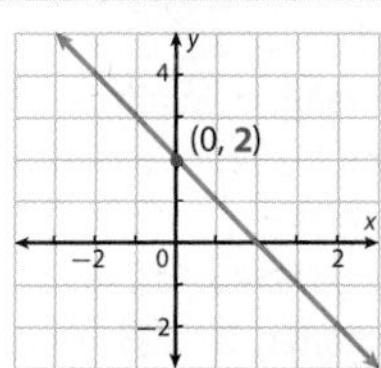 The *y*-intercept is 2.

Z

ENGLISH	SPANISH	EXAMPLES
zero exponent For any nonzero real number x, $x^0 = 1$.	**exponente cero** Dado un número real distinto de cero x, $x^0 = 1$.	$5^0 = 1$
zero of a function For the function f, any number x such that $f(x) = 0$.	**cero de una función** Dada la función f, todo número x tal que $f(x) = 0$.	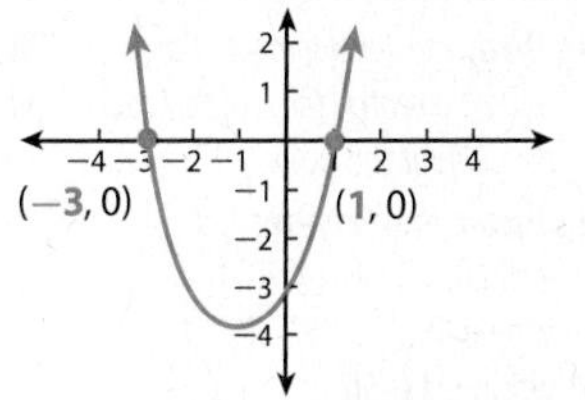 The zeros are −3 and 1.
Zero Product Property For real numbers p and q, if $pq = 0$, then $p = 0$ or $q = 0$.	**Propiedad del producto cero** Dados los números reales p y q, si $pq = 0$, entonces $p = 0$ o $q = 0$.	If $(x - 1)(x + 2) = 0$, then $x - 1 = 0$ or $x + 2 = 0$, so $x = 1$ or $x = -2$.

Index

A

B

C

Index

D

E

F

M

N

Q

R

S

T

U

V

W

X

Y

Z

TABLE OF MEASURES

LENGTH

1 inch = 2.54 centimeters
1 meter = 39.37 inches
1 mile = 5280 feet
1 mile = 1760 yards
1 mile = 1.609 kilometers
1 kilometer = 0.62 mile

MASS/WEIGHT

1 pound = 16 ounces
1 pound = 0.454 kilograms
1 kilogram = 2.2 pounds
1 ton = 2000 pounds

CAPACITY

1 cup = 8 fluid ounces
1 pint = 2 cups
1 quart = 2 pints
1 gallon = 4 quarts

1 gallon = 3.785 liters
1 liter = 0.264 gallons
1 liter = 1000 cubic centimeters

SYMBOLS

$\neq$	is not equal to
$\approx$	is approximately equal to
10^2	ten squared; ten to the second power
$2.\overline{6}$	repeating decimal 2.66666...
$\lvert -4 \rvert$	the absolute value of negative 4
$\sqrt{\ }$	square root
π	pi: (about 3.14)
$\overleftrightarrow{AB}$	line *AB*
$\overrightarrow{AB}$	ray *AB*
$\overline{AB}$	line segment *AB*
AB	the distance from *A* to *B*
$\triangle ABC$	triangle *ABC*
$\angle A$	angle *A*
$\angle ABC$	angle *ABC*
$^\circ$	degree
$\cong$	is congruent to
$m\angle A$	measure of angle *A*
A'	*A* prime
$\vec{AB}$	vector *AB*
$\langle a, b \rangle$	the component form of a vector

FORMULAS

Triangle	$A = \frac{1}{2}bh$
Parallelogram	$A = bh$
Circle	$A = \pi r^2$
Circle	$C = \pi d$ or $C = 2\pi r$
General Prisms	$V = Bh$
Cylinder	$V = \pi r^2 h$
Sphere	$V = \frac{4}{3}\pi r^3$
Cone	$V = \frac{1}{3}\pi r^2 h$

Pyramid	$V = \frac{1}{3}Bh$
Pythagorean Theorem	$a^2 + b^2 = c^2$
Quadratic Formula	$x = \frac{-b \pm \sqrt{b^2 - 4ac}}{2a}$
Arithmetic Sequence	$a_n = a_1 + (n - 1)d$
Geometric Sequence	$a_n = a_1 r^{n-1}$
Slope	$m = \frac{y_2 - y_1}{x_2 - x_1}$
Distance Formula	$\sqrt{(x_2 - x_1)^2 + (y_2 - y_1)^2}$
Midpoint Formula	$M\left(\frac{x_1 + x_2}{2}, \frac{y_1 + y_2}{2}\right)$